Developing E-Government Projects:

Frameworks and Methodologies

Zaigham Mahmood
University of Derby, UK & North West University, South Africa

A volume in the Advances in Electronic Government, Digital Divide, and Regional Development (AEGDDRD) Book Series

Information Science REFERENCE

Managing Director: Lindsay Johnston
Editorial Director: Joel Gamon
Book Production Manager: Jennifer Yoder
Publishing Systems Analyst: Adrienne Freeland
Development Editor: Monica Speca
Assistant Acquisitions Editor: Kayla Wolfe
Typesetter: Henry Ulrich
Cover Design: Jason Mull

Published in the United States of America by
Information Science Reference (an imprint of IGI Global)
701 E. Chocolate Avenue
Hershey PA 17033
Tel: 717-533-8845
Fax: 717-533-8661
E-mail: cust@igi-global.com
Web site: http://www.igi-global.com

Library of Congress Cataloging-in-Publication Data

Developing E-government projects : frameworks and methodologies / Zaigham Mahmood, editor.
pages cm
Includes bibliographical references and index.
Summary: "This book presents frameworks and methodologies for strategies toward the design, implementation, and adoption of e-government projects,
providing best practices in the successful adoption of e-government"--Provided by publisher.
ISBN 978-1-4666-4245-4 (hardcover) -- ISBN 978-1-4666-4246-1 (ebook) -- ISBN 978-1-4666-4247-8 (print & perpetual access) 1. Internet in public administration--Cross-cultural studies. 2. Electronic government information--Congresses--Cross-cultural studies. 3. Information technology--Political aspects--Cross-cultural studies. 4. Public administration--Information resources management--Cross-cultural studies. I. Mahmood, Zaigham.
JF1525.A8D47 2013
352.3'802854678--dc23
2013009729

This book is published in the IGI Global book series Advances in Electronic Government, Digital Divide, and Regional Development (ISSN: 2326-9103; eISSN: 2326-9111)

British Cataloguing in Publication Data
A Cataloguing in Publication record for this book is available from the British Library.

All work contributed to this book is new, previously-unpublished material. The views expressed in this book are those of the authors, but not necessarily of the publisher.

Advances in Electronic Government, Digital Divide, and Regional Development (AEGDDRD) Book Series

ISSN: 2326-9103
EISSN: 2326-9111

Mission

The successful use of digital technology to provide public services and foster economic development has become an objective for governments around the world. The development towards electronic government not only affects the efficiency and effectiveness of public services, but also has the potential to transform the nature of government interactions with citizens. Current research on the adoption of electronic/digital government in organizations around the world aims to emphasize the extensiveness of this growing field.

The **Advances in Electronic Government, Digital Divide & Regional Development (AEGDDRD) Book Series** presents all areas of research involved in these fields, including new applications and methodologies.

Coverage

- Digital Democracy
- E-Citizenship
- Electronic & Digital Government
- ICT Adoption in Developing Countries
- ICT within Government & Public Sectors
- Knowledge Divide
- Public Information Management
- Regional Planning
- Urban & Rural Development
- Web 2.0 in Government

IGI Global is currently accepting manuscripts for publication within this series. To submit a proposal for a volume in this series, please contact our Acquisition Editors at Acquisitions@igi-global.com or visit: http://www.igi-global.com/publish/.

The Advances in Electronic Government, Digital Divide, and Regional Development (AEGDDRD) Book Series (ISSN 2326-9103) is published by IGI Global, 701 E. Chocolate Avenue, Hershey, PA 17033-1240, USA, www.igi-global.com. This series is composed of titles available for purchase individually; each title is edited to be contextually exclusive from any other title within the series. For pricing and ordering information please visit http://www.igi-global.com/book-series/advances-electronic-government-digital-divide/37153. Postmaster: Send all address changes to above address.

Titles in this Series

For a list of additional titles in this series, please visit: www.igi-global.com

Developing E-Government Projects: Frameworks and Methodologies
Zaigham Mahmood (University of Derby, UK)
Information Science Reference • copyright 2013 • 346pp • H/C (ISBN: 9781466642454) • US $180.00 (our price)

Citizen E-Participation in Urban Governance Crowdsourcing and Collaborative Creativity
Carlos Nunes Silva (University of Lisbon, Portugal)
Information Science Reference • copyright 2013 • 353pp • H/C (ISBN: 9781466641693) • US $180.00 (our price)

E-Government Success around the World Cases, Empirical Studies, and Practical Recommendations
J. Ramon Gil-Garcia (Centro de Investigación y Docencia Económicas, Mexico)
Information Science Reference • copyright 2013 • 358pp • H/C (ISBN: 9781466641730) • US $180.00 (our price)

E-Government Success Factors and Measure Theories, Concepts, and Methodologies
J. Ramon Gil-Garcia (Centro de Investigación y Docencia Económicas, Mexico)
Information Science Reference • copyright 2013 • 352pp • H/C (ISBN: 9781466640580) • US $180.00 (our price)

E-Government Implementation and Practice in Developing Countries
Zaigham Mahmood (University of Derby, UK)
Information Science Reference • copyright 2013 • 348pp • H/C (ISBN: 9781466640900) • US $180.00 (our price)

Global Sustainable Development and Renewable Energy Systems
Phillip Olla (Madonna University, USA)
Information Science Reference • copyright 2012 • 354pp • H/C (ISBN: 9781466616257) • US $180.00 (our price)

City Competitiveness and Improving Urban Subsystems Technologies and Applications
Melih Bulu (Istanbul Sehir University, Turkey)
Information Science Reference • copyright 2012 • 322pp • H/C (ISBN: 9781613501740) • US $180.00 (our price)

International Exploration of Technology Equity and the Digital Divide Critical, Historical and Social Perspectives
Patricia Randolph Leigh (Iowa State University, USA)
Information Science Reference • copyright 2011 • 254pp • H/C (ISBN: 9781615207930) • US $180.00 (our price)

Regional Innovation Systems and Sustainable Development Emerging Technologies
Patricia Ordóñez de Pablos (Universidad de Oviedo, Spain) W.B. Lee (Polytechnic University of Hong Kong) and Jingyuan Zhao (Harbin Institute of Technology, China)
Information Science Reference • copyright 2011 • 276pp • H/C (ISBN: 9781616928469) • US $180.00 (our price)

To Ozair Hussain Mahmood:
Happy 18th

Editorial Advisory Board

Table of Contents

Section 4
E-Government Projects: Review and Assessment

Detailed Table of Contents

and citizens' participation, accessibility and power relationship ratios. It is clear from literature that e-Government is not a new phenomenon in most developed countries and some developing countries in Asia and Africa. These countries have already announced their Open Government Initiatives and data portals. However, e-Government leads to greater information asymmetry among citizens and government. There is also, institutionalization and diffusion asymmetry of the practice of the current Openness in e-Government models within developing countries in particular. The study presented in this chapter draws on organizational decision-making research and adopts an explorative research approach that is informed by grounded theory. The findings of the research are that the information asymmetry between citizens and government; asymmetry in institutionalization, and diffusion within developed and developing countries are widely attributed to socio-economic and political variations in developed and developing countries. Unless these differences are skilfully identified and accommodated as such into the development and use models, Openness in e-Government efforts would not help achieve the social and economic development goals by developing countries in particular.

E-Government is about using the tools and systems, made possible by Information and Communication Technology (ICTs), such as Decision Support Systems (DSSs) as a strategy to enhance human resources output in public sector organisations. The aim is to provide better public services to citizens and the business sector. ICTs are already widely used by government bodies, especially in developed countries, just as in enterprises. In Zimbabwe, and in many other developing countries, Public Sector Organisations have already started exploiting DSS, unlike the private sector where such systems have been in use for a long time. DSSs have subsequently improved decision making processes in the private sector. Service efficiency and improved effectiveness are the expected benefits of DSSs exploitation alongside increased stakeholder value. This chapter aims to provide the grounds for building an evaluation theory or a framework for assessing DSS adoption and exploitation in the context of public sector and public services provision. It discusses the results of a study that finds that, to a greater extent, decision support systems can be used as an e-Government strategy that will in turn be highly effective in assisting decision making in Public Sector Organisations.

Insight into the reasons why people adopt or reject technology is one of the most challenging issues in information technology research. This chapter draws on the Electronic Commerce Technology Acceptance (ECTA) framework, which is in turn based on Technology Acceptance Model (TAM) and examines Jordanian government's employees' attitudes towards adoption and use of Electronic Mailing systems within their job. This chapter is aimed at providing an overview of the current state of use, adoption and implementation of electronic mailing innovation within organisations, specifically governmental institutions in developing countries like Jordan. More precisely, we first quantify constructs relating to the current state of governmental institutions' beliefs and attitudes toward E-Mailing systems technology in Jordan, and then develop and validate the relationships between the various factors that drive the adoption and acceptance of such innovation. A quantitative survey is used to establish and illustrates employee's behavioural intention and decision to e-mailing systems. The main influencing issues discussed in this chapter that affect these employees imply perceived usefulness, perceived ease of use, employees' attitudes towards new technologies, and behavioural intentions to use. Whereas, these various issues are suggested in the Technology Acceptance Model (TAM), the enhanced Technology Acceptance Model extends them to include the external social factors proposed in this chapter such as trust, cultural beliefs, and sociology of technology. Eventually, the significant insight emanated from the findings identifies ways of assisting and spurring employees to make use of technology more effectively.

Section 2
E-Government Adoption: Frameworks and Policy

Over the last few years, many different definitions for the e-government term have appeared in the literature. This diversity of definitions created a conceptual multiplicity and divergence. While being understandable, taking into consideration the newness of the e-government field, this may be prejudicing the e government research and development. The aim of this chapter is to contribute to the clarification of the e government concept, by providing a framework that hopefully will help to understand its boundaries and main constituents, as well as the way in which many of the different related terms found in the literature, can be further articulated. The framework put forward in this chapter is based on a generic model of a democratic government system. Building on that model, six main spaces, where Information Technologies (ITs) can be deployed, are identified and discussed. The use of IT in all those spaces contributes to the overall development of a country's e government reality and maturity. By suggesting and arguing for a comprehensive, holistic and eclectic vision of e government, this framework provides a basis for achieving more sustained e-government research and development efforts.

Effective policy frameworks are essential when developing e-government projects. Participatory e-government practices that facilitate civic engagement depend upon a combination of direct and indirect information and communication technology (ICT) policies. Direct policies focus on infrastructure development and enhancing citizens' ICT adoption and use. Indirectly, ICTs can be used to support policy processes through, for example, information dissemination and the provision of spaces for deliberation. This chapter examines Australian e-government initiatives, suggesting that local governments provide a useful context for online civic participation and engagement. However, local initiatives are often developed on an ad hoc basis and are largely limited to the provision of one-way information and service delivery features. Conversely, federal documentation addresses both direct and indirect ICT policy areas and stresses the value of online civic participation. Yet, there is a significant disconnection between federal ideals of engagement and the actual implementation of two-way participatory practices, with service delivery mechanisms again prioritised. This chapter suggests that greater online civic engagement may be achieved through a policy approach that combines national guidance and resources with local knowledge, while using policies to support ICTs and ICTs to support policy processes.

There are two common strategies for the development of e-government projects. One approach is demand based e-government initiatives having no national level centralized Enterprise Architecture and the other approach is the development of projects under the shadow of a predefined set of guidelines following a given Enterprise Architecture at the national level. It is similar to developing a demand based unplanned city development verses a master plan based development. Complex electronic service deliveries need allied and synchronized output of all the projects. Architectural approach provides guidelines for project planning to technical development. It aligns all the e-government projects with some standard principles. A National Enterprise Architecture based approach provides a number of benefits, including institutionalization of top level strategic planning, standardized development across all levels of e-government, sustainability of e-government projects when governments change, cost reduction by sharing resources and better return on investment. There are many enterprise architectures for e-government development. Different countries are experimenting with different enterprise architectures. In this chapter, e-government projects and their devolution is discussed using Zachman Framework, Reference Model for Open Distributed Processing (RM-ODP), A Reference Model for Collaboration Networks (ARCON), The Open Group Architectural Framework (TOGAF), and Federal Enterprise Architecture Framework (FEAF). It is recommended that architectural implementation should be aligned with governing structure of a country such as centralized, devolved and decentralized. However large governments may use a decentralized architecture and devolve it to its sub-nationals such as sate/provincial level and city level as per their political, fiscal and administrative needs.

This study analyzes the legal framework of e-taxation in the Turkish Republic. Tax service is commonly provided by using ICT in many countries. In e-government applications in Turkey, provision of e-tax service is one of the leading projects. Among the members of OECD, electronic tax return, payment systems and tax automation systems generated in this area have gained an increasing importance. Taxpayers fill the declarations electronically and also pay tax debts without going to the tax offices. E-taxation system is becoming widespread in Turkey. Implementation of the system in Turkey started in 1998 with VEDOP I and continued with 2004 VEDOP II and 2007 VEDOP III Projects. These applications are legislated by the Tax Procedure Law in Turkey. Thus, legal regulations on electronic recording are established on a legal basis. In this study, e-government tax applications in the Turkish Tax Law (e-tax return, e-books, e-signature, e-audit) and legal base of this application is examined. Information is given on how it is implemented by means of information technologies in Turkey. The main purpose of the study is to examine what legal regulations were enacted for registering and taxation in the use of information technologies and to determine the current situation in Turkey.

Section 3
E-Government Implementation: Governance and E-Inclusion

Recent World Bank study shows that a 10% increase in mobile phone subscribers is associated with a 0.8% increase in economic growth while 10% increase in high speed Internet connections is related to a 1.3% increase in economic growth. Development of ICT infrastructure attracts foreign direct investment, generates fiscal revenues and creates employment opportunities especially for youth and women. Political, Cultural, Socio-economic developmental and behavioral decisions today rests on the ability to access, gather, analyze and utilize information. These remarkable advancements in technology and understanding of how it affects growth highlight a strategic shift in the way ICT can influence development. The distribution of this tool of wealth creation and knowledge are highly unequal amongst countries of the Globe. At the current rate of technological advancement, such disparities in access to ICT related developments are large and likely to become larger in adoption amongst the countries around the Globe. As more of the services in an economy come online, those without access to this technological advancement will be marginalized. The ubiquitous presence of Internet has penetrated every aspect of daily life. This chapter discusses the role of e-Governance in citizen centric e-Government as well as the various issues and challenges of implementation of e-Governance in general. Last part of the chapter is about the e-Governance in Indian context. This chapter is likely to give the reader an overview of e-Governance and the related issues.

This chapter presents and discusses the application of an analytical framework for managing digital innovation initiatives in the public sector. The chapter positions e-Government and digital innovation initiatives in the public sector within the broader framework of e-Governance (i.e. governance aided by ICT). It first introduces the conceptual framework on which the discussion is based, and then proposes a higher order conceptualization of the relationship between e-Governance and its underpinning value drivers of performance, openness and inclusion. In particular, the analysis focuses on the role that these value drivers plays in the enactment of digital governance initiatives such as the ones related to open government and smart cities. To this end, the chapter discusses its application to initiatives carried out in Barcelona and Tallinn. A typology of e-Governance 'attitudes' is then identified to provide evidence of further specific interventions required for an appropriate management of similar initiatives in other countries. The chapter concludes by highlighting the policy implications for administrative reform and offering practical recommendations for implementing digital governance initiatives.

In this chapter, five case studies of the implementation of contact centers in Swedish municipalities are described and discussed with a focus on inclusive e-government. The research methods used are mainly qualitative interviews with different categories of municipal personnel and also with some citizens. The

Preface

Electronic Government, or E-Government, is about harnessing the information revolution to improve the efficiency of government processes and the lives of citizens. It aims at a citizen centred approach to governance through effective use of the Internet and Information and Communication Technologies (ICTs). E-Government promotes transparency and effectiveness of a government's processes as well as citizens' participation (e-participation) in the affairs of the government.

E-government projects are huge undertakings that require long term commitment as well as correct planning and availability of financial resources. World governments are in the process of achieving full e-government, however, they are at different stages of e-government adoption. Advanced nations are well on the way to achieving inclusive and integrated horizontal and vertical e-government, including two-way government-to-citizen (G2C) and government-to-government (G2G) interactions as well as provision of e-commerce by the industry. However, developing nations are lagging behind due to political, cultural, financial and other resources issues. Developing countries often start with a web portal providing one-way G2C information via a set of governmental websites and then develop individual nation-wide projects, one at a time and independent of each other. This is highly inefficient and often results in duplication, waste of resources and the 'reinvention of the wheel'. In the short term, a government portal is fine but otherwise a long term strategy needs to be in place that first determines the e-readiness of the nation (government and the citizens) and conducts a gap analysis. It then fills the gap to ensure that the required infrastructure, financial support, citizens' computing requirements, public affordability of the ICT, etc are all in place. While, at the same time, the plan ensures that the overall framework and appropriate methodologies are also determined, within which the various e-government projects will be conducted and e-services delivered.

BOOK OBJECTIVE

The current publication, *Developing E-Government Projects: Frameworks and Methodologies*, aims to serve as a reference text and presents frameworks, methodologies, policies, techniques and technologies as well as case studies. The objective is to understand the courses of actions and best practices that provide successful strategies towards appropriate policy, design, implementation and adoption of e-government projects as well as transparent e-governance. To this end, the present text provides reports and discussions on the following:

- Current research and new ideas
- Frameworks, policies, and strategies

- Novel practices and diffusion of innovation approaches
- Technologies, tools, information systems and platforms
- E-governance, e-inclusion and e-democracy
- Inherent issues, limitations and barriers
- Best practices and recommendations
- Case studies highlighting practical experiences.

TARGET AUDIENCE

Developing E-Government Projects: Frameworks and Methodologies is a reference text that is aimed at several groups of readers, including the following:

- University students, lecturers and researchers in the field of e-government
- Software engineer, information system specialists and practitioners of ICT
- Decision makers in the e-government-related departments in governments
- Project managers developing e-services and managing e-government projects.

BOOK ORGANISATION

Developing E-Government Projects: Frameworks and Methodologies is organised in four sections with a total of 17 chapters, authored by 25 experts from around the world, as follows:

- **Section 1:** E-Government Development: Methodologies and Approaches (Chapters 1 through 4)
- **Section 2:** E-Government Adoption: Frameworks and Policy (Chapters 5 through 8)
- **Section 3:** E-Government Implementation: Governance and E-Inclusion (Chapters 9 through 13)
- **Section 4:** E-Government Projects: Review and Assessment (Chapters 14 through 17).

CHAPTER DESCRIPTIONS

Detailed abstracts of the book chapters appear in the Detailed Table of Contents. Here, very brief summaries of chapters' content are presented.

Chapter 1, entitled *E-Government Systems Development Methodologies, Tools and Platforms*, is authored by Jean, Magda, and Adegboyega. It provides an overview of the methods, tools and platforms for software development processes for e-government systems and discusses the methodological approaches. Stages of growth models, agile software engineering and Semantic Web techniques are also presented in some detail and illustrated with real world case studies. Emphasis is on the analysis, design and implementation of e-government systems and e-services deploying Semantic Web ontology languages, database management systems and semantic query languages. Systems integration techniques are also reviewed and discussed.

Chapter 2 is entitled *E-Government for Social and Economic Development: Asymmetric Information, Institutionalization and Diffusion Challenges*. Developed by Bongani Ngwenya, it posits that by leveraging economic development, e-government initiatives can help to streamline government services to more social-based values of citizens' participation. The chapter draws on organizational decision-making research and presents findings of an exploratory research. It is suggested that the information asymmetry between citizens and government, asymmetry in institutionalization, and diffusion within developed and developing countries are widely attributed to socio-economic and political variations in developed and developing countries.

Chapter 3 is entitled *Decision Support Systems: An E-Government Strategy to Enhance Human Resources Output in Public Sector Organisations*. Authored by Bongani Ngwenya, it focuses on decision support systems (DSS) as a strategy to enhance human resources output in public sector organisations. The aim is to provide more efficient e-services to citizens and the business sector. Discussing the benefits of service efficiency and improved effectiveness of DSS, the chapter provides the basis for building an evaluation theory or a framework for assessing DSS adoption and exploitation in the context of public sector and services provision. Results of a study are presented to suggest the effectiveness of DSS with reference to e-Government strategies and planning.

Chapter 4 is entitled, *Adopting E-Mailing System Technology: Challenges Confronting Government Institutions in Jordan*. Authored by Ahed Al-Haraizah, this chapter draws on the ECTA and TAM technologies to examine Jordanian government employees' attitudes towards adoption and use of e-mailing system. It provides an overview of the current situation and discussing the various influencing issues, the chapter validates the relationships between the relevant factors that drive the acceptance of such innovations. Additional factors such as trust, cultural beliefs and sociology of technology are also taken into account. The survey based approach also identifies ways of assisting employees to make use of technologies more effectively.

Chapter 5 is entitled *E-Government Concept: A Holistic and Eclectic Framework*. Authors, Delfina and Luis look at the many definitions and concepts relating to e-government and develop a holistic view. The chapter aims to contribute to the clarification of such concepts as well as to the way in which many of the different concepts are related. The framework put forward in the chapter is based on a generic model of a democratic government system. Building on that model, the authors identify and discuss *six spaces of IT,* where Information Technologies can be usefully deployed. The authors suggest that the use of IT in those *spaces* contributes to the overall development of a country's e-government reality and e-governance maturity.

Chapter 6 is written by Julie Freeman. Entitled *Evolving Local E-Government: A Cohesive Policy Approach*, it discusses Australian e-government initiatives. The chapter suggest that local governments can provide a useful context for online civic participation and engagement; however, the author maintains that local initiatives are often developed on an ad hoc basis and largely limited to the provision of one-way G2C information and service delivery. Discussing participatory e-government practices, the chapter concludes that online civic engagement may be more effectively achieved through a policy approach that combines national guidance and resources with local knowledge, while using policies to support ICTs and using ICTs to support policy processes.

Chapter 7, entitled *Enterprise Architectures for E-Government Development*, authored by Kashif, Shafay and Mian, looks at the Architectural approaches that provide guidelines for planning and technical development of complex projects. The chapter discusses the e-government projects and their devolution using well known architectural approaches such as: Zachman Framework, Reference Model for Open Distributed Processing (RM-ODP), Reference Model for Collaboration Networks (ARCON), TOGAF, and Federal Enterprise Architecture Framework. It is suggested that governments may usefully employ decentralized architectures and devolve them to provincial/city levels as per their political, fiscal and administrative needs and capacity.

Chapter 8 by Güneş Çetin Gerger is entitled, *Legal Framework for the E-Taxation in Turkey*. It discusses the existing legal framework for the e-taxation system in the Turkish Republic. The e-Tax project in Turkey was initiated in 1998 with subsequent updates in 2004 and 2007. The e-Tax applications are now legislated by the Tax Procedure Law, suggesting that legal regulations on electronic recording are established on a legal framework. The author examines the e-Tax applications to discuss: e-tax return, e-books, e-signature, e-audit as well as the legal basis for such applications. The chapter aims to examine the legal regulations that formed the basis for the said e-Tax e-services. The authors also discuss the legal framework for the use of ICTs.

Chapter 9 is entitled, *Role of E-Governance in Citizen Centric E-Government*. Developed by Ganesh Chandra Deka, it discusses the importance of three core elements viz e-Democracy, Ethics in Governance and e-Transparency as well as the effective role of ICT for the inclusion of these in the implementation of citizen centric e-governance. Additionally, the chapter introduces m-Governance (Mobile Governance) in relation to e-governance in the Indian context and discusses the G-Cloud project of the India government. Discussing the importance of standardization, the chapter also highlights the challenges of developing e-government projects and e-inclusion and presents solutions and recommendations.

Chapter 10 is developed by Gianluca and Gianluigi. Entitled, *Managing E-Governance: A Framework for Analysis and Planning*, the chapter looks at the management of e-governance and discusses an analytical framework for managing digital innovation initiatives in the public sector within the broader framework of e-Governance. It proposes a higher order conceptualization of the relationship between e-Governance and its underpinning value drivers of performance, openness and inclusion. The analysis focuses on the role of these value drivers in the enactment of digital governance initiatives in Barcelona and Tallinn in Spain. The chapter highlights the policy implications for administrative reforms and offers recommendations for implementing digital governance.

Chapter 11 is entitled *Towards Inclusive E-Government: The Development of Municipal Contact Centers in Sweden* and authored by Irene and Kerstin. Discussing the implementation of contact centers in Swedish municipalities, the chapter presents five case studies that focus on inclusive e-government. The authors conduct qualitative interviews with municipal personnel as well as citizens and conclude that implementation of contact centers contribute to increased accessibility of municipal e-services. The study also indicates that development towards increased equal treatment of citizens is highly correlated with the digital divide that exists and that implementation of municipal contact centers provides a useful step towards inclusive e-government.

Chapter 12 is authored by Mary and Sara. Entitled, *Malaysia's Internet Governance Dilemma*, it assesses the democratic, business and political challenges of Internet governance. The chapter presents the results of a study where media, business and government personnel were interviewed to assess their reactions to the explosion of diversity of critical public opinion that subsequently resulted in much tighter control of Internet usage by the government of Malaysia. The chapter concludes that support for the Internet to remain uncensored remains strong in Malaysia's professional elites, but this is primarily for economic and pragmatic, rather than democratic reasons. The authors also suggest solutions to the current situation in Malaysia.

Chapter 13 is entitled *Leveraging the Service Paradigm for Producing Next Generation E-Governance Applications* and authored by Pethuru Raj. The chapter focuses on service and cloud technologies as major drivers for new-generation digital governance. Suggestion is that *services* can stimulate the process-centric approach for application development and that programming models and mechanisms (agile, aspect, component, composite) are also gelling with the service paradigm in articulating and actuating dynamic, smart and sophisticated systems. The author discusses the service-oriented technology for designing, developing, deploying and delivering applications for many of the tasks associated with digitally inspired e-governance.

Chapter 14, developed by Haroula N. Delopoulos, is entitled *Evaluation and Metrics of E-Government: From eEurope2002 to Digital Agenda 2020*. It discusses the EU methodologies used for the evaluation of e-government related plans including: Action Plan 2002, Action Plan 2005, the Strategic Framework i2010 and the Digital Agenda 2020. The chapter highlights differences and similarities between these plans, suggesting that Europe should not focus mainly on the supply side (track availability and sophistication) but should also investigate indicators that might directly affect the adoption of eGovernment. The author also evaluates whether or not some of the targets of Digital Agenda 2020 will be accomplished by stated 2015.

Chapter 15 is authored by Sujana Adapa and entitled *E-Services Efficiency of Government Organizations in Asia*. It discusses the importance and benefits of ICTs for e-government and the business sector. Presenting the theoretical foundations, the chapter suggests the importance of inclusion and participation of various stakeholders. Case studies are provided to illustrate the effective planning and implementation of e-government-based strategies, especially with respect to e- services focusing on nine Asian countries. Factors that promote and hinder the e-services delivery are also discussed. The chapter also provides a comparison of how e-government is adopted in newly industrialized countries versus the developing nations.

Chapter 16 is written by Harekrishna Misra. Entitled, *E-Governance Projects for E-Inclusion in India: An Architectural Assessment Framework*, the chapter focuses on e-inclusion. In this chapter, e-governance architectural issues are discussed with three cases drawn from Indian scenarios. A conceptual framework is presented that examines the possibilities of architectural convergence for national level e-governance services with e-inclusion as a core attribute and assesses its validity using three case studies belonging to the Mission Mode Project (MMP), The studies refer to Watershed Project Initiatives (WPI), Mahatma Gandhi National Rural Employment Guaranty Scheme (MGNREGS) and National e-Governance Plan (NeGP).

Chapter 17 entitled *Rhetoric vs. Realities in Implementation of E-Government Master Plan in Nepal* is authored by Kiran and Almas. It discusses different facets of implementation of e-government in Nepal with a specific focus on the "e-government Master Plan". Core elements of e-government initiatives, namely infrastructure, human resources, institutions, and policy and legal aspects are looked into and considered in relation to Heeks's e-government success/failure model in terms of information, technology, process, objectives, values, staffing, skills, management systems, structures and resources. The authors also analyze the constraints in e-government implementation with respect to infrastructure, human resources, institutions, and policy and legal aspects.

Zaigham Mahmood
University of Derby, UK & North West University, South Africa

Acknowledgment

The editor acknowledges the support and efforts of a number of colleagues. First and foremost, I would like to thank the contributors to this book: the 25 authors and co-authors, from academia as well as industry from around the world that collectively developed and submitted a total of 17 chapters. Without their efforts in developing quality chapters conforming to the required guidelines and meeting often the strict deadlines, this text would not have been possible. Their names and expertise are listed in a separate section in this book.

Secondly, my grateful thanks are due to the members of the advisory and editorial board of this book who willingly volunteered their time in reviewing the book chapters and providing further advisory and editorial support. Their names and affiliations also appear in a separate section in this book.

Finally, I would like to thank members of my immediate family – Rehana, Zoya, Imran, Hanya and Ozair – for their encouragement and moral support – and for happily allowing me time to devote to the development of this 2nd in a series of reference books on electronic government. Initially, they thought I was developing yet another book on Cloud Computing but now they know better.

Thank you all.

Zaigham Mahmood
University of Derby, UK & North West University, South Africa

Section 1

E-Government Development: Methodologies and Approaches

Chapter 1
E-Government Systems Development Methodologies, Tools and Platforms

Jean Vincent Fonou-Dombeu
Vaal University of Technology, South Africa

Magda Huisman
North-West University, South Africa

Adegboyega Ojo
United Nations University International Institute for Software Technology, China

ABSTRACT

The analysis of e-government initiatives of various countries shows that the development and deployment of e-government systems for effective online service delivery to citizens remain a key priority in e-government development. On the other hand, given the complex nature of the public administration system with several departments and agencies, thousands of legislations and operating procedures, added to the high number of technologies needed for developing e-government systems, there is a need to learn about the software development practices in e-government. This chapter provides an overview of the methodologies, tools and platforms for software development processes of e-government systems. Firstly, the state-of-the-art software development practices in e-government are reviewed. Secondly, the methodological approaches employed for developing e-government systems including stage of growth models, agile software engineering and Semantic Web techniques are presented and illustrated with real world case studies for their application in e-government projects. Thirdly, the tools and platforms used for the analysis, design, implementation and deployment of e-government systems including traditional software engineering tools and platforms, Semantic Web ontology languages and platforms, database management systems and semantic query languages are analysed and discussed in detail. Finally, the state-of-the-art of e-government systems integration techniques are reviewed and discussed.

DOI: 10.4018/978-1-4666-4245-4.ch001

INTRODUCTION

An analysis of e-government initiatives of countries with successful e-government implementation such as Australia (Teicher & Dow, 2002), Singapore (Devadoss et al., 2003), Taiwan (Sang et al., 2005) and the United Kingdom (Beynon-Davies, 2005), shows that the development and deployment of e-government systems for effective online service delivery to citizens remain a key priority in e-government development. On the other hand, given the complex nature of the public administration system with several departments and agencies, thousands of legislations and operating procedures, added to the high number of technologies needed for developing e-government systems, there is a need to learn about the software development practices in e-government.

The current trends in e-government software systems development is geared towards the building of a single government web portal also called one-stop e-government portal (Wimmer, 2002). One-stop portals enable seamless citizens' access to relevant government services, without visiting each autonomous website of government departments and agencies to access these services. In other words, the building of a one-stop portal requires e-government services across all government departments and agencies to be re-engineered and integrated at a single access point. Then, when citizens request a service at the access point, all the required information is automatically gathered from various government entities integrated through the access point, to accomplish the requested service. This is transparent to the user (citizen) as he/she is not aware of the back-office operations such as services composition, merging, etc. that are performed to satisfy his/her request. Several one-stop e-government solutions have been proposed in the literature (Chatzidimitriou & Koumpis, 2008; Gouscos et al., 2002; Feldkamp et al., 2008). Chatzidimitriou and Koumpis (2008) present a one-stop e-government solution based on life-events or citizen's needs. The architecture for one-stop e-government services delivery is presented in Gouscos et al. (2002), whereas, the Switzerland one-stop e-government model is described by Feldkamp et al. (2008). The main challenge in building an efficient and interactive one-stop portal is the ability to integrate and interoperate various heterogeneous systems from different government departments and agencies. From the software development perspective, Web service standards and semantic technologies (Muthaiyah & Kerschberg, 2008) are currently employed to address these issues. At present, a number of countries have one-stop e-government portals.

E-government development broadly requires: (1) a legal framework that regulates the process, (2) the infrastructure and technologies for developing and deploying real world e-government applications for online service delivery to citizens, businesses and organizations, and (3) the readiness of citizens to embark into e-government. Thus presented, e-government development in a given country is a huge and complex task. To address this complexity, over the years, many companies and organizations (Deloitte & Touche, 2001; United Nations, 2003) have developed maturity or stage of growth models which provide a stepwise manner for adopting e-government through iterative stages. Meanwhile, traditional software engineering methodologies including structured analysis and design, object oriented and agile methods have been applied to develop e-government systems worldwide. And more recently semantic web technologies have emerged as useful tools for developing e-government software systems (Muthaiyah & Kerschberg, 2008). The following sections provide details on how the abovementioned methodologies and technologies have been used in e-government, the tools and platforms employed, as well as, sample case studies of their applications in different countries around the world.

METHODOLOGIES FOR E-GOVERNMENT SYSTEMS DEVELOPMENT

Methodologies Based on Maturity or Stages of Growth Models

Considerable research has been conducted by public administrators for e-government planning and implementation. They propose different stages for e-government development in maturity models or stage of growth models. A maturity model or stage of growth model is designed as a sequence of stages of e-government growth and constitutes a guiding and benchmarking tool for e-government planning and development. Each maturity model stage prescribes a list of web features that are needed online or mechanisms required to create changes at that particular stage of e-government development. Examples of existing maturity models are provided in Table 1. These maturity models are of three to six stages each; a summary of their stages is provided in Figure 1.

Examples of maturity models with four stages are presented in Layne and Lee (2001) and West (2004). The Layne and Lee (2001) model stages are cataloguing, transaction, vertical integration and horizontal integration. Another maturity model with nine stages namely: strategy development, building infrastructure, building trust, making portal, initial interaction and stimulation, prototyping, enrichment, integration and ICT industry development is proposed by Zarei et al. (2008). A similar work is presented in Bri (2009) in a stage of growth model with seventh stages namely legislative, structure and process, ICT, consolidated customer view, data mining and knowledge management, process improvement and flexible process, integral system and system dynamics. An example of e-government initiative that has used the Layne and Lee (2001) model is the Integrated Acquisition Environment (IAE) e-government project in the US (Sang et al. 2005).

Incremental and Iterative Methods

This category of e-government development methodologies includes software development methodologies such as the structured analysis and design, object-oriented and agile methods. This section presents some research and projects that have employed traditional software engineering techniques in e-government projects.

The Interoperability Framework (IF) of the Hong Kong Government is presented by Lee et al. (2009). The IF provides system analysts and developers with an integrated schema design methodology which covers modeling techniques including business process modeling, data modeling and XML schema definition. The technical specifications of the IF recommend Web Service Standards for the functional integration of applications. Lee et al. (2009) reported that many e-government projects have already applied the IF and that the Macao e-government project was in the process of adopting the IF.

Another e-government development experience from the Dubai Municipality (DM) is presented by Arif (2008). The e-government development team from the IT department of

Table 1. Examples of Maturity or Stage of Growth Models

Maturity Models	Number of Stages
Howard (2001)	3
World Bank (2003)	3
Layne & Lee (2001)	4
Baum & Maio (2000)	4
Chandler & Emanuel (2002)	4
West (2004)	4
United Nations (2003)	5
Hiller & Blanger (2001)	5
Moon (2002)	5
Asia Pacific (2004)	6
Deloitte & Touche (2001)	6

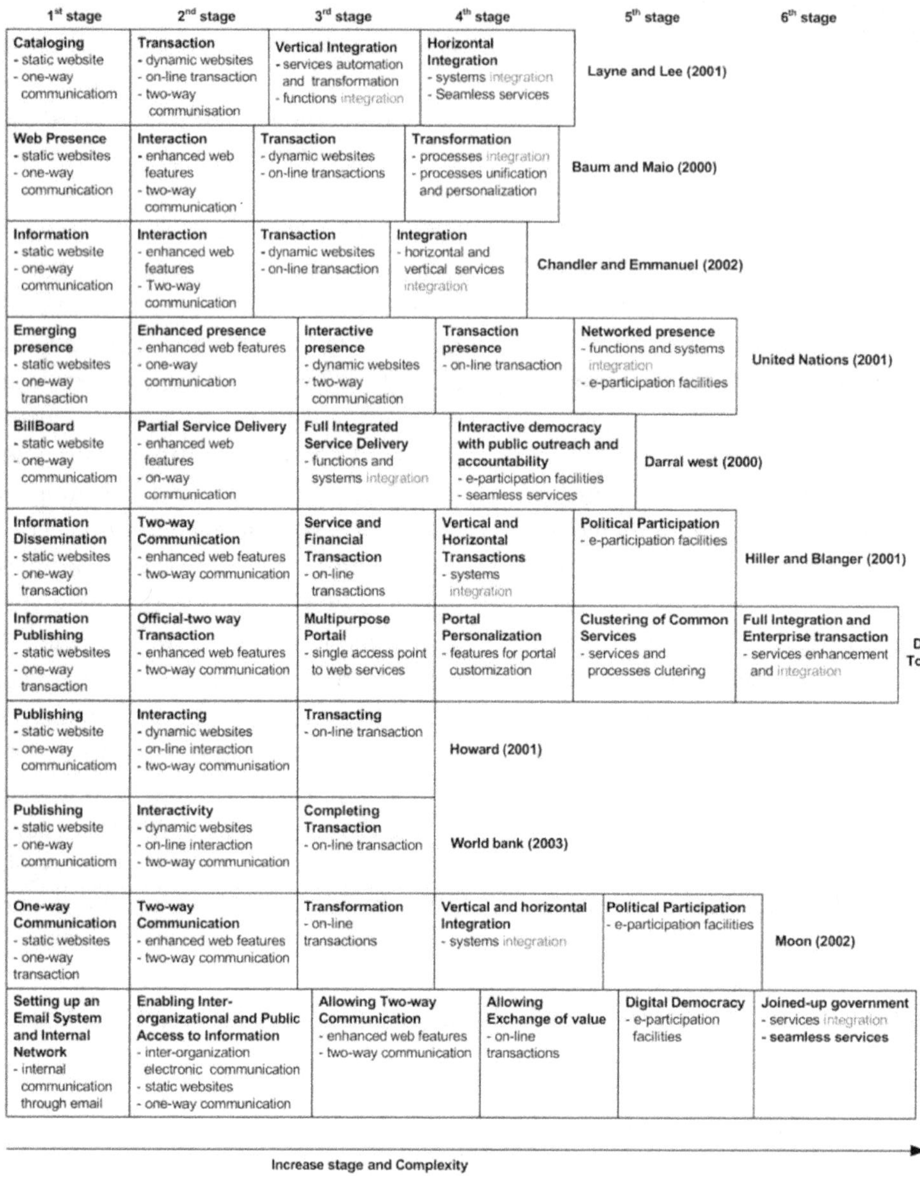

Figure 1. Summary of eleven existing e-government maturity models

the DM is composed of four major role players, namely: service custodian, business analysts, system analysts and programmers. The service custodian manages the entire process of converting a traditional DM service into an online service and oversees the maintenance of the online service after implementation. The business analysts are in charge of documenting the process flow of a service prior to system design and implementation in collaboration with the relevant department within the municipality. After documenting the process flow of a service, system analysts are responsible for designing the system; they create the data flow diagrams, entity relationship diagrams and UML diagrams. The implementation or coding of the system is carried out by the programmers after the design. Programmers also take care of any required modification post-implementation. Further, one of the functions of the system development section of the IT department of the DM is to prepare and determine the technical criteria and standards for the development of systems, databases and programming languages (Arif, 2008).

A well formalized framework for e-government development based on software engineering techniques is proposed by the e-government research team at the Centre of Electronic Government of the United Nations University in China (Janowski et al., 2007). Janowski et al. (2007) view an e-government project as an ensemble of activities: survey, training and development, dissemination, and research tasks. The development activity is carried out using a waterfall software development approach with four steps namely: requirements, modeling, design, and implementation.

Salhofer and Ferbas (2007) present the methodological approach they have used during the development of the city of Graz's e-government platform in Austria. At the beginning of the project, the most important goals, requirements and constraints were defined including intensive usage of open source software and integration of existing and upcoming standards in the e-government field. Thereafter, a spiral software engineering process model, adopted from Barry Boehms (Salhofer & Ferbas, 2007) was chosen for the iterative development of the e-government platform.

The experience of the Greek Ministry of Finance's e-services lifecycle is presented in Vassilakis et al. (2002). The authors describe how a software engineering approach was used to develop the electronic tax return system of the Ministry. The lifecycle of the project was comprised of the following steps: requirements analysis, design, implementation, and maintenance (Vassilakis et al., 2002).

The advantages of software engineering techniques is that they provide a large range of tools and mechanisms for analyzing and describing the requirements of the complex public administration systems and provides platforms for implementing and deploying web-based e-government applications.

Semantic Based Methods

During the past few years, Semantic Web technologies based on ontology have attracted e-government developers. A plethora of semantic e-government domain specific ontology models have been developed to describe and specify various aspects of e-government services delivery (government documents, laws and regulations, government structures and processes, life events of citizens with government, software processes, etc.); with ontology and Semantic Web ontology languages and platforms, it is possible to describe and specify e-services in such a way that they can be easily composed, mapped, matched and merged and facilitate their semantic integration and interoperability.

An example of an ontology that has been developed to address the interoperability problem in e-government is the Federal Enterprise Architecture Reference Model Ontology (FEA-RMO) presented in Allemang et al. (2004). The FEA-RMO ontology is a set of 5 modules, namely, Performance, Business, Services, Technology and Data reference models ontologies; these ontologies were developed to enable the interoperability of the US government's federal agencies; they basically provide common reference models for modelling federal agencies' business processes, thereby, supporting their interoperability.

Other examples of semantic-driven e-government programmes that have employed ontologies include: the Italian e-government architecture (Baldoni et al., 2007), the Estonian semantic interoperability architecture (Luts, 2004) and the Palestinian interoperability framework (Jarrar et al., 2011). The Italian e-government architecture (Baldoni et al., 2007) includes an ontologies repository, which is composed of a set of ontologies and schemas that describe the services and information semantics. The ontology component of the Estonian semantic interoperability architecture (Luts, 2004) is a set of domain ontologies that describe objects including web service operations, business processes and data structure. The Palestine interoperability framework (Jarrar et al., 2011) includes a government ontology formed of a set of 15 domain ontologies which describe data concepts, services and processes of the Palestine government.

Various aspects of e-government have been modeled in academic research studies using ontologies. Sanati and Lu (2009) use life-event ontology to model the e-services integration processes. In Chen et al. (2008), a framework for services integration based on specific ontologies is proposed, whereas, Gugliotta et al. (2005) established the mapping of various ontologies to a predefined e-government system reference model, with the purpose of achieving services integration and interoperability for one-stop portals. The issue of services interoperability is also addressed in Xiao et al. (2007), Sabucedo and Rifon (2006), and Sabucedo et al. (2010), with e-government specific ontology models. Another relevant literature by Puustjarvi (2006) proposes a process-document ontology model for the business process modeling in e-government. Fonou-Dombeu and Huisman (2012) proposed an ontology for e-government monitoring of development projects in Sub-Saharan Africa and the developing countries at large.

Several European based e-government projects employ ontologies to describe and specify the public administration domain as well as the e-government services delivery processes. Examples of these projects include:

- SmartGov (Fraser et al., 2003),
- OntoGov (Apostolou et al., 2005a; 2005b),
- TerreGov (Barthes & Moulin, 2005),
- Reimdoc (Ortiz-Rodriguez & Villazon-Terrazas, 2006),
- OneStopGov (Todorovski et al., 2007),
- SAKE (Butka et al., 2006),
- Estrella (Breuker et al., 2006),
- SemanticGov (Goudos et al., 2006; 2007) and
- Access-eGov (Hreno et al., 2011).

The OneStopGov project uses life-event ontology to model public services (Todorovski et al., 2006) while the issue of composition, re-configuration and evaluation of e-services is addressed in the OntoGov project (Apostolou et al., 2005a; 2005b) with various kinds of ontologies. The real-estate transactions are described with a set of ontologies in the Reimdoc project (Ortiz-Rodriguez & Villazon-Terrazas, 2006). Another set of ontologies is used in the SAKE project (Butka et al., 2006) to model the public administration workflow and business processes, and to describe the structure of information or metadata as well as the concepts related to the performance evaluation of the public administration's processes. The Government Enterprise Architecture (GEA) ontology (Goudos et al., 2007), created from the GEA object model (Peristeras & Tarabanis, 2006), is developed in the SemanticGov project to model the public administration semantic as well as the overall e-government domain; the reference ontology is also used to enable the automatically mapping of citizens' needs to suitable public services. The SmartGov project (Fraser et al., 2003) presents the e-government services ontology that models the business process and social aspects of e-government services delivery. Another interesting work is done in the Estrella project (Breuker et al., 2006) where the Legal Knowledge Interchange Format (LKIF) core ontology is built to describe basic legal concepts; aiming at supporting the translation, alignment and harmonization between national jurisdictions of European countries. The Access-eGov (Hreno et al., 2001) project uses a set of ontologies to model the e-services integration process. Semantic interoperability solutions for local governments are proposed in the TerreGov (Barthes & Moulin, 2005) project with a set of ontologies; these ontologies are used to describe services and documents, and enable the semantic Web services orchestration and discovery processes.

Perspective of Mixed Methods

The maturity models as presented above provide various stages for e-government development as well as web features or levels of sophistication of e-government systems at each stage of development. However, the specification of the maturity models' stages lack design guidelines and tools for the effective design and implementation of the prescribed web features. In the software engineering and Semantic Web domains, e-government development is not done according to prescribed stages or phases; which might make it extremely difficult to plan and implement a semantic-driven e-government project with these techniques, given the complex nature of the public administration system with several departments and agencies, thousands of legislations and operating procedures, added to the high number of technologies needed. Finally, Fonou-Dombeu and Huisman (2012) have argued that few guidelines are provided in the semantic based e-government researches and projects to enable the repeatability of the proposed ontology based solutions in other e-government projects.

To address the aforementioned challenges, Fonou-Dombeu and Huisman (2012) have amalgamated the methodological features from the maturity models, software engineering and Semantic Web domains to design and specify a semantic-driven methodology framework for e-government systems development. Figure 2 depicts the architecture of the proposed semantic-driven e-government development methodology framework; it displays and overlay of features from maturity models (top layer), traditional software engineering (middle layer) and semantic knowledge representation (bottom layer) domains.

In a software engineering perspective, e-government systems implementation entails gathering the requirements of the government service to be delivered online to citizens, design, implement, and deploy the e-service on the Web for online interaction with citizens; these processes could be carried out iteratively and incrementally with state-of-the-art software engineer-

Figure 2. The proposed three phase e-government development framework aligning the united nation maturity model stages with ontologies

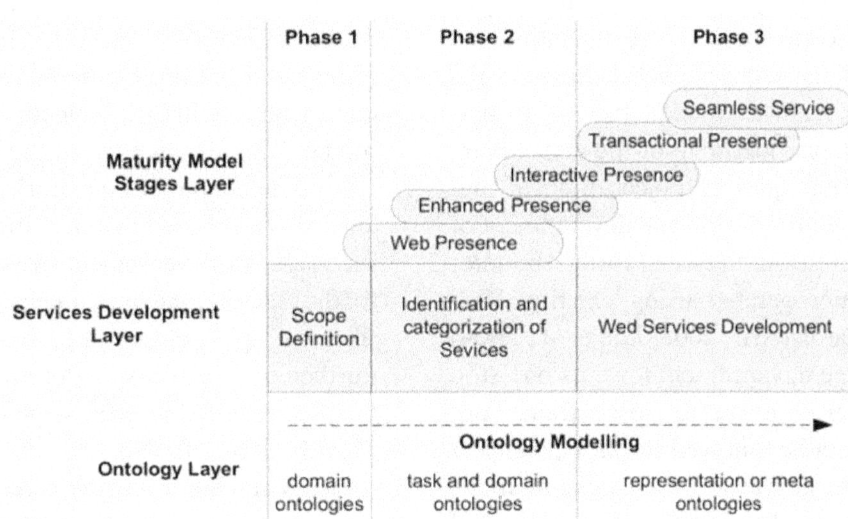

ing techniques. In view of the complexity of the public administration system, e-government implementation as described above requires (1), mechanisms for the planning and implementation of e-services at various stages or phases of e-government development, (2), state-of-the-art software engineering techniques and platforms for the design and implementation of e-services, as well as (3), emerging technologies as the Semantic Web technologies which have potential to facilitate the integration and interoperability of e-services towards one-stop e-government (Muthaiyah & Kerschberg, 2008). These three requirements are provided in the proposed methodology framework in Figure 2. The framework in Figure 2 is composed of three layers namely maturity model stages layer (MMSL), services development layer (SDL) and ontology layer (OL). The MMSL provides various stages for e-government development; each stage prescribes the web features that should be implemented and launch on the web site of the government department or agency for online interaction with citizens. The stages are complemented with software engineering and semantic-based tools and techniques at various phases of the framework to enable the effective design, implementation and deployment of the prescribed web features of maturity models. At each phase of the framework, the SDL and OL provides system analysis and design techniques as well as platforms for the implementation and deployment of the required web features at the corresponding maturity model stage(s). In particular, the SDL provides state-of-the-art software engineering techniques as object-oriented and agile methods for the design and development of e-services; these e-services can further be integrated and interoperated using existing Web services standards (Arif, 2008; Lee et al., 2009) and promote the advancement towards one-stop portals. Furthermore, the proposed framework phases might not be followed chronologically or in a linear order in practice, then, agile methods at SDL provide mechanisms for the iterative and incremental development of e-services through a continuous review of e-services requirements and prototyping to enable the quick development of required e-services (Greg et al., 2006). The OL provides various ontology models that capture at each phase of the framework the semantic content of e-services under development; the resulting e-services ontology models are implemented in Semantic Web ontology languages such as XML, Resource Description Framework (RDF) and/or Web Ontology Language (OWL) with Semantic Web platforms to enable their easy composition, matching, mapping and merging and facilitate their integration and interoperability towards one-stop e-government.

As shown in Figure 2, the service development layer provides the names of the framework phases: scope definition, identification and categorization of services, and web services development. It represents the process of e-services development, from the requirements of a government's business domain to the effective e-services implementation. Figure 3 depicts the flowchart of the business process model of the proposed framework in Figure 2; it describes the incremental and iterative process for realizing the web features prescribed by the maturity models stages, at each phase of e-government implementation. Table 2 describes the variables used in the flowchart.

The incremental and iterative process in Figure 3 follows the agile software development paradigm (Greg et al., 2006; Clutterbuck et al., 2009); it commences with the selection of a maturity model. This means that, at the beginning of an e-government project, a maturity model has to be chosen. The chosen maturity model will provide the stages of development as well as guidelines for the planning and implementation of the system from a simple web presence to a one-stop portal. Further, each maturity model will provide the web features required at each stage of e-government growth. After having chosen the appropriate maturity model, its stages need to be aligned to the framework as described later in this study.

Figure 3. Flowchart of the Business Process Model of the Methodology Framework

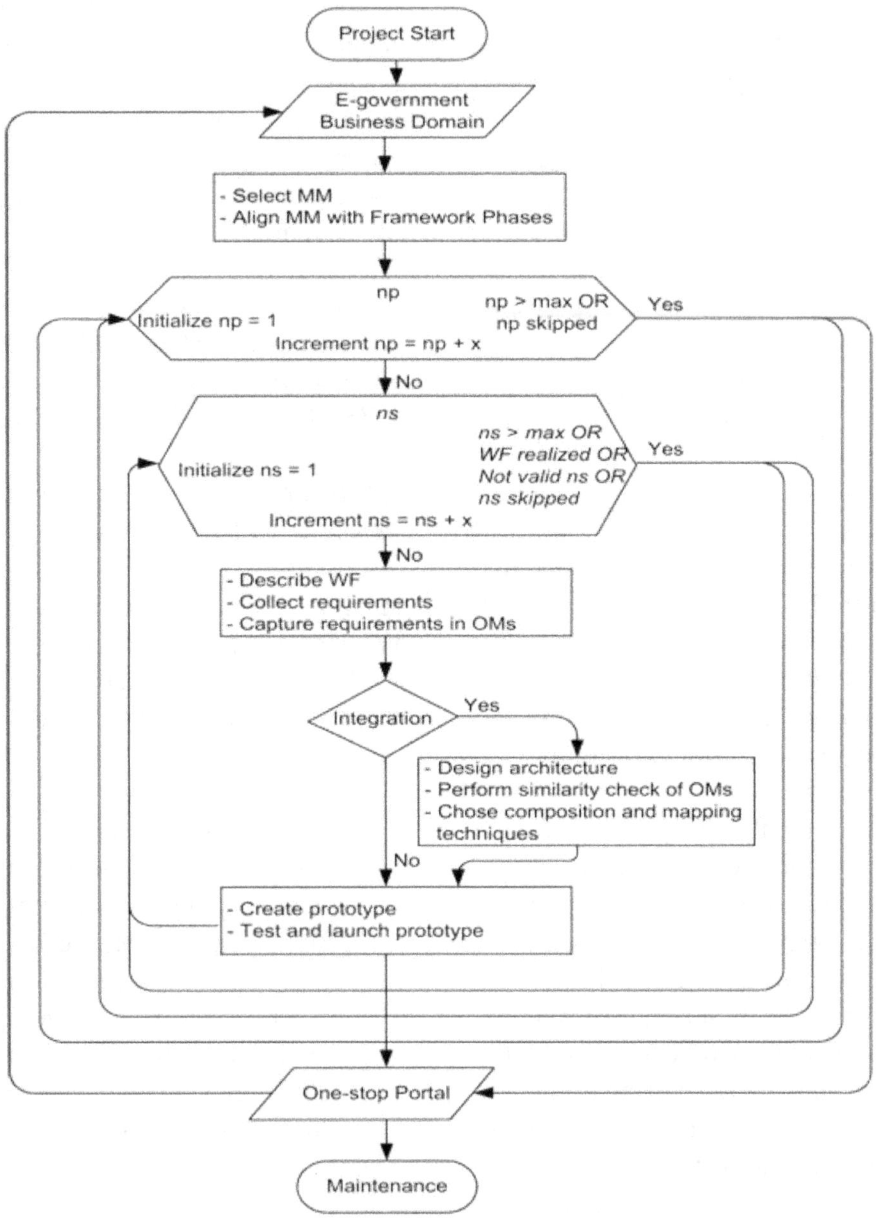

Thereafter, the iteration starts with the first phase of e-services development (see the outer loop in Figure 3).

At each phase of development, an iterative process is performed (see the inner loop in Figure 3) to realize and launch the web features required by the maturity model stages aligned to the corresponding phase of the methodology framework; at each iteration of the process (see the inner loop in Figure 3), the web feature under development should be described, its requirements collected in consultation with end-users who are the citizens and civil servants, and its semantic content captured with the prescribed semantic ontology models. Thereafter, if an integration is needed i.e. a government web portal exists and

Table 2. Variables of the Business Process Model Algorithm

Variables	Description
np	Number of framework phases (1 to 3)
ns	Maturity model's number of stages
max	Maximum number of phases or stages
WF	Web features
MM	Maturity model
OM	Ontology model
x	Pace of increment

the e-service being developed is to be integrated with the components of this existing system, the architecture of the integration must be designed, a similarity check of the e-services ontology models (those of the current system and the new e-service) performed and the mechanisms and techniques (composition, mapping, merging, etc.) for the integration chosen.

In all the cases (whether integration is needed or not), a prototype has to be developed, tested and launched onto the government web portal or the resulting prototype from the previous iteration has to be improved and tested. The iterative process is performed until the required web features are realized at that particular phase, or the required web features are to be completed in the next phase of the framework as shown in Figure 2 with the United Nations maturity model stages. After all the web features or changes required by the maturity model stages aligned to the current methodology framework phase have been realized, the iterative process continues to the next phase of the framework.

The requirements of the e-government business domain are revisited during iterations (See the inner loop in Figure 3) to ensure that the prototype systems developed meet the requirements of users who are the citizens and civil servants. The process is repeated until all the web features or changes prescribed by the maturity model are realized i.e. until a complete one-stop portal is implemented. The phases of the framework might not be followed in a linear order in practice; then, the business process model in Figure 3 allows a direct selection of a particular phase in order to implement and launch a desired web feature on the government web portal.

TOOLS AND PLATFORMS FOR E-GOVERNMENT SYSTEMS DEVELOPMENT

Software Engineering Tools and Platforms

A large range of software engineering tools, technologies and platforms are currently utilized to model, design and implement e-government systems. They mainly serve the following purposes:

- **Workflow Management:** Concerns technologies that support the reengineering, modelling, implementation and automation of public administration operations and processes (Mahapatra et al., 2008). Two workflow management systems are widely used in e-government development including: Workflow Management Coalition (WfMC) and Java Business Process Management (jBPM).
- **Web Services Development:** Web services are software components that are developed to establish communication between e-government systems and enable their interoperability. Three technologies are key in Web services development (Bouguettaya et al., 2006): Web Service Description Language (WSDL), Simple Object Architecture Protocol (SOAP) and Unified Description, Discovery and Integration (UDDI).

- **Document Management:** Entails creating, capturing, modifying, storing and propagating public administration's electronic documents. These operations are achieved with Document Management Systems (DMS). The widely used DMS include: Jakarta Slide and Subversion (Kunis et al., 2007).

The complete implementation and deployment of the aforementioned e-government systems workflows, web services and operations is achieved with programming platforms including: Java EE/J2EE, .NET, Apache and Lotus Notes.

Semantic Web Ontology Languages and Platforms

The Semantic Web domain provides various languages for the formal representation and description of e-government service workflow processes, Web services operations and documents processing using ontologies; they include Extensible Markup Language (XML), Resource Description Framework (RDF), DARPA Agent Markup Language (DAML), and OWL (Laclavik, 2005). OWL is the most widely used of these languages because of its high expressive power and the fact that it is the W3C standard ontology language for the Semantic Web (Singh & Malik, 2008). Several software tools are also used for ontology edition including WebODE, OntoEdit, KAON1, and Protégé (Calero et al., 2006). Ontology developers prefer Protégé for its ease of use and its abstraction capabilities; it has a graphical user interface which enables ontology developers to concentrate on conceptual modeling without any knowledge of the syntax of the output language (Singh & Malik, 2008). Furthermore, Protégé is open-source software which is downloadable from the Stanford Medical Informatics website. OWL is a common language employed for semantic knowledge representation in e-government. In particular, OWL ontologies allow the composition (Apostolou et al., 2005a; Sabucedo et al., 2010), searching, matching, mapping and merging (Apostolou et al., 2005b; Sanati & Lu, 2009) of e-government services and facilitate their integration (Apostolou et al., 2005a; 2005b; Salhofer et al., 2009), maintenance (Apostolou et al., 2005a) and interoperability (Xiao et al., 2007; Muthaiyah & Kerschberg, 2008; Sanati & Lu, 2009; Sabucedo et al., 2010).

Database Management Systems

As in any Information System, efficient, stable and permanent storage of information is of prime importance in e-government systems. Countries around the world store their e-government information at centre points namely registries/repositories and data warehouses (Sourouni et al., 2008; Hu, 2010; Liu & Luo, 2010; Bhanti et al., 2011). A repository is viewed as a centre location where all government data are stored and distributed amongst e-government systems. Government information may be partitioned and stored in separated data repositories, which constitutes a data warehouse. A data warehouse is composed of several physical data repositories; each of the repositories can be physically distributed on different servers and geographically in different places (Liu & Luo, 2010). The main purpose of a data warehouse is to serve as a central reporting and data distribution environment for e-government systems (Bhanti et al., 2011).

The e-government registries and data warehouses are built on the basis of traditional Database Management Systems (DBMS) such as Oracle, SQL Server, MySQL, etc. Bhanti et al. (2011) proposed data warehouse architecture for e-government applications in the higher education system in India. Although the authors did not mention any specific DBMS that may be used in such data warehouse architecture, they advised that any traditional DMBS may be suitable for the logical database design. Another architecture for a data warehouse solution for e-government is proposed in Liu and Luo (2010); the authors used an ensemble of technologies, applications and practices which provide facilities for integrating, analysing and presenting large amounts of data to build a data warehouse for e-government; the DBMS employed are MySQL and PostgreSQL, respectively. Hu (2010) describes the technologies they propose for the building of a data center based on data warehouse technology, for e-government in Nanhai city in China; the DBMS advised by the author included server databases, namely, Microsoft SQL Server, Oracle and IBM DB2. The specification of the ontology-driven knowledge-based registry/repository developed within the Interoperability Framework of the Greek government is presented in (Sourouni et al., 2008); the DBMS used in the development of the registry was Microsoft SQL Server 2005.

Semantic Query Languages and Mechanisms

Developing e-government systems using semantic technologies consists of modelling and specifying the public administration system, the services (tax return, social grants, etc.) that it delivers to the public (citizens, businesses, etc.) and the services delivery processes, using ontologies. In its simple representation, ontology is a graph where the vertices are objects, concepts, and entities of the domain and the edges are lines interconnecting pairs of vertices and representing the relationships between the constituents of the domain. These ontologies must be further written formally with semantic web ontologies languages such as XML, RDF, DAML, OWL (Laclavik, 2005) and Topic Maps (Bailey et al., 2009). The resulting formal ontologies should then be stored in a traditional DBMS such as Oracle, MySQL, PostgreSQL, etc. (Wilkinson et al., 2003) and query in the day to day running of e-governments applications interfacing them to provide answers to citizens' requests. The semantic web domain has developed a set of languages for the technical implementation of these semantic-based queries. These languages include: RDQL, nRQL, Semantic Web Rule Language (SWRL) (Zhang, 2005), XSLT, XPath, XQuery, SPARQL, SeRQL, TRIPLE, Xcert, tolog, AsTMA, Toma and OWL-QL (Bailey et al., 2009). Furthermore, these languages for querying ontology in semantic web are classified according to the ontology language employed as follows:

- **XML:** XSLT, XPath and XQuery.
- **RDF:** RDQL, SPARQL, SeRQL, nRQL, TRIPLE and Xcert.
- **Topic Maps:** AsTMA, tolog and Toma.
- **OWL:** OWL-QL and SPARQL.

In some of the above languages, queries are formulated in an SQL-like syntax, whereas, for others, queries are written with a combination of SQL and functional languages syntax (Bailey et al., 2009).

Perspective and Challenges

In light of the above, it is clear that there are a large and diverse number of tools and technologies that are being employed for the practical software implementation of e-government systems worldwide. Therefore, the main challenge may lie in the choice of the appropriate combination of all these diverse solutions when implementing a new e-government system. The availability of skilled and experienced people for the deployment of all these technologies may also be a challenge in e-government development in a given country. Therefore, there is need to develop new methodologies or frameworks that provide clear guidelines on the choice of appropriate tools and technologies in an incremental and iterative manner throughout the lifecycle of e-government projects.

E-GOVERNMENT SYSTEMS INTEGRATION METHODS

Current State of E-Government Systems Integration

All over the world, e-government has been largely implemented in the form of autonomous and heterogeneous web-based systems in government departments and agencies. This has given rise to the issue of integrating and interoperating these heterogeneous systems for a seamless service delivery to citizens.

Many e-government projects use Web services technology to address electronic services (e-services) integration and interoperability problems in e-government (Arif, 2008; Lee et al., 2009). However, it has been demonstrated that Web services standards provide only the syntactical representation and description of e-services; they lack the semantic features which are more efficient and reliable (Muthaiyah & Kerschberg, 2008). Therefore, Semantic Web technologies based on ontology have attracted e-government developers in the past seven years as alternative solutions to Web Services standards. A plethora of semantic e-government domain specific ontology models have been developed to describe and specify various aspects of e-government service delivery. With ontology and Semantic Web ontology languages and platforms, it is possible to describe and specify e-services in such a way that they can be easily composed, mapped, matched and merged to facilitate their semantic integration and interoperability (Fonou-Dombeu & Huisman, 2012).

Integration Based on Existing XML-Based Standards

Open XML-based standards such as UDDI, WSDL, SOAP have been used to implement Web services technology (Bouguettaya et al., 2006). The UDDI technology serves as a repository of existing Web services, the WSDL is a language used to describe and specify the Web services stored in the UDDI and the SOAP is the communication protocol between Web services (Marjit et al., 2009). There are three components of the Web services architecture: service provider, service broker and service requestor (Comert & Akinci, 2004; Elsas, 2002). The Web Services architecture is often referred to as Service-Oriented Architecture (SOA). The interactions among these components involve publishing, finding and binding Web services and are described as follows.

- **Service Provider:** Hosts Web services; defines a service description for the web service and publishes it to a service broker.
- **Service Broker:** Responsible for service registration and discovery of the Web services; lists various service types, descriptions, and locations of the services that help the service requestors find and subscribe to the required services.
- **Service Requestor:** Retrieves the service description locally or from the service broker and uses the service description to bind with the service provider and invoke the Web service implementation.

Web services provide solution to the integration and interoperability problem in e-government. They enable the automatic composition of e-services which include the automatic selection and interoperation of e-services; these enable e-government applications to process complex user queries.

Semantic Based Integration Algorithms

As mentioned earlier, the XML-based technologies for e-services integration described above provide only a syntactical representation of information; this limits their capacity in expressing information and automatically discovering web services. To address these shortcomings, semantic web technologies based on ontology have been used to address e-services integration problem in various e-government research and projects.

Salhofer et al. (2009) presented an ontological approach for service integration in e-government. A semantic objective and service discovery technique was used to illustrate how e-services could be derived from citizens' needs expressed in the form of simple phrases. The derived e-service ontologies were represented in OWL and the Web Service Modelling Language (WSML). Another ontological approach for semantic interoperability in e-government was proposed by Mathaiyah and Kershberg (2008). They used a shared hierarchal ontology in which knowledge is organized at different levels with local ontologies. A semantic bridging process methodology was described for the mapping, merging and integration of local ontologies represented in an OWL syntax. In Sabucedo et al. (2010), an intelligent platform to host e-government services in the form of a customer-oriented e-government Web portal was put forward. To facilitate services and related public administrations interoperability they introduced the concept of an intelligent document and a Life Event service both of which are semantically modelled with OWL ontology. These allow automatic services composition, advanced searching mechanisms and better usability from the user's point of view. A multilevel abstraction of life-events for e-government services integration was presented in Sanati and Lu (2009). In their work, a life-event is defined as a collection of actions needed to deliver a public service satisfying the needs of a citizen in a real-life situation and is modelled using three kinds of ontologies: e-government ontology, regulatory ontology and service ontology. The ontologies are represented in OWL to enable dynamic services integration through semantic searching and matching of concepts. Xiao et al. (2007) present yet another ontology-based approach for semantic interoperability in e-government. They describe the business process of e-government services using an E-government Business Ontology (EG-BOnt). Each business process is described in terms of its input, output, resource constraints and logical relations with other relevant businesses. Thereafter, each class of the EG-BOnt is defined using the OWL language for its strong semantic and logic relation expressiveness. Finally, an architecture describing a semantic interoperability framework between different government systems based on the proposed EG-BOnt was presented.

Perspective and Challenges

The main challenge in integrating and interoperating heterogeneous e-government systems at the country level may lie in the semantic mismatch between these systems. The semantic mismatch may come from the different formats used to represent information (software components, database structures, etc.) in these systems and/or the difficulties inherent to the practical supervision and coordination of such integration at the country level. To achieve successful integration of heterogeneous e-government systems, the government of each country should define and adopt an interoperability framework that specify the technologies and data format to be used as well as the rule of their combination across all government departments and agencies. A government body/ structure that oversees all e-government projects under implementation in the country that ensures compliance with the interoperability framework specification should be created as well.

CONCLUSION

This chapter has investigated and discussed the methodologies, technologies, tools and platforms currently used for e-government software systems development. The methodologies include maturity/stage of growth models, incremental and iterative software engineering, and semantic-based techniques. Maturity models prescribe the stages that should be followed when building e-government systems; the software engineering domain provide the methodologies and platforms for the design and implementation of e-government systems; cutting age techniques are provided with semantic technologies to enable the integration and interoperability of heterogeneous e-government systems. A large range of diverse tools and technologies are also used for the practical implementation of e-government systems; they are amongst others: workflows and documents management, and web services developments technologies and platforms. Workflow management concerns the technologies that support the reengineering, modelling, implementation and automation of public administration operations and processes; web services are software components that are developed to establish communication between e-government systems and enable their interoperability, whereas, document management entails creating, capturing, modifying, storing and propagating public administration's electronic documents. Various programming languages, database management systems and semantic query languages are employed as well. Web services and semantic technologies are being employed for addressing the integration and interoperability of heterogeneous e-government systems. With regards to the development of e-government systems, two main challenges remain: the choice of the appropriate combination of all the diverse solutions when implementing a new e-government system and the availability of skilled and experienced people for the deployment of these technologies in a given country. A solution to the first problem is to develop new methodologies or frameworks that provide clear guidelines on the choice of appropriate tools and technologies in an incremental and iterative manner throughout the lifecycle of e-government projects. The second problem could be dealt with in the long-term by (1) introducing courses on e-government studies in information technology, computer science, and software engineering programmes at academic institutions, (2) developing partnerships between academic institutions, industry and government for the efficient utilization of the trained graduates and (3) encouraging collaboration between countries with successful e-government implementation and those with skill shortages through exchange programmes and workshops.

REFERENCES

Allemang, D., Hodgson, R., & Polikoff, I. (2005). *Federal reference model ontologies (FEA-RMO)*. White Paper. Retrieved December 12, 2012, from http://www.topquadrant.com

Apostolou, D., Stojanovic, L., Lobo, T. P., Miro, J. C., & Papadakis, A. (2005). Configuring e-government services using ontologies. *IFIP Intl. Federation for Information Processing, 189*, 1571–5736.

Apostolou, D., Stojanovic, L., Lobo, T. P., & Thoensen, B. (2005). In Bohlen, M. (Ed.), *Towards a semantically-driven software engineering environment for e-government* (*Vol. 3416*, pp. 157–168). IFIP Intl. Federation for Information Processing.

Arif, M. (2008). Customer orientation in e-government project management: A case study. *The Electronic. Journal of E-Government, 6*(1), 1–10.

Bailey, J., Bry, F., Furche, T., & Schaffert, S. (2009). Semantic web query languages. Encyclopedia of Database Systems 2009 (pp. 2583-2586).

Baldoni, R., Fuligni, S., Mecella, M., & Tortorelli, F. (2007). The Italian e-government service oriented architecture - Strategic vision and technical solutions. In *Proc. of the 6th EGOV Conference* (pp. 79-88). Regensburg, Germany, 3-7 September.

Barthes, J. P., & Moulin, C. (2005). Impact of e-government on territorial government services. Deliverable No. 1.4. Retrieved December 6, 2012, from http://www.terregov.eupm.net

Beynon-Davies, P. (2005). Constructing electronic government: The case of the UK inland revenue. *International Journal of Information Management*, *25*(1), 3–20. doi:10.1016/j.ijinfomgt.2004.08.002.

Bhanti, P., Kaushal, U., & Pandey, A. (2011). E-government in higher education: Concept and role of data warehouse techniques. *International Journal of Computers and Applications*, *18*(1), 15–19. doi:10.5120/2249-2879.

Bhanti, P., Kaushal, U., & Pandey, A. (2011). E-governance in higher education: Concept and role of data warehousing techniques. *International Journal of Computers and Applications*, *18*(1), 15–19. doi:10.5120/2249-2879.

Bougettaya, A., Gracanin, D., Yu, Q., Zhang, X., Liu, X., & Malik, Z. (2006). Ubiquitous web services for e-government social services. In *Proc. of the Symposium Semantic Web meets eGovernment (2006 AAAI Spring Symposium Series)* (pp. 2-3).

Breuker, J., Hoekstra, R., & Boer, A. Van der berg, K., Sartor, G., Rubino, R., Palmirani, M. (2006). *OWL ontology of basis legal concepts (LKIF-Core)*. Deliverable 1.4. Retrieved December 12, 2011, from http://www.estrellaproject.org/doc/D1.4-OWL-Ontology-of-Basic-Legal-Concepts.pdf

Bri, F. D. (2009). An e-government stages of growth model based on research within the Irish revenue offices. *Electronic. Journal of E-Government*, *7*(4), 339–348.

Butka, P., Gabor, A., Ko, A., Mach, M., Ntioudis, S., Papadakis, A., & Zelinsky, T. (2006). *Semantic-enable, agile, knowledge-based e-government (SAKE)*. Deliverable No. 3. Retrieved December 13, 2011, from www.sake-project.org/fileadmin/filemounts/sake/DeliverableD6b.pdf

Calero, C., Ruiz, F., & Piattini, M. (Eds.). (2006). *Ontologies for software engineering and software technology*. Springer-Verlag Berlin Heidelberg. doi:10.1007/3-540-34518-3.

Chatzidimitriou, M., & Koumpis, A. (2008). Marketing one-stop e-government solutions: The European OneStopGov project. *International Journal of Computer Science*, *35*(1), 1–6.

Chen, D., Nie, G., & Liu, P. (2008). Research knowledge sharing of e-government based on automatic ontology mapping. In *Proc of the 6th Wuhan Intl. Conference on E-Business* (pp.105-111).

Clutterbuck, P., Rowlands, T., & Seamons, O. (2009). A case study of SME web application development effectiveness via agile methods. *The Electronic Journal of Information Systems Evaluation*, *12*(1), 13–26.

Comert, C., & Akinci, H. (2004). WEB services, NSDI and e-government. In *Proc. of the FIG Working Week* (pp. 1-13). 22-27 May. Athens, Greece.

Deladoss, P. R., Pan, S. L., & Huang, J. C. (2003). Structurational analysis of e-government initiatives: A case study of SCO. *Decision Support Systems*, *34*(3), 253–269. doi:10.1016/S0167-9236(02)00120-3.

Deloitte, & Touche. (2001). The citizen as customer. *CMA Management, 74*(10), 58.

Elsas, A. (2002). E-government: Integration with web services. In *Proc. of the 7th Intl. Scientific Conference – Summer School*. Frankfurt, Germany.

Feldkamp, D., Siberski, W., Thönssen, B., & Wache, H. (2008). E-government for distributed autonomous administrations. *AAAI-Symposium, AI Meets Business Rules and Process Management* (pp. 1-11). California, USA, 26-28 March.

Fonou-Dombeu, J. V., & Huisman, M. (2012). *A semantic content based methodology framework for e-government development.* (Doctoral Thesis). North-West University, South Africa.

Fraser, J., Adams, N., Mckay-Hubbard, A., Macintosh, A., & Canadas, R. (2003). *A framework for e-government services.* Deliverable No. 71. Retrieved December 14, 2011, from http://smartgov.e-gov.gr/index.php?category=results

Goudos, S. K., Peristeras, V., Lutas, N., & Tarabanis, K. (2007). A public administration domain ontology for semantic discovery of e-government services. In *Proc. of the 2nd IEEE Conference on Digital Information Management 2007 (ICDIM 2007)* (pp. 260-265). Lyon, France, 11-13 December.

Gouscos, D., Laskaridis, G., Lioulias, D., Mentzas, G., & Georgiadis, P. (2002). An approach to offering one-stop e-government services – Available technologies and architectural issues. In *Proc. of the Electronic Government, First International Conference (EGOV 2002)* (pp. 264-271). Aix-en-Provence, France, 2-5 September.

Grey, J., Huisman, M., & Goede, R. (2006). *An investigation of the suitability of agile system development methodologies for the development of data warehouses.* (Msc. Dissertation). North-West University, South Africa.

Gruber, T. R. (1993). Toward principles for the design of ontologies used for knowledge sharing. *International Journal of Human-Computer Studies, 43*, 907–928. doi:10.1006/ijhc.1995.1081.

Gugliotta, A., Cabral, L., Domingue, J., & Roberto, V. (2005). A conceptual model for semantically-based e-government portal. In *Proc. of the Intl. Conference on e-Government 2005 (ICEG 2005).* Ottawa, Canada, 2005.

Hreno, J., Bednar, P., Furdík, K., & Sabol, T. (2001). Integration of government services using semantic technologies. *Journal of Theoretical and Applied Electronic Commerce Research, 6*(1), 143–154.

Hu, X. (2010). *Data warehouse technology and application in data centre design for e-government* (pp. 371–383). E-learning, Experiences and Future. doi:10.5772/8800.

Janowski, T., Estevez, E., & Ojo, A. (2007). *A project framework for e-government.* Research Report No. 359. Centre for Electronic Government, United Nations University-International Institute for Software Technology (UNU-IIST), Macao, China.

Jarrar, M., Deik, A., & Farraj, B. (2011). Ontology-based data process governance framework – The case of e-government interoperability in Palestine. In *Pre-proc. of the IFIP International Symposium on Data-Driven Process Discovery and Analysis (SIMPDA'11)* (pp. 83-98). Campione, Italy, 30 June.

Kunis, R., Runger, G., & Schwind, M. (2007). A model for document management in e-government systems based on hierarchical process folders. *Electronic. Journal of E-Government, 5*(2), 191–204.

Laclavik, M. (2005). *Ontology and agent based approach for knowledge management.* (Doctoral Thesis). Slovak Academy of Sciences.

Layne, K., & Lee, J. (2001). Developing fully functional e-government: A four stage model. *Government Information Quarterly, 18*(2), 122–136. doi:10.1016/S0740-624X(01)00066-1.

Lee, T., Hon, C. T., & Cheung, D. (2009). XML schema design and management for e-government data interoperability. *Electronic. Journal of E-Government, 7*(4), 381–390.

Liu, X., & Luo, X. (2010). A data warehouse solution for e-government. [IJRRAS]. *International Journal of Research and Reviews in Applied Sciences*, *4*(1), 101–105.

Luts, M. (2004). *Estonian semantic interoperability initiative*. SEMIC. EU publications.

Mahapatra, S. K., Das, D. K., & Das, B. (2008). Workflow based e-government applications: Case study of Wf-Bhulekh. In Bhattacharya, J. (Ed.), *Towards next generation e-government* (pp. 220–228).

Marjit, U., Roy, R., Santra, S., & Biswas, U. (2009). A semantic web service based approach to e-governance. In *Proc. of the 2nd Intl. Conference on Applications of Digital Information and Web Technologies (ICADIWT 2009)* (pp. 232-237). 4-6 August, London, UK.

Murch, R. (2005). *Methodologies in IT: Comprehension, selection, and implementation*. IBM Press.

Muthaiyah, S., & Kerschberg, L. (2008). Achieving interoperability in e-government services with two modes of semantic bridging: SRS and SWRL. *Journal of Theoretical and Applied Electronic Commerce Research*, *3*(3), 52–63. doi:10.4067/S0718-18762008000200005.

Ortiz-Rodriguez, F., & Villazon-Terrazas, B. (2006). EGO ontology model: Law and regulation approach for e-government. In *Proc. of the Workshop on Semantic Web for E-government 2006, Workshop at the 3rd European Semantic Web Conference* (pp. 13-23). Budva, Serbia and Montenegro, 12 June.

Peristeras, V., & Tarabanis, K. (2006). Reengineering public administration through semantic technologies and the GEA domain ontology. *AAAI Spring Symposium, Semantic Web meets eGovernment (SWEG)*. 27-29 March, Stanford University, California.

Puustjarvi, J. (2006). Using knowledge management and business process in e-government. In *Proc. of the Information Integration and Web-based Applications and Services 2006 (iiWas2006) Conference* (pp. 331-339). Yogyakarta Indonesia, 4 - 6 December.

Sabucedo, L. A., & Rifon, L. A. (2006). *Semantic service oriented architectures for e-government platforms*. American Association for Artificial Intelligence.

Sabucedo, L. M. A., Rifon, L. E. A., Corradini, F., Polzonetti, A., & Re, B. (2010). Knowledge-based platform for e-government agents: A web-based solution using semantic technologies. *Journal of Expert Systems with Applications*, *37*(5), 3647–3656. doi:10.1016/j.eswa.2009.10.026.

Salhofer, P., & Ferbas, D. (2007). A pragmatic approach to the introduction of e-government. In *Proc. of the 8th Annual Intl. Digital Government Research Conference* (pp. 183-189). Philadelphia, Pennsylvania, USA, May 20-23.

Salhofer, P., Stadlhofer, B., & Tretter, G. (2009). Ontology driven e-government. *Electronic. Journal of E-Government*, *7*(4), 415–424.

Sanati, F., & Lu, J. (2009). Multilevel life-event abstraction framework for e-government service integration. In *Proc. of the 9th European Conference on E-government 2009 (ECEG 2009)* (pp. 550-558). London, UK, 29-30 June.

Sang, M. L., Tan, X., & Trimi, S. (2005). Current practices of leading e-government countries. *Communications of the ACM*, *48*(10), 99–104. doi:10.1145/1089107.1089112.

Singh, M., & Malik, S. K. (2008). Constructing ontologies in OWL using Protégé-2000. In *Proc. of the 2nd National Conference on Challenges and Opportunities in Information Technology (COIT 2008)* (pp. 1-4). Mandi Gobindgarh, Punjab, India.

Sourouni, A. M., Lampathaki, F., Mouzakitis, S., Charalabidis, Y., & Askouris, D. (2008). Paving the way to e-government transformation: Interoperability registry infrastructure development. In *Proc. of the 7th International Electronic Government Conference (eGov 2008)* (pp. 340-351). 3-7 September, Torino, Italy.

Teicher, J., & Dow, N. (2002). E-government in Australia: Promise and progress. *Information polity, 7*(4), 231-246.

Torodovski, L., Kunstelj, M., Cukjati, D., Vintar, M., Trochidis, I., & Tambouris, E. (2007). *OneStopGove: D13 – Life-event Reference Models. Deliverable No. 13*. Retrieved December 13, 2011, from http://islab.uom.gr/onestopgov/index.php?name=Deliverables.

United Nations. (2003). *UN global e-government survey 2003*. Retrieved March 28, 2011, from http://unpan1.un.org/intradoc/groups/public/documents/un/unpan016066.pdf

Vassilakis, C., Laskaridis, G., Lepouras, G., Rouvas, S., & Georgiadis, P. (2002). Transactional e-government services: An integrated approach. *Lecture Notes in Computer Science, 2456*, 276–279. doi:10.1007/978-3-540-46138-8_44.

West, D. M. (2004). E-government and the transformation of service delivery and citizen attitudes. *Public Administration Review, 64*(1), 15–27. doi:10.1111/j.1540-6210.2004.00343.x.

Wilkinson, K., Sayers, C., Kuno, H., & Reynolds, D. (2003). Efficient RDF storage and retrieval in Jena2. In *Proceedings of the First International Workshop on Semantic Web and Databases (SWDB)* (pp. 131-150). Berlin, Germany.

Wimmer, M. A. (2002). Integrated service modelling for online one-stop government. *Electronic Markets, 12*(3), 149–156. doi:10.1080/101967802320245910.

Xiao, Y., Xioa, M., & Zhao, H. (2007). An ontology for e-government knowledge modelling and interoperability. In *Proc. of IEEE Intl. Conference on Wireless Communications, Networking and Mobile Computing (WiCOM 2007)* (pp. 3600-3603). Shanghai, 21-25 September.

Zang, Z. (2005). *Ontology query languages for the semantic web: A performance evaluation*. (MSc Thesis). The University of Georgia.

Zarei, B., Ghapanchi, A., & Sattary, B. (2008). Toward national e-government development models for developing countries: A nine stage model. *The International Information & Library Review, 40*(3), 199–207. doi:10.1016/j.iilr.2008.04.001.

ADDITIONAL READING

Choudrie, J., & Weerrakody, V. (2007). Horizontal process integration in e-government: The perspective of UK local authority. *International Journal of Electronic Government Research, 3*(3), 22–39. doi:10.4018/jegr.2007070102.

Heeks, R. (2006). Implementing and managing e-government. *Book Review. Journal of Scientific and Industrial Research, 65*(10), 845–846.

Medjahed, B., Rezgui, A., Bouguettaya, A., & Ouzzani, M. (2003). Infrastructure for E-government Web Services. *IEEE Internet Computing, 7*(1), 58–65. doi:10.1109/MIC.2003.1167340.

KEY TERMS AND DEFINITIONS

E-Government: Use of information and communication technologies (ICT) for delivering government services to citizens; the ICT facilities and the Internet technologies are used to deploy web-based applications that support government processes; this support consists of: (1) providing a large range of government information and services (health care, education, social services, community development, taxes return, etc.) online, (2) facilitating online citizens' participation to government processes and decision making, and (3) streamlining and reorganizing government processes.

Methodology: A repeatable process with project-specific methods, best practices, rules, guidelines, templates, checklists, and other features for building quality e-government systems. The methodology can be used and reused any number of times (Murch, 2005).

Ontology: An explicit specification of a conceptualization. A conceptualization is an abstract and simplified view of a domain of knowledge one wish to represent for certain purposes; the domain could be explicitly and formally represented using existing objects, concepts, entities and the relationship that exists between them (Gruber, 1993).

Platform: Refers to computing platform; it is a framework on which e-government applications may be run.

System Integration: Also call horizontal integration (Layne and Lee 2001); it consists of building a single e-government system that serves as access point to all government services across different functional units.

Tool: Refers to software development tool; it is a program or application that e-government developers may use to create, debug, maintain, or otherwise support other e-government programmes and applications.

Web Service: Software components developed to establish communication between e-government systems and enable their interoperability.

Chapter 2
E-Government for Social and Economic Development: Asymmetric Information, Institutionalization and Diffusion Challenges

Bongani Ngwenya
Solusi University, Zimbabwe & North-West University-Mafeking, South Africa

ABSTRACT

This chapter posits that e-Government constitutes a critical context for social and economic development in both developed and developing countries. In addition to leveraging economic development, e-Government also helps to stream line government services to more social based values of inclusion and citizens' participation, accessibility and power relationship ratios. It is clear from literature that e-Government is not a new phenomenon in most developed countries and some developing countries in Asia and Africa. These countries have already announced their Open Government Initiatives and data portals. However, e-Government leads to greater information asymmetry among citizens and government. There is also institutionalization and diffusion asymmetry of the practice of the current Openness in e-Government models within developing countries in particular. The study presented in this chapter draws on organizational decision-making research and adopts an explorative research approach that is informed by grounded theory. The findings of the research are that the information asymmetry between citizens and government; asymmetry in institutionalization, and diffusion within developed and developing countries are widely attributed to socio-economic and political variations in developed and developing countries. Unless these differences are skillfully identified and accommodated as such into the development and use models, openness in e-Government efforts would not help achieve the social and economic development goals by developing countries in particular.

DOI: 10.4018/978-1-4666-4245-4.ch002

INTRODUCTION

E-Government is about using the tools and systems made possible by Information and Communication Technology (ICTs) to provide better public services to citizens and business. ICTs are already widely used by government bodies, just as in enterprises, but e-Government involves much more than just the tools (Ngwenya, Lubbe, & Klopper, 2010). Effective e-Government involves rethinking organizations and processes, and changing behavior so that public services are delivered more efficiently to the people who need to use them. Implemented well, e-Government enables all citizens, enterprises and organizations to carry out their business with government more easily, more quickly and at lower cost (Reding, 2006). Differing characteristics of local environments, both infrastructural and socio-economic, have created a significant level of variation in the acceptance and growth of e-government in different regions of the world (Rothschild & Stiglitz, 1976). This chapter posits that; e-Government constitutes a critical context for social and economic development in both developed and developing countries. The chapter also suggests that e-Government encompasses more than just technology, that is; it attempts to highlight the social and economic implications of changes that have occurred in recent years as a result of the transparency and accountability of government and how software usage can influence digital inclusion, trust and privacy and possible strategies to eliminate the digital divide by encouraging greater public and commercial use and re-use of government information through putting government data on the Web. There are documented differences between the success and failure factors in the developed and developing countries with regard to the adoption and embracing of Openness in e-Government practice models. In addition to leveraging economic development, e-Government also helps to stream line government services to more social based values of inclusion and citizens' participation, accessibility and power relationship ratios.

The main objectives of this chapter are: to explore the role of e-Government in social and economic development in both developed and developing countries with particular emphasis on developing countries, to explore the effects of information asymmetry among citizens and government; to explore the effects of the asymmetry in institutionalization and diffusion of e-Government models within developed and developing countries; and to advance the knowledge that the asymmetry in institutionalization and diffusion within developing and developed countries can be attributed to socio-economic and political variations in developing and developed countries.

In the sections that follow, the author discusses the existing literature on e-Government aspects and conceptual framework; information asymmetry between citizens and government, asymmetry in institutionalization, and diffusion within developed and developing countries. To this end, interpretive research conventions are used in this study. Finally, the conclusions are drawn and the chapter ends by the focus of the study, the study`s major findings and suggestions for further future research.

BACKGROUND TO CONCEPTUAL FRAMEWORK

A comprehensive insight into the literature that covers some aspects of e-Government, and models that have been developed from past research and studies conducted elsewhere, are highlighted in the following sub-section. Also covered in this section on literature review are related topics such as e-governance and the digital divide, information asymmetry and its problems, information asymmetry problems between government and business, and asymmetry in institutionalization and diffusion.

E-Government: Definitions and Aspects

The terms e-Government and e-Governance are often used synonymously and interchangeably. However, although they are similar, there is a slight, but important, difference. E-Government refers to the institution itself, whereas e-governance is a broader concept describing forms of governing which are not necessarily in the hands of the formal government. It is the application of ICT to the functioning of government. According to Keohane and Nye (2000) governance, means the processes and institutions, both formal and informal, which guide and restrain the collective activities of a group. Government is the subset that acts with authority and creates formal obligations. Governance need not necessarily be conducted exclusively by governments. Private firms, associations of firms, non-governmental organizations (NGOs) and associations of NGOs all engage in it, often in association with government bodies, to create governance; sometimes without governmental authority (Keohane & Nye, 2000). E-government, on the other hand, is the use of ICT's to promote a more efficient and effective government that is not only more accessible but one that is also more transparent and accountable to its citizens. The primary characteristics of e-Government include electronic service delivery and workflow.

E-Government refers to the delivery of government information and services online through the Internet or other digital means (Muir & Oppenheim, 2002). It is about delivering improved services to citizens, businesses, and other members of the society through drastically changing the way governments manage information (Accenture, 2004). However, the e-Government challenge is not a technological one. Rather, the challenge is to use technologies to improve the capacities of government institutions, while improving the quality of life of citizens by redefining the relationship between citizens and their government (Gautrin, 2004).

The section that follows details two case studies of e-Government in some developing countries, that is, Botswana and Zambia, adopted from literature by Kelvin Joseph Bwalya and Mike Healy in their article harnessing e-Government Adoption in the SADC Region: a Conceptual Underpinning.

Case Studies of E-Government in Developing Countries

Botswana

According to Bwalya and Healy (2010) Botswana has a dedicated agenda towards promoting e-Government because the leaders have understood the importance of e-Government to an appreciable extent. Quoting from Mmegi Newspaper (2009, September), they go further to suggest that the potential of e-Government on improving the governance value chain in Botswana is explicitly outlined. For the case of Botswana, e-Government delivers far greater stakeholder value when it is designed within the context of a broader service delivery reform agenda. This 'whole-of-government strategy' leverages infrastructure, reduces cost and improves the on-line experience for clients. This newspaper projected that by the end of 2009, all appropriate government services will be on-line by 2009 (Bwalya & Healy, 2010). Has this been achieved? This is the question the two authors ask. The two authors suggest that although Botswana does not have a formal e-Government strategy as do Tanzania, South Africa, Mauritius, it has scored positive gains on the e-Government Indexes. It is considered an emerging ICT-usage-powerhouse in Sub-Saharan-Africa (SSA). Recently Botswana has successfully implemented massive projects such as the construction of the Kgalagadi optical fibre network, full liberalizations of the telecommunications sector, putting in place sound ICT sector regulatory and institutional frameworks, dedicated ICT policy, setting up of Botswana IT hub, etc. These interventions have also been solidified with the convergence of wireless technologies which enable individuals of all statuses to use mobile technologies such as mobile phones, personal digital assistant (PDAs) etc to communicate, manage data and generally participate in the digital boom (Bwalya & Healy, 2010).

Gillwald and Stork (2008) have also done a study on Botswana and conclude that Botswana has emerged as one of the countries with a higher fixed-line penetration with 11 to 18% of households having a working fixed-line phone. By the end of March 2002, there were 278 000 mobile subscribers as compared to 142 000 fixed line subscribers (Monnane, 2003). In 2007, mobile penetration had grown to 87 per 100 inhabitants and 250 000 fixed line subscribers (Lazauskaite, 2008). Compared to other countries, Botswana's mobile penetration (teledensity) has been remarkable, from nothing in 1997 to 14.24/100 inhabitants in 2002 and 76 per 100 inhabitants in 2007 (Lazauskaite, 2008), only second to South Africa in the region. In terms of mobile lines as percentage of total lines, Botswana is behind Lesotho, South Africa and Tanzania only (Gillwald & Stork, 2008).

Pheko (2009) suggests that, with the introduction of cheap Taiwan or Chinese phones on the local telecommunications market, acquiring a handset is no longer a far-fetched dream for Botswana citizens (Batswana). Telecom operators for example, Mascom and Orange Botswana have started offering internet accessibility on mobile phones. People in the rural communities can also access internet or mobile signal coverage as appropriate ICT infrastructure is now being erected even in rural areas as guided by the rural telecommunications initiative. This initiative has brought modern telecommunications, including internet access, for the first time to 147 villages (Pheko, 2009). When fully implemented, the project will ensure that more than 50% of Batswana living in the remote areas of the country will be provided with basic telecommunications services. Further, the Botswana Telecommunications Corporation (BTC) has launched VSAT technology. It is hoped that the technology, will play a role in bringing services to remote areas through the use of satellite and overcome limitations placed on traditional services by vast distances and difficult terrain (Mesa, 2007). It is anticipated that Botswana's telecommunication industry is likely to record growth in the year 2009 placing it ahead of the telecoms market of South Africa and Nigeria in terms of teledensity. This forecast follows the launch of BeMobile by BTC in 2008 (Pheko, 2009).

A number of significant initiatives have been introduced in the telecoms sector to encourage the growth of this sector. Lewin et al. (2004) has noted that a Convergence Bill is under preparation to update the 1996 Telecommunications Act. Debate has focused on how far this Bill can include provisions that would extend liberalization. Another initiative has been the putting in place of the Cybercrime Bill, originally published in the Government Gazette in October 2007 (Mesa, 2007). The Convergence Bill encourages further liberalizations and convergence of both wireless and fixed technologies. Pheko (2009) notes that the effect of this has been the following: a) licensing of beMobile (the BTC mobile arm); b) rollout of product packages and price offerings to attract more customers by Orange Botswana and Mascom Wireless; c) establishment of own International Voice Gateways by Mascom Wireless and Orange Botswana; d) introduction of VoIP services by PTOs and VANS; e) upgrading of Public Land Mobile networks to introduce 3G services; and f) rollout of WiMax services to some urban areas; g) increase in the number of registered VANS. (In 2008, 25 VANS were registered and total number of VANS is now 43.). It is thought that a vibrant telecommunications sector may facilitate appropriate e-Government interactions (Pheko, 2009).

Despite these novel interventions to encourage e-Government, the limitations have been lack of trust and limited education levels of a greater portion of the population (Pheko, 2009). Due to lack of effective promotional and awareness campaigns of e-Government benefits, many ordinary citizens do not find the urge to engage in e-Government. Given this scenario, it is fair to state that there is a lot of potential of e-Government in Botswana as more and more people are having access to mobile phones which can further be used as platforms for internet access. This further allows citizens, government and businesses to interact constructively using interconnected technologies (Bwalya & Healy, 2010).

Zambia

Bwalya and Healy (2010) suggest that in the case of Zambia, very little has been done to encourage e-Government. Despite a poverty reduction strategy (PRS) in place, the country does not have a dedicated e-Government strategy. In fact, e-Government has only been mentioned once in Zambia's ICT policy launched in 2006 (Bwalya, 2009). Several government departments such as the Ministry of Home Affairs, Immigrations department, have tried to implement e-Government by encouraging online applications for resident/work permits; VISAs and so forth (Simenda, 2009). This however, has been met with a lot of resistance and the expected users have not given it a buy-in. This may be because strategic strategies that should have been undertaken, as outlined by Colesca (2009), have not been adopted.

The two authors further refer to 2008 e-Government Index computed by the United Nations DPEPA which recognized Zambia as a country with deficient e-Government capacity because its index was way below 1.00 (0.22) (Bwalya & Healy, 2010). Although this is the case, the country has shown massive improvement from lack of online presence in 2005 to occupying 158th position of the countries surveyed in 2008 (UN e-govt. report, 2008). Although Zambia is just at the emerging stage of e-Government implementation, there are several initiatives that are in the pipeline for e-Government development. The government is about to engage a consultant to help come up with the e-Government adoption and implementation strategy (Simenda, 2009). At an organizational level, Zambia enjoys massive support on e-Government implementation from regional groupings such as SADC and COMESA which have in place dedicated e-Government implementation action plans and roadmaps (Bwalya, 2009). The onus is on the country to adopt these different legal and regulatory framework guidelines and instruments and adapt them to the local culture (Bwalya & Healy, 2010).

Since access to the internet is also vital to let the different players in an e-Government environment interact, it is important that we first look at the internet (both broadband and wireless) penetration in Zambia as this gives a snapshot of e-Government adoption in general. The following table shows the number of internet subscribers (both broadband and wireless) in Zambia pitted against the levels of internet penetration in its neighbouring countries. Table 1 below shows internet penetration in Zambia and neighbouring countries region (2009).

The information shown in the table above demonstrates that, relatively speaking, Zambia has a sizeable number of people accessing the Internet. This means, that assuming everyone who accesses internet has adopted and uses the e-Government platform in continuance patterns, the government will only reach 6% of the total population. Given these statistics, it is fait to ask whether it is logically coherent for the government and other cooperating partners to engage into massive tasks of putting in place systems, institutional and legal frameworks that will create an enabling environment for e-Government to thrive. It is also worth investing the issues of lack of trust in online applications, low ICT literacy levels, exorbitant costs of internet access, scarcity of computers, etc., and how these impact on the adoption of e-Government in the case of Zambia. These issues can be taken care of by drawing e-Government implementation strategies by closely following a carefully drawn conceptual adoption model. As the Zambian government's

Table 1. Internet penetration in Zambia and neighboring countries region (2009) (Source: Internet World Stats (August, 2009) - http://www.internetworldstats.com/stats1.htm)

AFRICA	Population (2009 Est.)	Internet Users Dec/2000	Internet Users Latest Data	Penetration(% Population)	User Growth(2000-2009)	% Users in Africa
Angola	12,799,293	30,000	550,000	4.3%	1,733.3%	0.8%
Botswana	1,990,876	15,000	100,000	5.0%	566.7%	0.2%
Malawi	15,028,757	15,000	139,500	0.9%	830.0%	0.2%
Mozambique	21,669,278	30,000	350,000	1.6%	1,066.7%	0.5%
Namibia	2,108,665	30,000	113,500	5.4%	278.3%	0.2%
Tanzania	41,048,532	115,000	520,000	1.3%	352.2%	0.8%
Zambia	11,862,740	20,000	700,000	5.9%	3,400.0%	1.1%
Zimbabwe	11,392,629	50,000	1,421,000	12.5%	2,742.0%	2.2%

organs and line ministries have just started stamping their presence on the internet, with very few people accessing the internet and undeveloped ICT infrastructures, it can be aptly said that Zambia is at the emerging stage of e-Government implementation (Bwalya & Healy, 2010).

Bwalya and Healy (2010) refer to Mulozi (2008) who looks at the current connectivity issues in Zambia and suggests that they contribute to the poor development and adoption of e-Government services in Zambia. He goes further and mentions that Zambia's connectivity is characterized by a few major internet providers, high dependency on VSAT access to the internet, and a poor landline telecom system. The rural areas are most hit as most of these areas have dilapidated ICT infrastructure. Much of rural Zambia is not serviced by ground telephone and let alone fibre optic cables – the mainstay of communication – which are still being constructed. Zambia's ISP services are concentrated along the railway line from Livingstone to Chingola. The country depends on VSAT access as it is not yet connected to the international submarine cable which interconnects with the global Internet backbone. Mulozi (2008) further mentions that out of the eleven registered Internet Service Providers (ISPs) in Zambia, six provide services to rural areas with an estimated 17,800+ clients. More than 50% of the clients use dial-up services.

A look at these websites suggests that issues of usability have not been considered to any appreciable degree during their design. Also, since Zambia has 73 different languages, providing web content only in English may be disadvantageous to some of the citizens. These web pages do not cover even half of the services that the government offers in a conventional and ordinary setup. It is vital to mention that such issues need to be followed, especially in the testing stage of the conceptual e-Government adoption model proposed in this chapter. The two cases of ICT landscape in Botswana and Zambia provide a good illustration of e-Government in the region. Since the SADC bloc has countries which have almost the same contextual environment, a look at the aforementioned countries may be somewhat representative enough for the SADC bloc. With reference to these two cases and a look at the factors identified from different literature sources, (as in the background), it is now possible to compile a list of factors that may affect domestication of e-Government in the SADC bloc (Bwalya & Healy, 2010). The next section describes e-Government for social and economic development.

E-Government for Social and Economic Development

Initially, e-Government may seem like another option for communication with citizens. But in the face of rising demands from demographic, economic, social, and global trends, e-Government no longer appears to be a matter of choice, but a necessity for any country wishing to enter the 21st century as a competitive nation in the world arena. Governments have been viewed as complex, mammoth bureaucratic establishments with a set of information silos that erect barriers to the access of information and make the provision of services cumbersome and frustrating. With e-Government, the quality of services provided to citizens and businesses can be improved significantly while attaining greater efficiency for all participants. The provision of 24/7 services can improve the level of satisfaction among citizens and enhance their acceptance of the public sector (Gautrin, 2004).

E-Government can result in significant cost savings to governments and citizens alike. These potential huge savings are dependent on how quickly adoption rates increase (Eggers, 2004). The services offered by e-Government are categorised into three phases: publishing, interacting, and transacting. Government websites are primarily being used to obtain information; to date; limited progress has been made in interacting with citizens and online business transactions (Accenture, 2004). The potential of e-Government to reduce the cost of public service delivery, encourage social inclusion, encourage participatory and inclusive governance cannot be overemphasized. In addition, e-Government can be a prerequisite to strategic initiatives avoiding rampant corruption and red-tape that characterizes most Africa's government organs and thwarts effectiveness of public service delivery systems (Bwalya, 2009). E-Government offers a number of potential benefits to citizens; it gives citizens more control on how and when they interact with the government. Instead of visiting a department at a particular location or calling the government personnel at a particular time specified by the government, citizens can choose to receive these services at the time and place of their choice. The accessibility of government services also increases despite government's mammoth infrastructure. There are always a limited number of personnel interacting directly with the citizens and waiting times, even on the phone, can be long.

The electronic delivery of government services, especially the availability of different forms and the option of electronically submitting them, provides a considerable saving of time and money for individuals. Technology now makes it possible to personalise a website to a point where delivery of services could be tailored to meet the specific needs of an individual, thereby increasing the satisfaction of citizens from government services (Gilber & Balestrini, 2004). The adoption and usage of online government services has a special significance for developing countries. Unlike developed countries, the governments of developing countries have an incessant shortage of resources. They are always short of skilled personnel and facilities to provide adequate services to their citizens. The concept of information and service provision by telephone is non-existent in most of the developing countries. A personal visit to the department and face-to-face interaction with government personnel is mandatory to receive any type of service. Getting a form from a government department, so conveniently available online in a number of developed countries and taken for granted, costs citizens of developing countries significant time, effort, money, and untold frustration.

The online delivery of government services could tremendously increase accessibility; bring significant time and cost savings to citizens in developing countries. The element of transparency built in the online channel could also alleviate corruption, a serious problem in a number of developing countries. Therefore, e-Government could virtually revolutionise the provision of government services in developing countries.

Access to the Internet by citizens is a serious issue but it could be dealt with by providing public access terminals. Canada's effort, for example, to provide Internet access through public terminals is regarded as an important step in encouraging e-Government adoption (Government On-Line, 2004). E-Government involves the use of online information technologies by government agencies to provide services. E-government services are essentially concerned with the delivery of public services to citizens, employees, businesses, and government organizations through the use of information communication technology (ICT). Suggested are three aspects of e-government, that is; Government to Individuals (G2Is) also referred to as Government to consumer (G2C) (Arrow, 1984).On the other hand, suggestions are made for Government to Business as a Citizen (G2BC) and Government to Business in the Marketplace (G2BMKT) (Dolowitz & Marsh, 2000).Government to Individuals (G2Is) or Government to Consumer(G2C) takes public agencies to provide services to citizens such as issuance of national identity documents, drivers' licenses, tax return applications, or obtaining passport via online, etc.

Similarly, G2BC is involved with commercial transactions, such as institutional payment of taxes or fines by the commercial enterprises to public agencies. G2BMKT is concerned with the business transactions between government and businesses such as e-procurement, government hiring of contractors, and government acquisition of goods or services. The term "e-government" is a comprehensive term that is sometimes referred to as "on-line government" or "Internet-based government." The term denotes a multidimensional sense. It is also stated that it is "...the use of Internet technology to support government operations, engage citizens, and provide government services" (Elkins & Simmons, 2005, pp. 33-51). The first of these, government operations, primarily involves management practices that, although critical, are largely invisible to the public. Implementation of Internet technology in American state governments for example is taking place at a brisk pace (Eu Commission, 2006a). In this annual review of features available online in American federal and state websites, there are several documents changes that have occurred since the review began in 2000. In 2000 only two percent of government sites offered three or more services online; in 2007 that figure rose to 58 percent. It is noted that almost all sites now provide publications and databases (98 and 84 percent, respectively).

Almost half the sites (46 percent in 2007) now comply with the World Wide Web Consortium (W3C) standards for disability access. This is a phenomenal social development. The most common services offered by the states include; business registration, professional licensing, driver license and license plate renewal, filing and paying taxes, locating information on sex offenders and missing persons. This reflects considerable effort towards achieving socio-economic development. Many state legislatures offer bill and legislation search and live broadcasts of legislative sessions. In addition, many states offer unique services. For example, in New York and New Jersey, using Privacy Policy links, citizens may request any site information that is public record. Georgia citizens may search for the lowest gas prices in the state, and South Carolina legislators provide legislative broadcasts with closed captioning (Thomas & Streib, 2003). From 2007, for example, 89 percent of government sites allowed the public to e-mail public officials directly rather than simply e-mailing the webmaster (Thomas & Streib, 2003). While state implementation of digital services and outreach is changing quickly, there is considerable progress to be made. Most sites exceed the reading level of the average citizen. Many are poorly organized; portal pages make it difficult to navigate through the sites. Some sites have limited accessibility, while others have no apparent privacy provisions, leading to more challenges of digital divide.

The section that follows deals with the main focus of the chapter, that is, issues, controversies and problems underlying the motivation for conducting this study. The e-Government issues that affect the efficiency of e-Government services are discussed. The main focus of the chapter is; taking the view on the institutional theory`s account of diffusion further and extending it by premising that Open Government Initiatives and data portals also lead to greater information asymmetry among citizens and government and also, institutionalization and diffusion asymmetry of the practice of the current openness in e-Government models within developing countries in particular are widely attributed to socio-economic and political variations in developed and developing countries. This makes the main contribution of this study to the body of knowledge. The study also suggests rethinking of the classic institutional, framing and diffusion model.

ISSUES AND CONTROVERSIES

The section discusses the limitations and issues affecting the efficiency of e-Government services, such as e-Government and the Digital Divide, information asymmetry and its problems, information asymmetry problems between business and government, and asymmetry in institutionalization and diffusion.

E-Government and Digital Divide

Just because technology is available, it does not mean that it is also accessible. The term digital divide has been used since the 1990s to describe patterns of unequal access to ICTs — primarily computers and the Internet — based on income, ethnicity, geography, age, and other factors, such as lack of skills (Mishra, Raghunathan, & Yue, 2007).The realization of these goals requires that the digital divide be addressed (Liao & Cheung, 2001). In a study of e-Government use by citizens, the digital divide was found to be more pronounced among government web site visitors than among internet users in general (Akerlof, 1970). A lack of access to the Internet is a major element of the digital divide. Research consistently identifies ethnicity, income, age and education as significant predictors of access to technology. Sixty percent of white households had Internet access, while only 34 percent of African American and 38 percent of Latino households did (Akerlof, 1970). Also, roughly 78 percent of households with income between $50,000 and $75,000 by then had Internet access, while only 40 percent of those with household incomes between $20,000 and $25,000 had Web access. The research, found that ethnicity, education, income, and age discriminate Internet users from non-users (Jo¨rgens, 2004). The research concluded that among Internet users, ethnicity and education are important predictors of which Internet users will also utilize government Web sites, with those users more likely to be white and better educated. The perpetuation of digital exclusion in Zimbabwe and other developing countries for example is contradictory to citizens' constitutional right to access of information. This right is enshrined in most of these countries' constitutions, and as such, the right would have been violated. Notwithstanding the negative impact of information asymmetry, another critical challenge to e-Government is social and economic development, which is expected to be facilitated by e-Government.

In Zimbabwe, there is Access to Information and Protection of Privacy Act (AIPPA). The Act enshrines the citizens' rights to access to information, at the same time gives the government agents' authority to pry on individual citizens' use and dissemination of information. The whole thing is politically motivated, and used to curtail opposition to the ruling party. There is a clear contradiction here.

Information Asymmetry and Associated Problems

The theory of asymmetric information has been lively developed in the field of economic research for the last two decades. The prominent foundations for this theory were established in the following research (Fiala, 2005; Levi-Faur & Jordana, 2005; Garicano & Kaplan, 2001). Information asymmetry occurs when one party has more or better information than the other party; it assumes that at least one party to a transaction has better relevant information whereas the other(s) do not. This is typically with governments. Naturally, government would have more or better information about itself than its citizens. Information asymmetry has mass effect on the business networks, for example, supply chains. Information asymmetry is a key source of supply chain inefficiency and strategic partnerships and information sharing can help to cope with the "bullwhip effect," caused by the information asymmetry in supply chains (Kauffman & Mohtadi, 2003). Pointed out is that information distortion may reduce the benefit levels or even stop information sharing in supply chains (Naschold & Von Otter, 1996).

There are two typical problems asymmetric information may trigger, namely; moral hazard and adverse selection. Moral hazard refers to "situations where one side of the market can't observe the actions of the other. For this reason it is sometimes called a hidden action problem" (Naschold & Von Otter, 1996, pp. 49). In addition, it means the chance, or hazard, that a party in a transaction with more information about its intentions or actions behaves in a way that a party with less information would consider inappropriate, or in the extreme, "immoral." An example of moral hazard is when people are more likely to behave recklessly if insured, either because the insurer cannot observe this behaviour or cannot effectively retaliate against it, for example by failing to renew the insurance. On the other hand adverse selection generally refers to a market process in which bad results occur due to information asymmetries between buyers and sellers, where the "bad" products or customers are more likely to be selected and the "good" ones are driven out of the market (Varian, 2000). It has been discussed extensively in the fields of economics, insurance, and risk theory. An example of adverse selection in the insurance market is when people who are of high risk are more likely to buy insurance, because the insurance company cannot effectively discriminate against them. In some countries, for example, people living with Human Immunodeficiency Virus (HIV), and Acquired Immune Deficiency Syndrome (AIDS). The same premiums are set by the insurer for both groups with high risk and low risk. The insurance company anticipates or learns that the cost of the combined policy holders exceeds that of the general population, and sets the higher premiums accordingly. The result is that people with lower risks tend to go uninsured.

Another famous example illustrated is that for the second hand car market, which is referred to as the "lemon market", people buying used cars do not know whether they are "lemons" (bad cars) or "cherries" (good ones), so they are willing to pay an average price that lies in between the lemons and cherries (Wigand, Picot, & Reichwald, 1997). As a result, the same situation as in the insurance market happens here, the "cherries" will be driven out and "lemons" will dominate the market. The similar findings are also supported by the recent e-commerce research which concluded that, "poor vendor quality, especially as regards "lemons", is identified as a significant disincentive to virtual retailing over the Internet" (Rogers, 2003, pp. 56). Two terms are equated here, that is, moral hazard and adverse selection with hidden action and hidden information, respectively. Moral hazard arises when the action undertaken by the agent is unobservable and has a differential value to the agent as compared to the principal (Rogers, 2003). With the fast development of information technology (IT), more recently, the theory of asymmetric information has been expanded in the field of economics of information technology and discussed by various researches, such as, (Varian, 2002; Bennett, 1997; Benbasat, Goldstein, & Mead, 1987; Rubin & Rubin, 1995; Westpal & Zajac, 1994; Dacin, Goodstien, & Scott, 2002). In addition to "moral hazard" and "adverse selection" information asymmetry would also increase costs of acquiring information, such as transaction costs (which raise more in opaque situations). These could be: search costs; information costs; decision costs; policing costs; and enforcement costs.

Information Asymmetry Problems: Between Business and Government

Very little attention has been paid to the asymmetric information issues between profit driven businesses and public goods oriented government. However, the recent movement of the public sector transformation of forming public-private partnerships (PPP) by many countries in this world, where a government and a private entity collaboratively undertake traditionally public activity, has made the boundary between the government and private business become less and less obvious (Stiglitz, 2000). In this section the researcher puts his focal point on this transforming regime and discusses whether asymmetric information problems of moral hazard and adverse selection can also be triggered during the business and government interaction. One of the most important roles for government in the G2B relationship is the government control role.

A good example of such control is in Tax and Customs Administration, as it is directly related with the collection of government revenues. European Union (EU) governments for example have been experiencing severe losses from various tax frauds. According to EU Commission (Galliers, 1992), estimates of tax fraud of 2 to 2.5% of Gross Domestic Product (GDP) are mentioned, which is about 200 to 250 billion Euro per year at EU level and at unprecedented levels in developing countries, especially in Africa. Such tax fraud is a fitting example and can be interpreted as the moral hazard problem caused by the asymmetric information. An illustrative example is the value added tax (VAT) collection. Simply two parties are involved here: a private company who is obliged to declare VAT and pay the tax; and a Tax office as a government agency who audits the tax report and control the VAT collection. However in the real world, especially in developing countries the private company always, knows better about its own operating details and the real value of transactions, whereas the Tax office does not. Private company has better information than the Tax office and thus has motivation to hide and even falsify certain information from Tax office to get tax advantages. If such motivation is obvious and easy to achieve without tax office knowing, or the penalty of defaulting is not severer enough, the private company will choose to cheat - a moral hazard problem is caused that the tax office receives less VAT than it should have. The researcher posits that the problem of asymmetry does not only lie with information, in this case pertaining to e-Government but also with institutionalization and diffusion of organisational practices, such as e-Government.

Asymmetry Institutionalization and Diffusion

In accordance with the existing literature, diffusion is defined as a process by which policy innovations are communicated in the international system and adopted voluntarily by an increasing number of countries over time (Rubin & Rubin, 1995; Thompson, Locander, & Pollio, 1989; Meyer & Rowan, 1977). Diffusion refers to an international spread of policy innovations driven by information flows rather than by hierarchical or collective decision-making within international institutions. At the micro-level it is triggered by mechanisms of social learning, copying or mimetic emulation

(Westpal & Zajac, 1994). The essential feature of policy diffusion is that it occurs in the absence of formal or contractual obligation. Moreover, diffusion is basically a horizontal process whereby individually adopted policies and programmes add up to a decentralized regulatory structure (Dacin, Goodstien, & Scott, 2002). Unlike in the case of multilateral legal treaties, which are negotiated centrally between states and subsequently implemented top-down, with diffusion, decision-making procedures are decentralized and remain at the national level, at its own pace and ability to implement. In the absence of a centralized regulatory regime with highly visible and explicitly stated aims, international policy diffusion may thus result in a 'regulatory revolution by stealth' (Dacin, Goodstien, & Scott, 2002). While our understanding of diffusion follows the predominant use of this concept in the recent literature (Bennett, 1997; Howlett, 2000; Spiggle, 1994; Thompson, Locander, & Pollio, 1989; Westpal & Zajac, 1994), it contradicts those approaches that view diffusion as an outcome rather than a process. A prominent example for this body of literature is the understanding of diffusion as 'any pattern of successive adoption of a policy innovation' (Eyestone, 1977). This understanding of diffusion as the sum of all domestic adoptions of a policy innovation, regardless of the particular causal mechanisms through which these adoptions were brought about, certainly is legitimate.

Literature suggests that e-Government is not a new phenomenon in most developed countries such as the US, UK, Japan, most of the European countries and some developing countries in Asia and Africa which have already announced their Open Government Initiatives and data portals. E-Government is perceived to also lead to greater information asymmetry among citizens and government and also, institutionalization and diffusion asymmetry of the practice of the current openness in e-Government models within developed and developing countries (Perrow,1986). Drawing on organizational decision-making research and following the explorative and grounded based research approach the findings of this research are as follows. Information asymmetry between citizens and government and asymmetry in institutionalization and diffusion within developed and developing countries are widely attributed to socio-economic and political variations in developed and developing countries. Unless these differences are skillfully identified and accommodated as such into the development and usage of models, Openness in e-Government efforts would not help achieve the social and economic development goals by both developed and developing countries (Orenstein, 2003).

METHODOLOGY

At an early stage of investigation, the research was exploratory and to a large extent, it took the form of a grounded theory research, to bring in the element of scientific research approach, for which a single country case study was appropriate (Benbasat, Goldstien, & Mead, 1987; Galliers, 1992). The selection of Zimbabwe government departments i.e. Department of Information, Department of Local Government, Department of Registry and Zimbabwe Revenue Authority (ZIMRA) constituted this case study. At the same time, literature review sufficed to appreciate the similar developments in the developed countries, such as US and EU. The researcher conducted a purposeful sampling technique, which provided a total of 168 households, based on the community members surrounding these government departments, and as representative of the technologically disadvantaged. These represented the intended beneficiaries of e-Government services in Zimbabwe. Very few of the respondents possessed skills or training in computer technology or had any knowledge and information about on-line government services and some communities had virtually no access to computer technology. The author served as a volunteer within the community, which cultivated familiarity and trust necessary to collect data (Rubin & Rubin, 1995).

Any unintended influence of the author was minimized as the author was a volunteer among several other volunteers who were not even aware of the research objectives. In addition to households, the author interviewed some heads of these selected government departments, Members of Parliament of Zimbabwe, Permanent Secretaries and Principal Directors of some key ministries in the Zimbabwean government as well. The semi-structured interviews lasted between 30 minutes and 1.5 hours and all of them were recorded. Table 2, below shows the distribution of the sample.

The interviews were transcribed and their contents were analysed. The processing and analyses of the information had the following stages:

- Creation of a content analysis matrix segment
- Detailing the Data Collection and Analysis Procedures
- Discussion and Summary of Research Findings
- Conclusion and Suggestions for Future Studies

Table 2. Category of Respondents

Category	Number of Respondents	Male	Female
House holds	168	100	68
Members of Parliament	17	10	7
Principal Directors	11	5	6
Heads of Departments	8	3	5
Permanent Secretaries	7	4	3

Interview Script

A number of interviews were conducted. The script for the interview had some of the following "grand tour" questions or interview protocols:

- Do you have any knowledge and information about e-Government practices in Zimbabwe?
- What is your opinion and understanding of e-Government practice?
- What do you understand by the concept, "e-Government for social and economic development"?
- In your opinion how would e-Government enhance social and economic development in a developing country like Zimbabwe?
- What is information asymmetry?
- What is the government doing about information asymmetry within its departments?
- In your opinion how far is Zimbabwe in terms of Open Government Initiatives and data portals?
- What challenges is Zimbabwe facing with regard to adopting and implementing Openness in e-Government practices?
- To what extent has e-Government been institutionalized in Zimbabwe?
- What is your assessment of the digital divide levels in Zimbabwe?
- What is your assessment of the digital inclusion levels in Zimbabwe?
- Are there any plans to expand technology accessibility to rural areas as well?
- Do the promoters of technology usage participate readily? Where is there most resistance?
- What is your role in the implementation of e-Government practice?
- With increases in internet usage, is there improvement in terms of government service delivery?
- With increases in open government data portals and internet usage, is there changes

in social development of communities in the country?

- With increases in open government portals and internet usage, is there changes in economic development within the country?
- What are the areas in which the department has most difficulty in implementing the usage of technology?
- In terms of e-Government practices, can one say that there is a set of best practices which are transmitted by people?
- With e-Government data portals usage, have there been changes in the sharing and distribution of information within the stakeholders in the country?
- Is there an Intranet where the processes are managed within the departments?
- What kind of innovations have emerged with e-Government practices?
- Does the entire department staff have training?
- How is the know-how of employees transmitted? Orally? Written? Have there been changes with information technology usage?
- Is the government department well aware of its clients? How evident is it? How does the department try to meet the needs of its customers or clients?
- Are there partnerships with various organizations? Are they the same as those that existed before e-Government practices or improvements were made? What kind of partnerships are these?
- Does the department share knowledge and information in the network of openness in e-government organizations? What are the advantages?
- Do you consider that e-Government practice has made processes simpler or more bureaucratic?

The analysis of the interview protocol (questionnaire) was undertaken in a systematic format that is similar to previous interpretive research (Galliers, 1992). An extensive systematic and interpretive analysis employing categorization, abstraction, comparison, dimensionalization, integration, iteration, and refutation was conducted (Thompson, Locander, & Pollio, 1989). As interviews were conducted and transcribed notations were made regarding respondents' opinions and perceptions of the effectiveness of e-Government as leverage for social and economic development. The main approach to the analysis of the evidence obtained from this single country case study was to use content analysis, correspondence analysis and the reduction-data display technique. Because content analysis was used, a positivist approach was followed supported by a realist and interpretive approach to discuss the results and interpret it in order to apply the conclusions.

These techniques require the researcher to carefully comb through the extensive evidence collected from the case study interviews and supplied documents in order to find patterns that display general principles applying to the organizations studied in this singly country case study. As a result of detailed work, empirical generalizations and theoretical propositions described in the next paragraph were developed.

This chapter posits that e-Government constitutes a critical context for social and economic development in both developed and developing countries. However the findings of this study are that e-Government also leads to information asymmetry among citizens and government and also, institutionalization and diffusion asymmetry of the practice of the current Openness in e-Government models within developed and developing countries. An interpretive analysis was developed, refined, and reviewed by the researcher. First, an individual or ideographic understanding of each interview was sought. Secondly, separate interviews were related to each other as the researcher attempted to grasp, rather than impose meanings that emerged from the dialogue. In this way, the interpretations sought do describe common patterns of experience (Meyer & Rowan, 1977). Still further, the researcher formulated a classification analysis of the data to identify concepts, guided by the literature in what is prevailing in the developed countries. Next, the researcher elaborated on this analysis by integrating concepts and bringing into the picture a process analysis that the perceptions of Openness in e-Government institutionalization and diffusion asymmetry are subject to change over time.

Upon closer inspection of the e-Government, digital divide, information asymmetry and institutionalization and diffusion asymmetry literature and the transcriptions of the 211 interviews, this interpretive research analysis also grounded in theory revealed two underlying attributes to this "asymmetry challenge" in e-Government: (1) Socio-Economic Variation and (2) Political Variation in developed and developing countries. Unless these differences are skill fully identified and accommodated as such into the development and use models, Openness in e-Government efforts would not help achieve the social and economic development goals by both developed and developing countries. See Figure 1, below, that combines these elements to present potential adoption motivations in a simple matrix diagram.

In Figure 1, developing countries` motivations appear in the left and upper segment; this segment is characterized by high socio-economic and political variation, and high information, institutionalization and diffusion asymmetry and hence, high digital divide intensity. Developed countries` motivations appear in the right segment; this segment is characterized by low socio-economic and political variation, and low information, institutionalization and diffusion asymmetry and hence, high digital inclusion intensity.

SOLUTION AND RECOMMENDATIONS

This chapter offers a look at combining rational and social accounts of e-Government practice institutionalization and diffusion by asking whether a concern with "asymmetry problems" discussed before are necessarily influenced by the level of a country's development. The researcher's argument is that the higher the socio-economic and political variation in a country the greater the challenge and problem of asymmetric information and asymmetry in diffusion of innovation like e-Government models. This study's findings thus suggest that both developed countries based on previous studies and developing countries based on the results of this interpretive study are challenged by information asymmetry problems, digital divide and asymmetry in diffusion. As a result concerns with social and economic development gains driven by e-Government practice models are not as period-dependent as has been argued; rather, they may be more universally shared. On the basis of this study, the researcher can only suggest as to why this is the case, but it appears possible that aspirations to achieve social and economic gains may be, to some extent, independent of the diffusion process. For instance, if the theorization of e-Government as offering performance benefits of greater social and economic gain appears compelling to adopting organizations throughout a diffusion process, then one would not expect to see differences between developed and developing countries in terms of social and economic gains as a motive for adoption.

The findings of this interpretive research are that the information asymmetry between citizens and government and asymmetry in institutionalization and diffusion within developed and developing countries are widely attributable to socio-economic and political variations in developed and developing countries. These findings prompt rethinking of the classic institutional, and diffusion theory, to suggest e-Government models that will suit the socio-economic and political context of developing countries in particular. Specifically, this study has shown that both developed and developing countries report having both social and economic motivations for adopting openness in e-Government, albeit for

Figure 1. Motivations for Adopting Innovation and Diffusion

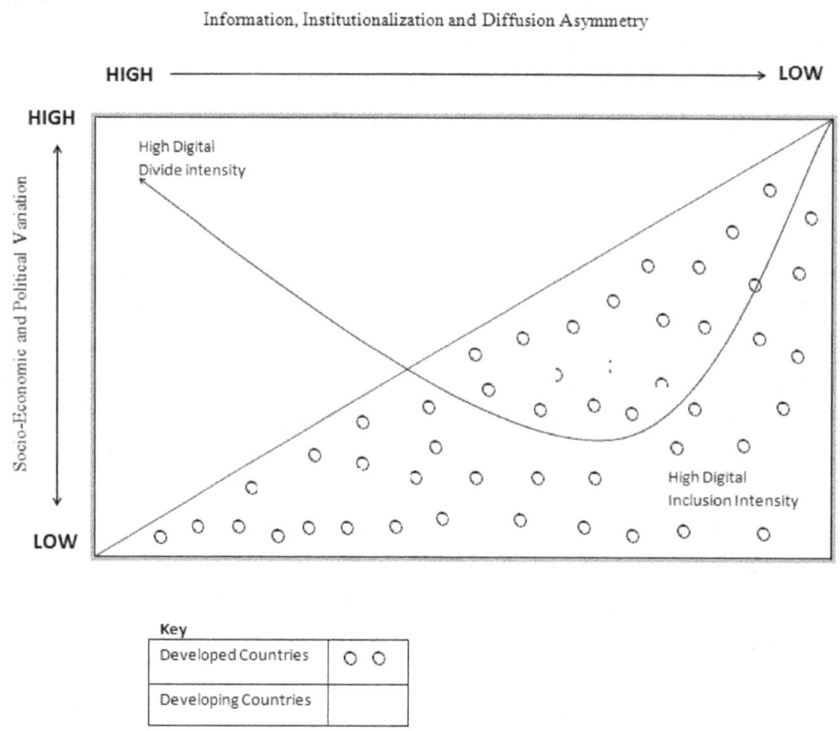

pursuing social gains and economic gains. Overall, the findings support rethinking the institutional diffusion theory's dichotomization of social and technical motivations for adopting innovations. Finally, this study deepens understanding of why the implementation of new practices is frequently shallow or even nonexistent-an area that has drawn increasing research attention (Westpal & Zajac, 1994; Dacin, Goodstien, & Scott, 2002). Developing countries, in this instance, are equally motivated by both social and economic gains for adopting innovation, however from the information gathered from the interviews conducted in this study, it became clear that developing countries have concern about their social, economic and political contexts and that they may not be ready to adopt the current e-Government models that are adopted by the rest of the world. The researcher suggests directions for further research in future in the next section.

FUTURE RESEARCH DIRECTIONS

However, connecting this part of the conventional diffusion model with theories of issue interpretation requires suggested hypotheses, which is not the focus of the current chapter. The author suggests further non interpretive research to consider sighting hypotheses and testing them. The findings and conclusions of this interpretive study could also be strengthened by hypothesizing and testing the assertions or propositions on "asymmetry challenges" in the future in addition to a full grounded theory study.

CONCLUSION

In this chapter, the author posits that e-Government constitutes a critical context for social and economic development in both developed and developing countries. The study also suggests rethinking of the role of motivations in the diffusion of practices among organization by extending the diffusion of practices and innovation to e-Government model. Specifically, this study has shown that both developed and developing countries report having both social and economic motivations for adopting e-Government models or practices, albeit for pursuing social gains and economic gains. Although organizations and managers or leaders are frequently subject to constraints that limit their ability to be mindful of practices or habits of thinking that are taken for granted in their institutional environments, the researcher believes that the extent of mindless imitation has been overstated. This study has taken considerable steps toward recognizing greater managerial or leadership rationality and agency (Dacin, Goodstien, & Scott, 2002). For instance in this research, the findings are that the information asymmetry between citizens and government and asymmetry in institutionalization and diffusion within developed and developing countries are widely attributed to socio-economic and political variations in developed and developing countries. Unless these differences are skill fully identified and accommodated as such into the development and use models, e-Government practice efforts would not help achieve the social and economic development goals by both developed and developing countries. These findings prompt rethinking of the classic institutional, framing and diffusion model, to suggest full grounded theory research in future, that would develop e-Government models that suit the social, economic and political context of developing countries in particular.

REFERENCES

Accenture. (2004). *The government executive series: E-government leadership – Realising the vision.* Retrieved July 14, 2006, from http://www.accenture.com/Global/Research_and_Insights/By_Industry/Government/EGovernmentVision.htm

Akerlof, G. A. (1970). The market for" lemons": Quality uncertainty and the market mechanism. *The Quarterly Journal of Economics, 84*(3), 488–500. doi:10.2307/1879431.

Arrow, K. J. (1984). *The economics of agency.* Institute for Mathematical Studies in the Social Sciences, Stanford University.

Benbasat, I., Goldstein, D. K., & Mead, M. (1987). The case research strategy in studies of information systems. *Management Information Systems Quarterly, 11*(3), 369–386. doi:10.2307/248684.

Bennett, C. J. (1991a). How states utilize foreign evidence. *Journal of Public Policy, 11*, 31–54. doi:10.1017/S0143814X0000492X.

Bennett, C. J. (1997). Understanding ripple effects: The cross-national adoption of policy instruments for bureaucratic accountability, and Governance. *An International Journal of Policy and Administration, 10*(3), 213–233. doi:10.1111/0952-1895.401997040.

Bwalya, K. J. (2009). Factors affecting adoption of e-government in Zambia. *Electronic Journal of Information Systems in Developing Countries, 38*(4), 1–13.

Bwalya, K. J., & Healy, M. (2010). Harnessing e-government adoption in the SADC region: A conceptual underpinning. *Electronic. Journal of E-Government, 8*(1), 23–32.

Colesca, S. (2009). Increasing e-trust: A solution to minimize risk in e-government adoption. [JAQM]. *Journal of Applied Quantitative Methods*, *4*(1), 31–44.

Commission, E. U. (2006a). *EU coherent strategy against fiscal fraud – frequently asked questions*. Retrieved from http://europa.Eu/rapid/pressreleasesaction.Do?Reference=memo/06/221&format=html&ag d=0&language=en&guilanguage=en. Brussels

Dacin, M. T., Goodstein, J., & Scott, W. R. (2002). Institutional theory and institutional change: Introduction to the research forum. *Academy of Management Journal*, *45*, 45–56. doi:10.5465/AMJ.2002.6283388.

Dolowitz, D., & Marsh, D. (2000). Learning from abroad: The role of policy transfer in contemporary policy making, governance. *An International Journal of Policy and Administration*, *13*(1), 5–24. doi:10.1111/0952-1895.00121.

Eggers, W. D. (2004). Boosting e-government adoption. *Deloitte Research Public Sector, FTA Annual Conference*.

Elkins, Z., & Simmons, B. (2005, March). On waves, clusters and diffusion: A conceptual framework. *The Annals of the American Academy of Political and Social Science*, *598*, 33–51. doi:10.1177/0002716204272516.

Eyestone, R. (1977). Confusion, diffusion and innovation. *The American Political Science Review*, *71*(2), 441–447. doi:10.2307/1978339.

Fiala, P. (2005). Information sharing in supply chains. *Omega (Oxford)*, *33*(5), 419–423. doi:10.1016/j.omega.2004.07.006.

Galliers, R. D. (1992). Choosing information systems research approaches. In Galliers, R. D. (Ed.), *Information systems research: Issues, methods, and practical guidelines* (pp. 144–162).

Garicano, L., & Kaplan, S. N. (2001). The effects of business-to-business e-commerce on transaction costs. *The Journal of Industrial Economics*, *49*(4), 463–485. doi:10.1111/1467-6451.00158.

Gautrin, H. F. (2004). *Connecting Quebec to its citizens. Report on E-Government for Verdun*. Parliamentary Assistant to the Premier.

Gilbert, D., Balestrini, P., & Littleboy, D. (2004). Barriers and benefits in the adoption of e-government. *International Journal of Public Sector Management*, *17*(4), 286–301. doi:10.1108/09513550410539794.

Gillwald, A., & Stork, C. (2008). *Towards evidence-based ICT policy and regulation: ICT access and usage in Africa*. 1(2). Retrieved June 9, 2009, from www.researchictafrica.net/.../ria-policy-paper_ict-access-and-usage-2008.pdf

Howlett, M. (2000). Beyond legalism? Policy ideas, implementation styles and emulation based convergence in Canadian and U.S. environmental policy. *Journal of Public Policy*, *20*(3), 305–329. doi:10.1017/S0143814X00000866.

Jörgens, H. (2004). Governance by diffusion – Implementing global norms through cross-national imitation and learning. In Lafferty, W. M. (Ed.), *Governance for sustainable development. The challenge of adapting form to function* (pp. 246–283). Cheltenham: Edward Elgar Publishing.

Kauffman, R. J., & Mohtadi, H. (2003). Analyzing interorganizational information sharing strategies in b2b e-commerce supply chains. In *INFORMS Conference on Information Systems and Technology*, Atlanta, GA.

Keohane, R. O., & Nye, J. S. (2000). Introduction. In Nye, J. S., & Donahue, J. D. (Eds.), *Governance in a globalizing world* (pp. 1–44). Washington: Brookings Institution Press.

Lazauskaite, V. (2008). *Internal gateway liberalization, WSIS facilitation meeting on action line C6 ITU headquarters*. Retrieved October 23, 2009, from http://www.itu.int/wsis/c2/docs/2008-May-19/mdocs/C6-session4-Lazauskaite-IGL.pdf

Levi-Faur, D. (2005). The global diffusion of regulatory capitalism. *The Annals of the American Academy of Political and Social Science*, *598*, 12–34. doi:10.1177/0002716204272371.

Levi-Faur, D., & Jordana, J. (2005, March). Preface: The making of a new regulatory order. *The Annals of the American Academy of Political and Social Science*, *598*, 6–9. doi:10.1177/0002716204272612.

Lewin, D., Hall, R., & Milne, C. (2004). *Further liberalization of Botswana's telecommunications industry*. Consultation document for interested parties issued by the Botswana Telecommunications Authority. Retrieved August 8, 2009, from www.bta.org.bw/pubs/Liberalisation%20Consult2.pdf

Liao, Z., & Cheung, M. T. (2001). Internet-based e-shopping and consumer attitudes: An empirical study. *Information & Management*, *38*(5), 299–306. doi:10.1016/S0378-7206(00)00072-0.

Mesa, A. (2007). Successes and challenges: E-governance in Tanzania. Retrieved from http://www.ftpiicd.org/iconnect/ICT4D_Governance/EN_Governance_TA.pdf

Meyer, J. W., & Rowan, B. (1977). Institutionalized organization: Formal structure as myth and ceremony. *American Sociological Review*, *83*, 340–363. doi:10.1086/226550.

Mishra, B. K., Raghunathan, S., & Yue, X. (2007). Information sharing in supply chains: Incentives for information distortion. *IIE Transactions*, *39*, 863–877. doi:10.1080/07408170601019460.

Mmegi Newspaper. (2009). E-government in Botswana. Retrieved from www.mmegi.bw

Monnane, M. (2003). *Botswana telecommunications services*. Southern African Trade Research Network (SATRN). Working Paper No. 3.

Muir, A., & Oppenheim, C. (2002). National information policy developments worldwide in electronic government. *Journal of Information Science*, *28*(3), 173–186. doi:10.1177/016555150202800301.

Mulozi, D. L. (2008). *Rural access: Options and challenges for connectivity and energy in Zambia*. International Institute for Communication and Development IICD thematic report. www.iicd.org/files/Zambia-Rural-Access-Report.pdf. Accessed 10 September 2009

Naschold, F., & Von Otter, C. (1996). *Public sector transformation: Rethinking markets and hierarchies in government*. John Benjamins.

Ngwenya, B., Lubbe, S., & Klopper, R. (2010, October). *Institutionalization, framing and diffusion: The logic of openness in egovernment and implementation decisions (a lesson for developing countries)*. Paper presented to the 6th International Conference on e-Government, Cape Peninsula University of Technology, South Africa.

Orenstein, M. A. (2003, August). *Mechanisms of diffusion. An interdisciplinary review*. Paper presented to the American Political Science Association Annual Meeting, Philadelphia.

Perrow, C. (1986). Complex organizations: A critical essay. New York.

Pheko, T. G. (2009). *Botswana telecommunications authority*. Botswana Country Report to CRASA. Retrieved August 15, 2009, from www.crasa.org/.../reports/.../Botswana%20Report%202009%20Presentation.pdf

Reding. (2006). *eGovernment in Europe 2006, eGovernment Action Plan, 2006*. Retrieved April 7, 2010, from ec.europa.eu/information-society/activites/egovernment/index_en.htm

Rogers, E. (2003). *Diffusion of innovations*. New York: Free Press.

Rothschild, M., & Stiglitz, J. (1976). Equilibrium in competitive insurance markets: An essay on the economics of imperfect information. *The Quarterly Journal of Economics, 90*(4), 629–649. doi:10.2307/1885326.

Rubin, H. J., & Rubin, I. S. (1995). *Qualitative interviewing, the art of hearing data*. Sage Publications London.

Simenda, K. (2009). Electronic/mobile government in Africa: Progress made and challenges ahead, Addis Ababa, Ethiopia. Retrieved from http://www.unpan.org/emgkr_africa

Spence, M. (1973). Job market signaling. *The Quarterly Journal of Economics, 87*(3), 355–374. doi:10.2307/1882010.

Spiggle, S. (1994). Analysis and interpretation of qualitative data in consumer research. *The Journal of Consumer Research, 21*, 491–503. doi:10.1086/209413.

Stiglitz, J. E. (2000). The contributions of the economics of information to twentieth century economics. *The Quarterly Journal of Economics, 115*(4), 1441–1478. doi:10.1162/003355300555015.

Thomas, J. C., & Streib, G. (2003). The new face of government: Citizen-initiated contacts in the era of e-government. *Journal of Public Administration: Research and Theory, 13*(1), 83–102. doi:10.1093/jpart/mug010.

Thompson, C., & Locander, W., & Pollio. (1989). Putting consumer experience back into consumer research: The philosophy and method of existential-phenomenology. *The Journal of Consumer Research, 16*, 133–146. doi:10.1086/209203.

United Nations Report. (2008). *UN E-government survey 2008: From e-government to connected governance*. UN White paper. ISBN 978 -92-1-123174. Retrieved October 24, 2009, from http://unpan1.un.org/intradoc/groups/public/documents/UN/UNPAN028607.pdf

Varian, H. R. (2002). *Intermediate microeconomics: A modern approach*. New York: WW Norton & Co..

Varian, H. R., Farrell, J., & Shapiro, C. (2004). *The economics of information technology: An introduction*. Cambridge University Press. doi:10.1017/CBO9780511754166.

Westphal, J. D., & Zajac, E. J. (1994). Substance and symbolism in CEOs long-term incentive plans. *Administrative Science Quarterly, 39*, 367–390. doi:10.2307/2393295.

Wigand, R. T., Picot, A., & Reichwald, R. (1997). *Information, organization and management: Expanding markets and corporate boundaries*. New York: Wiley.

ADDITIONAL READING

Accenture. (2002). The government executive series-egovernment leadership: High performance, maximum value. Retrieved July 14, 2006, from http://www.accenture.com/Global/Research_and_Insights/By_Industry/Government/HighValue.htm

Accenture. (2005). The government executive series-egovernment leadership: Leadership in customer service: New expectations, new experiences. Retrieved July 14, 2006, from http://www.accenture.com/Countries/Canada/Services/By_Subject/Customer_Relationship_Management/R_and_I/Le adershipNewExperiences.htm

Akinci, S., Aksoy, S., & Atilgan, E. (2004). Adoption of Internet banking among sophisticated consumer segments in an advanced developing country. *International Journal of Bank Marketing*, *22*(3). doi:10.1108/02652320410530322.

Atkin, D. J., & Jeffres, L. W. (1998). Understanding Internet adoption as telecommunications behaviour. *Journal of Broadcasting & Electronic Media*, *42*(4), 475–490. doi:10.1080/08838159809364463.

Bauer, K., & Hein, S. E. (2006). The effect of heterogeneous risk on the early adoption of Internet banking technologies. *Journal of Banking & Finance*, *30*(6), 1713–1725. doi:10.1016/j.jbankfin.2005.09.004.

Black, N. J., Lockett, A., Winklhofer, H., & Ennew, C. (2001). The adoption of Internet financial services: A qualitative study. *International Journal of Retail and Distribution Management*, *29*(8), 390–398. doi:10.1108/09590550110397033.

Bloemer, J. M. M., & Kasper, H. D. P. (1995). The complex relationship between consumer satisfaction and brand loyalty. *Journal of Economic Psychology*, *16*, 311–329. doi:10.1016/0167-4870(95)00007-B.

Brown, I., Hoppe, R., Mugera, P., Newman, P., & Stander, A. (2004). The impact of national environment on the adoption of internet banking: Comparing Singapore and South Africa. *Journal of Global Information Management*, *12*(2), 1–26. doi:10.4018/jgim.2004040101.

Carter, L., & Bélanger, F. (2005). The utilisation of e-Government services: Citizen trust, innovation and acceptance factors. *Information Systems Journal*, *15*(1), 5–25. doi:10.1111/j.1365-2575.2005.00183.x.

Chan, S. C., & Lu, M. T. (2004). Understanding internet banking adoption and use behavior: A Hong Kong perspective. *Journal of Global Information Management*, *12*(3), 21–43. doi:10.4018/jgim.2004070102.

Chiemeke, S. C., Evwiekpaefe, A. E., & Chete, F. O. (2006). The adoption of internet banking in Nigeria: An empirical investigation. *Journal of Internet Banking and Commerce*, *11*(3).

Cho, J. (2004). Likelihood to abort an online transaction: influences from cognitive evaluations, attitudes, and behavioural variables. *Information & Management*, *41*(7), 827–838. doi:10.1016/j.im.2003.08.013.

Citrin, A. V., Sprott, D. E., Sliverman, S. N., & Stem, D. E. Jr. (2000). Adoption of internet shopping: The role of consumer innovativeness. *Industrial Management & Data Systems*, *100*(7), 29–300. doi:10.1108/02635570010304806.

Cronin, J. J. Jr, & Taylor, S. A. (1992). Measuring service quality: A re examination and extension. *Journal of Marketing*, *56*(3), 55–68. doi:10.2307/1252296.

Davis, F. D. (1989). Perceived usefulness, perceived ease of use, and user acceptance of information technology. *Management Information Systems Quarterly*, *13*(3), 318–340. doi:10.2307/249008.

Dholakia, R. R., & Kshetri, N. (2004). Factors impacting the adoption of the internet among SMEs. *Small Business Economics*, *23*(4), 311–322. doi:10.1023/B:SBEJ.0000032036.90353.1f.

Doherty, N., Ellis-Chadwick, F., & Hart, C. (2003). An analysis of the factors affecting the adoption of the Internet in the UK retail sector. *Journal of Business Research*, *56*(11), 887–897. doi:10.1016/S0148-2963(01)00275-2.

Durkin, M., & O'Donnell, A. (2005). Towards a model of adoption in internet banking: Strategic communication challenges. *Service Industries Journal*, *25*(7), 861-878. Retrieved from http://www.accenture.com/Global/Research_and_Insights/By_Industry/Government/HighValue.htm

Rogers, E. (1983). *Diffusion of innovations* (3rd ed.). New York: Free Press.

Rogers, E. (1995). *Diffusion of innovation*. New York: The Free Press.

Rogers, E. M. (1995). *Diffusion of innovations*. New York: Free Press.

Sait, S., Al-Tawil et al. (2004). E-commerce in Saudi Arabia: Adoption and perspectives. *AJIS, 12*(1).

Schall, M. A. (1983). Communication –rules approach to organizational culture. *Administrative Science Quarterly, 28*(4), 557–581. doi:10.2307/2393009.

Schneiberg, M., & Soule, S.A. (2005). *Institutionalization as a contested, multilevel process: The case of rate regulation in American fire insurance.*

Scott, W. R. (1995). *Institutions and organizations*. Thousand Oaks, CA: Sage.

Scott, W. R., Ruef, M., Mendel, P., & Caronna, C. (2000). *Institutional change and healthcare organizations: From professional dominance to managed care*. Chicago: University of Chicago Press.

Singh, J. V., House, R. J., & Tucker, D. J. (1986). Organizational change and organizational mortality. *Administrative Science Quarterly, 31*, 587–611. doi:10.2307/2392965.

Spiggle, S. (1994). Analysis and interpretation of qualitative data in consumer research. *The Journal of Consumer Research, 21*, 491–503. doi:10.1086/209413.

Spinelli, R. (2008). The digital economy: A conceptual framework for a new economic paradigm. *Journal of E-Business, 8*(1, 2), 53-60.

Staw, B. M., Sandelands, L., & Dutton, J. E. (1981). Threat rigidity cycles in organizational behavior: A multi level analysis. *Administrative Science Quarterly, 26*, 501–524. doi:10.2307/2392337.

Thompson, C., & Locander, W. (1989). Pollio, putting consumer experience back into consumer research: The philosophy and method of existential-phenomenology. *The Journal of Consumer Research, 16*, 133–146. doi:10.1086/209203.

Thornton, P. H. (2004). *Markets from culture: Institutional logics and organizational decisions in higher education publishing*. Stanford, CA: Stanford University Press.

Tolbert, P. S., & Zucker, L. G. (1983). Institutional sources of change in the formal structure of organizations: The diffusion of civil service reform. *Administrative Science Quarterly, 28*, 22–39. doi:10.2307/2392383.

Venkatesh, V., & Davis, F. D. (2000). A theoretical extension of the technology acceptance model: Four longitudinal field studies. *Management Science, 46*(2), 186–204. doi:10.1287/mnsc.46.2.186.11926.

Venkatesh, V., Morris, M. G., Davis, G. B., & Davis, F. D. (2003). User acceptance of information technology: Toward a unified view. *Management Information Systems Quarterly, 27*(3), 425–478.

Westphal, J., Gulati, R., & Shortell, S. (1997). Customization or conformity? An institutional and network perspective on the content and consequences of TQM adoption. *Administrative Science Quarterly, 42*, 366–392. doi:10.2307/2393924.

Westphal, J. D., & Zajac, E. J. (1994). Substance and symbolism in CEOs' long-term incentive plans. *Administrative Science Quarterly, 39*, 367–390. doi:10.2307/2393295.

Westphal, J. D., & Zajac, E. J. (1998). The symbolic management of stockholders: Corporate governance reform and shareholder reactions. *Administrative Science Quarterly, 43*, 127–153. doi:10.2307/2393593.

Westphal, J. W., & Zajac, E. J. (1994). The costs and benefits of managerial incentives and monitoring in large U.S. corporations: When is more not better? *Strategic Management Journal*, *15*, 21–142.

World Bank. (2005). *Definition of e-government*. Retrieved from http://go.worldbank.org/M1JHE0Z280

KEY TERMS AND DEFINITIONS

Asymmetric Roles: Divergent or opposing roles.

Diffusion: Means the assimilation of organizational practices that have been adopted from elsewhere.

Digital Divide: A general lack of access to the internet.

E-Government: The practice of putting government information and data on the Web, so that users access it on line.

Information Asymmetry: Lack of knowledge of information about the other party by the other party.

Institutionalization: When organizational practices have attained a full buy-in within all organizational structures and functions, it is referred to have been institutionalized.

Social and Economic Development: Social and economic improvement of standards of living.

Chapter 3

Decision Support Systems:
An E-Government Strategy to Enhance Human Resources Output in Public Sector Organisations

Bongani Ngwenya
Solusi University, Zimbabwe & North-West University-Mafeking, South Africa

ABSTRACT

E-Government is about using the tools and systems, made possible by Information and Communication Technologies (ICTs), such as Decision Support Systems (DSSs) as a strategy to enhance human resources output in public sector organisations. The aim is to provide better public services to citizens and the business sector. ICTs are already widely used by government bodies, especially in developed countries, just as in enterprises. In Zimbabwe, and in many other developing countries, Public Sector Organisations have already started exploiting DSS, unlike the private sector where such systems have been in use for a long time. DSSs have subsequently improved decision making processes in the private sector. Service efficiency and improved effectiveness are the expected benefits of DSSs exploitation alongside increased stakeholder value. This chapter aims to provide the grounds for building an evaluation theory or a framework for assessing DSS adoption and exploitation in the context of public sector and public services provision. It discusses the results of a study that finds that, to a greater extent, decision support systems can be used as an e-Government strategy that will in turn be highly effective in assisting decision making in Public Sector Organisations.

DOI: 10.4018/978-1-4666-4245-4.ch003

INTRODUCTION

According to Yun and Opheim (2010), one of the most rapid innovations taking place in state governments today is the increased use of the Internet to provide services to be accessed by citizens: a practice referred to as e-Government. The two authors further cite a recent study by the PEW Research Centre in the States (2008a), which found that states are using the Internet to make it significantly easier for citizens to do business and transact on-line. They go further to cite an example that in Michigan, obtaining an air quality permit used to take from six to eighteen months, however, it now takes only a few days. In many states, a citizen is able to renew a drivers license or auto registration, pay a fine, or locate information on sex offenders or missing persons – all on-line (Yun & Opheim, 2010). The study suggests that in over 20 percent of the states the above mentioned services are provided in different foreign languages as well. States are also providing increasing opportunities for citizens and public officials to interact. This trend in public outreach and participation has made it easier for interested parties to seek information about specific issues, send comments to public officials, and even personalize communication.

While few studies show that increased Internet access improves citizens' basic trust in political institutions, digital or e-Government and through application of Decision Support Systems (DSS) does appear to improve perceptions of government processes (Tolbert & Mossberger, 2006; Larson & Rainie, 2002; Gibson, Lusoli, & Ward, 2007). All the states have made rapid progress in implementing Internet technology. For example, in 2000, 78 percent of the states did not offer on-line services; in 2007 only 14 percent of the states were without these services (West, 2007). However, implementation of digital services and outreach has taken place much more rapidly in some states (Yun & Opheim, 2010).

Yun and Opheim (2010) suggest that the term e-Government is a comprehensive one that is sometimes referred to as on-line government or Internet-based government. Dawes (2002) gives us a sense of the multidimensional nature of the term when she states that it is the *use of Internet technology to support government operations, engage citizens, and provide government services*. The first of these, government operations, primarily involves management practices that, although critical, are largely invisible to the public. Stahl's (2005, p. 4) use of the term e-government corresponds with the concept of e-service that includes those aspects of public administration that have to do with the tasks of the executive. Typically these tasks involve service delivery decision making, but they may also involve the interpretation or enforcement of laws. Public agencies employ an entrepreneurial model, that is, they strive to emulate the success of business in building efficiency and cutting costs. Governments seek to adopt approaches that are customer driven and are closely associated with the reinventing government reforms of the United States and the New Public Management reforms abroad (Tolbert & Mossberger, 2006; Ho, 2002).

According to Ngwenya et al. (2010), e-Government is about using the tools and systems made possible by Information and Communication Technology (ICTs) to provide better public services to citizens and business. ICTs are already widely used by government bodies, just as in enterprises, but e-Government involves much more than just the tools. Effective e-Government also involves rethinking organizations and processes, and changing behaviour so that public services are delivered more efficiently to the people who need to use them. Implemented well, e-Government enables all citizens, enterprises and organizations to carry out their business with government agencies more easily, more quickly and at lower cost (Reding, 2006). According to Reding (2006), *we are starting to see benefits from e-Government...but we need to be more active in learning lessons from each other and getting benefits of scale*. The purpose or objective of this chapter is, however, not to define the emerging concept of e-Government, but to generate a discussion and interest about using the tools and systems made possible by Information and Communication Technology (ICTs) such as Decision Support Systems (DSS) to provide better public services to citizens and business. Another aim is to explore the role of Decision Support Systems (DSS) as an e-Government strategy to enhance the human resources output in the public sector organisations. The chapter also seeks to advance the knowledge that DSS enhance human decision making capabilities within the public sector organisations.

In this context, the author first examines some insights from the literature from which the conceptual framework is drawn. Following the examination of the literature, the main focus of the chapter concentrates on issues, controversies and inherent problems. The research methodology employed in this study is explained, followed by the suggested solutions and recommendations. Finally, the conclusions are drawn and the chapter ends with the focus of the study, the major findings and suggestions for further future research.

BACKGROUND

Conceptual Framework and Literature Review

This section presents the review of literature that forms the basis for the conceptual framework discussed in the chapter. The review of the related scholarly views focuses on the structure of decisions and the benefits derived from the DSS. Important themes are derived from literature that provides the basis of the conceptual framework. Refer to Figure 1.

Hypothesis

From the above conceptual framework, we can draw the following hypotheses:

- ***H_1*:** Human resource output in the public sector organisations is significantly related to their application of Decision Support Systems e-Government strategy, methodology and framework and the moderating variables (age, years of experience and qualification).

Figure 1. Conceptual framework

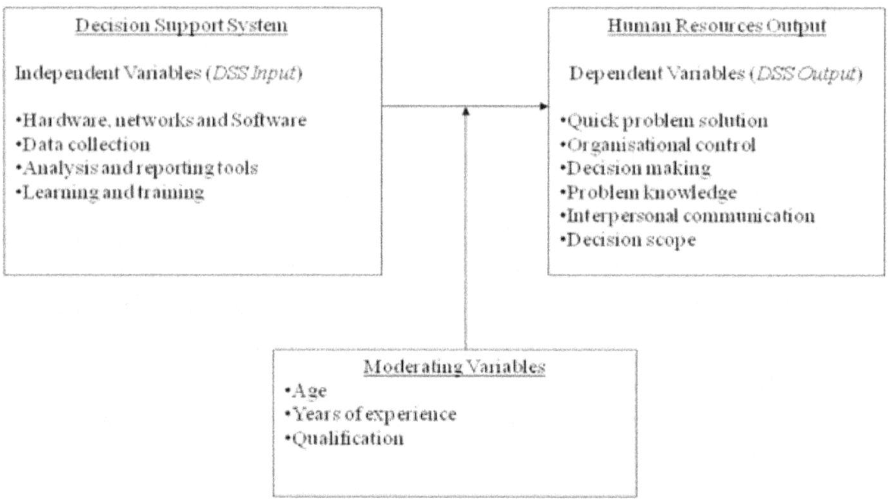

- H_2: Decision Support Systems application as e-Government strategy, enhance human decision making capabilities within the public sector organisations.

The following section deals with the following variables:

- **Independent Variable:** Decision Support System
- **Associated Dependent Variable:** Human resources output.

Decision Support Systems

A Decision support system (DSS) is a computer-based system that enables management to interrogate the computer system on an ad hoc basis for various kinds of information in the organisation and to predict the effect of potential decisions beforehand. Drawing on various definitions that have been suggested (Alter, 1996; Keen, 1978; Simon, 1965) a DSS can be described as a computer-based interactive human computer decision-making system that, supports decision makers rather than replace them, utilises data and models, solves problems with varying degrees of structure, non-structured (unstructured or ill-structured), semi-structured, and focuses on effectiveness rather than efficiency in decision processes (facilitating decision processes). DSS support technological and managerial decision making by assisting in the organisation of knowledge about ill-structured, semi-structured, or unstructured issues. A structured issue has a framework comprising elements and relations between them are known and understood (Cats-Baril & Huber, 1987). Structured issues are generally ones about which an individual has considerable experiential familiarity. A decision support system is not intended to provide support to humans about structured issues since little cognitively based decision support is generally needed. Emphasis in the use of a decision support system is upon provision of support to decision makers in terms of increasing the effectiveness of the decision-making effort (Galbraith, 1971). This support involves the systems engineering steps of formulation of alternatives, the analysis of their impacts, and interpretation and selection of appropriate options for implementations (Gachet, 2004).

DSS applications are classified in several different ways. Not every DSS fits neatly into one category, often there is a mix of two or more architectures. Some researchers have classified DSS into the following six frameworks: Text-oriented DSS, Database-oriented DSS, Spreadsheet-oriented DSS, Solver-oriented DSS, Rule-oriented DSS, and Compound DSS (Holsapple & Whinston, 1996). A compound DSS is the most popular classification for a DSS. It is a hybrid system that includes two or more of the five basic structures described, as described by Holsapple and Whinston. Furthermore, the support given by DSS can be separated into three distinct, interrelated categories: Personal Support, Group Support, and Organisational Support. As part of the functional inputs, a DSS is run and supported by good hardware, software requirements, a good network and operating system. Literature differs on which technologies to use depending on when the literature was written and what technologies in this area were present then. It is therefore a general consensus among scholars that the best hardware, software networks and operating systems that form the basis of every DSS will therefore depend on compatibility and what is latest technology for maximum output and utilisation; technology is evolving, it is not stationary (Holsapple & Whinston, 1996).

A DSS is not a single piece of technology, such as a database, file server, or network. Rather, it is a system for incorporating and integrating disparate data sources to better allow decision makers to access and compile data in a useful format (Sharda et al., 2002). The technology associated with a decision support system depends on the organisation`s pre-existing technologies and data architecture (how data are currently stored and accessed), as well as the organisation`s technical and functional requirements identified during planning efforts. In general, most decision support systems will include the hardware, networking technologies, and operating systems necessary for supplying and supporting databases and/or servers; a user interface with mechanisms for accessing, manipulating, and transferring data; and some type of repository for temporarily or permanently storing data. Key technical requirements often revolve around issues such as accessibility, processing and transfer speed, scalability, interoperability, cost effectiveness, and security (Stephen et al., 2004).

DSS operate effectively in a network of computers and other devices (such as printers) that are connected by some type of transmission media. Variations on the elements of a network and the way it is designed, however, are nearly infinite. Networks may be as small as two computers connected by a cable in a home office or as large as several thousand computers connected across the world via a combination of cable, phone lines, and satellite links. In addition to connecting personal computers, networks may link mainframe computers, printers, plotters, fax machines, and phone systems. They may communicate through copper wires, fibre-optic cable, radio waves, infrared, or satellite links (Hiquet, 2005). All networks offer advantages relative to using a standalone computer that is, a computer that is not connected to other computers and that uses software applications and data stored on its local disks. Most importantly, networks enable multiple users to share devices such as printers and data such as spreadsheet files, which are collectively known as the network`s resources (Laudon & Laudon, 2004). Sharing devices saves money. For example, rather than buying 20 printers for 20 staff members, an organisation can buy just one printer and have all the 20 staff members share it over a network.

Sharing devices also saves time. For example, it`s faster for co-workers to share data over a network than to copy data to a removable storage device and physically transport the storage device from one computer to another, an outdated file-sharing method commonly referred to as sneaker net. Before networks, transferring data via floppy disks was the only possible way to share data. Another advantage to networks is that they allow for management, or administration of resources on multiple computers from a central location. Imagine the Information Technology (IT) department of a multinational bank, for example has to verify that each of its 5000 employees around the globe uses the same version of a database program. Without a network, the IT personnel would have to visit every employee`s machine to check and install the proper software. With a network, however, one could check the software installed on these computers around the world from the comfort of their office, using the computer on their desk. Because networks allow for the sharing of devices and administration of the computers centrally, networks increase productivity. It is not surprising, then, that most businesses depend on their networks to stay competitive (Gupta, 2006; Sprague & Carlton, 1982).

According to Matsatsinis and Siskos (2002), data collection forms the foundation on which a DSS makes or derives its source of decision making. Tablin (1984) suggests that knowledge of the methods for collecting or compiling data at the DSS sites is essential because these methods influence the way that data are processed, analysed, and interpreted, making the right decisions in business is usually based on the quality of data. It is therefore essential on how data is captured at entry point; the expertise of those involved should be such that any data collection exercise requires advance planning, recruitment and training of staff (Power, 2002). It also involves the designing and printing of DSS forms and the preparation of training manuals. Individuals who meet minimum qualifications are normally recruited and training focuses on proper ways to use DSS. The training manuals clearly indicate the duties and responsibilities of the staff.

Staff may receive periodic training on how to use or operate equipment. Once data has been captured it follows therefore, that it has to be stored in a database of some sort. A Data warehouse is a repository of an organisation`s electronically stored data. Data warehouses are designed to facilitate reporting and analysis (Stair & Reynolds, 2001). A data warehouse houses a standardised, consistent, clean and integrated form of data sourced from various operational systems such as DSS in use in the organisation. It is structured in a way to specifically address the reporting and analytic requirements. Closely related to data warehouse is data aggregation which is a process in which information gathered in the database or data warehouse is expressed in a summary form, for purposes such as statistical analysis (Bairu, 2006). A data warehouse and data aggregators are major components of the DSS. They assist in the storage and analytical process (Tablin, 1984).

Power (2005) suggests that, given this participatory emphasis, DSS design methodology drew upon theories that recognised and encouraged new roles for the user. The Lewin-Schein change process mode and the representation oriented design methodologies dominate current approaches used to build and implement DSSs today. Current DSS technology with its command driven emphasis and importance given to the interface also support these methodologies. Embedded in this design concept is a strong view of the user as a learner. Traditional benefits of DSSs are often linked to improved understanding and task learning. Several researchers have pursued the notion of DSS as a learning support system. One justification for this perspective lies in the ability of a DSS to influence fundamental beliefs or assumptions held by the user as well as to improve their capability to take effective action (behaviour). For example, a DSS may be used to support choice in a complex and uncertain environment.

The "what if" capability, coupled with a powerful normative model, can aid the decision makers to reach a better (ideally, optimal) decision (Henderson, 1985). But does the DSS aid the user in challenging the appropriateness of making that decision in the first place? Better stated, is the decision maker focusing on the right problem or decision? Has the user established the appropriate context or frame of reference for the decision? Methodologically, a pragmatic means to cope with the need for learning has been to prototype the design of the DSS. While this methodology does provide for increased participation of the user and has been shown to help users converge to a system they feel meets their needs, there is nothing explicit in the approach that challenges the fundamental belief structures of the users. The researcher (Henderson, 1985) further points out the lack of a divergent thinking process induced by prototyping could lead to a poor DSS design. Learning can occur as a by-product of initial and ongoing use of a DSS. Two types of learning seem to occur: learning of new concepts and the development of a better factual understanding of the business and decision making environment. Some DSSs serve as "de facto" training tools for new employees.

The sub-sections that follow deals with the Dependent variable: Human Resource Output (DSS output) and its sub-variables, quick problem solution, organisational control, decision making, problem knowledge, interpersonal communication and decision scope.

Human Resources Output

There is a deeply-seated and pervasive notion among scholars that decision making in commercial settings is an individual activity: that isolated managers or analysts, often using personal computers, make business decisions. This notion confuses responsibility or accountability with process and activity; although it is quite common for a single, named individual to be responsible or accountable for the effects of a decision, almost all commercial decisions worth talking about are made by groups of people. Similarly, it is (Drucker, 1967) noted that most businessmen still believe that decisions are made by top management. But the business enterprise of today is no longer an organisation in which there are a handful of bosses at the top who make all the decisions while the workers carry out orders. It is primarily an organisation of professionals exercising autonomous, responsible judgment. Every one of them whether manager or individual expert contributor constantly makes truly entrepreneurial decisions, that is, decisions which affect the economic characteristics and risks of the entire enterprise. It is with this notion that this paper sought to review literature on several human resources issues that relate to DSS as an assessment of its effectiveness in the business environment.

Decision making is the process of sufficiently reducing uncertainty and doubt about alternatives to allow a reasonable choice to be made from among them. This definition stresses the information-gathering function of decision making. It should be noted here that uncertainty is reduced rather than eliminated. Very few decisions are made with absolute certainty because complete knowledge about all the alternatives is seldom possible. Thus, every decision involves a certain amount of risk (Harris, 2009). Many decision makers have a tendency to seek more information than required to make a good decision. When too much information is sought and obtained, one or more of several problems can arise (Power, 2007). (1) A delay in the decision occurs because of the time required to obtain and process the extra information. This delay could impair the effectiveness of the decision or solution. (2) Information overload will occur. In this state, so much information is available that decision-making ability actually declines because the information in its entirety can no longer be managed or assessed appropriately. A major problem caused by information overload is forgetfulness. (3) Selective use of the information will occur. That is, the decision maker will choose from all the information available only those facts which support a preconceived solution or position. (4) Mental fatigue occurs, which results in slower work or poor quality work. (5) Decision fatigue occurs, where the decision maker tire of making decisions. Often the result is fast, careless decisions or even decision paralysis-no decisions are made at all. The time savings that have been documented from using computerised decision support are often substantial (Power, 2007).

Increasingly, computers are being used to collect and store information for control purposes. Many organisations privately monitor each employee`s computer usage to measure employee performance, among other things. Some people question the appropriateness of computer monitoring. Managers must carefully weigh the benefits against the costs both human and financial before investing in and implementing computerised control techniques. Organisational control includes any process designed to assure that organisation plans are carried out the way they were designed. Traditionally, control processes were primarily quantitative in nature, which is, budgets, standard cost systems, market quotas. During the past decade, control systems have moved from strictly quantitative in nature to both quantitative and qualitative in nature, that is, from performance bonuses based on bottom-line net income to efforts that generate increased satisfaction of customers with the quality of products or services. The contemporary attitude of control and control systems is that such control efforts should motivate people toward desired organisational behaviour and not promote dysfunctional behaviour. To increase organisational control Data-driven DSSs often make business transaction data available for performance monitoring and ad hoc querying. Such systems can enhance management understanding of business operations and managers perceive that this is useful (Power, 2007). According to Power (2007), effective control systems share several common characteristics; these are common in DSSs.

DSS are a form of computer-based information systems (IS) that support individual decision makers in the decision-making process, with the goal of improving decision quality in recurring, low-structure tasks requiring human judgement (Kasper, 1996). They can provide information and decision making structures to an individual decision maker. In addition, DSS aided groups are found to make higher quality decisions and have lower variance in decision quality than groups without such support. There are several examples of DSS use in the decision making process. One such example is RealPlan, which is a DSS package for the commercial real estate industry. RealPlan analyses lease and rental terms, including cost-of-living adjustments, and makes forecasts for the future (O'Brien, 2005). Accordingly (Trull, 1996), the success of a decision is a function of its quality and of how it is implemented. Decision quality is judged by a decision`s compatibility with existing constraints, its timeliness, and its incorporation of the optimal amount of information.

A successful implementation of a decision results when managers avoid conflict of interest, make sure the decision is understood by those who must carry it out, and perceive the rewards of successful implementations are worth the risks of implementing the decision. Decision success is a measure of whether objectives sought when making a decision have been partially or completely attained. The distinction between effectiveness of decision-making and efficiency in decision-making helps DSS analysts understand the impact of DSS on decision behaviour. Literature (Keen & Scot-Morton, 1978) presents the following explanations of these important concepts. They suggest that effectiveness in decision-making requires addressing the process of identifying what should be done, efficiency in decision-making addresses the means for performing a given defined task in order to achieve outputs as well as possible, relative to some predefined performance criteria.

DSSs can improve communication and collaboration among decision makers. In appropriate circumstance, communication-driven and group DSS have had this impact. Model-driven DSS provide a means for sharing facts and assumptions. Data-driven DSS make "one version of the truth" about company operations available to managers and hence can encourage fact-based decision making. Improved data accessibility is often a major motivation for building a data-driven DSS. This advantage has not been adequately demonstrated for most types of DSS (Keen & Scot-Morton, 1978). The researcher goes further to suggest that people engage in interpersonal communication because they need to express and receive interpersonal needs and because of the different roles users play on the system and the dependability of one`s work on that of another it is inevitable that communication between the users will always improve mainly progress driven. Every decision is made within a decision environment, which is defined as the collection of information, alternatives, values, and preferences available at the time of the decision.

An ideal decision environment or decision scope would include all possible information, all of it accurate, and every possible alternative. However, both information and alternatives are constrained because the time and effort to gain information or identify alternatives are limited. The time constraint simply means that a decision must be made by a certain time. The effort constraint reflects the limits of manpower, money, and priorities. It's like spending three hours and half tank of gas trying to find the very best parking place at the mall (Harris, 2009). Since decisions must be made within this constrained environment, we can say that the major challenge of decision making is uncertainty, and a major goal of DSSs and decision analysis is to reduce uncertainty and enhance the decision scope. We can almost have all information needed to make a decision with certainty when using DSSs, although most decisions involve an undeniable amount of risk. It is therefore conclusive to suggest that DSSs provide an equivalent of hindsight to decision makers, the data that they store in the database keeps track of events past which help increase the basis upon which decisions can be made thus reducing uncertainty and increasing the decision environment or scope (Harris, 2009).

There is an ever present drive to make the decisions objective. Subjectivity is associated with incorrect, ill-conceived and poor decisions. However, some researchers (Gachet, 2004) argue that the managers are hired to make the subjective decisions. The managers are routinely called upon to sift the data available, that is, data not necessarily collected to support the decision question at hand to take decisions based on their personal judgement and biases. Ability to make these subjective decisions distinguishes a good manager from a novice. Computer databases have been in routine and common use for a few decades now. Organisations, all over the world, have accumulated data perceived to be relevant to their interests (Power, 2001). However, new applications and decision needs emerge continuously. Frequently, the data available in the database does not directly meet the data needs of the issue under consideration.

At the same time, the volume of the data at hand may preclude unaided manual decision processes; especially, if the process requires a long period of time from an important manager. In the process new approaches of thinking about a problem space are revealed. Knowledge driven DSSs can suggest or recommend actions to managers. These DSSs are person computer systems with specialised problem solving expertise. This expertise consists of knowledge about a particular domain, understanding of problems within that domain, and skill at solving some of these problems. A related concept is Data Mining. It refers to a class of analytical applications that search for hidden patterns in a database. Data mining is the process of sifting through large amounts of data to produce data content relationships. Tools used for building Knowledge Driven DSSs are sometimes called Intelligent Decision Support methods. They increase the decision makers problem space in coming up with solutions (Druzdzel & Flynn, 2005).

ISSUES AND LIMITATIONS

The increased usage of computer based decision support systems is perceived as transferring decision authority to software programs. This has led to the notion that decision making power has been somewhat transferred from human decision makers and over centralised on the machine in the decision loop. The pertinent questions are: Has DSS enhanced the human resource output in the Public Sector Organisations as an e-Government strategy, methodology or framework? How do we identify the areas where DSS introduction could greatly improve service quality and how to measure the resulting added stakeholder value?

Making decisions concerning complex systems, such as management of organisational operations, industrial processes, investment portfolios, the command and control of military units, or the control of nuclear power plants often strains our cognitive capabilities (Hemant & Power, 2007). Even though individual interactions among a system`s variables may be well understood, predicting how the system will react to an external manipulation such as a policy decision is often difficult (Druzdzel & Flynn, 2005).There is a substantial amount of empirical evidence that human intuitive judgment and decision making can be far from optimal, and it deteriorates even further with complexity and stress. Because in many situations the quality of decisions is important, aiding the deficiencies of human judgment and decision making has been a major focus of science throughout history (Forman & Selly, 2001). Disciplines such as statistics, economics, and operations research developed various methods for making rational choices. More recently, these methods, often enhanced by a variety of techniques originating from information science, cognitive psychology, and artificial intelligence, have been implemented in the form of computer programs, either as stand-alone tools or as integrated computing environments for complex decision making. Such environments are often given the common name of DSS (Druzdzel & Flynn, 2005).

It is suggested in literature that billions of business transactions are recorded in enterprise scale data warehouses every day hence, information by itself is no longer perceived as an asset, its acquisition, storage and management are commonplace and often automated (Ganguly & Gupta, 1996). The question increasingly faced by the scientific or business decision maker, is not how one can get more information or design better information systems, but what to make of the information and systems already in place. The challenge is to be able to utilize the available information, to gain a better understanding of the past, and predict or influence the future through better decision-making using DSS. A systematic review of the literature during the period 1990-2007 in the realm of initiating therapy found some indication of greater effectiveness of Clinical Decision Support Systems (CDSS) after, rather than before, drug selection. Also a critical appraisal of research on Clinical Decision Support Systems (Johnston et al., 1994) concluded that strong evidence suggests that some decision support systems can improve physician performance. Additional well-designed studies are needed to assess their effects and cost-effectiveness, especially on patient outcomes (Gordon & Gordon, 1996).

A study and publication on Management Science carried out in America found that the research subjects who used DSS made significantly more effective decisions than the subjects that did not have access to DSS (Power, 2008). The groups using DSS did take more time to make decisions at the start of the study than the non DSSs users, but decision making times were the same after a few weeks. While there is substantial empirical evidence on the improvements that information system have in supporting the decision making loop other scholars suggest that the human element is being overridden in the process, thus transferring decision making power to the computer (Power, 2000). The question however is, has this transferring of decision making power improved the decision making process in organisations, or made it efficient and effective? Building DSS, especially knowledge-driven DSS, may be perceived as transferring decision authority to a software program (Power, 1997). The researcher goes further to suggest that they advocate building computerised decision support systems because they want to see an improvement of decision making while keeping a human decision maker in the 'decision loop.'

In general, the need for human discretion and innovation in the decision making process is valued and it should be balanced and applied properly. Proper application of decision-making tools are said to increase productivity, efficiency, and effectiveness and gives many organisations a competitive advantage over their competitors, allowing them to make optimal choices for technological processes and their parameters, planning business operations, logistics, or investments (Druzdzel & Flynn, 2005). It is with this notion that the researcher sought to evaluate the impact of the DSS in Public Sector Organisations, in terms of the human resource efficiency that should be an outcome of their usage. The argument in this chapter is that Public Sector Organisations can also benefit from the use and application of DSS as an e-Governemnt strategy, methodology or framework.

RESEARCH METHODOLOGY

A questionnaire was developed and copies distributed to 43 people in management positions in the Information Technology (IT) departments of 13 Universities in Zimbabwe. The research used a quantitative descriptive method to assess the effectiveness of DSS, being study of Universities in Zimbabwe. The study focused on finding the relationship between DSS and human resource output and how they are affected by the moderating variables as depicted by the conceptual framework. The samples used for the questionnaire were picked and chosen according to their age, years of experience and qualification in order to guarantee that they had the necessary computer skills to use and they applied DSSs in their operations and decision making processes. Evaluation and scoring of responses on the questionnaire is as shown in Table 1.

SOLUTION AND RECOMMENDATIONS

The general information on the demographic characteristics of the population was gathered from personnel in management positions in the IT departments of the Universities that use DSSs in their operations. Table 2 summarises the distribution of respondents according to qualification.

A total of 90.8% of the respondents meets the basic minimum qualification of Higher Certificate/ Diploma to Masters/PhD levels. Because of this level of literacy, the researcher safely concluded that the respondents responded genuinely and without influence from other people as they did not necessarily have to look for an interpreter or reader. Their literacy level also means that they fully comprehended the instrument and answered knowledgeably. Table 3 below summarises the distribution of respondents according to age.

As part of the demographic data, information obtained about the ages of the respondents was distributed in such manner that 27.9% of the respondents were aged between 31 and 35 years of age, while 25.7% of the respondents were between 26 and 30 years of age. Only 11.6% were above 41 years of age which could be explained by that most of the respondents were in lower and middle management, higher level management were generally older and constituted a small portion of the respondents that is, 11.6% for those forty one and above. The Table 4 summarises the distribution of respondents according to years of experience.

The majority of the respondents were experienced as the results show that at least 80.6% had worked for at least 3 years and they should have understood better how the DSSs operate. Management positions in Zimbabwean Universities have a minimum requirement of between 3 to 5 years work experience. This therefore means that at least 80.6% of the respondents are well experienced for their jobs therefore give an opinion reflecting

Table 1. Evaluation and scoring of questionnaire

Scale	Responses	Verbal Interpretation	Scaled Interval
5	SA = Strongly Agree	Usual practice	4.51-5.00
4	A = Agree	Frequently but not usual practice	3.51-4.50
3	UD = Undecided	Not sure	2.51-3.50
2	D = Disagree	Infrequent, or rarely the practice	1.51-2.50
1	SD = Strongly Disagree	Not implemented at all	1.00-1.50

Table 2. Distribution of respondents according to qualifications

	Frequency	Percentage	Valid Percentage	Cumulative Percentage
Valid O Level	1	2.3	2.3	2.3
A Level	3	7.0	7.0	9.3
Higher Certificate/ Diploma/ HND	14	32.6	32.6	41.9
Degree	18	41.9	41.9	83.7
Masters/ PhD	7	16.3	16.3	100.0
Total	43	100.0	100.0	

Table 3. Distribution of respondents according to age

Age	Frequency	Percentage	Valid Percentage	Cumulative Percentage
21-25	5	11.6	11.6	11.6
26-30	11	25.7	25.7	37.2
31-35	12	27.9	27.9	65.1
36-40	9	21	21	86.0
41-50	5	9.3	9.3	97.7
56 and above	1	2.3	2.3	100.0

on what actually obtains in their organisations. This meant that their responses were more accurate and a true representation of what actually takes place in their organisations. Table 5 below summarises the opinion of respondents in regards to the effectiveness of DSSs.

Six Critical Success Factors or indicators of human resource output were selected according to their importance and effectiveness as a measure of the effectiveness of DSSs in the Public Sector Organisations in Zimbabwe. These factors were selected from the points of view of different authors as the output of DSSs use. As shown in the table 4 above the means of the opinions of the respondents on the effectiveness of the DSSs on human resource output were tabulated to measure the extent to which they agreed or disagreed. A mean between 3.51-4.50 was interpreted to mean that they agreed, a mean between 4.51-5.00 was taken to mean that they strongly agreed while a mean equal or less than 3.50 meant that the DSSs are not effective. The benchmark of 3.51 was therefore used as the minimum acceptable range in order to determine the extent of the opinion of the respondents on the effectiveness of the DSS.

The main research question was: to what degree is the human resource output affected by the DSS as an e-Government strategy, methodology or framework, and moderating variables as summarised by the alternate hypothesis? Human resource output is not significantly related to DSS and the moderating variables (age, years of experience and qualification. The regression analysis was used to find out which variables were related to the DSS and moderating variables. Years of age, quick problem solution, and data collection and decision scope were found to have significant relationships.

The following statistics summarise the regression analysis for the effect of DSSs and moderating variables on quick problem solution (Model Summary):

1. Predictors: (Constant), Years of Age
2. F=5.709
3. Significant level=0.024
4. Beta Value of 0.024 (Coefficients)
5. Adjusted R, squared=0.144

Table 4. Distribution of respondents according to years of experience

Years	Frequency	Percentage	Valid Percentage	Cumulative Percentage
1-2	7	16.3	19.4	19.4
3-5	17	39.5	47.3	66.7
6-10	8	18.7	22.3	89.0
11-15	3	7	8.4	97.2
16 and above	1	2.3	2.8	100.0
Total	36	83.7	100.0	
Missing	7	16.3		
Grand Total	43	100.0		

Table 5. Respondents opinion on effectiveness of DSS

	Dependent Variable		Statistic
		Mean	Std. Deviation
1	Organisational Control	3.6476	0.82380
2	Quick Problem Solution	3.9286	0.46711
3	Decision Making	3.7202	0.49756
4	Problem Knowledge	3.6071	0.60269
5	Interpersonal Communication	3.9286	0.54368
6	Decision Scope	3.5762	0.37011
	Overall Mean	3.7347	0.55082

From the statistics above, of all the DSS and moderating variables, only the age accounted for 14.4% of the variance in quick problem solution. The F Value of 5.709 was found to be significant at 0.05 level of significance. The positive Beta Value of 0.024 shows that the older the respondent the quicker they solve problems.

The following statistics summarises the regression analysis for the effect of DSS and moderating variables on decision scope (Summary Model):

1. Predictors: (Constant), data collection
2. F=6.632
3. Significant level=0.016
4. Beta Value of 0.259 (Coefficients)
5. Adjusted R, squared=0.167

From the above statistics, the regression analysis for the effect of DSS and moderating variables on decision scope shows that only data collection accounted for 16.7% of the variance in decision scope. The F Value of 6.632 was found to be significant. The positive Beta Value of 0.259 shows that the more accurate data are collected the better is the decision scope.

Future Research Directions

Recommendation is that the study be replicated in other sectors of the economy, such as the private sector and other organisations that use DSS on a longitudinal perspective. A grounded theory study can be conducted to develop a theory on the impact of DSS on human resource output as an e-Government strategy, methodology and framework.

CONCLUSION

This chapter premises that e-Government is about using the tools and systems made possible by Information and Communication Technology (ICTs) such as Decision Support Systems (DSS) as a strategy, methodology and framework to enhance human resources output in public sector organisations in order to provide better public services to citizens and business in general. ICTs are already widely used by government bodies, especially in developed countries, just as in enterprises. In Zimbabwe, and other developing countries, Public Sector Organisations started exploiting DSS only in recent years, compared to the private sector where such systems have been used for long time to improve decision making processes. Service efficiency and effectiveness improvement are the expected results of DSS exploitation, together with increased stakeholder value. This chapter aims at providing the ground for building an evaluation theory or framework in future, for assessing DSS adoption and exploitation in the context of public sector and public service provision.

Responses from the management were concentrated on the higher positive side showing that they agreed that most of the human resource elements were improved by use of the decision support systems in their operations in the Government departments that have adopted and institutionalised e-Government. It was recognised in this study that the older the respondent the quicker they solve problems and accurate data collection was found to increase the decision scope. To a greater extent DSS enhance the decision making process of its users and also enhance their output. While other scholars suggest that the human element is overridden in the decision making process, that is the DSS transfer decision making power in the decision loop from the human element and over centralise it on the machines as viewed by other researchers (Power, 1997). This study shows that DSS enhance human decision making capabilities within the Public Sector Organisations and DSS` s applicability as e-Government strategy, methodology or framework is justified.

REFERENCES

Alter, S. (1996). *Information systems: A management perspective* (2nd ed.). USA: The Benjamin.

Bairu, G. (2006). *National forum on education statistics: Forum guide to decision support systems*. A Resource for Educators.

Cats-Baril, W. L., & Huber, G. P. (1987). Decision support systems for ill-structured problems. *Journal of Decision Sciences*, *18*, 350–372. doi:10.1111/j.1540-5915.1987.tb01530.x.

Drucker, P. F. (1967). *Long-range planning in technology, management & society*. Harper & Row.

Druzdzel, J. M., & Flynn, R. R. (2005).. . *Information Science*.

Forman, E., & Selly, M. A. (2001). *Decision by objectives: How to convince others that you are right*. World Scientific Publishing.

Gachet, A. (2004). *Building model-driven decision support systems with dicodess*. VDF.

Galbraith, J. K. (1971). *The new industrial state*. Signet.

Ganguly, A. R., & Gupta, A. (2005). *Data mining and decision support for business and science: Encyclopaedia of data warehousing and mining*. Idea Group.

Gibson, R. K., Lusoli, W., & Ward, S. (2007). The Australian public and politics online: Reinforcing or reinventing representation? *Conference Proceedings, The Annual Conference of the UK Political Studies Association*. University of Bath, Bath, UK.

Gordon, S. R., & Gordon, J. R. (1996). *Information systems: A management approach*. Fort Worth, TX: Dryden Press.

Gupta, J. N. D. (2006). *Intelligent decision-making support system: Foundation, applications and challenges*. Springer.

Harris, R. (2009). *Introduction to decision making*. Springer.

Hemant, K. B., Power, D. J., & Daewon, S. (2007).. . *Decision Support Systems*, *43*(4).

Henderson, J. C. (1985). *A methodology for identifying strategic opportunities for DSS*. Massachusetts: Massachusetts Institute of Technology Cambridge.

Hiquet, S. L. (2005). *Network Plus*. Thompson Course Technology PTR.

Holsapple, C. W., & Whinston, A. B. (1996). *Decision support systems: A knowledge-based approach*. St. Paul: West Publishing.

Johnston, M. E., & Langton, K. B. Haynes., & Mathieu, A. (1994). Effects of computer-based clinical decision support systems on clinical performance and patient outcome: A critical appraisal of research. McMaster University, Hamilton, Ontario, Canada.

Kasper, G. M. (1996). A theory of decision support system design for user calibration. *Information Systems Research, 7*(2), 215–232. doi:10.1287/isre.7.2.215.

Keen, P. G., & Scott-Morton, M. S. (1978). *Decision support systems: An organisational perspective*. Reading, MA: Addison-Wesly.

Keen, P. G. W. (1978). *Decision support systems: An organisational perspective*. Reading, MA: Addison-Wesley Pub. Co..

Larson, E., & Rainie, L. (2002). *The rise of the e-citizen: How people use government agencies' web sites*. Washington, DC: Pew Internet and American Life Project.

Laudon, K. C., & Laudon, J. P. (2004). *Management information systems: Managing the digital firm* (8th ed.). Prentice hall.

Matsatsinis, N. F., & Siskos, Y. (2002). *Intelligent support systems for marketing decisions*. Kluwer Academic Publisher.

Ngwenya, B., Lubbe, S., & Klopper, R. (2010). Institutionalisation, framing and diffusion: The logic of openness in egovernment and implementation decisions (a lesson for developing countries). *6th International Conference on e-Government, Cape Peninsula University of Technology*. South Africa.

O'brien, J. A. (2005). *Introduction to information systems* (12th ed.). Tata Mcgraw Hill Publishing Company Limited.

PEW Research Centre for the People & the Press. (2008a). Grading the states. *The state management report card for 2008*. Retrieved from http://www.pewcenteronthestates.org/uploadedFiles/Grading-the-States-2008.pdf

Power, D.J. (1997). What is a DSS? *The On-Line Executive Journal for Data-Intensive Decision Support, 1*(3).

Power, D. J. (2000). Web-based and model-driven decision support systems: Concepts and issues. In *Proceedings of the American Conference on Information Systems*. Long Beach, California.

Power, D. J. (2001). *Supporting decision-makers: An expanded framework*. USA: University of Northern Lowa.

Power, D. J. (2002). *Decision support systems: Concepts and resources for managers*. Westport, CT: Quorum Books.

Power, D.J. (2005). Can computerised decision support systems impact, eliminate, exploit, or reduce cognitive biases in decision making? *Decision Support Systems News, 6*(20).

Power, D.J. (2007). *An empirical assessment of computer-assisted decision analysis*.

Power, D. J. (2008). *Can DSS impact decision outcomes?* Reding. (2006). eGovernment in Europe 2006, eGovernment Action Plan, 2006. Retrieved April 7, 2010, from ec.europa.eu/information-society/activites/egovernment/index_en.htm

Sharda, R., Barr, S. H., & McDonnell, J. C. (2002). Decision support systems effectiveness: A review and an empirical test. *Management Science*.

Simon, H. A. (1965). *The new science of management decision: The shape of automation for men and management*. Harper Torch Books.

Sprague, R. H., & Carlton, E. D. (1982). *Building effective decision support systems*. Englewood Cliffs, NJ: Prentice-Hall.

Stair, R. M., & Reynolds, G. W. (2001). *Principles of information systems: A managerial approach* (5th ed.). USA: Course Technology.

Stephen, H., Cummings, M., & McCubbrey, D. J. (2004). *Management information systems for the information age* (4th ed.). McGraw-Hill/Irwin.

Tablin, D. (1984). Comparison of single and multi-round surveys for measuring mortality in developing countries. In Vallin, J., Pollard, J., & Heligman, L. (Eds.), *Methodologies for the collection and analysis of mortality data*. Liege, Belgium: International Union for the Scientific Study of Population, Ordina Editions.

Tolbert, C. J., & Mossberger, K. (2006). The effects of e-government on trust and confidence in government. *Public Administration Review*, *66*(3), 354–370. doi:10.1111/j.1540-6210.2006.00594.x.

Trull, S. G. (1996). Some factors involved in determining total decision success. *Management Science*, B-270–B-280.

Turban, E., Aronson, J.E., & Liang, T. (2008). *Decision support systems and intelligent systems*. 574.

West, D. (2007). State and federal e-government in the United States. *Inside Politics*. Retrieved from http://www.insidepolitics.org

Yun, H. J., & Opheim, C. (2010). Building on success: The diffusion of e-government in the American States. *Electronic Journal of e-Government, 8*(1), 71 - 82. Retrieved from www.ejeg.com

ADDITIONAL READING

Beyle, T., & Ferguson, M. (2008). Governors and the executive branch. In Gray, V., & Hanson, R. L. (Eds.), *Politics in the American states: A comparative analysis*. Washington, DC: CQ Press.

Bolgherini, S. (2007). The technology trap and the role of political and cultural variables: A critical analysis of the e-government policies. *Review of Policy Research, 24*(3), 259–275. doi:10.1111/j.1541-1338.2007.00280.x.

Brudney, J. L., Hebert, F. T., & Wright, D. S. (1999). Reinventing government in the American states: Measuring and explaining administrative reform. *Public Administration Review, 59*(1), 19–30. doi:10.2307/977476.

Carter, L. E., & LaPlant, J. T. (1997). Diffusion of health care policy innovation in the United States. *State & Local Government Review, 29*(1), 17–26. doi:10.1177/0160323X9702900102.

Census, U. S. (2007). *State by age, sex, race, and hispanic origin*. Retrieved from http://www.census.gov/popest/datasets.html

Chadwick, A., & May, C. (2003). Interaction between states and citizens in the age of the Internet: E-government in the United States, Britain, and the European Union. *Governance: An International Journal of Policy, Administration and Institutions, 16*(2), 271–300. doi:10.1111/1468-0491.00216.

Council of State Governments. (2008). *Book of the states*. Lexington, KY: Council of State Governments.

Dawes, S. S. (2002). *The future of e-government*. University at Albany/SUNY: Center for Technology in Government.

Diggle, P. J., Heagerty, P., Liang, K., & Zeger, S. L. (2002). *Analysis of longitudinal data* (2nd ed.). New York: Oxford University Press.

Durning, D. (1995). Governors and administrative reform in the 1990s. *State and Local Government Review, 27*(1), 36–54.

Elazar, D. J. (1972). *American federalism: A view from the states*. New York: Harper and Row.

Gibson, R. K., Lusoli, W., & Ward, S. (2007). The Australian public and politics online: Reinforcing or reinventing representation? *Conference Proceedings, The Annual Conference of the UK Political Studies Association*. University of Bath, Bath, UK.

Gray, V. (2008). The socioeconomic and political context of states: A comparative analysis. In Gray, V., & Hanson, R. L. (Eds.), *Politics in the American states: A comparative analysis*. Washington, DC: CQ Press.

Grossback, L. J., Nicholson-Crotty, S., & Peterson, D. A. (2004). Ideology and learning in policy diffusion. *American Politics Research*, *32*(5), 521–545. doi:10.1177/1532673X04263801.

Grupp, F., & Richards, A. R. (1975). Variations in elite perceptions of American states as referents for public policy making. *The American Political Science Review*, *69*(3), 850–858. doi:10.2307/1958394.

Hayes, S. P. (1996). Influences on reinvention during the diffusion of innovations. *Political Research Quarterly*, *49*(3), 631–650.

Ho, A. T. (2002). E-government: Reinventing local governments and the e-government initiative. *Public Administration Review*, *62*(4), 434–444. doi:10.1111/0033-3352.00197.

Holbrook, T. M., & La Raja, R. (2008). Parties and elections. In Gray, V., & Hanson, R. L. (Eds.), *Politics in the American states: A comparative analysis*. Washington, DC: CQ Press.

Hwang, S., & Gray, V. (1991). External limits and internal determinants of state public policy. *The Western Political Quarterly*, *44*(2), 277–299. doi:10.2307/448779.

Karch, A. (2007). Emerging issues and future directions in state policy diffusion research. *State Politics & Policy Quarterly*, *7*(1), 54–80. doi:10.1177/153244000700700104.

Larson, E., & Rainie, L. (2002). *The rise of the E-citizen: How people use government agencies' web sites*. Washington, DC: Pew Internet and American Life Project.

Lieberman, R. C., & Shaw, G. M. (2000). Looking inward, looking outward: The politics of state welfare innovation under devolution. *Political Research Quarterly*, *53*(2), 215–240.

McNeal, R. S., Tolbert, C. J., Mossberger, K., & Dotterweich, L. J. (2003). Innovating in digital government in the American states. *Social Science Quarterly*, *84*(1), 52–70. doi:10.1111/1540-6237.00140.

Mooney, C. Z., & Lee, M. (1995). Legislating morality in the American states: The case of pre-roe abortion regulation reform. *American Journal of Political Science*, *39*(3), 599–627. doi:10.2307/2111646.

Mossberger, K. (2000). *The diffusion of innovations and the spread of enterprise zones*. Washington, DC: Georgetown University Press.

National Telecommunications and Information Administration (NTIA). (2007). *Households using the Internet in and outside the home, by selected characteristics: Total, urban, rural, principal city*. Retrieved from http://www.ntia.doc.gov/reports/2008/Table_HouseholdInternet2007.pdf

Nice, D. C. (1994). *Policy innovation in state government*. Ames, Iowa: Iowa State University Press.

Nugent, J. D. (2001). If e-democracy is the answer, what's the question? *National Civic Review*, *90*(3), 221–233. doi:10.1002/ncr.90303.

Opheim, C. (1996). Reinventing images: State legislative efforts to reach the public. *State and Local Government Review*, *28*(2), 135–146.

Osborne, D., & Gaebler, T. (1993). *Reinventing government: How the entrepreneurial spirit is transforming the public sector*. New York: Penguin.

Peters, B. G. (2001). *The future of governing: Four emerging models* (2nd ed.). Lawrence, Kansas: University Press of Kansas.

PEW Research Center for the People & the Press. (2000, February). The tough job of communicating with voters. *Survey Reports*. Retrieved from http://people-press.org/report/46/the-tough-job-of-communicating-with-voters

PEW Research Center for the People & the Press. (2008a). Grading the states. *The state management report card for 2008*. Retrieved from http://www.pewcenteronthestates.org/uploadedFiles/Grading-the-States-2008.pdf

PEW Research Center for the People & the Press. (2008b). Internet's broader role in campaign 2008. *Survey Reports*. Retrieved from http://people-press.org/report/384/internets-broader-role-in-campaign-2008.

Quinn, J. B. (1992). *Intelligent enterprise*. New York: Free Press.

Ranney, A. (1976). Parties in state politics. In Jacob, H., & Vines, K. (Eds.), *Politics in the American states: A comparative analysis*. Boston: Little Brown.

Squire, P. (2007). Measuring state legislative professionalism: The squire index revisited. *State Politics & Policy Quarterly*, *7*(2), 211–227. doi:10.1177/153244000700700208.

Stahl, B. C. (2005). The paradigm of E-commerce in E-government and E-democracy. In Huang, W., Siau, K., & Wei, K. K. (Eds.), *Electronic government strategies and implementation*. Hershey, PA: Idea Group Publishing.

Tolbert, C. J., & Mossberger, K. (2006). The effects of e-government on trust and confidence in government. *Public Administration Review*, *66*(3), 354–370. doi:10.1111/j.1540-6210.2006.00594.x.

Tolbert, C. J., Mossberger, K., & McNeal, R. S. (2008). Institutions, policy innovation, and e-government in the American states. *Public Administration Review*, *68*(3), 549–563. doi:10.1111/j.1540-6210.2008.00890.x.

Volden, C. (2006). States as policy laboratories: Emulating success in the children's health insurance program. *American Journal of Political Science*, *50*(2), 294–312. doi:10.1111/j.1540-5907.2006.00185.x.

Walker, J. L. (1969). The diffusion of innovation among the American states. *The American Political Science Review*, *63*(3), 880–889. doi:10.2307/1954434.

Ward, S., & Lusoli, W. (2005). From weird to wired' MPs, the Internet and representative politics in the UK. *Journal of Legislative Studies*, *11*(1), 57–81. doi:10.1080/13572330500158276.

West, D. (2005). *Digital government: Technology and public sector performance*. Princeton, NJ: Princeton University Press.

West, D. (2007). State and federal e-government in the United States, 2007. *Inside Politics*. Retrieved from http://www.insidepolitics.org

Wright, S. (2006). Electrifying democracy? 10 years of policy and practice. *Parliamentary Affairs*, *59*(2), 236–249. doi:10.1093/pa/gsl002.

KEY TERMS AND DEFINITIONS

Decision Scope: The spectrum for making decisions.

Decision Support Systems: Computer-based application systems that enables interrogation of computer systems.

E-Government Strategy: The operating tools or strategies used or employed to put government information and data on the Web, such as Internet, Decision Support Systems.

E-Government: The practice of putting government information and data on the Web, so that users access it on line.

Human Resources Output: The performance level and measures for employees in the Public Sector Organisations.

Public Sector: Government departments and organisations.

Stakeholder: Member with a vested interest in an organisation.

Chapter 4
Adopting E-Mailing Systems Technology:
Challenges Confronting Government Institutions in Jordan

Ahed S Al-Haraizah
Saudi Electronic University, Saudi Arabia

ABSTRACT

Insight into the reasons why people adopt or reject technology is one of the most challenging issues in information technology research. This chapter draws on the Electronic Commerce Technology Acceptance (ECTA) framework, which is in turn based on Technology Acceptance Model (TAM) and examines Jordanian government's employees' attitudes towards adoption and use of Electronic Mailing systems within their job. The chapter is aimed at providing an overview of the current state of use, adoption and implementation of electronic mailing innovation within organisations, specifically governmental institutions in developing countries like Jordan. More precisely, the author first quantify constructs relating to the current state of governmental institutions' beliefs and attitudes toward E-Mailing systems technology in Jordan, and then develop and validate the relationships between the various factors that drive the adoption and acceptance of such innovation. A quantitative survey is used to establish and illustrates employee's behavioural intention and decision to e-mailing systems. The main influencing issues discussed in this chapter that affect these employees imply perceived usefulness, perceived ease of use, employees' attitudes towards new technologies, and behavioural intentions to use. Whereas, these various issues are suggested in the Technology Acceptance Model (TAM), the enhanced Technology Acceptance Model extends them to include the external social factors proposed in this chapter such as trust, cultural beliefs, and sociology of technology. Eventually, the significant insight emanated from the findings identifies ways of assisting and spurring employees to make use of technology more effectively.

DOI: 10.4018/978-1-4666-4245-4.ch004

INTRODUCTION

The acceptance and adoption of e-mailing systems has been widely investigated in the case of developed countries. The Technology Acceptance Model (TAM) by Davis (1989) has been the basis for a vast amount of research into technology diffusion. Moreover, the most of examined studies were conducted in the USA and other developed countries, because of this exclusive nature of the use of TAM. It seems that there is a sort of significance to undertake a research into the adoption of new technology, for instance E-Mailing systems technology, in the circumstances of legging behind countries, such as Jordan.

There is no exaggeration to assert that there is no empirical evidence that information technology acceptance models, established in developed countries, can be applied equally to developing countries without bearing in mind some amendments to account for the variation in context. Nonetheless, it is not unreasonable to presume that the need for some modifications possibly the case. A globally applicable model must hold relevance across the broad field of information technology implementations and should also encompass a high probability of success in relocate of various technologies across economic and cultural boundaries.

The proposed chapter investigates the appropriateness of the TAM model for the study of electronic mailing technology in the Middle East countries with a specific focus on Jordan context. This is to be done by examine literature, which proposes that model of information technology adoption and use in advanced counties perhaps not be thoroughly applicable to developing countries. Besides, literature survey and research upshots will thereafter be analysed to recommend amendments to the technology acceptance model in order to make it more relevant for research on technological acceptance and adoption in the circumstance of developing countries such Jordan.

Noticeably, TAM is considered to be beneficial and then used as a theoretical foundation in developing a comprehensive research framework for this study. The framework of Electronic Commerce Technology Acceptance (ECTA) is developed to provide an extensive picture of individuals' behaviours towards the acceptance and use of electronic commerce technology in Jordan. The theoretical foundation for this research framework originated from Theory of Reasoned Action as the basis of TAM.

This chapter uses the Electronic Commerce Technology Acceptance framework to evaluate the effectiveness and efficiency of e-mailing systems technology adoption within governmental institutions in Jordan.

THEORETICAL BACKGROUND

The framework embarked in this study is based on the Electronic Commerce Technology Acceptance (ECTA) framework (Al-Haraizah & Choudhury, 2009), which is in turn built on Technology Acceptance Model (TAM) (Davis, 1989; Davis et al., 1989). The Technology Acceptance Model (TAM) was initially suggested as an instrument to predict the likelihood of new technology being adopted within a group or an organization. Fundamentally, it was originated from the theory of reasoned action (TRA) (Fishbein & Ajzen, 1975). In addition, it proposes that technology acceptance and its use can be explained in context of individual's internal beliefs, attitudes and intentions. The original TAM measured the impact of four internal variables upon the actual use of the technology. These being: perceived ease of use (PEU), perceived usefulness (PU), attitude toward use (A), and behavioral intention to use (BI). Theory of Reasoned Action (TRA) (Fishbein & Ajzen, 1975) focuses on two dependent factors for determining behavioral intention: the attitude towards behaviour and the attitude towards subjective norm. These determinants correspond to behavioral and normative beliefs where the former refers to the extent of the adopter's favourable or otherwise reaction (evaluation, appraisal, etc.) toward a given behaviour while normative beliefs considers the likelihood that referent persons approve or disapprove of performing a given behaviour. TRA with its robust nature lends itself well to generalization and has been applied to numerous areas consisting of the modelling of technology acceptance (Scannell, 1999).

The theory of reasoning action (TRA) as the basis of TAM is grounded on the assumption that humans are rational beings that systematically use or process the information available to them (Fishbein, 1980). Though TRA is concerned with the determinants of human consciously intended behaviour, it is a widely investigated model in social psychology (Fishbein & Ajzen, 1975).

Moreover, it has been utilized to develop a common frame of reference for comparison of independent research studies technology on social systems, these models (Davis, 1986, 1989, Davis et al, 1989). Much less specific than TRA, this model incorporates components from the Information Systems literature, and assumes two key determinants for describing technology adoption behaviour-the technology perceived usefulness and its perceived ease of use. Subjective norms are not taken as important factors in this model; Figure 1 shows the TRA model.

In this theory, an individual's performance of a particular behaviour is determined by his/her behaviour intention (BI) to perform the behaviour. The BI is determined by an individual's perception of personal factors; for example attitude (A) towards behaviour and Subjective Norm (SN); SN can be identified as what the consumer believes other people would think of the behaviour being performed, which is the social pressure of the behaviour in question (Fishbein & Ajzen, 1975; Fishbein, 1980).

Arrows in the TRA (Figure 1) indicate the direction of the influence. Conventionally, the theory of reasoned action can be presented as follows (Fishbein & Ajzen, 1975, p. 301):

$$B \sim BI = (AB)\,W1 + (SN)\,W2$$

Where B= a specific behaviour, I= consumer's intention to perform behaviour B, AB= consumer's attitude toward performing behaviour B, SN= subjective norm with respect to whether other people want the consumer to engage in that behaviour. W1 and W2= empirically determined weights that represent the relative influence of AB and SN, and the components of BI.

As per TRA, attitudes are a function of beliefs. The beliefs that performing an act would lead to a positive outcome makes individuals to hold a positive attitude towards performing the behaviour, while a person who believes that performing would lead to mostly negative outcomes would hold an unfavourable attitude. The belief that underlie individual attitude towards the behaviour is termed as behaviour beliefs (Fishbein, 1980).

Figure 1. Theory of Reasoned Action (Fishbein & Ajzen, 1975)

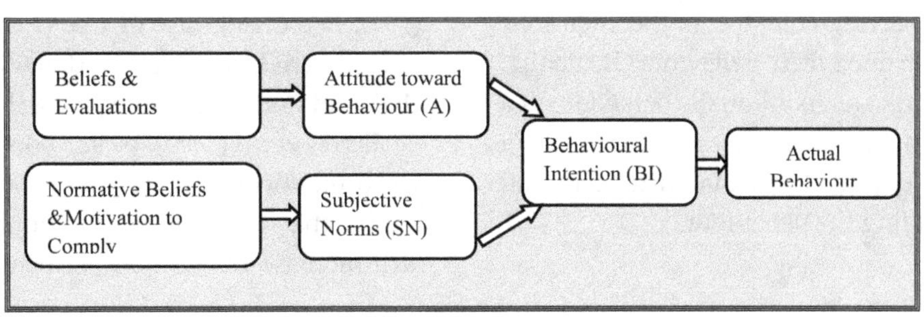

Subjective norms are the function of beliefs. That is, an individual believes that a specific group thinks he/she should or should not perform the behaviour. If the person believes that most referents think he/she should perform the behaviour, the perceived social pressure to perform would increase the more he/she is motivated to comply with each of referents. Vice versa, if an individual believes that most referents are opposed to his/her performing the behaviour, his/her perception of social pressure not to perform the behaviour will increase with the motivation to comply. Therefore, the belief underlying a person's beliefs is termed as the normative belief (Fishbein & Ajzen, 1975, p. 16; Ajzen & Fishbein, 1980, p. 7).

Ajzen and Fishbein (1980, p. 172) stressed that consumer attitudes towards an object might need not have a systemic relation to consumer intentions or behaviour. Furthermore, they modified and extended the model to better relate to consumer's beliefs and attitudes to their behavioural intentions. In addition, the theory assumes that consumers consciously consider the consequences of the alternative behaviour under the consideration and choose the one that leads to the most desirable consequences. The outcome of this selection process is an intention to engage in the selected behaviour. Specifically, the theory suggests that voluntary behaviour is determined by the intention to perform the behaviour (Fishbein & Ajzen, 1975). The TRA identifies the variables that underlie consumers' intentions to perform a specific behaviour. Likewise, the TRA looks at intentions rather than attitudes as the most significant predictors of overt behaviour. Nevertheless, the measures of consumers' intention perhaps not always are perfect indicators of the intentions that in fact determine their behaviour. Basically, TRA proposes that an individual's behaviour is a function of both the individual's attitude toward a specific behaviour and the social influences and norms surrounding the behaviour.

The Technology Acceptance Model (TAM) was suggested by Davis (1989) and Davis et al. (1989) as an instrument to predict the likelihood of new technology being adopted within a group or an organization. Fundamentally, it was originated from the theory of reasoned action (TRA) (Fishbein & Ajzen, 1975) and in addition it proposes that technology acceptance and use can be explained in the context of an individual's internal beliefs, attitudes and intentions. The original TAM measured the impact of four internal variables upon the actual use of the technology. Therefore, the internal variables in the original TAM are: perceived ease of use (PEU), perceived usefulness (PU), attitude toward use (A), and behavioural intention to use (BI). The model stresses that technology acceptance and usage is determined by intention to use, which determines the actual systems use. Davis et al. (1989) discussed that intention to use new technology can be explained in two ways: first, when both perceived usefulness and perceived ease of use are both positive, individuals will create intention to perform behaviours on the basis of positive attitude; second, individuals will provoke the intention toward behaviours that is believed to be useful for a job performance without concerning either the ease of use is negative or positive.

The objective of TAM is to provide an explanation of the determinants of computer acceptance that is commonly capable of explaining the behaviour of users across a broad range of end-user computing technology and user populations, while concurrently being both parsimonious and theoretically justified (Davis et al., 1989, p. 985). TAM uses TRA to identify causal linkages between relevant sets of constructs, Perceived Usefulness (PU), Perceived Ease of Use (PEOU), user Attitude toward Using (ATU), Behavioural Intention (BI), and Actual computer Usage behaviour (AU).

Davis et al. (1989, p. 985) defined Perceived Usefulness (PU) as the user's "subjective probability that using a specific application system will increase his/her job performance within an organisation context." Also, Perceived Ease of Use (PEOU) is defined as "the degree to which an individual believes that using a particular system would be free of physical and mental effort" (Davis et al., 1993, p. 447). Merely, the more useful and easier to use the technology is, the more likely the user would use it. Or, whereas, PU is concerned with the expected overall influence of system use on job performance (process and outcome), PEOU pertains only those performance impacts related to the process of using the system per se (Davis et al., 1993, p. 447).

The upshots of prior studies (Davis, 1989, p. 1000; Davis et al., 1989, p. 333) have confirmed that perceived usefulness is more strongly linked to IT adoption and usage than perceived ease of use as individuals may be willing to tolerate a complex technology to gain an advantage from IT adoption. As a result, it can be inferred that the perceived benefits from individual perception impact the decision-making process of IT adoption.

Both of the keys construct, PU and PEOU in the TAM paradigm, predict an individual's attitude towards using a computer system. PU and PEOU will influence an individual's AU. ATU will influence the BI, and in turn, Actual use of the system (AU). Actual Use (AU) will be predicted by the individual's BI. Davis (1986) and Davis et al. (1989) clarified that the arrows in the TAM model to demonstrate the probable causality, as illustrated in Figure 2.

The TAM model (Davis, 1986) has been extended to include various external social factors (e.g., Trust, Culture, and Sociology of Technology) that are required to present more comprehensive set of factors that determine the overall attitude of individuals to accept and use e-commerce technology. Both TAM and social external variables have been handled in many researches (Davis, 1993; Davis et al., 1989; Malhotra & Galletta, 1999; Venkatesh & Davis, 2000; Geffen et al., 2003; Mao, 2002; Jones-B & Hubona, 2005; Al Haraizah & Choudhury, 2009). Electronic Commerce Technology Acceptance (ECTA) framework is based on TAM, its social factors (trust) formulated from (Geffen et al., 2005; Geffen et al., 2003; Connolly & Bannister, 2007). While it's cultural dimensions were adopted from (Hofstede, 1980). Furthermore, sociology of technology adapted from (Qiao, 2008; Previte, 2005). These social external factors are explaining human behaviour towards the adoption and use of electronic mailing technology in Jordan.

Figure 2. Technology Acceptance Model based on Davis (1989)

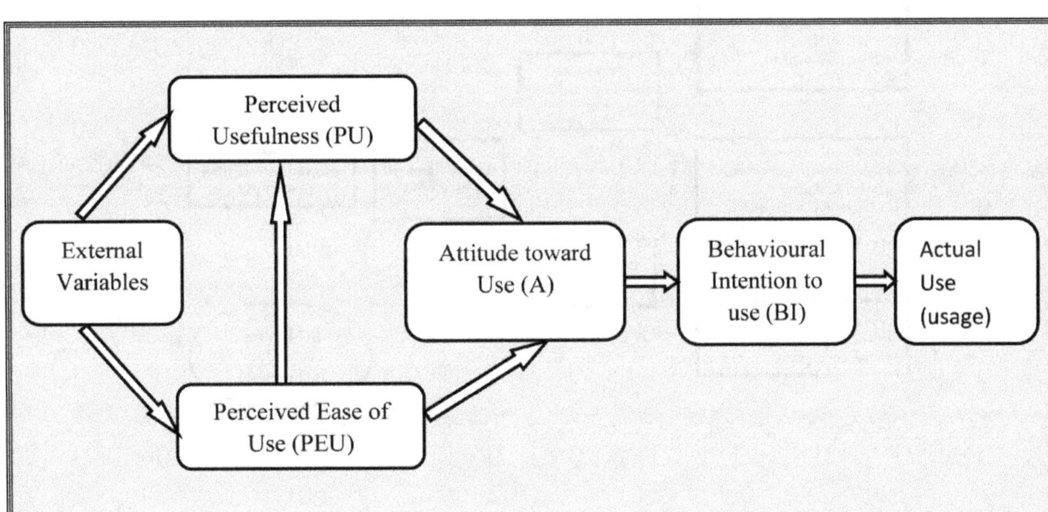

ECTA FRAMEWORK AND RESEARCH HYPOTHESES

E-mailing systems acceptance and adoption has been widely investigated in developed countries, which is created in, and for, those countries. Davis (1989) Technology Acceptance Model (TAM) has been the base of vast of the research into technology diffusion. Moreover, the most of examined studies were conducted in the USA and other developed countries, because of this exclusive of the use of TAM. It seems that there is a sort of significance to undertake a research into the adoption of new technology, for instance E-mailing systems technology, in the circumstances of developing countries such as Jordan, as presented in Figure 3. E-commerce technology framework is drawn to clarify the linkage between external and internal components of e-mailing technology acceptance model, the external factors presented by trust, culture, and sociology of technology. While the internal elements(TAM) presented by perceived usefulness of EC, perceived ease of use of EC, attitude toward using EC, behavioural intention to use EC, and actual use of EC technology. All mentioned factors either external/internal are affecting individuals' attitude toward performing a specific behaviour (adopting e-mailing systems technology).

The significance of the ECTA framework emanated from the incorporation of several factors that have already been demonstrated in respect to trust (Geffen et al., 2003; Geffen et al., 2005). This research has led to a comprehensive framework to include sets of factors that relate to the main determinants of attitude and behaviour in the acceptance and use of E-Mailing Systems technology. These factors presented by Culture (Hofstede, 1980; 2001; Geffen et al., 2005; Straub et al., 1997); and sociology of technology. In this framework, PA, PU, ECPA, and ATUEMT are intermediate states, dependent on other independent variables which can be determined in the context of the study and will be examined to inspect how they directly affect PA and PU.

Figure 3. ECTA framework for E-mailing systems adoption and use by government institutions in Jordan

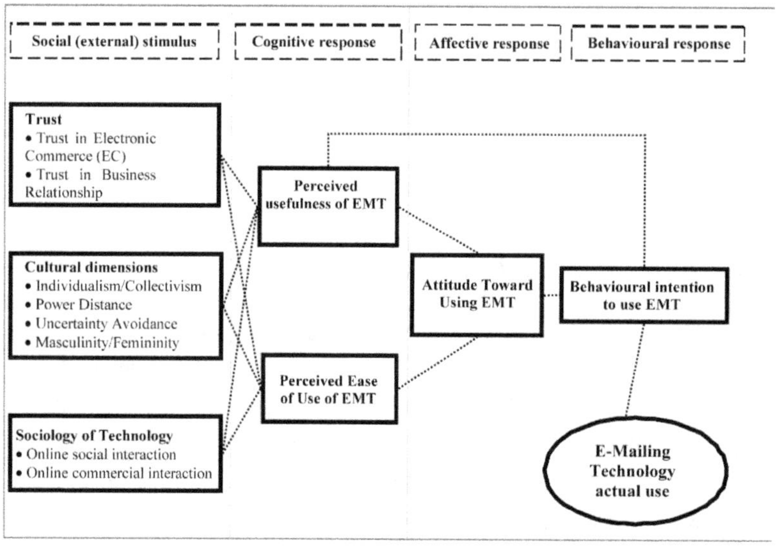

The adopted model forms the basis of this chapter and constructs based on a huge body of relevant research (Fishbein & Ajzen, 1975; Davis, 1986; Davis et al., 1989; Venkatesh et al., 2003; Jones & Hubona, 2005). Definition of various constructs now follows:

- **Attitude:** Refers to an individual's overall feeling of favourableness or unfavourableness toward some stimulus object (Fishbein & Ajzen, 1975, p. 216), which is specifically based on individuals' evaluation regarding a particular object. In e-mailing systems acceptance view, individuals generally have attitudes toward e-mailing systems application in their work processes, these attitudes might be positive or negative (accept/ reject). Attitudes contained the following components:
- **Cognition:** Reflects an individual's feelings toward and evaluation of some object, person, issue, or event (Fishbein & Ajzen, 1975, p. 12). Therefore, affects individual's beliefs, theories, expectancies, cause and impact beliefs, and perceptions related to the focal object. Their cognitive capacity has a great impact on the individuals' decision making they form feelings toward the acceptance and adoption of E-mailing systems.
- **Affection:** Represents the affective constituents that are demonstrating the individuals' feelings with regards to the focal object for instance liking, anxiety, or upset.
- **Behavioural Intention:** Symbolizes individuals' ambitions, expectations, goals, and predicted responses to the given object, which is forming the actual behaviour to use object. Actual behaviour directly affected by behavioural intention for the target of using technology such as E-mailing systems.
- **Evaluation:** Refers to an individual's judgment with respect to specific object and considered as core component of attitude. Evaluations implies the imputation of some degree of goodness or badness to an attitude object, positive or negative attitude toward an object referred to evaluative component. Evaluations are function of cognitive, affect and behavioural intention of the object.
- **External Stimulus:** These are the external factors (social affect) that influencing the internal components which are in turn affecting an individual attitude toward performing target behaviour. External factors for this research model are presented by trust, culture, and sociology of technology. In this research view, these factor influencing the acceptance and use of e-mailing systems technology in Jordan's government.

ECTA KEY FACTORS

Trust has been defined from various viewpoints according to its nature. It is a social phenomenon, which has varied definitions relying on the content (McKnight et al., 2002). Nevertheless, Geffen *et al* (2005) have stated the definition of trust in EC study as "the belief that another person or organization on whom one depends will behave in a socially acceptable manner-honest, caring and capable-in doing so will fulfil the trusting party's expectation". This chapter has used trust in internet to exchange information among employees within government's institutions.

The proposed chapter is based on Hofstede's cogitation of *culture* as*: the collective programming of the mind which distinguishes the members of one group or category of people from* another (1997, p. 5). Hofstede argued that people share a collective national character that reflects their cultural mental programming, which forms individual's values, beliefs, assumptions, expectations, attitudes, and behaviours. Additionally, identified five dimensions along which national culture differ: power distance, uncertainty avoidance, individualism vs. collectivism, femininity vs. masculinity, and long-term vs. short-term orientations (Hofstede, 1980). One assertion by Hofstede that is significant to the proposed research that is culture "is learned," not only "inherited." This sustains the belief theory that individuals can both learn and unlearn cultural traits based on environmental effects such as adopting e-mailing systems technology.

- **Sociology of Technology:** Is reflected by social aspect of technology (internet).in this chapter internet-based technology is used as an online social interaction tool.
- **Perceived Usefulness (PU):** Is the degree to which a person believes that using a particular system would improve his/her job performance (Davis et al., 1989). From e-mailing systems technology view, this would represent predicted advantages gained from acceptance and use of e- mailing systems technology by governmental institutions.
- **Perceived Ease of Use (PEOU):** Is the degree to which an individual believes that using a particular system would be free of effort (Davis, 1989; Davis et al., 1989). From mailing systems technology aspect, this reflects that e- mailing systems technology will be usable and acceptable if it is viewed as easy as painless.
- **Attitude Toward Using (ATU):** Defined as "An individual's positive or negative feelings (evaluative affect) about performing the target behaviour" (Fishbein & Ajzen, 1975, p. 216). ATU is a function of beliefs, favourably or unfavourably towards the behaviour (Fishbein & Ajzen, 1975, p. 216). Fishbein and Ajzen (1975) stressed that adopting behaviour is an indirect consequence of the beliefs related to the consequences of an evaluation of such behaviour and consequences. From e- mailing systems perspective, this would clarify an individual's attitude towards e- mailing systems technology acceptance and use will be based on their assessment and beliefs regarding this technology whether acceptable or refused.
- **Behavioural Intention to Use (BI):** Fishbein and Ajzen (1975, p. 12) defined behavioural intention (BI) as "a person's intentions to perform various behaviours". Ambitions, expectations, goals, and predicted responses to the attitude target are considerable factors in this respect (Pavlou, 2003).
- **Actual Use (AU):** Is behaviour. Theory of reasoned action (TRA) (Fishbein & Ajzen, 1975) proposed that beliefs lead to attitude, which leads to behavioural intention that leads to actual behaviour. With respect to e-mailing systems technology, actual use of e- mailing systems technology directly affected by behavioural intention, which is in turn influenced by attitude towards accepting and use of e- mailing systems that affected by the perception of e- mailing systems technology usefulness and ease of use.

The major question addressed within this chapter is: what are the relationships among these factors?

The proposed chapter posits that the application of Electronic Commerce Technology Acceptance framework will allow for more effective and efficient adoption of e-mailing systems within governmental institutions in Jordan. Accordingly, the following hypotheses, utterly formulated in the setting of the governmental institutions in Jordan, are predicted to be true. Hence, the questions employed in the questionnaire will attempt to sustain all of these hypotheses.

H1: There will be a positive relationship between trust and perceived usefulness of e-mailing systems technology.
H2: There will be a positive relationship between trust and perceived Ease of Use of e- mailing systems technology.
H3: There will be a positive relationship between culture and perceived usefulness of e- mailing systems technology.
H4: There will be a positive relationship between culture and perceived Ease of Use of e- mailing systems technology.
H5: There will be a positive relationship between sociology of technology and perceived Usefulness of e- mailing systems technology.
H6: There will be a positive relationship between sociology of technology and perceived Ease of Use of e- mailing systems technology.
H7: There will be a positive relationship between perceived usefulness and Attitude toward using e- mailing systems technology.
H8: There will be a positive relationship between perceived Ease of Use and Attitude toward using e- mailing systems technology.
H9: There will be a positive relationship between perceived Ease of Use and Perceived Usefulness of e- mailing systems technology.
H10: There will be a positive relationship between Perceived Usefulness and Behavioural Intentions to use e- mailing systems technology.
H11: There will be a positive relationship between Attitude and Behavioural Intentions to use e- mailing systems technology.
H12: There will be a positive relationship between Behavioural Intentions and Actual use of e- mailing systems technology.

RESEARCH METHOD

The objective of this study is to examine factors affecting electronic mailing systems technology adoption and acceptance in the governmental institutions in Jordan. Hence, work was made to keep the research method similarly fit with used earlier studies focused on TAM.

Topic of Study and Data Collection

The crucial point of this study is to investigate the e-mailing systems technology adoption behaviour in the governmental institutions in Jordan. Jordan has 25 ministries, 70 institutions, and 26 departments. A random sample was selected throughout these organisations. In this sampling procedures, sample components are selected because they are believed to be representatives of the population of interest and are expected to serve the research purpose of the study.

Initially, data collection was carried out in Jordan; the questionnaire was then translated into the official Jordanian language using back-translated method. This was undertaken within two steps. In the first step, the English version questionnaire was translated into the Arabic language by a professional translator. The concepts and terminologies used in the original version were critically discussed between the researcher and the translator. This was to ensure that the Arabic questionnaire was conceptually corresponding to the English version. It should be recognised that this was not a word-for-word or a literal translation. The aim of translation was to achieve the conceptual equivalent of a word or phrase which intended to produce a data collection tool that empirically performed the same way as the original version. In this phase, the questionnaire was translated from English to Arabic by professional translator from. A few revisions were made prior final version issued. The whole process of translation in this phase consumed approximately one week.

In the second step, the questionnaire was retranslated back into English by bilingual Jordanian working independently. The original English questionnaire and the second re-translated English questionnaire were then compared and discussed to ensure they were conceptually equivalent. The final versions afterwards used for this study. The second step took another week to finish. The completed questionnaire implied nine pages of A4 paper. Before conducting the survey, the questionnaire was pre-tested to determine the accuracy and consistency of the responses.

Data Collection

The survey research strategy is used and applied to conduct this study. Quantitative data is required to examine the comprehensive framework of E-mailing systems technology adoption through the associated factors of Electronic Commerce Technology Acceptance framework (ECTA). The questionnaire utilised in this chapter comprised of several types of questions. Each question has represented a component of the research model. All constructs were measured by using 7-points Likert type interval scales ranging from 'strongly disagree' to 'strongly agree.' Most constructs were adapted from existing scales, which have been visible to have a high reliability. Some constructs were newly developed because of its non-existence of some scales for examining the concepts in this study.

Construct Items of Social Stimulus Phase

The questions were selected for their conceptual significance and potential relevance to practice. Questionnaire has been designed in order to test the proposed hypotheses; several of theoretical measurement scales were developed. The scales were either acclimatised from existing scales in literature or lately developed for this study. Questionnaire consisted of the following major segments. The questions measuring the concepts within the trust context are demonstrated in the Table 1. The trust context consisted of trust in e-commerce technology and trust in business relationship.

Table 2, that appears below, illustrates five constructs within the cultural dimensions context implying individualism/collectivism(IC), power distance (PD), uncertainty avoidance (UA), masculinity/ femininity (MF), and long/short term orientation (LST). The construction of these items was based on Hofstede (1980). Several studies have confirmed the validity and reliability of Hofstede's system (e.g., Straub, 1994; Fernandez et al., 1997) and used to account for empirical observations (Earley, 1993; Hofstede, 2001). Identically, this study has utilized Hofstede's big five dimensions. The scale has employed the five cultural dimensions of culture beliefs context. Each dimension scaled within 5 items adopted from Hofstede's system.

Sociology of technology is the third social stimulus context, which has two major components: online social interaction and online commercial interaction. The online social interaction construct was based on Previte (2005). While the online commercial interaction construct was newly developed for this study. Each construct has been scaled within four items as showed in Table 3.

Construct Items of Cognitive Response

The components of cognitive response context included Perceived usefulness, Perceived ease of use. These scales for these constructs were adapted from prior studies, many of which have already established their reliability and validity (Davis, 1989; Moor & Benbasat, 1991; Taylor & Todd, 1995b; Malhotra & Galleta, 1999). The constructs of cognitive response are determining the Sentiment of individual toward accepting E-Mailing technology. Perceived Usefulness and perceived Ease of Use constructs contained 2 items for each as explained in Table 4.

Table 1. Theoretical measurements within trust context

Construct	Code	Statement	Measurement
Trust in E Commerce Technology (TECT) (Based on Connolly & Bannister, 2007)	TECT1	I trust the internet to do transactions such as buying, selling, and money transferring	1=strongly disagree to 7=strongly agree
	TECT2	Internet shopping is unreliable	
	TECT3	Internet shopping cannot be trusted, there are just too many uncertainties	
	TECT4	In general, I cannot rely on internet vendors to keep the promises that they make.	
Trust in Business Relationship (TBR) (based on Chow & Chan, 2008)	TBR1	I know that other organisational members will always try and help me out if I get into difficulties	
	TBR2	I can always trust other organisational members to lend me a hand if I need it	
	TBR3	I can always rely on other organisational members to make my job easier	
	TBR4	In general, I have a very good relationship with other organisational members	

Construct Items of Affective and Behavioural Response

The components of affective and behavioural response context contained Attitude toward EM Acceptance, behavioural Intention to use, and the Adoption of EM Innovation. These scales for these constructs were adapted from prior studies, many of which have already established their reliability and validity (Fishbein & Ajzen, 1975; Davis, 1989; Moor & Benbasat, 1991; Taylor & Todd, 1995b; Malhotra & Galleta, 1999). The constructs of affective and behavioural response are determining the actual adoption of EM innovation.

Attitude toward EM Acceptance constructs consisted of two items, EM Use Intention included two items, and finally the Adoption of EM Innovation contained two items (Table 5).

In addition, the internal consistency reliability method was used to verify the reliability of the scales employed in the questionnaire. Cornbach Alpha was used to measure internal consistency for survey and research variables based on sample estimation. Cronbach Alpha can be increased in either the average correlation or number of items (Zander & Kogout, 1995). Nunnally (1978) stressed that Cronbach Alpha must be greater than 0.7 to be considered good and acceptable for most research. Furthermore, value more than 0.6 is regarded as a satisfactory level (Dinev & Hart, 2002; Nunnally). Table 6 reflects the Cronbach's Alpha scores for modified scales together with the number of items used in the final scale of the study.

RESULTS AND DISCUSSION

The findings reported in this study are based on the analysis of 140 usable responses collected from the respondents. The questionnaire items tapped respondents'/employees' expectations of the use of

Table 2. Theoretical measurements within culture context

Construct	Code	Statement	Measurement
Individualism /Collectivism (IC) (Based on Hofstede, 1991)	IC1	Group success is more significant than individual success	1=strongly disagree to 7=strongly agree
	IC2	Individual rewards are not as important as group welfare	
	IC3	Being accepted as a member of a group is more important than being independent	
	IC4	Manager should encourage loyalty and a sense of duty in subordinates than it is to encourage individual initiative	
	IC5	In general, being loyal to a group is more valuable than individual gain.	
Power Distance (PD) (based on Hofstede, 1991)	PD1	Managers should make their decision without consulting subordinators	1=strongly disagree to 7=strongly agree
	PD2	Manager should be aware not to ask the standpoints of subordinators too frequently, otherwise the manager maybe considered to be a weak or incompetent	
	PD3	Employees should not comments their manager's decision	
	PD4	Higher level employees should have more power than the lower level employees	
	PD5	In general, the manager, not the employees should have the last word	
Uncertainty Avoidance (UA) (based on Hofstede, 1991)	UA1	It is better to work within an organisation with specific rules and regulations as opposed to a more flexible organisation	1=strongly disagree to 7=strongly agree
	UA2	Order and structure are very significant in a work environment	
	UA3	People should avoid making changes when their outcomes are uncertain.	
	UA4	Providing opportunities to be innovative is more important than requiring standardized work procedures.	
	UA5	In general, it is important that people take initiative in their work rather than following up step-by-step instructions.	
Masculinity/Femininity (MF) (based on Hofstede, 1991)	MF1	It is important for men to have a professional career than it is for women to have a professional career	1=strongly disagree to 7=strongly agree
	MF2	Women do not value recognition and promotion in their work as much as men do	
	MF3	It is preferable to have a man in high position rather than a woman	
	MF4	Men usually solve problems with logical analysis; women usually solve problems with intuition	
	MF5	In general, there are some jobs in which man can always do better than a woman.	
Long vs. Short-Term Orientation (LST) (Based on Hofstede, 2001)	LST1	It is important to have a conscience in business	1=strongly disagree to 7=strongly agree
	LST2	Respect for tradition hinders performance	
	LST3	Personal stability is not crucial to success in business	
	LST4	The exchange of favours and gifts is not necessary to excel	
	LST5	Upholding one's personal image makes little difference in goal achievement.	

Table 3. Theoretical measurements within sociology of technology context

Construct	Code	Statement	Measurement
Online Social Interaction (OSI) (Based on Previte, 2005)	OSI1	The value of internet is the social network, it makes us a global community	1=strongly disagree to 7=strongly agree
	OSI2	Most of my personal and social interactions with close friends are taking place electronically. It is a real frustration for me when I have a friend that's part of my immediate social group that does not have e-mail contact.	
	OSI3	By using the internet I keep in touch with people more than I ever would have done before	
	OSI4	In general, I've got a greater opportunity to meet more like-minded people online, than in my local community	
Online Commercial Interaction (OCI) (newly developed by the author)	OCI	The internet enables me to make several transactions such as buying, selling goods and services in a safe environment.	1=strongly disagree to 7=strongly agree
	OCI2	It would be preferred to inspect items physically rather than view it virtually on the internet	
	OCI3	The internet is empowering people to have more control over what they are seeing, or doing, or thinking about	
	OCI4	In general, internet facilitates people to do business in an online environment easily	

Table 4. Theoretical measurements within cognitive response context

Construct	Code	Statement	Measurement
Perceived Usefulness (PA) (based on Davis, 1989)	PU1	Using the internet in my job would enable me to accomplish tasks more quickly	1=strongly disagree to 7=strongly agree
	PU2	Using the internet would improve my job performance	
Perceived Ease of Use(PU) (Based on Davis,1989)	PEOU1	Learning to operate the internet would be easy for me	
	PEOU2	It would be easy for me to become skilful at using the internet	

Table 5. Theoretical measurements within affective and behavioural response context

Construct	Code	Statement	Measurement
Attitude toward using(ATU) (Based on Davis,1989; Taylor & Todd, 1995b)	ATU 1	Using the internet is a good idea	1=strongly disagree to 7=strongly agree
	ATU 2	Using the internet would be pleasant	
Behavioural Intention to Use (BI) (based on Liu & Ma, 2006)	BI 1	I am willing to use the internet for my work	
	BI 2	I do not mind spending some time to learn how to use the internet for my work	
Actual Use (AU)	AU 1	I am using Electronic Commerce Technology	
	AU 2	I am not using Electronic Commerce Technology	

Table 6. Cronbach Alpha test results of the main study

Variable	No. Of items	No. Of cases	Alpha %
Trust	2	140	62.2%
Culture	10	140	60.4%
Sociology of technology	2	140	65.3%
Perceived usefulness	2	140	80.4%
Perceived ease of use	2	140	70.9%
Attitude toward use	2	140	68.1%
Behavioural intention	2	140	63.2%
Total	22	140	67.2%

the e-mailing systems technology. This proposition appears reasonable bestowed that TAM considers behavioural intentions of the information systems users are reliable predictors of future system usage (Malhotra & Galletta, 1999).

Significantly, in this study it is very important to clarify the demographic variables results as it shows how demographics can be playing a crucial role the adoption process. Table 7 demonstrates the analysing demographic variable results.

The analysis process for the embarked framework is conducted within three phases: first, using multiple linear regressions for variables such as trust, culture, sociology of technology, perceived usefulness, perceived ease of use, and attitude toward using. While a simple linear regression used to explain the relationship between attitude toward using and behavioural intention, and on the other hand to demonstrate the correlation between perceived usefulness and behavioural intention. Finally, in the last phase, one-way ANOVA is used because Actual Use (AU) was a category variable with two items. To test the hypotheses associated with the predictors and dependent variables, the SPSS (17) compute package was used compute predictor variables entered/removed, model summary, analysis variance (ANOVA). The Figure 4 below shows these used analysis techniques classified within phases.

In the first phase, multiple regressions analysis is used to predict the relative contribution of trust, culture, and sociology of technology to the outcome variables, perceived usefulness (PU), and perceived ease of use (PEOU). Thus, trust, culture, and sociology of technology as independents variables predict the relationships with dependent variables (PU and PEOU). In addition, multiple regressions analysis is used to predict the relationships between PU, PEOU and attitude towards using (ATU). PU and PEOU as independent variables predict the relationships with the dependent variable (ATU).

In the second phase, simple linear regression analysis is used to figure the contribution of ATU to the outcome variable, behavioural intention (BI). Resemble, the independent variable ATU

Table 7. Analysing demographic variables results

Variable	Valid	Frequency	Percent %
Gender	Male	104	74.2%
	Female	36	25.8%
Age	From 18-25 year	41	29.2%
	From 26-35 year	52	37.2%
	From 36-45 year	33	23.6%
	More than 45 year	14	10%
Education level	High school	11	7.8%
	Diploma	23	16.4%
	Bachelor	80	57.2%
	Master	21	15 %
	Doctorate	3	2.1%
	Other	2	1.4%
Management position	Top management	24	17.2%
	Middle management	76	54.3%
	Lower management	40	28.6%
Use of internet	Yes	138	98.6%
	No	2	1.4%
Time period	Less than six months	3	2.3%
	6 months-12 months	8	5.7%
	1-3 year	23	16.4%
	4-6 year	34	24.2%
	More than 7 years	72	51.4%
Frequency of internet usage	Less than once a month	1	0.08%
	Once a month	2	1.4%
	Once a week	10	7.1%
	Once per 2-3 days	19	13.6%
	Every day	108	77.1%
Knowledge and skills	Beginner user	12	8.6%
	Moderate user	57	40.7%
	Advanced user	71	50.7%
Total		140	100

predicts the relationship with the dependent variable BI. Moreover, simple linear regression analysis is used to find the contribution of PU to the outcome variable, Behavioural Intention (BI). In other words, the independent variable PU predicts the relationship with the dependent variable BI.

Finally, in the third phase, one-way analysis of Variance (ANOVA) is used to find whether or not there is a significant difference in people behavioural Intention (BI) during actual Electronic Mailing systems use.

External Social Factors That Influence E-Mailing Systems Acceptance/Usage

The hypothesised relationships depicted in Figure3 were tested using multiple linear regressions to preserve consistency with prior studies that have been extended and developed TAM. The general form of the multiple regressions equation for the variables included in this study as follows:

$$Y= \beta 1+\beta 2\ X1+\beta 2\ X2+....+\beta n\ Xn+\epsilon,$$

Figure 4. Three phases' techniques of analysis

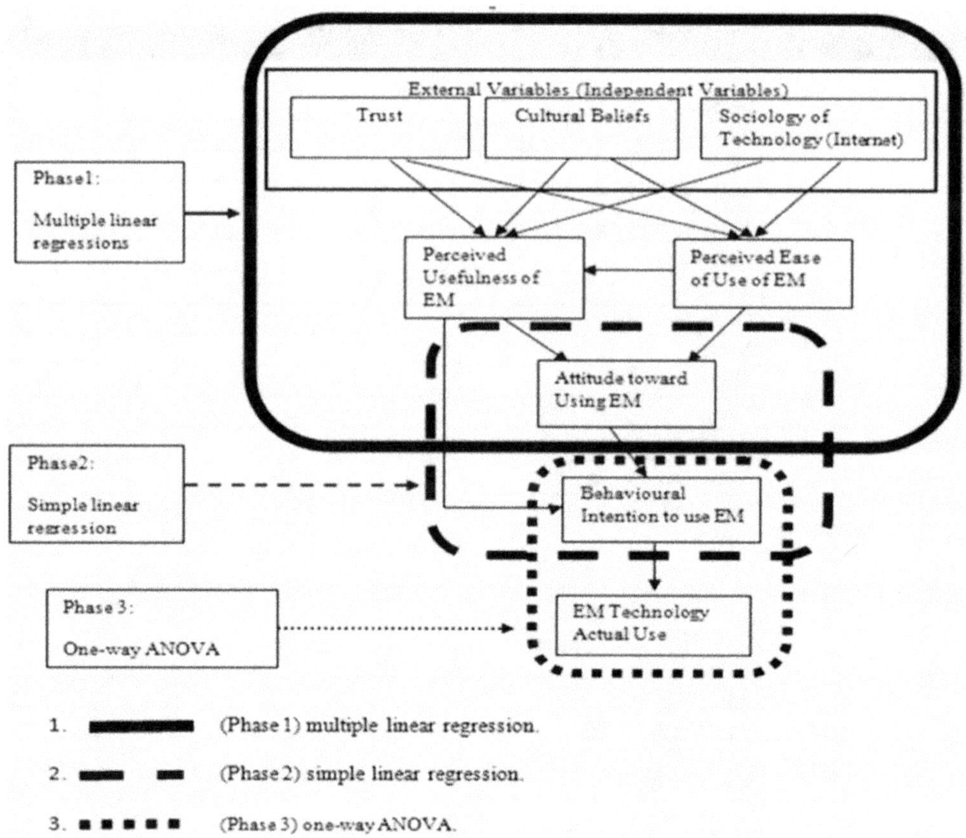

where y is the response variable; X1, X2.... Xn are the predictors variables; β1, β2, β3.... βn are the partial regression coefficients, net regression coefficients or just regression coefficients, also € is the error.

Hypotheses H1& H2: multiple regressions analysis was used between trust and perceived usefulness in the first hypothesis, and hypothesis 2 tested the relationship between trust and perceived ease of use, as PU and PEOU dependent variables. Based on this, the value of P for trust is positive and not significant ($P=0.204>0.05$), and thus does not support hypothesis H1. The value of P for trust in the internet is positive too but not significant ($P= 0.101>0.05$), and therefore does not support hypothesis H2.

H3 & H4, multiple regressions analysis was used between culture and perceived usefulness in the hypothesis H3, also hypothesis 4 tested the relationship between culture and perceived ease of use, as PU and PEOU dependent variables. The value of P for culture is positive but not significant ($P= 0.69> 0.05$), and thus does not support hypothesis H3. While, the value of P for culture is positive and not significant ($P= 0.022> 0.05$), and therefore it does not support hypothesis H4.

H5 & H6, multiple regressions analysis was used between sociology of technology and perceived usefulness in the hypothesis H5, also hypothesis 6 tested the relationship between sociology of technology and perceived ease of use, as PU and PEOU dependent variables. The value of P for sociology of technology is positive and significant ($P= 0.000< 0.05$), R^2 explains 12% of the variance related to PU, thus supports hypothesis H5. Whereas, the value of P for sociology of technology is positive but not significant (P= 0.012> 0.05), and hence it does not support hypothesis H6.

Influence on Attitudes

Multiple regressions analysis was used between perceived usefulness and attitude towards using in the hypothesis H7; also hypothesis 8 tested the relationship between perceived ease of use as the independent variable, and ATU as a dependent variable. The value of P for perceived usefulness is positive and significant (P= 0.000< 0.05), R^2 explains 17%of the variance related to ATU, and therefore supports hypothesis H7. In addition, the value of P for perceived ease of use is positive and significant (P=0.002> 0.05), R^2 explains 8.8% of the variance related to ATU, and consequently it does support hypothesis H8.

In other respect, simple linear regression analysis was used between perceived usefulness as the dependent variable, and PEU as the independent variable. The value of P for perceived ease of use is positive and significant (P=0.000>0.05), R^2 explains 8.8% of the variance related to PU, and thus support hypothesis H9.

Influence on Behavioural Intentions

H10, simple linear regression analysis was used between behavioural intention BI, as the dependent variable, and PU as the independent variable. The value of P for perceived ease of use is positive and significant (0.000>0.05), R^2 explains 14% of the variance related to BI, and therefore supports hypothesis H10.

For hypothesis H11, simple linear regression analysis was used between behavioural intention BI, as the dependent variable, and ATU as the independent variable. The value of P for attitude toward using is positive and significant (0.000>0.05), R^2 explains 2.9% of the variance related to BI, and therefore supports hypothesis H11.

Influence on Electronic Mailing Technology Use

To test the associated hypothesis (H12) between actual use (AU) of e-mailing systems technology (EM) and behavioural intention (BI) in this study, univariate Analysis of Variance (UANOVA) is used. This is because AU was a category variable and it gives the same results that supported H11. The hypothesis proposes that the actual use of e-mailing technology varies as per behavioural intention to use e-mailing systems technology. The mean, standard deviation and numbers of those actually use e-mailing systems technology is M=5.7500, SD=1.48917, N=121, while the mean, standard deviation, and numbers those who do not actually use e-mailing systems technology is M=2.4571, SD=1.84808, N=19. This clarified that there is a high proportion of behavioural intention to use e-mailing systems technology within governmental institution in Jordan. Table8 shows these means and standard deviations, and num-

Table 8. Descriptive statistics

Using e-mailing systems technology	Mean	Std. Deviation	N
Yes	5.7500	1.48917	121
No	2.4571	1.84808	19
Total	8.2071	3.33725	140

bers for individuals accept /reject using e-mailing systems technology in Jordan. Moreover, Table 9 illustrates the test between- subjects' effects.

CONCLUSION

The findings of this study suggest that social External factors impacts play a crucial role in determining the acceptance and usage behaviour of new information technologies. For example, culture is suggested to play an important role in explaining different patterns in information technology usage (Straub et al., 1997). Furthermore, cultural factors are a significant point of difference between individuals in the Middle East and those in the advanced countries. Culture beliefs are key independent variables in predicting the success or failure of technology acceptance (Straub et al., 2001). The finding of this study suggests that culture has a positive influence on PU and PEU but this influence is not significant. However, to determine the level influence of culture on PU and PEU, the grand mean was calculated as 4.65. When this was compared with the 7 point Likert scale, it was greater than the neutrality (mid) point (+4), and less than the agreement (+5) which means that there is only some perception of usefulness and ease of use by the respondents in the sample. Therefore, the mean (4.65) indicates that there is

Table 9. Tests of between- subjects effects

Dependent Variable:s7

Source	Type III Sum of Squares	df	Mean Square	F	Sig.
Corrected Model	107.960[a]	22	4.907	1.750	.030
Intercept	604.338	1	604.338	215.576	.000
gender	2.018	1	2.018	.720	.398
age	5.089	3	1.696	.605	.613
Education level	35.672	4	8.918	3.181	.016
Management position	18.119	4	4.530	1.616	.175
Time period	11.128	4	2.782	.992	.415
Frequency of internet usage	15.631	4	3.908	1.394	.240
Knowledge and skills	1.855	2	.928	.331	.719
Error	325.191	116	2.803		
Total	19571.000	139			
Corrected Total	433.151	138			

a. R Squared = .249 (Adjusted R Squared = .107)

a perceived usefulness and perceived ease of use of e-mailing systems (see Table 10).

The findings also suggest that trust has a positive influence on PU and PEU but this influence is not significant. To establish the level of trust in the internet, as perceived by respondents, the grand mean for trust calculated as 4.675. In comparison with 7 Likert scale, it was greater than the neutrality (mid) point (+4), and less than the agreement (+5), which reflects that there is some perception of usefulness and ease of use by the respondents in the sample. Thus, the mean (4.675) indicates that there is a perceived usefulness and perceived ease of use of e-mailing systems (see Table 10).

Sociology of technology is third external factor which in turn affect PU and PEU. Sociology of technology has a positive as well as a significant influence on PU. Whereas, it has a positive influence on PEU but this influence is not significant. In order to determine the level influence of Sociology of technology on PU and PEU, the grand mean was calculated as 4.4143. When this was compared with the 7 point Likert scale, it was greater than the neutrality (mid) point (+4), and less than the agreement (+5) which means that there is only some perception of usefulness and ease of use by the respondents in the sample. Therefore, the mean (4.4143) indicates that there is a perceived usefulness and perceived ease of use of e-mailing systems (see Table 10).

Consequently the consideration of social influences and how they impact the commitment of the individual toward acceptance and use of the information systems appears significant for insight, explaining, justifying, and predicting system usage and acceptance behaviour.

With respect to TAM inner components, the study findings revealed a significant, positive relationship between Perceived Usefulness (PU) and Attitude Toward Using (ATU), Perceived Ease of Use (PEU) and Attitude Toward Using(ATU), Perceived Ease of Use(PEU) and Perceived Usefulness(PU), Attitude Toward Using (ATU) and Behavioural Intention (BI), and Perceived Usefulness(PU)and Behavioural Intention(BI). The findings reported a high consistency with the findings from previous studies emphasising Technology Acceptance Model (TAM) (Davis, 1993; Hsu &Chiu, 2004; Saade et al., 2007; Bagozzi, 2007; Liu & Ma, 2006; Malhotra & Galletta, 1999). Table 10 explains the mean of these factors.

Based on the findings of this study, it seems that social influences have direct effects on the user's perceived usefulness and perceived ease of use, then in turn PU and PEU affect directly attitude toward using, which in turn affects be-

Table 10. Results of the respondents' categorisation for the study

Variables	Mean	The results
Trust	4.675	High
Culture	4.64713	High
Sociology of Technology	4.4143	High
Perceived Usefulness (PU)	5.08215	High
Perceived Ease of Use (PEOU)	5.75	High
Attitude Toward Using (ATU)	6.1536	High
Behavioural Intention (BI)	5.8607	High
Actual Use (AU)	4.10355	High

havioural intention to use. All mentioned factors are interrelated directly also PU and PEU mediate the relationship between social external factors and attitude toward using e-mailing technology. Furthermore, PU is mediated the relationship between social external factors and behavioural intention, and finally, BI has a direct effect on actual use of the system, which determined by attitude toward using the system.

Hence, it seems that the crucial point of innovation adoption and acceptance is developing individuals' attitudes that are spurring to effective usage and acceptance behaviour. More insight into these relationships needs to be promoted in the future research informed by the conceptual and theoretical facets developed in this study.

The study has important implications for enquiry often questioned that why individuals demonstrate ineffective acceptance and usage behaviour, and then resulting in negligible performance improvements resulting from technology application (Gillooly, 1998). Based on this, there might some factors affecting those individuals' decision to accept or use technologies; this could be affected by decision making process as the high proportion of employees are middle and lower management, so the decision making process is issued from high positioned people, then individuals mostly are not involved to contribute whether or not accepting or using new technologies within their job.

The second reason could be lack of awareness. Individuals do not have knowledge about specific technology will not be able to deal with it. In such scenario, these study findings suggest that expectations of future e-mailing system technology will be usable as well as acceptable within the governmental institutions. For more developed and enhanced used, government should bear the importance of this technology for employees in order to achieve their job with painless and performance speed of exchanging information among governmental institutions.

Future research is required to better understand how organisations can facilitate greater commitment of individuals to effectual use of new information technologies. Possibilities could be suggested regarding this are; first, the current topic can assist organisations to spur allowance and opportunities for users to participate in deploying the needed information quickly. Secondly, using e-mailing systems to exchange information will allow for cutting time and facilitate employees to achieve their tasks within a short time; thirdly, using this technology will offer a huge reduction of communications costs. Finally, convincing employees to use such innovation will allow for more spreading of information and thereafter deploying knowledge between users such as regulations, instructions, academic stuff, and informative.

REFERENCES

Ajzen, I., & Fishbein, M. (1980). *Understanding attitudes and predicting social behaviour*. New Jersey: Prentice-Hall, Inc..

Al Haraizah, A., & Choudhury, I. (2009). E-commerce technology acceptance (ECTA) framework for SMEs in the Middle East with reference to Jordan. In *Proceedings for the 14th UKAIS annual conference*. St Anne's College, University of Oxford, 31st March-1st April.

Bagozzi, R. (2007). The legacy of the technology acceptance model and a proposal for a paradigm shift. *Journal of the Association for Information Systems*, *8*(4), 244–254.

Burton-Jones, A., & Hubona, G. S. (2005). Individual differences and usage behavior: Revisiting a technology acceptance model assumption. *ACM SIGMIS Database*, *36*(2), 58–77. doi:10.1145/1066149.1066155.

Chow, W. S., & Chan, L. S. (2008). Social network, social trust and shared goals in organisational knowledge sharing. *Information & Management*, *45*, 458–465. doi:10.1016/j.im.2008.06.007.

Connelly, R., & Bannister, F. (2007). Consumer trust in electronic commerce: Social & technical antecedents. In Proceedings for world academy of science, engineering and technology, 25, 386-395.

Davis, F. D. (1986). A technology acceptance model for empirically testing new end-user information systems: Theory and results. In *MIT Sloan School of Management*. Cambridge, MA: Mit Sloan School of Management.

Davis, F. D. (1989). Perceived usefulness, perceived ease of use, and user acceptance of information technology. *Management Information Systems Quarterly*, *13*(3), 319–340. doi:10.2307/249008.

Davis, F. D. (1993). User acceptance of information technology: System characteristics, user perceptions and behavioral impacts. *International Journal of Man-Machine Studies*, *38*(3), 475–487. doi:10.1006/imms.1993.1022.

Davis, F. D., Bagozzi, R. P., & Warshaw, P. R. (1989). User acceptance of computer technology: A comparison of two theoretical models. *Management Science*, *35*(8), 982–1003. doi:10.1287/mnsc.35.8.982.

Dinev, T., & Hart, P. (2002). *Internet privacy concern and trade-off factors-empirical study and business implications*. Working paper. Florida Atlantic University.

Early, P. C. (1993). East meets west mind-east: Further explorations in collective versus individualistic work groups. *Academy of Management Journal*, *36*, 319–348. doi:10.2307/256525.

Fernandez, D., Carlson, D., Stepina, L., & Nicholson, J. (1997). Hofstede's country classification 25 years later. *The Journal of Social Psychology*, *137*(1), 43–54. doi:10.1080/00224549709595412.

Fishbein, M. (1980). A theory of reason action: Some applications and implications. In How, H., & Page, M. (Eds.), *Nebraska symposium on motivation* (pp. 65–116). Lincoln: NB University of Nebraska Press.

Fishbein, M., & Ajzen, I. (1975). *Belief, attitude, intention, and behaviour: An introduction to theory and research*. Addison-Wesley Pub. Co..

Gefan, D., Rose, G., Warkentin, M., & Pavlou, P. (2005). Cultural diversity and trust in IT adoption: A comparison of potential e-voters in the USA and South Africa. *Journal of Global Information Management*, *13*(1).

Gefen, D., Karahanna, E., & Straub, D. W. (2003). Trust and TAM in online shopping: An integrated model. *Management Information Systems Quarterly*, *27*(1), 51–90.

Gillooly, C. (1998). Disillusionment. *Information Week*, *16*, 46–56.

Hofstede, G. (1980). Culture's consequences: International differences in work-related values. *Sage (Atlanta, Ga.)*.

Hofstede, G. (1991). *Cultures and organisations: Software of the mind*. McGraw-Hill.

Hofstede, G. (1997). *Culture and organizations: Software of the mind*. London: Mc Graw Hill.

Hofstede, G. (2001). *Culture's consequences-Comparing values, behaviours, institutions, and organizations across nations* (2nd ed.). SAGE Publications.

Hsu, M. H., & Chiu, C. M. (2004). Internet self-efficacy and electronic service acceptance. *Decision Support Systems*, *38*(3), 369–381. doi:10.1016/j.dss.2003.08.001.

Liu, L., & Ma, Q. (2006). Perceived system performance: A test of an extended technology acceptance model. *The Data Base for Advances in Information Systems*, *37*(2-3), 51–59. doi:10.1145/1161345.1161354.

Malhotra, Y., & Galleta, D. (1999). Extending the technology acceptance model to account for social influence: Theoretical bases and empirical validation. In *Proceedings of the 32nd Hawaii International Conference on System Sciences IEEE.*

Mao, E. (2002). An investigation of IT usage over time. *Eight American Conferences on Information Systems* (pp. 1307-1312).

McKnight, D., Choudhury, V., & Kacmar, C. (2002). Developing and validating trust measures for e-commerce: An integrative typology. *Information Systems Research, 13*(3), 334–359. doi:10.1287/isre.13.3.334.81.

Moore, G. C., & Benbasat, I. (1991). Development of an instrument to measure the perceptions of adopting an information technology innovation. *Information Systems Research, 2*(3), 192–222. doi:10.1287/isre.2.3.192.

Nunnally, J. C. (1978). *Psychometric Theory* (2nd ed.). New York: Mc Graw-Hill.

Pavlou, P. A. (2003). Consumer acceptance of electronic commerce: Integrating trust and risk with the technology acceptance model. *International Journal of Electronic Commerce, 7*(3), 101–134.

Previte, J. (2005). *Understanding everyday internet experience: Applications to social marketing theory and practice.* (PhD thesis). Queensland University of Technology.

Qiao, Y. (2008). *Social networks and e-commerce.* Seminar on Internetworking.

Saade, R. G., Nebebe, F., & Tan, W. (2007). Viability of the technology acceptance model in multimedia learning environments: A comparative study. *Interdisciplinary Journal of Knowledge and Learning Objects, 3*, 175–182.

Scannell, T. V. (1999). *Behavioural models of advanced manufacturing technology selection.* (PhD Thesis). Michigan State University.

Straub, D., Loch, K. D., & Hill, C. (2001). Transfer of information technology to the Arab World: A test of cultural influence modeling. *Journal of Global Information Management, 9*(4), 6–28. doi:10.4018/jgim.2001100101.

Straub, D. W. (1994). The effect of culture on IT diffusion: E-mail and fax in Japan and the USA. *Information Systems Research, 9*(2), 16–29.

Straub, D. W., Keil, M., & Brenner, W. (1997). Testing the technology acceptance model across cultures: A three country study. *Information & Management, 33*(1), 1–11. doi:10.1016/S0378-7206(97)00026-8.

Taylor, S., & Todd, P. A. (1995b). Understanding information technology usage: A test of competing models. *Information Systems Research, 6*(2), 144–176. doi:10.1287/isre.6.2.144.

Venkatesh, V., & Davis, F. D. (2000). A theoretical extension of the technology acceptance model: Four longitudinal field studies. *Management Science, 46*(2), 186–204. doi:10.1287/mnsc.46.2.186.11926.

Venkatesh, V., Morris, M. G., Davis, G. B., & Davis, F. D. (2003). User acceptance of information technology: Toward a unified view. *Management Information Systems Quarterly, 27*(3), 425–478.

Zander, U., & Kogut, B. (1995). Knowledge and the speed of the transfer and imitation of organizational capabilities: An empirical test. *Organization Science, 6*(1), 76–92. doi:10.1287/orsc.6.1.76.

ADDITIONAL READING

Adams, D, A., Nelson, R. R., & Todd, P. A. (1992). Perceived usefulness, ease of use and usage of information technology: A replication. *Management Information Systems Quarterly, 16*(2), 227–247. doi:10.2307/249577.

Agarwal, R., & Prasad, J. (1997). The role of innovation characteristics and perceived voluntariness in the acceptance of information technologies. *Decision Sciences*, *28*(3), 557–582. doi:10.1111/j.1540-5915.1997.tb01322.x.

Agarwal, R., & Prasad, J. (1998). A conceptual and operational definition of personal innovativeness in the domain of information technology. *Information Systems Research*, *9*(2), 204–215. doi:10.1287/isre.9.2.204.

Agarwal, R., & Prasad, J. (1999). Are individual differences germane to the acceptance of new information technologies? *Decision Sciences*, *30*(2), 361–391. doi:10.1111/j.1540-5915.1999.tb01614.x.

Al-Bakri, A. (2007). *The adoption and diffusion of internet-electronic data interchange (I-EDI) by Jordanian SMEs*. (Master Thesis). University of Wollongong: Australia.

Al-gahtani, S. (2001). The applicability of TAM outside North America: An empirical test in the United Kingdom. *Information Resources Management Journal*, *14*(3), 37–46. doi:10.4018/irmj.2001070104.

Al-gahtani, S. (2008). Testing for the applicability of the TAM model in the Arabic context: Exploring an extended TAM with three moderating factors. *Information Resources Management Journal*, *21*(4), 1–26. doi:10.4018/irmj.2008100101.

Alam, S. S., Khatibi, A. A., Bin Ismail, H., & Ahmad, S. (2005). Perceived benefits of e-commerce adoption in the electronic manufacturing companies in Malaysia. *Journal of the Social Sciences*, *1*(3), 188–193. doi:10.3844/jssp.2005.188.193.

Algahtani, S. S., & King, M. (1999). Attitudes, satisfaction and usage: Factors contributing to each in the acceptance of information technology. *Behaviour & Information Technology*, *18*(4), 277–297. doi:10.1080/014492999119020.

Auger, P., & Gallaugher, J. M. (1997). Factors affecting adoption of an internet-based sales presence for small businesses. *The Information Society*, *13*(1), 55–74. doi:10.1080/019722497129287.

Baker-Eveleth, L., & Stone, R. W. (2008). Expectancy theory and behavioural intentions to use computer application. *Interdisciplinary Journal of Information, Knowledge, and Management*, *3*, 135–145.

Bingi, P., Leff, L., Shipchandler, Z., & Rao, S. (2000). Critical IT implementation issues in developed and developing countries. Information Strategy: The Executive Journal, pp. 25-34.

Bingi, P. A., & Khamalah, J. (2000). The challenges facing global e-commerce. *Information Systems Management*, *17*(4), 26–35. doi:10.1201/1078/43193.17.4.20000901/31249.5.

Boyd, D. M., & Ellison, N. B. (2007). Social network sites: Definition, history, and scholarship. *Journal of Computer-Mediated Communication*, *13*(1), 11. doi:10.1111/j.1083-6101.2007.00393.x.

Brian, J., Corbitt, T. T., & Han, Y. (2003). Trust and e-commerce: A study of consumer perceptions electronic commerce. *Research and Applications*, *2*, 203–215.

Chau, P. Y. K., & Hu, P. J. (2002). Examining a model for information technology acceptance by individual professionals: An exploratory study. *Journal of Management Information Systems*, *18*(4), 191–229.

Cheung, C. M. K., Zhu, L., Kwong, T., Chan, G. W. W., & Limayem, M. (2003). Online consumer behaviour: A review and agenda for future research. In *Proceedings of the 16th Bled eCommerce Conference*, Bled, 9-11 June.

Chin, W., & Todd, P. A. (1995). On the use, usefulness, and ease of use of structural equation modeling in MIS research: A note of caution. *Management Information Systems Quarterly*, *19*(2), 237–246. doi:10.2307/249690.

Dahlberg, T., Mallet, N., & Orni, A. (2003). A trust enhanced technology acceptance model: Consumer acceptance of mobile payment solutions. In *Proceedings of the 2nd Stockholm Mobility Roundtable*, May 22-23, Stockholm, Sweden.

Deroian, F. (2002). Formation of social network and diffusion of innovations. *Research Policy*, *31*, 835–846. doi:10.1016/S0048-7333(01)00147-0.

Dholakia, R. R., & Kshetri, N. (2004). Factors impacting the adoption of the internet among SMEs. *Small Business Economics*, *23*(4), 311–322. doi:10.1023/B:SBEJ.0000032036.90353.1f.

Doll, W., Hendrickson, A., & Xiandong, D. (1998). Using Davis's perceived usefulness and ease-of-use instruments for decision making: A confirmatory and multi-group invariance analysis. *Decision Sciences*, *29*(4), 839–869. doi:10.1111/j.1540-5915.1998.tb00879.x.

Fernandez, D., Carlson, D., Stepina, L., & Nicholson, J. (1997). Hofstede's country classification 25 years later. *The Journal of Social Psychology*, *137*(1), 43–54. doi:10.1080/00224549709595412.

Finin, T., Ding, L., Zhou, L., & Joshi, A. (2005). Social networking on the semantic web. *Learning Organisation Journal*, *12*(5), 418–435. doi:10.1108/09696470510611384.

Fuerst, W. L., & Cheney, P. H. (1982). Factors affecting the perceived utilisation of computer-based decision support systems in the oil industry. *Decision Sciences*, *13*, 554–569. doi:10.1111/j.1540-5915.1982.tb01182.x.

Gong, W., Li, Z. G., & Stump, R. L. (2007). Global internet use and access: Cultural considerations. *Asia Pacific Journal of Marketing and Logistics*, *19*(1), 57–74. doi:10.1108/13555850710720902.

Grandon, E., & Pearson, M. J. (2004a). E-commerce adoption: Perception of managers/owners of small and medium sized firms in Chile. *Communications of the Association for Information Systems*, *13*(81), 81–102.

Hall, E. T. (1989). *Beyond culture*. New York: Anchor Books Editions.

Hall, S. (1997). *Representation: Culture representations and signifying practice*. London: Sage.

Hee, S. P. (2000). Relationships among attitudes and subjective norms: Testing the theory of reasoned action across cultures. *Communication Studies*, *51*(2), 162–175. doi:10.1080/10510970009388516.

Herbig, P. R., & Miller, J. C. (1991). The effect of culture upon the sourcing of innovations: A case study of Japan and the US. *International. Journal of Consumer Marketing*, *3*(3).

Jackson, C. M., Chow, S., & Leitch, R. A. (1997). Toward an understanding of the behavioural intention to use information system. *Decision Sciences*, *28*(2), 357–389. doi:10.1111/j.1540-5915.1997.tb01315.x.

Kapurubandara, M., & Lawson, R. (2006). Barriers to adopting ICT and e-commerce with SMEs in developing countries: An exploratory study in Sri Lanka. CollECTeR. Adelaide.

Katz, J. E., & Rice, R. E. (2002). *Social consequences of Internet Use: Access, involvement, and interaction*. Cambridge, MA: MIT Press.

Kolekofski, K. E. J., & Heminger, A. R. (2003). Beliefs and attitudes affecting intentions to share information in an organizational setting. *Information & Management*, *40*, 521–532. doi:10.1016/S0378-7206(02)00068-X.

Lindsay, P. H., & Norman, D. A. (1977). *Human information processing: An introduction to psychology*. New York: Academic Press.

Lippert S.K. (2002). Contributing to a unified model of technology trust: Understanding trust in information systems technology. *Academy of Business and Information Technology meeting*, *2*(4), 343-364.

Lukas, H. C., & Spitler, V. K. (1999). Technology use and performance: A field study of broker workstations. *Decision Sciences*, *30*(2), 291–311. doi:10.1111/j.1540-5915.1999.tb01611.x.

Mao, E., & Palvia, P. (2006). Testing an extended model of IT acceptance in the Chinese cultural context. *The Data Base for Advances in Information Systems*, *37*(2-3), 20–32. doi:10.1145/1161345.1161351.

Mathieson, K. (1991). Predicting user intentions: Comparing the technology acceptance model with the theory of planned behaviour. *Information Systems Research*, *2*(3), 173–191. doi:10.1287/isre.2.3.173.

McKnight, D. H., Cummings, L. L., & Chervany, N. L. (1998). Initial trust formation in new organisational relationships. *Academy of Management Review*, *23*(3), 473–490.

Molla, A., & Licker, P. S. (2005a). eCommerce adoption in developing countries: A model and instrument. *Information & Management*, *42*, 877–899. doi:10.1016/j.im.2004.09.002.

Ratnasingam, P. (2005). Trust in inter-organisational exchange: A case study in business to business electronic commerce. *Decision Support Systems*, *39*(3), 525–544. doi:10.1016/j.dss.2003.12.005.

Rose, G., & Straub, D. (1998). Predicting general IT use: Applying TAM to the Arab world. *Journal of Global Information Management*, *6*(3), 39–46.

Sinkovics, R., Mo, Y., & Matthias, H. (2007). Cultural adaptation in cross border e-commerce: A study of German companies. *Journal of Electronic Commerce Research*, *8*(4), 221–235.

Szmigin, I., Canning, L., & Reppel, L. E. (2005). Online community: Enhancing the relationship marketing concept through customer bonding. *International Journal of Service Industry*, *16*(5), 480–496. doi:10.1108/09564230510625778.

Turban, E., Matthew, K., & Lee, O. (2001). A trust model for consumer internet shopping. *International Journal of Electronic Commerce*, *6*(1), 75–91.

Yeniyurt, S., & Townsend, J. D. (2003). Does culture explain acceptance of new products in a country? An empirical investigation. *International Marketing Review*, *20*(4), 377–396. doi:10.1108/02651330310485153.

KEY TERMS AND DEFINITIONS

Affection: Represents the affective constituents that are demonstrating the individuals' feelings with regards to the focal object for instance liking, anxiety, or upset.

Attitude: Refers to an individual's overall feeling of favourableness or unfavourableness toward some stimulus object (Fishbein & Ajzen, 1975, p. 216), which is specifically based on individuals' evaluation regarding a particular object. In e-mailing systems acceptance view, individuals generally have attitudes toward e-mailing systems application in their work processes, these attitudes might be positive or negative (accept/ reject).

Behavioural Intention: Symbolizes individuals' ambitions, expectations, goals, and predicted responses to the given object, which is forming the actual behaviour to use object. Actual behaviour directly affected by behavioural intention for the target of using technology such as E-mailing systems.

Culture: "The collective programming of the mind which distinguishes the members of one group or category of people from another" (Hofstede, 1997). People share a collective national character that reflects their cultural mental programming, which forms individual's values, beliefs, assumptions, expectations, attitudes, and behaviours.

Developing Countries: Nations with a low living standard, undeveloped economic base, and low Human Development Index relative to other countries.

ECTA: Electronic Commerce Technology Acceptance framework is a framework emanated from the incorporation of several factors. It is a comprehensive framework to include sets of factors that relate to the main determinants of attitude and behaviour in the acceptance and use of E-Mailing Systems technology. These factors presented by Trust, Culture and sociology of technology. In this framework, PA, PU, ECPA, and ATUEMT are intermediate states, dependent on other independent variables which can be determined in the context of the study.

E-Mailing Systems: Systems that allow the transmission of messages over communications networks.

Evaluation: Refers to an individual's judgment with respect to specific object and considered as core component of attitude. Evaluations implies the imputation of some degree of goodness or badness to an attitude object, positive or negative attitude toward an object referred to evaluative component. Evaluations are function of cognitive, affect and behavioural intention of the object.

External Stimulus: These are the external factors (social affect) that influencing the internal components which are in turn affecting an individual attitude toward performing target behaviour. External factors for this research model are presented by trust, culture, and sociology of technology. In this research view, these factor influencing the acceptance and use of e-mailing systems technology in the government institutions in Jordan.

Governmental Institutions: Institutions that are managed by the state according to plans and programs designed to serve the citizens.

Jordan: Is a state located in the heart of the Middle East, bordered to the north, Syria, Saudi Arabia to the south, Iraq to the east, the west by the West Bank.

Perceived Ease of Use (PEOU): The degree to which an individual believes that using a particular system would be free of effort (Davis, 1989; Davis et al., 1989). From mailing systems technology aspect, this reflects that e- mailing systems technology will be usable and acceptable if it is viewed as easy as painless.

Perceived Usefulness (PU): The degree to which a person believes that using a particular system would improve his/her job performance (Davis et al., 1989). From e-mailing systems technology view, this would represent predicted advantages gained from acceptance and use of e- mailing systems technology by governmental institutions in Jordan.

Sociology of Technology: Is reflected by social aspect of technology (internet).in this chapter internet-based technology is used as an online social interaction tool.

TAM: Technology Acceptance Model. The Technology Acceptance Model was developed by Davis (1986) to explain technology acceptance among its users. In formulating TAM, Davis used the TRA as the grand theory. According to Davis, using IT stemmed from the perception of its usefulness and ease of use of IT.

TRA: Theory of Reasoned Action The theory of reasoning action (TRA) is the basis of TAM which is based on the assumption that human beings are rational animals that systematically use or process the information available to them.

Trust: Trust in EC has been defined as "the belief that another person or organization on whom one depends will behave in a socially acceptable manner-honest, caring and capable-in doing so will fulfil the trusting party's expectation" (Geffen et al., 2005). This chapter has used trust in internet to exchange information among employees within government institutions in Jordan.

Section 2
E-Government Adoption: Frameworks and Policy

Chapter 5

E-Government Concept: A Holistic and Eclectic Framework

Delfina de Sá Soares
University of Minho, Portugal

Luis Amaral
University of Minho, Portugal

ABSTRACT

Over the last few years, many different definitions for the e-government term have appeared in the literature. This diversity of definitions created a conceptual multiplicity and divergence. While being understandable, taking into consideration the newness of the e-government field, this may be prejudicing the e-government research and development. The aim of this chapter is to contribute to the clarification of the e-government concept, by providing a framework that hopefully will help to understand its boundaries and main constituents, as well as the way in which many of the different related terms found in the literature, can be further articulated. The framework put forward in this chapter is based on a generic model of a democratic government system. Building on that model, six main spaces, where Information Technologies (ITs) can be deployed, are identified and discussed. The use of IT in all those spaces contributes to the overall development of a country's e-government reality and maturity. By suggesting and arguing for a comprehensive, holistic and eclectic vision of e-government, this framework provides a basis for achieving more sustained e-government research and development efforts.

INTRODUCTION

In the late 1990s, the term *e-government* was coined and started to be used around the world, both by practitioners as well as research communities. Since then, a significant number of research papers, books, reports, green books, white books, and other documents have been published on the subject. Although, those documents constitute valuable contributions to knowledge development and extension in the e-government field, several criticisms have been raised concerning the lack of scientific rigor, quality, and maturity still exhibited by the research undertaken in this emergent area (Andersen & Henriksen, 2005; Bolívar, Muñoz, & Hernández, 2010; Grönlund, 2004; Heeks & Bailur, 2007; Löfstedt, 2005; Rana, Williams, Dwivedi, & Williams, 2011). Some of the main criticism concerns the following:

DOI: 10.4018/978-1-4666-4245-4.ch005

- The disregard or lack of variability of the research paradigm adopted i.e. most of the works do not state explicitly nor it is easily or implicitly understandable to the reader, the authors' research paradigm standpoint;
- The type of research performed i.e. there is a predominance of descriptive work and a lack of either theoretical, theory generating or theory testing work);
- The type of outcomes generated by the studies (i.e. most of the works produce descriptions, lists or models; only a small percentage of them produce theories or frameworks.

Although some of these criticisms are understandable taking into consideration the newness of the field, it seems to be the time to leave this initiation and categorize research opportunities, characterized by the publication of many articles in a still unstructured and unorganized research domain. The aim is to provide a step forward towards an upper level of research maturity.

One of the problems and challenges that persist in the e-government research relates to the meaning of the e-government concept itself. Indeed, the review, analysis, and comparison of numerous e-government definitions found in literature show that different authors define e-government in slightly different ways, some giving it a narrow perspective in which e-government is a synonym of electronic services (e-services) provision, while others giving it a wider perspective, in which e-government includes much more than e-services provision initiatives. The analysis and comparison of e-government definitions also show that there is still some confusion, overlapping and disarticulation in the use of terms such as e-government, e-politics, e-administration, e-participation, and e-democracy.

The aim of this chapter is precisely to bring a contribution to the clarification of the e-government concept. The intent of the chapter is not simply to provide yet another e-government definition, but to provide and describe a framework for the e-government concept that helps to understand its boundaries, its main constituents and the way in which many of the different e-government definitions are articulated. The proposed framework, based on a generic model of a democratic government system, suggests and argues for a holistic and eclectic vision of the e-government concept. The framework may become a relevant frame of reference in the e-government field. It can be useful to the research community, as an instrument to guide and organize research activities, as well as to the community of practice, helping, for instance, in the definition of general long-term e-government development strategies and in the characterization of the evolution and the current status of e-government development efforts of a country.

This chapter is organized into five sections. After the introduction section, we set the background for the rest of the chapter. This background section starts by providing an historical context of e-government, where some of the major developments concerning the use and adoption of Information Technologies (IT) in government in the last few decades are described and the most relevant landmarks that fostered the emergence of the e-government term and the rising of the so-called *e-government era* are pointed out. After the historical context, the section proceeds with the review and comparison of multiple e-government definitions found in the literature. By the end of this section, it will be evident that there is still no universally accepted definition for the e-government term that is agreed by most researchers and practitioners. Instead, the terms are frequently used with slightly different meaning covering different scopes ranging from a narrower perspective (in which e-government is seen as e-services delivery) to a wider perspective (in which the term includes not only the e-services delivery but also elements such as the change and transformation of internal agencies operations and the renewal of participative and democratic processes). The next section starts with a brief description of a generic model of a democratic government system. Building on this generic model, a set of six "spaces of use," where IT can be adopted and used, are identified and described. The use and adoption of IT in each of those "spaces of use" contribute to the overall development of the e-government reality of a country. The section that follows systematizes the framework proposed in this chapter and enumerates a set of seven key ideas underlying the framework. The use of IT in each of the six "spaces of use" identified and described in section three give rise to the six main areas (electronic services (e-Services), electronic administration (e-Administration), electronic political-administrative relationships (e-PAR), electronic politics (e-Politics), electronic democracy (e-Democracy), and electronic society (e-Society)) that the authors defend should constitute and are relevant parts of the e-government concept. This holistic and eclectic perspective of the e-government concept is considered as essential to achieve a full, integrated, sustained and sustainable e-government development strategy in a state. The final section presents the main conclusions of the chapter and highlights the main contributions of the proposed framework.

BACKGROUND

Historical Context of E-Government

At the end of the 1980s and beginning of the 1990s, a new set of terms – *public sector revitalization, public sector reengineering*, and *government reinvention* – entered the vocabulary of politicians, public sector managers and employees, journalists and many other societal actors (Osborne & Gaebler, 1992). Although, these were new terms at that time, the truth is that they constituted a manifestation of a process of public sector reform that had already initiated for some time (Heeks, 2001a). In fact, taking into consideration a simplistic and general definition of public sector reform as being the "...change within public sector organizations that seeks to improve their performance" (Heeks, 2001a, p.10), it can be argued that public sector reform is a phenomenon almost as old as the existence of a public agency, thus already happening for several decades. Nevertheless, and adopting a narrower perspective, it was during the 1970s, as a result of the emergence of a new ideology in the public sector – the *New Public Management* – that the term *public sector reform* acquired all its prominence (Grande, Araujo, & Serna, 2002; Heeks, 2001a). According to Heeks (2001a), three main aspects motivated the rising of the public sector reform during the 1970s:

- **The Sector Crisis:** There were, at that time, significant and growing problems affecting the public sector operation and a general feeling that "something should be done" to overcome the crisis that those problems were generating;
- **The Emergence of a Renew Ideology in the Sector:** It was also clearly evident by those times the rising of neo-liberal ideas within the public sector, which sustain that "something could be done" to achieve a new operating way of the public sector;
- **The Power and the Politic Will:** Besides the recognition that "something should be done" and that "something could be done," there was also a growing of the political will to conduct the required reform, demonstrated by a positive attitude of politicians towards the principle that "something would be done."

Since then, governments have been defining, promoting, and implementing intensive programs in order to achieve the so-called public sector reform. Major parts of those programs and efforts have revolved around the use of IT to support and improve public sector activities. Consequently, IT spending in public sector has grown and started to be discriminated as part of the reform plans (Heeks & Davies, 2001).

In parallel with the raising of concern around the public sector reform, another relevant phenomenon happened: the emergence of terms and ideas such as "Information Age" and "Information Society." Toffler (1980) prophesied a new paradigm of society characterized by a growing and intensive usage of IT and in which information would assume a quintessential role. This prophecy has gradually gained the attention of managers and others, conquering in the 1990's, a fundamental presence in discussions and development of the society (Pérez-Villaplana, 2003).

Another remarkable phenomenon occurred during the 1990s decade: "Internet explosion" whose proliferation rhythm has remained accelerated until nowadays. Indeed, until the end of the 1980s, Internet existed but was only accessible to people working in some government agencies, universities and research centers (Anderson, 2011). Only by the early 1990s, did the "Internet explosion" occur as a consequence of two main events: i) the opening of the Internet for commercial use by the US government and ii) the invention of the World Wide Web, as an easy way to create, display, and link to Information on the Internet (Anderson, 2011). The massive widespread and use of the Internet and of a set of web-based technologies, completely revolutionized the operating of all society.

It should be noted that, despite the awareness and pressures associated with the idea of fostering the creation of an information society and despite the opportunity provided by new forms of technology and communications associated with the proliferation of the Internet, public agencies still kept using IT with the main purpose of improve ing the automation level of their intradepartmental tasks (Heeks, 2001b; Reynolds & Regio, 2001). In fact, IT usage was strongly associated with the almost exclusive idea of reaching internal efficiency gains, which would result from the substitution of manual procedures by equivalent digital data processing systems (García-Arribas & López-Crespo, 2003; Heeks & Davies, 2001; Valle, 2003). This means that there was not yet a full recognition of all the potential that IT could convey to government agencies' activities. This lack of recognizance prevented politicians from understanding the value that IT could represent, thus leading to the inexistence of strong and genuine political support to the use of IT as an instrument of modernization and transformation of all the governmental machinery (Lenk & Traunmüller, 2002).

This scenario suffered a reverse on March 3, 1993, when President Clinton initiated the movement known as *reinvention of government* and charged his Vice President Al Gore for streamlining the Federal Government administration functions. During the presentation of the *USA National Information Infrastructure Initiative*, Al Gore vividly stressed the role that Information Society could perform in the renovation of all the American society, specifically mentioning the relevance that creating a government able to work better, at a lower cost, through the massive incorporation of the IT could have to the country's evolution (USA, 2003). This constituted a turning point in the way politicians view and support IT initiatives in the public sector. Since then, countries all over the world started to develop and implement strategies to promote and develop Information Society and e-government.

The European Commission, itself, outlined a strategy to nurture Information Society development in Europe and created a working group for its implementation. This working group produced a document, known as *Bangemann report* (EC 1994a), which was made available on May 1994 and approved by the European Council on June 1994, based on which the action plan *Europe's Way to the Information Society* (EC 1994b) was later published. Since then, Europe started to valorize the potential that IT, and specially the Internet, could have to public sector and Information Society development (Lenk & Traunmüller, 2002). Such fact became even more evident when, in December 1999, the European Commission launched the *eEurope – An Information Society for All* initiative, in which e-government was set as one of the ten priority areas of action (EC, 1999). The need for a strong initiative and a strong commitment on the part of all European countries concerning their e-government development was reinforced in Lisbon and Feira summits that took place in March and June 2000, respectively.

From that moment onwards, many countries in the world started to develop e-government strategies and policies to the development and implementation of e-government action plans. Researchers attempted to establish structures for governance, implementation, monitoring, and evaluation of e-government initiatives, and to the creation of the infrastructure and support conditions to the gradual achievement of a true e-government reality. This was the beginning of the so-called *e-government era*.

Figure 1 presents the main landmarks, mentioned earlier, that led to the entry and progress in the e-government era.

E-Government Conceptual and Terminological Multiplicity

Since the advent of the *e-government era*, more than ten years have passed. During this time, a significant number of research papers, books, reports, green books, white papers and other documents have been produced by academics, researchers and practitioners. In spite of all these contributions and their value for the creation of a body of knowledge (that intends to support and strengthen the research and practice in the emergent and challenging area of e-government), there is still a very long way to go. This suggests that more deepen, more rigorous and more relevant research in the e-government area is needed.

One primary and fundamental ingredient for the development and maturity of knowledge in any research area is the clarification and shared understanding of its basilar concepts (Astley, 1985), and this is the point where stands one of the debilities of the e-government area. Indeed, extensive literature reviews conducted by authors such as Grönlund and Horan (2005), Hu, Pan, Lu, and Wang (2009), and Gil-Garcia (2012) clearly demonstrate the anarchy that still persists in the e-government research field concerning the conceptualization of the e-government term itself.

Figure 1. Main historical landmarks in the emergence of the e-government era

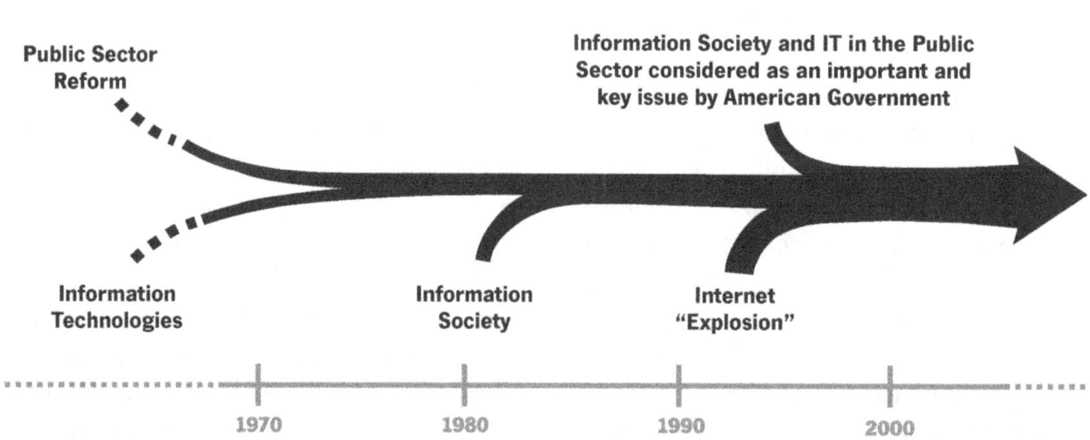

The analysis and comparison of e-government definitions show that different authors define e-government in different ways. Some provide a narrow perspective (Perri, 2001; Deloitte, 2000; Holden, Norris, & Fletcher, 2003; Norris, Fletcher, & Holden, 2001; Reynolds & Regio, 2001; Zweers & Planqué, 2001), while others give it a much broader perspective (Coleman, 2008; EzGov, 2000; Fraga, 2002; Gil-Garcia, 2012; Grönlund & Horan, 2005; Ho, 2002; Okot-Uma, 2000; Pablo & Pan, 2003). As Grant and Chau (2005, p. 2) stress, the e-government construct means different things to different people.

One of the earliest and most frequent conceptualizations of e-government considers it as synonym with electronic information and service delivery i.e. the use of IT (particularly the Internet and Web-based technologies) to deliver more efficient and effective government services and information to citizens (in this chapter, the term *citizen* is used in a broader sense, comprising not only individuals but also commercial, voluntary, civic, and social organizations that form the basis of a country's society). Norris, Fletcher, and Holden (2001, p. 5), for example, define e-government as being "the delivery of governmental services and information electronically, 24 hours per day, seven days per week." In the same line, OECD (2003, p. 23) defines e-government as "the use of information and communication technologies, and particularly the Internet, as a tool to achieve better government." Deloitte (2000), Grönlund (2003), Holden, Norris, and Fletcher (2003), Reynolds and Regio (2001), and Zweers and Planqué (2001) are other authors that share the same e-government perspective. To conceptualize e-government with a focus on services provision is understandable because the electronic delivery of public services is a key component of any e-government program. The implementation of electronic services delivery is also generally mentioned as the quicker and easier kind of efforts to implement when a country starts to pursue a strategy of e-government development, and last, but not the least, because electronic services delivery constitutes the most visible and appealing e-government component to citizens (Pérez-Villaplana, 2003; Reynolds & Regio, 2001).

While keeping the focus of e-government definition on the information and service delivery, EzGov (2000) and Jaeger and Thompson (2004) extend their definitions by considering the delivery of information and services not only to citizens (the "external audience"), but also to other government agencies and employees (the "internal audience"). The inclusion of these two types of audience is clear in EzGov (2000, p. 2). Here, e-government is presented as having "two primary dimensions: online-services (applications that serve a government agency's "external audience," including citizen-centric portals, community calendars, FAQs and transactional applications) and government operations (services that benefit government employees and other "internal" groups, including electronic procurement, Web-based document management, electronic forms and Intranet)."

A broader perspective of e-government is advocated by Grönlund and Horan (2005), Okot-Uma (2000), Palvia and Sharma (2007), and Relyea (2002). According to these authors, besides the electronic information and services delivery component, e-government also embraces the internal change and transformation of government agencies. This then sets the focus not only on the front-end perspective of services delivery, but also on the back-end reorganization that will be required to achieve the adequate levels of quality in services delivery and of efficiency and efficacy in internal agencies operation. This perspective is also shared by Pablo and Pan (2003, p. 289), to whom e-government is "…the transformation, through ICT use, of government business (processes, operations, and transactions)."

An even broader perspective is proposed by a number of authors: refer to Coleman (2008), Fraga (2002), Gil-Garcia (2012), Ho (2002), infoDev (2009), and Pablo and Pan (2003). For those authors, e-government encompasses not only information and services delivery and the internal transformation in the way public agencies operate, but also the quest of citizen engagement and participation in public discussions and decision-making processes. Gil-Garcia (2012, p. 16), for example, defines electronic government as the "selection, design, implementation, and the use of information and communication technologies in government to provide public services, improve managerial effectiveness, and promote democratic values and participation mechanisms."

A still more inclusive e-government definition was presented by Perri (2001). This author stresses another e-government component: the one related with the "support of policy making, decision making, group work between ministers and their juniors, senior civil servants working on policy formulation, development and management, and with policy advisors who are contracted to provide confidential policy support" (Perri, 2001, p. 7). This new component is also included in the definition by Gartner (2000), where e-government is described as "the continuous optimization of service delivery, constituency participation, and governance by transforming internal and external relationships through technology, the Internet, and new media as well as in the *The Role of eGovernment for Europe's Future* communication from the European Commission where e-government is defined as the "the use of ICT combined with organizational change and new skills in order to improve public services, democratic processes and public policies" (EC, 2003, p. 4). While additional works can be cited, like Lenk and Traunmüller (2002) and Batini and Mecella (2002), this new kind of element is neglected, or at least is not clearly stated, in most of the e-government definitions found in the literature (Perri, 2001).

An additional source of confusion and complexity surrounding the clarification of the e-government concept is introduced by the *e-governance* term. In fact, there are authors (such as Dawes (2009); Evangelidis, Akomode, Taleb-Bendiab, and Taylor (2002); Flak, Moe, and Saebo (2003); Grönlund and Horan (2005); Jayashree and Marthandan (2010); Pablo and Pan (2003); Riley (2003); and Saarenpää (2003)) to whom e-governance is a different and much broader concept than e-government. At the same time, there are others who use the term e-government and e-governance interchangeably, providing definitions for e-government that encompass almost the same elements as those argued to be in the realm of e-governance.

At this point, it seems evident that there are multiple conceptualizations and perspectives on e-government. Despite all them being legitimate, they feature partial perspectives of e-government that, while not being incompatible with each other, may convey conceptual ambiguity (Gil-Garcia, 2012; Grant & Chau, 2005; Hu, Pan, Lu, & Wang, 2009). Each one of those conceptualizations reflects the diversity of researchers' backgrounds, the intellectual pressure set by neighboring research fields (Astley, 1985; Hu et al., 2009) as well as the visions of different actors that, by having different interests, will see the way IT can be used in government in different ways: citizens and businesses wish to have better services; journalists wish to have access to more and better information; politicians wish to have more information on agencies performance and on social and economic tendencies; and constituencies wish to have better participation mechanisms (Lenihan, 2002). Although, these are valid conceptualizations, several authors have been calling the attention to the fact that the adoption of a partial and narrow perspective of e-government (for instance, the adoption of a definition exclusively centered in the services and information provision) can contribute to a distorted and limited vision of what could and should be the overall e-government realm (Dawes, 2009; Gil-Garcia, 2012; Grant & Chau, 2005; Lenk & Traunmüller, 2002). The existence of a more comprehensive conceptualization of e-government, that makes explicit and frames the multiple spaces where IT can be used to support and improve the overall state government activities inside the complex ecological system of which they are part, is absolutely invaluable and mandatory (Gil-Garcia, 2012; Grande et al., 2002). An incomplete perspective of e-government could restrain considerably all the potential opportunities and benefits that a wider perspective could provide, thus compromising both the research and the practical implementation and development of e-government (Caldow, 2001; Ndou, 2004).

"SPACES OF USE" FOR IT IN GOVERNMENT ACTIVITIES

Last section has finished arguing that a wide and comprehensive conceptualization of e-government is a mandatory issue for fully e-government achievement. The need for a wide e-government definition has already been noticed and stressed by authors such as Gil-Garcia (2012) and Grant and Chau (2005), which have made efforts to propose much broader e-government definitions. The efforts made by those authors involved (i) the collection, analysis and comparison of multiple e-government definitions found in literature, (ii) the identification of the relevant elements that stood from each of the definitions, and (iii) the congregation of all those relevant elements in a wider e-government definition.

Although being wider, useful, and interesting, those new definitions could still continue to be "not comprehensive enough," since they came out from a set of partial definitions. Indeed, there is a risk that if there is one component that is relevant to e-government but is not pointed out in none of the collected and reviewed definitions, this component will not surface in the new wider final proposed definition. It would thus be advisable to set a more stable, grounded and rational conceptualization of e-government. In order to do that a different and more structured approach is required. Thus, instead of following an approach in which wider e-government definitions are the result of the review, systematization, and juxtaposition of narrow definitions found in literature, a more sustained approach would be to base the e-government conceptualization on its nuclear element: government. Indeed, the essence in the e-government term is on "government" not on "e" (infoDev, 2009). Thus, if we want to use IT as a facilitator and a catalyzer for government renewal and transformation, it seems reasonable to ground the conceptualization of e-government on a generic model of a government system.

In a generic and intuitive way, a democratic representative government system can be represented, as shown in Figure 2, by three interrelated spheres: the *Politics* sphere, the *Administration* sphere, and the *Society* sphere. The *Politics* and *Administration* spheres represent "two primary or ultimate functions" in a state, respectively "the expression of the will of the state" and the "execution of that will" (Goodnow, 2003, p. 22). The specific purpose of the *Politics* sphere is to define and assure the general interest of the state (Amaral, 1994), being responsible for the establishment of the state's general public policies that pursue and assure the essential values of society, such as defense and security, justice, education, culture, and the economic and social well-being. The *Administration* sphere is associated to the implementation of these policies, thus constituting the instrument to achieve the purposes of the state. The third sphere represents the *Society*, which constitutes the state's reason of being and the ultimate aim of the state's governance (Nunes, 2004).

The arrows in Figure 2 suggest the basic set of relations that exist among the three spheres. Lenihan (2002, p. 29) calls this set of arrows the *governance triangle*. In a simplistic way, Lenihan describes the governance triangle as starting with citizens, who have the duty and right to choose their representatives, through an electoral process, giving them power to speak and act on their behalf. After elected, these representatives will be part of a formal political system that will work in order to interpret and set specific policies, direc-

Figure 2. Generic model of a democratic government system

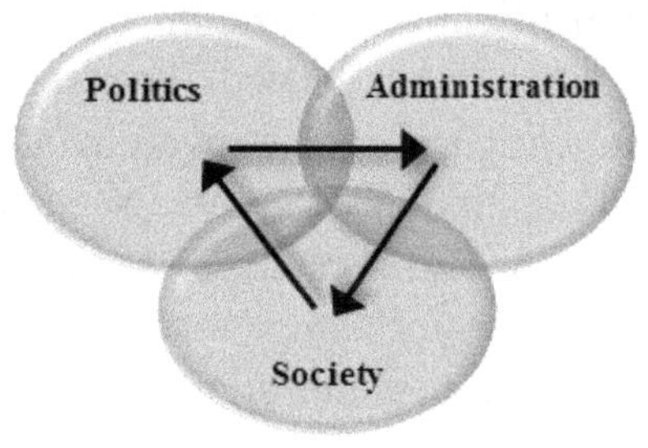

tions, and budgets that should persuade and fulfill the overall community needs. Public Administration agencies will take those policies, directions and budgets and turn them into programs, measures, and services provided to citizens.

Despite the simplicity of the description, the relationships that exist among the spheres are not so simple as they may seem. Instead, a quite intricate and complex set of mutual influences among them is in place. For example, voting is not the only way citizens (*Society* sphere) can influence the political power (*Politics* sphere). Many other forms can be used such as pressures from lobbying groups (Lenihan, 2002). Another example is that, although the administrative function is generally regarded as being under the political function influence (Goodnow, 2003), the truth is that, public managers (*Administration* sphere) can also exert some pressures and influences upon politicians (*Politics* sphere). Public managers have a thorough knowledge about how administration operates, about its problems, about its performance levels, that is fundamental and can limit and determine political decisions (Grönlund, 2005). In fact, the relationship between "politicians" and "bureaucrats," as is usually mentioned, is a subject frequently discussed by many authors, who alert to the fact that. "..*Politics* and *Administration* are not activities insensitive to one another..." (Amaral, 1994, p. 46). It should also be noted that the relationships and influences may have different intensity (Bannister, 2001) and that the intensity of each influence may change over time (Lenihan, 2002). For instance, the instability usually generated in situations of political crisis, may raise the "weight" and power that the *Administration* sphere has over the *Politics* sphere (Nunes, 2004).

Although a long discussion could be maintained around the multiple influences and interrelations among the spheres, this is outside the scope of this chapter. Our intent is just to stand out the broad and complex context in which any governmental system inevitably operates. It is our conviction that this "big picture" should frame the study, planning, development and implementation of the e-government phenomenon. Indeed, each of the spheres and each of the relationships identified in Figure 2 constitute a key intervention "space" in which IT can be used to facilitate and promote the overall government renewal, transformation, and modernization. Each of these "spaces" of use for IT, depicted in the Figure 3 by each of the six arrows, are now detailed in the next subsections.

Electronic Services (E-Services)

Interactions between the *Administration* and *Society* spheres constitute a relevant "space" of intervention when seeking the transformation and improvement of the overall state government activities (UMIC, 2003). As citizens are main actors directly involved in these interactions, all the changes and improvements that can be achieved at this level are extremely "visible" to citizens and can have an immediate and huge impact on their life. It is for this reason that relationships between *Administration* and *Society* are considered as a primordial space of use for IT in the process of creating and building better and renewed state government activities. Indeed, during the last years, we have been assisting to a paradigm shift on public agencies reformation efforts, from a purely internal and intra-agency perspective, focused on efficiency improvements of the internal operations of any particular agency, to an external perspective, strongly focused on citizens (Millard,

Figure 3. Main "spaces of use" for IT in the overall state government activities

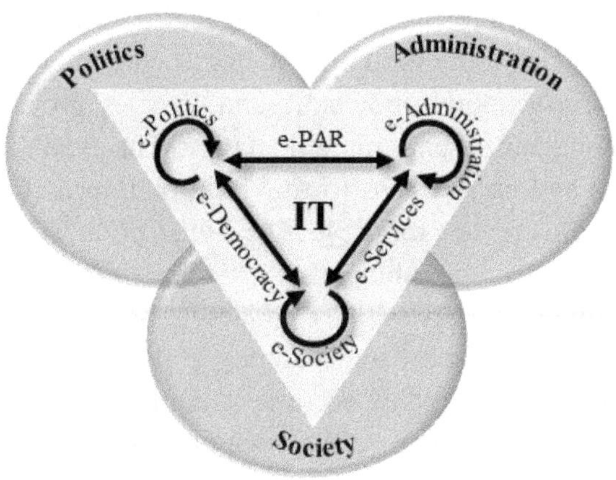

2003). This new "citizen-centered administration" vision aims to change the way government agencies deliver their services to citizens, and is an attempt to address the dissatisfaction that citizens have been expressing concerning their interactions with government agencies, as well as a way to react and answer to the increasingly expectations that citizens have been showing about public services delivery quality.

A great part of the dissatisfaction felt by citizens is due to the excessive bureaucracy that they came across when requiring for public services. Indeed, the only thing a citizen wishes, when he/she requires for a service, is to see his/her request executed in a quick, correct and streamlined way, without having to know details on which agencies are involved in it and on how it is conducted (EPAN, 2004; OECD, 2003; Reynolds & Regio, 2001; Santos & Amaral, 2003). Unfortunately, and despite the recent improvements introduced at this level, there is still some red tape that can and need to be cut in public agencies.

At the same time, citizens are becoming more and more demanding and expectant concerning the quality of public services. A study published by the *Economist Intelligence Unit* showed that the growth of citizens' expectations is one of the factors that will have deeper impact in the functioning and organization of government agencies (EIU, 2005). For instance, citizens increasingly expect to found the new and more sophisticated forms of interaction offered by private sector organizations also available in the public sector services (Budge, 2002; EIU, 2005; Tambouris & Tarabanis, 2005).

Citizens also increasingly expect to be able to access a public service at any time, from anywhere and through any channel (Srivastava & Teo, 2004; UMIC, 2003). Although desktop computers remain a privileged channel for accessing electronic public services, the use of alternative access channels, such as mobile phones, WAP devices, PDAs and digital television, is also being claimed by citizens (EIU, 2005; Ndou, 2005; Pérez-Villaplana, 2003). It should be noted that citizens also want to be able to keep using more traditional channels such as the telephone, fax, conventional mail, or even personal attendance places, to interact with agencies, particularly during some special services provision. In fact, there are specific services that, either because they cannot be fully electronically provided or because they involve aspects of a delicate and sensitive nature, can lose quality if delivered exclusively through new electronic means (Millard, 2003). The relevant point is to ensure that citizens are able to choose the interaction channel that best suits their needs (EPAN, 2004; OECD, 2003).

An additional expectation of citizens is to have personalized public services (EIU, 2005), what Millard calls the *Me-Government* (Millard, 2003). That is, citizens want to be able to customize the services provided by agencies according to their preferences, and to have "intelligent and self-learning" services that are able to, automatically and by themselves, adapt to user's interests and needs.

The term *Electronic Services (e-Services)*, adopted herein, refers precisely to the use of IT to support and promote the transformation and renewal of the interactions between *Administration* and the multiple *Society* agents, including citizens

(*Government-to-Citizen* (G2C) interactions) and businesses (*Government-to-Business* (G2B) interactions), in order to reduce the dissatisfaction of citizens and to fulfill their expectancies when dealing with government agencies.

Although the most publicized and discussed kind of interaction between *Administration* and *Society* concerns the delivery of services, other kind of interaction exists and should be considered: that which arises from the role that *Administration* assumes as provider of information. In fact, the process of reform and modernization should not be restricted to the notion of *service*; the *information* is also present, by itself or as part of the processes that are involved in services delivery (Budge, 2002). The terms *Electronic Service Delivery (e-SD)* and *Electronic Information Provision (e-IP)* are used in this chapter to denote each of these perspectives. Although one can argue that the information provision can be viewed as a service offered by *Administration*, the distinction between the provision of information and the delivery of services is important, since the impacts, challenges and strategies associated with the use of IT in each of these sub-aspects are distinct.

According to various evolutionary models of e-government (e.g. Gartner, 2000; Hiller & Bélanger, 2001; infoDev, 2009; Jayashree & Marthandan, 2010; Kho & Prybutok, 2003; Layne & Lee, 2001; Siau & Long, 2004; UN, 2012), the informational perspective of the relationship between *Administration* and *Society* is often where any global e-government development effort starts. This being the first area where Internet and Web-based technologies are used, resulting usually in the creation of agencies' Websites containing information such as the description of services provided, agencies working hours, location and contact information, and frequently asked questions (EzGov, 2000).

However, the informational perspective is much richer than this. It should involve not only the provision of simple and "innocuous" information, which generally corresponds to the information already available in brochures, leaflets and similar resources, but also the provision of a vast array of information about agencies' strategies, agencies' operation and management, agencies' socio-economic indicators, and agencies' projects management and implementation. The availability and easy access to this kind of information would create a more *open Administration*, which is clearly something that citizens want to see happening (EIU, 2005). Indeed, more openness would mean more transparency, giving the citizen the opportunity to become a kind of agencies "auditor" (Budge, 2002), which would lead to increased levels of citizen trust in *Administration*, thus contributing to a substantial improvement in the state's image. It should be noted that citizens that are more and better informed about the reality of their *Administration* are in a better position not only to claim and enjoy their rights but also to exercise their duties and play their roles in their relations with government (Davison, Wagner, & Ma, 2005; EIU, 2005). The benefits that IT can produce at this level are significant, allowing the collection, relationship and organization of information and its continuous availability in the appropriate format according to citizens' interests.

Electronic Administration (E-Administration)

The *Administration* sphere in Figure 3 is another major intervention "space" in the process of transforming and renewing the state government activities.

Continually challenged by restricted budgets, by higher levels of citizens' demand, by the growing rigor and discipline imposed by politicians, and by the accelerated pace of change, public administration has been adopting new management techniques and using IT to support and improve their internal and external operations (EIU, 2005; Gonçalves, 2000).

Although the successive reforming efforts done so far have produced some noticeable improvements, public administration still continues to be synonym of low levels of productivity and efficiency, low reliability, excessive bureaucracy and massive overspending (Gonçalves, 2000), which is a rather inconvenient situation, not only for public managers, but also for civil servants, politicians, citizens and the overall country's image. This unpleasant and inconvenient situation is widely justified by the insular nature that continues to characterize the way multiple government agencies keep operating. Indeed, when interacting with *Administration*, citizens continue to feel as if there were many public administrations and not one public administration in a country. This "silos problem," as Bannister (2001) calls it, is the legacy that resulted from decades of introspective developments done by agencies and constitutes the Achilles heel in the process of creating a fully renovated digital state (Prasad, 2005). As noted by Vidigal (2003), "the paraphernalia of clients, servers, storage devices, networks, databases and middleware, acquired by each agency along the last decades, instead of being a facilitator, ended up being a restraining force to provision of responsive and quality services."

In order to be able to work in a more integrated way and attain the adequate levels of efficiency and quality of services and operations, agencies must abandon their current introverted model of thinking, planning, implementing and managing their processes and information systems (Tambouris & Tarabanis, 2005). Agency collaboration, cooperation, coordination and interoperation are recognized as priority traits in the transformation of public administration (Ndou, 2004; Valle, 2003). According to Prasad (2005), integration of the multiple government agencies is the "right place" to start a sustained process of government transformation.

Information technologies assume, in this context, a fundamental role. The term *Electronic Administration (e-Administration)* is used herein to describe the phenomenon of using IT to support and promote the transformation and renewal of the internal operation of each agency and of the way the various agencies can work together (i.e. the so-called *Government-to-Government* (G2G) interactions).

Putting multiple agencies working together, i.e. to make their multiple heterogeneous and autonomous information systems to interoperate, is a Herculean challenge (Soares & Amaral, 2011), that tends to be as much difficult and complex as the number of agencies involved and the diversity of administration levels to which such agencies belong increases. Indeed, four different interoperability situations may happen in what concerns the administration level of the agencies involved in one initiative:

- **Intra-Agency Interoperability:** In this case only one agency is involved. The intention in these cases is to promote the interoperability of different systems that exist within the same agency, in order to eliminate the agency internal "silos;"
- **Horizontal Interagency Interoperability:** In this case more than one agency at the same administration level is involved. In such cases the challenge is to achieve interoperability among, for example, two or more systems from central administration level agencies or among two or more systems from local administration level agencies;
- **Vertical Interagency Interoperability:** In this case more than one agency from different administration levels are involved. In such cases the challenge is to achieve interoperability, for example, among systems from central government agencies and local government agencies;
- **International Interagency Interoperability:** In this case agencies from different countries are involved. Srivastava and Teo (2004) call this kind of interactions G2F (*Government to Foreign Government*). Although interoperability initiatives at

> national level can be considered a priority in the reform process, it is important to be aware that supranational efforts are being planned and implemented. European Commission, for instance, has been promoting and sponsoring a set of actions aiming the creation of a pan-European Public Administration able to provide cross-country electronic public services. This fact brings additional complexity to agencies, since the solutions they are adopting and developing at a national level should be compatible and flexible enough to easily interoperate in future interaction with the administrations of other member states.

As shown in Figure 4, and similarly to what was mentioned in the previous section, in the *Electronic Administration* "space" is also possible to identify two subareas of intervention, one having a more informational focus and the other a more procedural focus (Millard, 2003; Sakowicz, 2003; Srivastava & Teo, 2004).

The more procedural subarea, herein called *Electronic Administration Processes Integration (e-API)*, refers to the set of changes and alignments that need to be done in the agencies' internal processes and information systems in order to create the required conditions to provide completely integrated cross-agency electronic services. Indeed, only through reorganization of agencies' back-offices will government be able to deliver truly and fully "end-to-end" services to citizens (Valle, 2003). According to Millard, Iversen, Kubicek, Westholm, and Cimander (2004), the success of the creation and availability of renewed and technologically sophisticated front-offices can utterly fail if not supported by integrated back-offices. Integrated back-offices will not only allow for more streamlined and better services provision to citizens but also to improve agencies' efficiency, efficacy and productivity, as well as to lower agencies' expenditures. The need to rethink the *modus operandi* of government agencies' processes (Lenk & Traunmüller, 2002) and the way IT can be used in this purpose, thus assumes a prominent role in the renewal and transformation of the overall state government activities. For this reason, numerous initiatives, efforts, and debates have been launched over the last few years, by practitioners, academics and researchers in this area.

Unlike the procedural perspective, the more informational perspective – *Electronic Administration Information Integration (e-AII)* – has not got so much attention from practitioners, academics or researches (Batini & Mecella, 2002). The lack of interest and apparent apathy concerning this perspective is rather incomprehensible, since the existence of a comprehensive and articulated informational body in agencies is absolutely fundamental. Indeed, the creation of a properly structured network of accurate and update information (EIU, 2005), seems to be essential. This is not only for "internal consume," that is to support the proper functioning and management of the entire administrative structure, but also for "external consume," that is to feed the policy formulation and decision-making activities occurring in the *Politics* sphere, as well as the information provision mechanisms that should be available to citizens, as argued in the previous subsection. It is also expected that serious and profound interventions at this level may help to clarify the mission and responsibilities of each agency, as well as to identify and reduce informational redundancies that may exist in agencies.

Despite of being a mandatory issue, the integration of administration information, which will provide a global view of the informational entities manipulated by the multiple agencies, is a complex area of intervention. Indeed, the fragmentation and dispersion of information by the multiple agencies (Budge, 2002), the different and sometimes incompatible schemes and meanings of data in different agencies, the redundancy and replication of data by the agencies, and the fact that some information may not even be available

Figure 4. Processual and information perspectives in the Administration "space"

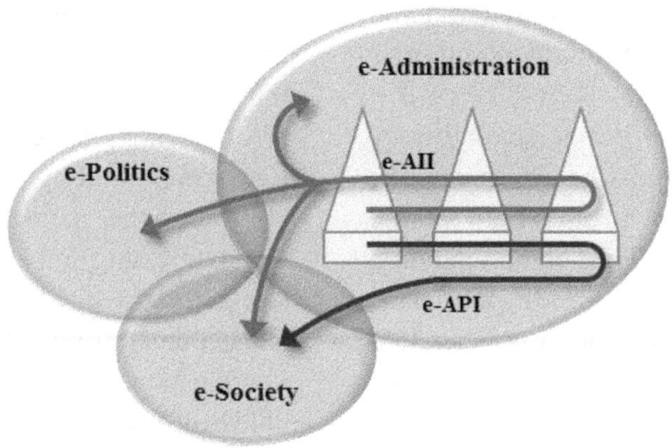

in digital format, are all factors that hamper the prosecution of information integration initiatives. Other factors related to knowledge management, security, and coordination, are also implied in the creation of new ways to gather, edit, forward, disseminate, integrate and conveniently organize the information of the numerous government agencies (Perri, 2001; Lenihan, 2002).

Whatever the intervention is considered, *e-API* or *e-AII*, the challenges involved are huge. Indeed, these are high complexity initiatives that implicitly demand for changes in established working routines. In fact, for each new practice that has to be adopted, older customary practices have to be abandoned. This is not easy or quick to achieve. A study by COMNET-IT (2002, p. 3) showed that "the real challenge in administrative systems reform is the inculcation of attitudes that acknowledge data and information to be a corporate resource – and therefore shareable and subject to standards – as well as introducing process and regulatory changes that fly in the face of established hierarchical decision-making structures." Notwithstanding the expected difficulties, the truth is that this process is irreversible: government agencies "are being forced," by today's conjuncture, to collaborate and cooperate, and IT will undoubtedly contribute to this intent (EIU, 2005).

Electronic Political-Administrative Relationships (E-PAR)

A third area of intervention in the process of government reformation and modernization are the relationships between the *Politics* and *Administration* spheres.

As previously mentioned, *Politics* and *Administration* spheres represent two essential functions of a state government system: *Politics* purpose is to define the general interest of the state collectivity and *Administration* purpose is to accomplish the general interest defined by *Politics* (Amaral, 1994; Goodnow, 2003).

Although, conceptually these functions can be differentiated, their execution can hardly be understood separately (Goodnow, 2003). Rather, they are closely related, being the success of each function highly dependent on the existence of a good matching and harmonization between them (Nunes, 2004). In fact, any decision taken by *Politics*, that express a will of the state, will have no effect at all unless it is executed by *Administration*. Similarly, the execution by *Administration* of a rule that is not the expression of a state will is not going to contribute to the creation of the desired state collectivity well-being (Goodnow, 2003). Although there are few indications of "how" and "what" to do to balance the rules, determinations and criteria of *Administration* and *Politics*, the intervention in this area is absolutely fundamental, when seeking the improvement, renewal and transformation of the overall government activities (Nunes, 2004).

To achieve the convenient balance and harmony between *Politics* and *Administration*, there must be a clear and fluid communication between the players of both spheres. This communication must be bidirectional: on one side politicians make decisions and define general policies that they communicate to public managers who then execute them (Nunes, 2004). On the other side public managers are the ones who best know their agencies, the way policies are implemented, and the effects of those policies implementation, that is, public managers possess relevant information that must be transmitted to politicians. In fact, the decision making and policy definition processes carried out by politicians must be strongly based on a thorough knowledge about how policies implementation is proceeding and performing (Goodnow, 2003). This knowledge is also fundamental to politicians because they need to be prepared to respond and report to the Chief of State and to the Parliament. According to Gonçalves (2000), along the 21st century, the rigor and discipline imposed by politicians on public managers will tend to increase even more, as a result of the growing pressures that politicians are being submitted to.

By all this, it is urgent to ensure the existence of a communication channel that allows a flow of correct, accurate, timely, and integrated information from the *Administration* to the *Politics* sphere.

Information technologies can play a prominent role in the *Politics-Administration* interaction "space." New IT can facilitate the creation and deployment of new communication channels between the two spheres. These channels will greatly enhance the quality of the communication process, making it more agile, more flexible and more convenient. Information technologies can also contribute to improve the quality of the exchanged and manipulated information by various actors. In addition, the use of IT may also produce considerable benefits concerning the management of the communication process itself, by facilitating the joint work of politicians and public managers, by making the communication process more transparent, and by allowing a greater accountability of the multiple communicating actors. One interesting and paradoxical aspect should be stressed at this point: although more transparency and accountability at the *Politics-Administration* relationships level seems to be important and desirable benefits, politicians may not look upon them favorably, since they will be much more espoused to the public manager's scrutiny. This though is also true for public managers, who may not look upon those benefits favorably, since they will be more espoused to politicians' scrutiny. These aspects may hamper and strongly jeopardize the prosecution of IT initiatives at this level. Finally, another interesting benefit of IT use at this level can be the increase of politicians' awareness about the role and importance that IT plays in the renewal and transformation of the overall state government activities. Indeed, since politicians will benefit and be directly affected by these initiatives, they will be more conscious and convinced about the value that IT can play also in all the remaining "spaces" of intervention indicated in Figure 3, and thus become supporters and sponsors of IT use in each one of those "spaces."

Electronic Politics (E-Politics)

As mentioned above, any of the spheres and any of the zones of interaction that are depicted in Figure 3 constitute intervention "spaces" where IT can be used to facilitate and catalyze the renewal and transformation of the overall state government activities. Thus, it seems understandable that the use of IT to support, restructure and innovate the way activities are conducted in the *Politics* sphere is considered as a relevant issue.

Defined broadly as the public activity of State that aim to define the general interest of society

(Amaral, 1994), the *Politics* function involves a huge amount of complex decision-making processes, which tend to become even more complex as social, environmental and financial pressures on government intensify. To be able to deal with such complexity, politicians must have access to accurate, updated, timely, reliable, and well-structured information (Bajpei, 2005). While, as mentioned previously, a large volume of those data comes from the *Administration* sphere, there is a whole set of additional data that come from other sources such as the private sector, the media, the voluntary civic and social organizations, and the international institutions. All this needs to be collected, cross-checked, structured and integrated in order to create a complete and quality informational base.

As important as having a complete and quality informational base to support decision-making is to have mechanisms that facilitate and support the articulation and coordination of the individual tasks and efforts of all the political actors involved in the decision-making and policy formulation processes. Indeed, it is expectable that the decisions made and the policies settled by the various governmental ministries are consistent and compatible among them, which will happen only if ministerial offices are able to act and decide in an articulated and coherent way. Hence, is essential to develop systems that enable the integrated operation of the various government departments (Lenk & Traunmüller, 2002).

The use of IT to transform and support the creation, management, provision, and use of adequate repositories, that contain the information generated and accumulated throughout the various ministerial offices (Lenk & Traunmüller, 2002), can significantly improve the *Politics* sphere' processes and outputs. Additionally, as stated at the end of the previous section, there is an indirect benefit that results from the successful implementation of IT-based reformation initiatives at this level. This is quite relevant, since the lack of politicians' awareness usually leads to a lack of political will and commitment to implement e-government initiatives, which is usually identified as a major impediment to the development of electronic government (Adams, Haston, Gillespie, & Macintosh, 2003; EC, 2006; Realini, 2004; Soares & Amaral, 2011; Srivastava & Teo, 2004).

Electronic Democracy (E-Democracy)

The interaction between citizens and government structures is being recognized as a primordial area in the complex process of reformation and transformation of state government activities.

In the previous *Electronic Services (e-Services)* subsection were already mentioned and stressed two kinds of relations that exist between citizens and governmental spheres: one where citizens play a role of "clients" or "consumers" of information and public services, and another where citizens play a role of "auditors" of *Administration*'s duties, rights, and performance. In both these cases the focus is placed on the relations between citizens and *Administration* (Davison et al., 2005). There is, however, another area where citizens interact with the governmental: one in which the citizens take the role of "owner" or "shareholder" (Tapscott & Agnew, 1999). In this case, the focus is set on the relations between citizens and *Politics*.

The way these relationships take place has been undergoing some changes during the last few years. For long years, these relationships had been almost exclusively limited to the electoral periods, during which candidates communicate to citizens their electoral programs and strategies and citizens took, through their vote in the elections day, a participatory action expressing their preferences and selecting their representatives. In the last years, this situation has been changing. Maybe as a result of recent educational, cultural, social, economic, and technological developments, we are witnessing to a sharp increase in the number and type of interactions that occur between citizens and political actors. In fact, citizens are stepping up pressure on political representatives, asking for more openness in their actions. Citizens not only want to have more information about the political processes, but also want to express their opinions, to propose their ideas, and to participate more directly in decision-making activities (Reynolds & Regio, 2001).

Information technologies are increasingly being seen as a useful and determinant instrument to transform the way citizens-representatives relations take place. By offering a whole range of alternative and flexible means to support and renew interactions between citizens and politicians, IT are extending the public space and contributing to the improvement of the democratic process' effectiveness and efficiency (Evangelidis, Akomode, Taleb-Bendiab, & Taylot, 2002). The use of IT to support the interactions between citizens and political power is generally called *Electronic Democracy (e-Democracy).*

It should be noted that the IT use in constituencies-elected representatives' relationships can have two different focuses. First, IT can be used to facilitate and enhance the participation and involvement of citizens in processes of deliberation, consulting, debating, and definition of governmental policies, strategies, and action plans (OECD, 2003; Sakowicz, 2003). The initiatives developed at this level are currently known as *Electronic Participation (e-Participation)* and constitute different mechanisms to "listen" and "talk to" citizens (Heeks, 2001b). Examples of these initiatives include the possibility of conducting meetings and discussions in a virtual environment (Sakowicz, 2003), the creation of community fora, and the creation of online consultation systems to facilitate the conduct of polls and make it possible to know and understand the positioning of citizens concerning to matters under discussion (Perri, 2001; Batini & Mecella, 2002). Indeed, the fundamental rationale underlying the creation of more and different participation mechanisms is to try to define and adopt public policies that reflect better and are more aligned with the real needs and interests of citizens (Heeks, 2001b). Second, IT can also be used as a facilitating and simplifying mechanism for the formal electoral processes (EzGov, 2000; OECD, 2003). Efforts at this level are usually associated with the creation of electronic voting systems (e-Voting) (Perri, 2001; Batini & Mecella, 2002), that allow voters to record their secret and secure ballot electronically.

Whichever the focus – e-participation or e-voting – any of these types of interventions is mostly presented as contributing to the revitalization of democracy and to the reinforcement of democratic values (Islam, 2008; Lenihan, 2002; OECD, 2001).

It should be noted that the use of IT in this context must be carefully planned, managed and implemented, since it raises not only new opportunities for democracy, but it also raises and brings huge concerns and challenges (Lenihan, 2002; Stahl, 2005). Knowing these opportunities and concerns is fundamental, in order to guarantee that these intervention processes are successful implemented and lead to the expected results. For example, it could be expected that the implementation of e-participation initiatives, by enabling the direct participation of constituents in government activities, may lead to the strengthening of participatory democratic models and to the weakening of representative democratic models. If this could mean, by one side, that there is an "empowerment of citizens" (EIU, 2005; Sakowicz, 2003), on the other side, it can mean "a free from responsibility" for politicians, since it is easier for them to argue that a particular decision was taken because it "was the people's will" (Lenihan, 2002). Authors such as Islam (2008), Lenhian (2002), and Stahl (2005) also argue that, if not very careful managed, e-democracy initiatives may end up having the contrary impact, creating an even lesser democratic state. This constitutes, indeed, a strongly debated subject, that has been catching the attention of politicians, practitioners, researchers and the general Society.

Electronic Society (E-Society)

Unlike the "spaces" described in the previous five subsections, the *Society* sphere is not, in itself, an obvious "space" of direct intervention when talking about e-government development efforts. However, since *Society* is the "reason of being" of the State and the ultimate end of its governance (Nunes, 2004), it ends to be indirectly implicated in the e-government implementation, playing in it a dual role, as suggested in Figure 5. On the one hand, *Society* influences how e-government is developed and determines how it is accepted and adopted by citizens (arrow 4) and, on the other hand, *Society* is conditioned and transformed by e-government development (arrow 2). Thus, it is expected that new e-government efforts developed in any of the previous five "spaces" (arrow 1), produce indirect interventions in the *Society* sphere (arrow 3).

For example, the decision to provide electronically a public service, for which there is a high demand and whose traditional supply conditions are unpleasant because of long waiting queues and very limited working hours seldom compatible with citizens' schedules, will bring huge convenience benefits to citizens. These benefits will end up attracting and convincing a large number of citizens, some of which hitherto not very IT enthusiasts, about the use of IT-based systems to interact with government, making them customary e-government users and even transforming them in e-government demanders. It is important to remark that an e-government initiative will only be valuable if it will be accepted and used by citizens, otherwise it will be a waste of time and resources. Thus, the success of a country's e-government strategy will depend, in great part, on the level of acceptance and predisposition of citizens to adopt this new ways of interaction with the overall government structures and activities.

Another example can be presented. The creation of an e-procurement system for public administration agencies, and the decision that only the goods and services proposals submitted through the e-procurement system will be eligible, is a strong motivation for the technological development of enterprises (infoDev, 2009). The opportunity to conduct electronic transactions with public agencies ultimately stimulates the use of IT and the improvement of their own internal operating procedures, thus contributing to increased businesses' competitiveness. Reciprocally, private sector businesses, mainly those using more advanced and sophisticated IT systems, tend to pressure government actors in order to have at their disposal new, more efficient, and more convenient ways to interact with them.

A third example is related to the fact that the implementation of some e-government initiatives could somehow "force" the launch of other *e-Society* initiatives. Indeed, it just makes sense that government provides online services, if citizens have at their disposal the necessary infrastructures to access those services and also if their computer literacy levels are adequate to use them. Thus, the implementation of e-government initiatives may implicitly lead to the launching of initiatives such as the development of a national infrastructural network and the creation of educational programs.

These examples make clear that e-government may have a key role in fostering competitiveness and Information Society development (Budge, 2002; UMIC, 2003), as well as in creating a favorable climate for the overall development of *Society* (Heeks, 2001b; Jayashree & Marthandan,

Figure 5. Duality of influences between Society and e-government development initiatives

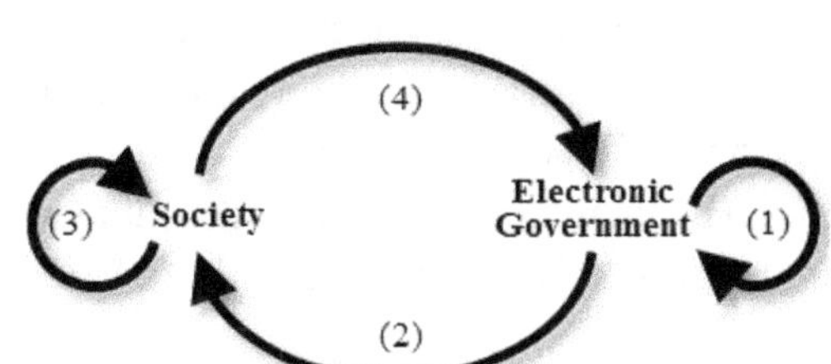

2010). In the same sense, examples also show that *Society*, and all the educational, cultural, social, economic, and technological changes that have been occurring, may influence – either positively, acting as an accelerator, or negatively, acting as a brake – the pursue of e-government development. Thus, to be aware of the reciprocal relationship that exists between *Society* and the overall governmental structures and activities seems to be something fundamental in the process of e-government development. Indeed, driving new efforts to reach e-government (arrow 1), will produce a set of effects on *Society* (arrow 2), which can lead to changes in its *statu quo* (arrow 3), which will end to have an effect in the e-government development process (arrow 4). In this sense, it seems appropriate that all interventions that are initiated in order to promote e-government are planned and implemented taking into account the multiple effects that may result from themselves.

A HOLISTIC AND ECLECTIC PERSPECTIVE ON E-GOVERNMENT CONCEPT

In the previous section, several "spaces," where IT can be used in order to support, renew, transform and modernize the state government activities, were described in detail. Only the joint development of IT initiatives in all those "spaces" will truly lead to the emergence and achievement of the overall and fully e-government country's reality. Consequently, and as evidenced in the framework presented in Figure 6, we argue in this chapter that the e-government concept should assume a comprehensive, holistic and eclectic perspective, and define it as being the conduction of the multiple government activities in a renewed, transformed, and strongly IT-supported way.

Briefly, there are seven main ideas underpinning the proposed framework, as listed below:

- The e-government concept is closely related to the implementation of initiatives aimed at contributing to the reform, transformation and modernization of the overall state government activities;
- The e-government concept is invariably associated with the use of IT as a facilitator and a catalyst of the intended reformation, transformation, and modernization of the overall state government activities;
- The e-government concept is eclectic, covering different and multiple intervention "spaces" in which IT can be used to foster the reformation, transformation, and modernization of the overall state government activities, including: the relationships between *Society* and *Administration*, the relationships between *Administration* and *Politics*, the relationships between *Politics* and *Society*, as well as the inner functioning of the *Administration* sphere, the inner functioning of the *Politics* sphere, and the inner functioning of the *Society* sphere;
- The e-government concept is holistic, requiring the ability to know and understand the whole set of relationships and interdependencies that exist among the various intervention "spaces;"
- The fully successful e-government development depends, considerably, on the existence of a vision of the overall "e-government ecology;"
- E-government development should be thought globally. This systemic thinking is of paramount importance in e-government development, since this will avoid the emergence of a mesh of unarticulated initiatives that will delay or preclude the achievement of a truly and genuinely renewed and transformed government;
- E-government development should be achieved gradually. E-government is not something that "is built," it is something that "is being built." While e-government

Figure 6. E-government conceptual framework

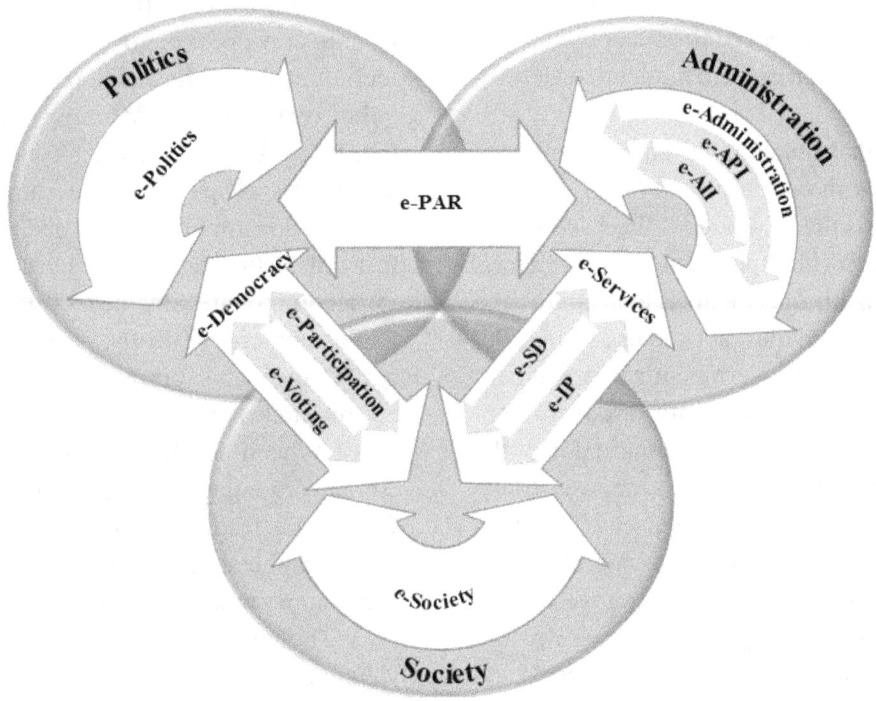

should be thought as a whole reality, it will be materialized and gain existence through the implementation of a successive set of specific initiatives, each one aimed at support, facilitate, innovate and transform the way multiple state government activities are performed.

Considering the wide scope and inclusiveness of the proposed framework, the trek to e-government is neither simple nor easy, but is an unavoidable challenge in today's society (Davison et al., 2005).

CONCLUSION

The existence of a clear and consensual conceptualization of e-government is a fundamental and relevant issue, not only for creating and for maintaining the identity and distinctiveness of the e-government research field, but also for nurturing its development and flourishing. Notwithstanding, as evidenced in the second section of this chapter, instead of clarity and consensus around the e-government concept, the e-government field is populated by a multiplicity of different and partially overlapping definitions that has been generating an uncomfortable and adverse ambiguity. Aware of those facts, several authors have made efforts in order to find out and provide wider and consensual e-government definitions. Those wider definitions were extracted from the analysis and comparison of a set of definitions that authors gathered from the literature through either more or less systematic and structured processes. Thus, while being wider, those definitions are dependent on, and biased by, the definitions already existent in the literature.

In this chapter, we also aimed to contribute to the clarification of the e-government concept but, unlike the efforts done so far, we haven't restricted our work on the existent definitions. Instead, we followed a different and more sustained approach, having grounded our conceptualization of e-government on a generic model of a government system.

Drawn on that model, an e-government conceptual framework was proposed. The framework comprehends six main "spaces" – the *Administration* sphere, the *Politics* sphere, the *Society* sphere, and the relationships between each one of them – on which we can and must act and use IT in order to promote an overall government's improvement and transformation. Consequently, e-government was herein defined as being the conduction of the multiple government activities in a renewed, transformed, and strongly IT-supported way. This definition suggests and argues for a comprehensive, holistic, and eclectic perspective of e-government. Thisencompasses the improvement, renewal and transformation of public information provision and services delivery (e-Services), of internal management and operation (e-Administration), of the politics-public servants interactions (e-PAR), of the functioning of political activities (e-Politics), of democratic processes (e-Democracy), of citizens' involvement and participation (e-Participation), of electoral voting acts (e-Voting), and of nuclear societal conditions namely of an educative and infrastructural nature (e-Society).

It is our conviction that the existence of such a comprehensive conceptualization (that articulates the multiple "spaces" where IT is used to support and improve the overall state government activities) is of paramount importance when seeking to achieve the idealized "dream vision" of a fully e-government reality in a country. An incomplete perspective of e-government could restrain considerably all the potential opportunities and benefits that a wider articulated perspective could provide, thus weakening both the research and the practical implementation and development of e-government.

It is also our conviction that the proposed framework is enough robust to constitute a stable conceptualization of e-government. This happens, first of all, because the framework is based on its core concept (i.e. government), thus naturally including all its relevant elements or components, being very unlikely that any additional element that might be suggested isn't already framed in any of the six "spaces" of the framework. Second, because it is not limited nor tied to any particular form of technology, being compatible and able to accommodate any new kind of technology that can emerge. Thirdly, because it has an open nature and being permeable to new and different research theories, methods, techniques, and tools, as well as ideas and knowledge that may come from adjacent fields. And fourth, because visually the framework has an intuitive, clear, and clean graphical representation that make it self-explanatory and very easy to understand and use.

We believe that this framework may become a valuable frame of reference in the e-government field, not only because it provides a wide, intuitive, and stable conceptualization of e-government, but also because it can be a useful working instrument.

For instance, possible work to be done would be to collect and analyze a collection of papers and plot them on the framework according to the "space" in which each paper is focused. This will give the e-government community a perspective of the *field's focus profile*, that is an integrated view of which have been the most and the least e-government areas or elements researched in the field. Similarly, if we populate the framework with the names of the articles' authors we will be able to trace *researcher profiles*, that is to know which authors have been researching and publishing in which area. In the same line, if we plot on the framework the theories, frameworks, or models that were used in those papers we will have a picture of what type of research instruments were used in which are of the field. Many other visions of the field may still be developed. Repeating this kind of works on a periodical base will provide the research community with a longitudinal picture that shows the overall evolution of the field along the time. Additionally, the framework will not only be useful to show what has been happening in the e-government field, but also do define a roadmap for future research, serving as the base for discussing and outlining future research agendas. All this enriching knowledge could contribute to strengthen the collective identity of the e-government research field and to its sustained and sustainable development.

The framework can also be used by scholars at a personal level to visualize how they have been orientating, or intend to orientate, their research interests and activity.

Finally, we also believe that this framework may become a useful instrument for practitioners. It will be particularly relevant for those responsible for the long-term overall strategy and development of e-government in a country. They could use it as a frame where they can note down the initiatives and projects that have been or are being planned or implemented. This would give them a broad and rich picture about what has already been done, what remains to be done, which are the areas that have caught less attention and investment, and so forth. This broad vision of the overall e-government development status will help them to reevaluate and redirect their strategies, priorities, and action plans.

The framework could also bring benefits at an international level and scale. Indeed, it would be possible to use it to depict the e-government development status of any country, and then compare and benchmark them in order to get an understanding of how countries have been organizing and directing their e-government efforts.

It is our hope that this framework will get the recognition and acceptance of the e-government scholars, and thus becoming a shared conceptualization in the field.

REFERENCES

Adams, N., Haston, S., Gillespie, N., & Macintosh, A. (2003). Conventional and electronic service delivery within public authorities: The issues and lessons from the private sector. In Traunmüller, R. (Ed.), *Electronic Government* (*Vol. 2739*, pp. 129–134). Lecture Notes in Computer Science Berlin: Springer-Verlag. doi:10.1007/10929179_23.

Amaral, D. F. (1994). *Curso de Direito Administrativo*. Coimbra: Livraria Almedina.

Andersen, K., & Henriksen, H. (2005). The first leg of e-government research: Domains and application areas. *International Journal of Electronic Government Research*, *1*(4), 26–44. doi:10.4018/jegr.2005100102.

Anderson, J. (2011). *Wikipedia – The company and its founders*. North Mankato: Technology Pioneers.

Astley, W. (1985). Administrative science as socially constructed truth. *Administrative Science Quarterly*, *30*(4), 497–513. doi:10.2307/2392694.

Bajpei, N. (2005). Knowledge based decision support systems in governance. In G. Nayak, M. Mishra & A. Das (Eds.), *Proceedings of the Eighth National Conference on e-Governance* (pp. 43-46). Bhubaneswar.

Bannister, F. (2001). Dismantling the silos: Extracting new value from IT investments in public administration. *Information Systems Journal*, *11*(1), 65–84. doi:10.1046/j.1365-2575.2001.00094.x.

Batini, C., & Mecella, M. (2002). Cooperative processes for e-Government. *European Research Consortium for Informatics and Mathematics*, *48*, 38–39.

Bolívar, M., Muñoz, L., & Hernández, A. (2010). Trends of e-government research: Contextualization and research opportunities. *The International Journal of Digital Accounting Research, 10*, 87–111. doi:10.4192/1577-8517-v10_4.

Budge, E. (2002). Foundations of e-government. In Smith, A. (Ed.), *Digital opportunities for development: A sourcebook for access and applications* (pp. 331–368). Washington: LearnLink.

Caldow, J. (2001). *Seven e-government leadership milestones*. Institute for Electronic Government. Retrieved May 13, 2012, from http://www-1.ibm.com/industries/government/ieg/pdf/Seven_E-Gov_Milestones.pdf

Coleman, S. (2008). Foundations of digital government. In Chen, H., Brandt, L., Gregg, V., Traunmüller, R., Dawes, S., & Hovy, E. et al. (Eds.), *Digital government: E-government research, case studies, and implementation* (pp. 3–19). New York: Springer.

COMNET-IT. (2002). *Country profiles of e-governance*. A report of The Commonwealth Network of Information Technology for Development Foundation (COMNET-IT). Retrieved June 3, 2012, from http://unesdoc.unesco.org/images/0012/001276/127601e.pdf

Davison, R., Wagner, C., & Ma, L. (2005). From government to e-government: A transition model. *Information Technology & People, 18*(3), 280–299. doi:10.1108/09593840510615888.

Dawes, S. (2009). Governance in the digital age: A research and action framework for an uncertain future. *Government Information Quarterly, 26*(2), 257–264. doi:10.1016/j.giq.2008.12.003.

Deloitte. (2000). *At the dawn of e-government: The citizen as customer*. A global public sector study by Deloitte Consulting and Deloitte & Touche. Retrieved March, 23, 2012, from http://epractice.eu/en/library/281462

EC. (1994a). *Europe and the global information society – Bangemann report recommendations to the European Council*. Retrieved April 19, 2012, from http://www.epractice.eu/files/media/media_694.pdf

EC. (1994b). *Europe's way to the information society – An action plan*. COM(94) 347 final. Retrieved April 19, 2012, from http://ec.europa.eu/archives/ISPO/docs/htmlgenerated/i_COM(94)347final.html

EC. (1999). *eEurope: An information society for all*. COM(1999) 687 final. European Commission. Retrieved February 10, 2012, from http://eur-lex.europa.eu/LexUriServ/LexUriServ.do?uri=COM:2002:0263:FIN:EN:PDF

EC. (2003). *The role of eGovernment for Europe's Future*. COM(2003) 567 final. Retrieved May 26, 2012, from http://eur-lex.europa.eu/LexUriServ/LexUriServ.do?uri=COM:2003:0567:FIN:EN:PDF

EC. (2006). *A legal and institutional analysis of barriers to egovernment – Draft deliverable 1b*. Breaking barriers to egovernment: Overcoming obstacles to improving European public services - modinis study (Contract n. 29172). Retrieved December 18, 2011, from http://www.egovbarriers.org/downloads/deliverables/Deliverable_1b_Aug_16_2006.pdf

EIU. (2005). *Business 2010: The Public Sector*. White Paper. Economist Intelligence Unit. Retrieved May 26, 2012, from http://graphics.eiu.com/files/ad_pdfs/Business_2010_Public_sector_WP.pdf

EPAN. (2004). *Key principles of an interoperability architecture*. European Public Administration Network – eGovernment Working Group. Retrieved January 7, 2012, from http://www.epractice.eu/en/library/281244

Evangelidis, A., Akomode, J., Taleb-Bendiab, A., & Taylor, M. (2002). Risk assessment & success factors for e-government in a UK establishment. In Traunmüller, R., & Lenk, K. (Eds.), *Electronic Government* (*Vol. 2456*, pp. 395–402). Lecture Notes in Computer Science Berlin: Springer-Verlag. doi:10.1007/978-3-540-46138-8_64.

EzGov. (2000). E-government: Making sense of a revolution. *Government Technology August* (Advertising Supplement). Retrieved March 14, 2012, from http://ebookbrowse.com/egovernment-making-sense-revolution-pdf-d291274249

Flak, L., Moe, C., & Saebo, O. (2003). On the evolution of e-government: The user imperative. In Traunmüller, R. (Ed.), *Electronic Government* (*Vol. 2739*, pp. 139–142). Lecture Notes in Computer Science Berlin: Springer-Verlag. doi:10.1007/10929179_25.

Fraga, E. (2002). *Trends in e-government: How to plan, design, secure and measure e-government.* Sante Fe, New Mexico: Gartner Consulting. Retrieved March 28, 2005, from http://www.gmis.org/documents/GMIS_2002_Gartner_LullBeforeStormSantaFe.pdf

García-Arribas, G., & López-Crespo, F. (2003). Landscape of e-government at the dawn of the 21st century. *UPGRADE – The European Journal for the Informatics Professional, 4*(2), 2-6.

Gartner. (2000). Key issues in e-government strategy and management. *Gartner Group Research Notes, Key Issues*. Retrieved from http://www.gartner.com/id=306621

Gil-Garcia, R. (2012). *Electronic government success: Definition, measures, and factors*. New York: Springer. doi:10.1007/978-1-4614-2015-6.

Gonçalves, J. (2000). Para uma Administração Pública do Século XXI: O Caminho das Causas das Buropatologias. In Bilhim, J. (Ed.), *Reforma do Estado e Administração Pública Gestionária* (pp. 87–95). Lisboa: Instituto Superior de Ciências Sociais e Políticas.

Goodnow, F. (2003). *Politics and administration: A study in government*. New Brunswick: Transaction Publishers.

Grande, I., Araujo, C., & Serna, S. (2002). Research on e-government: A proposal of theoretical framework. *European Group of Public Administration Conference*.

Grant, G., & Chau, D. (2005). Developing a generic framework for e-government. *Journal of Global Information Management, 13*(1), 1–30. doi:10.4018/jgim.2005010101.

Grönlund, A. (2003). Framing e-gov: e=mc3. In Traunmüller, R. (Ed.), *Electronic Government* (*Vol. 2739*, pp. 191–198). Lecture Notes in Computer Science Berlin: Springer-Verlag. doi:10.1007/10929179_36.

Grönlund, A. (2004). State of the art in e-gov research: A survey. In Traunmüller, R. (Ed.), *Electronic Government* (*Vol. 3183*, pp. 178–185). Lecture Notes in Computer Science Berlin: Springer-Verlag. doi:10.1007/978-3-540-30078-6_30.

Grönlund, A. (2005). What's in a field – Exploring the egovernment domain. *The 38th Hawaii International Conference on System Sciences*. Retrieved March 16, 2006, from http://ieeexplore.ieee.org/iel5/9518/30166/01385489.pdf

Grönlund, A., & Horan, T. (2005). Introducing e-gov: History, definitions, and issues. *Communications of the Association for Information Systems, 15*, 39.

Heeks, R. (2001a). Reinventing government in the information age. In Heeks, R. (Ed.), *Reinventing government in the information age – International practice in IT-enabled public sector reform* (pp. 9–21). London: Routledge.

Heeks, R. (2001b). *Understanding e-governance for development*. Retrieved March 13, 2012, from http://unpan1.un.org/intradoc/groups/public/documents/NISPAcee/UNPAN015484.pdf

Heeks, R., & Bailur, S. (2007). Analyzing e-government research: Perspectives, philosophies, theories, methods, and practice. *Government Information Quarterly*, *24*(2), 243–265. doi:10.1016/j.giq.2006.06.005.

Heeks, R., & Davies, A. (2001). Different approaches to information age reform. In Heeks, R. (Ed.), *Reinventing Government in the Information Age — International practice in IT-enabled public sector reform* (pp. 22–48). London: Routledge.

Hiller, J., & Bélanger, F. (2001). Privacy stategies for electronic government. In Abramson, M., & Means, G. (Eds.), *E-Government 2001* (pp. 162–198). Lanham: Rowman and Littlefield Publishers.

Ho, A. (2002). Reinventing local government and the e-government initiative. *Public Administration Review*, *62*(4), 434–444. doi:10.1111/0033-3352.00197.

Holden, S., Norris, D., & Fletcher, P. (2003). Electronic government at the local level: Progress to date and future issues. *Public Performance & Management Review*, *6*(4), 325–344. doi:10.1177/1530957603026004002.

Hu, G., Pan, W., Lu, M., & Wang, J. (2009). The widely shared definition of e-Government: An exploratory study. *The Electronic Library*, *27*(6), 968–985. doi:10.1108/02640470911004066.

infoDev. (2009). E-government primer. A report by *infoDev – Innovate. Connect. Transform, The World Bank*. http://www.infodev.org/en/Publication.823.html

Islam, M. (2008). Towards a sustainable e-participation implementation model. *European Journal of ePractice, 5*, 26-37. Retrieved 12 May, 2012, from http://www.epractice.eu/files/ePractice-Journal-Volume-5.pdf

Jaeger, P., & Thompson, K. (2004). Social information behavior and the democratic process: Information poverty, normative behavior, and electronic government in the United States. *Library & Information Science Research*, *26*(1), 94–107. doi:10.1016/j.lisr.2003.11.006.

Jayashree, S., & Marthandan, G. (2010). Government to e-government to e-society. *Journal of Applied Sciences*, *10*, 2205–2210. doi:10.3923/jas.2010.2205.2210.

Kho, C., & Prybutok, V. (2003). The three ring model and development of an instrument for measuring dimensions of e-government functions. *Journal of Computer Information Systems*, *43*(3), 34–39.

Layne, K., & Lee, J. (2001). Developing fully functional e-government: A four stage model. *Government Information Quarterly*, *18*(2), 122–136. doi:10.1016/S0740-624X(01)00066-1.

Lenihan, D. (2002). *Realigning governance: From e-government to e-democracy*. Centre for Collaborative Government. Retrieved May 2, 2012, from http://www.kta.on.ca/KTA_site_RVSD/pdf/cg6.pdf

Lenk, K., & Traunmüller, R. (2002). Electronic government: Where are we heading? In Traunmüller, R., & Lenk, K. (Eds.), *Electronic Government* (*Vol. 2456*, pp. 1–9). Lecture Notes in Computer Science Berlin: Springer-Verlag. doi:10.1007/978-3-540-46138-8_1.

Löfstedt, U. (2005). E-government – Assessment of current research and some proposals for future directions. *International Journal of Public Information Systems, 1*(1), 39–52.

Millard, J. (2003). The (r)e-balancing of government. *UPGRADE — The European Journal for the Informatics Professional, 4*(2), 48-51.

Millard, J., Iversen, J., Kubicek, H., Westholm, H., & Cimander, R. (2004). *Reorganisation of government back-offices for better electronic public services – European good practices*. Final report to the European Commission. Danish Technological Institute, University of Bremen. Retrieved January 5, 2012, from http://www.oeaw.ac.at/ita/ebene5/back_office_reorganisation_volume3.pdf

Ndou, V. (2004). E-government for developing countries: Opportunities and challenges. *The Electronic Journal on Information Systems in Developing Countries, 18*(1), 1–24.

Norris, D., Fletcher, P., & Holden, S. (2001). *Is your local government plugged in? Highlights of the 2000 electronic government survey*. Washington, DC: International City/County Management Association.

Nunes, P. (2004). *Sebenta de Organização e Gestão Pública*. Barcelos: Instituto Politécnico do Cávado e do Ave.

OECD. (2001). Citizens as partners: OECD handbook on information, consultation and public participation in policy-making. Retrieved June 2, 2012, from http://www.ecnl.org/dindocuments/214_OECD_Engaging%20Citizens%20in%20Policy-Making.pdf

OECD. (2003). The e-government imperative: main findings. *Policy Brief – Observer OECD*. Retrieved April 24, 2012, from http://www.epractice.eu/en/library/281285

Okot-Uma, R. (2000). *Electronic governance: Re-inventing good governance*. Commonwealth Secretariat, London. Retrieved May 3, 2012, from http://webworld.unesco.org/publications/it/EGov/wordbank%20okot-uma.pdf

Osborne, D., & Gaebler, T. (1992). *Reinventing government: How the entrepreneurial spirit is transforming the public sector*. Reading: Addison-Wesley.

Pablo, Z., & Pan, S. (2003). A multi-disciplinary analysis of e-governance: Where do we start? *The Seventh Pacific Asia Conference on Information Systems* (pp. 288-302). Retrieved October 26, 2011, from www.pacis-net.org/file/2002/105.pdf

Palvia, S., & Sharma, S. (2007). E-government and e-governance: Definitions/domain framework and status around the world. In A. Agarwal & V. Ramana (Eds.), *Foundations of e-government - 5th International Conference on E-Governance*. Retrieved from http://www.iceg.net/2007/books/book1.html

Pérez-Villaplana, J. (2003). Technology for e-government: A study case. *UPGRADE — The European Journal for the Informatics Professional, 4*(2), 33-38.

Perri. (2001). E-governance: Do digital aids make a difference in policy making? In J. Prins (Ed.), *Designing e-government: On the crossroads of technological innovation and institutional change* (pp. 7-27). The Hague: Kluwer Law International.

Prasad, S. (2005). What is wrong with e-governance projects in India? How to build the foundation for successful e-governance. In G. Nayak, M. Mishra, & A. Das (Eds.), *Proceedings of the Eighth National Conference on e-Governance* (pp. 28-32). Bhubaneswar.

Rana, N., Williams, M., Dwivedi, Y., & Williams, J. (2011). Reflecting on e-government research: Toward a taxonomy of theories and theoretical constructs. *International Journal of Electronic Government Research*, *7*(4), 64–88. doi:10.4018/jegr.2011100105.

Realini, A. (2004). *G2G e-government: The big challenge to Europe*. (Master Thesis). University of Zürich, Zürich.

Relyea, H. (2002). E-gov: Introduction and overview. *Government Information Quarterly*, *19*(1), 9–35. doi:10.1016/S0740-624X(01)00096-X.

Reynolds, M., & Regio, M. (2001). E-Government as a catalyst in the information age. In *Briefing book outline: E-government*. Advisory Committee to the Congressional Internet Caucus. Retrieved December 5, 2011, from http://www.netcaucus.org/books/egov2001

Riley, T. (2003). *E-government vs. e-governance: Examining the differences in a changing public sector climate*. Retrieved May 20, 2009, from http://www.electronicgov.net/pubs/research_papers/tracking03/IntlTrackRptMay03no4.pdf

Saarenpää, A. (2003). A legal framework for e-government. In Traunmüller, R. (Ed.), *Electronic Government* (*Vol. 2739*, pp. 377–384). Lecture Notes in Computer Science Berlin: Springer-Verlag. doi:10.1007/10929179_69.

Sakowicz, M. (2003). *How to evaluate e-government? Different methodologies and methodes*. Retrieved November 19, 2011, from http://unpan1.un.org/intradoc/groups/public/documents/NISPAcee/UNPAN009486.pdf

Santos, L., & Amaral, L. (2003). O e-Government. *inter.face. Administração Pública*, *17*, 28–31.

Siau, K., & Long, Y. (2004). Factors impacting e-government development. *The Twenty-Fifth International Conference on Information Systems, ICIS 2004* (pp. 221-233).

Soares, D., & Amaral, L. (2011). Information systems interoperability in public administration: Identifying the major acting forces through a delphi study. *Journal of Theoretical and Applied Electronic Commerce Research*, *6*(1), 61–94. doi: doi:10.4067/S0718-18762011000100006.

Srivastava, S., & Teo, T. (2004). A framework for electronic government: Evolution, enablers and resource drainers. *The Eighth Pacific Asia Conference on Information Systems, PACIS'2004* (pp. 2079-2085). Retrieved February 12, 2012, from www.pacis-net.org/file/2004/P04-003.pdf

Stahl, B. (2005). The ethical problem of framing e-government in terms of e-commerce. *The Electronic Journal of e-Government, 3*(2), 77-86. doi: http://www.ejeg.com/volume-3/vol3-iss2/StahlBernd.pdf

Tambouris, E., & Tarabanis, K. (2005). E-government and interoperability. In D. Remenyi (Ed.), *Proceedings of the 5th European Conference on E-Government* (pp. 399-407). UK: Academic Conferences Limited.

Tapscott, D., & Agnew, D. (1999). Governance in the digital economy. *Finance & Development, 36*(4), 34-37. Retrieved May 12, 2012, from http://www.imf.org/external/pubs/ft/fandd/1999/12/pdf/tapscott.pdf

Toffler, A. (1980). *The third wave*. New York: Morrow.

UMIC. (2003). *Plano de Acção para o Governo Electrónico – Qualidade e Eficiência dos Serviços Públicos*. Retrieved February 16, 2012, from http://www.umic.pt/images/stories/publicacoes/II_Plano_Accao_eGov.pdf

UN. (2012). *E-government survey 2012: E-government for the people*. United Nations. Retrieved July 23, 2012, from http://www.unpan.org/e-government

USA. (2003). *The national information infrastructure: An agenda for action*. Department of Commerce – The President's Information Infrastructure Task Force. Retrieved April 5, 2003, from http://www.ibiblio.org/nii/NII-Agenda-for-Action.html

Valle, R. (2003). E-government: A future of inter-administrative cooperation. *UPGRADE – The European Journal for the Informatics Professional, 4*(2), 11-13.

Vidigal, L. (2003). *O futuro pulsar electrónico da Administração Pública e o papel do Instituto de Informática*. Retrieved April 22, 2012, from http://luisvidigal.no.sapo.pt/html/o_futuro_pulsar_electronico_da.html

Zweers, K., & Planqué, K. (2001). Electronic government: From an organizational based perspective towards a client oriented approach. In Prins, J. (Ed.), *Designing e-government: On the crossroads of technological innovation and institutional change* (pp. 91–120). The Hague: Kluwer Law International.

ADDITIONAL READING

Almarabeh, T., & AbuAli, A. (2010). A general framework for e-government: Definition, maturity challenges, opportunities, and success. *European Journal of Scientific Research, 39*(1), 29–42.

Bekkers, V., & Homburg, V. (2005). E-Government as an information ecology: Backgrounds and concepts. In Bekkers, V., & Homburg, V. (Eds.), *The information ecology of e-government: E-government as institutional and technological innovation in public administration* (pp. 1–20). Amsterdam: IOS Press.

Cordella, A., & Iannacci, F. (2010). Information systems in the public sector: The e-Government enactment framework. *The Journal of Strategic Information Systems, 19*(1), 52–66. doi:10.1016/j.jsis.2010.01.001.

Fang, Z. (2002). E-government in digital era: Concept, practice, and development. *International Journal of The Computer. The Internet and Management, 10*(2), 1–22.

Finger, M., & Pécoud, G. (2003). From e-Government to e-Governance? Towards a model of e-Governance. *Electronic. Journal of E-Government, 1*(1), 1–10.

Frissen, V. (2005). The e-mancipation of the citizen and the future of e-government: Reflections on ICT and citizens' partnership. In Khosrow-Pour, M. (Ed.), *Practicing e-government: A global perspective* (pp. 163–178). Hershey: IDEA Group Publishing. doi:10.4018/978-1-59140-637-2.ch008.

Garson, G. (2006). *Public information technology and e-governance: Managing the virtual state.* Sudbury: Jones & Bartlett Learning.

Mishra, A., & Mishra, D. (2011). E-government: Exploring the different dimensions of challenges, implementation, and success factors. *ACM SIGMIS Database, 42*(4), 23–37. doi:10.1145/2096140.2096143.

Reddick, C. (2012). *Public administration and information technology*. Burlington: Jones & Bartlett Learning.

Wong, K., Fearon, C., & Philip, G. (2007). Understanding egovernment and egovernance: Stakeholders, partnerships and CSR. *International Journal of Quality & Reliability Management, 24*(9), 927–943. doi:10.1108/02656710710826199.

KEY TERMS AND DEFINITIONS

E-Democracy: Refers to the use of IT to support, renew, transform and modernize the traditional notion of democratic involvement.

E-Government: Refers to the use of IT to support, renew, transform and modernize the multiple state government activities.

E-Participation: Refers to the use of IT to support, renew, and transform and modernize the engagement of citizens, civil society organizations and other democratically constituted groups in processes of public deliberation, consulting, debating, and decision-making.

E-Politics: Refers to the use of IT to support, renew, transform and modernize the way activities are conducted in the *Politics* sphere.

E-Public Administration: Refers to the use of IT to support, renew, transform and modernize the internal operations of public administration agencies and the way they can interoperate with each other in order to provide better and streamlined public services.

E-Services: Refers to the use of IT to support, renew, transform and modernize the way public administration agencies provide information and deliver services to society agents (citizens, businesses, voluntary, civil and social organizations and institutions).

E-Society: Refers to the use of IT to support, renew, transform and modernize the way the multiple societal actors act, interact and interrelate.

E-Voting: Refers to the use of an IT system to support a voting act, by allowing the secure and secret record of voters' ballots.

Chapter 6
Evolving Local E-Government: A Cohesive Policy Approach

Julie Freeman
University of Canberra, Australia

ABSTRACT

Effective policy frameworks are essential when developing e-government projects. Participatory e-government practices that facilitate civic engagement depend upon a combination of direct and indirect information and communication technology (ICT) policies. Direct policies focus on infrastructure development and enhancing citizens' ICT adoption and use. Indirectly, ICTs can be used to support policy processes through, for example, information dissemination and the provision of spaces for deliberation. This chapter examines Australian e-government initiatives, suggesting that local governments provide a useful context for online civic participation and engagement. However, local initiatives are often developed on an ad hoc basis and are largely limited to the provision of one-way information and service delivery features. Conversely, federal documentation addresses both direct and indirect ICT policy areas and stresses the value of online civic participation. Yet, there is a significant disconnection between federal ideals of engagement and the actual implementation of two-way participatory practices, with service delivery mechanisms again prioritised. This chapter suggests that greater online civic engagement may be achieved through a policy approach that combines national guidance and resources with local knowledge, while using policies to support ICTs and ICTs to support policy processes.

DOI: 10.4018/978-1-4666-4245-4.ch006

INTRODUCTION

Information and communication technologies (ICTs) offer authorities the chance to develop the democratic quality of representative government through the provision of new avenues for civic participation in decision-making. Large-scale infrastructure improvements such as the Australian Federal Government's *National Broadband Network* (*NBN*) provide the frameworks for increased online interaction and are promoted as enhancing electronic government. It is intended that this Australian development will enable online engagement through opportunities for greater public involvement in policy and service delivery (Department of Broadband, Communications and the Digital Economy (DBCDE), 2011). A key aim of the Australian Federal Government's *National Digital Economy Strategy* is to have four out of five Australians engaging with governments online by the year 2020, with digitally aware state and local authorities driving this engagement (DBCDE, 2011). The Federal Government also recognises that advancing online participation requires action by and coordination through all levels of government (DBCDE, 2011). In addition to the provision of improved infrastructure, such a goal will require broad guidance and support for authorities implementing online practices. While the networked technology of the Internet allows for open-ended communication, the democratic quality of online mechanisms depends upon government application of the technology (see Catinat & Vedel, 2000), and the policies used to guide efforts undertaken.

The implementation of online spaces for citizen engagement by local, state and federal authorities calls for strong policy guidance, particularly to ensure equity of technology application throughout the country. A combination of direct and indirect policies facilitates civic access to ICTs, the development of appropriate digital skills, the provision of relevant content to which citizens can contribute, and helps to ensure that citizens' online political participation impacts decision-making processes (see Cohen, van Geenhuizen, & Nijkamp, 2005). Such considerable goals require resource and knowledge coordination between the different levels of government to optimise the development and use of the policies and practices employed. National-level governments can provide appropriate guidelines to create and implement e-government practices and fund infrastructure improvements. In contrast, local knowledge about an area's requirements and citizens' needs can be utilised by national governments to offer effective, appropriate and integrated policy approaches to ICT infrastructure development. Local governments also provide a useful context for digital skill development programs and targeted participatory e-government, particularly as municipalities occupy the spaces where the effects of state and national initiatives materialise and as increased civic interest in everyday local issues encourages active involvement (Margolis & Moreno-Riaño, 2009; Bradford, 2008). This chapter suggests that a cohesive policy approach is needed to offer long-term, sustainable frameworks for participatory e-government development.

This chapter focuses on e-government in Australia, highlighting the impact of national policies and initiatives on the development of local online participation methods. Australia has a three-tiered level of representative government that works within a parliamentary system of democracy. There are 562 local governments, with broad diversity in population and geographic sizes. Australian local governments have limited authority, with their responsibilities largely restricted to day-to-day services including: household waste collection; the provision and maintenance of parkland, play equipment, local libraries and community centres; local road developments; and town planning. State governments are responsible for education and policing, which often fall under the responsibility of local governments in other countries. Local e-government in Australia is currently advancing autonomously from federal guidance, with ad hoc

ICT applications frequently implemented without guiding policy documentation. The result has been a broad focus on one-way information dissemination and service delivery online, with many local authorities overlooking the potential use of ICTs as platforms for two-way civic involvement in policy processes and to aid civic connection with representatives. This chapter suggests that a cohesive policy approach with greater coordination between federal and local governments would facilitate the steady evolution of local participatory e-government practices, which offer contexts for civic discussions and engagement with government. First, however, this chapter outlines the importance of local e-government, and suggests how policies can be framed to facilitate participatory online practices.

BACKGROUND

ICTs and Australian Local Government

While local government structures and processes are frequently reformed and vary between countries, local governments traditionally have been responsible for a range of tasks. These tasks can be categorised within three broad, complementary roles: local democracy, public policy-making, and direct service delivery (Pratchett, 1999; O'Toole, 2009). In terms of local democracy, Pratchett (1999) recognises that, as the closest democratic institution to citizens, it is the responsibility of local governments to engender and enhance democratic practices and consciousness. As the majority of citizen transactions with government take place at the local level (Shackleton, 2010; Shackleton, Fisher, & Dawson, 2005), strengthening local democratic structures and providing new methods for participation may improve civic satisfaction with the political system. In terms of public policy-making, local governments are required to provide forums for resolution of territorial, economic and social conflicts, offer community leadership, pursue community wide goals, and develop (and ensure achievement of) strategic visions for their locality, such as sustainable development programs (Pratchett, 1999). Service delivery, such as public transport, aged care, and household waste collection, has traditionally been seen as the primary role of authorities and remains important in the organisational structure of local governments (Pratchett, 1999). If employed successfully, ICTs can be used to address and advance all three roles to help local authorities govern more effectively.

Traditional service tasks often provide the basis for local e-government development as offering electronic services brings several advantages for local authorities (O'Toole, 2009). A large proportion of local government operations depend upon the collection, processing and use of information. Digital networked technologies provide avenues for more efficient and effective data handling and improved organisational performance, generating financial savings for the government in the long-term by, for example, minimising the number of staff hours necessary for customer services practices (see Beynon-Davies & Martin, 2004; Silcock, 2001). With growing population levels, ICT-enabled service delivery methods help government bodies cope with increasing demand. This is an important development for several Australian local governments with populations larger than a small state or territory of Australia. For example, in the State of Queensland, Brisbane and Gold Coast City Councils both have greater populations than the State of Tasmania, the Northern Territory, or the Australian Capital Territory (ACT). With over one million residents (and only 27 local government councillors), Brisbane City Council's population is closer to the combined populations of Tasmania, the Northern Territory and the ACT (Australian Bureau of Statistics (ABS), 2010a; 2010b). Electronic service delivery methods help local governments like Brisbane manage high demand, and the time saved through electronic service delivery can theoretically be re-focused towards the government's other roles of fostering local democracy and public policy-making.

Services *alone* is no longer an adequate role for local governments (Pratchett, 1999; Kolsaker, 2005) as councils are increasingly under pressure to modernise their structures through ICTs (O'Toole, 2009). If ICTs are to be used to strengthen local government operations by addressing public policy-making and local democracy, opportunities for two-way online civic consultation through, for example, discussion boards, chat facilities, or wikis should be offered in addition to online services. This point has been recognised by select Australian local governments including the Brisbane City Council, which provides online discussion forums to encourage civic contributions to current consultations and utilises social media including *Twitter*, *Facebook*, and *YouTube* to further engage with citizens (see www.brisbane.qld.gov.au). Darebin City Council in the State of Victoria trialled an e-forum to facilitate greater civic involvement in decision-making and increased government transparency and accountability (see Walsh, 2009). Such forms of direct civic participation in policy processes utilise networked digital communications to reinforce the connection between citizens and their government, thereby strengthening local democracy through more open public policy-making.

Examples like Brisbane and Darebin, where the local governments are undertaking online efforts to develop public policy-making and local democracy, are scarce. Instead, information dissemination and service delivery remain the primary focus of local government ICT use (see O'Toole, 2009; Shackleton, 2010). This is a common situation for local governments, with online service delivery often prioritised over civic participation and engagement in other countries (see, for example, Jimenez, Mossberger, & Wu, 2012). There are currently no binding obligations for Australian local governments to develop their online practices to facilitate citizen participation and engagement, but councils are increasingly under internal and external pressures to do so (Shackleton, 2010). Compounded with these pressures, variations between councils in resources, knowledge and community demands have led to ad hoc e-government developments with diverse practices. This situation has created an often 'confused' approach to e-government development amongst Australian local governments (Shackleton, 2010).

The large geographic, demographic, and population diversity of Australian local governments make it difficult for many authorities to implement online participatory practices, and for citizens to use e-government mechanisms. Many local authorities struggle to develop and implement e-government practices due to, for example, insufficiently skilled staff or lack of funding (see Cohen et al., 2005; King, 2007; Norris, 2007). In stark contrast to Brisbane City Council, the 50,000 square kilometre Shire of Murchison to the north-east of Geraldton in Western Australia has six councillors representing a population of 112 (ABS, 2010b), equating to one representative for approximately every nineteen citizens. This small population suggests that the council would have limited financial resources available for e-government development. Conversely, residents of some local governments, particularly in rural and remote areas, do not have the Internet infrastructure necessary to access online government information and services (Eardley, Bruce, & Goggin, 2009). Australia has the largest local government area in the world, the Shire of East Pilbara (also in Western Australia), which spans more than 370,000 square kilometres and is home to just over 8,000 people. In this instance, citizens sparsely populating the remote desert regions of the municipality have limited Internet service availability and a lack of affordable access (see Eardley et al., 2009). In cases like these, local governments are unlikely to possess sufficient resources to ensure civic access to the Internet and to develop participatory e-government practices. Improvements to infrastructure availability often depend on national coordination in order to ensure equity of access for citizens. Planned developments under the Federal Government's *NBN* (scheduled for completion in 2020) should eventually aid civic access to ICTs in rural and remote regions. Here, additional guidance and support from the Federal Government would be useful to facilitate civic adoption of ICTs, and to aid local authorities in the development of online content and applications.

An integrated relationship between national governments and local authorities in the development and use of ICTs for participatory e-government necessitates strong policy frameworks (see Goggin, 2003; Jaeger & Thompson, 2003). Place-based policies enable local priorities to fall within national objectives (Bradford, 2008), and local knowledge can be used to effectively shape the outcomes of national policies (Wilson, Cornford, Baines, & Mawson, 2011). The importance of local governments in such a policy relationship should not be overlooked. Localities act as the primary setting for policy implementation (Chanan, 1997), with the manifestation of policies varying from place to place. Local governments possess the knowledge necessary to ensure national developments are the most appropriate for particular areas and citizens' needs, and are well positioned to administer programs addressing citizens' digital skill limitations. For example, local governments are able to take into consideration socio-economic divisions or infrastructure requirements that affect their locality, more effectively developing policies and practices to suit *their* citizens than larger scale government bodies (see Bradford, 2008). A local lens is therefore necessary for national policies to adequately consider spatial impacts and to maximise the benefits of policy outcomes for specific groups of citizens by, for example, ensuring social inclusion (Bradford, 2008; see also Goggin, 2003).

Additionally, online discourse and deliberation is more manageable on a smaller scale than that which takes place at state or national levels (see Jimenez et al., 2012). Using a municipality as a focus and foundation for online deliberation may encourage more participants in discussions through an increased interest in local issues, such as development proposals, rates, and council elections (Margolis & Moreno-Riaño, 2009). In this regard, utilising globally networked communication technologies is a way to help reassert the importance of specific locales, reinforcing the position of local governments as key providers of information and areas for discussion and decision-making (Tambini, 1999). In other words, policies that focus on local online participation improve the likelihood of citizen involvement in the issues and decision-making processes of direct relevance to citizens and their communities, which helps to provide a connection to government and enhance local democracy. These observations highlight the important place occupied by local governments in the facilitation of opportunities for digital engagement. The following section suggests how ICT policies can be framed to facilitate greater online civic participation in public policy-making.

ICT Policies to Facilitate Participatory E-Government

Government policies shape civic capacity to participate in politics and the subsequent influence of civic participation on policy decisions (Coleman & Blumler, 2009). Horrocks (2009) highlights the significance of the relationship between e-government and policy. He suggests that e-government underpins a broad range of policy domains as it offers "both the technical platform and conceptual rationale for ongoing and widespread institutional and cultural change in government and public services" (Horrocks, 2009, p. 123). Government ICT use requires policy frameworks that ensure democratic application of technology (see Catinat & Vedel, 2000). E-government policies help to provide contexts for civic participation, facilitate equity of civic capacity to access and contribute to these contexts, and ensure that civic contributions are considered in decision-making processes. Such broad goals are achieved through a combination of direct and indirect ICT policies (Cohen et al., 2005). Direct policies support ICT access and adoption, while indirect policies are concerned with the broader use of ICTs in government operations.

Cohen, van Geenhuizen, and Nijkamp (2005) analyse the experience of Dutch cities and suggest that local areas provide a key context for both direct and indirect ICT-related policies. Direct policies, in which the final goal relates specifically to ICTs, fall within two categories: policies that focus on infrastructure development, and policies that are intended to help enhance adoption and use of new technologies. Local governments are aware of the available infrastructure in their region and are in the best position to identify areas for development, particularly to cater for growing populations. Additionally, local governments have greater familiarity with the traditional participation methods used by their citizens and understand key issues pertaining to their locality that may limit ICT use, such as age, education levels, linguistic background and socio-economic status. This knowledge can be considered when developing policies to enhance ICT infrastructure and implementing adoption programs. Examples of direct, local ICT policies include requiring housing estate developers to install the appropriate infrastructure to support broadband Internet during construction, and the provision of free access terminals and educational programs in local libraries.

Governments also have indirect ICT policies that do not specifically have ICT-related goals, but instead use ICTs to achieve other defined goals (Cohen et al., 2005). For example, ICTs are used to collect and organise data relating to child care and voting registries. At the local level, indirect ICT policies often contribute to the one-way information dissemination and service delivery focus of e-government initiatives, as these types of functions offer councils the greatest chance of economic gains. Local applications may include using a website to provide information on services and upcoming events, offering online mechanisms to lodge planning permits, and enabling e-commerce transactions to pay rates and registrations. But indirect ICT policies also enable local governments to develop their public policy-making and local democracy roles. Using the Internet to provide, for example, discussion forums on key issues, guidance for community groups and projects, and increased information and feedback surrounding local developments are all ways that local governments can facilitate greater participation in public policy-making to enhance local democracy.

Figure 1 illustrates that effective e-government engagement mechanisms necessitate both direct and indirect ICT policies. On the one hand, government policies should support ICT development to enhance infrastructure and address problems related to civic adoption and use of new technologies. On the other hand, governments need to use ICTs to develop their policy processes. In this regard, ICTs increase information dissemination and provide new citizenship practices that create a sense of connection between representatives and citizens. In other words, participatory e-government requires the provision of ICT infrastructure, ensuring citizens can access and use ICTs, and providing opportunities for citizens to participate in policy discourse through ICTs. Taking such a dual focused approach to ICT policy-making – using policies to support ICTs and using ICTs to support policies – offers governments the best chance for successful e-government engagement mechanisms.

While localities provide a strong basis for e-government policy development, there are many factors that inhibit local government ICT-related policy-making. Constraints include a lack of recognition of the relevance of ICTs for governmental processes, uncoordinated initiatives, failure to recognise strategic goals, an inability to

Figure 1. Linking ICT policies and e-government (Adapted from Freeman, 2012)

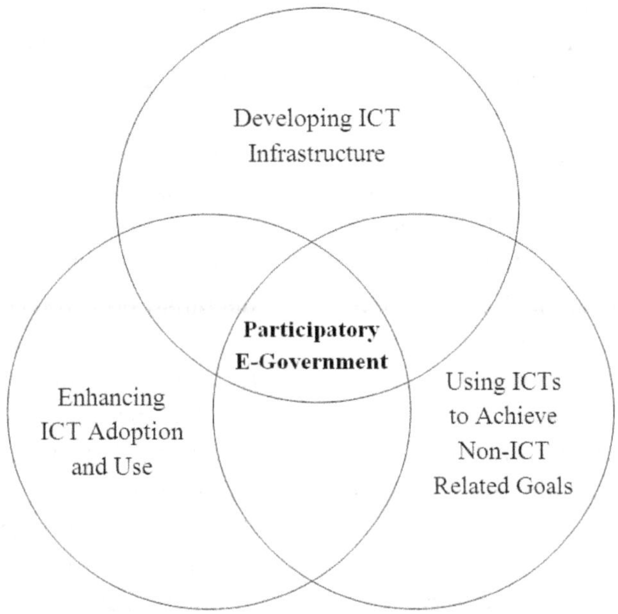

transfer visions into plans of action, a lack of proactive behaviour by local governments, and insufficient ICT education amongst policy-makers (Cohen et al., 2005; see also Chen, Gibson, Lusoli, & Ward, 2007). Additionally, e-government principles are often not embedded in local government processes, which may result in little emphasis on online participation (Damodaran, Nicholls, Henny, Land, & Farbey, 2005). These issues can lead to ad hoc ICT policy-making at the local level (Cohen et al., 2005).

ICTs hold promise for new methods of civic engagement, but the issues outlined above must be addressed if local governments intend to adapt existing online service delivery practices to successfully include civic participation in policy-making. Here, national policies could offer local governments assistance with the development of participatory online practices. The following section outlines e-government policies and initiatives at the federal level in Australia and highlights their impact on the participatory nature of local e-government.

E-GOVERNMENT IN THE AUSTRALIAN FEDERAL CONTEXT

Australian federal e-government policy initiatives illustrate that the government has long recognised the need to incorporate participatory online practices into its operations. However, there is currently a disconnection between the engagement ideals, strategies and goals set by the Federal Government and the actual implementation of two-way participatory e-government features. Federal initiatives instead reinforce a wide-spread governmental approach towards ICT use in Australian public sector operations, which privileges one-way information dissemination and simple service delivery functions over spaces for online discourse and deliberation.

Policy developments in communications infrastructure, online service delivery, and civic engagement demonstrate a commitment to e-government. Examples of past strategies include *Australia's Strategic Framework for the Information Economy 2004–2006: Opportunities and Challenges for the Information Age* (Department of Communications, Information Technology and the Arts (DCITA), 2004), which identified four broad objectives, four strategic priorities and sixteen associated strategies designed to provide "the policy platform needed to address new challenges to Australia's position as a leading information economy" (DCITA, 2004, p. 5). *Better Services, Better Government: The Federal Government's E-Government Strategy* (National Office for the Information Economy (NOIE), 2002) focused on citizens and proposed strategies to achieve greater efficiency, ensure convenient access, build user trust, and enhance citizen engagement. *Australia's National Broadband Strategy* (NOIE, 2004) concerned the coordination of broadband infrastructure availability across different levels of government.

Similarly, current infrastructure developments under the *National Broadband Network* are intended to provide ubiquitous, high speed broadband to all Australian premises. Connections of at least 12 megabits (and up to 100 megabits) per second will be offered to 93 percent of households through fibre optic infrastructure, with the remaining areas covered by fixed wireless and satellite technologies (see Corner, 2010; DBCDE, 2011; Given & Watkins, 2010; Tucker, 2010). However, the cost of accessing *NBN* infrastructure will be determined by retail providers, which may inhibit civic adoption and use. National coordination helps to ensure broad application of initiatives throughout the country, but the implementation and effects of such developments are distinctively local. This observation reinforces the suggestion that policies need to be explicit in recognising localities as the primary setting for implementation (Bradford, 2008; Chanan, 1997).

While the Australian Federal Government has introduced several e-government related policies and strategies over the past decade, these have had negligible impact on online operations in the different tiers of Australian government: "there remains a vast mismatch between electronic government as it actually is and as it is vividly imagined" (Thomas, 2004, p. 270). This mismatch raises the question of why the Federal Government's e-government policies and strategies are not leading to effective action. To assess this question, initiatives under the Federal Government's e-government strategy, *Responsive Government: A New Service Agenda* (Department of Finance and Administration, 2006), will be examined. This document was selected because it is the most recent Australian policy specifically for e-government and, unlike the documents mentioned above, it addresses both direct and indirect approaches including the need to improve existing infrastructure, service delivery and online civic engagement. It outlines issues, such as security and privacy, which hinder e-government advancement, and provides key priority areas for development with subsidiary strategies within each area. Overall, while the document's title appears to assume that responsiveness is related to service provision, the e-government strategy offers a basic framework for e-government implementation and encourages online engagement with government. To achieve this engagement, the Federal Government created principles to support a consistent experience for citizens communicating with governments online.

Principles for ICT-Enabled Citizen Engagement

The Federal Government's *Principles for ICT-Enabled Citizen Engagement* identifies "the potential to further promote a culture of democratic decision-making in Australia" (Department of Finance and Administration, 2007, p. 2). Eight online engagement principles were established from research on existing national and international principles and with input from representatives from all levels of Australian government. No indication is, however, provided by the government as to the form of representative input, how it was taken into account, and which other countries' principles were considered. The Federal Government recognises in the document that some government bodies have limited financial resources to engage citizens online. Subsequently, the principles are meant to act only as a "best practice guide for agencies wishing to engage with citizens using Information Communication Technology (ICT) as part of their policy making processes" (Department of Finance and Administration, 2007, p. 1).

The principles are (Department of Finance and Administration, 2007):

1. Commitment;
2. Community Focus;
3. Community Capability and Inclusiveness;
4. Mutual Respect, Confidence and Trust;
5. Interactivity and Flexibility;
6. Responsibility and Accountability;
7. Security and Privacy; and
8. Evaluation and Efficiency.

In general, these principles seek to enable two-way, responsive partnerships between governments and citizens through information access, knowledge sharing, and discussion. They recognise the need to facilitate broad involvement that reflects the diversity in citizen capabilities, locations, and socio-economic circumstances. It is furthermore suggested that community consultation is strengthened by informing citizens how their input is used in government policy-making. These processes require corresponding privacy protection, information security and identity authentication measures that comply with relevant legislation (Department of Finance and Administration, 2007).

These principles were designed as a guide for all levels of government to use when developing participatory e-government practices intended to strengthen community consultation and input into policy-making. However, as a best practice guide only, there are no explicit policies in place that require government agencies using ICTs to adhere to the principles. Without any binding obligations towards e-engagement, there is also no assurance that government ICT use will promote Australia's democratic decision-making culture, as the preamble to the principles suggests. As highlighted earlier, many Australian local governments prioritise service delivery in their e-government practices, which suggests that the federal documents are having little effect on locales. Moreover, while these principles were developed under the Federal Government's "online engagement with government" objective of its e-government strategy, many of the online initiatives implemented at the federal level do not actively engage citizens in two-way communications practices that promote ongoing dialogue. Instead, federal initiatives predominantly focus on further development of online service delivery mechanisms.

The Australian Government Entry Point

Under the e-government strategy, the Federal Government developed an online service point (australia.gov.au). This website provides the context through which the government addresses many of the priority areas set out in its e-government strategy, and offers a space for civic connection with government. The purpose of the entry point is to consolidate departmental websites to offer a streamlined online presence that simplifies access and use for citizens (Department of Finance and Administration, 2006). The website was to be designed to enable citizens to conduct transactions with various government departments without needing to reconfirm identity, simultaneously update citizen details across agencies, and provide pre-filled forms for improved service delivery. In May 2007, over AU$42 million was allocated to develop the online entry point (Turner, 2007).

The website currently allows citizens who register to log on to utilise customised settings, such as search topics and locations. It contains links to numerous government department websites, blogs, and publications, and is undergoing continual development. It has a 'Have Your Say' page on public consultations administered by different departments. However, the majority of these links to public consultations possess only limited two-way communication facilities, such as requests that individual submissions be posted or e-mailed to the government department. Moreover, it is government departments that retain control over the issues raised in these public consultations, meaning citizens are unable to create and participate in their own discussion topics.

While it is commendable that the Federal Government's online entry point makes citizen access to government information easier, the website does not currently enable advanced civic engagement processes or new forms of participation in policy discourse. Instead, the entry point provides an alternative means for citizens to carry out transactions with government departments. The website therefore reflects the service delivery focus of most e-government initiatives and understandings (Freeman & Hutchins, 2009), and partly contradicts the government's own principles for online engagement. If the Federal Government is unable to articulate the differences between service delivery and civic engagement clearly in its e-government practices, then it should come as little surprise that other tiers of Australian government appear to neglect online civic engagement mechanisms.

Government 2.0 Taskforce

The Australian Federal Government recognised the importance of advancing online practices to facilitate more active citizen involvement when it launched the *Government 2.0 Taskforce* (gov2.net.au) in June 2009. The taskforce was assigned the duty of investigating how the government could facilitate better services and greater engagement through the Internet's Web 2.0 capabilities. After six months of research, including the use of online public sphere forums and road shows, the taskforce released a report to the government entitled, *Engage: Getting on with Government 2.0*. The report provides thirteen recommendations for the Federal Government to adopt when developing its online practices. The central recommendation was the need for: "A declaration of open government by the Australian Government" (Government 2.0 Taskforce Report, 2009, p. xvii). In an increasingly common refrain, this recommendation emphasised the value of government transparency and citizen involvement in policy-making to facilitate a healthy democracy. It was also recognised that such reform must take place at all levels of government (Government 2.0 Taskforce Report, 2009).

In May 2010, the Federal Government produced a report in response to the taskforce's suggestions. The government agreed with the taskforce's central recommendation that it was desirable to change the culture of government to promote greater participation in Australia's democracy (Government Response to the Report of the Government 2.0 Taskforce, 2010). A *Declaration of Open Government* was subsequently issued on 16 July 2010 to demonstrate the government's commitment to an open government, based on a culture of engagement that enables better access to and use of government information, sustained through innovative technology use (Department of Finance and Deregulation, 2010). The declaration offered three key principles to support an open government: informing, engaging, and participating. This citizen-centric approach is a promising development for the future of e-government in Australia.

Since the release of the government's report, there has been little emphasis placed on developments to actively engage citizens online. In part, this is likely due to the media silence following the report's release, as the *Declaration of Open Government* was announced the day before the 2010 Australian Federal Election was called. While the election provided an opportune occasion to capitalise on open government to connect with citizens, the major political parties employed only limited use of online participatory tools in their election campaigns. While they offered the veneer of Web 2.0, there was little actually occurring behind it (Stilgherrian in Funnell, 2010). Even the two-way features that were utilised by candidates were often restricted and failed to facilitate any form of ongoing dialogue. Macnamara (2010) highlights that between the 2007 and 2010 Australian Federal Elections, use of online activities by federal politicians more than doubled. However, this use was heavily restricted to the broadcasting of messages, with negligible opportunities for two-way consultation and a lack of responsiveness by politicians (Macnamara, 2010). This type of Internet use has not advanced from the 2007 election, in which politicians frequently failed to use the interactivity features of Web 2.0 tools. Instead, political parties and their politicians chose to restrict dialogue by, for example, turning off options for comments or limiting public access on sites to supporters only (Macnamara, 2008). It was predominantly citizen-run websites that facilitated increased interaction and political participation (Macnamara, 2008). Changing the culture of government to be more receptive and responsive to online citizen participation is therefore unlikely to occur in the short-term.

The taskforce and declaration are important steps forward for e-government in Australia. Commitment to action is, however, dependent upon the willingness and ability of political representatives to support new forms of engagement. Collins (2010) notes that the will and capacity for governmental change will require broader reform of government operations, such as discontinuing the practice of blocking access to many Web 2.0 tools like *Twitter*. Moreover, effective e-government requires ongoing research and development, with online initiatives continually updated to suit changes in the communicative environment; a point overlooked by the six-month operation of the *Government 2.0 Taskforce*. Also noteworthy is that the government's declaration responds to *recommendations*, meaning essentially there is no new policy here that ensures commitment to action across the different tiers of Australian government. In essence, the Federal Government has done little to guarantee the actual development and implementation of mechanisms that facilitate new forms of two-way civic participation. The provision of effective policy frameworks requiring action and implementation is therefore a fundamental problem inhibiting Australian e-government development.

A COHESIVE E-GOVERNMENT POLICY APPROACH

The above observations highlight that, while federal documents stress the concept of online civic engagement, current e-government practices are predominantly limited to one-way information dissemination and service delivery applications. There are, however, many factors that inhibit the development of participatory e-government at the federal level including, for example, issues of scale and manageability (Jimenez et al., 2012). As previously highlighted and as recognised by the Australian Federal Government (DBCDE, 2011), local governments offer a key space for the development of online engagement opportunities. Despite this, there are no explicit federal requirements for local e-government development and, similarly to federal initiatives, Australian local governments are prioritising online information dissemination and service delivery practices. This suggests that the current policy framework is having little effect on the development and implementation of participatory e-government at the local level.

There are, however, some joint direct ICT policy initiatives that are likely to produce positive outcomes in the long-term. For example, the company (NBN Co.) responsible for coordinating broadband infrastructure development under the Australian Federal Government's *NBN* has recognised the importance of utilising local knowledge. To achieve optimal rollout results, NBN Co. is collaborating with local governments regarding site selection and deployment (see NBN

Co., 2012). This approach enables NBN Co. to take into consideration factors such as existing infrastructure, proposed developments and growth corridors, and the connection speed already available in particular areas.

The Federal Government is attempting to address ICT skill inequalities through its *Digital Communities* program. The government will invest AU$23.8 million over three years to establish digital hubs in the 40 communities that received *NBN* infrastructure in the initial rollout stage. In these hubs, citizens will be able to receive training to develop digital literacy skills (DBCDE, 2011). Additionally, under the Federal Government's *Digital Local Government* program, the local governments representing these 40 communities can also apply for competitive funding to develop online services. Eligible councils will receive a maximum of AU$375,000 for proposals and must contribute at least a quarter of the total project cost to gain funding (cash or in-kind) (DBCDE, 2012). This federal program emphasises the importance of these local governments developing replicable and scalable online services that other local governments can adapt (DBCDE, 2012). Here, it may be useful if the Federal Government facilitated coordination between local governments to maximise knowledge and resource use. Moreover, greater federal guidance in terms of the types of practices that should be developed will reduce the risk of local governments with limited knowledge and skills paying for ineffective or inappropriate initiatives (see Bertot & Jaeger, 2006; Horrocks, 2009). It should not be assumed that the issues faced by local governments as outlined earlier, such as failure to recognise strategic goals and insufficient ICT education amongst policy-makers (Cohen et al., 2005), have been overcome by access to improved infrastructure alone. Additional federal assistance may aid in reducing the impact of these types of issues.

These examples highlight various degrees of federal and local coordination surrounding infrastructure development, enhancing ICT adoption and use, and advancing local online services, which are important steps forward for local e-government. There is no doubt that these types of initiatives are needed in order to advance online engagement, but the current focus of these projects again appears to be on creating more efficient services rather than facilitating explicit opportunities for two-way digital participation. It will be difficult to increase online civic engagement throughout the country, as desired by the Federal Government (DBCDE, 2011), without more detailed indirect ICT policy guidance and support to shape the provision of such opportunities.

In their evaluation of e-government policy approaches in the United Kingdom (UK) and the Netherlands, Flowers, Tang, Molas-Gallart, and Davies (2006) found that the UK's top-down model offers a framework for development, with "general points of reference to frame and support specific initiatives developed closer to the context of application. In the absence of such generic guidelines, local initiatives may lack the necessary political and financial support to achieve their objectives" (Flowers et al., 2006, p. 78). This chapter suggests that to meet the Federal Government's goal of having four out of five Australians choosing to engage online by 2020, with local governments as key contexts in which to drive digital engagement (DBCDE, 2011), greater guidance is needed than what is provided by the current policy framework. In addition to general strategy documentation, specific recommendations would assist local governments in developing online practices that facilitate citizen participation in policy-making. This does not necessarily mean that all Australian local governments would comply with additional recommendations in federal policy, but it would offer starting points and support, or the building blocks for development.

A governmental strategy that combines federal and local knowledge, while using policies to support ICTs and using ICTs to support policies, would be beneficial in the advancement of e-government engagement. This coordinated approach offers guidance and support to local governments to increase the likely success of new participatory opportunities, and draws from local knowledge to develop the most appropriate opportunities for citizens and locales. Proximity matters in the development and implementation of policies and practices aimed to enhance participation and ensure democratic legitimisation (Borja & Castells, 1997). Local governments are well positioned to develop targeted initiatives as they are able to identify and address obstacles likely to hinder e-government progress in particular areas, which will vary depending on the type of online initiative, specific locales, government bodies, and citizens' needs. Local knowledge about citizens and infrastructure requirements can be utilised by national bodies to optimise policies and implement more effective, appropriate, and integrated developments aimed at enhancing ICT infrastructure and use (see Goggin, 2003; Wilson et al., 2011). As communication infrastructure developments lie beyond the control of local governments in Australia, conveying local knowledge is vital to ensure effective use of federal resources. In other systems of government, however, many local authorities take a more active role in initiatives that aim to improve ICT infrastructure and eliminate access and skill inequalities (see, for example, Wiklund (2005); Mossberger, Tolbert, & McNeal (2008); Aurigi (2005)). In Australia, integrated policy frameworks would be useful when developing e-government engagement projects in order to promote long-term sustainability of citizen-centric practices.

FUTURE DIRECTIONS

ICT policies are necessary to guide e-government and ensure effective use of resources when implementing citizen-centric practices. This chapter suggests that, within Australia, there is a need for greater coordination of e-government policy between federal and local governments to facilitate the development of online practices that enable civic participation and engagement. Such an approach has been undertaken elsewhere, which offers Australia and other countries seeking to advance e-government policy and practice an opportunity to draw from existing experiences. The UK, while a different system of government to Australia, offers one such example of a coordinated approach to e-government.

Under the UK's two-tiered, unitary system of government, central government documentation such as the *National Strategy for Local E-Government* offers a common framework with broad contexts and requirements for development. This approach privileges local authorities creating their own online initiatives to suit local priorities and the specific needs of their citizens, while backed by national resources (Morphet, 2009). Central government provides support to local authorities through, for example, supplying technical and legal standards, coordinating work between central and local governments, identifying and addressing barriers to development (such as skills gaps and training programs), and developing products to reduce costs for local governments (Office of the Deputy Prime Minister, 2002). 83 percent of UK local authorities indicated that the national strategy directly impacted on improvements to service delivery, and 64 percent highlighted that the policy influenced public engagement in local decisions (Downe & Martin, 2006).

The UK approach faced many challenges and received criticism (see, for example, Laffin, 2008; Birch, 2003; King, 2007; Beynon-Davies & Williams, 2003; Martin, 2008). Nevertheless, a comparison of differing policy contexts would enable identification of further recommendations and suggestions for improvement, and help to ensure effective use of resources in the development and implementation of new participatory practices. Both positive and negative experiences provide useful considerations when designing a policy approach intended to facilitate the steady evolution of local e-government contexts for civic engagement.

CONCLUSION

Methods for online engagement are fundamentally shaped by the e-government policy approach undertaken by authorities. While there are many short-term struggles associated with e-government development, particularly at the local level, online governmental transformations are gradual, ongoing processes (Senyucel & Stubbs, 2006). This should be recognised in both e-government policy and practice, and highlights why the facilitation of online participatory practices necessitates considerable, ongoing guidance. Both direct and indirect ICT policies are important to enhance civic participation in decision-making through e-government. Combining these types of policies facilitates access to ICTs, helps citizens develop appropriate digital skills, and assists governments to provide relevant content and spaces for civic participation and engagement. It is, however, worth noting that problems of civic engagement cannot be solved through policy alone (see Simone, 2010). Rather, strong policies facilitate and support more effective implementation of infrastructure and services, and shape how civic involvement influences policy-making.

At present, limited policy guidance for Australian local e-government is resulting in the autonomous development of ad hoc initiatives that predominantly reiterate the service delivery role of local governments. While several authorities have implemented or are experimenting with participatory e-government practices, these often lack policies guiding online content and applications. Improved opportunities for local online engagement require more effective policy frameworks. National guidance is useful in the provision of resources for improved infrastructure, and to educate and assist local bodies when developing online spaces for civic participation in decision-making to bolster local democracy. Initiatives like the *NBN*, *Digital Local Government* program, and *Digital Communities* bring promise of greater e-government engagement. But, like previous schemes that have stressed engagement, these federal-local government developments follow a predominantly service delivery trajectory. The problem lies in transforming visions of engagement into solid courses of action. In order to achieve e-engagement goals, there is a need for federal and local governments to more effectively intersect and develop an integrated e-government policy relationship to produce optimal online opportunities for civic participation and connection with representatives.

Jaeger and Thompson (2003) highlight that in order "to achieve effective e-governance, the different levels of government in a nation must work in cooperation to develop and implement an e-government strategy" (2003, p. 391). In Australia, federal policies, strategies, and principles address direct and indirect ICT policy approaches to e-government and are designed to encourage civic participation. However, challenges to the facilitation of online civic engagement remain. These include: providing specific recommendations and support to local governments on how to develop e-government practices to achieve the online engagement ideals portrayed in federal policy; encouraging local governments to realise the worth of utilising federal guidelines; and ensuring federal initiatives consider the needs of locales.

This chapter suggests that greater coordination of e-government policy and practice would benefit the development and implementation of civic engagement strategies. Participatory e-government practices are becoming increasingly important, particularly as opportunities for collaboration and exchange become more pervasive through Web 2.0 tools. A symbiotic approach to online citizen participation and engagement – combining federal guidance and support with local knowledge while using policies to support ICTs and using ICTs to support policies – promotes long-term sustainability of citizen-centric e-government practices designed to meet the needs of citizens in their locales, and provides thorough support for e-government engagement mechanisms.

REFERENCES

Aurigi, A. (2005). *Making the digital city: The early shaping of urban Internet space*. Aldershot, Hampshire: Ashgate Publishing Limited.

Australian Bureau of Statistics (ABS). (2010a). *Australian demographic statistics, March 2010 (No. 3101.0)*. Canberra, Australian Capital Territory: Australian Bureau of Statistics.

Australian Bureau of Statistics (ABS). (2010b). *Regional population growth, Australia (No. 3218.0)*. Canberra, Australian Capital Territory: Australian Bureau of Statistics.

Australian Government. (2012). *Australia.gov.au: Your connection with government*. Retrieved March 19, 2012, from http://australia.gov.au

Bertot, J. C., & Jaeger, P. T. (2006). User-centred e-government: Challenges and benefits for government Web sites. *Government Information Quarterly*, *23*(2), 163–168. doi:10.1016/j.giq.2006.02.001.

Beynon-Davies, P., & Martin, S. (2004). Electronic local government and the modernisation agenda: Progress and prospects for public service improvement. *Local Government Studies*, *30*(2), 214–229. doi:10.1080/0300303042000267245.

Beynon-Davies, P., & Williams, M. D. (2003). Evaluating electronic local government in the UK. *Journal of Information Technology*, *18*(2), 137–149. doi:10.1080/0268396032000101180.

Birch, D. (2003). *Local e-government: A survey of local authorities*. London: The Office of the Deputy Prime Minister.

Borja, J., & Castells, M. (1997). *Local and global: The management of cities in the information age*. London: Earthscan Publications Ltd.

Bradford, N. (2008). *Canadian social policy in the 2000s: Bringing place in*. Ottawa, Ontario: Canadian Policy Research Networks.

Brisbane City Council. (2012). *Brisbane City Council*. Retrieved April 20, 2012, from http://www.brisbane.qld.gov.au

Catinat, M., & Vedel, T. (2000). Public policies for digital democracy. In Hacker, K. L., & van Dijk, J. (Eds.), *Digital democracy: Issues of theory and practice* (pp. 184–208). London: Sage.

Chanan, G. (1997). *Active citizenship and community involvement: Getting to the roots*. Dublin: European Foundation for the Improvement of Living and Working Conditions.

Chen, P., Gibson, R., Lusoli, W., & Ward, S. (2007). Australian governments and online communication. In Young, S. (Ed.), *Government communication in Australia* (pp. 161–180). Port Melbourne, Victoria: Cambridge University Press.

Cohen, G., van Geenhuizen, M., & Nijkamp, P. (2005). ICT as a contributing factor to urban sustainable development: Policymaking in Dutch cities. In van Geenhuizen, M., Gibson, D. V., & Heitor, M. V. (Eds.), *Regional development and conditions for innovation in the network society* (pp. 99–117). West Lafayette, Indiana: Purdue University Press.

Coleman, S., & Blumler, J. G. (2009). *The Internet and democratic citizenship: Theory, practice and policy*. New York: Cambridge University Press. doi:10.1017/CBO9780511818271.

Collins, S. (2010, June 18). Government 2.0... It can be a reality. *The drum unleashed*. ABC News 24, Australian Broadcasting Corporation. Retrieved September 26, 2010, from http://www.abc.net.au/unleashed/stories/s2928556.htm

Corner, S. (2010). Australia's national broadband network: How it came to be and where it might be heading. *Telecommunications Journal of Australia, 60*(2), 31.1-31.9.

Damodaran, L., Nicholls, J., Henney, A., Land, F., & Farbey, B. (2005). The contribution of sociotechnical systems thinking to the effective adoption of e-government and the enhancement of democracy. *The Electronic Journal of E-Government, 3*(1), 1–12.

Department of Broadband, Communications and the Digital Economy (DBCDE). (2011). *#au20 national digital economy strategy: Leveraging the national broadband network to drive Australia's digital productivity*. Canberra, Australian Capital Territory: DBCDE.

Department of Broadband, Communications and the Digital Economy (DBCDE). (2012). *Digital local government program*. Retrieved August 3, 2012, from http://www.dbcde.gov.au/digital_economy/programs_and_initiatives/digital_local_government_program

Department of Communications, Information Technology and the Arts (DCITA). (2004). *Australia's strategic framework for the information economy 2004–2006: Opportunities and challenges for the information age*. Canberra, Australian Capital Territory: DCITA.

Department of Finance and Administration. (2006). *2006 e-government strategy, responsive government: A new service agenda*. Canberra, Australian Capital Territory: Australian Government Information Management Office.

Department of Finance and Administration. (2007). *Principles for ICT-enabled citizen engagement*. Canberra, Australian Capital Territory: Australian Government Information Management Office.

Department of Finance and Deregulation. (2010). *Declaration of open government*. Canberra, Australian Capital Territory: Australian Government Information Management Office.

Downe, J., & Martin, S. (2006). Joined up policy in practice? The coherence and impacts of the local government modernisation agenda. *Local Government Studies, 32*(4), 465–488. doi:10.1080/03003930600793045.

Eardley, T., Bruce, J., & Goggin, G. (2009). Telecommunications and community wellbeing: A review of the literature on access and affordability for low-income and disadvantaged groups (SPRC Report 9/09, prepared for the Telstra Low Income Measures Assessment Committee (LIMAC)). Sydney: Social Policy Research Centre, University of New South Wales.

Flowers, S., Tang, P., Molas-Gallart, J., & Davies, A. (2006). Contrasting approaches to the adoption of e-government. *Journal of E-Government, 2*(3), 51–83. doi:10.1300/J399v02n03_04.

Freeman, J. (2012). E-government engagement and the digital divide. In Parycek, P., Sachs, M., & Skoric, M. (Eds.), *CeDEM Asia 2012: Proceedings of the international conference for e-democracy and open government* (pp. 19-30). Krems: Edition Donau-Universität Krems.

Freeman, J., & Hutchins, B. (2009). Balancing the digital democratic deficit? E-government. *Media International Australia, 130*, 17–27.

Funnell, A. (2010, August 5). Our nod to the federal election campaign and an update on gov 2.0 initiatives. In Davies, A. (Producer), *Future tense*. Radio National, Australian Broadcasting Corporation. Retrieved September 26, 2010, from http://www.abc.net.au/rn/futuretense/stories/2010/2967969.htm

Given, J., & Watkins, J. (2010). Broadband: Policy, innovation, use. *Communication, Politics & Culture, 43*(1), 1–6.

Goggin, G. (2003). Wiring the country: Local telecommunications and Australian rural communities. *Southern Review: Communication, Politics & Culture, 36*(1), 34–47.

Government 2.0 Taskforce. (2010). *Government 2.0 taskforce*. Retrieved June 3, 2010, from http://gov2.net.au/

Government 2.0 Taskforce Report. (2009). *Engage: Getting on with government 2.0*. Canberra, Australian Capital Territory: Australian Government Information Management Office.

Government Response to the Report of the Government 2.0 Taskforce. (2010). *Government response to the report of the government 2.0 taskforce: Engage: Getting on with government 2.0*. Canberra, Australian Capital Territory: Department of Finance and Deregulation.

Horrocks, I. (2009). 'Experts' and e-government: Power, influence and the capture of a policy domain in the UK. *Information, Communication and Society*, *12*(1), 110–127. doi:10.1080/13691180802109030.

Jaeger, P. T., & Thompson, K. M. (2003). E-government around the world: Lessons, challenges, and future directions. *Government Information Quarterly*, *20*(4), 389–394. doi:10.1016/j.giq.2003.08.001.

Jimenez, B. S., Mossberger, K., & Wu, Y. (2012). Municipal government and the interactive Web: Trends and issues for civic engagement. In Manoharan, A., & Holzer, M. (Eds.), *E-governance and civic engagement: Factors and determinants of e-democracy* (pp. 251–271). Hershey, Pennsylvania: Information Science Reference. doi:10.4018/978-1-4666-1740-7.ch006.

King, S. F. (2007). Citizens as customers: Exploring the future of CRM in UK local government. *Government Information Quarterly*, *24*(1), 47–63. doi:10.1016/j.giq.2006.02.012.

Kolsaker, A. (2005). Third way e-government: The case for local devolution. In Böhlen, M., Gamper, J., Polasek, W., & Wimmer, M. A. (Eds.), *E-government: Towards electronic democracy* (pp. 70–80). Berlin: Springer. doi:10.1007/978-3-540-32257-3_7.

Laffin, M. (2008). Local government modernisation in England: A critical review of the LGMA evaluation studies. *Local Government Studies*, *34*(1), 109–125. doi:10.1080/03003930701795014.

Macnamara, J. (2008). Internet media and the public sphere: The 2007 Australian e-electioneering experience. *Media International Australia*, *129*, 7–19.

Macnamara, J. (2010). *E-electioneering 2010: Social media in the Australian Federal Election*. Sydney: Australian Centre for Public Communication.

Margolis, M., & Moreno-Riaño, G. (2009). *The prospect of Internet democracy*. Farnham, Surrey: Ashgate Publishing Limited.

Martin, S. (2008). *Meta-evaluation of the local government modernisation agenda, the state of local services: Performance improvement in local government.* Wetherby, West Yorkshire. Communities and Local Government Publications.

Morphet, J. (2009). E-government and local government. In Budd, L., & Harris, L. (Eds.), *E-governance: Managing or governing?* (pp. 197–212). New York: Routledge.

Mossberger, K., Tolbert, C. J., & McNeal, R. S. (2008). *Digital citizenship: The Internet, society and participation*. Cambridge, Massachusetts: MIT Press.

National Office for the Information Economy (NOIE). (2002). *Better services, better government: The Federal Government's e-government strategy*. Canberra, Australian Capital Territory: NOIE.

National Office for the Information Economy (NOIE). (2004). *Australia's national broadband strategy*. Canberra, Australian Capital Territory: NOIE.

NBN Co. (2012). *Local government*. Retrieved June 1, 2012, from http://www.nbnco.com.au/communities/local-government.html

Norris, D. F. (2007). Electronic democracy at the American grassroots. In Norris, D. F. (Ed.), *Current issues and trends in e-government research* (pp. 164–179). Hershey, Pennsylvania: IGI Global. doi:10.4018/978-1-59904-283-1.ch008.

O'Toole, K. (2009). Australian local government and e-governance: From administration to citizen participation? In Khosrow-Pour, M. (Ed.), *E-government diffusion, policy and impact: Advanced issues and practices* (pp. 171–184). Hershey, Pennsylvania: Information Science Reference.

Office of the Deputy Prime Minister (ODPM). (2002). *The national strategy for local e-government*. London: ODPM.

Pratchett, L. (1999). New technologies and the modernization of local government: An analysis of biases and constraints. *Public Administration*, *77*(4), 731–750. doi:10.1111/1467-9299.00177.

Senyucel, Z., & Stubbs, M. (2006). Towards e-government facilitation in UK local authorities. *Journal of E-Government*, *2*(2), 19–44. doi:10.1300/J399v02n02_03.

Shackleton, P. (2010). Engaging citizens through local e-government: An Australian experience. In Reddick, C. G. (Ed.), *Citizens and e-government: Evaluating policy and management* (pp. 418–434). Hershey, Pennsylvania: IGI Global. doi:10.4018/978-1-61520-931-6.ch023.

Shackleton, P., Fisher, J., & Dawson, L. (2005). From dog licenses to democracy: Local government approaches to e-service delivery in Australia. In Bartmann, D., Rajola, F., Kallinikos, J., Avison, D., Winter, R., Ein-Dor, P., Becker, J., Bodendorf, F., & Weinhardt, C. (Eds.), *Proceedings of the thirteenth European conference on information systems* (pp. 724-735). Regensburg, Germany: ECIS Standing Committee.

Silcock, R. (2001). What is e-government? *Parliamentary Affairs*, *54*(1), 88–101. doi:10.1093/pa/54.1.88.

Simone, M. A. (2010). Deliberative democracy online: Bridging networks with digital technologies. *Communication Review*, *13*(2), 120–139. doi:10.1080/10714421003795527.

Tambini, D. (1999). New media and democracy: The civic networking movement. *New Media & Society*, *1*(3), 305–329. doi:10.1177/14614449922225609.

Thomas, J. (2004). Horizons of expectation: Imaginary trajectories of electronic government. In Goggin, G. (Ed.), *Virtual nation: The Internet in Australia* (pp. 258–272). Sydney: University of New South Wales Press.

Tucker, R. S. (2010). Broadband facts, fiction and urban myths. *Telecommunications Journal of Australia*, *60*(3), 43.1-43.15.

Turner, A. (2007, May 8). Government single-user plan raises ID concerns. *The Age, Next*, p. 1.

Walsh, L. (2009). Online policy consultation: A case study of local government. In Khosrow-Pour, M. (Ed.), *E-government diffusion, policy and impact: Advanced issues and practices* (pp. 139–155). Hershey, Pennsylvania: Information Science Reference.

Wiklund, H. (2005). A Habermasian analysis of the deliberative democratic potential of ICT-enabled services in Swedish municipalities. *New Media & Society*, *7*(5), 701–723. doi:10.1177/1461444805056013.

Wilson, R., Cornford, J., Baines, S., & Mawson, J. (2011). New development: Information for localism? Policy sense-making for local governance. *Public Money & Management*, *31*(4), 295–299. doi:10.1080/09540962.2011.586243.

ADDITIONAL READING

Bekkers, V., & Homburg, V. (2007). The myths of e-government: Looking beyond the assumptions of a new and better government. *The Information Society: An International Journal, 23*(5), 373–382. doi:10.1080/01972240701572913.

Bowles, M., & Wilson, P. (2012). Appraising the importance of the National Broadband Network in Australia's race to compete in the digital economy. *The Australian Quarterly, 83*(1), 11–19.

Bradford, N. (2005). *Place-based public policy: Towards a new urban and community agenda for Canada*. Ottawa, Ontario: Canadian Policy Research Networks.

Budde, P. (2011). The NBN policy gap. *Telecommunications Journal of Australia, 61*(2), 16.1-16.5.

Burgess, S., & Houghton, J. (2006). E-government in Australia. In Hernon, P., Cullen, R., & Relyea, H. C. (Eds.), *Comparative perspectives on e-government: Serving today and building for tomorrow* (pp. 84–101). Lanham, Maryland: Scarecrow Press Inc.

Burns, A., & McGrail, S. (2012). Australia's potential internet futures: Incasting alternatives using a new technology images framework. *Journal of Future Studies, 16*(4), 33–50.

Cullen, R. (2006). E-Government and the digital divide. In Hernon, P., Cullen, R., & Relyea, H. C. (Eds.), *Comparative perspectives on e-government: Serving today and building for tomorrow* (pp. 289–313). Lanham, Maryland: Scarecrow Press Inc.

Eggers, W. D. (2005). *Government 2.0: Using technology to improve education, cut red tape, reduce gridlock, and enhance democracy*. Lanham, Maryland: Rowman & Littlefield Publishers, Inc.

Geiselhart, K., Griffiths, M., & FitzGerald, B. (2003). What lies beyond service delivery – An Australian perspective. In Curtin, G. G., Sommer, M. H., & Vis-Sommer, V. (Eds.), *The world of e-government* (pp. 213–233). Binghamton, New York: The Haworth Political Press. doi:10.1300/J199v02n03_12.

Hargittai, E., & Shafer, S. (2006). Differences in actual and perceived online skills: The role of gender. *Social Science Quarterly, 87*(2), 432–448. doi:10.1111/j.1540-6237.2006.00389.x.

Helbig, N. C., Gil-Garcia, J. R., & Ferro, E. (2009). Understanding the complexity in electronic government: Implications from the digital divide literature. *Government Information Quarterly, 26*(1), 89–97. doi:10.1016/j.giq.2008.05.004.

Henman, P. (2010). *Governing electronically: E-government and the reconfiguration of public administration, policy and power*. Basingstoke, Hampshire: Palgrave Macmillan.

Hernon, P. (2006). E-government in the United Kingdom. In Hernon, P., Cullen, R., & Relyea, H. C. (Eds.), *Comparative perspectives on e-government: Serving today and building for tomorrow* (pp. 55–65). Lanham, Maryland: Scarecrow Press Inc.

Ho, A. T.-K. (2002). Reinventing local governments and the e-government initiative. *Public Administration Review, 62*(4), 434–444. doi:10.1111/0033-3352.00197.

Homburg, V. (2008). *Understanding e-government: Information systems in public administration*. New York: Routledge.

Karakaya-Polat, R. (2005). The Internet and political participation: Exploring the explanatory links. *European Journal of Communication, 20*(4), 435–459. doi:10.1177/0267323105058251.

Leach, S., & Pratchett, L. (2005). Local government: A new vision, rhetoric or reality? *Parliamentary Affairs*, *58*(2), 318–334. doi:10.1093/pa/gsi025.

Livingstone, S., & Lunt, P. (2007). Representing citizens and consumers in media and communications regulation. *The Annals of the American Academy of Political and Social Science*, *611*(1), 51–65. doi:10.1177/0002716206298710.

Loader, B. D. (Ed.). (1998). *Cyberspace divide: Equality, agency and policy in the information society*. London: Routledge. doi:10.4324/9780203169537.

Lowndes, V., Pratchett, L., & Stoker, G. (2001). Trends in public participation: Part 1 – local government perspectives. *Public Administration*, *79*(1), 205–222. doi:10.1111/1467-9299.00253.

Martin, S., & Bovaird, T. (2005). *Meta-evaluation of the local government modernisation agenda: Progress report on service improvement in local government*. London: Office of the Deputy Prime Minister Publications.

Mayer-Schönberger, V., & Lazer, D. (2007). From electronic government to information government. In Mayer-Schönberger, V., & Lazer, D. (Eds.), *Governance and information technology: From electronic government to information government* (pp. 1–14). Cambridge, MA: MIT Press.

Pratchett, L. (2004). Electronic government in Britain. In Eifert, M., & Püschel, J. O. (Eds.), *National electronic government: Comparing governance structures in multi-layer administrations* (pp. 13–45). London: Routledge.

Pratchett, L., Wingfield, M., & Karakaya-Polat, R. (2008). Local democracy online: An analysis of local government Web sites in England and Wales. In Norris, D. (Ed.), *E-government research: Policy and management* (pp. 120–139). Hershey, PA: IGI Global. doi:10.4018/978-1-59904-947-2.ch267.

Verdegem, P., & Hauttekeete, L. (2010). A user-centric approach in e-government policies: The path to effectiveness? In Reddick, C. G. (Ed.), *Citizens and e-government: Evaluating policy and management* (pp. 20–36). Hershey, Pennsylvania: IGI Global. doi:10.4018/978-1-61520-931-6.ch002.

Warschauer, M. (2003). *Technology and social inclusion: Rethinking the digital divide*. Cambridge, MA: MIT Press.

KEY TERMS AND DEFINITIONS

Citizens: Individuals with the political right to reside in a region, vote and be represented by a government.

Direct ICT Policy: Policies with goals that specifically relate to ICTs, such as infrastructure development and educational programs to enhance adoption.

E-Government: Use of information and communication technologies as the interface for government-citizen communications.

Engagement: The active involvement of citizens in political issues, with the capacity to exert influence on government decision-making.

ICTs: Information and communications technologies that combine computing with telecommunications, such as the Internet and World Wide Web.

Indirect ICT Policies: Policies that intend to use ICTs to achieve goals that do not specifically relate to the technologies, such as data collection and organisation, information dissemination, or deliberative forums.

Local Government: An administrative level of government concerned with the civic affairs of a designated region.

Participation: Citizens' political involvement with government.

Chapter 7
Enterprise Architectures for E-Government Development

Muhammad Kashif Farooq
Punjab Information Technology Board (PITB), Pakistan

Shafay Shamail
Lahore University of Management Sciences (LUMS), Pakistan

Mian Muhammad Awais
Lahore University of Management Sciences (LUMS), Pakistan

ABSTRACT

There are two common strategies for the development of e-government projects. One approach is demand based e-government initiatives having no national level centralized Enterprise Architecture. The other is the development of projects under the shadow of a predefined set of guidelines following a given Enterprise Architecture at the national level. It is similar to developing a demand based unplanned city development verses a master plan based development. Complex electronic service deliveries need allied and synchronized output of all the projects. Architectural approach provides guidelines from project planning to technical development and operations. It aligns all the e-government projects with some standard principles. A National Enterprise Architecture based approach provides a number of benefits, including institutionalization of top level strategic planning, standardized development across all levels of e-government, sustainability of e-government projects when governments change, cost reduction by sharing resources and better return on investment. There are many enterprise architectures for e-government development. Different countries are experimenting with different enterprise architectures. In this chapter, e-government projects and their devolution is discussed using Zachman Framework, Reference Model for Open Distributed Processing (RM-ODP), A Reference Model for Collaboration Networks (ARCON), The Open Group Architectural Framework (TOGAF), and Federal Enterprise Architecture Framework (FEAF). It is recommended that architectural implementation should be aligned with governing structure of a country such as centralized, devolved and decentralized. However, governments may use a decentralized architecture and devolve it to its sub-nationals such as state/provincial level and city level as per their political, fiscal and administrative needs and capacity.

DOI: 10.4018/978-1-4666-4245-4.ch007

INTRODUCTION: NATIONAL ENTERPRISE ARCHITECTURES

Enterprise Architecture (EA) is a high level framework to standardize an organization's business strategy, Information Communication Technology (ICT) infrastructure, software, human resource, operations, and projects. It also defines how information technology will support the business operations and provide benefit to the business. Enterprise Architecture is a business issue and covers business process integration and business process standardization (Peter Weill & Ross, 2004). A National Enterprise Architecture (NEA) defines national strategy and the corresponding ICT infrastructure to run a government. It is also called as Federal Enterprise Architecture (FEA) or Government Enterprise Architecture (GEA). Main objectives of NEA are to reduce duplication and hence cost by encouraging reuse in public sector projects. A NEA helps cover gap between policy and its implementation (Janssen & Hjort-Madsen, 2007).

It is a global trend that governments are realizing the importance of enterprise architectures to improve public services and efficiencies. Figure 1 shows the similarity between town planning and EA. Town planning includes long-term plan of transportation and communication networks, provision of utilities, health and housing facilities, etc. A building owner may be interested in the aesthetics and comfort of living whereas a construction contractor would need guidelines about the water, electricity and other supplies in location. Local authorities interest would be facilitate and regulate expansion of a town. Its main responsibility would include provision of and availability of shared facilities such as schools, shopping areas, hospitals, graveyards, public transport and community centers. The establishment of services is a common investment, and the use of these services is regulated to achieve an acceptable investment cost. For example sky rising building would need extra resources. Without a town plan, there is a risk of disorder, chaos, and hence increased security threat. A town planner's job is not to construct or design the buildings, roads and under passes, they primarily provide the vision and master plan.

Similarly, NEA provides guidelines at the strategic level to design and implement ICT infrastructure starting from the top-level applications to lowest level of physical IT facilities, while keeping manpower, security and governance in view. Similar to a town planner, NEA architect provides a master plan in the form of a IT Architecture (ITA) covering e-governance strategy, e-applications, and IT infrastructure. This ITA also provides guidelines how different types of systems will integrate using common standards and protocols (Meersman & Vandenborre, 2006), (White-Paper, 2003).

An architectural approach for the e-government development projects has the following main characteristics:

Figure 1. Similarity between town planning and enterprise architecture

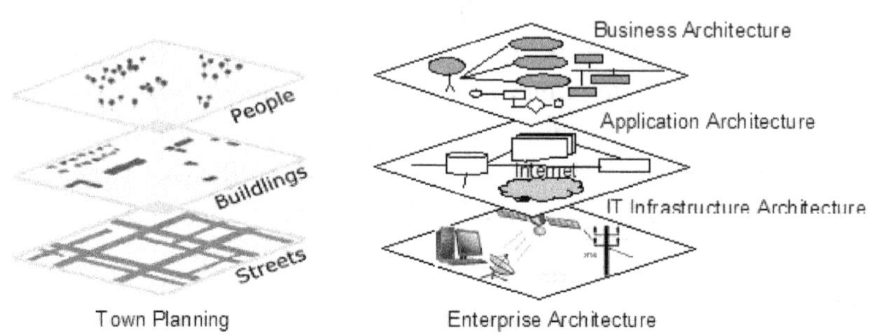

- **Institutionalization:** NEA based approach for e-government provides establishment of comprehensive documentation, support on legislative grounds, strategies specific to organizations' goals, target architecture based on a pre-defined baseline architecture, and transition plan for institutionalization (Song & Song, 2010).
- **Standardized Development:** NEA approach facilitates the standardized development across all the e-government initiatives.
- **Sustainability:** e-Government projects need sustainability. During long-term projects, political leadership may be changed and often new leadership may not agree with the aims and objectives of development projects. In this case, NEA based implementation plan plays an important role to sustain the aims of the e-government projects.
- **Cost Reduction Through Shared Resources:** NEA approach reduces the cost of e-government development by using the optimized shared resources and avoids any duplicate efforts (Rico, 2008). It also brings reliability in online services.
- **Return On Investment (ROI):** The overall Return On Investment and the ratio of benefits to costs improve due to shared resources and lower duplication (Christiansen & Gøtze, 2006).

The following section provides a summary of some international EA implementations by different countries.

INTERNATIONAL EXPERIENCE

In the last two decades, e-government leading countries moved from demand-based e-government projects to well-planned national enterprise architectures. At the same time, experts of enterprise architecture field made progress and introduced very comprehensive architectures and frameworks. There are many countries involved in implementing their NEA. A few of them are being discussed below.

United States is the pioneer in EA development and implementation. They started developments in 1980s with the adoption of Government Open Systems Interconnection Profile (GOSIP), Federal Information Processing Standard for data transfer. The law on public IT acquisitions (the Clinger-Cohen Act) supported the EA activities (Liimatainen, Hoffmann, & Heikkilä, 2007). In 1999, the Federal Chief Information Officer Council (CIOC) published the "Federal Enterprise Architecture Framework" (FEAF) (CIOC, 2001). It provides guidance in developing architectures for multi-organizational functional areas. FEA reference model was presented by the Office of Management and Budget (OMB) (Christiansen & Gøtze, 2006; Schekkerman, 2005; Saha, 2010). These EA efforts used standard EAs such as Zachman (Guijarro, 2007) and TOGAF (Liimatainen et al., 2007).

German Federal Administration (KBSt) issued guidelines including architecture models and standards for e-government initiatives, called Standards and Architectures for e-Government Applications (SAGA). It serves as the basis for the German NEA. SAGA was based on Reference Model-Open Distributed Processing (RM-ODP). SAGA has been progressed continuously and led towards the E-Government 2.0 and the Deutschland-Online programs (Liimatainen et al., 2007; SAGA, 2008). In a study (Daniel, 2009), it is concluded that there is positive acceptance of SAGA in German municipalities and is correlated with the size of municipality.

The British Government published e-Government Interoperability Framework (e-GIF) in 2001. The e-GIF encompasses government's technical policies and specifications for achieving interoperability and coherence of Information and Communication Technology (ICT) systems across the public sector. The e-GIF is a popular framework and has been adopted by some Commonwealth countries (Liimatainen et al., 2007). Scotland is using the Open Scotland Information Age Framework (OSIAF), which extends the e-GIF by making Scottish public sector services interoperable with UK government services. Northern Ireland has shown its commitment to the e-GIF and the Welsh Assembly Government is a voluntary partner of the e-GIF, (Schekkerman, 2005). In addition, New Zealand's own e-GIF is based on the British framework (Liimatainen et al., 2007).

UK Government has introduced a new cross-Government Enterprise Architecture (xGEA). The aim of xGEA is to develop a business and IT blueprint for government. In addition to this, the xGEA supports the better inter-working between agencies through the agreement of shared standards. The Reference Model of xGEA is xGEARM having repository of Architectures for administrative branches and their agencies to develop departmental EAs (Liimatainen et al., October 2007; Christiansen & Gøtze, 2006; Schekkerman, 2005).

The Swiss NEA was initiated in 2006 with the name eGovCH that is based on The Open Group Framework (TOGAF). The Federal Administration emphasized its viewpoint of using open-source, vendor-neutral and freely available tools. The Swiss IT Council approved The Open Source Software (OSS) and open standard strategy in 2004. The Swiss NEA is based on two different views the process view and the structural view and adopts its implementation guidelines from SAGA. eGovCH is service-oriented paradigm. It also takes care of political and legal constraints (Liimatainen et al., 2007), (Schekkerman, 2005), (Müller, 2005).

Canada has also initiated a federated architecture approach. The objective is to bring uniformity in the design, grouping, transformation, governance and interoperability of services and systems. An EA tool kit "Business Transformation Enablement Program (BTEP) was introduced with following two components:

1. **The Strategic Reference Models of Canadian Government:** It suggests a common modeling language for federal, provincial and municipal to map their processes.
2. **Transformation Methodology:** It involves step-by-step processes and implementation plans.

In 2004, Chief Information Officer Branch of the Treasury Board of Canada Secretariat developed Governments of Canada Strategic Reference Model (GSRM) under the shadow of BTEP (Liimatainen et al., 2007; Schekkerman, 2005; BTEP, 2004; CIO, 2008).

Netherlands or Dutch Government Reference Architecture (NORA) has been developed, though it is not a mandatory model for adoption across the government agencies. Organizations work with NORA on a voluntary basis. NORA enables better cohesion and collaboration among government bodies (Liimatainen et al., 2007; Schekkerman, 2005; NORA, 2007).

Australian Government initiated Australian Government Architecture Reference Models (AGA-RM) which is based on the FEAF of US (Schekkerman, 2005; Steward, 2011).

Singapore Government started EA program in 2002. In 2007, a set of reference models were introduced with the name Singapore Government Enterprise Architecture (SGEA) including Business Reference Model (SG-BRM); Data Reference Model (SG-DRM); Application Reference Model (SG-ARM); and Technology Reference Model (SG-TRM). Furthermore, a methodology was developed named as Methodology for AGency ENTerprise Architecture (MAGENTA) to enable agencies to align to and fully support the government's transformation objectives and outcomes (Saha, 2009; Pheng, 2007). The program is now called Whole-of-Government Enterprise Architecture (WOG EA) and aims for end to end service delivery with integration and shared approach (Schekkerman, 2005).

Denmark is Europe's leader in the use of NEA. Denmark's NEA was initiated in a white Paper in 2003. The Danish NEA implementation approach is based on incentives, i.e. there are no rules, regulations, governing standards and principles for NEA development in government. The implementation of NEA is based on voluntarism and it is up to each public organization to evaluate their need for NEA and take decisions related to it. This highly decentralized governance model provides liberty to municipalities to adopt it independently and get benefited from experience of mature and large size municipalities. NEA was initiated by the Ministry of Science, Technology and Innovation (MVTU) and is based on the Zachman framework (Liimatainen et al., 2007). It focuses more on the planning process as proposed by Spewak. Service-Oriented architecture (SOA) has been encouraged as the preferred architectural style for government (Janssen & Hjort-Madsen, 2007; White-Paper, 2003; Pheng, 2007).

Norwegian Government developed a centralized architecture and translated into domain and organizational architectures at the local level. It is mandatory for national agencies (Aagesen, Veenstra, Janssen, & Krogstie, 2011). There is a strong emphasis on open standards and open software. The Norwegian NEA comprises technical, conceptual, organizational and procedural standards. It also includes a shared component library (Liimatainen et al., 2007).

Finland's Ministry of Finance initiated NEA program in 1990s. Finnish Government has been a leader in introducing ICT based reforms in public administration and services. Many countries learn from Finnish experiences. The framework consists of four common viewpoints: business, information, application and technology. The framework is based on several famous frameworks such as FEA and TOGAF (Liimatainen et al., 2007).

United Nations Department of Economic and Social Affairs (UNDESA) have conducted surveys (UNDESA, 2012) of e-government implementation of different countries. According to these reports majority of the governments are trying to improve their e-governance. They are modernizing their developments, approaches and gaining trust in their online services. These efforts can be categorized in two approaches such as "demand-based e-government" and architecture based e-government. Many governments adopted enterprise architectures for providing planned, reliable and standardized e-services to stakeholders.

Based on the above discussion, it is observed that there are three types of NEA implementations:

- **Strongly Federated:** Countries having strong federated structure have implemented this type of centralized NEA. Usually, these are small countries needing no decentralization.
- **Weakly Federated:** Countries who have decentralized their structure at different sub-national levels implement a devolved NEA structure. Usually these countries are big in size and have large population. They may partially decentralize their NEA using devolved models.
- **Independent:** Countries having nearly independent states/sub-nationals do not have a mandatory or controlled NEA structure. They have very broad level guidelines and leave the actual implementation of EA to the respective states/sub-nationals.

Components of devolved e-Government architecture are now discussed.

DEVOLUTION/DECENTRALIZATION

Large size and generous governments believe in decentralized governing structure and provide autonomy to their local governments for better service delivery and governance. In the second half of the century, many countries embraced decentralization in terms of political, fiscal and administrative powers (Cheema & Rondinelli, 1983). The "Soufflé" theory of decentralization (Parker, 1995) described role of political, fiscal, and administrative decentralization. It proposed that only appropriate mixture of these types of decentralizations can produce results (Parker, 1995). Decentralization and devolution are considered to be same in nature. Devolution may be defined as: *Devolution to lower levels has to involve a meaningful transfer of authority to be acceptable and to work effectively. It also has to maintain horizontal equity by ensuring a fair distribution of fiscal and other resources across the units* (Ferguson & Chandrasekharan, 2004).

Generally, federal governments devolve their many powers to their sub-national levels such as state/province and local (city/district) levels for better governance.

Devolution in E-Government

E-Government is the largest enterprise system of a country. It works as a shadow of the government, and drives the e-government strategy and governing structure (federated, decentralized or independent) of a government (Farooq, Shamail, & Awais, 2006). Heeks categorized eight main areas of decentralization i-e planning, organizational structures and staffing, data management, computing and data management architecture, information systems development, information technology acquisition, training, and technical support (Heeks, 1999). A centralized approach requires very strong controls, whereas a partial decentralized approach in which few modules are centralized while few are decentralized can be cost effective and a better solution for both mature and undeveloped organizations. Richard Heeks recommended a 'core-periphery' approach to public information, a system that combines both central and local action, and is therefore most effective (Heeks, 1999). In Heeks (1999), the Core-Periphery solution is defined as: "... core-periphery approach that attempts to reconcile the push of the centralized approach with the pull of the decentralized approach."

Federal level may devolve many powers and service delivery operations to sub-nationals (local government and municipalities) while policy, enterprise applications and related databases may be kept centralized. In this way, integration, standardization, security, technical experience and investment can be utilized in optimum manner. As a result, multiple levels of government need to rearrange their roles and intergovernmental relationships. Devolution in e-governance facilitates the transfer of few powers related to e-government activity from central government to sub-national level with respect to other devolutions such as political, fiscal and administrative powers (Farooq et al., 2006). e-Devolution highly depends on the devolution of political representation, fiscal management and administrative control of the e-government functions.

Political Representation

In a democratic regime, public representation is essential at local level for electronic service delivery to public and business sector. Political ownership and "will" is also very important for the implementation set by central government. Federal and state/provincial governments may select technocrats and political leaders for effective launching of e-services. Local governments and municipalities may set targets for elected councilors for the mobilization and education of the people for usage of online services.

e-Government projects need business process re-engineering, change management and technology, first two components need strong political leadership (Furuholt & Wahid, 2008). There are two types of political roles in e-government activities: 1) Individual participation like polls for need of e-services, quality and reliability of e-services, and 2) owning of ruling party, audit by opposition, and mobilization through none governmental organizations (NGO) or civil society organizations (CSO). Trust in e-government services can be improved through these political participations (Shaun, Robin, & Peter, 2009). Political value chain is as significant in e-government as value chain in industrial business (Virili & Sorrentino, 2002).

Fiscal Management

Investment on online services is the subject of financial agencies of the government. They have to analyze the cost-benefit of the project in perspective of demand-supply of related services. They have to take care of public revenue for the development schemes and government operations. Fiscal devolution supports the political as well as administrative devolution and has major role in inter-governmental relations horizontally as well as vertically.

Economists have believed that fiscal autonomy can increase the efficiency and responsibility of sub-national governments. Many countries have granted greater fiscal autonomy to their sub-nationals for better planning, budgeting and revenue collection as per their socio-economic conditions (Darby, Muscatelli, & Roy, 2003). Fiscal devolution can provide liberty for the development projects as compared to the centralized fiscal regimes, however it poses considerable challenges for macroeconomic management (Shah, 2006).

Administrative Control

Reference to the scale of country and traditional administrative devolution, e-government devolution also needs a complete administrative role in delivering public services. Operations of e-services also need some degree of involvement of field staff, kiosks and back-offices. This requires administrative work-force at the local government level, hence requiring devolution in the administrative access of e-government portals or applications. High degree of collaboration is required between agencies at different levels, both horizontal as well as vertical to deliver e-services by using integrated information (Gil-Garcia & Luis Felipe, 2006; Bram & Marijn, 2008).

Adoption of Devolution Approach

In 2006, the IT University of Copenhagen, Copenhagen Business School and the Association of Enterprise Architects conducted a survey evaluating the governmental EA program. Sixteen governments participated in the survey. Figure 2 shows the governance model of participated governments in terms of centralized, devolved and decentralized approaches (Christiansen & Gøtze, 2006).

Estonia and Denmark have centralized governance. Taiwan has decentralized governance. Canada stated that they do not have any governance, as their EA program is not imposed while USA, Singapore, the Netherlands, Korea, Switzerland and Japan have all both centralized and decentralized or devolved governance (Christiansen & Gøtze, 2006).

International experience may be summarized into three categories: decentralized, devolved and centralized approaches. NEA may also be classified with respect to these approaches as shown in Figure 3. Columns from left to right show decentralization to centralization or weak NEA to strong NEA. Intermediate approach is the devolved approach i-e hybrid approach of decentralization

Figure 2. Governance Models (Source: Christiansen & Gøtze, 2006)

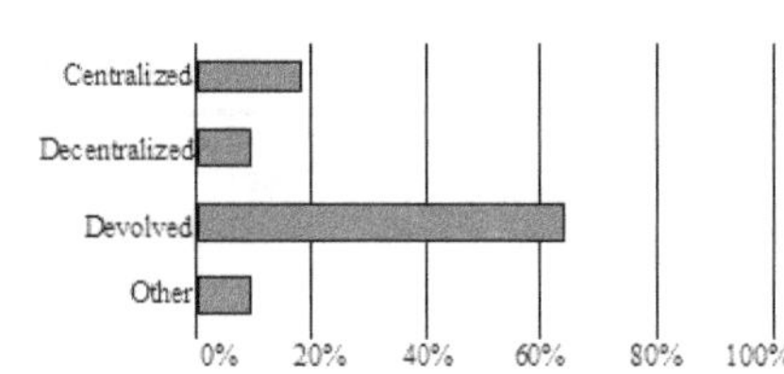

and centralization. These ten cells present the features and levels of NEA.

E-Government Architectural Framework

E-Government is a complex and multidimensional enterprise system, and needs comprehensive plan for development, implementation and operations. A National Enterprise Architecture integrates all the related initiatives. NEA can connect horizontal as well as vertical relationship among national and sub-national levels (Janssen & Hjort-Madsen, 2007). Enterprise Architecture is the basic instrument for transformation and reconstruction of government (Kristian, 2009).

There are many generic EAs available. A number of different Enterprise Architectures are selected for discussion in the light of devolution in e-government in the following sections, inclusing the following five: Zachman Framework (ZF), Reference Model for Open Distributed Processing (RM-ODP), A Reference model for COllaboration Networks (ARCON), The Open Group Architectural Framework (TOGAF), and Federal Enterprise Architecture Framework (FEAF).

Zachman Framework

John Zachman introduced Zachman Enterprise Architecture Framework (ZF) (Zachman, 1987). It is the most famous framework among public and private sectors. Majority of the enterprise architectures have been derived from John Zachman's original framework (Bellman & Rausch, 2004).

Figure 3. NEA and decentralization

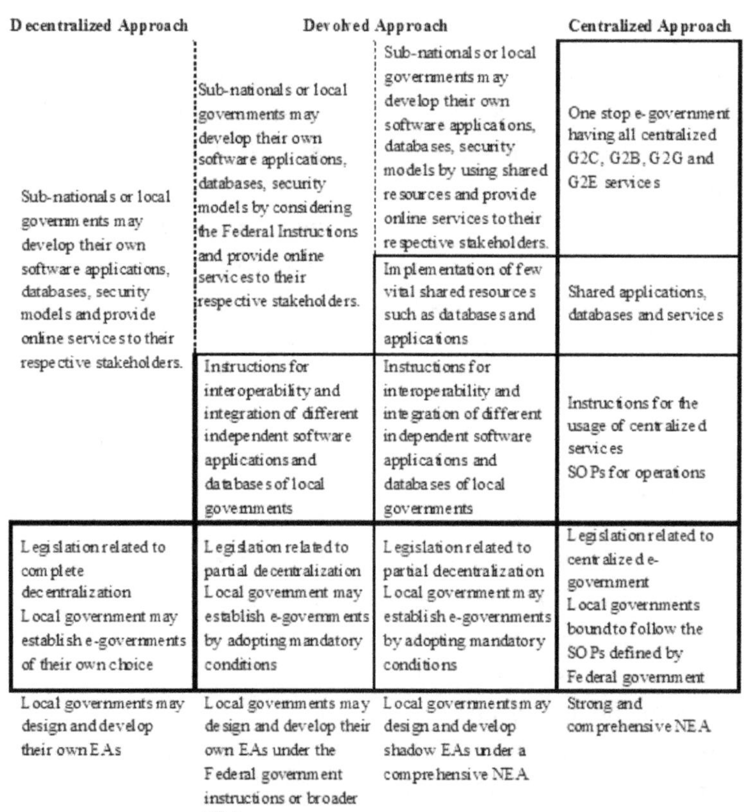

Zachman organized different information in an enterprise matrix. Each cell of this matrix represents the relation to certain viewpoint (data, function, network, people, time, and motivation) and of the perception (contextual, conceptual, logical, physical, and out of context). Each column estimates one of the Aristotelian questions: what, how, where, who, when and why. Each row corresponds to one of the roles: the planner, the owner, the designer, the builder, and the subcontractor (Guijarro, 2007; Zachman, 1987). This framework is initiated at the planning level and then it bridges with lower sections containing the technical architecture. Overall this framework delivers comprehensive knowledge about the business process and its technical development (Espadas, Romero, Concha, & Molina, 2008).

First row of five columns explained by Zachman present the planner view of the enterprise framework that exhibits the executive summary. It consists of the purpose, scope, cost and objectives of the system. The second row reflects user prospective in terms of operations and others without considering any technical details. This section encompasses people, resources, services and responsibilities. Third row is the system model that joins the top two rows with the bottom two rows. The last two rows are technical in nature regarding system development.

This framework has six columns representing dual perceptions. These columns explain the whole system with Aristotelian questions. First column having title "what" is associated with data of the whole system and also defines the scope of data to technical details. Second column having title "how" is associated with functions of the system. Its five-level detail starts from scope level and goes to application or program level. Third column "where" is responsible for location(s) of the system including centralized and decentralized infrastructure. This column starts from scope of locations and its bottom technical level represents detailed network architecture. Fourth column "who" associates with system stakeholders. Scope level mentions the category of people involved and the last technical level describes comprehensive organizational breakdown structure (OBS) with all roles and responsibilities. Fifth column "when" focuses on the business and operational occasions. At scope level it mentions major time lines while at the last level it includes detailed schedule. Sixth column "why" addresses the purpose, goals and strategy of enterprise (Bellman & Rausch, 2004).

It can also be elaborated by following levels of abstraction for six architecture descriptions (CIOC, 2001):

1. The Planner or Scope View
2. The Owner's or Enterprise Model View
3. The Designer's or System's Model View
4. The Builder's or Technology Model View
5. The Subcontractor's or Detailed Representation View
6. The Functioning Enterprise or Actual System View.

The six architecture descriptions and the interrogatives are (CIOC, 2001):

1. The Data Description - What
2. The Function Description - How
3. The Network Description - Where
4. The People Description - Who
5. The Time Description - When
6. The Motivation Description - Why.

E-Devolution and Zachman Framework

Zachman Framework (ZF) has capability to facilitate the devolution approach for a centralized e-government. Devolution in e-governance may be accommodated at fourth column "who" which can address organization, people and stakeholders (Farooq et al., 2006). This decentralization may be introduced among inter agencies or inter governments or sub-nationals. The devolved Zachman Framework is discussed below.

Upper two levels of the fourth column are significant for high-level executive summary including scope of decentralization. It also defines the ownership, partnership and collaborations of central administration and sub-nationals. Role of private sector and collaborative networks may also be defined there.

Decision makers devolve the powers or responsibilities at this section as shown in Figure 4. Level one is exclusive for the scope of the decentralization of whole enterprise, and may define the ownership of central or federal government agency of the e-government project. Moreover all main stakeholders of the EA such as sub-national governments and their agencies can be notified. At this level, roles may be defined superficially such as ownership, developing partners, executing partners at different levels of government, outsourcing requirements and the users of the e-government services.

Second level is reserved for enterprise modeling keeping in view the ownership and operational viewpoint. A comprehensive devolution model can be addressed at this point. The strategy for devolution in e-government should be aligned with the traditional devolution like political, fiscal and administrative devolutions.

Third level of "who" column is known as "system model." It integrates the above two strategic levels with lower technical levels. This model has details for the responsible stakeholders involved in the designing the solution for e-services. This role distribution is according to the responsibilities of federal and sub-national as per defined in level 1 and 2. System analysts gather requirements and then translate into technical language. They

Figure 4. Devolution Aspect in Zachman Framework - Column 4

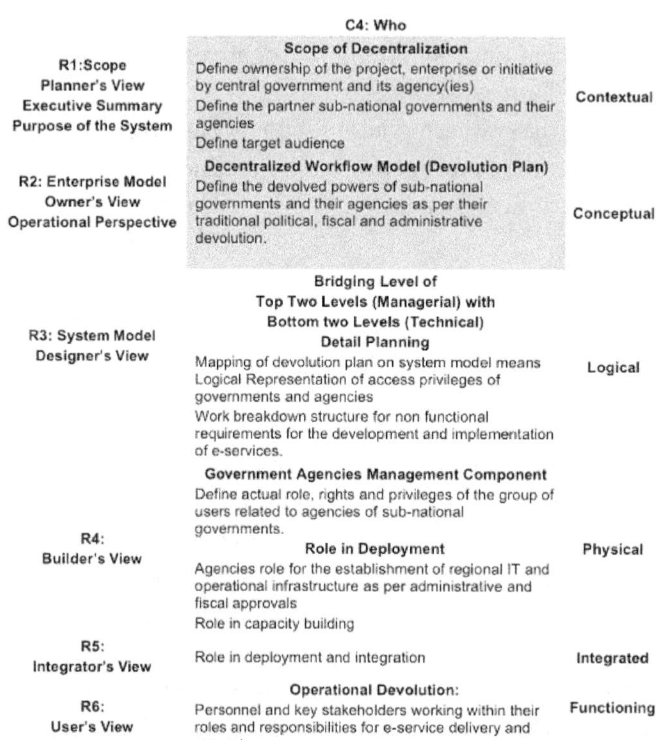

also propose solutions and prepare functional specifications.

Fourth level of "who" column is known as "Builder's View." It explains the role of developers including people, organizations or outsourcing involved in actual development of solutions. In case of e-government, different solutions may be outsourced to different organizations.

Fifth level of "who" column is known as "Integrator View." It is responsible for integration of different modules and deployment. At this level, integrating people and their responsibilities may be discussed.

Sixth level of "who" column is known as "User view." It addresses the operational responsibilities. This cell also corresponds to the responsibilities of a user. Role and responsibilities of support services may also be discussed here. Feedback of user is also an important task to further improve the online services.

Reference Model of Open Distributed Processing (RM-ODP)

Reference Model of Open Distributed Processing (RM-ODP) was introduced by International Organization for Standardization (ISO) and International Telecommunication Union (ITU). German government implemented it as NEA with the name known as SAGA (Standards and Architectures for e-Government Applications) (Liimatainen et al., 2007). RM-ODP is suitable for heterogeneous systems (Putman, 2001). This EA has five viewpoints to explain a complex enterprise system. These viewpoints describe the business model, technology, engineering, software and information (Meneklis, Kaliontzoglou, Polemi, & Douligeris, 2005). In each viewpoint, federal and local devolved powers have been addressed with respect to political, fiscal and administrative devolved powers. (Farooq, Shamail, & Awais, 2008).

E-Devolution and RM-ODP

Reference to RM-ODP, devolution in e-governance can be addressed first in enterprise viewpoint then other viewpoints accordingly. In each viewpoint, federal and local government powers can be addressed. All the micro details of devolved powers can be classified in the five viewpoints as shown in Figure 5.

Enterprise Viewpoint (Enterprise Devolution)

This viewpoint addresses the legislation, policies, rules and regulations related to e-government initiatives. The description may also define the responsibilities of federal government and local governments. This viewpoint correlates all devo-

Figure 5. Devolution Aspect in RM-ODP

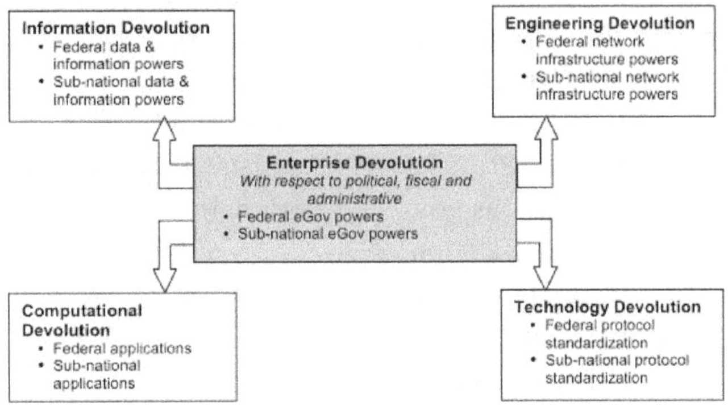

lutions in policy matters. Government is related with large, complex and heterogeneous structure, so comprehensive details are required in this viewpoint. Vertical and horizontal integration of multilevel government should be focused here. Remaining four viewpoints have technical details based on this enterprise devolution. Following are the salient features of the enterprise devolution.

- Scope and purpose of centralized and de-centralized functions
- Introduction of major stakeholders related to e-government devolutions
- Classification of powers and responsibilities related to federal and local governments and their agencies
- Alignment of e-government devolved powers with political, fiscal and administrative powers

Information Viewpoint (Information Devolution)

This viewpoint explains the information architecture for centralized and decentralized perspective. It describes the information owner, provider, user and auditor of information/data. All these roles, responsibilities with respect to devolved powers related to information may be dispersed among federal and local agencies.

Computational Viewpoint (Computational Devolution)

This viewpoint is responsible for setting open standards for integration of centralized and decentralized applications. Application sharing approach such as Application Service Provider (ASP) models can also be defined. Various government services need integration for verification, authorization and collaboration. Integration is also required for public and private applications. For example, a central agency of citizen registration and identification is valuable for other government applications and e-services to identify citizens.

Engineering Viewpoint (Engineering Devolution)

This viewpoint is responsible for the devolution in Information Communication Technology (ICT) infrastructure. There is a need of documented architecture for central and local arrangements to deliver the reliable, secure and swift e-services. There should be multi-channel service delivery such as web-based, mobile-based and call center based. To achieve these multi-mode services, many technologies should be engaged such as Kiosks, Public Switched Telephone Network (PSTN), broadband, wireless, cellular network and satellite services. Majority of buildings and public places should have Wi-Fi hotspots.

Technology Viewpoint (Technology Devolution)

E-government refers to the online public services including Government to Citizen (G2C), Government to Business (G2B), Government 2 Government (G2G) and Government to Employee (G2E). A government cannot impose one technology for all applications, security measures and integration. Therefore, it is very important to standardize the technology, protocols and formats. In this way, heterogeneous systems and applications can integrate with each other to provide the complex services. Open Source Software (OSS) also needs policy. Reference to the devolution plan, technology standardization may be addressed at federal level or at subnational level. Few standards should be mandatory and few should be optional as per their nature.

Relations Among Devolved Powers

There are many inter-relationships among devolved powers such as dependencies, constraints and prerequisites. Relations may occur within the same viewpoint or among different viewpoints. Many devolved powers are associated with political, fiscal and administrative devolutions. Figure 5 shows how these viewpoints can address devolution of e-governance.

Reference Model for Collaboration Networks (ARCON)

A Reference model for COllaboration Networks (ARCON) is a conceptual framework to facilitate the collaborative network. This consists of three perspectives (1) Life cycle perspective, (2) Environment characteristics perspective and (3) Model intents perspective (Camarinha-Matos & Afsarmanesh, 2006b), (Camarinha-Matos & Afsarmanesh, 2008). These dimensions may be incorporated to establish a virtual government by collaborative prospective: "Virtual government – an alliance of governmental organizations (e.g. city hall, tax office, cadaster office, and civil infrastructures office) that combine their services through the use of computer networks to provide integrated services to the citizen through a common front-end" (Camarinha-Matos & Afsarmanesh, 2008; UNINOVA & UvA, 2006).

Collaboration has three stages known as networking, coordination and cooperation while coordination covers networking; cooperation encompasses coordination; and collaboration leads cooperation (Camarinha-Matos & Afsarmanesh, 2006a).

- **Networking** is the initial stage having communication and exchange of information for common interest (Camarinha-Matos & Afsarmanesh, 2006a). All the sub-nationals and federal government have this kind of relation. They have communication and information exchange for the smooth administration and exchange of governing experience (Lazer & Binz-Scharf, 2004).
- **Coordinated Networking** is the aggregated step of simple networking. Alignment of administrative activities to achieve the common goals i-e good governance (Camarinha-Matos & Afsarmanesh, 2006a). For example, local governments and their agencies extend their relations in terms of inter agencies and municipalities for better service delivery. They may standardize their processes for uniform operations.
- **Cooperation**, the aggregated step of coordinated networking, defines the sharing of resources for achieving goals (L. Camarinha-Matos & Afsarmanesh, 2006a). Now this stage is the beginning of shared services. For example, the central e-government portal for G2C services available on one stop portal. In this way all the local governments may use the common portal application. Other example is the national database of citizens. All departments may verify the people for the service delivery.
- **Collaboration** is the superior relation having main features such as sharing information, resources and responsibilities under an agreed documented plan (Camarinha-Matos & Afsarmanesh, 2006a). Centralized e-government is the best example of collaboration. All centralized portals such as G2C, G2B, G2G and G2E are collaborative efforts of sub-nationals and agencies. To establish such centralized portal, sub-nationals have to achieve networking, coordinated networking, cooperation and collaboration. There are many countries having highly decentralized governing structure to establish collaborative network for e-services.

E-Devolution and ARCON

ARCON is a wide-range theoretical framework; it may be implemented as any kind of Collaborative Networks (CN). A decentralized government may give liberty to local governments to provide e-services of their own choice while local governments may not have homogeneous capacity, resources, investment and socio-economic conditions. Therefore, it is optimum approach to establish a collaborative enterprise system to deliver e-services at mass level and a number of local governments may join this enterprise system. In this way, the services may be cost effective by using shared resources (Farooq, Shamail, & Awais, 2008). ARCON is the three dimensional in nature as shown in Figure 6. One dimension is the life cycle perspective, second is environment characteristics and third is the modeling layer.

Life-Cycle Perspective

In a decentralized structure, e-government may be implemented in the form of a collaborative network. Figure 7 shows a presentation of the life cycle of a collaborative network including the stages creation, operation, dissolution and metamorphosis as explained below.

- **Creation:** Establishing of a collaborative network requires a comprehensive set of plans including scope, requirement analysis, standardized processes of each service, functional & none functional specifications, and required ICT infrastructure. Stakeholder analysis includes roles, rights and responsibilities of each stakeholder. This collaboration network may be developed at any sub-national level such as state/province, city or municipal level. This collaboration may be planned for whole e-government or for few e-services. This stage can be extended for legislation, contract management for CN members, required business process reengineering (BPR), development, deployment and change management.
- **Operation:** It is the second stage after finalization of a collaborative network. This stage needs comprehensive operational manual. All CN members (local governments or municipalities) need to re-engineer their business processes of traditional services as per defined standard processes. CN members need to train their staff for operations. Migration of historical data (if applicable) required for the initiation of services. Then each CN member starts operations of online services as per defined

Figure 6. Modeling perspective in ARCON (Source: (UNINOVA & UvA, 2006))

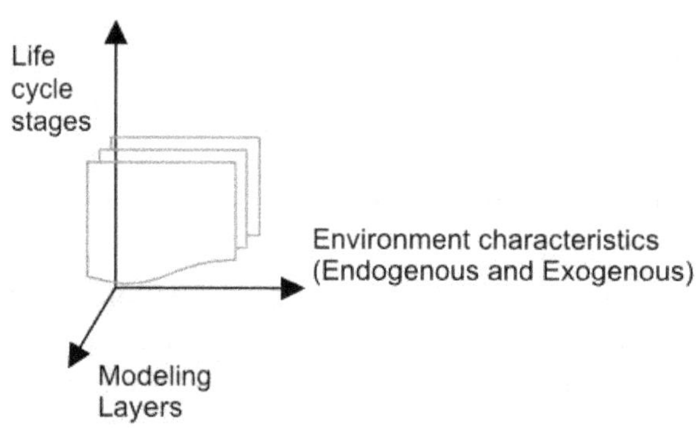

Figure 7. Devolution aspect in ARCON (Source: (UNINOVA & UvA, 2006))

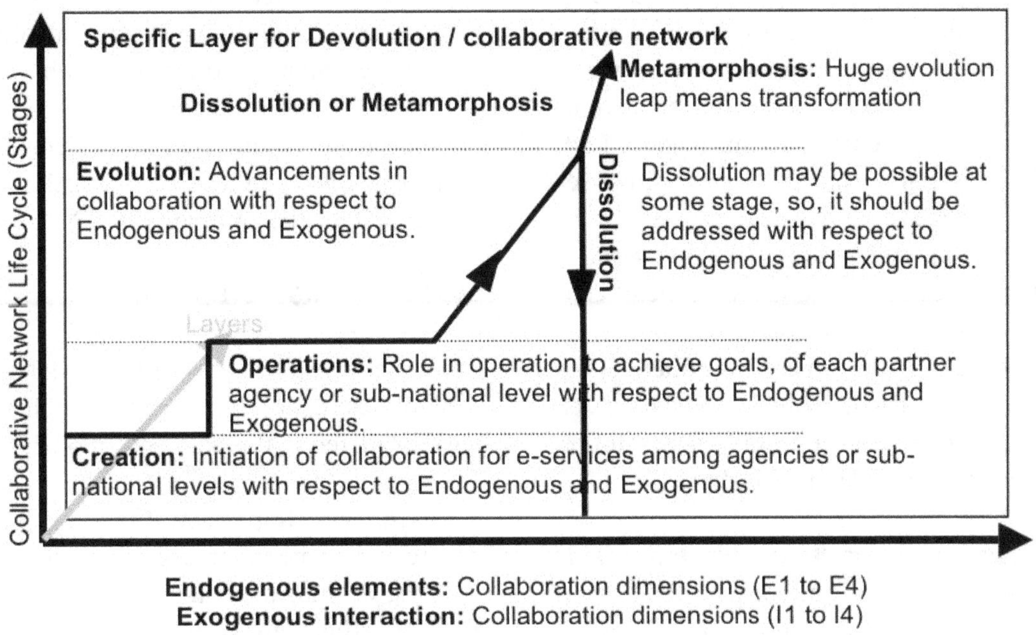

roles and responsibilities. Feedback is important for change request.

- **Evolution:** Modernization of services depends on technology advancements, feedback and user experience. Evolution is a continuous process. This process may be expedited by applying ranking systems among all collaborative networks of the same nature around the world.
- **Dissolution or Metamorphosis:** Generally, CNs have provisions that any member can leave from the membership. Detailed policy should be available for this situation. CN may move towards transformation.

Environment Characteristics Perspective

The second dimension of the ARCON is regarding environment characteristics. In this perspective internal and external factors can be addressed. Internal factors may be addressed at endogenous elements while external factors may be addressed at exogenous elements (UNINOVA & UvA, 2006). These two subspaces of the CN environment characteristics in the domain of e-governance are further discussed below.

- **Endogenous Elements Subspace:** This subspace addresses the internal relations of different entities. These are the relations among partner organizations such as local governments or municipalities and may be the relations among different services or functions. CN members have heterogonous characteristics such as resources, culture, literacy, infrastructure, size, population etc. Therefore, their requirements, issues and constraints are different.

Endogenous elements are classified by four variables: Structural (E1), Componential (E2), Functional (E3) and Behavioral (E4) (UNINOVA & UvA, 2006). Reference to the e-government related Collaborative Network Organization

(CNO), structural dimension E1 includes CNO partner's role, responsibilities and organizational details. The componential dimension E2 focuses on the readiness for the initiation of e-services, capacity building and IT literacy of the citizens for e-services. The functional dimension E3 addresses the re-engineering in business processes for the standardized e-services and service delivery channels such as web media, cellular interface, Interactive Voice Response (IVR) and call center services. And the behavioural dimension E4 is responsible for the principles, policies, and governance rules that regulate the CNO partners. Additionally, contracts and conflict resolution policies are also included in this dimension.

- **Exogenous Interactions Subspace:** This viewpoint shows an abstract illustration of the CNO from external side. There are many external factors that affect the e-government services such as literacy rate of general public, IT penetration in society, transparency in public services and decentralization in terms of political, fiscal and administrative manners. Legislative support also plays a vital role for joining the collaborative network. Political will is the most important factor for the e-government scope and services.

Exogenous elements have four dimensions that are defined as I1: Market, I2: Support, I3: Society and I4: Constituency (UNINOVA & UvA, 2006). Reference to the e-government perspective, the market dimension I1 covers the main consumer of e-government such as citizens, business sector, inter-agencies and government employees. The support dimension I2 includes the supporting edges such as political, fiscal and administrative decentralization by federal government. Furthermore, private sector may provide support in terms of ICT service providers such as telecommunication companies, Internet bandwidth providers and technology enablers. The societal dimension I3 comprises the interaction of e-government with society where many values may be involved such as trust, acceptance and socio-economic compatibility of e-services. The last one is constituency dimension I4 responsible for the joining of new partner in CNO and retiring of existing member from CNO for the continuity of CNO.

Model Intents Perspective

CNO reference model may further be defined in the form of abstraction layer. Following three layers are considered in this reference model.

- **General Representation Layer:** It includes general concepts, policies, processes, workflows applicable on all CNOs.
- **Specific Modeling Layer:** This intermediate layer may include some specific policies, processes, workflows for specific CNO. This flexible layer provides option to accommodate some specific features for a certain CNO. For example, largest CNO or the smallest CNO have some special cares for their services. In some cases, new technologies or approaches have to be introduced as pilot project for certain CNO and after positive feedback, these technologies or approaches would be implemented to whole network.
- **Implementation Modeling Layer:** Implementation of an EA is the key area of whole life cycle of architecture based e-government. This includes all procedures for the adoption of services offered by CN and data migration plans.

The Open Group Architecture Framework (TOGAF)

TOGAF initiated by the Architecture Forum of The Open Group and progressing since the mid-1990s. Initial version of TOGAF was introduced in 1995. TOGAF's objective is to facilitate a broad range framework to develop architectures for enterprises and specifically for e-governments (Boyce, 2008). A main area of TOGAF is Architecture Development Method (ADM) that describes the comprehensive processes from scratch to certain mature level (Sabine et al., 2009). Enterprise Continuum (EC) is very useful feature of TOGAF. ADM and EC facilitate the requirements of a large organization such as e-government where number of agencies and sub-national organizations are engaged. ADM is based on feedback of experienced architectural practitioners. It suggests an approach for developing the enterprise architecture, and integrates the components of TOGAF. The Enterprise Continuum is an important component for the communication and understanding. This is a "framework-within-a-framework."

e-Government requires enterprise continuum for its NEA implementation and also needs to develop common understanding among all the stakeholders.

E-Devolution and TOGAF

TOGAF is based on the following four architecture domains with respect to e-devolution.

- **Business Architecture** aims to address the strategy, policy, governance, organization, and business processes of the different government services. Reference to TOGAF as NEA, devolution architecture can also be easily explained here as shown in Figure 8. Roles of Federal Government and sub-national for e-government can be documented here by considering the political, fiscal and administrative decentralization (Perks & Beveridge, 2004).
- **Applications Architecture** is the showcase for the technical specifications of application systems to be deployed. Most important sub domain of this architecture is the integration specifications. Centralized applications at Federal level have to be integrated with applications that are used at local level as shown in Figure 8.
- **Data Architecture** includes the data sources of organization. In case of NEA, centralized and local databases should be documented with the comprehensive policies regarding data usage, ownership, updating and integration. Figure 8 shows that data architecture may be designed under the guidelines of business architecture.
- **Technical Architecture** focuses the ICT infrastructure including hardware, software and bandwidth necessary for electronic services to all stakeholders of e-government. Figure 8 shows all IT infrastructure resources of federal and sub-national governments under the perspective of business architecture. (Nakakawa, Bommel, & Proper, 2009).

Business architecture is the leading architecture among other architectures. Devolution plans, legislations policies and strategies can be addressed at this architecture level and data, application and technology architectures may be organized under the shadow of this business architecture.

Federal Enterprise Architecture Framework (FEAF)

United States is the pioneer in EA technologies that was triggered by the Clinger-Cohen Act (Liimatainen et al., 2007). Federal CIO (Chief Information Officers) Council of USA introduced "Federal Enterprise Architecture Framework"

Figure 8. Devolution aspect in TOGAF

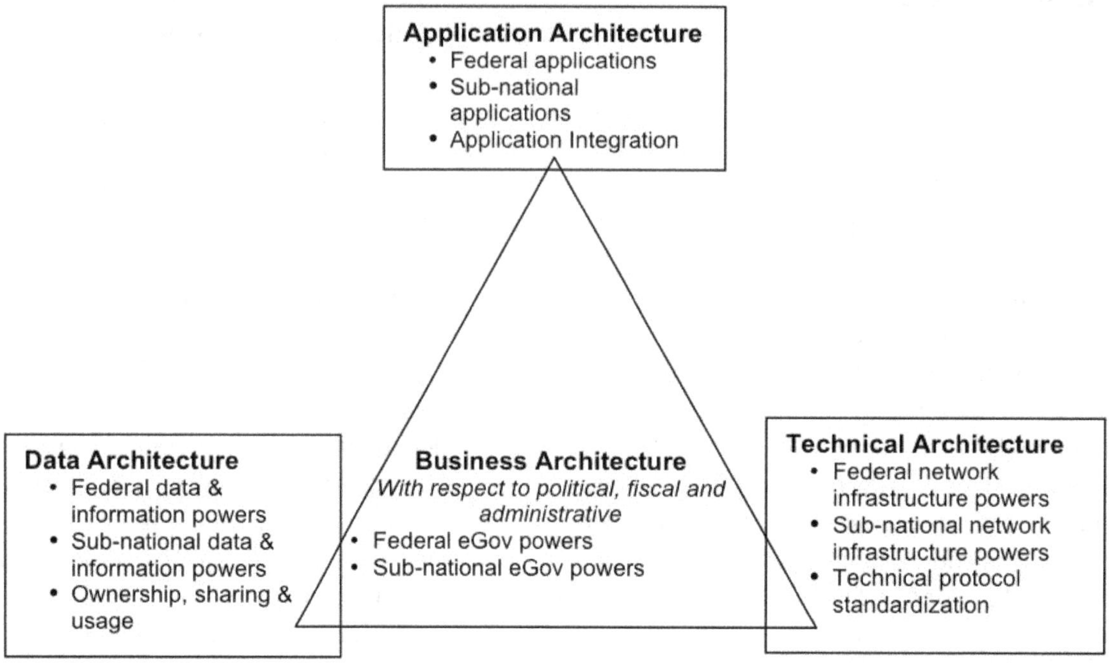

(FEAF) Version 1.1 (FEAF, 1999) for developing EA for federal agencies. The FEAF aims to provide a standard for developing and documenting architecture explanations.

A few countries are in the process to following this framework as NEA such as Australia. It evolved from Zachman framework. The FEAF currently includes the first three columns of the Zachman framework and the Spewak EA planning methodology. Table 1 shows FEAF matrix derived from Zachman Framework. There are three columns common in both frameworks i-e What: Data Architecture, How: Application Architecture and Where: Technology Architecture. The main objective of this framework is sharing information and resources across federal agencies, reduce costs, and improve citizen services.

FEAF architecture domains are business, data, applications, and technology. The Federal Enterprise Architecture Framework is built using fol-

Table 1. FEAF Architecture Matrix (Source: CIOC, 2001)

Zachman Columns	**What**	**How**	**Where**
FEAF Columns	**Data Architecture**	**Application Architecture**	**Technology Architecture**
Planner Perspective	List of Business Objects	List of Business Processes	List of Business Locations
Owner Perspective	Semantic Model	Business Process Model	Business Logistics System
Designer Perspective	Logical Data Model	Application Architecture	System Geographic Deployment Architecture
Builder Perspective	Physical Data Model	Systems Design	Technology Architecture
Subcontractor Perspective	Data Dictionary	Programs	Network Architecture

lowing reference models (Bellman & Rausch, 2004):

- Performance Reference Model (PRM)
- Business Reference Model (BRM)
- Service Component Reference Model (SCRM)
- Data Reference Model (DRM)
- Technical Reference Model (TRM)

BRM is the leading reference model among the other reference models. This reference model is responsible for the role of federal, state and local level governments and agencies to deliver services to citizens, providing support, adoption of service channels and management of government resources as shown in Figure 9. All other reference models should be aligned as per BRM.

E-Devolution and FEAF

Primarily FEAF has been designed and developed for federal agencies. However, it can be implemented for states and local government level. Following reference models may also support the effective decentralization.

Performance Reference Model (PRM)

PRM aims to assess the performance of key ICT funding and their role in organizational performance. The PRM has following three main purposes (OMB, 2007):

- Help produce enhanced performance information to improve strategic and daily decision-making;
- Improve the alignment and better articulate the contribution of inputs to outputs and outcomes, thereby creating a clear "line of sight" to desired results; and
- Identify performance improvement opportunities that span traditional organizational structures and boundaries (OMB, 2007).

Reference to the devolution approach, performance of federal and sub-national agencies

Figure 9. Devolution aspect in FEAF

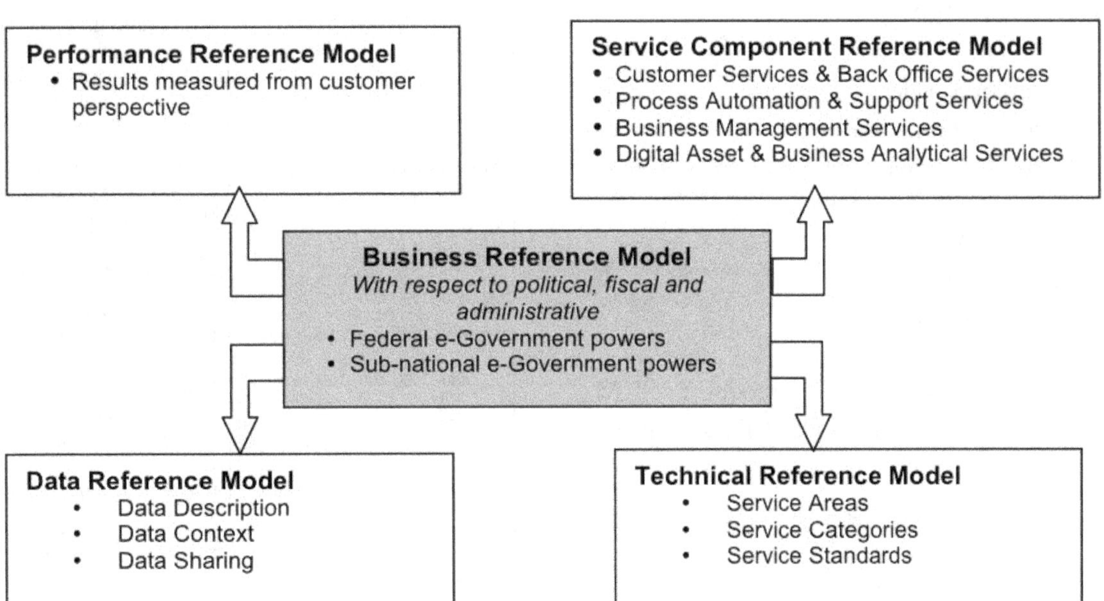

can easily be assessed by the implementation of the PRM.

Business Reference Model (BRM)

BRM is the leading reference model that explains all business operations of federal government and its agencies. This reference model consists of four areas (OMB, 2007):

- Services for Citizens
- Mode of Delivery
- Support Delivery of Services
- Management of Government Resources

Devolution of e-government can be addressed at this reference model. Role of federal and sub-national governments regarding Electronic Service Delivery (ESD) may be defined here as shown in Table 2.

Service Component Reference Model (SRM)

SRM is responsible for all domains including applications, modules and their integrations to deliver services. Following are the service domains of SRM (OMB, 2007):

- Customer Services
- Process Automation Services
- Business Management Services
- Digital Asset Services
- Business Analytical Services
- Back Office Services
- Support Services

Reference to the devolution model for SRM, all service domains can be distributed among central and sub-national level agencies as shown in Table 3.

Data Reference Model (DRM)

DRM is the technical reference model dedicated for all data management affairs. DRM's three standardization areas are (OMB, 2007):

- Data Description
- Data Context
- Data Sharing

Reference to decentralization, degree of devolution in superior layer BRM will reflect in the lower technical layers. Data architecture is significant in terms of data ownership, sharing, updating, integration and usage for federal and sub-national level.

Table 2. Functions of BRM

Function	Description
Services for Citizen	Selection of services to be online through centralized, decentralized or partial de-centralized (centralized online front end while Decentral-ized verifications, physical attendance, tariff of service charges and back office operation
Mode of Delivery	Centralized online mode of delivery or Decentralized of-fline mode of delivery Delivery mode on mobile, call center services, kiosks etc.
Support Delivery of Services	Centralized online support of services Call center services Technical support Decentralized offline support of services like legislative relations, planning, resource allocation
Management of Government Resources	Devolved administration powers Devolved financial powers

Table 3. Functions of SRM

Function	Description
Customer Services	Centralized Customer Relationship Management (CRM) Decentralized: Local Kiosks for customer services
Process Automation Services	Centralized tracking and workflows
	Decentralized operations and reports
Business Management Services	Decentralized organizational and investment management. Devolved Supply Chain Management (SCM) among central and sub-national agencies
Digital Asset Services	Devolved roles for content, document, knowledge and record management
Business Analytical Services	Centralized or decentralized analysis, statistics, visualization, knowledge discovery and business intelligence
Back Office Services	Decentralized including data updation, verification, human resources, financial management etc.
Support Services	Centralized online efforts
	Decentralized offline efforts

Technical Reference Model (TRM)

The TRM is a technical framework that classifies the standards and technologies to support and facilitate the e-services (OMB, 2007). The TRM consists of:

- Service Areas
- Service Categories
- Service Standards

This reference model explains the details about the services including categories and standards (mandatory and optional) for federal and sub-national levels.

Evaluation of NEA

Evaluation of NEA is the most important step of the EA implementation and its sustainability. Continuous assessment is a prerequisite for the improvement in EA program. Governments have to evaluate their investment and efforts spent for the implementation of NEA. There is a lack of a comprehensive model for the benefit evaluation. Governments face various problems in evaluation and measurement of costs and benefits (Liimatainen, 2008). Evaluation has been studied from many perspectives. Organization for Economic Co-operation and Development (OECD) has published several evaluations for distinct e-governments and country comparison reports. Surveys of NEA have been scattered and unrelated (Kostoska, Gusev, & Kiroski, 2010). Evaluation model may aim to assess the following objectives (Liimatainen, 2008):

- reduced costs (no duplication of efforts, sharing of common resources)
- providing a complete status of the enterprise,
- assessment of business-IT alignment,
- improved change management,
- improved risk management,
- improved interoperability and integration, and
- shortened cycle times

Above mentioned evaluation objectives are not limited. Referring to the "International Enterprise Architecture survey, 2006," approximately 45% of the countries are measuring EA performance including USA, Switzerland, Japan, Taiwan and Denmark (Christiansen & Gøtze, 2006).

SUMMARY

E-Government implementations can be categorized either demand-based or architecture based.

This chapter introduces the concept of National Enterprise Architecture (NEA) and emphasizes its importance. Adoption of NEA by different countries is also briefly discussed. A National Enterprise Architecture based approach provides a number of benefits, including institutionalization of top level strategic planning, standardized development across all levels of e-government, sustainability of e-government projects when governments change, cost reduction by sharing resources and better return on investment. A review of e-government implementations of different countries indicates that governments adopt either a centralized, decentralized or a devolved governing structure based on their strongly federated, weakly federated or independent governance models. Decentralized and devolved implementations require political, fiscal and administrative decentralization or devolution. In order to effectively reap the benefits of the National Enterprise Architecture it is recommended that consensus shall be built among all major stakeholders along with a legislative support at political, fiscal, and administrative levels.

This chapter also discusses five different enterprise architecture frameworks in light of devolved e-government. Zachman architecture is the pioneer and is reflected in the implementation of majority of the NEAs. All of these frameworks can be implemented for three different governance structures. RM-ODP and TOGAF are also generic architectures and frameworks that may be implemented on any governing structure. However the Collaborative Network approach is more appropriate for countries having decentralized or independent governing model.

The NEAs are approaching a maturity stage. It is now needed to evaluate these NEA investments and efforts and assess their maturity level.

ACKNOWLEDGMENT

Services of Sabahat Kashif, Farwa Ali and Shaista Atif are appreciated.

REFERENCES

Aagesen, G., van Veenstra, A. F., Janssen, M., & Krogstie, J. (2011). *The entanglement of enterprise architecture and IT-Governance: The cases of Norway and the Netherlands*. Paper presented at the Proceedings of the 2011 44th Hawaii International Conference on System Sciences.

Bellman, B., & Rausch, F. (2004). *Enterprise architecture for e-government* (pp. 48–56). Electronic Government.

Boyce, R. (2008). *TOGAF The open group architecture framework 100 success secrets - 100 most asked questions: The missing TOGAF guide on how to achieve and then sustain superior enterprise architecture execution*. Emereo Pty Ltd..

Bram, K., & Janssen, M. (2008). *Stage models for creating joined-up government: From local to nation-wide integration*. Paper presented at the Proceedings of the 2008 international conference on Digital government research, Montreal, Canada.

BTEP. (2004). *GSRM service reference patterns*.

Camarinha-Matos, L., & Afsarmanesh, H. (2006a). Towards a reference model for collaborative networked organizations. Information technology for balanced manufacturing systems (pp. 193-202).

Camarinha-Matos, L., & Afsarmanesh, H. (2006b). towards a reference model for collaborative networked organizations (pp. 193-202).

Camarinha-Matos, L. M., & Afsarmanesh, H. (2008). ARCON reference models for collaborative networks. Collaborative networks: Reference modeling (pp. 83-112).

Cheema, G. S., & Rondinelli, D. A. (Eds.). (1983). *Decentralization and development: Policy implementation in developing countries.* London: Sage Publications.

Christiansen, P. E., & Gøtze, J. (2006). *International enterprise architecture survey - Trends in governmental enterprise architecture on a national level.* Association of Enterprise Architects. Retrieved from http://www.easurvey.org

CIO. (2008). *Government of Canada profile of information technology (IT) services.*

CIOC. (2001). *A practical guide for federal enterprise architecture.*

Daniel, J. Veit. (2009). *Can national e-government standards find acceptance?* Paper presented at the 42nd Hawaii International Conference on System Sciences.

Darby, J., Muscatelli, A., & Roy, G. (2003). Fiscal decentralization in Europe: A review of recent experience. *Regional Public Finance: European Research in Regional Science, 13.*

Espadas, J., Romero, D., Concha, D., & Molina, A. (2008). Using the Zachman framework to achieve enterprise integration based-on business process driven modelling. On the move to meaningful internet systems: OTM 2008 workshops (pp. 283-293).

Farooq, M. K., Shamail, S., & Awais, M. M. (2006). *Devolution of e-governance among multilevel government structure.* Paper presented at the Innovations in Information Technology.

Farooq, M. K., Shamail, S., & Awais, M. M. (2008). Devolution in a virtual enterprise. In Camarinha-Matos, L., & Picard, W. (Eds.), *Pervasive collaborative networks* (*Vol. 283*, pp. 433–440). Springer Boston. doi:10.1007/978-0-387-84837-2_45.

Farooq, M. K., Shamail, S., & Awais, M. M. (2008). *Reference model for devolution in e-governance.* Paper presented at the Proceedings of the 2nd International Conference on Theory and Practice of Electronic Governance, Cairo, Egypt.

FEAF. (1999). *Federal enterprise architecture framework version 1.1.*

Ferguson, I., & Chandrasekharan, C. (2004). Paths and pitfalls of decentralization. *ITTO Tropical Forest Update*, *14*(3), 1–7.

Furuholt, B., & Wahid, F. (2008). *E-government challenges and the role of political leadership in Indonesia: The case of Sragen.* Paper presented at the Hawaii International Conference on System Sciences, Proceedings of the 41st Annual.

Gil-Garcia, J. R., & Luna-Reyes, L. F. (2006). *Enacting inter-organizational e-government in the Mexican federal government.* Paper presented at the Proceedings of the 2006 international conference on Digital government research, San Diego, California.

Goldfinch, S., Gauld, R., & Herbison, P. (2009). The participation divide? Political participation, trust in government, and e-government in Australia and New Zealand. *Australian Journal of Public Administration*, *68*(3), 333–350. doi:10.1111/j.1467-8500.2009.00643.x.

Guijarro, L. (2007). Interoperability frameworks and enterprise architectures in e-government initiatives in Europe and the United States. *Government Information Quarterly*, *24*(1), 89–101. doi:10.1016/j.giq.2006.05.003.

Heeks, R. (1999). Centralised vs. decentralised management of public information systems: A core-periphery solution. *Information Systems for Public Sector Management Working Paper Series*. Institute for Development Policy and Management.

Janssen, M., & Hjort-Madsen, K. (2007). *Analyzing enterprise architecture in national governments: The cases of Denmark and the Netherlands.* Paper presented at the System Sciences, 2007. HICSS 2007. 40th Annual Hawaii International Conference on System Sciences.

Kostoska, M., Gusev, M., & Kiroski, K. (2010). *Evaluation methodology for national enterprise architecture frameworks*. Paper presented at the ICT Innovations 2010. Hjort-Madsen, K. (2009). *Enterprise architecture in government: Fad or future?* Paper presented at the 42nd Hawaii International Conference on System Sciences.

Lazer, D., & Binz-Scharf, M. C. (2004). *Managing novelty and cross-agency cooperation in digital government*. Paper presented at the Proceedings of the 2004 annual national conference on Digital government research, Seattle, WA.

Liimatainen, K. (2008). *Evaluating benefits of government enterprise architecture*. Paper presented at the IRIS31 - The 31st Information Systems Research Seminar in Scandinavia, ÅRE SWEDEN. http://www.iris31.se/papers/IRIS31-059.pdf

Liimatainen, K., Hoffmann, M., & Heikkilä, J. (2007, October). *Overview of enterprise architecture work in 15 countries, Finnish enterprise architecture research project*. Ministry of Finance, Finland. Retrieved from www.vm.fi/julkaisut

Meersman, B., & Vandenborre, F. (2006). *The commission enterprise IT architecture framework (CEAF) Version 1.*

Meneklis, B., Kaliontzoglou, A., Polemi, D., & Douligeris, C. (2005). Applying the ISO RM-ODP standard in e-government. E-government: Towards electronic democracy (pp. 213-224).

Müller, W. (2005). *eGovCH – The Swiss egovernment architecture.*

Nakakawa, A., Bommel, P., & Proper, H. A. E. (2009). Quality enhancement in creating enterprise architecture: Relevance of academic models. In Practice advances in enterprise engineering II (pp. 109-133).

NORA. (2007). *Dutch government reference architecture [NORA].*

OMB. (2007). *FEA consolidated reference model version 2.3.*

Parker, A. N. (1995). *Decentralization: The way forward for rural development?* (1475). World Bank Policy Research Working Paper No. 1475 Retrieved from http://ssrn.com/abstract=620575

Perks, C., & Beveridge, T. (2004). Opportunities, solutions, and migration planning. Guide to enterprise IT architecture (pp. 360-391).

Pheng, T. (2007). *Enterprise architecture in the Singapore government. Handbook of enterprise systems architecture in practice* (pp. 129–143). IGI Global. doi:10.4018/978-1-59904-189-6.ch007.

Putman, J. R. (2001). *Architecting with RM-ODP*. Prentice Hall.

Rico, D. F. (2008). *Optimizing the ROI of enterprise architecture using real options. End user computing challenges and technologies: Emerging tools and applications* (pp. 48–56). IGI Global.

Sabine, B., Alexander, M. E., Florian, M., Ren, R., & Schweda, C. M. (2009). *Using enterprise architecture management patterns to complement TOGAF*. Paper presented at the Proceedings of the 2009 IEEE International Enterprise Distributed Object Computing Conference (edoc 2009) - Volume 00.

SAGA. (2008). *Standards and architectures for egovernment applications.*

Saha, P. (2009). *A methodology for government transformation with enterprise architecture. Advances in government enterprise architecture* (pp. 1–29). IGI Global.

Saha, P. (2010). Enterprise architecture as platform for connected government.

Schekkerman, J. (2005). Trends in enterprise architecture (1.0 ed.).

Shah, A. (2006). Fiscal decentralization and macroeconomic management. *International Tax and Public Finance*, *13*(4), 437–462. doi:10.1007/s10797-006-8948-1.

Song, H., & Song, Y.-T. (2010). *Enterprise architecture institutionalization and assessment*. Paper presented at the Proceedings of the 2010 IEEE/ACIS 9th International Conference on Computer and Information Science.

Steward, A. (2011). *Australian government architecture reference models version 3.0*.

UNDESA. (2012). United nations e-government survey 2012: E-government for the people. Retrieved December 4, 2012, from http://www.un.org/en/development/desa/publications/connecting-governments-to-citizens.html

UNINOVA, & UvA. (2006). *D52.2: Rough reference model for collaborative networks*. European Collaborative Networked Organizations Leadership Initiative (ECOLEAD).

Virili, F., & Sorrentino, M. (2002). Reconfiguring the political value chain: The potential role of web services. In Electronic government (pp. 227-230).

Weill, P., & Ross, J. W. (2004). *IT governance: How top performers manage it decision rights for superior results*. Harvard Business School Press.

White-Paper. (2003). *White paper on enterprise architecture*.

Zachman, J. A. (1987). A framework for information systems architecture. *IBM Systems Journal*, *26*(3). doi:10.1147/sj.263.0276.

ADDITIONAL READING

Bernus, P., Nemes, L., & Schmidt, G. (2003). *Handbook on enterprise architecture*. Springer. doi:10.1007/978-3-540-24744-9.

Frank, U. (2007). *Evaluation of reference models. Reference modeling for business systems analysis* (pp. 118–139). IGI Publishing.

Garson, G. D. (2004). The promise of digital government. Digital government: Principles and best practices (pp. 2-15).

Iyer, B., & Gottlieb, R. (2004). The four-domain architecture: An approach to support enterprise architecture design. *IBM Systems Journal*, *43*(3), 587–597. doi:10.1147/sj.433.0587.

Jonkers, H., Lankhorst, M. M., ter Doest, H. W. L., Arbab, F., Bosma, H., & Wieringa, R. J. (2006). Enterprise architecture: Management tool and blueprint for the organisation. *Information Systems Frontiers*, *8*(2), 63–66. doi:10.1007/s10796-006-7970-2.

McGovern, J. (2004). *A practical guide to enterprise architecture*. Prentice Hall.

Pereira, C. M., & Sousa, P. (2004). *A method to define an enterprise architecture using the Zachman framework*. Paper presented at the Proceedings of the 2004 ACM symposium on Applied computing.

Peristeras, V., & Tarabanis, K. (2000). Towards an enterprise architecture for public administration using a top-down approach. *European Journal of Information Systems*, *9*(4), 252–260. doi:10.1057/palgrave/ejis/3000378.

Rocheleau, B. A. (2006). *Public management information systems*. Idea Group Pub..

Saha, P. (2009). *Advances in government enterprise architecture*. Information Science Reference.

Schekkerman, J. (2003). *How to survive in the jungle of enterprise architecture frameworks: Creating or choosing an enterprise architecture framework*. Trafford Publishing.

Sessions, R. (2007). *Comparison of the top four enterprise architecture methodologies*.

Spewak, S. H., Hill, S. C., & Zachman, J. (1993). *Enterprise architecture planning: Developing a blueprint for data, applications, and technology*. QED Publishing Group.

Tambouris, E., & Wimmer, M. (2004). *Online one-stop government: A single point of access to public services. Electronic government strategies and implementation* (pp. 5–44). Hershey, PA: Idea Group Publishing.

Weerakkody, V., Janssen, M., & Hjort-Madsen, K. (2007). Integration and enterprise architecture challenges in E-government: A European perspective. [IJCEC]. *International Journal of Cases on Electronic Commerce*, *3*(2), 13–35. doi:10.4018/jcec.2007040102.

KEY TERMS AND DEFINITIONS

Architecture: Architecture is an approach to present structures at macro level. This structure masks all the detailed operational issues for the common user of the services that the structure can provide.

ARCON: A Reference Model for Collaboration Networks.

CN: Collaborative Network.

CNO: Collaborative Network Organization.

Devolution: It refers to meaningful transfer of authority to be acceptable and to work effectively. There types of devolutions are common such as political, fiscal and administrative.

Enterprise Architecture: This is a business issue and covers business process integration and business process standardization.

e-Services: Electronic or online services such as citizen registration, marriage certificate, death certificate, driving license, payment of taxes, utility bills etc.

FEAF: Federal Enterprise Architecture Framework.

G2B: Government to Business, group of services related to government and business sector such as taxes, NOCs, different registrations, import, export etc.

G2C: Government to Citizen, group of services related to government and citizen such as citizen registration, marriage certificate, death certificate, driving license, payment of taxes, utility bills etc.

G2E: Government to Employee, group of services related to government and government employee such as, recruitment, salary, allowances, leave, transfer, retirement, pension etc.

G2G: Government to Government, group of inter-governmental services such as development & non development funding, revenue collection, planning etc.

NEA: National Enterprise Architecture.

RM-ODP: Reference Model for Open Distributed Processing.

TOGAF: The Open Group Architectural Framework.

Viewpoint: One aspect of complex system (definition as per information systems).

Chapter 8
Legal Framework for the E-Taxation in Turkey

Güneş Çetin Gerger
Celal Bayar University, Turkey

ABSTRACT

This study analyzes the legal framework of e-taxation in the Turkish Republic. Tax service is commonly provided by using ICT in many countries. In e-government applications in Turkey, provision of e-tax service is one of the leading projects. Among the members of OECD, electronic tax return, payment systems and tax automation systems generated in this area have gained an increasing importance. Taxpayers fill the declarations electronically and also pay tax debts without going to the tax offices. E-taxation system is becoming widespread in Turkey. Implementation of the system in Turkey started in 1998 with VEDOP I and continued with 2004 VEDOP II and 2007 VEDOP III Projects. These applications are legislated by the Tax Procedure Law in Turkey. Thus, legal regulations on electronic recording are established on a legal basis. In this study, e-government tax applications in the Turkish Tax Law (e-tax return, e-books, e-signature, e-audit) and legal base of this application is examined. Information is given on how it is implemented by means of information technologies in Turkey. The main purpose of the study is to examine what legal regulations were enacted for registering and taxation in the use of information technologies and to determine the current situation in Turkey.

INTRODUCTION

E-Tax system is an important online service that enables citizens to file their tax returns online. These systems are particularly favorable for governments because they avoid many of the mistakes taxpayers make in manual filings. Also, through data matching, they help to prevent tax evasion. E-taxation is mostly common in countries such as the USA, Australia, Canada, Finland, France and Germany. The concept of electronic tax administration is a concept that was initially put forth by

DOI: 10.4018/978-1-4666-4245-4.ch008

the American Tax Administration (IRS-Internal Revenue Service). In 2000, IRS, which continued its activities within the framework of its strategic plan, sent returns to more than 35 million Americans in electronic form fast, reliably, accurately, and in an easy to reach way using the IRS electronic filing (e-file) system, which was an alternative to paper statement. Organizations such as OECD, WTO, G8 and EU also attach importance to the concept of e-government and e-governance. After all, this process has become a requirement of the democratic rule of law. E-democracy has led to the implementation of increasingly flourishing public projects. E-taxation enhances the efficiency of taxation in the realization of common practices of national and international platforms through the sharing of information. Taxpayers filling the declarations electronically and also paying tax debts without going to the tax offices have led e-taxation system to become highly desirable in Turkey. The general perspective of this chapter is to provide information about e-government applications and e-taxation system in Turkey in some detail, answering questions such as: how e-taxation legal regulations are organized in Turkish Tax Law and which e-taxation applications are mostly used in Turkey. The chapter discusses the legal regulations in some more detail.

BACKROUND

ICT helps to lead efficiency, transparency and contribute to the improvement of tax assessment and collection system. The implementation of ICT based tax assessment and collection system contributes to the improvement of good financial governance the transparent and responsible management of public resources (Napierala & Kiefer, 2009).

Electronic tax filing systems are defined as e-government applications that have now spread all over the word in a short time. In order to avoid a lot of mistakes of taxpayer in tax return fillings, governments especially prefer those systems helping them to prevent tax evasion by data matching. Using developed electronic tax filings, the data warehouses let tax inspectors to analyze declarations more intensively and enable policy makers to develop fairer and more effective tax policies (Dinara et al., 2012).

In order to give opportunity to enable the country to perform Information Society standards, e-Transformation Turkey project was started in 2003. The State Planning Organization (SPO) of Turkey was responsible for project coordination. The preparation and activation of Information Society Strategy (ISS) which includes 4 years period, from 2006 to 2010, is the main step towards the information society (Medeni, 2011, p. 1). In March 2005, the Short Term Action Plan was called e-Transformation Turkey. 2005 Action Plan was the second step of that. Different activities on international technology were either recommended or monitored for the progress. Another initiative definition of Information Society Strategy in connection with the short-term targets of the action plans of the e-Transformation Turkey Project was initiated in 2005. It was a step further to give opportunity to Turkey to get both the benefit from ICT and identify the middle and long term strategies and also goals for the realization of transformation.

Finally, the High Planning Council in July 2006 adopted Turkey's Information Society Strategy (2006-2010). The Strategy includes two main priorities regarding e-Government: one is citizen-oriented service transformation and the other is the modernization of Public Administration (E-Government Practice Editorial Team, 2010).

Law No. 877 dated 28 July 2006 is the law by which the Turkish Grand National Assembly approved the Ninth Development Plan (2007–2013) which constitutes Turkey's main policy document. In the section 'Ensuring the Dissemination and Effectiveness of e-Government Applications,' to ensure the provision of public services to citizens in a fast, continuous and large available manner, the plan sets out Turkey's high-level e-Government policy approach, emphasizing that information and communication technologies will be used at the highest level.

Electronic taxation applications constitute one of the important e-government projects in Turkey. VEDOP Project which was carried out by Ministry of Finance is the most important electronic taxation project. Ministry of Finance was adapted this project at 1998. Electronic taxation added effectiveness to the taxation processes in Turkey. Legal base of these applications are improving continuously. In this study we try to give information about legal improvements and IT innovations in case of taxation in Turkey.

E- GOVERNMENT APPLICATIONS IN TURKEY

E-government has become a key concept to renovate and modernize public services covering many activities (Baştan & Gökbunar, 2004). Developments in information and communication technologies in Turkey increased the importance of e-government applications. E-government applications are cost saving, efficient, transparent, and fast and effective tool both for the individual and the state. Developments of e-government applications began in 2000, in Turkey. The main highlighted projects in the field of e-government applications in Turkey are as follows: Central Population Administration System (MERNİS), Identity Sharing System (KPS), in the field of Finance Tax Offices Automation Project (VEDOP), e-Budget, Accounting Office Automation System (Say2000i), the Social Security field of e-disclosure, in the field of Customs and Foreign Trade Customs Modernization Project (GIMOP), Computerized Customs Activities (BİLGE), Customs Data Warehousing System (GÜVAS), Custom Doors Security Systems (GÜMBİS), in the field of Local Government Local Information and Local Net projects, in the field of Justice National Judiciary Network Project (UYAP), in the field of Security Police Information Network (POLNET), in the field of Health National Health Information System (USBS) (Hepaksaz, 2012).

The e-government applications in Turkey at institutions and establishments were classified with functional classification and their web sites were examined in the annex 1. The following classification related organizations, generally providing information from their websites, ability to downloading the required forms, books and reports from web sites, has the ability to make query on the internet. Also, some of them have the opportunity to realize the service completely over the internet (DPT, 2005, p. 141-203).

The "e-transformation Turkey project" was developed in 2003 for modernization of the public sector.

The e-Transformation Turkey Project aims to carry out the process of transformation into an information society in a harmonious and integrated structure all over the society with all citizens, enterprises and public segments (SPO, 2006, p. 1).

A lot of e-government projects can be succeeded in the context of the e-transformation policy in Turkey, and the official e-government portal (http://www.turkiye.gov.tr) was opened on 18th December 2008 by the Prime Minister of Turkey. Republic of Turkey Official E-Government Portal is prepared by TURKSAT: International cable and satellite operator (Yeloglu & Sagsan, 2009). Best practices are:

- **Tax Services:** www.gib.gov.tr
- **Social Security Premiums:** www.sgk.gov.tr
- **Judiciary SMS Information Services (UYAP):** www.uyap.gov.tr
- **Prime Ministry Communication Center (BİMER):** www.basbakanlik.gov.tr (SPO, 2011, p. 191).

E-Government Applications: Legal Basis in Turkey

Major regulations and recent changes in the Constitution and the laws related to e-government applications in Turkey are now discussed, as follows.

Right of Information Act

Right to Information Act (Law No: 4982) was enacted in October 2003 and went into effect on April 2004. It was initially prepared by the Ministry of Justice and was introduced to the Parliament on 25 June, 2003. The Act was supplemented by a circular on 'The exercise of the right of petition and access to information', issued by The Prime Ministry (No: 2004/12, Republic of Turkey, Official Gazette, 24 January 2004, Number: 25356).

Data Protection/Privacy Legislation

Section 5 of the 1982 Turkish Constitution is entitled, "Privacy and Protection of Private Life." Article 20 of the Turkish Constitution deals with "Privacy of the Individual's Life," and states: "Everyone has the right to demand respect for his private and family life. Privacy of individual and family life cannot be violated. Exceptions necessitated by judiciary investigation and prosecution are reserved. Unless there exists a decision duly passed by a judge in cases explicitly defined by law, and unless there exists an order of an agency authorized by law in cases where delay is deemed prejudicial, neither the person nor the private papers, nor belongings of an individual shall be searched nor shall they be seized." Article 22 states: "Secrecy of communication is fundamental. Communication shall not be impeded nor its secrecy be violated, unless there exists a decision duly passed by a judge in cases explicitly defined by law, and unless there exists an order of an agency authorized by law in cases where delay is deemed prejudicial. Public establishments or institutions where exceptions to the above may be applied will be defined by law."

E-Commerce Legislation

Due to the recent expansion in the global trend towards electronic commerce, new means for supporting e-Commerce have been introduced in Turkey. Particular arrangements regarding e-Commerce have been introduced within Law no. 4822 ("Law on Consumer Protection"), which came into force on the 23rd of June 2003. This law has basically enlarged the definition of "goods" for the purpose of Turkish Consumer Law to cover electronic products, and added distance-selling contracts (concluded through electronic means) into the scope of the Consumer Protection Law (Law no. 4077).

E-Communications Legislation

Electronic Communications Law, enacted and put into force on 10 November 2008, replaced most of the provisions in the current laws regarding electronic communications. The law provides the basis for alignment with the EU framework. According to this law, the former 'Telecommunication Authority' has been now renamed as 'Information Technologies and Communication Authority,' referred to as Law no. 4502.

E-Signatures Legislation

The Law no. 5070 on electronic signatures was enacted in 2004. The purpose of this law is to define the principles for the legal and technical aspects and application of electronic signatures. The law covers the legal status of electronic signatures, operations concerning electronic signatures and the activities of Electronic Certificate Service Providers (ECSPs). This establishes that qualified electronic signatures produced according to the identified procedures have the same legal impact with that of handwritten signatures.

E-Procurement Legislation

In accordance with Turkey's Information Society Strategy, the Public Procurement Agency has been granted the responsibility for establishing electronic public procurement and purchasing systems. The amendment of the Public Procurement Law with the Law No. 5812, that will enable the implementation of electronic public procurement, was published on 5 December 2008.

PUBLIC SECTOR ICT INVESTMENT: 2002-2011

E-Government applications and services are implemented through ICT investments made by public agencies. The ICT investments of central government agencies have been regularly monitored since 2002. An approximately 4-fold increase took place in central government ICT investments within a period of 10 years. The ICT investment allocation, which was about 526 million TL at 2011 prices, reached 2 billion TL in 2011. ICT investments have displayed a continuous increase compared to previous years, except for 2008 (Figure 1). Especially the projects in the education sector had a major influence in the rapid increase experienced in 2011. The total project amount of 210 projects included in the 2011 Investment Program is 4.9 billion TL (SPO, 2011, p. 74).

The electronic taxation which is based on the first three of 20 applications of e-government applications is according to the provisions of the European Union regulations, as presented in Table 1 and Table 2.

Income tax, corporate tax and value added tax online sophistication scores are high among the 20 basic public e-services in Turkey. Turkey's e-Services score 80% on usability and 100% on user satisfaction monitoring (as compared to the EU averages of 79% and 80% respectively). For e-Services, usability referring to SPO (2011, p. 195), we note the following:

- **Transparency of Service Delivery:** Rated at 89% (EU+: 52%)

Figure 1. Public ICT investment allowance (State Planning Organization, Information Society Statistics of Turkey, 2011)

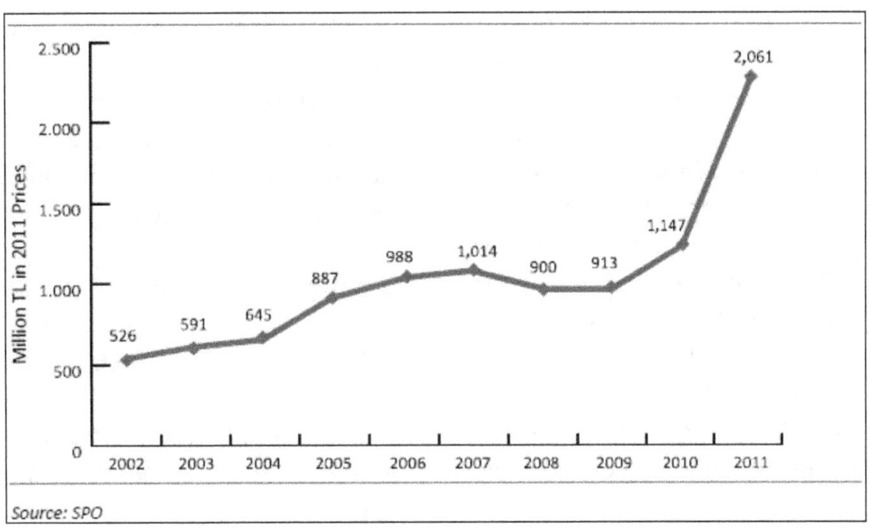

Table 1. E-taxation is among 20 basic public services in Turkey (SPO, 2011)

PUBLIC SERVICE DEFINITION SERVICES PROVIDED IN TURKEY	
SERVICES TO CITIZENS	
1.Income taxes	Declaration, accrual, and payment transactions can be done online using e-Declaration.
2.Corporate tax	Statement, accrual, and payment transactions can be done online within the scope of e-Declaration.
3.Value added tax	Statement, accrual, and payment transactions can be done online within the scope of e-Declaration.

- **Multi-Channel Service Provision:** Rated at 90% (EU+: 88%)
- **Privacy and Data Protection:** Rated at 78% (EU+: 90%)
- **Ease of Use of Services:** Rated at 94% (EU+: 80%)

E-TAXATION IN TURKEY

Tax and customs transactions are being offered at the maximum level possible, and work is in progress on an e-government portal where citizens will be offered integrated services from a single point (SPO, 2006, p. 13). E taxation is an e-government application which provides assessment and collection of taxes via online communication tools and internet connected computers without going to the tax office. In Turkey, Ministry of Finance effectively uses e-finance applications. Revenue Administration entered in the process of e-taxation with VEDOP I (1998), continued during VEDOP II (2004), VEDOP III (2007) projects and has followed many applications that is used in many OECD countries widespread such as e-statement, e-invoicing (Çetin, 2010, p. 80). Many new applications in the field of taxation like e-statement, e-books, e-billing, e-assessment, e-sheets, e-foreclosure were launched with these projects. These applications caused effective communication between taxpayers and tax administration. All of them create time and cost savings.

Development Process of E-Finance Applications: 2000-2012

E-finance applications emerged in Turkey in the early 2000s, and the development of it has made a huge acceleration during last ten years. The opening of e-government gate in 2007, both legal and IT infrastructure arrangements came to the fore in Turkey.

E-finance applications in Turkey began to be implemented with VEDOP projects. Table 3 shows the development of e-finance practices and legal infrastructure of e-taxation.

Classification of E-Finance Applications

E-taxation applications are listed below in Turkey. These are the backbone of e-taxation and VEDOP projects. These applications help to regulate tax system with ICT. There are short information and explanations in the Table 4.

E declaration system applications consist of two stages. Principally these are: the electronically submission of tax declaration indicating the amount of tax to Tax Office and paying the accrued tax via electronically devices without going to Tax Office Apart from those who do not have to go to Office to pay their taxes, national taxpayers who declare their tax, and are connected to fully-automated tax offices submit their tax declaration electronically.

Generally Electronic Bill Register System which enables the use of safe electronic e-bill in the context of some certain conditions and reduces obligation to archive the copy of the bill on a piece of paper, providing that the information on the bills arranged by the organizations in accordance with the identified standards transfers to Revenue Administration (GİB) on electronical

Table 2. Online sophistication scores of 20 basic public e-services in Turkey (SPO, 2011)

		Administration Level			
Services	Country Score	NUTS0	NUTS3	NUTS4	NUTS5a
		National	Provinces	Districts	Main Cities
Income taxes	100	100			
Job search services	100	100			
Social security benefits	90	100			
Unemployment benefits	100	100			
Child allowances	60				
Medical costs	100				
Student grants	100	100			
Personal Documents	80	100	25		
Passports	100	100			
Driver's license	60		25		
Vehicle registration	100	100	26		
Building license application	25		1	4	7
Corporate tax	100	100			
VAT	100	100			

environment. The arrangement in Tax Procedure Law Article 242 has been conducted in relation to e bill. In the context of Electronic bill Registration System (EFKS) which is the initial stage for e bill system, taxpayers involving in Electronic bill Registration System signed a protocol with revenue administration which both has to archive the bills organized in accordance and give the bills to recipients on paper environment or magnetic environment as well. Taxpayers involved in Electronic bill Registration System by means of signing protocol are brought to the public attention on website: http://www.efatura.gov.tr.

Finance Inspection Board Control Information System known "MTK DEBİS" is an electronic inspection (e- inspection) application inspecting works and operations of tax offices bookkeeping and national real estate offices more efficiently. MTK DEBİS, is an audit information system which is above sub-control systems, covers and also completes them (Kapanoglu et al., 2011).

DATA SECURITY IN E-GOVERNMENT APPLICATIONS

Data security is an important issue in e-government applications for users. Citizens are expected to protect their personal data when they pay tax, fulfilling legal obligations, and benefiting from social security services in the process. The main security problems in Turkey are presented in Figure 2.

Security problems are significant barriers for extensive use of ICT. The proportions of Internet users who experience security problems were 31%, 29%, 28.9%, and 46.8% in 2007, 2008, 2009, and 2010, respectively, as demonstrated in Figure 3. The high ratio of 2010 is striking. The security problems most frequently encountered by individuals were computer viruses and junk e-mail or e-mail spams that cause time and information losses (SPO, 2011, p. 31).

Table 3. Development process of e-finance applications in Turkey: 2000-2012 (Adapted from Hepaksaz, 2012)

01.01.2000	In the scope of Internet Tax Office related to taxpayer declarations; accrual, payment, debt, default fine, prohibition of foreign output data becomes questionable
01.09.2000	In the scope of Internet Tax Office, corporate taxpayers to be included
01.09.2001	In the scope of Internet Tax Office, income taxpayers to be included
30.12.2001 (24626 (Official Gazette)	Introduction of electronic book, electronic document and electronic records definitions (Arrangements made under Tax Procedure Code repeated 242/2 Article via 4731 of Law No. 4-E Article)
30.01.2003 (25009 Official Gazette)	SCT taxpayers' No. (I), (II) and (IV) declarations start sending out via internet tax office (SCT 3 Item No. General Communiqué)
04.12.2003 (25306 Official Gazette)	Entry into force of e-Transformation Turkey Project 2003-2004 (2003/48 by the Prime Ministry)
2004	Launching VEDOP II Project
23.01.2004 (25355 Official Gazette)	The Law of Electronic Signatures No 5070 adoption
23.01.2004 (25355 Official Gazette)	On Secure Electronic Signature regulation (The regulation in Law No 818 Code of Obligations Law No. 5070 article 22)
23.01.2004 (25355 Official Gazette)	About Secure Electronic Signature regulation (No. 1086 in accordance with Article 23 of the Civil Procedure Law, the regulations of Law No. 5070)
31.07.2004 (25539 Official Gazette)	E-Declaration on the implementation of legislation (Article 28 of the Law on Tax Procedure Paragraph added by Article 3 of Law No. 5228)
31.07.2004 (25539 Official Gazette)	The authorization of the Ministry of Finance on E-Declaration (Paragraph added with Article 8 of Law No. 5228 to Tax Procedure Law 257/4)
30.09.2004 (25599 Official Gazette)	Publication of the General Communiqué on Tax Procedure Law No. 340 related to E-Declaration return optionally via in electronic format.
Ocak-2005	The publication of SPO " e-Transformation Turkey Project Short-Term Action Plan Evaluation Report No. 4 "
03.03.2005 (25744 Official Gazette)	The publication of No. 346 Tax Procedure Law General Communiqué concerning obligatory e-declaration sending electronically.
21.07.2005 (25882 Official Gazette)	Demanding regret or spontaneously declarations regulation related granting in electronic form after the legal period pass (Tax Procedure Law 257/3. Amendment Law No. 5398 Article 23 / a)
21.07.2005 (25882 Official Gazette)	Failure to comply with the obligation tax returns are filed electronically related arrangements for special irregularity penalty has to be cut (Amendment with Law No. 5398 Article 23 in repeated 355 article of the Tax Procedure Law)
13.10.2005 (25965 Official Gazette)	Publication of Tax Code General Communiqué No. 351 concerning the declarations given after statutory period and penalty applications.
02.03.2006 (26096 Official Gazette)	Publication of 357 Tax Procedure Law General Communiqué concerning with declaration rates which must be given in electronic form for profits derived in 2005.
08.04.2006 (26133 Official Gazette)	E-foreclosure legislation on regulation (Amendment with Law No. 5479 Article 5 in No. 6183 Law on the procedures of collection of public receivables 79. article)
July-2006	Action entitled as" Practice of Electronic Book and Billing " in the No. 64 be included at "Information Society Strategy 2006-2010 Action Plan" .
11.07.2006 (26225 Official Gazette)	The publication of No. 361 Tax Procedure Law General Communiqué related with keeping on electronic Book, records and documents.
18.10.2007	Launching VEDOP-3 Project
30.01.2007 (26419 Official Gazette)	The publication of No. 440Tax Procedure Law General Communiqué concerning e-foreclosure

continued on following page

Table 3. Continued

01.02.2007 (26421 Official Gazette)	The publication of No. 367 Tax Procedure Law General Communiqué concerning Large Taxpayers Tax Administration Department of Istanbul taxpayers compulsory send all tax returns electronically.
01.03.2007 (26449 Official Gazette)	The publication of No. 368 Tax Procedure Law General Communiqué concerning issue the correction declarations electronically
28.06.2007 (26566 Official Gazette)	The publication of No. 373 Tax Procedure Law General Communiqué
30.06.2007 (26568 RG)	The publication of No. 1Collection General Communiqué concerning e- foreclosure
06.02.2008 (26779 Official Gazette)	The publication of No. 381 Tax Procedure Law General Communiqué concerning to send Ba and Bs Forms obligatory monthly
06.06.2008 (26898 Official Gazette)	Reorganization of the authority of Ministry of Finance about electronic books, documents and records (Arrangements made under Tax Procedure Law repeated 242/2-5 via Law No. 5766 Article17)
05.03.2010 (27512 Official Gazette)	The publication of No. 397 General Communiqué concerning implementation of e-invoicing and financial stamp
01.08.2010 (27659 Official Gazette)	Initiation of the practice of Electronic declaration (Law No. 107 / A added to Tax Procedure Law and Law No 6009 Article 7 added)
19.01.2011 (27820 Official Gazette)	Arrangements made in the Electronic Declaration (No. 7201 Changes to the law, Law No. 6099)
04.02.2011(27836 Official Gazette)	Regulation about safe electronic signature (The provision of No. 6098 New Turkish Code of Obligations article15)
25.02.2011 (27857 Official Gazette)	The regulation concerning the abolition of obligation of hanging tax board (Arrangements made by Law No. 6111 in Tax Procedure Law 5/4. article)

A decline was experienced in 2010 in the proportions of security problems most frequently mentioned in the whole year. However computer viruses and e-mail spam maintained their places on the first rank with 36.4% and 32%, respectively. As different from the other years, the problems concerning personal data were taken up with two separate answers and reservations about children were also included. According to this, the problems concerning personal data were stated to be "misuse of personal information sent over the Internet and other security violations" with 3.5% and "financial losses as a result of receiving fake messages or acquisition of personal data by being directed to fake websites" with 2.8%. The information security survey conducted by Tubitak Bilgem resulted as below.

Question: What do you think the most important lack of cyber security in our country is?

a. Institutions don't allocate enough manpower to ensure cyber security 27.66%

b. Cyber security is absence of an owner's supported by laws at the country level of 30%
c. Unconsciousness of end-users in this regard. 12.98%
d. Lack of sufficiently effective measures of service providers 5.96%
e. Cyber security not be addressed in our Education system 23.4%

Number of Voters: 470

A secure e-taxation in legal framework for operation in the field of cyber security will have a positive effect to users' e-taxation compliance.

Table 4. Classification of e-finance applications in Turkey

Internet Tax Office	It is a web- based application that all tax offices work as a unique tax Office in Turkey.
Electronic Declaration	E-declaration is transferred to the tax administration by those who prepare tax declaration or those who pay tax without using paper.
Tax Office Automation	All operations in Tax office are executed via computers.
Data Warehousing	On condition that the data provided by public institutions and the private sector through Directorate of Revenue Administration is processed and a system established to struggle with informal economy.
Electronic Banking Collections Processing System	Tax collection authority send the payments by banks and taxpayers to Directorate of Revenue Administration on electronic environment.
Tax Auditors Automation System	The exchange of information electronic environment operations to be done by audit staff in order to ensure the unity of application and efficient.
Electronic Lien	Taxpayer who has tax debt on condition that they have debt can notify garnishee order to collect.
E-Billing	e- Bill is a kind of bill system created on electronic environment. Revenue Administration (GİB) sets the standards.
E-Book	e- book, tax procedural law and within the scope of the Turkish Commercial Code, ensure keeping general ledger and journal which are necessarily typed on paper on electronic environment.
E-Notification	Taxpayers having valid e-mail can be informed all announcement and information about tax on electronic environment.
Electronic Tax Plate	E.T.P. is preparation of tax plate to hang in taxpayer's office on electronic environment.

Figure 2. Security problems experienced by internet users in Turkey (State Planning Organization, Information Society Statistics of Turkey, 2011)

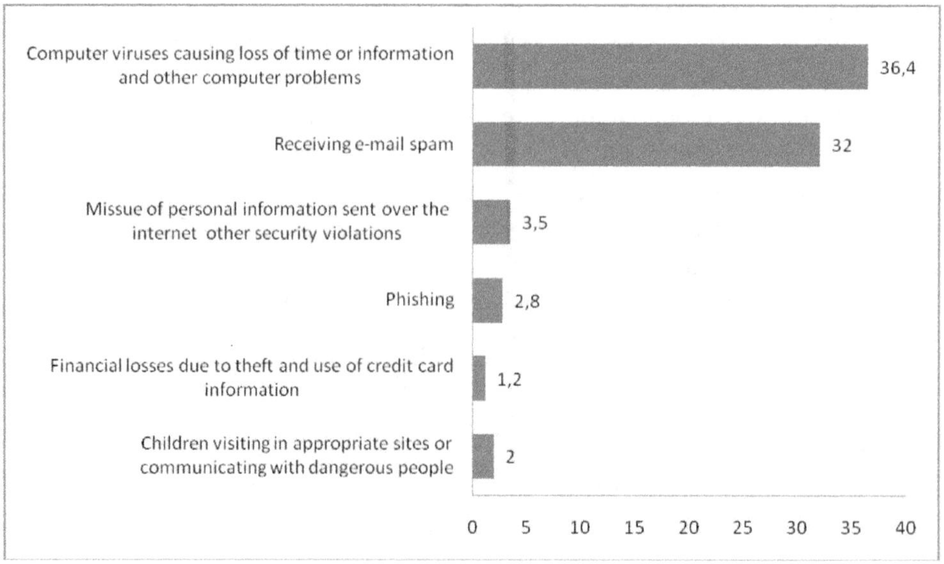

Figure 3. Security problems experienced by internet users in Turkey (State Planning Organization, Information Society Statistics of Turkey, 2011)

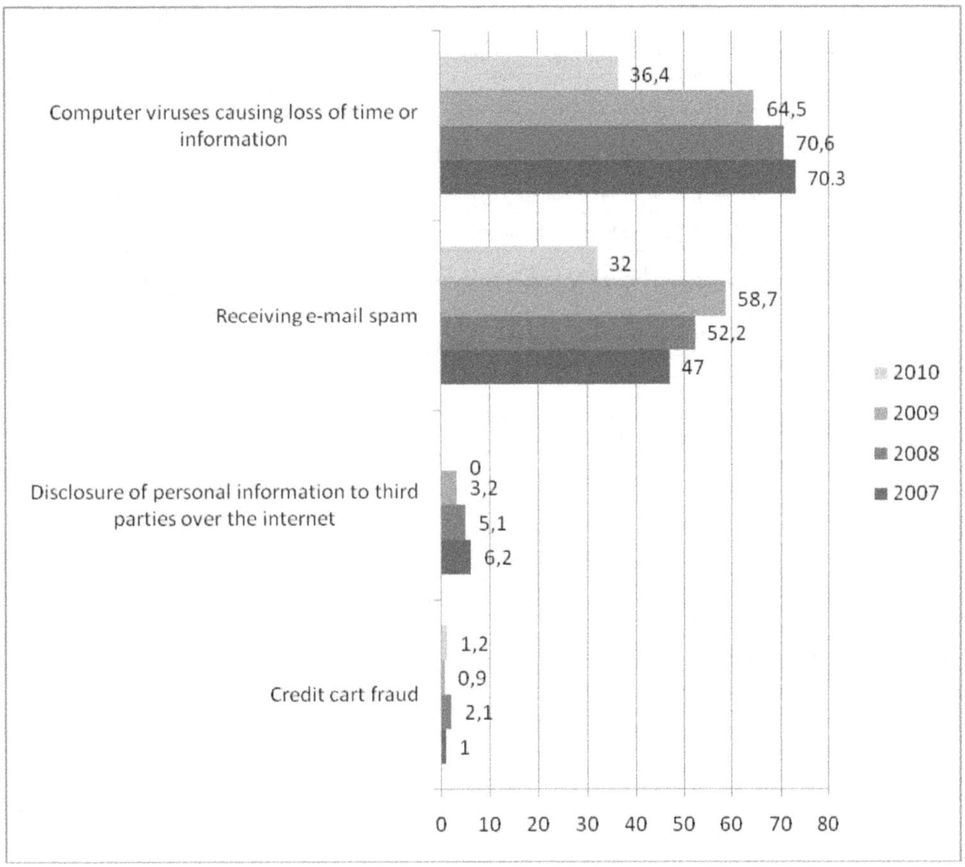

CONCLUSION

E-government applications result is being more reliable public institutions and more efficient operating institutions (Table 5). Nowadays, individuals are competing economically and socially in a highly competitive environment. E-government applications help to accelerate the compliance of individuals to the state regulations. Taxation operations that related to public finance area are one of the most intense areas of e-government applications. Electronic tax administration reduced significantly the cost of stationery of the state. It is also important in terms of taxation transparency. It provides to record informal economy. This will lead to an increase in tax capacity in the long run. It provides the application of legal and IT infrastructure such as e-statement, e-books, e-assessment, e-notification, e-tax plate, e-audit, e-inspection in Turkey. These applications are designed in tax procedural law and other laws. Such applications are developing as a part of the VEDOP project that is most important project related e-finance projects.

It is important that to ensure data security and privacy in order to establish an effective e-taxation system in e-finance applications. Furthermore human resource training for using e-taxation applications is another important aspect. Quality of personnel training, as well as tax compliance of taxpayers in the primary process will bring about a positive outcome. As well as employment of

Table 5. Classification of e-government applications in Turkey (DPT, 2005)

Legislative and Audit Services	Parliament, Prime Ministry, Ministry of Finance, Ministry of Justice, Ministry of Interior, Court of Auditors, Competition Board, Banking Regulation and Supervision Agency, Republic of Turkey Energy Market Regulatory Authority (EPDK).
Judicial Services	Constitutional Court, Supreme Court, Council of State, Ministry of Justice, Notaries Union of Turkey,
E-Transformation	Republic of Turkey Planning Organization (DPT), The Scientific and Technological Research Council of Turkey (TUBİTAK)
Population and Citizenship Affairs	General Directorate of Population and Citizenship Affairs, Ministry of Justice, Ministry of Justice, Criminal Records and Statistics Department, Ministry of Foreign Affairs, Ministry of Interior, Gendarmerie General Command
Tax Services	Ministry of Finance Revenue Administration
Economic Data and Services	Ministry of Finance, General Directorate of Budget and Fiscal Control, Ministry of Finance, Financial Crimes Investigation Board, State Planning Organization, Undersecretariat of Treasury, Central Bank of The Republic Of Turkey, Undersecretariat of Foreign Trade, Turkish Standards Institution, Istanbul Stock Exchange, Capital Market Board, Savings Deposit Insurance Fund (TMSF), Privatization Administration
Export Data Services	Undersecretariat of Foreign Trade, Foreign Trade Export Promotion Center of Turkish Cooperation and Development Agency,
Customs Services	Undersecretariat of Customs, General Administration of Customs Undersecretariat of Customs,
Foreign Policy	Ministry of Foreign Affairs, Secretariat General for EU Affairs, Ministry of Defense, Central Finance and Contracts Unit
Energy Market Services	Ministry of Energy and Natural Resources, Energy Market Regulatory Authority, Directorate General of Turkey Petroleum Corporation, BOTAS and so on
Agricultural Services	Ministry of Agriculture, Tobacco, Tobacco Products and Alcoholic Beverages Market Regulatory Authority, Soil Products Office
Environment and Forestry Services	Ministry of Environment and Forestry
Business Services	Ministry of Industry and Trade, Social Insurance Institution
Small and Medium Enterprises Service	Republic of Turkey Small&Medium Enterprises Development Organizations (KOSGEB), KOSGEB SME NET
Standard Services	Turkish Standards Institute,
Patent Services	Turkish Patent Institute
Procurement Services	Public Procurement Authority Ministries and Public Institutions
Electronic Sales Service	State Supply Office, Ministry of Finance, General Directorate of National of property, Ministry of Finance, Turkish Historical Society
Consumer Services	Ministry of Industry and Trade, Ministry of Health, Telecommunications Authority, Turk Telekom
Transportation Services	General Directorate of Highways, General Directorate of Turkish State Railways, General Directorate of State Airports Authority, Directorate General of Civil Aviation
Shipping Services	Undersecretariat for Maritime Affairs
Telecommunications and Communications Services	Telecommunications Authority, Radio and Television Supreme Council, Turk Telekom
Postal Services	General Directorate of Post and Telegraph Organization (PTT)
Science and Technology Facilities	State Planning Organization, The Scientific and Technological Research Council of Turkey (TUBITAK), Ministry of National Defense
Education Services	Ministry of National Education, General Directorate of Educational Technologies, Center for EU Education and Youth Programmes (National Agency), Higher Education Council Student Selection and Placement Center, Ministry of National Defense, Ministry of Culture and Tourism, Academy of Sciences of Turkey, Turkish Accreditation Authority of Civil Aviation Directorate General of Turkey Atomic Energy Agency, Republic of Turkey Small&Medium Enterprises Development Organizations (KOSGEB).
Language Services	Turkish Language Institution, Ministry of Justice, Telecommunications Authority
Religious Services	Presidency of Religious Affairs

continued on following page

Table 5. Continued

Culture and Tourism Services	Ministry of National Education, General Directorate of Educational Technologies, Center for EU Education and Youth Programmes (National Agency), Higher Education Council Student Selection and Placement Center, Ministry of National Defense, Ministry of Culture and Tourism, Turkish Academy of Sciences, Turkish Accreditation Authority of Civil Aviation Directorate General of Turkey Atomic Energy Agency, Republic of Turkey Small&Medium Enterprises Development Organizations (KOSGEB).
Safety Services	Security General Directorate, Ankara Security Directorate, Istanbul Security Directorate, İzmir Police Department, General Command of Gendarmerie, Coast Guard, Directorate General of Coastal Safety and Salvage Administrations
Health Services	Ministry of Health, Social Insurance Institution, Bag-Kur General Directorate of Ministry of Labour and Social Security, Social Insurance Institution, General Directorate of Retirement Fund, Bag-Kur, Turkey Business Council,
Social work	Social Services and Child Protection Agency, General Directorate of Foundations, Youth and Sports General Directorate, Academy of Sciences of Turkey, Credit and Hostels Institution
Deed Services	General Directorate of Land Registry and Cadastre
Housing Services	Mass Housing Administration, Ministry of Public Works and Settlement
Compulsory Earthquake Insurance	Natural Disaster Insurance Institution
Public Personnel Services	State Personnel Department
Recruitment Services	Turkey Business Council, Ministry of Education, Ministry of Interior, Ministry of Finance, Ministry of Health, Ministry of Industry and Trade, Ministry of Agriculture and Rural Affairs, Telecommunications Authority, General Directorate of State Meteorology Affairs, General Directorate of Civil Aviation, Turkish Patent Institute, Istanbul Metropolitan Municipality
Municipal Services	General Directorate of Local Authorities, Ankara Metropolitan Municipality, General Directorate of EGO, Ankara Water and Sewerage Administration (ASKI), Istanbul Metropolitan Municipality, Istanbul Water and Sewerage Administration, İGDAŞ, İETT, Istanbul Sea Buses, Izmir Metropolitan Municipality, Water and Sewerage Administration General Directorate of Izmir,
Weather Forecast Services	General Directorate of State Meteorological Service
Statistical Services	State Institute of Statistics, Population and Citizenship Affairs General Directorate, Ministry of Justice General Directorate of Judicial Records and Statistics, Ministry of Justice General Directorate of Prisons and Detention Houses, Ministry of Finance, General Directorate of Budget and Fiscal Control, Ministry of Finance Revenue Administration, Ministry of Finance, General Directorate of National Property, Research, Planning and Coordination Committee of the Ministry of Finance, Ministry of Health, Ministry of Labour and Social Security, Ministry of Culture and Tourism, Bag-Kur, Social Insurance Institution, General Directorate of Retirement Fund, Turkey Business Council, Treasury, Undersecretariat of Foreign Trade, Foreign Trade Export Promotion Center, Undersecretariat of Customs, General Administration of Customs Undersecretariat for Maritime Affairs, Police, Gendarmerie General Command, Ministry of Education, Ministry of National Education General Directorate of Educational Technologies, General Directorate of Libraries and Publications, Higher Education Council Student Selection and Placement Center, Turkish History Institution, Competition Authority, Telecommunications Authority, Public Procurement Agency, Radio and Television Supreme CouncilTobacco, Tobacco Products and Alcoholic Beverages Market Regulatory Authority, The General Directorate of PTT, (Post and Telegraph Organization), Turkish Patent Institute, TEIAS State Airports Authority, General Directorate of Libraries and Publications, National Library, Library Catalog Search Council of State, Court E-Library (Electronic Copy), Grand National Assembly of Turkey Parliamentary Library, Electronic Library Ministry of Foreign Affairs, Ministry of Finance, Ministry of Education, Ministry of Health, Refik Saydam Library e-Library of Ministry of Industry and Trade, Ministry of Agriculture and Rural Affairs Virtual Library, Library services, Ministry of Environment and Forestry.
Library Services	General Directorate of Libraries and Publications, National Library, Library Catalog Search the State Council, Court of Accounts e-Library, Parliament Library, Electronic Library Ministry of Foreign Affairs, Ministry of Finance, Ministry of National Education, Ministry of Health, Refik Saydam Library E-Library of the Ministry of Industry and Trade, Agriculture and Ministry of Environment and Forestry, Ministry of Culture and Tourism, State Planning Organization, Undersecretariat of Treasury, DTMİ, TUBITAK Marmara Research Center Cahit Arf Library, The Scientific and Technological Research Council of Turkey (TUBITAK), Istanbul Stock Exchange, Turkish History Institution, Directorate General of Press and Information, Presidency of Religious Affairs, Turkish Language Association, Central Bank of the Republic of Turkey, Competition Authority, the European Union, General Secretariat, the General Directorate of Foundations, Turkey Atomic Energy Agency, the General Directorate of State Hydraulic Works, Republic of Turkey Railways (TCDD) Library, Istanbul Electricity, Tramway and Tunnel General Amnagement (İETT) Transportation Library

continued on following page

Table 5. Continued

Press and Publication Services	Directorate General of Press and Information, Press Ad Agency, Constitutional Court, Council of State, Supreme Court, Court of Auditors, Board of Supreme Audit, General Directorate of State Archives, Ministry of Justice, Ministry of Justice General Directorate of Judicial Records and Statistics, Ministry of Defense, Ministry of Interior, General Directorate of Population and Citizenship Affairs, Ministry of Labour and Social Security, Environment and Ministry of Forestry, General Directorate of Budget and Fiscal Control, General Directorate of Accounting, Treasury, Undersecretariat of Foreign Trade Undersecretariat of Customs, Defense Industry Undersecretariat, TÜBİTAK, Telecommunications Authority, Capital Markets Board, Public Procurement Agency, Energy Market Regulatory Authority, Competition Authority, Savings Deposit Insurance Fund, Istanbul Stock Exchange, Presidency of Religious Affairs, Turkish Language Society, Student Selection and Placement Center (SSPC), Turkish Standards Institute, Bag-Kur General Directorate of Employment Status Report, State Personnel Department, Privatization Administration, GAP Regional Development Administration, Administration for Disabled People, General Directorate of Foundations Central Finance and Contracts Unit, Directorate General of Highways, General Directorate of State Airports Authority Publications, Directorate General for the Status of Women, Turkish Cooperation and Development Agency, General Directorate of State Meteorology Affairs, General Directorate of Foundations, Turkish Patent Institute, Republic of Turkey Small&Medium Enterprises Development Organizations (KOSGEB), PTT General Directorate, Turkey Petroleum Corporation Partnership, General Directorate of Electrical Power Resources, Survey and Development Administration, MTA, General Directorate of Mineral Research and Exploration, Istanbul Water and Sewerage Administration
Information Services	Constitutional Court, Prime Ministry, General Directorate of State Archives, Chairman of the Board of Supreme Audit, Ministry of Justice, Ministry of Interior, Ministry of National Defense Information, Ministry of Foreign Affairs, Ministry of Finance, Ministry of Education, Ministry of Labour and Social Security, Ministry of Health, Ministry of Industry and Trade, Ministry of Transport, Ministry of Public Works and Settlement, Ministry of Agriculture and Rural Affairs, Culture and Tourism Ministry, Ministry of Environment and Forestry, State Planning Organization, Undersecretariat of Foreign Trade, State Personnel Department, Foreign Trade Export Promotion Center of the Customs Undersecretariat of Treasury, Undersecretariat for Maritime Affairs, Defense Industry Undersecretariat Capital Markets Board of Turkey, Banking Regulation and Supervision Agency, Public Procurement Authority, Telecommunications Authority, Energy Market Regulatory Authority, Radio and Television Supreme Council, Competition Authority Tobacco, Tobacco Products and Alcoholic Beverages Market Regulatory Authority, Central Bank of Republic of Turkey, Savings Deposit Insurance Fund General Directorate of Security and Gendarmerie General Command, Coast Guard, Social Insurance Institution, General Directorate of Retirement Fund, Bag-Kur, Turkey Business Council, State Institute of Statistics, European Union General Secretariat, Center for EU Education and Youth Programmes (National Agency), TUBITAK, Department of Religious Affairs, GAP Regional Development Administration, Turkish Language Society, Turkish Cooperation and Development Agency, Turkish Patent Institute, Turkish Standards Institute, Privatization Administration, Administration for Disabled People, Public Housing Administration, KOSGEB, General Directorate of Highways, High- Education Council, Credit and Hostels Institution, TODAİE, Directorate General of Press and Information of State Hydraulic Works General Directorate of Land Registry and Cadastre General Directorate of Social Services and Child Protection Agency, PTT General Directorate of Foundations General Directorate of Mineral Research and Exploration Directorate of State Meteorology Affairs General Directorate of State Airports Management General Directorate of Youth and Sports General Directorate, General Directorate for the Status of Women, Istanbul Stock Exchange, National Productivity Centre, Soil Products Office, BOTAS, Electricity Generation AS (EUAS), machinery and Chemical Industry Corporation, Turkey Atomic Energy Agency, Turkey Electricity Distribution AS (TEDAS), Turkey Electricity Transmission AS (TEİAS), Turkey Petroleum Corporation, Turk Telekom Ankara Metropolitan Municipality, Istanbul Metropolitan Municipality of Izmir Metropolitan Municipality, Ministry of Energy and Natural Resources Undersecretariat for Maritime Affair

high quality personnel, taxpayers' training in the primary process will bring about a positive outcome about tax compliance. The legal system brought into line with the constitutional arrangements will help in solving legal problems. Lack of access to use of the Internet, the security concerns of citizens, due to deficiencies in the structure of e-government and e-taxation remained hesitant on the citizens. Therefore, technological and legal infrastructure must be created properly about e-taxation. The Ministry of Finance has accelerated the studies in this direction since the early 2000s. In our study, the legal status of these steps is given and they are defined.

Electronic tax system management provides advantages over the traditional tax system. These advantages are as follows: increasing efficiency in tax administration and controlling of the electronic tax payment system, reducing bureaucracy and reduce transaction costs, enabling online control, operations to increase the accuracy and precision rate, increasing quality of public service, spending less time, increasing the percentage of taxes to be paid on time, increasing public information and reduction of the informal economy, the reduction in the workload of tax practitioners.

The e-taxation requires the use of highest level of information technologies. To accomplish legal infrastructure of data security and data privacy issues accelerate the adaptation process of e-taxation. Giving tax courses and e-taxation practices for the elementary school children will make it more convenient to introduce the next generation compliance with this issue. Organizing training seminars for citizens concerning implementation of e-taxation and making user manuals about these applications will make e-taxation application more active. Turkey which is in the e-transformation process has made a long way since the beginning of the 2000s.

REFERENCES

Akdemir, T., & Öz, E. (2004). Elektronik Devlet ve Vergi Yönetimimi II. Vergi Sorunları, (188), 112.

Baştan, S., & Gökbunar, R. (2004). Kamu Hizmetlerinin Sunumunda E-Devletle İlgili Yeni Gelişmeler: Tümleşik E-Devlet Sistemlerine Doğru. DEÜ-İİBF, *19*(1).

Berdykhanova, D., Dehghantanha, A., & Hariraj, K. (2010). Trust challenges and issues of e-govemment: E-tax prospective. Information Technology (ITSim) 2010 International Symposium: Volume 3. (pp.1015-1019). IEEE.

Çetin, G. (2010). Bilişim Teknolojilerindeki Gelişmelerin Vergilemede Kayıt Düzeni ve Denetim Uygulamalarına Etkisi. Ekonomi Bilimleri Dergisi.2(1). ISSN: 1309-8020 (Online). Retrieved September 3, 2012, from http://www.sobiad.org/eJOURNALS/dergi_EBD/arsiv/2010_1/09gunes_cetin.pdf

DPT. (2005). E-Devlet Proje ve Uygulamaları 2005. Retrieved September 9, 2012, from http://www.bilgitoplumu.gov.tr

E-Government Practice Editorial Team. European Dynamıcs S.A. (2010). E-government in Turkey. E-government factsheets Turkey. Retrieved October 3, 2012, from http://epractice.eu

Hepaksaz, E. (2012). Türkiye'de Vergi Sisteminin Yeniden Yapılandırılmasında Muhtemel Fayda ve Maliyetleriyle VEDOP Projesi ve E-Maliye Uygulamaları. 27. Türkiye Maliye Sempozyumu. Retrieved October 3, 2012, from www.maliyesempozyumu2012.org/teblig-kitabi.html

Kapanoğlu, A., Sökmen, B., & Aykin, H. (2011). *Kayıtdışı Ekonomi ve Yolsuzlukla Mücadele Açısından Maliye Teftişkurulu Elektronik Denetim Uygulaması. Kamu Yönetimi ve Teknoloji. Vol:360*. Ankara: TODAIE.

Medeni, T., et al. (2011). *Information society strategy & e-government gateway development in Turkey: Moving towards integrated processes and personalized services. t*Gov Workshop 11. March 17 – 18 2011, UB8 3PH. Brunel University: West London.

Napierala, N., & Kiefer, A. (2009). *The use of ICT for tax administration*. GTZ. Federal Ministry of Economic Cooperation and Development. Retrieved October 3, 2012, from http://www.docstoc.com/docs/40251831/The-use-of-ICT-for-Tax-Administration

Republic of Turkey Official Gazette. (2004, January 24). Article. No: 2004/12. Number: 25356.

State Planning Organization. (2010). Information society strategy (2006-2010). Retrieved September 3, 2012, from http://www.bilgitoplumu.gov.tr/Documents/5/Documents/060700_InformationSocietyStrategy.pdf

State Planning Organization. (2011). *Information society statistics of Turkey*. Undersecretariat for State Planning Organization Information Society Department. SPO Publication No: 2829.

Tubitak, B. (2012). *Survey*. Retrieved October 3, 2012, from http://www.bilgiguvenligi.gov.tr/89.html?mosmsg=Oyunuz+i%E7in+te%FEekk%FCrler%21

Yeloğlu, H., & Sağsan, M. (2009). The diffusion of e-government innovations in Turkey: A conceptual framework. Serial No.50. USA. Journal of US-China Public Administration, *6*(7). ISSN 1548-6591.

ADDITIONAL READING

Dečman, M., Stare, J., & Klun, M. (2010). E-government and cost-effectiveness: E-taxation in Slovenia. *Transylvanian Review of Administrative Sciences*, No. 31e.

Efendioğlu, A., & Sezgin, E. (2007). E-Devlet Uygulamalarında Bilgi ve Paylaşım Güvenliği. Ç.Ü. Sosyal Bilimler Enstitüsü Dergisi. 16(2).

Gökbunar, R., & Utkuseven A. (2002). Elektronik Ticaretin Vergilendirilmesinde Yaşanan Gelişmeler: Yeni İpek Yolu Bir Vergi Cenneti Mi?. İ.Ü. Siyasal Bilgiler Fakültesi Dergisi. 27.

Öz, Ersan., & Bozdoğan, Doğan. (2012). Türk Vergi Sisteminde E-Maliye Uygulamaları. Suleyman Demirel University. *The Journal of Faculty of Economics and Administrative Sciences*, *17*(2).

Turan, A.H., & Özgen F.B. (2009). Türkiye'de E-Beyanname Sisteminin Benimsenmesi: Geliştirilmiş Teknoloji Kabul Modeli İle Ampirik Bir Çalışma. Doğuş Üniversitesi Dergisi, *10*(1).

KEY TERMS AND DEFINITIONS

E-Taxation: E taxation is an e-government application which provides assessment and collection of taxes via online communication tools and internet connected computers without going to the tax office.

E-Transformation Turkey Project: The e-Transformation Turkey Project aims to carry out the process of transformation into an information society in a harmonious and integrated structure all over the society with all citizens, enterprises and public segments.

ICT: ICT covers all forms of computer and communications equipment and software used to create, design, store, transmit, interpret and manipulate information in its various formats.

VEDOP: Turkish Revenue Administrations' Tax Office Automation Project started at 1998. Auditors have access to all existing information about taxpayers through VEDOP.

Section 3
E-Government Implementation: Governance and E-Inclusion

Chapter 9
Role of E-Governance in Citizen Centric E-Government

Ganesh Chandra Deka
DGE&T, Ministry of Labour & Employment, Government of India, India

ABSTRACT

Recent World Bank study shows that a 10% increase in mobile phone subscribers is associated with a 0.8% increase in economic growth while 10% increase in high speed Internet connections is related to a 1.3% increase in economic growth. Development of ICT infrastructure attracts foreign direct investment, generates fiscal revenues and creates employment opportunities especially for youth and women. Political, Cultural, Socio-economic developmental and behavioral decisions today rests on the ability to access, gather, analyze and utilize information. These remarkable advancements in technology and understanding of how it affects growth highlight a strategic shift in the way ICT can influence development. The distribution of this tool of wealth creation and knowledge are highly unequal amongst countries of the Globe. At the current rate of technological advancement, such disparities in access to ICT related developments are large and likely to become larger in adoption amongst the countries around the Globe. As more of the services in an economy come online, those without access to this technological advancement will be marginalized. The ubiquitous presence of Internet has penetrated every aspect of daily life. This chapter discusses the role of e-Governance in citizen centric e-Government as well as the various issues and challenges of implementation of e-Governance in general. The last part of the chapter is about the e-Governance in Indian context. This chapter is likely to give the reader an overview of e-Governance and the related issues.

DOI: 10.4018/978-1-4666-4245-4.ch009

INTRODUCTION

Social computing is playing a leading role in educating and sharing the views and opinion of the masses in an area of their interest both political and apolitical. Presently social networking websites such as Facebook, Twitter, Flickr, LinkedIn, YouTube etc has shown a phenomenal growth in number of users specifically in sharing their views in various contemporary issues. There has been an explosive growth of social networking for a variety of business functions including sales, marketing, customer service, entertainment, politics and government. The public sector, even though slower in adopting social media, is now accepting its potentials which can play the role of communications channels between government and users of government services.

The benefits gained in the different stages of usage of social computing are relative to the system complexity and effort that has to be made in order to advance e-Governmental processes by utilizing the benefits of ICT. Even though ICT is not substitute for good policy, it empowers the citizens to question the actions of regulators and brings systemic issues to the forefront.

Integration of e-Governance and ICT contributes to:

- Good governance
- Trust and Accountability
- Citizen's awareness and empowerment
- Citizen's welfare
- Democracy
- Nation's economic growth

This chapter discusses e-Democracy, Ethics in Governance and e-Transparency as well as the role of ICT for implementation of these three pillars of the democratic Governance for implementation of citizen centric e-Governance as well as the various issues and challenges of implementation of e-Governance, specifically in underdeveloped and developing countries. Another emerging e-Governance technology m-Governance (Mobile Governance) is also introduced in this chapter. Last part of the chapter is about the e-Governance in Indian context. Sufficient references are included for the benefit of advanced reader on e-Governance and G-Cloud (Government Cloud). This chapter is likely to give the reader an overview of e-Governance and the related issues.

ROLE OF ICT IN CITIZEN CENTRIC GOVERNANCE

ICT can augment government transparency and reduce corruption as well as build the foundation of e-Democracy. Transition from democracy to automated governance takes a revolutionary ICT development approach. In the following subsections, we discuss e-Democracy, Ethics in Governance and e-Transparency.

E-Democracy

The transition towards e-Democracy (Yrjö Neuvo et al., 2012) not only requires technological but also cultural and political changes in the mindset of government and the citizens. The followings are the 4 stages of implementation of e-Democracy:

- **Stage-1:** Web Presence: Most basic form of e-Government is web presence. In this stage, governments only provide relatively static information or regularly updated information online. Most of the underdeveloped and developing counties are still in the stage of e-Governance, either their web presence are poor or nonexistent. Most of the cases the websites are either not developed or not updated regularly. Non-availability of web contents in local languages too disappoints the citizens to visits the government websites in addition to poor network connectivity.

- **Stage-2:** Online Interaction: Second stage is Interaction i.e. providing the simplest mode of interaction between the government and citizens such as search information; inquire about public services etc.
- **Stage-3:** Onlie Transaction: 3rd stage is Transaction i.e. enabling citizens and organizations to complete online transactions such as filing of online applications etc.
- **Stage-4:** Transformation: 4th stage is Transformation which represents a major jump compared to the previous 3 stages. In this stage, the government has a more integrated view of online services and they are provided through a single portal instead of many fragmented services.

According to this model e-Democracy represents the most mature level of e-Government development for those countries which has achieved the fourth stage.

The governments which are in this stage utilize all kinds of ICT tools for increasing the interaction amongst the citizen and as well as organizational participation in governance ultimately leading to political transparency. ICT does away with paper and gives a real time faceless communication instantly flattening the hierarchical communication of traditional bureaucracy. By accessing Government services online instead of physically going down to the various government agencies, the citizens save time and adding convenience to their life. e-Governance has not only the ability to handle momentum and complexity of Governance but also to underpin the regulatory reform. It also refers to the citizen to government interface (C2G) including the feedback of policies.

ICT & Ethics in Governance

"Ethical Governance" is the term used to explain the performance issues in management and policy making in Business, Government, politics, International relations, health care, etc. Ethical Governance is integral to sustainable growth, stopping financial meltdowns and economic degradation, eradication of poverty, income inequalities also to achieve high standards of ethical conduct, in the areas of human rights, labour, surroundings and anti-corruption. A comprehensive hard work is necessary to fight deviations from ethical norms. There ought to be ethics in citizens' behavior because such behavior impinges directly on ethics in government and administration.

Corruption is thought about to be of the major roadblocks in developing and underdeveloped countries in their journey to a developed economy. Economist, the magazine, has classified corruption in to two categories:

- **Payment of Bribes for the work someone is supposed to do:** The corruption of first category takes place in the lower bureaucracy of Governance particularly in Government office/Organization where the victim has to pay bribe for getting some sort of certification etc. This type of corruption is organized in the peer groups.
- **Payment of Bribes** for the work someone is not supposed to do: The second type of corruption takes place in the higher level of bureaucracy/Government machinery which involves very high amount most of the cases in terms of millions.

Probability of corruption is more in a system with excessive discretion in the hands of the official machinery mostly at lower levels which can be curtail by reducing discretion and maximizing transparency in the system as well as introducing strict accountability for actions. Corruption and abuse of office has been aggravated by three factors (Sanwalka, 2011):

- First, there is a colonial legacy of unchallenged authority and tendency to exercise power arbitrarily. In a society which worships power; it is simple for public officials to deviate from ethical conduct;

- Second, there is an immense asymmetry of power in our society. Thus asymmetry of power reduces societal pressure on Government machinery to conform to ethical behavior and makes it simple to indulge in corruption;
- Third, as a conscious choice, the Indian state in the early decades after Independence selected a set of policies whose unintended consequence was to put the citizen at the mercy of the State. Over regulation, extreme restrictions on economic activity, excessive state control, near-monopoly of the government in plenty of sectors and an economy of shortage all created conditions conducive to unbridled corruption.

Furthermore, lots of state subsidies and beneficiary oriented programs are implemented with asymmetry of power giving the public servant the privilege of a patron and reduced most citizens in to mendicants. This without delay enhanced opportunities to indulge in corruption and reduced the citizen's capacity to resist extraordinary demands adequate dividends.

Fraud takes longer to detect in Asia (Sanwalka, 2011) as compared to anywhere else in the World. The period of fraud prior to detection in Asia is in average of 5 years, with 16% of frauds going undetected for 10 years or more compared to 4.2 years in United States and 3.7 years Western Europe. In India 88% of frauds are not communicated. Enforcement and disciplinary actions occur in 25% cases and resignation/voluntary retirement in 19%. Size of crime in Asia Pacific was $1.4 million, in the United States $1.1 million and in Europe the Middle East and Africa (EMA) $ 900,000 in 2011. The World Bank has identified corruption as the greatest obstacles to Economic and Social development. It is found in various surveys and case studies that countries with a higher perception of corruption not only deters financial institutions from long term investment but can actually lead to capital outflows, making a volatile economic surroundings. Capital inflows, international trade and private as well as public enterprise have helped contribute significantly to India's growth since liberalization.

Competition and decentralization definitely reduce corruption in definite sectors. But if the demand for corruption is fuelled by inexhaustible appetite for illegitimate money in politics, then other avenues of corruption will be forcibly opened up. As a result, even as corruption declines in definite areas, it shifts to other, sometimes more hazardous, areas in which competition cannot be introduced and the state exercises a natural monopoly. What is necessary with liberalization is corresponding political and governance reform to fine-tune the incentives in politics and public office and to promote integrity and ethical conduct.

The most successful anti-corruption reforms are those that seek to reduce discretionary benefits controlled by public officials. There are lots of governmental activities where discretion can be eliminated by. Wherever it is not possible to eliminate discretion the exercise of powers should be bound by clear guidelines to minimize discretion. Effective checks and balances should be built over exercise of discretion.

The second "Administrative Reforms Commission" of Government of India, in its 4th report entitled "Ethics in Governance," has made the following recommendations:

- All government offices having public interface should undertake a review of their activities and list out those which involve use of discretion. In all such activities, attempt should be made to eliminate discretion. Where it is not possible to do so, well-defined regulations should attempt to 'bound' the discretion. Ministries and Departments should be asked to coordinate this task in their organizations/offices and complete it within one year;

- Decision-making on important matters should be assigned to a committee rather than individuals. Care has to be exercised, however, that this practice is not resorted to when prompt decisions are required;
- State Governments should take steps on similar lines, especially in local bodies and authorities, which have maximum 'public contact.'

E-Transparency

When ICT is used for implementation of transparency of Government machinery, it is termed as e-Transparency. e-Transparency refers to the use of ICT to handle some or all of the transparency related information flow in Government machinery. There are various levels of e-Transparency (Heeks, 2008):

- **Publication:** Just providing basic information about a particular area of government;
- **Transaction:** Automating some public sector process and reporting on that process;
- **Reporting:** Providing specific details of public sector decisions and actions e.g. via performance indicators;
- **Openness:** Allowing users to compare public servant performance against pre-set benchmarks;
- **Accountability:** Allowing users some mechanism of control e.g. reward or punishment over public servants.

Global Corruption Barometer of Transparency International (gcb.transparency.org/gcb201011/results/) is the largest cross-country survey to gather the general public's views on and experiences of corruption. In 2011 the Barometer interviewed more than 100,000 people in 100 countries. Table 1 and Table 2 show the survey result of two important questions asked in seven countries of Asia pacific.

Transparency, openness, information flow, degree of resemblance in communication is the foundation for effective implementation of Ethical Governance in real sense. Where expertise and transparency is introduced, corruption has been considerably controlled. Computerization and access to information have made lots of services from railway reservation to issuing of driving licenses increasingly free from corruption in India. ICT has a big role to play in the transparency of functioning of Government machinery. e-Governance can also help fight corruption. The fact that it brings in a much-needed measure of transparency can act as a check against corruption. Aided by the political and administrative will, e-Governance can definitely battle corruption. But the traditional role of the media as a watchdog against corruption will not disappear in a digital democracy (Harshad Patil et al., 2008).

ICT AND E-GOVERNANCE

ICT is the conduit that transmits information and knowledge to individual to widen their choices for economic and social empowerment. By integrating technology into development more effective and speedy solutions can be found for sustainable human development and economic growth (Sanjaya Kannath, 2009). The association of the

Table 1. In past 3 years, how the level of corruption in this country has changed?

Country	Decreased	Increased	Same
India	10%	74%	16%
China	25%	46%	29%
Bangladesh	36%	46%	18%
Pakistan	7%	77%	17%
Nepal	19%	67%	14%
Sri Lanka	32%	19%	49%
Malaysia	19%	46%	35%
Singapore	32%	39%	35%

Table 2. How would you assess your current Government's action in the fight against corruption?

Country	Ineffective	Effective	Neither
India	44%	25%	31%
China	35%	36%	30%
Bangladesh	22%	62%	17%
Pakistan	73%	12%	15%
Nepal	27%	41%	32%
Sri Lanka	36%	52%	12%
Malaysia	20%	48%	32%
Singapore	31%	30%	40%

government with its constituents i.e. citizens and businesses as well as between its own organs can be enhanced by effective use of ICT. The ICT has the potential to transform and redefine processes and systems of governance. The most evident impact has been in access to information and data and electronic service delivery. e-Governance ensure wider participation and deeper involvement of citizens, institutions, civil society groups and the private sector in the decision making process of governance.

Even though ICT is not substitute for good policy, it empowers the citizens to question the actions of regulators and brings systemic issues to the forefront. Leading governments are transforming themselves into Flatter, Agile, Streamlined and Tech-enabled (FAST) organizations.

Flatter, Agile, Streamlined and Tech-Enabled Government

FAST governments (F.A.S.T. Government (Flat, Agile, Streamlined, Tech-enabled) for the 21st Century, Posted on 20 July 2012) develop innovative public services, effectively meet citizens' needs, care for scarce natural resources and create new public value. FAST does not necessarily mean speedy, although the time frame for many decisions may be shortened with the help of collaboration platforms, tools and analytics; nor does FAST mean ignoring the core government values of merit, equity, checks and balances, accountability and jurisdiction.

The following provides an outline of Flatter, Agile, Streamlined and Tech-enabled (FAST) government for political and government leaders everywhere.

Government Must be "Flatter"

This can be done by achieving the following:

- **Citizen Engagement:** Decreasing the distance between government and the people through the use of social media, mobile devices and mapping tools; increasing people's participation through online deliberation, consultations, surveys and other communication modes and committing to open data that provide citizens and businesses with access to much more public information in easy to use, searchable electronic formats.
- **Administrative Efficiency:** Decreasing layers in hierarchies between top management and line personnel and removing red tape, aided by collaborative work environments, business technique redesign and business analytics to foster evidence-based decision making.
- **Better Decision-Making:** Flattening of the decision-making method can be accomplished vertically as new information and analytical processes put information where it is necessary by policy-makers and others, and horizontally by building collaboration within and across government departments, agencies and ministries.
- **Intergovernmental and Cross-Sectoral Collaboration:** Networks that lie across public, private and nonprofit sector organizations and various government entities

will be critical in the 21st century to solve complex issues, gain economies of scale and scope, leverage innovative ideas and best practice.

Government Must be "Agile"

Agility and adaptability are critical to effective and innovative governments. Successful governments are able to organize themselves to marshal public and private resources quickly to address challenges. As important, governments must be able to de-organize themselves when specific structures and processes are no longer needed. This requires an agile workforce made up primarily of highly expert knowledge workers with broad problem-solving capabilities. Agility and adaptability include organizational structures, processes, and service delivery models. Civil servants and others employed in government works flexibility in regulatory and legal structures.

Government Must be "Streamlined"

Governments in the 21st century will be marked in lots of countries by reductions in the size of the civil service like diets, in lots of cases these 'crash' workforce reductions only show successful in the short run, if at all. Virtually all governments are reducing staffing levels, most often without any actual reduction in service levels.

Government Must be "Tech-Enabled and Tech-Savvy"

Governments of the future must be fully tech-enabled with a tech-savvy workforce. Legal and Regulatory frameworks and processes must be redesigned to align with the dynamics of the networked world. Knowledge infrastructures must support new modes of collaboration for knowledge intensive governance. Even in the poorest regions, brilliant examples of service innovation have been driven through the use of cheap mobile wireless technologies.

FASTer governments are likely to attract and retain new breed of civil servant who thrives on problem-solving, results and innovation. As governments become FASTer, the 21st century will witness a renaissance of government and public service, when the "best and the brightest" seek out public service-whether through government agencies, civil society organizations or businesses working in the civic sector.

Over the past few years, a paradigm shift has been emerging around how governments work use the Web and ICT to deliver better services to their constituencies. The new approach is called Open Government. It means rethinking how to govern, rethinking how the administrations ought to alter their procedures to meet the demands and necessities of the citizens.

Open Government

Open Government means a Cultural, Organizational, Procedural and Attitude adjustment in public servants and their relationship with the citizens. It is a new kind of understanding of political policies which are more legitimate and collaborative:

Open Government=Transparency+Efficiency+ Participation+Accountability

Open Government Data (OGD) is a pillar of an Open Government strategy. OGD (http://data.gov.uk/sites/default/files/Open_data_White_Paper.pdf) is when ministries and state agencies put their raw knowledge on the Web in readable formats (preferably, machine readable, open standard formats). The public can review and download the knowledge, and even generate new applications around the knowledge. The governments of the United States and United Kingdom are so far the most prominent practitioners of this new approach, and have established portals to knowledge catalogs. This knowledge is usable and freely exploitable by NGOs, activists, developers, IT companies, etc. to build and deliver services to people and organizations.

The Web Foundation has been deeply involved in the OGD domain from the outset, through founder Sir Tim Berners-Lee and director Nigel Shadbolt, who continue to advise the United Kingdom government on the realization of knowledge.gov.uk. This paradigm shift is taking hold in other countries, regions and cities, but chiefly, so far in the developed world. OGD programs have so far demonstrated multiple benefits:

- Increased transparency of governments;
- Increased number of services to people, due to an increased base of potential service providers;
- New business opportunities and jobs for application and service developers;
- New synergies between government, public administration, and civil society organizations;
- Increased citizen participation and inclusion through extended offers of services closer to people's needs;
- New, innovative uses of data in a ways that owners of data would never have thought of.

M-GOVERNMENT

According to London-based Informa Telecoms and Media's latest forecast (Jotischky, 2010), the mobile subscribers in India are likely to reach 1.159 billion by the end of 2013. As per the World Bank report, more than 90 percent of adults in most countries have access to a mobile phone. This penetration creates opportunities to use mobile phones as a service delivery platform for both public and private services. Basic phones can already transform how some services are performed (Jotischky, 2010). The m-Governance initiatives would primarily be aimed at the rural population which does not have access to e-governance schemes due penetration of Web and Broadband. M-Government is also known as "Unplugged Government" is basically used of all kinds of wireless and mobile technology to deliver the government services at the door step of the citizens. Considering the rapid penetration rate of mobile phones in rural areas the m-Government is having lots of scope to deliver a plethora of services to the rural poor.

The following are some of the advantages:

- Investment is very less
- Accessible is Rural areas
- Can be used in local language

As per the report of "Mobile Government in Europe" of "Mobile Government Consortium International, 15th March 2011, UK (United Nations e-Government Survey 2010-Leveraging e-government at a time of financial and economic crisis, 2010)," the countries like Estonia and Lithuania which are the leader in m-Governance has scored relatively high CPI score in the survey during 2010 (Estonia, 6.6 & Lithuania, 4.9). Denmark, New Zealand and Singapore topped the list by scoring 9.3. New Zealand by June 2010 has transferred the operation of Government through use of the Internet.

Danish e-Government and ICT policies are strongly linked, due both to the former having its origins in the latter, and the leadership role that the Ministry of Science, Technology and Innovation (MVTU) have undertaken.

In the case of Singapore, the citizens can do online filing of taxes, checking the availability of new HDB flats, registering for National Service or applying for a new passport with e-Citizen (https://www.singpass.gov.sg/sppubsvc/), the one-stop online portal for all government services and information. The citizens are given one password, SingPass which stands for "Singapore Personal Access," is the common password to access different government online services. To access the online services, a person requires the SingPass ID (which is the 9 character code "National Registration Identity Card (NRIC)" number for citizens and residents or Foreign Identification Number (FIN) for foreigners. SingPass protects privacy by giving citizens personal online identity and password to authenticate transactions online.

Only 7% of the total population in India has access to the Web, but as per the latest figures from Telecom Regulatory Authority of India (TRAI) the mobile penetration has reached 64.7%. Mobile phones has become increasingly affordable and reliable, thus creating the emergence of a mobile web and creating avenues for citizens to access key government services through their phones. m-Government cell is being created under the department of Information Technology's(DITs) e-Governance unit with a mix group of 1,500 officials, comprising members from the Academy, industry stake holder, civil society(non-Government organizations) and officials from DIT and department of telecommunication. The aim is to deliver all services presently available through computers through mobile technology. For effective implementation m-Governance there should be regularity regime so that there will be some discipline amongst the various mobile operators. Apart from this, the following are also crucial:

- Creating a mobile platform so that all these mobile applications can be relevant for the purposes of G2C services;
- Creating a Mobile Service Delivery Gateway (MSDG) so that all telecom service providers can converge on one platform.

E-Governance in India

The first step of e-Governance in India was the Computerization of Government Departments. Present e-Governance initiatives will be encapsulating the finer points of Governance for instance Citizen Centricity, Service Orientation and Transparency. Government of India is having an ambitious objective of transforming the citizen-government interaction at all levels by electronic mode by 2020.

For speeding up the e-Governance implementation across the various arms of Government at National, State and Local levels due cognizance has been taken to adopted common vision and strategy having the potential of huge costs savings in presenting a seamless view of Government to Citizens (G2C) by:

- Sharing of core and support infrastructure;
- Enabling interoperability through standards.

The followings are the recommendations of Second Administrative Reforms Commission, Government of India for application of ICT in Governance:

- Each Ministry/Department/Organization of government should draw up a plan for use of IT to improve governance. In any government process, use of Information Technology should be made only after the existing procedures have been thoroughly re-engineered;
- The Ministry of Information and Technology needs to identify certain governmental processes and then take up a project of their computerization on a nationwide scale.

Administrative Reforms Commission's 12th Report titled "Citizen Centric Administration-The Heart of Governance 7 step Model for Citizen Centricity is as following:

1. Define all services which are to be provided and identify the clients;
2. Set standards and norms for each service;
3. Develop capability to meet the set standards;

4. Perform to achieve the standards;
5. Monitor performance against the set standards;
6. Evaluate the impact through an independent mechanism;
7. Continuous improvement based on monitoring and evaluation of results.

On 18th May 2006, Government of India approved NeGP which consists of 20 Mission Mode Projects (MMPs) of State Governments & Central Government and 7 Integrated MMPs (www.negp.gov.in/Projects/Default.aspx). The theme of the NeGP is to "Make all Government services accessible to the common man in his locality through common service delivery outlets, and ensure efficiency, transparency and reliability of such services at affordable costs to realize the basic needs of the common man."

National e-Governance Plan (NeGP) has a clear vision, an approach, a well defined strategy, key components, Implementation methodology and an agreed management structure. Within the NeGP Plan, different accessible or continuing projects in the Mission Mode Project (MMP) category under the Central Ministries, States and State Departments would be improved and enhanced to align with the objectives of NeGP." The followings are some of the MMP project under the NeGP:

Central MMPs

1. Banking
2. Central Excise & Customs
3. Income Tax (IT)
4. Insurance
5. MCA21
6. National Citizen Database
7. Passport
8. Immigration, Visa and Foreigners Registration & Tracking
9. Pension
10. e-Office

State MMPs

1. Agriculture
2. Commercial Taxes
3. e-District
4. Employment Exchange
5. Land Records
6. Municipalities
7. Gram Panchayats
8. Police
9. Road Transport
10. Treasuries

Integrated MMPs

1. CSC
2. e-Biz
3. e-Courts
4. e-Procurement
5. EDI For e-Trade
6. National e-governance Service Delivery Gateway
7. India portal

ICT for Rural Community

India has been one of the best performers in the world economy in recent years but the fruits of this performance are not equally distributed to all. The urban centers and their surroundings have appeared as big pockets of development on its land while rural areas have been appeared as dark region on it. Villages have become symbol of poverty, unemployment, illiteracy, displacement of youth, etc and overall backwardness. This imbalance in the development process has forced the rural youth to migrate from their villages in search of employment and better living. Studies show that the demographical change caused by migration of rural youth has disturbed the socio- cultural and environmental harmony of rural life. In the 21st century, development of rural areas is a big question for economists and policy makers. Various rural e-Governance applications have confirmed the important role the ICT can play in the realm of rural development. Several e-Governance projects have attempted to improve the reach, enhance the base, minimize the processing costs, increase transparency, and reduce the cycle times. Following are the two Integrated MMPs specifically for rural community: e-Panchayat and Common Services Centres.

E-Panchayat

NeGP identify e-Panchayat (http://panchayat.gov.in/mopr/viewPortalPage.do?cToken=-1235127219) as one of its integrated MMP with the objective of bringing ICT to all 2,50,000 Panchayati Raj Institutions (PRIs) at the Gram Panchayat (village), Block (intermediate) and Zilla Parishad (district) levels. For planning and implementing the Centrally Sponsored Schemes(CSSs) i.e. the National Rural Health Mission, Mid Day Meal Scheme, Indira Awas Yozana (IAY), Pradhan Mantri Gram Sadak Yozana (PMGSY) and National Rural Employment Guarantee Scheme, one third of the central budget of INR 3,50,000 Crore is allocated to the Panchayats annually.

For effective implementation and monitoring of the money being spent on development and uplifting of masses, a complete Panchayat Enterprise Suite (PES) was developed to outline all function and services that Panchayats were expected and mandated to deliver. The core applications meet the pre-requisites for:

- De-centralize Database
- PRI budgeting and accounting
- Implementation and monitoring of central and State sponsored schemes
- Citizens centric services
- Unique codes to Panchayats
- Essential GIS based services
- Online self-learning medium for all 3 million elected representatives and around 1 million officials' of the Panchayats

Twelve core applications to be developed centrally through National Informatics Centre (NIC) were identified which will address majority of the needs of the stake holders. Out of 12 applications 4 of them namely PLANPlus, PRIASoft, National Panchayat Directory and Panchayat Profile (Partly) have been developed & deployed in all 2, 50,000 Panchayats and the rest 8 is likely to be rolled out in all the Panchayats by 2011.

Presently Bharat Sanchar Nigam Limited (BSNL) has provided Broadband connectivity to 70,000 Zilla Parishads, Block Panchayats and Gram Panchayats (GP). The 5000 GPs of North Eastern Region will be connected by satellite connectivity (VSAT). One time funding for filling ICT infrastructure gaps at GP level is available from Mahatma Gandhi National Rural Employment Guarantee Scheme (MGNREGS) fund over and above the permitted 6% administrative expenses.

Common Services Centers (CSC)

CSC is another important Integrated MMP of NeGP for common people. Objective of these CSC in rural areas are to introduce e-Governance on large scale at grassroots level. These CSCs will offer the following web-enabled e-Governance services to rural communities:

- Application forms;
- Certificates and utility payments such as electricity, telephone and water bills.

The proposed scheme under the Private Public Partnership (PPP) model will be consisting of a 3-tier structure:

- Village Level Entrepreneur (VLE) will be at the bottom of the structure also called the CSC operator;
- The 2nd layer above the VLE will be the Service Centre Agency (SCA) which will be responsible for a cluster of 500-1000 CSCs, and

- The topmost layer called State Designated Agency (SDA) identified by the State Government will be responsible for managing the implementation above the entire State.

The expansion of internet amongst the masses has added another dimension for transfer of the data and information over long distances at virtually no cost. The storage, retrieval, processing and transmitting power of IT if properly harnessed can make governmental processes more transparent and objective ultimately reducing the scope for corruption. However, before any introduction of IT, it is necessary that the existing procedures are properly re-engineered and made computer adaptable.

There were examples of several successful implementation of e-Governance (World Wide Web Foundation's, First ever Web Index reveals impact of Web around the worldweb, 2012). But the greatest challenges being their replicability and up-scaling. There are very few examples of e-Governance with a nationwide impact (e.g. the railway reservation system in India). Lack of good infrastructure and insufficient competence of the personnel have proved to be major bottlenecks in the spread of e-Governance. A good deal attention needs to be paid to familiarize Departmental officials with the relevant e-Governance processes and its capabilities (Table 3). Apart from imparting on-the-job training, the Departmental officials involved with planning and implementations of such strategies may be sent to organizations, including some in the private sector, where similar processes are already successfully implemented.

If the websites of the Government Departments/Ministries are updated regularly it will not only enhance the transparency but will also be saving the valuable time otherwise spent replying the enquiries of the citizens as well replying the questions relating the various services offered by the departments/Ministry concerned. Poor record keeping and limited use of ICT in Government offices are the main handicap for successful implementation of various development schemes implemented by Government.

There should be provision in the Website of the organization for filling Online Feedback. Department of Administrative Reforms and Public Grievances (DAR&PG), the nodal department for grievance handling in Government of India has put in place an online web enabled portal-Centralized Public Grievance Redress and Monitoring System (CPGRAMS), which helps in streamlining of the registration, transmission, and tracking and monitoring of grievances both at the citizen and departmental level. The website of the Government organizations should be linked to http://pgportal.gov.in so that the grievances arising out of unsatisfactory response or no response from the Ministry/Department concerned can be taken up by the Public Grievances officers of DAR&PG for close monitoring and expeditious resolutions.

The mobile subscribers in India are likely to reach 1.159 billion by the end of 2013(Jotischky, 2010) .Considering the rapid penetration rate of mobile phones in rural area, the integration of Mobile Services Delivery Gateway and UIDAI [Aadhaar] will be the foundation of the m-Government for the inclusive Development of India.

- As part of 100 day agenda, Ministry of Information Technology is planning to come up with an Electronic Service Delivery Act (ESDA) by the end of this year. This bill intends to make it mandatory for all government departments and ministries to deliver public services only in electronic mode from a cut date and that cut date will be fixed by the concerned department or the ministry depending upon their level of readiness
- Further there are lots of scope for study and research in the field of e-Governance, Administrative Reforms, Cyber law & implementation of Information Technology Act

Table 3. ICT acts dealing with the e-governance issues in India

Name of the Act	Purpose
Information Technology (Amendment) Act 2008, Section 69	This act authorize the Central Government/State Government/ its authorized agency to intercept, monitor or decrypt any information generated, transmitted, received or stored in any computer resource if it is necessary or expedient so to do in the interest of the sovereignty or integrity of India, defence of India, security of the State, friendly relations with foreign States or public order or for preventing incitement to the commission of any cognizable offence or for investigation of any offence.
Information Technology Act 2000.	a) To make the use of ICT effective the parliament of India has passed this Act. In this act the CHAPTER III represents the-ELECTRONIC GOVERNANCE where Section-8 indicates the b) Publication of rule, regulation etc. in Electronic Gazette. c) Any Rule, regulation, order, bye-law, notification or any other matter published in the Official Gazette should also be published in the Electronic Gazette. CHAPTER X represents THE CYBER REGULATIONS APPELLATE TRIBUNAL where Section-48 indicates the Establishment of Cyber Appellate Tribunal. a) The Central Government shall, by notification, establish one or more appellate tribunals to be known as the Cyber Regulations Appellate Tribunal. b) The Central Government shall also specify, in the notification referred to in subsection c) The matters and places in relation to which the Cyber Appellate Tribunal may exercise jurisdiction
Right to Information Act 2005	In this act the CHAPTER II (Sec-2 & Sec-4) represents the Right to Information and obligations of public authorities Section-2: It shall be a constant endeavour of every public authority to take steps in accordance with the requirements of clause (b) of sub-section (1) to provide as much information suo motu to the public at regular intervals through various means of communications, including Internet, so that the public have minimum resort to the use of this Act to obtain information. Section-4: All materials shall be disseminated taking into consideration the cost effectiveness, local language and the most effective method of communication in that local area and the information should be easily accessible, to the extent possible in electronic format with the Central Public Information Officer or State Public Information Officer, as the case may be, available free or at such cost of the medium or the print cost price as may be prescribed. Explanation-For the purposes of Sub-Sections-4 "disseminated" means making known or communicated the information to the public through notice boards, newspapers, public announcements, media broadcasts, the Internet or any other means, including inspection of offices of any public authority.

- The 12 digit Unique Identification (UID) number or Aadhaar issued by Unique Identification Authority of India to the citizen will not only clean the National citizens Database but also likely to be the master Database of NeGP. The Aadhaar can be used as one time password to access all e-Government services like SingPass (Singapore Personal Access) in Singapore for e-Citizen, the one-stop online portal for all Government services and information
- National Knowledge Network (NKN) was approved in March 2010 by the Cabinet with an outlay of US$ 1.21 billion (INR 599,000 millions) with an aim of establishing a strong and robust internal Indian network which will be capable of providing secure and reliable connectivity [http://nkn.in]. NKN will act as a super highway for integrating e-Governance infrastructure such as government data centers and networks by providing bulk data transfer facility required for e-Governance applications
- India's Telecom Commission proposal to create a US$ 4.5 billion National Optical Fibre Network (NOFN) has been approved by the Department of Telecom (DoT). This NOFN will extend the country's existing fibre optic network from the district level to the village level which will deliver e-

government services at the doorstep of the rural community

- The approach paper for 12th 5 year plan (2012-2017) seeks to reach growth rate to 9% up from 8.2%, desires to "Stimulate for wide spread development of ICT in the country to achieve inclusive growth." Draft National Telecom Policy-2011 released by Government of India has the ambition of providing affordable, reliable and secure telecommunication and broadband services across the country, envisioned to increase in rural tele-density from 35 to 100 by 2020 and 600 million broadband connections by 2020
- Department of Information Technology (DIT), Government of India will unveil G-Cloud policy by 2012
- There are 13 Data Centers are up and 26 State Wide Area Network (SWAN) are operational. However the States without have their own infrastructure can take the benefit of Cloud computing like the state of Jammu & Kashmir

STANDARDIZATION OF E-GOVERNANCE

Standardization of e-Governance will result in many positive results (Mahajan, 2012):

- Simplification of e-Governance service delivery mechanism
- Synchronization of activities of various wings of the Government machinery
- Synergy amongst various e-Governance business processes
- Utilization of standards as well as standardizing processes must be a commonplace practice
- Basic definitions and processes should be set up on the global level.

In standardizing activities for effective implementation of ICT in e-Governance 3 stakeholders i.e. Government, Business & Citizens must walk together in collaboration.

Well elaborated in different countries, interoperability frameworks considered mostly semantic, technical and organizational interoperability, focusing on open standards and open source software development. They receive quite good results in the development and implementation of open standards, however the administrative processes standardization is the most difficult effort and it demands further research.

Department of Electronics and Information Technology (DeitY) has identified 47 areas on the basis of interoperability requirements in e-Governance (Mahajan, 2012).

Standards formulations in pipeline include:

- Device Driver Policy for procurement of hardware in e-Governance applications
- Interoperability Framework for e-Governance (IFEG) in India
- Standards Release and Change Management
- Digital Preservation standards, policy and guidelines
- eForms
- Keyboard Layout Standard
- Mobile standards

CHALLENGES

The following are some of the challenges with respect to e-Governance in India:

- Implementation of IT Act 2000 is yet in a nebulous stage though the Act was enacted 10 years back. The biggest challenge of deploying e-Governance is not technology, but ability of various stakeholders to work together to manage the change introduced by ICT. There is an urgent need of ICT Act to address all the Legal issues pertaining to ICT.

- Most of the Government organizations in India either not developed their Website or the few which have developed their Websites were not updated regularly as a result the requisite information regarding the activities of the organizations is not readily available to the cliental group online. In most of the cases the websites of various department are neither identical nor user friendly. The standards and prototype for developing the websites are not followed in most of the cases.
- The 100,000+CSCs has a big role to plan in e-Governance as well as in bridging the digital divide in India. But the non-availability of the contents in local languages is a big handicap as most of the rural populations are not English literate. Connectivity especially high speed Internet connectivity in rural areas is also another challenge for e-Governance. The project in the PPP model specifically in the NE States will not be economically viable. In some cases it will be difficult to find Village Level Entrepreneur (VLE) to operate a CSC in remote areas.
- The challenge in e-Governance is not the Hardware, Software or the connectivity but organizational transformation including redefining rules and procedures. All the three stockholders of ICT i.e. Government, Business and Citizens must walk together for successful implementation of ICT in e-Governance. Departments, Agencies and Public bodies rarely re-use and adapt systems which are already been commissioned by another wing of the Government leading to wasteful replication.
- Poor network connectivity is the major challenge for implementation of e-Governance in the underdeveloped and developing country. The quality of Network, Broadband and Power Grid Capabilities are the main challenges for implementation of e-Governance in India.
- The challenges for e-Governance implementation, it is not only about the technical part, but also about Institutional arrangement, vested interest from existing work force and good old resistance to change that have to be dealt with.
- The main challenges m-Government is that the mobile handset using various OS is not compatible. Very few of mobile handsets available so far in the market which supports a few local languages. As of now, mobile can be used only to know the status, online processing capacity is limited. Mobile handsets having the Web compatibility are still costly. Sending vital information over mobile is not secure as the mobiles are easily traceable. Above all most of the mobile users are the first time users who have never ever used either the Desktop or Laptop computers.
- The Global Information Technology Report (World Economic Forum, Global Information Technology Report, 2012) tried to cast light on the evolution of ICT over the last decade as well as raising awareness about the importance of ICT diffusion and leveraging for increased development, growth, and better living conditions. The methodological framework of the Networked Readiness Index (NRI) has mapped out the enabling factors driving networked readiness, which is the capacity of countries to fully benefit from new technologies in their competitiveness strategies and their citizens' daily lives. The Index has allowed private and public stakeholders to monitor progress for an ever-increasing number of economies all over the globe as well as to identify competitive strengths and weaknesses in national networked readiness landscapes.

Networked Readiness Index (NRI) is a comprehensive assessment of the present state of networked readiness of the Country (Dutta et al., 2012). These relate to:

- The emerging Internet economy
- Communities to be built around digital highways
- The promise of technology
- ICT's growing impact on poverty reduction
- ICT's contribution to meeting the decade's challenges
- Localization 2.0
- ICT for an effective social strategy
- The creation of a fiber future and its regulatory challenge &
- Mobile banking in the emerging world

The following are some of the steps to overcome the challenges of e-Governance:

- To educate people through well designed training programs about the e-Governance
- To Explain the real benefits of use of e-Governance
- Executive orders and leadership support is critical
- In the Internet, there is a wider spectrum of cultures and a possible new international law governing the Internet needs to be based on the smallest common denominator shared by all humans. There is a need for strong ICT law having international jurisdiction.

DISCUSSION

The use of ICT in private sector has shown a tremendous growth in the past decade. ICT is already on roll in e-Commerce but e-Governance is yet to find its feet. It would be worthwhile to explore the possibility of using the e-Commerce solutions to deliver the citizen centric solutions of e-Governance services. The application of ICT by Government is essential for the deliverance of proficient and cost-effective public services which are responsive to the requirements of the citizens. The legislature, judiciary and administration may apply e-Governance in order to improve internal efficiency for the delivery of public services resulting to enhancement of the processes of democratic governance. For effective implementation of ICT in e-Governance the 3 stakeholders i.e. Government, Business and Citizens must walk together in collaboration. ICT is already on roll in e-Commerce but e-Governance is yet to find its feet. For successful computerization in Governance computer knowledge of departmental officers needs to be upgrade. Similarly, the NIC needs to be trained in department specific activities, so that they could understand each other's view point and also ensure that technology providers understand the anatomy of each department.

Many countries in the Asia-Pacific are focusing attention on how to collaborate more effectively across agencies and various levels of governments. However, the major hindrance that government must overcome is the dearth of gifted ICT manpower such as Chief Information Officers (CIOs). Solution is for governments to train local government staff so they can apply their acquired skills to new ICT tools (Bratt, 2010). Despite the potential benefits that can be offered by ICT, developing countries face significant obstacles to ICT connectivity.

The International Development agencies like World Bank, International Development Association (IDA) etc are having a big role to play. The World Bank project Moldova Governance e-Transformation had a Government Cloud component called "m-Cloud" was the first initiative by this International Development Agency; will focus not only on providing relatively inexpensive ICT solutions for a better Government resources management and service provision but will stimulate economic development, specially local IT Industries, create new business opportunities for Small and Medium Enterprises(SME), develop competences for the future and create resource and development opportunities for universities.

In fact, information from (Beinhocker et al., 2007) estimates that while the total population of India will increase by 30% between 2005 and 2025, the middle class population will increase about ten times or 1000% in the coursework of the same time period. In India, around 26 million births and 9 million deaths takes place every year. Around 6.6 million children went unregistered at birth in 2007 according to the Registrar General of India. Around 2.8 million deaths did not get registered. Only 11 states of India go for 100% record of births and only 5 states records all deaths. If the registration of birth and death is made mandatory to a central Database this will not only eliminate the mammoth task of decennial census but also give the exact picture of population of the country. These will also clan the national population Database which is having lots of duplicate entries.

The proliferation of social computing and social is having a high impact in the Socio-economic development of a country. Government agencies can utilize the potentials of social media through effective use of their e-Government platform. The emergence of mobile technology provides another launching pad for the facilitation of interactive governance through social media. The good news is that developing countries need not wait long for relieve from corruption. Civil society has expanded in strength and demands compliance from the government as well as rule makers. As a consequence by questioning the supply side of corruption, the demand side will involuntarily will reduce (Beinhocker et al., 2007).

CONCLUSION

ICT is the conduits that transmit information and knowledge to individual to widen their choices for Economic and social empowerment. Political, Cultural, Socio-Economic developmental and behavioral decisions today rests on the ability to access, gather, analyze and utilize information and knowledge.

The key challenges of e-Governance is not technological but organizational issues like defining rules and procedures, information transparency, legal issues, infrastructure, skill and awareness, access to right information at right time, inter-departmental collaboration and change of work culture. e-Governance is the key for eradication corruption, once everything becomes online, there will be little chance for corruption in Government machinery. However, effective strategies and legal frameworks can recompense significantly, even in least developed countries. Recently the percentage of middle people has reach around 40%. Governments of the future will require changes and continuously evolve to generate value for meeting the expectations of this class in the society. Higher the percentage of middle class people, lower the corruption rate. Government must be responsive to the quickly changing conditions to meet the citizen's expectations, build capacity to operate effectively in complex, interdependent networks of organizations and systems across the public, private and nonprofit sectors to co-produce public value. What is necessary today is flatter, agile, streamlined & Tech-enabled (FAST) government. The e-Panchayat if implemented successfully is like to bring mass awareness among the rural communities about ICT. The CSCs are likely to serve as Information Kiosks for easy and quick access for Information on Agriculture.

e-Governance is an emerging field of study and research. Plenty of developments are taking place in developing countries e.g. Malaysia has managed to achieve a lot in recent years.

REFERENCES

Beinhocker, E., et al. (2007, August). Tracking the growth of India's middle class. *McKinsey Quarterly*. Retrieved November 10, 2012, from www.mckinseyquarterly.com/Tracking_the_growth_of_ Indias_middle_class_2032

Bratt, S. (2010). *New project to assess potential of creating open government data initiatives in Chile, Ghana and Turkey*. Retrieved November 18, 2011, from http://www.webfoundation.org/2010/08/potential-of-open-government-data-in-chile-ghana-and-turkey/

Dutta, S., et al. (2012). *The global information technology report 2012. Living in a hyperconnected world*. World Economic Forum: Geneva, 2012.

Government, F. A. S. T. (2012, July 20). *(Flat, agile, streamlined, tech-enabled) for the 21st Century*. Retrieved August 2, 2012, from http://blog.mile.org/f-a-s-t-government-flat-agile-streamlined-tech-enabled-for-the-21st-century/

Government of India. (2007). *Ethics in governance, second administrative reforms commission 4th report*. Government of India. Retrieved December 17, 2012, from http://darpg.nic.in/darpgwebsite_cms/Document/file/ethics4.pdf

Government of India. (2012). *National e-governance plan*. Retrieved November 18, 2011, from http://www.negp.gov.in/Projects/Default.aspx

Government of India Ministry of Panchayati Raj. (2013.) Retrieved November 18, 2011, from http://panchayat.gov.in/mopr/ viewPortalPage.do?cToken=-1235127219

Heeks, R. (2008). *The use of ICTs in transparency projects*. Retrieved December 12, 2011, from http://www.egov4dev.org/transparency/

Jotischky, N. (2010). *India will overtake China as world's largest mobile market in 2013*. Press release Informa Telecoms & Media. Retrieved November 11, 2011, from http://blogs.informatandm.com/1475/press-release-india-will-overtake-china-as-worlds-largest-mobile-market-in-2013/

Kannath, S. (2009). *Ethical governance, building an ethical leadership*. Retrieved November 18, 2012, from http://ethicalgov.blogspot.in/

Mahajan, M. (2012). Standards for e-governance. In *Informatics* (pp. 26-27). National Informatics Centre. Retrieved August 2, 2012, from http://informatics.nic.in/uploads/pdfs/975f38cd_26-27_e-Gov_standards.pdf

Neuvo, Y., & Karvonen, E. (2012). *Bit bang IV–Future of the Internet: Societal, business, governance and technological aspects. Aalto University's Multidisciplinary Institute of Digitization and Energy*. MIDE.

Patil, H., et al. (2008). E-governance and white collar crime control. In *Proc. 6th Intl. Conference on E-Governance* (pp. 137-144).

Sanwalka, D. (2011). KPMG in India survey on bribery and corruption impact on economy and business environment. Retrieved November 20, 2012, from www.kpmg.com/IN/en/IssuesAndInsights/ThoughtLeadership/ KPMG_Bribery_Survey_Report_ new.pdf

Singapore Government. (2012). *Singapore Personal Access, SingPass*. Retrieved October 23, 2012, from https://www.singpass.gov.sg/sppubsvc/

Transparency International. (2012). *Global corruption barometer 2010/11*. Retrieved November 10, 2012, from http://gcb.transparency.org/gcb201011/results/

TSO. (2012). *Open data white paper unleashing the potential*. Retrieved November 18, 2011, from http://data.gov.uk/sites /default/files/Open_data_White_Paper.pdf

United Nations. (2010). *United Nations e-government survey 2010-Leveraging e-government at a time of financial and economic crisis*. Retrieved November 3, 2011, from http://www2.unpan.org/egovkb/documents/2010/E_Gov_2010_Complete.pdf

Web, W. W. (2012). *World Wide Web Foundation's first ever web index reveals impact of web around the worldweb*. Retrieved November 18, 2011, from http://www.webfoundation.org/projects/ogd/

World Economic Forum. (2012). *Global information technology report*. Retrieved October 1, 2012, from http://www.weforum.org/issues/global-information-technology

ADDITIONAL READING

Chandra, D. G. (2011). ICT its role in e-governance & rural development. In *International Conference on Advances in Computing and Communications (ACC 2011) April 22-24, 2011*. Retrieved from http://www.springerlink.com/ content/w860888557757h14/

Chandra, D. G. (2012). *Prospects of cloud computing in education and e-governance-An analytical study*. LAP LAMBERT Academic Publishing.

KEY TERMS AND DEFINITIONS

Aadhaar: Aadhaar is a 12 digit individual identification number issued by the Unique Identification Authority of India on behalf of the Government of India. This number will serve as a proof of identity and address, anywhere in India. Any individual, irrespective of age and gender, who is a resident in India and satisfies the verification process laid down by the UIDAI, can enroll for Aadhaar. Each individual needs to enroll only once which is free of cost. Each Aadhaar number will be unique to an individual and will remain valid for life. Aadhaar number will help you provide access to services like banking, mobile phone connections and other Govt and Non-Govt services in due course.

Administrative Reforms Commission: Organization and Method (O & M) Division was set up in Cabinet Secretariat in March, 1954, an as a follow up on one of the recommendations made by Paul H. Appleby. In March, 1964, a Department of Administrative Reforms was set up within the Ministry of Home Affairs and Organization and Method (O & M) Division was transferred to its charge from the Cabinet Secretariat. On 7th February, 1973, the work relating to Department of Administrative Reforms was transferred to Department of Personnel created under Cabinet Secretariat on 1st August, 1970 and was re-designated as Department of Personnel and Administrative Reforms. In April, 1977, Department of Personnel and Administrative Reforms was shifted from Cabinet Secretariat to the Ministry of Home Affairs. In March 1985, the Department of Personnel and Administrative Reforms was elevated to a fully fledged Ministry of Personnel and Training, Administrative Reforms, Public Grievances and Pensions. On December 10, 1985 Ministry of Personnel and Training, Administrative Reforms, Public Grievances and Pensions was re-designated as the Ministry of Personnel, Public Grievances and Pensions with three departments namely, Department of Personnel and Training (DOPT), Department of Administrative Reforms and Public Grievances and Department of Pension and Pensioners Welfare. This Ministry was placed under the overall charge of the Prime Minister assisted by a Minister of State.

E-Democracy: Is the use of ICT and strategies for effective implementation of democracy within the political processes of local communities, states/regions, nations and on the global stage."Democratic actors and sectors in this context include, in order of importance, citizens/voters, organizations, the elected officials, and

Governments. e-Democracy, like democracy in its ideal form, is a direct democracy.

E-Governance: It is the use of ICT such as Internet, Local Area Networks, mobiles etc. by Government to improve the effectiveness, efficiency, service delivery to promote democracy.

E-Panchayats: The Panchayat represents the first-level of government interaction for over 60% of the Indian populace, and provides a large number of basic services for millions of citizens living in rural locations across the nation. It is against this backdrop that the e-Panchayat MMP has been included in NeGP. This MMP aims to address and overcome the typical challenges faced in the villages, such as lack of reliable communication infrastructure, delay in delivery of services to citizens, low revenue mobilisation for implementing schemes at the Gram Panchayat level, and lack of monitoring mechanisms for schemes.

E-Transparency: e-Transparency is use of ICT to handle some or all of the transparency related information flow in Government machinery.

G-Cloud: G-Cloud is Internet based communications which enables public bodies to host, select and use computing services from secure, resilient and cost-effective IT service environment. The G-Cloud program's core benefits are cost reduction, improved services, faster delivery and progressive sustainability agenda. The citizen-centric data, services and applications will be stored, maintained and delivered from G-Cloud and a comprehensive government portal will be a part and parcel of this cloud-based service delivery. The latest trend on Government cloud seems to be following the agency-by-agency scenario.

ICT: Information and Communications Technology or Information and Communication Technology(ICT), is often used as synonym for Information Technology(IT) that stresses the role of unified communications and the integration of telecommunications(telephone lines and wireless signals), computers as well as necessary software, middleware, storage, and audio-visual systems, which enable users to access, store, transmit, and manipulate information. The phrase ICT had been used by academic researchers since the 1980s, but it became popular after it was used in a report to the UK government by Dennis Stevenson in 1997 and in the revised National Curriculum for England, Wales and Northern Ireland in 2000. The term ICT is now also used to refer to the convergence of audio-visual and telephone networks with computer networks through a single cabling or link system. There are large economic incentives to merge the audio-visual, building management and telephone network with the computer network system using a single unified system of cabling, signal distribution and management.

International Development Association: The International Development Association (IDA) is the part of the World Bank established in 1960, IDA aims to reduce poverty by providing loans (called "credits") and grants for programs that boost economic growth, reduce inequalities, and improve people's living conditions. IDA complements the World Bank's original lending arm-the International Bank for Reconstruction and Development (IBRD). IBRD was established to function as a self-sustaining business and provides loans and advice to middle-income and credit-worthy poor countries. IBRD and IDA share the same staff and headquarters and evaluate projects with the same rigorous standards. IDA is one of the largest sources of assistance for the world's 81 poorest countries, 39 of which are in Africa. It is the single largest source of donor funds for basic social services in these countries. IDA-financed operations deliver positive change for 2.5 billion people, the majority of whom survive on less than \$2 a day. m-Government can help make public information and government services available "anytime, anywhere" and that the ubiquity of these devices mandates their use in government functions such as use for sending short message service, or SMS, in the event of an emergency.

Mobile Government: m-Government, is the extension of e-Government to mobile platforms, as well as the strategic use of government services and applications which are only possible using cellular/mobile telephones, laptop computers, personal digital assistants (PDAs) and wireless internet infrastructure.

Mobile Service Delivery Gateway: A platform called Mobile Service Delivery Gateway (MSDG) will be set up on which all ministries and departments will be able to start their services, according to the document posted on the department's website for public comments. The distribution and retail infrastructure of mobile operators is likely to utilize for collecting and processing payments for mobile services, which can be leveraged for receiving payments for public services and delivery of basic financial services under the financial inclusion initiatives. Also in the plan is integration with Aadhaar so as to process the request for service made through mobile faster and easier. The policy envisions that the service will be delivered via SMS support by every handset using technologies such as 3G to deliver richer experience to those who can afford the technology.

Network Readiness Index: Networked Readiness Index (NRI) has mapped out the enabling factors driving networked readiness, which is the capacity of countries to fully benefit from new technologies in their competitiveness strategies and their citizens' daily lives. The Index has allowed private and public stakeholders to monitor progress for an ever-increasing number of economies all over the globe as well as to identify competitive strengths and weaknesses in national networked readiness landscapes.

Open Government: Open Government is the governing doctrine which holds that citizens have the right to access the documents and proceedings of the government to allow for effective public over sight. In its broadest construction it opposes reason of state and other considerations, which have tended to legitimize extensive state secrecy. The origins of open government arguments can be dated to the time of the European Enlightenment: to debates about the proper construction of a then nascent democratic society. Among recent developments is the theory of open source governance are application of the free software movement to democratic principles, enabling interested citizens to get more directly involved in the legislative process. Recently "Gov 2.0" (Government 2.0) has grown from being a name coined by William Eggers to now becoming the umbrella term for serious change in government, and not just here in the United States, but around the world. However, the openness and transparency that Gov 2.0 efforts around the world advocate for; driven by mobility and the cloud-have allowed people to be heard. To hear each other, those people whether in government or civic life, in business or entertainment.

SingPass: SingPass stands for "Singapore Personal Access," is a common password to transact with the Government online. As part of the ongoing effort to enhance the SingPass system, they have implemented the following security improvements that will take effect from 15 Sep 2012. The new password must be alphanumeric and contains 8-24 characters. SingPass passwords will expire every 2 years. Users will be prompted to change their password every 2 years. SingPass Users will need to enter a randomly-generated security codes after any failed login attempts.

Social Computing: Social computing is an area of computer science that is concerned with the intersection of Social behavior and computational systems. It has become an important concept for use in business. In the weaker sense of the term, social computing has to do with supporting any sort of social behavior in or through computational systems. It is based on creating or recreating social conventions and social contexts through the use of software and technology. Thus, blogs, email, instant messaging, social network services, wikis, social bookmarking and other instances of what is often called social software illustrate ideas from social computing, but also other kinds of software applications where people interact socially. Social computing has become more widely known because of its relationship to a number of recent trends. These include the growing popularity of social software and Web 2.0, increased academic interest in social network analysis, the rise of open source as a viable method of production, and a growing conviction that all of this can have a profound impact on daily life. A February 13, 2006 paper by market research company Forrester Research suggested that: "Easy connections brought about by cheap devices, modular content, and shared computing resources are having a profound impact on our global economy and social structure. Individuals increasingly take cues from one another rather than from institutional sources like corporations, media outlets, religions, and political bodies. To thrive in an era of Social Computing, companies must abandon top-down management and communication tactics, weave communities into their products and services, use employees and partners as marketers, and become part of a living fabric of brand loyalists." In the stronger sense of the term, social computing has to do with supporting "computations" that are carried out by groups of people, an idea that has been popularized in James Surowiecki's book, The Wisdom of Crowds. Examples of social computing in this sense include collaborative filtering, online auctions, prediction markets, reputation systems, computational social choice, tagging, and verification games. The Social Information Processing page focuses on this sense of social computing.

Chapter 10
Managing E-Governance: A Framework for Analysis and Planning

Gianluca Misuraca
European Commission, Institute for Prospective Technological Studies (JRC-IPTS), Spain

Gianluigi Viscusi
University of Milano-Bicocca, Italy

ABSTRACT

This chapter presents and discusses the application of an analytical framework for managing digital innovation initiatives in the public sector. The chapter positions e-Government and digital innovation initiatives in the public sector within the broader framework of e-Governance (i.e. governance aided by ICT). It first introduces the conceptual framework on which the discussion is based, and then proposes a higher order conceptualization of the relationship between e-Governance and its underpinning value drivers of performance, openness and inclusion. In particular, the analysis focuses on the role that these value drivers plays in the enactment of digital governance initiatives such as the ones related to open government and smart cities. To this end, the chapter discusses its application to initiatives carried out in Barcelona and Tallinn. A typology of e-Governance 'attitudes' is then identified to provide evidence of further specific interventions required for an appropriate management of similar initiatives in other countries. The chapter concludes by highlighting the policy implications for administrative reform and offering practical recommendations for implementing digital governance initiatives.

INTRODUCTION

The purpose of this chapter is to present and discuss an analytical framework for managing e-Governance issues in digital government initiatives. It positions e-Government and digital innovation initiatives in the public sector within the broader framework of e-Governance (i.e., governance with, and of, ICT) (Misuraca, 2007; Misuraca & Viscusi, 2010). Furthermore, the chapter considers e-Governance as strictly related to openness. Indeed, from a policy perspective,

DOI: 10.4018/978-1-4666-4245-4.ch010

the implementation of e-Governance requires that particular attention is paid to the governance dimension of interoperability (Misuraca, Alfano, & Viscusi, 2011a) in order to implement projects and initiatives that are not optimal but "satisficing" (Simon, 1996). For example, current interest in the implementation of open government calls for a representation of the complex configuration of policies, processes, human resource skills and training need to help policy makers and project managers. In addition, ICT infrastructure is needed for the adoption of innovative technologies and approaches. It is worth noting that though these issues may seem similar to previous e-Government initiatives, in fact they imply a change of perspective by Public Administrations (Di Maio, 2009; 2010; Harrison et al., 2011).

The chapter then discusses the application of a conceptual framework which resulted from the research activities of the authors and their experience in concrete projects. This framework proposes a higher order conceptualization of the relationship between e-Governance and openness. In particular, the analysis focuses on the role of e-Governance and its related dimensions as key factors for the enactment of digital governance initiatives (Dunleavy, Margetts, Simon, & Tinkler, 2006) such as the ones related to open government and smart cities. The relevance of the framework is demonstrated through a discussion of its application to case studies carried out in Barcelona and Tallinn in order to map their characteristics against this conceptual framework.

Then the chapter identifies a typology of e-Governance 'attitudes,' which results from the application of the framework. This typology aims to provide evidence of further specific interventions required for an appropriate management of similar initiatives and projects in other contexts. The main goal is to investigate the configuration of dimensions such as inclusion, transparency and accountability as necessary and sufficient conditions for mature e-Government and open government. The chapter concludes by highlighting the policy implications for governance and public administration reform and offers practical recommendations for strategy and project management of digital governance initiatives.

BACKGROUND AND MOTIVATION

The term *"governance"* originates from the need in economics and finance (as for *corporate governance*) and in political science (as for *state governance*), to convey diverse meanings not covered by the traditional term "government", which is only one of the actors involved in governance. Thus, the concept of governance has been studied from different perspectives and in different disciplines with evolving definitions and interpretations. As for political science and sociology, Jacquier (2005) points out that the concept of governance may refer to different issues such as enforcement of local democracy in a participative way, improvement of public-private partnerships, encouragement of cooperation between local authorities and the promotion of multi-level co-operation.

As a consequence, governance can also be described as a "process of transforming and reformulating approaches to public affairs which involves developing systems for ordering the various players at local level in societies" (Jacquier, 2008). The United Nations (UN) defines governance as "a multifaceted compound situation of institutions, systems, structures, processes, procedures, practices, relationships, and leadership behaviour in the exercise of social, political, economic, and managerial/administrative authority in the running of public or private affairs" (UNDESA, 2003). Taking these definitions into account, we consider governance to be *the process of decision-making and the process by which decisions are implemented, monitored and evaluated* (Misuraca, 2012). This process has multiple dimensions (the structures, roles and relationships governing how society functions), is constantly evolving and strongly conditioned by historical transformations in society's underlying values and organisational models, and has been analysed from several research perspectives (Misuraca et al., 2010).

Moving to information and communication technologies (ICTs), they are important and strategic tools which could be used to transform governance processes (Dunleavy et al., 2006; Misuraca et al., 2011a). However, although the concept of e-Governance is not commonly recognized or shared worldwide as a complementary activity inherently different from e-Government, we define e-Governance as the field of activity where policy design, decision-making, co-ordination, arbitration, networking and regulation, with ICTs, but also of ICTs, take place (Misuraca, 2007; Misuraca & Viscusi, 2010). e-Governance can therefore be considered as a broad framework to capture the co-evolution of ICTs' various stakeholders and the political institutions, at local, national and global level in what has been defined by Dunleavy et al. (2006) as *digital era governance*.

Current trends in open government and open data initiatives (Harrison et al., 2011; Lee & Kwak, 2011; McDermott, 2010) call for renewed focus on e-Governance with respect to traditional e-Government perspectives. Notwithstanding the current hype and interest in open data, we point out that open data is a means not an end, and releasing public data is a small step towards open government (Broster, Misuraca, & Bacigalupo, 2011). To achieve open government, we must go beyond the focus on accountability and transparency, which is typical of advanced phases of traditional e-Government maturity models (Andersen & Henriksen, 2006; Batini, Viscusi, & Cherubini, 2009; Lee, 2010). As a consequence, open government models of e-Governance call for several policy and research challenges to be solved. Broster et al.(2011) identify the following key challenges:

- The capacity of governments to survey the actual needs, expectations and desires of their target population;
- The establishment of a two-way dialogue between governments, individuals and collective agents;
- The technological evolution towards the virtualisation of processing and storage capacity enabled by cloud computing: decision makers must carefully evaluate the balance between efficiency and cost saving opportunities and uncertainties in terms of privacy and security (see Paquette & Wilson, 2010).

e-Governance in fact represents a relevant concept for addressing the emerging trends in the innovation of local public administration services, where openness, inclusion and performance are considered important quality dimensions (Misuraca et al., 2011a). In this regard, e-Governance must also be related to the concept of urban governance.

The notion of urban governance is often considered as an alternative to traditional approaches to government (centralised, hierarchical, top-down, bureaucratic). It promotes an approach based on public action networks and mechanisms aimed at cooperation, organisation and integration of different public and private stakeholders (Jacquier, 2005; 2008; OECD, 2001a). There are a number of different theories in the literature which explain the emergence of the concept of urban governance. These theories reflect the various problems and changes in society which the concept attempts to address, for example, from neo-liberalism theories to state transformation (OECD, 2001b; Perroux, 1960; 1990). Furthermore, the analysis of the literature on urban studies clearly shows, since the work of Castells (1992), that there is a growing awareness amongst scholars and urban actors on topics which reflect the interrelation of information society and urban development (Elling, Lentz, & de Jong, 2007). However, structural analysis of the linkages between the high value added assets of the digital economy (and particularly ICTs) is not considered by most research on urban governance and local development (Lévy & Jouyet, 2006). Nevertheless, several studies have shown how ICTs form the basis of a new technological revolution that will lead to a change of the technological paradigm with comprehensive impacts on economy, society and culture (Castells, 1997; Sassen, 1991).

Moreover, the rapid integration of ICTs in the public sector is transforming public administrations not only by increasing what people require and expect of governments in terms of efficiency and productivity but also by making governments more open to democratic control and social accountability. Indeed, social networks and user-driven technologies could transform government even further by changing power relationships and linking together all interested players more efficiently (Gatautis, 2008; Punie et al, 2009). In particular, the application of ICT-enabled solutions allows citizens to be included in the social and political life of a City more actively, facilitating decision-making for public institutions and improving public policy in local communities (Gatautis, 2008; Misuraca, 2011).

In order to address these challenges, city systems must find new models of governing, and ICTs can play a crucial role in this. Research in this domain has also been conducted from a practitioners' perspective. However, although many lessons can be learned from these practical experiences, there is a lack of information on e-Government at city level, where the missing dimensions concern e-Governance attributes in order to better understand how a city is progressing in the transformation process. Up until now, the most relevant studies about e-Government measurement to compare its evolution has been carried out at country level (Capgemini, IDC, Europe Rand, DTi, & Sogeti, 2010; UN, 2012). Regarding local level, benchmarking surveys mainly focus on the general aspects of the official websites. Although there are some exceptions such as results from the EUROCITIES network (Deloitte & Eurocities, 2005; Eurocities, 2011), a complete view of the e-Government process and progress at city level in e-Government, and open government cannot be found.

Taking these issues into account, it is our belief that considering various e-Governance dimensions represents a critical factor in the planning and management of effective e-Government initiatives. These will prepare and in some case lead the change towards open government. Furthermore, from both practitioner and academic perspectives, we found local government to be a relevant and interesting domain of analysis. Nevertheless, it is also our belief that a comprehensive analytical framework, which focuses on relevant dimensions, is a fundamental condition for effective interpretation of the type of context of intervention the planning activity aims to impact. Thus, in the following sections, we first discuss a theoretical framework for the analysis of e-Governance planning dimensions. We then apply the framework to the interpretative analysis of the case studies of smart city initiatives carried out in Barcelona and Tallinn. Finally, the results contribute to the production of a typology that can help to formulate policy through the elicitation of the e-Governance attitudes of (local) public administrations with respect to other actors (constituencies, other institutions, etc.) and (ICTs) resources.

THEORETICAL FRAMEWORK

ICT applications to support the transformation of governance processes and innovative forms of local service delivery have been developed in pioneering experiments and pilot projects in several large and middle-sized cities all over the EU. In this paper, we consider the findings of research conducted by the Information Society Unit at the Institute for Prospective Technological Studies (IPTS) of the European Commission's

Joint Research Centre, namely the Exploratory Research on emerging ICT-enabled governance models in EU cities (EXPGOV). Making reference to recent work in social studies, public policies and ICT (see e.g. Viscusi et al., 2010), the EXPGOV theoretical framework argues for the adoption of a wide definition of e-Government as a system of ICT-enabled innovation policies for public administration and related governmental functions. In this view, ICT-enabled projects and initiatives can be considered as high-level, context-sensitive interventions which aim to introduce and facilitate gradual changes. The EXPGOV project has identified three main *value drivers* that constitute the basis of a theoretical framework for ICT-enabled governance at the local level (Misuraca, 2010):

- **Performance:** I.E. effectiveness and efficiency (enabling optimal use of resources for citizens and tax payers in the service delivery); and also responsiveness (serving all citizens in a consistent and predictable way) as an indirect dimension.
- **Openness:** I.E. access to information as a proxy for participation (enabling the process of empowering citizens to legally control service delivery to their advantage) and transparency (bringing visibility to the service workflow for citizens by means of automated service delivery); and accountability (creating standards against which the individuals providing a service and the service delivery can be held accountable), that also serves the goal of ensuring consensus orientation (following democratic practices).
- **Inclusion:** I.E. equity and inclusiveness (referring to citizens receiving the service on an equal basis and providing services to disadvantaged and minority groups in society), which implicitly ensure respect for the rule of law (ensuring that laws and regulations governing the service are applied in an impartial way).

These value drivers represent the principles and the expected outcomes of e-Government initiatives, experiments and pilot projects taking place at different governance levels. However, while it is recognized that openness - and its crucial sub-dimension of interoperability - plays a key role in ICT-enabled governance, research into the non-technical dimensions of the phenomenon, and the relation between interoperability and governance processes is lacking.

Furthermore, scholars and public managers have few instruments that can give them a systemic perspective to face the challenges of the multiple facets of the openness dimension of e-Governance. For these reasons, we now discuss a conceptual model built on an analysis of state-of-the-art research and literature on ICT-enabled governance, and previous experiences of the authors in the implementation of specific projects.

The conceptual model represented in Figure 1 aims to support the elicitation of different configurations of ICT-enabled governance systems on the basis of the relationships between the following factors:

- Governance model characteristics (i.e. cultural administrative tradition and socio-economic characteristics of the context of intervention),
- Value drivers (i.e. performance, openness, inclusion).

This model aims to provide an interpretative instrument to deal with the multiple facets and layers of ICT-enabled governance and in particular, the impact and role of interoperability on the *value drivers*. These are influenced by *governance model characteristics* and related dimensions (see Figure 1), which can be evaluated in terms of quality dimensions associated with the considered value drivers. Thus, we provide a set of quality dimensions for each driver (see Table 1), which allows better interpretation of the type of contribution offered by ICT-enabled governance initiatives.

Figure 1. The conceptual model

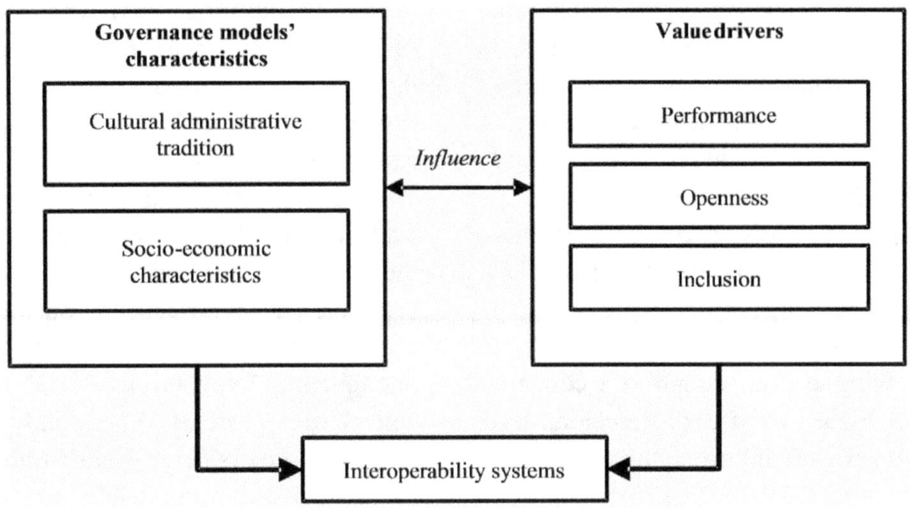

Table 1. Value drivers, governance and quality dimensions

Value Driver	Governance Dimension	Quality dimension
Performance	Efficiency	Economic
		Temporal
		Procedural (i.e. the obligations and constraints imposed by law on the administrative processes and on the interactions between administrations and users)
	Effectiveness	Service Reliability, including Accuracy and Completeness of information requested for the service provision in order to achieve the user's expectation
Openness	Access to information	Temporal
		Cultural
	Interoperability	Technological (i.e. diffusion of standards and technological infrastructures and systems for interoperability)
		Shared data / services (i.e. the ability of administrations to access data by means of the inter-administration back office, and the possibility for external users to access administrative data via ICTs)
	Accountability	Transparency (i.e. the volume of information that the public administration provide to users describing their internal functioning and informing users on what they can expect or claim while using the service)
		Participation (i.e. the effective level to which users' opinions reach the public administration in charge of the service and influence the provision)
Inclusion	Accessibility	Service accessibility for disabled people
		Technological (i.e. diffusion of the infrastructure and technologies which support the service provision) and channel accessibility (i.e. it focuses on the existence of different channels for service access and delivery, such as desktop PC, mobile phone, TV and radio, etc.).
	Equity	ease of access for minority groups
		ease of access for disadvantaged groups (e.g. poor, illiterate and elderly people)

The relevance of a systemic perspective on quality assessment to support strategic planning of e-Government initiatives has been discussed in Viscusi et al. (2010). These authors also propose a framework, which is further adapted to e-Governance issues in Misuraca, Alfano, and Viscusi (2011a; 2011b).

In this chapter, we apply aspects of the framework to the specific case of the elicitation of ICT-enabled governance targets and goals for each value driver considered (see Table 2).

In the following section, we apply the conceptual framework to the two cases of Barcelona and Tallinn, based on findings from the EXPGOV project (see Misuraca, 2012a; 2012b).

Case Study: Municipality of Barcelona

Barcelona is the capital of Catalonia, one of seventeen Spanish Autonomous Communities. In terms of population, it is the second largest city in Spain, after Madrid, with 1,621,537 inhabitants and a population density (inhabitants/Km^2) of 15,872 and a total of 655,302 households. Most of the households (182,729) have two adults with no minors. The birth rate is 8.7% and the death rate is 9.4%. In 2007, approximately 47% of the population was male and 53% was female. In 2008, life expectancy for men was 79 and for women 85.2.

Although Barcelona has a long and solid tradition of classic manufacturing activities, the city today has concentrated its activities on services. The significance of businesses and real estate agencies is noteworthy, making up nearly one fourth of total activity (24.3%), followed by collective services (20.7%), industry (12.7%), retail and repairs (11.5%), and transport (9.6%). More than one million jobs are located in the city and nearly 2.5 million jobs in the surrounding metropolitan area. At the end of 2007, there were 477,942 businesses located in the province of Barcelona. In terms of size, the vast majority of businesses with employees are small, or medium-sized enterprises with less than 200 workers, and 54% of active firms have no employees at all. 29% of companies and 48% of employees in the city work in knowledge-intensive sectors.

Table 2. Value drivers, quality dimensions and related level of application

ValueDriver	Dimension	Quality Level
Performance	Efficiency	Service
	Effectiveness	Organization
Openness	Transparency	Service
		Organization
	Accountability	Organization
		Legal
	Accessibility	Organization
		Technology
		Information
Inclusion	Accessibility	Service
		Technology
		Information

The Barcelona area has more than 210 technology parks and technology and research centres, as well as nine science and technology facilities that are international benchmarks. Around 700 new companies, that offer employment to more than 1,500 people, are created each year. Barcelona Activa, the municipal company that supports the design and execution of the employment, innovation and business-creation policies in the city, plays a key role in the promotion of entrepreneurship. In Barcelona, it only takes 48 hours to set a new company. Barcelona has a rich ecosystem of highly competitive business schools, foundations, and educational institutions, making it one of the most popular international destinations for business management studies.

Despite the global economic climate, characterized by the current recession, Barcelona has maintained its solid international position and very strong brand recognition. In 2010, the city was ranked the fifth best city for doing business by the European Cities Monitor.[1] Additionally, the publication 'Scorecard on Prosperity 2010' ranked Barcelona third in global prosperity, above metropolitan areas such as San Francisco, Paris, Madrid, Seattle, and Hong Kong.[2]

The above description of the socio-economic environment of Barcelona provides us with insights into the first set of dimensions of one of the main components of the Governance model's characteristics (see the conceptual model in Figure 1).

Table 3 shows the configuration of Barcelona's governance system, where socio-economic characteristics are influenced by *openness* and *inclusion* as major value drivers. The value-mediated implementation of the characteristics results in a focus on quality dimensions such as *transparency* (facilitating openness at service and organizational level) and *accessibility* (facilitating both openness and inclusion at service, technological, and information levels). Furthermore, openness and inclusion have influenced governance at

Table 3. Configuration of the governance system of Barcelona according to interoperability characteristics

Governance Models characteristics	Value drivers	Quality dimensions/level	Type of interoperability (enabling factor)
Cultural administrative traditions	Performance	Efficiency (Service) Effectiveness (Organization)	Organizational
	Openness	Transparency (Service) Transparency (Organization) Accountability (Legal framework) Accessibility (Information)	Technological
Socio-Economic Characteristics	Openness	Transparency (Service) Transparency (Organization) Accessibility (Service) Accessibility (Technology) Accessibility (Information)	Organizational
	Inclusion	Accessibility (Service) Accessibility (Technology) Accessibility (Information)	Technological

socio-economic level through the enforcement of productive interaction between organizational and technological interoperability, facilitating the emergence of creative and innovative businesses which rely on an effective technological infrastructure.

In the following paragraphs, we discuss the cultural and administrative traditions underlying the ICT-enabled city governance model of Barcelona (these are the other relevant characteristics shown in Table 3).

The Barcelona City Council is the local administration that represents, governs and administers the city's interests. State legislation and the Catalan Statute of Autonomy have given the municipal area of Barcelona a special regime, established by parliamentary law. The Barcelona City Council has the right to propose the modification of this regime and to participate in the elaboration of any changes to be made by law. Also, it must be consulted during the parliamentary process of any other legislative matters which affect it. The Municipal Charter of Barcelona, approved by the Parliament of Catalonia and by the Spanish Parliament, legally strengthens and guarantees the autonomy of the city. Its purpose is to facilitate efficient local management of the city for the citizens, and to reinforce the municipal powers in the area of collaboration with public administrations. Since 1984, Barcelona's local government has been organized in ten districts. Each district comprises several neighbourhoods and has autonomy regarding decision making and economic management. Finally, according to the Barcelona City Charter, one of the basic criteria in the organization of the city is that the political aspects of law making, policy making and control must be clearly differentiated from the administrative functions. For this reason, there are two levels of organization within the City Council: the political and the administrative. Other than the City Council, there are other actors that are part of the governance structure of the city:

- **Political Actors:** Mainly, other municipal political groups that are not governing the city as well as different administrative levels, and, sometimes, the European Union;
- **Economic Actors:** There are many business interests in the city and therefore some economic organizations that play an active role in the city governance (some of them are the Chamber of Commerce, the city hotel industry, the Economy Circle, Catalunya Caixa and La Caixa, financial institutions which are present in many city financial operations), construction companies, services companies, utilities companies (water, gas and electricity provision), and the knowledge-intensive companies in 22@;
- **Social Actors:** Some of the more relevant are the Third Sector Board (where organizations such as Cáritas or the Red Cross are present), the Social Welfare Council, the federation of neighbours' associations, unions, cultural organizations, universities, immigrants associations, the Alternative Space (for the last 10 years, there is a squatter tradition in the city that has given rise to alternative organizations), and economic and social actors, such as RACC (Royal Automobile Club of Catalonia) and the Barcelona Football Club;
- **Media Actors:** Particularly, the Catalan paper La Vanguardia.

Currently, reaching consensus on city matters is one of the main challenges for governance.

Taking these issues into account, 'transformation' is the term that best describes the Barcelona experience during the last thirty years. The challenge was to transform the economy and social profile, moving to a new age based on knowledge industries, modern city tourism and quality infrastructures for residents, investors and visitors. The City Council has been the driving force of these developments, the turning point being the organization of the Olympic Games in 1992. But at the same time, to be able to play this role, the municipal government has itself been forced to change. Since 1979, it has evolved to become a competent, citizen-centered public organization. Information and communication technologies have been an essential tool that has supported the multi-faceted innovation process. In 1995, the first municipal website was launched. From 1995 to 1998, the municipal website was changed five times, but it always focused on service. From 1999-2000 onwards, a third stage developed. At this time, the strategy was a multi-channel one and the goal was to integrate communication and electronic administration efforts in order to encourage users. As this strategy consolidated, there was a need to institutionalize ICT adoption; that is, to take measures to codify, formalize and thus boost the assimilation and "routinization" of ICT within the organization. Several changes were implemented from 2005 to 2007, including a change of the organizational structure, as will be described later.

The last phase started in 2008 with the Barcelona 2.0 management model, which aimed to take government to the citizens by offering them a more flexible, straightforward and efficient service. It therefore entailed a complete change in internal processes and in the relationship between the City Council and the citizens. As shown in Table 3, the main value driver of the Barcelona City Council's actions has been performance. Both efficiency and effectiveness have been prioritized at different stages for different reasons. This was the case back in the early nineties and is also the case today. Regarding openness, access to information has been emphasised, explaining why the municipal website has been subject to so many changes. A content tool to manage the website has now been successfully adopted. In addition, several interoperability initiatives have been carried out with other public administrations and also with professional bodies and financial institutions.

Inclusion has become a public value driver only recently in the Barcelona 2.0 framework. In particular, accessibility to technology has been prioritized with projects such as Barcelona WiFi (a Barcelona City Council service that allows the citizen to connect to the Internet through Wi-Fi access points, or hotspots, located in various municipal amenities). However, it does not seem that equity, understood here as ease of access for minority and disadvantaged groups, has been pursued in the different stages that have been described.

In general, inclusion is a strategic goal that currently results in the enforcement of the openness value driver quality dimensions through technological interoperability (see Table 3). The focus has been on *transparency* (at service and organizational level), *accountability* (at legal framework level), and *accessibility* of information. In the following paragraph, we will discuss the main steps in the implementation of each of these quality dimensions.

In June 2004, Professor Manuel Castells from the Open University of Catalonia (Universitat Oberta de Catalunya – UOC), published the results of a study conducted as part of the Project Internet Catalonia (PIC), an interdisciplinary research programme focused on the characteristics and development of the information society in Catalonia (Spain). This study emphasized the emergence of a city governance paradigm characterized by the institutional and conscious deployment of the Internet to increase efficiency in local government, of improving public services, and of rearticulating the city governance processes (Castells & Ollé, 2004).

After the local elections of June 2007, the organizational structure and the unit in charge of promoting ICT adoption in the city of Barcelona and within the Barcelona City Council experienced some changes. As a result, an ICT master plan was defined and implemented in September 2008. The ICT master plan was particularly important because it was seen as a key tool to enable the implementation of the new management model of the Barcelona City Council. Formally called Barcelona 2.0, this management model aimed to take government closer to citizens by offering them a more flexible, straightforward and efficient service, making Barcelona a smarter city by means of having a simple and effective, connected, ubiquitous, and innovative public (local) administration.

Three main areas were prioritized: infrastructures, smart services, and citizen interaction. Several infrastructure projects have been put in place: for example, Barcelona Wi-Fi (a Barcelona City Council service that allows the citizen to connect to the Internet through Wi-Fi access points, or hotspots, located in various municipal amenities) and the Wi-Fi mesh network (a municipal network for ubiquitous services, which is key to developing a smart city). Several smart services have also been implemented: for example, the Barcelona 3D city map, the use of PDAs by different actors within the City Council (such as the local police, inspectors, or those responsible for emergency services, and care of the elderly and the homeless), and the smart transport and mobility project. Finally, regarding citizen interaction, an integrated multichannel vision has been developed and citizen e-participation initiatives have been implemented. The most important was the electronic consultation on the transformation of the Diagonal Avenue, the city's main street, carried out in 2010.

Although the project started in 2000, the Barcelona 2.0 new management model has given it new life because infrastructures play an outstanding role. In this respect, the City Council has stated that the future development of Barcelona depends on its ability to integrate new information and communication technologies and, of course, to intensify its knowledge-driven industrial activities and profit from them. This is the main goal of 22@, a Barcelona municipal company, which aims to consolidate the role of Barcelona as an innovative city.

A specific and interesting line of action has lately been developed (since 2008): the 22@ urban lab project. It aims to use the city as an urban laboratory, as a testing ground for innovative solutions for companies that are in the pre-commercialization stage and are seeking to implement tests in any field. These initiatives, following the San Francisco model, aim to establish an 'open city', defined as one that invests in open government (i.e. open data, open applications and open services, and open infrastructures).

Moreover, ICT policy development has had different consequences in terms of regulation and organizational and administrative procedures. But the main implications that ICT policies have produced are the result of the strategy of the last two phases. On one hand, in Barcelona, major changes in regulation, like the approval of the Ordinance on Electronic Government and its procedural developments, have been critical for IT institutionalization. Formally, the Ordinance aimed to comply as effectively as possible with the principles of administrative accountability, transparency, proximity, and public service. Therefore, it set out to 1) establish the rights and responsibilities that must govern the relationship between citizens and the Barcelona City Council by way of electronic means, 2) establish the general principles for promoting and developing e-government in the local administration, and 3) regulate the conditions and legal effects of the use of electronic means for administrative procedures. In practice, this meant a shift from a (voluntary) service to a (mandatory) right to information and electronic services, fostering the need of general administration rules and procedures to adapt to the electronic means.

However, the regulatory and legal framework for ICT in Barcelona has developed beyond the Ordinance, for example:

- There is a Mayoral Decree that regulates the IT system for managing communications by members of the public reporting incidents and making claims, complaints, and suggestions (May 2009),

- Technical safety regulations were developed for the Barcelona City Council information system users, as were regulations on personal data processing at the Barcelona City Council (June 2009),
- Rules were passed on establishing electronic channels as a main way of receiving applications for selection procedures (December 2009),
- The electronic headquarters of Barcelona City Council were regulated, and
- Guidelines were developed for the running of the Barcelona City Council's electronic notice boards (January 2010).

The need to design new services based on ICTs has led to process reengineering. During the first years of the Internet and of electronic services, some initiatives aimed to transform procedures and workflows in specific departments and units such as the Guardia Urbana, the Barcelona police force, or the Tax Municipal Institute. With the implementation of Barcelona 2.0, the emphasis on the back office, on integration and on interoperability has grown stronger. The 'electronic report' ("expediente electrónico") has been the transversal tool to integrate the different modules designed such as e-documents, e-signatures, e-payments, e-contracts, or e-decrees. To sum up, it can be stated that, over the years, the public management model of the Barcelona City Council, regarding ICT, has changed from managing information (two first stages) to strengthening service delivery by the Internet (third stage) to prioritizing a complete change in internal processes. Decision making processes regarding online services or initiatives to be implemented have changed accordingly.

From the analysis carried out, it can be concluded that the Barcelona City Council has been an innovative and creative pioneer in ICT adoption throughout the years. In some areas, the results of the ICT strategy have proved really successful and Barcelona has become a reference to other cities not only in the same area but also in Spain as a whole and internationally. In other fields, the impact of the policies implemented still remains to be seen and further action is needed. In particular, it seems that there is a need to focus more on initiatives to facilitate participation and strengthen social inclusion.

Case Study: Municipality of Tallinn

Tallinn is the capital city of Estonia. According to the population register, the number of people living in Tallinn on 1 October 2010 was 411,880 which forms around 30% of the entire population of Estonia. The composition of the society is rather heterogeneous: more than half (52.2%) Tallinn's citizens are Estonians, Russian speakers account for nearly 40% and the remaining 10% of the population is made up of other nationalities (of which Ukrainians form approximately 4%). Tallinn has a tendency to urban sprawl, reflected in the emigration of people from Tallinn to close neighbourhoods in Harju County. More importantly, these are middle-aged citizens with higher education and well-paid jobs, who are therefore essential tax payers.

Tallinn, together with other local municipalities in Harju County, forms the most powerful economic region in Estonia. It is the centre that attracts most foreign capital and receives 4/5 of all investment made in Estonia. Furthermore, nearly half of the GDP of Estonia is produced in Tallinn. The employment structure of Tallinn has not undergone radical changes since 2005. The top 3 sectors of employment are the manufacturing sector, wholesale and retail trade, and the repair of motor vehicles and motorcycles. In addition, financial and insurance activities have been following a constant upward trend since 2005.

During the last 10 years since the inception of the ICT paradigm, figures for Internet penetration have been constantly growing. Tallinn has always been ahead of the other local municipalities in fostering ICT development. In 2009, the number of computer and Internet users in Tallinn reached 80% and the percentage of households with Internet connection at home is now relatively high (75%). Furthermore, there are 354 Wi-Fi areas in Tallinn and 7 Internet-providers.

The state's deep involvement in ICT development has inevitably influenced the economy and society of Tallinn city as the capital city. Estonia has put in place infrastructure successfully, i.e. digital databases, a data exchange layer enabling the databases "to communicate" (X-road) and digital identity provided by the ID card. The city uses this infrastructure to offer various kinds of e-services ranging from registration of place of residence to local government elections and e-tickets for public transport.

The above description of the socio-economic environment of Tallinn provides us with insights into the first set of dimensions of the Governance model characteristics (see the conceptual model in Figure 1). Table 4 shows the configuration of the governance system of Tallinn, where socio-economic characteristics are influenced by all three value drivers, with a special focus on *openness* and *inclusion*. The value-mediated implementation of the characteristics results in a focus on quality dimensions such as *efficiency* (facilitating performance at service level) and *accessibility/ equity* (facilitating both openness and inclusion at service, technological, and information levels).

Furthermore, openness and inclusion have influenced governance at a socio-economic level as these two drivers support growth in financial and insurance activities, which rely on an efficient and accessible technological infrastructure. In the following paragraph, we discuss cultural and administrative traditions (the other relevant governance model characteristics shown in Table 4).

Changes in the governance structure reflect not only the influence of new technologies but also political will and evolution in the underlying political culture. Estonia has a long tradition of local government. Before the establishment of independence in 1918, Estonia already had a functioning system of local administration. Local authorities were carrying out certain functions like collecting revenue and determining some expenditures. Estonia was the first of the Baltic States to begin re-establishing a local government system after the Soviet era. On 10 November 1989, an Act on the principles of local government was adopted. Specifically, it established primary level local authorities in towns in rural districts and rejected the empowerment of regional governments, mainly because of previous soviet experiences and links with Nordic countries. After regaining independence in August 1991, the new Constitution of the Republic of Estonia was adopted by a referendum on 28 June 1992. It conformed to the principles of the European Charter of Local Self-Government, establishing the legal basis for the existence of contemporary local government in Estonia.

The legislative framework regulating local governance also encompasses the Local Government Council Election Act and the Local Government Organisation Act. Whereas the former regulates local electoral procedures, the latter forms the basis for the functioning of local governments in Estonia (i.e. it establishes the jurisdiction, function, responsibilities and organizational structure of local authorities and their relationship with other local bodies and central government). In particular, the Constitution of Estonia states that the units of local governments in Estonia are towns and rural municipalities. However, Estonia is divided into 3 types of administrative entities: counties, towns and municipalities. County governments are in fact offices of the county governors who represent the central government at the regional level. Local self-government is exercised only at the municipal level (i.e. in towns and rural municipalities).

In Estonia, a parliamentary model is used as the form of governance (*cabinet model*). According to the Local Government Organisation Act, municipal institutions are comprised of a directly

Table 4. Configuration of the governance system of Tallinn according to interoperability characteristics

Governance Models characteristics	Value drivers	Quality dimensions/level	Type of interoperability (enabling factor)
Cultural administrative traditions	Performance	Efficiency (Service)	Technological
	Openness	Accountability (Organization) Accessibility (Information)	Organizational
	Inclusion	Accessibility (Service) Accessibility (Technology) Equity (Service)	Technological
	Openness	Accountability (Organization) Accessibility (Information)	Technological
Socio-Economic Characteristics	Performance	Efficiency (Service)	Technological
	Openness	Accessibility (Information)	Technological

elected council and a government composed of the council. Hence, the Tallinn city governance structure consists of 2 main bodies: the City Council and the City Government.

The *Tallinn City Council* is Tallin's representative body. It is elected on the basis of the Local Government Council Election Act in free elections for a term of four years. Tallinn City Council consists of 79 elected councillors. The exclusive competences of Tallinn City Council include making amendments to the budget, imposing local taxes, approving, amending and adopting development plans, electing a chairman and vice chairman of the council, electing and releasing the mayor of the city and fulfilling other functions provided by the laws. The everyday administration of the council's work is provided by the City Council Office. The City Council works in plenary sessions, fractions or committees which are created according to arising problems in need of solutions.

The *Tallinn City Government* is the local government's executive body. It consists of the Mayor and 6 Deputy Mayors who govern 13 departments, each of which is responsible for a special area of activity (e.g. environment department, sports and youth department, etc.). The organizational and technical work of the City Government is provided by the City Office. The latter is governed by the City Secretary appointed by the Mayor and composed of advisors, 8 services and 3 departments. In order to perform local government functions successfully, Tallinn has been divided into 8 city districts each with its own administration and council. City district administrations are governed by the City District Governor who is appointed and released by the City Administration on proposals from the Mayor. The city districts are administrative agencies whose competence and relationship with the city bodies are stated in their statutes approved by the City Council.

As for ICT Infrastructure, the emergence of Internet in the municipality of Tallinn dates back to 1996. At the outset, it was mainly used for exchanging e-mails between officials. It was, however, used on a rather informal level as the e-mails had no official power to either accept or reject any proposals. This provoked further development of internal management digitalization (i.e. the establishment of document registers and development of a document management system). In 1999, an Internet-based Tallinn Legislation Register (TÕR) emerged and in 2000 the City

Government Session Information System (LIIS) and the City Council Session Information System (AKTAL) were developed. In 2001, the Tallinn city authorities' common document management system for letters, contracts etc. labelled as "Postipoiss" (Postman) which provoked the emergence of Public Document Register was established. The 2000s were also characterized by the standardization of the infrastructure (e.g. by the creation of a wide area network and harmonization of various domains which had generated various e-mail addresses).

On the organizational side, strategic principles of ICT development were elaborated during several meetings of the IT Company Directors' Forum. The Government-to-Government (G2G) approach later moved to the Government-to-Citizen (G2C) perspective by delivering city services via Internet. The development of ICT-based city services began in 2007. A year later it was officially recognized as an important activity in the Tallinn public e-services development plan. The subsequent creation of an e-service working group has contributed much to the e-services development process.

Thus, the evolution of ICT in the city of Tallinn has been rather chaotic. In parallel with the gradual implementation of ICTs at state level, new services started emerging slowly in the city and their integration was more of an ad hoc activity than a carefully designed project.

Initially, there was a relatively high degree of fragmentation inside the governance structure of the city, which made coordination and control functions extremely complicated and eventually ineffective. Due to the ICT centralization process, which started in 2000, computers started to be purchased centrally through the ICT Service. The ICT Service under the City Office now serves all departments of the City Government: i.e. the computer support department (support of end user), the system support department (infrastructure) and the ICT systems and technical development department. The latter plays an active role in investigating the needs of the City Government departments in the ICT area. In addition, the head of the ICT service is constantly in contact with the heads of departments, city council members, and city district governors. At least once a year a general meeting takes place. Furthermore, centralization of ICT has also taken place in terms of services development.

Notwithstanding, there seems to be an information gap between city districts and city departments. For instance, the Social Department does not know anything about the social issues of any of the 8 city districts. The reason behind this gap is probably the high autonomy of city districts and the absence of any legislative act that could oblige city departments to be familiar with what is going on in the districts. This kind of problem seems to be partly resolved with the Development Service playing the role of a central institution gathering information about services and fostering their further development. Moreover, the central unit's closeness to the political level guarantees the development of services that may not be in the interests of a specific department, and gives it the ability to develop cross-department services such as the e-ticket.

The historical milestones of ICT evolution in the city of Tallinn (i.e. e-mail, G2G and finally G2C) did not develop on their own. One cannot underestimate the role of the Tallinn City Mayors who have been rather successful in fostering ICT changes in city governance. Tallinn City supports new ICT initiatives such as the ITL project "Estonian ICT cluster" and gives out ICT scholarships.

Moreover, Estonia has a well-developed communications network: all central and government agencies, educational and health institutions and most enterprises have an Internet connection. Approximately 90% of the Estonian population lives in areas with high availability of broadband Internet and the city of Tallinn is the best connected area in the country. At the end of 2010, 80% of people in Tallinn were using Internet. However, despite this fact, municipal government has recognized that there is a part of the population, in particular the economically underprivileged and elderly, for whom the access to the Internet is precluded. To foster broadband development and access to it, the City of Tallinn has compiled a Tallinn Public e-Services Development plan, which establishes the needed ICT environment for further development of public e-Services.

Innovation is in turn underpinned by active cooperation between public, private and non-governmental partners. This fosters the emergence of new modern approaches and solutions. In order to create new economic value through innovation, Tallinn has approved a long-term strategy - Tallinn Innovation Strategy 2009-2013. One of its target activities is to support partnerships.

Cooperation and networking require both public and private sectors to work in an active and trustworthy manner. Tallinn has elaborated a separate programme document that focuses on cluster development: Tallinn Cluster Development Programme, which applies to companies, umbrella organisations, and educational and research institutions. ICT, as one of the leading sectors, has the potential to be integrated in all clusters. Furthermore, Tallinn has provided grants for start-ups in the field of ICT since 2002 and since 2008, the City of Tallinn has also supported the students of Estonian Information Technology College who receive grants for innovative ideas in the field of local community development.

In addition to the infrastructure that has rapidly developed, there has been a determined effort from local governments to adapt to ICTs and integrate them into governance processes. On the legislative level, one of the mechanisms that has pushed the integration of "e" into "local government" has been the Public Information Act. The first Public Information Act in Estonia came into force in 2001. One of its basic principles, derived from the Constitution of the Republic of Estonia, states in § 44: "Everyone has the right to freely obtain information disseminated for public use."

Back in the 2001, this Act was quite revolutionary in terms of information accessibility in the public sector. It stipulates that *public information is all information created upon the performance of public duties*. Specifically, § 5 of the Act specifies the holders of the information, § 28 says what kind of information should be made public and § 29 obliges the holders of information to disclose it on a web site. There are 32 points altogether prescribing exactly what information should be disclosed on a web site, ranging from generalised economic statistics to document registers. The Public Information Act led to the digitalization of document management systems and also to the emergence of Internet-based document registers (on these issues, see the openness dimensions in Table 4).

As for services, in Tallinn there are in total 562 services listed in the public services database. These also include services that are provided by the state or private sector in cases where the city participates in their delivery. The services are divided into 2 categories: direct and indirect. The first group includes up to 400 services that can be directly applied. There are 162 indirect services which include public display of information or organizational activities in the city. The services are divided into 20 spheres, each with a service profile: short description, contacts of the service provider, the eligible service user, price, type of service delivery, contact details of the person responsible for the service, legislative acts concerning this service, and a link to the state portal for the submission of an application.

The city of Tallinn has become aware of the importance of ICTs and innovation, partly through the international interest that has been shown in e-Estonia development. Though the outside world may tie Tallinn city's identity to successful e-solutions and ICT companies, there is still a lot of work to be done within Estonia.

The development of the city of Tallinn provides us with a picture of how the developments and the influence of ICTs have affected municipal powers in transition economies. By and large, opening up from totalitarianism and the availability of ICTs for governance have coincided, sometimes speeding up and sometimes slowing down developments in the governance area. First, whereas municipalities in Western Europe are often beacons of progress, in the transition economies they tend to be more conservative than central government. Second, it was interesting to observe that the need to comply with central government legislation has provided quite a substantive influence on governance openness at the municipal level. Third, the influence of the European Union has played a major role in stabilizing the government.

As for the ICT-related developments themselves, what is important in governance terms is that Tallinn has been transformed. Back in the middle of the 20th century, it was a conglomerate of small satellite towns and quite decentralized. Parts of the city retained separate identities and responsibilties. Now, however, the ICT developments of the last decade have decidedly changed the direction of governance towards more centralization. Finally, as regards current developments, Tallinn seems to have overcome in transparency the public information and open government stages and is building ICT systems that allow full procedural transparency not only to civil servants and politicians but also potentially to any citizen. At the same time, the municipal government has a full overview of the services it provides to its stakeholders and also a variety of data needed for decision making, promising much better public management and policy planning.

CONCLUSION AND RECOMMENDATIONS

In this chapter, we have discussed the application and "instantiation" (Leydesdorff, 2011) of a conceptual model represented in Figure 1 to help the elicitation of different configurations of ICT-enabled governance systems. To this end, we have focused on the local level of governance and have taken two specific European cities, Barcelona and Tallinn, as case studies, on the basis of their emerging international relevance as best practices (the first as a creative industries cluster, the second for the development of open and accessible e-Government). The characteristics of these two cities make them comparable to autonomous institutional actors.

Figure 2 shows a typology of e-Governance attitudes as a result of the application of the framework. "Attitude" is a concept adopted to identify the current profile of a given institution. In project planning, it can provide evidence both at strategy and policy level of the alignment with AS-IS configuration of the proposed initiatives. Furthermore, the concept can support the identification of a TO-BE evolving path, on the basis of a desired "attitude" chosen at policy level.

Figure 2 shows that Tallinn (circle named T) currently has an *inclusive* attitude (focused on equity and accessibility) oriented towards *Openness* through a focus on accountability. Barcelona (circle named B), however, has a *performance* attitude (focused on effectiveness of services as described in Table 1) oriented towards *openness* through accountability).

In the case of Tallinn, it may be decided to focus policy more on openness and effective service provision, without losing in equity. As for Barcelona, the focus is already on qualities that support equity, without losing effectiveness in service provision.

In future work, we intend to further develop the functional relationship between the conceptual model, the quality dimensions, and the typology proposed. Furthermore, we will investigate the possible conceptualizations of "attitude" as an emerging concept which characterizes the attributes of policy making for public sector digital innovation. Finally, we will apply the framework to additional case studies to further develop the proposed typology. We will consider national

Figure 2. A typology of e-governance attitudes

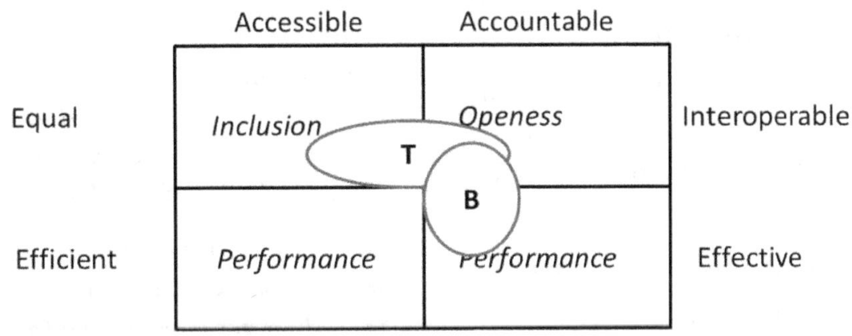

initiatives as well as local ones like those of Barcelona and Tallinn, analysed in this chapter.

DISCLAIMER

The views expressed in this chapter are purely those of the authors and may not in any circumstances be regarded as stating an official position of the European Commission.

ACKNOWLEDGMENT

This chapter has been partly drawn by research activity conducted by Gianluca Misuraca, as project leader of the EXPGOV project – Exploratory Research on Emerging ICT-enabled governance models in European cities, conducted for the European Commission Joint Research Centre, Institute for Prospective Technological Studies (JRC-IPTS). Special thanks go to Dr. Mila Gascó and Mr Ivar Tallo, who acted as local researchers for the analysis of the case studies of Barcelona and Tallinn, gathering relevant data and information and conducting interviews on behalf of the JRC-IPTS.

REFERENCES

Andersen, K. V., & Henriksen, H. Z. (2006). E-government maturity models: Extension of the Layne and Lee model. *Government Information Quarterly*, *23*, 236–248. doi:10.1016/j.giq.2005.11.008.

Batini, C., Viscusi, G., & Cherubini, D. (2009). GovQual: A quality driven methodology for e-government project planning. *Government Information Quarterly*, *26*(1), 106–117. doi:10.1016/j.giq.2008.03.002.

bot.com. (2013). Website. Retrieved from http://bot.com/Content/NavigationMenu/Policy/Scorecard/Scorecard_on_Prosperity_2010_FINAL.pdf

Broster, D., Misuraca, G., & Bacigalupo, M. (2011). Lifting off towards open government. A report from the EU Belgian Presidency Conference. *European Journal of ePractice*, 12 (March/April).

Capgemini, IDC, Europe Rand, DTi, & Sogeti. (2010). *Digitizing public services in Europe: Putting ambition into action - 9th Benchmark Measurement.*

Castells, M. (1992). *The informational city: Economic restructuring and urban development.* Wiley-Blackwell.

Castells, M. (1997). *The rise of the network society. The information age: Economy, society and culture* (*Vol. 1*). Oxford: Blackwell.

Castells, M., & Ollé Sanz, E. (2004). *The Barcelona model II. The Barcelona City Council in the Network Society*. Barcelona: Open University of Barcelona.

Deloitte, & Eurocities. (2005). *eCitizenship for all - European Benchmark Report 2005*.

Di Maio, A. (2009). *Moving from citizen-centric to citizen-driven government*. Gartner.

Di Maio, A. (2010). *Gartner open government maturity model*. Gartner.

Dunleavy, P., Margetts, H., Simon, B., & Tinkler, J. (2006). *Digital era governance – IT corporations, the state, and e-government*. London: Oxford University Press. doi:10.1093/acprof:oso/9780199296194.001.0001.

Elling, S., Lentz, L., & de Jong, M. (2007). Website evaluation questionnaire: Development of a research-based tool for evaluating informational websites. *6th International Conference, EGOV 2007*. Regensburg, Germany: Springer Berlin/Heidelberg. doi:10.1007/978-3-540-74444-3

Eurocities. (2011). *Eurocities annual report 2011 & work programme 2012*.

Europeancitiesmonitor.eu. (2013). Website. Retrieved from http://www.europeancitiesmonitor.eu/wp-content/uploads/2010/10/ECM2010-Full-Version.pdf.

Gatautis, R. (2008). E-government in transition economies. In A.-V. Anttiroiko & M. Mälkiä (Eds.), *Encyclopedia of digital government* (Vol. 1, pp. 554–559). Hershey, PA: Idea Group Reference. Retrieved from http://www.loc.gov/catdir/toc/ecip0611/2006010087.html

Harrison, T. M., Guerrero, S., Burke, G. B., Cook, M., Cresswell, A., Helbig, N., et al. (2011). Open government and e-government: Democratic challenges from a public value perspective. In *Proceedings of the 12th Annual International Digital Government Research Conference (dg.o 2011)* (pp. 245–253). College Park, MD, USA: ACM.

Jacquier, C. (2005). On relationships between integrated policies for sustainable urban development and urban governance. *Tijdschrift voor Economische en Sociale Geografie*, *96*(4), 363–376. doi:10.1111/j.1467-9663.2005.00469.x.

Jacquier, C. (2008). *Urban governance: Forging a path between complications and complexity*. Paper presented for the symposium "Towards New Territorial Governance" run by Urban-logement, 15 September 2008 Reims.

Lee, G., & Kwak, Y. H. (2011). Open government implementation model: A stage model for achieving increased public engagement. In *Proceedings of the 12th Annual International Digital Government Research Conference (dg.o 2011)* (pp. 254–261). College Park, MD, USA: ACM. Retrieved from http://doi.acm.org/10.1145/2037556.2037598

Lee, J. (2010). 10 year retrospect on stage models of e-Government: A qualitative meta-synthesis. *Government Information Quarterly*, *27*(3), 220–230. doi:10.1016/j.giq.2009.12.009.

Lévy, M., & Jouyet, J.-P. (2006). *L'économie de l'immatériel-La croissance de demain*.

Leydesdorff, L. (2011). "Meaning" as a sociological concept: A review of the modeling, mapping and simulation of the communication of knowledge and meaning. *Social Sciences Information. Information Sur les Sciences Sociales*, *50*(3-4), 391–413. doi:10.1177/0539018411411021.

McDermott, P. (2010). Building open government. *Government Information Quarterly*, *27*(4), 401–413. doi:10.1016/j.giq.2010.07.002.

Misuraca, G., (2007). *e-Governance in Africa from theory to action - A handbook on ICTs for local governance*. Africa World Press/IDRC.

Misuraca G. (2008). *Transforming government roles towards a digital state: Government reform as a key to success*. Background Paper to the 'Middle East e-Government Conference & Exhibition 2008', Riyadh, Kingdom of Saudi Arabia, 15-18 March 2008

Misuraca, G. (2009). Futuring e-government: Governance and policy implication for building an ICT-enabled knowledge society for all. In *Proceedings of the International Conference on Theory and Practice of e-Governance*, ICEGOV2009, Bogotá, Colombia 11-13 November.

Misuraca, G. (2009). e-Government 2015: Exploring m-government scenarios, between ICT-driven experiments and citizen-centric implications. In Technological Analysis & Strategic Management, 21(3).

Misuraca, G. (2010). Concept paper. *Theoretical framework and key principles towards the development of a policy assessment framework for ICT-enabled governance at city level*. Seville: European Commission JRC-IPTS.

Misuraca, G. (2012a). eGovernance 2.0: Implications of social computing on public services. In E. Downey and M. Jones (Eds.), *Public services, governance and web2.0 technologies: Future trends in social media*. Retrieved from http://www.igi-global.com/book/public-service-governance-web-technologies/56009

Misuraca, G. (2012b). Reinventing governance in the digital age. In Quebec, E. N. A. P. (Ed.), *Revue, Special Issue on L'Administration Publique a l'ere du numerique*.

Misuraca, G., Alfano, G., & Viscusi, G. (2011a). Interoperability challenges for ICT-enabled governance: Towards a pan-European conceptual framework. *Journal of Theoretical and Applied Electronic Commerce Research*, *6*(1), 95–111.

Misuraca, G., Alfano, G., & Viscusi, G. (2011b). A multi-level framework for ICT-enabled governance: Assessing the non-technical dimensions of "government openness." *Electronic. Journal of E-Government*, *9*(2), 152–165. Retrieved from www.ejeg.com.

Misuraca, G., Broster, D., & Centeno, C. (2010). Envisioning digital Europe 2030: Scenario design on ICT for governance and policy modelling. In *Proceedings of the 4th International Conference on Theory and Practice of Electronic Governance* (ICEGOV) (pp. 347–356). Beijing, China: ACM. doi:10.1145/1930321.1930392

Misuraca, G., & Viscusi, G. (2010). E-governance for development: Designing an operational roadmap for ICT-enabled public administration reform. In D. Piaggesi Sund and. E. Castelnovo (Ed.), Global strategy and practice of e-governance: Examples from around the world. IGI Global Publishing.

OECD. (2001a). Cities for citizens. Improving metropolitan governance. Paris.

OECD. (2001b). *Governance in the 21st Century*. Organisation for Economic Co-operation and Development.

Paquette, S., & Wilson, S. C. (2010). Identifying the security risks associated with governmental use of cloud computing. *Government Information Quarterly*, *27*(3), 245–253. doi:10.1016/j.giq.2010.01.002.

Perroux, F. (1960). *Economie et société*. Paris: Presses Universitaires de France.

Perroux, F. (1990). *Dictionnaire économique et social*. Paris: Haitier.

Rodríguez, J. R. B., Battle, M. J., & Esteban, D. A. (2007). European study of e-government city models. *IDP. Revista de Internet, Derecho y Política*, (5).

Sassen, S. (1991). *The global city*. New York: Princeton University Press.

Simon, H. A. (1996). *The sciences of the artificial* (3rd ed.). Cambridge, MA: The MIT Press.

UN. (2012). E-government survey 2012 - E-government for the people. New York.

UNDESA. (2003). *World public sector report.*

Viscusi, G., Batini, C., & Mecella, M. (2010). *Information systems for egovernment: A quality-of-service perspective*. Springer. doi:10.1007/978-3-642-13571-2.

ADDITIONAL READING

Misuraca, G. (2012). eGovernance: Past, present and future, in egovernance, a global journey. IOS Press.

KEY TERMS AND DEFINITIONS

E-Governance: The field of activity where policy design, decision-making, co-ordination, arbitration, networking and regulation with ICTs, but also of ICTs, takes place. This involves the relationships of all governance actors, the state representatives being however one of the main stakeholders, and the evolving dynamics resulting from these interactions, in terms of organisational forms, processes, outcomes and impacts from the perspective of both the government and the citizens. (European Commission, JRC-IPTS, Misuraca, 2010).

E-Government: Can be considered as the process of innovation of public administration in order to achieve innovative forms of government and governance through the use of ICTs (OECD, 2003).

Governance: The process of decision-making and the process by which decisions are implemented, monitored and evaluated (Misuraca, 2011).

ICT-Enabled Governance: The use of ICTs to: – comprehensively - simplify and improve the internal administrative operations of government; facilitate public service interaction between government, citizens and other stakeholders; enable citizen participation and ensure inclusiveness and equal opportunity for all (Misuraca, 2010).

ENDNOTES

1 See europeancitiesmonitor.eu. (2013).

2 See bot.com. (2013).

Chapter 11
Towards Inclusive E-Government:
The Development of Municipal Contact Centers in Sweden

Irene Bernhard
University West, Sweden

Kerstin Grundén
University West, Sweden

ABSTRACT

In this chapter, five case studies of the implementation of contact centers in Swedish municipalities are described and discussed with a focus on inclusive e-government. The research methods used are mainly qualitative interviews with different categories of municipal personnel and also with some citizens. The main conclusions are that the implementation of contact centers seems to contribute to increased accessibility of municipal services, even for those citizens who might have problems using Internet services. The study indicates that development towards increased equal treatment of citizens and a contribution to reducing problems is mainly related to the "digital divide." Municipal services became more adapted to citizens' needs by using citizen-centric methods and dialogue during the development process and in the daily work of the contact centers. The implementation of municipal contact centers can thus be seen as a step towards inclusive e-government, but there is still a need to go further in this direction.

INTRODUCTION

During the last 10-15 years, e-government has gradually been implemented in most countries. The main characteristic of the implementation of e-government has been the ambition to use information and communication technology (ICT) as a tool to achieve more efficient government and e-services for citizens. Although Internet use is high in most Western countries, recent statistics show a gap between the supply and use of e-government services, indicating problems

DOI: 10.4018/978-1-4666-4245-4.ch011

with user satisfaction regarding public e-services (OECD, 2009). In fact, around 30% of Europe's population still does not use any e-government services (European Commission, 2010). There is, however, a scarcity of studies providing a more qualitative understanding of the change of citizen – government relationships following the implementation of e-government.

The worldwide problem of the digital divide has contributed to a relatively low use of public e-services (OECD, 2009). Some citizen groups with low Internet use are the elderly (over age 65), citizens with limited education, and citizens on a low income. Immigrant users also face obstacles when accessing services due, for example, to a lack of technical and language skills. Ironically, many of the excluded citizens are those who need government services the most. The gap between those who regularly access and use the Internet and those who do not have access is part of the so-called "digital divide dilemma." In November 2007, the European Commission adopted the Communication "European i2010 initiative on e-Inclusion - to be part of the information society" (European Commission, 2010). The Communication is meant to contribute to increased awareness and to national efforts to improve the conditions for everyone to take part in the information society by increasing broadband accessibility and tackling competence deficiencies. Public services should be available on equal terms to everybody, and therefore public authorities need to take into account the interests of all potential service users, following the principle of inclusive e-government.

The Swedish government has worked extensively on e-government and there are several local and regional initiatives for increased use of ICT and provision of broadband infrastructures (Swedish official governmental reports (SOU, 1999, p. 85; SOU, 2002, p. 51; SOU, 2008, p. 97). The government formed a special delegation named "The 24/7 Agency Delegation" to promote and stimulate the development and use of public e-services (SOU, 2004, p. 56). The implementation of e-services in public administration is promoted by the national government (SOU, 2005, p. 19) and is a dimension of e-government (Grönlund, 2006; Giritli, Nygren, & Wiklund, 2010). The Swedish government defines the role of the new ICT programs on the national level in a recent action plan, where it stresses the importance of using ICT in order to effectively develop public administration (Regeringskansliet, 2008). This could be done by combining organizational changes and new skills within the municipalities, leading to improved accessibility and understanding for the citizens with the aim to "make it as simple as possible for as many as possible" (Regeringskansliet, 2008). One example of such a change on the local level is the implementation of a municipal Contact Centre (CC). There is a lack of studies regarding citizens' attitudes towards the services produced by contact centers in municipalities, and there are no specific studies made on public opinion regarding these e-government initiatives, except for studies on citizens' confidence in the Swedish public sector. According to these studies, Swedish citizens have a relatively high confidence in the public sector at both the local and regional level in comparison to other European countries (Statskontoret, 2011).

The overall aim of this study is to analyze the implementation of municipal CCs, focusing on inclusive local e-government aspects with the aim to contribute to an understanding of whether the implementation of CCs can facilitate citizens' municipal contacts due to increased internal effectiveness. We do so by forming the following research question:

Does the implementation of municipal contact centers facilitate citizens' municipal contacts and do they contribute to an increase in the number of citizens getting access to and using municipal services?

After this introduction, the chapter proceeds in eight sections. The next section presents the background followed by definitions and dimensions of e-government and a short discussion of the contact center concept. A more through presentation of a CC, in relation to New Public Management, follows in the next section. Then, Swedish settings and SAMBRUK are presented, followed by the research method and presentation of the case studied and results. These are then analyzed and discussed in the following section, after which conclusions are presented. The chapter ends with implications and suggestions for further research.

BACKGROUND

Municipalities in Sweden make up 70% of total public administration and are considered to be the closest to citizens' needs in terms of public service. However, there are groups in society that are not used to computers or the Internet, and who have difficulties or do not feel comfortable with this way of handling public service. Some aspects that are important from a citizen's perspective are the provision and awareness of the e-government services, access to and experience of the e-services, trust in the handling of sensitive information by the government, and the organization of e-government services such as integration and personalization of services (OECD, 2009). The relationship between citizens and the government is crucial and according to a study in the EEC countries (Blakemore et al., 2010); it is mediated through a process of understanding citizens' needs and the process of developing citizen trust in the use of e-services.

Five case studies on the implementation of CCs in Swedish municipalities are presented and discussed, focusing especially on inclusive e-government aspects. The case studies were part of a three-year research project, Innoveta (2009 – 2011), intended to support and evaluate the municipalities' efforts to implement contact centers and e-services (Bernhard, 2009; Bernhard, 2010; Bernhard & Grundén, 2010; Grundén, 2010). One of the motivation factors for the project stemmed from background aspects such as access problems with very long waiting times for citizens who needed to reach a relevant handling officer to resolve their issues. The bureaucratic structure of the municipal organizations also hampered citizens' understanding of the relationship between their needs and the organizational functions, a fact that has further complicated the contacts.

E-GOVERNMENT AND CONTACT CENTERS

There are many definitions of e-government which, though common, is still a broad and much diffused concept with no universally accepted definition (Halchin, 2004; Yildiz, 2007). The development of broad-band in the United States in the late 1990s enabled Internet communication for citizens, which facilitated the emergence of e-commerce and later e-government as well. The origins of e-government can be found not only in motives for cost-cutting, but also in the realization of new public management reforms. According to Heeks (2006, p. 1), e-government is defined as "all use of information technology in the public sector," not merely confined to the Web or Internet-based applications. He includes all use of digital information technology in the public sector, which means that it consists of technology, information, and human beings who give the system purpose and meaning and the work processes that are undertaken. Other scholars argue that e-government aims to make public administration more citizen-oriented, efficient, transparent and responsive to the needs of the public (Wihlborg, 2005; Bock Seegard, 2009). According to Homburg (2008, p. 87), e-government refers to "the strategic use of ICT in and around public administrations, for the purpose of creating a 'wired' or 'digital' government." Grant and Chau (2006, p. 80) define e-government as "A broad-based transformation initiative, enabled by leveraging the capabilities of information and communication technology. The aim is: 1) to develop and deliver high quality, seamless, and integrated public services; 2) to enable effective constituent relationship management; and 3) to support the economic and social development goals of citizens, businesses, and civil society at local, state, national, and international levels." E-government in this context is further referred to as the redesign of information relationships between the administration and citizens, in order to create added value. From the perspective of this study Heeks (2006) offers the most useful definition of e-government, as he summarizes almost all the various dimensions of e-government that are exemplified through municipal CCs. The CCs encompass the use of Web or Internet-based applications and digital information technology (including telephones), information, and human beings (citizens and public administrators). However, the concept of municipal CC also includes a broader way of communication, with the option of personal visits by citizens and reorganization within the municipalities.

Based on this discussion the key characteristics of e-government can be defined according to their relationship to different actors, as shown in Figure 1. These are e-democracy (relationships between the electorate and the elected, i.e. the political interplay of citizens and elected politicians), e-services (in the relationship between the public administration and the citizens), and finally e-administration for the internal usage of information technology tools within governmental organizations to provide reports and support for decision making (Wihlborg, 2005, p. 7; Bernhard & Wihlborg, 2012). These dimensions in e-government among different actors can be identified for both analytical and practical purposes in order to further understand the distinction and relationship between them. In practice it is hard to make a clear division between these dimensions (Jansson, 2011). The model was developed from the view of e-governance including both public and private actors. However, in order to analyze these cases, we will use the concept of e-government, since the focus is on the public sector. In this study, e-government initiatives are expressed by the establishment of municipal CCs and the analyses are based on the perspective of the citizens. Thus the analyses in this study focus on the views of citizens (e-services), as in many definitions e-democracy is excluded from e-government (Jansson, 2011).

The concept of a municipal CC can be understood as an organizational unit aiming to contribute to increased citizen access to municipal service

Figure 1. Three dimension of e-government (Source: Bernhard, (2011) based on Wihlborg (2005, p. 7))

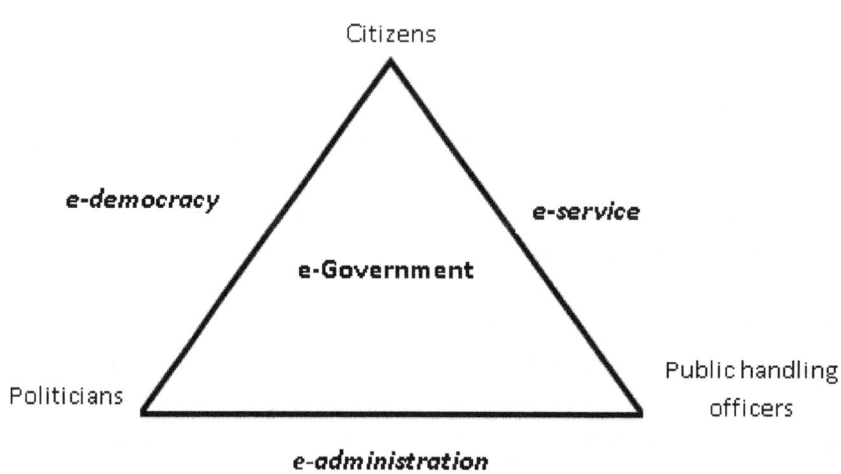

through multi-delivery channels like ICT in the form of telephone, Internet, municipal websites and Web-based applications (e-services), and generally with the option of personal visits. A broader description follows below.

A NEW PUBLIC MANAGEMENT AND CITIZEN-CENTRIC APPROACH

The theories of New Public Management (NPM) have inspired some changes in organization and administration when e-government is implemented. Some of the key features of NPM in practice are "customer orientation, improved responsibility to address client needs, focus on cost-efficiency and productivity and introducing market mechanisms" (Persson & Goldkuhl, 2010). Critics of practicing NPM in the public sector argue that there are key differences between public and private sectors, both in terms of overall purpose and structure of processes (e.g. Heeks, 1999). The use of lean and highly decentralized structures in public service is stressed, resulting in the breakdown of formerly unitary bureaucracies (Homburg, 2008). There is also emphasis on contract-like relationships and attention given to management strategies, performance indicators, and the service produced. The use of IT is essential for this organizational transformation. In a virtual organization, IT mediates the communication between different units in different geographical locations. What the citizens' roles are called reflects changes in the relationships between citizens and the government and refers to the NPM. Traditionally, citizenship in democratic countries refers to the rights of freedom, ownership, and justice, but also to democratic rights of participation in national elections and to a minimum standard of welfare. The implementation of e-government and new organizational paradigms has challenged the traditional citizen role and added new roles, such as clients, customers, and users (Lips, 2007; SOU, 2008, p. 97). The customer role is more market-oriented compared to the citizen role, for example (Collins & Butler, 2002; Michel, 2005; Wallström et al., 2009). A reason for using the customer concept could be that most e-applications originated as market tools in e-commerce, e-marketing, etc. However, by viewing citizens as customers, the perspective shrinks to only include customer relationships rather than participation in a political system and seeing the citizen as a holder of "rights" (Collins & Butler, 2002; Michel, 2005). When considering the citizen from a strict service perspective, it can be argued that using the concept of customer is useful (Lindblad-Gidlund et al., 2010). The definition of citizen in this chapter is, however, based on citizens having rights and duties rather than simply being customers interested in obtaining as much service as possible for the lowest costs achievable.

The concept of inclusive e-government implies within this context a new era of inclusive and accountable government aiming to involve all citizens within a municipality. An example of inclusive e-government is when municipal CCs and public e-services are implemented in order to meet the demand for increased citizen access to municipal services, and also to effectively develop public administration. Increased availability of municipal service via CCs and e-services could also contribute to more frequent dialogue between citizens and municipal service producers. Problems with the digital divide regarding Internet availability and understanding persist, however. In accordance with the role of citizenship, all citizens should have the right to equal possibilities to public services.

Although e-government usually is strongly related to a citizen-centric approach, at least in policy documents, there is still skepticism in regard to actual e-government achievements; becoming more user-focused could even be counter-cultural from the government's perspective and often fits poorly with "local" interests (OECD, 2005). There is a potential risk that internal efficiency aspects are prioritized over citizen-centric aspects when e-government is implemented (Grundén, 2009b). An increased focus on aspects of efficiency related to the implementation of e-government can be analyzed according to Ciborra's (2002) metaphor of "hospitality." This is an alternative metaphor for thinking critically about relationships between organizations, people, and technology. If management and developers are seen as hosts, and employees and clients as guests, then striving for increased internal efficiency can be seen as reasonable, according to the metaphor. As the management and development staff have the most control over the design and implementation, their internal goals can be given great attention, such as internal efficiency, according to traditional management philosophy. The risk then is that other goals become secondary.

In recent years, however, there has been a shift of paradigms, according to studies by the OECD (2009), changing focus from being government-centered to citizen-centered. Governments are paying more attention to social, organizational, and institutional aspects affecting the development and use of e-government services. Also, businesses and employees are included in the concept of users, but not citizens. Increasingly, governments no longer see a contradiction between a user-centric focus and a focus on internal efficiency aspects (OECD, 2009). Optimizing the development of e-government for the users can lead to higher use and higher user satisfaction of e-government, as well as to improved internal efficiency.

Contact Centers in the Public Sector

The use of ICT is one of the basic conditions and driving forces behind the development and implementation of call centers. The use of telemarketing in the United States was a precursor to the development of call centers (Norman, 2005), but the breakthrough came in the late 1980s when the use of computer-supported telephone calls spread (Tengblad et al., 2002). A call center receives and processes phone calls completely dependent on the use of IT. A call center can be an internal function of an organization or an outsourced detached function. There is no universal definition of the concept (Norman, 2005), but Andersson Bäck (2008, p. 3) defines a call center as "a 'new' type of organizational form, where the organization of actions and the use of technological tools are underpinned by the logics of cost-effectiveness and customer-focus." However, the organization of the inner workings of a call center can vary due to national context (Andersson Bäck, 2008). During the 1990s call centers were the most striking phenomenon in service work internationally (Frenkel et al., 1999). By the late 1990s there were 538 call centers established in Sweden, according to a study by Nutek (2000). In recent years, more and more CCs have been implemented in Swedish municipalities, influenced by the concept of "call centers," but there are still few research studies made. In Sweden, there are different names for service offices or centers providing municipal service to inhabitants, e.g. customer centers, contact centers, or service centers (Bernhard, 2010). In this study, we use the term CC. The concept of "contact center" indicates an extended function, not only focusing on phone calls, but also other contiguous work tasks (Andersson Bäck, 2008). The development of contact centers in the public sector is especially influenced by aspects such as increased service and availability from a citizen perspective and internal efficiency.

Figure 2 shows a conceptual model of the CC in the perspectives of citizens and businesses on the one hand and public administrators. Some e-services may also be directly connected to the handling officers in the back office.

Many Swedish municipalities have been inspired by the implementation of public CCs in other countries where it is common to have only one number to reach the contact center by phone. One example is from New York City (Rundle, 2009). The main function of Swedish municipal CCs is to supply services to the citizens more efficiently by primarily using the telephone and

Figure 2. A Conceptual model of a contact center in relation to citizens and public handling officers at the back office (Source: Bernhard (2011, p. 7))

ICT to handle citizen contacts. In some municipalities, it is also possible for citizens to visit the CC.

Although, the implementation of e-government often is associated with increased citizen accessibility to public e-services, it also means a fundamental organizational change within public organizations (Grönlund, 2001). The implementation of a CC should be seen as an example of organizational change. When CCs are implemented in municipalities, the work of the public administrative handling officers is supposed to become more efficient, as they will not be disturbed by phone calls regarding "simple questions" from citizens and some simple work processes are supposed to be transferred to the CC from the back office. The different organizational units are also supposed to cooperate in resolving citizen issues, in order to simplify citizens' contact with the municipality.

A related Swedish concept is a One-Stop Government Office (also known as a Civic Office), which is a common public service unit (front office) where personnel with general competencies provide services to citizens not only from the municipality but from other public authorities or sectors, which means across administration, authority and sector lines, hence the concept "one-stop" (SALAR, 1997; Björk & Bostedt, 2002). These "One-Stop-Government-Offices" are, according to the Swedish government, a tool for important dialogues between different public authorities and citizens and can thereby act as local democratic centers (Regeringskansliet, 1999; SOU, 2009). The "One-Stop Government Offices" are often implemented in municipalities with a high number of inhabitants having roots outside Sweden.

A related term is "one-stop shop" which, according to Karagiannaki (2005), is a European phenomenon and a single point of public contact to a front office providing public service from authorities on both national and local levels. However, the term is also used to refer to a single point of contact (welfare office) organized specifically as a partnership between the state and local municipalities as equal partners where the central government keeps responsibility for the national services and local governments keep responsibility for locally provided welfare services (Haugli Nyhuus & Thorsen, 2007).

SWEDISH MUNICIPALITIES AND SAMBRUK

The Swedish multi-level government system is based on three levels: national, regional and local. On the local level, there are 290 municipalities in Sweden responsible for providing community service in different areas (SKL, 2007). They are governed by elected local officials and have a high degree of autonomy.

The context of each municipality can vary considerably due to different geographical locations, population, social structures, and economic conditions (SKL, 2009). The service to inhabitants includes planning and environmental permits, matters regarding social services and schools, healthcare, daycare and welfare, as well as the booking of public halls (SOU, 2008, p. 97). The national government sets policies and directions, and municipalities do not have a regulated obligation to set up offices or similar service locations for their inhabitants. Swedish law mandates that all Swedish municipalities should provide individual service, e.g. meeting visitors and answering telephone calls from citizens. In the municipality this service should be of as high a quality as possible from an economic resources perspective (SFS, 1986, p. 223). The municipalities interpret their responsibility to provide services in varied ways, however. The development of e-government between municipalities also varies greatly.

To date, eighty municipalities are members of Sambruk, a non-profit association financed by its member municipalities (Sambruk, 2010). The vast majority of the municipalities in Sweden are too small to make big investments in the development of new e-services or re-engineering of internal business processes. One of the aims of Sambruk is to create a strong negotiating position with IT vendors and government bodies when creating solutions based on the use of ICT. Sambruk also participated in the Innoveta research project.

METHOD AND THEORETICAL FRAMEWORK FOR THE CASE STUDIES

In this section, five case studies from different municipalities which have implemented CCs are discussed. We name the municipalities A, B, C, D and E. The research methods of the studies are mainly qualitative (57 semi-structured recorded interviews with different personnel categories from the municipalities, telephone interviews with citizens, and document studies). The interviews with the different personnel categories took about an hour each and were tape-recorded. Quality content analysis was used for the analysis of the interviews. The interviews with different personnel categories in municipality A, B and C were made during the spring of 2009. The interviews in municipality D were made in spring 2010 and the interviews in municipality E were made in spring 2010 and winter 2011.

In one of the municipalities (A), municipal staff conducted customer surveys. In this study, we have reanalyzed the results from the surveys. The MOA model (Grundén, 2009a) was used as a reference model for the analysis of the results. The model focuses on important aspects that can be affected because of different designs of technology and organization. Such aspects are the staff's work situations, work processes, and services provided to the clients. Interrelated relationships between design of technology and organization are stressed in this model. Different consequences for work processes, work situations, and quality of services provided to the client could arise depending on the different designs of organization and technology. This chapter focuses on the quality aspects of the services provided to citizens. The municipalities in the case studies were selected to be as diverse as possible although there were not many CCs in Sweden to choose from. There were no statistics in Sweden about established CCs, for which reason we only selected CCs among municipalities in Sambruk.

The Pilot Citizen Study

In addition, an explorative citizen study was conducted in municipality D. The study was based on semi-structured telephone interviews, primarily using questions with predefined alternatives, to which some open-ended questions were added. Twenty-one citizens (14 female and 7 male) were asked about their attitudes to the newly established CC. The citizens differed in age; 6 respondents were elderly, i.e., over age 65; one was younger than 24 and the other 14 were between age 25 and 65. These interviews were held about four weeks after the CC was implemented in late 2009. When citizens who had been in contact with the public administrators at the CC ended their phone calls, they were asked if another person (a researcher) could call them back and conduct an interview regarding how well they were informed about this implementation, their opinions of the service delivered by the new municipal CC, if they had access to or used the Internet and public e-services, and about how this implementation has affected their access to local municipal service in general. However, most of the citizens asked were positive about participating in the survey, although some of them declined due to lack of time.

CASE STUDIES

In this chapter, we focus especially on a citizen perspective of the implementation and use of CCs in five Swedish municipalities. The case studies are already published (Bernhard, 2009; 2010; 2011; Bernhard & Grundén, 2010; Bernhard & Wihlborg, 2011; Grundén, 2010; 2011) and are therefore summarized in this section.

In Table 1, some characteristics of the five studied municipalities are described which are discussed further in the next section. The launching of the different CCs affected the different times for the interviews.

Results from the Case Studies from a Citizens' Perspective

According to the results of Table 1, the five municipalities that have implemented CCs have differences and similarities in their organizing of the CCs. One reason is the variation in the local context. The different contexts and organization of the CCs are described further in the following paragraphs.

Municipality A

The citizens use a single phone number to reach the CC for municipal services. Then they have to use touch-tone telephone technology to reach different service fields at the CC. The employees at the CC, who are called "customer service administrators," are specialists within specific areas and their work is organized in different response groups. The calls are connected via voicemail to these response groups depending on what field of activity they concern. Many work processes have been transferred from the different administrations within the municipality to the CC. The employees at the CC handle most of the simple questions from citizens and do not have much contact with the public administrators at the back office. Even if the municipality does not publicize the direct telephone numbers to back-office personnel externally, some citizens still use direct lines if they know the number. They could, for example, have been given the number during an earlier contact with a handling officer.

The CC is situated in the center of town and is open for visits by citizens. All issues and questions from citizens to the CC are registered. There is no One-Stop Government Office. The municipality has implemented several e-services. Focus groups with citizen participants have been used for the development of at least one e-service. Results from different customer surveys and citizen contacts with the CC have also been used in order to improve service to the citizens, for example the information on and design of the municipal website.

As a part of the implementation process of the CC, the management defined and launched a common citizen-centric value concept that was to permeate all contacts with citizens. In the interviews, a few respondents commented that there was still work to be done in order to use apply the concept in all contacts. One of the results of the work to increase the "citizen-in-focus concept" was that the information on the website was developed and made clearer with simple language

Table 1. Some characteristics of the studied municipalities

Municipality	A	B	C	D	E
Characteristics of the municipality	Medium-sized municipality which covers a large geographical area with rural areas and one bigger central city in which almost half of the inhabitants live	Medium-sized municipality which encompasses both densely populated urban and sparsely populated rural areas	Metropolitan area (includes 14 municipal districts that are responsible for most of the municipal services within their geographical area)	Bigger than medium-sized; consists of a variety of large and small population centers	Medium-sized municipality with both densely populated urban and sparsely populated rural area. Close to a metropolitan area.
Name of CC	Customer services	Contact center	Contact center	Contact center	Customer services
Start of CC	Stage 1: 2007, Stage 2: the whole municipality, 2009	2007	2005: 2 of their municipal districts. 2009: The whole municipality	December 2009	Stage 1: spring 2010, Stage 2 autumn 2010: Stage 3: December 2010
Main function of CC	Answer simple questions from citizens on the phone and provide support for public e-services. No calls are connected to handling officersat the back office. Registering of all issues	Answer simple questions from citizens on the phone and provide support for public e-services. Some calls are connected to the handling officers at the back office. Registering of all issues	Answer simple questions from citizens on the phone. Handle simple matters and provide support for simple e-services[REMOVED REF FIELD]. Registering of all issues	Answer simple questions from citizens on the phone, offering guidance and support for simple e-services. Direct numbers to handling officersat the back office. Registering of all issues	Answer simple questions and handling of simple issues from the citizens. Registering of all issues
Geographic location of CC	In the center of the municipality	Centre of the municipality	2 CCs at different locations of the municipality	Outside city center, but will move to city center in 2011	In the center of the municipality
CC open for personal visits	Yes	No	No	No, but will be in early 2011	Yes
One-Stop GovernmentOffice	No	5 (since 1987)	4	No	No
Organization of CC	Different response groups for different fields of activities	Divided in accordance with different fields of activities	One unit for "hard issues," one unit for "soft issues"	No division for different fields of activities	Different response groups for different fields of activities
Name of co-workers at CC	Customer service administrators	Society administrators	Service administrators	Municipality Guides	Service handling officers
Competence of co-workers at CC	Stage 1: Generalists. Stage 2: Specialists	Mainly Generalists	Specialists	Generalists	Specialists

in order to be more accessible to for all citizens. Specifically they wanted to improve the situation for citizens with disabilities and language problems. The management hired a reporter to write the information from the citizens' point of view, with "citizen eyes." The aim was to use clear, simple and non-bureaucratic language.

Municipality B

In this municipality, one-third of the inhabitants have roots in more than 100 countries around the world. The citizens use a single telephone number to the CC. The citizens have to use touch-tone technology in order to get in touch with employees at the CC, who are called society administrators. Most of the society administrators have a broad range of knowledge but some are also specialists within a certain area. Their competence profile could therefore be characterized as generalist rather than specialist. Some society administrators speak different languages. According to the management, one reason for this is that they want their services to be based on citizens' needs. The work is organized in different response groups and the telephone calls are connected to these response groups via voicemail, according to the field of activity they concern.

Many work processes have been transferred from the different administrations within the municipality to the CC. This process was quiet unproblematic, partly due to the fact that they had experience from earlier transfers of work processes from the back office to their civic offices. These working processes had been further developed and adjusted according to the needs of the citizens. Some respondents thought that their long experience of running One-Stop Government Offices contributed to awareness and knowledge of citizen preferences.

The CC is situated in the center of the municipality, but is not open for visits. On the other hand, there are five One-Stop Government Offices which have been open for personal visits for over twenty years. The society administrators at the CC do not handle that many questions from the citizens themselves. The citizens are invited to use e-services which the municipality has implemented, and some issues are forwarded either to the handling officers at the back office or to one of their civic offices. Still, the society administrators inform the citizens about the direct phone numbers to the handling officers within the back office, e.g. to schools. It is also possible for citizens to visit the handling officers in person or e-mail them directly.

The municipality has arranged dialogues with groups of citizens focusing on e-services, so-called "e-dialogues," and they plan to have a group of citizens involved in future e-service development process. There have also been dialogues with citizens via focus group discussions, and within some service fields they have established so-called "citizen panels." A citizen panel consists of a sample of the population in the municipality for collecting input on certain issues, usually participating via the Internet or SMS. The participants are selected randomly by gender, age, and population distribution. Furthermore, the management of the municipality has employed personnel who work as "service field developers." They are supposed to maintain a dialogue with citizens about different service fields in order to integrate their opinions in the development work. The information on the municipal website is partly developed on the basis of questions, comments and issues coming from citizens contacting the civic offices. All issues and questions that come from the citizens to the CC are registered.

When implementing the CC, the municipality worked on and developed a common citizen-centric concept for the whole organization of the municipality. Within the unit for dialogue and service, the management of the municipality decided that all employees should use the term "customer" in order to obtain increased service-mindedness and treat all citizens as customers who are entitled to receive the best service and ensure that everyone is treated equally.

Municipality C

In municipality C, two different CCs have been established. This municipality has a large population, a fact that has contributed to the municipal organization of several municipal districts responsible for service to citizens. The CCs are situated in different parts of the municipality and are not open to in-person visits. Anyone throughout the municipality who needs service for issues regarding the care of the elderly calls a single telephone number to a specific CC that provides service only for the elderly, and does not require the use of touch-tone technology. The municipality has another general telephone number for a CC that handles other municipal issues which requires touch-tone technology. The service administrators at the CC are specialists in different service fields.

Work processes have been transferred from the different administrations in the whole municipality to both CCs. According to the municipal e-strategy, the aim is to implement more e-services. The process of standardization of many work processes has facilitated the development of e-services. In this municipality, no citizens are involved yet in the development of e-services.

The service administrators at the CCs handle most of the questions from citizens, but it is still possible for citizens to communicate directly with back-office personnel (via phone, personal visits, or e-mail). There are four One-Stop Government Offices in different areas, located in districts with many immigrants. All issues and questions coming from citizens to the CC are registered.

When implementing the CC, the municipal managers worked on and developed a common citizen-centric concept for the whole organization of the municipality. They hired a consultant with communication skills to work with the consolidation of the common citizen-centric concept among the employees. According to a respondent, the greatest obstacle to the implementation of the CC has been negative attitudes from the administrative handling officers, and there were also some respondents who said that the implementation work could be improved.

Municipality D

There is a single telephone number to be used for all services at the CC in this municipality. They also still employ switchboard operators, whom they plan to incorporate into the CC in the near future when stage two is launched. The CC is currently situated in a peripheral part of the municipality and not open for citizen visits. The CC will, however, be moved into town in early 2011 and will then be open for citizen visits. The citizens who phone the CC use very simple touch-tone telephone technology with just one option. The municipal guides at the CC answer simple questions and often guide citizens to where to find the answers to their issues. Their work is not organized in different response groups and the municipal guides are generalists.

One work process has been transferred from one of the back-office administrations to the CC. According to some respondents, the ambition is to transfer policy-driven processes to the CC. For these work processes there are obvious, established criteria for what applies to each process and therefore they can be solved by the municipal guides without being sent to a handling officer at the back office. However, one respondent believes that there is great resistance from some of the handling officers in the back office. Even if just one work process is moved to the CC, the municipal guides answer many questions, even though many issues are still forwarded to the back-office handling officers. Sometimes citizens are called back by municipal guides after a few hours, when they have found the answer to the question. The municipal guides also encourage citizens to look for information and use e-services on the municipal website. It is still possible for citizens to communicate directly via telephone and personal visits with the back office handling officers, as their direct telephone numbers are available to the public.

There is no One-Stop Government office within the municipality. The municipality has implemented some e-services and plans to implement more. Citizens' opinions will be included in the implementation process when a citizen-advisory e-government board is established. The information on the municipal website is also to a great extent developed on the basis of questions, comments, and issues from citizen contacts with the CC. All issues and questions from citizens to the CC are registered.

When implementing the CC, the municipal managers worked on and developed a common, citizen-centric concept for the organization of the municipality. There seems, however, to be a deficiency in the implementation of the common citizen concept in the back-office administration. Some respondents stressed that there were deficiencies in internal communication regarding the implementation of the CC between the project management and administrative employees. One respondent stressed that the process of gaining approval of the CC implementation internally has revealed shortcomings. Another respondent mentioned that the implementation of the CC could result in a detour for the citizen and that the process had become more bureaucratic than necessary compared to previous methods when there was a direct connection to the handling officers at the back office.

Municipality E

Citizens use a single telephone number to the CC. Then, they use touch-tone technology with five options to get in touch with a service-handling officer at the CC in the response groups. Sometimes the direct numbers to the handling officers at the different authorities are given to citizens, but this possibility will be removed in the near future. A response group for social services was integrated in the CC in early 2011, and they were placed in a separate area of the office, due to privacy considerations for contacts with citizens. Since the beginning of 2011, there is a smaller office open for visits from citizens on the first floor of the building. The main CC is however located at the sixth floor of the building and not open for citizens' visits. This municipality is one of the municipalities in Sweden with the most developed e-services, but many of these are not used much by citizens.

The service handling officers are mainly specialists within different areas. They can use information in a wiki when they do not know the answer to a particular question from the citizens, but its use is voluntary. All calls from the citizens are registered in an information system. Some statistics are produced today, but the analysis and production of statistics will be further developed and used in the near future. Such statistics could then be used as a planning tool, to update information on the website according to the actual needs of the citizens, and to adjust staffing according to the number of incoming matters and calls within different areas.

The establishment of the municipal contact center with a single entrance to municipal service and with service-minded specialists employed at the CC has had a positive impact on democracy, according to a respondent who argues: "It has been a more democratic one-way entrance… and more time for each issue for the citizens compared to before when the handling officers at the back office were often stressed and at the same time had demands from above to cut back…."

Results from the Pilot Citizen Study

The results show that access to municipal service was good, as 18 of 21 citizens received answers to their questions immediately upon contacting the CC and three almost immediately. The citizens were also very pleased with the way they were treated and the attitudes of the municipal guides. Fifteen of the citizens had used the telephone to receive local governmental service from the municipality because they wanted to talk to a human being and six because they thought it was the easiest way to contact the municipality. The comments from the respondents regarding why they chose the phone mostly stated that they wanted quick feedback to their questions. Another comment was that they had not found the answers on the Internet, and a middle-aged citizen said, "I am not a computerized human being; I'd rather talk to a human being."

Half of the citizens had not visited the municipal website or used e-services. The reason mentioned was that they had no computer. One citizen comment was that in the future she would get information on the website as she had been guided and received knowledge in how to find information and use e-service on the municipal website by the public administrator at the CC. The reason why three had not visited the website was that they did not have access to the Internet. One respondent commented that he or she would do it later on, due to the fact that the handling officer at the CC had recently guided the respondent to where to find the information needed on the website. Another respondent had visited the website, but could not find the information needed; therefore that respondent used the phone instead to obtain the information.

All respondents, but one, were very pleased with the simple touch-tone technology with just one choice to make. One respondent commented that "the fewer choices the better, especially for elderly people, multiple choices are hard for older people." Another respondent, who was very pleased with the simple touch-tone technology, said that when there are many different choices, the respondent does not know what to answer (or which button to press). Another respondent (who at the time lived abroad) commented that this was very good and made a comparison to other touch-tone technology: "Much better than when there is multiple choices. Here in England we have more than a hundred choices. It is really tough!" The respondents were very pleased with the use of the simple touch-tone technology compared to other examples of more complicated touch-tone technology. One respondent, however, argued that it would have been better if there had been more choices, but not too many.

Two-thirds of the respondents were satisfied with the operating hours of the CC. The CC was open Monday to Friday from 7.a.m. until 5 p.m. Four respondents wished to get in contact with the CC in the evenings and on weekends. Three respondents did not have an opinion.

ANALYSIS AND DISCUSSION

Increased Access for Citizens to Municipal Services

According to the results of the case studies, accessibility to municipal services and inclusion of citizens increased in all cases due to the implementation of the CC. In municipality D, for example, the citizens were satisfied with the increased accessibility to the CC, and the municipal guides and handling officers at the back office also thought that citizens were satisfied with the attitude of the municipal guides. In all municipalities, the citizens to a certain extent still have the possibility to phone handling officers at the back office of the municipality directly.

Municipality B had a long tradition of dialogue and providing service to their inhabitants, mainly through having implemented One-Stop Government Offices many years ago. This aspect can be seen as contributing to an increased access to municipal services, making it somewhat easier to transfer work processes to the CC as the handling officers at the back office were used to this. A similar example is the organization of One-Stop Government Offices and CCs in municipality C which could contribute to the inclusion of more groups of citizens using municipal services. Personal contacts seem to be especially important for immigrants and disabled people.

The implementation of simple touch-tone technology in municipality D contributed to the fact that more citizens (for example those unwilling or unable to handle touch-tone technology) could contact the CC and access municipal services. This can be seen as one way of increasing the number of citizens using municipal services and a step towards inclusive e-government. A similar aspect of including more citizens by increasing their possibility to access municipal services was the establishing of a special CC solely for issues regarding care of the elderly as in municipality

C. These groups of citizens did not have to use the touch-tone technology in order to contact specialists on elderly issues.

Towards Citizen Governance

One common aspect of all five case studies was that all issues and questions coming from citizens to the CC, either via telephone, personal visits or email were registered and documented, e.g. via a digital registration tool in a common database. This statistical information implies knowledge about citizens' needs for municipal service. This assumes that the statistics are followed up and evaluated by municipal managers. The registration of every issue also means that it becomes obvious to municipal managers what type of service citizens need. This can be associated with power. In a democratic society citizens have influence on, and there is a transparency of, the activities carried out in the public sector. This may be referred to as a part of e-democracy. This new knowledge may also contribute to citizen governance of municipal services. The use of statistics could also be the basis for the continuous professional development of employees at the CC.

Citizens Improve Municipal E-Government

The implementation of CCs in municipalities means that citizens become part of the development of public administration, as the employees at the CCs can be aware of e.g. an e-service or a form that is awkward for citizens to fill out. It is obvious to them since many citizens call needing help to handle the e-service or fill out the form. This information or feedback will then be taken care of by the handling officers at the CCs or sent to the handling officers at the back office who are responsible for this particular e-service or form. The communication with citizens and employees at the front office could contribute to the development and implementation of inclusive e-government in the municipalities.

Increased Level of Equality for Citizens

To implement CCs that also allow for personal visits and to transfer more processes and more e-services to the CCs is a way of contributing to more equal treatment of citizens, provided that the municipalities clearly maintain other channels of communication as well, for example clear information on their website, fax, letters, information in newspapers, etc. Even the citizens who did not have a direct communication channel to the administrators within the municipality before now have the same opportunity to access the municipal service. The implementation of more e-services (which obviously requires access to and knowledge of how to use them) should be considered in light of the digital divide that still exists, which will be discussed in the following section.

Digital Divide Still Exists

To implement more public e-services can be seen as one way towards a broader use of e-services in Sweden as more than 84% of Sweden's inhabitants use the Internet today (not necessarily daily) (Findahl, 2011). There is still a need, however, for improvements in existing e-services as there are problems in using them; about 1.5 million Swedish citizens are still outside the world of the Internet. This implies that there is still a digital divide. The reason for this is first of all a lack of interest among those who are outside the Internet, above all the elderly (Findahl, 2011). Other reasons are technical adversities and not enough technical knowledge (Findahl, 2011). In 2008, 5% declared that they were, to some extent, unable to use the Internet due to various physical disabilities. Problems with bad eyesight and motor skills are the most common reasons, while dyslexia is another (Findahl, 2009; Hadenius et al., 2008). Furthermore, even in the year 2009 there was a connection between age, education, and income regarding the use of the Internet. This connection was strongest among elderly people (Findahl, 2009).

To enable citizens to choose a communication channel and to be able to communicate with the municipality through different channels are thus extremely important factors, at least from a democracy perspective. To establish CCs with "one simple path" via the phone and also allowing physical visits means enabling access to municipal services for groups outside the Internet as well. This is a further example of efforts to include more groups of citizens and a step towards an inclusive e-government municipality.

The results from municipality D show, however, that even if the municipal guides within the CC have access to a municipal local intranet information system, there are restrictions on what the municipal guides are allowed to respond to and perform depending on their level of expertise, for example when asked about certain legal matters. The main information source for their knowledge is the public information available on the Internet. One way to increase access to municipal service for citizens may be to transfer more decision-making processes regarding policies to the CC. Such a transfer could contribute to increasing the quality of work for handling officers at the back office as they would no longer handle as many routine matters. This would in turn provide an increased level of service to citizens as they would not have to contact other personnel at the back office, but would be answered directly by a person who has the authority to make decisions. Also, when there is an issue that needs to be answered by a handling officer at the back office, the handling officer would have more time to discuss this. Routine questions would be handled by the CC personnel.

CONCLUSION

Towards Inclusive E-Government

The implementation of CCs in municipalities and more public e-services seem to have contributed to increased access for citizens to municipal services within the municipalities studied. Citizens, including groups outside the world of Internet, now have increased possibilities to choose communication channels in order to gain access to municipal service which may reduce the digital divide. The use of simple touch-tone technology and establishing of a special CC solely for issues regarding the care of the elderly seem to contribute to the inclusion of more groups of citizens. To communicate directly and engage in dialogue with different groups of citizens, e.g. focus groups, citizen panels, and e-boards, can also be seen as an example towards inclusive e-government.

However, for citizens it is important to understand the values that characterize the "classic" public handling officer and what quality of service the citizens may demand. This may also have impact on the skills of the handling officers. A critical issue is the demand for learning within the municipalities. Due to the varying local context of each municipality there is no need to make "blueprints," even if it is important to be familiar with and share experience of various ways of organizing and working.

This study implies that the implementation may be viewed towards a citizen-centric approach in the respect of that all issues from citizens to the CC were registered. This may contribute to increased knowledge about the citizens' needs regarding municipality services. The municipal services could then be localized and adjusted to the citizens' needs (and to different communities of the citizens), and hence the production of municipal services became more citizen-governed than before the implementation of the CCs, it can be argued that this might contribute to citizen impact in the planning of municipal management developing issues.

The implementation of CCs may be seen as a way of contributing to more equal treatment of citizens. This depends on if the municipalities clearly maintaining other channels of communication as well. However, it is not only the quantity of e-services that matter. It is still a problem that a number of public e-services are used to a low extent. A reason for this may be the quality of the e-services. Many citizens seem to be dissatisfied with the design of the e-service. Also, the implementation of more e-services (which obviously requires access to and knowledge of how to use them) should be considered in the light of the digital divide that still exists. Citizen-centric development work could make developers more aware of municipal service needs, especially from citizen groups that do not use Internet services.

To conclude, the implementation and development of municipal CCs (which is a new phenomenon within the Swedish municipal e-government context) may be viewed as one practical result of Swedish e-government policy. However even if the results indicate and increased accessibility to municipal service for citizens, this study does not offer enough evidence of whether the policy objectives to "make it as simple as possible for as many as possible" have been achieved by implementing CCs, although the study does indicate that this will lead to improved municipal accessibility for citizens.

FURTHER RESEARCH DIRECTIONS

Recent studies show a gap between the supply and demand sides of e-government services (OECD, 2009). In fact, users of e-government services in the EU declined in 2008 compared to 2007 (Codagnone & Osimo, 2010). According to the study, 46.9% used the Internet in 2007 for obtaining information from public sector websites compared to 41.8% in 2008. 19.2% used the Internet for sending completed forms to public authorities compared to 21.9% in 2007. Recent studies of digital inclusion also show that individuals and communities facing conditions of multiple social disadvantages are unlikely to become proficient users of the Internet and e-government services, at least in the short term (Codagnone & Osimo, 2010). There are obviously still challenges to be met in order to fulfill the goals of the EU Ministerial e-Government Declaration (2005) of inclusive e-government focusing on increased transparency, accessibility, accountability, and participation of the citizens. It is still a challenge to have a real citizen-centric approach when developing and implementing e-government. There is for example a need to improve our knowledge of qualitative aspects of citizen characteristics and preferences regarding the use and non-use of the Internet and of e-government services as a complement to the quantitative studies made, in order to design the services according to the needs of citizens. There are some tentative approaches for classifications of users of e-government services, which could be useful for further empirical studies. For example, Codagnone and Osimo (2010) identify the following groups: dropouts (digitally excluded and lacking intellectual and material resources to use ICT); digital reluctant (lacking in motivation, confidence and/or trust); potential climbers (have the potential to become e-government users); basics (simple users, search mainly e-government information); trendy and mobile (have a high degree of IT competence and sophistication); digital natives (have grown up with ICT).

A further methodological challenge is to identify the complex diversity of different citizen groups who have different needs for municipal service. It is also a challenge to reach all these groups of citizens in order to investigate their understanding and experiences of e-governance and e-services as well as their willingness to use such services.

REFERENCES

Bäck, A. Monica (2008). *Conceptions, conflicts and contradictions at the introduction of a Swedish Health Call Centre.* (Doctoral thesis). Göteborg: Gothenburg University.

Bernhard, I. (2009). Evaluation of customer centre and e-services in a Swedish municipality with focus on the citizens' perspective. In D. Remenyi (Ed.), *Proceedings of the 3rd European Conference on Information Management and Evaluation (ECIME)* (pp. 34-41). 17-18 Sept. Reading, UK: Academic Press Ltd.

Bernhard, I. (2010). Establishment of customer centres in the public sector in Sweden – The citizens' views. In D. O'Donnell (Ed.), *Proceedings of the 10th European Conference on e-Government* (pp. 63-70). National Centre for Taxation Studies, University of Limerick, Ireland, 17-18 June 2010. Intellectual Capital Research, Limerick, Ireland, Academic Publishing International.

Bernhard, I. (2011, August). *Local e-government in Sweden – Establishment of municipal contact centers with focus on the citizens and the public administrators.* Paper presented at the 51st European Congress of Regional Science Association International, Barcelona, Spain.

Bernhard, I., & Grundén, K. (2010). Kompetensstrategier vid införande av kundcenter i kommuner. In Lagrosen, S., Lundh Snis, U., & Nehls, E. (Eds.), *Lärande i och för det nya arbetslivet* (pp. 31–46). Lund: Studentlitteratur.

Bernhard, I., & Wihlborg, E. (2011). Municipal contact centers. A slower approach towards sustainable local development. In I. Bernhard (Ed.), *Uddevalla Symposium 2011. Entrepreneurial Knowledge, Technology and Transformation of Regions.* (pp. 111-125). Revised papers presented at the 14th Uddevalla Symposium, 16-18 June 2011, Bergamo, Italy. Research reports 2011:05, University West.

Bernhard, I., & Wihlborg, E. (2012). Trust in secure public e-services – Translating policies into use. In Karlsson, C., Johansson, B., & Stough, R. R. (Eds.), *Entrepreneurship, social capital and governance directions for the sustainable development and competitiveness of regions* (pp. 241–262). Cheltenham, UK & Northampton, MA, USA: Edward Elgar.

Björk, P., & Bostedt, G. (2002). *Avsektoriserad lokal offentlig service: Organisationsteoretiska perspektiv på försöksverksamhet med medborgarkontor 1995-2000*, Stockholm: Svenska kommunförbundet och Landstingsförbundet/SALAR.

Blakemore, M., Mc Donald, N., Hall, N., & Jucuite, R. (2010). Delivering citizen-centric public services through technology in Europe - Facilitated organizational change. In P. G. Nixon., V. N. Koutrakou, & R. Rawal (Eds.), Understanding e-government in Europe. Issues and challenges (pp. 19-37). Oxon: Routledge.

Bock Seegard, S. (2009). *Veje til lokalt e-demokrati – organisering, mål, virkmidler og resurser.* Oslo: Oslo University Press.

Ciborra, C. (2002). *The labyrinths of information: Challenging the wisdom of systems.* Oxford: Oxford University Press.

Codagnone, C., & Osimo, D. (2010). Beyond i2010: E-Government current challenges and future scenarios. In Nixon, P. G., Koutrakou, V. N., & Rawal, R. (Eds.), *Understanding e-government in Europe. Issues and challenges* (pp. 38–59). Oxon: Routledge.

Collins, N., & Butler, P. (2002). When marketing models clash with democracy. *Journal of Public Affairs, 3*(1), 52–62. doi:10.1002/pa.133.

EU. (2005). EU ministerial declaration on e-government 2005. *Manchester, Ministerial eGovernment Conference* (pp. 2). 24. Nov. Transforming Public Services. Retrieved December 9, 2010, from www.egov2005conference.gov.uk/documents/proceedings/pdf/051124declaration.pdf

European Commission. (2010). Europeans Information Society Thematic Portal. *Inclusive eGovernment – no citizen left behind.* Retrieved December 27, 2010, from http://ec.europa.eu/information_society/activities/einclusion/policy/egov/index_en.htm

Findahl, O. (2009). *Svenskarna och Internet 2009* (The Swedes and the Internet 2009). World Internet Institute. Retrieved December 12, 2009, from http://www.wii.se

Findahl, O. (2011). *Äldre svenskar och Internet 2010.* World Internet Institute &. SE (The Internet Infrastructure Foundation). Retrieved June 10, 2011, from http://www.wii.se

Frenkel, S., Korczynski, M., Shire, K., & Tam, M. (1999). Beyond bureaucracy? Work organization in call centres. *International Journal of Human Resource Management, 9*(6), 957–979. doi:10.1080/095851998340694.

Giritli Nygren, K., & Wiklund, H. G. (2010). En IT-styrd förvaltning – en fjärde förvaltningsdoktrin? In K. Lindblad-Gidlund, A. Ekelin, S, Eriksén & A. Ranerup (Eds.), Förvaltning och medborgarskap i förändring (Ongoing change in public administration and citizenship – Established practice and critical perspectives) (pp. 215-228). Lund: Studentlitteratur.

Grant, G., & Chau, D. (2006). Developing a generic framework for e-Government. In Hunter, G., & Tan, F. (Eds.), *Advanced topics in global information management* (*Vol. 5*, pp. 72–101). London: Idea Group. doi:10.4018/978-1-59140-923-6.ch004.

Grönlund, Å. (2001). En introduktion till electronic government. In Grönlund, Å., & Ranerup, A. (Eds.), *Elektronisk förvaltning, elektronisk demokrati. Visioner, verklighet, vidareutveckling*. Lund: Studentlitteratur.

Grönlund, Å. (2006). Electronic government – What's in a word? Scope, status and future of the field. In EuroSpace (Ed.), E-government: European Strategies compared. EuroSpace S.r.1.

Grundén, K. (2009a). MOA – An evaluation model for implementation and use of IT in organisations. In D. Remenyi (Ed.), *Proceedings of the 3rd European Conference on Information Management and Evaluation (ECIME)* (pp. 187-194). *17-18 Sept.* Reading, UK: Academic Press Ltd.

Grundén, K. (2009b). A social perspective on implementation of eGovernment - A longitudinal study at the County Administration of Sweden. *The Electronic Journal of e-Government (EJEG), 7*(1), 65-76.

Grundén, K. (2010). Evaluation of contact centre implementation in a Swedish municipality with focus on social aspect. In D. O'Donnell (Ed.), *Proceedings of the 10th European Conference on e-Government* (pp. 199-206). National Centre for Taxation Studies, University of Limerick, Ireland, 17-18 June, Intellectual Capital Research, Limerick, Ireland: Academic Publishing International.

Grundén, K. (2011). Implementation of contact centre in a Swedish municipality. In M. Klun, M. Decman, and T. Jukic (Eds.), *11th European Conference on eGovernment (ECEG 2011).* Faculty of Administration, University of Ljubljana, Ljubljana, Slovenia, 16-17 June 2011.

Hadenius, S., Weibull, L., & Wadbring, I. (2008). *Massmedier. press, radio och tv i den digitala tidsåldern*, 9:e upplagan, reviderad 2008. Stockholm: Ekerlids förlag.

Halchin, L. E. (2004). Electronic government: Government capability and terrorist resource. *Government Information Quarterly, 21*, 406–419. doi:10.1016/j.giq.2004.08.002.

Haugli Nyhuus, K., & Thorsen, T. (2007). *Partnerskap: Intensjon og virkelighet i NAV reformens velferdskontor*. Karlstads Universitet & Högskolen i Hedmark.

Heeks, R. (1999). *Reinventing government in the information age – International practice in IT-enabled public sector reform*. London: Routledge. doi:10.4324/9780203204962.

Heeks, R. (2006). *Implementing and managing egovernment: An international text*. Thousand Oaks, CA/London: Sage Publications.

Homburg, V. (2008). *Understanding e-government. Information systems in public administration*. Abingdon, Oxon: Routledge.

Jansson, G. (2011). *Local values and e-government - Continuity and change in public administration. Implementing public e-Services on two Swedish municipalities' administration*. Sweden: Linköping University.

Karagiannaki, E. (2005). *Jobcentre plus or minus? Exploring the performance of Jobcentre Plus for nonjobseekers. CASEpaper 97. Centre for Analysis of Social Exclusion*. London School of Economics.

Lindblad-Gidlund, K., Ekelin, A., Eriksén, S., & Ranerup, A. (Eds.). (2010). *Förvaltning och medborgarskap i förändring (Ongoing change in public administration and citizenship – Established practice and critical perspectives)* (pp. 21–30). Lund: Studentlitteratur.

Lips, M. (2007). E-government under construction. Challenging traditional conceptions of citizenship. In Nixon, P. G., & Koutrakou, V. N. (Eds.), *E-government in Europe. Re-booting the state* (pp. 33–47). London: Routledge Advances in European Politics.

Michel, H. (2005). E-administration, e-government, e-governance and the learning city: A typology of citizenship management using ICTs. *The Electronic Journal of e-Government (EJEG), 3*(4), 213-218. Retrieved February 15, 2009, from www.ejeg.com

Norman, K. (2005). *Call centre work – Characteristics, physical and psychosocial exposure and related outcomes*. (Doctoral dissertation). Linköping: The University of Linköping. Division of Industry Ergonomics.

Nutek. (2000). *En marknadsstudie av callcentre i Sverige hösten 1999*. Report 2000:10.Stockholm: Närings- och utvecklingsverket.

OECD. (2005). *E-government for better government. OECD Government Studies* (p. 42). Paris: OECD Publishing.

OECD. (2009). *Rethinking e-government services. User-centric approaches*. Paris: OECD Publishing.

Persson, A., & Goldkuhl, G. (2010). Government value paradigms – Bureaucracy, new public management, and e-government. *Communications of the Association for Information Systems, 27*(1). Article 4, July, 45-62. Retreived June 27, 2012, from http//aisle.aisnet.org/cias/vol27/iss1/4

Regeringskansliet. (1999). *Medborgarkontor i utveckling* Departementsserien (Ds) *Ds1999:26*, [One-Stop-Government-Offices in development] Justitiedepartementet [Swedish Ministry of Justice], Stockholm.

Regeringskansliet. (2008). *Handlingsplan för eFörvaltning. Nya grunder för IT-baserad verksamhetsutveckling*. Retrieved March 23, 2010, from http://www.regeringen.se/content/1/c6/07/49/95/2c28b30b.pdf

Rundle, E. (2009). New York City Streamlining 911 Call Talking Process. In *Government Technology* (p. 1). Retrieved October 5, 2010, from http://www.govtech.com/gt/articles/663164

SALAR. (1997). [The Swedish Association of Municipalities and Regions] *Samtjänst vid medborgarkontor*, 1997:122, 26.08.1997.

Sambruk. (2010). *Municipal e-services*. Retrieved October 13, 2010, from http://www.sambruk.se/inenglish.4.76e8b1c6112f078db498000144852.html

SFS. (1986). *Förvaltningslag* (1986:223), (Administrative Law). Retrieved January 14, 2010, from http://www.notisum.se/rnp/SLS/LAG/19860223.HTM

SKL. (2007). Om kommuner. (About municipalities). Stockholm: Sveriges kommuner och landsting (SKL). (Swedish Association of Local Authorities and Regions).

SKL. (2009). e-förvaltningsutveckling i Sveriges kommuner 2006-2008. Delrapport 3. (The development of e-government in Swedish municipalities 2006-2008). Stockholm: Sveriges kommuner och landsting (SKL) (Swedish Association of Local Authorities and Regions).

SOU. (1999). Statens offentliga utredningar SOU1999:85. Bredband för tillväxt i hela landet. [Broadband for nationwide growth] Swedish official governmental reports Näringsdepartementet, betänkande från IT-infrastrukturutredningen, Stockholm.

SOU. (2002). *Statens Offentliga utredningar SOU 2002:51. Breddtjänster - ett nytt skede i IT-politiken, Näringsdepartementet, IT-kommissionens rapport 3/2002, Statens offentliga utredningar*. Stockholm: Fritzes.

SOU. (2004). Statens offentliga utredningar SOU 2004:56 e-tjänster för alla [e-services for everyone] Swedish official governmental reports. Finansdepartmenetet. 24-timmars delegationen. Stockholm: Fritzes.

SOU. (2005). *Statens offentliga utredningar SOU 2005:19. e-tjänster för ett öppnare samhälle. Slutbetänkande av 24-timmarsdelegationen. Swedish official governmental reports* [e-services for a more open society]. Stockholm: Fritzes.

SOU. (2008). *Statens offentliga utredningar SOU 2008:97. Styr samverkan - För bättre service till medbor*garna. Socialdepartementet, Utveckling av lokal service i samverkan, Swedish official governmental reports Stockholm: Fritzes.

SOU. (2009). *Statens offentliga utredningar SOU 2009:92, Se medborgarna – för bättre offentlig service. Slutbetänkande av Utveckling av lokal service i samverkan*. Stockholm: Fritzes.

Statskontoret. (2011). *Den offentliga sektorns utveckling. En samlad redovisning 2011*. Statskontoret, Stockholm. (The Swedish Agency for Public Management). Retrieved June 29, 2011, from http://www.statskontoret.se/publikationer/2011/den-offentliga-sektorns-utveckling-en-samlad-redovisning-2011/

Tengblad, P., Wiberg, A., Herrman, L., & Backström, M. (2002). *Hållbart arbete i informationssamhället. Call centre i utveckling. Final report from the project "Call centre i utveckling – långsiktigt hållbart arbete med kunder på distans." Vinnova report VR 2002:7*. Stockholm: VINNOVA.

Wallström, Å., Engström, A., Salehi-Sangari, E., & Ek Styvén, M. (2009). Public e-services from the citizens' perspective – Adopting a market orientation. *International Journal of Public Information Systems*, *5*(2), 123–134.

Wihlborg, E. (2005). *Offentliga e-tjänster i medborgarens tjänst*. [Public e-services for the citizens] Stockholm: 24-timmarsdelegationen.

Yildiz, M. (2007). E-government research: Reviewing the literature, limitations, and ways forward. *Government Information Quarterly*, *24*(3), 646–665. doi:10.1016/j.giq.2007.01.002.

ADDITIONAL READING

Axelsson, K., Melin, U., & Lindgren, I. (2010). Exploring the importance of citizen participation and involvement in e-government projects. Practice, incentives, and organization. *Transforming Government: People. Process and Policy*, *4*(4), 299–321.

Carter, L., & Bélanger, F. (2005). The utilization of e-government services: Citizen trust, innovation and acceptance factors. *Information Systems Journal*, *15*, 5–25. doi:10.1111/j.1365-2575.2005.00183.x.

Grundén, K., & Bernhard, I. (2012). Implementation of a contact centre – A local e-government initiative. In M. Gascó (Ed.), *Proceedings of the 12th European Conference on e-Government* (pp. 329-335). ESADE Ramon Llull University, Barcelona, Spain 14-15 June. Reading, UK: Academic Publishing International Limited.

Meijer, A., & Bannister, F. (2011). The coming of age of e-government studies. *Information Polity*, *16*, 1–3.

Norris, D., & Reddick, C. (2012). eGovernment among US local governments: Current status and recent trends. In M. Gascó (Ed.), *Proceedings of the 12th European Conference on e-Government* (pp. 537-545). ESADE Ramon Llull University, Barcelona, Spain 14-15 June. Reading, UK: Academic Publishing International Limited.

Rabiaiah, A., & Vandijck, E. (2011). A strategic framework of e-government: Generic and best practice. In Worrall (Ed.), Leading issues in e-government research. Reading: Academic Publishing Internationals.

Rose, W. R., & Grant, G. G. (2010). Critical issues pertaining to the planning and implementation of e-government initiatives. *Government Information Quarterly*, *27*(1), 26–33. doi:10.1016/j.giq.2009.06.002.

Saad-Sulonen, J., & Horelli, L. (2010). The value of community informatics to participatory urban planning and design: A case-study in Helsinki. *The Journal of Community Informatics*, *6*(2).

Schwester, R. (2011). Examining the barriers to e-government adoption. In Worrall, L. (Ed.), *Leading issues in e-government research*. Reading, UK: Academic Publishing International.

Worral, L. (Ed.). (2011). *Leading issues in e-government research*. Reading, UK: Academic Publishing International Ltd..

KEY TERMS AND DEFINITIONS

Citizen-Centric Approach: To have a citizen-centric approach means to put the citizens' interests in the center of municipal service production. The establishment of focus groups with citizens as participants or citizen panels can contribute to integrating the citizens' needs into the development and implementation work of e-government. The concepts of good governance and citizen-centric municipal administration are intimately connected.

Digital Divide: The concept "digital divide" generally refers to the socio-economic gap between communities that have access to computers and the Internet and those that do not. The term could also refer e.g. to aspects affecting availability to quality, useful digital content such as ICT literacy, and technical skills.

Inclusive E-Government: The concept inclusive e-government implies a new era of inclusive and accountable government aiming to involve all citizens within a municipality. We still have problems with the digital divide regarding Internet availability and understanding. In accordance with the role of citizenship, all citizens should have the right to equal possibilities in accessing public services.

Municipal Contact Center: The use of the term "contact centre" indicates an extended function, not only focusing on phone calls, but also on other contiguous work tasks. The main function of Swedish municipal CCs is to supply services to citizens more efficiently by primarily using the telephone and ICT (e.g. e-services) to handle citizen contacts. The development of municipal contact centers is especially influenced by aspects such as increased service and availability from a citizen perspective and internal efficiency. When a municipal contact centre is implemented, there are usually also organizational changes such as increased process orientation inspired by, for example, New Public Management theories.

New Public Management (NPM): NPM is frequently described as an umbrella term of management ideas from the business sector implemented in a public sector context. NPM is both a practice and a theoretical conceptualization rooted in different research fields with diverse directions. There is emphasis on contract-like relationships and attention given to management strategies, performance indicators, and the service produced. The use of IT is essential for this organizational transformation where IT mediates the communication between different units in different geographical locations. The theories of NPM have inspired some changes of organization and administration when e-government is implemented and the use of lean and highly decentralized structures in public service is stressed, resulting in the breakdown of formerly unitary bureaucracies (Homburg, 2008).

"One-Stop Government Office" or Civic Office: A "One-Stop-Government-Office" is a public front-office public service unit where personnel with general competencies provide services across levels of governance, administration, authority and sector. This sets it apart from a contact centre, as the service provided to citizens concerns issues not only from the municipality but instead from more than one public authority or sector, hence the term "one-stop."

Chapter 12
Malaysia's Internet Governance Dilemma

Mary Griffiths
University of Adelaide, Australia

Sara Chinnasamy
University of Technology Mara, Malaysia

ABSTRACT

After the unexpected result of the 2008 General Election in Malaysia, the political potential of an uncensored Internet was recognized by political and social elites. The 'tsunami' of criticism of government triggered a reconsideration of tighter Internet regulation, despite Vision 2020's guarantee that e-government and multimedia business development would be unrestricted by Internet censorship. Through a study of the role of Independent News Portals (INPs), particularly the Malaysiakini.com, this chapter assesses the democratic, business, and political challenges of Internet governance. The perspectives of key media, business and government personnel are included in a small nested study of elite reactions to the explosion of diversity of critical opinion online, and the subsequent consideration of tighter Internet regulation. The interview findings conclude that support for the Internet to remain uncensored remains strong in Malaysia among members of the professional elites, but this is primarily for economic and pragmatic, rather than democratic reasons. Suggested solutions include increasing cross-silo discussions between government agencies about ICT development and outcomes in Malaysia.

INTRODUCTION

The Internet is recognized as a productive communications technology in that it has the capacity to anchor, change and disrupt existing economic, political and social relations. This succinct comment from the 'future issues' workshop at the Internet Governance Forum (2008) concisely sums up the significance of its transformational impact on the governance of relations both internal to a nation, and internationally with others around the globe:

DOI: 10.4018/978-1-4666-4245-4.ch012

The Internet is the most important piece of infrastructure of our time and that it underpins our economies, our cultures, and our communities. And it is also beginning to underpin our governance, how we understand, how we need to interact with each other in a much more networked way around the world. How the Internet is beginning to break down the silos between sectors. How you have governments talking with each other across regions. How you have governments working with the private sector, the engagement of civil society and so on… (Creech, 2008)

This chapter focuses on a study of the Internet's governance debates in Malaysia, as public awareness grew of the political impact of the unregulated circulation of news during, and following, the 2008 General Election. In the aftermath of voting, some establishment responses crystallized in expressions of the need to reconsider Internet governance issues. Others, more committed to political change, rested their arguments on the initial guarantee of no Internet censorship. Still others pointed to the economic drivers needed to achieve an information economy, pointing out that the success of e-government projects required a liberal approach to governance of the Internet. Thus, Malaysia's Internet governance dilemma began as mutually exclusive development goals clashed: the aim for an information economy and national business untrammeled by Internet restrictions, versus the preservation of existing political power through tighter regulatory control of online communications. In late 2012, the question seemed provisionally resolved, and this study highlights key features of the long process.

The next section contextualizes global Internet governance issues and notes the international regulatory bodies' moves from adjudicating on technology issues, to a deeper engagement with emerging social, political and democratic issues. It notes the complexity of policy formation in developing a national information economy. The chapter then outlines relevant Malaysian e-government initiatives. It describes the impact of the independent news portals (INPs) reporting during the 2008 'Internet Election.' Findings are reported from the nested study of qualitative data derived from in country interviews with ten key informants from government, information hub, and urban elites. It puts forward recommendations about cross-silo discussions and engagement with civil society organizations, prior to future consideration of regulatory frameworks. The chapter concludes by discussing the significance of a research study on Internet governance to future e-government and e-democracy research.

INTERNET GOVERNANCE AND INFORMATION ECONOMY DEVELOPMENT

Studies of interactive communications technology, its protocols, and its impact on changing relationships between governments and citizens are central to scholarship on democracy, e-government and e-participation. In the latter two fields, e-government and e-democracy, research foci routinely include access issues, population readiness, inclusiveness, the means of engagement, the scaling-up of citizen participation in policy-making, and descriptive analyzes of the practicalities of instances of e-government activity. The documenting of such enabling processes has been illustrative of the scale and ubiquity of global uptake by governments of Internet-based communications and the redefinition of the relationship between governments and citizens.

There is less of a research focus on the foundational question of how each state operates its terms and conditions of Internet use within a developing international governance framework. In the area of comparative studies of Internet-related governance, international modeling offers useful scoping and ranking data, but gives scant information about the specific contextual factors driving each nation's Internet governance as it pertains to e-government trajectories, and policy agenda priorities. In Malaysia, for example, in 2008 ranked 17 in terms of UN web measures as reported in a paper arguing for greater e-government efforts to increase and diversify public participation (Salamat et al., 2011), the Internet and e-government initiatives have been resourced primarily to enable less-restricted, more competitive business practices in a developing information society (Evers et al., 2010).

The Malaysian government guaranteed an Internet free of regulatory interference on the inception of the Multimedia Super Corridor (MSC) in 1997. The business hubs and e-government pilots were expected to flourish under a light-touch regulatory framework. Other Malaysian communications businesses such as print and broadcast news platforms are however subject to tight government controls over ownership, operating licenses and content. This has created an imbalance in styles, diversity and approach in news reporting. The Internet's development was unrestricted by a similar regulatory environment, as it appears to have been conceptualized and resourced from the beginning as if it were an information silo, operating solely for commercial advantage in a socio-political vacuum.

The potential socio-political outcomes of allowing unrestricted access and content distribution were not so easily foreseen in the 1990s. Before the so-called 'Arab Spring' of revolutionary social-media mobilization and a decade earlier, 'People Power 11' texting helped removed Estrada from office in the Philippines, the connection between many-to-many communications technologies and direct political change seemed a tenuous one to make. New phenomena and disruptive trends were used to argue for the democratizing power of the Internet as each event instance of popular Internet-enabled expression was reported. The claims made for ICTs can be exaggerated; but the diversification of alternative sources of information, and the mobilization of resistant or minority interests, have proved universally challenging to power elites, since Internet and mobile communications have put communicative aggregation potential into the hands of previously powerless individuals and groups.

A key focus of Internet development in countries in the Asia Pacific region has been on growing national economic potential through competitive engagement in a global economy. Singapore, Indonesia, India, Australia, New Zealand and Malaysia all have established information economy agendas, but each nation has to face compelling and different issues to achieve their aims: geography, Internet penetration and uptake rates, costs, patterns of partnerships with the private sector, and literacy and digital literacy issues. A shared ambition is maximizing national wealth creation by capitalizing on the new business opportunities afforded by the development and clustering of 'intelligent' workforces seen to create a competitive edge in the global digital economy. In the last twenty years, the whole region has seen rapid, though uneven, ICT infrastructure construction and development. Greater access and participation have been encouraged by governments, the private sector, education, ICT training programs, and varied levels of support for information and multimedia business. Market ideology prioritizes non-compulsion and ease of information flow, as reflected in the principles standing behind many global governance organizations like WSIS or ICANN. Yet, as policy research has argued, even apparently non-political issues such as domain name extensions can trigger deep-seated and emotional forms of nationalism (Shlovski & Struthers, 2010). The politics of the Internet are embedded in nascent attempts at gaining agreement to simple issues in international governance, let alone more complex ones. At the national level, in developing democracies especially, ensuring an Internet-enabled openness to business opportunities also delivers a - sometimes less welcome - free market in ideas, the increased opportunity for individual exchanges of ideologies and beliefs and, ultimately, the potential for political mobilization.

Internet access, modes of participation and governance are thus critical policy issues for governments and for e-government research. Studies of e-government 'transactional' exchanges between government agencies and citizens, i.e., the concept of providing services and information to citizens, have been prolific and have often focused on micro-level technical issues such as web-design ease of use, or the stream-lining of business administration processes. E-government research also assumes the power of the nation state, and describes the economies gained by the introduction of e-government and the transparency of online transactions within a relatively unquestioned progressive development and information economy framework (Yilditz, 2007). On the connections to democracy and politics, e-government work can be vaguer, or non-specific, or silent.

However, with the interconnectivity of most countries' global Internet and mobile network participation, governments are presented with fresh and more interconnected technology governance issues. At the global governance level, debates on future issues at the World Summit on Internet Governance recognize that Internet governance is more than the provision of domain classifiers through ICANN, and establishment of agreements on trade exchanges. The Internet crosses borders in unexpected ways in the lives of a nation's citizens. The global sociopolitical issues such as the right to Internet access, protection from Internet crime, a citizen's right to protection from government, and the global problems of terrorism and crime at a supra-national level are consequently becoming harder to detach from state e-government regulatory or governance fields. In addition, non-government organizations seeking to democratize more broadly, and open information movements, also exert pressures on a nation-state's internal Internet policies. New international reporting considerations attract concomitant internal controversies about local regulation of the Internet, privacy legislation and to citizens' rights to freedom of speech.

Governments' responses to these burgeoning and less manageable phenomena range - at an authoritarian point on the spectrum - from the Chinese and North Korean practice of instituting national firewalls and full control over citizens' domestic Internet uses, to Australia's failed proposal of mandatory filtering in 2009, and its struggling proposals for data retention and heightened online security powers in 2012. National policy responses to the democratizing potential of the Internet highlight the significant political contrasts in framing normative approaches to e-governance. Malaysia is facing culturally specific but familiar dilemmas in finding the policy balance between national, business and political interests, and what 'netizens' want.

MSC Malaysia and E-Governance

The implementation of the e-government agenda by Malaysia's ruling regime, the BN government, was seen as a core application of the MSC Malaysia project (Yusoff & Radzi, 2002). A range of initiatives became flagship developments under MSC implementation. These included high-technology projects such as Telemedicine, Smart School, Multipurpose Smart Card System, Research and Development Cluster, e-Business and Technopreneur Development (MyGovernment, 2012). Under the e-government badge, many well-resourced projects have been implemented. With allocations of RM5.2 billion under 8th Malaysia Plan (2000-2005), they have received high -priority status from the Barisan Nasional (BN) government (Salmah, 2012). The administrative structure is complex: under the eight MSC flagship applications, the combined government agencies consist of more than 219 Federal departments and 346 departments, with 142 local authorities involved. This complex organization works within an e-government framework between business sectors and citizens to 'transform administration process and service delivery through the extensive utilization of ICT and multimedia' (MAMPU, 2012).

From the beginning, ICT development was focused more on information economy and business. It is now expanding to E-services, e-procurements, generic office environments, project monitoring systems (SPP II), human resource management. Still further development will see expansion to electronic labor exchanges, and to e-syariah (the Islamic justice portal), e-court and e-land. From the Malaysian Administrative Modernization and Management Planning Unit (MAMPU) record, it can be concluded that the government has expanded its ICT infrastructure initiatives to enhance government's multiple delivery channels based on ICT-enabled human capital development. Policies and legislation related to e-government have been implemented, such as Digital Signature Act 1997, Copyright (Amendment) Act 1997, Computer Crimes Act 1997, Telemedicine Act 1997, and Communication & Multimedia Act 1999. Plans have been made for developing the Electronic Government Activities Act (EGAA), Electronic Transactions Act (ETA) and Personal Data Protection Act (Salmah, 2012) to manage privacy settings in e-government applications and related matters. Overall, the ICT and e-government has been adopted as a fundamental component of achieving government's agenda in enhancing and broadening service delivery. The development of this sector appears to work without much cross-silo policy discussion of broader societal policy considerations. The role of confronting new socio-political dilemmas created by a new information environment is seen as one that the realm of politics can manage apparently without recourse to the growing knowledge base of those involved in e-government development.

The MSC initiatives were launched to create a geo-located multimedia utopia and knowledge hub for innovative producers and users of multimedia technology. Consortia comprised of local and foreign companies collaborating with multiple government agencies, departments and ministries to enhance the socio-economic development of Malaysia. The initial idea was that the MSC would transform Malaysia to a knowledge-based economy, as envisaged in the high-level policy statement, Vision 2020. The establishment of the MSC program was crucial to accelerating the objectives of Vision 2020, and to transforming Malaysia into a modern state by the year 2020, with the adoption of a knowledge-based society framework (Jeong, 2007). Supported personally by then Prime Minister, Dr Mahathir Mohammad, its core purpose was seen as exploratory and creative, 'MSC is paramount to leapfrog (Malaysia) into the 21st century and to achieve Malaysia's Vision 2020; the MSC was created to endeavor the best environment to harness the full potential of the multimedia without any artificial limits. MSC is a global test bed (hub), where the limits of the possible can be explored and new ways of living, working, and playing in the new area of the Information Age' (Ibrahim & Goh, 2000; Jeong, 2007). The visionary rhetoric insists on innovation, change and MSC's freedom to explore 'new ways of living, working and playing.' Yet with all liberalizing changes come unexpected and unplanned-for aspects in other sectors of a country's development, as the rest of the chapter demonstrates.

Initial e-government implementation began in 1997. Vision 2020 set out to achieve a fully developed country in the next 23 years (Seng et al., 2010). The government's initiative resulted in more than half of the population accessing the Internet by the end of 2009 (ITU, 2009), and since then, a 2012 telecommunications report indicates an increasing rate of broadband uptake, while mobile communications are exploding (Budde, 2012). As noted, a feature of e-government in Malaysia has been government support for ICT development, and opening up to the market. In e-government applications to improve transparency and achieve efficiency, the emphasis was also on opening up to more accountable business processes. The Malaysian Administrative Modernization and

Management Planning Unit (MAMPU) oversees most e-government projects. It operates as part of the Prime Minister's Department. MAMPU initiated the *My Government* portal (http://www.gov.my) for citizens to access government information and online services. The site recorded nearly 6.5 million visitors in May 2008 (Ahmad, 2008) and grew to 11.2 million visitors in September 2012 (http://www.malaysia.gov.my).

MAMPU also oversees the monitoring of online media space. A founding principle of MSC Malaysia was that the BN government would not censor the Internet. This was thought necessary to empower innovation and enable market forces to operate more effectively and innovatively. Seeing a regulatory loophole, former mainstream media journalists and those frustrated with mainstream reportage, such as Steven Gan and Premesh Chandran, established an independent news portal (INP), www.malaysiakini.com in November 1999.

Malaysiakini operated free of the regular controls that appeared to restrict the freedom of mainstream media (PBS News Hour, 2000). A year after it began, *Malaysiakini* was internationally recognized as one of Malaysia's most popular websites (BBC News, 2000). As a mark of its international impact, the site was awarded a Free Media Pioneer award from the International Press Institute in 2001 (International Consortium of Investigative Journalists, 2001). Gan was awarded one of the 2000 CPJ International Press Freedom Awards for his work with the site (Committee to Protect Journalists, 2000). *Malaysiakini* reported important and controversial events concerning the former deputy Prime Minister Anwar Ibrahim's dismissal. When Ibrahim was jailed on corruption charges, mainstream media gave rare headlines to the corruption scandals, and was accused of biased reporting against Anwar Ibrahim by opponents. *Malaysiakini* fuelled broad demand for greater political transparency, as there was a public interest in information on Anwar Ibrahim's case. The INPs were seen as linked to critique of government, rather than – as the international awards demonstrated – in its self-nominated role as a 'government watchdog'. The 4th estate role conception of journalism depends on the right to freedom of expression, and INPs disrupted the development journalism expectations of press-government relations embedded in the country's established, influential mainstream practices. After nearly a decade, *Malaysiakini* again came to prominence by reporting on major political events before the 2008 General Election, and it gained more popularity during the election (Times, 2008).

After the election result, the 'free' Internet which supported INPs was perceived as having created a more complex and challenging information environment in Malaysia for the ruling party, the BN. 2008 produced election polls showing significant BN losses, for the first time since 1969, and the Internet was blamed for the opposition's electoral gains (Asia Sentinel, 2010). It was seen as significant that control of five of the thirteen states with relatively high Internet penetration had switched political allegiance, including Penang and Selangor states.

The 2008 General Election was regarded as a political tsunami (Rajaratnam, 2009) and a political earthquake for the BN (Mohamad, 2009). The former Prime Minister, Abdullah Badawi realized unrestricted Internet political commentary critical of the BN had contributed to the results. This included the key leading INP, Malaysiakini. It is still widely read, even though many INPs came into existence after the post 2008 vote. The late realization by political leaders is expressed in this comment by Abdullah Badawi, as quoted in the New Straits Times, March 2008, in a story titled 'Internet served a painful lesson', he states, 'We didn't think it was important. It was a serious misjudgment. We thought newspapers; the print media, the televisions were important but the influence of alternative media was painful.' In the aftermath of the election, Malaysian observers and analysts noted the government's determination to reconsider Internet regulation.

Internet as a Political Threat

The battles over online freedom of expression emerge when almost one third of the world's population are connected in different affiliations than those defined by geography or nationally defined restrictions. Many governments are responding to the increased influence of social networking and news websites. Regimes can tighten online surveillance by monitoring and controlling online activities and restricting free flow information, which infringes users' rights according to international democracy watchdogs (Freedom House, 2012). In Malaysia's case, the freedom of the media is already restricted by the Federal Constitution under the Article 10 since reactions to the 1969 riots gave national stability in a multi-racial state a higher priority than the public airing of alternative, resistant or minority voices. Stringent laws such as the Sedition Act, the Internal Security Act (ISA), and Defamation Act are used regularly to impose restrictions on the press and other critics, and all transgressions are punishable by several years in prison, in some cases without trial.

2008 triggered a high number of online regulation discussions after the recognition of the Internet's election role (Janet, 2009; Kensaku, 2008: Stodden, 2008). Yet, in 2009, several Ministers gave press statements, including the Prime Minister Najib Tun Razak, that the Internet would not be regulated. Additionally, in 2009, the government announced greater flexibility with regard to the most stringent laws impinging upon freedom of speech: the Internal Security Act (ISA), the Police Act and the Communications and Multimedia Act 1998. Further, the Information, Communication, and Culture Minister Rais Yatim stated that the Police Act would include provisions allowing peaceful assembly in certain designated places such as stadiums, without the need to obtain a permit from the police (Kuek, 2009).

However, the review of restrictions on the freedom of the Internet still has an uncertain status, as the BN government, while hesitating to implement censorship legislation, is using other means to manage the challenge. Since the government currently chooses not to restrict the Internet, other measurements like the passing of the Peaceful Assembly Act 2012 and Section 114A of the Evidence Act 2012 have taken place. These reduce the possibilities of political threat emerging from Internet-enabled protest and publication of critique. On 13 Jan 2011, a statement issued by the Prime Minister (PM) Najib Tun Razak indirectly hinted at the dangerous nature of the Internet if it remained unfettered. He argued that online negative influence could destroy Asian values and heritage. He urged for greater regulation of the internet stating that 'indecency and anarchy can seep into any environment that is not anchored on cultural roots and our values' (Centre for Independent Journalism, 2010). Examples of the PM's concerns on Internet development include, 'Civil society must be aware of cyber threats that are causing harm to the nation's sovereignty and society's interest' (Themalaysiainsider.com, 2009) and 'Bloggers and Internet users have to "draw the line" and online media or digital democracy has made it more difficult to win in the election' (Themalaysiainsider.com, 2011)

Contradictory as the instances cited are, they reflect the policy dilemma. It is notable that many of the BN's efforts were focused on suppressing the INPs in particular, which continue to hold a unique position in a tightly controlled mainstream media landscape. For the government and its allies in mainstream media, the pattern of alternative news sources with potential to generate more diverse political participation through news coverage was an unwelcome new feature of the public sphere. Information about upcoming rallies, coverage of the rallies, and memos about participation events organised by city councils and community centre and NGOs are now more readily available. By offering coverage to groups of people with non-BN political agendas, the alternative news sources gained popularity, simultaneously strengthened older political networks and helped establish new ones. Attempts were made to impose mainstream media laws on one of the most powerful independent news sources, Malaysiakini.com. Eventually, the Kuala Lumpur High Court quashed the Home Ministry's decision not to grant a publishing permit to the INP on 1 October 2012 (Malaysiakini, 2012). The government is nevertheless tightening up on freedom of expression by controlling protest rallies with the Peaceful Assembly Act (2012). The Internet Security Act (ISA) has been replaced by the Security Offences (Special Measures) Act 2012, which strengthens police powers to detain citizens. The Security Offences (Special Measures) Act 2012 was passed by Parliament and given royal assent on 18 June 2012. However, the law is not yet in force as of July 2012 (Official Portal e-Government Gazette, 2012) as it is awaiting the announcement of the Minister of Home Affairs.

Current Online Media Controversies

More stringent measures are becoming evident as the 2013 election approaches. These include including surveillance of online space, book banning, the harassment and intimidation of bloggers, show cause letters, the denial and cancelation of permits, and interference with radio and television organizations. A draft bill to regulate online media has been proposed by the Ministry of Home Affairs. These formal policy suggestions and more reactive practices indicate that party political goals may be being prioritized ahead of other national and democratic considerations. Cases of bloggers being harassed or charged under vaguely worded security laws continue. In 2008, the detention and arrest of a political website founder of Malaysia Today, Raja Petra Kamaruddin, followed his criticism of BN politicians. The procedures were affected under ISA law. The country has no federal freedom of information legislation, and officials are reluctant to share controversial data with journalists for fear of being charged under the colonial-era Official Secrets Act (OSA). The significant feature of the Malaysia's media environment is that mainstream media is predominantly privately owned by government representatives. Mainstream media is further controlled by the Printing Presses and Publications Act (PPPA) 1984, which requires all publishers and printing firms to obtain an annual operations' permit. This provides the Prime Minister with the power to revoke licenses at any time without judicial review. As has happened, 'show cause' letters may also be issued by the Home Minister, which require the news agency to explain certain articles, or face suspension or revocation of their permits.

Censorship takes many forms and is responsive to media laws that are a result of the country's mixed ethnic, religious and cultural values and traditions. For instance, in February 2010, the Star's editor, Gunasegaran, was issued a 'show cause' letter for an article criticizing the caning of three women for illicit sex under Sharia (Islamic law). The Star issued an apology after several police reports accused the editor of insulting Islam. In another example, the license of the Opposition's newspaper, Suara Keadilan, was not renewed. 'Show cause' letters were issued to the two opposition newspapers, the Rocket (owned by the Democratic Action Party), and Harakah (affiliated with the Islamic Party of Malaysia). Each of these licenses was eventually renewed. In other case, at least 25 books were banned, seized, or detained under the the Printing Presses and Publications Act (PPPA) 1984. This included a number of books published by a political cartoonist, Zulkiflee Anwar Haque, popularly known as Zunar. The cartoon compilations were published by Malaysiakini through its subsidiary, Kinibooks. In August 2010, Zunar and Malaysiakini filed a legal challenge to the Ministry of Home affairs' ban. One month later, 66 copies of Zunar's books were seized from his office, and Malaysiakini's premises were searched (Freedom House, 2012). These cases have again brought Malaysia to the attention of global watchdogs for the protection of journalists and international monitors of the democratic health of a country. Just as the international ranking a country receives for Internet development and access issues is important to a developing nation, the question of how well a country ranks in terms of ensuring stability, and allowing freedom of expression and diversity of political opinion is considered relevant to continued and confident foreign investment.

Another illustration: INPs like Malaysiakini and Malaysia Insider actively criticized the arrest of demonstrators and journalists on the Bersih's 3.0 rally on the 28 April 2012. The event was organized by the Coalition for Free and Fair Elections, Bersih, an alliance of civil society groups, NGOs and political parties calling for a variety of election reforms. The rally, which drew reportedly around 80,000 participants, took place at the Dataran Merdeka, and historic Public Square in Kuala Lumpur. A court order prevented demonstrators from entering the square, but they broke through the barricades in protest. Police responded by firing tear gas and water cannons at the protesters. More than 500 demonstrators were arrested. The group argued that through the recently-approved Peaceful Assembly Act, police may impose conditions on planned assemblies, but are not allowed to bar them outright. The Bersih's April rally was the third major protest since their 2011's and 2007's rallies. In the 2011 protest, more than 1,600 people, including nine prominent human rights activists and Bersih leaders, were arrested and the rally further suppressed by roadblocks, preemptive arrests of participants, and attacks with tear gas, batons, and water cannons (Malaysiakini, 2012). These events also draw international attention. However, the Peaceful Assembly Act places new restrictions on public demonstrations, including a ban on street protests and new powers for police forces to arrest participants. Many local and international organizations have urged the government to allow peaceful assemblies to proceed without further disruption or harassment. The demonstrations reflect the increasingly vocal desire in the Malaysian polity for a more transparent and fair electoral system. Yet, authorities continue to attempt to curb freedom of expression and association. Further, Malaysiakini's journalists were attacked by authorities to prevent media coverage on the police violence against protesters. Online editors are harassed. For instance, the Malaysiakini chief editor Steven Gan was questioned for his INP reporting on Prime Minister Najib Abdul Razak's speech during the 2010 annual meeting of United Malays National Organization (UMNO) party.

The government has made a concerted effort to influence public opinion by establishing its own presence online. In addition to the e-government information projects noted in 2.0 above, citizen-to-government participation is being added to the emerging policy development agenda. This could be seen as a contradictory development in light of the previous discussion of repression of new kinds of democratic participation, as ICT literacy works across all sectors. Thus, if citizens are being enabled in one area, their expectations tend to migrate to other fields of everyday activity online. A growing number of Malaysians communicate via advanced web applications such as the Facebook social-networking site, Twitter's micro blogging service, and the video-sharing site, YouTube. Facebook continues to flourish, and hosts vigorous debates on political issues, such as the government's proposed ban on the use of the word 'Allah' by non-Muslims. Media observers were concerned, however, about an announcement from the Home Ministry that a new law would be introduced to govern sedition in cyberspace. Although this had not yet occurred by the end of 2010, advocacy groups such as the Centre for Independent Journalists viewed it as a deliberate attempt to censor the Internet (Centre for Independent Journalism, 2010). However, the country remains formally committed to a policy of refraining from censorship of the medium, as guaranteed in Section 3(3) of the Communications and Multimedia Act (CMA) and the Multimedia Bill of Guarantees. Malaysia, with 65% percent of the population accessing the internet in 2010 (World Internet Stats, 2012) hosts many sources of news to compete with official sources. Bloggers were still required to tread carefully. In September 2010, Irwan Abdul Rahman, better known as Hassan Skodeng, was arrested and charged with allegedly publishing false information on his blog. Although he was later released on bail, if convicted he could have been fined up to RM 5,000 (approximately $1,600), jailed up to a year, or both.

Mahathir, who led the development of ICT initiatives so optimistically, stated recently that the government should rethink the current absolute freedom on the Net (themalaysiainsider, 2012). The government's indecision about Internet governance is evidenced by the interventions described: policy directions available to the BN seem to present stark choices, with a general election looming as the impetus for a rapid decision.

CASE STUDY: ELITE PERSPECTIVES ON INTERNET GOVERNANCE ISSUES

Industry and government voices also demonstrate concern about whether and how the Internet can be regulated in future, as the final phase of the MSC Malaysia project finishes, and ones on the digital economy begin.

Recently, the Multimedia Development Corporation (MDeC) announced further growth in the third phase (2011-2020) of MSC Malaysia with ICTs expected to contribute RM42 billion to gross domestic income (GDP) of the country by 2015 (Bernama, 2012). There are political as well as economic reasons for the success of the MSC and ICT development in Malaysia. The Prime Minister's department administers them and the political factor could be regarded as one of the important drivers in renewed discussion of Internet governance. After the 2008 General Election, the debate about the outcome continued in policy and practitioner circles. As e-government stakeholders translate political will into action, we thought it important to explore the key players' perspectives on regulating the Internet in the future.

Relevant data was extracted from a larger study on news media and political culture where broader questions about news discourses had been collected from a bigger sample of respondents. The in-depth interviews described here were conducted with key informants from the ICT, e-government and non-governmental organization (NGOs) sectors in 2011.

Focus of the Interviews

All 10 interviewees are from Cyberjaya, Putrajaya and Kuala Lumpur and have diverse backgrounds, political values and expertise. They represent educated urban elite, some of whom have a stakeholder investment in ICT, e-government and the progress of the information economy.

For the purposes of this research, the interviewees are referred to as Respondent R1 to R10 to ensure anonymity. Respondents were asked open-ended questions on four themes:

- The impact of the election on the future progress of MSC.
- Perspectives on Internet censorship
- Assessing public acceptance of Internet censorship
- The Internet's potential for divisiveness, complexity and conflict

Data was coded using Nvivo software, and delivered the results reported and discussed below. The general findings indicate that the confusions of the public debates are also being played out in elite circles of expert citizens with a professionally informed knowledge of technology, and ICT policy.

Impact of the 2008 General Election on MSC

The interviewees gave mixed reactions when questioned about the impact of the 12th General Election on the future progress of the MSC Malaysia and ICT development in the country. In 2011, most respondents from the MSC Malaysia and ICT industries believed that the 2008 General Election results had not had any impact on their work routines. They continue to promote ICT projects as initiated by the Prime Minister's office in the same ways, and individuals confirm their sense of the gradual achievement of Vision 2020 goals. As a group, they recognize the importance of the 2008 watershed event, but see its impact as generating more activity and pressure to succeed with the nation's economic Vision 2020 objectives.

R1 comments at some length, 'After the 2008 general election, particularly now with the Prime Minister Najib is very active, doing a good job and aggressively pushing the Economic Transformation Program (ETP) and all these factors involved ICT infusion, where we are very much heavily involved in. Also when it comes to the budget announcement by Prime Minister Najib also during the RMK 10, we have taken more active role when taking the drive to pushing ICTs and have been doing so in any ways in the past few years. Right now we are taking a more active role. We have recently wrapped phase I and phase II, and now we are in the phase III of the last MSC Malaysia project that is moving to realize Vision 2020. We are moving towards an innovative digital economy'(R1).

For R4, there is no connection between the politics on the Internet as seen during 2008, potential censorship measures, nor ICT investment in the country. Respondent R6 agreed. He notes that no matter how many people wanted to utilize the Internet for political discussions, it would not affect ICT income and investments to the country, 'Nobody thinks the MSC Malaysia is making money. Do you believe that it bring billions money to Malaysia every year. It does. How do you want to stop it? That's why the government wants to educate the people to understand the alternative media. No matter what they do, today they do, tomorrow another one will come. The capacity for the government to stop it is there. The only way out is to get the media together and not to affect the ICT because it has brought billions to the country.'

Further, he suggests that the BN government should evaluate the potential of the Internet for political purposes and differentiate the Internet's policies as they affect MSC Malaysia programs aiming for a less drastic outcome in the following way, 'Whatever law that been applied to the traditional media, should be applied to the independent news portals (INPs) otherwise then the regulation that affects the MSC needs to be changed. The government should create the balance: what's effective the industry in order to strengthen the alternative media.'(R6).

R9's replies also pointed to the inherent policy contradictions, stressing that the main factor with the potential to affect MSC Malaysia, or even the progress of ICT development, is the active role of the independent media. In turn, the respondent thinks, government feels pressured to control the Internet. Given the investment in the multimedia hubs, that seems unlikely given the well-known practical difficulties of governing the Internet. He comments, 'Whether Internet should be regulated: it is very hard to do that, because we have MSN and Cyberjaya. Government always says that they wanted to control the Internet, but they never do that. Internet media is not under anyone's command' (R9).

Overall, respondents recognize government's dilemma, but also reaffirm that business investment requirements, and see that the need for ICT development to support e-government projects, and the hubs, is the pragmatic block to the introduction to tighter Internet controls being imposed.

Perspectives on Internet Censorship

When asked directly about the concept of the Internet filtering or censoring the Internet, all respondents reaffirm the view that such policies could have an impact on the growth of the ICT and its investment to the country. For instance, R1 argues that a country like Malaysia should not take a similar step to China in strict monitoring of the Internet. The most important issues are the ICT and foreign investment factors, rather than a consideration of likely political outcomes should the Internet continue unrestricted. R1 states unequivocally '... (censorship) will definitely impact on the ICT (sector) because, for example, like in American companies, our role in AMDEC is to drive the investment. It also depends on the political point of view. Now Google wants to invest in Malaysia, how about if there are censorship guidelines? Maybe they would, but they might invest more if it is a freer society. As much as we see this as political issue but it's also the matter of investment as well.' R2 is in general agreement, commenting, 'Internet censorship will have impact on ICT when come to the investment' (R2).

In contrast, R3 argues that there could be some basis for setting ground rules for the users online, but not for completely regulating the Internet. 'I don't mind that there are some ground rules. Ground rules that the Netizens could use. But if it is totally regulated, I think it can be stifling and we don't want to be to a certain degree turned off by using the technology and the technology is supposed to help'(R3).

R4, an expert in the country's media law, states that censoring the Internet is not the solution to the governance issues that Malaysia faces. Further, R4 argues that no matter to what extent the Internet regulation has been implemented in other countries, there will always be ways for people to voice their demands and interests online. Thus, the respondent suggests that the BN government should apply a different and more rational policy approach. R4 suggests that legislation already exists to tackle illegal online activity, reproducing an argument heard internationally about the conundrum of politically-driven regulation of the Internet explaining, 'I would like to see a more rational approach such as what is the danger of the Internet. It's not about regulating it, if you want to regulate, it's already regulated with the laws that exist. The challenge remains. As for traditional crimes, you look for footprints and fingerprints but online media you still look for prints as well but it is in digital environment. It's again about the skills and ability of law enforcement agency, how able they tract and trace the prospectors. The law remains the same' (R4).

R5, located at Ministry level, states that Internet policy research and observations are taking place, to study the impact of the Internet on the socio-political environment. Government is also reportedly checking international policy, and benchmarking. From R5's point of view, the government is only scoping ways of controlling the Internet, and not seeking ways of censoring it completely because it could affect investment. This reflects a more pragmatic and also more reactive approach to the scale of online activity, 'I think online regulation is important and it must be based on the realities. If we propose a law and a strong filtering, the investors will not come to Malaysia. This is bad for our country. The important thing is the public interest. What do the people need? If our people are mature, then we don't require censorship. If they still trust on wrong information, then we have to take filtering action'(R5).

R5's comments raise the 'user-readiness issue' faced by legislators and policy-makers accustomed to setting the terms on which citizens interact, for example, with government in e-government portals. However, the comments demonstrate a strong awareness of how mass communication tools are changing the rules of engagement but, for R5, it is a simple matter: illegal activity requires a better enforcement of existing laws.

R6, a highly-placed official in the government sector, rejects the idea of regulating the Internet, agreeing with R5 that the existing of laws allows people to take legal actions against the others, if they are being impacted negatively by adversarial online comment. This is similar advice to that given by R6 to the politicians who object to online political discussion linked to them. 'I don't think the Internet can be regulated. PM Najib has mentioned that he is not going to regulate the Internet. But anybody who is not happy with what is going on the Internet can take his or her own action. People are free to take any legal action on anybody. Even, in the case of Wikileaks that involved the politician, Rais Yatim. We still couldn't do anything. Two things, which can't be separated,: one is the industry involved and if you put measures to stop all these alternate media or Internet access for whatever excuse, it will directly affect the ICT industries' (R6). R6 concludes by supporting the cross group refrain of the importance of ICTs to the country.

While most of the respondents presented the same argument that online filtering could lead to a negative impact on ICT investment in the country, R7 had a different and more personal response.

R7 had some direct experience of hostile online attacks, as a target of online discussions. The respondent subsequently made suggestions to government for a change in Internet policy. R7 states that his idea was rejected many times by authorities. Following his experience online attacks, R7 wanted to propose Internet censorship, but realized the climate in the electorate was unlikely to find such a measure acceptable, as the following comment illustrates, 'Censoring the Internet will not be received in Malaysia, I think. At one time, I suggested there must be some kind of censorship on the Internet; even then the authorities said nothing much it can do. Even people commented about me on the Internet. They attack me, and say 'you are murderer' … I can't run away from these things or ask for censorship (of them). If I start to talk about the censorship then all the bloggers will start to attack on me' (R7).

These respondents' comments show that online activities, they personally might find unacceptable, hostile, naive or lacking in 'maturity,' cannot be governed through blanket censorship of the Internet. There is too much at stake nationally, and in getting existing legal frameworks right, for that to happen.

Public Acceptance of Internet Censorship

When answering a question about public acceptance of the Internet, most of the respondents thought that the public view would be in sharp contrast to that of the ruling government. R1 notes the general popular resistance to Internet regulation. Asked if there should be Internet censorship, the reply is blunt, 'Definitely not. I have seen people and I have seen tweets that say if Malaysia starts to regulate the Internet or imposes stricter censorship guidelines they will go out of the country' (R1).

Just as R5 in the previous section on personal perspectives on censorship raised issues about the polity's acceptance of misinformation online, R4's answers here raise issues of the need for public IT literacy and the limited usefulness of blanket filtering when trying to target, for example, illegal uses, 'The reality now is the media literacy. It's no longer accepted to do regulatory action. I think filtering might work for the common good, such as for (the prevention of) pornography. One thing about filtering is you tar everybody with a brush, because you don't allow the opportunity to engage at all. Perhaps you type something and will be filtered out. Sometimes filtering is not effective anyway. That's why at SKMM we are firm believers more in terms of enhancing our ability to investigate and creating the more public awareness' (R4).

R3 argues that the government has to evaluate the mindset of the people before making policy changes. This is essential to understand the history behind the population's acceptance of a free

Internet for fifteen years, in order to assess its likely acceptance of new restrictions. R3 draws a comparison with Malaysia's regional neighbor and rival in the expansion of information hubs, Singapore, 'Like Singapore, (Malaysia) is a small island and developed from early on. They probably can achieve it because their nature is like that. They can implement like that but at the same time there are a lot of threats. There is (more) availability in the Singapore. For an example, they have other channels to express. At the certain level they understand better. The rural area in Singapore is aware but in Malaysia, it is different thing' (R3).

Further comparisons are made between Malaysia and China, one of the countries well known for strict government control of the Internet, at ISP firewall and user data surveillance level: 'While, China is strict and managed to implement (censorship) because of the government has that power. They are not a democratic society but they are a very liberal communist state. They bringing business, and inviting people to come in. China's power broadly rising and they have the power to say 'Google, you don't show this' and the people accept it. It depends how many people are using the technology. Not all of them are really savvy, probably from the urban. They know their country and they operate in such way' (R3).

R6 confirms the general view that the ruling government will not in the end pursue policy that has strong popular opposition, 'I think people will not accept it whether it's from the Opposition or the BN itself. We are living in the information era where you couldn't stop the information. If you stop that, it's like you're curbing the country's economy and growth. Now, we cannot see Internet as a threat' (R6).

The rest of respondents argue any Internet regulation would not be acceptable. For instance, R8 comments: 'The moment you say you want to regulate, then they will say one year permits and so on. People will not be happy.' Here there is a belief - which is not limited to the Malaysian context - that once the first step in the concept of Internet regulation is conceded, further measures will be taken to increase political control of freedom of speech. The reference to one-year permits shows an awareness of the general connection being drawn in many comments about the incremental inevitability of increased regulation leading to politicization of the regulatory framework.

Internet's Potential for Divisiveness, Complexity and Conflict

Respondents recognise the disruptive nature of the Internet, and suggest that the Internet's role in the future of Malaysia requires that a policy balance be found between the needs of the ICT sector and management of the Internet's potential threat against the government. The biggest perceived political threat is the rise of minority voices and more active participation in political culture.

Most respondents admitted that increased Internet use has potential to create complexity in terms of the country's goal of multi-ethnic national unity. For instance, R1's agreement 'Yes, of course, it has potential to create complexity' and R4's bald comment 'It can split the people', are complemented by more extended discussions, as in R3's comment which notes the difficulty of being understood clearly in a new medium.

In online political debate, this respondent argues, some communicative signs are missing and this creates in itself, the potential for conflict, 'You don't see the expression online and you are not in the web cam all the time. Even those don't become dangerous. Amazingly one sentence said in the joking manner and one said in the hushed manner, you can't specially translate when come to the text unless you want to put smiley face. But if you want to talk political facts, do you want to put smiling face at the end of the sentences? Those are things that can be misinterpreted and (create) missed conclusions as such. That is the danger, and you can put up anything or if you want to make any statement if it is factual in nature then you should have the fact. If you are queried, then you have to answer it. It can be simple as that. If not and if you want to make your point across, there are some many ways of going about it. The Internet can be a launching pad but if you want to make your point across you have make physical. Why not?' (R3).

Here, the respondent notes the notorious limitations of online as opposed to face-to-face interactions. R4 agrees about the potential for divisiveness in translating political conversation to an online medium, 'It does create the potential of complexity. If you are racist you can say anything that you want in the Internet, even sometimes for the comfort of their community as in Facebook groups. If there are issues they will be shocked, because that is their way; how they have been communicating. For me, it is the awareness in terms of how you said and how it impacts others.' (R4).

R9 and R10 are less sure about new media's impact, and point to the importance of considering levels of access, and the established racial issues in Malaysia, for which new media can hardly be blamed in their view. R9 states, 'You have to see the Internet penetration and ownership whether the Internet really brings complexity among the society' (R9). R10 states, 'It is not true to say that the new media is creating complexity. People have been doing that for a long time even in traditional media. It is a double standard; the traditional media still spur up the racial issues. It is not fair if you are blaming the new media for the same thing. Utusan Malaysia is very racist which I read, compulsory' (R10).

DISCUSSION AND FUTURE RESEARCH

The consensus drawn from these interviews is that amongst this group of well-informed urban elite and expert citizen-observers, whose work activities may make them stakeholders in the information economy agenda, the governance issues are clear: Internet censorship is impractical, not what the polity would support, and would detract from Malaysia's capacity to achieve Vision 2020. The political issues are largely ignored, and no respondent directly mentions the connections between achieving e-government objectives and the enhanced democracy, which could be the result of encouraging a freer, more engaged and better informed polity.

The multi-stakeholder, multi-level, multi-agency nature of Internet use compounds the impasse that the BN government faces in confronting Internet governance matters. There appears to be little internal political consensus on the matter, if the variety of statements emanating from spokepersons indicates at different times since 2008. Solutions for the BN could include consideration of a unified approach to public statements on their reconsideration of Internet regulation. BN politicians have reportedly already adopted alternative means of engaging constituents (for example, social networking), as the opposition did in 2008.

Thus, if 2008 triggered the governance discussion, it has not yet been resolved, despite the political exigencies of a forthcoming election. Other legal frameworks have been used to curtail online publication of critiques of government. In terms of maximising on the collective efforts of the many e-government agencies involved in promoting the information economy, a solution for consideration is the implementation of regular cross-agency discussions for internal knowledge transfer about the broader implications of Internet regulation or light-touch policies and their outcomes.

Future research might focus on a larger scale study of the agencies responsible for related information economy development work, including the canvassing of the perspectives of officials on wider democratic governance issues.

CONCLUSION

Internet governance challenges continue in Malaysia as the 2013 General Election approaches.

The government may be demonstrating policy uncertainty about finding ways of controlling the Internet's disruptive potential as online news and bloggers become pockets of resistance and political mobilization in Malaysia. The government and e-government workers prioritize the ICT sector and its key players as essential in meeting the ICT project goals. Elite stakeholders in the information hubs and government ministries understand the policy dilemma, and – perhaps unsurprisingly – regard economic priorities as paramount, as well as recognize the difficulty of internal Internet governance.

The chapter has shown that other legislation is being used to manage the phenomena of online dissent, without recourse to a full-blown Internet censorship law.

The rhetoric of public engagement by citizens is part of e-government policy implementation, and there are signs of much public information being placed online, and e-transactions are developing in a variety of directions simultaneously. These in themselves will create new relationships and expectations in citizens. Not least will be the increased sense of entitlement to know about and comment on government and politicians in other public domains where government control is less intrusive. The democratizing of information in civil society in Malaysia is happening more quickly than government can cordon off e-government behind a barrier of solely economic development rhetoric. As the breadth and variety of online transactions between governments and citizens increases, e-government will be productive of change in more than just the e-government field, though some of those who implement facilitate its operations seem unaware of its wider impact on society. It will become the foundation for a growing awareness of new possibilities in relations for and between citizens, and between citizens and government. A liberal flow of some information in one domain leads to popular expectations of unrestricted communication flows everywhere, including by INPs.

The chapter has illustrated the complex challenges of internal governance of the Internet in Malaysia. These may be similar to the difficulties shared by many countries, but Malaysia's challenges are historically and culturally specific, and derive in part from the utopian beginnings of an information economy, and from the belief that it can be achieved in a political and democratic vacuum. For e-government research more generally, the study indicates that instrumentally focused, technology application-based research can usefully be augmented by broader considerations of a country's underpinning cultural, social and political frameworks and practices.

REFERENCES

Ahmad, B. A. B. (2008). *Evaluation offederal and state e-government websites in Malaysia*. Paper presented at the 4th International Conference on e-Government. Academic Conferences Limited. RMIT, Melbourne. Australia

Asia Sentinel. (2010, August 17). Malaysia's uneasy dance with the web. *Asia Sentinel*. Retrieved from http://asiasentinel.com/index.php?option=com_content&task=view&id=2645&Itemid=178.html

Bernama. (2012, April 20). ICT to contribute RM42 billion to Malaysia's GDP by 2015. *Bernama*. Retrieved from http://www.outsourcingmalaysia.org.my/news-flash/424-ict-to-contribute-rm42-billion-to-malaysia-s-gdp-by-2015.php

Blackstone, E., Bognanno, A. M., & Hakim, S. (2005). *Innovations in e-government: The thoughts of governors and mayors*. Rowman and Littlefield.

Budde, P. (2012). *Malaysia*. Telecommunications Research. Retrieved from http://www.budde.com.au/Research/Countries/Malaysia/

Centre for Independent Journalism. (2010). *Freedom of expression in Malaysia 2010. An Annual Review*. Retrieved from http://www.scribd.com/doc/49753546/Freedom-of-Expression-in-Malaysia-2010.html

Committee to Protect Journalists. (2000). Retrieved October 1, 2012, from http://cpj.org/asia/2000/

Creech, H. (2008). International institute for sustainable development. Retrieved October 18, 2012, from http://www.intgovforum.org.html

Evers, H. D., Nordin, R., & Nienkemper, P. (2010). *Knowledge cluster formation in peninsular Malaysia: The emergence of an epistemic landscape. Centre for Policy Research, University Sains Malaysia and International Studies (CenPRIS) and Center for Development Research (ZEF).* University of Bonn.

Freedom House. (2011). *Freedom on the net: Malaysia.* Retrieved October 10, 2012, from http://www.freedomhouse.org/report/freedom-net/freedom-net-2012.html

Freedom House. (2012). *New report: Governments grow increasingly repressive online, activists fight back.* Retrieved October 10, 2012, from http://www.freedomhouse.org/article/new-report-governments-grow-increasingly-repressive-online-activists-fight-back.html

Ibrahim, A., & Goh, C. C. (2000). *Multimedia super corridor.* Leeds Publication.

International Consortium of Investigative Journalists. (2001). Retrieved October 1, 2012, from http://www.icij.org/awards

International Telecommunications Union (ITU). (2009). *ICT statistics 2009—Internet.* Retrieved November 20, 2010, from http://www.itu.int/ITUD/icteye/Reporting/ShowReportFrame.html

Janet, S. (2009). Professionalism online: How Malaysiakini challenges authoritarianism. *The International Journal of Press/Politics, 14*(1), 91–111.

Jeong, C. H. I. (2007). *Fundamentals of development administration.* Selangor: Scholar Press.

Kensaku, N. (2008). *The power of Internet in Malaysia's recent election.* Retrieved June 28, 2010, from http://www.helium.com/items.com.html

Kuek, S. K. K. (2009). Coming soon: A lenient ISA, rallies without permits. *Malaysiakini.* Retrieved from http://malaysiakini.com/news/110939.html

Malaysiakini. (2012). Evidence act's 114A - yet another flip-flop. *Malaysiakini.* Retrieved from http://www.malaysiakini.com/news/207600.html

Malaysiakini. (2012b). Malaysiakini wins court battle over print license. *Malaysiakini.* Retrieved from http://www.malaysiakini.com/news/210454.html

MAMPU. (2012). *Malaysian administrative modernisation and management planning unit.* Retrieved from http://www.mampu.gov.my

Mohamad, M. (2008). Malaysia-democracy and the end of ethnic politics? *Australian Journal of International Affairs, 62*(4), 441–459. doi:10.1080/10357710802480691.

Mohsin, A. (2006). Implementation of electronic government in Malaysia: The status and potential for better service to the public. *Public Sector Management Review, 1*(1).

MyGovernment. (2012). *Multimedia super corridor.* Retrieved October 5, 2012, from http://www.malaysia.gov.my.html

News, B. B. C. (2000, November 20). Malaysia's first online paper. *BBC News.* Retrieved from http://www.bbcnews.com.html

Official Portal e-Government Gazette. (2012). *Attorney-general's chambers.* Retrieved October 10, 2012, from http://www.federalgazette.agc.gov.my

PBS NewsHour. (2000). Steven Gan - editor Malaysiakini. *PBS News.*

Rajaratnam, U. D. (2009). Role of traditional and online media in the 12th general election, Malaysia. *Journal of the South East Asia Research Centre, 1*(1), 33–58.

Salamat, M., Hassan, S., & Muhammad, M. S. (2011). Electronic participation in Malaysia. Journal of e-Government Studies and Best Practices, Vol. 2011.

Salmah, K. (2012). *Electronic government in Malaysia. Malaysian administrative modernisation and management planning unit (MAMPU)*. Prime Minister's Department. Malaysia Government.

Seng, W. M., Jackson, S., & Philip, G. (2010). Cultural issues in developing E-Government in Malaysia. *Behaviour & Information Technology. Queen's University Management School, 29*(4), 423–432.

Shkovski, I., & Struthers, D. (2010). Of states and borders on the Internet: The role of domain name extensions in expressions of nationalism online in Karzakhstan. *Policy and Internet, 2*(4), 107–129.

Siau, K., & Long, Y. (2006). Using social development lenses to understand e-government development. *Journal of Global Information Management, 14*, 47–62. doi:10.4018/jgim.2006010103.

Stodden, V. (2008). *The Internet drives election results in Malaysia*. Message posted to http:www.blogs.law.harvard.edu/idblog.com/

Themalaysiainsider. (2009). Civil society must be aware of cyber threats that are causing harm to the nation's sovereignty and society interest. *Themalaysiainsider*. Retrieved from http://www.themalaysianinsider.com

Themalaysiainsider. (2011, April 24). Bloggers and Internet users have to "draw the line" and online media or digital democracy had made it more difficult to win in the election. *Themalaysiainsider.* Retrieved from http://www.themalaysianinsider.com.

Themalaysianinsider. (2012, June 3). Dr M.: Rethink absolute freedom on net. Retrieved from http://www.themalaysianinsider.com

Times, N.S. (2008, March 9). Internet served a painful lesson. *New Straits Times*.

World Internet Stats. (2012). *World internet statistics report*. Retrieved from November 26, 2012, from http://www.internetworldstats.com/stats.htm

Yildiz, M. (2007). E-government research: Reviewing the literature, limitations, and ways forward. *Government Information Quarterly, 24*, 646–665. doi:10.1016/j.giq.2007.01.002.

Yusoff, M., & Radzi, M. (2002). *E-government opportunities and challenges: Malaysia's experience*. Retrieved August 10, 2012, from http://egovaspac.apdip.net/topics/country/my/radzi-yusoff.html

ADDITIONAL READING

Allen, S., & Thorsen, E. (2009). *Citizen journalism*. NY: Peter Lang.

Castells, M. (2000). *The rise of the network society*. Oxford, MA: Blackwell.

Castells, M. (2001). *The Internet galaxy: Reflections on the internet, business and society*. Oxford, UK: OUP.

Castells, M. (2004). *The information age: Economy, society and culture*. Oxford, MA: Blackwell.

Coleman, S., & Blumler, J. (2009). *The Internet and democratic citizenship: Theory, practice & policy*. Cambridge, MA: Cambridge University Press. doi:10.1017/CBO9780511818271.

Crick, B. R. (2003). *Democracy: A very short introduction*. Oxford: Oxford UP.

Held, D. (2006). *Models of democracy* (3rd ed.). Cambridge: Polity.

Hindman, M. S. (2009). *The myth of digital democracy*. Princeton, NJ: Princeton University Press.

Norris, P. (2011). *Democratic deficit: Critical citizens revisited.* MA: Cambridge University Press. doi:10.1017/CBO9780511973383.

Pole, A. (2010). *Blogging the political: Politics & participation in a networked society*. NY: Routledge.

KEY TERMS AND DEFINITIONS

Barisan Nasional (BN): Malaysia's ruling government party.

Bloggers: Independent content providers publishing online commentary on hyperlinked web logs.

Censorship: Suppression of free speech by governments or other bodies.

Cyberjava: A science park located in Sepang Malaysi, which forms a key feature of MSC Malaysia.

Democracy: A form of political arrangement which depends on power-sharing, and is underpinned by characteristics such as free elections, fair representative government, an independent judiciary, a public service free of interference and a free press.

E-Government: The use of information and communication technologies to enhance delivery of government services for benefit of citizens.

General Election 2008: Malaysia 12th General Election which occurred in 2008; the previous election was held in 2004.

Global Internet Governance: The rules and principles made by global agreements for the organization of the Internet.

Governance: The institutional arrangements which support and manage human relations in organizations, and which enable and anchor organizational outcomes.

Independent News Portals (INPs): News portals established online independent of government ownership or finance.

Information Economy: An economy supported by activities with an emphasis on exchange of information and communication, and on globalization.

Information Silos: The concept that information may not flow freely between different national sectors or agencies of government.

Internet as Disruptive Technology: The concept that global access to information impacts on a society's traditional practices and politics.

Internet Development: The infrastructure of global communications technology and the growth of online publications, networks and consumption patterns.

Internet Governance: An approach on how to managing the Internet and matters related to it.

Internet Regulation: Restrictions that applied to the access of the Internet.

Malaysia: A multi-ethnic federal constitutional monarchy in SE Asia with a population of over 27.5 million.

Malaysiakini.com: An INP established during the1990's by two former mainstream media journalists.

Multimedia Supercorridor (MSC): An ICT project initiated by the former Malaysian Prime Minister Mahathir Mohamad co-located to support multimedia industries and attract global investment in business and research.

Policy: Government's establishment of rules or principles to guide the writing of legislation.

Politics: The art and practice of running a state's affairs.

WSIS: World Summit on the Information Society was set up by the UN General Assembly and meets regularly to garner the political support to ensure that the information society will be available to all.

Chapter 13
Leveraging the Service Paradigm for Producing Next Generation E-Governance Applications

Pethuru Raj
Wipro Technologies, India

ABSTRACT

The 21st century is aptly being termed as e-age. This is with the arrival of a suite of path-breaking and trend-setting computational and communication technologies and tools besides the grand and global installation of wired as well as wireless network infrastructures. As many of yesterday's concepts, ideas, dreams, vision and desires are being translated into reality today through a host of resilient and robust software, hardware, networking, sensing, perception, and decision-enabling technologies and best practices, it is natural for the total human society to embrace IT and enjoy its direct as well as indirect fruits in a big way with a tinge of assurance. In this context, e-governance methods, platforms, processes and practices also became the cornerstone for effective, efficient, energetic, fast, timely, transparent, and people-centric governance. In this chapter, the author brings forth a new promising, matured, proven, dependable and easy-to-use service technology for designing, developing, deploying, and delivering applications for many of the tasks associated with digitally inspired e-governance. The author has zeroed down on service and cloud technologies as the major drivers for new-generation digital governance. This chapter throws more light on these technologies. Services are stimulating the process-centric approach for application development, modifiability and sustainability. Further on, all kinds of programming models, methods and mechanisms (agile, aspect, component, composite, and event model building blocks) are easily gelling with the supple service paradigm and principles in articulating and actuating dynamic, real-time, instant-on, smart and sophisticated systems.

DOI: 10.4018/978-1-4666-4245-4.ch013

E-GOVERNANCE: INTRODUCTION

Every industry domain aspires to grow drastically and decisively with the smart adoption and adaptation of potential and prominent information and communication technologies (ICT). That is, technology assimilation has been a routine affair for any business organization in order to be competitive and cognitive in its operations, outputs and outlooks. IT is being widely accepted as the top business enabler and hence it is being successfully leveraged to accomplish the goals of business automation, acceleration, and augmentation. There are a number of new buzzwords emerging and evolving with businesses joyfully joining hands with all kinds of improvements and improvisations of IT. All the prime industry domains are rebranded as e-commerce, e-business, e-market / e-auction, e-supply chain, e-cash, e-voting and so on. Students, scientists and scholars are very much contributive in unearthing high-performance and assurance techniques, tips and technologies in simplifying and streamlining the transition from ordinary to extraordinary IT-inspired business applications. E-governance is a kind of highly popular and pervasive subject of study, research and embrace. Worldwide governments are showing an exemplary interest in analyzing and accommodating all kinds of matured and stabilized technologies in order to ensure speedy delivery of citizen-centric services to the authenticated and authorized in time with all the quality entrenched.

Holistic visions of digital government have emerged over the past decade. Digital government or following the current techno linguistic conventions, e-government can be defined as the civil and political conduct of government including service provision, using information and communication technologies (ICT). Nowadays, government transcends all sectors in a society. It provides the legal, political, security and economic infrastructure to support other sectors, apart from exerting significant influence on the social factors that contribute immensely to other development. E-government, as a result, has the potential to profoundly transform citizen's conceptions of civil and political interactions with their governments. Unlike, commercial service offerings, digital government services must be made accessible to all the citizens in an impartial fashion.

Digital government systems can generally be characterized along two major dimensions:

- The architectural relationship they have with their clients;
- The type of service they can provide to their clients.

Architectures include intranets to support intergovernmental as well as intra-governmental processes, public network access to facilitate government-citizen interactions, and extranets for supporting interactions between the government and non-governmental organizations. Generally, current e-government system designs provide one of four service levels:

- First-level services provide one-way communication for displaying information about a given agency or aspect of government;
- Second-level services provide simple two-way communication capabilities usually for uncomplicated types of data collection such as registering comments;
- Third-level services facilitate complex transactions that may involve intra-governmental workflows and legally binding procedures. Examples of such services include voter and motor vehicle registration;
- Fourth-level services seek to integrate a wide range of services across a whole government administration, as characterized by the many emerging government portals.

E-GOVERNANCE: WHY

A 'joined up' government-community-citizen infrastructure has its own significance. A strong and effective information chain, comprising a choice of practical, accessible and manageable channels of communication has a dual benefit. Citizens enjoy a fast and convenient 'service', whilst government not only becomes more integrated into the community itself, but also can focus its resources where they are needed most. Moreover, a culture of self-service enables citizens to 'help themselves' wherever possible, saving time and money for all concerned.

In fact, Information Technology and Information Highways are going to dominate the next century. Government therefore has to take this fact into account and create SMART governance (simple, moral, accountable, responsive and transparent government). Various States have framed their IT policies and have started implementing the same. Citizens themselves are becoming increasingly demanding. They expect high standards of service, instant access to information, efficient transactions, and support, whenever and wherever they need it. There are already numerous e-governance initiatives by our states and countries outside. There are a number of services being accomplished through electronic infrastructure products to the masses as an initial and foundational step. Simultaneously IT solutions and services organizations have invested quite a significant amount in unfolding a series of e-governance enabling and facilitating solutions and services besides a focused research is going on in worldwide labs in unearthing technologies, mechanisms, tools, and other tangible and intangible stuff in making e-governance an easy and routine affair. Finally the market research and analyst groups have forecast a rosy picture for venture capitalists and other innovators in e-governance.

E-GOVERNANCE: CHALLENGES

Any activity has its own challenges to be tackled. In the same way for ushering an era of e-governance, there are some critical challenges ahead in the form of unbreakable security, broadband communication, scalability, high performance, availability, reliability, dependability, and anytime, anywhere computing. The other requirements that are veering around include innovative input / output systems and software such as easily navigable systems, touch screens, ATMs, Web and micro browsers, stand-alone client applications, tiny clients, Human Machine interface (HMI), Human-computer interaction (HCI) and other appliances, systems, gadgets, and instruments through which people can connect, collect, correspond, coordinate, collaborate, communicate, consume information and services offered by their government and for interacting with governmental authorities. Consequently, human factors, geography, organization, Ontologies, security, data quality, service delivery, timely and correct information, and other issues must all be dealt with in ways possibly more complex than other application domains require. Real-time information and a sort of dynamism will surely creep into the functioning of governments with red tape and other inefficiencies will vanish into the thin air.

Thus with a brief of what is all about e-governance, we would like to plunge into a promising and trustworthy technology that helps immensely in bringing out a host of innovative web services that will bring a sharp change in the way people all over the world interact.

E-GOVERNANCE: THE ROLE OF INTERNET

With the emergence of Web as a perspective platform for not only providing right location and device-independent information at any time to anyone but also the one for providing community, business, computation, transactional, and communication services in a highly cost effective and simple manner. Thus, there comes a strong need for a range of Web sites, integrated e-portals and e-applications by composing, assembling, integrating, orchestrating a suite of logically related e-services so that citizens and others concerned can easily connect, click and retrieve valuable parliament records and happenings inside, appropriate information about government organizations, institutions, galleries, agencies, departments, ministries' activities, forms, statues, rules and regulations, policies from their 24/7 online Web sites.

Further on, the implementation of a public service often requires the integration of intra-government ICT. The current vision of e-government is being dominated by the Web like most other IT areas. Commercial Web services have clearly raised citizens' expectations of the service level that government agencies' Web-enabled offerings must provide.

XML-BASED SERVICES TECHNOLOGY

There are many analysis, design, development, testing, deployment and administration technologies such as intelligent and smart mobile agents, Sun Microsystems' J2EE technologies and services, Microsoft Web technologies besides a whole lot of open source software technologies for e-governance and digital government.

In the recent past, we've been barraged with messages and case studies from the press, analysts, vendors, and others about possible useful applications of Web services. Almost all of these messages envision Web services in a transactional world, sometimes as a medium for application integration. Web services, being hailed by industry analysts, as the next technology focus, will speed the design, development and deployment of enterprise and business applications, reducing time to market and costs. Web Services are self-contained, modular business applications based on open standards that allow streamlined integration among multiple disparate applications and environments through a common channel - the Internet. Through the use of common standards, primarily XML and SOAP, Web Services dramatically diminish integration costs making it feasible to share bits and pieces of software functionality over the Internet. Basically, Web services are applications that call other routines dynamically using standard Internet protocols. Through Web services, IT departments will be able to speed up the deployment of applications that expedite effective decision-making.

XML for the Enterprise IT

Extensible Markup Language (XML) is very hot in business IT. XML is universally accepted as the most common and compact mechanism for representing, persisting and exchanging data across diverse and distributed systems.

- XML is a platform-independent, non-proprietary, and web-oriented way of sharing textual data. The type of hardware or operating system used is immaterial.
- It is fast becoming the de-facto standard for sharing data between heterogeneous applications across different organizations.
- XML provides extreme flexibility in organizing data yet the XML data can be manipulated relatively easily. There are several methods such as XSLT, XML-FO and other customized tools in order facilitate the transition from XML to MS Word, PDF, Image, and other well-versed data formats. That is, XML is being positioned as the universal data format. It is a kind of a hub from which all kinds of data formats can be programmatically created as associates on the fly.

- XML is not only machine-readable but also human-readable. Scores of domain-specific as well as generic markup languages have been derived out of XML. Web content markup languages such as XHTML are very popular.
- The XML document structure and design makes it ideal for hierarchically structured data, which fits the meta-model of the database perfectly.
- There are access, navigation, processing, querying, and report generation technologies and tools in plenty in order to derive something useful and usable from XML content.

XML Options

Choosing XML is only a first step. In a way, the choice of XML is akin to choosing to saying that one chooses the ".MDB" format (the database format used by Microsoft Access). There is still the important and often tedious step of defining the actual database structure i.e. the tables, their various fields, the meaning of the fields and the relationships between tables. This is done by specifying the tags and the relationships between them i.e. the definition of the XML data elements. A number of options are available to define the allowable data tags or schema to describe the vocabulary and the structure of the XML data. There are research publications that list out proven procedure for converting a conventional database into an XML database quickly.

The original and oldest method is by using a DTD (Data Type Definition) schema. Although this can be embedded in the document, the preferred method is the construction of a separate, external .DTD file. There are a number of drawbacks to using DTDs and the main one is the lack of (attribute) inheritance support in the hierarchical structure (as per meta-model). There exist a number of alternatives, the most important one being the XML Schema, with the SOX (Schema for Object-Oriented XML) specification of XML Schema probably the most suitable contender. However XML Schema still lacks popular tool support, is more complex and waits for final standardization.

WEB SERVICES TECHNOLOGY: ORIGIN

The evolution of software development has been a long climb from the primordial ooze of machine language to the higher ground of object-oriented, component-based, agent and aspect-based application development and distributed computing. Web services stand at the top of this evolutionary chain—as discrete, self-describing, reusable software components that can be developed, registered, identified, accessed, assembled, orchestrated automatically and linked together into full-blown smart enterprise and business applications for various domains using a suite of middleware tools, execution environments, and products through the standard and lightweight Internet protocols.

These days, software applications developed using business objects, and components turn to be services-oriented applications. That is, applications are being provided as subscriptions-based (free or fee) services over the Internet, intranet and extranet using the standard protocols. As services-oriented architecture (SOA) and management (SOM) are being both effective and beneficial for both the providers as well as the consumers, it is logical that future applications will be built with services orientation.

Web Services

Web services are the latest, most powerful example of distributed, enterprise-scale, Internet-ready, reusable software components. The difference with the existing distributed computing technologies are that instead of incorporating component code directly into application, the users or applications can simply access the services over the Web, and pass his parameters along with it and let the remote services do the work for him. It is an industry-wide response to the need for a more flexible and efficient business collaboration environment. Web services are self-contained, modular business applications that have open, Internet-oriented, standards-based interfaces. The core concepts behind Web services are as follows:

- Integration between software applications should be loosely coupled to allow maximum flexibility to businesses.
- Service interfaces should be published and discovered by business partners.
- Assembling, aggregating, composing, orchestrating or combining one or more Web services can develop smart and business Web services.

Web Services: Vision

The vision of Web services technology is to make it as the most powerful model for unifying disparate and diverse systems and applications through the two styles of integration: request-response and messaging. Typically many integration approaches have selected either tightly coupled request-response approach or loosely coupled one-way messaging. As companies move into complex Web integration, they came to the realization that they need both styles of communication and hence the adoption of web services. Web services technology is to facilitate e-business on demand, utility and grid computing models and collaborative commerce a reality.

Web Services: Unique Features

IT Applications development yearns for programming language, platform-independent technology due to the heterogeneous nature of platforms, languages, protocols, and other infrastructure solutions. Thus platform independence and near-universal agreement on standards clearly distinguish Web services from its previous and existing distributed component architectures, such as OMG's CORBA, Microsoft's DCOM, Java Jini technology, RMI and EJB. Primarily Microsoft and IBM led the development of the three main protocols that underlie Web services, which are now being supported throughout the industry. Web services protocols are themselves lightweight, text-based XML schema. And because Web services use HTTP as the transport, firewall issues quietly evaporate. Thus though web services technology has its roots in the above-mentioned distributed computing technologies, it surely stands tall among them. Web Services are Internet-based modular applications that perform a specific business task and conform to a particular technical format. The technical format ensures that each of these self-contained business service applications will integrate easily with other services to create a complete and robust business process. This interoperability allows businesses to dynamically publish, find, access, aggregate, compose, orchestrate and manage a new range of complex and smart web services through the ever expanding Web. Finally apart from development of innovative, flexible and bug free software components as services and integration of modern, packaged, monolithic and other legacy applications, web services technology is based on service-oriented architecture (SOA).

Web Services Technology: Motivations

Businesses today face a rapidly changing and ultra-competitive landscape. To face this challenge head on, business houses require a highly flexible, service-oriented and scalable IT infrastructure that cleanly facilitates them to transform their currently running business processes into accessible services and share those services among their employees, partners, suppliers and their perspective customers. This setup will make customer's relationships tight, will facilitate improved business collaboration, and will generate new revenue opportunities by exposing existing software assets and leveraging them into new business models through expanded distribution channels.

Web services also can quickly respond to changing market conditions and customer preferences by utilizing loosely coupled and modular services. Finally, return on investment (ROI) is to be protected by avoiding technology lock-in via a standards-based architecture and hardware, operating environment and programming language neutrality.

Secondly, there is a tremendous effort going on to connect computer and information systems, information, Web, consumer, communication appliances and consumer electronics, devices, sensors, gadgets, instruments and equipments inside a network as well as in the Internet (both wired and wireless). There are two primary reasons behind this gigantic effort. The first one is due to phenomenal growth of e-business, which is motivating companies to expose their business services and information over the Web as this exposition has its own material benefits. This makes the task of linking their core business systems to their Web site mandatory, as the Web has become the hot platform these days for executing businesses.

The other primary reason is integration of enterprise applications and business processes and their management (BPM), which is the systematic automation of everyday business by integrating core systems. BPM requires a change in the way of applications are viewed. Monolithic applications are reevaluated as a set of components and services that are then aggregated into new flexible and durable processes. The focus of BPM is driven by the need to expose processes to Web users efficiently and effectively in a secured manner so that processes use can scale if the Web site attracts many users.

Web services provide dependability and integrity for Internet commerce through the following:

- Subscription to known good services,
- Benefits of transactions and transactional services,
- Online contracts and verifiable transactions
- Availability of Services,
- Standardization of Web and consumer interaction,
- Standards acceptance for Internet commerce,
- Code stability.

Web Services: Technical Benefits

The integration task with partners outside of firewalls has become a tough one due to various reasons such as heterogeneous environment, hardware, software and diverse technologies and hence the ability of businesses to communicate and collaborate came struck. Thus came the realization for standards-based approach for the sake of sharing business services and infrastructure. Web services technology represents application-to-application connectivity. The term "Web service" describes specific business functionality exposed by a company, organization or any provider, usually through an Internet connection, for the purpose of providing a solution in the form of information, business, transaction and computational services for another company, organization, customer or software program to use the specified service. Thus Web services are functional software components for any business process or activity that can be accessed over the public net. They combine the best aspects of component-based development and the Web, delivering the distributed "peer-to-peer" computing. Based on open Internet standards, Web Services enable the construction of Web-based applications using any platform, object model, or programming language.

Web Service applications can vary in function from simple requests (for example, the retrieval of a stock price) to complex business systems that access and combine information from multiple sources. For example, one company calls other's service to send a purchase order directly via an Internet connection. Once a Web Service is deployed, then the other applications and Web Services can discover and invoke that service. Web services are faster and cheaper to develop, easier to deploy and be discovered, and offer more flexibility and interoperability.

WEB SERVICES: BUSINESS CASES

It has become a practice for business houses these days to make sure about the extraordinary business benefits of any technology before applying it. Here is a list of factors such as:

- Greater Availability, reliability and security of data.
- Maximizing customer Access and higher productivity.
- International Commerce and Global business.
- Perfect, guaranteed and precise streamlining transaction completion.
- Return on investment (ROI) gets preserved
- Revenue Base Expansion and customer relationship maintained.
- Customers feel simplicity, availability, and convenience.
- Easy to develop and deploy, integrate, assemble, orchestrate and Web-based management.
- Business processes are increasingly global, complex, and intertwined between organizations.
- Touch-points across all entities must be seamless, information-rich, and timely.
- Excess capacity and pressures to reduce costs drive the need for higher productivity, better information, and reduced cycle times.

Web services bring tremendous benefits to IT community, for example:

- Save time, the code can be reused and the development cycles accelerated.
- Free up programming resources for more intellectually stimulating work.
- Save money, freeing up budgets for innovation.
- Enable investments in legacy applications to accrue a higher return.
- Extend reach to global markets by enabling "strangers" to trade, collaborate and exploit new opportunities.
- Enable higher levels of personalization.
- Enable internal collaboration between corporate departments, thereby increase efficiencies and reduce operating costs.
- Enable external collaboration between partners across firewalls and support cross fertilization of ideas and support alliance building.
- Enable higher levels of automation and machine-to-machine processing.

Service-Oriented Architecture (SOA)

The service-oriented model builds on software components that are deployed as services (Behara, 2009). Such components are then described in *WSDL* format and the descriptions are published in a registry (UDDI) or made available for discovery (*WSIL*). When another enterprise component needs a service that satisfies some functionality, then a query is made against the registry to find the *WSDL* of an available service or the *WSDL* is discovered by some mechanism. Once the service is located, the service client binds to the service provider and exchanges messages in some format/protocol such as SOAP to solve the problem.

The service-oriented vision offers many benefits to enterprises, and the creation of a class of enterprise services allows us to create services that are modular, accessible, well described, implementation-independent and interoperable. Thus Web services are bound to integrate legacy systems with present-day enterprise systems.

Web services as mentioned above, are self-contained, modular and component-based business software applications that have open, Internet-oriented, and standards-based interfaces. Web services are inherently able to initiate communication with them towards collaboration. The standards-based technologies permit Web services to be accessed by customers, partners, suppliers, and retailers irrespective of hardware, software, and even operating environment. Thus Web services bring an environment wherein businesses can expose their business applications as Web services that can be easily discovered and consumed by any external applications (Figure 1). Web services bring down the total cost of ownership, facilitate inventory and reduction in transaction cost, and provide both faster integration and quicker time-to-market.

The Web Service Provider publishes (advertises) the particular services on the Web. The Service Consumer/Customer will make use of the services dynamically, in real time, from the Web. Towards automating the process of locating published and registered web services, two important things have to be considered:

- There should be a common and elegant way to describe the Web service.
- There should be an affordable public registry to keep all the available Web services in the Web

The common way to describe the Web service is by using the Web Service Definition Language (WSDL). The public registry to define all the available Web services is the Universal Description, Discovery and Integration (UDDI).

From the above picture, we can understand that the following steps are the pivotal for Web Services:

- The service provider exposes the actual service in the Web.
- The service provider describes the service using *WSDL.*
- The service provider publishes the service in the *UDDI.*
- The service consumer will search (query) the service information in the *UDDI* using the search template.
- The service consumer will then access the service using the service information obtained from *UDDI.*

Figure 1. Interactions between service provider and customer

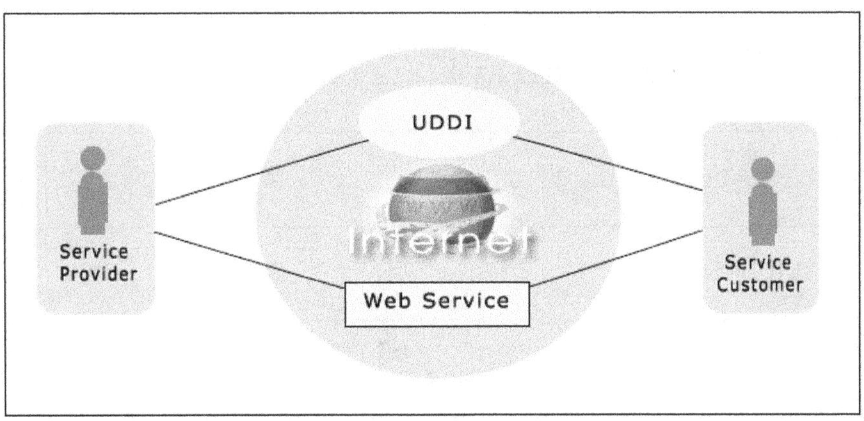

Web Services Stack

We have discussed, in the previous section, the fundamental operations: publish, find and bind in a Web services environment. In order to make that possible, we need a basic web services stack that will be present in each application that wishes to play a certain role in the Web services system.

Refer to Figure 2. On the left side of the diagram, the layered blocks are simply conceptual. The labels shown on the right side of each layered blocks are the actual technologies that are present in each layer. Each of the blocks builds upon the block beneath it.

Transport Layer is responsible for making the Web services accessible by using any of the transport protocols available like HTTP, SMTP, FTP and so forth. Web services are built on existing communication standards that make them transport-independent. HTTP, being the ubiquitous communication protocol, is the preferred one for web services. Within an organization, JMS is the preferred network protocol for web services.

XML Messaging is the next layer in the web services stack. This defines the message format that is used for application communication and the standard commonly used by web services is SOAP, an XML-based lightweight protocol for exchanging information between application regardless of the operating environment, development language and object model.

The Service Description layer provides a viable mechanism for the service provider to describe the functionality that the Web service provides. WSDL through XML grammar describes the web service. A well-written WSDL describes a web service as having a collection of endpoints or ports operating independently on both document-oriented and procedure-oriented messages. At an abstract level, a Web service definition contains the following elements.

1. Port Types
2. Messages
3. Types
4. Bindings

Web Services: Standards and Protocols

XML-based Technologies that Enable Communication with Web Services are:

- Universal Description, Discovery, and Integration (UDDI)

Figure 2. The web service stack

SERVICE PUBLICATION/DISCOVERY	UDDI
Service Description	WSDL
XML Messaging	SOAP
Transport Network	HTTP; SMTP; FTP; HTTPs over TCP/IP

- Web Services Description Language (WSDL)
- Simple Object Access Protocol (SOAP)
- Web services Inspection Language (WSIL)

Universal Description, Discovery and Integration (UDDI)

The specification defines a way to publish and discover information about web services. It creates a global, platform independent and open framework, to enable businesses to:

- Discover each other;
- Define how they interact over the net;
- Share information in a global registry that will more rapidly accelerate the global adoption of B2B commerce.

Web Services Definition Language (WSDL)

It has the ability to describe the mandatory inputs and outputs of a Web service. It facilitates a server to publish the interface of a service, so a client on getting the interface details, can connect with the server and communicate for the sake of the prescribed services to be done. WSDL carries two main benefits. Firstly, it enforces a logical separation between the interface and implementation and secondly it is inherently extensible.

There are software tools that help to automate the process of creation of proxies that can communicate and use Web services, and also the implementation of skeletons or templates for implementing a Web service within a specific programming model. The proxies and skeletons offer a simple programming model to use Web services and do not require any knowledge on manipulation of the raw SOAP or XML messages. Using XML and message models for communication allows message broker products such as IBM Web Sphere MQ (Integrator) to observe in-flight messages and perform transparent addition of capability.

Simple Object Access Protocol/Service-Oriented Architecture Protocol (SOAP)

This is a typical request-response (RPC) mechanism based on HTTP. SOAP is much simpler than HTTP and starts out as just XML message format an envelope, which contains the destination address, some headers and a message body. The body normally contains one or more elements and each element may be encoded using a standard SOAP encoding. That is, using a standard way of capturing programming language data elements – integers, doubles, strings – in a common interoperable format.

The SOAP message may be part of an RPC operation, in which case the parameters are encoded as child elements of a common parent, whose name indicates the operation and whose namespace indicates the service. SOAP can be sent over any application protocol such as HTTP and RMI / IIOP, Instant messaging, and IBM WebSphere MQSeries. SOAP is the key to interoperability as every major vendor supports it. And major B2B standards such as ebXML and RosettaNET are to embrace SOAP as the primary messaging protocol.

Web Services Inspection Language (WSIL)

This language complements the discovery features of UDDI. It provides for a global or wide-scale directory of services and helps to find and identify services. But it becomes essential to identify which local services are available at a particular site. The inspection standard offers this ability to query a given site or server and retrieve a list of available services. The list of services includes pointers to either WSDL documents or UDDI service entries. WSIL is a useful lightweight way of accessing a service description without requiring access to a UDDI server.

WEB SERVICES: DEVELOPMENT TECHNOLOGIES AND TOOLS

There are primarily two approaches for Web Services development. They are Sun Microsystems J2EE and Microsoft .NET Framework. The present development challenges of Web Services are Service Description, Implementation, Publishing, Discovery, Binding, Invocation and Execution.

Java Enterprise Edition, Sun ONE Architecture and Application Server

Over the past few years, the enterprise application engineering standard Java Enterprise Edition (JEE) has emerged as the dominant standard for serving up information on the Web. A large number of standards have evolved, of which Web services is one of the most recent, to place application functionality behind Web front ends. First there were Servlets and JSP, as well as stateless session Enterprise Java Beans. Over time, the EJB specification changed and grew to support stateful bean, then entity bean, and eventually message-based semantics. The JEE application server could be expanded to provide native support for deploying, managing, and accessing Web services in a standard fashion.

JEE is a set of specification for various enterprise technologies implementation and services. In the recent past, there are a number of innovative well thought specifications for smoothening Web services development and deployment. JEE-enabled Web Services exchange information with interested parties using WSDL to come to an agreement on the proper format for each transferred XML document. Third parties who want to transact businesses with a JEE-enabled Web Service company can look up information about the company's Web Services in a registry.

Existing Java classes and applications can be wrapped using the Java API for XML-based RPC (JAX-RPC) and exposed as Web Services. JAX-RPC uses XML to make remote procedure calls (RPC) and exposes an API for marshaling (packing parameters and return values to be distributed) and un-marshaling arguments and for transmitting and receiving procedure calls. With JEE, business services written as Enterprise Java Beans are wrapped and exposed as Web Services. The resulting wrapper is a SOAP-enabled Web Service that conforms to a WSDL interface based on the original EJB's methods

The JEE Web Services architecture is a set of XML-based frameworks, providing infrastructures that allow companies to integrate business-service logic that was previously exposed as proprietary interfaces. Currently, JEE supports Web Services via the Java API for XML Parsing (JAXP). This API allows developers to perform any Web Service operation by manually parsing XML documents.

Sun Microsystems is positioning its Java API for XML Registries (JAXR) as a single general purpose API for interoperating with multiple registry types. JAXR allows its clients to access the Web Services provided by a Web Services implementer exposing Web Services built upon an implementation of the JAXR specification. There are three types of JAXR providers: The JAXR Pluggable Provider, the Registry-specific JAXR Provider, and JAXR Bridge Provider. J2EE uses the Java API for XML-based RPC (JAX-RPC) to send SOAP method calls to remote parties and receive the results. JAX-RPC enables Java developers to build Web Services incorporating XML based RPC functionality according to the SOAP 1.1 specification.

Once a JAX-RPC service has been defined and implemented, the service is deployed on a server-side JAX-RPC runtime system. The deployment step depends on the type of component that has been used to implement the JAX-RPC service. For example, an EJB based service is deployed in an

EJB container. During the deployment of a JAX-RPC service, the deployment tool configures one or more protocol bindings for this JAX-RPC service. A binding, ties an abstract service definition to a specific XML based protocol and transport.

Microsoft .NET Framework

Microsoft .NET is the latest novel and revolutionary offer from Microsoft and is being defined as a revolutionary new computing platform, built on open Internet protocols and standards, with tools and services that meld computing and communications in a new ways. In other words, .NET framework specifies a new environment for developing and running software applications like Web-based services, rich standard run-time services available to components written in a variety of programming languages, and inter-language and inter-machine interoperability.

The .NET applications are no longer directly executed in native machine code. All programs are compiled to an intermediate binary code called the Microsoft Intermediate Language (MSIL). This portable binary code is then compiled to native code using a Just in Time compiler (JIT) at run time and run in a virtual machine called the Common Language Runtime (CLR). This is similar to the way that Java works, except .NET encompasses several languages. Each is translated to MSIL, which is executed in the CLR using the JIT. With the .NET platform, Microsoft will provide several languages based on the Common Language Infrastructure (CLI), such as Managed C++, JScript, VB.NET and C#.

Tools to Develop .NET Applications

Microsoft .NET Framework SDK: The SDK is free and includes command-line compilers for C++, C#, and VB.NET and various other utilities to aid development.

- **Microsoft ASP.NET Web Matrix:** This is a free ASP.NET development environment from Microsoft.
- **Microsoft Visual Studio.NET Professional:** Visual Studio.NET includes support for all the MS languages (C#, C++, VB.NET) and has extensive wizard support.

A Sample E-Governance Application: Citizens Medical Insurance Web Service

Governments have the huge responsibility of providing appropriate health care to its people. Medical insurance has become the prominent insurance service as the part of national health care today. Thus with the opening of insurance services sector to private organizations, it is keenly anticipated that many national and international players will come into the lucrative insurance services offering a variety of value-added features and other benefits for their customers.

A health insurance company is the one with whom a customer signs up for medical coverage. The company provides consumers with several health plans, varying in premiums, insurance coverage and so on, and the consumer signs up for one of those plans. A health insurance company is thus more of a broker. Hospitals, physician offices, and private medical clinics join as health care providers to this broker. By a care provider, we mean the actual places where the customer will go if they have a medical issue that needs to be addressed. This application is being developed using Web services standards and technologies.

- The subscriber will visit the insurance Web site and navigate to their reservation section
- The subscriber can then search for the providers who have registered with this site depending on several search criteria like city, specializations, Qualifications, appointment date and time, and so on.

- Once the subscriber selects a particular provider, they should be presented with a list of appointment slots to choose from by communicating with the providers' back-end reservation systems

From the details supplied, the customer will choose a particular slot and sends the request for making the reservation. The insurance site then dispatches the request to the provider's back-end system and confirms the reservation back to the subscriber. We have used the following software:

- Java Development Kit 1.4
- Apache Tomcat 3.2 and SOAP toolkit 2.2
- IBM Web Services Toolkit (WSTK) 2.3
- JDOM Xerces XML Parser
- JavaMail and Java Beans Activation Framework (BAF)

The workflow architecture is presented in Figure 3.

SERVICE-ORIENTED E-GOVERNANCE

E-governance is the purposeful use of powerful and pioneering information and communication technologies and infrastructures to cost-effectively and efficiently deliver citizen-specific services. That is, timeliness, efficiency, transparency and affordability are the prominent quality of service (QoS) attributes being insisted while formulating and providing a variety of government services to people. As indicated above, service computing is a trendsetting phenomenon towards simplifying and streamlining complex and change-centric business services and applications. Here is an attempt to leverage the promising SOA concepts and constructs for seamlessly and spontaneously incorporating productivity, simplicity, modifiability and nimbleness into government services. This assumes significance as today's delivery system is totally flawed with a number of drawbacks and holes that are being cunningly exploited by those in power and authority.

An SOA approach to e-governance aligns IT with service delivery goals and enables various government departments to reuse their current people-centric applications. As widely known,

Figure 3. The web service workflow architecture

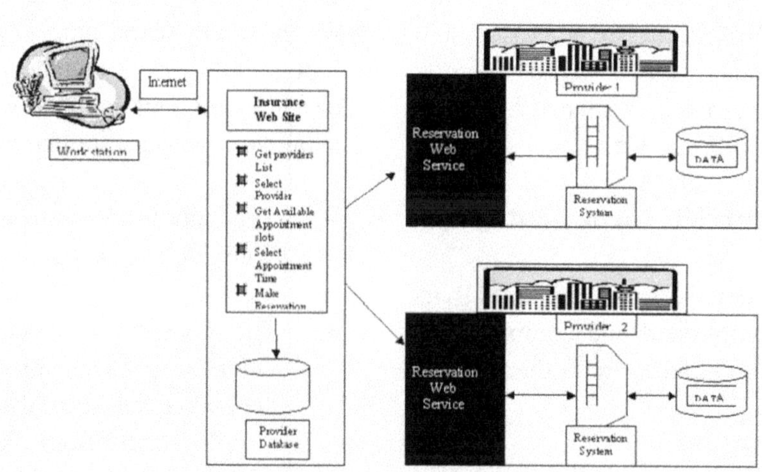

modernization, integration and composition are the top three unique selling factors of SOA. That is, modifying the existing IT assets to be service-centric applications, migrating the upgraded artifacts to service-centric platforms, unifying with other service-centric applications, and managing from there are the typical steps for service-enablement and delivery. As per the paper titled as "Service Oriented Architecture for E-Governance" authored by Gopala Krishna Behara, Vishnu Vardhan Varre and Madhusudhana Rao, an SOA based solution reduces the dependency on back-end applications and the need to write code every time there is a change in policy, and introduces new software that promotes the direct collaboration of citizens and government departments irrespective of the delivery model. The various steps involved in executing SOE are (1) service identification, (2) identification of forms, (3) business process modeling/re-engineering, (4) services solution architecture, (5) integrating various departments, (6) deployment (centralized or decentralized).

Service Identification and Classification

There are a wider variety of government services emerging and evolving. Their contributions vary and the usage patterns too differ. A number of local and cultural factors need to be taken into account in order to identify, index, prioritize, catalogue and manage. Following are the various categories of the services to be identified and classified:

- Government Services
- Data / Information Services
- Interactive / Portal / Dashboard Services
- Middleware Services (Aggregation, Mining, Dissemination, etc.)
- Process, Performance & Transactional Services
- Government Intelligence (GI) Services
- IT Services (Support, Access, Utility, Security, Payment, etc.)

Government-to-citizen (G2C) services include providing information and facilitating transitions such as electronically applying for passport, paying utility bills, making appointments, and renewing licenses. Providing financial assistance directly to people is emerging as a viable option for the Indian government (Das & Patra, 2009; Prabhu, 2012) to plug the gap.

It is about giving citizens the convenience of choosing when and where they access public services. It is about changing the way people view the government. And it is about being transparent and efficient rather than bureaucratic. The government services to business organizations include e-procurement, supply chain, and conducting transactions, such as electronic quotations and company registrations. This government-to-business (G2B) relationship is about making interactions, transactions, and communication faster, clearer, and easier for business.

The government-to-employee (G2E) services are between government employees and government departments and divisions. The well-known services include information and knowledge management (documents, policies, and other relevant content). There are collaborative and communication services (e-mail facilities). Finally there are specific services between governments in a federal setup or among various national governments across the globe.

E-Form

This helps the government departments to maintain a structured and streamlined process. Also, with e-forms, government departments process forms more efficiently, timely, and securely, helping achieve cost savings and meeting the demands of people more proactively and programmatically. The e-forms are being categorized as follows:

- Information gathering forms
- Transaction processing forms
- Regulatory compliance forms

The metadata of these forms is important as it specifies the structure of e-forms. Constructing electronic forms from metadata promotes the reuse of metadata across forms, which in turn reduces form authoring costs, and facilitates harmonization across forms. The e-governance initiatives within the government employ XML as a core technology to enable data interoperability, exchange, and reuse.

Business Process Redesign (BPR)

The current government application workflows and processes need to be critically upgraded as such a makeover will go a long way in having consolidated, lean and optimized workflows and processes. Business process modeling, simulation, engineering / reengineering, integration and management enables in arriving at competent and comprehensive processes bringing value to governments and people. The main stages in BPR methodology are:

- Map existing processes
- Define end-state
- Gap analysis
- Redesign of workflow and processes
- Adoption of BPR in e-governance helps to
- Lower cost
- Increase revenue
- Enhance effectiveness, efficiency, and re-usability
- Increase customer satisfaction

Service-Oriented Solution Architecture

The following are the important features and processes of the e-Governance portal and middleware solution (Misra, 2010):

- Adopt service oriented architecture (SOA).
- Develop business functionality as services.
- Provide web-based interface.
- Extensible to support multiple access devices such as desktop computer, IVRS, mobiles, CSCs, etc.
- Ensure confidentiality of citizen's data
- Achieve interoperability between state portals and national portal.
- Integrate with departmental applications for services.
- Integrate with websites of government departments and organization for content.

E-Governance portal allows the citizens to access government information easily and to enjoy one-stop government services. It enhances the customer focused service delivery channels. E-governance portal allows a department to present information, applications, and services in a single consolidated browser view. It provides a secure and individualized view of multiple online resources and interactive services. It offers a single access point to critical information and the primary applications necessary for an individual to avail the services. In a simple way, e-governance portal acts like an interface between the government and the citizens.

E-Governance portal is built based on SOA, which is defined as a dynamic pool of diverse services that communicate with each other through data-passing or messages. This communication enables the participating services to accomplish the desired business activity through collaboration. All the services will be realized by the technology platform, which has the following architectural building blocks:

- Web server
- Application server
- Enterprise service bus (ESB) & service delivery platform (SDP)
- LDAP server
- Email Exchange Server

In any typical e-governance portal application, there are several layers for enforcing flexibility.

Predominantly there are client / presentation layer, government application logic layer, data / information management layer, data layer, security, governance, and infrastructure layers. The resources can be logically or physically separated in order to simplify modifiability and maintainability.

CLOUD-BASED E-GOVERNANCE SERVICE DELIVERY PLATFORM

Simpler Service Interaction

With increasing number of choices, customers expect more cost effective offerings. Customer centricity has become the uncompromising norm these days and hence there are new buzzwords such as customer loyalty, intimacy and delight doing rounds in the IT circle. Customers' preferences need to be understood precisely in order to artfully design and build basic services. This infuses the need for an innovation environment to be successful in a knowledge-driven competitive market. Then right services are being identified and subjected to the aggregation process. The services being aggregated are with distributed and decentralized suppliers, retailers, partners, and others. This clustering is to roll out premium and people-centric products and services quickly and cost effectively to meet ever-changing customer needs and preferences. In short, customer engagement and management are very critical to succeed.

Unified View and Access

For any kind of service organizations (small, medium or large), a standardized service delivery platform (SDP) has become the core and central module for intelligent service delivery and management. High-quality services could be quickly defined, developed, assembled and deployed using the unique capabilities of the hot service paradigm. There is a strong tool support for service engineering and delivery, which is getting accentuated and accelerated with the emergence of scores of standards-compliant service modeling, design, development, mining, orchestration, and execution and delivery platforms. The service ecosystem consistently breeds delectable and decisive innovations and improvisations thereby business houses are able to attract new customers and retain the existing customers quiet convincingly.

Service Authentication, Authorization and Aggregation

Newer avenues are being explored in order to enhance the revenue as there are consistent and conscious efforts underway to move from the product to the service space with all ease. The business agility, autonomy and affordability are the top three advantages with the overwhelming embarkation on the transformative, disruptive and augmentative service discipline. That services are highly consumable, amenable and adept are doing a lot of good things for growing enterprises these days in proactively visualizing and understanding peoples' pulses and needs in order to quickly develop and deliver original services to users.

Innovation

Another noteworthy factor is that Internet Protocol (IP) has become the ubiquitous protocol for communication. Ad hoc networks via mesh networking could be temporarily created for emergent functionalities and disbanded once the purpose is fully over. The convergence of data, voice, and video over the IP network is another remarkable point. The communication (wireless as well as wired) service providers, media companies, application service providers (ASPs), security and storage vendors, cloud service providers (CSPs), and high-tech industries are seemingly the first in using multi-faceted and multichannel SDPs to be ahead of their competitors. In a nutshell, SDP represents the recognition and renaissance in the service world. SDPs have definitely emerged as the strategic element for the ensuing service era. SDPs are bound to play a very distinctive and disruptive role in introducing novel solutions and services quicker in the market and shaping up the service industry. Any competitive SDP directly and indirectly impacts on the aspects such as the return on investment (RoI) and total cost of ownership (TCO) of service-centric applications. In a nutshell, it is all about Sense and Respond (S & R) enterprises.

Next-Generation Platform

An SDP is a composite platform in the sense that there are several modules inside collaborating and contributing for the projected success. Integration backbone, process manager, aggregation engine, governance tool, event processor, access, identity, and infrastructure modules, a set of common services, etc. clearly capture and enhance the market share and mindshare too. The unique benefits of such an open software solution are that it creates a dynamic developers and users community. This open-ended community leads to huge public subscription, consumption and creation of new services. The well-known examples are Apple and Android application stores.

With an effective SDP, operators have the opportunity and wherewithal to reduce service creation costs, accelerate the development cycle for novel mobile applications, increase the variety, richness, and reach of applications, promote service reuse, and reduce their proportionate business risks within their total application portfolio. If an SDP is to continue to help service organizations to meet their tactic as well as strategic needs, such platform solutions ought to adapt to the changes in the technologies, emerging business realities and consumers' expectations. Thus convergence is an important ingredient in realizing next-generation SDPs that are capable of meeting various needs of diverse domains and disciplines.

Significance of SDP for the Service Era

Why SaaS-enablement? - The service paradigm has made a huge impact on ICT resources (software as well as hardware) and hence we often hear and read about Service-Driven Infrastructures (SOIs) and Service-Driven Enterprises (SOEs). Resource optimization, collaboration, sharing and utilization get a new lease of life and gain immense momentum with the smooth stability of service orientation concepts, technologies, and methodologies. The service orientation principles guarantee the much-wanted features and functionalities of the futuristic IT. Being technology-agnostic, services can be deployed, executed, and maintained on any standards-compliant container. These remarkable characteristics have clearly elevated the value and verve of SOA in effortlessly assimilating newer concepts, modernizing languishing and sagging applications, integrating disparate and distributed systems, realizing exciting and elegant composites and building pragmatic service-oriented systems. The near as well as the long-term implications are that the complicated, closed, and costly business IT is definitely destined for a major overhaul and turnaround into affordable, adaptive, and agile IT. SOA, being the first and foremost business-driven technology, promises for a closer and tighter alignment between business and IT as executives and managers are struggling and stretching consistently to find implementable and intelligent ways and means to do more with less.

Significantly service-orientation is process-centric and this helps business and process consultants to revisit, refine and make resilient and robust business processes to achieve process excellence. Business process innovation (BPI) through effective process modeling, enhanced visibility, effective consolidation, governance, and integration has been a stable and spectacular contribution towards taking SOA to greater heights. That is, we are all set to have elastic, lean, and integrated processes that in turn would lead to integrated and intelligent systems. Further on, the task of creation of composite services is getting simplified with open standards and corresponding techniques. In other words, SOA facilitates building and manipulation of composite data, views, and services that in turn lead to business-centric processes and applications, which considerably ease decomposition, substitution, extensibility, separation of concerns, etc. It is no exaggeration that the origin and the growth story of SOA are incredibly and inspiringly phenomenal.

Finally, SOA has the wherewithal to lease unbelievably enormous amount of assistance and assurance for cloud and ultimately to the promised knowledge era. The service revelation and revolution is catching up fast and as a striking consequence, the new subject of service science is spreading its wings wider and deeper. Service engineering is another intriguing discipline going through a meteoric rise among students and scholars. Precisely speaking, service-orientation has brought in a dazzling array of innovations and improvisations in forming and formulating nimbler business, development, delivery, consumption and pricing models. Best practices, design metrics, key guidelines, proven methodologies, and extensible processes are being brought out very frequently. Software as a service (SaaS), the hotly discussed and debated deployment and delivery model, rekindles a sense of hope and buoyancy among industry veterans and newcomers alike.

SDP for the SaaS World

Giving users the applications and services they need is very critical to ensure success in almost every modern business. That is, ubiquitous service access (USA) is the latest buzzword. But the inefficiencies resulting from globalization, server management, and changes in the business, consumer and technology ecosystems can raise costs and frustrate users. Precisely speaking, today's business reality demands that the underlying Information and Communication Technology (ICT) infrastructures have to adequately be adaptive. With an increasing array of common as well as specific services getting accumulated in distributed and decentralized service environments, the need for converged SDPs is being felt across in strengthening the imminent service era.

Importance of Cloud-Based SDP

Cloud computing has been making waves and buzzes in the business-enabling IT arena and its impacts on both business and IT are definitely multifaceted and mesmerizing. Conceptually, the cloud style has ignited scores of original business, consumption and pricing models. On the infrastructural side, clouds have emerged as the elastic infrastructure for optimally hosting, managing, and delivering next-generation services and applications. In a way, clouds are being positioned as the consolidated, virtualized, automated, shared, and quality of service (QoS)-compliant infrastructures. Having understood its strategically sound business and technical benefits, global enterprises are very much forthcoming in embracing this pioneering IT paradigm. Following the footsteps of enterprise IT, embedded IT (the device space) too jumps into the cloud bandwagon very positively and progressively.

There are several transnational and transformational initiatives for producing competent and open architectures and frameworks that facilitate seamless connectivity and service-level integration between infinitesimal embedded devices and cloud. Every worthwhile domain is contemplating, competing and completing the Cloud modernization and migration enthusiastically. Market onlookers are very categorical in their forecast that the ingenious cloud idea is to be massively adopted across the globe and adapted accordingly by IT services and solutions providers. The cloud model has opened up fresh possibilities for the scores of unresolved problems and limitations of current IT and brings forth innumerable opportunities to sustain the IT dynamism and momentum.

Cloud is being recognized as the most powerful, potential and promising technology for future IT. Along with the enterprise and the embedded IT, the cloud IT is to support the IT evolution and revolution continuously and consistently for the years to unfold. In a nutshell, with the grand arrival and overwhelming reception of the cloud paradigm, philosophies and principles, the stagnant, expensive, costly and closed IT is getting smoothly and seamlessly transitioned into elastic, green, clean and catalytic IT. The brewing cloud idea has demonstrably brought in tectonic and tremendous shifts in the way IT is being approached, applied, and articulated.

Cloud Infrastructures

With enterprise IT infrastructures (servers, storages, and network solutions) are being made ready for the future IT challenges extensively leveraging cloud technologies (consolidation, virtualization, and automation), all kinds of web, consumer, and enterprise applications and services are being accurately and adequately remedied and moved to clouds. Next in line for the goal of cloud-enablement are nonetheless the IT platforms (development, deployment, management, integration, aggregation, analytics, dissemination, delivery etc.). As explained elsewhere, the SDP is the comprehensive and converged platform for next-generation service delivery. That is, SDPs are being taken to and deployed in cloud infrastructures to be globally accessed and used to craft and deliver extended cloud services to worldwide consumers with all the requirement service qualities embedded. Also cloud-based SDP is for integrating diverse cloud services spread across geographically distributed cloud servers.

With the surging popularity for Cloud Brokerage Services (CBS), the need for new-generation SDP is steadily growing. The next-generation SDP will act as a viable and valuable broker, integrator, composer, orchestrator, mediator, aggregator, etc. All kinds of enrichment and empowerment tasks are being silently and successfully done by the SDP. With the concepts of federated clouds and the Intercloud are picking up fast, services that are hosted and maintained in different, distributed and decentralized cloud-based platforms, corporate networks, web application servers, private and personal clouds, etc. are also getting linked up in order to produce smart and sophisticated cloud services. Thus for the ensuing cloud era, the relevance of SDPs is really great. The ultimate goal of cloud-based service delivery is to rely on a variety of thin and trendy clients (smart phones, tablets, TVs, web appliances, car multimedia, infotainment and home integration devices, etc.) that seamlessly connect with and access remote networked storage, compute, content, and application resources.

The Converged SDP

The converged SDP makes it easier to build and deliver rich and converged applications and services that incorporate network assets and revenue-sharing partnerships with developer and content communities. This has the additional capabilities of addressing governance, management and quality across the network, IT, and Web-based service delivery models comprehensively. With SOA, addressing the end-to-end service lifecycle and workflow across business and operational systems get greatly simplified. With Web 2.0, the power of personal, community and enterprise service innovations is being realized.

Cost Reduction

Service innovation is a continuous process involving huge costs. The SDP 2.0 can hugely offset the cost. These savings are achieved through the simplification of the service delivery infrastructure, which reduces the capital, integration, operational and maintenance costs associated with multiple and complex service delivery systems. The cost of maintaining a silo-based service delivery system drains human and financial resources, and hinders the vital business agility necessary to stay ahead of the competition.

Risks Mitigation

Services are thoroughly tested across multiple systems and refined. By enabling the reuse of functionality across multiple systems, companies can lower their risks of service creation. SOA principles enable companies to reflect their business priorities in the service delivery process.

Faster Time-to-Market

Collaboration is the key for any noteworthy success. With SDP 2.0, distributed teams and even third-parties can collaborate effectively and easily to come out with a cornucopia of new and revenue-generating services. The time-to-market gets halved with next-generation SDPs.

Breeds Innovation

Converged SDP can introduce path-breaking and profitable services, quickly and efficiently across wireless and wire line systems forcing major changes to CSPs' business models. This allows the combination of multiple business models between subscribers, service providers, and application developers by building and delivering services that are more relevant to subscribers, service providers can improve the likelihood that these services are continually consumed, as well as increase network traffic, improve the revenue level, and reduce churn. Context-aware services also can be delivered, which further enhances subscriber loyalty and differentiation. Better targeted services also can reduce the amount of money spent on retention, while making new customer acquisitions easier and less costly.

On concluding, the market for cognition-attached, composite and converged services is rapidly expanding. All kinds of service providers in the hot communications, media, and entertainment, web and enterprise application spaces have been meticulously modernizing and empowering their IT services infrastructures to profitably meet the growing demands delectably and to enhance the customer experience substantially. An essential part of this evolution has been the implementation of a SDP. These SOA-centric platforms enable operators to cost-effectively develop, deliver and manage converged digital services. SDPs help to break down the inefficient, redundant and siloed infrastructures and to sharply improve the much-needed collaboration across the services ecosystem. New services can be developed and rolled-out to customers faster and more reliably, shortening the time to revenue whereas lessening any risks and controlling flaring costs.

The service landscape is being continuously empowered with the transformative, disruptive and innovative ideas of the cloud paradigm. On the other hand, IT infrastructures and platforms are being service-enabled for remote discoverability, accessibility and leveragability. The ability to rapidly create, deliver and manage new and compelling customer-centric services is more important than ever. Businesses are driving high performance in their business operations through a series of innovations in service deployment, delivery, governance and enhancement. SDP is very effective in reducing the costs and risks of new product development while supporting a more collaborative development environment. The demand for Web 2.0, rich-media content, vide on-demand (VoD), IPTV, mobile TV, collaborative business tools, on-demand services, and Tele-Presence is radically changing the landscape of 21st century service delivery.

The requirements for SDPs are going beyond the horizon. Today, new service delivery requirements have been crystallized. New-generation platforms need to address governance, management and quality across the network, IT, and web-based services. The quality of service (QoS) (Non-functional requirements) attributes need to be ensured in service interactions and delivery. There is not iota of doubt that SDP occupy the prominent and dominant portion of the approaching service era.

CONCLUSION

As worldwide central, state and federal governments are pumping in quite a big amount of money in setting up a full-fledged e-governance infrastructure and processes in order to serve their citizens better and faster, and in framing appropriate rules, regulations, and policies, the e-governance domain and discipline is to become a lucrative and luscious opportunity for IT solution and services providers. Regulatory bodies and monitoring mechanisms are also simultaneously being established and evolved to meet up soaring expectations of governors as well as common people. In this chapter, we have analyzed the effectiveness and efficiency of XML-centric services technology in providing interoperable, extensible, composable, reliable and adaptive services. These services are bound to facilitate designing, building, deploying and delivering next-generation e-governance applications. The uniqueness of service technology is its wide industry acceptance and XML as the universal data representation, exchange and persistence language. All kinds of structural, schematic, symbiotic, and syntactic differences and deficiencies are getting wiped out in a single stroke with the adoption and adaption of service technology. All kinds of dependencies are being decimated to ensure any software runs on any hardware. Data translation and protocol transformation adaptors, connectors, drivers and other key enabling modules are thriving in the service world. With the emergence of cloud infrastructures for hosting service platforms and service-oriented systems fluently and fluidly, the days of empowered e-governance services and applications thriving incessantly are very near.

In a nutshell, service and cloud computing models are to meet up the growing e-governance expectations as well as needs in a secure and safe manner. The people-centric governments across the globe are to deliver e-governance facilities and functionalities to their citizens in a affordable and affable fashion. Welcome XML-based Web services for the burgeoning e-governance era!

REFERENCES

Behara, G. K., Varre, V. V., & Rao, M. (2009). *Service oriented architecture for e-governance*. Retrieved from http://www.bptrends.com/publicationfiles/10-09-art-%20soa-e-govermance-behara-final.pdf

Das, R. K., & Patra, M. R. (2009). *SOA for e-governance in India: Potentials and pitfalls*. Retrieved from http://delivery.acm.org/10.1145/1700000/1693050/p36-das.pdf?ip=203.91.193.5&acc=active%20service&cfid=67638877&cftoken=19183172&__acm__=1330070104_a44cefd8a5f3d7314baf868a4502e406

Misra, H. (2010). *Understanding SOA perspective of e-governance in Indian context*. Retrieved from http://www.intechopen.com/source/pdfs/10809/intech-understanding_soa_perspective_of_e_governance_in_indian_context_case_based_study.pdf

Prabhu, C. S. R. (2010). *Towards an e-governance grid for India (E-GGI): An architectural framework for citizen services delivery*. Retrieved from http://www.csi-sigegov.org/1/7_266.pdf

Section 4
E-Government Projects: Review and Assessment

Chapter 14
Evaluation and Metrics of E-Government:
From eEurope 2002 to Digital Agenda 2020

Haroula N. Delopoulos
National and Kapodistrian University of Athens, Greece

ABSTRACT

This chapter discusses EU methodologies used for the evaluation of a number of e-government related strategies including: Action Plan e-Europe 2002, Action Plan e-Europe 2005, the Strategic Framework i2010 as well as the Digital Agenda 2020. It highlights differences and similarities between these plans. It is suggested that Europe should not focus mainly on the supply side (track availability and sophistication), but should also investigate indicators that might directly affect the eGovernment adoption. To this end, we have searched Eurostat Database in order to demonstrate some of the eGovernment evaluation metrics that affect the use and availability of eGovernment (eGov) in European Union concerning individuals and enterprises. We processed the row data and estimated the annual average and the annual average change of eighteen eGovernment indicators for the years 2005-2010. Furthermore, the chapter determines whether or not some of the targets of Digital Agenda 2020 will be accomplished by stated 2015. The author's estimates are based according to existing trends to determine how these indicators will affect, if nothing changes, in or by 2015.

DOI: 10.4018/978-1-4666-4245-4.ch014

INTRODUCTION

eGovernment (eGov) Strategy of European Union (EU) is outlined in Action Plan eEurope 2002, Action Plan e-Europe 2005, the Strategic Framework i2010 and the Digital Agenda 2020. In this study, the availability & sophistication of twenty basic public services was looked at in the evaluation frameworks of Action Plan e-Europe 2002, Action plan e-Europe 2005, and strategic framework i2010. For this, a four stage evaluation model was adopted. In the last decade, Europe evaluated mainly the supply side of the eGov by evaluating the availability of 20 basic public services by estimating the indicator "Online availability and interactivity of public services."

In this chapter, we have demonstrated the evaluation of Europe's frameworks Action Plan e-Europe 2002 to Digital Agenda and conducted a data analysis of Eurostat Database (Eurostat - Your key to European Statistics). We processed row data and estimated the annual average and the annual average change of 18 eGov indicators for the years 2005-2010. Among these indicators are some that might affect the use of eGov. We found that availability of eGov in EU-27 for the years 2005-2010 is high (see Table 1). Here, EU-27 refers to the following countries: Austria [AT], Belgium [BE], Bulgaria [BG], Cyprus [CY], Czech Republic [CZ], Denmark [DK], Estonia [EE], Finland [FI], France [FR], Germany [DE], Greece [EL], Hungary [HU], Iceland [IS], Italy [IT], Latvia [LV], Lithuania [LT], Luxembourg [LU], Malta [MT], Netherlands [NL], Poland [PL], Portugal [PT], Romania [RO], Slovakia [SK], Slovenia [SI], Spain [ES], Sweden [SE], United Kingdom [UK]. Nevertheless, eGov usage by individuals for obtaining information from public authorities, for downloading official forms from public authorities, or for sending filled forms is very low at the same period. This indicates that it is not enough to evaluate mainly the supply side, but Europe should investigate the reasons why eGov use is low.

We note that, eGov usage by enterprises is high for the years 2005-2010 concerning usage of Internet: for obtaining information from public authorities, or for obtaining forms from public authorities, or for returning filled in forms to public authorities but it is low concerning interaction with public authorities for full electronic case handling. On the contrary, eGov usage by enterprises for interaction with public authorities for e-procurement is low. Internet purchases of goods or services, over the Internet, by individuals for private use is low as well as, online purchases in the last 3 months for the period 2005-2010. Online sales of small to medium enterprises (SMEs), not within the financial sector, 10-249 persons employed, with at least 1% of turnover, is again low for the years 2005-2010.

EU, in the evaluation of frameworks of eGov, did not give a deep focus on some indicators that might affect directly the use of eGov or might play the role of "prerequisites" for eGov adoption. These indicators may include the use of Internet. A major proportion of individuals in EU-27 had never used Internet for the period 2005-2010. This might have happened because the access or the equipment costs are too high, or access is not needed (content is not useful, not interesting, etc.), or there is lack of skills, or their content is harmful.

It is very important that, before EU implements a new eGov strategy, we see the trends of those indicators that affect directly the adoption or use of eGov services by individuals and enterprises .This will help EU to track down a strategy with more realistic targets.

In this study, we will highlight 18 eGov indicators and suggest that they be taken seriously in consideration before Europe implements a new eGov strategy. We have calculated the annual average for the years 2005-2010, as well as the annual change of these indicators. We concluded that some targets of Digital Agenda are very ambitious and might not become reality by 2015, for all European countries member states of EU27, and we found out that major differences appear in some indicators.

Table 1. Online availability and interactivity of public spaces services (supply side) of European Countries-EU27 for period 2005-2010 (Source: Eurostat row data (isoc_bde15ess))

Online availability and interactivity of public services (supply side)- Indicator 1			
Percentage of 20 basic services			
countries	annual average for the years 2005-2010	countries	annual average change for the years 2005-2010
BG	38	EE	3
SK	42	AT	4
EL	43	CY	4
PL	43	EL	4
RO	47	HU	4
CY	48	FR	5
LV	49	MT	5
LU	50	SE	6
HU	52	DK	7
LT	52	LT	7
CZ	57	SI	7
BE	65	BE	8
EU-27	**70**	FI	8
IS	70	RO	8
NL	70	UK	8
DE	72	**EU-27**	**9**
IT	73	CZ	10
FR	75	IT	10
ES	75	NL	10
DK	76	PT	10
FI	77	ES	10
UK	84	SK	11
EE	85	DE	12
SE	86	IS	12
PT	87	LU	13
SI	89	PL	15
MT	93	BG	19
AT	97	LV	21

DIFFERENT APPROACHES TO EGOV EVALUATION

There are different approaches to eGov evaluation. Assessment of eGov is a complex and multidimensional task. Different views for eGov assessment exist among the scientific community. eGov measures can be categorized (Gupta & Jana, 2003) as follows:

- Hard measures or Quantitative methods e.g. Cost Benefit Analysis, comparative evaluation in eGov ie benchmarking
- Soft measures or Qualitative methods e.g. Rating method e-score, e-government stages, social effects) or a mixture of methodologies can be used for eGov evaluation (Gupta & Jana, 2003).

Depending on the methodology, some researchers treat eGov as a system (holistic approach) (Wimmer & Tambouris, 2002) others give priority to customer needs and treat citizens as customers or focus on the value of eGov (Flak et al., 2009). Some researchers evaluate the performance of eGov (Gupta & Jana, 2003) or the reengineering of the public organization (Jeremy Millard et al., 2004), or try to measure eGov in economic terms (*eGovernment Economics Project (eGEP) Measurement Framework*, 2006), or eGov readiness (United Nations, 2003; 2004), or deal with the evaluation of the supply side of eGov services (Gemini, Ernst, & Young, 2002a; 2002b; 2004; 2007) or benchmarking specific life sectors such as eHealth (i2010 High Level Group, 2009).

Other benchmarking reports give focus on readiness, availability, uptake and impact of eGov (Heeks, 2006). A variety of methods is used for sample data gathering and they try to measure among others: the telecommunication infrastructure, the presence of eGov strategy, the government expenditure on IT, the quality of government websites, the general features of eGov websites, the participation-specific features of government websites, the government website maturity, the government-specific infrastructure, the prospective attitude towards use of eGov by citizens, the adoption of best practices, use of eGov by citizens, the use of eGov by businesses, the experience of eGov use by citizens, the retrospective attitude towards use of eGov by citizens, the benefits for citizens, the financial benefits, the back office changes.

A method to evaluate, to compare and to find the best practices in information technology between similar organizations which offer similar services is "e-score" (Kaylor, Deshazo, & Van Eck, 2001). They attempted to rank eGov implementation among cities and they tried to encapsulate the functions (e.g. images, audio/video, documents, applications, e-procurements) and services (e.g. payments, registration, permits, customer service, communication, licenses) that municipalities provide. It was an effort to set standards in the implementation of eGov and to try to evaluate the degree of sophistication by comparing the on line presence of an organization. The evaluation was done using a four stage model as follows:

- **1st Stage:** In the website, there is static information concerning a given topic
- **2nd Stage:** A link exists at the website for communication details (e.g. email address, telephone number)
- **3rd Stage:** There are available forms that the user can download on a given topic
- **4th Stage:** Any transaction or interaction can be completed in real time and on line,

For the implementation and the completion of e-government, a four stage eGov model was also proposed by Layne and Lee (2001). The stages are:

- **1st Stage:** Cataloguing: online presence, catalogue presentation, downloadable forms
- **2nd Stage:** Transaction: services and forums on line, working database supporting online transactions

- **3rd Stage:** Vertical integration: local systems linked to higher level systems, within similar functionalities
- **4th Stage:** Horizontal integration: systems integrated across different functions, real one stop shopping for citizens.

In other researches, eGov is evaluated using a series of mature stages (Accenture, 2003) such as:

- **Stage 1:** Networks: e.g. The information must be public to the web
- **Stage 2:** Basic ability: e.g. Development of a main plan and establishment of laws
- **Stage 3:** Availability of services: e.g. Basic gateways and more service delivery
- **Stage 4:** Mature distribution/delivery: e.g. Bundled services.

Tangible and intangible benefits of eGov are evaluated by following a mixed methodology or a "multi-methodology" (Gupta & Jana, 2003) evaluation. The proposed multi-methodology was composed of the following: a) cost benefit analysis, b) benchmarking eGov, c) scoring method, d) stages of eGov, e) sociological angle, and f) hierarchy of measures. This gives us a 6-level stage model. Cost benefit analysis is a way to measure/evaluate tangible benefits. Usually, the goods offered by the government are public goods and every citizen can acquire and consume them in a price below the marginal social cost and the offered quantity is a decision made by the government and not made by the laws of demand. All the social effects should be considered in the evaluation, such as the employees' early retirement due to the new information and communication technologies. A measurement hierarchy of 6 measures was used that is attributable to "Return on eGov" which is relevant to "assessing return of information." This constitutes of following levels: *Level 1*: return on investment, *Level 2*: total costs & revenues, *Level 3*: improvement in quality of planning & control, Level 4: quality of decisions, *Level 5*: value of information, *Level 6*: system characteristics (Gupta & Jana, 2003).

We must also note that for the development of a useful one-stop shop e-government platform, according to "holistic approach" (Wimmer & Tambouris, 2002), we should fulfil, among others, the following requirements:

- All the classic procedure should be adopted smoothly to the new technologies,
- All public services should be offered by just one portal/link even if the services belong to different public divisions and organizations,
- It should be accessed available through different channels and devices (connections) (e.g. Internet, PDA, WAP, call centres, etc.),
- The one-stop shop platform needs an efficient security, identification and privacy system, especially in eGov services regarding personal data and highly sensitive information,
- All internal (internal networks, data bases) and external (information and communication services with the citizen through the web) functions should in the public sector,
- The user should have access to public services without knowing the hierarchy of the public sector,
- The user should be able to watch the progress of his/hers application and understand the different stages of service delivery (information, interaction with the public authorities, on line applications, service delivery and financial transactions, complaints, necessary feedback, etc),
- All eGov services should be user friendly, so that any user, citizen or business, can understand and use them.

The holistic approach considers the public administration as a combined system of social and technological factors. The system includes:

citizens, employees in the public sector, social groups, information systems, laws and restrictions, social and cultural policies, national identity, ethics, environmental issues (Wimmer & Tambouris, 2002).

In Digital Europe's measurements, eGov services are treated as "advanced services" and conclude that a "main category at risk of exclusion from eGov usage and from internet use" is the low level of education" (European Comission, 2010), that "may lack the skills for the use of "advanced services" (European Comission, 2010), and finally, "the mere provision of a service does not guarantee its usage" (European Comission, 2010).

Europe followed specific measurement frameworks beginning with the evaluation framework of e-Europe 2002 until the evaluation framework of Digital Agenda 2020. In the Action Plans e-Europe2002 (Gemini, Ernst, & Young, 2002a; 2002b; Comission of the European Communities, 2002b; Commission of the European Communities, 2001), e-Europe2005 (Gemini, Ernst, & Young, 2004; Comission of the European Communities, 2002a; 2002b; Commission of the European Communities, 2002) and, in the Strategic Framework i2010 evaluation frameworks (Gemini, Ernst, & Young, 2007; Commission of the European Communities, 2005), the stages of eGov played an important basic role in the evaluation of eGov indicators.

The concept of stages in eGov evaluation is common place in many evaluation methods (Kaylor et al., 2001; Gupta & Jana, 2003) as well as the idea of fully or partially integrated on line eGov services (West Darrell, 2000). Also, all the above mentioned evaluation methodologies were taking place after eGov services were produced and gave focus on supply side of eGov services. Are Digital Agenda's targets feasible? How easy are key performance targets of Digital Agenda 2020 to be easily accomplished by 2015? when the proportion of individuals that had never used a computer rose to 50% in Romania but decreased in Sweden to 4%, in 2011, and the proportion of households who have internet access rose rose to 94% in Netherlands and decreased to 45% in Bulgaria in 2011 (Delopoulos, 2012).

In the present research, we demonstrate the methodologies of evaluation frameworks that have been used by Europe and pointed out that in the applied Europe's measurement Frameworks a 4rth or a 5th stage scale is used to evaluate the availability (supply side) and the sophistication of eGov services. Also we highlight some major similarities and differences in the evaluation methodologies. We evaluated and highlighted specific indicators of eGov that might directly affect the use of eGov in EU-27. We draw specific questions that should be answered by politicians, policy as well as decision makers before eGov strategy is implemented in EU.

We searched Eurostat and estimated that eGov availability is high in 2005-2010, in EU-27 (see Table 1). Also, following the existing trends, approximately all countries in EU-27 intend to have 100% availability of 20 public services that are on line by 2015. We found that the use of eGov by individuals has been very low in 2005-2010 in EU-27 (see Table 2) and also varies a lot among countries members states in EU-27. Following the existing trends, major differences will exist among countries member states in EU-27 in 2015 (see Table 7). Also, the use of eGov by enterprises in EU-27 for the years 2005-2010 is high in EU-27 (see Table 5), but the usage for e-procurement is low (see Table 5) and following the existing trend will remain low and great differences appear in countries member states in 2015 (see Table 7). The proportion of individuals that have never used Internet for some countries is high and is very low for other countries for the years 2005-2010, in EU-27 (see Table 3), and will still remain low in 2015 and great differences will exist for some countries (see Table 7).

Table 2. Individuals use Internet to interact with public authorities for the period 2005-2010 in EU-27 (Source: Eurostat row data (isoc_ci_ac_i))

Internet use: obtaining information from public authorities-Indicator 2				Internet use: downloading official forms from public authorities-Indicator 3				Internet use: sending filled forms to public authorities-Indicator 4			
Percentage of individuals											
countries	annual average for the years 2005-2010	countries	annual average change for the years 2005-2010	countries	annual average for the years 2005-2010	countries	annual average change for the years 2005-2010	countries	annual average for the years 2005-2010	countries	annual average change for the years 2005-2010
RO	5	**EU-27**	**1**	RO	3	IT	0	RO	3	LU	-1
BG	7	FI	1	EL	4	BE	1	BG	4	AT	0
EL	9	FR	1	BG	5	BG	1	CZ	4	EL	0
CZ	14	EL	1	CZ	7	CZ	1	EL	4	IT	0
PL	14	IT	1	LV	8	DE	1	IT	5	BG	1
IT	15	LT	1	BE	10	EL	1	PL	5	CY	1
CY	16	LU	1	PL	10	LV	1	LV	6	CZ	1
LT	16	MT	1	CY	11	LU	1	CY	7	**EU-27**	**1**
PT	16	PL	1	IT	11	PL	1	SI	7	FR	1
HU	20	RO	1	LT	11	PT	1	BE	8	DE	1
LV	20	AT	2	PT	12	RO	1	MT	8	HU	1
MT	20	BE	2	MT	14	SK	1	ES	8	LV	1
IS	21	BG	2	**EU-27**	**15**	ES	1	HU	10	MT	1
BE	22	CY	2	ES	15	SE	1	SK	10	PL	1
EU-27	**25**	CZ	2	UK	15	AT	2	**EU-27**	**11**	RO	1
SK	26	DE	2	HU	16	CY	2	LT	11	SK	1
ES	27	HU	2	SK	17	**EU-27**	**2**	DE	12	SI	1
SI	29	IS	2	SI	17	FR	2	AT	13	ES	1
UK	29	PT	2	IS	19	HU	2	PT	13	BE	2
AT	31	SK	2	AT	20	IS	2	UK	13	IS	2
FR	31	ES	2	DE	20	LT	2	FR	17	LT	2
EE	34	SE	2	FR	21	MT	2	IS	17	PT	2
DE	34	UK	2	EE	25	FI	3	LU	17	SE	2
LU	42	NL	3	FI	30	NL	3	FI	19	FI	3
FI	45	EE	4	NL	30	SI	3	EE	24	NL	3
NL	48	LV	4	SE	31	UK	3	SE	26	UK	3
SE	49	SI	4	DK	32	EE	4	NL	31	EE	4
DK	54	DK	7	LU	35	DK	5	DK	32	DK	8

Table 3. Individuals never used Internet for the period 2005-2010 in EU-27 (Source: Eurostat row data (isoc_ci_ifp_iu))

Individuals never used Internet Indicator 5			
Percentage of individuals			
countries	annual average for the years 2005-2010	countries	annual average change for the years 2005-2010
SE	10	CZ	-7
DK	11	FR	-7
NL	13	HU	-6
FI	16	IS	-6
LU	19	BG	-5
UK	21	LT	-5
DE	22	PL	-5
BE	28	SK	-5
AT	29	BE	-4
EE	29	CY	-4
FR	30	EL	-4
SK	30	IT	-4
EU-27	**35**	LV	-4
IS	37	LU	-4
LV	38	MT	-4
SI	39	RO	-4
ES	41	SI	-4
CZ	42	ES	-4
HU	44	AT	-3
PL	46	EE	-3
LT	47	**EU-27**	**-3**
MT	49	PT	-3
IT	52	UK	-3
CY	55	FI	-2
PT	55	DE	-2
BG	59	NL	-2
EL	60	DK	-1
RO	65	SE	-1

EUROPE'S MEASUREMENT FRAMEWORKS: FROM ACTION PLAN E-EUROPE 2002 TO DIGITAL AGENDA 2020

Action Plan e-Europe 2002 and eGov Evaluation Framework

In March 2001, in Brussels, the European committee announced the first evaluation of the Action plan e-Europe 2002. The evaluation measured how the action plan can contribute in the development of the knowledge society and how it can be realized.

In the initiative Action Plan e-Europe 2002, the Internal Market Board of the EU in November 2000 defined 23 progress indicators (Commission of the European Communities, 2001). These indicators were representative of the initiative's e-Europe 2002 progress. One of the indicators was the development rate of e-government. For this indicator the member states agreed on a common list of 20 basic public services available, twelve of these services were related to the citizens:

1. Income taxes: declaration, notification of assessment
2. Job search services by labour offices
3. Social security contributions (3 out of the following 4): Unemployment benefits-Family allowances-Medical costs (reimbursement or direct settlement)- Student grants
4. Personal documents (passport and driver's license)
5. Car registration (new, used and imported cars)
6. Application for building permission
7. Declaration to the police (e.g. in case of theft)
8. Public libraries (availability of catalogues, search tools)
9. Certificates (birth, marriage): request and delivery
10. Enrolment in higher education / university
11. Announcement of moving (change of address)
12. Health related services (e.g. interactive advice on the availability of services in different hospitals; appointments for hospitals.)

Eight of them were related to businesses:

1. Social contribution for employees
2. Corporation tax: declaration, notification
3. VAT: declaration, notification
4. Registration of a new company
5. Submission of data to statistical offices
6. Customs declarations
7. Environment-related permits (incl. repo incl. reporting)
8. public procurement

Twice a year, the progress of the list's application (if the services were applicable in electronic environment) was examined in all 15 member states of the E.U including Norway and Iceland. The examination took place through the following 4 stage development framework:

- **Stage 1:** Information
- **Stage 2:** On way interaction (downloadable forms)
- **Stage 3:** Two way interaction
- **Stage 4:** Transaction (Full electronic case handling)

There was a major need to adopt an efficient method of eGov, so that eGov can be applied successfully. All the countries/members of EU were looking for the "best eGov practice." This was done by considering the three steps as follows: a) choosing the best practical model (best practice) worldwide, b) some best practices could be applied more widely, and c) the best practices should be disseminated widely. Mechanisms were established to diffuse the best practice among member EU states such as workshops, by supporting networks and World Wide Web.

In order to choose the best practices, a comparative analysis was needed. For the statistics regarding the information society, a common evaluation base was necessary. They decided to follow two stages for the comparative analysis:

- Definition of indicators: accomplishment of a supporting indicator's policy, renewal of indicators, new lists of indicators
- Measurement and analysis: the measurement of the indicators was taken by the official statistics of each national statistic service or by Eurostat.

Benchmarking was about "the percentage of available public services on line" and "the average rate of the services' development, of the member states" for (15+2) member states.

Action Plan e-Europe 2005 and eGov Evaluation Framework

The comparative evaluation of the Action plan e-Europe 2005 followed the same methodology as the evaluation of Action Plan e-Europe 2002. A four stage evaluation model was followed on the sample of 20 basic public services available. In Action plan e-Europe 2002, eGov evaluation, the index measured "the percentage of the available public e-service." In Action Plan e-Europe 2005 eGov index was redefined as "the number of basic electronic public services, available on line" (European Commission DG Information Society, 2004). There were some methodology problems as well such as: a) the developed methodology was about the availability of public services, through the Internet, which meant that all the other available public services distributed in other ways should not be evaluated (e.g. call centres, DTV, mobile devices), b) only the public electronic services that were available on line were evaluated, and c) only the supply side was evaluated.

The comparative evaluation of the Action plan e-Europe 2005 followed three stages/phases (refer to Table 4):

- **Defining the Indicators:** The indicators should be updated so that they follow the goals of the Action plan e-Europe 2005. The indicators were supported by the Internal Market Board/Council in November 2000. In the end of the Action plan e-Europe 2005, after the year 2004, a new list of indicators was used for the candidate countries, and new regional indicators were created.
- **Measurement and Analysis:** A reliable statistic survey regarding the web has a short life-time, while all the measurements for the indicators are available instantly, due to their importance for strategic planning. For the quality improvement of the results, all indicators decided to be measured by each National Statistic Service or by Eurostat. Naturally, the measures should be comparable, comparison between 2 different things is impossible, for this reason a common base (for the statistics regarding the information society of EU) was needed.
- **Benchmarking:** The indicators were based on certain factors, the analysis of these factors was crucial because the policy planning was depending on these indicators and factors. By benchmarking analysis could (Comission of the European Communities, 2002b) every member state have the necessary information to make its own analysis. The Committee and all member states were supporting the idea of creating regional indicators, in order to promote regional benchmarking, especially in less developed regions.

The EU decided that for the evaluation of the new index, same methodology will be used as before in researches in October 2001, April 2001

Table 4. Reasons why households do not have access to Internet at home for the period 2005-2010 in EU-27 (Source: Eurostat row data (isoc_pibi_rni))

Households without access to Internet at home, because the access costs are too high (telephone, etc.) – Indicator 6				Households without access to Internet at home, because the equipment costs are too high – Indicator 7				Households without access to Internet at home, because access is not needed (content is not useful, not interesting, etc.) – Indicator 8				Households without access to Internet at home, because of lack of skills – Indicator 9				Households without access to Internet at home, because access is not wanted (content is harmful, etc.) – Indicator 10			
Percentage of households																			
countries	annual average for the years 2005-2010	countries	annual average change for the years 2005-2010	countries	annual average for the years 2005-2010	countries	annual average change for the years 2005-2010	countries	annual average for the years 2005-2010	countries	annual average change for the years 2005-2010	countries	annual average for the years 2005-2010	countries	annual average change for the years 2005-2010	countries	annual average for the years 2005-2010	countries	annual average change for the years 2005-2010
LU	1	PT	-5	LU	1	PT	-5	NL	7	FR	-5	DK	2	RO	-3	LT	0	FR	-5
NL	1	EE	-4	NL	1	EE	-4	E	7	AT	-4	NL	2	ES	-3	IT	1	EE	-3
DK	2	SK	-4	DK	2	LT	-4	UK	9	LT	-4	LU	4	CY	-2	BE	2	PT	-3
IS	3	HU	-3	MT	3	SK	-4	DK	10	MT	-4	SE	4	PT	-2	DE	2	IS	-2
MT	3	PL	-3	SE	3	BG	-3	CZ	11	PT	-4	LT	5	EE	-1	PL	2	BE	-1
SE	3	BG	-2	AT	5	HU	-3	FI	11	BE	-3	AT	6	FR	-1	DK	3	DK	-1
AT	5	FR	-2	IS	6	PL	-3	FR	12	EE	-3	UK	6	DE	-1	LU	3	DE	-1
IT	5	LT	-2	IT	6	ES	-3	IS	12	EL	-3	BE	8	EL	-1	BG	4	EL	-1
UK	5	EU-27	-1	UK	6	FR	-2	LU	14	IT	-3	CZ	8	HU	-1	CZ	4	HU	-1
BE	7	DE	-1	FI	7	AT	-1	DE	15	LU	-3	FI	8	IS	-1	NL	4	LU	-1
FI	7	EL	-1	CY	9	BE	-1	BE	16	SK	-3	DE	8	LT	-1	SK	4	MT	-1
EL	7	MT	-1	DE	9	EU-27	-1	EU-27	16	BG	-2	IS	8	LU	-1	UK	4	SI	-1
CZ	8	RO	-1	EL	9	DE	-1	RO	16	CY	-2	SK	10	SI	-1	EU-27	5	ES	-1
CY	9	SI	-1	BE	10	EL	-1	IT	17	EU-27	-2	EU-27	11	UK	-1	MT	5	SE	-1
EU-27	9	UK	-1	CZ	10	MT	-1	MT	18	DE	-2	PL	11	AT	0	AT	6	AT	0
DE	9	AT	0	EU-27	11	RO	-1	AT	19	HU	-2	FR	13	BE	0	RO	6	BG	0
LT	10	BE	0	FR	14	SI	-1	LV	21	PL	-2	MT	13	BG	0	IS	7	CY	0
ES	10	CY	0	LT	14	CY	0	EE	22	SI	-2	IT	15	DK	0	SE	7	EU-27	0
BG	12	CZ	0	SK	14	DK	0	SK	22	ES	-2	HU	16	EU-27	0	FI	8	FI	0
FR	12	DK	0	ES	14	FI	0	PL	24	DK	-1	LV	16	IT	0	FR	8	IT	0
SK	14	FI	0	SI	16	IS	0	BG	25	IS	-1	ES	17	MT	0	LV	8	LT	0
SI	15	IS	0	PL	17	IT	0	SI	25	LV	-1	SI	18	NL	0	ES	9	NL	0
PL	16	IT	0	LV	21	LU	0	ES	25	NL	-1	EL	19	PL	0	SI	10	PL	0
LV	17	LU	0	BG	22	NL	0	HU	27	RO	-1	RO	20	SK	0	EL	12	RO	0
HU	22	NL	0	HU	27	SE	0	CY	30	UK	-1	EE	26	SE	1	HU	13	SK	0
RO	22	ES	0	PT	27	UK	0	EL	30	SE	0	BG	27	CZ	2	CY	14	LV	1
PT	24	SE	0	RO	27	CZ	2	PT	34	FI	2	CY	29	FI	2	PT	14	UK	1
EE	26	LV	2	EE	29	LV	2	LT	35	CZ	3	PT	32	LV	2	EE	20	CZ	3

and October 2002. By the year 2002, the research took place twice a year. For the e-Europe 2002 action plan the comparative analysis was done only once a year. This research analyzed the results of the fourth evaluation taken in October 2003. Once again 20 services were evaluated.

In the evaluation of e-Europe 2005, the same stages are used as in e-Europe 2002, with some small differences in the first stage. These differences want to prevent two possibilities: a) the provider of the public services does not have an available web site, and b) the public provider has

Table 5. Enterprises using Internet for interaction with public authorities in EU-27 for the period 2005-2010 (Source: Eurostat row data (isoc_pibi_egov))

Enterprises using Internet for obtaining information from public authorities- Indicator 11				Enterprises using Internet for obtaining forms from public authorities– Indicator 12				Enterprises using Internet for returning filled in forms to public authorities- Indicator 13				Enterprises using Internet for interaction with public authorities - for full electronic case handling– Indicator 14				Enterprises using Internet for interaction with public authorities - for e-procurement- Indicator 15			
Percentage of enterprises All, without financial sector (10 employed persons or more)																			
countries	annual average for the years 2005-2010	countries	annual average change for the years 2005-2010	countries	annual average for the years 2005-2010	countries	annual average change for the years 2005-2010	countries	annual average for the years 2005-2010	countries	annual average change for the years 2005-2010	countries	annual average for the years 2005-2010	countries	annual average change for the years 2005-2010	countries	annual average for the years 2005-2010	countries	annual average change for the years 2005-2010
RO	44	EL	-3	RO	42	FR	-2	CY	14	FR	-8	CZ	19	FR	##	FI	0	EL	-2
BG	46	FR	-2	BG	43	EL	-2	RO	29	EL	0	CY	25	EL	-8	CY	1	CZ	-1
DE	48	LT	0	CY	46	LT	-1	BG	34	MT	1	NL	26	PT	-7	ES	5	BG	0
LV	49	BE	0	LV	48	AT	0	LV	34	CY	2	PL	28	LT	-4	LV	6	FI	0
UK	54	FI	1	BE	50	FI	1	CZ	38	PL	2	LV	30	AT	-2	SK	6	FR	0
CY	55	DK	1	DE	51	SE	2	ES	42	NL	2	BG	31	DK	1	BE	7	IS	0
PL	56	SE	2	UK	51	DK	2	UK	43	LT	3	RO	31	MT	1	NL	7	UK	0
ES	56	ES	2	PL	56	ES	2	IT	45	AT	3	SE	33	SK	1	DK	8	AT	1
BE	57	CZ	2	ES	56	BE	3	DE	46	ES	3	**EU -27**	38	CZ	2	SI	8	BE	1
HU	57	EE	2	HU	58	EE	3	MT	46	DK	3	DE	38	IS	4	BG	9	CY	1
EU -27	**60**	AT	3	**EU -27**	**59**	CZ	4	BE	48	FI	3	HU	38	BG	4	PL	9	EE	1
FR	60	IT	3	FR	61	IT	4	**EU -27**	48	EE	4	MT	38	ES	4	**EU -27**	10	**EU -27**	1
AT	64	**EU -27**	**3**	EL	65	**EU -27**	4	LU	48	SE	4	ES	39	UK	4	HU	10	DE	1
PT	65	SI	3	PT	65	LU	4	SK	48	CZ	5	UK	39	EE	5	MT	10	HU	1
EL	68	NL	4	CZ	67	IS	4	HU	49	**EU -27**	5	AT	40	**EU -27**	5	CZ	11	LT	1
NL	68	IS	4	MT	69	NL	4	FR	53	BE	7	IT	43	SE	6	FR	11	MT	1
CZ	72	MT	4	NL	69	SI	5	AT	54	SI	7	DK	46	BE	7	EL	11	SK	1
EE	73	UK	4	EE	71	UK	5	SE	57	LV	7	BE	47	CY	7	RO	11	SI	1
IT	74	CY	4	IT	72	MT	5	EE	59	UK	7	SK	48	FI	8	UK	11	ES	1
LT	74	PL	4	AT	74	PL	5	PL	60	PT	7	FI	49	SI	8	DE	12	DK	2
MT	74	BG	6	LT	76	PT	5	DK	62	IT	8	LU	49	LV	8	IT	12	LV	2
SK	75	PT	6	SK	76	SK	7	NL	63	BG	8	PT	49	IT	13	PT	12	NL	2
IS	79	LU	6	SI	76	BG	7	SI	63	IS	9	FR	50	PL	14	SE	13	PT	2
SI	79	DE	7	IS	79	DE	7	EL	65	SK	9	EE	51	HU	16	AT	14	SE	2
SE	80	HU	7	SE	79	HU	7	IS	65	DE	10	LT	53	RO	16	EE	14	PL	3
LU	82	SK	7	DK	83	CY	8	LT	66	HU	10	EL	55	NL	17	LU	14	IT	4
DK	84	RO	8	LU	85	LV	8	PT	67	RO	13	IS	57	DE	22	LT	15	RO	4
FI	89	LV	8	FI	91	RO	9	FI	80	LU	15	SI	60	LU	31	IS	21	LU	5

an available web side, but the web site does not have any relevant information, one way or two way communication, for the evaluating public e-service. A scoring framework of Action Plan e-Europe 2005 was defined as follows:

- **Stage 1 (Electronic Publication of the Necessary Information):** All the necessary information should be available on the public services' web site

- **Stage 2 (One Way Interaction):** On the web site should be available all the printable forms and applications (but not e-applications)
- **Stage 3 (Two Way Interaction):** All applications and forms should have on line delivery to the user. The user should be able to fill in the applications and forms electronically. In this stage authentication and identification of the user are needed.
- **Stage 4 (Complete Electronic Transactions):** On the web site should be available fully (electronically) executable services, such as payments, application responses, with no further procedures.
- **Stage 0:** Either there is not a freely available web site of the public service or there is one but it is not qualified.

The same methodology problems appeared in the evaluation framework, that of Action plan e-Europe's 2002: a) the developed methodology is about the availability of public services, through the Internet, which means that all the other available public services distributed in other ways should not be evaluated (e.g. call centers, DTV, mobile devices), and b) only the public electronic services that are available on line are evaluated.

Strategic Framework i2010 and eGov Evaluation Framework

In September 2007, according to the 7th Measurement (European Commission, 2007) of Strategic Framework i2010, an unchanged eGov indicator on the number of public services fully available on line, continued to be measured on the existing 4 level model and the same sample of 20 public services (see Table 1 & Table 2) was evaluated. The 7th measurement has extended the existing Framework by including a fifth level of sophistication that was dealing with pro-activity and personalization and the new online sophistication eGov indicator was based on a renewed 5 level model. This 5th stage, sophistication (personalization) level, included the idea of pro-active service delivery. It was an indication of the extent to which the government pro-actively performs actions to enhance delivery quality and user friendliness. Also in this level the idea of automatic service delivery was included, which meant that the government automatically provides specific services linked to a certain condition of the user, without the user to request the service. The sophistication of online services was measured by using the following five stages:

- **Stage 1:** Information
- **Stage 2:** One way interaction (downloadable forms)
- **Stage 3:** Two way interaction (electronic forms)
- **Stage 4:** Transaction (Full electronic case handling)
- **Stage 5:** Personalization (pro-active, automated)

Among other things, they tried to identify: a) if the online provision of the 20 services (see Table 1 & Table 2) was based on reengineering of front and back offices, and b) if available data are reused, and if the "idea of a proactive delivery exists." Proactive delivery means that for certain services, citizen/customer receives the services automatically based on a previous registration of an event and no other physical action is required on behalf of the citizen.

In this benchmark, the following indicators have been measured:

- The old indicator which measured "the number of public services fully available online," based on the existing 4 level model as the previous measurements that of e-Europe 2002 and e-Europe2005. This happened in order for evaluation to continue to have a historical base.
- User centricity indicators which are a composition of four sub-indicators

- National portals were assessed in order to evaluate if European Governments concerning 20 services, had personalized (my portal) and consistent layout

The main change in this measurement method was with respect to: i) sophistication indicator and ii) full online availability by indicator as well as country rankings and analysis of services cluster.

Additionally, an effort to categorize countries has been made, and countries were ranked according to sophistication and availability and some countries appeared to be "Fast Movers." Four service baskets (service clusters) were evaluated, such as: income generating (for government); registration; service returns; and permits and licenses. An indicator of user-Centricity was composed of elements of: data security, reducing administrative burden, multichannel access, and compliance with accessibility standards. A composite indicator for user centricity was structured. Citizens were treated as customers and the main idea was "if governments seek to engage customers they must enable not only the services that deliver funds into government, but also those that deliver value to customers" (European Commission, 2007, p. 6). The sample of 20 services was the same as in previous measurements, 31 countries participated (27 member states plus Iceland, Norway, Switzerland, and Turkey).

At that time, EU mainly focused on the supply side and started to monitor the demand side, after the strategic Framework i2010, by measuring the percentage of individuals and enterprises using the Internet for interacting with public authorities. In the i2010 benchmarking framework (i2010 High Level Group, 2006) mix indicators were measuring the different aspects of the objectives that should be achieved. Focus was given on impact and usage of technologies. Therefore, a special module was measured: a) skills & digital literacy and b) ICT adoption for enterprises. Also, inclusion metrics evaluated: a) the reasons for not having internet access at home and the reasons for not having broadband at home and b) the different places for accessing internet (e.g. at home, at place of work, at place of education, at another person's home, at public Internet Access Points).

Concerning the public services (i2010 High Level Group, 2006), eGov needs to be benchmarked according to supplementary indicators:

- **Availability and Sophistication:** By using the eGov indicator "Number of Basic (20 services) Public services fully available on line. The data were collected by using the same methodology which was used in eEurope 2002 measurement framework.
- **Take-Up of Online Public**: Services by using one eGov indicator for individuals" Percentage of Individuals using the Internet for interacting with public authorities broken down by purpose (purposes: obtaining information, obtaining forms, returning filled in forms) and, one eGov indicator for enterprises "Percentage of enterprises using the Internet for interacting with public authorities broken down on purpose (purposes: obtaining information, obtaining forms, returning filled in forms, full electronic case, submitted proposal in an electronic tender system (e-procurement)).
- **Impact:** Back offices restructuring and impact on users.

Digital Agenda 2020 and eGov Evaluation Framework

For the evaluation of Digital Agenda 2020, EU created an evaluation mechanism called Score-Board (Scoreboard), where graphs, progress by country and progress by target are available, on line. For the first time in Digital Agenda 2020 EU establishes key performance targets and an evaluation system (Scoreboard) closely related to its pillars. The pillars of Digital Agenda are:

- **Pillar I:** Digital Single Market
- **Pillar II:** Interoperability & Standards
- **Pillar III:** Trust & Security
- **Pillar IV:** Fast and ultra-fast Internet access
- **Pillar V:** Research and innovation
- **Pillar VI:** Enhancing digital literacy, skills and inclusion
- **Pillar VII:** ICT-enabled benefits for EU society

Priority was given to the Internet but there are seven obstacles that prevent the exploitation of ICT including: 1) fragmented digital markets, 2) lack of interoperability, 3) rising of cybercrime and the risk of low trust in networks, 4) lack of investment in networks, 5) insufficient research and innovation efforts, 6) lack of digital literacy and skills, 7) missed opportunities in addressing societal challenges. (Comission of the European Communities, 2010). Also, key performance targets of Digital Agenda 2020 (European Comission, 2012) are the following:

1. The entire EU to be covered by broadband by 2013,
2. The entire EU to be covered by broadband above 30 Mbps and 50% of the EU to subscribe to broadband above 100Mbps by 2020,
3. 50% of the population to buy online by 2015,
4. 20% of the population to buy online cross-border by 2015,
5. 32% of SMEs to make online sales by 2015,
6. The difference between roaming and national tariffs to approach zero by 2015,
7. To increase regular usage from 60% to 75% by 2015 and from 41% to 60% among disadvantaged people,
8. To halve the proportion of the population that has never used the Internet from 30% to 15% by 2015,
9. 50% of citizens to use eGov by 2015 and 25% of citizens returning completed forms,
10. All key cross-border public services, to be agreed by Member States in 2011, to be available online by 2015,
11. To double public investment in ICT R&D to 11bn Euro by 2020.

DATA ANALYSIS OF EGOV EVALUATION INDICATORS IN EU-27

We surveyed Eurostat Database and gathered data concerning eGov that to help us to recognize if the ambitious targets of Digital Agenda 2020 set realistic and feasible targets for all countries member states of EU-27. We estimated the annual average as well the annual average change for the years 2005-2010 for 18 eGov indicators for years 2005-2010, as follows:

- eGov usage Indicator concerning services (supply side):

Indicator 1: "Online availability and interactivity of public services (supply side)"

- eGov usage Indicators concerning Individuals (Demand side):

Indicator 2: Internet use: obtaining information from public authorities,
Indicator 3: Internet use: downloading official forms from public authorities
Indicator 4: Internet use: sending filled forms

- Internet use by Individuals:

Indicator 5: Internet use: Individuals never used Internet

- Reasons for not having Internet access at home

Indicator 6: Households without access to Internet at home, because the access costs are too high (telephone, etc.)

Indicator 7: Households without access to Internet at home, because the equipment costs are too high

Indicator 8: Households without access to Internet at home, because access not needed (content is not useful, not interesting, etc.)

Indicator 9: Households without access to Internet at home, because of lack of skills

Indicator 10: Households without access to Internet at home, because access is not wanted (content is harmful, etc.)

- eGov usage Indicators concerning enterprises (Demand side):

Indicator 11: Enterprises using Internet for obtaining information from public authorities

Indicator 12: Enterprises using Internet for obtaining forms from public authorities

Indicator 13: Enterprises using Internet for returning filled in forms to public authorities

Indicator 14: Enterprises using Internet for interaction with public authorities for full electronic handling

Indicator 15: Enterprises using Internet for interaction with public authorities for e-procurement

- Indicators concerning Usage of Internet for economic purposes by individuals and enterprises:
- Internet purchases by Individuals:

Indicator 16: Individuals who never ordered goods or services, over the Internet, for private use

Indicator 17: Last online by individuals purchase: in the last 3 months

- Internet Sales by Enterprises

Indicator 18: Enterprises selling online (at least 1% of turnover), SMEs (10-249 persons employed), without financial sector

eGov Availability in EU-27 for the Years 2005-2010

What is the Level of "Online Availability and Interactivity of Public Services"?

In all Action plans, Europe mainly evaluated the indicator of online availability and interactivity of public services (supply side)/the Percentage of 20 basic services. The annual average of "Online availability and interactivity of public services-the Percentage of 20 basic services" for the years 2005-2010 is very low for some countries and very high for some others (see Table 9, Figure 2). E-government online availability is an indicator that shows the percentage of the 20 basic services (see Table 1 & Table 2) which are fully available online, i.e. for which it is possible to carry out full electronic case handling. For example if in a country 13 of the 20 services were measured as being 100% available online and one service was not relevant (e.g. does not exist), the indicator is 13/19 which is 68.4%. Measurement is based on a sample of URLs of public web sites agreed among Member States to be relevant to each service.

The annual average of "online availability and interactivity of public services-the percentage of 20 basic services" for the year 2005-2010 for EU-27 the annual average is 70%, and rose to 97% in Austria and decreases to 38% in Bulgaria. The annual average change of the percentage of 20 basic services is positive for the years 2005-2010 for all European countries in EU-27 and varies from 3% in Esthonia to 21% in Latvia (see Table 1, Figure 1).

Figure 1. Annual change of online availability and interactivity of public services (supply side) of European Countries-EU27 for the years 2005-2010

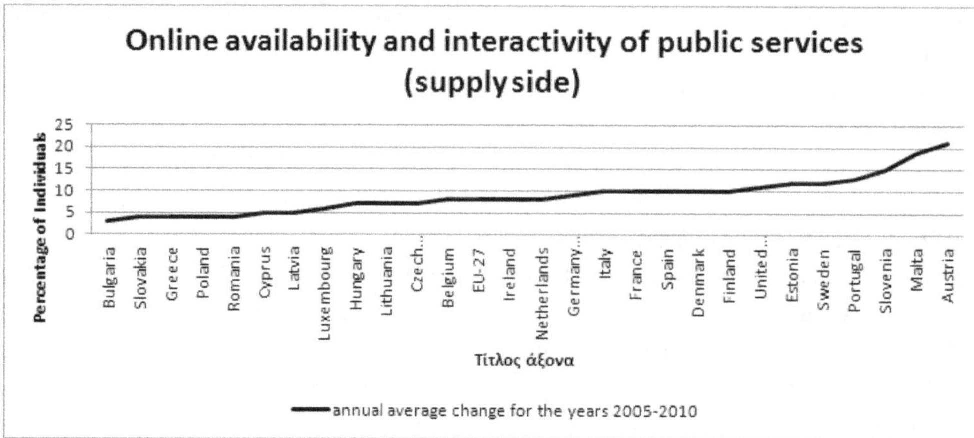

eGov use by Individuals in EU-27 for the Years 2005-2010

How Many Europeans Used eGov Services for Obtaining Information from Public Authorities?

Eventhough, availability is high the use of eGov for the years 2005-2010 is very low, the annual average of "individuals who used internet obtaining information from public authorities" for the years 2005-2010, rose 54% (5 individuals in every 10 individuals) in Denmark and decreased to 5% (1 individual in every 10 individuals) in Romania. The total annual average for EU-27 in this period is 25%, which means that approximately 3 individuals in every 10 individuals obtained information from public authorities every year. The annual average change of individuals who "used internet obtaining information from public authorities" for the years 2005-2010, rose 7% to Denmark and decreased to 1% to Finland. The annual average change of EU-27 is 1% for this period (see Table 2, Figure 2).

How Many Europeans Used eGov Services for Downloading Official Forms from Public Authorities?

The annual average of "individuals who used internet downloading official forms public authorities" for the years 2005-2010, rose 35% (4 individuals in every 10 individuals) in Luxembourg and decreased to 3% (no individual in every 10 individuals) in Romania. The total annual average for EU-27 in this period is 15%, which means that approximately 2 individuals in every 10 individuals download official forms from public authorities every year. The annual average change of individuals who "used internet downloading information from public authorities" for the years 2005-2010, rose 5% in Denmark and decreased to 5% in Finland. The annual average change of EU-27 is 2% for this period (see Table 2, Figure 2).

How Many Europeans Used eGov Services for Sending Filled Forms to Public Authorities?

The annual average of "individuals who are sending filled forms to public authorities" for the years 2005-2010, rose 32% (3 individuals in every 10

Figure 2. Annual change of use of Internet by Individuals for interaction with public authorities for the period 2005-2010 in EU-27

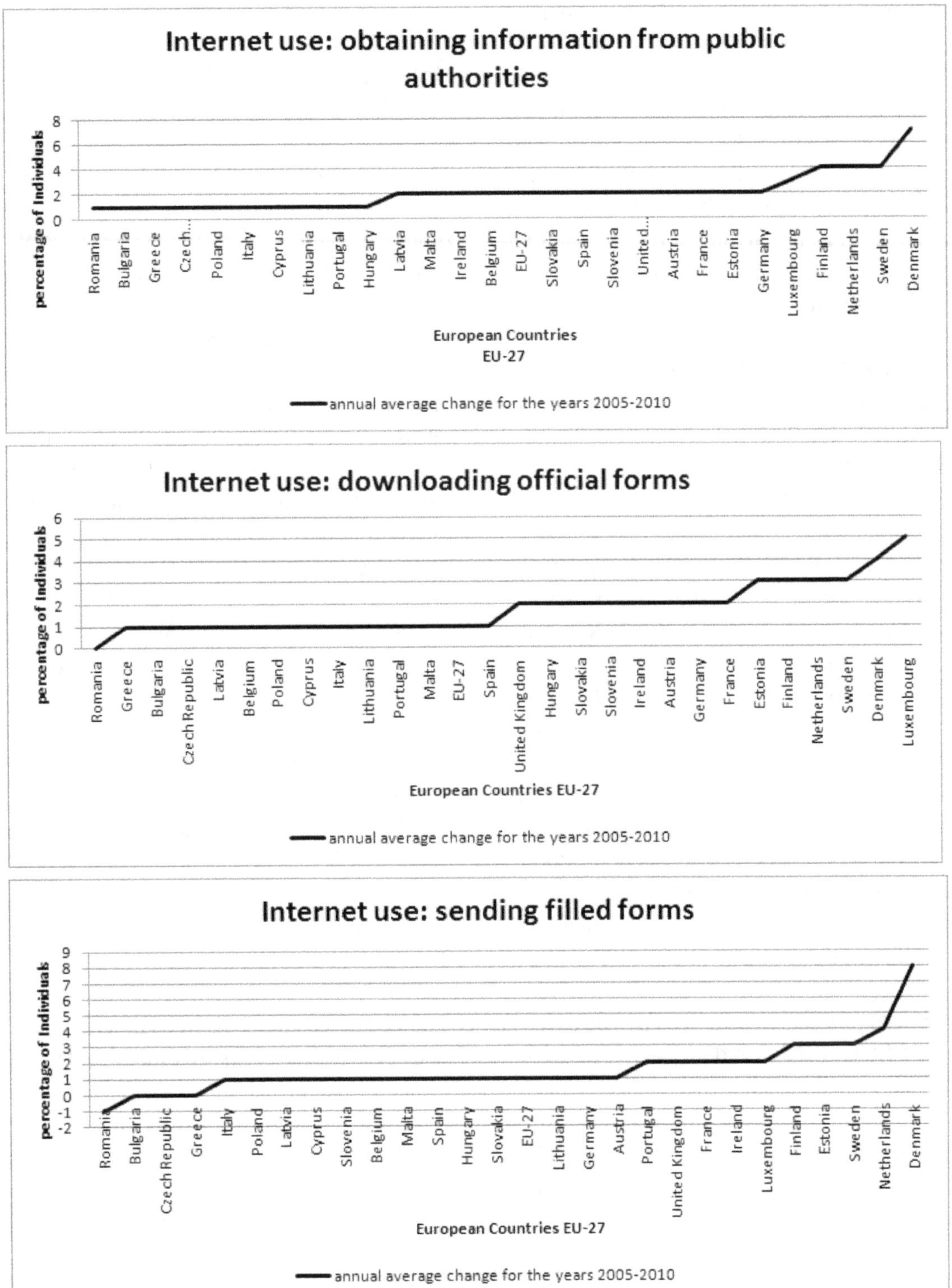

individuals) in Denmark and decreased to 3% (1 individual in every 10 individuals) in Romania. The total annual average for EU-27 in this period is 11%, that means that approximately 1 individual in every 10 individuals download official forms from public authorities every year in EU-27. The annual average change of individuals who are sending filled forms to public authorities for the years 2005-2010, rose 8% in Denmark and decreased to -1% in Luxembourg. The annual average change of EU-27 is 1% for this period (see Table 2, Figure 2).

Use of Internet in EU-27 for the Years 2005-2010

Are there Europeans That Never Used the Internet?

The annual average of "individuals who had never used Internet" for the years 2005-2010, rose 65% (7 individuals in every 10 citizens) in Romania and decreased to 10% (1 individual in every 10 individuals) in Sweden. The total annual average for EU-27 in this period is 35%, that means that approximately 4 individuals in every 10 individuals had never used internet in EU-27. The annual average change of individuals who sending filled forms to public authorities for the years 2005-2010, rose -1% in Denmark and decreased to -7% in Checz Republic. The annual average change of EU-27 is -3% for this period (see Table3, Figure 3).

Why Some Individuals Never Used Internet in EU-27 for the Years 2005-2010?

Europe must investigate the reasons why eGov usage is very low. One reason might be that individuals do not have internet at home. There are European citizens that do not have access at home because they estimate that: access cost is too high (telephone, etc), or there is lack of skills, or the content is not useful, or the equipment costs are too high, or content is harmful.

How Many Europeans do not have Internet at Home, Because They Think Access Cost is Too High?

The annual average of "individuals who don't have internet access because the access costs are too high (telephone, etc.)" for the years 2005-2010, rose 26% (3 individuals in every 10 individuals) in Esthonia and decreased to 1% (no citizen in 10 citizens) in Luxembourg. The total annual average for EU-27 in this period is 9%, which means that approximately 1 individual in every 10 individuals don't have internet access because the access costs are too high (telephone, etc.) every year in EU-27. The annual average change of individuals who don't have internet access at home because the access costs are too high (telephone, etc.) for the years 2005-2010, rose 2% in Latvia and decreased to -5% in Portugal. The annual average change of EU-27 is -1% for this period (see Table 4, Figure 4).

How Many Europeans do not have Internet at Home, Because they Estimate that the Equipment Costs are too High?

The annual average of "individuals who don't have Internet at home because the equipment costs are too high" for the years 2005-2010, rose 29% (3 individuals in every 10 individuals) in Esthonia and decreased to 1% in Luxembourg. The total annual average for EU-27 in this period is 11%, that means that approximately 1 individual in every 10 individuals don't have Internet at home because the equipment costs are too high every year in EU-27. The annual average change of individuals who don't have Internet at home because the equipment costs are too high for the years 2005-2010, rose 2% in Latvia and decreased to -5% to Portugal.

Figure 3. Annual change of individuals that have never used Internet in EU-27 for the period 2005-2010

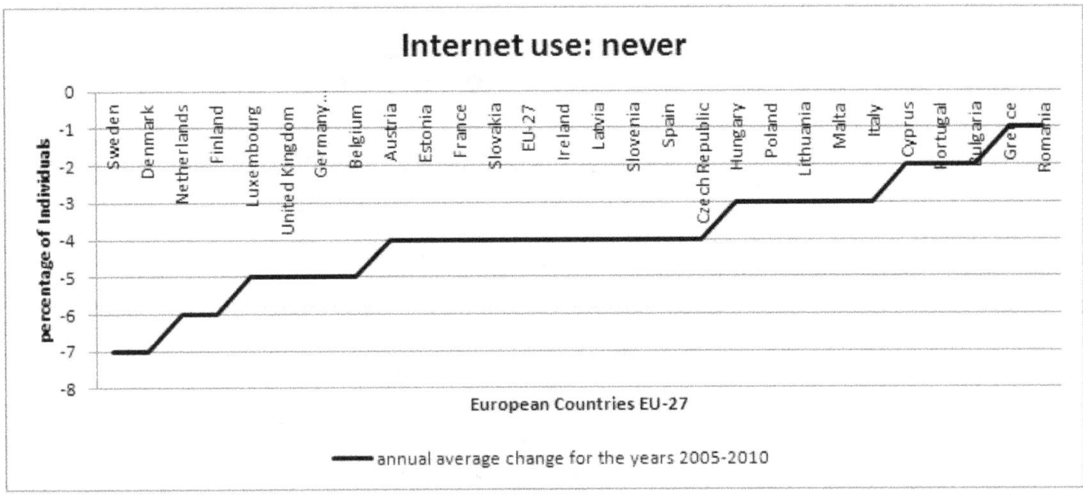

The annual average change of EU-27 is -1% for this period (see Table 4, Figure 4).

How Many Europeans do not have Internet at Home, Because They Think Content is not Useful or Interesting?

The annual average of *individuals who don't have Internet at home* because access not needed (content is not useful, not interesting, etc.) for the years 2005-2010, rose 35% (4 individual in every 10 individuals) in Lithouania and decreased to 7% (1 individual in every 10 individuals) in Netherlands. The total annual average for EU-27 in this period is 16%, which means that approximately 2 individuals in every 10 individuals don't have Internet at home because access is not needed (content is not useful, not interesting, etc.) every year in EU-27. The annual average change of individuals who don't have Internet at home because access is not needed (content is not useful, not interesting, etc.) for the years 2005-2010, rose 3% to Chech Republic and decreased to -5% in France. The annual average change of EU-27 is -2% for this period (see Table 4, Figure 4).

How Many Europeans do not have Internet at Home, Because They Think There is lack of Skills?

The annual average of *"individuals who don't have Internet at home* because of lack of skills" for the years 2005-2010, rose 32% (3 individuals in every 10 individuals) in Potugal and decreased to 2% (1 individual in every 10 individuals) in Denmark. The total annual average for EU-27 in this period is 11%, which means that approximately 1 individual in every 10 individuals don't have Internet at home because of lack of skills every year in EU-27. The annual average change of individuals who don't have Internet at home because of lack of skills for the years 2005-2010, rose 2% in Latvia and decreased to -3% in Romania. The annual average change of EU-27 is 0% for this period (see Table 4, Figure 4).

How Many Europeans do not have Internet at Home, Because They Think the Content is Harmful?

The annual average of "individuals who don't have Internet at home Households because access not wanted (content is harmful, etc.)" for the years

Figure 4. Annual change of reasons why households do not have Internet at home in EU-27 for the period 2005-2010

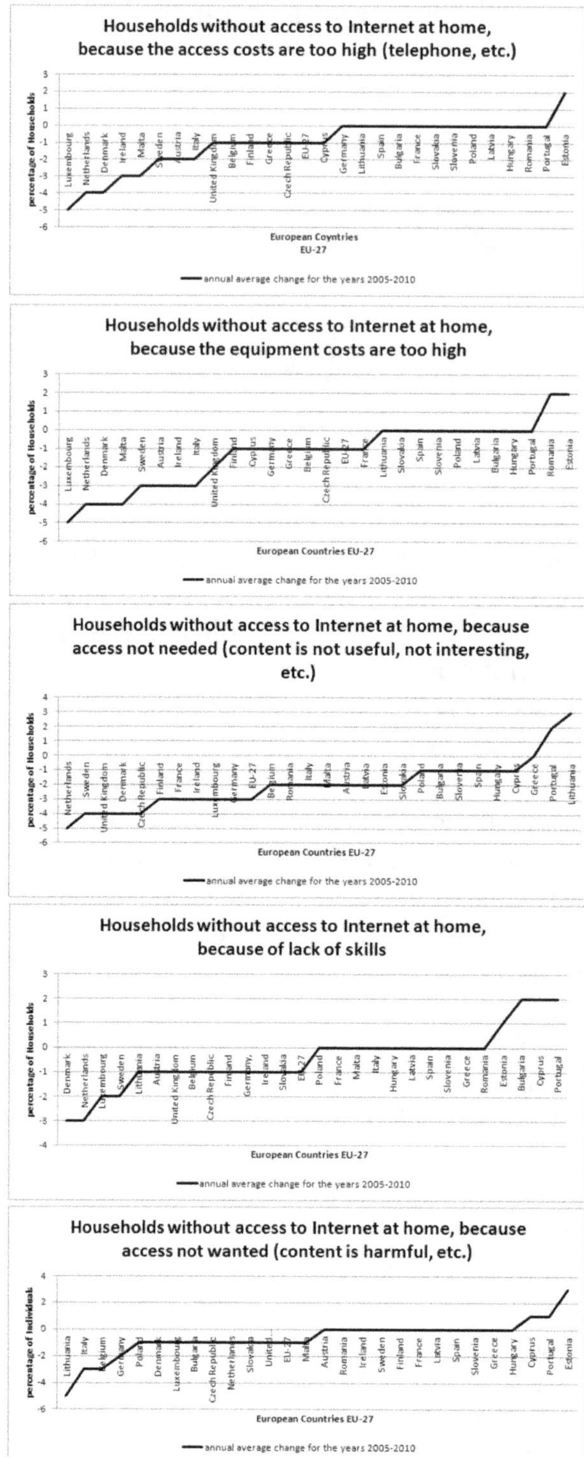

2005-2010, rose 20% (2 individuals in every 10 individuals) in Estonia and decreased to 0% (no individual in every 10 individuals) in Lithuania. The total annual average for EU-27 in this period is 5%, that means that approximately 1 individual in every 10 individuals don't have Internet at home because access is not wanted (content is harmful, etc.) every year in EU-27. The annual average change of individuals who don't have Internet at home because access not wanted (content is harmful, etc.) for the years 2005-2010, rose 3% in Chech Republic and decreased to -5% in France. The annual average change of EU-27 is 0% for this period (see Table 4, Figure 4).

Use of eGov Services by Enterprises in EU-27 for the Years 2005-2010

How Many Enterprises use Internet for Obtaining Information from Public Authorities?

The annual average of *"enterprises* using Internet for obtaining information from public authorities" for the years 2005-2010, rose 89% (9 individuals in every 10 individuals) in Finland and decreased to 44% (5 enterprises in every 10 enterprises) in Romania. The total annual average for EU-27 in this period is 60%, which means that approximately 6 enterprises in every 10 enterprises use Internet for obtaining information from public authorities every year in EU-27. The annual average change of enterprises using Internet for obtaining information from public authorities for the years 2005-2010, rose 8% to Latvia and decreased to -3% to Greece. The annual average change of EU-27 is 3% for this period (see Table 5, Figure 5).

How Many Enterprises use Internet for Obtaining Forms from Public Authorities?

The annual average of "enterprises using Internet for obtaining forms from public authorities" for the years 2005-2010, rose 91% (9 individuals in every 10 individuals) in Finland and decreased to 42% (4 enterprises in every 10 enterprises) in Romania. The total annual average for EU-27 in this period is 59%, which means that approximately 6 enterprises in every 10 enterprises using Internet for obtaining forms from public authorities every year in EU-27. The annual average change of enterprises using Internet for obtaining forms from public authorities for the years 2005-2010, rose 9% in Romania and decreased to -2% in France. The annual average change of EU-27 is 4% for this period (see Table 5, Figure 5).

How Many Enterprises use Internet for Returning Completed Forms to Authorities?

The annual average of "enterprises using Internet for returning filled in forms to public authorities" for the years 2005-2010, rose 80% (8 enterprises in every 10 enterprises) in Finland and decreased to 14% (1 enterprise in every 10 enterprises) in Cyprus. The total annual average for EU-27 in this period is 48%, that means that approximately 5 enterprises using Internet for returning filled in forms to public authorities every year in EU-27 The annual average change of enterprises using Internet for returning filled in forms to public authorities for the years 2005-2010, rose 15% in Luxembourg and decreased to -8% in France. The annual average change of EU-27 is 5% for this period (see Table 5, Figure 5).

How Many Enterprises use Internet for Interaction with Public Authorities for Full Electronic Case Handling?

The annual average of "enterprises using Internet for interaction with public authorities for full electronic case handling" for the years 2005-2010, rose 60% (6 enterprises in every 10 enterprises) in Slovenia and decreased to 19% (2 enterprises in evewry 10 enterprises) in Czech Republic. The

Figure 5. Enterprises using Internet for interaction with public authorities in EU-27 for the period 2005-2010

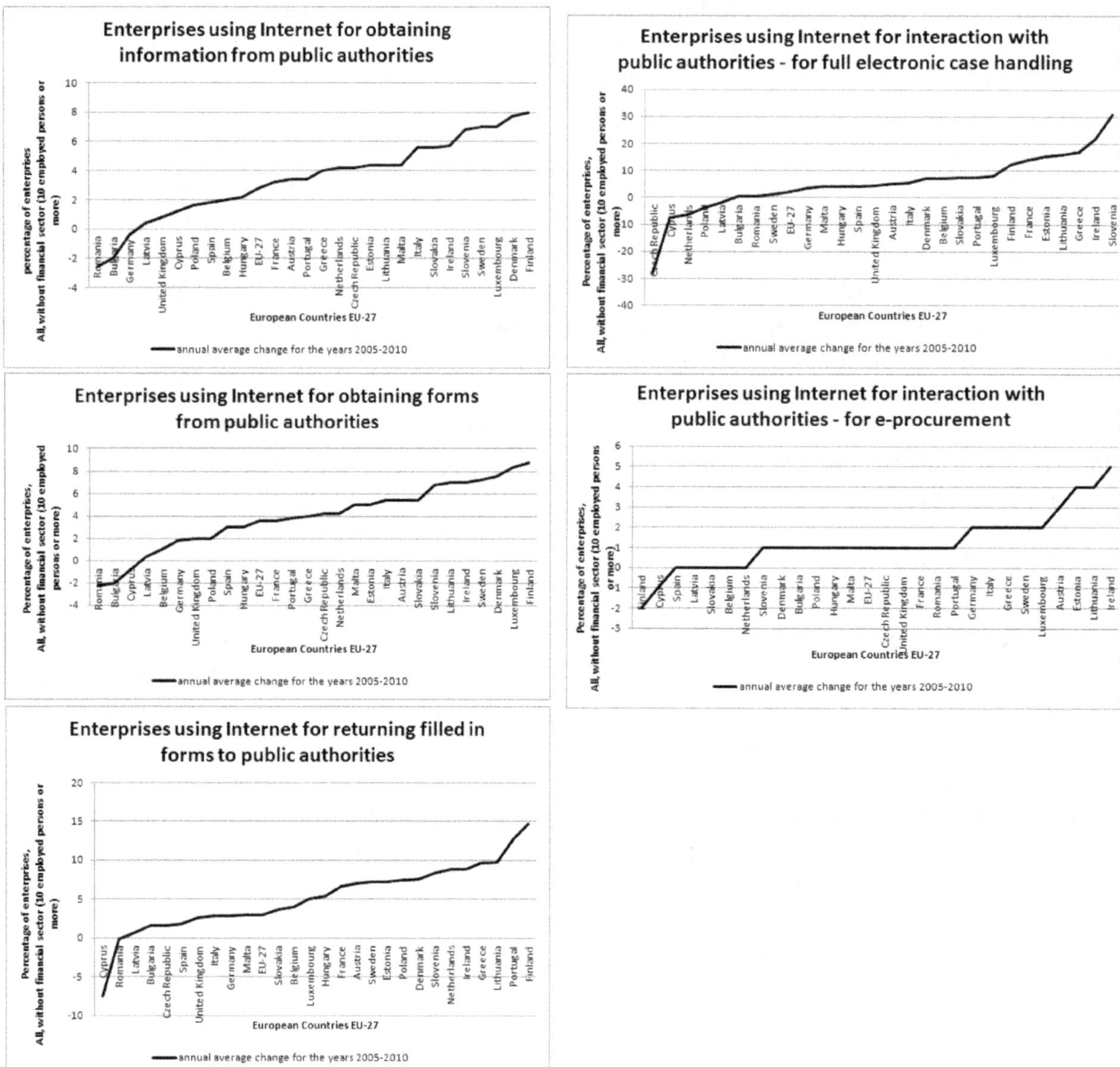

total annual average for EU-27 in this period is 38%, which means that approximately 4 enterprises in every 10 enterprises are using Internet for interaction with public authorities for full electronic case handling every year in EU-27. The annual average change of enterprises using Internet for interaction with public authorities for full electronic case handling for the years 2005-2010, rose 31% in Luxembourg and decreased to -28% in France. The annual average change of EU-27 is 5% for this period (see Table 5, Figure 5).

The annual average of "enterprises using Internet for interaction with public authorities for e-procurement" for the years 2005-2010, rose 21% (2 enterprises in every 10 enterprises) in Ireland and decreased to 0% (no enterprise in every 10 enterprises) in Finland. The total annual average for EU-27 in this period is 10%,which means that approximately 1 enterprise enterprise is using Internet for interaction with public authorities for e-procurement every year in EU-27. The annual average change of enterprises using Internet for interaction with public authorities for e-procurement for the years 2005-2010, rose 5% in Luxembourg and decreased to -2% in Greece. The annual average change of EU-27 is 4 for this period (see Table 5, Figure 5).

Use of Internet for Economic Purposes by Individuals and Enterprises in EU-27 for Years 2005-2010

Are There Europeans that have Never Used Internet to Buy/Order Online Goods or Services?

It concerns "individuals never having ordered/bought goods or services for private use over the internet in the last three months." This indicator covers all individuals aged 16 to 74. Financial investments are excluded.

The annual average of individuals never having ordered/bought goods or services for private use over the internet in the last three months for the years 2005-2010, rose 56% (6 individuals in every 10 individuals) in Estonia and decreased to 20% (2 individuals in every 10 individuals) in Germany. The total annual average for EU-27 in this period is 29%, which means that approximately 3 individuals have never ordered/bought goods or services for private use over the internet in the last three months every year in EU-27. The annual average change of individuals that have never ordered/bought goods or services for private use over the internet in the last three months for the years 2005-2010, rose 4% in Bulgaria and decreased to -3% in Denmark. The annual average change of EU-27 is 0 for this period (see Table 6, Figure 6).

Do Europeans Usually Buy Online Goods or Services via Internet?

It concerns "individuals bought goods or services for private use over the internet in the last three months." This indicator covers all individuals aged 16 to 74. Financial investments are excluded.

The annual average of individuals bought goods or services for private use over the internet in the last three months for the years 2005-2010, rose 48% (5 individuals in every 10 individuals) in United Kingdom and decreased to 2% (no individual in every 10 individuals) in Bulgaria. The total annual average for EU-27 in this period is 24%, which means that approximately 2 individuals bought goods or services for private use over the internet in the last three months every year in EU-27. The annual average change of individuals bought goods or services for private use over the internet in the last three months in the last three months for the years 2005-2010, rose 6% in Denmark and decreased to 3% in Bulgaria. The annual average change of EU-27 is 0 for this period (see Table 6, Figure 6).

Do SMEs Usually Sell Online (at Least 1% of Turnover) via Internet?

It concerns the percentage of "SMEs (10-249 persons employed), without financial sector selling online (at least 1% of turnover)"

The annual average of "SMEs (10-249 persons employed), without financial sector that selling online (at least 1% of turnover) for the years 2005-2010, rose 24% (2 individuals in every 10 individuals) in Sweden and decreased to 4% (no individuals in every 10 individuals) in Bulgaria. The total annual average for EU-27 in this period is 13%, that means that approximately 1 enterprise in every 10 enterprises sells online every year in EU-27. The annual average change of enterprises selling online for the years 2005-2010, rose 7% in Denmark and decreased to -4% in Bulgaria.

Table 6. Usage of Internet for economic purposes by individuals and enterprises in EU-27 for the period 2005-2010 (Source: Eurostat data (isoc_bde15dec))

Internet purchases by individuals Individuals who never ordered goods or services, over the Internet, for private use- Indicator 16				Internet purchases by individuals Last online purchase: in the last 3 months- Indicator 17				SMEs (10-249 persons employed), without financial sector Enterprises selling online (at least 1% of turnover)-Indicator 18 (data available 2010-2011)			
Percentage of individuals											
countries	annual average for the years 2005-2010	countries	annual average change for the years 2005-2010	countries	annual average for the years 2005-2010	countries	annual average change for the years 2005-2010	countries	annual average for the years 2005-2010	countries	annual average change for the years 2005-2010
DE	20	DK	-3	BG	2	BG	0	BG	4	BE	-4
UK	20	NL	-3	RO	2	RO	0	IT	4	AT	-3
DK	22	SE	-3	LT	4	EL	1	RO	5	DK	-3
SE	25	BE	-2	EL	6	HU	1	CY	7	PT	-3
MT	26	FI	-2	HU	7	IT	1	EL	7	FR	-2
NL	26	FR	-2	IT	7	LV	1	HU	8	EL	-2
LU	27	DE	-2	LV	7	LT	1	LV	8	NL	-2
FR	28	SK	-2	PT	7	PT	1	SK	10	RO	-2
IS	28	AT	-1	EE	8	CY	2	EE	11	BG	-1
EU-27	**29**	LU	-1	CY	9	CZ	2	FR	11	**EU-27**	**-1**
FI	29	MT	-1	CZ	10	EE	2	SI	11	LT	-1
RO	29	PL	-1	SI	11	SI	2	AT	12	MT	-1
AT	31	UK	-1	SK	12	ES	2	ES	12	ES	-1
EL	31	EE	0	PL	13	AT	3	**EU-27**	**13**	CY	0
IT	32	**EU-27**	**0**	ES	13	BE	3	UK	14	IT	0
PL	32	LV	0	BE	18	**EU-27**	**3**	LU	15	SE	0
CY	33	SI	0	MT	18	FI	3	FI	16	UK	0
PT	34	ES	0	**EU-27**	**24**	DE	3	MT	16	EE	1
BG	36	CY	1	IS	25	IS	3	PT	17	FI	1
CZ	37	IS	1	AT	27	LU	3	NL	20	LU	1
ES	37	PT	1	FR	29	PL	3	CZ	22	SI	1
SI	39	CZ	2	FI	33	SK	3	IS	22	HU	2
BE	41	EL	2	LU	39	SE	3	LT	22	IS	3
HU	42	IT	2	DE	41	MT	4	BE	23	LV	3
SK	43	HU	3	SE	41	NL	4	DK	24	CZ	6
LV	44	LT	3	DK	42	FR	5	SE	24	SK	7
LT	46	RO	3	NL	42	UK	5	DE	*	DE	*
EE	56	BG	4	UK	48	DK	6	PL	*	PL	*

*data not available

Figure 6. Online purchases by Individuals in the last 3 months and individuals who never ordered goods or services over the internet in EU-27 for the period 2005-2010

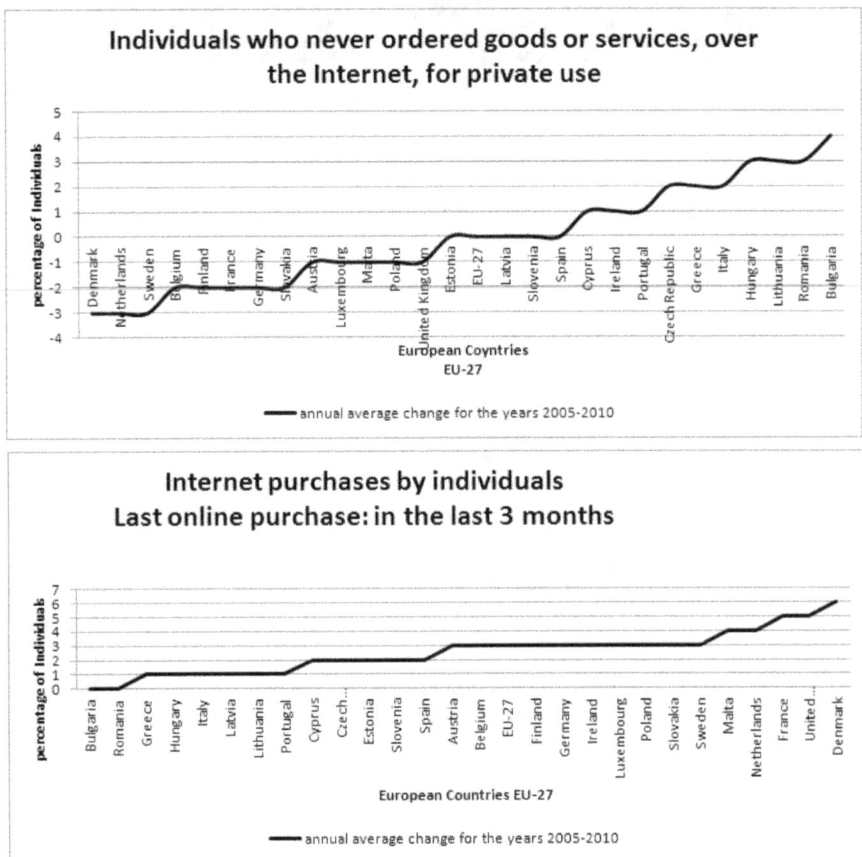

The annual average change of EU-27 is -1 for this period (see Table 6, Figure 7).

Digital Agenda 2010 Targets Accomplishment by 2015 - Predictions of eGov Indicators

How easy is it for 50% of the population to buy online by 2015 and 20% of the population to buy online cross-border by 2015 (key performance targets of digital agenda 2020?)

Europe, according to existing trends, will reach this target by 2015, but major differences will exist among member states of EU-27. We estimate that the proportion of individuals that purchase online will vary between 2% to 85% in 2015 and the average total of EU-27 will be 46%. Also the proportion of individuals never used Internet will vary from 0% to37% and the average total of EU-27 will be 12% in 2015 (see Table 7).

A main target of digital agenda 2020 is that 50% of citizens use eGov by 2015, with more than half returning completed forms (key performance targets of digital agenda 2020). is it possible that at least 50% of citizens use eGov by 2015 and at least 25% of citizens return completed forms?

This target is difficult to be accomplished if the trends do not change. The proportion of individuals that used Internet sending filled forms to

Table 7. Predictions of eGov indicators in 2015

INDICTATORS	Lowest value in 2015	highest valuea in 2015	Average total EU-27 in 2015
Indicator 1: Online availability and interactivity of public services (supply side)	68	100	97
Indicator 2: Internet use: obtaining information from public authorities ,	11	100	33
Indicator 3: Internet use: downloading official forms from public authorities	9	64	28
Indicator 4: Internet use: sending filled forms	4	90	18
Indicator 5: Internet use: Individuals never used Internet	0	37	12
Indicator 6: Households without access to Internet at home, because the access costs are too high (telephone, etc.)	32	0	2
Indicator 7: Households without access to Internet at home, because the equipment costs are too high	0	33	3
Indicator 8: Households without access to Internet at home, because access not needed (content is not useful, not interesting, etc.)	0	26	12
Indicator 9: Households without access to Internet at home, because of lack of skills	0	28	10
Indicator 10: Households without access of Internet at home, because access not wanted (content is harmful, etc.)	0	28	4
Indicator 11: Enterprises using Internet for obtaining information from public authorities	40	100	85
Indicator 12: Enterprises using Internet for obtaining forms from public authorities	39	100	87
Indicator 13: Enterprises using Internet for returning filled in forms to public authorities	0	100	87
Indicator 14: Enterprises using Internet for interaction with public authorities for full electronic handling	0	100	74
Indicator 15: Enterprises using Internet for interaction with public authorities for e-procurement	0	55	17
Indicator 16: Individuals who never ordered goods or services, over the Internet, for private use	0	65	27
Indicator 17: Last online by individuals purchase: in the last 3 months	2	85	46
Indicator 18: Enterprises selling online (at least 1% of turnover), SMEs (10-249 persons employed), without financial sector	0	49	8

public authorities 3% to 32% for the years 2005 -2010 and we estimate that this proportion will vary between 4% to 90% in 2015 and the average total of EU-27 will be 18% (see Table 7). This indicates that major differences will exist among member states of EU-27 in 2015.

Is it possible to halve the proportion of the population that has never used internet from 30% to 15% by 2015 (key performance targets of digital agenda 2020)?

How feasible is it for these key performance targets of Digital Agenda to be accomplished, when the proportion of individuals who had never had internet access vary between 10% to 65% for the years 2005 -2010. We estimate that this proportion will vary between 0% to 37% in 2015

Figure 7. Enterprises sell online in EU-27 for the period 2005-2010

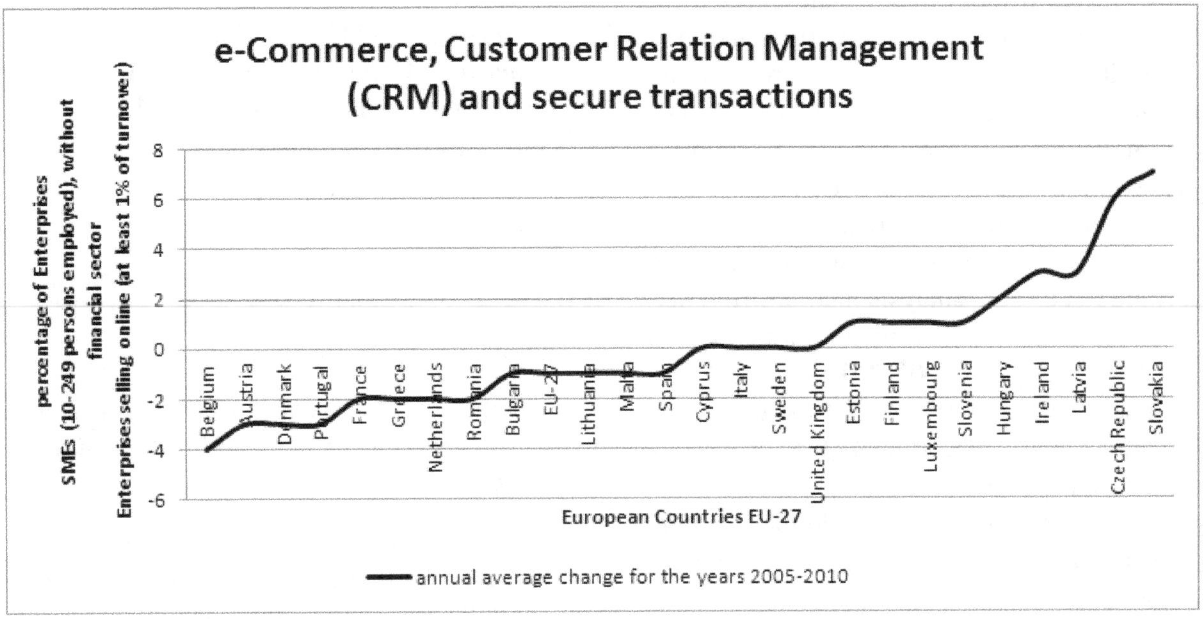

and the average total of EU-27 will be 12%.This indicates that major differences will exist among member states of EU-27 in 2015 (see Table 7).

FUTURE RESEARCH DIRECTIONS

If nothing changes, the same indicators' trends for the years 2005-2010 will probably appear for the next 5 years (2011-2015). If this happens, according to our data analysis, some countries will be under the key performance targets of Digital Agenda 2020. Also, for the years 2005-2010 trends of the same indicator are negative for some countries of EU-27 and for others are positive. Future research is needed to investigate the reasons why this is happening.

Also, we found that major differences exist for the same indicator among countries member states of EU-27. Europe should find out the reasons that cause these differences.

CONCLUSION

Undoubtedly, in order for individuals to interact with government via Internet, they need to: a) know how to use a computer and b) have access to a computer, c) know how to use Internet and d) have access to Internet, e) to estimate that the access costs of Internet are not too high (telephone etc), f) to estimate that they have the adequate skills to use Internet, g) to estimate that Internet content is not harmful, h) to estimate that Internet content is useful and interesting, and i) dismiss privacy or security concerns. So, all the above mentioned might constitute some of the prerequisites for adoption of eGov services for individuals. Moreover, some countries face difficulties in following the ambitious targets of Digital Agenda 2020. EU must find a mechanism to track down why great differences exist among member countries in EU-27.

Europe used to focus mainly on the supply side. We found out that eGov usage by individuals in EU-27 is low as well as the usage of enterprises for e-procurement for the years

2005-2010. We propose that eGov usage EU must take into consideration the eGov usage by individuals and enterprises (demand side) before it sets an eGov strategy. Europe should establish a framework that should track down the reasons why eGov usage is low in some countries and why it is high in other countries. EU may group countries according to its eGov readiness or maturity of adoption of eGov services. According to our data analysis, major differences exist concerning specially for individuals in EU-27 for the years 2005-2010.

Also, in the framework, it must be defined which indicators affect directly the use of eGov e.g. is it Internet use? Is it computer use? etc. If these indicators are correctly defined, a more realistic European strategy could be outlined for all member states of EU-27.

It is important that Europe first sets targets of eGov and then evaluates them. In order for the targets of Digital Agenda to be successfully accomplished, EU should produce eGov services that will be evaluated at the phase of design. In the design stages, the services will be personalized accordingly to a) citizens' needs of each country, and b) the prerequisites of adoption of eGov services. This could be materialized if a "Common Framework of Pre-evaluation" is taking in consideration the prerequisites of adoption of eGov services and is followed by all countries at the stage of design of e-government services.

Furthermore, EU could find out which of the prerequisites are via Questionnaires answered by citizens among countries member states of EU-27 or by using other techniques.

Finally, EU should find ways to co-design eGov services with citizens in view. If this happens, there is a greater possibility that produced eGov services are adopted by citizens.

REFERENCES

i2010 High Level Group. (2006). *Benchmarking framework.* Conducted for i2010 Information Space, Innovation & Investment in R&D, Inclusion, European Commission.

i2010 High Level Group. (2009). *Benchmarking digital Europe 2011-2015 a conceptual framework.* Conducted for i2010 Information Space, Innovation & Investment in R&D,Inclusion, European Commission.

Accenture. (2003). *The government executive series egovernment leadership: Engaging the customer.*

Comission of the European Communities. (2002b). *eEurope Benchmarking Report eEurope 2002*. Brussels: Comission of the European Communities.

Delopoulos, H. (2012). Objectives and barriers of implementation of egovernment European strategy: From Lisbon strategy to digital agenda. *European Journal of ePractice, 17.*

eGovernment Economics Project (eGEP) Measurement Framework. (2006). Luiss management RSO SPA prepared for the egovernment unit DG information society and media European Commission.

European Comission. (2010). Europe's digital competitiveness report 2010 (No. ISBN 978-92-79-15829-2). Publications Office of the European Union.

European Comission. (2012). *Commission staff working document digital agenda scoreboard 2012.*

European Commission. (2007, September). *The user challenge benchmarking the supply of online public services, 7th Measurement*. Report conducted for Directorate General for Information Society and Media. Retrieved January 10, 2009, from http://ec.europa.eu/information_society/eeurope/i2010/docs/benchmarking/egov_benchmark_2007.pdf

European Commission DG Information Society. (2004). *Online availability of public services: How is Europe progressing? Web based survey on electronic public services, report of the fourth measurement*. Retrieved March 15, 2012, from http://ec.europa.eu/information_society/eeurope/2005/doc/highlights/whats_new/capgemini4.pdf

European Council. (2002). *eEurope 2005: An information society for all*. An action plan to be presented in view of the Sevilla European Council.

European Parliament. (2001). *eEurope2002 impact and priorities*. Communication from the Commission to the Council the European Parliament the European Economic and Social Committee and the Committee of the Regions.

European Parliament. (2002a). eEurope 2005: Benchmarking indicators, 655 final. Brussels, Belgium: European Parliament.

European Parliament. (2005). *i2010 – A European information society for growth and employment, {SEC(2005) 717}, COM(2005) 229 final*. Communication from the Commission to the Council the European Parliament the European Economic and Social Committee and the Committee of the Regions.

European Parliament. (2010). *A digital agenda for Europe, COM(2010) 245 final/2*. Communication from the Commission to the Council the European Parliament the European Economic and Social Committee and the Committee of the Regions.

Eurostat. (2013). Website. Retrieved from http://epp.eurostat.ec.europa.eu/portal/page/portal/statistics/themes

Flak, L. S., Dertz, W., Jansen, A., Krogstie, J., Spjelkavik, I., & Ølnes, S. (2009). What is the value of eGovernment - and how can we actually realize it? *Transforming Government: People. Process and Policy*, *3*(3), 220–226.

Gemini, C. Ernst, & Young. (2002a). Summary report web-based survey on electronic public services (Results of the second measurement: April 2002), results of the second measurement. Conducted for European Commission DG Information Society.

Gemini, C. Ernst, & Young. (2002b). Web-based survey on electronic public services, results of the third measurement. Conducted for European Commission DG Information Society.

Gemini, C. Ernst, & Young. (2004). Online availability of public services: How is Europe progressing? Web based survey on electronic public services, report of the fourth measurement. Conducted for European Commission DG Information Society.

Gemini, C. Ernst, & Young. (2007). The user challenge benchmarking the supply of online public services, 7th measurement. Conducted for Directorate General for Information Society and Media, European Commission.

Gupta, M. P., & Jana, D. (2003). E-government evaluation: A framework and case study. *Government Information Quarterly*, *20*(4), 365–387. doi:10.1016/j.giq.2003.08.002.

Heeks, R. (2006). *Benchmarking egovernment: Improving the national and international measurement, evaluation and comparison of egovernment*. Development Informatics Group Institute for Development Policy and Management University of Manchester.

Kaylor, C., Deshazo, R., & Van Eck, D. (2001). Gauging e-government: A report on implementing services among American cities. *Government Information Quarterly, 18*(4), 293–307. doi:10.1016/S0740-624X(01)00089-2.

Layne, K., & Lee, J. (2001). Developing fully functional e-government: A four stage model. *Government Information Quarterly, 18*(2), 122–136. doi:10.1016/S0740-624X(01)00066-1.

Millard, J., Iversen, J. S., Kubicek, H., Westholm, H., & Cimander, R. (2004). *Reorganisation of government back offices for better electronic public services – European good practices (Back - office reorganisation). Danish Technological Institute & Institut für Informationsmanagement GmbH.* University of Bremen.

United Nations. (2003). *World public sector report 2003: E-government at the crossroads (No. ST/ESA/PAD/SER.E/49).* New York: United Nations.

United Nations. (2004). *Global e-government readiness report 2004- Towards access for opportunity. No: UNPAN/2004/11.* New York: United Nations.

West Darrell, M. (2000). Assessing e-government: The internet, democracy, and service delivery by state and federal governments. Retrieved October 1, 2008, from http://www.insidepolitics.org/egovtreport00.html

Wimmer, M., & Tambouris, E. (2002, August 26-30). *Online one-stop government: A working framework and requirements.* Paper presented at the IFIP World Computer Congress, Montreal.

ADDITIONAL READING

Akman, I., Yazici, A., Mishra, A., & Arifoglu, A. (2005). E-government: A global view and an empirical evaluation of some attributes of citizens. *Government Information Quarterly, 22*(2), 239–257. doi:10.1016/j.giq.2004.12.001.

Andersen, K. V., & Henriksen, H. Z. (2006). E-government maturity models: Extension of the Layne and Lee model. *Government Information Quarterly, 23*(2), 236–248. doi:10.1016/j.giq.2005.11.008.

Andersson, A., & Grönlund, Å. (2003). *E-society accessibility: Identifying research gaps* (pp. 15–20). Lecture Notes in Computer Science Electronic Government.

Anthopoulos, L. G., Siozos, P., & Tsoukalas, I. A. (2007). Applying participatory design and collaboration in digital public services for discovering and re-designing e-Government services. *Government Information Quarterly, 24*(2), 353–376. doi:10.1016/j.giq.2006.07.018.

Bertot, J. C., & Jaeger, P. T. (2006). User-centered e-government: Challenges and benefits for government Web sites. *Government Information Quarterly, 23*(2), 163–168. doi:10.1016/j.giq.2006.02.001.

Cegarra Navarro, J. G., Dewhurst, F. W., & Briones Penalver, A. J. (2007). Factors affecting the use of e-government in the telecommunications industry of spain. *Technovation, 27*(10), 595–604. doi:10.1016/j.technovation.2007.03.003.

Chen, Y.-C., & Gant, J. (2001). Transforming local e-government services: The use of application service providers. *Government Information Quarterly, 18*(4), 343–355. doi:10.1016/S0740-624X(01)00090-9.

Cheverie, J. F. (1999). U.S. government information on the web: Getting the information you need. *Journal of Academic Librarianship, 25*(6), 496–497. doi:10.1016/S0099-1333(99)00115-9.

Chou, T.-C., Chen, J.-R., & Pu, C.-K. Exploring the collective actions of public servants in e-government development. *Decision Support Systems, In Press, Corrected Proof,* 124.

Delopoulos, H. (2010). *Barriers and opportunities for the adoption of egovernance services*. Paper presented at the Conference of Waset World Academy of Science, Engineering And Technology Retrieved from http://www.waset.org/journals/waset/v42.php

Dias, G. P., & Rafael, J. A. (2007). A simple model and a distributed architecture for realizing one-stop e-government. *Electronic Commerce Research and Applications*, *6*(1), 81–90. doi:10.1016/j.elerap.2006.02.001.

Esteves, J., & Joseph, R. C. (2008). A comprehensive framework for the assessment of eGovernment projects. *Government Information Quarterly*. doi:10.1016/j.giq.2007.04.009.

Evans, D., & Yen, D. C. (2005). E-government: An analysis for implementation: Framework for understanding cultural and social impact. *Government Information Quarterly*, *22*(3), 354–373. doi:10.1016/j.giq.2005.05.007.

Gil-Garcia, J. R., & Pardo, T. A. (2005). E-government success factors: Mapping practical tools to theoretical foundations. *Government Information Quarterly*, *22*(2), 187–216. doi:10.1016/j.giq.2005.02.001.

Gouscos, D., Kalikakis, M., Legal, M., & Papadopoulou, S. (2007). A general model of performance and quality for one-stop e-Government service offerings. *Government Information Quarterly*, 124.

Guijarro, L. (2007). Interoperability frameworks and enterprise architectures in e-government initiatives in Europe and the United States. *Government Information Quarterly*, *24*(1), 89–101. doi:10.1016/j.giq.2006.05.003.

Gupta, M. P., & Jana, D. (2003). E-government evaluation: A framework and case study. *Government Information Quarterly*, *20*(4), 365–387. doi:10.1016/j.giq.2003.08.002.

Heeks, R., & Bailur, S. (2007). Analyzing e-government research: Perspectives, philosophies, theories, methods, and practice. *Government Information Quarterly*, *24*(2), 243–265. doi:10.1016/j.giq.2006.06.005.

Johnson, C. L. (2007). A framework for pricing government e-services. *Electronic Commerce Research and Applications*, 124.

Layne, K., & Lee, J. (2001). Developing fully functional E-government: A four stage model. *Government Information Quarterly*, *18*(2), 122–136. doi:10.1016/S0740-624X(01)00066-1.

Mitra, R. K., & Gupta, M. P. A. (2008). Contextual perspective of performance assessment in e-government: A study of Indian Police administration. *Government Information Quarterly*, 124.

Picci, L. (2006). The quantitative evaluation of the economic impact of e-government: A structural modelling approach. *Information Economics and Policy*, *18*(1), 107–123. doi:10.1016/j.infoecopol.2005.08.001.

Reddick, C. G. (2004). A two-stage model of e-government growth: Theories and empirical evidence for U.S. cities. *Government Information Quarterly*, *21*(1), 51–64. doi:10.1016/j.giq.2003.11.004.

Stephen, S. (2006). eGovernment is dead: Long live transformation. *Computer Law & Security Report*, *22*(1), 1–2. doi:10.1016/j.clsr.2005.12.002.

Torres, L., Pina, V., & Acerete, B. (2005). E-government developments on delivering public services among EU cities. *Government Information Quarterly*, *22*(2), 217–238. doi:10.1016/j.giq.2005.02.004.

Vassilakis, C., Laskaridis, G., Lepouras, G., Rouvas, S., & Georgiadis, P. (2003). A framework for managing the lifecycle of transactional e-government services. *Telematics and Informatics*, *20*(4), 315–329. doi:10.1016/S0736-5853(03)00011-X.

Vassilakis, C., Lepouras, G., & Halatsis, C. (2007). A knowledge-based approach for developing multi-channel e-government services. *Electronic Commerce Research and Applications*, *6*(1), 113–124. doi:10.1016/j.elerap.2006.07.004.

Wang, Y.-S., & Liao, Y.-W. (2008). Assessing egovernment systems success: A validation of the DeLone and McLean model of information systems success. *Government Information Quarterly*. doi:10.1016/j.giq.2007.06.002.

Wimmer, M., Schneider, C., & Shaddock, J. (2007). *Framework and methodology to turn barriers and challenges of eParticipation into research themes and actions. Expanding the knowledge society: Issues, applications, case studies. Part1* (pp. 189–196). Amsterdam: IOS Press.

KEY TERMS AND DEFINITIONS

4 Stage Model: The model used to estimate the availability of eGovernment services.

Barriers to eGov Adoption: What prevents citizens and enterprises of using eGovernment services.

Benchmarking eGovernment: E.g. to compare eGovernment metrics among different countries.

eGov Usage by Enterprises: a) Enterprises using Internet for obtaining information from public authorities, b) Enterprises using Internet for obtaining forms from public authorities, c) Enterprises using Internet for returning filled in forms to public authorities, d) Enterprises using Internet for interaction with public authorities for full electronic handling e) Enterprises using Internet for interaction with public authorities for e-procurement.

eGov Usage by Individuals: a) Internet use for obtaining information from public authorities b) internet use for downloading official forms from public authorities, and c): Internet use for sending filled forms to public authorities.

eGovernment Adoption: eGovernment use.

eGovernment Availability: eGovernment supply or provision of 20 basic public services.

eGovernment Evaluation/Assessment: To define indicators in order to evaluate the success of eGovernment implementation.

Chapter 15
E-Services Efficiency of Government Organisations in Asia

Sujana Adapa
The University of New England, Australia

ABSTRACT

This chapter discusses the importance of Information and Communication Technologies (ICTs) and highlights the benefits of embracing the aforesaid in the government and the business sector. It presents a discussing on eGovernment and the theoretical foundations associated with it. The chapter also suggests the importance of inclusion and participation of various stakeholders. A number of short case studies are provided that relate to the effective planning and implementation of eGovernment-based strategies, especially with respect to e- services offerings focusing on the Asian countries context. Case studies refer to 9 countries in Asia. Factors that promote and obstacles that hinder the eGovernment services delivery are also discussed. The chapter provides an in-depth analysis of the differences between the effective implementation and the uptake of eGovernment by newly industrialised countries and developing nations. Furthermore, important recommendations are provided that, hopefully, the developing countries on the road to full implementation of eGovernment will find useful.

INTRODUCTION

The Information and Communication Technologies (ICTs) have revolutionised the traditional mode of operations of the world governments. These technological advancements have brought in many advantages such as operational efficiency, reduction in cost, delivering quality services, convenience, innovations, and learning opportunities in several countries. Existing literature indicates that the private organisations responded and embraced the technological innovations at a faster

DOI: 10.4018/978-1-4666-4245-4.ch015

pace compared to their public counterparts. Consequently, governments as public sector organisations in various countries have taken initiatives to integrate technological enhancements in their day to day operations partly for the convenience of their citizens and themselves and partly to keep up with the rest of the world.

Developed and Newly Industrialised Countries (NICs) have well developed eGovernment models due to their affordability to invest in infrastructures and their receptiveness to technological innovations. As a result, a majority of the public sector related services are available to citizens in developed countries and NICs through online channels via the Internet, thus leading to the fast and efficient processes and mechanisms in place. On the contrary, in the developing and subsistence countries, lack of proper infrastructure and low awareness levels of the governments and citizens to eGovernment implementation are the major obstacles in opening up these nations for technological innovations. eGovernment offers many benefits to their citizens by streamlining several public sector related operations and offering them to their citizens on a technological platform, thus reducing the time lag associated with the aforesaid. This feature has inherent advantages associated such as keeping their citizens satisfied with the services, offering the service to the required in a more efficient and effective manner, reducing citizens waiting times and increasing self-service options.

Though, developing countries in Asia are exhibiting astounding performance with regard to their economic growth and gross domestic product, the divide between the social classes in such nations is high and the transparency, accountability and corruption levels are at a questionable level. The receptiveness of the technological innovations by the governments, their employees and their citizens is just another issue in front of these countries in order to focus on reaping benefits from implementing eGovernment. However, once the different stakeholders associated with eGovernments are aware of the actual and potential benefits associated, there are expected to be enormous opportunities within these countries.

This chapter sets out to describe the economic situation, the technological advancements and the receptiveness levels of various stakeholders associated with the eGovernment mechanisms in the Asian context. The main focus of the chapter is to look at the nascent eGovernment processes offering e-services to their citizens and evaluating the effectiveness of these programs. For example, detailed information in the form of a case study *eSeva* in India will be provided. Similarly, factors influencing the effective eservices implementation by eGovernment in order to cater to the needs of their citizens such as political instability, trust in government, economic structure, type of government structure and the impact of the prevailing legal framework of the country would be discussed. This chapter also outlines and discusses the various challenges associated with the effective e-services implementation through the eGovernment projects. Practical implications are also discussed and workable recommendation presented.

BACKGROUND

The advent of the internet resulted in many information and communication related technological innovations that appealed to citizens, businesses and governments alike. However, the uptake of the aforesaid technological innovations was very different between the private and public sectors in many countries. Private sector was fast in embracing these technological innovations and has set certain standards by eliciting the positives associated. This has resulted in the revolution of service offerings by the businesses and resultant changes in the processes of supply chain management and value change management. The key factors that promoted to the faster uptake of information and communication technologies by the private sector relate to the availability of resources, ability to attract funds from other sources in an efficient manner, involvement of less number of players in the process of service offerings and the presence of a relatively simplistic decision-making process (Riley, 2001). On the other hand, public sector in a way is lagging behind the private sector and is struggling to catch with the private sector with the use and implementation of these information and communication technologies. This sort of digital divide between the private and public sectors is evidently visible even today in many countries. The main reasons that relate to the lag of the public sector in embracing information and communication technologies include the presence of complex networks, involvement of various agencies, presence of a sophisticated level of integration between these agencies and networks, lack of appropriate infrastructure, non-availability of funds and so on. Consequently private sector has raised the expectations of the businesses and citizens through the provision of efficient service delivery mechanisms (Saxena, 2005). As a result, public sector has to focus on the incorporation of technological enhancements and raise the level of service offerings to its citizens and businesses. Therefore the governments operating in many countries focused on integrating various services that they offer by effective implementation of technological innovations (World Market Research Centre, 2001). More over the economic liberalisation and changes to the existing telecommunication policies in many countries paved the way for the use of information and communication technologies use by respective governments. Furthermore the emergence of economic globalisation critically focuses on the effective interconnectedness of businesses and economies in various regional areas and countries on the basis of geographical proximity.

Though the digital divide exists between the private and public sectors, developed countries took a lead role in the implementation of eGovernment based systems in place. This basically involved the computerization of the several government agencies, data and process automation and increasing the efficiency of the government service offerings. eGovernments transformed the relations with citizens, businesses and other governments by bringing in changes in administration, service and participation areas. Governments typically offer services to three important categories such as citizens, businesses and other governments. Therefore eGovernments focus on combining several government agencies through technological advancements, integrating multiple services under a single portal system, reducing corruption, increasing accountability and transparency for citizens. Similarly, eGovernments tend to focus on electronic delivery of service offerings, reducing the turnaround time and increasing the efficiency and convenience to access various services for the businesses (Lovelock & Cartledge, 1999). Government to government interaction through technological upgrades focus largely on policy changes and analysis related issues from the external perspective and benchmarking employee performance, productivity gains and retrieval of historical data from the internal perspective. Therefore the interaction of government with three categories such as citizens, businesses and other governments is manyfold. The acceptance of the eGovernment also to a larger extent depends on the readiness index as well as the intention to adopt from the citizens, business and other governments perspective.

The emergence of eGovernment is not sudden; however, it has been an evolutionary process. As mentioned earlier, governments operate in a complex environment that requires cohesion between many agencies and networks (Lovelock et al., 1996). The phenomenon of eGovernments in developed countries through the implementation of information and communication technologies have demonstrated four phases such as emergence, interaction, transaction and transformation. In the emergence phase governments simply focus on creating a website and communicating their offerings and available services to the general public, businesses and other governments through web presence. In the interaction phase citizens, businesses and other governments can interact with the eGovernment through online and access various service offerings. In the transaction phase various categories or stakeholders actually focus on performing two way transactions and benefit through the service delivery offerings. The transformation phase focuses on integrating various departments and services under one specific category, thus providing a holistic approach. However, in the developing countries, the emergence of eGovernment and the associated service offerings are still considered to be novel phenomena. Many developing countries have surpassed the emergence stage which means that the initial phase of the eGovernment focused on successful launch of websites and enhanced their web presence. Moreover, many developing countries are also successfully passing through the interaction and transaction phases. Transformation stage is yet to be achieved by the developing countries. Through the eGovernment sites, the various services offered are categorised under eServices, eParticipation and eAdministration.

CASE STUDIES

This chapter focuses on the emergence of eGovernment in developing countries specifically relating to the Asian context. Therefore, the key strategies related to the adoption of eGovernment in the Asian countries are discussed. Considering the differences between NICs and other developing nations, case studies relating to nine countries as now presented.

Singapore

Singapore focused on 'Many agencies one government' vision in 2001 with the aim of interagency collaboration and knowledge sharing. As a result, an eCitizen portal was created, whereby citizens could update their information to several government agencies by filling in a single form. The visibility of the eGovernment in Singapore is evident through the creation of eCitizen portal whereby around 1600 services are offered to various stakeholders via online. eCitizen portal is a single point of contact with effective integration of front-end applications and back-end systems. The presence of a central facility Public Service Infrastructure is critical in the deployment of efficient eServices in Singapore. The first steps of the Singaporean government to align with eGovernment strategy focused on computerisation of the civil service programme. Later in 2003, the Singaporean government focused on initiating the SingPass that allows the eCitizens in Singapore to access a wide range of government services via online and perform transactions with the government through this unique Singapore Personal Access. Singaporean government further promoted a specific government to business portal that serves as an entry point for all of the local and international businesses (West, 2001). The government also developed action plans in phases for delivering public services with a customer centric approach and developing robust information and communication technologies framework. Currently, eGovernment in Singapore aims to achieve value addition through eServices and increasing the networked efficiency of the government agencies. More recently through the iGov2010 master plan, focused on the energy and innovation capabilities of the Singapore's mobile cellular market and further increasing the satisfaction rates of the citizens and businesses.

The success of the Singapore eGovernment strategies can be attributed to their citizen and customer centric focus. Various programs implemented by the Singaporean government involved customer interactions and customer feedback in order to improve their service efficiency. This invaluable customer feedback helped the government strategy refinement and thus ensured that customer satisfaction is guaranteed through better service offering and integrated service delivery management. Thus Singaporean government moved away from the tradition top down management approaches and bureaucratic leadership styles of the organisations and fostered on change management strategies. Effective change management strategies were implemented throughout the Singaporean government sector. These changes were not only implemented across the public sector, but the government also focused on educating Singaporean citizens about the benefits of eGovernment services, technological advancements and time efficiency through massive marketing communications. By liaising with the citizens throughout the strategy implementation phases eGovernment service efficiency has been improved. Therefore in this case study, Singaporean eGovernment stands as an exemplar to many of the Asian and Western countries by following a balanced and well blended approach.

Malaysia

The Malaysian government has a national portal that aligns with the country's eGovernment strategy *mygov*. Malaysian government focused on vision2020 with an aim to reinvent the government sector through the effective use of multimedia technologies and fostering the collaborative environment. The Malaysian government also created Multimedia Super Corridor (MSC), which denotes a paradigm shift towards the new information age with the effective implementation of information and communication technologies. Malaysian government also focused on certain structural changes and invested heavily in developing the country's infrastructure. All the government administrative buildings are located now in Putrajaya often communicated to the public as the administrative capital of Malaysia. Smart Local Government Governance Agenda was initiated in order to align the regional government organisations with those in the capital city (Madon, 2004). Today the eGovernment in Malaysia offers various services such as inquiry, payments, submissions, feedback, rental payments, property assessments etc., via online. eGovernment in Malaysia also features on offering Interactive Voice Response (IVR) based features to its general public and business customers. More recently, the Malaysian government is aiming to create an international cyber court for justice.

Malaysian government today offers several eGovernment services to its citizens. The eGovernment focus of Singapore is quite different to that of Malaysia. In case of Singapore, the eGovernment efficiency is largely attributed to the government organisations readiness, formulation of effective change management strategies and citizen's readiness. However, in case of Malaysian context, eGovernment efficiency focus has been mainly concentrated on infrastructure development with an intention to enhance the visibility of the public sector within the eyes of the citizens, private sectors and other multi or transnational corporations. The development of the government organisation infrastructure and the creation of MSC largely related to the top down approach and the leadership vision of the Malaysian then Prime Minister. Effective policy changes and embracing the opportunities with the information and communication technologies quickly complemented and enhanced the eGovernment's service efficiency in Malaysia.

Korea

The Republic of Korea is proactive in providing effective eServices and associated tools to its citizens and businesses. The eGovernment strategies in Korea also focus on integrating the service offerings of various ministries such as health, education and social welfare. The eGovernment website which is a national portal offers useful information related to the government services and is user-friendly. The eGovernment in Korea focused on the creation of ePeople, whereby users can access the integrated services of various government departments via online through a secure login. The strategies that the government focused on with the aforesaid relate to the improvement of citizen engagement, reduction of the corruption levels and provision of efficient service delivery through the coordination of information and communication technologies. Around 400 public services are currently accessed by the general public from the government web sites including tax refunds, social welfare payments, permits, authorizations and so on (Jho, 2005).

Although, evidently, there are significant cultural changes and constant tension between North Korea and South Korea, The Republic of Korea, focused on uplifting its service efficiency of the public sector by embracing information and communication technologies related advancements. The Republic of Korea moved a step forward by focusing on a holistic approach of integrating several government-based services. As part of this, the Korean government focused on reducing the corruption levels and enhancing the citizen centric approaches by fostering citizen engagement and active participation in accessing the eGovernment-based services. The eGovernment in The Republic of Korea focused on enhancing the government web site quality by driving its efforts to improve the interaction quality and citizen engagement. Therefore, one of the critical success factors for the eGovernment in The Republic of Korea is the user-friendly nature of the eGovernment portals.

Taiwan

The Taipei government established GOV.TW, a centralised government portal that integrates all government related services and information. This information is available in Chinese and in English languages. Also this portal provides interactive communications to take place between citizens and government departments or agencies and allows for feedback and queries. Taiwan developed Government Service Network in 1998 in order to coordinate all the government units at all levels. Privacy and security policies developed by the government also gained recognition due to the presence of strong technical infrastructure. These policies were identified to be the primary measure of performance by government agency web portals. Several services such as finance, taxation, tariff systems and inter-government systems were integrated on Government Service Platform (RDEC, 2008). Later the government in Taiwan also developed Inter-Agency Electronic Document Exchange Project and Government Employee Identity Authentication IC Card projects. The ubiquitous government network promoted i-gov service that fosters integrated, innovative, interactive, individualised and instant services to the citizens. eTaiwan project developed later focused on bridging the digital divide and developed programs for remote areas and individuals with disabilities. Though the eInfrastructure, eGovernment and eBusiness initiatives developed by the government in Taiwan gained recognition, the eParticipation of all the local governments yet need to gain sufficient recognition.

The major focus of the eGovernment in Taiwan has been to increase the transparency of its operations with the various stakeholders involved in the process. The eGovernment strategies in Taiwan therefore focused on enhancing the fairness with the delivery of the public sector services, increase the reputation for government organisations, create a brand image for government organisations eService portal and thus gain citizen/customer's acceptance to use eGovernment services. The focus of Taipei government has been on reducing the corruption levels within the government-based agencies and gained the citizen's willingness to access the government-based online services. Reduction in the corruption levels increased the monetary resources for the government and therefore the government organisations were proactive in embracing advanced information and communication technologies and lured the opportunity to integrate several public sector services. Due to the citizen's willingness, acceptance and adoption of eGovernment services in Taiwan, Taipei government focused on extending these services to rural and remote areas.

China

The government of China focused on the Government Online Project by critically embedding three stages. Stage one related to enabling the technologies by connecting all government office and agencies to the internet. Stage two related to the aspect of information sharing whereby, the government looked at the feasibility of implementing the electronic data files. Stage three related to the creation of a paperless office by reducing the amount of paperwork in the government offices and agencies (Moon, 2002). The eGovernment strategy in China focused on initiating 17 Golden Projects such as Golden Customs, Golden Bridge and Golden Tax to name a few. These projects integrating foreign businesses, unified payment systems, national information knowledge hub etc. Similarly, the eGovernment in China approach was identified to be a leap-frog development model. Today various services that can be utilised by the citizens and businesses in China through eGovernment programme relate to online procurement bidding, electronic information exchange, welfare payments, electronic taxes and creation of digital identification cards (Yang, 2001). Several trends that relate to the implementation of eGovernment activities in China include the development of service-oriented government online services, automation of several departmental and agency services, defining intranet and extranet boundaries at different levels of the government and increasing the legal environment by enforcing Electronic Significant Law. The aim of the eGovernment in China is to foster democratic participation, promote authentic leadership and strengthen the surveillance of the central and provincial government networks. More recently the eGovernment in China has initiated Enterprise Online and Family Online projects. Although China focused on the implementation of eGovernment strategies across many domains, results indicate that these projects are superficial and calls for collaborative integration of many departments and agencies in order to provide efficient service delivery.

As mentioned although the eGovernment emergence in China has been in various phases, because of the population, corruption and leadership related aspects still the government in China is working towards integrated service delivery. Poor infrastructure and low citizen acceptance are identified to be the main hurdles for eGovernment strategies in China. Therefore now the Chinese government is focusing on citizen education about eGovernment and eService efficiency through its Golden projects. The eGovernment strategies at this stage follow the top down approach in China and calls for citizen acceptance and citizen adoption of these government-formulated strategies. The eGovernment service efficiency in China calls for collaboration, cooperation and integration of various agencies in order to cater for the needs of the citizens.

India

India's government structure was highly bureaucratic and was built on rationale principles. In 1990 Indian government started to realise the benefits of eGovernance strategy. At the same point, there was a pressure from several foreign operating businesses delivering quality customer-oriented services to the citizens. Today India has gained reputation in offering Business Process Outsourcing (BPO) services and software services. Evidently at the central level Indian government initiated a National eGovernance Action Plan from 2003-2007 to deliver right governance through quality institutional mechanisms. Also, the eGovernment strategy focused on creating a 'one stop shop' or a 'single window' for citizens, businesses and other governments to access the government services (Bhatnagar, 2004). Furthermore, the eGovernment strategy in India currently is focusing on coordinating the central, state and local level government-based agencies to become more citizen-centric and business-centric in nature. Smart Government Programme focused on creating a paperless file processing system. The eSeva programme initiate din the state of Andhra Pradesh serves the citizens through integrated citizen service centres (Gupta, 2004). Public private partnerships were critical in initiating this programme whereby, the priority is to provide services such as utility payments; sale of property, registrations etc., The Andhra Pradesh Smart Government (Smartgov) programme has been initiated at the secretarial level and elicited the internal efficiency of the government organisations. The Bhoomi programme initiated by the Karnataka state focused on the online delivery of land records and initiated computer-based transactions. Around 20million land records were computerised since the Bhoomi programme was launched (Kaushik, 2004). The Gyandoot programme initiated in the state of Madhya Pradesh serves as an important link between the government and the remote villages. Similarly in the state of Tamilnadu, the Indian government launched the public access internet kiosks for improving the engagement of the citizens with the government.

India suffers from several complex problems such as lack of authentic leadership, lack of adequate infrastructure, lower levels of citizen education and literacy levels, lower levels of citizen self-efficacy levels with information and communication technologies, several government-based organisations and agencies and lack of coordinated services. Several states in India adopted and experimented with eGovernment-based programmes in order to enhance the integrated citizen service. Some of these programmes have been very successful and are further implemented on a wider range. On the other hand, several programmes in many states are in pilot phase. For the eGovernment in India to deliver better-integrated services and enhance their service efficiency, the visibility of these programmes needs to be increased by massive advertising to gain citizen acceptance. Similarly, the various benefits associated with accessing eGovernment services need to be communicated to citizens through social marketing programs that enhances their awareness levels. Furthermore, government needs to focus on reducing the corruption levels at various organisation and agency levels in order to promote transparent and fair transaction processes.

Bangladesh

The emergence of eGovernment in Bangladesh is at the initial stages. The digital era started in the 1990s and the government in Bangladesh started to focus on information and communication technologies in 2001. Bangladesh is focusing on the concept of vision2021 in order to create a more resourceful and modern country with the effective implementation of information and communication technologies. The Bangladeshi government is mainly prioritising the automation of several internal processes related to the government organisations, electronic birth registration, electronic ticketing process, and so on. The installation of village phone in Grameen Banks in the villages of Bangladesh met with success. The government in Bangladesh also established National Identity Registration Authority (NIRA) and developed voter and citizen identification cards. Various acts initiated by the government in Bangladesh relate to the ICT Act 2009, Right to Information Act 2009 and National Identification Registration Law 2010. Other success stories relate to the effective launch of Online Hajj Information Management by the Ministry of Religious affairs in 2002. Since then the web site generated rapid interest and received accolades from national and international citizens. The initiation of the automation of the services of the Department of Roads and Highways also adds to the eGovernment set up model in Bangladesh (Hasan, 2003). The website created has portrayed a personalised access to the general public and businesses accessing the portal with effective service delivery mechanisms. More recently, Bangladesh government is focusing on electronic voting system whereby, citizens can vote via online through electronic voting machines and data can be retrieved in a fast and efficient manner.

The concept of eGovernment is still in its infancy in Bangladesh. The common obstacles for eServices efficiency of government organisations in Bangladesh relate to poor infrastructure, lack of adequate knowledge and awareness about accessing eServices and lack of appropriate resources. Therefore, in order to coordinate the services of various government organisations and agencies into a single platform, Bangladeshi government need to focus on educating its citizens about the advantages and ease of using eServices. Government may need to focus on initiatives such as advertising the benefits of coordinated public services that might enhance the awareness levels of the citizens towards the adoption and use of government-based eServices. Similarly, the government also need to set measures to improve the infrastructure and also work closely with the service providers to enhance service provision, citizen satisfaction and integrated service offering.

Sri Lanka

Sri Lanka is a developing country and has multiple constraints in the effective implementation of information and communication technologies by the government. However, the Sri Lankan government is focusing on a holistic long-term development driven view with eVision, eStrategy and eProgram initiatives. After the long prone war and ethnic tensions, Sri Lankan government is focusing on coalition building, institutional development and bottom-up initiatives. The notable challenges associated in the effective implementation of technologies by the government in Sri Lanka relate to highly fragmented and poorly managed political structure, weak leadership and coordination, low levels of digital literacy and uneven access to information infrastructure (Shelton, 2000). The National Chamber of Commerce in Sri Lanka worked closely the United States Agency for Institutional Development to promote the communications and technologies cluster. Later the technology implementation fastly spread to the banks and the key focus was to build local capacity and ownership. Dialog Telekom offers telecommunication and media services in Sri Lanka with integrated fixed, mobile, television and internet services. Several strategic projects are in the pilot phases and in early stages in Sri Lanka. Therefore, the focus today in Sri Lanka is on eGovernment, eBusiness and eSociety with development of human resources, information infrastructure and anticipated cohesion of vision, leadership, policies and institutions (Shahid, 2003). The government is also strategically focusing on funding quick-result projects, knowledge-based partnerships and software industry with institutional support and public private partnerships.

Although, Sri Lanka has abundant resources, long history of war and prevailing ethnic tensions hinder the prosperity of the country. As such the foreign direct investments suffered to a greater extent and the infrastructure of the country-lacked progress. Sri Lanka in order to keep up its pace on par with the other developing countries in the region with its eService delivery strategies of the public sector is focusing more on developing public private partnerships. Sri Lankan government is also trying to catch up with the rapid growth of information and communication technologies in order to offer a coordinated public sector service. Political motives need to be pushed to minimum in order to obtain maximum outputs with regards to the coordinated public sector service delivery. Similarly, citizens need to educated about the benefits associated with the integrated service delivery and their self-efficacy levels need to be enhanced.

Nepal

Nepal is also a developing country and at its infancy in the adoption of eGovernment practices and policies. The number of fixed telephone lines in Nepal has increased at a dramatic rate although the use and adoption of the Internet, emails and computers are scarce. The government in Nepal developed eGovernment Master Plan (eGMP) with the support of Korea Information Technology Agency (KITA) and completed the plan in the end of 2006. The aim of eGMP was to realise the benefits of good governance and identify the prospects of socio-economic development through effective, systematic and productive eGovernment practices. The Nepalese government in 2000 announced the first information technology policy 'IT Policy 2000'. Government also focused on the Establishment of High Level Communication and Information Technology Act (2003) and the enactment of Electronics Transaction Act (2007). Since then, the eGovernment initiatives in Nepal relate to the development of Integrated Voters Registration System, Document Management System, Finance Management System, Automated System for Customs Data, ePAN (electronic Permanent Account Number) and eIncome Tax Returns System (Pariyar, 2007). The government also focused on rural eConnectivity recently by developing village network, telecentres and wireless broadband network opportunities with the help of Ministry of Information and Communication. However the success rate obtained so far is not as anticipated due to issues such as poverty, inequity and social exclusion. Several projects are still in the pilot phase and the challenges ahead relate to the political transformation, resistance to change and effective management of the transition. Also the success rate with some of the projects can be attributed to specific Ministry's initiatives and proactive nature in their adoption of information and communication technologies. Therefore the primary area for the government in Nepal is attend to and integrate the services of various Ministries in order to enhance the overall service efficiency and offer good governance.

Nepalese government is also in its infancy with several pilot projects in place in its eService delivery. Several factors such as strong political motives, corruption levels, lack of transparency and fairness in processes, lack of citizen awareness, poor infrastructure and lesser investments. Similar to the context of other developing countries, Nepalese government need to focus on increasing the self-efficacy levels of its citizens, particularly of those living below the poverty line by providing adequate government-based services. Government organisations also need to be proactive in Nepal in embracing information and communication technological advancements and need to publicise to its citizens the benefits of the aforesaid through marketing communications.

DISCUSSION

Evidently, significant differences exist in the rate of adoption of eGovernment practices between newly industrialised and developing countries in the Asian context. These differences span around issues such as those presented in the following sections.

Budget

Newly industrialised countries are more proactive and are willing to spend finances in the investment of information and communication technologies. Added to this, the advanced nature of the countries, with better infrastructure, economic prosperity, lower levels of poverty, political stability, reduced levels of inequity and inclusion foster the public organisations to be more open to any innovations (Shelton, 2000). Leadership is also critical in diversification of service offerings by government organisations through electronic mode of delivery. Reduced levels of bureaucracy, openness to innovations and lower corruption rates allow for the effective disbursement of the available finances genuinely.

Knowledge

The variable of knowledge is critical and has a bidirectional influence. Firstly, the citizens residing in the country should be favourable to changes and show the readiness to accept these innovations that are embedded in the government systems. Secondly, the governments themselves need to be proactive in embracing information technology related changes and focus on coordination of various services through better integration. Better knowledge management practices and knowledge sharing activities are evident in the newly industrialised countries in the Asian context (West, 2001). These countries evidently are focusing on coordination and integration aspects in centralising all of their government services and making them available to their citizens under a single portal. Additionally these countries are also extending their strategic focus in reducing the amount of process work at various levels of the government. This is the stage that has yet to be attained in many newly industrialised countries and developing countries in the Asian context.

Web Navigation

Newly industrialised countries focused on developing web sites with necessary, relevant and accurate information. Additionally these web sites provided web links connecting different departments and agencies operating under specific government organisations providing better navigation opportunities (Yang, 2001). These web sites are therefore perceived by the citizens as easy to use and easy to retrieve better information. Also the newly industrialised countries in the Asian context took utmost care to implement security and privacy policies ensuring their citizens that information provided will be used for right purpose. All of the aforesaid has increased the citizens self-efficacy and confidence levels with the eGovernment sites and enhanced their participation in accessing eGovernment services.

Content Management

Apart from providing easy to understand eGovernment web sites, newly industrialised countries also focused on revamping the information content of various government services. Only relevant information has been highlighted on the eGovernment site that is easily understood by the citizens. Similarly, respective government organisations were also proactive in providing upfront information about their services and managing technical difficulties that citizens face whilst accessing their sites in the form of frequently asked questions. Newly industrialised countries also focused on providing interactive services for the benefit of rural or remote citizens, first time users, mature age customers etc.

Relationship Management

Presence of these interactive services in place fosters personalisation of the service offerings by the government organisations. Newly industrialised countries implemented interactive facilities to their citizens with an aim of providing tailor-made services and enhancing their satisfaction rates with the use of eGovernment sites (Jho, 2005). Better relationship management practices foster citizen retention on a long-term basis and also attract new citizens to access their service offerings. This particular aspect also fosters service recovery and enhances effective formulation of electronic channel management strategies.

Service Failure

Newly industrialised countries focused on implementing strategies in place in order to mitigate any unforeseen service failures through interactive communication, provision of 24/7 toll free numbers, available personnel etc., Citizens are considered to be their priority and are served immediately (West, 2001). The focus on better service management system in place allowed the success rate of eGovernment sites in case of newly industrialised countries.

The benefits that are associated with the implementation of eGovernment systems in developing countries relate to reduction in the gap between the citizens and/or businesses with the government. The government systems with the implementation of advanced information and communication technologies can deliver fast services to its various stakeholders (Riley, 2004). Similarly, the corruption levels can be reduced, accountability associated with various parties for any act related to the eGovernment is readily visible to all of the stakeholders involved and transparency levels associated to various acts can be enhanced. All of the abovementioned can increase the operational efficiencies of the government-based activities and increase the efficiency associated with the government-based service offerings. Coordination of the central, state and local government organisations and agencies would result in a simple decision-making process by reducing the complexities and may provide a 'one stop shop' for its citizens and businesses. eGovernment fosters convenience, speed in service delivery and direct interaction thus empowering people to participate directly in the political system, which may lead to important policy changes that would benefit all of the stakeholders involved in the process (West, 2001). Enhancing the eAdministration would foster effective sharing of the network data and creation of a paperless office thus contributing to the aspect of sustainability.

The main obstacle relates to the readiness associated with the governments, citizens and businesses to shift to the electronic mode of service delivery as well as access to the information. Citizens from low socio-economic background, less education and marginalised communities may not be familiar with how to access the information from the electronic modes and may prefer to have the traditional personalised contact with the personnel working in the government offices (Shelton, 2000). Even within the organisation the readiness levels of the employees to accept this major shift is questionable in many countries. Also the initial implementation and set-up costs associated with streamlining the information and communication technologies across various government organisations and agencies are tedious and costly. Coordination and integration of various agencies and organisations in the government sector depends on the organisational context and values and similarly the leadership role. Power complexities may hinder the whole process and may not generate sufficient interaction between various stakeholders (Osborne & Gaebler, 1992). Consequently, these factors may turn as a major obstacle for the effective implementation of eGovernment and may generate frictions between various stakeholders. In a majority of the developing countries the eGovernment based services are accessed to the full extent by the citizens and businesses operating in the urban context. Access of eGovernment services by the citizens residing in remote or rural areas is minimal due to lack of appropriate infrastructure and resources (Lovelock et al., 1996). Changes in policies related to the various sectors might impede the effective alignment of these sectors in the eGovernment based strategy.

Therefore, in order to increase the service efficiency as well as the service delivery attributes of the public sector, government-based organisations need to be proactive in embracing advanced information and communication technologies. There are important lessons that developing countries need to learn and share from the newly industrialised countries in terms of offering effective eService efficiency with their public sector (Zouridis & Thaene, 2002). The political responsiveness, responsible leadership practices, investment in infrastructure, self-efficacy and awareness levels of the citizens, transparency and fairness in the processes, readiness of the government-based organisations and shared learning are the common attributes that fostered the eService efficiency in government-based organisations in Singapore, Malaysia and Korea (West, 2001). As a result foreign direct investments poured into these countries, making these countries conducive for better infrastructure development. Thus newly industrialised countries focused on better service provision strategies and the government-based organisations in these countries embraced the technological advancements in order to offer better services to its citizens. The government-based organisations in newly industrialised countries also focused on coordination of various public sector services in order to enhance their service efficiency and increased citizen satisfaction (Riley, 2004). A step further now the newly industrialised countries are focusing on developing a holistic model and extending the eGovernment strategies to rural and remote areas.

On the other hand, developing countries such as India, China, Bangladesh, Sri Lanka and Nepal due to lack of appropriate infrastructure are still in their infancy in offering eGovernment services to its citizens. Lack of political transparency, lack of good governance models and poor infrastructure contributes to less coordination amongst the government-based organisations and agencies in developing countries (Shelton, 2000). Therefore in a majority of the developing countries the eGovernment based approaches are in pilot phases and are restricted to the state capitals. The developing countries need to focus on developing strategies to develop public private partnerships in order to develop their infrastructure in the first place to provide better service provision. Respective governments also need to focus on enhancing the readiness of both the government-based organisations as well as the citizens (West, 2001). Rather than following a top down approach or the bottom up approach, government organisations need to focus on developing a blended approach in order to enhance their service provision. Governments in developing countries also need to be proactive in setting up community training centres in order to increase the self-efficacy levels of its citizens.

RECOMMENDATIONS

It is evident that newly industrialised countries focused on the development of vast and modern infrastructure and thus had the ability to immediately embrace the information and communication technologies when readily available. Similarly, the readiness and the acceptance levels of the citizens, businesses and other governments are paramount in the emergence and effective implementation of various eGovernment-based strategies (Salem, 2003). Thus the eGovernment today in many newly industrialised countries is similar to those of the developed nations. All of the aforesaid have ushered greater benefits such as high satisfaction rates, value generated processes, economic profits and internal efficiencies. Now these countries are moving a step ahead and are focusing on incorporating the sustainability principles to address the environmental issues (Yang, 2001). Although the implementation rates of the information and communication technologies by respective governments in the developing nations is not in line with those of the developed and newly industrialised nations, yet most of the governments have taken the initial step towards eGovernment strategy. As evident through the various case studies presented earlier in this chapter, developing nations are at various phases of development with reference to their eGovernment strategies and associated eServices delivery. Firstly, these nations need to focus on the development of the infrastructure (Shahis, 2003). Then the credibility associated with the provision of accurate information from the government-based websites need to be highlighted.

This may need to use marketing communication tools to attract the interest of various stakeholders. Success stories from countries with similar infrastructure and economic status need to be widely publicized, so that similar projects may be implemented by other. Unsuccessful projects need to be revisited in order to identify where the potential gap exists and the possible focus needs to be on rectifying the errors.

Leadership is critical in carrying out the innovations associated with technological advancements and their effective integration across the government sector. Therefore possibility towards corruption need to be eliminated and governments and citizens need to focus on authentic leadership styles. In order to increase the internal efficiency and improve the operational efficiencies, the employees in the government sector need to be trained through workshops, seminars and webinars (Kaushik, 2004). This may include the efficiency levels and confidence of the employees with the eAdministration system. Also effective coordination of the service offerings via online will be achieved through streamlining of the central, state and local government agencies and networks. Government may focus on setting up internet kiosks and provide interactive help to enhance the readiness of the citizens to access online services (Jho, 2005). Citizens from the low socio-economic backgrounds need to be certain incentives for accessing online services and if applicable certain rebates may be provided, which may eventually motivate these citizens to access the government services via online on a more continued and frequent basis. It is also important to focus on the possible public private partnerships that offer mutual benefit to both the parties.

CONCLUSION

This chapter has highlighted the importance of eGovernment and various factors associated with the eGovernment-based strategy decisions. This chapter also elicited the importance of eGovernment from the theoretical perspective and also provided explanation on the factors that promote and obstacles that hinder eGovernment formation and implementation. The aforementioned discussion also provided short case studies that relate to the various projects initiated by the government sector in newly industrialised and developing nations. These case studies indicated the level of success in each of these countries particularly with the government sector with the effective coordination of information and communication technologies. These case studies also showcase the stages at which the eGovernment operates in respective countries. Furthermore, recommendations were also provided highlighting the importance associated with various stakeholders. eGovernment in developing nations has the potential to streamline various service offering, which will foster a value generated system. This study may be further extended by taking a comparative analysis of eGovernment operations in developed nations to those of the developing nations would further provide value addition.

REFERENCES

Bhatnagar, S. (2004). *E-government from vision to implementation*. Sage Publications.

Chadwick, A., & May, C. (2003). Interaction between states and citizens in the age of the Internet: e-government in the United States, Britain, and the European Union. *Governance: An International Journal of Policy and Administration*, *16*(2), 271–300. doi:10.1111/1468-0491.00216.

Cleary, R. E. (2000). The public administration doctoral dissertation re-examined: An evaluation of the dissertations of 1998. *Public Administration Review*, *60*(5), 446-455.

De, R. (2004). E-government systems in developing countries: Some research issues. *Pre-ICIS workshop on eGovernment.* Washington, December.

Devadoss, P. R., Pan, S. L., & Huang, J. C. (2002). Structurational analysis of e-government initiatives: A case study of SCO. *Decision Support Systems*, (34): 253–269.

Dubé, L., & Paré, G. (2003). Rigor in information systems positivist case research: Current practices, trends and recommendations. *Management Information Systems Quarterly*, *4*(27), 597–635.

Eisenhart, K. M. (1989). Building theories from case study research. *Academy of Management Review*, *4*(4), 532–550.

Electronic government. Third International Conference, EGOV 2004 (pp. 178-185). Berlin: Springer.

EU. (2004). *eGovernment research in Europe. European Commission.* Retrieved from http://europa.eu.int/information society/programmes/egov_rd/text_en.htm

EU. (2004b). *IST egovernment research in FP6 (2003-2006).* Retrieved November 15, 2004, from http://europa.eu.int/information_society/programmes/egov_rd/fp6/text_en.htm,visited

Giddens, A. (1984). *The constitution of society.* Berkeley, CA: University of California Press.

Golden, W., Hughes, M., & Scott, M. (2003). The role of process evolution in achieving citizen-cantered e-government. *Ninth Americas Conference on Information Systems.* Tampa, Florida.

Grönlund, Å. (2002). *Electronic government – Design, applications, and management.* Hershey, PA: Idea Group.

Grönlund, Å. (2004). *State of the art in e-gov research – A survey* (Traunmüller, R., Ed.). doi:10.1007/978-3-540-30078-6_30.

Gupta, M. P. (2004). *Towards e-government management challenges.* New Delhi: Tata McGraw-Hill Publishing Company Limited.

Hasan, S. (2003). Introducing e-government in Bangladesh: Problems and prospects. *International Social Science Review*, *78*(3&4), 111–125.

Hawaii. (2003). *Proceedings of the 36th Hawaii International Conference on System Sciences 2003.* New York: Wiley-IEEE Press.

Ho, A. T.-K. (2002). Reinventing local government and the e-government initiative. *Public Administration Review*, *4*(62), 434–444.

Ho, K. W. (2003, May 10). Cyber-war on terror: The checks in the e-mail. *The Straits. Times (London, England).*

Holden, S., Norris, D. F., & Fletcher, P. D. (2003). Electronic government at the local level. *Public Performance and Management Review*, *4*(26), 325–344. doi:10.1177/1530957603026004002.

Jho, W. (2005). Challenges for e-governance: Protests from civil society on the protection of privacy in e-government in Korea. *International Review of Administrative Sciences*, *71*(1), 151–166. doi:10.1177/0020852305051690.

Kaushik, P. D. (2004). E-governance: Government initiatives in India. In Debroy, B. (Ed.), *Agenda for improving governance.* New Delhi: Academic Foundation in Association with Rajiv Gandhi Institute for Contemporary Studies.

Kriebel, L., & Lapham, L. (2008). Transition to electronic resources in undergraduate social science research. A study of honour theses: Bibliographies, 1999-2005. *College & Research Libraries*, *69*(3), 268–283.

Krippendorff, K. (1980). *Content analysis: An introduction to its methodology.* Sage Publications, Inc..

Lovelock, P., & Cartledge, S. (1999). Special subject: E-China. *China Economic Quarterly, 3*(1), 19–35.

Lovelock, P., Clark, T., & Petrazzini, B. A. (1996, May 10). China's golden projects: Re-engineering the national economy. *Harvard Business School case study (N9-396-283).*

Molin, B., Månsson, L., & Strömberg, L. (1975). *Offentlig förvaltning (Public Administration).* Stockholm: Bonniers.

Moon, M. J. (2002). The evaluation of e-government among municipalities: Rhetoric or reality? *Public Administration Review, 62*(4), 424–433. doi:10.1111/0033-3352.00196.

Muhammad Rais, A. K., & Nazariah, M. K. (2003). *E-government in Malaysia.* Pelanduk Publications.

Myers, M. D. (2003). The IS core – VIII: Defining the core properties of the IS disciplines: Not yet, not now. *Communications of the AIS, 38*(12).

Norris, D., & Kraemer, K. (1996). Mainframe and PC computing in American cities: Myths and realities. *Public Administration Review, 6*(56), 568–576. doi:10.2307/977255.

Norris, D., & Lloyd, B. (2004). *The scholarly literature on e-government: Characterizing a nascent field.* SIG eGov workshop at ICIS, Washington DC, December 12.

OECD. (2003). *The e-government imperative.* Paris: OECD e-Government Studies.

Osborne, D., & Gaebler, T. (1992). *Reinventing government: How the entrepreneurial spirit is transforming the public sector.* Addison-Wesley.

Pan, S. L. (2004). *Managing strategic enterprise systems and e-government initiatives in Asia – A casebook.* World Scientific Publishing Co. Pty. Ltd.

Pariyar, M. P. (2007). EGovernment initiatives in Nepal: Challenges and opportunities. ACM International Conference Proceedings, *Proceedings of the First International Conference on Theory and Practice of Electronic Governance* (pp. 280-282).

RDEC. (2008). Research, development and evaluation commission. Electronic government 2007 Report: Taipei.

Rice, T. W., McCormick, J. M., & Bergmann, B. D. (2002). Graduate training, current affiliation and publishing books in political science. *Public Science and Politics, 35*(4), 751–755.

Riley, B. T. (2001). Electronic governance and electronic democracy: Living and working in the connected world. Commonwealth Centre for Electronic Governance, 2. Australia: Brisbane.

Riley, T. B. (2004). *E-Governance vs. E-Government.* Information for Development. Retrieved November 11, 2004, from http://www.i4donline.net/issue/nov03/ egovernance

Sachdeva, S. K. (2004). Quantifying and assessing e-governance. *Information for Development.* Retrieved November 11, 2004, from http://www.i4donline.net/issu/nov03/ /quantifying.htm

Salem, J. A. (2003). Public and private sector interests in e-government: A look at the DOE's PubSCIENCE. *Government Information Quarterly, 20,* 13–27. doi:10.1016/S0740-624X(02)00133-8.

Saxena, K. B. C. (2005). Towards excellence in e-governance. *International Journal of Public Sector Management, 18*(6), 498–513. doi:10.1108/09513550510616733.

Shahid, Y. (2003). *Innovation East Asia: The future of growth.* New York, NY: Oxford University Press.

Shelton, G. (2000). *Sri Lanka: In handbook of the media in Asia.* New Delhi: Sage.

West, D. M. (2001). *An assessment of city government websites.* Brown University Urban E-Government.

World Market Research Centre. (2001). *Global e-government survey*. USA: Brown University.

Yang, D. L. (2001). *The great net of China*. MFC Internet Update. Retrieved from www.mfcinsight.com/article/010209/oped4.html

Zouridis, S., & Thaens, M. (2002). eGovernment: Towards a public administration approach. In Proceedeings of Global e-Policy eGov Forum Seoul, Korea, Nov 6-7. Seoul: SungKyunKwan University, Global e-Policy eGovernment Institute.

ADDITIONAL READING

Brachman, R. J., Khabaza, T., Kloesgen, W., Piatetsky-Shapiro, G., & Simoudis, E. (1996). Mining business databases. *Communications of the ACM*, *39*(11), 42–48. doi:10.1145/240455.240468.

Chung, H. M., & Gray, P. (1999). Data mining. *Journal of Management Information Systems*, *16*(1), 11–16.

Dragulanescu, N. (2002). Website quality evaluations: Criteria and tools. *The International Information & Library Review*, *34*(3), 247–254. doi:10.1006/iilr.2002.0205.

Fayyad, U., & Uthurusamy, R. (1996). Data mining and knowledge discovery in databases. *Communications of the ACM*, *39*(11), 24–26. doi:10.1145/240455.240463.

Fjermestad, J., & Hiltz, S. R. (1998). An analysis of communication mode in group support systems research. Decision support systems. *Proceedings of the 31st Hawaii International Conference on System Sciences*, I, 17-26.

Fuchs, C., & Horak, E. (2008). Africa and the digital divide. *Telematics and Informatics*, *25*, 99–116. doi:10.1016/j.tele.2006.06.004.

Gilbert, D., Balestrine, P., & Littleboy, D. (2004). Barriers and benefits in the adoption of eGovernment. *International Journal of Public Sector Management*, *17*(4), 286–301. doi:10.1108/09513550410539794.

Jones, Q., & Rafaeli, S. (2000). Time to split, virtually: 'Discourse Architecture' and 'Community Building' as means to creating vibrant virtual metropolises. Electronic markets. *International Journal of Electronic Commerce & Business Media*, *10*(4), 214–223.

Kandelin, N. A., Lin, T. W., & Muntoro, K. R. (1998). A study of the attitudes of Indonesian managers toward key factors in information system development and implementation. *Journal of Global Information Management*, *6*(3), 17–26.

Kelegai, L., & Middleton, M. (2004). Factors influencing information systems success in Papua New Guinea organisations: A case analysis. *Australasian Journal of Information Systems*, *11*(2), 57–69.

Mujahid, Y. (2002). Digital opportunity initiative for Pakistan. *The Electronic Journal on Information Systems in Developing Countries*, *8*(6), 1–14.

Nair, K. G., & Prasad, P. N. (2002). Development through information technology in developing countries; Experiences from an Indian state. *The Electronic Journal on Information Systems in Developing Countries*, *8*(2), 1–13.

Vroom, C. A. V. S. R. (2004). Towards information security behavioral compliance. *Computers & Security*, *23*, 191–198. doi:10.1016/j.cose.2004.01.012.

Ward, J., & Elvin, R. (1999). A new framework for managing IT-enabled business change. *Information Systems Journal*, *9*(3), 197–221. doi:10.1046/j.1365-2575.1999.00059.x.

KEY TERMS AND DEFINITIONS

Developing Countries: The economic growth of the developing countries is less than the developed countries and the newly industrialised countries.

eGovernment: Government organisations focusing on delivering their services electronically through embracing information and communication technological advancements.

eServices: Coordination of the government-based services that are delivered to the users electronically.

Integrated Service: Effective coordination and implementation of various government based services for the maximum user satisfaction.

Newly Industrialised Countries (NICs): NICs in their economic growth and investment nature position between the developed countries and the developing countries.

Service Delivery: The way the intended service is channelled from the service provider to the service accessor.

Service Efficiency: An evaluation tool that reiterates the channel formulation strategies with the end user's satisfaction levels.

Chapter 16
E-Governance Projects for E-Inclusion in India:
An Architectural Assessment Framework

Harekrishna Misra
Institute of Rural Management Anand, India

ABSTRACT

Globally, e-governance systems have evolved towards wider acceptance. Almost all the countries have embraced e-governance as part of their long term policy. Contemporary e-governance systems argue in favour of convergence with scale up strategies. These strategies include convergence among the business sector, government and the civil society in the country and aim to connect with international agencies for better networking. E-inclusion has also been an integral part of the national e-governance strategies to spur citizen participation. In case of European Union (EU), e-governance, e-inclusion and such convergence have become very important because of the member-driven common interests and benefits. In the case of developing countries, similar efforts are being made to incubate and rollout converged services to citizens in rural and semi-urban areas with e-inclusion imperatives. Notwithstanding these varied approaches, there are pitfalls in translating the strategies into actions at the national level. Implementation of strategies at the national level calls for appropriate architectural analyses. This is because e-governance efforts need huge capital investments, require longer life development cycles and involve multi-agent service orientation to address the barriers of e-inclusion. In this chapter, e-governance architectural issues are discussed with three cases drawn from Indian scenarios through a conceptual framework. This framework aims to examine the possibilities of architectural convergence for national level e-governance services with e-inclusion as an important attribute.

DOI: 10.4018/978-1-4666-4245-4.ch016

INTRODUCTION

E-governance initiatives, despite acceptance to an extent in the form of e-government systems, have so far remained a hype in many parts of the world. Failure stories abundantly reflect that such initiatives with development perspectives have not yielded encouraging results. Surveys indicate that 35 per cent of these projects have been total failures, 50 per cent are partial failures, and 15 per cent of these have been successful in developing and transitional countries (Heeks, 2003). It is argued that e-governance initiatives are often on project mode and each project forms island for deliveries creating an overwhelming gap between project design and on-the-ground reality (known as design-reality gaps). This gap contributes to failures. Despite such discouraging outcomes, e-government initiatives in developing countries have evolved to a level of acceptance among government agencies and backend service provisioning organizations (Mishra, 2010). Most countries are now in the phase of assessing the "impact" on issues related to "efficiency," "effectiveness," and "equity." This is because most of e-governance efforts are now beyond the initial phases of addressing primary challenges of "digital divide," "setting up infrastructure," and "spreading awareness" to deliver citizen-centric e-governance services. Most of the countries are now able to showcase their e-governance services and declare the "availability" of these services uninterrupted crossing the spatial challenges (Bhatia, 2005; Bovaird, 2005). E-governance systems in many countries have evolved to the level of maturity. However, uses of such services have been a challenge for these countries. E-governance systems have so far remained supply-driven in most countries and their actual use largely depends on the type of services rendered. E-government services are now "mandatory" in nature and citizens are expected to use them. However, usage of many services which have development perspectives like income generation, health and education depends largely on the success of these services related to citizen needs. Though it is argued that readiness, availability, and uptake phases of e-governance systems are not contemporary anymore for evaluation of success in managing such projects, most of the developing countries still grapple with this phenomenon (Heeks & Molla, 2009). There are many challenges like use divide, low latent demand, and sub-optimal usage of e-governance services.

E-inclusion has emerged as a critical contributor to address digital divides. Thus e-governance and e-inclusion are expected to provide complementing support structures and processes for citizen centered services. It is contemplated that such synergy would overcome the barriers in adoption of e-governance services and in fostering social development. It is often argued that e-inclusion aims to transform the very approach to contemporary e-governance frameworks with focus on inclusive governance. It means citizen collaboration in addition to the existing strategies to include business, market and other stakeholders in the overall societal development (UN, 2005). In its e-governance readiness report for the year 2005 (UN, 2005), UN assessed various barriers of e-inclusion which are primarily the variants of digital divides.

It is a call to developing countries for shedding the emphasis on connectivity and access and substituting it with a focus on inclusion for all groups in the population. It is a call to focus on programmes and policies aimed at the diversification of the ICT base, such that those with low income, women, disadvantaged groups and those living in rural areas are systematically included in the impending benefits from newer technologies. The Framework propounds the notion that to build an inclusive society, e-government should expand to e-inclusion. (UN, 2005)

It is apparent that e-inclusion needs to influence e-governance strategies adopted at all the levels of national development policies. This means e-inclusion is a multi-dimensional and complex phenomenon. It is also posited that e-exclusion should be considered as one impediment to inclusive governance and this is a better measure for successful governance. E-exclusion measurements favour all the factors related to deprivations in providing perfect market and related services to deprived stakeholders in the society. This deprivation provides relativity in exercising individual power (information asymmetry) in various steps to have a good information society. This is argued to be best addressed with the help of suitable e-infrastructure in the access layer of the society (Mancinelli, 2007; Murray et al., 2004). It is therefore, necessary for the e-governance policy makers of a nation to ensure establishment of mechanisms to support e-inclusion. E-inclusion being multi-dimensional in nature should have effective methods for establishment of usable e-infrastructure and create enabling environment to foster participation, social inclusion, political trust in inclusive growth and transparency in e-governance services alongwith usable infrastructure for e-access (UN, 2006; UN, 2007a; Jörg Becker et al., 2008).

In this chapter, understanding on global e-governance initiatives is discussed while providing reflections on Indian e-governance scenario. Based on this understanding, a conceptual and analytical framework is developed to provide architectural perspectives with specific focus on e-inclusion and convergence. In India, citizens are influenced by the broad spectrum of development dimensions leading to various livelihood security challenges. In this framework, these dimensions are included for better appreciation of e-inclusions in Indian e-governance scenario. Through this architectural framework it is argued that all e-governance efforts need to converge for the benefit of common citizen and provide an environment for e-inclusion. In order to achieve this objective, due care should be taken to ensure that projects include common elements of the service-orientation mechanisms and add appropriate value. Projects should minimize redundancy in terms of infrastructure, networks and interfaces irrespective of their priorities in improving e-governance.

Organization of the chapter is as follows. In the next section, an overview of the e-governance efforts in global scenario is provided with references to e-inclusions. The following section includes the rationale behind studying architectural perspectives in e-governance. Subsequently Indian e-governance is discussed to appreciate the genesis and its present form in terms of policies, design and implementation. A conceptual framework is presented in the next section to argue in favour of architectural interfaces among various e-governance efforts in India keeping in view the e-inclusion imperatives. Three cases are drawn up to validate the conceptual framework. All these cases are under Mission Mode Project (MMP) mode and have their own focused deliveries to contribute to overall livelihood security of Indian citizens while providing scope for e-governance services. These cases are Watershed Project Initiatives (WPI), Mahatma Gandhi National Rural Employment Guaranty Scheme (MGNREGS) and National e-Governance Plan (NeGP). In the concluding section, results of evaluation exercises are discussed and directions for further research are presented.

ARCHITECTURAL PERSPECTIVES

E-governance has been a global phenomenon and is not limited to only developed countries. Proliferation of e-governance efforts across the globe has been well appreciated in government, business and citizen centric services. Due to this proliferation, e-governance issues have received due attention of academia, researchers and various government and non-government bodies, private and public sector organizations. E-government systems have transformed to reality in most of the countries with clear policies, and mandates to transform the functioning of governments at all levels of governance. The main focus is now towards consolidation of the services to promote collaboration of citizen. Thus convergence among back end applications, infrastructure and preparedness of government business has been a priority.

Global Scenario

Organization for Economic Co-operation and Development (OECD) has recognized this convergence as a major contributor to the success of e-governance systems globally. OECD argues in favour of delivering services for citizens, business, stimulate the information society and encourage governments to create an environment where business can thrive. United Nations (UN), in its survey for the year 2010, urges that e-enablement needs to go beyond the normal methods of optimizing government efficiency (e-government) and citizen engagements to build trust in the economy, business and market (UN, 2010) and social inclusions (UN, 2005). UN also recognizes that e-governments can support the Millennium Development Goals (MDGs) that aims at enhancing citizen services by the year 2015 and suggests connected governance with the benefits of enterprise architecture principles (Misra, 2012).

Contemporary e-governance efforts have provided desired impetus in overall development of society. Various standards, architectures are evolving for e-governance systems across the globe for effective replication and interoperability (Archmann & Kudlacek, 2008). For example, European Union (EU) has been working on e-governance architectures/standards for its member countries (EC, 2007a). "E-Inclusion" is being contemplated in EU countries keeping in view the desired services for workers, Small and Medium Enterprises (SMEs), children, doctors, artists, authors, musicians, disabled people, environment (carbon foot prints) etc. (Riga Declaration, 2006; EC, 2007b; EC, 2010). The set target is to reduce gaps in internet usage, increase digital literacy and make all government websites accessible to these stakeholders. However, study indicates that the steps taken are not free from challenges and recommends that ICT capabilities within communities is of prime importance in order to foster expected growth. Local populations need to be encouraged to accept and use the innovative use of ICT. It also pointed out that innovative and sustainable use of ICT would largely depend on appreciation and motivation of local people. Pro-poor policies are needed to keep these segments of people in the society engaged with e-governance services for better e-inclusions (Heeks, 2008). It is also recognized that "one-size-fit-for-all" is not the balanced approach for e-governance applications and services since localization is a major challenge. One of the approaches to address to foster the process of having an "Inclusive Information Society" in order to provide "right infrastructure," enhance "e-skills" and create an "accessible e-Government" for any good e-governance system with an expectation to improve upon the results and outcomes (Riga Declaration, 2006). It is also recognized that "e" part of "e-governance" is quite less critical in terms of assessing its success than the governance systems which need to adopt the right approach for process re-engineering, better interface with citizens and productive use of the process through innovation (Heeks, 2009).

Global e-government efforts strongly recognize "e-inclusion" framework that considers essential to ensure extension of benefits to those who do not have access to ICT or even do not know how to use ICT enabled services. United States of America (USA) established a "Federal Enterprise Architecture' (FEA) to foster speedy implementation of e-governance services. It recognized the importance of FEA to reduce redundancy, facilitate vertical and horizontal information sharing, support citizen – centered services and customer-focused government. It also argued in favour of FEA to provide services related to "government to citizen," "government to business," "government to government" and "internal efficiency and effectiveness" (ARC, 2008). European Commission's "e-Government Action Plan for 2010" seeks to ensure that "no citizen is left behind, by promoting inclusive e-Government, under which specific measures are developed to connect and deliver public services to vulnerable groups at risk of exclusion" (EC, 2007). It is also recognized that ICT is being increasingly embedded into local and regional level government processes to deliver public services with a view to reduce the complexities in citizens' dealing with administration and its intermediaries. The emphasis is now towards extending e-government services on equal terms to all and focusing on including interests of potential service users and not the administrators. Increased attention is now towards tuning the e-government services to meet specific demand of users, enabling front-end dialoguing through ICT in lieu of traditional face-to-face modes and ensure these processes are available at the users' domestic, community or institutional contexts. Despite these focused efforts to re-engineer government processes, there are enormous challenges like widening gap among policy makers, practitioners and ICT enabled service providers to converge to a common understanding and deliver desired services, fragmented efforts with "information silos and service islands" at local and regional level with fewer efforts to provide the desired "grid." This situation has led the citizens to prefer using the traditional channels instead of e-governance mediated services (EC, 2007). Therefore, in global e-governance scenario, efforts are in place to provide services through alternate channels, to focus on easing the citizen interfaces with public administration, increase better access to education, training and skill enhancement of citizens and social networks. This approach has recognized the importance of increase in coherence in e-governance policies with action plans. As per the e-government survey report of UN (UN, 2008), contemporary global e-governance systems emphasize on knowledge management, provisioning of better services and more choices to citizens and increase systems accountability.

Global efforts in e-governance have delivered mixed results. Some countries (depending on size, socio-political complexity, and government) have been able to derive appreciable results. United Nations (UN), European Union (EU), and other global entities have embraced e-governance practices and have given importance to citizen-centered services (Misra, 2009). UN recognizes the fact that under e-governance efforts have transformed to realizable phenomenon. Recent economic and financial crisis has emphasized emergence of global e-governance systems with more transparency and collaboration keeping in view the deadlines of MDG (UN, 2010). EU has also showcased the relevance of standards in e-governance practices and also demonstrated the way collaboration can be achieved among its various participating member countries. Thus there is need to examine the architectural perspectives of the e-governance efforts to minimize redundancy, information islands and inter-operability among services.

Indian Scenario

Discussion on global e-governance systems suggests a clear direction to policy makers and implementers on inclusive e-governance (Heeks, 2008; Misra, 2012). Globally, e-governance argues in favour of Enterprise Architectures (EA) which calls for provisioning of converged and value added services to citizens with least cost, time, and effort (EC, 2010; ARC, 2008). It is also evident that e-governance systems need to evolve to "connected governance" through establishment of robust infrastructure, backend integration with all stakeholders, and transforming the government itself through innovation and value addition. It needs a concerted effort to graduate any e-government effort to connected governance. In the context of Indian e-governance efforts, the situation is not different when compared to global e-governance scenarios, experiences, and trends.

In the context of e-governance in India, EA principles have gained much importance over the years. Department of Information Technology (DIT) of Government of India has accepted the EA as part of its core implementation strategy like other countries. It has focused on creation of meta-data standards; artifacts of EA based models and pilot them across the country as feasible. It has focused on an EA which could leverage the strengths of technologies in the areas of language interfaces, key-board layouts, content creation and browser supports with best practices (ARC, 2008). NeGP a national level MMP has been based on EA with three layers in order to accomplish the complex task relating to citizen-services and customer-focused government. These three layers are Common Service Centers (CSC) as front-end, State Data Centers (SDC) and twenty seven MMPs. The MMPs are part of various EA components such as "functional," "technical," "contextual" and "solution" architectures. These architectural components deal with specific services orientation (DIT, 2011).

ARCHITECTURAL PRINCIPLES

Enterprise systems architectural principles are quite contemporary since enterprises are more likely to adopt IT for adding value to their businesses (Ward & Peppard, 2002). These value additions are mainly due to optimization of transaction cost, agency cost, (leading to optimized use of factors of production), and making available the desired information to the stakeholders on demand. All these dimensions of organizational challenges are reflected through IS architectures and planning. IS architecture interfaces between organizational architecture dealing with various resources and the IT architecture being planned or acquired. It is therefore, considered important to align these architectures suitably. There is scope for e-governance architectures to learn from enterprise architectures and reuse the artifacts.

There are various approaches to understand, conceptualize and develop architectural principles. But, the two important premises which lead to a robust architecture are views and relationships (Garlan & Shaw, 1994). Views are considered important since they reflect on structural, behavioral and execution. Structural views reflect on organizational arrangement to understand the functional arrangement to support all its activities, and coordinate among them to achieve desired results. Organizational structure is an example through which structural views can be presented. One of the critical factors could be citizen satisfaction and e-inclusion. Another dimension of this structural view is to capture the strategic insights for the organizational existence. An example of this insight is collaborative e-governance with the support from local citizen whose critical success factor depends on functioning of Panchayat Raj Institutions (PRIs).

Behavioral view extends the structural views to a lower level in the organization through which view points of all stakeholders are presented. Besides, it also includes the views of the standard processes which are organized to carry out the plans defined at the structural level. An example to appreciate this view is to include process rules, process logics for a particular project that can be executed by the PRI. Views of rural households, PRI, government officials, and civil society could be included could be part of this exercise. Execution view is the critical link between the intended deliveries and the process through which the deliveries are made. In this IT architecture would come under scrutiny through the IS architecture. In this execution view, software engineering principles, IT component management (hardware, operating systems, applications) are mapped to support the views described structural as well as behavioral levels.

Execution views are emerging as standards in many areas to reflect on the architectures. Quality standards like ANSI/IEEE Standard 1471-2000, ISQA 4100/8106 (CIST3100- Organizations, Applications & Technology, ISQA3310– Managing the Database Environment, or ISQA8050– Data Organization & Storage) provide insights to the architectural treatment to the execution views (Misra, 2010; Misra, 2009; Ward & Peppard, 2002; Zachman, 1987; Eoin, 2006). Service oriented architecture (SOA) also includes execution views in order to brokerage and orchestrate the services demanded and supplied by the stakeholders in the organization. Discussions on execution views of the architectures provide insights to adopt computing scenarios in an organization. Broadly few architectural scenarios can be built for examinations i.e., "agent based computing," "service oriented computing" and combinations of both the architectures (Griffiths & Chao, 2010). These are the variants of the specifications of Object Management Group (OMG) which advocates for distributed computing including cloud computing. The main purpose behind such an approach is to provide thin-client environment to the common users and to facilitate seamless growth in agents and services without compromising the quality of services. Agent-based commuting and service-oriented computing architectures provide their own modeling techniques for the benefit of the common users. In e-governance scenarios, such an approach is quite essential since e-governance efforts need longer life cycles, seamless growth and demand-driven user interfaces.

One of the major considerations for effective e-governance is related to "convergence." Convergence of services forms integral parts of architectures related to agent-based computing and service-oriented computing. Convergence argues in favour of identifying agents in the form of government, business, entrepreneurs, and citizens. Besides, convergence also needs service orchestration in the lowest layer of the hierarchy in the citizen-centric service delivery systems. In this Chapter, various layers are listed to understand the hierarchical nature of agents and service-orientation of e-governance paradigms.

Figure 1 presents such layering. It is argued that the layering within the organization who can take the forms of government, business houses, civil society, etc. These are the agents who engage themselves in the process of rendering services. Information systems are built on the principles of SoA. These two architectures need to collaborate with each other to add services in the network for better citizen centric benefits. These two architectures are broadly termed in this chapter are Organization Architecture (OA) and Information Systems Architecture (ISA). OA describes three layers as its constituents and they are "strategic," "tactical" and "operational." These layers are mostly agent specific. ISA maps these three layers of OA into "core," "distribution and network," and "access" in order to provide synergy (Luftman, 2003). These layers map the agent specific service orientation to deliver to meet the demand. It is argued that e-inclusion can be effective with active support from all the stakeholders identified in each layer of the OA and ISA.

ARCHITECTURAL DIMENSIONS

Various agents collaborate in OA to deliver services through ISA. Since there is a need to collaborate between these two architectures it is imperative to understand various dimensions of OA, and ISA.

OA Dimensions

Treatment through OA principles includes understanding organizational strategies and its roadmap for information symmetry. This approach relates organization to systems for establishing technology interfaces. OA also considers "people" and "processes" as constituents to contribute to overall value additions at the enterprise level (Maier et al., 2009; Ward & Peppard, 2002). OA considers

Figure 1. Organizational Architecture Mapping

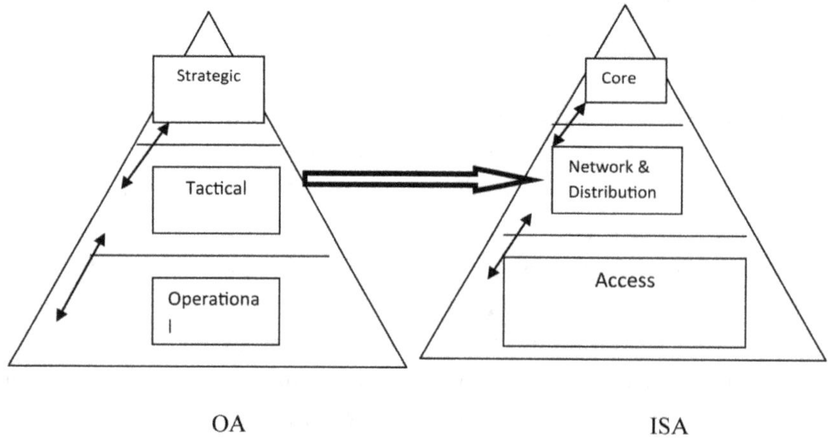

two important dimensions for a robust architecture which are "views' and "relationships" (Garlan & Shaw, 1994). Structural Views include "structural', "behavioral" and "execution" dimensions to reflect on organizational arrangement. Behavioral views extend the structural views to other areas in the organization like the people who are involved in the organization and customers who receive services from the organizational effort. Execution views of OA include the way strategies are translated into action. As regards "relationships" between the OA and ISA, it is essential to stratify the organizational layers and these are "strategic," "tactical" and "operational" as explained in Figure 1.

The operational layer in the organization is very critical since all the "transactions" occur in this layer. Databases generated to manage these transactions in this layer play a pivotal role. Event log management, tracking transaction owners (citizens/ customers/ internal employees/ other stakeholders like suppliers) and supporting their demands are deliveries in this layer. ISA terms it as "access layer" and transforms the deliveries through "user interfaces" and the medium is "Points of Services" (PoS). For ISA, this is the vital layer since success of all backend services/infrastructure lies in this layer. Some of the applications through IT intervention in this layer are Automated Teller Machine (ATM) and Personal Digital Assistant (PDA). These interventions provide avenues for on-line services in the access layer. This access layer of ISA grows independently and is mostly demand driven. Unique Identification Authority of India (UIDAI) aims to support this access layer in terms of authenticating the citizen who intends to access the services (UIDAI, 2010).

The tactical layer interacts with strategic and operational layers of OA. Most of the e-government applications are planned in this layer. These applications are met directly with the help of "domain experts" to the network and distribution layer of ISA. These domain experts take care of all processes, rules and logics and are responsible for establishing Standard Operating Procedures (SOPs) in order to manage the transactions successfully in the operational layer. Critical success factors in this layer include systems planning for aligning with organizational objectives, establishing inter-functional interface procedures and performance measurement standards. All these attributes of OA are mapped to the "network and distribution layer" of ISA. Data warehouses, web applications, n-tier applications for databases with user centered designs are examples of this layer which are in fact designed for supporting access and core layers.

The strategic layer functions at the apex of the organization and establishes directions for functioning of the organization. It also looks after polices, long term plans and directs for achieving short term achievements while maintaining the link to its mission statement. Chief Executive

Officer (CEOs) and board of governors constitute this layer. In e-government parlance heads of the state constitute this layer. Strategic layer exists in the governance paradigm to ensure that ultimate stakeholders (citizens/customers/shareholders) are benefited out of the organizational designs. Mostly these stakeholders are in operational layer. In ISA parlance, this layer belongs to the Chief Information Officer (CIO), engaged in formulating IT strategy, IT acquisitions, and establishing the desired information infrastructure for the stakeholders. The core layer of ISA formulates all these strategies to enable the access layer to render desired services.

View of OA and ISA find a common element during the mapping process which is related to inter- layer communications. Since there are various stakeholders in all these three layers of OA and ISA there is a need to capture the views of these stakeholders.

ISA Dimensions

ISA reflects the strategic behavior in three distinct layers in consonance with the organizational framework (Garlan & Shaw, 1994; Van & Leah, 2006). These are "core," "network and distribution," and "access." ISA, in access layer, deals with "user interfaces" and the medium is "Points of Services" (PoS). This is the vital layer since success of all backend services/infrastructure lies in this layer. In "network and distribution layer" of ISA, movement of data across various agencies is taken care of to provide seamless user services. In ISA the core layer belongs to the strategy group in the organization. This layer engages the strategic planners to formulate strategy for information systems, technology and establish a road map for creation of desired information infrastructure. Enterprise dashboards are conceptualized, recommended and implementing agencies are empowered to track the issues covered under dashboards. Examples included trend on budget, customer satisfaction, latency, connectivity and sourcing services for PoS orientation. One of the feasible architectures is adopt SoA principles for the purpose.

ITA Dimensions

It is noted that execution views are very important with the perspective of having good architectures in computing environment. This approach needs to emerge from strategically deployed ITA. ITA is expected to follow ISA and OA in sequence. Information Technology Architecture (ITA) provides the appropriate medium and mode to deliver desired user services "on demand." Thus ISA has a role to play in establishing architectural views for the ITA. ITA includes standards, protocols, quality management related to IT components and service orientation which are parts of software engineering principles and IT component management (hardware, operating systems, and applications). ITA aims to describe principles for mapping OA and ISA imperative, support their views described in structural as well as behavioral levels. In Figure 2 dimensions of ITA are presented to understand the complexity of the issues of convergence.

ITA for Access Layer of ISA aims to provide client-centric technology interfaces. The best practices under this architectural treatment are to have the thin-clients under n-tier architectures. SoA principles also advocate in its favour since in most the cases mobile computing with wireless application protocols are emerging as standards. This is because of the mobile penetrations in global scenario and developing countries are no exceptions. Ensuring citizen participation and catering to their demands at the POS are few challenges that ITA needs to take care of. This

Figure 2. ITA Dimensions to leverage ISA and OA Deliverables

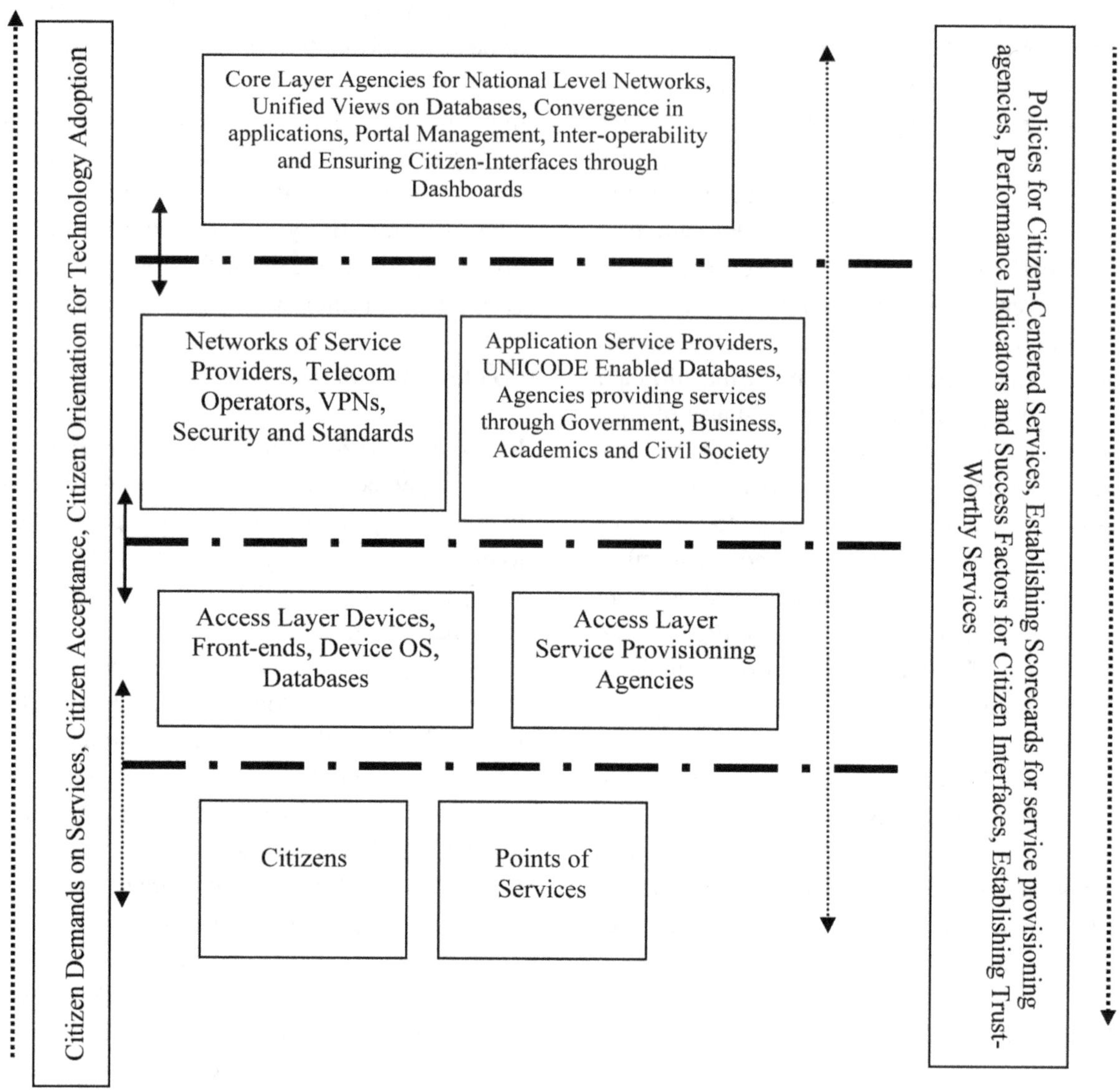

access layer needs to be transparently / logically linked to the service provisioning agencies and managers in the core layer in order to establish dashboard centric management and monitoring systems to ensure citizen satisfaction.

ITA for Network and Distribution Layer of ISA strives for establishing robust backend IT infrastructure to ensure secured networks of systems, databases and inter-operable services as planned in the core layer. This layer needs to be responsive to the dynamic needs and ensure life cycles of investment in infrastructure are of longer duration. In addition, cost of computing and sharing services through convergence are optimized to a larger extent.

ITA for Core Layer of ISA intends to form policies for national level networks, plans for scaled up services with unification and convergence so that redundancy in services is minimized. This layer also needs to establish a control mechanism to interface with citizens to measure the desired performance levels of the service providers networked. Dashboard centric evaluation systems are encouraged in this layer to capture architectural views of the ISA and OA discussed. This core layer aims to bind all the views spanning across the entire spectrum of stakeholders including the citizens. The idea of such collation is to free the common citizen from the complexities of the internal processes and provide them the desired service with ease and on demand (Paul et al., 2009).

E-INCLUSION AND CONVERGENCE

In order to make a technology general purpose, it has to be widely used and user should understand the benefits at large. This general purpose technology should be adopted in such a way that citizens accept it as a way of life. E-inclusion treats this aspect as one of its important success factors. E-governance in India has many complex problems related to diversities in society, culture, language, politics, education and democratic governance. Challenges in rural areas enhance these complexities in governance with e-inclusion imperatives. Because of the disconnect between setting up e-governance infrastructure and e-inclusion strategies India has not been able to scale up many pilot projects though successfully show cased. Therefore, it is important to consider policy level implications with specific reference to convergence and business use (Planning Commission, 2001). While studying the policies in India that are relevant to e-governance, one can conveniently divide these in four areas viz.: "Indian telecommunication Policy," "Indian IT policy," "Indian Infrastructure Policy" and "Policy on Convergence." As per the working group (GoI, 2001) for e-governance and convergence, the convergence in India has been defined as "Convergence of Content" and "Convergence of Carriage."

Indian Scenario

In India, foundation of e-governance was laid during 1954 when the Planning Commission introduced computers followed by setting up of the Department of Electronics (DoE) in 1970 and establishment of the National Informatics Centre in 1970 as a national agency to make available necessary infrastructure across all states to provide required connectivity with the central government. OA, ISA and ITA in Indian scenario did not follow the ideal sequences to formulate, develop and implement architectural views and contexts. Recent efforts indicate focus on ISA. However, an insight to OA and ISA indicates that the core layer is actively considering policies targeted at network/distribution layers. Tactical layers include state data centers, state level agencies and they are working towards delivering services demanded by the access layer. Access layer has remained disjointed.

These events provide the scope to explain architectural perspectives of e-governance efforts in India. Indian e-governance scenario considers the core layer of OA as one of the major contributors to the MMPs. The core layer is actively considering policies that are targeted at network/distribution and access layers of ISA to render services as planned. Tactical layers of OA are mapped to the ITA and ISA by including state data centers, state level agencies. Access layer of ISA has remained disjointed in Indian context. Various agencies in the spectrum of development, government and civil society are striving for extending support to Indian citizens. In the current context, Indian e-governance systems have seen prolific growth in terms of Point of Service (PoS) in the villages/ group of villages. Various forms of such entities also include Common Service Centers (CSC), Village Resource Centers (VRC), and other mechanisms. Convergence among these entities to establish a framework services for unified PoS for citizens are in the horizon like UIDAI.

Figure 3. Proposed Architecture Framework (Misra,2010b)

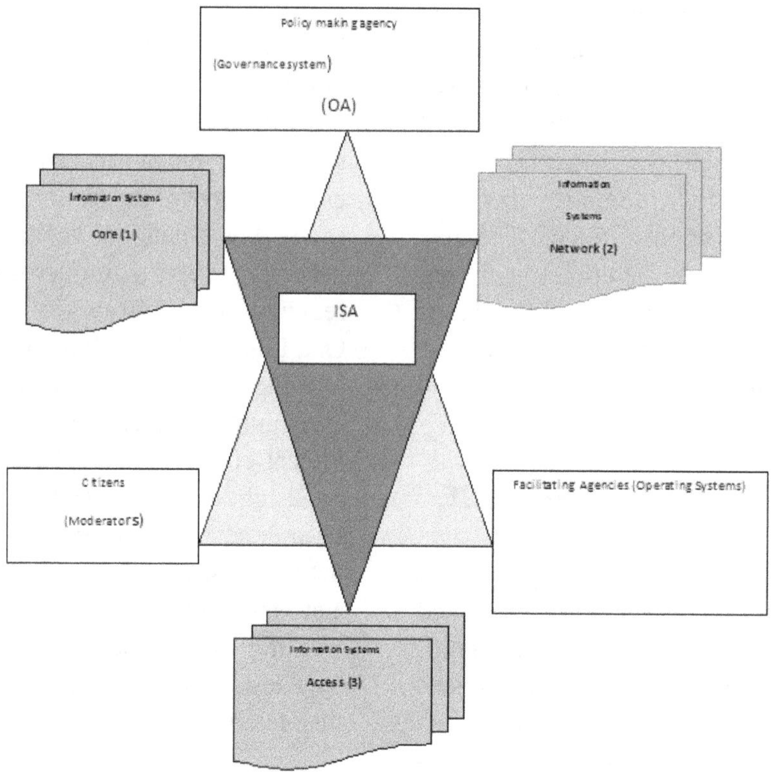

THE CONCEPTUAL FRAMEWORK

A conceptual framework (Misra, 2010; Misra, 2011) is designed to appreciate the convergence of architectural views and contexts which are discussed in the previous section. This is relevant because of the emergence of UIDAI which aims at establishing unified tracking of citizen centered services. This calls for a seamless architectural interface among OA, ISA and ITA. In Figure 3 this framework is proposed. The inverted triangle presents "ISA" which draws inputs and directions from "OA." These two triangles provide layered relationships with views of OA and ISA. Each layer in ISA has a specific task to accomplish while maintaining the integrity among relationships, views and contexts planned. The framework suggests a "triangular" presentation of architecture in order to discuss the focus. ISA aims to focus on "access layer" whereas OA considers governance system as the focal point. As explained in section 2, ISA needs to align with OA. OA components are governance systems, operating systems and citizens. Governance systems include elected bodies in the entire spectrum, government agencies, funding agencies and civil society. Citizens form a critical component in OA framework that "moderates" the existence of governance and operating systems.

As per ISA framework, Information Systems-1 (IS-1), IS-2 and IS-3 need to interface between OA components. This desired linkages among the organizational components together with that of ISA are termed as alignment. Such alignment needs to collectively adhere to the enabling factors for e-inclusion of ISA framework. It may be seen here that ISA focuses on access layer whereas OA focuses on governance systems. ITA is considered complimentary to this framework.

Table 1. ISA Framework for E-Governance Assessment

ISA Framework for E-Governance (Conceptual Deliveries)			
Information System Layer	**Views**	**Enabling Factors for E-Inclusion Under SoA**	**E-Inclusion stakeholders**
IS-3 (Operational Layer)	Citizen Interfaces -Citizens are Transaction Owners -Time, cost and convenience are important	**IS Imperatives** -Ease of use, Usability and Citizens' acceptance **IT Imperatives** -Convergence among Services	Citizens, Business Correspondents, CSC supported Village Level Entrepreneurs, Village level government representatives, PRIs etc.
IS-2 (Network/Distribution Layer)	Interfaces with Citizens -Standardized service Provisioning -Capturing latent demand -Preparation of Guidelines -Capacity Building	**IS Imperatives** -Building Information Infrastructure -Convergence among systems, processes **IT Imperatives** -Intranets, extranets -Unified Views of applications, databases and services	District level government administrators, CSC supported District Level Agencies and State Level Agencies, National Informatics Centre Administrators, State Wide Area Network Administrators, Data Warehousing Agencies.
IS-1 (Core Layer)	Interfaces with Citizens -Mandates designed for citizen benefits -Collaboration with citizens to design systems	**IS Imperatives** -Information management policy -Convergence Policy **IT Imperatives** -Common Procedures for Infrastructure	Union Government Ministries, National E-Governance Plan Authority, Planning Commission, Parliament, Department of Information Technology

In Table 1, information systems views and the critical success factors of the contexts (indicative, not exhaustive) for interfaces are discussed. Identifying enabling factors for e-inclusion are contextual since they describe the ways views are captured through ISA and SoA principles. Agents in this architecture are the stakeholders who are expected to collaborate in the process of e-inclusion. In Table 1these stakeholders are listed.

Three Cases are presented in this section to apply the concepts of architectural convergence in implementing e-governance services in Indian context.

EVALUATION CASE I: MGNREGS

Mahatma Gandhi National Rural Employment Guarantee Services (MGNREGS) is an act notified in the year 2005. It envisages 100 days of employment annually for a rural household whose adult members volunteer for this wage based unskilled work. It aims "to foster conditions for inclusive growth ranging from basic wage security and recharging rural economy to a transformative empowerment process of democracy (NREGA, 2008; Mehdi, 2005). Commencing its operation of the scheme in the year 2006 covering 200 districts, by the year 2008, the scheme is called up to reach all the districts in India. MGNREGS works on the principles of inclusive growth with transparency, collaboration of all stakeholders through established and well organized processes, and accountability of the delivering agencies involved at all levels. State level agencies are empowered to ensure decentralized planning with active involvement of rural citizens, PRIs and other stakeholders. Stakeholders include Wage seekers, Gram Sabha, PRIs (specially the gram panchayat), Programme Officer at the block level, District Programme Coordinator, State Government and Ministry of Rural Development. E-governance systems are being considered as a superset of e-government

Table 2. IS planning in MGNREGS

IS Planning Process Analysis as per ISA Framework			
Information System	**Views**	**Critical Success Factors for E-Inclusion (Contexts)**	**Challenges for E-Inclusion**
IS-3 (Access Layer)	Citizen Interfaces Workers Entitlement information Information on demand for work Stages of work in progress or completed Funds availability	1. Job card based information to the person engaged in the scheme. 2. Eligibility is verified through Gram Sabha (Village level PRI meetings) 3. UID is to support authentication process	1.Literacy among poor in the access layer 2. Information asymmetry still persists 3. Common PoS is yet to emerge in the access layer 4. Seamless language interfaces are yet to be in pace for portals
IS-2 (Network/ Distribution Layer)	Interfaces with Citizens 1. Roles and responsibilities of PRIs, Citizens are available in the guideline. 2. Capturing Physical and Financial Progress Interfaces with Agencies 1. Guidelines suggest the collaboration with state level agencies, PRIs, District Level Agencies. 2. Modules to be available in the public domain. 3. Convergence with other schemes	IS Imperatives 1. Availability of MIS in the public domain 2. Modules of applications related to have - a. Standard Estimates b. Quality of Work c. Worker Management, Fund Management, Labour Budgeting, Social Audit, Grievance Redressal, Alerts, Knowledge Network 3. Monthly Progress Reports at all levels in the operating system	Still irrelevant for the beneficiary. But government machinery and RTI activists are major beneficiaries.
IS-1 (Core Layer)	Interfaces with Citizens 1. Policy to converge 2. Policy to enhance to income of rural household 3. Plan for enhancing livelihood security 4. Analyze trends and planning for future at village level	IS Imperatives 1. Tracking funds utilization at national level with focus on individual household, Panchayat 2. Alerts for unfulfilled demand	Strategic planning and forecasting are possible now, but intended beneficiary in the access layer is oblivious due to poor access to information and low literacy

efforts. In other words it is essential to appreciate that e-government solutions need to contribute to the large issues related to governance (Misra, 2009; Heeks, 2003). MGNREGS provides all the shades of governance since its mission statement aims to enhance livelihood security of rural households. Concurrently, all state governments, PRIs and other agencies including civil society are involved to support this scheme.

IS Planning in MGNREGS

A careful analysis of the planning process of MGNREGS indicates existence of standard operating procedures for executing the scheme at a national level. Operational guidelines are reflecting these procedures in detail. The scheme recognizes the importance of IS planning during its inception. Existence of a website with url http://www.nrega.nic.in and links to the Ministry of Rural Development portal is an indication of the organized planning process. The website contains information on gram panchayats, blocks, districts and states. Job card number centric queries are possible through the website. In Table 2 critical success factors and challenges for e-inclusion are listed.

It may be noted that access layer is the most affected layer in terms of e-inclusion. This challenge is not limited to technologies, but is mostly influenced by various contributing factors including literacy, information asymmetry and imperfect market conditions.

Table 3. IT Planning in MGNREGS

IT Planning Process Analysis as per ISA Framework			
Information System	**Views**	**Critical Success Factors for E-Inclusions (Contexts)**	**Challenges for E-Inclusion**
IS-3 (Access Layer)	Citizen Interfaces 1. Grant ownership to Citizen 2. Provide local language based interaction 3. Make available information at least cost, low latency and accurate	1. Job card based information to the person engaged in the scheme. 2. Crediting job card holders' bank account in certain places (financial inclusion) 3. VKC, VRC, CSC are available 4. Bio-metric based beneficiary authentication and GPS enabled site authentication	1. Establishment of mechanisms for seamless convergence of services and provisioning of mobile PoS 2. Databases with convergence and unique identifications 3. Acceptance of device oriented mobile governance 4. Trust in e-governance services
IS-2 (Network/ Distribution Layer)	1. Interfaces with State Wide Area Networks 2. Web interfaces for citizens and stakeholders listed 3. Exception Handling Alerts	1. Web based NREGAsoft is available 2. Unicode enabled software for local language interfaces 3. Microsoft technology and Open source compatibility 4. Validation with rural household survey BPL census 2002 5. Convergence among other schemes under Ministry of Rural Development (Pilots)	1. Unification of e-governance services especially with e-government and domain specific service convergence. 2. Federated information systems with interoperable IS applications and IT back backbones
IS-1 (Core Layer)	1. Convergence among data sources 2. Unified views for all stakeholders 3. Common operating procedures and guidelines for implementation	Procedures available for IT Infrastructure acquisition and deployment	1. Unification of e-governance services especially with e-government and domain specific service convergence. 2. Federated information systems with interoperable IS applications and IT back backbones

IT Planning in MGNREGS

IT planning is an event that follows the IS planning (Ward & Peppard, 2002). It is essential for the national level agencies to provide a holistic view during execution of IT infrastructure projects that follow the IS planning process. In Table 3 below such a view is taken to understand the status of contexts met so far.

It is noted that the challenges in inclusive e-governance in this case are related to trust and acceptance of e-services. However, it is encouraging to note the advancements in technology interfaced transparent transactions.

EVALUATION CASE II: WATERSHED PROJECT INITIATIVES

Watershed Project Initiatives (WPI) in India came into force in the year 1994. Though initially, the project aimed at addressing issues related to drought, the government treated the initiative with multidimensional approach in the year 2008 to meet the challenges of drop in water table, reduction in forest cover, non-availability of fuel, fodder and drinking water (MoRD, 2010). The concept of watershed project took this shape with a holistic view. Common guidelines consider the issues important in rain fed areas like poverty, productivity, fragile ecosystems, land degradation, low rain water use efficiency and high population pressure. WPI also aims to improve rural livelihood through participatory watershed development to focus on integrated farming systems (Misra, 2011).

E-governance systems are considered as a superset of e-government efforts. In other words, it is essential to appreciate that e-government solutions need to contribute to the large issues related to governance (Misra, 2009). WPI is a national level initiative having a huge financial outlay to create infrastructure at the village level. WPI provides the mandate to village level institutions to own, operate and manage the watershed structures through active citizen participation which is in line with the agenda set by NeGP. Thus there is a scope to leverage the architectural benefits that NeGP provides and WPI looks for.

The framework considers the "WPI guidelines" to be the base document, an open document available. Framework was discussed and validated in a workshop arranged by Ministry of Agriculture and Cooperation which was attended by representatives from "National Rain Fed Authority of India," State agencies including social planners, financing and accounting officials and engineers. WPI guidelines were analyzed based on OA, ISA and ITA. The focus of the paper is to prepare a document showcasing the rationale for having an architectural analysis and understand the deliverables, and scope to improve upon the IT management.

OA of WPI

Organizations under the WPI are designed to have specific delivery mechanisms for meeting the common objectives. In Table 4, these are analyzed. It is noted here that village level institutions are given due importance to manage the resources and infrastructure. This is definite step towards social inclusion and thus has the potential for e-inclusion.

ISA in WPI

A careful analysis of the planning process of WPI indicates existence of standard operating procedures for executing the scheme at a national level. Operational guidelines are reflecting these procedures in detail. The scheme recognizes the importance of IS planning during its inception. Existence of a Ministry of Rural Development portal is an indication of the organized planning process. The website contains information on gram panchayats, blocks, districts and states. An analysis based on the architectural framework discussed provides following details (Table 5).

It may be noted that WPI needs to carefully implement the standards enumerated in the policy document with active considerations for convergence at national level.

Table 4. OA for WPI

OA for WPI		
Layer	**Organizations Planned**	**Objectives**
Operational Layer	Joint Forest Management Committee, Watershed Committee/ Self Help Groups/ User Groups, Gram Sabha/PRI	Management of Watershed resources and the structures at the village level
Tactical Layer	District Watershed Development Units, Implementing Agencies, Planning Committee	Integration of schemes with Watershed Project; Project Management
Strategic Layer	Ministry of Rural Development, Department of Land Resources	Funding for Projects at National Level; IT infrastructure creation
	National Data Centre	
	National Rain-fed Area Authority	Project resource standardization, coordination, Monitoring, Evaluation

ITA in WPI

IT planning is an event that follows the IS planning (Ward & Peppard, 2002). It is essential for the national level agencies to provide a holistic view during execution of IT infrastructure projects that

Table 5. ISA in WPI

IS Planning Process Analysis as per ISA Framework			
Information System Layer	**Views**	**Critical Success Factors for E-Inclusions (Contexts)**	**Challenges for E-Inclusion**
IS-3 (Access Layer)	Citizen Interfaces Citizens' Entitlement, Local demand, work in progress or completed, Funds availability	1. Information on the Citizen rights, privileges and WPI deliveries 2. Emergence of Village Institutions to manage resources and assets	1. Establishment of mechanisms for seamless convergence of services and provisioning of mobile PoS 2. Databases with convergence and unique identifications 3. Acceptance of device oriented mobile governance 4. Trust in e-governance services
IS-2 (Network/Distribution Layer)	Interfaces with Citizens 1. Roles and responsibilities of PRIs, Citizens are available in the guideline 2. Capturing Physical and Financial Progress Interfaces with Agencies 1.Modules to be available in the public domain 2.Convergence with other schemes	**IS Imperatives** **1.**Availability of MIS in the public domain 2. Modules of applications related to have Standard Estimates, Quality of Work, Fund Management, etc. 3. Monthly Progress Reports at all levels in the operating system	1. Unification of e-governance services especially with e-government and domain specific service convergence. 2. Federated information systems with interoperable IS applications
IS-1 (Core Layer)	Interfaces with Citizens 1. Policy to converge 2. Policy to enhance to income of rural household 3. Plan for enhancing livelihood security 4. Analyze trends and planning for future at village level	**IS Imperatives** 1. Tracking funds utilization at national level with focus on individual household, Panchayat 2. Alerts for unfulfilled demand	1. Unification of e-governance services especially with e-government and domain specific service convergence. 2. Federated information systems with interoperable IS applications and IT back backbones

follow the IS planning process. In Table 6 below such a view is taken to understand the status of contexts met so far.

WPI has recognized the relevance of technology interventions and IS-1 layer in the ISA has listed technology driven resources for the projects. The list includes rain gauges (automatic/manual), soil monitoring equipments (digital), Global Positioning Systems (GPS) units, personal computers and other IT infrastructures (MoRD, 2010).

EVALUATION CASE III: NATIONAL E-GOVERNANCE PLAN

National e-governance Plan (NeGP) has provided the platform to render effective services at the national and state levels through organized backbones, data centers and MMPs as a part of three layered EA. NeGP has been included 100,000 CSCs with an aim to provide the platform for convergence of various services through Private-Public-Partnership (PPP) modes. NeGP recognizes the scope for large-scale implementation of application under Mission Mode Projects (MMPs) with emphasis on integrated services. Under NeGP, national level MMPs and state level MMPs are identified for implementation on scale up mode as presented in Figure 4 (DIT, 2011).

Besides providing the MMPs for states, centre and integrated services the backbone network is one of the deliveries of NeGP. Every interested state government is now under State Wide Area Network plan (SWAN). Each state is now in the process of having SDCs under the NeGP policy. It envisages provisioning of services through CSCs

Table 6. ITA in WPI

IT Planning Process Analysis as per ISA Framework			
Information System Layer	**Views**	**Critical Success Factors for E-Inclusions (Contexts)**	**Challenges for E-Inclusion**
IS-3 (Access Layer)	Citizen Interfaces Grant ownership to Citizen, Provide local language based interaction, Make available information at least cost, low latency and accurate	IT orientation is not available as per the guidelines	1. Establishment of mechanisms for seamless convergence of services and provisioning of mobile PoS 2. Databases with convergence and unique identifications 3. Acceptance of device oriented mobile governance 4. Trust in e-governance services
IS-2 (Network/Distribution Layer)	Interfaces with State Wide Area Networks, Web interfaces for citizens and stakeholders listed, Exception Handling Alerts	Web based Portal for MoRD	1. Unification of e-governance services especially with e-government and domain specific service convergence. 2. Federated information systems with interoperable IS applications and IT back backbones
IS-1 (Core Layer)	Convergence among data sources, Unified views for all stakeholders, common operating procedures and guidelines for implementation	Procedures available for IT Infrastructure acquisition and deployment	1. Unification of e-governance services especially with e-government and domain specific service convergence. 2. Federated information systems with interoperable IS applications and IT back backbones

Figure 4. MMPs under NeGP (Source: DIT, 2011)

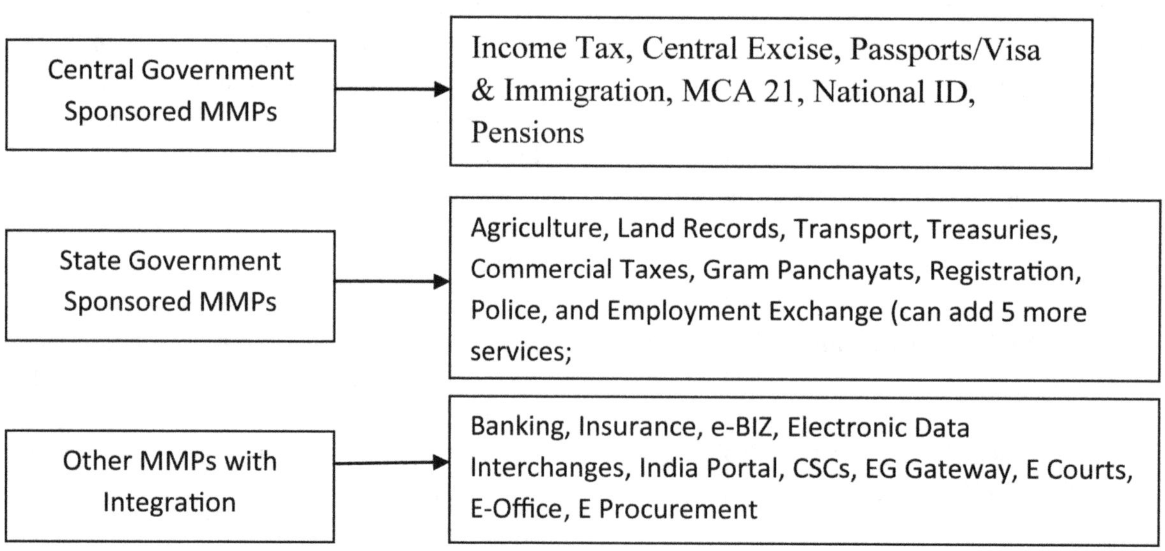

Figure 5. NeGP Approach for Integration (Source: DIT, 2011)

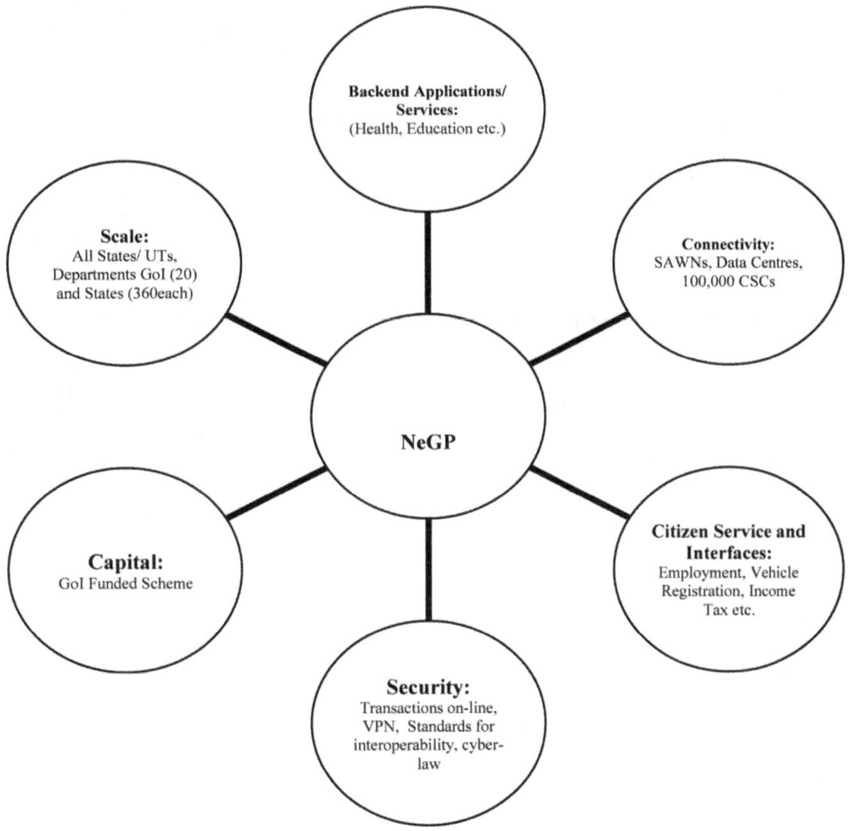

planned to be made available in every sixth village across the country and these services include district administration and citizen centric government services (DIT, 2011).

NeGP has now laid emphases on deploying MMPs at the levels of state and central government and provided the desired attention to integrate them so as to generate citizen centric services on demand and to increase the latent demand. In Figure 5 the approach to integrate various services is presented. In this integrated approach NeGP intends to provide a service grid through adequate connectivity, increased influx of capital with focused deliveries, increase in the capacity and capabilities of service provisioning agencies in the government, providing adequate content in local languages, establishing required policies and legal frameworks to encourage convergence of services and service providers, establish security standards and lastly channel the grid based services to the citizens through and established "channel of interface."

OA of NeGP

Organizations under the NeGP are designed to have specific delivery mechanisms for meeting the common objectives to render services to the citizens. In Table 7, these are analyzed.

It may be noted that organizationally, the strategic direction has been to outsource the e-governance services to various agencies engaged at levels of states and CSCs. This needs serious convergence policies to direct e-services to the CSCs.

Table 7. OA of NeGP

OA for NeGP		
Layer	**Organizations Planned**	**Objectives**
Operational Layer	CSCs owned by private entrepreneurs. Village Level Entrepreneurs are engaged to render services at a price	Citizens will get services in their vicinity
Tactical Layer	District Level Agencies (DLA) organize their work in coordination with district governments and liaise with business partners to render services to CSCs	Integration of services for providing services to citizens on demand
Strategic Layer	State Level Agencies (SLA) to coordinate at the state level and liaise with government agencies and business entities to provide services at the CSCs in collaboration with and DLAs.	Convergence of services at state level. National Level Agency (NLA) also plays a vital role to render desired services to SLAs.
	State Data Center, National Data Centre	

ISA in NeGP

A careful analysis of the planning process of NeGP indicates existence of standard operating procedures for executing the scheme at a national level. Operational guidelines are reflecting these procedures in detail. The scheme recognizes the importance of IS planning during its inception. Existence of a Ministry of Information Technology (DIT) and National Informatics Centre (NIC) are part of the architectural plan. Updates on CSCs and their implementations at state levels are presented for public views. An analysis based on the architectural framework provides the following details (Table 8).

Table 8. ISA in NeGP

IS Planning Process Analysis as per ISA Framework			
Information System Layer	**Views**	**Critical Success Factors for E-Inclusions Addressed (Contexts)**	**Challenges for E-Inclusion**
IS-3 (Access Layer)	1. Citizen Interfaces 2. Citizens' Entitlement, Local demand 3. Enabling environment for citizens to collaborate, place their demands and identify the needs	1.Information on the Citizen rights, privileges and converged services for citizen 2. Establishment of alternate channels for e-government services	1.Citizen service orientation 2.Trust in e-government services 3.Trust in service agents 4. Enhance quality of services
IS-2 (Network/ Distribution Layer)	Interfaces with District level and State Level government agencies, Business entities	**IS Imperatives** Availability of services in the public domain	1. Unification of e-governance services especially with e-government and domain specific service convergence. 2. Federated information systems with interoperable IS applications
IS-1 (Core Layer)	Interfaces with Citizens 1. Policy to converge 2. Policy to enhance to income of rural household 3. Plan for enhancing livelihood security 4. Analyze trends and planning for future at village level	**IS Imperatives** 1. Tracking citizen services planned and rendered 2. Alerts for unfulfilled demand	1. Unification of e-governance services especially with e-government and domain specific service convergence. 2. Federated information systems with interoperable IS applications and IT back backbones

An analysis on the e-inclusion challenges indicates that e-services available at the CSCs are mostly business oriented and there is service specific acceptance among the citizens. Because of this acceptance, there is scope to leverage these efforts for rolling out e-governance services with active collaborations of PRIs and citizens. But there are many challenges including unification

Table 9. ITA in NeGP

IT Planning Process Analysis as per ISA Framework			
Information System Layer	**Views**	**Critical Success Factors for E-Inclusions Addressed (Contexts)**	**Challenges for E-Inclusion**
IS-3 (Access Layer)	Citizen Interfaces, Create demand for Citizen services, Provide local language based interaction, Make available information related to other interventions – convergence	Alternate channel for e-government service provisioning	1.To provide e-government services on demand 2. Enhancing citizen trust in agents engaged
IS-2 (Network/ Distribution Layer)	Interfaces with State Wide Area Networks, Web interfaces for citizens and stakeholders.	Web based Portal for DIT, NIC and other agencies need to converge.	1. Unification of e-governance services especially with e-government and domain specific service convergence. 2. Federated information systems with interoperable IS applications and IT back backbones
IS-1 (Core Layer)	Convergence among data sources, Unified views for all stakeholders, common operating procedures and guidelines for implementation	Procedures need to be deployed for IT Infrastructure acquisition and deployment	1. Unification of e-governance services especially with e-government and domain specific service convergence. 2. Federated information systems with interoperable IS applications and IT back backbones

of services at the state and central levels of governments for e-inclusion.

ITA in NeGP

IT planning is an event that follows the IS planning (Luftman, 2003). It is essential for the national level agencies to provide a holistic view during

Table 10. Convergence in E-Governance Architecture

Layers	Attributes as per Framework	Convergence Status for NeGP, WPI and MGNREGS		Explanations
		Content	**Carriage**	
OA	Operational	Missing	Missing	Organizational arrangements are in islands of service provisioning. Need to converge in all these layers.
	Tactical	Missing	Missing	
	Strategic	Missing	Missing	
ISA	Access Layer	Missing	Missing	In the operational, tactical and core layers, convergence entirely missing. This needs immediate attention for the benefit of service providers and citizens.
	Network/ Distribution Layer	Missing	Missing	
	Core Layer	Missing	Missing	
ITA	Access	Missing	Missing	Except in tactical layer, where SWAN is deployed for service provisioning, other layers are in islands of technology infrastructure.

execution of IT infrastructure projects that follow the IS planning process. In Table 9 below such a view is taken to understand the status of contexts met so far.

It is noted that CSCs have merged as hubs of business activities for the entrepreneurs in the village. Trust for e-services, capturing the needs of citizens and collating their demands on e-services are some of the challenges for e-inclusion.

Table 11. Degree of E-Inclusion in three Cases

Architectural Assessment Layers	Layers in the Architecture	Case		
		MGNREGS	WPI	NeGP
OA	Operational	+++	+++	+
	Tactical	++++	+++	+
	Strategic	+++	+++	+++
ISA	Access Layer	+++	+++	++
	Network/Distribution Layer	+++	+	+
	Core Layer	++	++	++
ITA	Access Layer	+++	++	++
	Network/Distribution Layer	+++	++	++
	Core Layer	++	++	++

Note: + -> poor, ++ -> Average, +++ -> Satisfactory, ++++ -> Good, +++++ -> Excellent

DISCUSSION

Architectural treatment to e-governance needs a holistic approach. Global EA argues in its favour and Indian government is supporting this approach as well. However, convergence is not seen as an important contributor to this EA. In these three cases, convergence at all the layers of framework proposed is found missing. In Table 10, these dimensions are discussed with respect to convergence.

In Table 11, degree of e-inclusion available in three cases is presented. It is noted that MGNREGS is displaying the promises for e-inclusion across OA, ISA and ITA of the architecture. WPI and NeGP have shown promises of e-inclusion strategically.

CONCLUSION

The conceptual framework applied in understanding architectural perspectives to achieve convergence among various agencies and service oriented deliveries has provided some insights to the scope for value additions. It also provided insights to the e-inclusion challenges that are available in e-governance strategies discussed in three cases adopted. It is argued that agent-based computing architecture needs to converge with service-oriented architecture in e-governance scenario in Indian context. In many critical layers of the framework, convergence and e-inclusion seem to be inadequate across all the three cases discussed. Especially the MMPs designed for national level scale up in Indian context need convergence with e-inclusion strategies. In most of the cases OA and ISA do not converge and there many similar agents in the OA to deliver similar sets of services. This convergence is likely to reduce redundancy, improve upon protection in investments and provisioning of services to citizens. Reduction in redundancy is also expected to enhance degrees of e-inclusion. Nevertheless, there are attempts in the DIT and NIC in India to provide portal based services to meet the emerging need of convergence. There are many attempts to converge in the carriage element of convergence. NeGP provides necessary platform to consider convergence in addition to having "functional," "technical," "contextual" and "solution" architectures. In Table- 1 various agents under agent-based computing architecture are expected to be common to all the three cases discussed. Unfortunately, these commonalities are not visible during implementation of the programmes despite availability of tools under ITA. Thus there is a dire need for all the ministries in Indian government to converge the content element of convergence through organized agent-based and SOA based computing architectures.

The framework presented in this chapter is conceptualized to examine the convergence of architectures being planned for Indian e-governance systems with e-inclusion. The future agenda is to focus on its large scale applications to showcase the areas of improvements in convergence and e-inclusion in Indian context. The aim is also to document the findings for establishing best practices available globally and assess the areas in national e-governance plan for further value additions.

FURTHER RESEARCH

This chapter presents a conceptual framework to capture architectural perspectives to showcase its applicability during large scale e-governance projects. The future work aims to apply the dimensions of e-governance architectural framework and build a model and develop a tool to assess and predict possible voids during conceptualization of e-governance projects. This intends to help bridge the design-reality gaps that e-governance projects normally display.

REFERENCES

Administrative Reforms Commission (ARC). (2008). *Eleventh report of ARC, promoting e-governance, smart way forward*. Government of India.

Archmann, S., & Kudlacek, I. (2008, February). Interoperability and the exchange of good practice cases. *European Journal of ePractice*, 2. ISSN: 1988-625X.

Becker, J., Niehaves, B., Bergener, P., & Räckers, M. (2008). Digital divide in eGovernment: The einclusion gap model. In Wimmer, M. A., Scholl, H. J., & Ferro, E. (Eds.), *EGOV 2008, LNCS 5184* (pp. 231–242). Springer-Verlag.

Bhatia, D. (2005, April). *Designing and implementing e-government: Key issues, best practices and lessons learned*. World Bank.

Bovaird, T. (2005). E-government and e-governance: Organizational implications, options and dilemmas. In Practicing e-government: A global perspective. ISSBN 1-59140-637-4.

Clements, P., Bachmann, F., Bass, L., Garlan, D., Ivers, J., & Little, R. et al. (2009). *Documenting software architectures, views and beyond*. Boston, MA: Pearson Education, Inc..

Department of Information Technology (DIT). (2011). *Saaransh, a compendium of mission mode projects under NeGP*.

EC. (2007a). *Measuring progress in e-inclusion*. Riga Dashboard, European Commission, DG Information Society and Media, e-Government unit.

EC. (2007b, December). *Inclusive e-government: Survey of status and baseline activities*. European Commission, DG Information Society and Media, e-Government unit.

EC. (2010). European i2010 initiative on e-Inclusion "*To be part of the information society*." European Commission, DG Information Society and Media, e-Government unit.

Garlan, D., & Shaw, M. (1994). *An introduction to software architecture*. Carnegie Mellon University Technical Report CMU-CS-94-166.

Government of India. (2001, November). *Report of the working group on convergence and e-governance for tenth five year plan* (2002-2007, pp. 6-25). Planning Commission, New Delhi.

Government of India. (2013). *MoRD*. Retrieved May 29, 2010, from http://www.rural.nic.in

Government of India. (2013). *MGNREGS*. Retrieved April 29, 2010, from http://nrega.nic.in/netnrega/home.aspx

Griffiths, N., & Chao, K.-M. (2010). *Agent-based service-oriented computing*. Springer-Verlag. doi:10.1007/978-1-84996-041-0.

Harekrishna, M. (2009a). Understanding SOA perspective of e-governance in Indian context: Case based study. *22nd Bled Conference, eEnablement: Facilitating an Open, Effective and Representative eSociety*, June 14 - 17, Bled, Slovenia.

Harekrishna, M. (2009b). *Governance of rural information and communication technology: Opportunities and challenges. ISBN: 13*. New Delhi: Academic Foundation.

Harekrishna, M. (2010a). Citizen-centric service dimensions of Indian rural e-governance systems: An evaluation. In Rahman, H. (Ed.), *Cases on adoption, diffusion, and evaluation of global e-governance systems: Impact at the grass roots*. IGI Global Publishing.

Harekrishna, M. (2010b). Role of information systems architecture in e-governance: The case of MGNREGS in India. *ICEGOV2010*, October 25-28, Beijing, China.

Heeks, R. (2003). *Most e-government projects-for-development fail: How can risk be reduced?* Working Paper 14, IDPM, University of Manchester.

Heeks, R. (2008). ICT4D 2.0: The next phase of applying ICT for international development. IEEE Computer Society, 0018-9162/08.

Heeks, R., & Molla, A. (2009). *Impact assessment of ICT-for-development projects: A compendium of approaches*. Working Paper 36, Institute for Development, Policy and Management (IDPM), University of Manchester.

Khosrow-Pour, M. (2005). *Practicing e-government-A global perspective*. Idea Group Publishing. doi:10.4018/978-1-59140-637-2.

Luftman, J. (2003). Assessing IT/business alignment. *Information Systems Management*, *20*(4), 9–21. doi:10.1201/1078/43647.20.4.20030901/77287.2.

Maier, M. W., & Eberhardt, R. (2009). *The art of systems architecting* (3rd ed.). Taylor & Francis, Inc, CRC Press.

Mancinelli, E. (2007). E-Inclusion in the information society. Network for Information Society. Harekrishna, M. (2012). The role of software architectures in managing citizen-centric e-governance initiatives in India: An evaluation framework. Working Paper 231, Institute of Rural Management Anand.

Harekrishna, M. (2011). Role of information systems architecture in e-governance: The case of watershed management in India. ICACT Conference, Phoenix Park, South Korea, February, 13-16.

NREGA. (2008). The national rural employment guaranty act, 2005, (3rd ed.). Operational Guidelines, Ministry of Rural Development, Government of India, New Delhi.

Planning Commission. (2001). Government of India. Indian Communication Convergence Bill 2000 (pp. 2).

Riga Declaration. (2006). *Internet for all: EU ministers commit to an inclusive and barrier-free information society*. Press release of June, IP/06/769.

Scott, M., Golden, W., & Hughes, M. (2004). A click and bricks strategy for e-government. *17th Bled eCommerce Conference, eGlobal,* Bled, Slovenia, June 21 - 23

UIDAI. (2010, April). *Unique identification authority of india strategic overview*. Unique Identification Authority of India, Planning Commission, Government of India, New Delhi.

UN. (2005). *Global e-governance e-readiness report, from e-government to e-inclusion*. New York.

UN. (2006). *E-Participation and e-government: Understanding the present and creating the future, report of the ad hoc expert group meeting*. Budapest, Hungary, 27 – 28 July.

UN. (2008). *UN e-government survey, from e-government to connected e-governance*. New York.

UN. (2010). *United Nations e-government, survey 2010, Leveraging e-government, at a time of financial and economic crisis. UN Publishing Section*. New York: ISBN.

Van Vliet, P. J. A., & Pietron, L. R. (2006). Information systems development education in real world – A project methodology and assessment. *Journal of Information Systems Education, 17*(3). Retrieved May 5, 2010, from http://www.isqa.unomaha.edu/vanvliet/pvvresearch.htm

Ward, J., & Peppard, J. (2002). *Strategic planning for information systems*. England: John Wiley and Sons.

Woods, E. (2006). Experiences using viewpoints for information systems architecture: An industrial experience report. Artechra Limited, Hamilton House, 6th Floor, 111 Marlowes, Hemel Hempstead, HP1 3HY, UK.

Zachman, J. A. (1987). A framework for information systems architecture. *IBM Systems Journal, 26*(3). doi:10.1147/sj.263.0276.

ADDITIONAL READING

Ahen, D. M., Clouse, A., & Turner, R. (2001). *CMMI Distilled: A practical introduction to integrated process improvement* (pp. 6–17). New York: Addison-Wesley.

Arsanjani, A. (2004). *Service oriented modeling and architecture*. Web Service Centre of Excellence, IBM.

Asian Development Bank. (2008). Strategy 2020, the long-term strategic framework of the Asian Development Bank, 2008–2020. ISBN 978-971-561-680-5.

Benamou, N. (2006). Bringing e-government interoperability to local governments in Europe. egovInterop'06 Conference, Bordeaux, France.

Chandrashekhar, R. (2006). *Common services centres: A strategic cornerstone of NeGP*. Workshop on Knowledge Centre Initiatives, Jaipur, April, 19.

Clarke, J., Newman, J., Smith, N., Vidler, E., & Westmarland, L. (2007). *Creating citizen consumers*. London: Sage Publications.

Drake, P., & Shanks, G. (1997). User viewpoint modelling: Understanding and representing user viewpoints during requirements definition. *Information Systems Journal, 7*(3), 213. doi:10.1046/j.1365-2575.1997.d01-19.x.

Gallivan, M. J., & Keil, M. (2003). The user-developer communication process: A critical case study. *Information Systems Journal, 13*(1), 37. doi:10.1046/j.1365-2575.2003.00138.x.

Garland, J., & Anthony, R. (2003). *Large-scale software architecture: A practical guide using UML* (pp. 35–56). New Delhi: Wiley Dreamtech India.

Gordon, D. B., & Olson, M. H. (2000). *Management information systems: Conceptual foundations, structure and development* (2nd ed.). Singapore: McGraw-Hill.

Grady, R. B. (1992). *Practical software metrics for project management and process improvement* (pp. 30–38). New Jersey: Prentice Hall.

Grimsley, M., & Meehan, A. (2007). e-Government information systems: Evaluation-led design for public value and client trust. *European Journal of Information Systems, 16*(2), 134–148. doi:10.1057/palgrave.ejis.3000674.

Herron, D. (2002). *IT measurement: Practical advice from experts, international function point user group- Part-I* (pp. 27–28). Boston: Addison-Wesley Professional.

Huff, S. L., & Munro, M. C. (1985, December). Information technology assessment and adoption: A field study. *Management Information Systems Quarterly*, 327–340. doi:10.2307/249233.

Irani, Z., & Elliman, T. (2007). *Project VIEGO: Towards a virtual institute for research into e-government*. London: Brunel University.

Irani, Z., & Love, P. E. D. (2002). Developing a frame of reference for ex-ante IT/IS investment evaluation. *European Journal of Information Systems, 11*(1), 74–82. doi:10.1057/palgrave/ejis/3000411.

Jan Vom, B., Schenk, B., & Sonnenberg, C. (2009). *Classification criteria for governing the implementation process of service-oriented ERP systems – An analysis based on new institutional economics*. Americas Conference on Information Systems (AMCIS 2009). Retrieved October 23, 2009, from http://aisel.aisnet.org/amcis2009/316

Jansen, A. (2005). *Assessing e-governance progress- Why and what*. Department of e-government studies. University of Oslo, Norway. Retrieved July 11, 2006, from http://www.afin.uio.no/om_enheten/folk/ansatte/jansen.html

Kaul, U. (2008). *Common service centres: Slow progress*. Retrieved September 19, 2008, from http://dqindia.ciol.commakesections.asp/08061901.asp

Kelly, G., Mulgan, G., & Muers, S. (2002). *Creating public value: An analytical framework for public service reform. Strategy Unit discussion paper*. London: Cabinet Office.

Kelly, J. M. (2005). The dilemma of the unsatisfied customer in a market model of public administration. *Public Administration Review, 65*(1), 76–84. doi:10.1111/j.1540-6210.2005.00432.x.

Klecun, E., & Cornford, T. (2005). A critical approach to evaluation. *European Journal of Information Systems, 14*, 229–243. doi:10.1057/palgrave.ejis.3000540.

Lee, C. S. (2001). Modeling the business value of information technology. *Information & Management, 39*(3), 191–210. doi:10.1016/S0378-7206(01)00090-8.

Mishra, D. C. (2007). *Select aspects of conceptual foundations of e-government, clearing the fog for better vision*. International Conference of E-Governance (ICEG 2007), Hyderabad, 29-30 December.

Prabhu, C. S. R. (2004). *E-governance – Concepts and case studies*. Prentice Hall.

Prabhu, C. S. R. (2007). *Towards an e-governance grid for India (E-CGI): An architectural framework for citizen service delivery*. International Conference of E-Governance (ICEG 2007), Hyderabad, 29-30 December.

Rai, A., Lang, S. S., & Welker, R. B. (2002). Assessing the validity of IS success models: An empirical test and theoretical analysis. *Information Systems Research, 13*(1), 50–69. doi:10.1287/isre.13.1.50.96.

Ravichandran, T., Leong, Y.-X., Teo, H.-H., & Oh, L.-B. (2007). *Service-oriented architecture and organizational integration: An empirical study of IT-enabled sustained competitive advantage*. International Conference on Information Systems (ICIS). Retrieved October 23, 2009, from http://aisel.aisnet.org/icis2007/92

Riley, T. B. (2003). E-governance vs e-government. *I4D, 1*(4).

World Bank. (1994). *Governance the world bank's experience*. Washington, DC: The World Bank.

KEY TERMS AND DEFINITIONS

Architecture: Architecture is an approach to present structures at macro level. This structure masks all the detailed operational issues for the common user of the services that the structure can provide. This helps in understanding the behavior of the processes and provides the scope for reuse the benefits of structures already made for certain services.

Citizen Centric E-Governance: This provides a platform to establish cohesive relationships between citizens, business and government systems. It relates to convergence.

Convergence: Convergence aims to provide unified and aggregated views for the common user in which various architectures can be grouped. Convergence can happen in the content which ensures that tools like UNICODE are promoted for local language interfaces independent of applications, databases and platforms. Convergence is also related to the carriage which ensures interoperability among service providers in the areas of systems, hardware, networks and communication infrastructure developed. This is intended to provide seamlessly integrated services to the common citizen.

Dashboards: Dashboards are the fact oriented performance measures which are designed for providing multimedia enabled indicators to the users in access, network and core layers of the organizations. These are necessary to ensure that services are rendered as desired and also to provide the scope for improvements in the performance levels.

E-Governance: Electronic form of citizen interfaces and citizen service delivery.

E-Government: Electronic form of back end and formalized services for citizens.

E-Inclusion: Electronic form of inclusion in which equity of access to information and services is ensured.

Enterprise: Enterprises are built by people who come together to render services, produce goods and manage resources to add value to their investments collectively.

Governance: Participation of citizens in availing services of government.

Government: Formalized bureaucracy for provisioning of citizen services.

Information Systems: Information systems are the interfaces between the organizations like enterprises and the technology enabled tools to ensure that desired services are rendered with a common objective set by the organizations. Information systems developed provide the avenues to establish standard operating procedures and performance measures for efficient interfaces among users, technology and processes available in the organization.

Information: Processed data for the benefit of users or intended recipients.

Latency: Minimum delay in a system to render services.

Panchayat Raj Institution (PRI): Is an elected body at the village level that is empowered to provide services to the rural households and government machinery extend all support to this institution.

Personal Digital Assistant: This is a device that provides local computing facilities, storage space and ability to provide wireless/wire based communication to have access to remote servers on demand.

Point of Service: This is regarded as a spatial dimension of service that identifies the location where the service is made available.

Scorecards: Scorecards are used in the operational and tactical layers to provide controls in data acquisitions, validating the data architectures and ensure that information flow is maintained for effective implementations of dashboards.

Chapter 17
Rhetoric vs. Realities in Implementation of E-Government Master Plan in Nepal

Kiran Rupakhetee
Purbanchal University, Nepal

Almas Heshmati
Sogang University, Seoul, South Korea

ABSTRACT

This study discusses different facets of implementation of e-government in Nepal. With the background theoretical information about e-government in general, the Nepalese case of e-government initiatives is discussed with a specific focus on the "e-government Master Plan." Important pillars of any e-government initiatives, namely infrastructure, human resources, institutions, and policy and legal aspects are looked into from the perspective of feasibility of e-government implementation in Nepal. While doing so, Heeks's e-government success/failure model has been taken into consideration accounting for different dimensions, namely information, technology, process, objectives and values, staffing and skills, management systems and structures, and other resources, which are responsible to create design reality gap thereby jeopardizing the success of e-government projects. This study is the first in the Nepalese perspective, which tries to analyze the constraints in e-government implementation resulted from shortcomings in infrastructure, human resources, institutions, and policy and legal aspects. The authors believe that failure of e-GMP to achieve targeted objectives by the end of 2011 can also be attributed to these factors. The insights inferred can be useful in facilitating a smoother implementation of the master plan related to e-government.

DOI: 10.4018/978-1-4666-4245-4.ch017

INTRODUCTION

It is widely accepted that governments in the developing countries in general and the least developed countries in particular are costing too much and delivering too little. There is also a common belief that those governments are not responsive or accountable to the people to the extent they are supposed to be. The use of ICT, in this context, for the purpose of transforming conventional government to e-government has largely been accepted as one of the remedies of these problems. E-government not only simplifies and improves processes of governance, but also networks itself with citizens and business communities. It is, therefore, acknowledged as a powerful tool to ensure effective and affordable service delivery to its different stakeholders, namely, government organizations, business people and common citizens.

There is a tendency of pursuing e-government in narrow sense, i.e., providing limited services to the people online, especially in developing and the least developed countries. Making service online, therefore, is one of the prerequisites today for good governance, but it can't be a luxury any more. While integrating ICT in development process, some developing countries have achieved significant progress. Such progress has remained in the form of rapid economic development, improved administrative efficiency and greater opportunities for participation by the citizens in the affairs of government. E-Government these days is accepted as one of the fundamental rights of the citizen. e-Government needs to be understood, therefore, as much more substantial transformation than only e-Service delivery. It incorporates public sector, as well as the private institutions, people and processes. It is obviously not only about technology; it is about reinventing the way in which governments interact with citizens, governmental agencies, businesses, employees, and other stakeholders. It is about enhancing democratic processes and also about using new ideas to make lives easier for the citizen by transforming government processes, enabling economic development, and renewing the role of government itself in society (Lofsted, 2005).

Nepal, one of the least developed countries in the world, is also trying to have e-government in place, but without having concerted efforts. Specifically, for the last decade or so Nepal has been making effort in the development of ICT sector thereby promoting e-government through different plans, policies and programmatic interventions. Those efforts have remained shallow not bringing any encouraging result either because of institutional rigidity and inefficiency or because of not having concerted serious efforts towards this end. The implementation of e-Government Master Plan (e-GMP) (2007-2011) of Nepal was a hope to materialize the dream of e-government into reality. However, the deadline for its implementation (2011) is already over without achieving anything substantial . Against this backdrop, the purpose of this paper is to provide a foundation for future research in the field of e-government in Nepal. This paper is an attempt to analyze different hindering factors related to four important pillars of e-government, namely infrastructure, human resources, institutional aspects and policy and legal dimensions. In doing so, we have discussed different factors responsible to create design reality gap as proposed by Heeks (2004) in his e-Government success/failure model, namely information, technology, processes, objectives and values, staffing and skills, management systems and structures and other resources. E-Government Master Plan (e-GMP) of Nepal is presented as a case study in this regard to show that different factors mentioned above create a design reality gap thereby causing dismally low progress in the implementation of e-government in general and e-GMP in particular. Different research papers, which have been written previously on e-government in Nepal have not dealt with these factors from the perspective of implementation of e-GMP.

This study at the outset reviews relevant literature related to e-government focusing primarily on infrastructure, human resources, institutional, and policy and legal aspects. The paper also explains in brief the Heeks's e-government success/failure model. The next segment of the paper mentions about Nepal's demographic, economic, and industrial front in brief with a motive to link those factors with e-government implementation status of the country. Different aspects of the e-GMP have been explained at length as a case study by aligning it with Heeks's success/failure model. Before concluding the paper, some policy measures for the successful implementation of the e-Government are also suggested.

REVIEW OF LITERATURE

Since, process and structures are two basic factors in the delivery of online services to the common people and businesses (Backus, 2001), a number of variables are believed to be associated with these two aspects, namely human resources, institutional settings, policy and legal provisions and state of infrastructure. Hence, these factors are considered while reviewing the literature. Moreover, theoretical aspects of different stages of e-government implementation and Heeks's e-Government success/failure model are also presented under this heading.

Theoretical Understanding

There is no universally accepted model and definition of e-government as every country and society has its own priorities and needs. The necessary condition for e-government system to implement varies from country to country depending on their requirements and objectives of e-government system to be implemented along with the level of infrastructure development, arrangement of policy and legal provisions, and availability of human capital as a prerequisites (Pacific Council on International Policy, 2002).

Heeks (2001) defines e-government as the use of ICT to improve all activities of public sector or organizations. It establishes a relationship between government officials and citizens providing greater access to government information and services by making government accessible through online mechanism. Moreover, it enhances peoples' participation by enabling them to interact more conveniently with government officials thereby reducing corruption.

E-government is more than just a government website on the internet. In this context, Backus (2001) has defined e-government as a sort of e-business in governance and refers to the processes and structures pertinent to the delivery of electronic services to the people collaborating with businesses partners and carrying electronic transactions within and outside organizational entity. Curtin et al. (2004) in this regard have opined that it is an important agent for government in having better governance.

Lenk and Traunmuller (2000, as cited in Lofstedt, 2005)) accepting the wider scope of e-government assert that e-government is a powerful guiding vision for the transformation, which governments must adapt. E-Government, therefore, is the term that reflects the use of information and communication technology (ICT) in public administration to change structures and processes of government organizations. According to the UN (2003), there are three prerequisites that affect the potential of e-government; a minimum threshold level of technological infrastructure, human capital, and e-connectivity for all.

Gartner (2000, as cited in Zhiyuan, 2002) defines e-government as "the continuous optimization of service delivery, constituency participation and governance by transforming internal and external relationships through technology, the internet and the new media."

E-government is thought as luxury today in most of the developing world. However, such way of consideration is a very narrow thinking. E-government can be perceived as a basic necessity of every government; something like Any Time Money (ATM). Caldow (2001) is of the opinion that given the low and poor quality of public service provision, contemporary governments do not have another option other than embracing online service delivery by abandoning conventional system of governance. In failing to do so, most of these governments cannot provide basic minimum standard to the lives of common people.

Pacific Council on International Policy (2002) maintains the view that e-government can not be a quick remedy for economic growth, clean and efficient government. Moreover, big reforms through it is not possible overnight. It implies, therefore, that it is a evolution or process having financial and political costs and risks.

Heek's E-Government Success/Failure Model

Heeks (2003) is of the opinion that most e-government projects, both in industrialized and developing countries, fail either totally or partially. Lack of "e-readiness" and the oversize gaps between project design and on-the-ground reality, known as "design-reality gaps," are the most important factors behind such failure. He opines that these failures cost too much for the world's poorer countries and there is no single established way and no "best practice" that would lead to successful e-government. E-Government cannot be ensured with the mere purchase of advanced technology or the direct automation of complex procedures until and unless it can increase participation level of the citizen thereby bringing about effectiveness of government.

Despite the fact that successes of e-government projects are very important for the efficiency and effectiveness of public sector organizations, the majority of such projects fail. Heeks (2003) has categorized such failure into three parts: total failure, partial failure and not failure (success). He has defined total failure as the situation in which "the initiative was never implemented or was implemented but immediately abandoned." Partial failures are explained as "major goals for the initiative were not attained and/or there were significant undesirable outcomes." Lastly, success refers to a situation in which most stakeholders achieved their major goals and did not experience significant undesirable outcomes.

On the basis of his study, Heeks has estimated that out of total e-government projects in developing and transitional countries, 35% are total failures, 50% are partial failures, and 15% are success. He is of the opinion that e-Government success and failures, therefore, depends on the size of gap that exists between "current realities" and "design" of the e-government project. It is obvious, therefore, that the larger the gap the greater the risk of e-government failure and smaller the gap, the greater the chance of success.

Figure 1 depicts Heeks model showing different dimensions responsible for design reality gap thereby causing e-government failure. Seven dimensions summarized by the ITPOSMO acronym have been used by Heeks to explain design reality gaps. They are: (i) Information; (ii) Technology; (iii) Processes; (iv) Objectives and values; (v) Staffing and skills; (vi) Management systems and structures; and (vii) Other resources including time and money. He is of the opinion that putting these dimensions together with the notion of gaps produces the model for understanding success/failure of e-government as shown in the diagram above.

It is argued that ITPOSMO dimensions can be accommodated under four different dimensions, namely infrastructure, human resources, institution, legal and policy aspects, which have been considered for the purpose of this study. To be specific, information, technology and other resources of Heek's model can be included under infrastructure. Under human resources, staffing

Figure 1. Heeks's success/failure model for e-Government

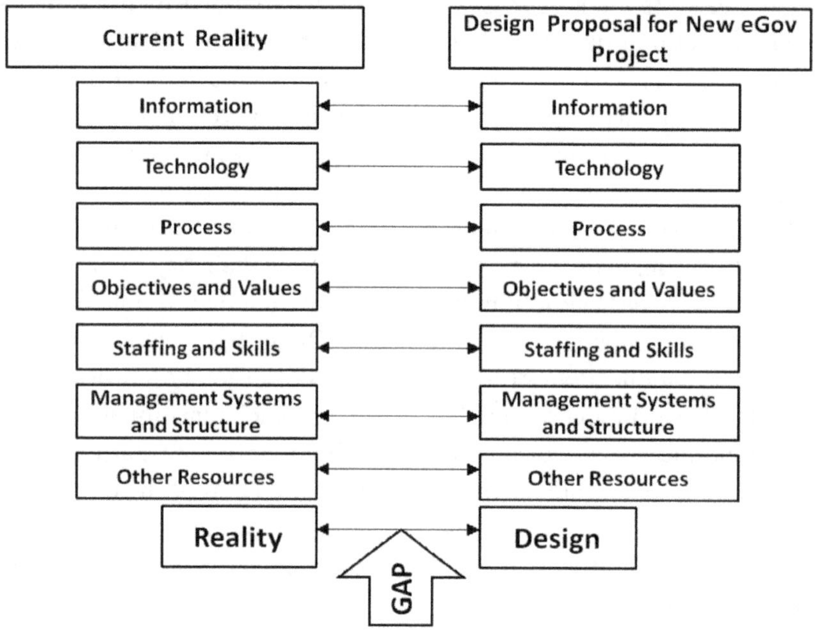

and skill dimension of Heek's design reality gap model can be accomodated.Under institution different dimensions of Heek's model's namely, management systems and structures and process can be incorporated .In addition, the objectives and values dimension of Heeks's model can be included under policy and legal aspects of our analysis.

Implementation of E-Government

E-government is a major opportunity to bring public services to all citizens, but one must consider its associated challenges as well. Seifert (2003) has mentioned some of the issues to be considered while implementing e-governments. They are, among others, technical, interoperability, privacy, security, affordability, accessibility, usability and issue of acceptance. It is accepted that implementation of e-government is not a technical issue rather it is policy and management issue incorporating different stakeholders addressing the problems of non-cooperation and non-collaboration among each other in the pursuit of implementation of a particular e-government project.

According to Wood-Harper et al. (2004), people, systems and processes must interact for the successful implementation of e-government. The interconnection between these success factors is shown in Figure 2. People refer to government officials and public (business and citizens) . System denotes ICT applications and tools to enable and support e-Government applications. It makes a strong foundation to build e-Government service. System supports the relationship and interaction between stakeholders. The process refers to management technique that reestablishes and implements the present process. It involves the reengineering of all governmental processes such as business, organization, corporate culture in order to capitalize on the potential benefit of e-government. It promotes reliability in service delivery.

For the success of e-government initiatives, peoples' participation is the must, which can be ensured by their trust on the government and its

Figure 2. Interconnected success factors for e-Government

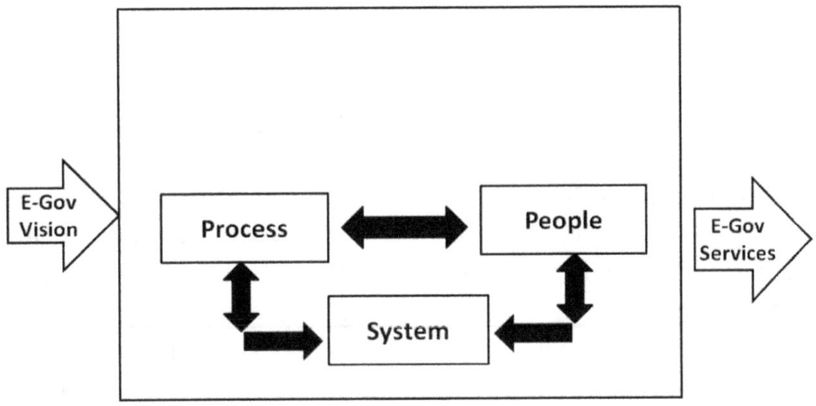

machineries for their expertise and technical capability to run e-government system. Recurrent non-performance from the government and corrupt behavior from government officials and employees decrease confidence among people and ultimately causing increased resistance against e-government programs (Carter & Weerakkody, 2008) . In totality, factors like political stability, government structure in terms of its centralized or decentralized nature, level of economic development, level of trust on government, and demand of the people are determining factors for the success of e-government (Backus, 2001).In the succeeding paragraphs, we have reviewed literature relevant to infrastructure; HRD; institutional aspects; and, policy and legal aspects, which are important ingredients of any e-government system. Moreover, they are the factors incorporating process, people and system as prescribed by Wood-Harper et al. (2004).

Infrastructure

There are two important parts of infrastructure: back office and front office. Back office includes system and infrastructure, where services and information are prepared to present in front office. Front office includes access channels through which stakeholders such as citizens, business, employees etc. receive e-government services. The good balance between the back and front offices leads to the effective and successful e-government service provision (Shakya, 2007).

Bertot et al. (1999) maintain that for the successful implementation of e-government consistent and reliable electricity, telecommunications, and internet are fundamental. The view is shared with Jaeger et al. (2003), who are of the opinion that without having necessary technological infrastructure e-government cannot succeed .

Digital divide has remained a major problem of the developing countries, especially in their effort of implementing e-government system The government of those countries have to ensure that all of their citizens have access to ICT facilities through different means such as different forms of phones, satellite receivers, kiosks, etc. for implementing e-government in practice. E-readiness and ICT literacy are very important to be able to harness whatever ICT infrastructures are available (Ndou, 2004).

Only having technology does not always solve the existing service delivery problem. The ease of use and system usability are important factors to be considered (Davis, 1989). Perceived usefulness, perceived ease of use and user acceptance of information technology largely determines the success of any e-government initiative.

Human Resources Development (HRD)

Human resources are the most important components of an e-government process. However, most of the developing countries lack qualified professionals having necessary skills to successfully implement e-government. ICT related human resources are necessary for installation, maintenance, designing and implementation of ICT infrastructure (Davis, 1989). Human resources are also needed for change management as possibility of resistance to changes in organization and procedures has to be managed through these qualified management experts. Once the service goes online, the queries of the people have to be responded by knowledgeable staff. Availability of such staff can be ensured through knowledge management.

Institutional Aspects

Backus (2001) is of the opinion that a clear cut vision, mission and strategy of an institution are necessary to implement the principles of e-government in practice. In this regard, instead of confining e-government into online service delivery to different stakeholders, it should be accepted as enabler for innovation in the public sector (Dovifat, 2004). Dawes and Nelson (1995) are also of the opinion that frequent mismatch between organizational goal and IT project is one of the challenges in the implementation of e-government.

Sound institutional base is a very important factor for the success of e-government system, but mere institution cannot deliver result and efficiency without reducing cost and minimizing layers of organizational processes. Such action is possible only through reengineering and streamlining operating procedures (Seifert, 2003).

e-business climate within institution concerned is very important to develop readiness of that very institution to go to the e-government system. Magnitude of resistance, legal framework and information security are some of the factors that determine such climate (Anderson, 1991).

Policy and Legal Aspects

Before implementing any IT project, public manager must consider whether required legal arrangements have already been made (Dawes & Nelson, 1995). E-government involves complex process of combining technology with legal and policy provisions. Lunching of e-government demands policies, laws, regulations and other required legislative changes to accommodate electronic activities, namely digital signature, electronic archiving, data protection, cybercrime, copyright, intellectual property rights, etc. (Ndou, 2004). Seifert (2003) maintains the view that e-government "intersects many legislative issues, including privacy, digital divide, public access to government information, service delivery, and information security" (p.1). According to Pacific Council on International Policy (2002), implementation of e-government requires legal reforms to ensure privacy, security and legal recognition of electronic interactions and electronic signatures.

Stages of E-Government Implementation

It is worthwhile to mention about different phases of e-government implementation because each phase is characterized by different activities and they require different physical infrastructure, institutional, legal and human resources related supply arrangements. Such categorization into different phases also provides some advance knowledge on possible hindrances each stage has to encounter. It is urgent, therefore, for the policymakers and e-government project implementers to be vigilant as to which stage their project is at the moment and what the expected stage is in future.

Classification of e-government implementation has been tried by many scholars and institutions, but there is no consensus, however, regarding sequence of such phases. There are many scholars who try to categorizes such phases, but a very few of them are really acclaimed by the academic circle. One of them is Gartner's Four Phases of e-Government. It classifies the e-government implementation into phases, namely presence, interaction, transaction and transformation(Baum & Di Maio, 2000). United Nations Division for Public Economics and Public Administration and American Society of Public Administration (UN-ASPA) (2002) have categorized e-government in five different stages, namely emerging, enhanced, interactive, transactional and seamless (UN/ASPA, 2002). "Emerging," implies presence of government on the web through a few independent official sites with limited, basic and static information. In the "enhanced" stage government sites not only increase and information becomes more dynamic, but also content and information is updated with greater regularity. One can download forms, email officials, interact through the web and make appointments and requests in the "interactive stage." The fourth stage is "transactional" referring to the stage in which users can pay for services or conduct financial transactions online. The last stage is about "full integration" of e-services across administrative boundaries with total integration of e-functions and services having all services and links are provided on a single governmental portal ensuring the processing of all the administrative services on- line (GoN, 2006).

Hiller and Belanger (2000, as cited in Coursey & Noris, 2008) has proposed five–stage model with different progression and end point [31]. Information dissemination/catalogues and two-way communication are first and second stages of this model. Service and financial transformation, vertical and horizontal integration, and political participation are stage 3, stage 4 and stage 5, respectively .

Layne and Lee (2001) propound a four stage model to develop a fully functional e-government. Based on technical, organizational and managerial feasibilities, he mentions that e-government is an evolutionary phenomenon, and posits four stages of a growth model for e-government: (1) cataloguing, (2) transaction, (3) vertical integration, and (4) horizontal integration. Coursey and Norris (2008) has considered Layne and Lee model as outlier compared to other models. The model is similar to other's e-government implementation model up to the level 2. However, from third stage the model diverges from the other models. The third stage, vertical integration, involves upper and lower levels of government sharing data and information online. The final step is horizontal integration enabling e-government system sharing of data and information online across departments within governments (Coursey & Noris, 2008).

On the basis of different maturity stages propounded by different scholars and institutions mentioned above, one can broadly categorize the maturity stages of e-government into: (i) online presence, (ii) interaction, (iii) transaction and (iv) full integration. In the first stage, government starts towards e-government and publish useful information. In the second stage, governments go further and citizen can be interactive with government by downloading forms, emailing to officials. In the transaction phase typical services such as tax filling and payment, drivers' license renewal are available. The last stage has to do with redefinition of government service by providing a single point of contact to constituents.

It is to be noted that the models mentioned above presented the linear stepwise and progressive development of e-government, which may not be always true (ibid).Moreover, these models do not tell us how this progression or evolution occurs or how long it takes to graduate from each stage or phase. Not having this kind of information may pose government in troublesome position as it may not be able to overcome problems related to financial, legal, organizational, technological, and political factors. Coursey and Norris (2008) research on local e-government in the US local government unveiled that fact that "e-government is not linear. Late adopters of e-government need not start at the most basic level of e-government. They can and do learn from the experiences of other governments and the private sector begins with more sophisticated offerings."

DEVELOPMENT STATUS OF NEPAL

Nepal is a South Asian landlocked country sandwiched between India and China. It shares border with China to the north whereas she has border with India to the south, east and west. Stretching from east to west it spreads over 1,47,181 square Km. The country is divided into 14 zones and 75 administrative districts. Ecologically it is divided into three regions, namely the mountain region, the hill region and Terai region (plain area of Nepal near to Indian border). Each ecological region has distinct climatic conditions and the mountain region is full of snowcapped mountains around the year and hilly region consists of valleys and terrains. Therefore, Nepal is a mountainous and hilly country making lives of the people difficult as many parts of the country are still out of reliable telecommunication, electricity and transportation facilities. Moreover, such areas are also depriving of education and health facilities. Shortage of such facilities have been hampering in the effort of converting conventional governance system to e-governance.

Over the decades, the population of Nepal has rapidly been growing. It will be around 30 million by 2014. Increasing population means more and more services and facilities that need to be provided by the government, which is not possible through the present form of governance and hence compulsion can be realized for a rapid transformation to the e-government service delivery.

The population growth is not commensurated by economic growth. Nepal is one of the least developed countries in the world where around 25.2% of its population are below poverty line defined by the World Bank, namely $1 per day. Agriculture is still the largest contributing sector to the Nepalese economy. The agriculture is having around 35 percent share in the GDP and it is giving employment to more around 80% of the population (MoF, 2012).As the Nepalese economy is characterized by heavy reliance on agriculture, low growth rate and is very small in volume, it is difficult for her to finance a full implementation of e-government with her own resources.

In a bid to transform conventional governance system into e-governance, the role of education and specifically qualified human resources is immense. There is no doubt that the country has progressed a lot in education sector, but still around 13.0% of children are deprived of education. Moreover, education facilities (both school and university) are not equally accessible by gender, class and regions. The education sector is characterized as high rate of repetition and drop out and low rate of graduation (NPC, 2008). Despite the fact that orientation towards the importance of education has been increased massively among the populace, still the country is not in a position to produce a sizable amount of ICT manpower. There are a very few colleges and universities which carry out academic course related ICT, IT or computer engineering or computer science, but they are grossly insufficient to meet the ICT manpower demand with in the country.

The situation of human development in Nepal is not encouraging in comparison to that of other countries in South Asian region (UNDP, 2011). Nepal is slightly above than Afghanistan in HDI ranking. It can be improved through e-governance in place. Underdevelopment of Nepal is characterized also by its present condition of weak industrial base. Despite the fact that industrial sector can play an important role in increasing employment opportunity and also in alleviating poverty, the share of industry sector in Nepal's GDP is also very less (around 15%) in comparison to other countries in South Asian region (MOF, 2012).The present state of industrial development in Nepal can also be attributed to the low level of ICT development in the country. Moreover, conventional governmental set up has also been constraining to create favorable industrial development environment.

ANALYSIS OF E-GOVERNMENT SITUATION IN NEPAL

Efforts Towards E-Government Implementation

This part tries to analyze the present condition of e-government in Nepal through a few indicators, namely infrastructure, human resources, organizational capacity, and policy and regulation etc. in order to capture the ITPOSMO factors as envisaged by Heeks (2004). In this regard, at the outset past initiatives are presented.

E-governance is still not a popular concept in Nepal. Despite the fact the Nepal has been putting emphasis on science and technology since the very beginning of first five year plan in 1956, its achievement in that sector is not up to the expectation. The use of ICT for the purpose of e-governance is very limited and present status in this area clearly demands putting extra effort to ensure its contribution in the overall development of Nepal.

The year 1971 can be regarded as a Landmark Year in terms of Nepal's exposure to ICT. In that very year, the Nepalese Government used computers (IBM 1401) to process National Population Census data followed by the establishment of National Computer Center (NCC) in 1974 with the objective of imparting IT trainings within Nepal. The NCC developed software for various government agencies, processed examination results for School Leaving Certificate (SLC) Board, and Tribhuvan University (http://www.enrd.org/egovernance.php).

1971 was also the year when the first telecom project was executed to modernize Nepal's telecommunication sector. Private sector began its activity in early eighties after the introduction of Personal Computers. In 1992 Mercantile Communication Pvt. Ltd. (MCPL) started commercial e-mail through Internet as First Internet Service Provider (ISP). Since 1999 Government liberalized its policy to use VSAT. Since then the number of ISPs have increased to 29 and currently around 74,140 Internet Subscribers exists in the country (NTA, 2012).

Although Nepal entered into information technology arena almost at the same time as in other countries, real progress was not witnessed until 1995. It was during this time that a large number of offices went for automation, universities and colleges started computer science and computer engineering courses. Likewise, developments in computer hardware and software business, IT related training and desktop publication took a shape during the period. Such development was possible through the aggressive participation of the private sector in the ICT sector rather than through the government planning and efforts alone.

During the period from 1997 to 2004, a number of policy and regulatory measures were prepared and implemented in the information and communication sectors. It is the same period in which the notion of e-governance got importance in Nepal. The Telecommunication Act was enacted in 1996; Nepal Telecommunication Authority was constituted in 1997 as an independent telecom regulatory body; the Information Technology Policy 2000 (revised 2010) and Cyber Law, 2004 and Electronic Transaction Act, 2006 was introduced. ICT sector was given a major thrust with the then constitution of the High Level Commission for Information Technology (HLCIT) in 2003.

The liberalization of the communication sector mentioned above facilitated the rapid growth in

IT business with the dominant participation of the private sector. Likewise, with the announcement of the Telecommunication Policy 2004, a broad institutional framework for the development of ICT has been in place. It is believed that this framework has provided conductive environment for the development of ICT in the urban areas with thriving business in ICT hardware, software, ISPs, land and mobile telephone, cyber cafe etc. The urban educated population is in the position to have access to information required for various needs (Chapagain, 2006).

Different Dimensions of E-Government Implementation

In this portion of the study, we have explained four main pillars of e-government, namely physical infrastructure, human resources, organizational capacity, policy and legal initiatives.

Physical Infrastructure

Considering low per capita income (around US$742 in 2012) and wide spread poverty (around 25.2%) still a sizable population are not in a position to afford facilities like telephone (both land line and mobile) and internet . Contrarily, those who can afford are also underserved. Out of total population only 3.15% has access to fixed telephone and around 58.70% has access to mobile telephone facilities. Total penetration rate of telecommunication and related services is around 66.14% and internet penetration rate is around 19.32 percent (NTA, 2012). Refer to Table 1, Table 2 and Table 3.

The most encouraging result is in the use of mobile phone. There was no mobile telephone facility in the country until about 1998 and now around 15.6 million people are using it. The first year of implementation of e-GMP, i.e., 2007 alone witnessed subscription of around additional 1 million mobile phones. As far as landline telephone line is concerned, the growth is not as encouraging as the growth of mobile. Over the period 1997-2007, the landline increased by 475%. However, the whole telephone line subscribers are only around 0.83 million, which is very less in comparison of population of about 26.62 million (CBS, 2003). Over the same period, the internet users have grown from around 5,000 in 1997 to 397,500 in 2007 (around 784% increments). Again this number was just around 1.38% of the total population. At present, data/internet subscribers are about 5.1 million covering around 19 percent of the total population showing significant progress in this front (NTA, 2012). Refer to Table 4.

Human Resources

Most public institutions have no concrete programs for training in ICT or e-governance. The importance of HRD in ICT and e-governance areas is neither seriously perceived nor planned. Fifteen central level training centers operating under different ministries in different fields have

Table 1. Present Status of ICT Facilities in Nepal

Telecom Statistics (in number)	
Fixed Line	839,067
Mobile	15,627,188
Others(LMS and GMPCS)	1,141,107
Total	17,607,362
Source: NTA,2012	

Table 2. Service Penetration Rate

Service Penetration of ICT Facilities (in %)	
Fixed telephone	3.15
Mobile service	58.70
Others(LMS and GMPCS)	4.28
Total	66.14
Source: NTA,2012	

Table 3. Data/Internet Subscribers

Data/Internet subscribers (in number)	
Services	**Subscribers**
Dialup (PSTN+ISDN)	15,037
Wireless Modem, Optical Fibre Ethernet	45,612
Cable Modem, Cable etc.	17,981
ADSL	88,058
GPRS	4,782,322
CDMA IX	196,183
Total	5,145,193
Internet Penetration Rate (%)	19.32
Source: NTA,2012	

not substantially incorporated ICT components in their curricula.

It is not only because of low use of ICT facilities that obstruct to materialize the notion of e-governance in the country, but also because of a low number of ICT related educational institutions which fail to produce enough number of ICT professionals who can be really instrumental to materialize the dream of e-government. There are only 5 universities in the country but none of them is established solely to deal with ICT related education. There are a good number of private sector institutions imparting ICT related training, but their coverage in terms of geography and

Table 4. Progress Sheet of E-Government Master Plan

Priority	Projects	Sector	Executing Agency	Progress % Evaluation
1	Government Portal	G2C	HLCIT	90
2	Group Ware	G2G	NITC/MoEST	50
3	Enterprise Architecture	Infra.	HLCIT	100
4	GIDC	Infra.	NITC/MoEST	100
5	NID	G2C	MoHA	30
6	e-Education	G2G		20
7	e-Authentication	G2G		80
8	PKI	Infra.	OCCA/MoST	80
9	e-Tax	G2G	IRD/MoF	20
10	e-Customs	G2B	DoC/MoF	70
11	e-Vehicle	G2C	DoTM	30
12	e-Drivers License	G2C	DoTM	30
13	Community Network	Infra	NTA	30
14	e-Land	G2G	DoLRM	30
15	e-Procurement	G2B		30
16	e-Passport	G2C	MoFA	0
17	Immigration	G2G	MOFA	0
18	Business Registration & Approval Management System	G2B	-	0
19	e-Health	G2C	MoPH	30
20	e-Commerce	G2B		0
21	e-Agriculture	G2C		30
Source:NITC,2012				

number of participants is not worth mentioning largely serving only urban people. Government is the main actor to ensure e-governance in the country, but they have only around 500 IT graduates working for them .

On the one hand, the absorptive capacity of ICT manpower is very low and on the other hand, there is a shortage of skilled ICT personnel in the public sector. This problem is prominent at the ministry level of government and severe at the district and local levels.

Organizational Capacity

Ministry of Science and Technology, National IT Centre (NITC), and Ministry of Information and Communication are the main organizations responsible for the implementation of e-government in Nepal. The role of other Ministries and organizations under them can also not be undermined as the success of e-government lies on the ownership, initiative and participation of all government organizations. Moreover, the role of private sector is also important since without their support e-government goal cannot be materialized. The role of NITC, however, is immensely important as it has been entrusted important role to coordinate all the activities of implementing partners made responsible by the e-GMP.

NITC which was established in 2002 in line with IT Policy 2000 has got objective to build knowledge-based society by supporting knowledge-based institutions and industries as well as promoting and developing information technology accessible to the public (Bhattarai, 2008).

These institutions listed above have not been effective as they fail to meet their objectives because of different reasons, namely overlapping responsibilities, inadequate administrative and political commitment, political instability and inadequate resources. Most importantly, these institutions are supposed to take lead roles to strengthen the capability of all other concerned governmental agencies through various programs to make them ready to implement e-Government Master Plan in full swing. However, they have yet to initiate these activities.

Policy and Legal Initiatives

While dealing with e-government in Nepal, IT Policy, 2000; IT Policy, 2010; Telecommunication Policy, 2004; and Electronic Transaction; and Digital Signature Act, 2006 have to be considered. These policies and legal provisions have contributed directly or indirectly in the promotion of e-governance in the country. However, they are not being implemented in true spirit.

The main objectives of the Information Technology Policy, 2010 are: to make IT accessible to the general public and increase employment through this means; to build a knowledge-based society; and to establish knowledge-based industries. The policy reaffirms IT sectors as a prioritized sector, and emphasizes to create a conductive environment to attract private sector investment. The main objective of the Telecommunication Policy, 2004 is to make telecommunication services reliable and accessible to all in collaboration with the private sector and to use ICT for poverty alleviation and development of the rural areas. Electronic Transaction and Digital Signature Act, 2006 is a breakthrough in this regard. It validates and gives legal recognition to electronic documents, electronic signature and electronic transactions. It penalizes unauthorized access to information.

CASE STUDY: THE E- GOVERNMENT MASTER PLAN (E-GMP)

Rationale for the Plan

Because of meager economic condition of the country, government's capacity to provide quality, timely and reliable service is questionable. The problem is further aggravated because of scattered human settlement in far-flung remote areas. Lack of robust ICT infrastructure has added fuel to the fire leaving a large mass out of reach of government services. In such situation, it was urgent need on the part of Nepali government to change its governance system to e-governance to make service delivery of the government cost effective, reliable and timely. The e-Government Master Plan (e-GMP)came into being to fulfill that gap.

The e-GMP, which was prepared in July 2006 with the assistance of Korea IT Industry Promotion Agency (KIPA) has provided a framework for moving towards full-fledged e-government in the country. It has sought to establish the vision, lead applications and management framework including required legislation. (GoN, 2006) in order to deliver convenience in administrative services for citizens and enhance national competitiveness through more efficient administrative process. Moreover, it aims to facilitate employment through promotion of the domestic IT industry; diversify profit structure through expansion of the cutting-edge industry; and ultimately improve the average living standards of the people.

Vision, Mission and Goal of the Plan

The e-GMP has set vision as the creation of "the value networking in Nepal through citizen-centered service; transparent service; networked government; and knowledge based society" (ibid). In order to achieve the stated vision, the mission of the plan is to improve the quality of people's life without any discrimination, transcending regional and racial differences, and materialize socio-economic development by building a transparent government and providing value added quality services through ICT.

The main goal of the project is to achieve good governance and social and economic development by establishing effective, systematic, and productive e-government through Government to citizen (G2C), Government to Business (G2B) and Government to Government(G2G) and infrastructure development.

Proposed Projects and Legal Requirements

In order to materialize the goals mentioned above the e-GMP has proposed different strategies and projects under G2G, G2B, and G2C. For example, under G2C different projects, namely National ID, Government Representative Portal, Passport Registration System, Social Insurance Information System, e-health, e-Election, e-Vehicle, e-Driver License, e-Petition, e-Pension, e-Post and e-Agriculture are proposed. Recruitment and Employment Information System, e-Customs, e-Procurement, Business Registration and Approval Management System, e-Patent, e-Tourism and e-Commerce are the projects proposed under G2B. G2G component includes projects like e-Tax, Immigration Management System, e-Education, e-Land, e-MIS, Groupware, e-Pollution, e-Authentication, Knowledge Management System and GIS. As far as projects under infrastructure development are concerned, they are: Enterprise Architecture, Communication Network, Government Integrated Data Centre and Public Key Infrastructure (GoN, 2006).

To implement aforesaid projects and also to continue e-government related reform activities as an ongoing activity of the country, there are three categories of legal framework which Nepal needs to institutionalize. They are: Laws on National Informatisation Promotion, Laws on ICT Industry Promotion, and Laws on ICT Infrastructure Construction.

E-Government Promotion Model of Nepal

The e-GMP document has based its promotion model on UN-ASPA (2002) model of five stages of e-Government implementation. According to the plan document, Nepal is in first level since it has been providing limited services through the websites and being unable to keep its contents up-to-date. Nepal, however, has already possessed some of the features of third stage, for example, the use of electronic formats by some of the departments. Therefore, from the perspective of UN-ASPA model, Nepali e-government status can be stretched from level 1 to level 3 (ibid). On this ground, the e-GMP has devised 4 stages e-government promotion model instead of 5 stages as that of UN-ASPA model. The first stage includes computerization of internal process of the government. In the second stage, more comprehensive and citizen-centric services through Business Process Reengineering is made possible along with connection of government agencies. Availability of integrated on line services through connection of government agencies and to handle the citizen's requests online through web is ensured in the third stage. In the fourth stage, all processes are integrated with ubiquitous environment where citizens and businesses can get all the services they want wherever they are.

Implementation Strategy and Prerequisites

Implementation of e-government is a not a onetime business; rather it is an on-going process. The e-GMP envisions that the objective of such strategy is to provide the foundation needed for Nepal to continuously pursue the e-government plan. The plan document has acknowledged three implementation strategies, namely, informatisation through process innovation; project implementation and management structure ensuring effective monitoring and evaluation; and promotion of the IT through the e-government.

The plan has spoken also about organizational, human resources development, infrastructure and financial requirements as prerequisites for the successful implementation of the plan. Considering the ill fate of previous policies and projects, the plan has emphasized on the clear cut role of government agencies to secure budget, human resources development (HRD), and to establish national ICT infrastructure.

HRD is an area where the e-GMP really put emphasis on. It states that HRD is an essential element for successful implementation of the e-government and at the same time it is the biggest obstacle faced by Nepal in introducing the e-government. Range of targets, such as computer trainings to public servants, citizens and students are suggested to be covered under the HRD program.

According to the plan document, informatisation of administration service must be the first and foremost priority. Without informatisation of administration service, connectivity itself has no meaning because there will be no intending contents to utilize.

Roadmap for Implementation

On the basis of stipulated vision, mission, and objectives, the plan has recommended 33 projects in sectors comprising G2C, G2B, G2G and infrastructure. The plan has confessed that all the projects are vital to Nepal, but there is a limitation of time, budget, human resources and capability of implementing such projects. Therefore, considering the availability of technologies, institutional readiness, emergency handling capacity as well as environmental impact, only 8 projects were chosen as priority projects, namely building groupware systems for government, government portal, national identification, e-education, communication network, enterprise architecture, and integrated data center. However, the roadmap for the implementation of all those projects has also been proposed in the e-GMP.

The plan document has clearly mentioned that full implementation of e-GMP is a long term project and it requires more than 10 years. Considering the urgency, the project period is set for five years, from 2007 to 2011 (GoN, 2006).The e-GMP has also presented roadmap to implement it. According to the roadmap, Nepal at the moment being in first stage will jump to third stage by 2011, which is the final year to implement the plan. In order to realize the e-government, not only the implementation of target projects is required, but also the creation of e-government organization, preparation of laws/systems, and training of ICT personnel.

Achievements Made So Far

One has to confess that e-GMP was an ambitious project considering techno-socio-economic condition of the country. In order to implement it, the Nepalese government with the assistance of Asian Development Bank has prepared and started implementing ICT Development Project. The project is designed on the premise that information and knowledge are essential ingredients for effective community participation, good governance, poverty alleviation and economic development (ADB, 2007). The main executing agency of the project is Office of the Prime Minister and Council of Ministers (OPMCM). The deadline for the completion of the project is June 2014. Seven different activities are currently underway on different phases of implementation under ICT Development Project. They are: (i) Enterprise Architecture; (ii) Government Groupware; (iii) National ID; (iv) e-Vehicle and e-Driver License; (v) Community Network; and (vi) e-Land (ibid).

The government seems to provide high priority to the ICT development project as overall project implementation is supervised by a Project Steering Committee consisting of the Chief Secretary (Committee Chair) of government of Nepal. Secretaries of the Ministry of Industry (MOI), Ministry of Science and Technology (MoST), and Executive Director of NITC (Committee Secretary) who are member of steering committee. A project management unit (PMU) established under the Office of the Prime Minister and Council of Ministers (OPMCM), headed by a Chief Project Director (Secretary) and other two project directors, each for administration and technical aspects of the project implementation and a treasurer are also provisioned. However, ICT development project as a major tool to implement e-GMP has not taken a major headway.

Referring to the e-GMP, by the end of 2011, all projects related to G2C, G2B, G2G and infrastructure respectively must have been completed. However, achievements made are not up to the expectation. In order to implement e-GMP, altogether 21 different projects under G2G, G2B, G2C, and Infrastructure have been proposed and implemented (NITC, 2012), as shown in Table 4. Even if e-GMP was supposed to be completed by 2011, some of the project activities are found to be proposed by setting timeline up to the end of 2013.For example, Government Integrated Data Centre (GIDC), e-customs, e-procurement and e-health project are projected to be completed within 2013 (ibid). Interestingly, e-passport will be introduced by 2014. It is to be noted that by 2012 November project entitled Government Portal under G2C; Enterprise Architecture and GIDC under Infrastructure all have remained best performer among all 21 proposed projects. All of them have around 90 percent progress. Other projects, namely e-authetication,and e-procurement have around 80 percent progress in their implemenation. Other projects' progress ranges from 20 percent to 70 percent. Moreover, e-commerce; business registration and approval management system; and e-commerce don't have any definite projects so far for their implementation(ibid).In totality, as of November 2012, overall progress in e-GMP implementation is around 27 percent (ibid).

In totality, except major headway in the construction of Data Centre, GIDC, and enterprise architecture, the implementation of the e-GMP is not that encouraging. Government of Korea, through Korea International Cooperation Agency (KOICA), provided assistance for establishing GIDC. It is constructed as high grade data center at a national level aimed to be used by all entities of the government. With this background, we argue that there is a need to revisit the whole e-GMP and set out new implementation plan as the relevance of the plan is still there.

ISSUES TO BE ADDRESSED

The Nepalese government is not in a position to undermine the global wave of digitization and e-governance . It has been trying to make e-governance in reality, but not with concerted efforts. However, its efforts have not been matched with resource allocations and policy enforcement. Most of the central offices have websites, but either they are not maintaining with up-to-date data or are not operating in a proper way. The major breakthrough in this regard is Electronic Transaction and Digital Signature Act, 2006, which has already come into effect (Bhattarai et al., 2008).

Nepal, no doubt, is gradually progressing in this sector, but not to the level of expectation. The use of IT in governance is very low although awareness regarding the importance of IT is gradually increasing. Some successful initiatives are there, especially in Ministry of General Administration and General Post Office. The distinct problem felt, however, is the lack of process ownership contributing towards comprehensive reform. Moreover, some efforts have not been successful because the reform was focused on technology part only without giving due consideration to change management. Moreover, there is not a strong culture of technology within many parts of government. Communications between ministries is by paper and correspondence with email is regarded as having only an informal role to be followed by paper. E-transactions legislation is in place but the implementation is not as expected.

According to e-GMP Nepal is in stage 1 and by the end of 2011 Nepal must have reached stage 3. To move from the second stage to the third stage, there should have been two-way transactions, access to services through various channels, knowledge-based administrative processes, and pan-governmental collaborative network for knowledge sharing. However, nothing remarkable had happened towards this direction.

The reasons for being failure to achieve the desired goal by 2011 is also because of the lack of demand from the citizen for the use of computer system in the service delivery. In addition, civil service in Nepal is still traditional. Many regulations and workflow are traditional obstructing the introduction of IT. Applications are developed in individual initiation basis and organization does not feel ownership of the product. Most importantly, IT is treated as separate department and whole bureaucracy is separate from that. Only IT department is responsible for entering data, processing and reporting. IT does not seem to be a part of process workflow (ibid).

Inadequate human resources, lack of necessary legal framework, little public awareness about ICT, poor ICT infrastructure across the nation are the other factors that are hindering to implement e-governance successfully in the country. Ironically ICT resources in the government offices are not fully utilized. Most of the government officials have a mindset of losing their jobs, if ICT is introduced in their working environment and hence they are resistant to the proposed changes (Bhattarai et al., 2008).

The lack of integrated approach in the planning is another area to be considered. Sectoral plans, policies and strategies are yet to be aligned with e-GMP. In doing so, Business Process Reengineering (BPR) should have been the most important tasks to be carried out, which involves modification of legislation and policies in line with e-governance, arrangement of massive training, coordination among different responsible agencies, as well as resource arrangement (ibid). However, there is no enough attention towards this end.

HRD and infrastructure are important issues to be considered. There is absence of HRD planning in Nepal along with non-existence of capable training institutions within the government sector developing human resources for e-governance. In addition, there is inadequate infrastructure for meaningful information sharing among the central government and local governments, citizens and businesses. Enactment of relevant legislations are important factor in this process. However, the Nepalese government has not been able to bring legislations as recommended by the e-GMP. Accountability is another factor to be dealt with as authorities need to be accountable with clear mandate.

Economic and social issue should also be considered while dealing with e-government. The implementation of E-Govement Master Plan demands a lot of financial resources, which government may not be able to manage. The interface must be usable by disabled or elderly people, understandable by low literacy on non-native language people.

In a nut shell, plan documents, policies and legal provisions have given emphasis on different components of ICT in isolation without putting concerted and integrated efforts for the purpose of e-governance in particular. As a result, e-GMP could not be implemented in stipulated time frame.

According to the deadline set by the e-GMP, e-government in Nepal had to attain level 3 of e-government maturity model proposed by UN-ASPA by 2011. The implementation of the plan was started in 2007 implying that five years have already been spent for the implementation of the plan. It is natural to expect that at least all preparatory background works that are necessary to graduate from level 1 to level 2 and from level 2 to level 3 must have been completed. Nepal is in stage 1 currently and to be in level 2, there should be regular updating of the websites and provide more comprehensive and citizen-centric services through innovation in administrative process via business process engineering and connection of government agencies. According to the plan document, years 2007 and 2008 have been considered as the phase 1 and designated as the "year for the improvement in fundamentals" and the rest three years from 2009 to 2011 have been considered as the phase 2 showing the year for "Enhancement of realization." However, gathered information entailed that there is no major achievement so far except construction of GIDC as mentioned before.

In totality, the implementation of e-GMP is marred by implementation lag resulted in because of political and bureaucratic apathy, frequent transfer of human resources related to the implementation of the plan, and financial constraints.

IMPLEMENTATION GAP FROM THE PERSPECTIVE OF HEEK'S MODEL

Heeks (2003) opines in his model as explained before that different dimensions, namely information, technology, processes, objectives and values, staffing and skills, management systems and structures and time and money may create a design reality gap thereby causing e-government failure. In fact, the model was proposed by Heeks on the basis of his experience on East Africa, where a Scientific Information System was intended to support strategic decision making in a Natural Resource Ministry. However, there were gaps between system design and the Ministry's reality. Though the model was devised in African country's perspective, it is firmly believed that this can be fitted in the Nepalese perspective with reference to e-GMP.

The information dimension has created a gap between reality and design. Non-compliance of most of the targets set by the e-GMP by the end of 2011 show that the information collected in course of designing the plan was either inadequate or inaccurate. Moreover, it seems that decision makers' gut feeling and informal information have also helped create such gap. For example, most of the projects in G2C, G2B and G2G warrant business process reengineering in the beginning before going for implementation of the project. However, business process reengineering related activities are hardly carried out in the Nepalese case so far.

The Nepalese bureaucracy is still conventional relying on old technologies like type writers and manual system of file and notes preparation. Most of the high level bureaucrats and politicians are still not familiar with computer and its usage. However, the technology which e-GMP envisioned during and after its implementation is quite advanced and new in the Nepalese perspective. The plan desires to have transformation of bureaucracy in a rapid pace. However, there is enough inertia in the Nepalese bureaucracy to resist such transformation. This has caused serious problem in its implementation.

The successful implementation of e-GMP requires scientific work process which is free of corruption, non-transparency and red tapism. Moreover, it also desires to have a rational model of structured decision making within the particular organizations responsible for the implementation of the plan and also in overall bureaucracy. However, the Nepalese bureaucracy is still suffered from all of these diseases. This has caused the implementation gap and hence the e-GMP could not achieve desired goal as was planned.

The e-GMP was designed to be implemented in a scientific environment which believes in a "role culture" that values rules and logic. However, the implementation of the plan is being tried in a political environment which has a "power culture" that values self-interest and other hidden vested agenda. The political instability in the country has further aggravated the situation. During 2009-2010, the Ministry of Environment of Science Technology, which was a key player in the preparation of e-GMP was partitioned into two ministries, namely Ministry of Science and Technology and Ministry of Environment. Recently the HLCIT has been dissolved. The availability of the qualified staff for the implementation of the plan has been taken as granted. However, the plan has been witnessing the shortage of qualified human resources in a range of activities of projects prescribed by the plan. Moreover, frequent transfer of staff associated with the plan, placement of staff who is not familiar with the ICT and insufficient number of staff made available to the cause of implementation of the plan are other problems to be considered.

The management systems and structures dimension is also worth mentioning here. The implementation of e-GMP warrants such a management system and structure which support strategic decision making. However, such management system and structure are yet to be established.

The assumption made by e-GMP for its implementation seems not to be correct. The timeline set for shifting from present level 1 to level 3 of UN-ASPA definition is only 5 years and it has already been elapsed. The time frame set was too short considering ground reality of the Nepalese ICT sector. Moreover, shortage of resources is definitely a problem of the government as its economy is downturn after massive fall of remittance income. Donors have provided financial assistance to implement the plan but the assistance is not sufficient to implement the plan in full scale.

THE WAY FORWARD

Nepal's desire to have e-governance is not matched with its resources available, efforts and commitments towards it. Different policies and legal arrangements mentioned under heading 4.1 have largely been neglected and lacks alignment problem while formulating national periodic development plans and other sectoral plans. The fate of e-GMP is also the same like many development plans, programs and projects. Unfortunately, e-GMP also moved in a direction where it has witnessed a fate in the word of Heeks (2003), "implementation failure." The e-GMP was only hope for Nepal at the moment to turn Nepal at stage 3 of what UN-ASPA model of e-government has envisioned. However, there are different problems caused by the design reality gap. The gap can be minimized either by changing the design of the e-government project to make it more matching with reality and or changing current reality to make it more matching with the requirements with the project design (Heeks, 2003). Since the project is highly relevant to the Nepalese perspective, it has to be implemented with new time line.

The shortcomings we have mentioned above can be addressed by taking care of different dimension which we rely on for the analysis of our study, namely infrastructure, human resources, institution, and ultimately policy and legal aspects. We believe that improvement on these aspects can contribute in minimizing the gaps caused by shortcomings resulted in various dimensions, as postulated by Heeks (2003). We also do believe that addressing these dimensions definitely help improve the qualitative interaction among people, system and processes for the successful implementation of the e-government as envisioned by Wood-Harper et al. (2004).

Even if we have not been able to implement e-Government Master Plan in stipulated time frame, the relevance of the plan is still there. Therefore, it is wise to implement all the immaterialized activities of plan with new time frame after revisiting the plan with analysis of causes of failure of the plan in order to implement it as scheduled originally. Action plan and activities may be changed as per the changing need of time. While doing so, the following aspects need to be duly considered.

Infrastructure

Implementation of e-government in any country is a costly affair - it necessitates prioritizing existing programs and investment pattern and to make available more resources to e-government related activities. Heeks (2003) suggested to use "one for all" contracts that are reusable and to use project management techniques to reduce possible waste and delays. Scholars in this field widely believe that IT designers understand technology but not the realities of the government and public officials and politicians understand the realities of the government but not the technology. In Heeks language to solve problem like this "hybrid"/"tribrids" profession who understand both perspectives is needed. Apart from these, the following core infrastructure related activates be also performed.

More than half of the VDCs in the country have no access to national grid electricity. Urban areas are also facing severe power shortage and compelled to accept power cut more than 12 hours a day. This badly hampered the mission of putting e-government in place by 2011.This should be done by promoting affordable power supply through alternative energy sources such as solar PV systems with subsidy scheme to use in ICT enabled services in rural areas not covered by national grid electricity.

Considering the fact that without basic ICT infrastructure, the notion of e-government cannot be even initiated, basic ICT infrastructure including telephone, PC, internet and email facilities should be expanded with utmost priority.

Human Resources

There is a dearth of qualified experts in different fields of ICT and management to implement e-government in Nepal. In the short run, outsourcing, hiring new staff to expand the volume of current competencies and make use of external consultants can be some of the solutions. In the long run, however, efforts need to be undertaken to formulate a comprehensive HRD plan, encompassing all areas of ICT, primarily focusing on the implementation of e-GMP by ensuring availability of qualified ICT focused human resource in adequate number. In this regard, Nepal should introduce an ICT-related curriculum right from primary education to higher education, expand provision of e-learning, provide ICT training to bureaucrats, and improve computer literacy (www.egovonline.net). Moreover, the continuity of human resources who are involved in the implementation of the e-GMP should be ensured.

Institution

One of the major reasons for failure of e-GMP is the lack of credible institution which can own e-GMP and implement it with concerted efforts. The remedial measures under management systems and structures dimension is that instead of going for overhauling the system, it is better to retain the existing management systems and structures within e-government application design. It is because massive change at one shot may destabilize even the system functioning currently. According to Heeks (2004), e-government project fail also because they try to change too many things at once. To address this problem he suggests to adhere to the principle of "KISS: Keep it Small and Simple." It can be done by retaining the same information, same processes and same management system and structures, but merely change them from manual to computerized operations (Heeks, 2004). Same principle can be applied in case of implementation of e-GMP in Nepal. In this reference, there should be a strong policy level institution with a core mandate to develop coordination among different institutions responsible for the ICT development namely, MoEST, NITC, NTA and MoIC by ensuring their capacity development. In doing so, political leaders need to support modernization initiatives basically through e-government both with words and with actions.

Policy and Legal Aspects

The successful implementation of e-government in Nepal demands not only resources, technology and institutions, but also legal and policy provisions, which create favorable environment to implement such system. Such provision should ensure application of a reward and punishment system.

Accordingly, new acts, namely laws on the National Informatisation Promotion, Laws on ICT industry Promotion, and Laws on ICT infrastructure construction need to be enacted urgently to transform the present conventional governance system into e-governance. Lastly, different acts and aforesaid "Policy to promote e-governance in Nepal" should ensure participatory process.

CONCLUSION

The concept of e-government is not that old and it is still in evolutionary process. However, there is a general consensus that it has to do with reengineering and reinventing the business processes and procedures of government to interact with different stakeholders, namely people, businesses, different governmental agencies and employees in order to improve the quality of the service to be delivered by the government. It should not be confined only to technological adoption; rather it has also to do with enhancing democratic processes and making lives of the people more comfortable and easier (Lofstedt, 2005).

E-governance as a condition for sustainable development requires genuine commitment from political leadership, a proper regulatory framework to ensure information exchanges within and between government, positive attitude of citizens and businesses people, knowledge and skills, proper resource planning, investment in sound technological infrastructure, and proper management systems.

There is no doubt that the prosperity and development of Nepal will depend on its speedy transformation to e-governance from conventional bureaucracy by using state of the art information and communication technologies. However, the implementation of the e-GMP is severely affected by non-compliance of targets set by it. Inadequate political and administrative commitment, resource crunch, dearth of IT professionals, delay in drafting required acts and most importantly weak institutional capacity to implement the e-GMP are the factors responsible for dismal performance of the e-government in Nepal. Moreover, serious shortcoming related to four pillars of e-government (infrastructure, human resources, institutions and policies/laws) mentioned above have also resulted in implementation problem.

Addressing the abovementioned implementation problems contribute in improving the readiness for e-government thereby smoothen the e-government implementation process. In this context, capacity development is one of the areas to be considered seriously when we talk of attaining e-GMP. At the micro level, it constitutes the system under which civil servants will be able to involve in a continuous process of learning to ensure that the institutional capacity exists to implement, monitor and evaluate program/projects related to the e-GMP. Capacity development at the macro level, on the other hand, is required to evolve and maintain a more responsive bureaucracy that responds to the needs of the general people and improves and modernizes itself based on the feedback from the people. Moreover, there should be honest and strenuous efforts to improve the situation of infrastructural facilities, to formulate recommended policies and legislation and enhance institutional capacity .It is believed these policies and programmatic intervention definitely helps minimize the design-reality gaps to avoid failure of e-government in general and reformed e-GMP in particular in future.

To sum up, the key word in e-government is "government" but not "electronic." That's why e-government is still government, not electronics. Most importantly, implementation of e-governance is not a technical issue; instead it is a management issue (Shakya, 2007). Failure in e-government and its effective and timely implementation is not only harming provision of public services to citizens, but also it hampers the private firms' ability in taking advantage of ICT in production of good and services and their participation in the recent wave of liberalization and globalization processes.

REFERENCES

Anderson, D. F., & Dawes, S. S. (1991). *Government information management- A primer and casebook*. Englewood Cliffs, NJ: Prentice Hall.

Asian Development Bank. (2007). *TA No. 4833-NEP: Preparing the information and communications technology development project -A program of modernization for Nepal*. Kathmandu: Asian Development Bank, Resident Mission.

Backus, M. (2001). E-governance in developing countries. *IICD Research Report No 3*. Retrieved November 29, 2009, from http://scholar.google.com/scholar?q=Backus,+M.(+2001).+E-Governance+in+Developing+Countries&hl=en&as_sdt=0&as_vis=1&oi=scholart&sa=X&ei=VjujULfNHcWPrgfhnoDICw&ved=0CCgQgQMwAA

Baum, C., & Di Maio, A. (2000). *Gartner's four phases of e-government model*. Stamford, CT: Gartner, Inc..

Bertot, J. C., McClure, C. R., & Owens, K. A. (1999). Universal service in a global networked environment: Selected issues and possible approaches. *Government Information Quarterly*, *16*(4), 309–327. doi:10.1016/S0740-624X(00)86837-9.

Bhattarai., et al. (2008). Implementation of e-government in Nepal: Prospects, opportunities and threats. In T. Janowski & T.A. Pardo (Eds.), *ICEGoV'08 Proceedings of the 2nd International Conference on Theory and Practice of Electronic Governance* (pp. 483-484). New York: ACM New York.

Carter, L., & Weerakkody, V. (2008). E-government adoption: A cultural comparison. *Information Systems Frontiers*, *10*(4), 473–482. doi:10.1007/s10796-008-9103-6.

CBS. (2003). *Population monograph of Nepal (Vol. I)*. Kathmandu: Central Bureau of Statistics.

Chapagain, D. P. (2006). *PPP Led ICT enabled services in Rural Nepal-A policy paper prepared for economic policy network No 14*. Kathmandu: Ministry of Finance, Government of Nepal and Asian Development Bank, Nepal Resident Mission.

Coursey, D., & Norris, D. F. (2008). Models of e-government: Are they correct? An empirical assessment. *Public Administration Review*, *68*(3), 523–536. doi:10.1111/j.1540-6210.2008.00888.x.

Curtin, G. G., Sommer, M. H., & Vis-Sommer, V. (Eds.). (2004). *The world of e-government*. New York: Haworth Press.

Davis, F. D. (1989). Perceived usefulness, perceived ease of use and user acceptance of information technology. *Management Information Systems Quarterly*, *13*, 319–330. doi:10.2307/249008.

Dawes, S. S., & Nelson, M. R. (1995). Pool the risks, share the benefits: Partnerships in IT innovation. In Keyes, J. (Ed.), *Technology trendliness*. New York: Van Nosttrand Reinhold.

Dovifat, A., Kubisch, D., Bruggemeier, M., Lenk, K., & Reichard, C. (2004). *Explaining successes and failures of e-government implementation with micro politics* (*Vol. 3183*, pp. 308–312). Electronic Government Lecture Notes in Computer Science.

GoN. (2006). e-Government master plan consulting report. Kathmandu: Korean IT Industry Promotion Agency (KIPA) and Government of Nepal.

Gray, P. (2000). Knowledge management overview. *CRITO Working Paper*. Irvine: University of California.

Heeks, R. (2001). *Understanding e-governance for development. Precinct Centre, Manchester, M13 9GH*. UK: Institute for Development Policy and Management University of Manchester.

Heeks, R. (2003). *Most e-government –for-development project fail: How can risks be reduced. Precinct Centre, Manchester, M13 9GH*. UK: Institute for Development Policy and Management, University of Manchester.

Heeks, R. (2004). E-Government as a carrier of context. *e-Government Working Paper Series, Paper No.15*. Manchester: Institute for Development Policy and Management, University of Manchester.

Jaeger, P. T., & Thompson, K. M. (2003). E-Government around the world: Lessons, challenges, and future directions. *Government Information Quarterly*, *20*, 390–391. doi:10.1016/j.giq.2003.08.001.

Layne, K., & Lee, J. (2001). Developing fully functional e-government: A four stage model. *Government Information Quarterly*, *18*(2), 122–136. doi:10.1016/S0740-624X(01)00066-1.

Lofstedt, U. (2005). E-government: Assessment of current research and some proposals for future directions. *International Journal of Public Information Systems, 2005*(1), 39-52.

MoF. (2012). *The economic survey: Fiscal year 2011-2012*. Kathmandu, Nepal: Ministry of Finance, Government of Nepal.

Ndou, V. (2004). E-government for developing countries: Opportunities and challenges. [EJISDC]. *The Electronic Journal of Information System in Developing Countries*, *18*(1), 1–24.

NITC. (2012). *Progress sheet of e-GMP. National Information Centre, Singhadurbar, Kathamndu: Technology Centre*. NITC.

NPC. (2008). *Three year interim plan (2008-2011)*. Kathmandu, Nepal: National Planning Commission, Government of Nepal.

NTA. (2012). *Management information system, X Year, 93(45)*. Kathmandu, Nepal: Nepal Telecommucation Authority.

Pacific Council on International Policy. (2002). *Roadmap for e-government in the developing world: 10 questions e-government leaders should ask themselves*. Los Angeles, USA: The working Group on E-Government in the Developing World, The Western Partner of the Council on Foreign Relations.

Seifert, J. W. (2003). *A primer on e-government: Sectors, stages, opportunities, and challenges of online governance*.USA: Report for Congress, Congressional Research Service, The Library Congress. Retrieved January 10, 2010, from http://www.fas.org/sgp/crs/RL31057.pdf

Shakya, R. (2007). *Current issues and challenges in e-governance implementation in Nepal. A paper presented to the training course on Advanced course on Management and development*. Jawalakhel, Nepal: Nepal Administrative Staff College.

UN/ASPA. (2002). *Benchmarking e-government: A global perspective- Assessing the progress of the UN member states*. UN Division for Public Economics and Public Administration and American Society for Public Administration. Retrieved Feb 2, 2010, from http://unpan1.un.org/intradoc/groups/public/documents/UN/UNPAN021547.pdf

UNDP. (2011). *Nepal human development report 2011: State transformation and human development*. Kathmandu, Nepal: United Nations Development Program.

Wood-Harper, T., Ibrahim, O., & Ithnin, N. (2004). An interconnection success factor approach for service functional in Malaysian electronic government. In *ICE'04, Proceedings of the 6th International Conference on Electronic Commerce* (pp. 446-450).

Zhiyuan, F. (2002). E-government in digital era: Concept, practice, and development. *International Journal of the Computer and Management*, *10*(2), 1–22.

ADDITIONAL READING

Aikins, S. K. (2012). *Managing e-government projects: Concepts and best practices*. IGI Global.

Brentzen, L., & Olsen, M. G. (2009). Benchmarking e-government: A comparative review of three international benchmarking studies. *3rd International Conference on Digital Society* (pp. 77-82), Cancun, Mexico, February 1-7.

Caldow, J. (2001). *Seven e-government leadership milestones*. Institute for Electronic Government, IBM Corporation, USA. Retrieved October 22, 2009, from http://www-01.ibm.com/./government/ieg/./seven_egov_milestones.pdf

Chen, Y. N., Chen, H. M., Huang, W., & Ching, R. K. H. (2006). E-Government strategies in developed and developing countries: An implementation framework and case study. *Journal of Global Information Management*, *14*(1). doi:10.4018/jgim.2006010102.

Dwivedi, Y., Weerakkody, V., & Janssen, M. (2011). Moving towards maturity: Challenges to successful e-government implementation and diffusion. *ACM SIGMIS Database*, *42*(4), 11–22. doi:10.1145/2096140.2096142.

Hall, N. (2008). *How do socially disadvantaged citizens prefer to access public services? MC-eGov Study on Multichannel Delivery Strategies and Sustainable Business Model for Public Services Addressing Socially-Disadvantaged Groups, think paper 5*. Prepared by ECOTEC Consulting Ltd. for the DG Information Society of the European Commission.

Hamner, M., Negron, M. A., Taha, D., & Brahimi, S. (2012). e-Government implementation in a developing country: A case study. *Journal of Global Information Management*, *14*(1).

La Vigne. (2001). *Five kinds of "know-how" make e-government work*. Centre for Technology in Government. Retrieved November 15, 2009, from: www.netcaucus.org/books/egov2001/pdf/e-govtkn.pdf/

Moon, M. J. (2002). The evolution of e-government among municipalities: Rhetoric or reality? *Public Administration Review*, *62*(4), 424–433. doi:10.1111/0033-3352.00196.

Rose, W. R., & Grant, G. G. (2010). Critical issues pertaining to the planning and implementation of e-government initiatives. *Government Information Quarterly*, *27*(1), 26–33. doi:10.1016/j.giq.2009.06.002.

Shareef, M. A., Archer, N., & Dutta, S. (2012). *E-Government service maturity and development: Cultural, organisational and technological perspectives*. Information Science References.

UN. (2003). *UN world public sector report 2003: E-Government at the crossroads*. New York: United Nations.

UN. (2012). *E-Government survey 2012*. Department of Economic and Social Affairs, UN.

Wagner, C., Cheung, K., & Lee, F., & IP, R. (2003). Enhancing e-government in developing countries: Managing knowledge through virtual communities. [EJISDC]. *The Electronic Journal of Information System in Developing Countries*, *14*(4), 1–20.

Welch, E. W., & Pandey, S. (2006). E-Government and bureaucracy: Toward a better understanding of intranet implementation and its effect on red tape. *Journal of Public Administration: Research and Theory*, *17*(3), 379–404. doi:10.1093/jopart/mul013.

Wolfensohn, J. (2001). *Wolfensohn on e-government and the world bank*. Retrieved November 27, 2009.

KEY TERMS AND DEFINITIONS

ADB: Asian Development Bank.

DoC: Departmetn of Commerce.

DoLRM: Department of Landreform and Management.

DoTM: Department of Transport Management.

e-GMP: e-Government Master Plan.

E-Governance: It implies denotes technology or ICT driven governance with a motive of providing goods and services to the common populace in effective and efficient way.

E-Government Master Plan: It is a comprehensive visionary document with a long term e-government planning. It includes vision, mission, goals and objectives along with strategies to achieve stated goals and objectives.

E-Government: It refers to delivery of government information and services to the people by using internet, intranet, worldwide web and other latest means of ICT.

GDP: Gross Domestic Product.

GIDC: Government Integrated Data Centre.

HDI: Human Development Index.

HLCIT: High Level Commission for IT.

HRD: Human Resources Development.

Human Resource Development: It is a sort of framework referring to induction, development and enhancement of skills, knowledge and abilities of employees working in any organization. It is a comprehensive concept including performance management, training, succession planning, and mentoring etc.

ICT: Information and Communication Technology.

Infrastructure: It refers to a prerequisite for an organization to materialize its intended objectives. It can be either in hardware (equipment, road, bridge etc.) form or in software (human resources) form. Proper combination and utilization of hardware and software can greatly contribute an organization to materialize the dream of converting conventional governance into e-governance.

Institution: An organization established as per prevailing legal provision with an aim of achieving targeted objective is an institution. It is a wider term, which can incorporate a custom, practice, relationship, norms, values etc.

IT: Information Technology.

ITPOSMO: Information, Technology, Processes, Objectives and values, Staffing and skills, Management systems and structures; and other resources.

KIPA: Korea IT Industry Promotion Agency.

KOICA: Korea International Cooperation Agency.

MoEST: Ministry of Environment, Science and Technology.

MoF: Ministry of Finance.

MoFA: Ministry of Foreign Affairs.

MoH: Ministry of Home Affairs.

MoI: Ministry of Industry.

MoPH: Ministry of Population and Health.

MoST: Ministry of Science and Technology.

NITC: National IT Centre.

NPC: National Planning Commission.

NTA: Nepal Telecommunication Authority.

OPMCM: Office of the Prime Minister and Council of Ministers.

Policy: A policy is a particular course of action of the government to achieve an intended goal. It may be in the form of acts, regulations, status document, constitution, commitment of the government etc. Policy normally intends to influence public by making certain decisions.

PPP: Purchasing Power Parity.

UN-ASPA: UN and the American Society of Public Administration.

VDC: Village Development Committee.

Compilation of References

Aagesen, G., van Veenstra, A. F., Janssen, M., & Krogstie, J. (2011). *The entanglement of enterprise architecture and IT-Governance: The cases of Norway and the Netherlands*. Paper presented at the Proceedings of the 2011 44th Hawaii International Conference on System Sciences.

Accenture. (2003). *The government executive series egovernment leadership: Engaging the customer*.

Accenture. (2004). *The government executive series: E-government leadership – Realising the vision*. Retrieved July 14, 2006, from http://www.accenture.com/Global/Research_and_Insights/By_Industry/Government/EGovernmentVision.htm

Adams, N., Haston, S., Gillespie, N., & Macintosh, A. (2003). Conventional and electronic service delivery within public authorities: The issues and lessons from the private sector. In Traunmüller, R. (Ed.), *Electronic Government* (*Vol. 2739*, pp. 129–134). Lecture Notes in Computer ScienceBerlin: Springer-Verlag. doi:10.1007/10929179_23.

Administrative Reforms Commission (ARC). (2008). *Eleventh report of ARC, promoting e-governance, smart way forward*. Government of India.

Ahmad, B. A. B. (2008). *Evaluation of federal and state e-government websites in Malaysia*. Paper presented at the 4th International Conference on e-Government. Academic Conferences Limited. RMIT, Melbourne. Australia

Ajzen, I., & Fishbein, M. (1980). *Understanding attitudes and predicting social behaviour*. New Jersey: Prentice-Hall, Inc..

Akdemir, T., & Öz, E. (2004). Elektronik Devlet ve Vergi Yönetimimi II. Vergi Sorunları, (188), 112.

Akerlof, G. A. (1970). The market for" lemons": Quality uncertainty and the market mechanism. *The Quarterly Journal of Economics*, *84*(3), 488–500. doi:10.2307/1879431.

Al Haraizah, A., & Choudhury, I. (2009). E-commerce technology acceptance (ECTA) framework for SMEs in the Middle East with reference to Jordan. In *Proceedings for the 14th UKAIS annual conference*. St Anne's College, University of Oxford, 31st March-1st April.

Allemang, D., Hodgson, R., & Polikoff, I. (2005). *Federal reference model ontologies (FEA-RMO)*. White Paper. Retrieved December 12, 2012, from http://www.topquadrant.com

Alter, S. (1996). *Information systems: A management perspective* (2nd ed.). USA: The Benjamin.

Amaral, D. F. (1994). *Curso de Direito Administrativo*. Coimbra: Livraria Almedina.

Andersen, K. V., & Henriksen, H. Z. (2006). E-government maturity models: Extension of the Layne and Lee model. *Government Information Quarterly*, *23*, 236–248. doi:10.1016/j.giq.2005.11.008.

Andersen, K., & Henriksen, H. (2005). The first leg of e-government research: Domains and application areas. *International Journal of Electronic Government Research*, *1*(4), 26–44. doi:10.4018/jegr.2005100102.

Anderson, J. (2011). *Wikipedia – The company and its founders*. North Mankato: Technology Pioneers.

Anderson, D. F., & Dawes, S. S. (1991). *Government information management- A primer and casebook*. Englewood Cliffs, NJ: Prentice Hall.

Apostolou, D., Stojanovic, L., Lobo, T. P., Miro, J. C., & Papadakis, A. (2005). Configuring e-government services using ontologies. *IFIP Intl. Federation for Information Processing*, *189*, 1571–5736.

Apostolou, D., Stojanovic, L., Lobo, T. P., & Thoensen, B. (2005). In Bohlen, M. (Ed.), *Towards a semantically-driven software engineering environment for e-government* (*Vol. 3416*, pp. 157–168). IFIP Intl. Federation for Information Processing.

Archmann, S., & Kudlacek, I. (2008, February). Interoperability and the exchange of good practice cases. *European Journal of ePractice*, 2. ISSN: 1988-625X.

Arif, M. (2008). Customer orientation in e-government project management: A case study. *The Electronic. Journal of E-Government*, *6*(1), 1–10.

Arrow, K. J. (1984). *The economics of agency*. Institute for Mathematical Studies in the Social Sciences, Stanford University.

Asia Sentinel. (2010, August 17). Malaysia's uneasy dance with the web. *Asia Sentinel*. Retrieved from http://asiasentinel.com/index.php?option=com_content&task=view&id=2645&Itemid=178.html

Asian Development Bank. (2007). *TA No. 4833-NEP: Preparing the information and communications technology development project -A program of modernization for Nepal*. Kathmandu: Asian Development Bank, Resident Mission.

Astley, W. (1985). Administrative science as socially constructed truth. *Administrative Science Quarterly*, *30*(4), 497–513. doi:10.2307/2392694.

Aurigi, A. (2005). *Making the digital city: The early shaping of urban Internet space*. Aldershot, Hampshire: Ashgate Publishing Limited.

Australian Bureau of Statistics (ABS). (2010a). *Australian demographic statistics, March 2010 (No. 3101.0)*. Canberra, Australian Capital Territory: Australian Bureau of Statistics.

Australian Bureau of Statistics (ABS). (2010b). *Regional population growth, Australia (No. 3218.0)*. Canberra, Australian Capital Territory: Australian Bureau of Statistics.

Australian Government. (2012). *Australia.gov.au: Your connection with government*. Retrieved March 19, 2012, from http://australia.gov.au

Bäck, A. Monica (2008). *Conceptions, conflicts and contradictions at the introduction of a Swedish Health Call Centre*. (Doctoral thesis). Göteborg: Gothenburg University.

Backus, M. (2001). E-governance in developing countries. *IICD Research Report No 3*. Retrieved November 29, 2009, from http://scholar.google.com/scholar?q=Backus,+M.(+2001).+E-Governance+in+Developing+Countries&hl=en&as_sdt=0&as_vis=1&oi=scholart&sa=X&ei=VjujULfNHcWPrgfhnoDICw&ved=0CCgQgQMwAA

Bagozzi, R. (2007). The legacy of the technology acceptance model and a proposal for a paradigm shift. *Journal of the Association for Information Systems*, *8*(4), 244–254.

Bailey, J., Bry, F., Furche, T., & Schaffert, S. (2009). Semantic web query languages. Encyclopedia of Database Systems 2009 (pp. 2583-2586).

Bairu, G. (2006). *National forum on education statistics: Forum guide to decision support systems*. A Resource for Educators.

Bajpei, N. (2005). Knowledge based decision support systems in governance. In G. Nayak, M. Mishra & A. Das (Eds.), *Proceedings of the Eighth National Conference on e-Governance* (pp. 43-46). Bhubaneswar.

Baldoni, R., Fuligni, S., Mecella, M., & Tortorelli, F. (2007). The Italian e-government service oriented architecture - Strategic vision and technical solutions. In *Proc. of the 6th EGOV Conference* (pp. 79-88). Regensburg, Germany, 3-7 September.

Bannister, F. (2001). Dismantling the silos: Extracting new value from IT investments in public administration. *Information Systems Journal*, *11*(1), 65–84. doi:10.1046/j.1365-2575.2001.00094.x.

Barthes, J. P., & Moulin, C. (2005). Impact of e-government on territorial government services. Deliverable No. 1.4. Retrieved December 6, 2012, from http://www.terregov.eupm.net

Baştan, S., & Gökbunar, R. (2004). Kamu Hizmetlerinin Sunumunda E-Devletle İlgili Yeni Gelişmeler: Tümleşik E-Devlet Sistemlerine Doğru. DEÜ-İİBF, *19*(1).

Batini, C., & Mecella, M. (2002). Cooperative processes for e-Government. *European Research Consortium for Informatics and Mathematics*, *48*, 38–39.

Batini, C., Viscusi, G., & Cherubini, D. (2009). GovQual: A quality driven methodology for e-government project planning. *Government Information Quarterly*, *26*(1), 106–117. doi:10.1016/j.giq.2008.03.002.

Baum, C., & Di Maio, A. (2000). *Gartner's four phases of e-government model*. Stamford, CT: Gartner, Inc..

Behara, G. K., Varre, V. V., & Rao, M. (2009). *Service oriented architecture for e-governance*. Retrieved from http://www.bptrends.com/publicationfiles/10-09-ART-%20 SOA-E-Govermance-Behara-FINAL.pdf

Beinhocker, E., et al. (2007, August). Tracking the growth of India's middle class. *McKinsey Quarterly*. Retrieved November 10, 2012, from www.mckinseyquarterly.com/ Tracking_the_growth_of_ Indias_middle_class_2032

Bellman, B., & Rausch, F. (2004). *Enterprise architecture for e-government* (pp. 48–56). Electronic Government.

Benbasat, I., Goldstein, D. K., & Mead, M. (1987). The case research strategy in studies of information systems. *Management Information Systems Quarterly*, *11*(3), 369–386. doi:10.2307/248684.

Bennett, C. J. (1991a). How states utilize foreign evidence. *Journal of Public Policy*, *11*, 31–54. doi:10.1017/ S0143814X0000492X.

Bennett, C. J. (1997). Understanding ripple effects: The cross-national adoption of policy instruments for bureaucratic accountability, and Governance. *An International Journal of Policy and Administration*, *10*(3), 213–233. doi:10.1111/0952-1895.401997040.

Berdykhanova, D., Dehghantanha, A., & Hariraj, K. (2010). Trust challenges and issues of e-govemment: E-tax prospective. Information Technology (ITSim) 2010 International Symposium: Volume 3. (pp.1015-1019). IEEE.

Bernama. (2012, April 20). ICT to contribute RM42 billion to Malaysia's GDP by 2015. *Bernama*. Retrieved from http://www.outsourcingmalaysia.org.my/newsflash/424-ict-to-contribute-rm42-billion-to-malaysia-s-gdp-by-2015.php

Bernhard, I. (2009). Evaluation of customer centre and e-services in a Swedish municipality with focus on the citizens' perspective. In D. Remenyi (Ed.), *Proceedings of the 3rd European Conference on Information Management and Evaluation (ECIME)* (pp. 34-41). 17-18 Sept. Reading, UK: Academic Press Ltd.

Bernhard, I. (2010). Establishment of customer centres in the public sector in Sweden – The citizens' views. In D. O'Donnell (Ed.), *Proceedings of the 10th European Conference on e-Government* (pp. 63-70). National Centre for Taxation Studies, University of Limerick, Ireland, 17-18 June 2010. Intellectual Capital Research, Limerick, Ireland, Academic Publishing International.

Bernhard, I. (2011, August). *Local e-government in Sweden – Establishment of municipal contact centers with focus on the citizens and the public administrators*. Paper presented at the 51st European Congress of Regional Science Association International, Barcelona, Spain.

Bernhard, I., & Wihlborg, E. (2011). Municipal contact centers. A slower approach towards sustainable local development. In I. Bernhard (Ed.), *Uddevalla Symposium 2011. Entrepreneurial Knowledge, Technology and Transformation of Regions*. (pp. 111-125). Revised papers presented at the 14th Uddevalla Symposium, 16-18 June 2011, Bergamo, Italy. Research reports 2011:05, University West.

Bernhard, I., & Grundén, K. (2010). Kompetensstrategier vid införande av kundcenter i kommuner. In Lagrosen, S., Lundh Snis, U., & Nehls, E. (Eds.), *Lärande i och för det nya arbetslivet* (pp. 31–46). Lund: Studentlitteratur.

Bernhard, I., & Wihlborg, E. (2012). Trust in secure public e-services – Translating policies into use. In Karlsson, C., Johansson, B., & Stough, R. R. (Eds.), *Entrepreneurship, social capital and governance directions for the sustainable development and competitiveness of regions* (pp. 241–262). Cheltenham, UK & Northampton, MA, USA: Edward Elgar.

Bertot, J. C., & Jaeger, P. T. (2006). User-centred e-government: Challenges and benefits for government Web sites. *Government Information Quarterly*, *23*(2), 163–168. doi:10.1016/j.giq.2006.02.001.

Bertot, J. C., McClure, C. R., & Owens, K. A. (1999). Universal service in a global networked environment: Selected issues and possible approaches. *Government Information Quarterly*, *16*(4), 309–327. doi:10.1016/S0740-624X(00)86837-9.

Beynon-Davies, P. (2005). Constructing electronic government: The case of the UK inland revenue. *International Journal of Information Management*, *25*(1), 3–20. doi:10.1016/j.ijinfomgt.2004.08.002.

Beynon-Davies, P., & Martin, S. (2004). Electronic local government and the modernisation agenda: Progress and prospects for public service improvement. *Local Government Studies*, *30*(2), 214–229. doi:10.1080/0300303042000267245.

Beynon-Davies, P., & Williams, M. D. (2003). Evaluating electronic local government in the UK. *Journal of Information Technology*, *18*(2), 137–149. doi:10.1080/0268396032000101180.

Bhanti, P., Kaushal, U., & Pandey, A. (2011). E-government in higher education: Concept and role of data warehouse techniques. *International Journal of Computers and Applications*, *18*(1), 15–19. doi:10.5120/2249-2879.

Bhatia, D. (2005, April). *Designing and implementing e-government: Key issues, best practices and lessons learned.* World Bank.

Bhatnagar, S. (2004). *E-government from vision to implementation.* Sage Publications.

Bhattarai., et al. (2008). Implementation of e-government in Nepal: Prospects, opportunities and threats. In T. Janowski & T.A. Pardo (Eds.), *ICEGoV'08 Proceedings of the 2nd International Conference on Theory and Practice of Electronic Governance* (pp. 483-484). New York: ACM New York.

Birch, D. (2003). *Local e-government: A survey of local authorities.* London: The Office of the Deputy Prime Minister.

Björk, P., & Bostedt, G. (2002). *Avsektoriserad lokal offentlig service: Organisationsteoretiska perspektiv på försöksverksamhet med medborgarkontor 1995-2000*, Stockholm: Svenska kommunförbundet och Landstingsförbundet/SALAR.

Blackstone, E., Bognanno, A. M., & Hakim, S. (2005). *Innovations in e-government: The thoughts of governors and mayors.* Rowman and Littlefield.

Blakemore, M., Mc Donald, N., Hall, N., & Jucuite, R. (2010). Delivering citizen-centric public services through technology in Europe - Facilitated organizational change. In P. G. Nixon., V. N. Koutrakou, & R. Rawal (Eds.), Understanding e-government in Europe. Issues and challenges (pp. 19-37). Oxon: Routledge.

Bock Seegard, S. (2009). *Veje til lokalt e-demokrati – organisering, mål, virkmidler og resurser.* Oslo: Oslo University Press.

Bolívar, M., Muñoz, L., & Hernández, A. (2010). Trends of e-government research: Contextualization and research opportunities. *The International Journal of Digital Accounting Research*, *10*, 87–111. doi:10.4192/1577-8517-v10_4.

Borja, J., & Castells, M. (1997). *Local and global: The management of cities in the information age.* London: Earthscan Publications Ltd..

bot.com. (2013). Website. Retrieved from http://bot.com/Content/NavigationMenu/Policy/Scorecard/Scorecard_on_Prosperity_2010_FINAL.pdf

Bougettaya, A., Gracanin, D., Yu, Q., Zhang, X., Liu, X., & Malik, Z. (2006). Ubiquitous web services for e-government social services. In *Proc. of the Symposium Semantic Web meets eGovernment (2006 AAAI Spring Symposium Series)* (pp. 2-3).

Bovaird, T. (2005). E-government and e-governance: Organizational implications, options and dilemmas. In Practicing e-government: A global perspective. ISSBN 1-59140-637-4.

Boyce, R. (2008). *TOGAF The open group architecture framework 100 success secrets - 100 most asked questions: The missing TOGAF guide on how to achieve and then sustain superior enterprise architecture execution.* Emereo Pty Ltd..

Bradford, N. (2008). *Canadian social policy in the 2000s: Bringing place in.* Ottawa, Ontario: Canadian Policy Research Networks.

Bram, K., & Janssen, M. (2008). *Stage models for creating joined-up government: From local to nation-wide integration*. Paper presented at the Proceedings of the 2008 international conference on Digital government research, Montreal, Canada.

Bratt, S. (2010). *New project to assess potential of creating open government data initiatives in Chile, Ghana and Turkey*. Retrieved November 18, 2011, from http://www.webfoundation.org/2010/08/potential-of-open-government-data-in-chile-ghana-and-turkey/

Breuker, J., Hoekstra, R., & Boer, A. Van der berg, K., Sartor, G., Rubino, R., Palmirani, M. (2006). *OWL ontology of basis legal concepts (LKIF-Core)*. Deliverable 1.4. Retrieved December 12, 2011, from http://www.estrellaproject.org/doc/D1.4-OWL-Ontology-of-Basic-Legal-Concepts.pdf

Bri, F. D. (2009). An e-government stages of growth model based on research within the Irish revenue offices. *Electronic. Journal of E-Government*, *7*(4), 339–348.

Brisbane City Council. (2012). *Brisbane City Council*. Retrieved April 20, 2012, from http://www.brisbane.qld.gov.au

Broster, D., Misuraca, G., & Bacigalupo, M. (2011). Lifting off towards open government. A report from the EU Belgian Presidency Conference. *European Journal of ePractice*, 12 (March/April).

BTEP. (2004). *GSRM service reference patterns*.

Budde, P. (2012). *Malaysia*. Telecommunications Research. Retrieved from http://www.budde.com.au/Research/Countries/Malaysia/

Budge, E. (2002). Foundations of e-government. In Smith, A. (Ed.), *Digital opportunities for development: A sourcebook for access and applications* (pp. 331–368). Washington: LearnLink.

Burton-Jones, A., & Hubona, G. S. (2005). Individual differences and usage behavior: Revisiting a technology acceptance model assumption. *ACM SIGMIS Database*, *36*(2), 58–77. doi:10.1145/1066149.1066155.

Butka, P., Gabor, A., Ko, A., Mach, M., Ntioudis, S., Papadakis, A., & Zelinsky, T. (2006). *Semantic-enable, agile, knowledge-based e-government (SAKE)*. Deliverable No. 3. Retrieved December 13, 2011, from www.sake-project.org/fileadmin/filemounts/sake/DeliverableD6b.pdf

Bwalya, K. J. (2009). Factors affecting adoption of e-government in Zambia. *Electronic Journal of Information Systems in Developing Countries*, *38*(4), 1–13.

Bwalya, K. J., & Healy, M. (2010). Harnessing e-government adoption in the SADC region: A conceptual underpinning. *Electronic. Journal of E-Government*, *8*(1), 23–32.

Caldow, J. (2001). *Seven e-government leadership milestones*. Institute for Electronic Government. Retrieved May 13, 2012, from http://www-1.ibm.com/industries/government/ieg/pdf/Seven_E-Gov_Milestones.pdf

Calero, C., Ruiz, F., & Piattini, M. (Eds.). (2006). *Ontologies for software engineering and software technology*. Springer-Verlag Berlin Heidelberg. doi:10.1007/3-540-34518-3.

Camarinha-Matos, L. M., & Afsarmanesh, H. (2008). ARCON reference models for collaborative networks. Collaborative networks: Reference modeling (pp. 83-112).

Camarinha-Matos, L., & Afsarmanesh, H. (2006a). Towards a reference model for collaborative networked organizations. Information technology for balanced manufacturing systems (pp. 193-202).

Camarinha-Matos, L., & Afsarmanesh, H. (2006b). towards a reference model for collaborative networked organizations (pp. 193-202).

Capgemini, IDC, Europe Rand, DTi, & Sogeti. (2010). *Digitizing public services in Europe: Putting ambition into action - 9th Benchmark Measurement*.

Carter, L., & Weerakkody, V. (2008). E-government adoption: A cultural comparison. *Information Systems Frontiers*, *10*(4), 473–482. doi:10.1007/s10796-008-9103-6.

Castells, M. (1992). *The informational city: Economic restructuring and urban development*. Wiley-Blackwell.

Castells, M. (1997). *The rise of the network society. The information age: Economy, society and culture (Vol. 1)*. Oxford: Blackwell.

Castells, M., & Ollé Sanz, E. (2004). *The Barcelona model II. The Barcelona City Council in the Network Society*. Barcelona: Open University of Barcelona.

Catinat, M., & Vedel, T. (2000). Public policies for digital democracy. In Hacker, K. L., & van Dijk, J. (Eds.), *Digital democracy: Issues of theory and practice* (pp. 184–208). London: Sage.

Cats-Baril, W. L., & Huber, G. P. (1987). Decision support systems for ill-structured problems. *Journal of Decision Sciences*, *18*, 350–372. doi:10.1111/j.1540-5915.1987.tb01530.x.

CBS. (2003). *Population monograph of Nepal* (*Vol. I*). Kathmandu: Central Bureau of Statistics.

Centre for Independent Journalism. (2010). *Freedom of expression in Malaysia 2010. An Annual Review*. Retrieved from http://www.scribd.com/doc/49753546/Freedom-of-Expression-in-Malaysia-2010.html

Çetin, G. (2010). Bilişim Teknolojilerindeki Gelişmelerin Vergilemede Kayıt Düzeni ve Denetim Uygulamalarına Etkisi. Ekonomi Bilimleri Dergisi.2(1). ISSN: 1309-8020 (Online). Retrieved September 3, 2012, from http://www.sobiad.org/eJOURNALS/dergi_EBD/arsiv/2010_1/09gunes_cetin.pdf

Chadwick, A., & May, C. (2003). Interaction between states and citizens in the age of the Internet: e-government in the United States, Britain, and the European Union. *Governance: An International Journal of Policy and Administration*, *16*(2), 271–300. doi:10.1111/1468-0491.00216.

Chanan, G. (1997). *Active citizenship and community involvement: Getting to the roots*. Dublin: European Foundation for the Improvement of Living and Working Conditions.

Chapagain, D. P. (2006). *PPP Led ICT enabled services in Rural Nepal-A policy paper prepared for economic policy network No 14*. Kathmandu: Ministry of Finance, Government of Nepal and Asian Development Bank, Nepal Resident Mission.

Chatzidimitriou, M., & Koumpis, A. (2008). Marketing one-stop e-government solutions: The European OneStopGov project. *International Journal of Computer Science*, *35*(1), 1–6.

Cheema, G. S., & Rondinelli, D. A. (Eds.). (1983). *Decentralization and development: Policy implementation in developing countries*. London: Sage Publications.

Chen, D., Nie, G., & Liu, P. (2008). Research knowledge sharing of e-government based on automatic ontology mapping. In *Proc of the 6th Wuhan Intl. Conference on E-Business* (pp.105-111).

Chen, P., Gibson, R., Lusoli, W., & Ward, S. (2007). Australian governments and online communication. In Young, S. (Ed.), *Government communication in Australia* (pp. 161–180). Port Melbourne, Victoria: Cambridge University Press.

Chow, W. S., & Chan, L. S. (2008). Social network, social trust and shared goals in organisational knowledge sharing. *Information & Management*, *45*, 458–465. doi:10.1016/j.im.2008.06.007.

Christiansen, P. E., & Gøtze, J. (2006). *International enterprise architecture survey - Trends in governmental enterprise architecture on a national level*. Association of Enterprise Architects. Retrieved from http://www.easurvey.org

Ciborra, C. (2002). *The labyrinths of information: Challenging the wisdom of systems*. Oxford: Oxford University Press.

CIO. (2008). *Government of Canada profile of information technology (IT) services*.

CIOC. (2001). *A practical guide for federal enterprise architecture*.

Cleary, R. E. (2000). The public administration doctoral dissertation re-examined: An evaluation of the dissertations of 1998. *Public Administration Review, 60*(5), 446-455.

Clements, P., Bachmann, F., Bass, L., Garlan, D., Ivers, J., & Little, R. et al. (2009). *Documenting software architectures, views and beyond*. Boston, MA: Pearson Education, Inc..

Clutterbuck, P., Rowlands, T., & Seamons, O. (2009). A case study of SME web application development effectiveness via agile methods. *The Electronic Journal of Information Systems Evaluation*, *12*(1), 13–26.

Codagnone, C., & Osimo, D. (2010). Beyond i2010: E-Government current challenges and future scenarios. In Nixon, P. G., Koutrakou, V. N., & Rawal, R. (Eds.), *Understanding e-government in Europe. Issues and challenges* (pp. 38–59). Oxon: Routledge.

Cohen, G., van Geenhuizen, M., & Nijkamp, P. (2005). ICT as a contributing factor to urban sustainable development: Policymaking in Dutch cities. In van Geenhuizen, M., Gibson, D. V., & Heitor, M. V. (Eds.), *Regional development and conditions for innovation in the network society* (pp. 99–117). West Lafayette, Indiana: Purdue University Press.

Coleman, S. (2008). Foundations of digital government. In Chen, H., Brandt, L., Gregg, V., Traunmüller, R., Dawes, S., & Hovy, E. et al. (Eds.), *Digital government: E-government research, case studies, and implementation* (pp. 3–19). New York: Springer.

Coleman, S., & Blumler, J. G. (2009). *The Internet and democratic citizenship: Theory, practice and policy.* New York: Cambridge University Press. doi:10.1017/CBO9780511818271.

Colesca, S. (2009). Increasing e-trust: A solution to minimize risk in e-government adoption.[JAQM]. *Journal of Applied Quantitative Methods*, *4*(1), 31–44.

Collins, S. (2010, June 18). Government 2.0... It can be a reality. *The drum unleashed.* ABC News 24, Australian Broadcasting Corporation. Retrieved September 26, 2010, from http://www.abc.net.au/unleashed/stories/s2928556.htm

Collins, N., & Butler, P. (2002). When marketing models clash with democracy. *Journal of Public Affairs*, *3*(1), 52–62. doi:10.1002/pa.133.

Comert, C., & Akinci, H. (2004). WEB services, NSDI and e-government. In *Proc. of the FIG Working Week* (pp. 1-13). 22-27 May. Athens, Greece.

Comission of the European Communities. (2002b). *eEurope Benchmarking Report eEurope 2002*. Brussels: Comission of the European Communities.

Commission, E. U. (2006a). *EU coherent strategy against fiscal fraud – frequently asked questions*. Retrieved from http://europa.Eu/rapid/pressreleasesaction.Do?Reference=memo/06/221&format=html&ag d=0&language=en&guilanguage=en. Brussels

Committee to Protect Journalists. (2000). Retrieved October 1, 2012, from http://cpj.org/asia/2000/

COMNET-IT. (2002). *Country profiles of e-governance.* A report of The Commonwealth Network of Information Technology for Development Foundation (COMNET-IT). Retrieved June 3, 2012, from http://unesdoc.unesco.org/images/0012/001276/127601e.pdf

Connelly, R., & Bannister, F. (2007). Consumer trust in electronic commerce: Social & technical antecedents. In Proceedings for world academy of science, engineering and technology, 25, 386-395.

Corner, S. (2010). Australia's national broadband network: How it came to be and where it might be heading. *Telecommunications Journal of Australia, 60*(2), 31.1-31.9.

Coursey, D., & Norris, D. F. (2008). Models of e-government: Are they correct? An empirical assessment. *Public Administration Review*, *68*(3), 523–536. doi:10.1111/j.1540-6210.2008.00888.x.

Creech, H. (2008). International institute for sustainable development. Retrieved October 18, 2012, from http://www.intgovforum.org.html

Curtin, G. G., Sommer, M. H., & Vis-Sommer, V. (Eds.). (2004). *The world of e-government.* New York: Haworth Press.

Dacin, M. T., Goodstein, J., & Scott, W. R. (2002). Institutional theory and institutional change: Introduction to the research forum. *Academy of Management Journal*, *45*, 45–56. doi:10.5465/AMJ.2002.6283388.

Damodaran, L., Nicholls, J., Henney, A., Land, F., & Farbey, B. (2005). The contribution of sociotechnical systems thinking to the effective adoption of e-government and the enhancement of democracy. *The Electronic Journal of E-Government*, *3*(1), 1–12.

Daniel, J. Veit. (2009). *Can national e-government standards find acceptance?* Paper presented at the 42nd Hawaii International Conference on System Sciences.

Darby, J., Muscatelli, A., & Roy, G. (2003). Fiscal decentralization in Europe: A review of recent experience. *Regional Public Finance: European Research in Regional Science, 13.*

Das, R. K., & Patra, M. R. (2009). *SOA for e-governance in India: Potentials and pitfalls*. Retrieved from http://delivery.acm.org/10.1145/1700000/1693050/p36-das.pdf?ip=203.91.193.5&acc=ACTIVE%20SERVICE&CFID=67638877&CFTOKEN=19183172&__acm__=1330070104_a44cefd8a5f3d7314ba-f868a4502e406

Davis, F. D. (1986). A technology acceptance model for empirically testing new end-user information systems: Theory and results. In *MIT Sloan School of Management*. Cambridge, MA: Mit Sloan School of Management.

Davis, F. D. (1989). Perceived usefulness, perceived ease of use, and user acceptance of information technology. *Management Information Systems Quarterly*, *13*(3), 319–340. doi:10.2307/249008.

Davis, F. D. (1993). User acceptance of information technology: System characteristics, user perceptions and behavioral impacts. *International Journal of Man-Machine Studies*, *38*(3), 475–487. doi:10.1006/imms.1993.1022.

Davis, F. D., Bagozzi, R. P., & Warshaw, P. R. (1989). User acceptance of computer technology: A comparison of two theoretical models. *Management Science*, *35*(8), 982–1003. doi:10.1287/mnsc.35.8.982.

Davison, R., Wagner, C., & Ma, L. (2005). From government to e-government: A transition model. *Information Technology & People*, *18*(3), 280–299. doi:10.1108/09593840510615888.

Dawes, S. (2009). Governance in the digital age: A research and action framework for an uncertain future. *Government Information Quarterly*, *26*(2), 257–264. doi:10.1016/j.giq.2008.12.003.

Dawes, S. S., & Nelson, M. R. (1995). Pool the risks, share the benefits: Partnerships in IT innovation. In Keyes, J. (Ed.), *Technology trendliness*. New York: Van Nosttrand Reinhold.

De, R. (2004). E-government systems in developing countries: Some research issues. *Pre-ICIS workshop on eGovernment.* Washington, December.

Deladoss, P. R., Pan, S. L., & Huang, J. C. (2003). Structurational analysis of e-government initiatives: A case study of SCO. *Decision Support Systems*, *34*(3), 253–269. doi:10.1016/S0167-9236(02)00120-3.

Deloitte, & Eurocities. (2005). *eCitizenship for all - European Benchmark Report 2005*.

Deloitte, & Touche. (2001). The citizen as customer. *CMA Management, 74*(10), 58.

Deloitte. (2000). *At the dawn of e-government: The citizen as customer.* A global public sector study by Deloitte Consulting and Deloitte & Touche. Retrieved March, 23, 2012, from http://epractice.eu/en/library/281462

Delopoulos, H. (2012). Objectives and barriers of implementation of egovernment European strategy: From Lisbon strategy to digital agenda. *European Journal of ePractice, 17*.

Department of Broadband, Communications and the Digital Economy (DBCDE). (2011). #au20 national digital economy strategy: Leveraging the national broadband network to drive Australia's digital productivity. Canberra, Australian Capital Territory: DBCDE.

Department of Broadband, Communications and the Digital Economy (DBCDE). (2012). *Digital local government program.* Retrieved August 3, 2012, from http://www.dbcde.gov.au/digital_economy/programs_and_initiatives/digital_local_government_program

Department of Communications, Information Technology and the Arts (DCITA). (2004). *Australia's strategic framework for the information economy 2004–2006: Opportunities and challenges for the information age*. Canberra, Australian Capital Territory: DCITA.

Department of Finance and Administration. (2006). *2006 e-government strategy, responsive government: A new service agenda*. Canberra, Australian Capital Territory: Australian Government Information Management Office.

Department of Finance and Administration. (2007). *Principles for ICT-enabled citizen engagement*. Canberra, Australian Capital Territory: Australian Government Information Management Office.

Department of Finance and Deregulation. (2010). *Declaration of open government*. Canberra, Australian Capital Territory: Australian Government Information Management Office.

Department of Information Technology (DIT). (2011). *Saaransh, a compendium of mission mode projects under NeGP.*

Devadoss, P. R., Pan, S. L., & Huang, J. C. (2002). Structurational analysis of e-government initiatives: A case study of SCO. *Decision Support Systems*, (34): 253–269.

Di Maio, A. (2009). *Moving from citizen-centric to citizen-driven government.* Gartner.

Di Maio, A. (2010). *Gartner open government maturity model.* Gartner.

Dinev, T., & Hart, P. (2002). *Internet privacy concern and trade-off factors-empirical study and business implications.* Working paper. Florida Atlantic University.

Dolowitz, D., & Marsh, D. (2000). Learning from abroad: The role of policy transfer in contemporary policy making, governance. *An International Journal of Policy and Administration*, *13*(1), 5–24. doi:10.1111/0952-1895.00121.

Dovifat, A., Kubisch, D., Bruggemeier, M., Lenk, K., & Reichard, C. (2004). *Explaining successes and failures of e-government implementation with micro politics* (*Vol. 3183*, pp. 308–312). Electronic Government Lecture Notes in Computer Science.

Downe, J., & Martin, S. (2006). Joined up policy in practice? The coherence and impacts of the local government modernisation agenda. *Local Government Studies*, *32*(4), 465–488. doi:10.1080/03003930600793045.

DPT. (2005). E-Devlet Proje ve Uygulamaları 2005. Retrieved September 9, 2012, from http://www.bilgitoplumu.gov.tr

Drucker, P. F. (1967). *Long-range planning in technology, management & society.* Harper & Row.

Druzdzel, J. M., & Flynn, R. R. (2005).. . *Information Science.*

Dubé, L., & Paré, G. (2003). Rigor in information systems positivist case research: Current practices, trends and recommendations. *Management Information Systems Quarterly*, *4*(27), 597–635.

Dunleavy, P., Margetts, H., Simon, B., & Tinkler, J. (2006). *Digital era governance – IT corporations, the state, and e-government.* London: Oxford University Press. doi:10.1093/acprof:oso/9780199296194.001.0001.

Dutta, S., et al. (2012). *The global information technology report 2012. Living in a hyperconnected world.* World Economic Forum: Geneva, 2012.

Eardley, T., Bruce, J., & Goggin, G. (2009). Telecommunications and community wellbeing: A review of the literature on access and affordability for low-income and disadvantaged groups (SPRC Report 9/09, prepared for the Telstra Low Income Measures Assessment Committee (LIMAC)). Sydney: Social Policy Research Centre, University of New South Wales.

Early, P. C. (1993). East meets west mind-east: Further explorations in collective versus individualistic work groups. *Academy of Management Journal*, *36*, 319–348. doi:10.2307/256525.

EC. (1994a). *Europe and the global information society – Bangemann report recommendations to the European Council.* Retrieved April 19, 2012, from http://www.epractice.eu/files/media/media_694.pdf

EC. (1994b). *Europe's way to the information society – An action plan.* COM(94) 347 final. Retrieved April 19, 2012, from http://ec.europa.eu/archives/ISPO/docs/htmlgenerated/i_COM(94)347final.html

EC. (1999). *eEurope: An information society for all.* COM(1999) 687 final. European Commission. Retrieved February 10, 2012, from http://eur-lex.europa.eu/LexUriServ/LexUriServ.do?uri=COM:2002:0263:FIN:EN:PDF

EC. (2003). *The role of eGovernment for Europe's Future.* COM(2003) 567 final. Retrieved May 26, 2012, from http://eur-lex.europa.eu/LexUriServ/LexUriServ.do?uri=COM:2003:0567:FIN:EN:PDF

EC. (2006). *A legal and institutional analysis of barriers to egovernment – Draft deliverable 1b.* Breaking barriers to egovernment: Overcoming obstacles to improving European public services - modinis study (Contract n. 29172). Retrieved December 18, 2011, from http://www.egovbarriers.org/downloads/deliverables/Deliverable_1b_Aug_16_2006.pdf

EC. (2007a). *Measuring progress in e-inclusion.* Riga Dashboard, European Commission, DG Information Society and Media, e-Government unit.

EC. (2007b, December). *Inclusive e-government: Survey of status and baseline activities*. European Commission, DG Information Society and Media, e-Government unit.

EC. (2010). European i2010 initiative on e-Inclusion "*To be part of the information society*." European Commission, DG Information Society and Media, e-Government unit.

Eggers, W. D. (2004). Boosting e-government adoption. *Deloitte Research Public Sector, FTA Annual Conference*.

eGovernment Economics Project (eGEP) Measurement Framework. (2006). Luiss management RSO SPA prepared for the egovernment unit DG information society and media European Commission.

E-Government Practice Editorial Team. European Dynamics S.A. (2010). E-government in Turkey. E-government factsheets Turkey. Retrieved October 3, 2012, from http://epractice.eu

Eisenhart, K. M. (1989). Building theories from case study research. *Academy of Management Review*, *4*(4), 532–550.

EIU. (2005). *Business 2010: The Public Sector*. White Paper. Economist Intelligence Unit. Retrieved May 26, 2012, from http://graphics.eiu.com/files/ad_pdfs/Business_2010_Public_sector_WP.pdf

Electronic government. Third International Conference, EGOV 2004 (pp. 178-185). Berlin: Springer.

Elkins, Z., & Simmons, B. (2005, March). On waves, clusters and diffusion: A conceptual framework. *The Annals of the American Academy of Political and Social Science*, *598*, 33–51. doi:10.1177/0002716204272516.

Elling, S., Lentz, L., & de Jong, M. (2007). Website evaluation questionnaire: Development of a research-based tool for evaluating informational websites. *6th International Conference, EGOV 2007*. Regensburg, Germany: Springer Berlin/Heidelberg. doi:10.1007/978-3-540-74444-3

Elsas, A. (2002). E-government: Integration with web services. In *Proc. of the 7th Intl. Scientific Conference – Summer School*. Frankfurt, Germany.

EPAN. (2004). *Key principles of an interoperability architecture*. European Public Administration Network – eGovernment Working Group. Retrieved January 7, 2012, from http://www.epractice.eu/en/library/281244

Espadas, J., Romero, D., Concha, D., & Molina, A. (2008). Using the Zachman framework to achieve enterprise integration based-on business process driven modelling. On the move to meaningful internet systems: OTM 2008 workshops (pp. 283-293).

EU. (2004). *eGovernment research in Europe. European Commission*. Retrieved from http://europa.eu.int/information society/programmes/egov_rd/text_en.htm

EU. (2004b). *IST egovernment research in FP6 (2003-2006)*. Retrieved November 15, 2004, from http://europa.eu.int/information_society/programmes/egov_rd/fp6/text_en.htm,visited

EU. (2005). EU ministerial declaration on e-government 2005. *Manchester, Ministerial eGovernment Conference* (pp. 2). 24. Nov. Transforming Public Services. Retrieved December 9, 2010, from www.egov2005conference.gov.uk/documents/proceedings/pdf/051124declaration.pdf

Eurocities. (2011). *Eurocities annual report 2011 & work programme 2012*.

European Comission. (2010). Europe's digital competitiveness report 2010 (No. ISBN 978-92-79-15829-2). Publications Office of the European Union.

European Comission. (2012). *Commission staff working document digital agenda scoreboard 2012*.

European Commission DG Information Society. (2004). *Online availability of public services: How is Europe progressing? Web based survey on electronic public services, report of the fourth measurement*. Retrieved March 15, 2012, from http://ec.europa.eu/information_society/eeurope/2005/doc/highlights/whats_new/capgemini4.pdf

European Commission. (2007, September). *The user challenge benchmarking the supply of online public services, 7th Measurement*. Report conducted for Directorate General for Information Society and Media. Retrieved January 10, 2009, from http://ec.europa.eu/information_society/eeurope/i2010/docs/benchmarking/egov_benchmark_2007.pdf

European Commission. (2010). Europeans Information Society Thematic Portal. *Inclusive eGovernment – no citizen left behind*. Retrieved December 27, 2010, from http://ec.europa.eu/information_society/activities/einclusion/policy/egov/index_en.htm

European Council. (2002). *eEurope 2005: An information society for all*. An action plan to be presented in view of the Sevilla European Council.

European Parliament. (2001). *eEurope2002 impact and priorities*. Communication from the Commission to the Council the European Parliament the European Economic and Social Committee and the Committee of the Regions.

European Parliament. (2002a). eEurope 2005: Benchmarking indicators, 655 final. Brussels, Belgium: European Parliament.

European Parliament. (2005). *i2010 – A European information society for growth and employment, {SEC(2005) 717}, COM(2005) 229 final*. Communication from the Commission to the Council the European Parliament the European Economic and Social Committee and the Committee of the Regions.

European Parliament. (2010). *A digital agenda for Europe, COM(2010) 245 final/2*. Communication from the Commission to the Council the European Parliament the European Economic and Social Committee and the Committee of the Regions.

Europeancitiesmonitor.eu. (2013). Website. Retrieved from http://www.europeancitiesmonitor.eu/wp-content/uploads/2010/10/ECM2010-Full-Version.pdf.

Eurostat. (2013). Website. Retrieved from http://epp.eurostat.ec.europa.eu/portal/page/portal/statistics/themes

Evangelidis, A., Akomode, J., Taleb-Bendiab, A., & Taylor, M. (2002). Risk assessment & success factors for e-government in a UK establishment. In Traunmüller, R., & Lenk, K. (Eds.), *Electronic Government* (*Vol. 2456*, pp. 395–402). Lecture Notes in Computer ScienceBerlin: Springer-Verlag. doi:10.1007/978-3-540-46138-8_64.

Evers, H. D., Nordin, R., & Nienkemper, P. (2010). *Knowledge cluster formation in peninsular Malaysia: The emergence of an epistemic landscape. Centre for Policy Research, University Sains Malaysia and International Studies (CenPRIS) and Center for Development Research (ZEF)*. University of Bonn.

Eyestone, R. (1977). Confusion, diffusion and innovation. *The American Political Science Review*, *71*(2), 441–447. doi:10.2307/1978339.

EzGov. (2000). E-government: Making sense of a revolution. *Government Technology August* (Advertising Supplement). Retrieved March 14, 2012, from http://ebookbrowse.com/egovernment-making-sense-revolution-pdf-d291274249

Farooq, M. K., Shamail, S., & Awais, M. M. (2006). *Devolution of e-governance among multilevel government structure*. Paper presented at the Innovations in Information Technology.

Farooq, M. K., Shamail, S., & Awais, M. M. (2008). *Reference model for devolution in e-governance*. Paper presented at the Proceedings of the 2nd International Conference on Theory and Practice of Electronic Governance, Cairo, Egypt.

Farooq, M. K., Shamail, S., & Awais, M. M. (2008). Devolution in a virtual enterprise. In Camarinha-Matos, L., & Picard, W. (Eds.), *Pervasive collaborative networks* (*Vol. 283*, pp. 433–440). Springer Boston. doi:10.1007/978-0-387-84837-2_45.

FEAF. (1999). *Federal enterprise architecture framework version 1.1*.

Feldkamp, D., Siberski, W., Thönssen, B., & Wache, H. (2008). E-government for distributed autonomous administrations. *AAAI-Symposium, AI Meets Business Rules and Process Management* (pp. 1-11). California, USA, 26-28 March.

Ferguson, I., & Chandrasekharan, C. (2004). Paths and pitfalls of decentralization. *ITTO Tropical Forest Update*, *14*(3), 1–7.

Fernandez, D., Carlson, D., Stepina, L., & Nicholson, J. (1997). Hofstede's country classification 25 years later. *The Journal of Social Psychology*, *137*(1), 43–54. doi:10.1080/00224549709595412.

Fiala, P. (2005). Information sharing in supply chains. *Omega (Oxford)*, *33*(5), 419–423. doi:10.1016/j.omega.2004.07.006.

Findahl, O. (2009). *Svenskarna och Internet 2009* (The Swedes and the Internet 2009). World Internet Institute. Retrieved December 12, 2009, from http://www.wii.se

Findahl, O. (2011). *Äldre svenskar och Internet 2010.* World Internet Institute &. SE (The Internet Infrastructure Foundation). Retrieved June 10, 2011, from http://www.wii.se

Fishbein, M. (1980). A theory of reason action: Some applications and implications. In How, H., & Page, M. (Eds.), *Nebraska symposium on motivation* (pp. 65–116). Lincoln: NB University of Nebraska Press.

Fishbein, M., & Ajzen, I. (1975). *Belief, attitude, intention, and behaviour: An introduction to theory and research.* Addison-Wesley Pub. Co..

Flak, L. S., Dertz, W., Jansen, A., Krogstie, J., Spjelkavik, I., & Ølnes, S. (2009). What is the value of eGovernment - and how can we actually realize it? *Transforming Government: People. Process and Policy*, *3*(3), 220–226.

Flak, L., Moe, C., & Saebo, O. (2003). On the evolution of e-government: The user imperative. In Traunmüller, R. (Ed.), *Electronic Government* (*Vol. 2739*, pp. 139–142). Lecture Notes in Computer ScienceBerlin: Springer-Verlag. doi:10.1007/10929179_25.

Flowers, S., Tang, P., Molas-Gallart, J., & Davies, A. (2006). Contrasting approaches to the adoption of e-government. *Journal of E-Government*, *2*(3), 51–83. doi:10.1300/J399v02n03_04.

Fonou-Dombeu, J. V., & Huisman, M. (2012). *A semantic content based methodology framework for e-government development.* (Doctoral Thesis). North-West University, South Africa.

Forman, E., & Selly, M. A. (2001). *Decision by objectives: How to convince others that you are right.* World Scientific Publishing.

Fraga, E. (2002). *Trends in e-government: How to plan, design, secure and measure e-government.* Sante Fe, New Mexico: Gartner Consulting. Retrieved March 28, 2005, from http://www.gmis.org/documents/GMIS_2002_Gartner_LullBeforeStormSantaFe.pdf

Fraser, J., Adams, N., Mckay-Hubbard, A., Macintosh, A., & Canadas, R. (2003). *A framework for e-government services.* Deliverable No. 71. Retrieved December 14, 2011, from http://smartgov.e-gov.gr/index.php?category=results

Freedom House. (2011). *Freedom on the net: Malaysia.* Retrieved October 10, 2012, from http://www.freedomhouse.org/report/freedom-net/freedom-net-2012.html

Freedom House. (2012). *New report: Governments grow increasingly repressive online, activists fight back.* Retrieved October 10, 2012, from http://www.freedomhouse.org/article/new-report-governments-grow-increasingly-repressive-online-activists-fight-back.html

Freeman, J. (2012). E-government engagement and the digital divide. In Parycek, P., Sachs, M., & Skoric, M. (Eds.), *CeDEM Asia 2012:Proceedings of the international conference for e-democracy and open government* (pp. 19-30). Krems: Edition Donau-Universität Krems.

Freeman, J., & Hutchins, B. (2009). Balancing the digital democratic deficit? E-government. *Media International Australia*, *130*, 17–27.

Frenkel, S., Korczynski, M., Shire, K., & Tam, M. (1999). Beyond bureaucracy? Work organization in call centres. *International Journal of Human Resource Management*, *9*(6), 957–979. doi:10.1080/095851998340694.

Funnell, A. (2010, August 5). Our nod to the federal election campaign and an update of gov 2.0 initiatives. In A. Davies (Producer), *Future tense.* Radio National, Australian Broadcasting Corporation. Retrieved September 26, 2010, from http://www.abc.net.au/rn/futuretense/stories/2010/2967969.htm

Furuholt, B., & Wahid, F. (2008). *E-government challenges and the role of political leadership in Indonesia: The case of Sragen.* Paper presented at the Hawaii International Conference on System Sciences, Proceedings of the 41st Annual.

Gachet, A. (2004). *Building model-driven decision support systems with dicodess.* VDF.

Galbraith, J. K. (1971). *The new industrial state.* Signet.

Galliers, R. D. (1992). Choosing information systems research approaches. In Galliers, R. D. (Ed.), *Information systems research: Issues, methods, and practical guidelines* (pp. 144–162).

Ganguly, A. R., & Gupta, A. (2005). *Data mining and decision support for business and science: Encyclopaedia of data warehousing and mining.* Idea Group.

García-Arribas, G., & López-Crespo, F. (2003). Landscape of e-government at the dawn of the 21st century. *UPGRADE – The European Journal for the Informatics Professional, 4*(2), 2-6.

Garicano, L., & Kaplan, S. N. (2001). The effects of business-to-business e-commerce on transaction costs. *The Journal of Industrial Economics, 49*(4), 463–485. doi:10.1111/1467-6451.00158.

Garlan, D., & Shaw, M. (1994). *An introduction to software architecture*. Carnegie Mellon University Technical Report CMU-CS-94-166.

Gartner. (2000). Key issues in e-government strategy and management. *Gartner Group Research Notes, Key Issues*. Retrieved from http://www.gartner.com/id=306621

Gatautis, R. (2008). E-government in transition economies. In A.-V. Anttiroiko & M. Mälkiä (Eds.), *Encyclopedia of digital government* (Vol. 1, pp. 554–559). Hershey, PA: Idea Group Reference. Retrieved from http://www.loc.gov/catdir/toc/ecip0611/2006010087.html

Gautrin, H. F. (2004). *Connecting Quebec to its citizens. Report on E-Government for Verdun*. Parliamentary Assistant to the Premier.

Gefan, D., Rose, G., Warkentin, M., & Pavlou, P. (2005). Cultural diversity and trust in IT adoption: A comparison of potential e-voters in the USA and South Africa. *Journal of Global Information Management, 13*(1).

Gefen, D., Karahanna, E., & Straub, D. W. (2003). Trust and TAM in online shopping: An integrated model. *Management Information Systems Quarterly, 27*(1), 51–90.

Gemini, C. Ernst, & Young. (2002a). Summary report web-based survey on electronic public services (Results of the second measurement: April 2002), results of the second measurement. Conducted for European Commission DG Information Society.

Gemini, C. Ernst, & Young. (2002b). Web-based survey on electronic public services, results of the third measurement. Conducted for European Commission DG Information Society.

Gemini, C. Ernst, & Young. (2004). Online availability of public services: How is Europe progressing? Web based survey on electronic public services, report of the fourth measurement. Conducted for European Commission DG Information Society.

Gemini, C. Ernst, & Young. (2007). The user challenge benchmarking the supply of online public services, 7th measurement. Conducted for Directorate General for Information Society and Media, European Commission.

Gibson, R. K., Lusoli, W., & Ward, S. (2007). The Australian public and politics online: Reinforcing or reinventing representation? *Conference Proceedings, The Annual Conference of the UK Political Studies Association*. University of Bath, Bath, UK.

Giddens, A. (1984). *The constitution of society*. Berkeley, CA: University of California Press.

Gilbert, D., Balestrini, P., & Littleboy, D. (2004). Barriers and benefits in the adoption of e-government. *International Journal of Public Sector Management, 17*(4), 286–301. doi:10.1108/09513550410539794.

Gil-Garcia, J. R., & Luna-Reyes, L. F. (2006). *Enacting inter-organizational e-government in the Mexican federal government*. Paper presented at the Proceedings of the 2006 international conference on Digital government research, San Diego, California.

Gil-Garcia, R. (2012). *Electronic government success: Definition, measures, and factors*. New York: Springer. doi:10.1007/978-1-4614-2015-6.

Gillooly, C. (1998). Disillusionment. *Information Week, 16*, 46–56.

Gillwald, A., & Stork, C. (2008). *Towards evidence-based ICT policy and regulation: ICT access and usage in Africa*. 1(2). Retrieved June 9, 2009, from www.researchictafrica.net/.../ria-policy-paper_ict-access-and-usage-2008.pdf

Giritli Nygren, K., & Wiklund, H. G. (2010). En IT-styrd förvaltning – en fjärde förvaltningsdoktrin? In K. Lindblad-Gidlund, A. Ekelin, S, Eriksén & A. Ranerup (Eds.), Förvaltning och medborgarskap i förändring (Ongoing change in public administration and citizenship – Established practice and critical perspectives) (pp. 215-228). Lund: Studentlitteratur.

Given, J., & Watkins, J. (2010). Broadband: Policy, innovation, use. *Communication. Politics & Culture, 43*(1), 1–6.

Goggin, G. (2003). Wiring the country: Local telecommunications and Australian rural communities. *Southern Review: Communication. Politics & Culture, 36*(1), 34–47.

Golden, W., Hughes, M., & Scott, M. (2003). The role of process evolution in achieving citizen-cantered e-government. *Ninth Americas Conference on Information Systems*. Tampa, Florida.

Goldfinch, S., Gauld, R., & Herbison, P. (2009). The participation divide? Political participation, trust in government, and e-government in Australia and New Zealand. *Australian Journal of Public Administration*, *68*(3), 333–350. doi:10.1111/j.1467-8500.2009.00643.x.

GoN. (2006). e-Government master plan consulting report. Kathmandu: Korean IT Industry Promotion Agency (KIPA) and Government of Nepal.

Gonçalves, J. (2000). Para uma Administração Pública do Século XXI: O Caminho das Causas das Buropatologias. In Bilhim, J. (Ed.), *Reforma do Estado e Administração Pública Gestionária* (pp. 87–95). Lisboa: Instituto Superior de Ciências Sociais e Políticas.

Goodnow, F. (2003). *Politics and administration: A study in government*. New Brunswick: Transaction Publishers.

Gordon, S. R., & Gordon, J. R. (1996). *Information systems: A management approach*. Fort Worth, TX: Dryden Press.

Goudos, S. K., Peristeras, V., Lutas, N., & Tarabanis, K. (2007). A public administration domain ontology for semantic discovery of e-government services. In *Proc. of the 2nd IEEE Conference on Digital Information Management 2007 (ICDIM 2007)* (pp. 260-265). Lyon, France, 11-13 December.

Gouscos, D., Laskaridis, G., Lioulias, D., Mentzas, G., & Georgiadis, P. (2002). An approach to offering one-stop e-government services – Available technologies and architectural issues. In *Proc. of the Electronic Government, First International Conference (EGOV 2002)* (pp. 264-271). Aix-en-Provence, France, 2-5 September.

Government 2.0 Taskforce Report. (2009). *Engage: Getting on with government 2.0*. Canberra, Australian Capital Territory: Australian Government Information Management Office.

Government 2.0 Taskforce. (2010). *Government 2.0 taskforce*. Retrieved June 3, 2010, from http://gov2.net.au/

Government of India Ministry of Panchayati Raj. (2013.) Retrieved November 18, 2011, from http://panchayat.gov.in/mopr/ viewPortalPage.do?cToken=-1235127219

Government of India. (2001, November). *Report of the working group on convergence and e-governance for tenth five year plan* (2002-2007, pp. 6-25). Planning Commission, New Delhi.

Government of India. (2007). *Ethics in governance, second administrative reforms commission 4th report*. Government of India. Retrieved December 17, 2012, from http://darpg.nic.in/darpgwebsite_cms/Document/file/ethics4.pdf

Government of India. (2012). *National e-governance plan*. Retrieved November 18, 2011, from http://www.negp.gov.in/Projects/Default.aspx

Government of India. (2013). *MGNREGS*. Retrieved April 29, 2010, from http://nrega.nic.in/netnrega/home.aspx

Government of India. (2013). *MoRD*. Retrieved May 29, 2010, from http://www.rural.nic.in

Government Response to the Report of the Government 2.0 Taskforce. (2010). *Government response to the report of the government 2.0 taskforce: Engage: Getting on with government 2.0*. Canberra, Australian Capital Territory: Department of Finance and Deregulation.

Government, F. A. S. T. (2012, July 20). *(Flat, agile, streamlined, tech-enabled) for the 21st Century*. Retrieved August 2, 2012, from http://blog.mile.org/f-a-s-t-government-flat-agile-streamlined-tech-enabled-for-the-21st-century/

Grande, I., Araujo, C., & Serna, S. (2002). Research on e-government: A proposal of theoretical framework. *European Group of Public Administration Conference*.

Grant, G., & Chau, D. (2005). Developing a generic framework for e-government. *Journal of Global Information Management*, *13*(1), 1–30. doi:10.4018/jgim.2005010101.

Grant, G., & Chau, D. (2006). Developing a generic framework for e-Government. In Hunter, G., & Tan, F. (Eds.), *Advanced topics in global information management* (*Vol. 5*, pp. 72–101). London: Idea Group. doi:10.4018/978-1-59140-923-6.ch004.

Gray, P. (2000). Knowledge management overview. *CRITO Working Paper*. Irvine: University of California.

Grey, J., Huisman, M., & Goede, R. (2006). *An investigation of the suitability of agile system development methodologies for the development of data warehouses*. (Msc. Dissertation). North-West University, South Africa.

Griffiths, N., & Chao, K.-M. (2010). *Agent-based service-oriented computing*. Springer-Verlag. doi:10.1007/978-1-84996-041-0.

Grönlund, A. (2005). What's in a field – Exploring the egovernment domain. *The 38th Hawaii International Conference on System Sciences*. Retrieved March 16, 2006, from http://ieeexplore.ieee.org/iel5/9518/30166/01385489.pdf

Grönlund, Å. (2006). Electronic government – What's in a word? Scope, status and future of the field. In EuroSpace (Ed.), E-government: European Strategies compared. EuroSpace S.r.1.

Grönlund, Å. (2001). En introduktion till electronic government. In Grönlund, Å., & Ranerup, A. (Eds.), *Elektronisk förvaltning, elektronisk demokrati. Visioner, verklighet, vidareutveckling*. Lund: Studentlitteratur.

Grönlund, Å. (2002). *Electronic government – Design, applications, and management*. Hershey, PA: Idea Group.

Grönlund, A. (2003). Framing e-gov: e=mc3. In Traunmüller, R. (Ed.), *Electronic Government* (*Vol. 2739*, pp. 191–198). Lecture Notes in Computer ScienceBerlin: Springer-Verlag. doi:10.1007/10929179_36.

Grönlund, A. (2004). State of the art in e-gov research: A survey. In Traunmüller, R. (Ed.), *Electronic Government* (*Vol. 3183*, pp. 178–185). Lecture Notes in Computer ScienceBerlin: Springer-Verlag. doi:10.1007/978-3-540-30078-6_30.

Grönlund, A., & Horan, T. (2005). Introducing e-gov: History, definitions, and issues. *Communications of the Association for Information Systems*, *15*, 39.

Gruber, T. R. (1993). Toward principles for the design of ontologies used for knowledge sharing. *International Journal of Human-Computer Studies*, *43*, 907–928. doi:10.1006/ijhc.1995.1081.

Grundén, K. (2009a). MOA – An evaluation model for implementation and use of IT in organisations. In D. Remenyi (Ed.), *Proceedings of the 3rd European Conference on Information Management and Evaluation (ECIME)* (pp. 187-194). *17-18 Sept.* Reading, UK: Academic Press Ltd.

Grundén, K. (2009b). A social perspective on implementation of eGovernment - A longitudinal study at the County Administration of Sweden. *The Electronic Journal of e-Government (EJEG), 7*(1), 65-76.

Grundén, K. (2010). Evaluation of contact centre implementation in a Swedish municipality with focus on social aspect. In D. O'Donnell (Ed.), *Proceedings of the 10th European Conference on e-Government* (pp. 199-206). National Centre for Taxation Studies, University of Limerick, Ireland, 17-18 June, Intellectual Capital Research, Limerick, Ireland: Academic Publishing International.

Grundén, K. (2011). Implementation of contact centre in a Swedish municipality. In M. Klun, M. Decman, and T. Jukic (Eds.), *11th European Conference on eGovernment (ECEG 2011)*. Faculty of Administration, University of Ljubljana, Ljubljana, Slovenia, 16-17 June 2011.

Gugliotta, A., Cabral, L., Domingue, J., & Roberto, V. (2005). A conceptual model for semantically-based e-government portal. In *Proc. of the Intl. Conference on e-Government 2005 (ICEG 2005)*. Ottawa, Canada, 2005.

Guijarro, L. (2007). Interoperability frameworks and enterprise architectures in e-government initiatives in Europe and the United States. *Government Information Quarterly*, *24*(1), 89–101. doi:10.1016/j.giq.2006.05.003.

Gupta, J. N. D. (2006). *Intelligent decision-making support system: Foundation, applications and challenges*. Springer.

Gupta, M. P. (2004). *Towards e-government management challenges*. New Delhi: Tata McGraw-Hill Publishing Company Limited.

Gupta, M. P., & Jana, D. (2003). E-government evaluation: A framework and case study. *Government Information Quarterly*, *20*(4), 365–387. doi:10.1016/j.giq.2003.08.002.

Hadenius, S., Weibull, L., & Wadbring, I. (2008). *Massmedier. press, radio och tv i den digitala tidsåldern*, 9:e upplagan, reviderad 2008. Stockholm: Ekerlids förlag.

Halchin, L. E. (2004). Electronic government: Government capability and terrorist resource. *Government Information Quarterly*, *21*, 406–419. doi:10.1016/j.giq.2004.08.002.

Harekrishna, M. (2009a). Understanding SOA perspective of e-governance in Indian context: Case based study. *22nd Bled Conference, eEnablement: Facilitating an Open, Effective and Representative eSociety*, June 14 - 17, Bled, Slovenia.

Harekrishna, M. (2010b). Role of information systems architecture in e-governance: The case of MGNREGS in India. *ICEGOV2010*, October 25-28, Beijing, China.

Harekrishna, M. (2009b). *Governance of rural information and communication technology: Opportunities and challenges. ISBN: 13*. New Delhi: Academic Foundation.

Harekrishna, M. (2010a). Citizen-centric service dimensions of Indian rural e-governance systems: An evaluation. In Rahman, H. (Ed.), *Cases on adoption, diffusion, and evaluation of global e-governance systems: Impact at the grass roots*. IGI Global Publishing.

Harrison, T. M., Guerrero, S., Burke, G. B., Cook, M., Cresswell, A., Helbig, N., et al. (2011). Open government and e-government: Democratic challenges from a public value perspective. In *Proceedings of the 12th Annual International Digital Government Research Conference (dg.o 2011)* (pp. 245–253). College Park, MD, USA: ACM.

Harris, R. (2009). *Introduction to decision making*. Springer.

Hasan, S. (2003). Introducing e-government in Bangladesh: Problems and prospects. *International Social Science Review*, *78*(3&4), 111–125.

Haugli Nyhuus, K., & Thorsen, T. (2007). *Partnerskap: Intensjon og virkelighet i NAV reformens velferdskontor*. Karlstads Universitet & Högskolen i Hedmark.

Hawaii. (2003). *Proceedings of the 36th Hawaii International Conference on System Sciences 2003*. New York: Wiley-IEEE Press.

Heeks, R. (1999). Centralised vs. decentralised management of public information systems: A core-periphery solution. *Information Systems for Public Sector Management Working Paper Series*. Institute for Development Policy and Management.

Heeks, R. (2001b). *Understanding e-governance for development*. Retrieved March 13, 2012, from http://unpan1.un.org/intradoc/groups/public/documents/NISPAcee/UNPAN015484.pdf

Heeks, R. (2003). *Most e-government projects-for-development fail: How can risk be reduced?* Working Paper 14, IDPM, University of Manchester.

Heeks, R. (2004). E-Government as a carrier of context. *e-Government Working Paper Series, Paper No.15*. Manchester: Institute for Development Policy and Management, University of Manchester.

Heeks, R. (2008). ICT4D 2.0: The next phase of applying ICT for international development. IEEE Computer Society, 0018-9162/08.

Heeks, R. (2008). *The use of ICTs in transparency projects*. Retrieved December 12, 2011, from http://www.egov4dev.org/transparency/

Heeks, R. (1999). *Reinventing government in the information age – International practice in IT-enabled public sector reform*. London: Routledge. doi:10.4324/9780203204962.

Heeks, R. (2001). *Understanding e-governance for development. Precinct Centre, Manchester, M13 9GH*. UK: Institute for Development Policy and Management University of Manchester.

Heeks, R. (2001a). Reinventing government in the information age. In Heeks, R. (Ed.), *Reinventing government in the information age – International practice in IT-enabled public sector reform* (pp. 9–21). London: Routledge.

Heeks, R. (2003). *Most e-government –for-development project fail: How can risks be reduced. Precinct Centre, Manchester, M13 9GH*. UK: Institute for Development Policy and Management, University of Manchester.

Heeks, R. (2006). *Benchmarking egovernment: Improving the national and international measurement, evaluation and comparison of egovernment*. Development Informatics Group Institute for Development Policy and Management University of Manchester.

Heeks, R. (2006). *Implementing and managing egovernment: An international text*. Thousand Oaks, CA/London: Sage Publications.

Heeks, R., & Bailur, S. (2007). Analyzing e-government research: Perspectives, philosophies, theories, methods, and practice. *Government Information Quarterly*, *24*(2), 243–265. doi:10.1016/j.giq.2006.06.005.

Heeks, R., & Davies, A. (2001). Different approaches to information age reform. In Heeks, R. (Ed.), *Reinventing Government in the Information Age — International practice in IT-enabled public sector reform* (pp. 22–48). London: Routledge.

Heeks, R., & Molla, A. (2009). *Impact assessment of ICT-for-development projects: A compendium of approaches*. Working Paper 36, Institute for Development, Policy and Management (IDPM), University of Manchester.

Hemant, K. B., Power, D. J., & Daewon, S. (2007).. . *Decision Support Systems*, *43*(4).

Henderson, J. C. (1985). *A methodology for identifying strategic opportunities for DSS*. Massachusetts: Massachusetts Institute of Technology Cambridge.

Hepaksaz, E. (2012). Türkiye'de Vergi Sisteminin Yeniden Yapılandırılmasında Muhtemel Fayda ve Maliyetleriyle VEDOP Projesi ve E-Maliye Uygulamaları. 27. Türkiye Maliye Sempozyumu. Retrieved October 3, 2012, from www.maliyesempozyumu2012.org/teblig-kitabi.html

Hiller, J., & Bélanger, F. (2001). Privacy stategies for electronic government. In Abramson, M., & Means, G. (Eds.), *E-Government 2001* (pp. 162–198). Lanham: Rowman and Littlefield Publishers.

Hiquet, S. L. (2005). *Network Plus*. Thompson Course Technology PTR.

Ho, A. (2002). Reinventing local government and the e-government initiative. *Public Administration Review*, *62*(4), 434–444. doi:10.1111/0033-3352.00197.

Ho, A. T.-K. (2002). Reinventing local government and the e-government initiative. *Public Administration Review*, *4*(62), 434–444.

Hofstede, G. (1980). Culture's consequences: International differences in work-related values. *Sage (Atlanta, Ga.)*.

Hofstede, G. (1997). *Culture and organizations: Software of the mind*. London: Mc Graw Hill.

Hofstede, G. (2001). *Culture's consequences- Comparing values, behaviours, institutions, and organizations across nations* (2nd ed.). SAGE Publications.

Ho, K. W. (2003, May 10). Cyber-war on terror: The checks in the e-mail. *The Straits. Times (London, England)*.

Holden, S., Norris, D. F., & Fletcher, P. D. (2003). Electronic government at the local level. *Public Performance and Management Review*, *4*(26), 325–344. doi:10.1177/1530957603026004002.

Holden, S., Norris, D., & Fletcher, P. (2003). Electronic government at the local level: Progress to date and future issues. *Public Performance & Management Review*, *6*(4), 325–344. doi:10.1177/1530957603026004002.

Holsapple, C. W., & Whinston, A. B. (1996). *Decision support systems: A knowledge-based approach*. St. Paul: West Publishing.

Homburg, V. (2008). *Understanding e-government. Information systems in public administration*. Abingdon, Oxon: Routledge.

Horrocks, I. (2009). 'Experts' and e-government: Power, influence and the capture of a policy domain in the UK. *Information Communication and Society*, *12*(1), 110–127. doi:10.1080/13691180802109030.

Howlett, M. (2000). Beyond legalism? Policy ideas, implementation styles and emulation based convergence in Canadian and U.S. environmental policy. *Journal of Public Policy*, *20*(3), 305–329. doi:10.1017/S0143814X00000866.

Hreno, J., Bednar, P., Furdík, K., & Sabol, T. (2001). Integration of government services using semantic technologies. *Journal of Theoretical and Applied Electronic Commerce Research*, *6*(1), 143–154.

Hsu, M. H., & Chiu, C. M. (2004). Internet self-efficacy and electronic service acceptance. *Decision Support Systems*, *38*(3), 369–381. doi:10.1016/j.dss.2003.08.001.

Hu, G., Pan, W., Lu, M., & Wang, J. (2009). The widely shared definition of e-Government: An exploratory study. *The Electronic Library*, *27*(6), 968–985. doi:10.1108/02640470911004066.

Hu, X. (2010). *Data warehouse technology and application in data centre design for e-government* (pp. 371–383). E-learning, Experiences and Future. doi:10.5772/8800.

i2010 High Level Group. (2006). *Benchmarking framework.* Conducted for i2010 Information Space, Innovation & Investment in R&D, Inclusion, European Commission.

i2010 High Level Group. (2009). *Benchmarking digital Europe 2011-2015 a conceptual framework.* Conducted for i2010 Information Space, Innovation & Investment in R&D,Inclusion, European Commission.

Ibrahim, A., & Goh, C. C. (2000). *Multimedia super corridor.* Leeds Publication.

infoDev. (2009). E-government primer. A report by *infoDev – Innovate. Connect. Transform, The World Bank.* http://www.infodev.org/en/Publication.823.html

International Consortium of Investigative Journalists. (2001). Retrieved October 1, 2012, from http://www.icij.org/awards

International Telecommunications Union (ITU). (2009). *ICT statistics 2009—Internet.* Retrieved November 20, 2010, from http://www.itu.int/ITUD/icteye/Reporting/ShowReportFrame.html

Islam, M. (2008). Towards a sustainable e-participation implementation model. *European Journal of ePractice, 5,* 26-37. Retrieved 12 May, 2012, from http://www.epractice.eu/files/ePractice-Journal-Volume-5.pdf

Jacquier, C. (2008). *Urban governance: Forging a path between complications and complexity.* Paper presented for the symposium "Towards New Territorial Governance" run by Urban-logement, 15 September 2008 Reims.

Jacquier, C. (2005). On relationships between integrated policies for sustainable urban development and urban governance. *Tijdschrift voor Economische en Sociale Geografie, 96*(4), 363–376. doi:10.1111/j.1467-9663.2005.00469.x.

Jaeger, P. T., & Thompson, K. M. (2003). E-Government around the world: Lessons, challenges, and future directions. *Government Information Quarterly, 20,* 390–391. doi:10.1016/j.giq.2003.08.001.

Jaeger, P., & Thompson, K. (2004). Social information behavior and the democratic process: Information poverty, normative behavior, and electronic government in the United States. *Library & Information Science Research, 26*(1), 94–107. doi:10.1016/j.lisr.2003.11.006.

Janet, S. (2009). Professionalism online: How Malaysiakini challenges authoritarianism. *The International Journal of Press/Politics, 14*(1), 91–111.

Janowski, T., Estevez, E., & Ojo, A. (2007). *A project framework for e-government.* Research Report No. 359. Centre for Electronic Government, United Nations University-International Institute for Software Technology (UNU-IIST), Macao, China.

Janssen, M., & Hjort-Madsen, K. (2007). *Analyzing enterprise architecture in national governments: The cases of Denmark and the Netherlands.* Paper presented at the System Sciences, 2007. HICSS 2007. 40th Annual Hawaii International Conference on System Sciences.

Jansson, G. (2011). *Local values and e-government - Continuity and change in public administration. Implementing public e-Services on two Swedish municipalities' administration.* Sweden: Linköping University.

Jarrar, M., Deik, A., & Farraj, B. (2011). Ontology-based data process governance framework – The case of e-government interoperability in Palestine. In *Pre-proc. of the IFIP International Symposium on Data-Driven Process Discovery and Analysis (SIMPDA'11)* (pp. 83-98). Campione, Italy, 30 June.

Jayashree, S., & Marthandan, G. (2010). Government to e-government to e-society. *Journal of Applied Sciences, 10,* 2205–2210. doi:10.3923/jas.2010.2205.2210.

Jeong, C. H. I. (2007). *Fundamentals of development administration.* Selangor: Scholar Press.

Jho, W. (2005). Challenges for e-governance: Protests from civil society on the protection of privacy in e-government in Korea. *International Review of Administrative Sciences, 71*(1), 151–166. doi:10.1177/0020852305051690.

Jimenez, B. S., Mossberger, K., & Wu, Y. (2012). Municipal government and the interactive Web: Trends and issues for civic engagement. In Manoharan, A., & Holzer, M. (Eds.), *E-governance and civic engagement: Factors and determinants of e-democracy* (pp. 251–271). Hershey, Pennsylvania: Information Science Reference. doi:10.4018/978-1-4666-1740-7.ch006.

Johnston, M. E., & Langton, K. B. Haynes., & Mathieu, A. (1994). Effects of computer-based clinical decision support systems on clinical performance and patient outcome: A critical appraisal of research. McMaster University, Hamilton, Ontario, Canada.

Jörgens, H. (2004). Governance by diffusion – Implementing global norms through cross-national imitation and learning. In Lafferty, W. M. (Ed.), *Governance for sustainable development. The challenge of adapting form to function* (pp. 246–283). Cheltenham: Edward Elgar Publishing.

Jotischky, N. (2010). *India will overtake China as world's largest mobile market in 2013*. Press release Informa Telecoms & Media. Retrieved November 11, 2011, from http://blogs.informatandm.com/1475/press-release-india-will-overtake-china-as-worlds-largest-mobile-market-in-2013/

Kannath, S. (2009). *Ethical governance, building an ethical leadership*. Retrieved November 18, 2012, from http://ethicalgov.blogspot.in/

Kapanoğlu, A., Sökmen, B., & Aykin, H. (2011). *Kayıtdışı Ekonomi ve Yolsuzlukla Mücadele Açısından Maliye Teftişkurulu Elektronik Denetim Uygulaması. Kamu Yönetimi ve Teknoloji. Vol:360.* Ankara: TODAIE.

Karagiannaki, E. (2005). *Jobcentre plus or minus? Exploring the performance of Jobcentre Plus for nonjobseekers. CASEpaper 97. Centre for Analysis of Social Exclusion.* London School of Economics.

Kasper, G. M. (1996). A theory of decision support system design for user calibration. *Information Systems Research*, *7*(2), 215–232. doi:10.1287/isre.7.2.215.

Kauffman, R. J., & Mohtadi, H. (2003). Analyzing interorganizational information sharing strategies in b2b e-commerce supply chains. In *INFORMS Conference on Information Systems and Technology*, Atlanta, GA.

Kaushik, P. D. (2004). E-governance: Government initiatives in India. In Debroy, B. (Ed.), *Agenda for improving governance*. New Delhi: Academic Foundation in Association with Rajiv Gandhi Institute for Contemporary Studies.

Kaylor, C., Deshazo, R., & Van Eck, D. (2001). Gauging e-government: A report on implementing services among American cities. *Government Information Quarterly*, *18*(4), 293–307. doi:10.1016/S0740-624X(01)00089-2.

Keen, P. G. W. (1978). *Decision support systems: An organisational perspective*. Reading, MA: Addison-Wesley Pub. Co..

Keen, P. G., & Scott-Morton, M. S. (1978). *Decision support systems: An organisational perspective*. Reading, MA: Addison-Wesly.

Kensaku, N. (2008). *The power of Internet in Malaysia's recent election*. Retrieved June 28, 2010, from http://www.helium.com/items.com.html

Keohane, R. O., & Nye, J. S. (2000). Introduction. In Nye, J. S., & Donahue, J. D. (Eds.), *Governance in a globalizing world* (pp. 1–44). Washington: Brookings Institution Press.

Kho, C., & Prybutok, V. (2003). The three ring model and development of an instrument for measuring dimensions of e-government functions. *Journal of Computer Information Systems*, *43*(3), 34–39.

Khosrow-Pour, M. (2005). *Practicing e-government-A global perspective*. Idea Group Publishing. doi:10.4018/978-1-59140-637-2.

King, S. F. (2007). Citizens as customers: Exploring the future of CRM in UK local government. *Government Information Quarterly*, *24*(1), 47–63. doi:10.1016/j.giq.2006.02.012.

Kolsaker, A. (2005). Third way e-government: The case for local devolution. In Böhlen, M., Gamper, J., Polasek, W., & Wimmer, M. A. (Eds.), *E-government: Towards electronic democracy* (pp. 70–80). Berlin: Springer. doi:10.1007/978-3-540-32257-3_7.

Kostoska, M., Gusev, M., & Kiroski, K. (2010). *Evaluation methodology for national enterprise architecture frameworks*. Paper presented at the ICT Innovations 2010. Hjort-Madsen, K. (2009). *Enterprise architecture in government: Fad or future?* Paper presented at the 42nd Hawaii International Conference on System Sciences.

Kriebel, L., & Lapham, L. (2008). Transition to electronic resources in undergraduate social science research. A study of honour theses: Bibliographies, 1999-2005. *College & Research Libraries*, *69*(3), 268–283.

Krippendorff, K. (1980). *Content analysis: An introduction to its methodology*. Sage Publications, Inc..

Kuek, S. K. K. (2009). Coming soon: A lenient ISA, rallies without permits. *Malaysiakini*. Retrieved from http://malaysiakini.com/news/110939.html

Kunis, R., Runger, G., & Schwind, M. (2007). A model for document management in e-government systems based on hierarchical process folders. *Electronic. Journal of E-Government*, *5*(2), 191–204.

Laclavik, M. (2005). *Ontology and agent based approach for knowledge management*. (Doctoral Thesis). Slovak Academy of Sciences.

Laffin, M. (2008). Local government modernisation in England: A critical review of the LGMA evaluation studies. *Local Government Studies*, *34*(1), 109–125. doi:10.1080/03003930701795014.

Larson, E., & Rainie, L. (2002). *The rise of the e-citizen: How people use government agencies' web sites*. Washington, DC: Pew Internet and American Life Project.

Layne, K., & Lee, J. (2001). Developing fully functional e-government: A four stage model. *Government Information Quarterly*, *18*(2), 122–136. doi:10.1016/S0740-624X(01)00066-1.

Lazauskaite, V. (2008). *Internal gateway liberalization, WSIS facilitation meeting on action line C6 ITU headquarters*. Retrieved October 23, 2009, from http://www.itu.int/wsis/c2/docs/2008-May-19/mdocs/C6-session4-Lazauskaite-IGL.pdf

Lazer, D., & Binz-Scharf, M. C. (2004). *Managing novelty and cross-agency cooperation in digital government*. Paper presented at the Proceedings of the 2004 annual national conference on Digital government research, Seattle, WA.

Lee, G., & Kwak, Y. H. (2011). Open government implementation model: A stage model for achieving increased public engagement. In *Proceedings of the 12th Annual International Digital Government Research Conference (dg.o 2011)* (pp. 254–261). College Park, MD, USA: ACM. Retrieved from http://doi.acm.org/10.1145/2037556.2037598

Lee, J. (2010). 10 year retrospect on stage models of e-Government: A qualitative meta-synthesis. *Government Information Quarterly*, *27*(3), 220–230. doi:10.1016/j.giq.2009.12.009.

Lee, T., Hon, C. T., & Cheung, D. (2009). XML schema design and management for e-government data interoperability. *Electronic. Journal of E-Government*, *7*(4), 381–390.

Lenihan, D. (2002). *Realigning governance: From e-government to e-democracy*. Centre for Collaborative Government. Retrieved May 2, 2012, from http://www.kta.on.ca/KTA_site_RVSD/pdf/cg6.pdf

Lenk, K., & Traunmüller, R. (2002). Electronic government: Where are we heading? In Traunmüller, R., & Lenk, K. (Eds.), *Electronic Government* (*Vol. 2456*, pp. 1–9). Lecture Notes in Computer ScienceBerlin: Springer-Verlag. doi:10.1007/978-3-540-46138-8_1.

Levi-Faur, D. (2005). The global diffusion of regulatory capitalism. *The Annals of the American Academy of Political and Social Science*, *598*, 12–34. doi:10.1177/0002716204272371.

Levi-Faur, D., & Jordana, J. (2005, March). Preface: The making of a new regulatory order. *The Annals of the American Academy of Political and Social Science*, *598*, 6–9. doi:10.1177/0002716204272612.

Lévy, M., & Jouyet, J.-P. (2006). *L'économie de l'immatériel-La croissance de demain.*

Lewin, D., Hall, R., & Milne, C. (2004). *Further liberalization of Botswana's telecommunications industry*. Consultation document for interested parties issued by the Botswana Telecommunications Authority. Retrieved August 8, 2009, from www.bta.org.bw/pubs/Liberalisation%20Consult2.pdf

Leydesdorff, L. (2011). "Meaning" as a sociological concept: A review of the modeling, mapping and simulation of the communication of knowledge and meaning. *Social Sciences Information. Information Sur les Sciences Sociales*, *50*(3-4), 391–413. doi:10.1177/0539018411411021.

Liao, Z., & Cheung, M. T. (2001). Internet-based e-shopping and consumer attitudes: An empirical study. *Information & Management*, *38*(5), 299–306. doi:10.1016/S0378-7206(00)00072-0.

Liimatainen, K. (2008). *Evaluating benefits of government enterprise architecture*. Paper presented at the IRIS31 - The 31st Information Systems Research Seminar in Scandinavia, ÅRE SWEDEN. http://www.iris31.se/papers/IRIS31-059.pdf

Liimatainen, K., Hoffmann, M., & Heikkilä, J. (2007, October). *Overview of enterprise architecture work in 15 countries, Finnish enterprise architecture research project*. Ministry of Finance, Finland. Retrieved from www.vm.fi/julkaisut

Lindblad-Gidlund, K., Ekelin, A., Eriksén, S., & Ranerup, A. (Eds.). (2010). *Förvaltning och medborgarskap i förändring (Ongoing change in public administration and citizenship – Established practice and critical perspectives)* (pp. 21–30). Lund: Studentlitteratur.

Lips, M. (2007). E-government under construction. Challenging traditional conceptions of citizenship. In Nixon, P. G., & Koutrakou, V. N. (Eds.), *E-government in Europe. Re-booting the state* (pp. 33–47). London: Routledge Advances in European Politics.

Liu, L., & Ma, Q. (2006). Perceived system performance: A test of an extended technology acceptance model. *The Data Base for Advances in Information Systems*, *37*(2-3), 51–59. doi:10.1145/1161345.1161354.

Liu, X., & Luo, X. (2010). A data warehouse solution for e-government.[IJRRAS]. *International Journal of Research and Reviews in Applied Sciences*, *4*(1), 101–105.

Lofstedt, U. (2005). E-government: Assessment of current research and some proposals for future directions. *International Journal of Public Information Systems, 2005*(1), 39-52.

Lovelock, P., Clark, T., & Petrazzini, B. A. (1996, May 10). China's golden projects: Re-engineering the national economy. *Harvard Business School case study (N9-396-283).*

Lovelock, P., & Cartledge, S. (1999). Special subject: E-China. *China Economic Quarterly*, *3*(1), 19–35.

Luftman, J. (2003). Assessing IT/business alignment. *Information Systems Management*, *20*(4), 9–21. doi:10.1201/1078/43647.20.4.20030901/77287.2.

Luts, M. (2004). *Estonian semantic interoperability initiative*. SEMIC. EU publications.

Macnamara, J. (2008). Internet media and the public sphere: The 2007 Australian e-electioneering experience. *Media International Australia*, *129*, 7–19.

Macnamara, J. (2010). *E-electioneering 2010: Social media in the Australian Federal Election*. Sydney: Australian Centre for Public Communication.

Mahajan, M. (2012). Standards for e-governance. In *Informatics* (pp. 26-27). National Informatics Centre. Retrieved August 2, 2012, from http://informatics.nic.in/uploads/pdfs/975f38cd_26-27_e-Gov_standards.pdf

Mahapatra, S. K., Das, D. K., & Das, B. (2008). Workflow based e-government applications: Case study of Wf-Bhulekh. In Bhattacharya, J. (Ed.), *Towards next generation e-government* (pp. 220–228).

Maier, M. W., & Eberhardt, R. (2009). *The art of systems architecting* (3rd ed.). Taylor & Francis, Inc, CRC Press.

Malaysiakini. (2012). Evidence act's 114A - yet another flip-flop. *Malaysiakini*. Retrieved from http://www.malaysiakini.com/news/207600.html

Malaysiakini. (2012b). Malaysiakini wins court battle over print license. *Malaysiakini*. Retrieved from http://www.malaysiakini.com/news/210454.html

Malhotra, Y., & Galleta, D. (1999). Extending the technology acceptance model to account for social influence: Theoretical bases and empirical validation. In *Proceedings of the 32nd Hawaii International Conference on System Sciences IEEE.*

MAMPU. (2012). *Malaysian administrative modernisation and management planning unit*. Retrieved from http://www.mampu.gov.my

Mancinelli, E. (2007). E-Inclusion in the information society. Network for Information Society.

Mao, E. (2002). An investigation of IT usage over time. *Eight American Conferences on Information Systems* (pp. 1307-1312).

Margolis, M., & Moreno-Riaño, G. (2009). The prospect of Internet democracy. Farnham, Surrey: Ashgate Publishing Limited.

Marjit, U., Roy, R., Santra, S., & Biswas, U. (2009). A semantic web service based approach to e-governance. In *Proc. of the 2nd Intl. Conference on Applications of Digital Information and Web Technologies (ICADIWT 2009)* (pp. 232-237). 4-6 August, London, UK.

Martin, S. (2008). *Meta-evaluation of the local government modernisation agenda, the state of local services: Performance improvement in local government. Wetherby, West Yorkshire.* Communities and Local Government Publications.

Matsatsinis, N. F., & Siskos, Y. (2002). *Intelligent support systems for marketing decisions.* Kluwer Academic Publisher.

McDermott, P. (2010). Building open government. *Government Information Quarterly, 27*(4), 401–413. doi:10.1016/j.giq.2010.07.002.

McKnight, D., Choudhury, V., & Kacmar, C. (2002). Developing and validating trust measures for e-commerce: An integrative typology. *Information Systems Research, 13*(3), 334–359. doi:10.1287/isre.13.3.334.81.

Medeni, T., et al. (2011). *Information society strategy & e-government gateway development in Turkey: Moving towards integrated processes and personalized services.* *t*Gov Workshop 11. March 17 – 18 2011, UB8 3PH. Brunel University: West London.

Meersman, B., & Vandenborre, F. (2006). *The commission enterprise IT architecture framework (CEAF) Version 1.*

Meneklis, B., Kaliontzoglou, A., Polemi, D., & Douligeris, C. (2005). Applying the ISO RM-ODP standard in e-government. E-government: Towards electronic democracy (pp. 213-224).

Mesa, A. (2007). Successes and challenges: E-governance in Tanzania. Retrieved from http://www.ftpiicd.org/iconnect/ICT4D_Governance/EN_Governance_TA.pdf

Meyer, J. W., & Rowan, B. (1977). Institutionalized organization: Formal structure as myth and ceremony. *American Sociological Review, 83*, 340–363. doi:10.1086/226550.

Michel, H. (2005). E-administration, e-government, e-governance and the learning city: A typology of citizenship management using ICTs. *The Electronic Journal of e-Government (EJEG), 3*(4), 213-218. Retrieved February 15, 2009, from www.ejeg.com

Millard, J. (2003). The (r)e-balancing of government. *UPGRADE — The European Journal for the Informatics Professional, 4*(2), 48-51.

Millard, J., Iversen, J., Kubicek, H., Westholm, H., & Cimander, R. (2004). *Reorganisation of government back-offices for better electronic public services – European good practices.* Final report to the European Commission. Danish Technological Institute, University of Bremen. Retrieved January 5, 2012, from http://www.oeaw.ac.at/ita/ebene5/back_office_reorganisation_volume3.pdf

Millard, J., Iversen, J. S., Kubicek, H., Westholm, H., & Cimander, R. (2004). *Reorganisation of government back offices for better electronic public services – European good practices (Back - office reorganisation). Danish Technological Institute & Institut für Informationsmanagement GmbH.* University of Bremen.

Mishra, B. K., Raghunathan, S., & Yue, X. (2007). Information sharing in supply chains: Incentives for information distortion. *IIE Transactions, 39*, 863–877. doi:10.1080/07408170601019460.

Misra, H. (2010). *Understanding SOA perspective of e-governance in Indian context.* Retrieved from http://www.intechopen.com/source/pdfs/10809/InTech-Understanding_soa_perspective_of_e_governance_in_indian_context_case_based_study.pdf

Misuraca G. (2008). *Transforming government roles towards a digital state: Government reform as a key to success.* Background Paper to the 'Middle East e-Government Conference & Exhibition 2008', Riyadh, Kingdom of Saudi Arabia, 15-18 March 2008

Misuraca, G. (2009). e-Government 2015: Exploring m-government scenarios, between ICT-driven experiments and citizen-centric implications. In Technological Analysis & Strategic Management, 21(3).

Misuraca, G. (2009). Futuring e-government: Governance and policy implication for building an ICT-enabled knowledge society for all. In *Proceedings of the International Conference on Theory and Practice of e-Governance*, ICEGOV2009, Bogotá, Colombia 11-13 November.

Misuraca, G. (2010). Concept paper. *Theoretical framework and key principles towards the development of a policy assessment framework for ICT-enabled governance at city level.* Seville: European Commission JRC-IPTS.

Misuraca, G. (2012a). eGovernance 2.0: Implications of social computing on public services. In E. Downey and M. Jones (Eds.), *Public services, governance and web2.0 technologies: Future trends in social media*. Retrieved from http://www.igi-global.com/book/public-service-governance-web-technologies/56009

Misuraca, G., & Viscusi, G. (2010). E-governance for development: Designing an operational roadmap for ICT-enabled public administration reform. In D. Piaggesi Sund and. E. Castelnovo (Ed.), Global strategy and practice of e-governance: Examples from around the world. IGI Global Publishing.

Misuraca, G., (2007). *e-Governance in Africa from theory to action - A handbook on ICTs for local governance*. Africa World Press/IDRC.

Misuraca, G., Broster, D., & Centeno, C. (2010). Envisioning digital Europe 2030: Scenario design on ICT for governance and policy modelling. In *Proceedings of the 4th International Conference on Theory and Practice of Electronic Governance* (ICEGOV) (pp. 347–356). Beijing, China: ACM. doi:10.1145/1930321.1930392

Misuraca, G. (2012b). Reinventing governance in the digital age. In Quebec, E. N. A. P. (Ed.), *Revue, Special Issue on L'Administration Publique a l'ere du numerique*.

Misuraca, G., Alfano, G., & Viscusi, G. (2011a). Interoperability challenges for ICT-enabled governance: Towards a pan-European conceptual framework. *Journal of Theoretical and Applied Electronic Commerce Research*, *6*(1), 95–111.

Misuraca, G., Alfano, G., & Viscusi, G. (2011b). A multi-level framework for ICT-enabled governance: Assessing the non-technical dimensions of "government openness." *Electronic. Journal of E-Government*, *9*(2), 152–165. Retrieved from www.ejeg.com.

Mmegi Newspaper. (2009). E-government in Botswana. Retrieved from www.mmegi.bw

MoF. (2012). *The economic survey: Fiscal year 2011-2012*. Kathmandu, Nepal: Ministry of Finance, Government of Nepal.

Mohamad, M. (2008). Malaysia-democracy and the end of ethnic politics? *Australian Journal of International Affairs*, *62*(4), 441–459. doi:10.1080/10357710802480691.

Mohsin, A. (2006). Implementation of electronic government in Malaysia: The status and potential for better service to the public. *Public Sector Management Review*, *1*(1).

Molin, B., Månsson, L., & Strömberg, L. (1975). *Offentlig förvaltning (Public Administration)*. Stockholm: Bonniers.

Monnane, M. (2003). *Botswana telecommunications services*. Southern African Trade Research Network (SATRN). Working Paper No. 3.

Moon, M. J. (2002). The evaluation of e-government among municipalities: Rhetoric or reality? *Public Administration Review*, *62*(4), 424–433. doi:10.1111/0033-3352.00196.

Moore, G. C., & Benbasat, I. (1991). Development of an instrument to measure the perceptions of adopting an information technology innovation. *Information Systems Research*, *2*(3), 192–222. doi:10.1287/isre.2.3.192.

Morphet, J. (2009). E-government and local government. In Budd, L., & Harris, L. (Eds.), *E-governance: Managing or governing?* (pp. 197–212). New York: Routledge.

Mossberger, K., Tolbert, C. J., & McNeal, R. S. (2008). *Digital citizenship: The Internet, society and participation*. Cambridge, Massachusetts: MIT Press.

Muhammad Rais, A. K., & Nazariah, M. K. (2003). *E-government in Malaysia*. Pelanduk Publications.

Muir, A., & Oppenheim, C. (2002). National information policy developments worldwide in electronic government. *Journal of Information Science*, *28*(3), 173–186. doi:10.1177/016555150202800301.

Müller, W. (2005). *eGovCH – The Swiss egovernment architecture*.

Mulozi, D. L. (2008). *Rural access: Options and challenges for connectivity and energy in Zambia*. International Institute for Communication and Development IICD thematic report. www.iicd.org/files/Zambia-Rural-Access-Report.pdf. Accessed 10 September 2009

Murch, R. (2005). *Methodologies in IT: Comprehension, selection, and implementation*. IBM Press.

Muthaiyah, S., & Kerschberg, L. (2008). Achieving interoperability in e-government services with two modes of semantic bridging: SRS and SWRL. *Journal of Theoretical and Applied Electronic Commerce Research*, *3*(3), 52–63. doi:10.4067/S0718-18762008000200005.

Myers, M. D. (2003). The IS core – VIII: Defining the core properties of the IS disciplines: Not yet, not now. *Communications of the AIS, 38*(12).

MyGovernment. (2012). *Multimedia super corridor*. Retrieved October 5, 2012, from http://www.malaysia.gov.my.html

Nakakawa, A., Bommel, P., & Proper, H. A. E. (2009). Quality enhancement in creating enterprise architecture: Relevance of academic models. In Practice advances in enterprise engineering II (pp. 109-133).

Napierala, N., & Kiefer, A. (2009). *The use of ICT for tax administration*. GTZ. Federal Ministry of Economic Cooperation and Development. Retrieved October 3, 2012, from http://www.docstoc.com/docs/40251831/The-use-of-ICT-for-Tax-Administration

Naschold, F., & Von Otter, C. (1996). *Public sector transformation: Rethinking markets and hierarchies in government*. John Benjamins.

National Office for the Information Economy (NOIE). (2002). *Better services, better government: The Federal government's e-government strategy*. Canberra, Australian Capital Territory: NOIE.

National Office for the Information Economy (NOIE). (2004). *Australia's national broadband strategy*. Canberra, Australian Capital Territory: NOIE.

NBN Co. (2012). *Local government*. Retrieved June 1, 2012, from http://www.nbnco.com.au/communities/local-government.html

Ndou, V. (2004). E-government for developing countries: Opportunities and challenges. *The Electronic Journal on Information Systems in Developing Countries*, *18*(1), 1–24.

Neuvo, Y., & Karvonen, E. (2012). *Bit bang IV–Future of the Internet: Societal, business, governance and technological aspects. Aalto University's Multidisciplinary Institute of Digitization and Energy*. MIDE.

News, B. B. C. (2000, November 20). Malaysia's first online paper. *BBC News*. Retrieved from http://www.bbcnews.com.html

Ngwenya, B., Lubbe, S., & Klopper, R. (2010). Institutionalisation, framing and diffusion: The logic of openness in egovernment and implementation decisions (a lesson for developing countries). *6th International Conference on e-Government, Cape Peninsula University of Technology*. South Africa.

NITC. (2012). *Progress sheet of e-GMP. National Information Centre, Singhadurbar, Kathamndu: Technology Centre*. NITC.

NORA. (2007). *Dutch government reference architecture [NORA]*.

Norman, K. (2005). *Call centre work – Characteristics, physical and psychosocial exposure and related outcomes*. (Doctoral dissertation). Linköping: The University of Linköping. Division of Industry Ergonomics.

Norris, D., & Lloyd, B. (2004). *The scholarly literature on e-government: Characterizing a nascent field*. SIG eGov workshop at ICIS, Washington DC, December 12.

Norris, D. F. (2007). Electronic democracy at the American grassroots. In Norris, D. F. (Ed.), *Current issues and trends in e-government research* (pp. 164–179). Hershey, Pennsylvania: IGI Global. doi:10.4018/978-1-59904-283-1.ch008.

Norris, D., Fletcher, P., & Holden, S. (2001). *Is your local government plugged in? Highlights of the 2000 electronic government survey*. Washington, DC: International City/County Management Association.

Norris, D., & Kraemer, K. (1996). Mainframe and PC computing in American cities: Myths and realities. *Public Administration Review*, *6*(56), 568–576. doi:10.2307/977255.

NPC. (2008). *Three year interim plan (2008-2011)*. Kathmandu, Nepal: National Planning Commission, Government of Nepal.

NREGA. (2008). The national rural employment guaranty act, 2005, (3rd ed.). Operational Guidelines, Ministry of Rural Development, Government of India, New Delhi.

NTA. (2012). *Management information system, X Year, 93(45)*. Kathmandu, Nepal: Nepal Telecommucation Authority.

Nunes, P. (2004). *Sebenta de Organização e Gestão Pública*. Barcelos: Instituto Politécnico do Cávado e do Ave.

Nunnally, J. C. (1978). *Psychometric Theory* (2nd ed.). New York: Mc Graw-Hill.

Nutek. (2000). *En marknadsstudie av callcentre i Sverige hösten 1999*. Report 2000:10.Stockholm: Närings- och utvecklingsverket.

O'brien, J. A. (2005). *Introduction to information systems* (12th ed.). Tata Mcgraw Hill Publishing Company Limited.

O'Toole, K. (2009). Australian local government and e-governance: From administration to citizen participation? In Khosrow-Pour, M. (Ed.), *E-government diffusion, policy and impact: Advanced issues and practices* (pp. 171–184). Hershey, Pennsylvania: Information Science Reference.

OECD. (2001). Citizens as partners: OECD handbook on information, consultation and public participation in policy-making. Retrieved June 2, 2012, from http://www.ecnl.org/dindocuments/214_OECD_Engaging%20Citizens%20in%20Policy-Making.pdf

OECD. (2001a). Cities for citizens. Improving metropolitan governance. Paris.

OECD. (2001b). *Governance in the 21st Century*. Organisation for Economic Co-operation and Development.

OECD. (2003). *The e-government imperative*. Paris: OECD e-Government Studies.

OECD. (2005). *E-government for better government. OECD Government Studies* (p. 42). Paris: OECD Publishing.

OECD. (2009). *Rethinking e-government services. User-centric approaches*. Paris: OECD Publishing.

Office of the Deputy Prime Minister (ODPM). (2002). *The national strategy for local e-government*. London: ODPM.

Official Portal e-Government Gazette. (2012). *Attorney-general's chambers*. Retrieved October 10, 2012, from http://www.federalgazette.agc.gov.my

Okot-Uma, R. (2000). *Electronic governance: Re-inventing good governance*. Commonwealth Secretariat, London. Retrieved May 3, 2012, from http://webworld.unesco.org/publications/it/EGov/wordbank%20okot-uma.pdf

OMB. (2007). *FEA consolidated reference model version 2.3*.

Orenstein, M. A. (2003, August). *Mechanisms of diffusion. An interdisciplinary review*. Paper presented to the American Political Science Association Annual Meeting, Philadelphia.

Ortiz-Rodriguez, F., & Villazon-Terrazas, B. (2006). EGO ontology model: Law and regulation approach for e-government. In *Proc. of the Workshop on Semantic Web for E-government 2006, Workshop at the 3rd European Semantic Web Conference* (pp. 13-23). Budva, Serbia and Montenegro, 12 June.

Osborne, D., & Gaebler, T. (1992). *Reinventing government: How the entrepreneurial spirit is transforming the public sector*. Reading: Addison-Wesley.

Pablo, Z., & Pan, S. (2003). A multi-disciplinary analysis of e-governance: Where do we start? *The Seventh Pacific Asia Conference on Information Systems* (pp. 288-302). Retrieved October 26, 2011, from www.pacis-net.org/file/2002/105.pdf

Pacific Council on International Policy. (2002). *Roadmap for e-government in the developing world: 10 questions e-government leaders should ask themselves*. Los Angeles, USA: The working Group on E-Government in the Developing World, The Western Partner of the Council on Foreign Relations.

Palvia, S., & Sharma, S. (2007). E-government and e-governance: Definitions/domain framework and status around the world. In A. Agarwal & V. Ramana (Eds.), *Foundations of e-government - 5th International Conference on E-Governance*. Retrieved from http://www.iceg.net/2007/books/book1.html

Pan, S. L. (2004). *Managing strategic enterprise systems and e-government initiatives in Asia – A casebook*. World Scientific Publishing Co. Pty. Ltd.

Paquette, S., & Wilson, S. C. (2010). Identifying the security risks associated with governmental use of cloud computing. *Government Information Quarterly, 27*(3), 245–253. doi:10.1016/j.giq.2010.01.002.

Pariyar, M. P. (2007). EGovernment initiatives in Nepal: Challenges and opportunities. ACM International Conference Proceedings, *Proceedings of the First International Conference on Theory and Practice of Electronic Governance* (pp. 280-282).

Parker, A. N. (1995). *Decentralization: The way forward for rural development?* (1475). World Bank Policy Research Working Paper No. 1475 Retrieved from http://ssrn.com/abstract=620575

Patil, H., et al. (2008). E-governance and white collar crime control. In *Proc. 6th Intl. Conference on E-Governance* (pp. 137-144).

Pavlou, P. A. (2003). Consumer acceptance of electronic commerce: Integrating trust and risk with the technology acceptance model. *International Journal of Electronic Commerce, 7*(3), 101–134.

PBS NewsHour. (2000). Steven Gan - editor Malaysiakini. *PBS News*.

Pérez-Villaplana, J. (2003). Technology for e-government: A study case. *UPGRADE — The European Journal for the Informatics Professional, 4*(2), 33-38.

Peristeras, V., & Tarabanis, K. (2006). Reengineering public administration through semantic technologies and the GEA domain ontology. *AAAI Spring Symposium, Semantic Web meets eGovernment (SWEG)*. 27-29 March, Stanford University, California.

Perks, C., & Beveridge, T. (2004). Opportunities, solutions, and migration planning. Guide to enterprise IT architecture (pp. 360-391).

Perri. (2001). E-governance: Do digital aids make a difference in policy making? In J. Prins (Ed.), *Designing e-government: On the crossroads of technological innovation and institutional change* (pp. 7-27). The Hague: Kluwer Law International.

Perroux, F. (1960). *Economie et société*. Paris: Presses Universitaires de France.

Perroux, F. (1990). *Dictionnaire économique et social*. Paris: Haitier.

Perrow, C. (1986). Complex organizations: A critical essay. New York.

Persson, A., & Goldkuhl, G. (2010). Government value paradigms – Bureaucracy, new public management, and e-government. *Communications of the Association for Information Systems, 27*(1). Article 4, July, 45-62. Retreived June 27, 2012, from http//aisle.aisnet.org/cias/vol27/iss1/4

PEW Research Centre for the People & the Press. (2008a). Grading the states. *The state management report card for 2008*. Retrieved from http://www.pewcenteronthestates.org/uploadedFiles/Grading-the-States-2008.pdf

Pheko, T. G. (2009). *Botswana telecommunications authority*. Botswana Country Report to CRASA. Retrieved August 15, 2009, from www.crasa.org/.../reports/.../Botswana%20Report%202009%20Presentation.pdf

Pheng, T. (2007). *Enterprise architecture in the Singapore government. Handbook of enterprise systems architecture in practice* (pp. 129–143). IGI Global. doi:10.4018/978-1-59904-189-6.ch007.

Planning Commission. (2001). Government of India. Indian Communication Convergence Bill 2000 (pp. 2).

Power, D. J. (2000). Web-based and model-driven decision support systems: Concepts and issues. In *Proceedings of the American Conference on Information Systems*. Long Beach, California.

Power, D. J. (2008). *Can DSS impact decision outcomes?* Reding. (2006). eGovernment in Europe 2006, eGovernment Action Plan, 2006. Retrieved April 7, 2010, from ec.europa.eu/information-society/activites/egovernment/index_en.htm

Power, D.J. (1997). What is a DSS? *The On-Line Executive Journal for Data-Intensive Decision Support, 1*(3).

Power, D.J. (2005). Can computerised decision support systems impact, eliminate, exploit, or reduce cognitive biases in decision making? *Decision Support Systems News, 6*(20).

Power, D.J. (2007). *An empirical assessment of computer-assisted decision analysis*.

Power, D. J. (2001). *Supporting decision-makers: An expandedframework*. USA: University of Northern Lowa.

Power, D. J. (2002). *Decision support systems: Concepts and resources for managers*. Westport, CT: Quorum Books.

Prabhu, C. S. R. (2010). *Towards an e-governance grid for India (E-GGI): An architectural framework for citizen services delivery*. Retrieved from http://www.csi-sigegov.org/1/7_266.pdf

Prasad, S. (2005). What is wrong with e-governance projects in India? How to build the foundation for successful e-governance. In G. Nayak, M. Mishra, & A. Das (Eds.), *Proceedings of the Eighth National Conference on e-Governance* (pp. 28-32). Bhubaneswar.

Pratchett, L. (1999). New technologies and the modernization of local government: An analysis of biases and constraints. *Public Administration*, *77*(4), 731–750. doi:10.1111/1467-9299.00177.

Previte, J. (2005). *Understanding everyday internet experience: Applications to social marketing theory and practice*. (PhD thesis). Queensland University of Technology.

Putman, J. R. (2001). *Architecting with RM-ODP*. Prentice Hall.

Puustjarvi, J. (2006). Using knowledge management and business process in e-government. In *Proc. of the Information Integration and Web-based Applications and Services 2006 (iiWas2006) Conference* (pp. 331-339). Yogyakarta Indonesia, 4 - 6 December.

Qiao, Y. (2008). *Social networks and e-commerce*. Seminar on Internetworking.

Rajaratnam, U. D. (2009). Role of traditional and online media in the 12th general election, Malaysia. *Journal of the South East Asia Research Centre*, *1*(1), 33–58.

Rana, N., Williams, M., Dwivedi, Y., & Williams, J. (2011). Reflecting on e-government research: Toward a taxonomy of theories and theoretical constructs. *International Journal of Electronic Government Research*, *7*(4), 64–88. doi:10.4018/jegr.2011100105.

RDEC. (2008). Research, development and evaluation commission. Electronic government 2007 Report: Taipei.

Realini, A. (2004). *G2G e-government: The big challenge to Europe*. (Master Thesis). University of Zürich, Zürich.

Reding. (2006). *eGovernment in Europe 2006, eGovernment Action Plan, 2006*. Retrieved April 7, 2010, from ec.europa.eu/information-society/activites/egovernment/index_en.htm

Regeringskansliet. (1999). *Medborgarkontor i utveckling* Departementsserien (Ds) *Ds1999:26*, [One-Stop-Government-Offices in development] Justitiedepartementet [Swedish Ministry of Justice], Stockholm.

Regeringskansliet. (2008). *Handlingsplan för eFörvaltning. Nya grunder för IT-baserad verksamhetsutveckling*. Retrieved March 23, 2010, from http://www.regeringen.se/content/1/c6/07/49/95/2c28b30b.pdf

Relyea, H. (2002). E-gov: Introduction and overview. *Government Information Quarterly*, *19*(1), 9–35. doi:10.1016/S0740-624X(01)00096-X.

Republic of Turkey Official Gazette. (2004, January 24). Article. No: 2004/12. Number: 25356.

Reynolds, M., & Regio, M. (2001). E-Government as a catalyst in the information age. In *Briefing book outline: E-government*. Advisory Committee to the Congressional Internet Caucus. Retrieved December 5, 2011, from http://www.netcaucus.org/books/egov2001

Rice, T. W., McCormick, J. M., & Bergmann, B. D. (2002). Graduate training, current affiliation and publishing books in political science. *Public Science and Politics*, *35*(4), 751–755.

Rico, D. F. (2008). *Optimizing the ROI of enterprise architecture using real options. End user computing challenges and technologies: Emerging tools and applications* (pp. 48–56). IGI Global.

Riga Declaration. (2006). *Internet for all: EU ministers commit to an inclusive and barrier-free information society*. Press release of June, IP/06/769.

Riley, B. T. (2001). Electronic governance and electronic democracy: Living and working in the connected world. Commonwealth Centre for Electronic Governance, 2. Australia: Brisbane.

Riley, T. (2003). *E-government vs. e-governance: Examining the differences in a changing public sector climate.* Retrieved May 20, 2009, from http://www.electronicgov.net/pubs/research_papers/tracking03/IntlTrackRpt-May03no4.pdf

Riley, T. B. (2004). *E-Governance vs. E-Government.* Information for Development. Retrieved November 11, 2004, from http://www.i4donline.net/issue/nov03/ egovernance

Rodríguez, J. R. B., Battle, M. J., & Esteban, D. A. (2007). European study of e-government city models. *IDP. Revista de Internet, Derecho y Política*, (5).

Rogers, E. (2003). *Diffusion of innovations.* New York: Free Press.

Rothschild, M., & Stiglitz, J. (1976). Equilibrium in competitive insurance markets: An essay on the economics of imperfect information. *The Quarterly Journal of Economics, 90*(4), 629–649. doi:10.2307/1885326.

Rubin, H. J., & Rubin, I. S. (1995). *Qualitative interviewing, the art of hearing data.* Sage Publications London.

Rundle, E. (2009). New York City Streamlining 911 Call Talking Process. In *Government Technology* (p. 1). Retrieved October 5, 2010, from http://www.govtech.com/gt/articles/663164

Saade, R. G., Nebebe, F., & Tan, W. (2007). Viability of the technology acceptance model in multimedia learning environments: A comparative study. *Interdisciplinary Journal of Knowledge and Learning Objects, 3*, 175–182.

Saarenpää, A. (2003). A legal framework for e-government. In Traunmüller, R. (Ed.), *Electronic Government* (*Vol. 2739*, pp. 377–384). Lecture Notes in Computer ScienceBerlin: Springer-Verlag. doi:10.1007/10929179_69.

Sabine, B., Alexander, M. E., Florian, M., Ren, R., & Schweda, C. M. (2009). *Using enterprise architecture management patterns to complement TOGAF*. Paper presented at the Proceedings of the 2009 IEEE International Enterprise Distributed Object Computing Conference (edoc 2009) - Volume 00.

Sabucedo, L. A., & Rifon, L. A. (2006). *Semantic service oriented architectures for e-government platforms.* American Association for Artificial Intelligence.

Sabucedo, L. M. A., Rifon, L. E. A., Corradini, F., Polzonetti, A., & Re, B. (2010). Knowledge-based platform for e-government agents: A web-based solution using semantic technologies. *Journal of Expert Systems with Applications, 37*(5), 3647–3656. doi:10.1016/j.eswa.2009.10.026.

Sachdeva, S. K. (2004). Quantifying and assessing e-governance. *Information for Development.* Retrieved November 11, 2004, from http://www.i4donline.net/issu/nov03/ /quantifying.htm

SAGA. (2008). *Standards and architectures for egovernment applications.*

Saha, P. (2010). Enterprise architecture as platform for connected government.

Saha, P. (2009). *A methodology for government transformation with enterprise architecture. Advances in government enterprise architecture* (pp. 1–29). IGI Global.

Sakowicz, M. (2003). *How to evaluate e-government? Different methodologies and methodes.* Retrieved November 19, 2011, from http://unpan1.un.org/intradoc/groups/public/documents/NISPAcee/UNPAN009486.pdf

Salamat, M., Hassan, S., & Muhammad, M. S. (2011). Electronic participation in Malaysia. Journal of e-Government Studies and Best Practices, Vol. 2011.

SALAR. (1997). [The Swedish Association of Municipalities and Regions] *Samtjänst vid medborgarkontor*, 1997:122, 26.08.1997.

Salem, J. A. (2003). Public and private sector interests in e-government: A look at the DOE's PubSCIENCE. *Government Information Quarterly, 20*, 13–27. doi:10.1016/S0740-624X(02)00133-8.

Salhofer, P., & Ferbas, D. (2007). A pragmatic approach to the introduction of e-government. In *Proc. of the 8th Annual Intl. Digital Government Research Conference* (pp. 183-189). Philadelphia, Pennsylvania, USA, May 20-23.

Salhofer, P., Stadlhofer, B., & Tretter, G. (2009). Ontology driven e-government. *Electronic. Journal of E-Government, 7*(4), 415–424.

Salmah, K. (2012). *Electronic government in Malaysia. Malaysian administrative modernisation and management planning unit (MAMPU).* Prime Minister's Department. Malaysia Government.

Sambruk. (2010). *Municipal e-services.* Retrieved October 13, 2010, from http://www.sambruk.se/inenglish.4.76e8b1c6112f078db498000144852.html

Sanati, F., & Lu, J. (2009). Multilevel life-event abstraction framework for e-government service integration. In *Proc. of the 9th European Conference on E-government 2009 (ECEG 2009)* (pp. 550-558). London, UK, 29-30 June.

Sang, M. L., Tan, X., & Trimi, S. (2005). Current practices of leading e-government countries. *Communications of the ACM, 48*(10), 99–104. doi:10.1145/1089107.1089112.

Santos, L., & Amaral, L. (2003). O e-Government. *inter. face. Administração Pública, 17*, 28–31.

Sanwalka, D. (2011). KPMG in India survey on bribery and corruption impact on economy and business environment. Retrieved November 20, 2012, from www.kpmg.com/IN/en/IssuesAndInsights/ThoughtLeadership/KPMG_Bribery_Survey_Report_ new.pdf

Sassen, S. (1991). *The global city.* New York: Princeton University Press.

Saxena, K. B. C. (2005). Towards excellence in e-governance. *International Journal of Public Sector Management, 18*(6), 498–513. doi:10.1108/09513550510616733.

Scannell, T. V. (1999). *Behavioural models of advanced manufacturing technology selection.* (PhD Thesis). Michigan State University.

Schekkerman, J. (2005). Trends in enterprise architecture (1.0 ed.).

Scott, M., Golden, W., & Hughes, M. (2004). A click and bricks strategy for e-government. *17th Bled eCommerce Conference, eGlobal,* Bled, Slovenia, June 21 - 23

Seifert, J. W. (2003). *A primer on e-government: Sectors, stages, opportunities, and challenges of online governance.* USA: Report for Congress, Congressional Research Service, The Library Congress. Retrieved January 10, 2010, from http://www.fas.org/sgp/crs/RL31057.pdf

Seng, W. M., Jackson, S., & Philip, G. (2010). Cultural issues in developing E-Government in Malaysia. *Behaviour & Information Technology. Queen's University Management School, 29*(4), 423–432.

Senyucel, Z., & Stubbs, M. (2006). Towards e-government facilitation in UK local authorities. *Journal of E-Government, 2*(2), 19–44. doi:10.1300/J399v02n02_03.

SFS. (1986). *Förvaltningslag* (1986:223), (Administrative Law). Retrieved January 14, 2010, from http://www.notisum.se/rnp/SLS/LAG/19860223.HTM

Shackleton, P., Fisher, J., & Dawson, L. (2005). From dog licenses to democracy: Local government approaches to e-service delivery in Australia. In D. Bartmann, F. Rajola, J. Kallinikos, D. Avison, R. Winter, P. Ein-Dor, J. Becker, F. Bodendorf & C. Weinhardt (Eds.), *Proceedings of the thirteenth European conference on information systems* (pp. 724-735). Regensburg, Germany: ECIS Standing Committee.

Shackleton, P. (2010). Engaging citizens through local e-government: An Australian experience. In Reddick, C. G. (Ed.), *Citizens and e-government: Evaluating policy and management* (pp. 418–434). Hershey, Pennsylvania: IGI Global. doi:10.4018/978-1-61520-931-6.ch023.

Shah, A. (2006). Fiscal decentralization and macroeconomic management. *International Tax and Public Finance, 13*(4), 437–462. doi:10.1007/s10797-006-8948-1.

Shahid, Y. (2003). *Innovation East Asia: The future of growth.* New York, NY: Oxford University Press.

Shakya, R. (2007). *Current issues and challenges in e-governance implementation in Nepal. A paper presented to the training course on Advanced course on Management and development.* Jawalakhel, Nepal: Nepal Administrative Staff College.

Sharda, R., Barr, S. H., & McDonnell, J. C. (2002). Decision support systems effectiveness: A review and an empirical test. *Management Science.*

Shelton, G. (2000). *Sri Lanka: In handbook of the media in Asia.* New Delhi: Sage.

Shkovski, I., & Struthers, D. (2010). Of states and borders on the Internet: The role of domain name extensions in expressions of nationalism online in Karzakhstan. *Policy and Internet, 2*(4), 107–129.

Siau, K., & Long, Y. (2004). Factors impacting e-government development. *The Twenty-Fifth International Conference on Information Systems, ICIS 2004* (pp. 221-233).

Siau, K., & Long, Y. (2006). Using social development lenses to understand e-government development. *Journal of Global Information Management*, *14*, 47–62. doi:10.4018/jgim.2006010103.

Silcock, R. (2001). What is e-government? *Parliamentary Affairs*, *54*(1), 88–101. doi:10.1093/pa/54.1.88.

Simenda, K. (2009). Electronic/mobile government in Africa: Progress made and challenges ahead, Addis Ababa, Ethiopia. Retrieved from http://www.unpan.org/emgkr_africa

Simone, M. A. (2010). Deliberative democracy online: Bridging networks with digital technologies. *Communication Review*, *13*(2), 120–139. doi:10.1080/10714421003795527.

Simon, H. A. (1965). *The new science of management decision: The shape of automation for men and management*. Harper Torch Books.

Simon, H. A. (1996). *The sciences of the artificial* (3rd ed.). Cambridge, MA: The MIT Press.

Singapore Government. (2012). *Singapore Personal Access, SingPass*. Retrieved October 23, 2012, from https://www.singpass.gov.sg/sppubsvc/

Singh, M., & Malik, S. K. (2008). Constructing ontologies in OWL using Protégé-2000. In *Proc. of the 2nd National Conference on Challenges and Opportunities in Information Technology (COIT 2008)* (pp. 1-4). Mandi Gobindgarh, Punjab, India.

SKL. (2007). Om kommuner. (About municipalities). Stockholm: Sveriges kommuner och landsting (SKL). (Swedish Association of Local Authorities and Regions).

SKL. (2009). e-förvaltningsutveckling i Sveriges kommuner 2006-2008. Delrapport 3. (The development of e-government in Swedish municipalities 2006-2008). Stockholm: Sveriges kommuner och landsting (SKL) (Swedish Association of Local Authorities and Regions).

Soares, D., & Amaral, L. (2011). Information systems interoperability in public administration: Identifying the major acting forces through a delphi study. *Journal of Theoretical and Applied Electronic Commerce Research*, *6*(1), 61–94. doi: doi:10.4067/S0718-18762011000100006.

Song, H., & Song, Y.-T. (2010). *Enterprise architecture institutionalization and assessment*. Paper presented at the Proceedings of the 2010 IEEE/ACIS 9th International Conference on Computer and Information Science.

SOU. (1999). Statens offentliga utredningar SOU1999:85. Bredband för tillväxt i hela landet. [Broadband for nationwide growth] Swedish official governmental reports Näringsdepartementet, betänkande från IT-infrastrukturutredningen, Stockholm.

SOU. (2002). *Statens Offentliga utredningar SOU 2002:51. Breddtjänster - ett nytt skede i IT-politiken, Näringsdepartementet, IT-kommissionens rapport 3/2002, Statens offentliga utredningar*. Stockholm: Fritzes.

SOU. (2004). Statens offentliga utredningar SOU 2004:56 e-tjänster för alla [e-services for everyone] Swedish official governmental reports. Finansdepartmenetet. 24-timmars delegationen. Stockholm: Fritzes.

SOU. (2005). *Statens offentliga utredningar SOU 2005:19. e-tjänster för ett öppnare samhälle. Slutbetänkande av 24-timmarsdelegationen. Swedish official governmental reports* [e-services for a more open society]. Stockholm: Fritzes.

SOU. (2008). *Statens offentliga utredningar SOU 2008:97. Styr samverkan - För bättre service till medborgarna.* Socialdepartementet, Utveckling av lokal service i samverkan, Swedish official governmental reports Stockholm: Fritzes.

SOU. (2009). *Statens offentliga utredningar SOU 2009:92, Se medborgarna – för bättre offentlig service. Slutbetänkande av Utveckling av lokal service i samverkan*. Stockholm: Fritzes.

Sourouni, A. M., Lampathaki, F., Mouzakitis, S., Charalabidis, Y., & Askouris, D. (2008). Paving the way to e-government transformation: Interoperability registry infrastructure development. In *Proc. of the 7th International Electronic Government Conference (eGov 2008)* (pp. 340-351). 3-7 September, Torino, Italy.

Spence, M. (1973). Job market signaling. *The Quarterly Journal of Economics*, *87*(3), 355–374. doi:10.2307/1882010.

Spiggle, S. (1994). Analysis and interpretation of qualitative data in consumer research. *The Journal of Consumer Research*, *21*, 491–503. doi:10.1086/209413.

Sprague, R. H., & Carlton, E. D. (1982). *Building effective decision support systems*. Englewood Cliffs, NJ: Prentice-Hall.

Srivastava, S., & Teo, T. (2004). A framework for electronic government: Evolution, enablers and resource drainers. *The Eighth Pacific Asia Conference on Information Systems, PACIS'2004* (pp. 2079-2085). Retrieved February 12, 2012, from www.pacis-net.org/file/2004/P04-003.pdf

Stahl, B. (2005). The ethical problem of framing e-government in terms of e-commerce. *The Electronic Journal of e-Government, 3*(2), 77-86. doi: http://www.ejeg.com/volume-3/vol3-iss2/StahlBernd.pdf

Stair, R. M., & Reynolds, G. W. (2001). *Principles of information systems: A managerial approach* (5th ed.). USA: Course Technology.

State Planning Organization. (2010). Information society strategy (2006-2010). Retrieved September 3, 2012, from http://www.bilgitoplumu.gov.tr/Documents/5/Documents/060700_InformationSocietyStrategy.pdf

State Planning Organization. (2011). *Information society statistics of Turkey*. Undersecretariat for State Planning Organization Information Society Department. SPO Publication No: 2829.

Statskontoret. (2011). *Den offentliga sektorns utveckling. En samlad redovisning 2011*. Statskontoret, Stockholm. (The Swedish Agency for Public Management). Retrieved June 29, 2011, from http://www.statskontoret.se/publikationer/2011/den-offentliga-sektorns-utveckling-en-samlad-redovisning-2011/

Stephen, H., Cummings, M., & McCubbrey, D. J. (2004). *Management information systems for the information age* (4th ed.). McGraw-Hill/Irwin.

Steward, A. (2011). *Australian government architecture reference models version 3.0.*

Stiglitz, J. E. (2000). The contributions of the economics of information to twentieth century economics. *The Quarterly Journal of Economics, 115*(4), 1441–1478. doi:10.1162/003355300555015.

Stodden, V. (2008). *The Internet drives election results in Malaysia*. Message posted to http:www.blogs.law.harvard.edu/idblog.com/

Straub, D. W. (1994). The effect of culture on IT diffusion: E-mail and fax in Japan and the USA. *Information Systems Research, 9*(2), 16–29.

Straub, D. W., Keil, M., & Brenner, W. (1997). Testing the technology acceptance model across cultures: A three country study. *Information & Management, 33*(1), 1–11. doi:10.1016/S0378-7206(97)00026-8.

Straub, D., Loch, K. D., & Hill, C. (2001). Transfer of information technology to the Arab World: A test of cultural influence modeling. *Journal of Global Information Management, 9*(4), 6–28. doi:10.4018/jgim.2001100101.

Tablin, D. (1984). Comparison of single and multi-round surveys for measuring mortality in developing countries. In Vallin, J., Pollard, J., & Heligman, L. (Eds.), *Methodologies for the collection and analysis of mortality data*. Liege, Belgium: International Union for the Scientific Study of Population, Ordina Editions.

Tambini, D. (1999). New media and democracy: The civic networking movement. *New Media & Society, 1*(3), 305–329. doi:10.1177/14614449922225609.

Tambouris, E., & Tarabanis, K. (2005). E-government and interoperability. In D. Remenyi (Ed.), *Proceedings of the 5th European Conference on E-Government* (pp. 399-407). UK: Academic Conferences Limited.

Tapscott, D., & Agnew, D. (1999). Governance in the digital economy. *Finance & Development, 36*(4), 34-37. Retrieved May 12, 2012, from http://www.imf.org/external/pubs/ft/fandd/1999/12/pdf/tapscott.pdf

Taylor, S., & Todd, P. A. (1995b). Understanding information technology usage: A test of competing models. *Information Systems Research, 6*(2), 144–176. doi:10.1287/isre.6.2.144.

Teicher, J., & Dow, N. (2002). E-government in Australia: Promise and progress. *Information polity, 7*(4), 231-246.

Tengblad, P., Wiberg, A., Herrman, L., & Backström, M. (2002). *Hållbart arbete i informationssamhället. Call centre i utveckling. Final report from the project "Call centre i utveckling – långsiktigt hållbart arbete med kunder på distans." Vinnova report VR 2002:7.* Stockholm: VINNOVA.

Themalaysiainsider. (2009). Civil society must be aware of cyber threats that are causing harm to the nation's sovereignty and society interest. *Themalaysiainsider*. Retrieved from http://www.themalaysianinsider.com

Themalaysiainsider. (2011, April 24). Bloggers and Internet users have to "draw the line" and online media or digital democracy had made it more difficult to win in the election. *Themalaysiainsider.* Retrieved from http://www.themalaysianinsider.com.

Themalaysianinsider. (2012, June 3). Dr M.: Rethink absolute freedom on net. Retrieved from http://www.themalaysianinsider.com

Thomas, J. (2004). Horizons of expectation: Imaginary trajectories of electronic government. In Goggin, G. (Ed.), *Virtual nation: The Internet in Australia* (pp. 258–272). Sydney: University of New South Wales Press.

Thomas, J. C., & Streib, G. (2003). The new face of government: Citizen-initiated contacts in the era of e-government. *Journal of Public Administration: Research and Theory*, *13*(1), 83–102. doi:10.1093/jpart/mug010.

Thompson, C., & Locander, W., & Pollio. (1989). Putting consumer experience back into consumer research: The philosophy and method of existential-phenomenology. *The Journal of Consumer Research*, *16*, 133–146. doi:10.1086/209203.

Times, N.S. (2008, March 9). Internet served a painful lesson. *New Straits Times*.

Toffler, A. (1980). *The third wave*. New York: Morrow.

Tolbert, C. J., & Mossberger, K. (2006). The effects of e-government on trust and confidence in government. *Public Administration Review*, *66*(3), 354–370. doi:10.1111/j.1540-6210.2006.00594.x.

Torodovski, L., Kunstelj, M., Cukjati, D., Vintar, M., Trochidis, I., & Tambouris, E. (2007). *OneStopGove: D13 – Life-event Reference Models. Deliverable No. 13.* Retrieved December 13, 2011, from http://islab.uom.gr/onestopgov/index.php?name=Deliverables.

Transparency International. (2012). *Global corruption barometer 2010/11*. Retrieved November 10, 2012, from http://gcb.transparency.org/ gcb201011/results/

Trull, S. G. (1996). Some factors involved in determining total decision success. *Management Science*, B-270–B-280.

TSO. (2012). *Open data white paper unleashing the potential.* Retrieved November 18, 2011, from http://data.gov.uk/sites /default/files/Open_ data_White_Paper.pdf

Tubitak, B. (2012). *Survey*. Retrieved October 3, 2012, from http://www.bilgiguvenligi.gov.tr/89.html?mosmsg=Oyunuz+i%E7in+te%FEekk%FCrler%21

Tucker, R. S. (2010). Broadband facts, fiction and urban myths. *Telecommunications Journal of Australia, 60*(3), 43.1-43.15.

Turban, E., Aronson, J.E., & Liang, T. (2008). *Decision support systems and intelligent systems*. 574.

Turner, A. (2007, May 8). Government single-user plan raises ID concerns. *The Age, Next*, p. 1.

UIDAI. (2010, April). *Unique identification authority of india strategic overview*. Unique Identification Authority of India, Planning Commission, Government of India, New Delhi.

UMIC. (2003). *Plano de Acção para o Governo Electrónico – Qualidade e Eficiência dos Serviços Públicos.* Retrieved February 16, 2012, from http://www.umic.pt/images/stories/publicacoes/II_Plano_Accao_eGov.pdf

UN. (2005). *Global e-governance e-readiness report, from e-government to e-inclusion.* New York.

UN. (2006). *E-Participation and e-government: Understanding the present and creating the future, report of the ad hoc expert group meeting*. Budapest, Hungary, 27 – 28 July.

UN. (2008). *UN e-government survey, from e-government to connected e-governance*. New York.

UN. (2010). *United Nations e-government, survey 2010, Leveraging e-government, at a time of financial and economic crisis. UN Publishing Section*. New York: ISBN.

UN. (2012). *E-government survey 2012: E-government for the people*. United Nations. Retrieved July 23, 2012, from http://www.unpan.org/e-government

UN/ASPA. (2002). *Benchmarking e-government: A global perspective- Assessing the progress of the UN member states*. UN Division for Public Economics and Public Administration and American Society for Public Administration. Retrieved Feb 2, 2010, from http://unpan1.un.org/intradoc/groups/public/documents/UN/UNPAN021547.pdf

UNDESA. (2003). *World public sector report.*

UNDESA. (2012). United nations e-government survey 2012: E-government for the people. Retrieved December 4, 2012, from http://www.un.org/en/development/desa/publications/connecting-governments-to-citizens.html

UNDP. (2011). *Nepal human development report 2011: State transformation and human development.* Kathmandu, Nepal: United Nations Development Program.

UNINOVA, & UvA. (2006). *D52.2: Rough reference model for collaborative networks.* European Collaborative Networked Organizations Leadership Initiative (ECOLEAD).

United Nations Report. (2008). *UN E-government survey 2008: From e-government to connected governance.* UN White paper. ISBN 978 -92-1-123174. Retrieved October 24, 2009, from http://unpan1.un.org/intradoc/groups/public/documents/UN/UNPAN028607.pdf

United Nations. (2003). *UN global e-government survey 2003.* Retrieved March 28, 2011, from http://unpan1.un.org/intradoc/groups/public/documents/un/unpan016066.pdf

United Nations. (2003). *World public sector report 2003: E-government at the crossroads (No. ST/ESA/PAD/SER.E/49).* New York: United Nations.

United Nations. (2004). *Global e-government readiness report 2004- Towards access for opportunity. No: UNPAN/2004/11.* New York: United Nations.

United Nations. (2010). *United Nations e-government survey 2010-Leveraging e-government at a time of financial and economic crisis.* Retrieved November 3, 2011, from http://www2.unpan.org/egovkb/documents/2010/E_Gov_2010_ Complete.pdf

USA. (2003). *The national information infrastructure: An agenda for action.* Department of Commerce – The President's Information Infrastructure Task Force. Retrieved April 5, 2003, from http://www.ibiblio.org/nii/NII-Agenda-for-Action.html

Valle, R. (2003). E-government: A future of inter-administrative cooperation. *UPGRADE – The European Journal for the Informatics Professional, 4*(2), 11-13.

Van Vliet, P. J. A., & Pietron, L. R. (2006). Information systems development education in real world – A project methodology and assessment. *Journal of Information Systems Education, 17*(3). Retrieved May 5, 2010, from http://www.isqa.unomaha.edu/vanvliet/pvvresearch.htm

Varian, H. R. (2002). *Intermediate microeconomics: A modern approach.* New York: WW Norton & Co..

Varian, H. R., Farrell, J., & Shapiro, C. (2004). *The economics of information technology: An introduction.* Cambridge University Press. doi:10.1017/CBO9780511754166.

Vassilakis, C., Laskaridis, G., Lepouras, G., Rouvas, S., & Georgiadis, P. (2002). Transactional e-government services: An integrated approach. *Lecture Notes in Computer Science, 2456*, 276–279. doi:10.1007/978-3-540-46138-8_44.

Venkatesh, V., & Davis, F. D. (2000). A theoretical extension of the technology acceptance model: Four longitudinal field studies. *Management Science, 46*(2), 186–204. doi:10.1287/mnsc.46.2.186.11926.

Venkatesh, V., Morris, M. G., Davis, G. B., & Davis, F. D. (2003). User acceptance of information technology: Toward a unified view. *Management Information Systems Quarterly, 27*(3), 425–478.

Vidigal, L. (2003). *O futuro pulsar electrónico da Administração Pública e o papel do Instituto de Informática.* Retrieved April 22, 2012, from http://luisvidigal.no.sapo.pt/html/o_futuro_pulsar_electronico_da.html

Virili, F., & Sorrentino, M. (2002). Reconfiguring the political value chain: The potential role of web services. In Electronic government (pp. 227-230).

Viscusi, G., Batini, C., & Mecella, M. (2010). *Information systems for egovernment: A quality-of-service perspective.* Springer. doi:10.1007/978-3-642-13571-2.

Wallström, Å., Engström, A., Salehi-Sangari, E., & Ek Styvén, M. (2009). Public e-services from the citizens' perspective – Adopting a market orientation. *International Journal of Public Information Systems*, *5*(2), 123–134.

Walsh, L. (2009). Online policy consultation: A case study of local government. In Khosrow-Pour, M. (Ed.), *E-government diffusion, policy and impact: Advanced issues and practices* (pp. 139–155). Hershey, Pennsylvania: Information Science Reference.

Ward, J., & Peppard, J. (2002). *Strategic planning for information systems*. England: John Wiley and Sons.

Web, W. W. (2012). *World Wide Web Foundation's first ever web index reveals impact of web around the world-web*. Retrieved November 18, 2011, from http://www.webfoundation.org/projects/ogd/

Weill, P., & Ross, J. W. (2004). *IT governance: How top performers manage it decision rights for superior results*. Harvard Business School Press.

West Darrell, M. (2000). Assessing e-government: The internet, democracy, and service delivery by state and federal governments. Retrieved October 1, 2008, from http://www.insidepolitics.org/egovtreport00.html

West, D. (2007). State and federal e-government in the United States. *Inside Politics*. Retrieved from http://www.insidepolitics.org

West, D. M. (2001). *An assessment of city government websites*. Brown University Urban E-Government.

West, D. M. (2004). E-government and the transformation of service delivery and citizen attitudes. *Public Administration Review*, *64*(1), 15–27. doi:10.1111/j.1540-6210.2004.00343.x.

Westphal, J. D., & Zajac, E. J. (1994). Substance and symbolism in CEOs long-term incentive plans. *Administrative Science Quarterly*, *39*, 367–390. doi:10.2307/2393295.

White-Paper. (2003). *White paper on enterprise architecture*.

Wigand, R. T., Picot, A., & Reichwald, R. (1997). *Information, organization and management: Expanding markets and corporate boundaries*. New York: Wiley.

Wihlborg, E. (2005). *Offentliga e-tjänster i medborgarens tjänst*. [Public e-services for the citizens] Stockholm: 24-timmarsdelegationen.

Wiklund, H. (2005). A Habermasian analysis of the deliberative democratic potential of ICT-enabled services in Swedish municipalities. *New Media & Society*, *7*(5), 701–723. doi:10.1177/1461444805056013.

Wilkinson, K., Sayers, C., Kuno, H., & Reynolds, D. (2003). Efficient RDF storage and retrieval in Jena2. In *Proceedings of the First International Workshop on Semantic Web and Databases (SWDB)* (pp. 131-150). Berlin, Germany.

Wilson, R., Cornford, J., Baines, S., & Mawson, J. (2011). New development: Information for localism? Policy sense-making for local governance. *Public Money & Management*, *31*(4), 295–299. doi:10.1080/09540962.2011.586243.

Wimmer, M., & Tambouris, E. (2002, August 26-30). *Online one-stop government: A working framework and requirements*. Paper presented at the IFIP World Computer Congress, Montreal.

Wimmer, M. A. (2002). Integrated service modelling for online one-stop government. *Electronic Markets*, *12*(3), 149–156. doi:10.1080/101967802320245910.

Wood-Harper, T., Ibrahim, O., & Ithnin, N. (2004). An interconnection success factor approach for service functional in Malaysian electronic government. In *ICE'04, Proceedings of the 6th International Conference on Electronic Commerce* (pp. 446-450).

Woods, E. (2006). Experiences using viewpoints for information systems architecture: An industrial experience report. Artechra Limited, Hamilton House, 6th Floor, 111 Marlowes, Hemel Hempstead, HP1 3HY, UK.

World Economic Forum. (2012). *Global information technology report*. Retrieved October 1, 2012, from http://www.weforum.org/issues/global-information-technology

World Internet Stats. (2012). *World internet statistics report*. Retrieved from November 26, 2012, from http://www.internetworldstats.com/stats.htm

World Market Research Centre. (2001). *Global e-government survey*. USA: Brown University.

Xiao, Y., Xioa, M., & Zhao, H. (2007). An ontology for e-government knowledge modelling and interoperability. In *Proc. of IEEE Intl. Conference on Wireless Communications, Networking and Mobile Computing (WiCOM 2007)* (pp. 3600-3603). Shanghai, 21-25 September.

Yang, D. L. (2001). *The great net of China*. MFC Internet Update. Retrieved from www.mfcinsight.com/article/010209/oped4.html

Yeloğlu, H., & Sağsan, M. (2009). The diffusion of e-government innovations in Turkey: A conceptual framework. Serial No.50. USA. Journal of US-China Public Administration, *6*(7). ISSN 1548-6591.

Yildiz, M. (2007). E-government research: Reviewing the literature, limitations, and ways forward. *Government Information Quarterly*, *24*, 646–665. doi:10.1016/j.giq.2007.01.002.

Yun, H. J., & Opheim, C. (2010). Building on success: The diffusion of e-government in the American States. *Electronic Journal of e-Government, 8*(1), 71 - 82. Retrieved from www.ejeg.com

Yusoff, M., & Radzi, M. (2002). *E-government opportunities and challenges: Malaysia's experience*. Retrieved August 10, 2012, from http://egovaspac.apdip.net/topics/country/my/radzi-yusoff.html

Zachman, J. A. (1987). A framework for information systems architecture. *IBM Systems Journal*, *26*(3). doi:10.1147/sj.263.0276.

Zander, U., & Kogut, B. (1995). Knowledge and the speed of the transfer and imitation of organizational capabilities: An empirical test. *Organization Science*, *6*(1), 76–92. doi:10.1287/orsc.6.1.76.

Zang, Z. (2005). *Ontology query languages for the semantic web: A performance evaluation*. (MSc Thesis). The University of Georgia.

Zarei, B., Ghapanchi, A., & Sattary, B. (2008). Toward national e-government development models for developing countries: A nine stage model. *The International Information & Library Review*, *40*(3), 199–207. doi:10.1016/j.iilr.2008.04.001.

Zhiyuan, F. (2002). E-government in digital era: Concept, practice, and development. *International Journal of the Computer and Management*, *10*(2), 1–22.

Zouridis, S., & Thaens, M. (2002). eGovernment: Towards a public administration approach. In Proceedeings of Global e-Policy eGov Forum Seoul, Korea, Nov 6-7. Seoul: SungKyunKwan University, Global e-Policy eGovernment Institute.

Zweers, K., & Planqué, K. (2001). Electronic government: From an organizational based perspective towards a client oriented approach. In Prins, J. (Ed.), *Designing e-government: On the crossroads of technological innovation and institutional change* (pp. 91–120). The Hague: Kluwer Law International.

About the Contributors

Zaigham Mahmood is a researcher and author. He has an MSc in Mathematics, MSc in Computer Science and PhD in Modelling of Phase Equilibria. Dr Mahmood is a Senior Technology Consultant at Debesis Education UK, a researcher at the University of Derby UK and Professor Extraordinaire at the North West University in South Africa. He is, currently, also a Foreign Professor at NUST Islamabad Pakistan. Professor Mahmood has published over 100 articles in international journals and conference proceedings in addition to four books on cloud computing and two reference texts on e-government viz: *E-Government Implementation and Practice in Developing Countries* and *Developing E-Government Projects: Frameworks and Methodologies*. He is also the Editor-in-Chief of the *Journal of E-Government Studies and Best Practices* and Series Editor-in-Chief of the IGI book series on *Advances in Electronic Government, Digital Divide & Regional Development* (AEGDDRD). Professor Mahmood is an active researcher; he also serves as editorial board member of several journals, books and conferences; guest editor for journal special issues; organiser and chair of conference tracks and workshops; and keynote speaker at conferences. His research interests encompass subject areas including software engineering, project management, enterprise computing, e-government studies and cloud computing. Dr Mahmood can be reached at *z.mahmood@debesis.co.uk*. He welcomes your views and comments.

***

Sujana Adapa has a PhD and is currently a Lecturer in Management (Strategy & Marketing) in the UNE Business School at the University of New England (UNE), Armidale, Australia. Sujana teaches Introduction to Marketing, Marketing Strategy & Management, Services Marketing and International Marketing units at UNE for undergraduate and postgraduate students. Her research interests relate to the adoption of technological innovations, corporate social responsibility, sales management, destination visitations and branding. She has published research papers in reputed journals and presented her research in national and international journals.

Ahed Al-Haraizah has a PhD. He worked as an assistant Professor at Al-Ahliyya Amman University in MIS department from 2010 to 2011. In 2011, he shifted to Middle East University for higher studies in the department E-Business (Teaching and supervising MEB students). Currently, he is working for Saudi Electronic University as Training Consultant and Lecturer for MBA program. Dr. Al-Haraizah has acted as Primary supervisor for the successful completion of a postgraduate research candidature in the fields of E-Business and Knowledge Management.

Luis Amaral holds a PhD in Information Systems obtained at University of Minho in 1994. He is Associate Professor at Department of Information Systems of University of Minho where he teaches information systems management and information systems planning. Since 2005 is the President of the board of directors of CCG - Centro de Computação Gráfica. Pró-Rector of University of Minho between July 2006 and October 2009. President of the National College of Informatics (Order of Engineers) since March 2010.

Mian Muhammad Awais received his Ph.D. from Imperial College, University of London. Prior to joining LUMS, Dr. Awais conducted European Union research and development projects for a UK based SME. His Ph.D. work related to the development of on-line models for parametric estimation of solid fuel-fired industrial boilers. Dr. Awais has also conducted research work on a class of iterative methods pertinent to Krylov subspaces for optimisation, such as the oblique projection and implicitly restarted model reduction methodologies. Research Interests: Artificial Intelligence, Inverse Modeling, Data Management, Fuzzy Logic, Soft Computing and e-Government Architecture.

Iréne Bernhard is a lecturer in media- and communication studies at the University West, Trollhättan, Sweden and a PhD Candidate at the Royal Institute of Technology, Stockholm, Sweden. Her research focuses on local e-government and sustainable development. She was a part of a research project within eGovernment 2009-2011. The aim of the research project was to support and evaluate the development of municipal contact centres in Sweden. Besides this she has extensive experience in applied organisational communication on research issues e.g. she is coordinator for international research symposia.

Sara Chinnasamy is a final year PhD student in Media, at the University of Adelaide. Her thesis deals with media discourse and political participation in Malaysia. From 1999-2005, she was a broadcast journalist for the public broadcaster, Radio Television Malaysia, Kuala Lumpur, where her role focused on parliamentary reporting, political assignments and related analyses. In 2006, she began lecturing on broadcast journalism in the Faculty of Media and Communication Studies, University of Technology Mara, Malaysia, before coming to Australia in 2009 on a Malaysian government international scholarship.

Haroula N. Delopoulos is Adjunct Teaching Staff, since 1989, in the Department of Economic Sciences, National and Kapodistrian University of Athens (UOA), Greece. She is a member of the Scientific Team of the Laboratory of Informatics at the School of Law, Economics and Political Science of UOA. She is teaching a number of courses on topics such as: eGovernance, eCommerce, Computer Applications in the Economy, Data Base Systems. Her early interests include eGovernance, ecommerce, eparticipation, edeliberation, e-learning, management of new technologies.

Ganesh Chandra Deka started his carrier as Programmer, Nowgong Polytechnic, Nagaon, Assam. He was Consultant (Computer Science) National Institute of Rural Development, India during 2003-2006. He is now Assistant Director of Training in Directorate General of Employment & Training, India since 2006. He has published more than 30 research papers in "e-Governance, Cloud Computing, Speech Processing & Data Mining" in various National & IEEE International Conferences held in India and served as Technical Program Committee member in more than 29 IEEE International conferences. He has authored 2 books in Cloud Computing and delivered keynote address at various national conferences and served as session chair in 6 IEEE International Conferences so far.

Muhammad Kashif Farooq is a researcher and practitioner. He has fifteen years job experience at different organizations of public and private sectors. Currently, he is doing job at Punjab Information Technology Board (PITB) as Program Manager. He was Research Associate at Computer Science department of Lahore University of Management Sciences (LUMS) Pakistan. He has experience in e-government, e-governance, enterprise architectures & frameworks, policy making, e-learning and ICT based social media, Public Private Partnership.

Jean Vincent Fonou Dombeu received his PhD in Computer Science at the North-West University in 2012. He also holds a MSc. in Computer Science from the University of KwaZulu-Natal. Dr. Fonou-Dombeu is currently a Senior Lecturer in the Department of Software Studies at the Vaal University of Technology where he teaches programming languages to IT and Engineering students, and provides leadership in research at postgraduate level. His current research interests are in Semantic Web and its application in E-Government.

Julie Freeman is a Postdoctoral Research Fellow in Communication and Media Studies at the University of Canberra, Australia. Julie received her PhD from Monash University in 2011 for a thesis entitled *Local E-Government: Politics and Civic Participation.* Her research interests include e-government, ICT-enabled citizen participation and engagement, e-democracy, the digital divide, and the policy contexts of government 2.0.

Güneş Çetin Gerger is As. Prof. Dr. at School of Applied Sciences. Her research mostly focuses on taxpayer's rights, tax compliance behaviour, tax amnesties and electronic taxation. She has a BA and MA degree in Public Finance. She has lectured for two years about Public Finance and Turkish Tax System in Manisa Celal Bayar University.

Mary Griffiths is Associate Professor in the Discipline of Media at the University of Adelaide. She is a regular chair at ECEG e-participation tracks. Research interests: e-participation, digital citizens, online and offline governance, digital humanities, and participatory media. 2012 publications include: 'Empowering citizens: A constructivist assessment of the impact of contextual and design factors on the concept of shared governance'; 'Real time political news: Designing information flows in an online scenario'; and guest editing of 'China', *Communications, Politics and Culture*, 45.2, 2012.

Kerstin Grundén is a professor in informatics at the University West, Trollhättan, Sweden. She has also a background as a sociologist. Kerstin has developed the MOA model for evaluation of implementation of IT and e-learning systems in organizations. She has made several studies in organizations using the model within the fields of e-learning and e-government for example. During 2009 – 2011 she participated in the research project Innoveta for the study of customer centres implementation within municipalities in Sweden.

Almas Heshmati is Professor of Economics at Sogang University. He held similar positions at the Korea University, Seoul National University, University of Kurdistan Hawler, RATIO Institute (Sweden) and the MTT Agrifood Research. He was Research Fellow at the World Institute for Development Economics Research (WIDER), The United Nations University during 2001-2004. From 1998 until 2001, he was an Associate Professor of Economics at the Stockholm School of Economics. He has a Ph.D. from the University of Gothenburg (1994). His research interests include applied microeconomics, globalization, development strategy, productivity and growth with application to manufacturing and services. In addition to more than 100 scientific journal articles, he has published books on EU Lisbon Process, Global Inequality, East Asian Manufacturing, Chinese Economy, Technology Transfer, Information Technology, Water Resources, Power Generation, and Development Economics.

Magda Huisman is a Professor of Computer Science and Information Systems at the North-West University (Potchefstroom Campus) where she teaches software engineering, IT project management, management information systems, and decision support systems. She received her Ph.D degree in Computer Science and Information Systems at the Potchefstroom University for CHE in 2001. Prof. Huisman is actively involved in research projects regarding systems development methodologies. Her current research interests are in the use and effectiveness of systems development methodologies and the diffusion of information technologies.

Harekrishna Misra is currently Professor, in the area of IT & Information Systems Group at the Institute of Rural Management Anand, India. He holds a doctorate degree in the area of Information Systems Management. He has around 31 years of experience in industry and academia in the fields of ICT. His research interests include software engineering, e-governance, ICT for Development, and ICT enabled value chain in rural enterprises. He is member of IEEE, Association of Computing Machinery (ACM) and Association of Information Systems, USA.

Gianluca Misuraca is a Senior Scientist at the Information Society Unit of the European Commission's Joint Research Centre, Institute for Prospective Technological Studies (IPTS) based in Seville, Spain. Before joining IPTS, he was the Managing Director of the Global Executive Master in e-Governance at the Ecole Polytechnique Fédérale de Lausanne (EPFL). Previously he held several positions as policy advisor for International Organizations and bilateral cooperation agencies as well as working with consulting and industrial organizations in the area of e-Government, regional development, research and innovation. His background is in economics with focus on the interface between ICTs and public administration. He also holds a Diploma of Specialization in European Union Economics and Law, a specialization in Security Management, an Executive Master in e-Governance and a PhD in Management of Technology from EPFL.

Bongani Ngwenya is Dean, Faculty of Business, MBA Thesis Defense Panel Chair, Lecturer and Master's thesis supervisor at Solusi University, in Zimbabwe. Has twenty-seven years of work experience, both in the public and private sector. Currently studying for a PhD in Business Management and Administration, with specialization in Strategic Management (A Grounded Theory Research), with North West University, Mafeking Campus in South Africa. My research interests are mainly in the areas of Organisational Decision-Making Research and in Business in general.

Adegboyega Ojo currently leads the E-Government Unit at the Digital Enterprise Research Institute (DERI). At DERI, his research and development work focuses on how governments can effectively leverage Linked Open Government Data for public service and policy innovation. Before his current role, he worked as academic program officer and post-doctoral fellow at the Center for Electronic Governance, United Nations University - International Institute for Software Technology (UNU). He gained a doctorate degree in 1991 from the University of Lagos in Nigeria.

Pethuru Raj is an enterprise architecture (EA) consultant in Wipro Consulting Services (WCS) division. Having obtained the competitive UGC research fellowship, Pethuru Raj successfully obtained the PhD degree from Anna University, Chennai, India. He then obtained the CSIR fellowship to work as a postdoctoral researcher in the Department of Computer Science and Automation (CSA), Indian Institute of Science (IISc), Bangalore. Thereafter, he was granted a couple of international fellowships (JSPS and JST) to work as a research scientist for 3 years in two leading Japanese universities. Dr. Raj worked as a lead architect in the corporate research (CR) division of Robert Bosch India for 1.5 years.

Kiran Rupakhetee is a PhD graduate from Seoul National University under Technology, Management, Economics and Policy Program. While pursuing PhD, he conducted research on the microcredit support effect on enterprise development for poverty reduction. Nowadays he is teaching in Purbanchal University, ACME Engineering College, Masters in Engineering Management Program in Nepal. He has been associating with government of Nepal for the last two decades or so as a midcareer policy and decision maker. His area of research interest includes innovation, monitoring and evaluation, microcredit, microenterprise development and e-governance.

Delfina de Sá Soares is an Assistant Professor at the Department of Information Systems of University of Minho. Delfina has a graduation in Systems and Informatics Engineering and a Master in Informatics. She's got a PhD in Information Systems and Technologies, with the thesis *Information Systems Interoperability in Public Administration*. Delfina's research interests are among information systems interoperability, electronic government, and information systems management. She has been participating and supervising national/international research projects in the area of IST in Government.

Shafay Shamail completed his BSc Electrical Engineering from UET Lahore, MSc Electronics from University of Wales, UK, and Ph.D. degree in Electrical Engineering from University of Bath U.K. Before joining LUMS Dr. Shamail worked in both the software industry as well as in the academia. During his stay at software industry, he gained experience in e-commerce technologies, especially those from Microsoft. Dr. Shamail has taught at public as well as private sector intuitions and has a vast experience of curriculum design and implementation. He was Chair Department of Computer Science LUMS from 2004 to 2009. He is a Senior Member of IEEE and chaired IEEE Lahore Section for the session 2010-2011. His research interests include software engineering, information technology, and e-government.

Gianluigi Viscusi has a PhD and is post-doc research fellow at the Department of Informatics, Systems and Communication (DISCo) of the University of Milan Bicocca. Research interests concern methodologies for policy Dr.iven information systems planning, e-Government, convergence and information growth impacts on information systems design, digital information asset evaluation (Information Value), business modelling and IS strategy alignment, data reverse engineering. He has published more than 50 referred papers in books, conference proceedings, and journals as Data & Knowledge Engineering and Government Information Quarterly. In 2010 he co-authored with Carlo Batini and Massimo Mecella the book "Information Systems for eGovernment: a quality of service perspective" (Springer, Heidelberg).

Index

www.ingramcontent.com/pod-product-compliance
Lightning Source LLC
LaVergne TN
LVHW062137200926
848484LV00007B/1828

UCLA COTSEN INSTITUTE OF ARCHAEOLOGY PRESS

MONOGRAPH SERIES

CONTRIBUTIONS IN FIELD RESEARCH AND CURRENT ISSUES
IN ARCHAEOLOGICAL METHOD AND THEORY

MONOGRAPH 74

ROCK ART AT LITTLE LAKE: AN ANCIENT CROSSROADS IN THE CALIFORNIA DESERT

Jo Anne Van Tilburg, Gordon E. Hull, and John C. Bretney

MONOGRAPH 73

THE HISTORY OF THE PEOPLES OF THE EASTERN DESERT

Hans Barnard and Kim Duistermaat (eds.)

MONOGRAPH 71

CRUCIBLE OF PUEBLOS: THE EARLY PUEBLO PERIOD IN THE NORTHERN SOUTHWEST

Richard H. Wilshusen, Gregson Schachner, and James R. Allison (eds.)

MONOGRAPH 70

CHOTUNA AND CHORNANCAP: EXCAVATING AN ANCIENT PERUVIAN LEGEND

Christopher B. Donnan

The Dead Tell Tales

The Dead Tell Tales:

Essays in Honor of Jane E. Buikstra

Edited by

María Cecilia Lozada and Barra O'Donnabhain

Monograph 76

Cotsen Institute of Archaeology Press

University of California, Los Angeles

The Cotsen Institute of Archaeology Press is the publishing unit of the Cotsen Institute of Archaeology at UCLA. The Cotsen Institute is a premier research organiza¬tion dedicated to the creation, dissemination, and conservation of archaeological knowledge and heritage. It is home to both the Interdepartmental Archaeology Graduate Program and the UCLA/Getty Master's Program in the Conservation of Archaeological and Ethnographic Materials. The Cotsen Institute provides a forum for innovative faculty research, graduate education, and public programs at UCLA in an effort to positively impact the academic, local and global communities. Established in 1973, the Cotsen Institute is at the forefront of archaeological research, education, conservation and publication and is an active contributor to interdisciplinary research at UCLA.

The Cotsen Institute Press specializes in producing high-quality academic volumes in several different series, including *Monographs*, *World Heritage and Monuments*, *Cotsen Advanced Seminars*, and *Ideas, Debates and Perspectives*. The Press is committed to making the fruits of archaeological research accessible to professionals, scholars, students, and the general public. We are able to do this through the generosity of Lloyd E. Cotsen, longtime Institute volunteer and benefactor, who has provided an endowment that allows us to subsidize our publishing program and produce superb volumes at an affordable price. Publishing in nine different series, our award-winning archaeological publications receive critical acclaim in both the academic and popular communities.

This book is set in 10.2-point Janson Text, with titles in 24-point Janson Text.
Copyediting: Peg J. Goldstein
Layout: William Morosi

Library of Congress Cataloging-in-Publication Data

The dead tell tales : essays in honor of Jane E. Buikstra / edited by
María Cecilia Lozada and Barra O'Donnabhain.
ISBN-13: 978-1-931745-68-0 (hardcover)
pages cm -- (Monograph / Cotsen Institute of Archaeology ; 76)
1. Human remains (Archaeology)--Case studies. 2. Paleopathology--Case
studies. 3. Funeral rites and ceremonies--Case studies. I. Lozada,
María Cecilia, author, editor of compliation. II. O'Donnabhain, Barra,
author, editor of compilation. III. Buikstra, Jane E., honouree.
CC79.H85D43 2013
930.1--dc23

2012048970

Contents

PART IV. BIOARCHAEOLOGICAL RESEARCH IN EUROPE, AFRICA, AND THE MIDDLE EAST

About the Editors

María Cecilia Lozada is a Peruvian bioarchaeologist who has been conducting archaeological research in the South Central Andes for the last 20 years, and holds a PhD degree in Anthropology from the University of Chicago. She uses a multidisciplinary approach to study the past, combining archaeology, human osteology and ethnohistory, which is exemplified in her book, *El Señorío de Chiribaya en la Costa Sur del Perú* (2002) and multiple publications that showcase her integrated social and biological reconstructions of past Andean societies. For the past 7 years, Lozada has been the main field archaeologist and human osteologist for several multidisciplinary and collaborative projects in northern Chile co-sponsored by the Cotsen Institute of Archaeology at UCLA and La Universidad de Chile. In 2009, she initiated a new archaeological project in the Vitor valley in southern Peru. As the Principal Investigator of the Vitor Archaeological Project, Lozada leads a multinational team that includes Peruvian investigators as well as numerous American students and researchers from institutions such as UCLA, the Field Museum of Natural History in Chicago and The University of Chicago. Her close professional and personal ties to the archaeological community in Peru has helped garner support from the Ministerio de Cultura del Perú which, in turn, has helped the project to flourish. She is currently a Research Associate in the Department of Anthropology at the University of Chicago, and has been actively working to promote collaborations between local universities in Peru and the United States through her projects.

Barra O'Donnabhain, who holds a PhD degree in Anthropology from the University of Chicago, is an Irish bioarchaeologist who has been conducting archaeological research in Ireland and other parts of the world for over 25 years. His publications cover a wide temporal span as well as a broad range of themes but are characterized by an integrative approach in their reconstructions of past lives. This is exemplified by recent papers dealing with the political use of the ritualized violence of executions (2011) and the use of bone chemistry to characterize diet and identity in Viking Age Dublin (2012). He has also challenged in print the traditional narrative of "Celtic Ireland." O'Donnabhain has directed and collaborated in archaeological projects in a number of world areas. His recent focus has been on institutional confinement. From 2009 to 2011, he directed excavations at a putative leper hospital in south west Ireland and in 2012 he began excavations at a 19th century prison. Also in 2012, he directed the mortuary component of excavations at an Inca outpost in southern Peru in collaboration with researchers from UCLA and USC. He is currently on the faculty of the Department of Archaeology at University College Cork and is on the Board of Directors of the Los Angeles-based Institute for Field Research.

About the Contributors

DAVE AFTANDILIAN is Assistant Professor of Anthropology at Texas Christian University and co-chair of the Animals and Religion Consultation for the American Academy of Religion. He is the editor of *What Are the Animals to Us? Approaches from Science, Religion, Folklore, Literature, and Art* (Tennessee, 2007), and his research and teaching focus on animals and religion, Native American religion and ecology, food justice, and Illinois archaeology.

DANIEL H. AGUILAR holds a M.Sc. in material chemistry, and is currently working as a research assistant at Cinvestav-Mérida, Yucatan, Mexico. He possesses experience in the applying the techniques of X-ray diffraction, X-ray fluorescence and small angle X-ray scattering, which he has applied to organic and inorganic materials, such as ceramics, archaeological sustrates, and semiconductors.

IVAN OLIVA ARIAS obtained his PhD in Material Sciences and currently work as a Researcher at Cinvestav, IPN (Unidad Mérida), Mexico. His research area is related to the preparation and characterization of films of metals, alloys, and semiconductors for nanotechnology applications.

MARÍA DEL ROSARIO DOMÍNGUEZ CARRASCO is a researcher at the Centro de Investigaciones Históricas y Sociales of the Universidad Autónoma de Campeche. Her research on Maya archaeology has centered in archaeometry, specifically in the study of ceramics, pigments, lithic and limestone materials.

JUAN V. CAUICH-RODRÍGUEZ received his PhD in the IRC in Biomedical Materials at Queen Mary and Westfield College (London, UK) in 1997 and the MSc in Polymer Science and Technology at UMIST (Manchester, UK) in 1994. After obtaining his degree, he has worked as a researcher at the Centro de Investigación Científica de Yucatán A.C. developing biomaterials for orthopedic applications. Currently, he is developing polymers for cardiovascular applications such as biodegradable polyurethanes and CTN composites.

WILLIAM J. FOLAN is a Director, professor, emeritus researcher and cofounder of the Centro de Investigaciones Históricas y Sociales of the Universidad Autónomo de Campeche. His interdisciplinary research on Maya archaeology, coupled with paleoclimatology, has centered around the Maya centers of Calakmul, Oxpemul, and Champoton.

GEORGE R. MILNER'S (Professor of Anthropology, The Pennsylvania State University) osteological research currently focuses on age estimation and trauma, and his archaeological work mostly pertains to the prehistory of eastern North America. He has conducted archaeological field work in the United States, Egypt, and Micronesia, and as part of various projects has examined ancient and modern skeletal remains from North America, Europe, and Africa.

PATRICIA QUINTANA OWEN holds a PhD in chemistry of ceramic materials, and is currently working as a researcher at Cinvestav-Mérida, Yucatan, Mexico. Her research is directed toward studying the chemistry and characterization of materials (ceramics, biomaterials, karstic rocks and archaeological) with electrical and photocatalytic applications; and identification of clay materials present in soils of the Yucatan Peninsula.

CHRISTOPHER STOJANOWSKI is Associate Professor in the School of Human Evolution and Social Change at Arizona State University. He is a specialist in the bioarchaeology of the Southeast with an emphasis on dental anthropology and biodistance analysis.

VERA TIESLER holds a PhD in anthropology and is employed as a research professor at the Autonomous University of Yucatán, Mérida, Mexico. Her research has centered on Caribbean and Mesoamerican, specifically prehispanic and colonial Maya bioarchaeology and mortuary archaeology emphasizing interdisciplinary approaches.

LORI WRIGHT is Professor of Anthropology at Texas A&M University. Her research examines ancient Maya diet, health, and migration using stable isotope geochemistry of skeletal remains and paleopathology.

INTRODUCTION

MARÍA CECILIA LOZADA
DEPARTMENT OF ANTHROPOLOGY, UNIVERSITY OF CHICAGO

BARRA O'DONNABHAIN
DEPARTMENT OF ARCHAEOLOGY, UNIVERSITY COLLEGE CORK

THIS VOLUME OF ESSAYS IS OFFERED TO Professor Jane E. Buikstra to honor her sixty-fifth birthday, which she celebrated in 2011. The volume began life in a symposium entitled "The Dead Tell Tales: Jane E. Buikstra and Narratives of the Past," held in San Juan, Puerto Rico, in 2006 at the seventy-first annual meeting of the Society for American Archaeology and organized by the editors of this volume. Both of us are active in bioarchaeological research and teaching. As a result, we have always been keenly aware of Buikstra's pioneering work in the development of the discipline, her leadership role in its ongoing development, and her important contributions to other aspects of anthropological research. The SAA symposium marked the first time that multiple generations of Buikstra's former doctoral students and other colleagues gathered to discuss the impact of her mentorship, and the session was remarkable for its breadth, both in terms of the topics discussed and the geographical range they covered. Despite the diversity and scope of the contributions, they were united by the integrative cross-disciplinarity that has always been a hallmark of Jane E. Buikstra's anthropology. The aim of the current volume is to disseminate the contributions to a wider audience and to thereby reinforce this approach. Like the SAA symposium, this volume celebrates more than three decades of scholarship by Jane E. Buikstra and the professional and personal relationships she has built in the process. Buikstra's mentorship has been marked by generosity. She has been a consistent advocate for her students, who have tended to move smoothly from pupil to colleague (see Rakita this volume). She has fostered generations of young scholars, not only from the United States but also from many of the countries in which she has conducted research and beyond. Her foreign students were drawn from countries where formal training in bioarchaeology was not available, and through her personal involvement and mentorship, she has played a direct role in seeding the discipline in a number of different world areas. This pioneering spirit has its roots very early in Buikstra's career.

Jane E. Buikstra's interests in archaeology and human biology can be traced to her childhood. She is from southern Indiana, an area rich in archaeological remains, where she grew up in a medical household. Her undergraduate training in anthropology was at DePauw University. She moved to the University of Chicago for her postgraduate studies. While gaining a strong background in biological anthropology under the tutelage of Dr. Charles Merbs, and others, she had an equally strong background in archaeological fieldwork with Stuart Struever due to her participation in excavations at the Koster Site in southern Illinois. In 1976, four years after she obtained her Ph.D., in a paper delivered to the Southern Anthropological Society, she advocated a new approach that sought to find common ground between these interests and to live up to the aspiration of anthropology to be a holistic endeavor. Bioarchaeology, as defined by Buikstra, sought to integrate the previously distinct areas of study of biological anthropology and archaeology (Buikstra 1977:69). This was in keeping with the ethos of the New Archaeology of the time, stressing as it did the place of humans in broader cultural and ecological systems. Proposing a new modus operandi is easier than giving it a reality. Equally critical to the development of bioarchaeology has been Buikstra's leadership in nurturing the discipline by means of a prodigious research output, much of it collaborative, characterized both by the integration of narratives from a range of discourses and by its dynamism, informed as it is by changing directions in theory, method, and practice (see chapters in this volume by Patterson and Charles).

Jane E. Buikstra's innovative and pioneering approach is also apparent in her career-long involvement with the Center for American Archaeology at Kampsville, Illinois. This involvement grew from the Koster excavations, which played a formative role for many anthropologists of her generation. From its earliest days, one of the distinguishing features of the CAA has been its community involvement. Dialogue with local communities is now commonplace in archaeological research projects, but Buikstra and the CAA anticipated this by decades at Kampsville. The center has played an important role in fostering students of archaeology and bioarchaeology but has always had a broader vision of involving the wider community through its various activities and outreach programs. Under Buikstra's leadership, the CAA has been characterized by its respect for local identities and by the creation of a space for open dialogue between the local and scientific communities.

Buikstra's commitment to sharing knowledge has been a characteristic of her career since her earliest academic appointment at Northwestern University. While also undertaking substantial administrative duties, Buikstra pioneered the integration of osteological data in funerary archaeology, which had lasting implications for both mortuary theory and bioarchaeology. She also collaborated in a number of groundbreaking studies across a range of topics, including bone chemistry and methods of assessing heritability of nonmetric traits in primates. Furthermore, she made important contributions in paleopathology. Her 1981 volume *Prehistoric Tuberculosis in the Americas* set a new standard for paleopathological studies and, true to the roots of bioarchaeology in the New Archaeology, established a new population-based approach that moved beyond the clinically oriented, descriptive case-study methodology of earlier studies. The 1981 volume was also notable for its integration of narratives from different disciplines.

Combining these elements of close collaborations between academic disciplines, and also between anthropologists and local communities, Buikstra was instrumental in establishing centers of bioarchaeological research outside North America. In particular, her work in Peru was critical in the seeding of her vision of bioarchaeology in the Andes. As the discipline developed in Peru, it was again characterized by its interdisciplinarity and its engagement with, and sensitivity to, the wider community. Her significant record of publications is testament to her enduring commitment to the region. She also played a personal role in establishing bioarchaeological research in Spain, where she was drawn by the culture of dialogue and inclusiveness fostered by the leaders of the Gatas Project. Her involvement marked a decisive break from previous approaches in the region and resulted in a broadening of research agendas regarding mortuary contexts. Buikstra has also worked in Argentina, Brazil, Mexico, and Honduras, and through her students she has indirectly influenced the development of the discipline in a number of countries, including Greece, Indonesia, and Ireland.

Buikstra's ability to recruit graduate students from the United States and abroad was enhanced by her move in 1986 to the University of Chicago, where she created a rich learning and research environment characterized by cultural and intellectual diversity. Her term at Chicago was marked by a number of honors. In 1987 Buikstra was elected to the National Academy of Sciences. Two years later she was elected to the presidency of the American Anthropological Association, becoming the sixth woman to hold that post since the organization was founded in 1902. These honors were an affirmation of her standing in the anthropological community but also an acknowledgment of the place of bioarchaeology within the broader discipline. This came at a time of potential crisis for the discipline, as the passing of the Native American Graves and Repatriation Act (NAGPRA) in 1990 allowed for the possible return of cultural items and human remains to their respective peoples and for their reburial. With the prospect of the repatriation of many collections of archaeologically retrieved human skeletons, there was concern about the lack of a standardized approach to analysis and reporting and the need to gain the maximum amount of information from remains that might no longer be available for scientific study. A series of meetings initiated by the Paleopathology Association sought to develop standards for the collection of osteological data. This resulted in a workshop held in 1991 at the Field Museum of

Natural History in Chicago that was supported by the National Science Foundation. The resulting publication (Buikstra and Ubelaker 1994) became a key resource for researchers and students alike.

In 1995 Buikstra moved to the University of New Mexico, where her work was marked by an increase in evaluative and synthetic publications. Her international interests expanded to include studies of the ancient Maya, where she collaborated on population-based studies of hard tissue biochemistry while also generating individual osteobiographies that traced residence changes and the personal, physical cost of wielding political power (see chapters in this volume by Wright and by Tiesler et al.). She also began a productive collaboration with colleagues in Britain, where bioarchaeology, or human osteoarchaeology as it is usually called there, had come of age in the 1980s and 1990s (Roberts this volume). This work was marked by a return to a long-standing interest, the bioarchaeology of tuberculosis. Debates about the coevolution of humans and the pathogens that produce TB are critical to research aimed at mitigating the global threat to modern populations posed by this reemerging disease.

This focus on the relevance of bioarchaeology to contemporary society anticipated Buikstra's move in 2005 to Arizona State University, where she became the first director of the newly established Center for Bioarchaeological Research. The high value placed on bioarchaeology at ASU and the manner in which the center is integrated into the broader research strategies of the School of the Human Environment and Social Change are models of research and higher education that Buikstra has advocated throughout her career. At ASU Buikstra is in an innovative environment that explicitly seeks to move beyond the scope that traditionally defined the study of anthropology and that balances sociocultural and biologically based approaches to humanity. In the years since her move to Arizona, Buikstra has collaborated on three important volumes that, characteristically, span a range of interests—mortuary practices (Rakita et al. 2005), forensic anthropology (Komar and Buikstra 2008), and bioarchaeology (Buikstra and Beck 2006)—with each volume including an assessment of the current status of the topic. In the last few years, Buikstra's accomplishments have been recognized in the form of a number of awards, including the T. Dale Steward Award from the physical anthropology section of the American Academy of Forensic Sciences (2008) and the Charles Darwin Lifetime Achievement Award by the American Association of Physical Anthropology (2008). Her multidisciplinary study of past societies, the hallmark of her research, was further acknowledged by the Fryxell Award by the Society for American Archaeology in 2010. Her service to academia has also been continued through her role in the establishment of the *International Journal of Paleopathology*, providing an international forum for the study of health and disease in the past.

Organization of This Volume

The organization of this volume reflects the extent of Buikstra's influence in the discipline and her advocacy for a bioarchaeology that is embedded in and in constant dialogue with broader anthropological praxis. An opening section devoted to her theoretical impact is followed by papers organized geographically and reflecting the breadth of Buikstra's reach. Part I of this volume specifically addresses Buikstra's contributions to anthropology. Patterson (chapter 1) charts the dynamic interplay between theory and practice that has characterized her career, and he locates her approach within developments in the broader discipline, both in the United States and in other countries. One of the most direct ways to understand an individual's contribution to a discipline is to examine his or her body of published works. Rakita's analysis of Buikstra's bibliography (chapter 2) provides an insight into her signature multidisciplinary approach, her breadth of subject matter spanning the biological and social sciences, and the many geographical areas in which she has worked. Furthermore, the collaborative nature of much of her output reflects the collegiality of her approach and the altruism of her mentorship. In chapter 3, Charles takes up the theme of the dynamic nature of the study of archaeological human remains and notes the development of a diversity of approaches since the 1970s. He eloquently highlights the challenges inherent in attempts to straddle the physical sciences/social sciences divide, and he notes the malleability of Buikstra's bioarchaeology, which has allowed it to mature in the context of shifting theoretical landscapes. Buikstra has been particularly sensitive to these changing paradigms, and this sensitivity is reflected across the spectrum of her engagement with the human body, past and present. Buikstra's concern with advancing methods provided the inspiration for Lewis and Tung's contribution (chapter

4). In the context of new research technologies that feed growing demands for osteological samples, this is a timely reminder of the need to develop and adhere to protocols designed to facilitate research but also the long-term conservation of human remains.

The focus of the papers in Part II is on North America, where Buikstra's academic life has been based and where, through her continuing fieldwork at Kampsville, her anthropological life is anchored. Over the last two decades, NAGPRA has posed serious challenges for the praxis of bioarchaeology in North America. Goldstein (chapter 5) uses reports from the Smithsonian Institution Repatriation Office to examine the nature of relationships between researchers and native peoples in the context of negotiations concerning the repatriation of archaeological artifacts and human remains. Goldstein reflects on the multiscalar nature of identity and the importance of the oral tradition in the formation of collective memory. The emotive connection between living peoples and ancient human remains is also evoked in Watson's detective work concerning the discovery and subsequent histories of mummified remains from Kentucky (chapter 6). She follows the development of popular narratives concerning the biographies of these remains, which are contrasted with results of more recent bioarchaeological analyses. Watson highlights how human remains, both ancient and modern, have an interest beyond the scientific, and she charts the different social lives that dead bodies can have through time. The relevance of archaeological approaches to both ancient and modern contexts is also apparent in the paper by Ubelaker (chapter 7), who notes that in bioarchaeology, contexts with commingled human remains present particular challenges in terms of excavation and analysis. Ubelaker uses the ossuaries of Maryland to address these issues. He presents a rigorous approach to the proper recovery and documentation of secondary deposits of multiple individuals, as well as a systematic methodology that allows for the spatial analysis of remains, their demographic profiles, and the details of burial practices in the past. These approaches are not only relevant to archaeological contexts but could also be adopted for forensic investigations of more recent mass graves. A similarly rigorous methodology is proposed by Aftandilian (chapter 8) with regard to the analysis of animal effigies deposited as grave goods in Mississippian burials from Illinois. This method and analysis provide a good example of the integrative approach espoused in bioarchaeology as it draws together material cultural symbolism within mortuary ritual to document a relationship between specific motifs and particular cohorts of the population, such as infants and children. The integrative approach is also central to the paper by Stojanowski (chapter 9), which examines the fluid relationship between biology and social identity among human groups. In his discussion of the use of morphological distance as a means for drawing inferences about community self-definition, Stojanowski situates biodistance studies within a broad social framework, and he argues for historically contingent reconstructions of the formation and transformation of group identities in the past.

In Part III, the focus shifts to Central and South America, where Buikstra has made a number of important direct contributions since the early 1980s. Tiesler et al. (chapter 10) note that investigations of Maya elites have benefited over the last decade from multidisciplinary studies that seek to integrate bioarchaeological and other data sets with more traditional approaches. These authors present sophisticated analyses of residues found adhering to two royal skeletons from Calakmul, Mexico, the results of which are discussed in the context of other aspects of the burial record to provide new insights into details of the complex funerary treatments of individuals from the Mayan elite. Wright's contribution (chapter 11) also has an individual focus as it takes an osteobiographical approach using stable isotopes to document age-specific changes among elite skeletons from Copan, Honduras. While acknowledging the challenges presented by such chemical analyses, her studies provide an enriched narrative of individual life histories and allow her to chart mobility, rainfall seasonality, weaning, and social differences in diet. Keeping with ancient Maya society but in contrast to the usual situation encountered in bioarchaeology, Ashmore (chapter 12) examines situations where archaeologists have encountered spaces that were prepared as if to receive the dead, but where no bodies were found. The chapter considers inferences about such "absences" to examine not only instances in which bodies may have been moved but also circumstances where interment never took place. These absences are situated within current thinking about past mortuary programs and Maya beliefs relating to the dead and to the deceased's physical remains.

In South America, Andean archaeologists have the benefit of a rich ethnohistorical record of the precolonial period. Lozada and Rakita (chapter 13) use such accounts to interpret social and biological transitions among the Chiribaya of coastal Peru. (The Chiribaya project was directed by Buikstra.) They integrate the analysis of skeletal data, grave goods, ethnohistory, and funerary patterns as a means of drawing inferences about gender construction and attitudes toward key transitions in the life cycle of an individual. Nystrom also seeks to integrate narratives from bioarchaeology, ethnohistory, and material culture studies (chapter 14). In one of the first investigations of the biological impact of the Inca expansion, he documents the effects of the process of imperial domination on local populations that reflect the context-specific strategies used to build Inca hegemony.

The focus of Part IV is on the Old World, where a number of different approaches to archaeologically retrieved human remains developed in parallel to the emergence of bioarchaeology in the Americas. Paleopathology has been central to the emergence of a number of these developments. In chapter 15, Aufderheide considers the long history of the study of pathological lesions in mummified human remains, where the presence of soft tissues has both fascinated and challenged researchers. He documents how the integration of clinical and bioarchaeological approaches in the last few decades has broadened the agenda beyond paleopathology and has led to the emergence of mummy studies as vibrant scientific endeavors that have moved beyond their traditional home in Egypt. In her discussion of leprosy in medieval Europe and particularly Britain (chapter 16), Roberts combines the clinical approach to the malady with historical and bioarchaeological perspectives and concludes that to achieve a more complete understanding of the impact of disease, it is necessary to move beyond biological dimensions and to consider the social context of such afflictions. Perry et al. use bioarchaeological approaches to contest the validity of historical narratives of mine workers in Byzantine-period Jordan (chapter 17). Using bone chemistry analysis and other lines of evidence, they identify a hitherto invisible cohort of the mining population, providing more complete and representative biographies of the laborers behind the production of metal. In chapter 18, Lull et al. follow similar methodologies to those outlined by Ubelaker in Part III and also consider the importance of taphonomic issues in the formation of the funerary record. They argue that categories such as collective burial have a homogenizing effect that masks diachronic variability in mortuary behavior. They advocate the adoption of historically contingent approaches where variability is related to broader socioeconomic factors. Historical contingency is also central to the contribution by O'Donnabhain and Hallgrímsson, who, like Stojanowski in Part II, examine the relationship between biology and social identity. Using morphological distance studies to interrogate the nature of the colonial encounter in Viking Age Ireland, they argue that cultural responses to biological syncretism varied and that material culture and habituated practices were critical to identity construction. In chapter 20, Milner demonstrates that it is unsafe to make broad assumptions about the relationship between health status and social organization by examining the connection between trauma, sex, and longevity in medieval Denmark. He concludes that bioarchaeological research should be historically contingent, and he questions a number of conventional wisdoms regarding temporal and geographical variations in health.

In conclusion, our hopes for this volume can be distilled into two points. First, we hope that the volume documents the degree to which bioarchaeological approaches have become normalized and integrated into anthropological research. It is apparent from this collection of essays that Buikstra's vision of bringing the osteologist out of the lab and into the field, and thereby out of the appendix and into the interpretation of archaeological data, has been achieved. This is testament to the success of Buikstra's pioneering work and her subsequent evangelical approach to the promotion of the discipline both within the United States and internationally. Secondly, we hope this volume serves to highlight the dynamism of bioarchaeology, which owes so much to the strong foundations laid down over the last few decades. New perspectives have emerged, partly in response to broader theoretical changes within anthropology but also as a result of the engagement of the broader discipline with bioarchaeology. Engagement with the broader community has also had a transformative effect on the discipline and has contributed to forging new avenues of research. We anticipate further exciting developments and a long-lasting role for bioarchaeological approaches in furthering our knowledge of the human experience in the past. Such narratives deepen our understanding of the human career and have a significant relevance to our present and future.

REFERENCES CITED

Buikstra, Jane E.

1977 Biocultural Dimensions of Archeological Study: A Regional Perspective. In *Biocultural Adaptation in Prehistoric America*, edited by Robert L. Blakely, pp. 67–84. Southern Anthropological Society Proceedings No. 11. University of Georgia Press, Athens.

Buikstra, Jane, E. (editor)

1981 *Prehistoric Tuberculosis in the Americas.* Northwestern University Archeological Program, Evanston, Illinois.

Buikstra, Jane E., and Lane A. Beck (editors)

2006 *Bioarchaeology: The Contextual Analysis of Human Remains.* Academic Press, New York.

Buikstra, Jane E., and Douglas H. Ubelaker (editors)

1994 *Standards for Data Collection from Human Skeletal Remains: Proceedings of a Seminar at the Field Museum of Natural History.* Arkansas Archaeological Survey Press, Fayetteville.

Komar, Debra, and Jane E. Buikstra

2008 *Forensic Anthropology: Contemporary Theory and Practice.* Oxford University Press, New York.

Rakita, Gordon F. M., Jane E. Buikstra, Lane A. Beck, and Sloan R. Williams (editors)

2005 *Interacting with the Dead: Perspectives on Mortuary Archaeology for the New Millennium.* University Press of Florida, Gainesville.

PART I

BUIKSTRA'S GENERAL CONTRIBUTIONS TO ANTHROPOLOGY

1

The Anthropological Praxis of Jane Buikstra

Thomas C. Patterson
Department of Anthropology, University of California–Riverside

Jane E. Buikstra is fascinated with human skeletons. By the time she received her doctorate from the University of Chicago, she already knew at least four things well: (1) human beings live in society; (2) there is a metabolism between human beings in society and the milieus in which they live; (3) how they live and the webs of relations in which they are enmeshed are inscribed both in their bodies and in the demographic structures of those communities; and (4) there are often significant differences within societies as well as between different kinds of society. She soon learned about inequality and the differential treatment of women and minorities in the academy, perhaps as a result of gendered career advice and having to pour tea for male colleagues at faculty meetings (Buikstra 2003). These understandings—based on observation, insight, intuition, and personal experience—are not trivial. Entire careers have been built on a lot less. Buikstra has continued to learn new things and to grow intellectually throughout her career. For example, she is now trying to master saying no when asked to do something; however, it is not clear whether her only modest success so far stems from difficulties with the consonant or the vowel.

My goal in this paper is to explore Jane E. Buikstra's anthropological praxis. By this I mean broadly the creative activity through which she has come to understand the world and to change both her and our understanding of what happened in that world. This exploration involves looking at how she practices anthropology and the theoretical framework that buttresses her practical activity.

Buikstra was a graduate student in the late 1960s when the "new" or processual archaeology was coming of age and being institutionalized. Her early work is recognizably a part of this intellectual tradition, which advocated hypothesis testing, ecological thinking, and a regional approach to the study of societal development, among other things. Lamenting that bioanthropologists were "too often limited to a study of bones for their own sake—far removed from either their burial or their living context," she early argued for an integrating and integrative methodology that would provide those contexts and overcome some of the limitations imposed by hierarchically organized or technical divisions in labor in research projects (Buikstra 1976:3, 1991). This ran counter to long-accepted descriptions of the scientific method and how scientific research should be organized, as well as to then-current practices in multidisciplinary archaeological research projects (Dickson 1979). Her perspective called into question distinctions between those who gathered and assembled information and those who interpreted its significance. Noteworthy in this regard are the collaborative projects in which she has engaged and the large number of papers she has coauthored during her career, often as a junior author, with students and colleagues both inside and outside the field.

A second feature of Buikstra's perspective has been the methodical way in which she and her collaborators approached problems. While methods of multiple working hypotheses and hypothesis testing were long-time features of archaeological research, they received renewed emphasis in the late 1960s. In one sense, Buikstra's work was not exceptional in that she made use of these techniques to address problems defined by archaeologists. What was noteworthy, however, were (1) the clarity with which she dissected and stated hypotheses; (2) the rigor with which she tested them against empirical evidence and theoretically derived models; and (3) her use of diverse lines of evidence to construct "cables" of interpretation composed of a number of independent but mutually supportive strands of argumentation rather than merely additive "links in a chain" logical sequences or forms of reasoning (e.g., Buikstra and Konigsberg 1985; Konigsberg and Buikstra 1995; Konigsberg et al. 1989). Also noteworthy was that the lines of argumentation she used often derived from different fields, that they frequently exposed the limitations of models cherished by the practitioners of one field or another, and that they often argued for the importance of historical processes in ordering particular social forms (e.g., Buikstra and Mielke 1985; Buikstra et al. 1986).

A third feature of Jane E. Buikstra's point of view was that it increasingly threatened to cross not only the subfield boundaries that were being actively promoted in anthropology after World War II but also the chasms that separated anthropology from other disciplines (e.g., Buikstra 1991). It quickly necessitated drawing on steadily widening ranges of evidence, models, and theories to formulate hypotheses. This was not necessarily typical of the interdisciplinary projects of the time. Here, archaeologists tended to define the research problems. The findings of specialists from other fields were typically reported in appendices or data chapters. Their comments were either treated in isolation or used selectively to support the conclusions of the larger project. Often, what else the specialists had to say was not considered at all. From the beginning of her career, Buikstra was reading and incorporating techniques and ideas from fields ranging from physical chemistry and geology to physiology and genetics to history and cultural anthropology. Her appropriations were not relegated to appendices but appeared instead in the body of the text as well as in conclusions. Reading widely and thoughtfully in diverse fields can increase our understanding of a problem by drawing attention to the possible associations of seemingly unrelated data and by forcing us to think seriously about their significance and implications. Buikstra certainly takes into consideration a much wider range of evidence, models, and theories now than she did earlier in her career.

However, reading widely and attentively is also potentially destabilizing. She argued forcefully on more than one occasion that archaeologists should be clear about the assumptions implicit in the methods and theories they use. For example, in their discussion of the interrelations of demography, diet, and health, Buikstra and James Mielke issued a word of caution about the facile transfer of ideas from one field to another and the need to clarify the underlying presuppositions of the fields involved:

> Contemporary demographers use demographic parameters as measures of community health in human groups. This strategy is appropriate for past populations as well. However, the adaptation of demographic methods to paleodemographic study must be accompanied by an explicit appreciation of assumptions made about the uniformity of biological processes in our species—in the past and in the present—as well as the biases introduced by the nature of the archaeological record [Buikstra and Mielke 1985:361].

Making assumptions explicit can be simultaneously revelatory and complicating: revelatory in the sense that the assets and liabilities implicit in particular frameworks are brought into high relief, and complicating in the sense that the problem being investigated suddenly acquires unexpected, unpredicted, and inexplicable texture.

A fourth feature of Buikstra's praxis is that she never really adopted the neoevolutionary arguments of some strands of the New Archaeology. This was partly a consequence of her concern with what happened in a particular region—such as the lower Illinois River valley or the far south coast of Peru (e.g., Buikstra 1976; Lozada and Buikstra 2005). Thus her focus has always been history, which involves a concern with both the succession of historical forms and the historical processes that underwrote their formation rather than an embryonic-like unfolding of society or the emergence of new levels of societal development. She and Douglas Charles have advocated narratives as a means of connecting events in the archaeological record and of entry into the past of particular regions and peoples. In her view, this allows us to see more clearly the intersection of structure and agency in those communities and to understand more fully the transformations of the landscapes inhabited and created by those peoples (Charles and Buikstra 2002:15–17).

Jane E. Buikstra began her career with the tools of the New Archaeology, which informed her practice of archaeology; ultimately, her practice allowed her to hone and refine her theoretical understanding of the peoples with whose remains she worked. Perhaps another way of saying this is that practice destabilized her theoretical base. It forced her to reconceptualize those theoretical foundations and to reconsider what she knew and understood about those societies (e.g., Buikstra and Charles 1999:203–204). In Buikstra's case, this has been an ongoing dialectical process. Her continual reassessment has not resulted in either a theoretical eclecticism or an "add theory X and stir" approach to problems. It has instead led to a much more integrative and integrating view of anthropology and social theory than she held in the mid-1970s. Let us look briefly at some of the ways in which the theoretical foundations have been reworked.

In 1983 Jane E. Buikstra and Douglas Charles noted that the Archaic mortuary sites of the central Mississippi drainage contradicted received wisdom about the occurrence of formal disposal areas of the dead. While sedentary agricultural communities had cemeteries, these were not supposed to exist in foraging societies, which were widely viewed at the time as mobile. From Charles and Buikstra's perspective, the apparent contradiction was a product of bias in the ethnographic sample. They began their chapter on this topic with a lengthy discussion of their basic assumption about ancestor cults: "[T]he occurrence of formal cemetery areas is associated with corporate lineal inheritance of crucial and restricted resources" (Charles and Buikstra 1983:117). This discussion built on notions of property and territoriality (as the practice of defending or marking an area), one derived directly from liberal political thought and the other indirectly from it via ecological theory (Macpherson 1978; Ryan 1984). Both concepts are concerned with relations among peoples (communities) expressed in terms of things (land, resources, places) and behavior (competition). They concluded not only that the Archaic populations of the region were more sedentary than previously assumed but also that "the functioning corporate unit . . . was apparently the village" (Charles and Buikstra 1983:140). This emphasis on community rather than the individual or the family is a theoretically informed statement that builds on diverse currents of communitarian thought that emphasize the social nature of the individual rather than the atomized individual of liberalism.

In 1999 Buikstra and Charles turned their attention once again to the mortuary sites in the mid-continent. This time, their focus encompassed not only the Archaic but also the Woodland and Mississippian phases as well. Here, they distinguished ancestor cults from mortuary rituals. The former referred to "rituals which provide continued access to the deceased in the afterworld," while the latter "separate[d] the living from the deceased" (Buikstra and Charles 1999:204). While ancestor cults reflected defined power relations, mortuary rituals were sites of activity where those relations were contested. They also distinguished between exclusive ancestral cults, often located within or adjacent to villages, and earth/fertility cults, which ethnographically were both more inclusive and located in peripheral positions. In this paper, they argued that ancestor cults had a long history in the lower Illinois Valley. The mortuary rituals associated with them became increasingly elaborate during Middle Woodland times and "served to re-create social and political inequalities among the living" (Buikstra and Charles 1999:221). The transition from Late Woodland to Mississippian times witnessed the resolution of existing contradictions and the emergence of new forms of social inequality. As Buikstra and Charles put it, the "older, more fragile tensions between kin groups . . . [gave way to] institutionalized inequalities" (Buikstra and Charles 1999:221). Their view of social stratification is not based on claims that inequality exists in all societies or that it always develops in the same direction, but rather on the idea that it is socially constructed and historically contingent (e.g., Davis and Moore 1998 [1945]; Gailey 1987:248–266).

In 2002 Buikstra and Charles turned their attention once again to the processes of societal change and history in the lower Illinois Valley (Charles and Buikstra 2002:13, 17). This time they focused on the social and political-economic structures that provided the contexts of funerary practices in the region as well as on the historical transformations that occurred when those structures changed and new conditions developed. Any theory of history must have a theory of structure, a theory of transformation, and a theory of directionality (Callinicos 1995:95–140). The theory of structure they elaborate combines Weberian notions of power and domination with Marxist concerns about property relations. The theory of transformation they develop recognizes the importance of the mechanisms responsible for the changes that occurred in a particular society and for the ways in which one structure was dissolved and replaced by another. They do not attempt to explain all changes by the same mechanism and imply instead that different mechanisms were operative in different historical epochs (for example, Middle Archaic, Early Woodland, Middle Woodland, Late Woodland, and Mississippian), or alternatively that if the same mechanisms were operative, their effects varied from one society or historical epoch to another. This is a neo-Weberian theory of transformation that puts historical contingency at center stage combined with a Marxist theory of transformation that focuses on the development and resolution of contradictions within the domain of social production. Together with Julieann van Nest, they write,

> The end of Hopewell in the lower Illinois River valley corresponds to the slowing down and eventual cessation of this demographic transformation of the landscape. . . . Biological distance measures suggest that kinship networks had stabilized geographically and had begun to expand by this time. Simply put, the previous Middle Woodland level of negotiation among individuals and communities, utilizing the media of Hopewell was no longer necessary. Social, political and economic interaction in a more stable demographic landscape was now being conducted along kinship webs visible only through biological, rather than archaeological, analyses [Charles et al. 2004:49].

Finally, they do not elaborate a clear-cut theory of directionality that accounts for the overall pattern of historical transformation that occurred in the region, since their arguments are not evolutionist in a developmental sense; nor do they seem to rely on notions of progress, decline, or cyclicity. In their words: "The appearance of Hopewell indicates not a rise in social complexity *per se*, but rather the onset of a period of marked social and political activity" (Charles et al. 2004:48).

In conclusion, let us pull together the main strands of Jane E. Buikstra's anthropological praxis. First, her practical activity involves hypothesis testing, both deductive and inductive reasoning, blurring the boundaries between established disciplines, and listening carefully and thoughtfully to the arguments of others before she incorporates their insights into her own work. This has had destabilizing effects on the practical knowledge and methods she brought to the field in the 1970s; it has led her to hone and refine methods, to look at evidence in new ways, and to ask new questions that she probably would have thought unanswerable earlier in her career. Second, the continually evolving nature of her practical activity forced her to clarify the theoretical frameworks she used, to make explicit their presuppositions, and ultimately to explore new theoretical frameworks as she reframed research questions. Third, the destabilizing effects combined with new questions and theoretical insights underwrote the development of new forms of practical activity and fueled further changes in her praxis and understanding of the peoples with whom she worked. Fourth, her praxis has become increasingly historicized in the sense that she argues that a proper understanding of culture is necessarily always historical and involves the concepts of both process and succession. In a real sense, her praxis is a process: theory informs her practical activity; this practical activity allows her to hone and refine theory; and theory permits her to devise new forms of practical activity. Fifth, her concerns are not limited to a past that is hermetically sealed off from the present. Tuberculosis and gender inequities in the sciences, two problems she has addressed in her writings, continue to have impacts on society today. In her view, it is essential to know how they came to be and how they operate today in order to change them (Buikstra 2003; Roberts and Buikstra 2003).

There are two more strands of Jane E. Buikstra's praxis that need to be emphasized. First, while I have focused on her bioarchaeological investigations in the mid-continental United States, she has also carried out research from Honduras to Chile in the Americas, well as in various parts of Europe. In every instance, she has contributed in significant ways to our understanding of the past in all the regions where she has worked and to the intellectual development of students and junior colleagues in all the countries where she has worked. The second and most important aspect of her praxis is that she is a superb mentor to students and junior colleagues. She guided her own students and junior colleagues, as well as those of others, through the often difficult early years of their careers, and she championed their visibility at this stage of their professional development by publishing important papers with them, usually as the junior author. No one can ask for more. Unfortunately, this kind of mentoring, while not unique, is all too rare in the profession today.

Acknowledgments

I want to thank María Cecilia Lozada and Barra O'Donnabhain for the invitation to participate in this volume honoring Jane E. Buikstra. The chapter has profited from the thoughtful insights and comments of Wendy Ashmore.

References Cited

Buikstra, Jane E.

1976 *Hopewell in the Lower Illinois River Valley: A Regional Approach to the Study of Human Biological Variability and Prehistoric Behavior.* Scientific Papers No. 2. Northwestern University Archeological Program, Evanston, Illinois.

1991 Out of the Appendix and into the Dirt: Comments on Thirteen Years of Bioarchaeological Research. In *What Mean These Bones? Studies in Southeastern Bioarchaeology*, edited by Mary L. Powell, Patricia S. Bridges, and Ann Marie W. Mires, pp. 172–189. University of Alabama Press, Tuscaloosa.

2003 Advice and Cautionary Tales: A Case Study from a Career in Bioarchaeology. Paper presented at the twelfth annual Women in Science and Engineering conference, Texas A&M University, College Station.

Buikstra, Jane E., and Douglas K. Charles

1999 Centering the Ancestors: Cemeteries, Mounds, and Sacred Landscapes of the Ancient American Midcontinent. In *Archaeologies of Landscape: Contemporary Perspectives*, edited by Wendy Ashmore and A. Bernard Knapp, pp. 201–228. Blackwell Publishers, Oxford.

Buikstra, Jane E., and Lyle Konigsberg

1985 Paleodemography: Critiques and Controversies. *American Anthropologist* 87(2):316–333.

Buikstra, Jane E., Lyle Konigsberg, and Jill Bullington

1986 Fertility and the Development of Agriculture in the Prehistoric Midwest. *American Antiquity* 51(4):528–546.

Buikstra, Jane E., and James H. Mielke

1985 Demography, Diet, and Health. In *The Analysis of Prehistoric Diets*, edited by Robert I. Gilbert Jr. and James H. Mielke, pp. 360–422. Academic Press, Orlando.

Callinicos, Alex

1995 *Theories and Narratives: Reflections on the Philosophy of History.* Duke University Press, Durham, North Carolina.

Charles, Douglas K., and Jane E. Buikstra

1983 Archaic Mortuary Sites in the Central Mississippi Drainage: Distribution, Structure, and Behavioral Implications. In *Archaic Hunters and Gatherers in the American Midwest*, edited by James L. Phillips and James A. Brown, pp. 117–146. Academic Press, New York.

2002 Siting, Sighting, and Citing the Dead. In *The Space and Place of Death*, edited by Helaine Silverman and David B. Small, pp. 13–26. Archaeological Papers No. 11. American Anthropological Association, Arlington, Virginia.

Charles, Douglas K., Julieann van Nest, and Jane E. Buikstra

2004 From the Earth: Minerals and Meaning in the Hopewellian World. In *Soils, Stones and Symbols: Cultural Perceptions of the Mineral World*, edited by Nicole Boivin and Mary Ann Owoc, pp. 43–70. UCL Press, London.

Davis, Kingsley, and Wilbert E. Moore

1998 [1945] Some Principles of Stratification. In *Social Class and Stratification: Classic Statements and Theoretical Debates*, edited by Rhonda F. Levine, pp. 86–98. Rowman and Littlefield, Lanham, Maryland.

Dickson, David

1979 Science and Political Hegemony in the Seventeenth Century. *Radical Science Journal* 8:7–37.

Gailey, Christine W.

1987 *Kinship to Kingship: Gender Hierarchy and State Formation in the Islands.* University of Texas Press, Austin.

Konigsberg, Lyle W., and Jane E. Buikstra

1995 Regional Approaches to the Investigation of Past Human Biocultural Structure. In *Regional Approaches to Mortuary Analysis*, edited by Lane Beck, pp. 191–219. Plenum Press, New York.

Konigsberg, Lyle, Jane E. Buikstra, and Jill Bullington

1989 Paleodemographic Correlates of Fertility: A Reply to Corruccini, Brandon, and Handler and to Handler. *American Antiquity* 54(4):626–636.

Lozada, María C., and Jane E. Buikstra

2005 *Pescadores* and *Labradores* Among the *Señorío* of Chiribaya in Southern Peru. In *Us and Them: Archaeology and Ethnicity in the Andes*, edited by Richard M. Reycraft pp. 206–225. Monograph 53. Cotsen Institute of Archaeology Press, UCLA.

Macpherson, Crawford B.

1978 *Property: Mainstream and Critical Positions.* University of Toronto Press, Toronto.

Roberts, Charlotte A., and Jane E. Buikstra

2003 *The Bioarchaeology of Tuberculosis: A Global View on a Reemerging Disease.* University Press of Florida, Gainesville.

Ryan, Alan

1984 *Property and Political Theory.* Basil Blackwell, Oxford.

2

LIFE IN PRINT: THE PUBLICATION RECORD OF JANE E. BUIKSTRA

GORDON F. M. RAKITA
DEPARTMENT OF SOCIOLOGY & ANTHROPOLOGY, UNIVERSITY OF NORTH FLORIDA

IN 1976, AT THE SOUTHERN ANTHROPOLOGICAL Society meetings in Atlanta, Jane E. Buikstra first used the term *bioarchaeology* to define "a new form of regionally based, interdisciplinary research in mortuary site archaeology and human osteology" (Buikstra 1977a:69). With her paper in 1976 and the publication of an expanded version the following year, Buikstra initiated a novel research perspective in archaeology. The bioarchaeological approach is regional and diachronic in scope, is based in the analysis of populations rather than individuals, is biocultural in outlook, is explanatory rather than simply descriptive, and, above all, emphasizes answering anthropological research questions not simply archaeological or physical anthropological ones. More than anything else, the approach is concerned with understanding humanity through archaeological remains, human skeletal biology, and that uniquely social aspect of humanity, funerary and ritual behavior.

In defining bioarchaeology, Buikstra emphasized that prehistoric mortuary practices and the excavation strategies of archaeologists can have a profound effect on interpretations of osteologically derived data. In a similar fashion, biological anthropology and the analyses of osteologists can provide incredible insights to archaeologists seeking to understand the human condition of prehistoric populations. Thus it is imperative that archaeologists and physical anthropologists work cooperatively in developing research strategies. In this way, Buikstra encouraged a generation of physical anthropologists to learn the methods and theories of archaeology so as to more fully contextualize their results. Furthermore, bioarchaeology had the effect of enriching the research results of both archaeologists and physical anthropologists. In this way, the bioarchaeological approach advocates moving sterile osteological descriptions out of appendices of archaeological site reports and synthetically integrating them with archaeological interpretations. Thus the inspiration of the bioarchaeological perspective was its explicit multidisciplinary viewpoint, which brought together facets of both physical anthropology and archaeology. In this way Buikstra has significantly enhanced multidisciplinary awareness and cooperation within anthropology. Moreover, the role of bioarchaeology and bioarchaeologists in contemporary archaeology (in both academia and the private sector) is testament to the enduring impact her multidisciplinary approach has had and continues to have on the field. More than thirty years later, Buikstra's definition has fundamentally changed how archaeologists view the research potential of human remains.

Far from simply defining the bioarchaeological approach, Buikstra has been instrumental in publishing the foundational works in that approach. Her impressive publication record includes more than 150 individual articles and chapters and more than a dozen edited or authored volumes, spanning more than 35 years and covering a tremendous range of topics, including paleopathology, paleodemography, prehistoric diet, health reconstruction, soil chemistry, bone microstructure, biological distance and ancient DNA, ethnicity, forensic anthropology, mortuary ritual, and general archaeology. She has published on materials from the American midcontinent and Southwest, as well as from the Andes, Spain, and Mesoamerica. Her publications also span a wide range of contributions, including theoretical, methodological, and empirical. Finally, she has coauthored with more than 125 different people in a range of fields. Clearly, part of her influence on the discipline, in terms of publications, is her demonstrated commitment to collaborating with a wide range of scholars on an equally wide range of topics and materials. She leads here by eminent example.

Many of her publications are considered seminal works within the diverse range of her expertise. For example, her publication (with Douglas Ubelaker in 1994) of *Standards for Data Collection from Human Skeletal Remains* presciently saw the impending need for consistent, uniform data collection standards in the era of NAGPRA. However, she has also published fundamental works in paleopathology (with Della Cook in 1980) and has continued to pursue this work both on specific disease conditions (for example, her work with Charlotte Roberts on tuberculosis in 2003) and on general methods in paleopathology such as differential diagnosis (e.g., Buikstra 1977b). Her work in paleodemography (for example, with Lyle Konigsberg in 1985) has been instrumental in moving the approach through a period of stagnation and critique and into a more promising era. Starting with her dissertation and continuing throughout her career, Buikstra has been on the cutting edge of biological distance studies. This focus has continued and in recent years has moved into the complex process of ancient DNA methods. Equally consistent has been her interest in the use of chemical analysis of human bone for reconstructing prehistoric lifeways. Indeed, she has collaborated with Joseph Lambert and others to develop models of dietary reconstruction using both trace elemental and stable light isotopes data. More recently, she has been on the vanguard (Buikstra et al. 1989) in using heavy isotope ratios to identify prehistoric migration patterns. Her work with materials at the origins of agriculture revolutionized our thinking on this important transition for humanity. As noted in the citation for her election to the National Academy of Sciences in 1987,

> Buikstra developed new and more rigorous methods for assessing, from osteological remains, the health and demographic characteristics of prehistoric populations. By the application of these methods to skeletal remains she demonstrated that, contrary to current theory, intensive agriculture in prehistoric American societies often resulted in declining health and longevity.

Buikstra has had a long-standing interest in human ritual behavior, particularly mortuary practices. She has contributed centrally to each of the major mortuary archaeology volumes published in the last thirty years (Beck 1995; Chapman et al. 1981; Rakita et al. 2005). She has also contributed to the emerging interest in ethnicity in archaeology with her recent publication on Andean ethnogenesis. One final example of her influential publication record is that she literally published the book on bioarchaeology (with Lane Beck in 2006): *Bioarchaeology: The Contextual Analysis of Human Remains*. No matter which aspect of bioarchaeology a researcher might be interested in, Buikstra's publications have been foundational.

In this chapter I present my examination of the trends and patterns in Buikstra's publication record. I give special attention to the nature of her publications, be they theoretical, methodological, or empirical, and the geographic and topical coverage of each publication. I drew my inspiration for this study from Buikstra herself. Having been her student and research assistant, and now her colleague, I know that she has made use of the historical examination of publishing trends within the field. Indeed, I remember days spent in library reference sections checking the Social Sciences Citation Index and making hash marks next to lists of particular publications. She has made use of citation and publication data to examine the history and development of biological distance studies (Buikstra et al. 1990), human osteology (Stojanowski and Buikstra 2005), approaches to ritual and religion in American archaeology (Rakita and Buikstra 2008), the careers of colleagues (Buikstra and Maples 1999), and the field of bioarchaeology itself (Buikstra et al. 2003).

DATA SET

To examine Buikstra's publishing record, I began with a copy of her curriculum vitae. From her vitae, I coded into a database file characteristics of each of her publications. Specifically, I entered data on all monographs, books, articles, and book chapters published by Buikstra between 1973 and 2005. I did not include book reviews or technical reports in my examination. Nor did I examine the dozen-plus publications listed as "in press," "in preparation," or "accepted for publication" on her vitae as of May 2005. Subsequently, I imported the data into the Statistical Package for the Social Sciences (SPSS). As a further window into Buikstra's publication patterns, I collated a list of all her coauthors for the 1973 to 2005 period and noted how often they had published with her. Finally, I obtained a list of all her doctoral students up to 2005 and calculated how many times each one had published with her, noting each person's sex and from which institution he or she had received a doctorate. The charts and tables presented below are drawn from this data set.

In coding each of Buikstra's publications, I examined a set of characteristics for each work (Table 2.1). To begin, I coded the year, decade, and half decade that each work was published. Second, I identified the type of publication—that is, journal article, book, book chapter, or other type of publication. I coded Buikstra's authorship role, be it editor, single author, first author of a multiple-author work, or secondary author of a multiple-author work. I coded each publication in terms of scope: whether it is primarily an empirical, methodological, theoretical, or historical contribution to the literature. In some cases, works crossed these various scopes, so a "mixed" category was included. Similarly, I made a determination of the primary topical focus of each work. I developed seven topical categories, including biodistance, chemical analysis, demography, forensics, mortuary analysis, nutrition or diet, and pathology and disease. To these were added another "mixed" category (as with the scope variable) and an "other" category. Finally, I coded the regional focus of each publication, be it European, Mesoamerican, South American, or U.S. mid-continental. (Another

Table 2.1. Basic Publishing Patterns of Jane E. Buikstra.

		1970s	1980s	1990s	2000s	Total
Type	Article	10 (66.7%)	29 (56.9%)	15 (39.5%)	15 (37.5%)	69 (47.9%)
	Book	2 (13.3%)	3 (5.9%)	3 (7.9%)	5 (12.5%)	13 (9.0%)
	Chapter	3 (20.0%)	17 (33.3%)	20 (52.6%)	19 (47.5%)	59 (41.0%)
	Other	0 (0.0%)	2 (3.9%)	0 (0.0%)	1 (2.5%)	3 (2.1%)
Authorship	Editor	0 (0.0%)	3 (5.9%)	2 (5.3%)	3 (7.5%)	8 (5.6%)
	Multiple (first author)	2 (13.3%)	12 (23.5%)	11 (28.9%)	7 (17.5%)	32 (22.2%)
	Multiple (secondary author)	6 (40.0%)	28 (54.9%)	17 (44.7%)	26 (65.0%)	77 (53.5%)
	Single	7 (46.7%)	8 (15.7%)	8 (21.1%)	4 (10.0%)	27 (18.8%)
Scope	Empirical	6 (40.0%)	20 (39.2%)	14 (36.8%)	10 (25.0%)	50 (34.7%)
	Historical	1 (6.7%)	2 (3.9%)	3 (7.9%)	4 (10.0%)	10 (6.9%)
	Methodological	3 (20.0%)	17 (33.3%)	8 (21.1%)	8 (20.0%)	36 (25.0%)
	Mixed	3 (20.0%)	12 (23.5%)	12 (31.6%)	14 (35.0%)	41 (28.5%)
	Theoretical	2 (13.3%)	0 (0.0%)	1 (2.6%)	4 (10.0%)	7 (4.9%)
Topic	Biodistance	2 (13.3%)	6 (11.8%)	3 (7.9%)	1 (2.5%)	12 (8.3%)
	Chemical	3 (20.0%)	9 (17.6%)	5 (13.2%)	3 (7.5%)	20 (13.9%)
	Demography	0 (0.0%)	4 (7.8%)	1 (2.6%)	1 (2.5%)	6 (4.2%)
	Forensics	0 (0.0%)	3 (5.9%)	3 (7.9%)	2 (5.0%)	8 (5.6%)
	Mixed topic	3 (20.0%)	17 (33.3%)	13 (34.2%)	14 (35.0%)	47 (32.6%)
	Mortuary analysis	1 (6.7%)	3 (5.9%)	6 (15.8%)	8 (20.0%)	18 (12.5%)
	Nutrition/diet	1 (6.7%)	1 (2.0%)	0 (0.0%)	0 (0.0%)	2 (1.4%)
	Other	0 (0.0%)	5 (9.8%)	1 (2.6%)	1 (2.5%)	7 (4.9%)
	Pathology/disease	5 (33.3%)	3 (5.9%)	6 (15.8%)	10 (25.0%)	24 (16.7%)
Region	Europe (Spain)	0 (0.0%)	1 (2.0%)	6 (15.8%)	1 (2.5%)	8 (5.6%)
	Mesoamerica (Maya)	0 (0.0%)	0 (0.0%)	1 (2.6%)	5 (12.5%)	6 (4.2%)
	Mid-continental (Illinois)	7 (46.7%)	17 (33.3%)	5 (13.2%)	11 (27.5%)	40 (27.8%)
	Other	8 (53.3%)	28 (54.9%)	17 (44.7%)	9 (22.5%)	62 (43.1%)
	South America (Andes)	0 (.0%)	5 (9.8%)	9 (23.7%)	14 (35.0%)	28 (19.4%)
Total		**15 (100.0%)**	**51 (100.0%)**	**38 (100.0%)**	**40 (100.0%)**	**144 (100.0%)**

Note: Percentages represent proportion for the decade.

"other" category was included here.) In all, I coded 144 publications.

For example, the well-known *Standards* volume edited by Buikstra and Douglas Ubelaker (Buikstra and Ubelaker 1994) was coded as Type: *Book*, Authorship: *Editor*, Scope: *Methodological*, Topic: *Mixed*, Region: *Other*. Her 1976 article in the *American Journal of Physical Anthropology* on Caribou Eskimo disease was coded as Type: *Article*, Authorship: *Single*, Scope: *Empirical*, Topic: *Pathology*, Region: *Other*. Finally, her 1979 contribution to the *Hopewell Archaeology* volume was coded as Type: *Chapter*, Authorship: *Single*, Scope: *Historical*, Topic: *Mixed*, Region: *Mid-Continental*.

It is important to recognize that these are my own interpretations of these publications. Other individuals, perhaps more familiar with specific publications, would code them differently. Indeed, Buikstra herself would surely disagree with some of the categories in which I have placed her publications. Moreover, by selecting only one topic, region, or scope for each publication, I am obscuring meaningful variation and nuance in many of her publications. However, I believe the data as gathered are useful for the broad approach I take here.

BASIC PUBLISHING PATTERNS

Table 2.1 presents frequency data for all publications in the data set for the basic categories coded. For example, most of Buikstra's publications have either been journal articles (48 percent) or chapters in books (41 percent). She has been the editor of eight books and a first or only author for 59 publications (41 percent of all her publications). In terms of publication scope, empirical, methodological, and mixed-approach works are most common. Mixed-topic publications dominate, as would be expected of an interdisciplinary bioarchaeologist who regularly integrates various biological and cultural data to understand the human condition. Finally, as she has worked longest in the U.S. mid-continent, this region is the most common geographic focus of her publications, though South America runs a close second.

A series of bivariate comparisons of the five characteristics of Buikstra's works provides further information about her publishing patterns. For example, a comparison of the frequencies of the various types of publication by scope shows that her methodological papers are more often published as journal articles. Alternatively, book chapters are the overwhelming venue for those publications with mixed scope. Cross-tabulating her authorship roles across the various publication scopes demonstrates

Table 2.2. Scholars with Buikstra Numbers of 1.

Allison, M.
Alon, D.
Ambrose, S.
Anton, S.
Arriaza, B.
Asch, D.
Aufderheide, A.
Autry, W.
Baker, B.
Beck, L.
Ben Itzhak, S.
Ben Yosef, A.
Blom, D.
Boldsen, J.
Bradtmiller, D.
Braunstein, E.
Breitberg, E.
Bullington, J.
Burgi, P.
Burton, J.
Cartmell, L.
Casto M., P.
Chapman, R.
Charles, D.
Cheverud, J.
Clark, N.
Condon, K.
Conrad, G.
Cook, D.
DeRousseau, C. J.
Dijema, J.
Dittmar, K.
Eisenberg, L.
Ekberg, F.
Ericson, J.
Fornaciari, G.
Frankenberg, S.
Gale, N.
Goldberg, P.
Goldstein, L.
Goldstein, P.
Gonzalez M., P.
Gordon, C.
Grant, A.
Grigson, C.
Guhl, F.
Guillen, S.
Hallgrimmsson, B.
Hanson, D.
Ho, J.
Holcomb, T.
Holl, A.
Hoshower, L.
Indriati, E.
Janusek, J.
Johnson, D.
Jones, M.
Keng, L.
King, J.
Knudson, K.
Komar, D.
Konigsberg, L.
Krueger, H.
Lambert, J.
Leigh, S.
Levy, T.
Lozada C., M. C.
Lull, V.
Madden, M.
Magennis, A.
Maples, M.
Martinson, E.
McGrath, J.
McLaughlin, C.
Mico, R.
Mielke, J.
Milner, G.
Nystrom, K.
Picazo, M.
Price, T. D.
Ragsdale, B.
Rakita, G.
Rathbun, T.
Reinhard, K.
Renier, C.
Rice, D.
Richtsmeier, J.
Risch, R.
Roberts, C.
Rose, J.
Rosen, S.
Rowan, Y.
Ruiz, M.
Sabari, P.
Salo, W.
Sanahuja, M.
Shater, S.
Shoreman, E.
Simpson, S.
Smith, P. Springfield, A.
Stevens-Tuttle, D.
Stojanowski, C.
Stos-Gale, S.
Streitz, J.
Swegle, M.
Szpunar, C.
Thomet, A.
Tomczak, P.
Torres P., E.
Twichell, E.
Ubelaker, D
van der Merwe, N.
van der Sman, P.
van Vark, G.
van Nest, J.
Vinh, T.
Vlasak, S.
Webster, A.
Weems, C.
Weiner, S.
Weydert, J.
Wilbur, A.
Williams, S.
Wittmers, L.
Wright, L.
Xue, L.

that on empirical and methodological papers, she is often a secondary author, while she is a single or first author of theoretical or historical papers. Moving on to type of publication by topic, Buikstra's publications dealing with biodistance, chemical analysis, forensics, and disease are frequently journal articles. In contrast, mixed-topic and mortuary analysis papers are more likely to be chapters in books or books themselves. Only two publications were recorded as dealing with nutrition or diet, and both of these were book chapters. In terms of authorship by topic, she was overwhelmingly a secondary author on publications dealing with biodistance and chemical analysis. As to type of publication by region of focus, there is a wider range of publication types in those regions where Buikstra has been working longest, especially the U.S. mid-continent and South America. Comparing topical focus and region, there is also a great variety of publication topics for these two regions, in contrast to those publications dealing with Mesoamerican and European materials.

Temporal Trends

Table 2.1 also breaks down these various publication characteristics over time, specifically decades. The table provides a temporal perspective on Buikstra's work. For example, book chapters have been a significant portion of her publication types over the last three decades. Indeed, in the last two decades, they represent approximately half of all her publications. Journal articles were the largest proportion of her publications during the 1970s and 1980s. Their frequency within the last two decades has declined, but they still remain a large portion of her publications (more than 35 percent in both decades). Books are becoming an increasing portion of her written works, with the 1990s seeing her publish five, amounting to 12.5 percent of her publications that decade. In terms of authorship, while edited books and single-author works have always been a portion of Buikstra's publications, what stands out most significantly is that she has definitely been a collaborative publisher, whether as a first or secondary author on multiple-author works. Multiple-author works have constituted more than 70 percent of her publications in the last three decades.

In terms of scope, Buikstra has always been a proponent of publishing empirical data; she sees this as one of the most fundamental contributions she can make to the discipline. In each of the four decades, empirical reports represented at least one-quarter of all her publications, and even more during the 1970s and 1980s. Methodological works are also a perennial aspect of her publishing. At least one-fifth of her publications were methodologically focused; in the 1980s this focus jumped to one-third. Buikstra's theoretical publications cluster in the 1970s, at the beginning of her career, and in the current decade. Her historical publications have witnessed a steady increase through time. As expected for an interdisciplinary researcher, her publications of a mixed empirical, methodological, historical, and theoretical scope represent anywhere from one-fifth to one-third of her publications in any given decade.

The most interesting trends, to my view, are those of the topic and regional focuses of Buikstra's publications. Topically, there are numerous trends, and these are shown best in Figure 2.1, which displays counts of her various publications by topic across the four decades. Chemical and biodistance studies saw their peak in the 1980s, yet these topics still represent a significant part of her work. Demographic studies were also most common during the 1980s. Over the past three decades, she has maintained a publishing agenda in the forensic sciences. Publications coded as dealing with nutrition and diet, on the other hand, have been absent for the past twenty years. This may be an artifact of my coding of certain works or it may be that Buikstra's paleodietary work is embedded within those publications coded as having a mixed topic. These mixed-focus publications are by far the most common, especially in the past three decades. Mortuary analyses and publications on diseases or pathologies are on the rise, reaching their highest frequency in the 2000s.

Figure 2.2 displays counts of Buikstra's publications broken down by regional focus and decade. Given her early interest and work in the lower Illinois River valley, it is not surprising to see that she has always been active in publishing on the U.S. mid-continental region. In particular, the 1980s and 2000s show surges of publications related to this region. Clearly, she has not had her final say on prehistoric Hopewell and Mississippian cultures. Since beginning work in southern Peru, she has also had an increasing role in Andean archaeology. Her publication record in this regard shows an ever-increasing publishing agenda. Publications relating to Spanish materials peaked in the 1990s, highlighting her involvement in research related to Bronze Age settlements in southern Spain. Finally, the 2000s show a sharp upswing in publications related to the Mayan

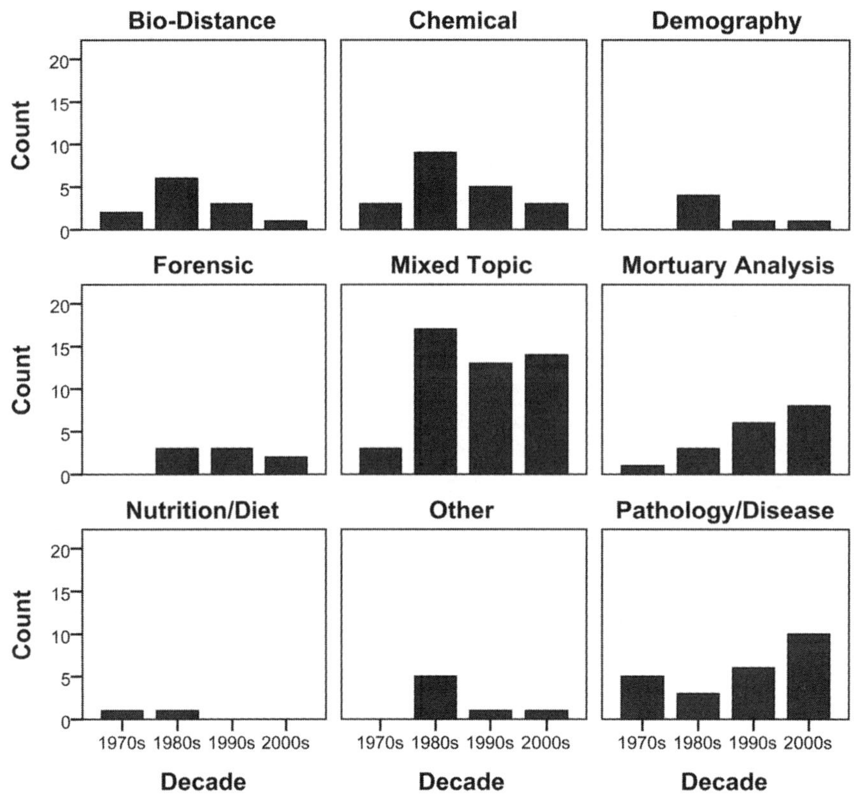

Figure 2.1. Counts of Buikstra's publications by topic and decade.

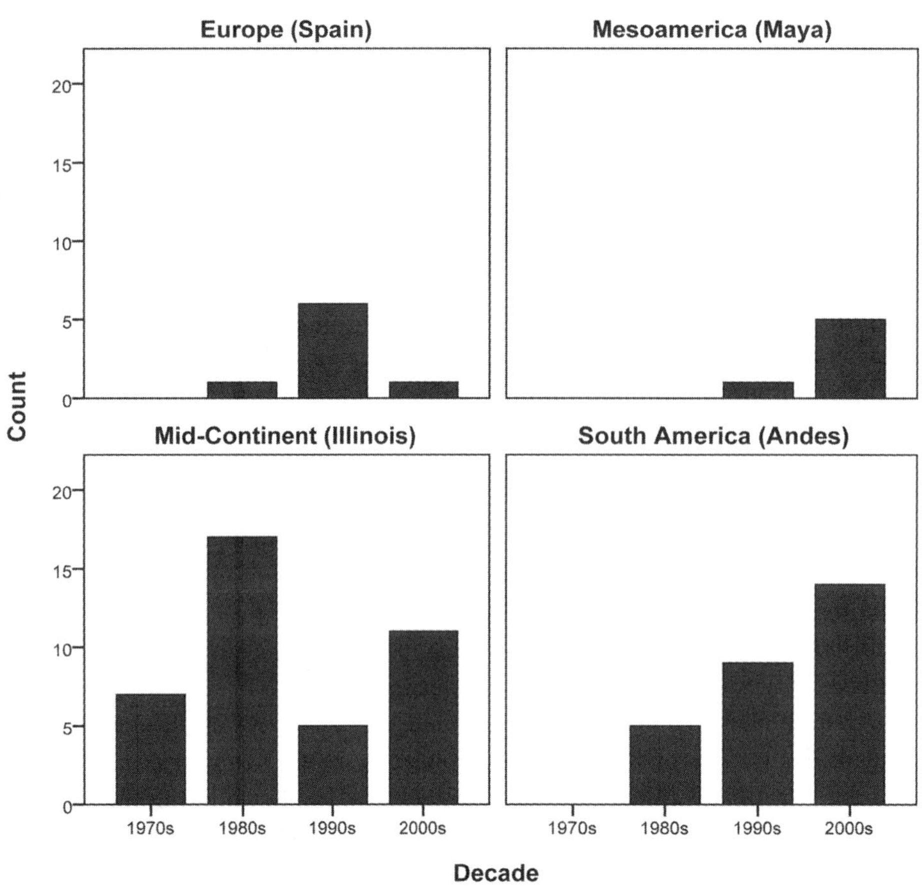

Figure 2.2. Counts of Buikstra's publications by region and decade.

region, illustrating Buikstra's more recent engagement in research in that area.

COLLABORATING AND COAUTHORING

More than 75 percent of Buikstra's publications explored in this study were multiple-author works. By May 2005 she had coauthored with 127 different people. Clearly part of her influence on the discipline, in terms of publication, is her willingness to collaborate with a wide range of scholars on an equally wide range of topics and materials. To casually explore this aspect of her publishing, I would like to introduce a numerical publishing statistical method.

Here I suggest the "Buikstra number"—that is, a simple count of how many times an individual has published with Buikstra (Tables 2.2 and 2.3). High Buikstra numbers indicate a stronger publishing connection with her. Table 2.3 provides lists of scholars with Buikstra numbers over 2 as of May 2005. For example, Paula Tomczak has twice coauthored with Buikstra; thus her Buikstra number is 2. Joseph Lambert has the highest Buikstra number at 15, with Doug Charles as the second most frequent coauthor with 14.

These Buikstra numbers also allow us to assess a variety of other aspects of Buikstra's coauthoring. For example, the data show that publishing a book with her is slightly predictive of a higher number of coauthored articles or chapters. Those who have coauthored or coedited two books with Buikstra have an average of 8.5 other publications with her; those who have published one book with her have an average of 3.00 other publications; and those who have not published a book with her have an average of 1.96. Buikstra seems to publish more frequently with her Ph.D. students, although there are exceptions. Those who coauthored with Buikstra and were her doctoral students published with her an average of 3.68 times. Nonstudent coauthors, on the other hand, published with her an average of 1.91 times. These data can also be used to explore how much she has published with her students from the various institutions at which she has taught. The data show that on average, she published slightly more often with Northwestern (2.47) students than with her New Mexico (1.75) or Chicago (1.00) students. However, these averages are being draw upward by outliers such as Doug Charles, Sloan Williams, Lyle Konigsberg, María Cecilia Lozada Cerna, and Deborah Blom because of multiple collaborations. Thus a more accurate estimate would be the median number of coauthorships for students from each school. In this case, New Mexico ranks first (1.50), followed by Northwestern (1.00) and finally Chicago (.00). It should be noted that she also had many more students at the latter two institutions, and many of them did not coauthor with her, thus decreasing both means and medians for these samples. Additionally, I examined whether she was more likely to have published with male or female students. A student's T-test and a nonparametric Mann-Whitney Test do not indicate a statistically significant difference between the number of publications she coauthored with females and males. Indeed, of the twelve former students who have the most coauthored publications with Buikstra (two or more publications), six are females and six are males.

Table 2.3. Scholars with Buikstra Numbers over 1.

Buikstra Number > 3	Buikstra Number of 3	Buikstra Number of 2
Lambert, 15	Arriaza	Alon
Charles, 14	Bullington	Braunstein
Cheverud, 10	Casto M.	Cartmell
Aufderheide, 8	Chapman	Eisenberg
Konigsberg, 7	Clark	Goldberg
Williams, 7	Condon	Grigson
Cook, 6	Frankenberg	Hanson
Lozada C., 6	Goldstein	Holl
Simpson, 6	Gonzalez M.	Keng
Blom, 5	Lull	Knudson
Nystrom, 5	Picazo	Levy
Szpunar, 5	Price	Roberts
Gordon, 4	Rakita	Rose
Hoshower, 4	Reinhard	Salo
Milner, 4	Risch	Smith
Xue, 4	Sanahuja	Tomczak
	Springfield	Torres P.
	Stojanowski	Van Nest
		Weems

CONCLUSIONS

The publications listed on Buikstra's 22-page curriculum vitae demonstrate the incredible quantity, scope, and scale of her scholarship in bioarchaeology. Her wide-ranging list of works spans the full breadth of bioarchaeological topics, including chemical analysis, mortuary practices, paleodemography and paleopathology, forensic anthropology, and biodistance studies. Her work deals with data from three continents. She has been equally comfortable making empirical, methodological, theoretical, and historical contributions. She has more than 140 publications to her credit, with more than 125 coauthors.

However, far from simply publishing in the field, Buikstra has nurtured the bioarchaeological approach. She has consistently sought funding for her research and collaborative efforts. Her curriculum vitae shows that she has served as principal or co-principal investigator on 14 separate National Science Foundation research grants (from both the archaeology and physical anthropology directorates). She has also been a supervisor on more than a dozen NSF dissertation improvement grants. She has received funding from the Wenner-Gren Foundation, the National Geographic Society, and the Federal Emergency Management Agency, to name but a few. As successful grant proposals are reviewed by disciplinary peers, Buikstra's success in this regard is a tangible measure of the approval of her research strategies by fellow anthropologists. Moreover, the financial support these various grants provided allowed her and her colleagues to develop novel methodological approaches and to bridge disciplinary boundaries.

Buikstra's impact upon the field of archaeology and her nurturing of multidisciplinary cooperation perhaps can best be seen in the students she has trained. In her recent remarks upon receiving the American Association of Physical Anthropology's Darwin Award, she noted that it was her students who have most influenced her career. She has advised 42 students through their Ph.D. studies. While each student's specific research may fall within either the archaeological or physical anthropology subfield, each has been trained to be a multidisciplinary researcher. Each is continuing in that same vein to train the next generation of bioarchaeologists. Indeed, it is testament to her influence that she currently works collaboratively with Anne Stone (at Arizona State University), who is herself a student of George Milner (Buikstra's fourth Ph.D. student).

Buikstra has also contributed throughout her career with dedicated and consistent service to both the public and the four subfields of anthropology. Her curriculum vitae shows her service to the American Anthropological Association in a variety of capacities, including as president from 1989 to 1991, shepherding the association through turbulent times. She has likewise served as president of the American Association of Physical Anthropologists (1985 to 1987), the Paleopathology Association (2003 to 2005), and the Illinois Archaeological Survey (1977 to 1978). She has served on the American Association for the Advancement of Science's nominations committee and on the ethics committee and executive board of the American Board of Forensic Anthropology. She served on the board of directors of the Archaeological Conservancy from 1986 to 1991 and on the search committee for the executive director of the Society for American Archaeology in 1992. She has also served as a forensic consultant for numerous local medical examiner offices and has served as an external reviewer for more than 25 academic departments. She has served on the editorial boards of more than seven professional journals, including the *Journal of Anthropological Research*, the *Journal of Forensic Anthropology and Archaeology*, the *International Journal of Osteoarchaeology*, *Evolutionary Anthropology*, and the *Journal of Anthropological Archaeology*. She was a founding member and served on the board of directors of the Society for Professional Archaeologists (now the Register of Professional Archaeologists) and was recently the founding editor of the new *International Journal of Paleopathology*.

Perhaps most illustrative of her nurturing both archaeology and bioarchaeology is her involvement with two important research centers. She is the director of the Center for American Archaeology in Kampsville, Illinois, and the founding director of the Center for Bioarchaeological Research at Arizona State University. Buikstra sees the CBR as an interdisciplinary anthropological endeavor with strong links to the physical and natural sciences, biomedicine, the social sciences, and the humanities. When asked about the CBR she stated, "I am very excited about building a research center focused upon issue-based bioarchaeological investigations. One of our challenges is to bring knowledge of the deep past to problems that face humankind today and tomorrow" (Rakita 2005:10).

Buikstra's career defining, building the foundations of, and nurturing the interdisciplinary field of bioarchaeology exemplifies the important spirit and role of multidisciplinary cooperation in archaeology. Her work has significantly increased the awareness and application of interdisciplinary research in archaeology. Buikstra once was described (in a series of biographies of past AAA presidents) as "remain[ing] committed to the breadth of anthropology as a discipline whose core value is tolerance—both of multiple approaches within the field and of the diversity of humankind" (Darnell 2002:284). Her call for "mutually designed research strategies" in which bioarchaeologists are able to develop and implement research that uses theories and techniques from archaeology, physical anthropology, and numerous other scientific disciplines and that seeks to answer broadly anthropological questions is one of the most significant contributions to interdisciplinary archaeology in America. Her definition of the approach, her fundamental publishing in the field, and her continued meaningful service to the field have extensively increased awareness of interdisciplinary studies in archaeology.

REFERENCES CITED

Beck, Lane A. (editor)
1995 *Regional Approaches to Mortuary Analysis*. Plenum Press, New York.

Buikstra, Jane E.
1976 The Caribou Eskimo: General and Specific Disease. *American Journal of Physical Anthropology* 45(3):351–367.
1977a Biocultural Dimensions of Archeological Study: A Regional Perspective. In *Biocultural Adaptation in Prehistoric America*, edited by Robert L. Blakely, pp. 67–84. Southern Anthropological Society Proceedings No. 11. University of Georgia Press, Athens.
1977b Differential Diagnosis: An Epidemiological Model. *Yearbook of Physical Anthropology* 20:316–328.
1979 Contributions of Physical Anthropologists to the Concept of Hopewell: A Historical Perspective. In *Hopewell Archaeology: The Chillicothe Conference*, edited by D. S. Brose and N. Greber, pp. 220–233. Kent State University Press, Kent State, Ohio.

Buikstra, Jane E., and Lane A. Beck (editors)
2006 *Bioarchaeology: The Contextual Analysis of Human Remains*. Academic Press, New York.

Buikstra, Jane E., and Della C. Cook
1980 Palaeopathology: An American Account. *Annual Review of Anthropology* 9:433–470.

Buikstra, Jane E., Susan R. Frankenberg, Joseph B. Lambert, and Liang Xue
1989 Multiple Elements: Multiple Expectations. In *The Chemistry of Prehistoric Human Bone*, edited by T. D. Price, pp. 155–210. Cambridge University Press, Cambridge.

Buikstra, Jane E., Susan R. Frankenberg, and Lyle W. Konigsberg
1990 Skeletal Biological Distance Studies in American Physical Anthropology: Recent Trends. *American Journal of Physical Anthropology* 82:1–7.

Buikstra, Jane E., Jason L. King, and Kenneth C. Nystrom
2003 Forensic Anthropology and Bioarchaeology in the American Anthropologist: Rare but Exquisite Gems. *American Anthropologist* 105(1):38–52.

Buikstra, Jane E., and Lyle W. Konigsberg
1985 Paleodemography: Critiques and Controversies. *American Anthropologist* 87(2):316–333.

Buikstra, Jane E., and Margaret K. Maples
1999 The Life and Career of William R. Maples, Ph.D. *Journal of Forensic Sciences* (July):677–681.

Buikstra, Jane E., and Charlotte Roberts
2003 *The Bioarchaeology of Tuberculosis: A Global View on a Reemerging Disease*. University Press of Florida, Gainesville.

Buikstra, Jane E., and Douglas H. Ubelaker (editors)
1994 *Standards for Data Collection from Human Skeletal Remains: Proceedings of a Seminar at the Field Museum of Natural History*. Arkansas Archaeological Survey Press, Fayetteville.

Chapman, Robert, I. Kinnes, and Klavs Randsborg (editors)
1981 *Approaches to the Archaeology of Death*. Cambridge University Press, Cambridge.

Darnell, Regna
2002 Jane Buikstra 1990–1991. In *Celebrating a Century of the American Anthropological Association: Presidential Portraits*, edited by Regna Darnell and Frederick Wright Gleach, pp 281–284. American Anthropological Association, Arlington, Virginia.

Lambert, Joseph B., Carole B. Szpunar, and Jane E. Buikstra
1979 Chemical Analysis of Excavated Human Bone from Middle and Late Woodland Sites. *Archaeometry* 21:115–129.

Rakita, Gordon F. M., and Jane E. Buikstra (editors)
2008 *An Archaeological Perspective on Ritual, Religion, and Ideology from American Antiquity and Latin American Antiquity*. SAA Press, Washington, D.C.

Rakita, Gordon F.M.
2005 The Nature of Training in Bioarchaeology. *Society for Archaeological Sciences Bulletin* 28(4): 10–11.

Rakita, Gordon F. M., Jane E. Buikstra, Lane A. Beck, and Sloan R. Williams (editors)
2005 *Interacting with the Dead: Perspectives on Mortuary Archaeology for the New Millennium*. University Press of Florida, Gainesville.

Roberts, Charlotte A., and Jane E. Buikstra
2003 *The Bioarchaeology of Tuberculosis: A Global View on a Reemerging Disease*. University Press of Florida, Gainesville.

Stojanowski, Christopher M., and Jane E. Buikstra
2005 Research Trends in Human Osteology: A Content Analysis of Papers Published in the American Journal of Physical Anthropology. *American Journal of Physical Anthropology* 128(1):98–109.

3

Grave Concerns:
The Intersection of Biological and Social Approaches to the Archaeology of Cemeteries

Douglas K. Charles
Department of Anthropology, Wesleyan University

When Jane E. Buikstra was conducting her graduate research in the early 1970s, it seemed quite natural to analyze all aspects of cemeteries from the perspective of a comprehensive Darwinian metaphor. One domain was straightforward human biology; the other envisioned culture as part of the human phenotype, an "extrasomatic means of adaptation." Illustrative of this initiatory period of bioarchaeology are the title of the published version of Buikstra's dissertation, *Hopewell in the Lower Illinois Valley: A Regional Study of Human Biological Variability and Prehistoric Mortuary Behavior* (Buikstra 1976), and its chapter headings: "Introduction," "Age and Sex Determination," "Demography," "Status and Social Complexity," "Biological Distance," and "Summary and Conclusions." In the work of one researcher, we have biological analysis of skeletal remains (chapters 2, 3, and 5) and sociocultural analysis of funerary practices (chapter 4).

During the course of the last quarter century, cemeteries have increasingly been approached by one of two metaphors. Darwin is still with us when it comes to the skeletal material, but the sociocultural elements of mortuary behavior—in particular, the *meanings* of facility preparation, grave goods, and the spatial organization of a cemetery—are being explored by many archaeologists through a metaphor of interpretive sociology ultimately derived, directly or indirectly, from Marx. The use of these two metaphors has created a tension in the analysis of cemeteries. Should we seek to redefine a single framework, or is a dual approach preferable, or even possible?

Biology

In the preface to the recent volume *Bioarchaeology: The Contextual Analysis of Human Remains* (Buikstra and Beck 2006), Buikstra (2006a:xvii) asks, "What is 'bioarchaeology?'" The term was first used in Great Britain in the title of Graham Clark's (1972) *Starr Carr: A Case Study in Bioarchaeology*, where it referred to the study of archaeologically recovered biological materials (such as animal bones, mollusk shells, and plant remains). The term independently surfaced in the United States five years later in a volume titled, with a more or less synonymous first word, *Biocultural Adaptation in Prehistoric America* (Blakely 1977), which in turn echoed the title of an earlier paper by Van Gerven and coauthors (1974). In her contribution, Buikstra (1977:69) defined bioarchaeology as a multidisciplinary approach by which to address questions such as social organization, geography of genetic pools, diet, population density, health, and levels of interpersonal violence. She particularly emphasized the joint participation of human osteologists and archaeologists in all phases of research into cemeteries, even, as in her own practice, to the extent of the osteologist being the archaeologist. Thus *bio* meant biological anthropology in either terminology, while *archaeology* (or *cultural*) invoked the study of past cultures. By the early 1980s in Britain, the term *osteoarchaeology* had gained currency, referring to the study of both human and animal remains from archaeological contexts (Roberts 2006). For other perspectives on the development of these terms, see Armelagos (2003, 2008).

More recently, Larsen's (1997, 2002, 2006) conception of bioarchaeology has been widely adopted. For him, bioarchaeology is the study of past human biology, incorporating methods and specialists from other disciplines, such as geology, chemistry, physics, and engineering—although not necessarily archaeology. The involvement of archaeologists tends to end with their excavation of the skeletons (Goldstein 2006). Goldstein (2006:376) further notes that bioarchaeology has returned to a more explicit physical or biological anthropology, becoming "more science and laboratory oriented." Not surprisingly perhaps, Sofaer (2006) wishes to reunite osteology and archaeology, not as a collaborative enterprise in Buikstra's sense but as a synthetic "theoretical osteoarchaeology." While one can sympathize with Sofaer's (see also Goldstein 2006) frustration with the interpretative divide between a biologically based osteology and a humanities-derived interpretative archaeology, there are other possible resolutions.

Running through this brief history of conceptions of bioarchaeology (or biocultural study or osteoarchaeology) are several obvious dualities: American versus British disciplinary histories; scientific versus social or cultural analytical approaches; human versus animal. More broadly conceived, these oppositions reflect the deep structure of Cartesian dualism that purportedly haunts Western thought: science versus humanities; process versus structure; explanation versus understanding. Astuti (2001:430), directly addressing this phenomenon and the attempts to counter it, adds:

> consciousness vs. unconsciousness, thought vs. emotion, object vs. subject. In anthropology, of course, the mind-body dichotomy has been cast in terms of a dichotomy between culture and biology, or the many derivatives, such as the distinction between sex and gender, person and organism, individual and society. There are, therefore, as many anthropological claims for "monism" as there are versions of dualistic reasoning.

ARCHAEOLOGY

The history of funerary archaeology over the past 50 years parallels the more general history of Anglo-American archaeology. During roughly the first half of that period, prior to 1980, one grand theoretical framework sufficed for both biological and sociocultural interpretations of cemeteries. In the 1950s, the neo-Darwinian synthesis drove the transformation of physical anthropology into biological anthropology, instigated in large part by Washburn's (1951, 1953) call for a "new physical anthropology" based on population biology rather than typological approaches. Shortly thereafter, in the 1960s, Lewis Binford and others (Binford 1962; Binford and Binford 1968; Clark 1968) initiated what came to be called the New Archaeology (or processual archaeology), rejecting the classification focus of culture-historical archaeology typified by the work of James B. Griffin and others (e.g., Griffin 1952). Central to New Archaeology was White's (1949) concept of culture as *Homo sapiens*' "extra-somatic means of adaptation." The underlying paradigm or metaphor for both biological anthropology and processual archaeology was derived from Darwin's theory of evolution by natural selection. Integral to this project were concepts such as ecology, systems theory, sampling and statistical distributions, and the hypothetico-deductive model, in addition to adaptation (Johnson 2010; Trigger 2006; Willey and Sabloff 1993).

The archaeology of cemeteries was defined in this period by two works: Arthur Saxe's (1970) unpublished Ph.D. dissertation from the University of Michigan, "Social Dimensions of Mortuary Practices," and Binford's (1971) article "Mortuary Practices: Their Study and Their Potential." In line with the adaptive systems model of culture underwriting the New Archaeology, Binford argued that mortuary customs were not "random" culture-historical phenomena. That is, variation in funerary practices among different societies did not result from historical accidents. Patterns in burial treatments were systematically related to other variables. Based on the analysis of a cross-cultural sample of 40 societies classified in terms of organizational complexity as hunters and gatherers, shifting agriculturalists, settled agriculturalists, and pastoralists (following Murdock 1957), Binford (1971:23) concluded that (1) the number and (2) the specific dimensions of the *social persona* varied with social complexity, and (3) the "forms which differentiations in mortuary ritual take vary significantly with the dimensions of the *social persona* symbolized." Saxe's (1970) theoretical framework was more elaborately developed, but his sample included only three societies. His first seven hypotheses are largely elaborations on Binford's conclusions cited above. Saxe's (1970:119) Hypothesis 8—that the extent to which corporate control of resources is tied to lineal descent is correlated with the probability that formal places for the dead will be established—points in another direction (and has taken on a life of its own). The Saxe-Binford approach dominated mortuary archaeology in the United States for two decades.

Beginning in 1980, the Saxe-Binford model became a focal point for a postprocessual critique of archaeological theory and practice (e.g., Hodder 1980, 1982; Pader 1980, 1982; various authors in Hodder ed. 1982). Parker Pearson (1999) provides perhaps the most comprehensive Saxe-Binford critique and postprocessual reworking of an archaeology of death. The range of postprocessual approaches to funerary analysis does not lend itself to concise characterization, but early illustrations include Shanks and Tilley (1982) and Hodder (1984). Recent examples are seen in Arnold and Wicker (2002) and Gowland and Knüsel (2006b). As Parker Pearson concludes (1999:197):

> Archaeology has grown beyond attempts to explain all human life according to universal laws of behaviour. We now move towards the understanding and explanation of the past through more subtle ideas about human experience and perception. Archaeology can range across space and time to excavate and understand the many paths we make but, immanent in the diversity of life, there is one universal—death. We are all ultimately going in the same direction.

But are we—at least in the shorter haul?

DARWIN AND MARX

Darwin wrote *The Origin of Species* in England, and its subsequent development was predominantly in the English-speaking world. The Darwinian metaphor has been a strong presence in archaeology, especially during the last half of the twentieth century, notably in the processual concern with adaptation in the 1960s and 1970s (e.g., Binford 1962, 1968) and in the "roots" movement of the more recent selectionist approach (e.g., Barton et al. 1997; Dunnell 1980; O'Brien and Lyman 2000). In his later life, Marx also worked in England, although he wrote in German and was inspired by continental European thought. The Marxian metaphor is the more transformed of the two, having drifted from an early focus on materialism through the ideological bent of the Frankfurt School of critical theory to, in archaeology in particular, a concern with agency, meaning, context, the notion of material culture as text, and, most recently, phenomenology (e.g., Bender 1998; Hodder 1986; Shanks and Tilley 1987). Marxism occasionally inspired Anglo-American archaeology—the historical materialism of V. Gordon Childe in England in the early twentieth century and more subtly the incorporation of Leslie White's thought into the work of Binford and others (Patterson 2003; Trigger 2006). In general, however, the Marxian tradition resided on the continent, and it became a significant component of Anglophone archaeology only after 1980 (e.g., Hodder 1982b).

In practice, the antithetical positions that define much of Western thought have taken the form of the Darwinian and Marxian paradigms, or the biological and interpretative sociology metaphors, as Giddens (1984:1–2) identifies them, as expressed, for example, in the processual/postprocessual debates in Anglo-American archaeology in the final decades of the last century. The Darwinian metaphor is characterized by atomistic, ahistorical, abstract deductive, and prescriptive modes of Enlightenment thought; the Marxian metaphor embodies anti-Enlightenment sentiments, with holistic, historical, particularistic, and descriptive concerns (Charles 1992:909–910; see also Bloor 1976:54–57; Gibbon 1989:129–134). This paradigmatic opposition of Darwin and Marx developed in the twentieth century as others used their writings. Materialism and evolutionary change were central to both Darwin's and Marx's thought, and they did not see their work as antithetical (Foster 2000). Marx's conceptions are as modernist as Darwin's, and much of what now differentiates the two metaphors lies in postmodernist revisions of Marxian thought.

Questions thus arise: Are the Darwinian and Marxian metaphors now mutually exclusive? If this is the case, how does (or can) one researcher effectively shift between these two very distinctive manners of thought? Is the individual successfully compartmentalizing the use of the two metaphors, or are we witnessing cases of dissociative identity disorder, the condition associated with *Sybil* and *The Three Faces of Eve*? Alternatively, if the incompatibility of Darwinian and Marxian approaches has evolved over the course of the twentieth century, does a resolution lie in a new way of viewing Darwin and Marx?

To make what should be a very long discussion very short, we confront the distinction between nature and culture. In particular, we face the question of whether or not human social life can be studied scientifically. A Darwinian would answer yes; a Marxian would reply in the negative.[1] In the most extreme constructivist formulations of the latter, science in fact loses its privileged claim to knowledge. Not only is it inappropriate to apply Darwinian models to social behavior, it is problematic to use what can be argued to be a nineteenth-century economic model to describe nature. It was my attempt to imagine a constructivist of this ilk even engaging in a biological analysis of a skeletal population that led me to consider the relevance of dissociative identity disorder. Conversely, is a postmodern theory of evolution possible?

BIOLOGY AND ARCHAEOLOGY

Sofaer's (2006) goal is to unite osteoarchaeology and interpretative archaeology as a singular "theoretical osteoarchaeology." Osteoarchaeology is defined as the study of human bones alone and, significantly, "should be taken to include biological and physical anthropology" (Sofaer 2006:xvi). Interpretative archaeology is invoked in the sense of Hodder (e.g., 1991:15–16)—that is, an archaeology of meaning incorporating the material (real) nature of the past; a privileging of "emic" (not the term used by Hodder) perspectives but thereby making meaning local and public; and self-reflexivity and dialogue. Sofaer covers a wide range of topics—too wide to discuss in this chapter. I will focus on the main thrust of her argument: that there should be a theoretical archaeology, a synthesis of osteoarchaeology and interpretative archaeology.

Sofaer (2006:31–61) describes the differences between a science-oriented osteoarchaeology and a humanist-oriented interpretative archaeology (Table 3.1). The culminating nature–culture opposition mirrors the dualisms noted earlier in this chapter. She opposes an atheoretical osteoarchaeology against a theoretical interpretative archaeology. Gowland and Knüsel (2006a:ix) propagate this same formulation where they discuss science and *social* theory, but in a section actually titled "Science/theory divide." From this perspective, osteoarchaeology as science means that it is empirical and technical: "The osteological specialist is seen as being a dry technician . . . on the basis that the study of the physical body is mechanical in nature and executed according to a prescribed 'recipe book' of ideas and methods" (Sofaer 2006:33). This may seem an apt characterization in describing the relations between osteoarchaeologists and archaeologists in the United Kingdom and for that matter in the United States (Goldstein 2006). Larsen's (1997, 2002, 2006) view of bioarchaeology certainly reinforces this notion. To the extent that this is true, Sofaer's unification project is well considered. At the same time, as noted, Sofaer collapses biological/physical anthropology into osteoarchaeology. I (and I suspect most American biological anthropologists) view osteology (which would include its application to mortuary archaeology and its overlap with paleopathology) as one aspect of biological anthropology, alongside studies of human variability and adaptation, human and primate evolution, and primatology. In other words, biological anthropologists are generally and more appropriately perceived as biologists than as anthropologists. (In the United States, anthropology also includes archaeology and, less so now, linguistics.) This is so much the case that the lack of communication Sofaer sees between osteoarchaeologists and archaeologists really extends across anthropology and has led to severe rifts in the discipline in recent years (Holden 1993). This is not due to the fact that biological anthropologists are atheoretical, however. The failure to communicate relates to the fact that biological anthropology is highly theoretized, but it is Darwinian theory, not Marxian.

Table 3.1. Dualities of Osteoarchaeology Versus Interpretative Archaeology

Osteoarchaeology	Interpretative Archaeology
Atheoretical	Theoretical
Dead	Living
Inside (unfleshed)	Outside (fleshed)
Nature	Culture

Note: After Sofaer 2006:31.

Some sort of biocultural rapprochement is clearly in order. A dialectical and political economic approach is one means (e.g., Goodman and Leatherman 1998). Sofaer's move is to absorb osteoarchaeology into theoretical archaeology by dissolving the distinction between bodies (people) and objects. This is accomplished through a focus on the materiality of the body, particularly the skeleton, in an archaeological context (Sofaer 2006:64). While I have little argument with archaeologists "borrowing" bodies for their interpretative endeavors, Sofaer's project is part of a broader attempt to transcend a perceived Western tendency toward dualistic constructions. The Cartesian mind/body duality is problematic, particularly as it invariably leads to hierarchy, but attempts to negate it tend to be prescriptive rather than descriptive.

Cast about for attempts at monistic revisions of theoretical approaches to human life, and they are filled with dualistic terminology. Latour (1993) seeks to redefine modernity, which at its base rests on various distinctions: modern versus premodern specifically, but ultimately meaning culture versus nature, as in modern "cultured" Europe of the eighteenth and nineteenth centuries versus those "natural" societies encountered in the course of European expansion. In his conception, modernity rests on *two* dichotomies: nonhumans/nature versus humans/culture and purity versus hybrids. We (as moderns) conceive of things as either natural or cultural while at the same time refusing to acknowledge the cultural construction of "natural" objects, the natural constraints on "cultural" constructions, or, to make it symmetrical, the interpenetration (but with retained identity) of the natural and the cultural. In the latter case, in a chemical analogy, we would see mixtures, not solutions. Latour contrasts this modern outlook with the worldview of premoderns, who are very aware of the "danger" of hybrids and who monitor their creation and existence: magic, trees and rocks with souls, spirits that inhabit everyday objects, dead ancestors present at ceremonies of the living. Likewise, Franklin (2002) sees not a separation between nature and society but a deep interpenetration—but again, mixture not solution. Ingold (1998) is bent on dissolving the boundaries between social anthropology on the one hand and biological anthropology, archaeology, and psychology on the other. In this effort, he systematically discusses each pair, never actually developing an integrative terminology. Each of these endeavors, and the many others one could cite, are laudable. Given their aims, why are they never able to transcend the dualities?

Underlying Latour's, Franklin's, and Ingold's conundrum is the presumption that we are needlessly imposing Western dualisms on what should be unitary objects or processes. It may not be, however, a "needless" imposition. Dualistic thought may not be an exclusively Western phenomenon; it may instead be in the nature of being human, whether Western or non-Western (e.g., Astuti 2001; Bering 2006). Astuti (2001) specifically addresses the issue of whether or not dualistic thinking is confined to Western people, the heirs of Plato and Descartes. Cognitive experiments involving inferential reasoning by the non-Western Vezo of Madagascar, children and adults, indicate that, in contrast to their normative accounts, which appear to be devoid of dualism, the Vezo reason within a dualistic framework. Astuti is well aware of the implication for traditional ethnographic methods that follows from her findings: People's descriptions of what they think may not be accurate renderings of how they think.

Gell (1992), building on McTaggart (1908), distinguishes between A-series and B-series time and thereby lays a foundation for understanding the dualism inherent in biological versus interpretive approaches to cemeteries. Essentially, A-series time is that experienced by the individual, characterized by an anticipated future, a present, and a remembered past. This is a dynamic relationship, however, as anticipated future and remembered past structure the present. Time is experienced as passage, the world and the self as becoming. An event can be in the future; it can be now; it can be in the past. And it will be all those things. B-series time relates to calendrical reckoning: an event has a unique temporal assignment, and it is always before, at the same time as, or after another event with a different date. Time is about being (at a particular point on a scale). "Truth" cannot exist in A-series time. An event may be in the future, but at another time it will be in the past. In the B-series, an event that occurs on May 25, 1762, will always be tied to that date (barring, of course, a revision [translation] of the calendar). For example, for Bourdieu (1977), working in the Marxian tradition, time is A-series:

> It is essential to note the deep affinity between the A-series concept of time, and the concept of time implicit in the Marxist historical dialectic of the production of man by history and the production of history by man. This "history" is not the unchanging, inaccessible, B-series "past," but a past that is dynamically interconnected to the present, and that changes as the present changes. It is not a simple accretion of new events (changes) at the temporal front-line demarcated by the "now"; instead the change initiated in the now-moment occurs in depth. The whole history changes as the present changes, because of the continual interactions of historical residues in the current situation, which is centered in the "now," but which embraces the past and the future as well [Gell 1992:267].

Note, however, that the "accretion of new events (changes) at the temporal front-line demarcated by 'now'" reasonably describes Darwinian evolution. For a Marxian, time is A-series; for a Darwinian, time is B-series. To identify—to discuss an object, a process, a person, an event—we must place it in time (and space, but that is another matter), and to place it in time, we have to choose a time series—A or B. In other words, to study a phenomenon one must first commit to a time perspective, and to do that commits one to one side of a duality.

Things are not that simple, of course. Darwinian models—evolutionary archaeology, evolutionary psychology, sociobiology—readily offer B-series accounts of broad ranges of human behavior. Likewise, an A-series perspective can be brought to bear in a dialectical model of evolution (Levins and Lewontin 1985), and much of the inspiration for the structure of change incorporated in punctuated equilibria models (Eldredge and Gould 1972; Gould and Eldredge 1977) sprung from familiarity with the Hegelian and Marxian dialectic (Gould 2002:1017–1018). Nonetheless, the distinctness of A- and B-series time remains. A-series time is that experienced by the conscious individual or "experienced" by the evolving organism. The latter case refers, for example, to situations where a morphological modification creates a new niche with new selection pressures or where a structure selected for at some time in the past becomes a constraint on subsequent change in the face of altered selection pressures. B-series time is a method of measurement imposed from outside an event—that is, by the conscious person viewing an external process or sequence of events. Thus fossils and potsherds are pegged to particular times. Dinosaurs that lived in the Jurassic will always have lived before there were any *Homo sapiens* on the planet.

CONCLUSION (IN THE MESOLITHIC)

One area of common interest in which the distinction between explanations arising from social theory and those based in biology—that is, between A-series and B-series time frames—becomes paramount is the investigation of hominid evolution and early human history. The study of primate evolution is the same as the study of the evolution of any other mammalian group, or for that matter any animal group (or group of organisms from any of the kingdoms of life on earth). Dialectical biology and punctuated equilibria are revisions of, or additions to, Darwin's theory, not substitutes. Evolutionary psychology can provide some insight into human behavior, but in the end, it primarily produces ideologically embedded just-so stories. Evolution happened, and people are different from other animals. As yet, we do not have a theoretical framework from which to talk about both concepts. To understand Australopithecines we need modern evolutionary theory. To understand the situation in Iraq in the first decade of the twenty-first century, we require an array of postmodern perspectives. Between Olduvai Gorge and Babylon there is a huge gray area not served by either theoretical framework alone.

This tension plays out in the Mesolithic, or in its equivalent in eastern North America, the Archaic and Woodland periods. For Buikstra (1977, 2006a), biological theory is essentially the same.[2] Archaeological theory has changed, however:

> Since it has been repeatedly demonstrated (e.g., Saxe 1970; Binford 1971) that the mortuary activity associated with the individual directly reflects the sum of his socially defined roles (though certain roles may assume primacy), the analysis of Middle Woodland mortuary sites should focus upon (1) a definition of the range of burial behaviors appropriate to the individual at death and (2) the extent to which this variability is readily explicable in terms of age, sex, and other biological attributes. Then, the degree of complexity thus defined may be compared to models derived through the study of extant populations [Buikstra 1976:30].

Compare that to a recent passage (in Buikstra's words, although from a coauthored work) that invokes a very different sense. Note the shift from objective and prescriptive language in the previous quotation to an emphasis on a subjective view, and note the qualifying words like *may* and *interpreted.*

> Later mounds include "empty" tombs and are positioned near open spaces where audiences may have viewed the rituals staged from elevated ramps that encircled tomb structures. . . . These rituals served to anchor the Middle Woodland world, moving the dead across lofty platforms representing the upper world, through the flat disk of this world, into the dark, subsurface underworld. A thin layer of light-colored sediments encircling the tomb at ground level is interpreted to represent this world [Buikstra and Charles 1999:214].

So what is, or should be, bioarchaeology? Good question.

NOTES

1. It is worth remembering, however, that Marx himself was attempting to develop a science of historical materialism, a scientific socialism (Tucker 1978:xx).

2. Somewhat ironically for a "postprocessual" theoretical osteoarchaeology that would treat bones as objects, in North America NAGPRA has greatly altered bioarchaeological practice (Buikstra 2006b; Martin 1998). The treatment of skeletons as archaeological objects was seen as desecration and was deeply insulting to Native Americans. Biological anthropologists have had to develop cultural sensitivities not normally associated with "science."

REFERENCES CITED

Armelagos, George J.

2003 Bioarcheology as Anthropology. In *Archaeology Is Anthropology*, edited by Susan D. Gillespie and Deborah Nichols, pp. 27–41. Archaeological Papers No 13. American Anthropological Association, Arlington, Virginia.

2008 Biocultural Anthropology at Its Origins: Transformation of the New Physical Anthropology in the 1950s. In *The Tao of Anthropology*, edited by Alec J. Kelso, pp. 269–282. University of Florida Press, Gainesville.

Arnold, Bettina, and Nancy L. Wicker (editors)

2002 *Gender and the Archaeology of Death*. Altamira Press, Walnut Creek, California.

Astuti, Rita

2001 Are We All Natural Dualists? A Cognitive Developmental Approach. *Journal of the Royal Anthropological Institute*, n.s., 7:429–447.

Barton, C. Michael, Geoffrey A. Clark, and Douglas B. Bamforth (editors)

1997 *Rediscovering Darwin: Evolutionary Theory and Archaeological Explanation*. Archeological Papers of the American Anthropological Association No. 7. American Anthropological Association, Arlington, Virginia.

Bender, Barbara

1998 *Stonehenge: Making Space*. Berg, Oxford.

Bering, Jesse M.

2006 The Folk Psychology of Souls. *Behavioral and Brain Sciences* 29:453–498.

Binford, Lewis R.

1962 Archaeology as Anthropology. *American Antiquity* 28(2):217–225.

1968 Post-Pleistocene Adaptations. In *New Perspectives in Archaeology*, edited by Lewis R. Binford and Sally R. Binford, pp. 313–341. Aldine, Chicago.

1971 Mortuary Practices: Their Study and Their Potential. In *Approaches to the Social Dimensions of Mortuary Practices*, edited by James A. Brown, pp. 58–67. Memoir 25. Society for American Archaeology, Washington, D.C.

Binford, Sally R., and Lewis R. Binford (editors)

1968 *New Perspectives in Archaeology*. Aldine, Chicago.

Blakely, Robert L. (editor)

1977 *Biocultural Adaptation in Prehistoric America*. Southern Anthropological Society Proceedings No. 11. University of Georgia Press, Athens.

Bloor, David

1976 *Knowledge and Social Imagery*. Routledge and Kegan Paul, London.

Bourdieu, Pierre

1977 *Towards a Theory of Practice*. Cambridge University Press, Cambridge.

Buikstra, Jane E.

1976 *Hopewell in the Lower Illinois Valley: A Regional Study of Human Biological Variability and Prehistoric Mortuary Behavior*. Scientific Papers No. 2. Northwestern University Archeological Program, Evanston, Illinois.

1977 Biocultural Dimensions of Archeological Study: A Regional Perspective. In *Biocultural Adaptation in Prehistoric America*, edited by Robert L. Blakely, pp. 67–84. Southern Anthropological Society Proceedings No. 11. University of Georgia Press, Athens.

2006a Preface. In *Bioarchaeology: The Contextual Analysis of Human Remains*, edited by Jane E. Buikstra and Lane A. Beck, pp. xvii–xx. Academic Press, Amsterdam.

2006b Repatriation and Bioarchaeology: Challenges and Opportunities. In *Bioarchaeology: The Contextual Analysis of Human Remains*, edited by Jane E. Buikstra and Lane A. Beck, pp. 389–415. Academic Press, Amsterdam.

Buikstra, Jane E., and Douglas K. Charles

1999 Centering the Ancestors: Cemeteries, Mounds and Sacred Landscapes of the Ancient North American Midcontinent. In *Archaeologies of Landscape: Contemporary Perspectives*, edited by Wendy Ashmore and A. Bernard Knapp, pp. 201–228. Blackwell Publishers, Oxford.

Buikstra, Jane E., and Lane A. Beck (editors)

2006 *Bioarchaeology: The Contextual Analysis of Human Remains*. Academic Press, Amsterdam.

Charles, Douglas K.

1992 Shading the Past: Models in Archeology. *American Anthropologist* 94:905–925.

Clark, J. G. D.

1972 *Starr Carr: A Case Study in Bioarchaeology*. Addison-Wesley Modular Publications 10. Addison Wesley, New York.

Clarke, David L.

1968 *Analytical Archaeology*. Methuen, London.

Dunnell, Robert C.

1980 Evolutionary Theory and Archaeology. In *Advances in Archaeological Method and Theory*, vol. 3, edited by Michael B. Schiffer. Academic Press, New York.

Eldredge, Niles, and Stephen J. Gould

1972 Punctuated Equilibria: An Alternative to Phyletic Gradualism. In *Models in Paleobiology*, edited by T. J. M. Schopf, pp. 82–115. Freeman, Cooper and Company, San Francisco.

Foster, John Bellamy

2000 *Marx's Ecology: Materialism and Nature*. Monthly Review Press, New York.

Franklin, Adrian

2002 *Nature and Social Theory*. Sage Publications, London.

Gell, Alfred

1992 *The Anthropology of Time: Cultural Constructions of Temporal Maps and Images*. Berg, Oxford.

Gibbon, Guy

1989 *Explanation in Archaeology*. Basil Blackwell, Oxford.

Giddens, Anthony

1984 *The Constitution of Society: Outline of a Theory of Structuration*. University of California Press, Berkeley.

Goldstein, Lynne

2006 Mortuary Analysis and Bioarchaeology. In *Bioarchaeology: The Contextual Analysis of Human Remains*, edited by Jane E. Buikstra and Lane A. Beck, pp. 375–387. Academic Press, Amsterdam.

Goodman, Alan H., and Thomas L. Leatherman (editors)

1998 *Building a New Biocultural Synthesis: Political-Economic Perspectives on Human Biology*. University of Michigan Press, Ann Arbor.

Gould, Stephen Jay

2002 *The Structure of Evolutionary Theory*. Belknap Press of Harvard University Press, Cambridge.

Gould, Stephen Jay, and Niles Eldredge

1977 Punctuated Equilibria: The Tempo and Mode of Evolution Reconsidered. *Paleobiology* 3:115–151.

Gowland, Rebecca, and Christopher J. Knüsel

2006a Introduction. In *Social Archaeology of Funerary Remains*, edited by Rebecca Gowland and Christopher J. Knüsel, pp. ix–xiv. Oxbow Books, Oxford.

2006b *Social Archaeology of Funerary Remains*. Oxbow Books, Oxford.

Griffin, James B. (editor)

1952 *Archeology of Eastern United States*. University of Chicago Press, Chicago.

Hodder, Ian

1980 Social Structure and Cemeteries: A Critical Appraisal. In *Anglo-Saxon Cemeteries, 1979: The Fourth Anglo-Saxon Symposium at Oxford*, edited by Philip A. Rahtz, Tania Dickinson, and Lorna Watts, pp. 161–169. British Series Vol. 82. BAR, Oxford.

1982 *Symbols in Action*. Cambridge University Press, Cambridge.

1984 Burials, Houses, Women and Men in the European Neolithic. In *Ideology, Power and Prehistory*, edited by Daniel Miller and Christopher Tilley, pp. 51–68. Cambridge University Press, Cambridge.

1986 *Reading the Past*. Cambridge University Press, Cambridge.

1991 Interpretive Archaeology and Its Role. *American Antiquity* 56(1):7–18.

Hodder, Ian (editor)
1982 *Symbolic and Structural Archaeology*. Cambridge University Press, Cambridge.

Holden, Constance
1993 Failing to Cross the Biology-Culture Gap. *Science* 262:1641–1642.

Ingold, Tim
1998 From Complementarity to Obviation: On Dissolving the Boundaries Between Social and Biological Anthropology, Archaeology and Psychology. *Zeitschrift für Ethnologie* 123:21–52.

Johnson, Matthew
2010 *Archaeological Theory: An Introduction*. 2nd ed. Blackwell, Oxford.

Larsen, Clark Spencer
1997 *Bioarchaeology: Interpreting Behavior from the Human Skeleton*. Cambridge University Press, New York.
2002 Bioarchaeology: The Lives and Lifestyles of Past People. *Journal of Archaeological Research* 10(2):119–166.
2006 The Changing Face of Bioarchaeology: An Interdisciplinary Science. In *Bioarchaeology: The Contextual Analysis of Human Remains*, edited by Jane E. Buikstra and Lane A. Beck, pp. 359–374. Academic Press, Amsterdam.

Latour, Bruno
1993 *We Have Never Been Modern*. Translated by C. Porter. Harvard University Press, Cambridge.

Levins, Richard, and Richard Lewontin
1985 *The Dialectical Biologist*. Harvard University Press, Cambridge.

Martin, Debra L.
1998 Owning the Sins of the Past: Historical Trends, Missed Opportunities, and New Directions in the Study of Human Remains. In *Building a New Biocultural Synthesis: Political-Economic Perspectives on Human Biology*, edited by Alan H. Goodman and Thomas L. Leatherman, pp. 171–190. University of Michigan Press, Ann Arbor.

McTaggart, John Ellis
1908 The Unreality of Time. *Mind*, n.s., 17(68):457–474.

Murdock, George P.
1957 World Ethnographic Sample. *American Anthropologist* 59(4):664–687.

O'Brien, Michael J., and R. Lee Lyman
2000 *Applying Evolutionary Archaeology: A Systematic Approach*. Kluwer Academic/Plenun Publishers, New York.

Pader, Ellen-Jane
1980 Material Symbolism and Social Relations in Mortuary Studies. In *Anglo-Saxon Cemeteries, 1979: The Fourth Anglo-Saxon Symposium at Oxford*, edited by Philip A. Rahtz, Tania Dickinson, and Lorna Watts, pp. 143–159. British Series 82. BAR, Oxford.
1982 *Symbolism, Social Relations, and the Interpretation of Mortuary Remains*. International Series 130. BAR, Oxford.

Parker Pearson, Michael
1999 *The Archaeology of Death and Burial*. Texas A&M University Press, College Station.

Patterson, Thomas C.
2003 *Marx's Ghost: Conversations with Archaeologists*. Berg, Oxford.

Roberts, Charlotte A.
2006 A View from Afar: Bioarchaeology in Britain. In *Bioarchaeology: The Contextual Analysis of Human Remains*, edited by Jane E. Buikstra and Lane A. Beck, pp. 417–439. Academic Press, Amsterdam.

Saxe, Arthur A.
1970 Social Dimensions of Mortuary Practices. Unpublished Ph.D. dissertation, Department of Anthropology, University of Michigan, Ann Arbor.

Shanks, Michael, and Christopher Tilley
1982 Ideology, Symbolic Power and Ritual Communication: A Reinterpretation of Neolithic Mortuary Practices. In *Symbolic and Structural Archaeology*, edited by Ian Hodder, pp. 129–154. Cambridge University Press, Cambridge.
1987 *Reconstructing Archaeology*. Cambridge University Press, Cambridge.

Sofaer, Joanna R.
2006 *The Body as Material Culture*. Topics in Contemporary Archaeology. Cambridge University Press, New York.

Trigger, Bruce G.
2006 *A History of Archaeological Thought*. 2nd ed. Cambridge University Press, Cambridge.

Tucker, Robert C.
1978 Introduction. In *The Marx-Engels Reader*, 2nd ed., edited by Robert C. Tucker, pp. xix–xxxviii. W. W. Norton, New York.

Van Gerven, Dennis P., David S. Carlson, and George J. Armelagos
1974 Racial History and Bio-cultural Adaptation of Nubian Archaeological Populations. *Journal of African History* 14(4):555–564.

Washburn, Sherwood L.
1951 The New Physical Anthropology. *Transactions of the New York Academy of Sciences, Series II* 7:298–304.
1953 The New Physical Anthropology. *Yearbook of Physical Anthropology* 7:124–130.

White, Leslie A.
1949 *The Science of Culture: A Study of Man and Civilization*. Farrar, Strauss, New York.

Willey, Gordon R., and Jeremy A. Sabloff
1993 *A History of American Archaeology*. 3rd ed. W. H. Freeman, New York.

4

Methodological and Ethical Considerations When Sampling Human Osteological Remains

Cecil M. Lewis Jr.
Department of Anthropology, University of Oklahoma
Tiffiny A. Tung
Department of Anthropology, Vanderbilt University

We highlight several considerations that must be made when embarking upon destructive analyses of human remains. We view this as a step toward the creation of widely implemented standards within this particular methodological branch of bioarchaeological research. Thus it is fitting that this work is situated in a volume dedicated to Jane E. Buikstra, who, with her colleague Douglas Ubelaker, published the indispensable and oft-cited book *Standards for Data Collection from Human Skeletal Remains* (Buikstra and Ubelaker 1994). *Standards*, as it is known in shorthand throughout the discipline, integrated relevant methodological techniques compiled by a multidisciplinary team of experienced researchers and graduate students. That standardized compilation has contributed to more reliable comparisons of skeletal data sets collected by different researchers.

In its nine printings, *Standards* has found its place in anthropology and criminal justice departments in North, Central, and South America; Europe; and the Middle East (Deborah Sabo, Arkansas Archeological Survey Publications, personal communication 2010). We do not presume that this short paper is within the realm of the comprehensive volume created by Buikstra and Ubelaker. Yet we have taken our cue from those impressive scholars, noting that standardized methodological rigor will aid in improving our discipline. In this chapter we suggest research considerations and procedural practices intended to limit bone and tooth destruction and to maximize research potential and long-term posterity.

Background on Destructive Sampling

Gross observation of diagnostic features on human skeletal and dental remains, including natural, pathological, and anthropogenic traits, provides a means to reconstruct demographic profiles, population morbidity, biological relationships within and between populations, and frequencies of violence and cultural practices such as bodily expressions of identity (for example, cranial modification and tooth ablation) (Buikstra and Beck 2006; Walker 2005). Further details of one's health status and lifeways can be obtained through biochemical and molecular tests, which typically require the extraction and destruction of a small skeletal and/or dental sample. Those samples can provide a wealth of data for dietary reconstruction (Lambert et al. 1984; Schoeninger 1989), radiocarbon dating (Piotrowska and Goslar 2002), assessing migration (Knudson and Price 2007; Price et al. 1994), and documenting physiological adaptations (Bridges 1996), ontogenetic patterns (Dean 2006), demographic details (Wittwer-Backofen et al. 2004), and genetic variation within and among populations (Pääbo et al. 2004).

Because a sample of bone or tooth must be destroyed or altered, a cost-benefit analysis regarding the amount of destruction required for the amount of information to be gained must be evaluated. Sampling procedures should minimize destruction and enhance the quality of data obtained. There is a conspicuous absence of presenting such procedures in research articles. This leaves such vital considerations and procedures to individuals with a broad range of backgrounds, not all of whom will be specialists in bioarchaeology.

RESEARCH CONSIDERATIONS

Given the significant ethical concerns involved in the destructive analysis of human skeletal remains (Larsen and Walker 2005), serious consideration should be given to the potential insights to be gained vis-à-vis the material that will be lost and the concerns the process may bring to descendant communities. In the many world regions where indigenous descendant populations reside, there are conflicting views regarding the utility of the scientific study of human skeletons. As Larsen and Walker (2005:111) note:

> The traditional perspective of scientists who study ancient remains has been to consider human remains as valuable objects full of research potential. Many descendants of the people whose remains bioarchaeologists study, in contrast, view ancestral remains as objects of veneration that should be protected from what they see as the indignity of examination by scientists whose motivations they consider suspect at best and immoral at worst.

In light of these potentially disparate perspectives regarding the treatment of human remains, and after consultation with appropriate descendant communities (and see questions 7 and 8, below), the authors suggest that at least the following questions be considered before conducting any kind of destructive analysis:

1. Do I have a clear research question that can be addressed by this analysis?
A research question should always be articulated prior to data collection and analysis, especially if the data collection procedures lead to the destruction of the material under study. If any of the destructive analyses are outside the scope of the research questions to be addressed, they should be avoided. If it is concluded that destructive analysis will be conducted, consider ways to maximize the amount of information to be gained by the sample (see question 2).

2. Have I consulted with other specialists who plan to obtain data from this extracted sample?
Because several kinds of data may be obtained from one specimen, consulting a histologist, an archaeological chemist, and a molecular anthropologist, among others, is advised. These specialists can assess the feasibility of sectioning the sample for different studies. For example, it is typically possible to use a dental sample for multiple studies such that casts are made for microwear analysis, enamel is used for isotopic analyses (of both light and heavy isotopes, which may need to be conducted in different labs, thus requiring detailed planning), and roots are used to obtain ancient DNA. The order in which the specialists handle the samples is an important consideration. For instance, ancient DNA studies are vulnerable to modern contamination from handling, so it may be wise to conduct DNA extraction before other analyses. (In our experiences, removal of the root does not significantly interfere with making casts of the enamel crown.)

3. Is an experienced person or lab providing and analyzing the data?
Many laboratories will conduct analyses of your samples for a fee. Before consulting a lab, consider doing a background check on its reputation and the qualifications of its personnel. Review publications produced from the lab. Be explicit when discussing fees and author order (if applicable) for the resultant publications. It is strongly advised to employ a method of quality control (see below).

4. Is a system in place for quality control?
There are two effective approaches for quality control: the independent lab strategy and the blind sample strategy.

The independent lab strategy is standard for high-profile ancient DNA studies, but the strategy applies equally well to most destructive analyses. Duplicate samples are sent to independent (unaffiliated) laboratories, which report the results directly to the primary investigator, who then assesses whether results from the two labs are consistent.

The blind sample strategy is best used when the laboratory requires no identifying contextual information, only an identification code number. Each sample, regardless of whether it is a duplicate, has a unique identification number that can be linked to the contextual information only by the primary investigator. The laboratory is never given any information regarding which samples are duplicates. In fact, the laboratory may be unaware that duplicate samples are included.

Consequently, the primary investigator assesses whether results from the duplicate samples are consistent.

The independent lab strategy and the blind sample strategy work equally well when the primary investigator of the project and the director of the laboratory conducting the analysis are the same individual. Laboratory directors may wish to include duplicate blind samples to evaluate whether their lab is producing consistent results. Alternatively, laboratory directors may wish to send duplicate samples to a colleague for independent tests.

5. Will I be able to contribute to the conservation of the remaining skeletal material?

Often, monetary support for conservation material is limited. Researchers should consider including a budget for skeletal conservation. At the most basic level, human remains should be stored in an acid-free environment, with padding for the more delicate elements, and all elements should be stored in sturdy, well-labeled containers for long-term preservation.

The environmental conditions of the storage space are a critical aspect of proper conservation. In particular, humidity can lead to decay of skeletal elements. Removing moisture from the air using a dehumidifier will aid in protecting the bones. Pollutants in the air can also contribute to degradation or contamination of the skeletal material. In particular, insecticides, pollution from cars and factories, and even cleaning supplies will hinder conservation efforts. Researchers can protect human remains from contaminants by placing bones in rooms that are adequately sealed.

6. Are there additional samples or contextual information that would complement the skeletal samples?

In addition to the skeletal material, nonhuman samples and contextual information may be required to address questions posed in the study. For instance, samples from local soils, flora, or fauna may be needed for isotope studies on dietary reconstruction or residential mobility (Price 1989; Schoeninger 1989). For molecular studies, the principal investigator may need to obtain permission to acquire biological samples from project members who have handled remains, as they may be sources of modern contamination (Sampietro et al. 2006). Such samples would require informed consent from the participants.

7. Have I obtained the proper permission to conduct a destructive analysis?

National and local guidelines related to repatriation and cultural property rights must be met, and all relevant permissions should be obtained in writing. In addition to getting permission from the person or institution in charge of the material, you may need permission from the original excavator, the repository holding the material, the close relatives or descendants of the individuals studied, and relevant government agencies, such as those involved in cultural resource management. Additional permits from government agencies may be required for shipping samples out of the country from which they originated.

8. Have I considered the impact of this study on related individuals or communities?

While most destructive analyses can be conducted on relatively small bone samples and/or on teeth, any destructive analysis on human bone involves a serious ethical decision. The impact of your study requires careful consideration of the long-term conservation of the skeletal material. Importantly, the impact the study will have on living individuals closely connected with the material, both biologically and culturally, must be carefully considered. There are several well-written reviews on this subject (Larsen and Walker 2005; Walker 2000, 2005).

9. Have I attempted a pilot project to assess the feasibility of the study?

It is possible that postdepositional processes have made certain destructive analyses unfeasible. This is especially a concern for many ancient DNA studies. As a proof of principle, it is wise to begin with a pilot project on a limited number of individuals. The researcher first gauges what level of DNA preservation would be considered acceptable to continue the project. Applying a simple probability calculation can be informative. For example, if the researcher decides that a 50 percent DNA recovery rate is acceptable to continue the project, then, all things being equal, the probability of having a successful DNA extraction within three, four, or five samples is .875, .937, and .968, respectively, calculated as $p = 1 - (1 - r)^n$, where r is the hypothetical success rate and n is the number of samples examined. Thus, if after five samples no DNA preservation is observed, it is likely that the overall recovery rate will be less than 50 percent.

PROCEDURAL PRACTICES

The following procedural standards are intended for someone well trained in identifying a variety of dental and skeletal lesions and standard skeletal and dental traits. Such identifications are best made through hands-on experience rather than photographs.

Handling Bone

Destructive analyses for ancient DNA are particularly sensitive to modern contamination. As a result, minimizing direct contact with the skeleton is ideal. Nevertheless, there are in-house laboratory techniques that reduce modern DNA contamination (Kemp and Smith 2005; Yang and Watt 2005). Consequently, a permanent record of the skeletal material outweighs the potential added complication of having to purge modern contamination from a sample. Still, there are standard procedures that reduce modern contamination during the handling of human remains.

One should wear gloves to avoid passing oils, salts, and other contaminates to the specimen. Disposable sterile nitrile gloves are ideal. These gloves greatly reduce contamination when compared to reused cotton gloves, and they are smoother than disposable latex gloves, so they are less prone to snagging.

If possible, do not wash the skeletal material or treat it with any preservatives before sampling. If a consolidant needs to be applied to a skeleton to excavate it, treat one side only or at least leave a small portion clean for future testing.

In many cases, researchers may want to use museum specimens for isotope studies, and those are sometimes covered in PVAc glue (polyvinyl acetate with acetone solution). A recent study showed that if the PVAc is removed with organic solvents, researchers will still get reliable results for the analysis of carbon ($\delta^{13}C$) and nitrogen ($\delta^{15}N$) isotopes in bone collagen, for carbon isotopes in carbonate from bone hydroxyapatite, and for oxygen ($\delta^{18}O$) isotopes from phosphate in hydroxyapatite (France et al. 2011). However, oxygen isotopes from carbonates exhibit variable results and should not be used in investigations (France et al. 2011).

Data Collection Before Destructive Analyses

Osteological and pathological data should be recorded before samples are cut or extracted. We recommend using the data collection standards as outlined by Buikstra and Ubelaker (1994). This work should include at least the following:

1. Recording of:
- Dental calculus
- Enamel hypoplasias, hypocalcifications
- Dental caries
- Dental wear
- Dental chipping
- Dental and skeletal measurements
- Dental and skeletal nonmetric traits
- Dental and skeletal modifications
- Cut marks or other anthropogenic alterations to the specimen
- Stains from copper or other elements (for example, ochre, cinnabar)

2. Observations of pathological lesions (for example, periostitis, osteoarthritis, bone fractures, porotic hyperostosis)

3. Taphonomic descriptions (for example, color, sun or water damage, burning, rodent or other animal chew marks)

4. Creation of dental casts or a digital rendering of the element

5. Photographs of all views of dental and skeletal specimens (mesial, distal, lingual, buccal, occlusal, and inferior views of teeth; anterior, posterior, medial, and lateral views of bones), with a metric scale in the photos

6. Additional photos after sample extraction (for example, of the alveolar bone where a tooth was removed)

Selecting the Specimen

Selecting a Tooth. Teeth are among the most informative parts of a skeleton. Gross observation alone can provide insights into dental health (caries, abscesses, periodontal disease, antemortem tooth loss), developmental health status (linear enamel hypoplasias and metrics), diet (caries, dental wear, and calculus), genetic relationships (metric and nonmetric traits), and cultural affiliation (dental modifications). As noted above, all teeth should be photographed and an accurate cast or digital rendering should be made prior to sampling. When casting teeth, it is important to use a high-resolution casting material such as vinyl polysiloxane.

There are a number of reasonable tips for selecting a tooth to sample. Choose a tooth that has a lateral counterpart (left and right present) to reduce loss of valuable information in future studies. Lateral counterparts may differ somewhat, particularly in terms of pathological status, and while some studies prefer bilateral comparisons, selecting a tooth with a lateral counterpart is the most sensible.

Teeth with carious lesions or severe dental wear should be avoided as samples because of their potentially useful cultural information and, with respect to molecular studies, the increased risk of modern contamination. Of course, this advice does not apply if the research question itself relates to related studies on caries or dental wear.

Researchers should avoid destroying teeth that exhibit rare nonmetric traits in a particular population (for example, a protostylid), even if the tooth was caste or digitally rendered. Consult an osteologist with in-depth knowledge of the skeletal population to ensure that you are not destroying the one example of a rare trait in that study group.

Teeth with calculus (plaque) should be avoided because they can be used for noninvasive studies such as phytolith analysis (see Fox et al. 1996 for an example). If a tooth with calculus is selected, bag a sample of the calculus, noting its origin and the reason for removing it. Leave the labeled calculus sample with the original skeleton or arrange to have a phytolith specialist analyze it.

Selecting the appropriate tooth is a negotiation between the questions to be addressed, the teeth available, and the information stored in that tooth. Teeth are not equal in terms of the information they yield. For example, canines are much more likely to exhibit enamel hypoplasia and are well suited for histological analysis. In contrast, molars provide many more nonmetric traits than do canines. Nevertheless, it is straightforward to document dental traits before tooth destruction. Consider the pros and cons of each potential tooth sample before the final selection is made.

Selecting a Bone. The type of bone sample necessary for the destructive analysis may vary; consultation with the laboratory conducting the analysis is essential. As with the selection of dental specimens, select a sample that is free of pathological lesions (unless the research question is centered on analysis of such a pathology), and select a bone element that is present on both the left and right sides. As always, photograph and record the presence or absence of nonmetric traits and record all metric data.

There is a better chance of DNA preservation in denser material, such as long bone shafts. Yet long bones provide a wealth of morphological data. If long bones are sampled, every attempt should be made to keep the bone intact while taking the smallest excision required for the analysis. Although, from a conservation standpoint, it might be good to select an already fragmented piece of bone, this might not be ideal for the laboratory because exposed broken edges (especially exposed trabecular bone) often have soil and other contaminants integrated into the trabeculae, requiring additional cleaning. Bone freshly cut with a clean blade (see below) might be better. Ribs and phalanges are common alternatives to long bones in DNA studies and also work very well for isotope studies. For isotope studies, if comparisons are being made within and between skeletal populations, every effort should be made to sample the same element. Standardization is essential for reliable intra- and interpopulation comparisons because isotopic incorporation varies from bone to bone. Thus the sampling of a rib or a phalanx is encouraged because there are 24 ribs and 56 phalanges from which to choose. It is also worth noting that permitting agencies are typically more willing to allow destructive analysis of ribs and phalanges than femora and tibiae.

Sample Extraction

If a sample needs to be cut, do so with a sterilized tool. We suggest manual saws or multiple-speed rotary drills (Dremel, for example) with mini-carbon disks and engraving cutters. Always wear gloves, goggles, and a mask to protect both yourself and the sample. A rotary drill typically has disposable attachments (such as disks and cutters) that must be changed for each sample extraction to avoid cross-contamination. When using a rotary drill, check voltage requirements (110 or 220 volts) in the country where you are conducting the extraction. While manual saws disperse less bone dust, automated saws typically require less direct pressure on fragile materials. For molecular studies, one concern with rotary tools is the heat they generate, which may reduce DNA preservation (Adler et al. 2011); Adler et al. found that using lower speeds (100 rpm) resolves much of this issue.

Obtaining Dental Samples. Teeth are often free or loose in the alveoli (sockets). In these circumstances, extraction requires minimal invasive procedures. Unfortunately, this is not always the case. If a tooth is affixed in the socket, pull it gently to evaluate the degree of resistance. Sometimes a light wiggling of the tooth may free it. If not, determine whether an alternative tooth is available, assuming that your research question is not dependent on extracting that particular tooth type.

Evaluate whether curators or a previous researcher glued the teeth in their sockets. If so, the glue can sometimes be reversed with water or acetone (depending on the type of glue used) or by picking away glue chunks with tweezers and a drill. Obtain permission from the curator to reverse the gluing, and be sure to inform the laboratory if you used any water or acetone (or other reversing agent) to extract the tooth.

If the tooth is tightly affixed in the alveolar bone, additional tools will be required to extract it. Check with the curator, excavation director, or other responsible agent to ensure that you have permission to destroy some of the alveolar bone for extraction. Maxillary molars are much more difficult to extract, owing to their three-pronged root structure, so single- or double-rooted teeth may be better options. Using a drill with a cutting disk or engraving cutters, carefully cut away tiny portions of the alveolar bone surrounding the tooth. (This procedure is not advised if there is an abscess at the socket location.) After removing a small bit of bone, gently wiggle the tooth to extract it. Repeat this process until the tooth comes free. Do not yank the tooth, as excessive force will result in a fractured root, fractured enamel, and/or fractured bone.

Obtaining Skeletal Samples. Ribs and phalanges may be taken whole. For large bones, some cutting will likely be needed. If the bone is already broken, cut off a section from the broken end, ensuring that you have enough intact bone that is free of contamination. If a bone is intact, remove a rectangular piece, as if cutting a window into the skeletal element. This technique is preferred over cutting off the proximal or distal end of the bone, as that destroys the entire integrity of the bone. If you're using a rotary tool, you might need multiple cut disks to complete the removal of the bone sample, and the use of protective eyewear becomes even more essential.

Storing and Transport of Samples

Bone samples that are to be used for radiocarbon dating should not be wrapped in paper; rather, they should be wrapped in aluminum foil. All extracted samples should be individually wrapped in sterile bags. Each sample bag should then be placed inside another bag or container with an accompanying sample tag. The tag should be labeled with a permanent marker. Each tag should be marked with identification information (site name/number, excavation unit, feature, burial number, specimen number, and so on). Excavators on different projects often use different coding systems, so it is the responsibility of the osteologist to learn each project's coding system. Be sure to include all identification information with the extracted sample. Also include details of the sampled element (for example, "shaft fragment from distal end of left femur" or "mandibular right molar 2") and the weight of the specimen in micrograms. Finally, leave a tag in the original bag noting the following information for researchers who may study the skeletal collection 5 or 50 years later: (1) sample taken; (2) tests being performed and at which labs; (3) gross observations made on the element; (4) name; (5) date. Business cards are also good to leave with the original bag.

The loss or mixing of contextual information can have dire consequences for current and future studies of skeletal materials. It is a good practice to complete the sampling process one skeleton at a time. This helps prevent mislabeling samples or mixing skeletal elements from more than one individual. It is important that once someone begins the sampling process, that same person completes the process before moving on to another skeleton.

CONCLUDING REMARKS

The considerations and procedures presented here provide a foundation for studies of human remains that require the destruction of samples. Inevitability, different types of analyses will involve unique challenges for sample extraction, quality control, and skeletal conservation. We ask that papers presenting novel destructive analyses include brief descriptions of how the research assured quality control and conservation efforts. We hope that this brief description helps in establishing and maintaining responsible research agendas and provides guidance to those wishing to add these novel approaches to their own research design.

Acknowledgments

We are very grateful to Chris Stojanowski for detailed comments on an earlier draft of this chapter. Support for Dr. Lewis's research comes from the National Institutes of Health (R01 HG005172-01 and R01 GM089886-01A1) and the National Science Foundation (NSF 0845314). Support for Tung's research comes from the Wenner Gren Foundation for Anthropological Research (8169) and Vanderbilt University.

REFERENCES CITED

Adler, Christina J., Wolfgang Haak, D. Donlon, Alan Cooper, and Genographic Consortium
2011 Survival and Recovery of DNA from Ancient Teeth and Bones. *Journal of Archaeological Science* 38(5):956–964.

Bridges, Patricia S.
1996 Skeletal Biology and Behavior in Ancient Humans. *Evolutionary Anthropology* 4:112–120.

Buikstra, Jane E., and Lane A. Beck (editors)
2006 *Bioarchaeology: The Contextual Analysis of Human Remains.* Academic Press, New York.

Buikstra, Jane E., and Douglas H. Ubelaker (editors)
1994 *Standards for Data Collection from Human Skeletal Remains: Proceedings of a Seminar at the Field Museum of Natural History.* Arkansas Archaeological Survey Press, Fayetteville.

Dean, M. Christopher
2006 Tooth Microstructure Tracks the Pace of Human Life-History Evolution. *Proceedings of the Royal Society B* 273(1603):2799–2808.

Fox, Carles Lalueza, Jordi Juan, and Rosa M. Albert
1996 Phytolith Analysis on Dental Calculus, Enamel Surface, and Burial Soil: Information about Diet and Paleoenvironment. *American Journal of Physical Anthropology* 101(1):101–113.

France, Christine A. M., Jennifer A. Giaccai, and Nadia Cano
2011 The Efects of PVAc Treatment and Organic Solvent Removal on δ13C, δ15N, and δ18O Values of Collagen and Hydroxyapatite in Modern Bone. *Journal of Archaeological Science* 38:3387–3393.

Kemp, Brian M., and David Glenn Smith
2005 Use of Bleach to Eliminate Contaminating DNA from the Surface of Bones and Teeth. *Forensic Science International* 154(1): 53–61.

Knudson, Kelly J., and T. Douglas Price
2007 Utility of Multiple Chemical Techniques in Archaeological Residential Mobility Studies: Case Studies from Tiwanaku- and Chiribaya-Affiliated Sites in the Andes. *American Journal of Physical Anthropology* 132(1):25–39.

Lambert, Joseph, Sharon Vlasak Simpson, Carole Bryda Szpunar, and Jane E. Buikstra
1984 Ancient Human Diet from Inorganic Analysis of Bone. *Accounts of Chemical Research* 17:298–305.

Larsen, Clark Spencer, and Phillip L. Walker
2005 The Ethics of Bioarchaeology. In *Ethical Issues in Biological Anthropology*, edited by Trudy Turner, pp. 111–119. State University of New York Press, Albany.

Pääbo, Svante, Hendrick Poinar, David Serre, Viviane Jaenicke-Després, Juliane Hebler, Nadin Rohland, Melanie Kuch, Johannes Krause, Linda Vigilant, and Michael Hofreiter
2004 Genetic Analyses from Ancient DNA. *Annual Review of Genetics* 38:645–679.

Piotrowska, N., and T. Goslar
2002 Preparation of Bone Samples in the Gliwice Radiocarbon Laboratory for AMS Radiocarbon Dating. *Isotopes Environmental Health Studies* 38(4):267–275.

Price, T. Douglas
1989 *The Chemistry of Prehistoric Human Bone*. School of American Research Advanced Seminar Series. Cambridge University Press, Cambridge.

Price, T. Douglas, Clark M. Johnson, Joseph A. Ezzo, Jonathan Ericson, and James H. Burton
1994 Residential Mobility in the Prehistoric Southwest United States: A Preliminary Study Using Strontium Isotope Analysis. *Journal of Archaeological Science* 21:315–330.

Sampietro, María Lourdes, M. Thomas P. Gilbert, Oscar Lao, David Caramelli, Martina Lari, Jaume Bertranpetit, and Carles Lalueza-Fox
2006 Tracking Down Human Contamination in Ancient Human Teeth. *Molecular Biology and Evolution* 23(9):1801–1807.

Schoeninger, Margaret J.
1989 Reconstructing Prehistoric Human Diet. In *The Chemistry of Prehistoric Human Bone*, edited by T. Douglas Price, pp. 38–67. Cambridge University Press, Cambridge.

Walker, Phillip L.
2000 Bioarchaeological Ethics: A Historical Perspective on the Value of Human Remains. In *Biological Anthropology of the Human Skeleton*, edited by M. Anne Katzenberg and Shelley R. Saunders, pp. 3–39. Wiley Liss, Wilmington, Delaware.
2005 Bioarchaeological Methods. In *Handbook of Archaeological Methods*, vol. 2, edited by Herbert D. G. Maschner and Christopher Chippindale, pp. 871–918. Altamira Press, Walnut Creek, California.

Wittwer-Backofen, Ursula, Jutta Gampe, and James W. Vaupel
2004 Tooth Cementum Annulation for Age Estimation: Results from a Large Known-Age Validation Study. *American Journal of Physical Anthropology* 123(2):119–129.

Yang, Dongya Y., and Kathy Watt
2005 Contamination Controls When Preparing Archaeological Remains for Ancient DNA Analysis. *Journal of Archaeological Science* 32:331–336.

PART II

Bioarchaeological Research in North America

5

Negotiating the Gateway: Working with Multiple Lines of Evidence to Determine Identity

Lynne Goldstein
Department of Anthropology, Michigan State University

Until the advent of the Native American Graves Protection and Repatriation Act (NAGPRA) in 1990 and other recent legislation on local, state, and international scales, modern physical anthropologists did not necessarily focus their research on determining ethnic or tribal identities. Indeed, much work over the last 40 years has been devoted to issues of health, disease, and more precise determinations of age and sex. Some work focused on biological distance between groups, not as a way of linking past groups with living tribes or nations but instead as an approach to determining interrelationships between groups living at the same time in the past (cf. Buikstra et al. 1990). Beyond the fact that research took different directions, one reason for this lack of attention to the relationship between the bones of the past and living groups is the difficulty of making such links over what can be hundreds or thousands of years. Another reason is the not unwarranted concern that if one states that there *may* be a relationship, someone could take that statement of possibility for certainty and assume that there is indeed a relationship.

This reluctance to pursue such research has been unfortunate in many ways and was most notable when NAGPRA became U.S. law. NAGPRA requires museums and other institutions holding human remains to make determinations of relationships between those remains and living Native American tribes. The research on how to make these links and on how to determine identity was not well developed, and archaeologists and physical anthropologists did not have sophisticated or mature approaches to address this issue. Because the question had largely been avoided for so many years, researchers approached it with caution, at best. The best current research takes a multidimensional and multivariate approach to answering the question of identity, and indeed NAGPRA requires this. However, how many people or institutions actually go through the time and trouble of taking these steps?

My original intention in writing this paper was to employ case studies to examine what happens when archaeologists and physical anthropologists do and do not work with native peoples in determining identity when conducting repatriation studies. One major line of evidence in identity determination comes from native people, yet this can often be the most difficult kind of data to incorporate and collect. In conceiving this project, I was more than aware that there were biases, set views, and several different sides regarding this particular issue. Some saw archaeologists, physical anthropologists, and some ethnographers as gatekeepers in controlling and legitimating identity; others saw native peoples as having taken total control of the situation in recent years; and still others saw a general leveling of the playing field. To my knowledge, as of this writing, no one has examined real data to see what has actually happened in repatriation cases.

There is little question that anthropologists have traditionally been considered authorities on identity, but over the last 15 years, this view has shifted and changed rather dramatically. The organizers at a Society for American Archaeology symposium in 2007 stated:

> Laws and public opinion have traditionally empowered anthropologists as the authorities on Native American identity. More recently, Native Americans have asserted the right to establish their own identity. They embrace oral history and tradition in opposition to "scientific data" for determining identity. These conflicts have real consequences in debates over repatriation, land claims, and government recognition. This session examines the rights and autonomy of indigenous people in determining their own identity and the role of archaeologists as gatekeepers in legitimating that identity [Atalay and McGuire 2007].

Although a number of people and specific tribes may view the situation this way, one issue is that the law, at least in the United States under NAGPRA, has not changed, and *both* kinds of evidence (as well as other kinds of data) are equally valid. Further, this need not be an either/or debate, since many native people commonly use different kinds of evidence in documenting and determining their identities. Similarly, many anthropologists include and integrate oral histories in determining identity. Nonetheless, my sense in beginning this project was that archaeologists and physical anthropologists, and even cultural anthropologists, were not very consistent or clear about *how* they used oral history and oral traditions in determining identity. In addition, I did not think researchers purposely ignored oral tradition; but I thought they did not necessarily know how to incorporate the data, were uncomfortable doing so, or considered such data too "messy" or problematic. My sense of this situation came from my experience working with many archaeologists and physical anthropologists struggling to determine the potential identities of the archaeological and human remains in their possession. It also comes back to the problem of scholars not having addressed this kind of research for so many years.

Although this particular paper uses examples from the United States, the issue is not limited to the United States; it is a worldwide problem that is increasing as more and more countries wrestle with issues of repatriation and native identities. The focus of the problem is on identity and the kinds of evidence scholars use to make identity determinations from human remains, funerary objects, mortuary contexts, and oral and written histories. These kinds of determinations are made throughout the world, and the best analyses take into consideration every kind of data, as well as the potential biases of every data set. For example, in her case study from the classical Near East, Perry (2007) looks at textual data in addition to bioarchaeological data to answer research questions in Near Eastern archaeology. One of the important points Perry makes—a point also made by Buikstra et al. (2000) for a historic cemetery in Grafton, Illinois—is that it does not matter *whether* the historical and biological data differ but "*why* the texts provide a divergent history from the skeletons" (Perry 2007:490). The associations and interrelationships can be examined to let us better understand larger cultural and political processes.

Outline of the Project: The Smithsonian, Burials, and Repatriation

To examine these issues in a more systematic way, I looked to the Repatriation Office of the Smithsonian Institution National Museum of Natural History (SI). Even though the Smithsonian does not operate under NAGPRA, it is a good choice for this project for several reasons: (1) the SI has chosen to follow NAGPRA policies, and its law was subsequently amended in 1996 to follow NAGPRA more closely; (2) the SI has the financial and personnel resources to attend to repatriation in ways that most other institutions do not; (3) its reports are of high quality, are reasonably consistent in format, and are accessible;[1] (4) the SI has repatriated more human remains and objects from more sites and geographic areas than any other museum (see Table 5.1); and (5) because I served on the SI Repatriation Review Committee for 15 years, I had copies of most of its reports, although these reports are available to anyone who requests them.

For this project, I examined 45 reports—not all the reports produced by the SI Repatriation Office (I eliminated most reports dealing with only one or two items, for example) but a sufficient sample for this purpose. Geographically, the reports cover the United States—from Alaska to the Northwest Coast, from the Southwest to the Plains, from the Midwest to the Southeast to the Northeast (see Table 5.1).

Coincidentally, in 2005 Stephen Ousley, William Billeck, and Eric Hollinger published a long discussion and description of physical anthropology's role in repatriation at the Smithsonian, focusing on consultation between tribes and the SI, the SI's documentation of human remains, and especially the issue of cultural affiliation and the many ways that affiliation can be

Table 5.1. Smithsonian Institution Museum of Natural History Record of Repatriation: 1989–2005.

	Human Remains		Archaeological Items		Ethnographic Materials	
Region	**Returned**	**Not Returned**	**Returned**	**Not Returned**	**Returned**	**Not Returned**
Alaska	3,171	85	751	127	527	10
Northwest Coast	182	68	177	0	10	3
Hawaii	190	0	12	0	624	0
California	2	0	0	0	0	0
Great Basin	50	17	0	0	0	0
Plains	1,695	49	14,961	0	1	1
Plateau	83	8	2,225	15	1	2
Southwest	299	14	0	0	3	0
Northeast	16	37	3	28	2	1
Southeast	0	120	13	0	0	0
Totals	**5,688**	**398**	**18,142**	**170**	**1,168**	**17**

approached from the perspective of physical anthropology in particular. Ousley et al. (2005:9) make the point that the mandate to consider all available evidence and all relevant information is both reasonable and obvious. They go on to say: "The assumption that this process of consideration of evidence somehow pits archaeology against oral tradition, or scientists vs. Native Americans, is generally false." Because their focus is on physical anthropology, they really do not provide examples of oral histories or traditions that have helped inform cultural affiliation determinations. Indeed, their examples of interactions with tribes have to do with consultations on reburials, traditional care requests, and improved relationships, all of which are important but do not directly speak to the issue of determination of identity per se.

In a close reading of Ousley et al. (2005), it is clear that because of the quantity of human remains in the Smithsonian, much of the physical anthropology team's time is spent in documentation and sorting accession and other catalog problems. There were originally approximately 18,000 Native American human remains at the National Museum of Natural History; well over 5,000 human remains had been returned as of 2005. Once catalog problems are sorted, physical anthropologists focus their efforts on determining cultural affiliation and identity through various osteological data points and comparisons to known groups. They see their work as being especially helpful when other data sources are absent or ambiguous. However, in their 2005 paper, Ousley et al. do not discuss how they integrate other kinds of data, including oral traditions and oral histories, with biological data.

It is useful at this juncture to say something about the massive amount of work involved in documentation of the materials at the Smithsonian. While it is true that most of the human remains and objects at the Smithsonian have been there for a very long time, and while it is also true that people have been coming to the Smithsonian to study its collections for many years, comparable information is not available for all collections. In other words, beyond some basic catalog data, the Smithsonian does not have the same information for everything in its holdings. No large museum does. This is especially true when a museum and many different individuals have been collecting items over a long period and in many different contexts.

When it became clear that museums across the country would likely have to repatriate most of the human remains in their collections, a group of physical anthropologists met to determine a minimum set of standard measurements and observations that should be recorded for each set of human remains, whenever possible. These sets of observations came to be called the Standards, and ideally they will allow physical anthropologists to conduct comparative research using this information in the future, whether or not the particular remains have been repatriated. Buikstra and Ubelaker

(1994) compiled and edited the volume outlining the Standards. The Smithsonian has used a version of this system for all its human remains and has a digital version of these data available. Other institutions have done the same thing, in the United States and internationally. The comparability is not perfect, but it is far better than anything that would have been possible otherwise. The Standards have also created increased comparability in discussion and in print; they have become a reference tool.

What is most unfortunate is that nothing similar to the physical anthropology Standards was made for archaeology. Granted, physical anthropologists have the luxury of dealing only with human remains, which are certainly complicated, but archaeologists did not even try to decide at a general level what kinds of data and documentation should be recorded and kept. There were no comparable discussions about data.[2] This lack of attention to the problems of data and the overwhelming amounts of data is clear in the inconsistencies one sees in repatriation reports and in the lack of reports in many cases. This case study would not be possible for most institutions because the information does not exist.

Figure 5.1 shows the distribution of all the reports produced by the Smithsonian Repatriation Office from 1989 through 2005 by region of the country (the regions were labeled by the Repatriation Office). A total of 82 reports were produced during this period, and Figure 5.1 illustrates that the geographic distribution is not even. There are several reasons for this biased distribution: (1) Priority was first given to remains of named individuals and those with known descendants; and (2) priority was next given to tribes that had filed for the return of specific remains and/or collections. The distribution reflects both the collecting histories of the institution and the specific requests that tribes made.

Figure 5.1 shows clear bias or preference for Alaska and Northwest Coast regions, as well as for the Plains. The source of some of this bias is relatively easy to explain. First, most of the cases in the sample are historic in nature and are from collections that were originally in the Army Medical Museum; in 23 of the 45 reports examined, one or more individuals had originally been

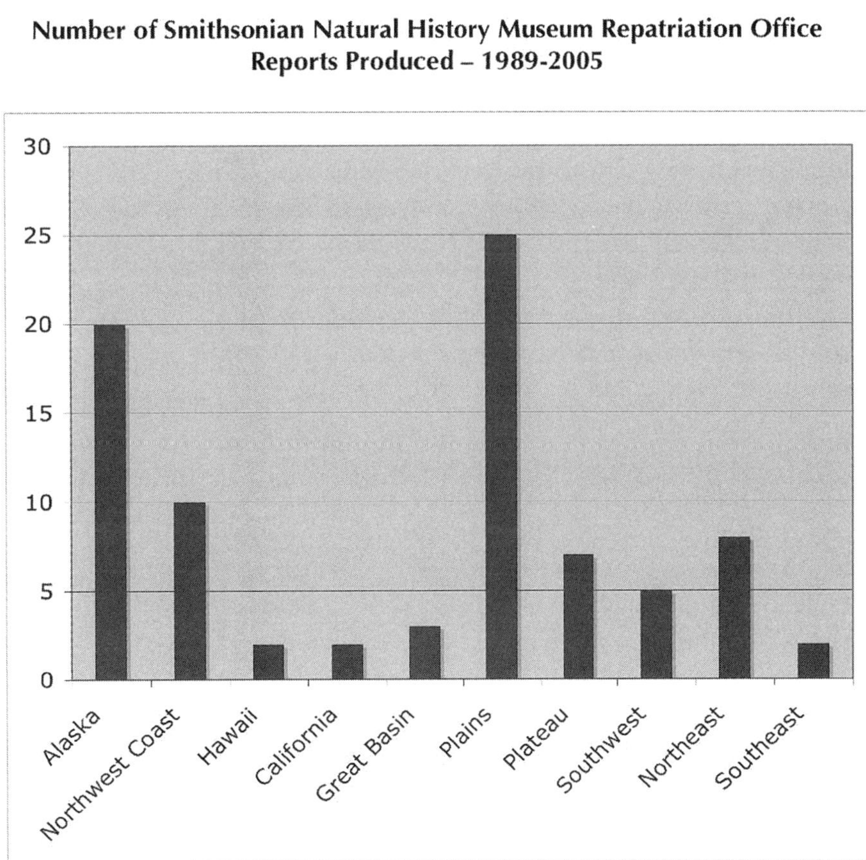

Figure 5.1. Number of Smithsonian Natural History Museum Repatriation Office reports produced from 1989 to 2005.

donated to the Army Medical Museum and were associated with army forts or army operations. Since many army operations in the middle to late nineteenth century occurred on the Plains, the correlation is not surprising.

A majority of the materials in Alaska and the Northwest Coast came to the Smithsonian from the expeditions of Smithsonian researchers, often from the expeditions of Aleš Hrdlička. Hrdlička was an important figure in the history of physical anthropology, but his field techniques were sometimes problematic from a modern perspective, and he documented his own excavations of graves of known individuals. Some sites he excavated were historic sites with clear links to peoples currently living in modern villages.

Hrdlička and other Smithsonian researchers in the first half of the twentieth century were especially interested in issues of migration from Siberia into Alaska. Other Smithsonian researchers during this time included Henry Collins, James Ford, and T. Dale Stewart. Their research included questions about how many waves of migration occurred; how the waves accounted for the present distribution of cultures, languages, and physical types; and whether or not one could identify the areas of origin of these peoples. The major research issues were New World origins and relationships between groups. The researchers excavated major sites and areas throughout Alaska.

Although the Plains have a large representation due to the presence of the army in the nineteenth century, another reason for the region's popularity in the Smithsonian collections is that the Smithsonian houses many materials from the River Basin Surveys (RBS). The importance and extent of the surveys warrant a short, separate discussion.

The RBS came out of the work of the Committee for the Recovery of Archeological Remains, a group of anthropologists sponsored by the American Anthropological Association, the Society for American Archaeology, and the American Council of Learned Societies, with liaisons from the Smithsonian and the National Research Council. These groups wanted to preserve archaeology threatened by post–World War II programs such as dam and reservoir construction. The ultimate result of the committee's work was the Inter-Agency Salvage Program, an arrangement among the Smithsonian, National Park Service, Army Corps of Engineers, Bureau of Reclamation, many universities, and other public and private organizations. It was particularly active in the Missouri River basin, West Coast states, southeastern states, and Texas.

In two articles in *Science* (Johnson 1966; Wedel 1967), the accomplishments of the program are outlined. Wedel, who at the time was the senior archaeologist in anthropology at the Smithsonian and had also been field director of the RBS, focused his discussion on the Smithsonian work in the Missouri River basin. For our purposes, it is significant to note that Wedel outlines the many contributions of the Missouri Basin project, especially since if the work had not been done, all this information would have been lost through flooding and construction. Instead, "[g]reat quantities of artifacts and important collections of skeletal material have been gathered under controlled conditions; and rigidly selected representative samples, with full provenience data, have been added to the national collections" (Wedel 1967:592). Wedel (1967) goes on to note that more than 200 sites were tested or extensively excavated, whereas prior to the program, fewer than a dozen sites in the region had received professional attention. More than 800 historic Arikara burials were excavated, as well as burials from the Central Plains and Woodland traditions.

Through most of its existence, the RBS was a unit of the Bureau of American Ethnology (BAE), with headquarters in Washington, D.C., and with field offices. One major field office was in Lincoln, Nebraska, and that office directed the work in the Missouri Basin. When the BAE was disbanded in 1965, the RBS joined the Smithsonian Office of Anthropology. In 1966 the headquarters moved to Lincoln, and in 1968 the RBS was placed administratively under the director of the National Museum of Natural History. In 1969 the Smithsonian transferred the RBS to the National Park Service, but provision was made for the deposit of records and manuscripts in the Smithsonian. The relationship between the RBS and the Smithsonian is a long and close one.

ANALYSIS OF REPATRIATION OFFICE REPORTS

The Repatriation Office reports I examined for this exercise include assessments of human remains only, as well as assessments of human remains and funerary objects. The report dates range from 1992 through 2004. Unfortunately, this range excludes one of the major reports and repatriations conducted by the SI—the Arikara collection, consisting of 1,288 individuals and 14,449 funerary objects—but since I did not have immediate access to the completed report, I could not include it in this analysis (although it is included in both Figure 5.1 and Table 5.1).

The reports are biased in terms of when they were prepared; 33 of the 45 were written prior to 1998. This is *not* because the Smithsonian was productive in the earlier years of the Repatriation Office and is not productive now, but the difference likely reflects several factors: (1) a decrease in staff due to an overall decrease in budget; (2) the 1996 change in the Smithsonian law, which changed what the SI had to report and when it had to report it; and (3) a shift in work to some of the larger collections, such as the Arikara collection, which required significantly more time to complete. The time bias is particularly relevant because not only did the reports improve in quality over time, but as case officers gained confidence and experience in working with tribes, their reports became more sophisticated and inclusive.

Reports fall into one of three categories: (1) human remains only; (2) human remains and funerary objects; and (3) objects only (the objects may be cultural patrimony, sacred, or unassociated funerary). Of the reports, 20 reports fall into the first category; 19 fall into the second; and 6 fall into the third. Although it is fairly easy to divide reports into these categories, there is a great deal of diversity within each group.

The first category—assessment of human remains only—is the least diverse group and the one that is least likely to include a discussion of oral histories and oral traditions. Of the 20 reports in this category, 16 did *not* include any mention of oral histories or traditions. Of the 651 individuals considered for repatriation in this group, 454, or 69.7 percent, were offered to tribes for repatriation. I do not know how many reports tribes subsequently challenged, but I am certain that at least a few reports were challenged.[3] Seventeen of the reports examined were completed between 1992 and 1998.

In the second category of human remains and funerary objects, of the 19 reports in this category, 13 did *not* include a specific discussion of oral traditions or oral histories. Of the 2,184 individuals reported here, 2,096 (or 95.9 percent) were offered for repatriation, along with 1,103 of the 1,447 objects considered (76.2 percent). Of the 19 reports, 8 were completed from 1997 through 2004. Several tribes have challenged the decisions of the Smithsonian in this category, and in more than one case these challenges ended in a reversal of the initial SI decision. The tribes brought forward additional evidence, sometimes in the form of oral histories, sometimes other kinds of evidence, but always information that the Smithsonian did not have or did not interpret properly because case officers did not have as extensive or intensive knowledge of the specific area or region.

In the category of objects only, there are six case reports. In three of these reports, the authors did not use oral traditions or histories in their discussions, either because historic and/or archaeological evidence was sufficient to establish the identity and/or because such oral evidence did not exist. The Smithsonian returned objects in four cases; in another case, it returned one object and retained the other. In the sixth case, the Smithsonian used oral tradition and oral histories extensively. The museum established that the tribe requesting the object had a cultural affiliation to the object but had not demonstrated that it was a sacred object or an object of cultural patrimony. Various scholars at the Smithsonian thought the object should be returned, and people worked very hard and deliberately over several years to document that the object had been used historically in ceremonies and/or rituals but found that they could not demonstrate that this had been the case. Indeed, interviews with tribal elders documented that if the object were returned, it would not necessarily be used in a ceremony today. Further, the Smithsonian was able to document that the museum had clear title to the object.

I have deliberately not been specific in outlining these cases because my purpose is to provide only a sense of the kinds of information available and the kinds of cases that have been processed. However, at the end of this paper I have listed a separate and complete bibliography of all the case reports that I used in this analysis.

In terms of the use of oral histories and oral traditions, with a few notable exceptions, the report authors tend to outline what the traditions and histories say, indicate how they agree or disagree with each other and the other data, and then continue. In other words, they either do not appear to know what to do with these data or have decided not to use them. Unlike "messy" archaeological data, which authors might discuss, dissect, or sort, the discrepancies here often seem to be sufficient for authors to set all the data aside. When oral histories and traditions do not agree with archaeological and other data, they are dismissed. Roger Echo-Hawk (2000) and others have discussed specific and systematic ways to approach such problems, but none of the case officers used these methods in the reports I examined. In a few reports, oral histories were used extensively, but these were exceptions; most of the time, the histories were simply outlined.

Indeed, archaeologists and physical anthropologists do not tend to eliminate archaeological or osteological data when they find an errant sherd or an unusual bone, so why eliminate oral history when it doesn't quite fit with other data? Rather than automatically assigning a malevolent cause, I think the reason is likely much simpler: We have not been taught what to do with the data. Few graduate anthropology programs specifically train students in how to incorporate oral traditions and oral histories into archaeological, ethnographic, historic, geographic, and other data. As we desire to be more scientific, we tend to like messy data less and less. This is unfortunate since reality is more and more messy, and more and more interesting. Data that fit a neat pattern are never as interesting as data that have some rough edges. If we really want our students to do better in these circumstances in the future, it would be to our benefit to focus training on such issues.

At the outset, I said I wanted to examine what happens when archaeologists do and do not work with native peoples in determining identity. I am not certain that this examination of using oral traditions in reports gets directly (or even indirectly) to this question, but I can say that since the Repatriation Office at the Smithsonian has been in existence, and as the case officers have gotten more experience, not only has the quality of the reports improved, but the level and degree of interaction with tribes have also improved.

Appropriate to this discussion, we can look at the overall pattern of case reports and record of returns. Table 5.1 provides this information. It is organized by region in the same way as Figure 5.1 and is divided by categories of information—human remains, archaeological items, and ethnographic materials. For each category for each region, I have tallied how many of the items requested and reported were returned (through 2005) and how many were not returned. The human remains represent individuals, but the archaeological numbers are a bit misleading; beads are sometimes counted individually, leading to very large numbers in places like the Plains. The lack of returns of archaeological and ethnographic items in some regions relates to the circumstances of the original report; the return of historic human remains had highest priority, so it was done before everything else.

Table 5.1 demonstrates that the Smithsonian has returned a significant number of human remains, archaeological items, and ethnographic objects and that it has rarely refused to return items. Indeed, in the reports I examined, it returned 93.5 percent of the human remains it considered, 90.7 percent of the artifacts considered, and 98.6 percent of the ethnographic items considered. These numbers may be misleading, however, since the SI has a long way to go in processing all its collections and all the requests it may receive from tribes; the reports I examined represent what can be termed the easiest requests to fulfill.

Buikstra (2006:400–401) discusses the fact that ethnologists, archaeologists, and historians have made strong arguments that Native American oral traditions may reflect ancient historical events. As noted earlier, especially useful is the fact that several scholars have developed methods to validate the substance of these oral traditions (Echo-Hawk 2000; Vansina 1985; Whiteley 2002).

Especially relevant to the subject here, Echo-Hawk (1994, 1997) presented to the Smithsonian Institution a meticulous approach to using information from both oral traditions and archaeology to determine whether or not the Pawnee were culturally affiliated with the prehistoric Central Plains tradition and thus had rights to repatriation. This was the topic of one of the SI reports that tribes challenged. The Repatriation Office did not accept the challenge, so the Pawnee asked that the secretary of the Smithsonian send their appeal to the Repatriation Review Committee for a hearing. It was the first time a hearing was requested by any tribe. The committee accepted Echo-Hawk's approach as well as his interpretations, and human remains from the prehistoric Steed-Kisker site were transferred to the Pawnee (Echo-Hawk 1997).

CONCLUSIONS

To my knowledge, this report data set, as crudely outlined here, is the most complete documentation of how any institution (or even set of institutions) has or has not used evidence to repatriate human remains and funerary objects. But what does it actually tell us? Very little by itself. For the most part, if we look carefully into the reports, we find that the early case reports from the Smithsonian did not use oral traditions and oral histories because the remains and objects being returned were historic and came largely from the Army Medical Museum. Many of these items were from battlefields, forts, or other unsavory collection spots. The Smithsonian case officers rightly focused attention in their reports on specific collectors and their particular histories. Indeed, many of these reports are fascinating accounts of the early development of the Smithsonian and somewhat uncomfortable accounts of how collections got to the museum. If one reads several case reports, one comes to understand that some collectors are more trustworthy than others and that some designations as Kiowa, or Arapaho, or Sioux are more reliable than others.

In other instances, the case officers do not look to oral traditions and histories because the cases are nineteenth century or early twentieth century in nature, and there is ample documentation of exactly what happened, even if it is not a gruesome army situation. This is the case for many groups in Alaska, where Hrdlička and others excavated historic cemeteries, and the documentation of what was done is explicit and specific.

However, it is the third kind of case that should use oral traditions but does not. In these instances, oral traditions are mentioned or discussed, but they are not integrated or analyzed the way that other data are used. It is here that we have to look to improving our relationships with tribes and our knowledge of how to work with these kinds of data. It is here that we must become more comfortable with messy data and try to figure out *why* the oral traditions may not agree with some of the other data, if that is the case. As noted earlier, this kind of analysis may teach us much more about larger cultural and political processes.

Anthropologists may be gatekeepers in that they control access to the collections, but it is relevant to note that, in the Smithsonian case, they also help many native people gain access to a wealth of information stored by the federal government across Washington, D.C. For those tribes who are making or are planning to make a request, the Smithsonian Repatriation Review Committee, on which I sat for 15 years, had (and still has) a travel grant program to bring two tribal representatives per tribe to the Smithsonian to consult with case officers, get oriented to existing documentation, and examine collections containing items that may be subject to repatriation. Further, as a case officer works on a request, it is the policy, at least at the Natural History Museum, to call and consult with relevant tribes. None of the decisions or reports has been made in a vacuum, and there have been significant improvements in these consultations over the last 15 years.

Finally, as I read in more than one report in comments made by tribes, tribes have learned over the years that they get better results if they request specific items or kinds of items rather than asking for "everything." Where does one begin with a request for "everything"? Even if archaeologists are gatekeepers in some ways and in certain senses of the word, it is difficult to respond adequately and promptly to such a request. This increase in sophistication on all sides suggests that perhaps a number of us have learned to work more productively with others.

As long as people see themselves in opposition, I don't think the dialogue or the work will be especially productive or useful. We may not agree on a number of issues, and we may profoundly disagree on others, but there are potentially many ways in which we can move forward. It will, however, require real, open, and honest discussion, as well as new kinds of training for us and for our graduate students.

NOTES

1. It is quite startling to discover that most institutions have not documented or prepared written reports on collections subject to repatriation. They have prepared lists for tribes but not necessarily reports on their decisions whether or not to repatriate and on how these decisions were reached. This is a disturbing and troubling discovery that should be addressed by the profession.

2. All comments about data recording assume that the institution has permission from the appropriate group to record, take, and keep such measurements.

3. When a tribe challenges or questions a report, the Repatriation Office may work out the problem or issues with the tribe without the involvement of any other office or individuals. The tribe may present additional evidence, the Repatriation Office may provide a satisfactory explanation, or both. If the tribe is not satisfied, it can request that the secretary of the Smithsonian review the decision, and this review can include bringing in the Repatriation Review Committee for a formal or informal hearing.

REFERENCES CITED

Atalay, Sonya, and Randall McGuire
2007 Abstract for symposium "Archaeologists as Gatekeepers of Native American Identity." Society for American Archaeology annual meetings, Austin, Texas.

Buikstra, Jane E.
2006 Repatriation and Bioarchaeology: Challenges and Opportunities. In *Bioarchaeology: The Contextual Analysis of Human Remains*, edited by Jane E. Buikstra and Lane A. Beck, pp. 389–415. Academic Press, Amsterdam.

Buikstra, Jane E., Susan R. Frankenberg, and Lyle W. Konigsberg
1990 Skeletal Biological Distance Studies in American Physical Anthropology: Recent Trends. *American Journal of Physical Anthropology* 82:1–7.

Buikstra, Jane E., Jodie A. O'Gorman, and Cynthia Sutton (editors)
2000 Never Anything So Solemn: An Archeological, Biological, and Historical Investigation of the Nineteenth-Century Grafton Cemetery. Kampsville Studies in Archeology and History No. 3. Center for American Archeology, Kampsville, Illinois.

Buikstra, Jane E., and Douglas H. Ubelaker (editors)
1994 *Standards for Data Collection from Human Skeletal Remains: Proceedings of a Seminar at the Field Museum of Natural History.* Arkansas Archaeological Survey Press, Fayetteville.

Echo-Hawk, Roger C.
1994 Kara Katit Pakutu: Exploring the Origins of Native America in Anthropology and Oral History. Unpublished master's thesis, Department of History, University of Colorado, Boulder.
1997 Forging a New Ancient History for Native America. In *Native Americans and Archaeologists: Stepping Stones to Common Ground*, edited by Nida Swindler, Kurt E. Dongoske, Roger Anyon, and Alan S. Downer, pp. 88–102. AltaMira Press, Walnut Creek, California.
2000 Ancient History in the New World: Integrating Oral Traditions and the Archaeological Record in Deep Time. *American Antiquity* 65(2):267–290.

Johnson, Frederick
1966 Archaeology of Emergency. *Science* 152(329):1592–1597.

Ousley, Stephen, William T. Billeck, and R. Eric Hollinger
2005 Federal Repatriation Legislation and the Role of Physical Anthropology in Repatriation. *Yearbook of Physical Anthropology* 48:2–32.

Perry, Megan A.
2007 Is Bioarchaeology Handmaiden to History? Developing a Historical Bioarchaeology. *Journal of Anthropology Archaeology* 26:486–515.

Vansina, Jan
1985 *Oral Tradition as History*. University of Wisconsin Press, Madison.

Wedel, Waldo R.
1967 Salvage Archaeology in the Missouri River Basin. *Science* 156(3775):589–597.

Whiteley, Peter M.
2002 Archaeology and Oral Traditions: The Scientific Importance of Dialogue. *American Antiquity* 67(3):405–415.

REPORTS NOT CITED BUT USED IN ANALYSIS

Aronsen, Gary P., and Javier Urcid, with Tamara L. Bray
1997 *Inventory and Assessment of Human Remains and Funerary Objects from the Lower Columbia River Valley, Oregon and Washington States (Confederated Tribes of the Grande Ronde) in the National Museum of Natural History*. Case Report 91-010-A. Repatriation Office, National Museum of Natural History, Smithsonian Institution, Washington, D.C.

Aronsen, Gary P., and Javier Urcid
1996 *Inventory and Assessment of Human Remains and Funerary Objects from the Puget Sound and Grays Harbor Regions of Washington State in the National Museum of Natural History*. Case Report 92-007. Repatriation Office, National Museum of Natural History, Smithsonian Institution, Washington, D.C.

Baugh, Timothy G., Stephanie Makseyn-Kelley, and John W. Verano
1993 *With a Lock of Hair for Remembrance: Nakota and Central Dakota Legacy at the Smithsonian Institution*. Repatriation Office, National Museum of Natural History, Smithsonian Institution, Washington, D.C.

Billeck, William T., with Parvene Hamzavi, Elizabeth Miller, and Douglas Owsley
1997 *Inventory and Assessment of Human Remains and Funerary Objects Potentially Affiliated with the Ponca in the National Museum of Natural History*. Repatriation Office, National Museum of Natural History, Smithsonian Institution, Washington, D.C.

Billeck, William T., and Beverly S. Byrd (with contributions by others)
1996 *Inventory and Assessment of Human Remains and Funerary Objects Potentially Affiliated with the Mandan and Hidatsa of the Three Affiliated Tribes in the National Museum of Natural History*. Repatriation Office, National Museum of Natural History, Smithsonian Institution, Washington, D.C.

Billeck, William T., Erica B. Jones, Stephanie A. Makseyn-Kelley, and John W. Verano
1995 *Inventory and Assessment of Human Remains and Associated Funerary Objects Potentially Affiliated with the Pawnee in the National Museum of Natural History*. Case Report 88-007. Repatriation Office, National Museum of Natural History, Smithsonian Institution, Washington, D.C.

Billeck, William T., and Javier Urcid
1995 *Assessment of the Cultural Affiliation of the Steed-Kisker Phase for Evaluation by the National Museum of Natural History Native American Repatriation Review Committee*. Repatriation Office, National Museum of Natural History, Smithsonian Institution, Washington, D.C.

Bray, Tamara L., Javier Urcid, and Gary P. Aronsen
1993 *Inventory and Assessment of Human Remains from Upper and Lower Memaloose Islands and Adjacent Areas of the Middle Columbia River, Oregon and Washington, in the National Museum of Natural History*. Repatriation Office, National Museum of Natural History, Smithsonian Institution, Washington, D.C.

Bray, Tamara L., Gary P. Aronsen, and Javier Urcid
1996 *Inventory and Assessment of Human Remains from Northwest Oregon in the National Museum of Natural History*. Case Report 91-010. Repatriation Office, National Museum of Natural History, Smithsonian Institution, Washington, D.C.

Bray, Tamara L., Javier Urcid, and Gary P. Aronsen
1994a *Inventory and Assessment of Human Remains from Clallam County, Washington in the National Museum of Natural History*. Repatriation Office, National Museum of Natural History, Smithsonian Institution, Washington, D.C.
1994b *Inventory and Assessment of Human Remains from Northeastern Washington and Northern Idaho in the National Museum of Natural History*. Case Report No. 92-017. Repatriation Office, National Museum of Natural History, Smithsonian Institution, Washington, D.C.

Bray, Tamara, with Gary P. Aronsen, Javier Urcid, and John Verano
1992 *Inventory and Assessment of Native American Human Remains from the Western Great Basin, Nevada Sector in the National Museum of Natural History*. Repatriation Office, National Museum of Natural History, Smithsonian Institution, Washington, D.C.

Burgess, Laurie E., and William T. Billeck
2004 *Assessment of a Brass Patu Traded by Captain Cook in 1778 and an Anthropomorphic Stone Carving from Northeast Oregon in the National Museum of Natural History, Smithsonian Institution*. Repatriation Office, National Museum of Natural History, Smithsonian Institution, Washington, D.C.

Hollinger, R. Eric
2001 *Inventory and Assessment of Human Remains Potentially Affiliated to the Winnebago/Ho-Chunk Tribes in the National Museum of Natural History, Smithsonian Institution*. Repatriation Office, National Museum of Natural History, Smithsonian Institution, Washington, D.C.
2003 *Inventory and Assessment of Human Remains and Funerary Objects Potentially Affiliated with the Menominee Tribe in the National Museum of Natural History, Smithsonian Institution*. Repatriation Office, National Museum of Natural History, Smithsonian Institution, Washington, D.C.

Hollinger, R. Eric, and Elizabeth Eubanks
2003 *Inventory and Assessment of Human Remains Potentially Affiliated with the Miami Tribe in the National Museum of Natural History, Smithsonian Institution*. Repatriation Office, National Museum of Natural History, Smithsonian Institution, Washington, D.C.

Hollinger, R. Eric, Elizabeth Eubanks, and Stephen Ousley
2004 *Inventory and Assessment of Human Remains and Funerary Objects from the Point Barrow Region, Alaska, in the National Museum of Natural History, Smithsonian Institution*. Repatriation Office, National Museum of Natural History, Smithsonian Institution, Washington, D.C.

Killion, Thomas W., Scott Brown, and Stuart Speaker
1992 Naevahoo'ohtseme—*Cheyenne Repatriation: Human Remains*. Repatriation Office, National Museum of Natural History, Smithsonian Institution, Washington, D.C.

Killion, Thomas W., Elizabeth Eubanks, and William T. Billeck
2002 *Inventory and Assessment of Human Remains from the Salinas Pueblos of Gran Quivira and Quarai, New Mexico, in the National Museum of Natural History, Smithsonian Institution*. Repatriation Office, National Museum of Natural History, Smithsonian Institution, Washington, D.C.

Killion, Thomas W., and J. Stuart Speaker, with Javier S. Urcid and Beverly Byrd
1994 *Inventory and Documentation of Skeletal Remains from the Prince William Sound in the Physical Anthropology Collections of the Department of Anthropology, National Museum of Natural History*. Repatriation Office, National Museum of Natural History, Smithsonian Institution, Washington, D.C.

Lippert, Dorothy
2002 *Inventory and Assessment of Human Remains and Funerary Objects from Kauwerak, Akavingayak and Port Clarence, Alaska, in the National Museum of Natural History, Smithsonian Institution*. Repatriation Office, National Museum of Natural History, Smithsonian Institution, Washington, D.C.

Makseyn-Kelley, Stephanie A.
1999 *Inventory and Assessment of Human Remains and Funerary Objects Potentially Affiliated with the Brule Sioux in the National Museum of Natural History*. Case Report N93-026. Repatriation Office, National Museum of Natural History, Smithsonian Institution, Washington, D.C.

Makseyn-Kelley, Stephanie A., and Beverly Spriggs Byrd
1995 *Inventory and Assessment of Human Remains and Associated Funerary Objects Affiliated with the Cheyenne River Sioux Tribe in the National Museum of Natural History*. Case Report 91-011. Repatriation Office, National Museum of Natural History, Smithsonian Institution, Washington, D.C.
1997 *Inventory and Assessment of Human Remains and Funerary Objects Potentially Affiliated with the Oglala Sioux Tribe in the National Museum of Natural History*. Case Report N88-002. Repatriation Office, National Museum of Natural History, Smithsonian Institution, Washington, D.C.

Makseyn-Kelley, Stephanie A., and Erica Bubniak Jones
1996 *Inventory and Assessment of Human Remains from the Historic Period Potentially Affiliated with the Eastern Dakota in the National Museum of Natural History*. Repatriation Office, National Museum of Natural History, Smithsonian Institution, Washington, D.C.

Merrill, William L., Edmund J. Ladd, and T. J. Ferguson
1993 The Return of the *Ahayu:da:* Lessons for Repatriation from Zuni Pueblo and the Smithsonian Institution. *Current Anthropology* 34(5)1–79.

Molloy, Paula
2000 *Inventory and Assessment of a Stone Pendant (A017905) Requested by the Mohegan Tribe*. Repatriation Office, National Museum of Natural History, Smithsonian Institution, Washington, D.C.

Molloy, Paula, and Beverly S. Byrd, with John W. Verano
1995 *Inventory and Assessment of Human Remains from the State of Connecticut in the National Museum of Natural History*. Case Report 93-014. Repatriation Office, National Museum of Natural History, Smithsonian Institution, Washington, D.C.

Molloy, Paula, and Juliet Cleaves, with John W. Verano
1995 *Inventory and Assessment of Human Remains from North-Central Montana in the National Museum of Natural History*. Case Report 90-004. Repatriation Office, National Museum of Natural History, Smithsonian Institution, Washington, D.C.

Molloy, Paula, Phillip E. Minthorn, Gary P. Aronsen, and Javier Urcid, with Elizabeth Miller
1996 *Inventory and Assessment of Human Remains Identified as Nez Perce in the National Museum of Natural History*. Repatriation Office, National Museum of Natural History, Smithsonian Institution, Washington, D.C.

Molloy, Paula, and Ashley Wyant
1997 *Inventory and Assessment of Funerary Objects in Accession No. 325070, "The Pierite Collection."* National Museum of Natural History. Repatriation Office, National Museum of Natural History, Smithsonian Institution, Washington, D.C.

Mudar, Karen
1998 *Inventory and Assessment of Human Remains from Cape Denbigh, Bering Straits Native Corporation, Alaska, in the National Museum of Natural History*. Repatriation Office, National Museum of Natural History, Smithsonian Institution, Washington, D.C.
1999 *Inventory and Assessment of Human Remains and Funerary Objects from Unalakleet, Bering Straits Native Corporation, Alaska, in the National Museum of Natural History*. Repatriation Office, National Museum of Natural History, Smithsonian Institution, Washington, D.C.

Mudar, Karen M., Erica Bubiak-Jones, and Stuart Speaker
1995 *Inventory and Assessment of Human Remains and Associated Funerary Objects from Wainwright, Alaska, in the National Museum of Natural History*. Repatriation Office, National Museum of Natural History, Smithsonian Institution, Washington, D.C.

Mudar, Karen M., Erica B. Jones, and John W. Verano
1994 *Inventory and Assessment of Human Remains from the Hand Site (44SN22), Southampton County, Virginia, in the National Museum of Natural History*. Case Report 87-003. Repatriation Office, National Museum of Natural History, Smithsonian Institution, Washington, D.C.

Mudar, Karen M., Kathrine Nelson, Stuart Speaker, Richard Scott, Steven Street, and Elizabeth Miller
1996 *Inventory and Assessment of Human Remains and Associated Funerary Objects from Northeast Norton Sound, Bering Straits Native Corporation, Alaska, in the National Museum of Natural History*. Repatriation Office, National Museum of Natural History, Smithsonian Institution, Washington, D.C.

Mudar, Karen M., Stuart Speaker, and Erica Bubniak-Jones
1996 *Inventory and Assessment of Human Remains and Funerary Objects from Point Hope, Arctic Slope Native Corporation in the National Museum of Natural History*. Repatriation Office, National Museum of Natural History, Smithsonian Institution, Washington, D.C.

Mudar, Karen M., Stuart Speaker, and Elizabeth Miller
1996 *Inventory and Assessment of Human Remains and Associated Funerary Objects from St. Lawrence Island, Bering Straits Native Corporation, Alaska, in the National Museum of Natural History*. Repatriation Office, National Museum of Natural History, Smithsonian Institution, Washington, D.C.

Smythe, Charles W.
1995 *Assessment of the Six Nations Iroquois Confederacy Request to the National Museum of Natural History to Repatriate Two Wampum Items*. Repatriation Office, National Museum of Natural History, Smithsonian Institution, Washington, D.C.
2000 *Assessment of Request for the Repatriation of the Ontonagon Boulder by the Keweenaw Bay Indian Community*. Repatriation Office, National Museum of Natural History, Smithsonian Institution, Washington, D.C.

Speaker, Stuart, Beverly S. Byrd, John W. Verano, and Gretchen Stromberg
1994 *Inventory and Assessment of Human Remains Potentially Related to the Apache and Yavapai Tribes in the National Museum of Natural History*. Case Report 91-007. Repatriation Office, National Museum of Natural History, Smithsonian Institution, Washington, D.C.

Speaker, Stuart, Beverly S. Byrd, Javier Urcid, and John W. Verano
1994 Inventory and Assessment of Human Remains Potentially Related to the Kiowa Tribe in the National Museum of Natural History. Case Report 91-008. Repatriation Office, National Museum of Natural History, Smithsonian Institution, Washington, D.C.

Speaker, Stuart, Thomas W. Killion, and John W. Verano
1993 *Arapaho Repatriation: Human Remains*. Repatriation Office, National Museum of Natural History, Smithsonian Institution, Washington, D.C.

Speaker, Stuart, Erica Jones, and Karen M. Mudar
1995 *Inventory and Assessment of Human Remains and Associated Funerary Objects from Anaktuvuk Pass, Alaska in the National Museum of Natural History*. Case H 000008. Repatriation Office, National Museum of Natural History, Smithsonian Institution, Washington, D.C.

Speaker, Stuart, Deanna Kingston, and Karen M. Mudar
1996 *Inventory and Assessment of Human Remains and Associated Funerary Objects from Nunivak Island, Alaska in the National Museum of Natural History*. Case Report 93-025. Repatriation Office, National Museum of Natural History, Smithsonian Institution, Washington, D.C.

6

An Ancient Cave Mummy from Kentucky

Patty Jo Watson
Department of Anthropology, Washington University

Unlike the elaborately treated mummies of ancient Egypt or Peru, the human remains addressed here were preserved by natural factors in their burial environments: primarily dryness and lack of weathering. Exsiccation (drying) by minerals in the sediments or on rocky surfaces with which they were in contact also enhanced soft tissue preservation.

The prehistoric individual discussed below was found in Salts Cave, Kentucky, by Euro-Americans in 1875 (Figure 6.1). The remains were known as Little Alice for nearly a century, until their examination by physical anthropologist Louise Robbins (1971). Robbins established that the body was a Native American boy rather than a Euro-American girl or an Indian princess, as some had claimed. Details of Robbins's other findings are summarized, as well as the complex and imperfectly understood history of the discovery and subsequent itinerary of the Salts Cave boy to the present day. In the final section of this paper, I offer comments about the manner in which the boy's body was thought of and treated by the nineteenth- and twentieth-century Euro-Americans who had custody of the remains for various periods of time, concluding with some suggestions about what he might teach us in the future.

The Salts Cave Mummy

During a summer trip to Mammoth Cave National Park in Kentucky, circa 1955–1957, I made a casual visit to a small museum in the old Mammoth Cave post office near the visitor center. Then a graduate student in Near Eastern prehistory at the University of Chicago, I had no thought of undertaking archaeological research in Kentucky. Having recently married a caver (Richard A. Watson), however, a central member of a small group then exploring and mapping big caves in Flint Ridge within the park, I had been drawn into caving there and often joined weekend or summer vacation expeditions.

Included among the arrays of projectile points, ground stone tools, and other artifacts in the old museum was the body of a small person known as Little Alice, who had reputedly been found in one of the nearby caves—Salts Cave in Flint Ridge—in the late nineteenth century. By the time I had committed myself seven or eight years later to an archaeological project in Salts Cave, the mummy was no longer at the park. Eventually I tracked it to the University of Kentucky in Lexington, where the remains had been transferred from Mammoth Cave National Park in 1958. In 1969 the physical anthropologist in the University of Kentucky's Anthropology Department, Louise Robbins, undertook analysis (including X-rays) and dating of the body (Robbins 1971, 1974). As soon as she relocated the remains, one close look was sufficient to overturn nearly a century of folkloric belief that this mummy was female: the external genitalia were still present and unequivocally male.

Other results of Robbins's examination included two radiocarbon determinations on tissue from the lower thoracic and abdominal regions (the uncalibrated dates are 1960 +/- 160 B.P. [M-2258] and 1920 +/- 160 B.P.

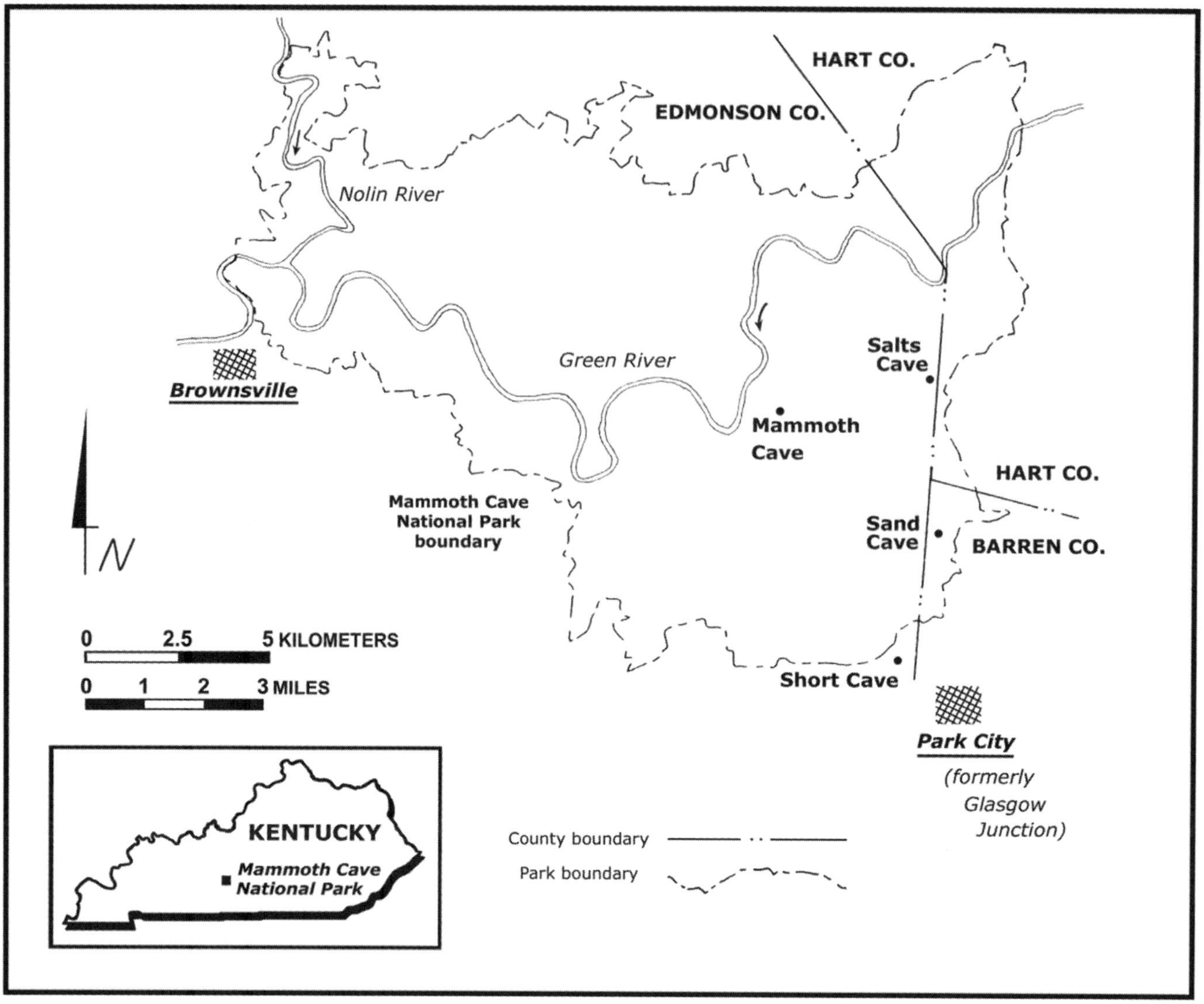

Figure 6.1. Map showing sites mentioned in this paper.

[M-2249]), as well as the little boy's age at death (nine years), the primary components of his last meal or meals (identified by Eric O. Callen and Richard A. Yarnell as hickory nuts, sumpweed, and chenopod; Yarnell 1974, 1978), and an assessment of his general health (good, except for a blood clot in the thoracic region). Robbins suggested that the boy "probably died rather suddenly from an internal hemorrhage resulting from a fall or a blow to the thoracic area" (Robbins 1974:144).

During the initial stages of fieldwork in Salts Cave in the 1960s, Robbins led a crew to the locale where the mummy was supposed to have been found.[1] Soon after the group began careful examination of the passage, one of them noticed a limestone rock bearing a penciled inscription (Watson 1974:25):

> Sir
> I have found one of the Grat wonders of the
> world in this cave, whitch is a muma
> Can all seed hearafter
> found March the 8
> T.E. lee J.L. lee 1875
> an W.d. cutliff
> dicuvers

What has come to be called the discovery rock was found on April 9, 1969, by Kim Dale, a Joint Venturer of the Cave Research Foundation (CRF). Across the passage from the discovery rock, a CRF group recording historic names and dates in the same general part of Salts Cave had previously found another inscribed rock (Stanley Sides, personal communication 2007), which they showed me on May 31, 1969. The message on this rock runs as follows:

> How are you grave robbers. What is it you would not do. They is nothing too mean for you to do. You low down scoundrls. What is it you wouldn't do. Just think for a sec of men to steal the dead [unclear; perhaps "Just speculate on it"]
> Sir you are worse than a murderer. Are you not afraid it will follow you in your paths of a day and your bed at night. You low down dirty damed thief of hell yours most [unclear, perhaps "respectfully"] J M Smith
> P.S. Call again you honest fellows when you get hard up for a few dimes or call at some other grave yard.

The second inscription, known as the damnation rock, is undated, but J. M. Smith left his name elsewhere in upper-level passages of Salts Cave with associated dates in the 1870s. Hence, we know he was a contemporary of Cutliff and the Lees.

During the mid-1980s and early 1990s, Tankersley et al. (1994) made further observations at the traditional mummy find-spot in Salts Cave, as well as on the mummy's physical remains at the Museum of Anthropology, University of Kentucky–Lexington. They agreed in general with Robbins's conclusions about cause of death but provided evidence (from SEM examination) for more extensive internal hemorrhaging than she was able to detect, supporting her suggestion that the boy died from internal bleeding, which they thought resulted from a severe fall in the cave. They concluded that he had climbed to a high point in the adjacent breakdown pile, from which he had slipped and fallen to his death. Other members of his group subsequently placed his body on a nearby ledge and left it in the cave.

Postdiscovery History of the Salts Cave Mummy: The Received View (1970s–1980s)

When the CRF Archeological Project was first engaging in research within Salts Cave, a lawyer and avocational historian from Shelbyville, Indiana, Harold Meloy, was pursuing the tangled histories of the various mummies from Mammoth Cave and the surrounding region. What follows here is drawn from Meloy's published accounts (Meloy 1977; Meloy and Watson 1969), with additional reference to an undated newspaper clipping brought to our attention by Cave City resident Ellis Jones.[2]

In 1875 the land including Salts Cave Sink (and the natural entrance to Salts Cave at the bottom of the sink) was widely believed to belong to the Mammoth Cave Estate. Much of Upper Salts Cave, however, underlay the property of Louis Vial. According to his daughter, author of the newspaper story preserved in Ellis Jones's clipping, Vial and his friends explored Salts Cave extensively via a "side entrance known only to themselves." It was during one of these trips that the Salts Cave mummy was discovered. Vial's daughter said that the mummy was found by her father and Bill Cutliff "about 1874." Meloy's information (obtained from archives and local folk traditions) indicated that the mummy was taken from Salts Cave and sold to a local show-cave manager, Larkin J. Proctor, who exhibited it in one of the caves he owned or leased, probably Wright's Cave, also known as Long Cave. At some point during the 1880s or 1890s, show-cave entrepreneur Henry C. Ganter, then managing Mammoth Cave and the Mammoth Cave Hotel, bought the Salts Cave mummy from Proctor and exhibited it as an Indian princess whose mortal remains had been found in Mammoth Cave. According to local oral tradition, the mummy was sent to the Chicago World's Fair in 1893 and was displayed at other exhibitions to promote tourist interest in Mammoth Cave. This may well have been the case, but the 1893 World's Fair mummy is now known to have been "Fawn Hoof," an adult female from Short Cave, not the little boy from Salts Cave.[3]

After Ganter's retirement in 1915, he collaborated briefly with another cave-region promoter, George D. Morrison, who in 1921 opened an artificial entrance to passages of Mammoth Cave that extended beyond the boundaries of the Mammoth Cave Estate. Morrison called his show cave the New Entrance to Mammoth Cave and engaged in fierce rivalry with the post-Ganter Mammoth Cave management for tourist and other public attention. One of the attractions advertised for the New Entrance Cave was the Salts Cave mummy (formerly the Mammoth Cave mummy), now identified as a young white (that is, Euro-American) girl. Meloy succeeded in locating a 1922 brochure that describes New Entrance Cave and refers to

> The Lady of the Cave. The little girl turned to stone; the most interesting and wonderful of all cave phenomena; a little girl, petrified or mummified by the action of the cave air; a mummy that was found in Salts Cave in 1875; that during the 47 years since the discovery, it had been exhibited in the Smithsonian Institution and at various other places by Mr. H.C. Ganter, the former owner and now exhibited at the New Entrance. It is believed that the little girl had been captured by Indians, and rather

> than endure their torture she sacrificed her life [Meloy 1977:12].

During the New Entrance exhibition period, the Salts Cave mummy began to be called Little Alice, a nickname that stuck for many decades. In 1931, when Morrison sold New Entrance Cave to the National Park Commission, which was acquiring property to form Mammoth Cave National Park, the mummy went with the cave, although it was displayed above ground after the government-managed Mammoth Cave was opened to the public. In 1958 the body was transferred to the University of Kentucky, where it remained until Louise Robbins sought it out some 10 years later.

Postdiscovery History of the Salts Cave Mummy: Revised View (1990s–Early 2000s)

After Harold Meloy's death in 1985, several other people developed interest in various aspects of nineteenth-century Mammoth Cave–area history. Three of them—Angelo George of Louisville, Kentucky; Stanley Sides of Cape Girardeau, Missouri; and Norman Warnell of Brownsville, Kentucky—focused to a greater or lesser degree on the discovery and subsequent travels of the Salts Cave mummy. George authored two publications detailing his views (1990, 1994), and Sides and Warnell generously discussed their ideas and interpretations with me.

George suggests that the original discoverers of the mummy may not be the three men whose names appear on the discovery rock. Other claims were made in 1875 by those involved in the cave business (exploration and commercialization) at other locales nearby, especially Grand Avenue Cave (also known as Long Cave or Wright's Cave) near what is now Park City (formerly Glasgow Junction), Kentucky. According to George, Grand Avenue Cave was then owned and managed by George M. Proctor. According to Warnell, who has worked through the actual deeds and titles (archived in the Edmonson County Courthouse, Brownsville, Kentucky), George Proctor's name is indeed on the 1875 Grand Avenue Cave deed, together with the names of his brother and sister-in-law, Larkin J. Proctor and Mary E. Proctor. But George Proctor was actually legally insolvent at the time and in debt to two men who held his promissory note. To settle this debt, the Edmonson County Court eventually intervened and put George Proctor's half interest in Grand Avenue Cave up for sale. In September 1877, Larkin and Mary Proctor paid off George Proctor's note, becoming sole owners of Grand Avenue Cave.[4]

These claims and counterclaims, as well as the entire swirl of events centering upon George Proctor's publicity efforts for the newly commercialized Grand Avenue Cave, and later entrepreneurial efforts by other men for other caves (for example, Mammoth Cave and New Entrance to Mammoth Cave), are quite complex (George 1994:106–121). Because the Salts Cave mummy was a major focus of some of this publicity for more than 50 years (from 1875 to around 1931), I provide a summary of George's interpretation.

George's main point is that "Little Al's 'history' from his 1875 discovery to 1958 is manufactured for publicity purposes to advertise commercial caves. . . . The actual persons who removed Little Al from Salts Cave are not definitely known" (George 1994:120–121). As part of the argument leading to this conclusion, George says, "The inscribed veracity on the 'Discovery Stone' with a date of March 8, 1875 is challengeable. There is no supporting documentation to better frame the event as this point in time" (George 1994:119). George then quotes extensively from an article entitled "That Pickled Squaw," printed in the Louisville *Courier-Journal* on September 27, 1875 (George 1994:112–114, 119–120). The author, unnamed but writing under the byline Fawn, apparently went to Mammoth Cave in September 1875, in a spirit of satirical investigative journalism (as indicated by the title and general tone of the article), to get a firsthand impression of the continuing controversy over the mummy's find-spot: Was it "a cave near Glasgow Junction" (Grand Avenue Cave) or Salts Cave? Fawn seems to have visited Mammoth Cave more than once during that summer of 1875. He says (George 1994:113):

> Early in this summer, during one of my visits to Mammoth Cave, a mummy was offered for sale to the proprietor. The owners of it refused to tell where it had been discovered, but described it as a female lying in a sleeping position with one hand laid across the chin, the other extended, but so nearly decomposed that it would have to be removed with a great deal of care to prevent it falling off. After some deliberation, it was concluded not to make the purchase, and the matter ended. The incident, then, was in a measure forgotten until the recent announcement of the discovery of a mummy in another cave near by revived the subject, while the similarity in every respect to the one which had been found in the summer gave rise to the surmise that the two were one and the same. The intense interest manifested by every

> one caused some of the more curious to make a visit to Salt's cave [*sic*] a few days since.

Fawn then briefly describes the trip made by "some of the more curious" to Salts Cave, culminating in what this group believed to be the place where the mummy had originally lain (George 1994:114):

> Leaving the main avenue you enter a side route, and after climbing over the roughest of roads for a hundred and fifty yards, reach the spot where a mummy was discovered, and from whence it has been recently removed. An indentation in the ground, under a shelving rock, corresponds precisely with that of the disputed mummy, while the mold formed around the body in all these years is still perceptible, with a few locks of its hair, which time has changed to a dark auburn. There can be no doubt that a mummy was here, the dryness of the atmosphere preserving it, as no water is found within the cave excepting at the extreme end of one of the routes.

George (1994:114) says that this is "the first and earliest published description of the discovery site for Little Al." I cannot agree because the description is too vague to establish a specific find-spot anywhere within the main trunk passage of Upper Salts Cave, which is 1.5 to 2 miles long and must be traversed by climbing over, around, and through masses of tumbled breakdown rock (Watson ed. 1969:2–4, 32, Plate 7). There are innumerable niches and rooms of various sizes throughout this jumbled breakdown, as well as so many cut-around and other side passages leading off the main trunk that Fawn's account—like that of Putnam (1875 [1973]), also quoted by George—is useless for pinpointing a specific locale within Upper Salts Cave.

George describes the discovery rock, suggesting that it was "back dated to establish priority" (George 1994:115). He adds (115), "Perhaps both inscriptions are authentic or are forgeries concocted when the cave [Salts] was commercialized in the 1920s."

In the course of his research on Mammoth Cave history, Warnell (2006) has found a number of relevant documents (personal communications 2007). These letters, exchanged among various claimants to Salts Cave and the Salts Cave tract during the 1920s and early 1930s, demonstrate that the Mammoth Cave Estate did not have clear title to Salts Sink or Salts Cave, a fact that emerged in 1896. Further, a local man named Lark (Larkin) Burnett, who made some efforts to commercialize Salts Cave in the mid-1920s (Watson ed. 1969:9; Watson ed. 1974:25), did not have clear title either. Given the long-standing ambiguity about title and ownership, it is not surprising that late-nineteenth- and early-twentieth-century attempts to make the Salts Sink entrance the gateway to a show cave were not very impressive. Whether the rather feeble efforts included forging one or both of the inscribed rocks discussed above is unknown. It is certainly the case that owners of show caves and their employees would literally stop at nothing to catch and retain the attention of tourists (the late nineteenth and early twentieth century in the Mammoth Cave region is still referred to as the "cave wars" period), hence—although I think that Cutliff and the Lees truly were authors of the discovery rock—forging a couple of inscriptions to attract and entertain visitors from near or far is a plausible suggestion.

As noted earlier, the authors of the discovery rock dated their inscription, but the damnation rock is undated. There is some further information relevant to the missing date (assuming the author was indeed J. M. Smith). According to Warnell, archives at Brownsville, Kentucky, and the *Register of Prisoners Confined in the Kentucky Penitentiary* show that on December 23, 1873, J. M. Smith was jailed in Brownsville on charges of murder (Warnell, personal communications 2007; see also Warnell 2006:35–36). On March 20, 1874, he was released on bail. On March 19, 1875 (11 days after Cutliff and the Lees found the Salts Cave mummy, according to the discovery rock), J. M. Smith's case came up for hearing, but it was postponed and he was released on bond. Six months later, on September 21, 1875, J. M. Smith was tried by jury, found guilty of voluntary manslaughter, and sentenced to four years in the Kentucky State Penitentiary. He entered prison on September 27, 1875 (coincidentally, this is the same day Fawn's article appeared in the Louisville *Courier-Journal*), and remained there until September 27, 1879.

Therefore, if the Salts Cave mummy was found on March 8, 1875, by Cutliff and the Lees, and if J. M. Smith did indeed author the undated damnation rock inscription (that is, if the inscription and/or his name was not forged or counterfeited by someone else as a move in the cave wars), then he had to have been in Salts Cave between March 8 and September 20, 1875 (excepting the few days between March 15 and March 19, 1875, when he would have been in custody while his case came up for hearing). Hence, assuming that the mummy was removed from the cave soon after discovery, the inscription date for the damnation rock was most likely mid- to late March 1875. One can readily understand the anger expressed by Smith in his inscription if—in the midst of his legal problems—he found that his sometime caving companions had completely excluded him from a sensational discovery they had made in his absence.

Given the above contextual details, I think it more likely that the contents of the two inscriptions are authentic than that they were both faked decades later to create a tale for such few tourists as may have visited Salts Cave prior to 1931. However, whatever the true status of these two inscriptions vis-à-vis empirical events in and around Salts Cave, Mammoth Cave, and Glasgow Junction in the spring and summer of 1875, the rocks are historic documents vividly conveying the cave wars atmosphere of late-nineteenth-/early-twentieth-century west-central Kentucky.

Discussion

The most striking theme with respect to the Salts Cave boy's nineteenth- and twentieth-century history is clearly the manner in which he was perceived and how the personae attributed to him were created and manipulated by those who made the original discoveries or gained control of the physical remains. Even the much more recent find of an adult male mummy in Mammoth Cave (Neumann 1938; Pond 1935, 1937; Robbins 1974) was viewed by the management more as a publicity gimmick and tourist attraction than as a valuable source of knowledge about an ancient individual and his time and place. Upon discovery in 1875, the Salts Cave mummy was immediately viewed as a commodity to be sold to the highest bidder, the bidders being primarily interested in the body for its cash value as an exhibit attractive to tourists.

Commodification of human remains, especially the nineteenth-century travels of the Salts Cave mummy and of Fawn Hoof from Short Cave, might simply be attributed to ethnocentrism and racial prejudice, but in fact there are striking similarities between what happened to these pre-Columbian bodies and what happened to the historic Euro-American body of Floyd Collins. Collins died in 1925 after having been trapped in Sand Cave, a short distance east of Mammoth Cave (Crothers 1983, Collins and Lehrberger 2001, Halliday 2004, Murray and Brucker 1979). His body was eventually recovered and buried in his family's cemetery, now inside Mammoth Cave National Park but on privately owned land at the time. When the Collins property, including Great Crystal Cave (discovered by Floyd Collins in 1917 and developed into a not-very-successful show cave by the Collins family), was purchased in 1927, the new owner was granted the right to exhume Floyd Collins's coffin and place it within the cave. This was clearly a move calculated to capitalize on the nationwide publicity attending the long-drawn-out and ultimately unsuccessful attempts to rescue Collins, whose reembalmed remains were then shown (through a glass lid with which the coffin was provided by the new cave owners) to those purchasing cave tour tickets between the late 1920s and early 1940s. The story of Floyd Collins's entrapment and death in Sand Cave is still very much alive and still attracts tourists to the area surrounding Mammoth Cave National Park (Benton 2009, Watson 2009:151).

Commodification of human remains from royal or otherwise famous individuals is a venerable theme in European history, perhaps best exemplified by the medieval trade in bones taken from the skeletons of saints and martyrs (Weiss-Krejci 2005). Weiss-Krejci relates, for example, what happened to the osteological remains of King Louis IX, who died in 1297 and was buried in the monastery of St. Denis north of Paris. His grandson, Philippe le Bel, wanted to transfer the body to Paris, but the monks refused to give it up. In 1304, however, Philippe was able to send one of Louis's finger joints to the king of Norway, and in 1306 other portions of the skeleton were taken to Paris. The mandible remained in St. Denis, but the cranium went to the Sainte-Chapelle and one rib to Notre Dame. Although Louis IX was not yet officially a saint (he was canonized in 1324), his mortal remains were highly desirable trophies. Possession and display of such relics not only enhanced the visitation rate and holiness quotient of abbeys, monasteries, and churches but also brought in more and larger donations than would otherwise have been received. Like the cave mummies just discussed, the relics had significant cash value and exemplify one of the many ways in which postfunerary populations profit by interacting with the dead (Rakita et al. 2005; see especially sections 2 and 3).

In spite of all the vicissitudes endured by the Kentucky cave mummies, they have taught us something about themselves and about the communities they represent. Basic information concerning sex, age at death, manner of death, and when death occurred (years before present) is known for each of them. Radiocarbon determinations on tissue indicate that the Short Cave mummy, Fawn Hoof, is approximately a millennium older than the Salts Cave and Mammoth Cave mummies (Horton 2003). Fawn Hoof's tissue date places her at the Archaic/Early Woodland boundary, whereas the other two are in or near the transitional period between Early and Middle Woodland. The Salts Cave mummy was a little boy no more than nine years old at the time of his death. Fawn Hoof, a mature female, was roughly the same age as the Mammoth Cave man, about 45. Fawn Hoof was buried with a considerable quantity and diversity of grave goods (which have recently provided a significant amount of technological and other cultural information), possibly in a cave dark zone but near the entrance, whereas the other two died accidentally far back in the dark zones of their respective caves. There is some indication that both the Salts Cave boy and the Mammoth Cave man may have been engaged in ceremonial activities when they died (Crothers 2012, Crothers et al. 2002, Munson et al. 1989)—the boy from a bad fall; the man crushed by a boulder he had undermined while digging the sediment beneath it. The archaeological context for the Salts Cave and Mammoth Cave mummies is fairly well-known (Crothers 2012, Crothers et al. 2002; Watson ed. 1969, 1974), but saltpeter mining of the early nineteenth century and several activities in Short Cave during the late nineteenth and early to mid-twentieth century (including laying an asphalt road leading to a bandstand built inside the cave, and blasting and bulldozing in an attempt to create a second opening at the far end) have destroyed the original cultural deposits (George 1994:55–56, Horton 2003, O'Malley 1986). Even so, careful attention to artifacts curated for more than a century at the Harvard Peabody and the Smithsonian Institution museums has recently yielded valuable information about the Short Cave mummy and her social role in life. Fawn Hoof's grave goods indicate that she was a woman of accomplishment, possibly a healer, wise woman, or shaman (Horton 2003).

Empirical dietary evidence has been obtained from the intestinal tracts of the Salts Cave and Mammoth Cave individuals, but there is no such comparable evidence for Fawn Hoof and cannot be because only her bones remain. Robbins was able to get X-rays of the Salts Cave mummy, but there are none for the Mammoth Cave and Short Cave bodies. Further radiographic work using modern techniques such as CT scanning would surely enable better age estimates as well as more detailed biohistories for each of these individuals (Komar and Buikstra 2008:258–281; Lynnerup 2007:170–173). If the requisite permissions were forthcoming, it would also be highly desirable to secure more AMS dates from soft or hard tissue samples for all three individuals. Equally important would be comparative isotopic and DNA analyses of the three mummies and of other individuals from the same, earlier, and later time periods in west-central Kentucky. Because artifactual remains in cave dark zones are not often directly comparable to those found above ground in rockshelters or open sites, we do not know whether those who spent long periods in cave interiors were members of local populations or came from other locales. Isotopic, biochemical, trace element, and DNA analyses might provide relevant information, and stable isotope data (e.g., Buikstra et al. 2005; see also Wright and Perry et al. this volume) could furnish additional evidence for health and diet, especially important for the Short Cave mummy. There is no scalp hair available for any of the three mummies, so high-resolution stable light isotopic analyses of their individual life histories (e.g., Wilson et al. 2007) is not possible.

Clearly, none of the Kentucky cave mummies provides an ideal bioarchaeological case study. Two of the three were removed from their primary contexts 201 and 137 years ago, respectively, before archaeology in the United States was professionalized. The other was documented by professionals at the time of discovery (Neumann 1938; Pond 1935, 1937), but that was 40 years prior to Jane E. Buikstra's first discussions of what she came to call bioarchaeology (Buikstra 1977, 2006). Nevertheless, painstaking historic research and physical anthropological and archaeological study during the 1960s, 1970s, and later have furnished significant pre- and postrecovery information for each individual. Thanks to conceptual and technological advances in bioarchaeological inquiry during the past three decades, there is now considerable potential for future interactions with these cave mummies by specialists in the subdiscipline defined by Buikstra and so well exemplified by her own work and that of her students.

Acknowledgments

Thank you, Nene and Barra, for inviting me to contribute a paper to this volume. I am grateful to Patrick Payne for creating the map appearing here as Figure 6.1. I am deeply indebted to Stanley Sides and Norman Warnell, both experts on early Euro-American history in the Mammoth Cave region, above ground and below. Drawing upon their own research, they promptly answered a long series of my questions about nineteenth-century people, land claims, and commercial caves. Norman kindly sent me many details from his encyclopedic knowledge of local genealogies and countless records pertaining to land patents, deeds, and titles. Stan, a valued consultant at every stage of the CRF Archeological Project's research (he was centrally involved in helping Louise Robbins secure X-rays of the Salts Cave mummy in 1969 and was also a member of the CRF group that rediscovered J. M. Smith's damnation rock inscription), speedily obtained via the Internet a copy of the 1973 reprint publication containing F. W. Putnam's account of his 1874 visit to Salts Cave. Thanks to P. Willey, who sent me a copy of Lynnerup's 2007 synthesis of mummy research, past and present. Finally, I am grateful to Angelo George for his stimulating publications concerning caves, mummies, and early commercialization efforts in the Mammoth Cave region. His suggestions concerning nineteenth- and early-twentieth-century activities in and around Salts and Mammoth caves caused me to revisit and rethink earlier understandings concerning key events and personnel surrounding the cave mummies discussed in this paper.

NOTES

1. The Cave Research Foundation Archeological Project (which I had the privilege of directing for 40 years) was initiated in 1963, with some financial support obtained by Joseph Caldwell, then head curator of archaeology at the Illinois State Museum. Caldwell also arranged for his assistant curator, Robert Hall, to participate in that first summer's fieldwork (Salts Cave 1963). See Watson ed. 1969, 1974, 1997 and Watson 2012 for project results.

2. The reference for this newspaper article, "Reminiscences of Mammoth Cave" by M. Carrie Morgan, *Glasgow Times*, is provided by Angelo George (1994:149, Note 9).

3. As indicated here, the Salts Cave mummy was provided with varying proveniences and identities to suit the needs of those controlling the physical remains at any specific time. Meloy (1977:9–10) notes that the Salts Cave mummy was often confused—sometimes deliberately—with another mummy, Fawn Hoof, found around 1811 in nearby Short Cave (Horton 2003). The mummy at the 1893 Chicago World's Fair (and at the 1876 Philadelphia World's Fair, as well as at the Smithsonian) was the Short Cave mummy.

4. Angelo George (1994:119, 121) also thinks it was George M. Proctor rather than his brother Larkin J. Proctor who purchased the Salts mummy. Meloy (1977:7, 9) says it was Larkin, as do Stanley Sides and Norman Warnell (personal communications 2008), although Sides notes that George Proctor might have bought the Salts Cave mummy while acting for his brother Larkin. At any rate, Warnell's data make it quite clear that George Proctor was legally in debt and insolvent in 1875, so he had no disposable income of his own.

REFERENCES CITED

Benton, Henry
2009 The Presence of Floyd Collins in the Mammoth Cave (Kentucky) Area Today. *Proceedings of the Fifteenth International Congress of Speleology* 3:1947–1948.

Buikstra, Jane E.
1977 Biocultural Dimensions of Archeological Study: A Regional Perspective. In *Biocultural Adaptation in Prehistoric America*, edited by Robert L. Blakely, pp. 67–84. Proceedings of the Southern Anthropological Society No. 11. University of Georgia Press, Athens.
2006 Preface. In *Bioarchaeology: The Contextual Analysis of Human Remains*, edited by Jane E. Buikstra and Lane A. Beck, pp. xvii–xx. Academic Press-Elsevier, London.

Buikstra, Jane E., Paula D. Tomczak, María Cecilia Lozada Cerna, and Gordon F. M. Rakita
2005 Chiribaya Political Economy: A Bioarchaeological Perspective. In *Interacting with the Dead: Perspectives on Mortuary Archaeology for the New Millennium*, edited by Gordon F. M. Rakita, Jane E. Buikstra, Lane A. Beck, and Sloan R. Williams, pp. 66–80. University Press of Florida, Gainesville.

Collins, Homer, and John L. Lehrberger
2001 *The Life and Death of Floyd Collins*. Cave Books, St. Louis.

Crothers, George M.
1983 Archaeological Investigations in Sand Cave, Kentucky. *National Speleological Society Bulletin* 45(2):19–33.
2012 Early Woodland Ritual Use of Caves in Eastern North America. *American Antiquity* 77(3):524–541.

Crothers, George M., Charles H. Faulkner, Jan K. Simek, Patty Jo Watson, and P. Willey
2002 Woodland Cave Archaeology in Eastern North America. In *The Woodland Southeast*, edited by David Anderson and Robert Mainfort, pp. 502–524. University of Alabama Press, Tuscaloosa.

Fawn
1875 That Pickled Squaw. *Courier-Journal* 27 September:3. Louisville, Kentucky.

George, Angelo
1990 *Prehistoric Mummies from the Mammoth Cave Area: Foundations and Concepts*. George Publishing Company, Louisville, Kentucky.
1994 *Mummies, Catacombs, and Mammoth Cave*. George Publishing Company, Louisville, Kentucky.

Halliday, William R.
2004 *Floyd Collins of Sand Cave: A Photographic Memorial*. Byron's Printing and Graphics, Louisville, Kentucky.

Horton, Elizabeth T.
2003 Investigation of Perishable Materials Associated with Fawn Hoof, a Desiccated Burial in Short Cave, Kentucky. Unpublished master's thesis, Department of Anthropology, Washington University, St. Louis.

Komar, Debra A., and Jane E. Buikstra
2008 *Forensic Anthropology: Contemporary Theory and Practice*. Oxford University Press, Oxford.

Lynnerup, Niels
2007 Mummies. *Yearbook of Physical Anthropology* 50:162–190.

Meloy, Harold
1977 *Mummies of Mammoth Cave: An Account of the Indian Mummies Found in Short Cave, Salts Cave, and Mammoth Cave, Kentucky*. 2nd ed. Micron Publishing Company, Shelbyville, Indiana.

Meloy, Harold, and Patty Jo Watson
1969 Human Remains: "Little Alice" of Salts Cave and Other Mummies. In *The Prehistory of Salts Cave, Kentucky*, edited by Patty Jo Watson, pp. 65–70. Reports of Investigations 16. Illinois State Museum, Springfield.

Morgan, M. Carrie
1929 Reminiscences of Mammoth Cave. *Glasgow Times* 22 December. Glasgow, Kentucky.

Munson, Patrick J., Kenneth B. Tankersley, Cheryl Ann Munson, and Patty Jo Watson
1989 Prehistoric Selenite and Satinspar Mining in the Mammoth Cave System, Kentucky. *Midcontinental Journal of Archaeology* 14(2):119–145.

Murray, Robert K., and Roger W. Brucker
1979 *Trapped!* G. P. Putnam's Sons, New York.

Neumann, George
1938 The Human Remains from Mammoth Cave. *American Antiquity* 3:339–353.

O'Malley, Nancy
1986 Cultural Materials from Short Cave. *National Speleological Society News* 44(2):35–36.

Pond, Alonzo
1935 Report of Preliminary Survey of Important Archaeological Discovery at Mammoth Cave, Kentucky. *Wisconsin Archeologist* 15:27–35.
1937 Lost John of Mummy Ledge. *Natural History* 39(3):176–184.

Putnam, Frederic Ward
1875 Archaeological Researches in Kentucky and Indiana, 1874. *Proceedings of the Boston Society of Natural History* 17:314–331.
1973 Archaeological Explorations in Kentucky and Indiana. Eighth Annual Report, 1875. In *The Archaeological Reports of Frederic Ward Putnam, Selected from the Annual Reports of the Peabody Museum of Archaeology and Ethnology, Harvard University 1875–1903*, edited by Philip Phillips, pp. 165–170. AMS Press, New York.

Rakita, Gordon F. M., Jane E. Buikstra, Lane A. Beck, and Sloan R. Williams (editors)
2005 *Interacting with the Dead: Perspectives on Mortuary Archaeology for the New Millennium*. University Press of Florida, Gainesville.

Robbins, Louise M.
1971 A Woodland "Mummy" from Salts Cave, Kentucky. *American Antiquity* 36(2):200–206.
1974 Prehistoric People of the Mammoth Cave Area. In *Archeology of the Mammoth Cave Area*, edited by Patty Jo Watson, pp. 137–162. Academic Press, New York.

Tankersley, Kenneth B., Samuel S. Frushour, Frank Nagy, Stephen L. Tankersley, and Kevin O. Tankersley
1994 The Archaeology of Mummy Valley, Salts Cave, Mammoth Cave National Park, Kentucky. *North American Archaeologist* 15(2):129–145.

Warnell, Norman
2006 *Mammoth Cave: Forgotten Stories of Its People*. 2nd ed. Eastern National, Fort Washington, Pennsylvania.

Watson, Patty Jo
1969 Recent History of Salts Cave. In *The Prehistory of Salts Cave, Kentucky*, edited by Patty Jo Watson, pp. 7–11. Reports of Investigations 16. Illinois State Museum, Springfield.
1974 Observation and Recording in Salts Cave. In *Archeology of the Mammoth Cave Area*, edited by Patty Jo Watson, pp. 25–29. Academic Press, New York.
2009 The World of the Past in the World Underground. *Proceedings of the Fifteenth International Congress of Speleology* 1:147–152.
2012 Forty Years' Pursuit of Human Prehistory in the World Underground. In *In the Dark Zone: A Global Perspective on the Ritual Use of Caves*, edited by Holley Moyes. University of Colorado Press, Boulder.

Watson, Patty Jo (editor)
1969 *The Prehistory of Salts Cave, Kentucky*. Reports of Investigations 16. Illinois State Museum, Springfield.
1974 *Archeology of the Mammoth Cave Area*. Academic Press, New York.
1997 *Archeology of the Mammoth Cave Area*. Reprint with a new foreword and supplemental bibliography. Cave Books, St. Louis.

Watson, Patty Jo, and Richard A. Yarnell
1986 Lost John's Last Meal. *Missouri Archaeologist* 47:241–255.

Weiss-Krejci, Estella
2005 Excarnation, Evisceration, and Exhumation in Medieval and Post-Medieval Europe. In *Interacting with the Dead: Perspectives on Mortuary Archaeology for the New Millennium*, edited by Gordon F. M. Rakita, Jane E. Buikstra, Lane A. Beck, and Sloan R. Williams, pp. 135–172. University Press of Florida, Gainesville.

Wilson, Andrew S., Timothy Taylor, Maria Constanza Ceruti, José Antonio Chavez, Johan Reinhard, Vaughan Grimes, Wolfram Meier-Augenstein, et al.
2007 Stable Isotope and DNA Evidence for Ritual Sequences in Inca Child Sacrifice. *Proceedings of the National Academy of Sciences* 104(42):16456–16461.

Yarnell, Richard A.
1974 Intestinal Contents of the Salts Cave Mummy and Analysis of the Initial Salts Cave Flotation Series. In *Archeology of the Mammoth Cave Area*, edited by Patty Jo Watson, pp. 109–112. Academic Press, New York.
1978 Domestication of Sunflower and Sumpweed in Eastern North America. In *The Nature and Status of Ethnobotany*, edited by Richard I. Ford, pp. 289–299. Anthropological Papers No. 67. Museum of Anthropology, University of Michigan, Ann Arbor.

7

OSSUARY III FROM THE JUHLE SITE, NANJEMOY, MARYLAND: BIOARCHAEOLOGICAL FEATURES

DOUGLAS H. UBELAKER
DEPARTMENT OF ANTHROPOLOGY, SMITHSONIAN INSTITUTION

AS NOTED BY BUIKSTRA AND BECK (2006) and Larsen (2001), the dynamic field of bioarchaeology involves complex interpretations that integrate data from the analysis of human remains with those from history, archaeology, and other related scholarly areas. Such research leads to key information relating to human remains in their archaeological context and the complex social factors that can be associated with them (Chacon and Dye 2007). Although the scope of research within bioarchaeology is extremely broad (Buikstra and Beck 2006), problems relating to the analysis of commingled human remains are among the most challenging (Adams and Byrd 2008). In such cases, standard approaches to analysis (Buikstra and Ubelaker 1994) frequently must be supplemented with problem-specific methodology. Complexity of analysis is enhanced when deposits of commingled remains contain many individuals with extensive skeletal disarticulation. Ossuaries from the mid-Atlantic area of the United States represent such complex deposits.

Mortuary procedures varied extensively among the late prehistoric and early historic American Indians in the mid-Atlantic area of the United States (Boyd and Boyd 1992). These customs included secondary burial, which in some areas resulted in ossuary deposits (Turner 1992). As noted by Ubelaker (1974:8), the term *ossuary* has been applied very generally to burials of multiple individuals. Following Ubelaker 1974, the term is used here to describe largely secondary deposits of multiple individuals.

Ossuary burial is well-known and documented for the mid-Atlantic area of the United States. Although thorough, direct descriptions of the detailed ossuary burial practice are not available in the ethnohistorical record, considerable indirect evidence, summarized in Ubelaker (1974), references the practice of temporary placement of the dead on scaffolds and/or in death houses, systematic cleaning of the bones, and final interment in ossuaries, especially in the coastal plain area of Maryland and Virginia.

Ubelaker's summary of reports of ossuary burial in the mid-Atlantic area lists 34 possible deposits in Virginia, Maryland, and southern Delaware (1974). Although detailed information is lacking for many of these sites, the number of individuals in each deposit varies considerably, with some containing more than 100 individuals. Curry (1999) summarizes that more than 30 ossuaries have been reported from the Maryland area. Ubelaker (1974) and Curry (1999) note that the Maryland ossuaries include evidence of burning on bones, ceremonial fires associated with burials, cut marks on bones likely associated with defleshing, variation in arrangement of bones within pits, the use of crania as containers, and variable artifact presence.

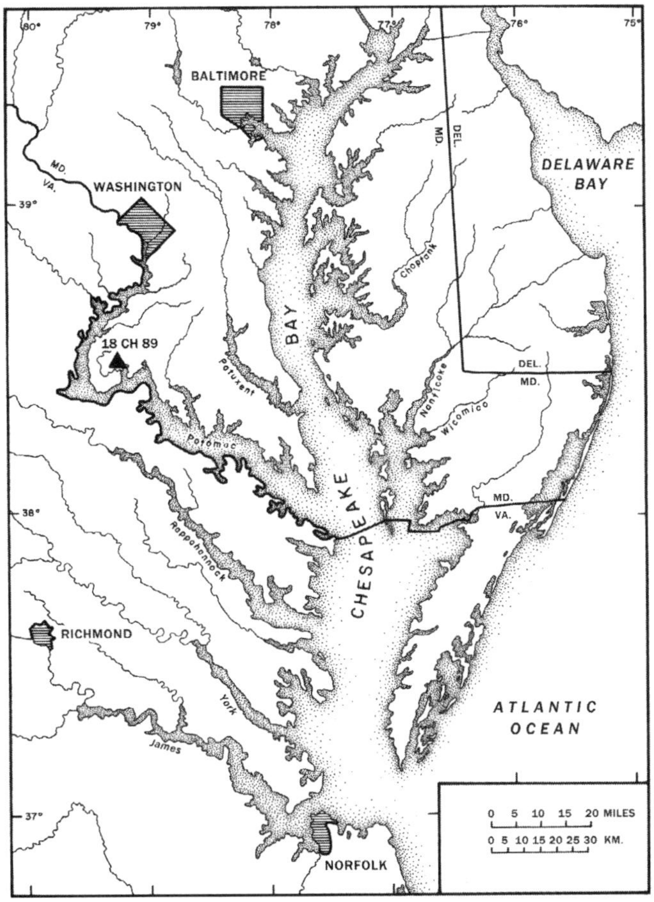

Figure 7.1. Location of Juhle Site, 18CH89.

Ossuaries from Nanjemoy Creek

Two ossuaries have been reported in detail from the Juhle Site (18CH89), dating from the late Woodland period in Charles County, Maryland (Figure 7.1). Both of these ossuaries were located on a bluff overlooking Nanjemoy Creek, a tributary of the Potomac River, and they appeared to be associated with a small habitation area (Ubelaker 1974). The first ossuary was excavated by T. D. Stewart between 1953 and 1955 and contained relatively few artifacts and at least 131 individuals (Ubelaker 1974).

The second ossuary from this site was excavated in 1971–1972 by Stewart and D. H. Ubelaker (Ubelaker 1974). This ossuary was located approximately 30.5 m northwest of Ossuary I and measured about 5.2 m long by about 2.1 m wide. At least 188 individuals were represented in the sample. As with the first ossuary, relatively few artifacts were present. Analysis noted that some remains were articulated, and some evidence of burning was present on the bones.

Ossuary III

In the autumn of 1979, the Juhle family contacted the Smithsonian Institution, reporting that an animal burrow had been found just southeast of the second ossuary, which was excavated in the early 1970s. Bones were detected within the backdirt of the animal burrow.

On November 16, 1979, Stewart and Ubelaker visited the site to recover the disturbed remains associated with the animal burrow and to explore any archaeological features. They noted that the bones recovered included human remains, and they excavated sufficiently to determine that the animal disturbance appeared to be associated with a third ossuary from that site.

The total weight of the disturbed material recovered from the animal burrow was 2,340 g and included four nonhuman animal bones, 15 shells, two wood fragments, 10 stones, and two pottery shards. Human remains in the disturbed sample included fragments representing at least three adults and one immature individual, with the largest fragment (from a left femur) weighing 117 g.

Intensive excavation of Ossuary III began on June 2, 1980, and continued until about September 19, 1980. Initially, excavation concentrated on the removal of topsoil to reveal the entire pit outline, detected at depths ranging from 20 to 22 cm. Once the entire pit outline was exposed, a 1-m grid system with a north-south orientation was organized over it (Figure 7.2). The ossuary intersected 15 of the 1-m squares. Excavation was complicated by the invasion of roots from a tree stump on the southwestern side of the ossuary. The area of disturbance caused by the animal burrow that led to the discovery of the ossuary was located in Square 5 on the east side.

Once the entire pit outline was visible, excavation proceeded downward within the grid system. Soil was carefully removed and screened to reveal bone and related material in situ. All bone concentrations were carefully cleaned for documentary photography and note taking. Any evidence of articulation was noted and given an articulation number. All crania were also noted and given individual numbers. Human remains removed from the ossuary, including the articulated bones and crania, were placed in bags labeled with the squares they were found in, dates of removal, and other relevant information. Excavation began in squares 1 and 2 on about June 12 and proceeded generally sequentially to Square 15.

When all the ossuary contents had been excavated and removed, the remaining pit was photographed

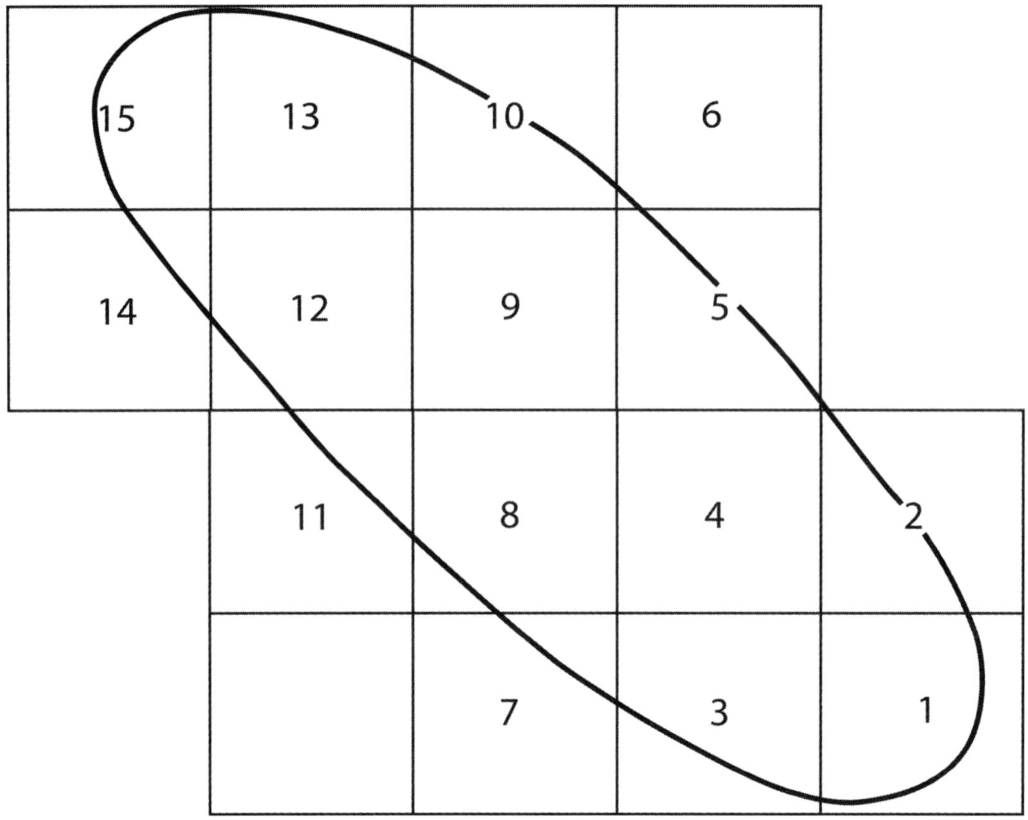

Figure 7.2. The 1-m grid system utilized in the excavation of Ossuary III.

(Figure 7.3) and the entire area was filled in with screened backdirt. Small particles of charcoal and occasionally burned bone were noted on the pit floor.

Location and Orientation of Crania

Seventy-seven crania were detected and given individual numbers during the excavation of Ossuary III. Of these, 14 (18 percent) were found resting on their left sides; 20 (26 percent) were found resting on their bases; 8 (10 percent) on their facial areas; 15 (19 percent) on their vertexes, and 16 (21 percent) on their right sides. Information on position is not available for four of the crania. Thus the crania were found in many different positions, and no evidence of placement in a particular position was detected.

Facial orientations of the crania (the direction each was facing) within the ossuary also were varied. Of the 77 crania, facial orientation was listed as 6 (8 percent) north, 8 (10 percent) northwest, 8 (10 percent) west, 7 (9 percent) southwest, 6 (8 percent) south, 10 (13 percent) southeast, 13 (17 percent) east, 5 (6 percent) northeast, 6 (8 percent) of unknown orientation, 6 (8 percent) face down, and 2 (3 percent) face up.

Articulations

As noted above, all evidence of skeletal articulation was recorded during excavation. Each observed articulation was given a number, documented as to location, and packaged separately for later analysis. In contrast to Ossuary II (Ubelaker 1974), no completely articulated individuals were observed during the excavation. A total of 197 examples of partial articulation were noted, and each was analyzed separately in the laboratory.

Inventory of the individual bones represented by the articulations provides detailed information on the areas of the skeleton and the individuals represented. For immature remains, three individuals were represented by right femora. Two individuals were represented by frontals, right maxillae, sacra, right ilia, vertebrae, ribs, humeri, and the right radius. Single individuals were represented by the mandible, left clavicle, manubrium and gladiolus of the sternum, right scapula, left ilium,

Figure 7.3. Ossuary III pit following excavation and removal of contents.

right pubis, left radius, left ulna, right femur, right tibia, right fibula, and foot bones.

Sorting of the immature bones from the articulations by bone type and age suggests that at least six individuals are present. Two newborns are represented by the left humerus. Two children, likely between the ages of three and four, are represented by left femora. A seven- to eight-year-old child is represented by a cranium and mandible. A 10- to 15-year-old individual is represented by vertebrae and sternum segments.

Immature articulated remains were recovered from eight of the 1-m squares within the ossuary: squares 1, 2, 3, 4, 8, 9, 10, and 13. These squares are distributed throughout the ossuary; thus the distribution of the immature articulations does not present any spatial clustering.

Of the articulated bones of adults, 13 individuals were represented by thoracic vertebrae, 11 by lumbar vertebrae, 6 by crania, mandibles, right radii, right ulnae, left tibiae, and left fibulae, 5 by the third through seventh cervical vertebrae, right tibiae, and foot bones, 4 by left radii, right fibulae, sacra, and hand bones, 3 by left ulnae and first cervical vertebrae, 2 by right femora, second cervical vertebrae, and right innominates, and 1 by a left femur and ribs.

Both sexes are represented by the articulated remains of both young and old adults. Although sex was not apparent for most of the articulated remains, the crania from two articulations were judged to likely represent females. The leg bones as well as the crania of two articulations were thought to represent males.

Articulated adult remains were found in nearly all the squares that had skeletal content. Specifically, articulated adult remains were recovered from squares 1, 2, 3, 4, 5, 7, 8, 9, 10, 11, 12, 13, and 14. As with the immature articulated remains, the adult articulated deposits were distributed throughout the ossuary and showed no clustered pattern.

Bone Weights

As noted above, a 1-m grid system was employed within the ossuary to examine spatial issues. Skeletal remains were found within 15 squares. Depth from the surface to the highest bone ranged from about 26 cm in Square 7 to 35 cm in Square 2. The deepest area of bone concentration (about 71 cm) was in the area of the junction of squares 4, 5, 8, and 9.

Table 7.1 presents the distribution of bone weight in grams from the various 1-m squares within the ossuary. Note that 3,711 g of bone (2.42 percent of the total) could not be associated with any particular square. These remains mostly represent those initially recovered from the disturbed area associated with the animal burrow, and they most likely originate from Square 5.

Table 7.1 reveals that the greatest concentration of remains was found in squares 3, 8, 9, and 12—squares located near the center of the ossuary. The total bone weight of 153,432 g represents approximately 67 percent of the 233,900 g of bone recovered from Ossuary II (Ubelaker 1974:22).

Table 7.1. Distribution of Bone Weight Within Ossuary III.

Square	Weight (g)	% Total Weight
1	3,886	2.53
2	4,242	2.76
3	23,484	15.31
4	14,565	9.49
5	5,742	3.74
6	1,420	.93
7	5,510	3.59
8	21,264	13.86
9	25,387	16.55
10	8,114	5.29
11	3,924	2.56
12	16,279	10.61
13	14,963	9.75
14	769	.50
15	172	.11
Other	3,711	2.42
Total	153,432	100.0

Spatial Distribution of Types of Bones

To investigate if any nonrandom spatial patterning of the remains could be detected, all recovered remains were labeled with the number of the square in which they were found. All remains were then sorted by bone type, with mature remains separated from those showing evidence of immaturity (for example, lack of epiphyseal union), and were weighed.

Tables 7.2 and 7.3 present the percentages of the total weight distribution of each bone category present in each square for adults and subadults. For example, of the total weight of adult femora in the ossuary, 2.5 percent was in Square 1, 1.9 percent in Square 2, and so on. Comparison of these values with the percentage of all bone weight in each square assists in detecting any nonrandom distribution patterns within the ossuary. Square 1 contained 2.5 percent of all bone weight within the ossuary but 6.7 percent of the weight of adult first cervical vertebrae and only .1 percent of the adult innominate weights. Although some variation is apparent, perusal of these data suggests no clear clustering by age or type of bone.

Minimum Number of Individuals

Tables 7.4 and 7.5 present the minimum number of individuals represented by each type of bone for both subadults and adults. The numbers were established by examining all bones of each type and sorting them by size and shape. For example, all mature left femora were compared with each other to establish the minimum number of individuals represented by that bone type. Fragments were assumed to relate to a single bone if no anatomical aspects were duplicated and if the size and shape were consistent. For subadults, this process suggested that at least 37 individuals were represented by the right femur and the right ilium (Table 7.4). In contrast, no immature coccygeal vertebrae were found, and only two individuals were represented by carpal and tarsal bones. Adults were most commonly represented by the right temporal (74), followed by the left temporal (66) and the right femur (65). Only 9 individuals were represented by middle and distal foot phalanges, and 17 individuals were represented by the left triquetral of the hand.

Sex Distribution

Since sex cannot be estimated reliably from immature remains, such estimates in this study were confined to mature individuals. Since the remains were commingled and for the most part not separated into individuals, estimates of sex had to be made from individual bones. Of all the bones of the skeleton, those of the pelvis provide the most reliable indicators of sex. For the ossuary remains, all mature bones of the pelvis were separated into left and right sides and then assessed for sex indicators, considering all available evidence. This procedure suggested that at least 14 males and 27 females were present, represented by mature left pelvic

Table 7.2. Distribution of the Percentage of the Total Square Bone Weight Represented by the Weight of Adult Bone Categories Within Ossuary III.

	Square Number															
Skeletal Element	**1**	**2**	**3**	**4**	**5**	**6**	**7**	**8**	**9**	**10**	**11**	**12**	**13**	**14**	**15**	**Other**
Femur	2.5	1.9	17.5	11.0	4.1	.4	1.6	17.6	9.9	4.5	2.5	12.8	11.0	.4	NDA[1]	2.4
Tibia	1.5	1.7	13.2	8.7	3.2	1.0	3.3	15.4	15.2	6.6	3.7	11.8	11.3	.7	NDA	2.9
Fibula	3.4	2.4	10.2	9.3	3.9	NDA	5.4	15.1	16.1	5.4	2.9	11.2	10.2	.5	NDA	3.9
Humerus	4.4	2.0	13.8	7.8	1.6	1.8	.4	15.1	16.2	4.9	1.3	11.6	14.4	.9	NDA	3.8
Radius	1.5	2.3	14.5	9.9	1.5	NDA	4.9	9.1	21.3	6.1	1.5	9.9	12.9	NDA	NDA	4.6
Ulna	.6	1.7	15.4	10.4	2.8	1.1	4.4	14.3	14.8	9.3	1.1	10.4	10.4	1.1	NDA	2.2
Clavicle	1.9	.9	22.4	11.2	1.9	.9	1.9	11.2	16.8	5.6	.9	11.2	11.2	.9	NDA	.9
Patella	3.3	1.3	15.7	14.5	5.3	3.9	2.3	9.8	15.2	7.8	2.7	5.1	8.0	NDA	NDA	5.2
Scapula	1.3	2.0	12.4	13.1	2.0	.7	7.2	13.7	17.7	5.2	1.3	13.7	7.8	NDA	NDA	2.0
Hand/foot bones	4.3	4.3	19.1	10.1	4.3	1.6	6.1	9.9	14.4	6.5	1.4	7.9	8.1	.5	NDA	2.0
Atlas	6.7	3.8	11.4	7.1	3.4	3.9	4.8	10.9	20.6	5.5	3.6	12.6	2.0	.3	NDA	3.5
Axis	1.9	3.1	16.2	7.8	1.7	2.7	1.8	9.8	31.4	9.6	2.6	7.4	2.1	NDA	NDA	1.9
Cervical	4.0	2.0	18.0	12.0	4.0	2.0	4.0	8.0	12.0	6.0	2.0	12.0	10.0	NDA	NDA	4.0
Thoracic	3.9	2.8	16.9	9.0	2.3	1.1	4.5	12.4	20.8	7.3	1.7	9.0	7.9	.3	NDA	.3
Lumbar	1.7	4.6	23.9	8.6	2.9	.6	4.0	10.3	18.2	5.1	2.9	9.1	7.4	.3	NDA	.6
Other vertebra	4.2	4.2	20.8	8.3	2.1	2.1	6.3	8.3	10.4	8.3	2.1	6.3	6.3	6.3	NDA	4.2
Innominate	.1	4.9	22.8	8.2	.8	.3	4.9	14.6	11.6	7.8	2.4	10.5	10.5	.1	NDA	.5
Cranium	1.9	2.9	14.0	8.5	5.4	.5	4.2	14.2	22.4	3.2	2.4	8.1	8.7	< .1	NDA	3.6
Mandible	1.9	NDA	22.4	4.7	3.7	3.7	1.9	16.8	17.8	5.6	.9	11.2	8.4	NDA	NDA	.9
Total	2.5	2.8	15.3	9.5	3.7	.9	3.6	13.9	16.6	5.3	2.6	10.7	9.8	.5	.1	2.4

1. NDA = no data available.

Table 7.3. Distribution of the Percentage the Total Square Bone Weight Represented by the Weight of Immature Bone Categories Within Ossuary III.

	Square Number															
Skeletal Element	**1**	**2**	**3**	**4**	**5**	**6**	**7**	**8**	**9**	**10**	**11**	**12**	**13**	**14**	**15**	**Other**
Femur	5.1	3.3	4.7	5.4	.7	.6	.5	8.8	36.0	4.2	10.0	16.3	4.0	NDA[1]	NDA	.3
Tibia	4.2	.6	3.5	7.9	6.3	.5	.6	13.4	12.9	.6	8.9	30.2	7.4	.2	NDA	2.8
Fibula	NDA	NDA	3.4	4.9	7.4	NDA	.6	21.2	21.3	11.5	7.0	8.3	7.4	NDA	NDA	6.8
Humerus	.5	.2	1.2	10.9	1.7	.7	.5	9.6	22.5	4.5	8.4	28.7	8.1	NDA	NDA	2.5
Radius	10.1	.2	2.3	13.4	7.0	.1	NDA	22.6	22.5	3.6	3.2	9.2	4.6	NDA	NDA	1.3
Ulna	2.8	.1	3.1	13.3	9.7	1.4	NDA	21.9	20.9	NDA	5.7	9.0	4.1	NDA	NDA	8.1
Clavicle	5.2	.2	5.6	14.6	6.8	.8	1.6	8.6	24.2	2.1	5.4	12.5	12.3	NDA	NDA	.2
Patella	NDA	NDA	NDA	NDA	4.5	NDA	NDA	NDA	17.3	3.8	NDA	60.9	13.5	NDA	NDA	NDA
Scapula	1.1	.2	4.6	9.7	7.4	1.6	.7	18.6	35.1	3.6	8.2	4.9	4.3	NDA	NDA	.1
Hand/foot bones	3.0	.5	2.0	9.0	6.9	6.6	.1	13.4	20.9	6.4	3.3	19.4	7.1	NDA	NDA	1.5
Atlas	NDA	4.8	11.2	16.3	NDA	NDA	NDA	5.2	37.9	NDA	6.8	10.8	4.0	NDA	NDA	3.2
Axis	9.0	NDA	NDA	17.4	NDA	8.0	NDA	30.6	23.2	6.8	NDA	3.6	NDA	NDA	NDA	1.4
Cervical	NDA	NDA	.6	17.2	10.5	.4	NDA	9.1	45.1	1.4	1.3	10.1	4.3	NDA	NDA	NDA
Thoracic	3.5	3.7	12.8	20.3	8.4	.8	.2	7.1	22.8	2.0	.9	9.0	4.9	3.2	NDA	.6
Lumbar	5.7	NDA	5.3	16.7	7.9	.5	1.2	11.7	20.2	.5	.3	12.2	16.4	NDA	NDA	1.2
Other vertebra	5.2	1.4	6.8	8.9	6.4	3.7	2.7	18.9	20.9	3.9	2.6	9.3	6.6	.1	NDA	2.8
Innominate	1.2	8.6	16.6	17.0	8.5	1.7	.3	15.8	16.7	1.7	.5	9.3	2.1	NDA	NDA	.2
Cranium	8.3	6.2	9.1	9.3	2.0	.1	5.2	4.3	20.3	2.8	.1	2.4	13.7	NDA	5.1	11.2
Mandible	2.4	.1	5.7	20.5	7.5	NDA	.3	12.0	20.5	NDA	1.0	19.5	10.5	NDA	NDA	.1
Total	2.5	2.8	15.3	9.5	3.7	.9	3.6	13.9	16.6	5.3	2.6	10.7	9.8	.5	.1	2.4

1. NDA = no data available.

Table 7.4. Minimum Number of Individuals Represented by Immature Bone Types.

Bone	Left		Right
Humerus	36		32
Radius	26		23
Ulna	31		33
Femur	36		37
Tibia	32		29
Fibula		36	
Clavicle	29		31
Scapula	25		32
Temporal	28		32
Maxilla	13		15
Mandible	26		27
Gladiolus		8	
Manubrium		7	
Ilium	34		37
Ischium	23		23
Pubis	18		17
Patella	5		5
Rib		14 (311)[1]	
Vertebrae[2]		17 (249)	
Sacrum		8	
Coccyx		0	
Calcaneus	13		11
Talus		13 (25)	
Other tarsals		2 (29)	
Carpals		2 (21)	
Metatarsals or metacarpals		10 (186)	
Phalanges		5 (225)	

1. Numbers in parentheses indicate actual number of bones.
2. Cervicals, thoracics, lumbars.

bones. Consideration of cranial morphology, coupled with pelvic analysis, suggested the presence of 25 males.

Estimation of Age at Death

For the mature remains, important information on age at death can be derived from the bones of the pelvis and skull. All mature pelvic bones were separated into left and right sides and then arranged in order of increasing age. In this procedure, the age progression was first established by arranging those bones that presented evidence of pubic symphysis. Next, bones that contained an auricular area were added to the sequence. The result was a progressive age sequence of pelvic bones extending from young adult to old adult. This sequence was then divided into five-year age intervals using standard methods of appraising pubic symphysis, auricular area, and related morphological indicators (Buikstra and Ubelaker 1994). The maximum age was judged to be between 65 and 70 years, consistent with the maximum age established from the previous study of ossuaries from this site (Ubelaker 1974). Noting the sex distribution of these bones as well, estimates from the left and right sides were compared.

A similar sorting procedure was employed for bones of the adult skulls. After separation into male, female, and sex-undetermined groups, the remains were assigned the most likely age at death. The resulting information was compared with the sex and age profile produced from the pelvic information, and the nonduplicated information was merged with it to produce a combined comprehensive sex and age-at-death profile. This process produced age-at-death information for 60 individuals between the ages of 15 and 70 years. Note that the minimum number of individuals in this adult age group was 74, established from the total bone inventory.

Although the sex of individuals less than 15 years of age could not be established, the minimum number of individuals in this age group was determined through comparative bone inventory procedures to be 38 (Table 7.6). Of these, 37 individuals were represented by right femora, and an additional individual in the 10-to-14-year category was suggested by cranial and pelvic data. Assessment of long bone lengths and the cranial/pelvic information suggested the following age distribution: newborn to six months: 16; .5 to 1.5 years: four; 1.5 to 2.5 years: eight; 2.5 to 3.5 years: three; 3.5 to 4.5 years: one; 5.5 to 6.5 years: two; 6.5 to 7.5 years: one; 8.5 to 9.5 years: one; and 10 to 14 years: two.

Table 7.5: Minimum Number of Individuals Represented by Adult Bone Types.

Bone	Left		Right
Long bones			
Humerus	58		53
Radius	54		50
Ulna	59		60
Femur	59		65
Tibia	59		63
Fibula	54		48
Irregular bones			
Clavicle	53		47
Scapula	52		55
Temporal	66		74
Maxilla	45		46
Mandible	51		47
Gladiolus		26	
Manubrium		30	
Innominate	43		41
Patella	43		45
Rib	32 (434)[1]		32(434)
Vertebrae			
Cervical 1		53	
Cervical 2		45	
Cervical 3–7		37 (189)	
Thoracic 1–9		53 (473)	
Thoracic 10		19	
Thoracic 11		55	
Thoracic 12		16	
Thoracic 10–11		0	
Thoracic 10–12		10	
Lumbar		61 (301)	
Sacrum		38	
Hand bones			
Carpals			
Navicular	25		32
Lunate	25		24
Triquetral	17		19
Pisiform		25 (49)	

1. Numbers in parentheses indicate actual number of bones.

Bone	Left		Right
Hand bones			
Carpals			
Greater multangular	25		24
Lesser multangular	19		24
Capitate	29		30
Hamate	25		27
Metacarpal 1	38		41
Metacarpal 2	33		40
Metacarpal 3	33		34
Metacarpal 4	19		37
Metacarpal 5	26		30
Phalanges			
Proximal 1–5		30 (294)	
Middle		24(191)	
Distal 1–5		13 (124)	
Foot bones			
Tarsals			
Calcaneus	44		46
Talus	60		54
Cuboid	41		45
Navicular	40		48
Cuneiform 1	47		43
Cuneiform 2	40		38
Cuneiform 3	40		39
Metatarsal 1	52		49
Metatarsal 2	32		31
Metatarsal 3	49		46
Metatarsal 4	40		44
Metatarsal 5	38		47
Phalanges			
Proximal 1–5		31 (303)	
Middle		9 (67)	
Distal 1–5		9 (81)	

Table 7.6. Minimum Number of Individuals Under 15 Years of Age.

Age in Years	MNI
.0–.5	16
.5–1.5	4
1.5–2.5	8
2.5–3.5	3
3.5–4.5	1
4.5–5.5	0
5.5–6.5	2
6.5–7.5	1
7.5–8.5	0
8.5–9.5	1
10–14	2
Total	38

Discussion

Although Ossuary III is smaller than the other two ossuaries reported from this site, its bioarchaeological details are similar, suggesting representation of all the deceased in the community for a fixed period of time. The paucity of artifacts and the egalitarian nature of the assemblage are consistent with Jirikowic's suggestion (1990) that the elite controlled wealth and the ossuaries represent the non-elite population. As with Ossuary II, Ossuary III presented a variety of cranial positions and orientations, with all ages, sexes, and skeletal parts distributed throughout the assemblage. As with both previous ossuaries, some articulated remains were noted, in addition to the secondary nature of most. Although no completely articulated individuals were found in Ossuary III, in contrast to the three such individuals in Ossuary II, 197 examples of partial articulation were noted. These represented at least six immature individuals and 13 adults. Ossuary III contained at least 112 individuals, fewer than the 131 found in Ossuary I and the 188 of Ossuary II.

Analysis of the Ossuary II sample noted that about 20 percent of the adults were represented by individuals with articulated lower leg bones and vertebrae. This figure was used to assist in the estimation of the length of time represented by the ossuary deposit (accumulation of the dead over a period of approximately three years). In Ossuary III, about 13 (18 percent) of the 74 adults maintained vertebrae articulation at the time of burial. Thus the Ossuary III data are consistent with those of Ossuary II in suggesting a time interval of about three years (actually 3.9 years for Ossuary III). In both ossuaries I and II, subadults comprised about 47 percent of the total sample. Within Ossuary III, the immature constituted only 34 percent of the sample, suggesting a slightly lower immature death rate and/or birth rate.

The Ossuary III analysis, coupled with those of the previous two ossuaries excavated from this site, reveals a consistent pattern of mortuary behavior, as well as biological profiles of the people represented. The bioarchaeological approach utilized in this analysis reflects a methodological orientation championed by Jane E. Buikstra over her long and accomplished career.

Acknowledgements

The author thanks Smithsonian Institution National Museum of Natural History staff Sally Graver, for her assistance in data collection, and Kristin Montaperto, for her assistance in manuscript preparation.

References Cited

Adams, Bradley J., and John E. Byrd
2008 *Recovery, Analysis, and Identification of Commingled Human Remains.* Humana Press, Totowa, New Jersey.

Boyd, Donna C., and C. Clifford Boyd Jr.
1992 Late Woodland Mortuary Variability in Virginia. In *Middle and Late Woodland Research in Virginia: A Synthesis*, edited by Theodore R. Reinhart and Mary Ellen N. Hodges, pp. 249–275. Special Publication No. 29. Archeological Society of Virginia, Richmond.

Buikstra, Jane E., and Lane A. Beck (editors)
2006 *Bioarchaeology: The Contextual Analysis of Human Remains.* Academic Press, New York.

Buikstra, Jane E., and Douglas H. Ubelaker (editors)
1994 *Standards for Data Collection from Human Skeletal Remains: Proceedings of a Seminar at the Field Museum of Natural History.* Arkansas Archaeological Survey Press, Fayetteville.

Chacon, Richard J., and David H. Dye
2007 *The Taking and Displaying of Human Body Parts as Trophies by Amerindians.* Springer, New York.

Curry, Dennis C.
1999 *Feast of the Dead: Aboriginal Ossuaries in Maryland.* Archeological Society of Maryland and Maryland Historical Trust Press, Crownsville.

Jirikowic, Christine
1990 The Political Implications of a Cultural Practice: A New Perspective on Ossuary Burial in the Potomac Valley. *North American Archaeologist* 11(4):353–374.

Larsen, Clark Spencer
2001 *Bioarchaeology of Spanish Florida: The Impact of Colonialism.* University Press of Florida, Gainesville.

Turner, E. Randolph, III
1992 The Virginia Coastal Plain During the Late Woodland Period. In *Middle and Late Woodland Research in Virginia: A Synthesis*, edited by Theodore R. Reinhart and Mary Ellen N. Hodges, pp. 97–136. Special Publication No. 29. Archeological Society of Virginia, Richmond.

Ubelaker, Douglas H.
1974 *Reconstruction of Demographic Profiles from Ossuary Skeletal Samples: A Case Study from the Tidewater Potomac.* Smithsonian Contributions to Anthropology No. 18. Smithsonian Institution Press, Washington, D.C.

8

INTERPRETING ANIMAL EFFIGIES FROM PRECONTACT NATIVE AMERICAN SITES:

APPLYING AN INTERDISCIPLINARY METHOD TO ILLINOIS MISSISSIPPIAN ARTIFACTS

DAVE AFTANDILIAN
DEPARTMENT OF SOCIOLOGY AND ANTHROPOLOGY, TEXAS CHRISTIAN UNIVERSITY

IN THIS CHAPTER I USE AN INTERDISCIPLINARY method that I modified from existing approaches to help archaeologists move from representations of animals on artifacts to an understanding of the socioreligious meanings of those animals in a given culture. The method has five steps—formal, functional, and material analysis; contextual analysis; natural history; ethnographic and ethnohistoric analogy; and finally interpretation—all of which will be discussed in detail below. I will also illustrate the method's use by applying it to several different kinds of animal artifacts made by Illinois Mississippian peoples. (For another such example, see Aftandilian 2007b.)

The larger study on which this chapter is based (Aftandilian 2007a) focused on interpreting Illinois Mississippian animal effigy artifacts recovered from an area bounded by Fulton and Peoria counties in central Illinois to the north, Madison and St. Clair counties in the American Bottom to the southwest, and Massac and Pope counties in southern Illinois. Key sites in each of these regions are noted in Figure 8.1.

Although comparatively few Mississippian artifacts have been recovered from the lower Illinois Valley (which includes the lower 70 miles of the Illinois River's drainage through Calhoun, Greene, Jersey, and Pike counties), that region is rich in Woodland-period remains and has been the subject of intensive archaeological study since the 1930s. Jane E. Buikstra has made a number of key contributions to the archaeology of this region since she began excavating there in 1966.

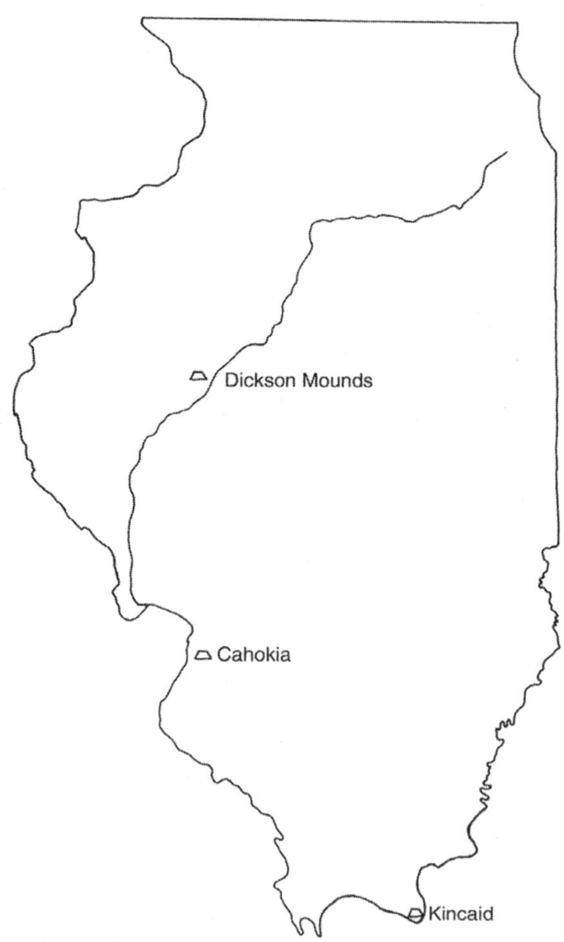

Figure 8.1. Illinois study area and key sites (after Perino 1971:Figure 1).

She has authored or coauthored dozens of articles on the archaeology of the lower Illinois Valley. Through these publications, Buikstra has established the key importance of bioarchaeology, viewed in both diachronic and regional perspectives, to understanding relationships among past cultural groups in this region (Buikstra 1976; Konigsberg and Buikstra 1995). For the purposes of this chapter, Buikstra's most important contributions to Illinois archaeology may have been her long-standing focus on multidisciplinary and interdisciplinary approaches to understanding the past, and on contextual analysis of human skeletal remains and the artifacts associated with them. As we will see, both of these contributions helped inspire my work on the research method presented here.

This approach is based on the research of a number of other scholars, each of whom has employed one or more of the steps discussed below to interpret archaeological materials. For example, it has become fairly common in recent decades for archaeologists to use ethnographic and ethnohistoric analogy. Part of the credit for the rising interest in such approaches is due to Ian Hodder. His ethnoarchaeological work on interpreting decorations on Ilchamus calabashes in Kenya demonstrated the crucial importance of researching the social and contextual contexts within which artifacts are used if we want to understand their functions and meanings to the people who made them (Hodder 1991:107–120). Karl Taube combined artistic, linguistic, and modern ethnographic evidence to interpret the meanings of the maize tamale in Classic Maya culture (Taube 1989). Kent Flannery and Joyce Marcus have also shown how ethnohistoric information, coupled with primary data on archaeological find contexts, can help us better understand ancient Zapotec religious practices in Mesoamerica (Flannery and Marcus 1993; Marcus and Flannery 1994).

The scholars who have employed methods most similar to the one I describe in this chapter are Olga Linares, Scott O'Mack, and those involved in the Mississippian Iconography Workshop at Texas State University–San Marcos. In her interdisciplinary analysis of burial vessels from high-status graves in central Panama (1500–500 B.P.), Linares (1977) used formal analysis of the vessels, natural history of the tropical animal species represented on the vessels, the archaeological contexts within which the vessels were discovered, and ethnohistoric analogy to interpret the meaning of the vessels' iconography to their makers. In his study, O'Mack (1991) drew on natural history, ethnohistoric analogy, and formal analysis to interpret the meanings of Yacateuctli and Ehecatl-Quetzalcoatl among the Aztec of central Mexico. And the participants in the Mississippian Iconography Workshop collectively developed a four-pronged approach that involves "recognition of style regions, visual structural analysis, archaeological content, and ethnographic analogy" (Reilly and Garber 2007:6; see also Reilly et al. 2011:xiii).

In developing my approach to interpreting Mississippian animal effigies, I offer several significant modifications to existing methods. First and foremost, I conduct in-depth studies of the natural history of the animals most frequently represented on the artifacts. While others have worked with biologists to identify the species represented and their habitats (e.g., Jett and Moyle 1986), very few archaeologists have researched the appearance, behavior, and other aspects of the lives of the animals whose representations they are analyzing. This is an unfortunate oversight, because it is precisely these aspects of the lives of real animals that partly inspired the Mississippians and other archaeologically known peoples to use the animals as symbols on their artifacts. I argue, then, that if we truly want to understand what representations of animals meant to the peoples who made them, we must devote serious attention to the natural history of these animals. Second, I apply each of the five steps in this method in a consistent manner to each kind of effigy artifact I analyze. And third, I develop my final interpretations in a manner consistent with Native American ways of knowing. (I will expand on this last point in the conclusion.)

Formal, Functional, and Material Analysis

The first step in this study involves formal, functional, and material analysis of animal images and the objects that bear them. I start the analysis here because these representations are our primary data; they constitute a visible record of symbolism that was important enough to the Illinois Mississippians that they chose to represent it in durable media such as ceramic pots and stone pipes.

The first question I ask of any animal image is: What kind of animal does it represent? And ideally: What species does it represent? Sometimes identifying the kind of animal is not difficult, but sometimes it can be quite challenging. In such cases, when I was unable to identify the animal myself, I sought the assistance of experts in the biological study of that kind of animal in Illinois.

Next I conduct a formal, art historical analysis of the animal image. What aspects of the representation are most detailed and specific? Picking out what seem to be the key features of a representation may help us identify particular aspects of an animal's appearance or behavior that intrigued the object's makers. Especially when the same traits are accentuated in nearly every image of a particular animal, we can assume that there is something about that feature worth looking into further. For instance, while Illinois Mississippian beaver bowls differ in whether they represent just the beaver's forelegs or also its back legs, and whether individual toes are marked off, nearly all the images share a single common feature: a narrow, cylindrical object gripped within the mouth and held by the two forepaws (Figure 8.2). Similarly, owl bottles may or may not represent an owl's face, wings, or feet, but they always include two prominent ear tufts that look like horns atop the head (Figure 8.3).

It is also important to consider the materials of which an object was made and to think about how the object might have been used by its makers. Certain materials have religious significance as materials, regardless of what they are made into. Copper is one example; shell another; and the same was likely true for various types of stone (Boivin and Owoc 2004; Claassen 1998:203–211; Trevelyan 1987:289–358). Several aspects of materials such as these, including their colors, shapes, or sources, might incite special interest.

Finally, we need to think about how a given object might have been used. For example, pipes were obviously smoked, and given their relative rarity in Illinois Mississippian archaeological collections, they were probably smoked only on important ceremonial occasions.[1]

Figure 8.2. Beaver bowl from St. Clair County/Madison County, Illinois (ISM 803/163; courtesy Illinois State Museum).

Figure 8.3. Owl bottle from Jackson County, Illinois (ISM 1997/178.0001; courtesy Illinois State Museum).

CONTEXTUAL ANALYSIS

The next step involves familiarization with the archaeological contexts within which an animal artifact is found. Most generally: Where in Illinois was the object found? Where have objects with similar animal images been found?

Next, was the object found in a house, a grave, or somewhere else? Were any other items found in association with the animal artifact? If the object was found in a burial, was it found with a man or a woman? An adult or a child? Knowing the answers to these contextual questions can help tremendously in interpreting the meanings of animal artifacts. For instance, nearly all the owl effigy bottles in Illinois come from graves, and in the cases where we know the age of the person they were buried with, they were nearly always buried with children or infants.[2] As we will see, that contextual information provides crucial clues for interpreting the meaning of horned owl bottles to the Illinois Mississippians.

Finally, whenever possible, I draw on the insights of zooarchaeologists to determine whether the type of animal depicted on an artifact lived in Illinois at the time the artifact was made, how common it was, and whether the animal was used for more than symbolism by the Illinois Mississippians. Was it hunted for food or other purposes? Were its bones used for tools or ritual objects? Were the animal's bones spread widely at major sites, or were they found only in certain restricted areas?

NATURAL HISTORY

Once I have found as much contextual information for a given animal artifact as possible, the next step is to delve into the natural history of the animal represented on the artifact. What sort of habitat is the animal usually found in? What does it look like? Also, how does the animal behave? What does it eat? How does it move? And finally, what about the animal's appearance and/or behavior might have made it particularly interesting to the Illinois Mississippians? What about its natural history might have especially fired their cultural imagination?

For instance, one unique aspect of beaver behavior is that they build things, such as lodges, dams, and canals. Animals that display humanlike behaviors often incite human interest, and this has certainly been true for beavers and their building habits, for both Native Americans and Europeans (Aftandilian 2007a:222–226). More importantly, in terms of interpreting the meaning of the imagery on the beaver bowls, beavers in the wild often grasp sticks between their forepaws and gnaw off the bark with their teeth—just as they are depicted doing on Illinois Mississippian bowls (compare Figures 8.2 and 8.4).

Figure 8.4. Beaver carrying stick in mouth (photo by and courtesy of Fran West).

Animals that move between different realms—anomalous or liminal animals—also seemed to be of special interest to the Illinois Mississippians, and indeed to many other Native American groups (Hudson 1976:139–148). Here again, the beaver is an excellent example, since it goes on land to cut trees but spends much of its time in the water. Owls are another example, gliding on soundless wings across the crepuscular boundaries between day and night.

ETHNOGRAPHIC AND ETHNOHISTORIC ANALOGY

The next step in this method involves ethnographic and ethnohistoric analogy.[3] The idea here is to use ethnographic information recorded from living or historically known peoples to try to understand what animals might have meant to the Illinois Mississippians. It is important to include collections of stories and folklore in this stage of the analysis, as well as standard ethnographies. Not only do animals often appear more frequently in such stories than in ethnographies, but sacred stories often provide crucial interpretive clues for understanding the history, function, and use of particular ceremonies involving animals (Bowers 2004:340–341). In employing ethnographic analogy to interpret Mississippian symbolism, I follow in the distinguished footsteps of many other scholars (see, e.g., Emerson 1989, 1997, 2003; Hall 1977a, 1977b, 1989, 1997; Howard 1968; Lankford et al. 2011; Reilly and Garber 2007; Townsend 2004; Waring 1968; Willoughby 2000).

Obviously, the use of ethnographic analogy is somewhat problematic and must be approached carefully.[4] We need to keep in mind such issues as the biases of the observer who recorded the ethnographic data we are using, the specific circumstances under which the data were recorded, and whether the data refer to a mythic or historical past (Barber and Berdan 1998:148–177; Galloway 1986). On the other hand, we have little choice but to use ethnographic analogy if we hope to understand what Illinois Mississippian animal representations may have meant to their makers. As Gordon Willey has pointed out, "there are some aspects of past life, principally those in the ideological realm, that can be satisfactorily explained only with the aid of specific historical analogy" (that is, ethnographic analogy; Willey 1990:303).

For my survey of ethnographic and ethnohistoric data, I focused especially on customs recorded from Dhegiha and Chiwere Siouan–speaking tribes of the central Plains who are likely most closely related to the Illinois Mississippians, including the Osage, Omaha, Kansa, and Ho-chunk, or Winnebago (Dorsey 1885; Howard 1956, 1995:4–5; La Flesche 1995:28–29, 284; Unrau 1971:15–16). Also included were data from tribes likely descended from other (non-Illinois) Mississippian groups, such as the Pawnee, Arikara, and Caddo in the southern Plains and the Creeks, Choctaw, and Seminole in the Southeast. In addition, ethnographies of some central Algonkian peoples whose ancestors might have lived near the Illinois Mississippians, such as the Ojibwe and Fox, were consulted. Finally, animal beliefs of the Pueblo peoples of the Southwest were reviewed, since maize probably came to the Illinois Mississippians from the Southwest (Fritz 1992:28; Smith 1995:184) and related ritual beliefs were likely passed along as well (Taube 2000:297; Young 1994:108). In my research on these tribes, I explored the roles played by each animal portrayed on Illinois Mississippian artifacts, including utilitarian uses, such as for food; social uses, such as for clan names; ritual uses; and uses in sacred stories, folklore, and cosmology.

For example, it is difficult to think of a creature that has had more contradictory beliefs associated with it among Native Americans than the owl (Aftandilian 2007a:433–482). On the one hand, owls are seen as bringers of healing medicine and spiritual power for warriors, hunters, and medicine people. On the other hand, certain kinds of owls, especially great horned and screech owls, are believed to be the familiars of witches and the bringers of ill omens of death or serious illness, or they are thought to be ghosts, transformed human spirits doomed to wander the earth. Perhaps the most consistent spiritual association of owls in many tribes, though, is with death and the afterlife.

INTERPRETATION

The final step in the method involves synthesizing all the data gathered from the other steps into the most likely interpretations of what each animal meant to the Illinois Mississippians. Let's finish our owl example to see how this works. Formal analysis of the owl images revealed that the one feature common to all owl bottles were the "horns" or ear tufts atop the head. From natural history, we learn that three owls found in Illinois have prominent ear tufts—great horned, screech, and long-eared owls (Aftandilian 2007a:418). Since long-eared owls are found in Illinois only in winter, I believe it more likely that great horned or screech owls, or both, were being represented on the owl bottles. From ethnographic analogy, we learn that these two tufted owls, great horned and screech, are also considered the most spiritually charged owls among many Native American tribes. As mentioned earlier, there is a wide range of owl beliefs in any one tribe, let alone among all Native American tribes. We can help narrow down which ethnographic information might be most relevant by relying on the archaeological contexts within which Mississippian owl bottles have been found in Illinois. First, all the owl bottles for which contextual information is available were found in graves. Secondly, most of the owl bottles were found buried with infants or children (see note 2 for details).

So what do we make of all this? We have already said that the most consistent spiritual association of owls in most Native American tribes is with death and the afterlife. Since all the owl bottles were found in mortuary contexts, this suggests that Illinois Mississippians associated owls with death. To be more specific than that, we need to rely on ethnographic analogy. It turns out that an owl or owl-human supernatural being serves as gatekeeper along the path to the afterlife among the Oglala Lakota, the Cheyenne, and the Ojibwe (Baraga 1966:198; Barnouw 1977:18–19; Cowdrey 2003; Jones 1919:311–313, 531–545; Lame Deer and Erdoes 1972:101, 198; Powers 1982:53, 1986:101; Sparks and Soper 1989:199). This owl being stands at the fork in the Milky Way, the road in the sky that leads to the land of the dead, letting some souls pass but condemning others to roam the earth as ghosts forever. I suggest that the owl or owl-human creature depicted on the Illinois Mississippian bottles represents such a being.

One aspect of the archaeological context just mentioned remains unexplained: Why were these owl bottles found most often with children and infants? Two potential interpretations can be offered. First, among the Lakota, a tattoo on the wrist signified to the Owl Woman, who guarded the path to the afterlife, that the spirit who wore it was a Lakota and thus should be allowed to pass to the land of the dead (Lame Deer and Erdoes 1972:101, 198). In many Native American tribes, tattoos are not given to children but only to adults who have earned the honor of a tattoo. Children and infants, then, would probably not have been tattooed yet. Therefore, when they died, the Owl Woman would not have recognized their spirits as qualified to proceed on to the afterlife. Perhaps in this case, the owl bottles were buried with the children to serve as passports to allow the children access to the land of the dead, just as tattoos did for adults.

A second possibility rests on the analogy of these owl bottles with gourd vessels, which were also frequently used to hold liquids among Native American tribes and likely were used for this purpose among the Illinois Mississippians.[5] The shapes of certain varieties of bottle gourds and of Illinois Mississippian owl bottles are nearly identical. This is likely not a coincidence. Among the Yuchi of Georgia and South Carolina, for instance, the shapes of gourds and squashes served as models for the shapes of pottery vessels (Speck 2004:27–28). Among the Yuchi, Pawnee, and Iroquois, gourd bottles and rattles sometimes also functioned in rituals and sacred stories as containers for souls (Hewitt 1895:109, Speck 2004:144–146, Weltfish 1977:466). Perhaps, then, the owl bottles buried with Illinois Mississippian children served as containers for their souls as well. How this might have worked in detail is difficult to know, but we might speculate that since owls are often considered the spirits of humans by Native American groups, perhaps the children's spirits became owls once they flowed into the owl bottles and the children then made their way to the land of the dead in the form of owls.[6]

Conclusion

This study has demonstrated how to apply an interdisciplinary analytical method to move from archaeologically recovered animal artifacts to the religious and social meanings the animals represented on them might have had for the peoples who made them. While this is not the first study to apply any of the various steps described above to interpreting Mississippian artifacts, truly *interdisciplinary* studies of Mississippian worldviews and symbolism, conducted in a systematic fashion, remain rather rare.[7] Guy Prentice's analysis of the Birger Figurine (Prentice 1986) is one key exception, as is the work conducted by participants in the Mississippian Iconography Workshop (Lankford et al. 2011; Reilly and Garber 2007). Natural histories of animals, in particular, have seldom been investigated by archaeologists and others attempting to interpret precontact representations of animals (but see Morphy 1989 for several welcome exceptions). This relative lack of interdisciplinary approaches to understanding precontact animal symbolism is unfortunate, since it is only through such approaches that we can hope to make the conceptual leap from representations of animals on Mississippian artifacts to the meanings of those animals in Mississippian worldviews.

Furthermore, if we truly want to understand Mississippian views of animals, we would do well to employ Native American ways of knowing in our analyses of animal effigies, since the Mississippians were precontact Native American peoples. In other words, I suggest that archaeologists use Native Americans not just as objects of study but as sources of the theoretical and analytical approaches we use in our studies of artifacts made by Native Americans and other peoples, as Christopher Ronwanien:te Jocks has argued scholars of Native American religions should do (Jocks 2000:72). One key aspect of Native American ways of knowing includes a holistic approach to understanding (Cajete 2000; Kawagley 2006); this is another reason to emphasize the importance of a wide-ranging interdisciplinary approach to interpreting precontact Native American artifacts.

There is another important lesson to be learned from Native American ways of knowing in relation to archaeological interpretations of animal effigy artifacts: a given symbol does not mean just one thing to members of a specific tribe, but rather it evokes a range of meanings depending on the circumstances within which the symbol is encountered, as well as one's clan, age, gender, individual experience, level of spiritual knowledge, and so on (in other words, symbols are polysemous and multivocal for Native Americans; cf. Turner 1967:50). Therefore, in our interpretations of animal effigies, we would do well to seek not just one reductive meaning of each effigy as a symbol but rather a range of potential meanings. By doing so, we are more likely to capture some of the wide array of meanings each animal effigy artifact would have had among the people who made and used it. This is why several possible interpretations have been offered for the Mississippian owl effigy bottles discussed earlier.

Finally, although the examples presented in this study were all drawn from Illinois Mississippian artifacts and peoples, such a method could certainly be applied to work on other peoples from other times and places. Depending on the specific context and the data available, various steps in the method would need to be reworked or perhaps dropped entirely, but the overall process would remain the same. Key to this process is the interdisciplinary approach, involving in this case art history, archaeology, natural history, folklore studies, history of religion, and ethnohistory. I hope that my demonstration of how such a method can be used will encourage other archaeologists to apply this or similar interdisciplinary approaches more frequently in the future.

Notes

1. However, pipes were not necessarily *just* smoked. A number of Illinois Mississippian sandstone frog pipes, for instance, have deep grooves on various surfaces (not just in their bowls or stem holes), which suggests that they were used as both pipes and abraders (Aftandilian 2007a:187).

2. Of the 14 Illinois Mississippian owl bottles I studied from definite mortuary contexts, 6 were found associated with infants or children, 1 was associated with a young adult female, and 1 was found near the surface in a possible crematory or charnel structure. The age and sex of the burials is unknown for the other 6 bottles. See Aftandilian 2007a:369–377 for detailed provenience information and references.

3. Technically speaking, ethnographic analogy refers to analogies with living peoples, while ethnohistoric analogy refers to analogies with historically known peoples who may or may not still be living today. In the New World, these techniques are also often referred to as the direct historical approach (see, e.g., Galloway 1986; Marcus and Flannery 1994; Wonderley 2005).

4. This difficulty probably explains at least some of the extreme discomfort with ethnographic analogy expressed by Lewis Binford and other processualist New Archaeologists during the 1960s and 1970s (Binford 1967:1, 1968:13; Willey and Sabloff 1980:205–207; Wylie 1985:84–87).

5. Linguistic data from Central Algonkian peoples suggest that the original Native American use of both gourds and squashes was as containers rather than as foods. The same word stem used for *squash* and *gourd* was also used for *container* and *receptacle* (as well as *spoon* and *dipper*; Munson 1973:119–120).

6. This would help explain a puzzling element in the stories that many tribes tell about the trip to the land of the dead—that the road is fraught with dangers and that the very old and the very young often cannot make it to the journey's end. Perhaps, by transforming into owls, the spirits of Illinois Mississippian children could make that journey unscathed.

7. In addition to the studies that have employed the ethnographic analogy cited above, a number of others in recent years have focused on formal analysis of effigy artifacts or have constructed folk taxonomies based on faunal remains and artistic representations. For selected references, see Aftandilian 2007a:60–61.

REFERENCES CITED

Aftandilian, Dave

2007a Animals, Agriculture, and Religion Among Native Americans in Precontact Illinois: An Interdisciplinary Analysis of Perception and Representation. Unpublished Ph.D. dissertation, Department of Anthropology, University of Chicago.

2007b Frogs, Snakes, and Agricultural Fertility: Interpreting Illinois Mississippian Representations. In *What Are the Animals to Us? Approaches from Science, Religion, Folklore, Literature, and Art*, edited by Dave Aftandilian, Marion W. Copeland, and David Scofield Wilson, pp. 53–86. University of Tennessee Press, Knoxville.

Baraga, Bishop

1966 *A Dictionary of the Otchipwe Language, Explained in English*. Reprinted. Ross & Haines, Minneapolis. Originally published 1878, Beauchemin and Valois, Montreal.

Barber, Russell J., and Frances F. Berdan

1998 *The Emperor's Mirror: Understanding Cultures Through Primary Sources*. University of Arizona Press, Tucson.

Barnouw, Victor

1977 *Wisconsin Chippewa Myths and Tales and Their Relation to Chippewa Life*. University of Wisconsin Press, Madison.

Binford, Lewis R.

1967 Smudge Pits and Hide Smoking: The Use of Analogy in Archaeological Reasoning. *American Antiquity* 32(1):1–12.

1968 Archeological Perspectives. In *New Perspectives in Archaeology*, edited by Sally R. Binford and Lewis R. Binford, pp. 5–32. Aldine, Chicago.

Boivin, Nicole, and Mary Ann Owoc (editors)

2004 *Soils, Stones, and Symbols: Cultural Perceptions of the Mineral World*. UCL Press, London.

Bowers, Alfred W.

2004 *Mandan Social and Ceremonial Organization*. Reprinted. University of Nebraska Press, Lincoln. Originally published 1950, University of Chicago Press, Chicago.

Buikstra, Jane E.

1976 *Hopewell in the Lower Illinois Valley: A Regional Approach to the Study of Human Biological Variability and Prehistoric Behavior*. Scientific Papers No. 2. Northwestern University Archeological Program, Evanston, Illinois.

1980 Epigenetic Distance: A Study of Biological Variability in the Lower Illinois River Region. In *Early Native Americans: Prehistoric Demography, Economy, and Technology*, edited by David L. Browman, pp. 271–299. Mouton, The Hague.

1984 The Lower Illinois River Region: A Prehistoric Context for the Study of Ancient Health and Diet. In *Paleopathology at the Origins of Agriculture*, edited by Mark Nathan Cohen and George J. Armelagos, pp. 215–234. Academic Press, New York.

Buikstra, Jane E., and Douglas K. Charles

1999 Centering the Ancestors: Cemeteries, Mounds, and Sacred Landscapes of the Ancient North American Midcontinent. In *Archaeologies of Landscape: Contemporary Perspectives*, edited by Wendy Ashmore and A. Bernard Knapp, pp. 201–228. Blackwell, Malden, Massachusetts.

Buikstra, Jane E., and Della C. Cook

1981 Pre-Columbian Tuberculosis in West-Central Illinois: Prehistoric Disease in Biocultural Perspective. In *Prehistoric Tuberculosis in the Americas*, edited by Jane E. Buikstra, pp. 115–139. Northwestern University Archeological Program, Evanston, Illinois.

Buikstra, Jane E., and George R. Milner

1991 Isotopic and Archaeological Interpretations of Diet in the Central Mississippi Valley. *Journal of Archaeological Science* 18(3):319–330.

Buikstra, Jane E., Douglas K. Charles, and Gordon F. M. Rakita

1998 *Staging Ritual: Hopewell Ceremonialism at the Mound House Site, Greene County, Illinois*. Kampsville Studies in Archeology and History No. 1. Center for American Archeology, Kampsville, Illinois.

Buikstra, Jane E., Jerome C. Rose, and George R. Milner

1994 A Carbon Isotopic Perspective on Dietary Variation in Late Prehistoric Western Illinois. In *Agricultural Origins and Development in the Midcontinent*, edited by William Green, pp. 155–170. University of Iowa, Office of the State Archaeologist, Iowa City.

Cajete, Gregory

2000 *Native Science: Natural Laws of Interdependence*. Clear Light Publishers, Santa Fe, New Mexico.

Charles, Douglas K., Jane E. Buikstra, and Lyle W. Konigsberg

1986 Behavioral Implications of Terminal Archaic and Early Woodland Mortuary Practices in the Lower Illinois Valley. In *Early Woodland Archeology*, edited by Kenneth B. Farnsworth and Thomas E. Emerson, pp. 458–474. Center for American Archaeology Press, Kampsville, Illinois.

Charles, Douglas K., Julieann van Nest, and Jane E. Buikstra

2004 From the Earth: Minerals and Meaning in the Hopewellian World. In *Soils, Stones and Symbols: Cultural Perceptions of the Mineral World*, edited by Nicole Boivin and Mary Ann Owoc, pp. 43–70. UCL Press, London.

Claassen, Cheryl

1998 *Shells*. Cambridge Manuals in Archaeology. Cambridge University Press, Cambridge.

Cowdrey, Mike

2003 The Turtle Hangs Before: Celestial Templates in Cheyenne Cosmology. *The European Review of Native American Studies* 17(2):1–10.

Dorsey, J. Owen

1885 Mourning and War Customs of the Kansas. *American Naturalist* 19(7):670–680.

Emerson, Thomas E.

1989 Water, Serpents, and the Underworld: An Exploration into Cahokian Symbolism. In *The Southeastern Ceremonial Complex: Artifacts and Analysis*, edited by Patricia Galloway, pp. 45–92. University of Nebraska Press, Lincoln.

1997 *Cahokia and the Archaeology of Power.* University of Alabama Press, Tuscaloosa.

2003 Materializing Cahokia Shamans. *Southeastern Archaeology* 22(2): 135–154.

Flannery, Kent V., and Joyce Marcus

1993 Cognitive Archaeology. *Cambridge Archaeological Journal* 3:260–270.

Fritz, Gayle J.

1992 "Newer," "Better" Maize and the Mississippian Emergence: A Critique of Prime Mover Explanations. In *Late Prehistoric Agriculture: Observations from the Midwest,* edited by William I. Woods, pp. 19–43. Studies in Illinois Archaeology No. 8. Illinois Historic Preservation Agency, Springfield.

Galloway, Patricia K.

1986 The Direct Historical Approach and Early Historical Documents: The Ethnohistorian's View. In *The Protohistoric Period in the Mid-South: 1500–1700,* edited by David H. Dye and Ronald C. Brister, pp. 14–23. Archaeological Report No. 18. Mississippi Department of Archives and History, Jackson.

Hall, Robert L.

1977a An Anthropocentric Perspective for Eastern United States Prehistory. *American Antiquity* 42(4):499–518.

1977b In Search of the Ideology of the Adena-Hopewell Climax. In *Hopewell Archaeology: The Chillicothe Conference,* edited by David S. Brose and N'omi Greber, pp. 258–265. Kent State University Press, Kent, Ohio.

1989 The Cultural Background of Mississippian Symbolism. In *The Southeastern Ceremonial Complex: Artifacts and Analysis,* edited by Patricia Galloway, pp. 239–278. University of Nebraska Press, Lincoln.

1997 *An Archaeology of the Soul: North American Indian Belief and Ritual.* University of Illinois Press, Urbana.

Hanson, Douglas B., and Jane E. Buikstra

1987 Histomorphological Alteration in Buried Human Bone from the Lower Illinois Valley: Implications for Paleodietary Research. *Journal of Archaeological Science* 14:549–563.

Hewitt, John Napoleon B.

1895 The Iroquoian Concept of the Soul. *Journal of American Folklore* 8(29):107–116.

Hodder, Ian

1991 *Reading the Past: Current Approaches to Interpretation in Archaeology.* 2nd ed. Cambridge University Press, Cambridge.

Howard, James H.

1956 The Persistence of Southern Cult Gorgets Among the Historic Kansa. *American Antiquity* 21(3):301–303.

1968 *The Southeastern Ceremonial Complex and Its Interpretation.* Memoir No. 6. Missouri Archaeological Society, Columbia.

1995 *The Ponca Tribe.* Reprinted. University of Nebraska Press, Lincoln. Originally published 1965, Bulletin No. 195, Bureau of American Ethnology, Smithsonian Institution, Washington, D.C.

Hudson, Charles

1976 *The Southeastern Indians.* University of Tennessee Press, Knoxville.

Jett, Stephen C., and Peter B. Moyle

1986 The Exotic Origins of Fishes Depicted on Prehistoric Mimbres Pottery from New Mexico. *American Antiquity* 51(4):688–720.

Jocks, Christopher Ronwanien:te

2000 Spirituality for Sale: Sacred Knowledge in the Consumer Age. In *Native American Spirituality: A Critical Reader,* edited by Lee Irwin, pp. 61–77. University of Nebraska Press, Lincoln.

Jones, William

1919 *Ojibwa Texts.* Publications of the American Ethnological Association Vol. 7, Pt. 2. G. E. Stechert, New York.

Kawagley, Angayuqaq Oscar

2006 *A Yupiaq Worldview: A Pathway to Ecology and Spirit.* 2nd ed. Waveland Press, Long Grove, Illinois.

Konigsberg, Lyle W., and Jane E. Buikstra

1995 Regional Approaches to the Investigation of Past Human Biocultural Structure. In *Regional Approaches to Mortuary Analysis,* edited by Lane Anderson Beck, pp. 191–219. Plenum Press, New York.

La Flesche, Francis

1995 *The Osage and the Invisible World: From the Works of Francis La Flesche.* Edited by Garrick A. Bailey. University of Oklahoma Press, Norman.

Lambert, Joseph B., Carole B. Szpunar, and Jane E. Buikstra

1979 Chemical Analysis of Excavated Human Bone from Middle and Late Woodland Sites. *Archaeometry* 21:115–129.

Lame Deer, John (Fire), and Richard Erdoes

1972 *Lame Deer: Seeker of Visions.* Pocket Books, New York.

Lankford, George E., F. Kent Reilly III, and James F. Garber (editors)

2011 *Visualizing the Sacred: Cosmic Visions, Regionalism, and the Art of the Mississippian World.* University of Texas Press, Austin.

Linares, Olga F.

1977 *Ecology and the Arts in Ancient Panama: On the Development of Social Rank and Symbolism in the Central Provinces.* Studies in Pre-Columbian Art and Archaeology No. 17. Dumbarton Oaks, Washington, D.C.

Marcus, Joyce, and Kent V. Flannery

1994 Ancient Zapotec Ritual and Religion: An Application of the Direct Historical Approach. In *The Ancient Mind: Elements of Cognitive Archaeology,* edited by Colin Renfrew and Ezra B. W. Zubrow, pp. 55–74. Cambridge University Press, Cambridge.

Milner, George R., Jane E. Buikstra, and Michael D. Wiant

2009 Archaic Burial Sites in the American Midcontinent. In *Archaic Societies: Diversity and Complexity Across the Midcontinent,* edited by Thomas E. Emerson, Dale L. McElrath, and Andrew C. Fortier, pp. 115–136. State University of New York Press, Albany.

Morphy, Howard (editor)

1989 *Animals into Art.* Unwin Hyman, London.

Munson, Patrick J.

1973 The Origins and Antiquity of Maize-Beans-Squash Agriculture in Eastern North America: Some Linguistic Implications. In *Variation in Anthropology: Essays in Honor of John C. McGregor,* edited by Donald W. Lathrap and Jody Douglas, pp. 107–135. Illinois Archaeological Survey, Urbana.

O'Mack, Scott

1991 Yacateuctli and Ehecatl-Quetzalcoatl: Earth-Divers in Aztec Central Mexico. *Ethnohistory* 38(1):1–33.

Perino, Gregory H.

1971 The Mississippian Component at the Schild Site (No. 4), Greene County, Illinois. In *Mississippian Site Archaeology in Illinois I: Site Reports from the St. Louis and Chicago Areas,* edited by James A. Brown, pp. 1–148. Illinois Archaeological Survey, Urbana.

Powers, Marla N.

1986 *Oglala Women.* University of Chicago Press, Chicago.

Powers, William K.

1982 *Oglala Religion.* University of Nebraska Press, Lincoln.

Prentice, Guy

1986 An Analysis of the Symbolism Expressed by the Birger Figurine. *American Antiquity* 51:239–266.

Reilly, F. Kent, III, and James F. Garber

2007 Introduction. In *Ancient Objects and Sacred Realms: Interpretations of Mississippian Iconography,* edited by F. Kent Reilly III and James F. Garber, pp. 1–7. University of Texas Press, Austin.

Reilly, F. Kent, III, and James F. Garber (editors)

2007 *Ancient Objects and Sacred Realms: Interpretations of Mississippian Iconography.* University of Texas Press, Austin.

Reilly, F. Kent, III, James F. Garber, and George E. Lankford

2011 Introduction. In *Visualizing the Sacred: Cosmic Visions, Regionalism, and the Art of the Mississippian World,* edited by George E. Lankford, F. Kent Reilly III, and James F. Garber, pp. xi–xviii. University of Texas Press, Austin.

Schaafsma, Polly
1989 Supper or Symbol: Roadrunner Tracks in Southwest Art and Ritual. In *Animals into Art*, edited by Howard Morphy, pp. 253–269. Unwin Hyman, London.

Shepherd, Deborah J.
1995 Bear, Elk, and Fish Symbolism in Finnish Contexts. In *The Symbolic Role of Animals in Archaeology*, edited by Kathleen Ryan and Pam J. Crabtree, pp. 27–37. MASCA Research Papers in Science and Archaeology Vol. 12. MASCA, University of Pennsylvania Museum of Archaeology and Anthropology, Philadelphia.

Smith, Bruce D.
1995 *The Emergence of Agriculture*. Scientific American Library, New York.

Sparks, John, and Tony Soper
1989 *Owls: Their Natural and Unnatural History*. Facts on File, New York.

Speck, Frank G.
2004 *Ethnology of the Yuchi Indians*. Reprinted. University of Nebraska Press, Lincoln. Originally published 1909, Anthropological Publications Vol. 1, No. 1. University Museum, Philadelphia.

Taube, Karl A.
1989 The Maize Tamale in Classic Maya Diet, Epigraphy, and Art. *American Antiquity* 54(1):31–51.
2000 Lightning Celts and Corn Fetishes: The Formative Olmec and the Development of Maize Symbolism in Mesoamerica and the American Southwest. In *Olmec Art and Archaeology in Mesoamerica*, edited by John E. Clark and Mary E. Pye, pp. 296–337. Studies in the History of Art 58. National Gallery of Art, Washington, D.C.

Townsend, Richard F. (editor)
2004 *Hero, Hawk, and Open Hand: American Indian Art of the Ancient Midwest and South*. Art Institute of Chicago and Yale University Press, Chicago.

Trevelyan, Amelia Margaret
1987 Prehistoric Native American Copperwork from the Eastern United States. Unpublished Ph.D. dissertation, Department of Art History, University of California, Los Angeles.

Turner, Victor
1967 *The Forest of Symbols: Aspects of Ndembu Ritual*. Cornell University Press, Ithaca, New York.

Unrau, William E.
1971 *The Kansa Indians: A History of the Wind People, 1673–1873*. University of Oklahoma Press, Norman.

Van Dyke, Ruth M.
2003 Memory and the Construction of Chacoan Society. In *Archaeologies of Memory*, edited by Ruth M. Van Dyke and Susan E. Alcock, pp. 180–200. Blackwell, Malden, Massachusetts.

Van Nest, Julieann, Douglas K. Charles, Jane E. Buikstra, and David L. Asch
2001 Sod Blocks in Illinois Hopewell Mounds. *American Antiquity* 66(4):633–650.

Waring, Antonio J., Jr.
1968 The Southern Cult and Muskhogean Ceremonial. In *The Waring Papers: The Collected Works of Antonio J. Waring, Jr.*, edited by Stephen Williams, pp. 30–69. Peabody Museum and University of Georgia Press, Cambridge.

Weltfish, Gene
1977 *The Lost Universe: Pawnee Life and Culture*. University of Nebraska Press, Lincoln.

Willey, Gordon R.
1990 Mesoamerican Art and Iconography and the Integrity of the Mesoamerican Ideological System. In *New World Archaeology and Culture History: Collected Essays and Articles*, by Gordon Randolph Willey, pp. 297–303. University of New Mexico Press, Albuquerque.

Willey, Gordon R., and Jeremy A. Sabloff
1980 *A History of American Archaeology*. 2nd ed. W. H. Freeman, New York.

Willoughby, Charles C.
2000 Notes on the History and Symbolism of the Muskhogeans and the People of Etowah. In *Explorations of the Etowah Site in Georgia: The Etowah Papers*, edited by Warren King Moorehead, pp. 7–66. Reprinted. University Press of Florida, Gainesville. Originally published 1932, Yale University Press, New Haven.

Wonderley, Anthony
2005 Effigy Pipes, Diplomacy, and Myth: Exploring Interaction Between St. Lawrence Iroquoians and Eastern Iroquois in New York State. *American Antiquity* 70(2):211–240.

Wylie, Alison
1985 The Reaction Against Analogy. In *Advances in Archaeological Method and Theory*, vol. 8, edited by Michael B. Schiffer, pp. 63–111. Academic Press, New York.

Young, M. Jane
1994 The Interconnection Between Western Puebloan and Mesoamerican Ideology/Cosmology. In *Kachinas in the Pueblo World*, edited by Polly Schaafsma, pp. 107–120. University of New Mexico Press, Albuquerque.

9

Ethnogenetic Theory and New Directions in Biodistance Research

Christopher M. Stojanowski
Arizona State University

Biodistance analysis uses phenotypic skeletal and dental variation to infer evolutionary processes in past populations. The approach is heavily quantitative and based on the assumption that cranial, dental, and (less commonly) postcranial size, shape, and morphology are genetically conditioned (not narrow-sense heritable per se; Vitzthum 2003). Thus the mathematical properties of these traits measured in populations (central tendency and variance) are subject to rules of intergenerational inheritance, quantitative genetics, and evolutionary mechanisms such as gene flow, genetic drift, and natural selection. Focus on "distance" a priori emphasizes relationships between objects (either individuals or samples) in multidimensional space. However, increasingly biodistance analysis refers to any investigation of evolutionary process or genetic inheritance in past populations, whether based on means and frequencies, explicit inferences of patterns of variances, or more cladistic approaches utilizing rare anomalies and their expression within biological lineages.

Defined so broadly, biodistance research can be dated to the nineteenth century, when issues of racial taxonomy considered populational differences in cranial and brain size volume (see a readable account in Marks 1995). *Distance* referred to "degeneration" along the *scala naturae*. During the early half of the twentieth century, taxonomic issues continued to dominate biodistance research through the work of noted scholars such as W. W. Howells (Howells 1989). Global surveys of craniometric variation sought answers to questions of modern human emergence and subsequent expansion throughout the Old and New Worlds. Turner's groundbreaking work with dental morphology was within the same vein, with an emphasis on Pacific Rim and New World population relationships and migrations (see Scott and Turner 1997). As recent scholarship indicates (e.g., Manica et al. 2007), interest in broad-scale questions of migration and virgin soil population expansion has not abated, a fact that has not escaped some critics (Armelagos and Van Gerven 2003).

Nonetheless, the advent of the New Archaeology, with its emphasis on social systems, initiated a regional focus in biodistance research, as exemplified by the work of Buikstra and colleagues on Middle and Late Woodland–period populations from the Illinois Valley (Buikstra 1976, 1977, 1980). Buikstra's research established the groundwork for most subsequent regional biodistance analyses, mine included (Stojanowski 2005a). Contributions were both methodological and theoretical. For example, Buikstra (1976, 1980) presented an explicit analytical framework for minimizing the effects of nongenetic variation on resulting biodistances, now familiarly known as preanalysis data treatments (sex effects, age-related variation, intertrait correlation). These tests are performed *de rigueur*. In addition, Buikstra highlighted the importance of a sample's archaeological context for interpreting the meaning of the resulting microevolutionary analyses. This approach was in direct contrast to global biodistance surveys, which often reified archaeological assemblages as biological populations and used phenetic similarity as the global proxy of population relatedness. Thus a more nuanced view of prehistory emerged from Buikstra's research program through goals that were multiscalar and multifaceted—understanding site formation processes, reconstructing community interrelationships, documenting interaction scales and boundaries, and providing a demographic basis for health inferences. However, the most important development to come out of the Illinois Valley research program was the emphasis on contextualization. Microevolutionary research was linked to the social world of past peoples, allowing modern scholars to "'flesh out' the image of our mound builder as a cultural individual: one who inherited or acquired wealth and status, who perhaps buried his dead with his mother's people, and whose family may have lived in one village long enough to become biologically distinct from contemporaries up the river" (Buikstra 1980:271). The present chapter proceeds within this realm of scholarship.

The multiscalar, context-specific inferences of biodistance analysis (Stojanowski and Schillaci 2006), combined with increasing concern for population genetic variance parameters (Relethford 2003; Relethford and Lees 1982), counter claims that biodistance analysis remains grounded in nineteenth-century typology as proposed by Armelagos and Van Gerven (2003). However, biodistance analysis does generally focus on inferring basic historical facts: Who is related to whom? From where did population x migrate? While I disagree with various elements of their critique (Stojanowski and Buikstra 2005), on this point Armelagos and Van Gerven are largely correct. The point is *not* that historical issues are unimportant but rather that other things can be learned through anthropological analysis of past populations—insights that inform the modern world directly and have contemporary relevance within a broader social sciences perspective. Nonetheless, criticism (pedantic or iconoclastic) for its own sake is not productive unless alternatives are presented. Therefore, rather than further critique historical evolutionary anthropology, in this chapter I discuss a new research domain in biodistance analysis—the study of ethnogenesis.

An Ethnogenetic Research Focus in Anthropology

In the simplest terms, ethnogenesis is "the establishment of group distinctiveness" (Sturtevant 1971:92). The group, in this case, is a social collective, one of many forms of human identities based on class, ethnicity, tribe, community, nationality, religion, or political affiliation. In this sense, ethnogenesis is clearly a diachronic (not evolutionary) process of group emergence or redefinition. However, ethnogenetic processes also manifest synchronically through intertribal or intercommunity exchange, whether that entails the movement of people, genes, or material objects. Ethnogenesis, then, is a diffusionary process in which people violate "normative rules" of an endogamous tribal society. People can and often do move across social boundaries, assume new social identities, or manipulate social interactions with a multitude of identities that are called upon situationally (Moore 1994a, 1994b, 2001; Quinn 1993; Terrell 2001a, b, c). These processes effectively decouple biological and social identities in evolutionary time and defy simple reification. Such a dynamic view of human societies has long-term and broad implications for how we view human prehistory. Proponents of an ethnogenetic view posit periodic, wholesale reshuffling of peoples among social units such that "resulting new social formations are likely to have their 'roots' or 'origins' in several antecedent societies" (Terrell 2001a:31). Thus the cladistic, branching models implicit within taxonomic anthropological genetics are inappropriate given the recurrent (repeatedly separating and recombining) realities of how human societies *actually* work and persist in a historical sense. It is important to note that synchronic (diffusionary) and diachronic (formative) aspects of ethnogenetic theory are part of the same sociohistorical process. Bioarchaeology, by virtue of the temporal resolution afforded archaeological assemblages, has the ability to elucidate both synchronic and diachronic elements of ethnogenesis in past populations—the former by considering patterns of genetic/phenetic variation against socially defined criteria of group distinction; the latter by reconstructing patterns of gene flow among populations through time.

The appeal of ethnogenetic theory as an emerging research focus is its ubiquity and simultaneous invisibility. We apply it all the time in bioarchaeology and bioanthropology but without specific recognition of this fact. Its significance is far-reaching; thus it unifies anthropology and the broader social sciences within a common research theme. Transnational migrations of ethnic minorities, ethnic-based modern political movements, ethnic cleansing and genocide, genetic models of population history, race, ethnic nepotism, and the multiregional model of modern human emergence all share in this ethnogenetic focus. This emphasis encapsulates complexities of "self" (emic) and "other" (etic) group identification, historical development of social forms, transcendence of identity categories (the "idea" of what a people are), and processes of biological and social integration across population boundaries. To study ethnogenetic theory in its many faces is to study the basis of the human condition, from Pleistocene hunter-gatherer band exogamy to ethnic enclaves and disenfranchisement within multiethnic modern cities.

In this chapter, I outline the range of research orientations that fall within the purview of ethnogenetic theory and propose a specific bridging model linking human biology to the social and cultural realms of the human experience. I specifically propose that biodistance analysis can contribute to our understanding of the development of social identities (ethnogenesis in a temporal sense) and can do so in a unique manner because of our ability to study temporal changes related to transformations in social identities through time. I make no appeal to sociobiological motives, isometry between ethnic groups and breeding populations, or the conflation of race and ethnic identity. Rather I propose that human biological variation can be interpreted within the social context that created the pattern of variation as signaling changes in social group composition. Phenotypic variation, as affected by patterns of mate exchange, is an indelible imprint of human agency and action; it is an invisible (and hence passive) marker of identity symbolism manifest within the sphere of reproduction. However, I eschew Darwinian sociobiological linkages between biology and culture, which are deterministic and based on notions of fitness driving biocultural evolution in a hyper-rational model of human behavior. Instead, I draw an operational analogy from practice scholarship (Bentley 1987; Lightfoot et al. 1998; Orser 2004; Pauketat 2001) and the archaeological analysis of material culture variation and "style" (particularly Bell 2005; Voss 2005; see also Sofaer 2006).

Ethnogenesis: Forms and Definitions

Ethnogenesis is ultimately about social group composition and construction—that is, how human social groups are organized, interrelated, and defined in a historical sense (Arutiunov 1994). Ethnogenesis can result from differentiation or fissioning of social groups, thus increasing diversity (Horowitz 1975). This cladistic, bifurcating process anchors nearly all anthropological genetic research that is historical in focus (Moore 2001), as well as evolutionary archaeological approaches that consider the relative importance of phylogenetic (differentiating through descent) versus ethnogenetic (diffusion, sharing, borrowing) mechanisms of cultural evolution (Collard et al. 2006; Guglielmino et al. 1995; Mace and Holden 2006; Mace et al. 2005; O'Brien et al. 2001). Ethnogenesis can also result from assimilation or fusion (Horowitz 1975), a process that describes many examples from indigenous colonial North and South American contexts (e.g., Albers and James 1986; Davis 2001; Galloway 1995; Haley and Wilcoxon 2005; Hickerson 1996; Hill 1996; Moore 1994a, 1994b, 2001; Sharrock 1974) and perhaps most dramatically from African maroon settlements in the New World (Bilby 1996; Kopytoff 1976). In these cases, multiple historically distinct groups coalesce to form a new social identity, often within a drastically different political-economic context.

Researchers of ethnogenesis differ significantly in their orientation, depending in large part on their commitment to the uniformitarian application of ethnogenetic theory into the remote (prehistoric, not colonial) past. The differences between perspectives result in a degree of inferential coarseness, reflective of a micro versus macro scale of analysis. Historical ethnographic approaches provide a social platform for expressing the rights of modern indigenous populations and decrying the repercussions of colonialist hegemonic policies (Ferguson and Whitehead 1992; Hill 1996). For these scholars, ethnogenesis as a process of ethnic emergence and reformulation is a *known* fact. It is not to be debated. The primary focus is describing historical cases and promoting the social significance of the inferences. As a matter of law, understanding the complexities of recent colonial histories of indigenous peoples is extremely important (Davis 2001; Haley and Wilcoxon 2005; Quinn 1993; Sider 1976) because economic and political positioning is intimately linked with membership in emerging pan-ethnic identities (Espiritu 1992; Tefft 1999). In a similar vein, ethnogenesis figures prominently in the modern migration and transnationalism literatures (e.g., Roosens 1989) and also explains many of the woes in developing nations with recent colonial histories (e.g., MacEachern 2000; Vail 1989). This is an entirely postcolonial discussion engaged in by ethnographers, historians, and the traditional peoples subjected to colonial rule.

The extrapolation of ethnogenetic processes to prehistoric contexts changes the research orientations significantly. Case studies cannot be developed within a specific historical context and therefore lack some of the nuanced details of historic research. Furthermore, there is no element of activism in prehistoric ethnogenetic research. Rather, researchers are more interested in theoretical issues about the nature of human societies in the past and present: Are human societies monolithic well-bounded aggregates (Wolf's billiard ball model), or are social boundaries ephemeral and permeable (Moore's braided stream model)? How well do patterns of social interaction coincide with biological integration? How do biosocial coevolutionary processes contribute to understanding patterns of biological and social diversity in the past? These perspectives are represented by the research of John Moore, an ethnographer (1994a, 1994b, 2001); a well-defined group of archaeologists, most visibly John Terrell (e.g., Bellwood 1996; MacEachern 2000; Terrell 1988, 2001a, 2001b, 2001c; Terrell and Stewart 1996; Terrell et al. 1997); and an inordinate number of anthropological geneticists. These scholars are more concerned with the long-term importance of ethnogenetic processes in human history—how often massive reorganizations occurred in the past, the rate at which reorganizations occur, and in what contexts they occur. A key component of these discussions is the relative importance of societal collapses and reconstructions compared to group fissioning events based on demographic expansion. That ethnogenesis occurred in contexts of colonial rule is uncontested. The causes were increased mortality (often epidemic), capitalist economic systems, and the power imbalances that resulted. Uniformitarian extrapolation of these same processes into the deep past is contentious but of ultimate importance for understanding the history of the human species. Did early modern humans devolve into primitive, isolated, and xenophobic "human hordes" (Terrell 2001a:21), or were we always "involved with other aggregates . . . in weblike, netlike connections" (Lesser 1961:42) such that "[h]ardly any people can speak of their 'purity of blood' and of their 'immemorial occupation' of their present territory" (Arutiunov 1994:91). This is the essence of the race debate in anthropology; it is inherently an ethnogenetic one.

ETHNOGENESIS AND HUMAN BIOLOGY

One primary difference between human and nonhuman evolutionary biology is the impact of cultural factors on patterns of human mate exchange (gene flow) and population size limits (genetic drift). Human biologists have long recognized this and adopted research strategies accordingly. Biological anthropologists consider ethnogenetic theory (rarely in name) by addressing the age-old question about the relationship between biological, cultural, and linguistic patterns of variation. Strategies include examining within- versus between-cultural-group genetic variability, comparing the distributional limits of cultural and biological populations across space, or comparing the degree of cultural and genetic diversity within a region under the assumption that signals should be proportional. The use of the general term *cultural* reflects the myriad ways in which social data are constructed in comparative analyses: intertribal, interethnic, interpolity (nation, state, province), and interreligion. However, by far, genetic comparison with language group affiliation has been most common, beginning with classic studies in the 1970s and 1980s (Rhoads and Friedlaender 1975; Serjeantson et al. 1983) and continuing today on issues such as agricultural demic diffusion in Europe (Barbujani and Sokal 1990; Sokal 1988) and global patterns of genetic-linguistic covariation (Cavalli-Sforza 1997; Cavalli-Sforza et al. 1988, 1992; McMahon 2004).

These synchronic approaches study the effects of ethnogenesis (its residual) but not the process itself, which requires temporal resolution. However, here again bioathropologists have considered ethnogenesis directly for some time now. I would argue, however, that this literature is ethnogenetic in name only. It rarely considers or incorporates social processes into the inferential framework. This work, produced both by bioarchaeologists and molecular anthropologists, often reconstructs population origins not in geographical terms (such as peopling of the New World or peopling of Polynesia) but in terms of the biological composition of an often nebulously defined contemporary social aggregate. In fact, the prose indicates that *ethnogenesis* is used as a synonym for *formation*, and any study that considers the origin of a modern population in terms of the mixing of distinct antecedent populations fits this definition of ethnogenesis equally as well (e.g., Ioviţă and Schurr 2004; North et al. 2000). Similar anthropological investigations focusing on population composition and the contributing origin of represented types have been published for decades. Most visible within the bioarchaeological literature is the dual-origin hypothesis of Japanese ethnogenesis (Hudson 1999; Ossenberg et al. 2006).

An Ethnogenetic Research Agenda in Bioarchaeology

It should be clear from the preceding discussion that bioarchaeological data sets have the potential to contribute to both synchronic and diachronic ethnogenetic perspectives. Most accessible, but I would argue the least interesting, is providing a basis for understanding the patterning of synchronic biosocial variation in the past, contexts often beyond the reach of molecular anthropologists using modern DNA. Such work compares patterns of phenotypic data against a cultural analog, such as material culture design variation, to reconstruct the extent to which they are coterminous and presumably coevolved. On the other hand, temporal approaches investigate how identities formed and changed through time and identify those conditions that affect the historical trajectory of specific social identities within specific historical and cultural contexts. This focus has a direct link to modern political discourse in which issues of identity form the core of major world conflicts, ethnocides, and genocides. It is within this realm of inquiry that socially relevant knowledge that bridges the evolutionary and social sciences can be produced.

I have previously indicated that the intersection of human biology and social identity has traditionally fallen within the purview of sociobiological explanations, an approach I reject as too deterministic. Rather, I propose that the intensity of social interaction in the past can be inferred from the degree of biological integration among communities within a regional interaction sphere. That is, migration and gene flow reflect human behavior and action at the community level and therefore serve as proxies for communal recognition of "us" and "other." In other words, gene flow, intermarriage, or mate exchange between populations reflects changing emic (subjective) definitions of the people themselves. Genetic and phenotypic signatures *passively* signal ethnic emergence. Homogenization of genetic exchange networks may reflect a broadening basis of identity that may ultimately lead to ethnogenesis in a reticulate manner. It is important to stress that this association between social and biological variation is temporal in structure and focuses on *changes* in the intensity of biological integration, not the static level of integration at any particular point in time. Interpreting patterns of phenotypic variation in a temporally static framework tells us very little about ethnogenesis or ethnic group composition. Only by seeing how *patterns* of mate exchange changed through time can we infer similar changes in community sentiments, and this is the true benefit of bioarchaeological approaches to ethnogenesis.

This theoretical model departs from past biological or evolutionary consideration of ethnic identity often based in ethnic nepotism theory and a strict interpretation of evolution as Darwinian in nature (James and Goetze 2001). Instead, this work draws its operational framework from historical archaeology and the analysis of material culture variation. The work of Barbara Voss (2005) is exemplary of this approach. Voss documented the emergence of a unified "Californio" identity at El Presidio de San Francisco through an analysis of material culture, architectural structures, and dietary practices by documenting the increasing homogenization of the material world despite the biologically diverse population in residence there. In particular, the residents made an increasingly similar material culture repertoire, including plain ware ceramics, similarity in cooking implements and techniques, and similar architectural styles, and also focused on gruels that were not ethnically coded. From this, Voss (2005) inferred that ethnogenesis was occurring as the community self-referent *gente de razón* replaced the divisive "mixed-race" structure of the *sistema de castas*. Over several decades, the residents of El Presidio de San Francisco eschewed the *castas* categorizations, which objectified them and also minimized the use of material symbols of local indigenous populations, thus signaling their burgeoning sense of community solidarity. Ethnogenesis in this case constructed a community identity not an ethnic group, tribe, or nation—distinctions of scale far beyond the scope of this chapter.

This example also highlights the importance of practice in building community identities, linking quotidian actions to macro-scale patterns and processes (see also Lightfoot et al. 1998; Pauketat 2001; Shennan 1989). In addition, it is clear that elements of the debate about the interpretation of style are being applied here (Conkey 1990; Hegmon 1992; Sackett 1982; Wiessner 1990. See also Jones 2002; Shennan 1989). The major difference is the diachronic focus adopted by Voss (2005) and others interested in ethnogenesis (e.g., Bell 2005; McGuire 1982, 1983). These studies do not equate a material culture pattern with an ethnic group; they equate homogenization of material culture and life experiences with ethnogenesis. Similarly, I am not interested in identifying ethnic groups through the application of genetic/phenotypic analyses, but in documenting the process of ethnogenesis by normalizing the study of human skeletal remains within the broader realm of research on residues of the past. However, phenotypic variation is completely passive, unlike most material symbols of group identity. It is not symbolic in any active sense of the word because individuals have no knowledge of the material expression of these underlying social actions (reflected in your cranium and dentition). Rather, phenotypic variation is merely reflective of the choices one makes within the social constraints established by your community with respect to reproduction (or marriage). And, stated this way, it is evident that phenotypic variation is the product of a specific "production sequence" as well, laden with inherent meaning to the participants in the social processes. Thus it is easy to envision the complexity of social meaning imbued within something so simple as changing patterns of genetic variation within an extended breeding network.

It is important to stress that this approach to microevolutionary data is not based on racial or typological models, patterns of genetic ancestry and descent (who is related to whom), population origins (from where did Native Americans migrate), or sociobiology and ethnic nepotism theory (interest groups arise due to shared alleles). The focus is on gene flow, not natural selection. The underlying basis of patterns of biological variation is social process not subconscious psychological motivation. However, this shift to a biosocial approach (contrasted with a sociobiological one) remains uncommitted as to the actual causal linkage between behaviors and their material manifestations. In the sociobiological model it is selection for behavioral phenotypes (nepotism, altruism) that explains patterns of behavior and the formation of distinct social groups. The biosocial approach adopted here remains nonspecific as to middle-range linkages, however. Gene flow can assume a more active form and be seen as actually contributing to the ethnogenetic process, and many colonial ethnographers would seemingly agree (Albers 1996; Hickerson 1996; Sharrock 1974). However, a completely passive bridging argument could also be used. Increasing biological integration could be reflective of changing attitudes among interacting communities but contribute no causality to the process itself. Thus gene flow is not a *cause* of ethnogenesis but a *result* of it. It is the behavior itself, the process of mate choice, that signals a change in emic sentiment that may signal a redefinition of "us" but not necessarily "them." This approach rejects any a priori notion that biological homogenization necessarily *causes* feelings of shared ethnic solidarity among previously distinct ethnic groups and also eschews notions that ethnic groups are genetically cohesive biological populations. Both could be true, but neither is requisite for ethnogenesis to occur.

ETHNOGENESIS IN SPANISH COLONIAL FLORIDA

I have previously published biodistance analyses for seventeenth-century mission communities in Spanish colonial La Florida (Figure 9.1) (Stojanowski 2004, 2005a, 2005b). These peoples were subject to intense sixteenth-century Spanish and French intervention, followed by a protracted period of missionary activity during the seventeenth century, which ultimately led to ethnocide for most precontact populations. Declining health combined with an increasingly maize-centric diet exacerbated mortality rates elevated by epidemics, frontier slave raiding, and the abuses of the Spanish labor draft system (see Larsen 2001 for a bioarchaeological summary). Model-bound population genetic analyses (R-matrix analysis) were used to describe the evolutionary signatures of the missionization process in La Florida, initially focusing on the expected effects of demographic collapse and genetic drift within increasingly smaller native populations. The results, as it turned out, were not so straightforward.

Biodistance analyses of odontometric (tooth size and shape) variation indicated that the transition from the precontact (circa 1400–1550) to the immediate postcontact period (circa 1600–1650) witnessed an increase in diversity among different ethnolinguistic communities subject to Spanish missionization. (Apalachee, Guale, and numerous Timucua-speaking tribes resided in northern Florida and southern Georgia during the pre- and postcontact periods; Figure 9.1.) This result is contrary to the expectations of a strict, stochastic drift model in which genetic diversity decreases within a mating network due to allele fixation and loss. Clearly, then, the populations of Florida and Georgia were not biologically integrated during the precontact period and would become less so after missionization. The transition from the early mission period (circa 1600–1650) to the late mission period (circa 1650–1700) witnessed a

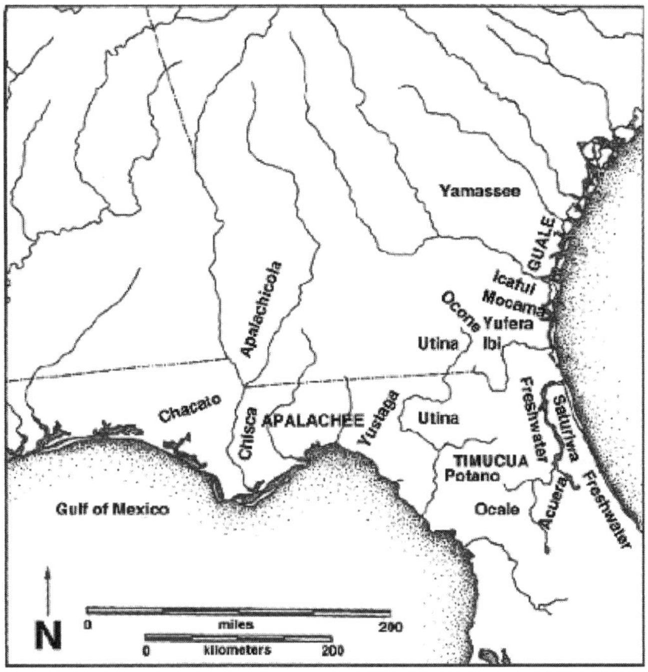

Figure 9.1. Map of Florida and Georgia showing the approximate locations of the primary ethnic groups or tribes discussed in the text. Names in bold represent the primary tribal distinctions recognized by the Spanish.

stark reversal in this pattern, however. Between-sample phenotypic variability decreased significantly, to the point that a single biological population was resident throughout the Spanish sphere of influence during the second half of the seventeenth century. From an evolutionary perspective, then, the pre- to postcontact transition is consistent with genetic drift operating within local populations not united into a single mate exchange network. In addition, migration decreased during the early mission period despite the widespread assumption of a Catholic quotidian existence. To the contrary, during the late mission period, the dramatic decline in among-population genetic variability concurrent with absolute demographic collapse can be explained only by the development of an extended pattern of migration and gene flow among formerly distinct ethnolinguistic communities.

These results are easy enough to interpret within an evolutionary theoretical context, but this is not what a "contextual analysis" of human remains prescribes (Buikstra and Beck 2006). Characterizations of migration patterns, gene flow, and genetic drift are not the most interesting things to say about these peoples, and I argue that the pattern is also reflective of changing social relations among these communities. Indeed, the diachronic changes are consistent with Nancy Hickerson's (1996) life cycle model of ethnogenetic transformation: an initial severing of ethnic ties (phase 1) precedes an exploratory phase in which new social connections are established among participating communities (phase 2), which ultimately results in nominal and mythological reification of a newly emerging social identity (phase 3).

In this chapter I proposed that ethnic realignments manifest in patterns of gene flow through either an active or passive bridging model linking the realm of social experience to the realm of human reproductive behavior (mate choice). However, to fully interpret these biodistance results, they must be further incorporated into their appropriate historical, archaeological, and social contexts. Otherwise, documentation of decreasing biological distances between distinct social communities becomes synonymous with fusion-based ethnogenesis. Such a 1:1 mapping is far too simplistic. Indeed, documenting that ethnogenesis was occurring in the past, in the absence of direct paleographic evidence for this, requires a careful reconstruction detailing historical actors, their motives, economic and political disparities, and changes in the social and material lives of the affected communities. I now turn to these data in an attempt to corroborate the biodistance analyses summarized above. I incorporate social theoretical perspectives on colonialism and ethnic identity, archaeological information on material culture patterns, and historical data on the economic and political contexts in which ethnogenetic changes are expected to occur.

Contextualization of Biodistance Analyses

I first consider why the early mission period was a time of decreasing biological integration among Christian communities. I propose that the first half of the seventeenth century was a time of "integrative devolution" as communities slowly were welcomed into the fold of the Catholic Church. Peace among soon-to-be Christian villages always immediately preceded their receiving friars (Geiger 1937:67; Oré 1936:114–117). One would think that gene flow would be more widespread once communities were united in religion and joined by amicable relationships. In fact, the opposite was documented in these analyses. This only makes sense when the role of warfare in integrating populations and chiefdoms is considered. Southeastern indigenous warfare prior to contact was characterized by two biologically meaningful practices: (1) the capture of prisoners, especially women and children, who were initially kept as slaves but eventually married into their adoptive societies; and (2) strategic alliances secured by the bestowal of brides and the establishment of fictive kinship relationships among chiefs. This was a ubiquitous feature of precontact southeastern chiefdoms. When intercommunity conflict subsided, so did the residual reshuffling of populations across social boundaries, as documented in the protohistoric chronicles (DePratter 1991. See also Bennett 1975:11, 85, 91, 105–106; Varner and Varner 1951:439, 487–489).

At the same time, Hickerson's model suggests that ethnic sentiments lose saliency during the initial phase of ethnogenesis. This second point is more theoretical and relates to the perception by scholars of ethnic units as tribes—monolithic, bounded entities. Since Barth (1969), social anthropology has embraced the notion that ethnic groups exist due to the very interactions that define their boundaries. There is no ethnicity without some degree of antagonism because "ethnic identities do not 'naturally' persist, but need to be maintained" (Banks 1996:32). Such views of ethnic groups as components within an interaction sphere rather than as isolated culture-bearing units have not permeated into biological anthropology or anthropological genetics. Nonetheless, this view does explain the decline in biological integration documented here. With the drastic changes in the sociopolitical world effected by the Spanish, old antagonisms may have lost meaning. Certainly, warfare and conflict were redefined in ways that precluded the movement of peoples among Catholic communities—indigenous-on-indigenous warfare was redefined into social revolts of the disenfranchised against the Spanish. In addition, while population sizes declined during the early seventeenth century, there is no reason to believe that widespread, massive epidemics created truly dysfunctional communities (see Kelton 2007 for one take on this). In other words, mate exchange was not expanding because the local population base, while surely smaller, was still large enough to maintain existing practices of marriage. The initial phase of ethnogenesis, therefore, was a matter of scale of political interaction. A more myopic modus may have prevailed.

The initiation of an exploratory, liminal phase of ethnogenesis is here marked by a dramatic increase in biological integration among Spanish, Christian communities. The reversal in the trajectory is stark and indicates that extensive migration and gene flow had become the norm. But what changed circa 1650 to dramatically alter the course of community engagement? The answer, as expected, is complex and multifaceted. First, the most obvious reason is that all mission communities had now experienced the effects of epidemics and were living in a postdemographic collapse environment characterized by smaller communities, rampant fugitivism, and in-migrations of peoples from the interior of Georgia and parts beyond. Small local population size generated a motive of necessity—gene flow *had* to become more expansive due to the effects of demographic collapse, regardless of any smoldering ethnic resentment among antecedent communities. However, this view by itself is mechanistic and does not afford any agency to the ethnogenetic process. That is, focus on gene flow alone assumes that people embrace a homogenous social identity because of demographic group dynamics (marriage and migration), and this is clearly an insufficient explanation. Rather, to fully appreciate the complexity of the ethnogenetic process, we must also consider the political context and scale from the top down, as well as the social environment from the bottom up. Social identities are both created by objectifying political forces and embraced and redefined by those subjected to the power imbalance.

I note first that the Spanish, through a number of actions and practices, reified a racial distinction between themselves and "Indians," who were expected to be good Christians and Catholics but always within their own *republica*—the *republica de indios* (Bushnell 2006). However, Spanish objectification of their indigenous allies does not explain the timing of the transition to the liminal phase of ethnogenesis (phase 2), in which new social connections are established among formerly distinct communities. For the Florida natives, the objectification suffered at the hands of the Spanish intensified as hemispheric geopolitics reignited the intense competition between Britain and Spain for control of eastern North America. After a protracted war with the Powhatans, the English at Jamestown began a process of frontier trade expansion. This occurred around 1644, concurrent with the initiation of the liminal phase of ethnogenesis. The Virginians were soon joined by Carolinians with mercantile roots in the Caribbean. The resources of the East Coast were aggressively pursued by the English without the encumbrances of an ecumenical charter. A plantation economy expanded, as did the trade in deerskins and Indian slaves to be sold to plantations in the Caribbean (where early-sixteenth-century epidemics had already devastated the local island populations). English traders plied their allies with superior firearms, improving hunting efficiency and establishing a debt economy that expanded in balloon-like fashion. Why is all this relevant? Because the Spanish missions were intensively targeted by slave raiders, some from as far away as the Great Lakes (the Westo; Bowne 2005). The debts encumbered in pursuit of European goods in many ways enslaved the enslavers, creating a basic distinction between well-armed, English-allied slave raiders (Westo, Yamassee, Cherokee, Creek/Uchise) and poorly armed, Spanish-allied Catholics. This dynamic situation most visibly unfolded in the expanding tribal zone of the Georgia interior and would give rise to the Creek "nation." During the latter half of the seventeenth century, indigenous populations in Florida experienced intense objectification in which ethnic nuance mattered little and a culture of fear pervaded the missions, as threats of mass suicide attest (Worth 1995:33).

At the same time, intense objectification from above does not guarantee that ethnogenesis will commence. Those participating in the dynamic must submit to the process itself and actively forge the components of a new burgeoning identity. It is here that practice scholarship is most informative (Bentley 1987). In bridging the divide between the primordial and situational theories of ethnic identity, the practice theory of ethnicity focuses on how shared experiences foster feelings of affinity among individuals. (Bentley draws from Bourdieu's *habitus* concept, a source of some criticism; Yelvington 1991.) Late-seventeenth-century Floridians had grown up within the Catholic Church, embraced a modified landscape centered around the mission *doctrina*, assumed Spanish surnames and Spanish attire, shared in the psychological devastation caused by slave raiders, and lived as fugitives or had relatives who had done so. Archaeologically, pottery types homogenized throughout the provinces, bow and arrow was traded for Spanish musket, and funerary customs coalesced toward formal Christian interments (extended, supine, with hands folded) within the *campo santo* or, more often, under the floor of the church (see Deagan and Thomas 2009; McEwan 2001). Bioarchaeologically, we see evidence for widespread morbidity, increasingly similar lifestyles and occupational practices, and a homogenization of diets (highly charged with identity symbolism)—maize-centric with the occasional input of European-imported food items (Larsen 2001). Following Bentley's approach (1987) to ethnic identity, then, Catholic Indians living during the latter half of the seventeenth century would have experienced increasingly similar lives regardless of what language they spoke or the precontact tribal identities of their ancestors. Therefore, in a context of intense objectification (by non-Catholic, English-allied tribes), we also see evidence for a region-wide shared life experience among Catholic Indian communities living in the missions, which provides indirect evidence for the emic, subjective construction of a new, broader identity through the symbolism in their material world.

I propose that these processes of ethnic amalgamation were preempted during this liminal phase, however, never to reach full reintegration in which a new ethnonym and mythological charter is adopted (Hickerson 1996). Between 1704 and 1706, a series of English and Creeks raids destroyed the mission chain stretching from Saint Augustine west into the Florida panhandle. These raids culminated a half century of escalating violence between Britain and Spain, a regional dynamic that helped define the Catholic indigenous communities in Florida. Whether a new ethnonym was ever constructed may never be known. Nothing of the sort appears in the ethnohistoric annals, and this creates the historical invisibility that leads to ethnocide and the denial of aboriginal rights for those descendant communities that had a new name chosen for them. Indeed, Patricia Wickman, a historian of the modern Seminole, noted: "The act of naming is also the act of creation and the 'right' to create is inherently the assumption of a profound power" (Wickman 1999:183). Nonetheless, I have shown here that discovery of nascent ephemeral identities is possible through the kinds of nuanced interdisciplinary analyses that bioarchaeology affords. The results presented came in a surprising form: microevolutionary analysis. However, these inferences were bolstered by appropriate contextualization within social theoretical and historical literatures. The result is a much more interesting evolutionary narrative of Florida's native peoples, one of many unheralded diasporic communities whose detachment from traditional lands perpetuates the degree of historical invisibility that anthropologists attempt to correct.

CONCLUSIONS

Ethnogenetic theory is ubiquitous in anthropology, although it is rarely identified as such. Nonetheless, a concern with variation and group definition permeates anthropological discourse, both biological and social. In this chapter I have presented a bridging model that links evolutionary mechanisms to the social world of humans by drawing an operational analogy with archaeological analyses of material culture. In the past, biodistance analyses have been used to reconstruct patterns of mate exchange within a microevolutionary framework. I would argue that such patterns provide powerful inferences about specific reproductive choices people made in the past, and these choices are heavily laden with social significance. Biodistance analysis can contribute to the literature on ethnic identity by exploring contexts in which fission or fusion forms of ethnogenesis occur. Only by understanding how social phenomena develop can we truly understand their function, and bioarchaeology—specifically biodistance analysis—can provide unique perspectives on this topic with saliency in the modern world.

REFERENCES CITED

Albers, Patricia C.

1996 Changing Patterns of Ethnicity in the Northeastern Plains, 1780–1870. In *History, Power, and Identity: Ethnogenesis in the Americas, 1492–1992*, edited by Jonathan D. Hill, pp. 90–118. University of Iowa Press, Iowa City.

Albers, Patricia C., and William R. James

1986 On the Dialectics of Ethnicity: To Be or Not to Be Santee (Sioux). *Journal of Ethnic Studies* 14:1–27.

Armelagos, George V., and Dennis J. Van Gerven

2003 A Century of Skeletal Biology and Paleopathology: Contrasts, Contradictions, and Conflicts. *American Anthropologist* 105: 53–64.

Arutiunov, Sergei

1994 Ethnogenesis: Its Forms and Rules. *Anthropology and Archaeology of Eurasia* 33:79–93.

Banks, Marcus

1996 *Ethnicity: Anthropological Constructions*. Routledge, London

Barbujani, Guido, and Robert R. Sokal

1990 Zones of Sharp Genetic Change in Europe Are Also Linguistic Boundaries. *Proceedings of the National Academy of Sciences USA* 87:1816–1819.

Barth, Fredrik

1969 Introduction. In *Ethnic Groups and Boundaries. The Social Organization of Cultural Differences*, edited by Fredrik Barth, pp. 9–28. Universitetsforlaget, Oslo.

Bell, Alison

2005 White Ethnogenesis and Gradual Capitalism: Perspectives from Colonial Archaeological Sites in the Chesapeake. *American Anthropologist* 107:446–460.

Bellwood, Peter

1996 Phylogeny vs. Reticulation in Prehistory. *Antiquity* 70:881–890.

Bennett, Charles E.

1975 *Three Voyages: René Laudonnière*. University Press of Florida, Gainesville.

Bentley, G. Carter

1987 Ethnicity and Practice. *Comparative Studies in Society and History* 29:24–55.

Bilby, Kenneth

1996 Ethnogenesis in the Guianas and Jamaica: Two Maroon Cases. In *History, Power, and Identity: Ethnogenesis in the Americas, 1492–1992*, edited by Jonathan D. Hill, pp. 119–141. University of Iowa Press, Iowa City.

Bowne, Eric E.

2005 *The Westo Indians: Slave Traders of the Early Colonial South*. University of Alabama Press, Tuscaloosa.

Buikstra, Jane E.

1976 *Hopewell in the Lower Illinois Valley: A Regional Study of Human Biological Variability and Prehistoric Mortuary Behavior*. Scientific Papers No. 2. Northwestern Archeological Program, Evanston, Illinois.

1977 Biocultural Dimensions of Archeological Study: A Regional Perspective. In *Biocultural Adaptation in Prehistoric America*, edited by Robert L. Blakely, pp. 67–84. University of Georgia Press, Athens.

1980 Epigenetic Distance: A Study of Biological Variability in the Lower Illinois Valley. In *Early Native Americans*, edited by David L. Browman, pp. 271–300. Mouton, New York.

Buikstra, Jane E., and Lane A Beck.

2006 *Bioarchaeology: The Contextual Analysis of Human Remains*. Academic Press, Oxford.

Bushnell, Amy T.

2006 Ruling "the Republic of Indians" in Seventeenth-Century Florida. In *Powhatan's Mantle: Indians in the Colonial Southeast*, edited by Gregory A. Waselkov, Peter H. Wood, and Tom Hatley, pp.195–213. University of Nebraska Press, Lincoln.

Cavalli-Sforza, Luigi Luca

1997 Genes, Peoples, and Languages. *Proceedings of the National Academy of Sciences USA* 94:7719–7724.

Cavalli-Sforza, Luigi Luca, Eric Minch, and Joanna Mountain

1992 Coevolution of Genes and Languages Revisited. *Proceedings of the National Academy of Sciences USA* 89:5620–5624.

Cavalli-Sforza, Luigi Luca, Alberto Piazza, Paolo Menozzi, and Joanna Mountain

1988 Reconstruction of Human Evolution: Bringing Together Genetic, Archaeological, and Linguistic Data. *Proceedings of the National Academy of Sciences USA* 85:6002–6006.

Collard, Mark, Stephen J. Shennan, and Jamshid Tehrani

2006 Branching, Blending, and the Evolution of Cultural Similarities and Differences Among Human Populations. *Evolution and Human Behavior* 27:169–184.

Conkey, Margaret W.

1990 Experimenting with Style in Archaeology: Some Historical and Theoretical Issues. In *The Uses of Style in Archaeology*, edited by Margaret Conkey and Christine Hastorf, pp. 5–17. Cambridge University Press, Cambridge.

Davis, Dave D.

2001 A Case of Identity: Ethnogenesis of the New Houma Indians. *Ethnohistory* 48:473–494.

Deagan, Kathleen, and David H. Thomas

2009 From Santa Elena to St. Augustine: Indigenous Ceramic Variability (A.D. 1400–1700). Proceedings of the Second Caldwell Conference. Anthropological Papers No. 90. American Museum of Natural History, New York.

DePratter, Charles B.

1991 *Late Prehistoric and Early Historic Chiefdoms in the Southeastern United States*. Garland Publishing, New York.

Espiritu, Yen

1992 *Asian American Panethnicity: Bridging Institutions and Identities*. Temple University Press, Philadelphia.

Ferguson, R. Brian, and Neil L. Whitehead

1992 *War in the Tribal Zone: Expanding States and Indigenous Warfare*. School of American Research, Santa Fe.

Galloway, Patricia

1995 *Choctaw Ethnogenesis: 1500–1700*. University of Nebraska Press, Lincoln.

Geiger, Maynard

1937 The Franciscan Conquest of Florida (1573–1618). Unpublished Ph.D. dissertation, Catholic University of America, Washington, D.C.

Guglielmino, C. R., C. Viganotti, B. Hewlett, and L. L. Cavalli-Sforza
1995 Cultural Variation in Africa: Role of Mechanisms of Transmission and Adaptation. *Proceedings of the National Academy of Sciences USA* 92:7585–7589.

Haley, Brian D., and Larry R. Wilcoxon
2005 How Spaniards Became Chumash and Other Tales of Ethnogenesis. *American Anthropologist* 107:432–445.

Hegmon, Michelle
1992 Archaeological Research on Style. *Annual Review of Anthropology* 21:517–536.

Hickerson, Nancy P.
1996 Ethnogenesis in the South Plains: Jumano to Kiowa? In *History, Power, and Identity: Ethnogenesis in the Americas, 1492–1992*, edited by Jonathan D. Hill, pp. 70–89. University of Iowa Press, Iowa City.

Hill, Jonathan D.
1996 *History, Power, and Identity: Ethnogenesis in the Americas, 1492–1992*. University of Iowa Press, Iowa City.

Horowitz, Donald L.
1975 Ethnic Identity. In *Ethnicity: Theory and Experience*, edited by Nathan Glazer and Daniel P. Moynihan, pp. 111–140. Harvard University Press, Cambridge.

Howells, William W.
1989 *Skull Shapes and the Map: Craniometric Analyses in the Dispersion of Modern Homo*. Papers of the Peabody Museum of Archaeology and Ethnology Vol. 79. Harvard University Press, Cambridge.

Hudson, Mark J.
1999 *Ruins of Identity: Ethnogenesis in the Japanese Islands*. University of Hawaii Press, Honolulu.

Hunley, K., and J. C. Long
2005 Gene Flow Across Linguistic Boundaries in Native North American Populations. *Proceedings of the National Academy of Sciences USA* 102:1312–1317.

Hunley, Keith L., Graciela S. Cabana, D. Andrew Merriwether, and Jeffrey C. Long
2007 A Formal Test of Linguistic and Genetic Coevolution in Native Central and South America. *American Journal of Physical Anthropology* 132:622–631.

Ioviţă, Radu P., and Theodore G. Schurr
2004 Reconstructing the Origins and Migrations of Diasporic Populations: The Case of the European Gypsies. *American Anthropologist* 106:267–281.

James, Patrick, and David Goetze
2001 *Evolutionary Theory and Ethnic Conflict*. Praeger, Westport, Connecticut.

Jenkins, Richard
1997 *Rethinking Ethnicity: Arguments and Explorations*. Sage Publications, London.

Jones, Sîan
2002 *The Archaeology of Ethnicity*. Routledge, London.

Kelton, Paul
2007 *Epidemics and Enslavement: Biological Catastrophe in the Native Southeast 1492–1715*. University of Nebraska Press, Lincoln.

Kopytoff, Barbara
1976 The Development of Jamaican Maroon Ethnicity. *Caribbean Quarterly* 22:33–50.

Larsen, Clark S.
2001 *Bioarchaeology of Spanish Florida: The Impact of Colonialism*. University Press of Florida, Gainesville.

Lesser, Alexander
1961 Social Fields and the Evolution of Society. *Southwestern Journal of Anthropology* 17:40–48.

Lightfoot, Kent G., Antoinette Martinez, and Ann M. Schiff
1998 Daily Practice and Material Culture in Pluralistic Social Settings: An Archaeological Study of Culture Change and Persistence from Fort Ross, California. *American Antiquity* 63:199–222.

Mace, Ruth, and Clare J. Holden
2006 A Phylogenetic Approach to Cultural Evolution. *Trends in Ecology and Evolution* 20:116–121.

Mace, Ruth, Clare J. Holden, and Stephen Shennan
2005 *The Evolution of Cultural Diversity: A Phylogenetic Approach*. UCL Press, London.

MacEachern, Scott
2000 Genes, Tribes, and African History. *Current Anthropology* 41: 357–371.

Manica, Andrea, William Amos, François Balloux, and Tsunehiko Hanihara
2007 The Effect of Ancient Population Bottlenecks on Human Phenotypic Variation. *Nature* 448:346–349.

Marks, Jonathan
1995 *Human Biodiversity: Genes, Race, and History*. Aldine de Gruyter, New York.

McEwan, Bonnie G.
2001 The Spiritual Conquest of Florida. *American Anthropologist* 103:633–644.

McGuire, Randall
1982 The Study of Ethnicity in Historical Archaeology. *Journal of Anthropological Archaeology* 1:159–178.
1983 Ethnic Group, Status and Material Culture at the Rancho Punta de Agua. In *Forgotten Places and Things: Archaeological Perspectives on American History*, edited by Albert E. Ward, pp. 193–203. Center for Anthropological Studies, Albuquerque.

McMahon, Robert
2004 Genes and Languages. *Community Genetics* 7:2–13.

Moore, John H.
1994a Ethnogenetic Theory. *National Geographic Research and Exploration* 10:10–23.
1994b Putting Anthropology Back Together Again: The Ethnogenetic Critique of Cladistic Theory. *American Anthropologist* 96:925–948.
2001 Ethnogenetic Patterns in Native North America. In *Archaeology, Language, and History: Essays on Culture and Ethnicity*, edited by John E. Terrell, pp. 31–56. Bergin and Garvey, Westport, Connecticut.

North, Karie E., Lisa J. Martin, and Michael H. Crawford
2000 The Origins of the Irish Travellers and the Genetic Structure of Ireland. *Annals of Human Biology* 27:453–465.

O'Brien, Michael J., John Darwent, and R. Lee Lyman
2001 Cladistics Is Useful for Reconstructing Archaeological Phylogenies: Palaeoindian Points from the Southeastern United States. *Journal of Archaeological Science* 28:1115–1136.

Oré, Luis Geronimo
1936 *The Martyrs of Florida*. Joseph F. Wagner, New York.

Orser, Charles E.
2004 *Race and Practice in Archaeological Interpretation*. University of Pennsylvania Press, Philadelphia.

Ossenberg, Nancy S., Yukio Dodo, Tomoko Maeda, and Yoshinori Kawakubo
2006 Ethnogenesis and Craniofacial Change in Japan from the Perspective of Nonmetric Traits. *Anthropological Science* 114: 99–115.

Pauketat, Timothy R.
2001 Practice and History in Archaeology: An Emerging Paradigm. *Anthropological Theory* 1:73–98.

Quinn, William W.
1993 Intertribal Integration: The Ethnological Argument in *Duro v. Reina*. *Ethnohistory* 40:34–69.

Relethford, John H.
2003 Anthropometric Data and Population History. In *Human Biologists in the Archives: Demography, Health, Nutrition, and Genetics in Historical Populations*, edited by D. Anne Herring and Alan C. Swedlund, pp. 32–52. Cambridge University Press, Cambridge.

Relethford, John H., and Francis C. Lees
1982 The Use of Quantitative Traits in the Study of Human Population Structure. *Yearbook of Physical Anthropology* 25:113–132.

Rhoads, John G., and Jonathan S. Friedlaender
1975 Language Boundaries and Biological Differentiation on Bougainville: Multivariate Analysis of Variance. *Proceeding of the National Academy of Sciences USA* 72:2247–2250.

Roosens, Eugeen E.
1989 *Creating Ethnicity: The Process of Ethnogenesis*. Sage Publications, Newbury Park, California.

Sackett, James R.
1982 Approaches to Style in Lithic Archeology. *Journal of Anthropological Archaeology* 1:59–112.

Scott, G. Richard, and Christy G. Turner II.
1997 *The Anthropology of Modern Human Teeth: Dental Morphology and Its Variation in Recent Human Populations*. Cambridge University Press, Cambridge.

Serjeantson, S. W., R. L. Kirk, and P. B. Booth
1983 Linguistic and Genetic Differentiation in New-Guinea. *Journal of Human Evolution* 12:77–92.

Sharrock, Susan R.
1974 Crees, Cree-Assiniboines, and Assiniboines: Interethnic Social Organization on the Far Northern Plains. *Ethnohistory* 21:95–122.

Shennan, Stephen J.
1989 Introduction: Archaeological Approaches to Cultural Identity. In *Archaeological Approaches to Cultural Identity*, edited by Stephen J. Shennan, pp. 1–32. Unwin Hyman, London.

Sider, Gerald M.
1976 Lumbee Indian Cultural Nationalism and Ethnogenesis. *Dialectical Anthropology* 1:161–172.

Sofaer, Joanna R.
2006 *The Body as Material Culture: A Theoretical Osteoarchaeology*. Cambridge University Press, Cambridge.

Sokal, Robert. R.
1988 Genetic, Geographic, and Linguistic Distances in Europe. *Proceedings of the National Academy of Sciences USA* 85:1722–1726.

Stojanowski, Christopher M.
2004 Population History of Native Groups in Pre- and Postcontact Spanish Florida: Aggregation, Gene Flow, and Genetic Drift on the Southeastern U.S. Atlantic Coast. *American Journal of Physical Anthropology* 123:316–322.
2005a The Bioarchaeology of Identity in Spanish Colonial Florida: Social and Evolutionary Transformation before, during, and after Demographic Collapse. *American Anthropologist* 107:417–431.
2005b Spanish Colonial Effects on Native American Mating Structure and Genetic Variability in Northern and Central Florida: Evidence from Apalachee and Western Timucua. *American Journal of Physical Anthropology* 128:273–286.

Stojanowski, Christopher M., and Jane E. Buikstra
2005 Research Trends in Human Osteology: A Content Analysis of Papers Published in the *American Journal of Physical Anthropology*. *American Journal of Physical Anthropology* 128:98–109.

Stojanowski, Christopher M., and Michael A. Schillaci
2006 Phenotypic Approaches for Understanding Patterns of Intracemetery Biological Variation. *Yearbook of Physical Anthropology* 49:49–88.

Sturtevant, William C.
1971 Creek into Seminole. In *North American Indians in Historical Perspective*, edited by Eleanor B. Leacock and Nancy O. Lurie, pp. 92–108. Random House, New York.

Tefft, Susan K.
1999 Perspectives on Panethnogenesis: The Case of the Montagnards. *Sociological Spectrum* 19:387–400.

Terrell, John E.
1988 History as Family Tree, History as Entangled Bank. Constructing Images and Interpretations of Prehistory in the South Pacific. *Antiquity* 62:642–657.
2001a *Archaeology, Language and History: Essays on Culture and Ethnicity*. Bergin and Garvey, Westport, Connecticut.
2001b Introduction. In *Archaeology, Language and History: Essays on Culture and Ethnicity*, edited by John E. Terrell, pp. 1–10. Bergin and Garvey, Westport, Connecticut.
2001c The Uncommon Sense of Race, Language, and Culture. In *Archaeology, Language and History: Essays on Culture and Ethnicity*, edited by John E. Terrell, pp. 11–30. Bergin and Garvey, Westport, Connecticut.

Terrell, John E., Terry L. Hunt, and Chris Gosden
1997 The Dimensions of Social Life in the Pacific. *Current Anthropology* 38:155–195.

Terrell, John E., and Pamela J. Stewart
1996 The Paradox of Human Population Genetics at the End of the Twentieth Century. *Reviews in Anthropology* 25:13–33.

Vail, Leroy (editor)
1989 *The Creation of Tribalism in Southern Africa*. University of California Press, Berkeley.

Varner, John G., and Jeannette J. Varner
1951 *The Florida of the Inca*. University of Texas Press, Austin.

Voss, Barbara L.
2005 From *Casta* to *Californio*: Social Identity and the Archaeology of Culture Contact. *American Anthropologist* 107:461–474.

Vitzthum, Virginia J.
2003 A Number No Greater Than the Sum of Its Parts: The Use and Abuse of Heritability. *Human Biology* 75:539–558.

Wickman, Patricia
1999 *The Tree That Bends: Discourse, Power, and the Survival of the Maskókî People*. University of Alabama Press, Tuscaloosa.

Wiessner, Polly
1990 Is There a Unity to Style? In *Uses of Style in Archaeology*, edited by Margaret Conkey and Christine Hastorf, pp. 105–112. Cambridge University Press, Cambridge.

Worth, John E.
1995 *The Struggle for the Georgia Coast: An Eighteenth-Century Spanish Retrospective on Guale and Mocama*. Anthropological Papers No. 75. American Museum of Natural History, New York.

Yelvington, Kevin
1991 Ethnicity as Practice? A Comment on Bentley. *Comparative Studies in Society and History* 33:158–168.

PART III

Bioarchaeological Research in Central and South America

10

What's on the Bone?

Interdisciplinary Approaches in Reconstructing the Posthumous Body Treatments of the Ancient Maya Aristocracy of Calakmul, Campeche, Mexico

Vera Tiesler
Facultad de Ciencias Antropológicas, Universidad Autónoma de Yucatán
Andrea Cucina
Facultad de Ciencias Antropológicas, Universidad Autónoma de Yucatán
Patricia Quintana Owen
Cinvestav-Mérida, Depto. de Física Aplicada, Mérida
Daniel H. Aguilar
Cinvestav-Mérida, Depto. de Física Aplicada, Mérida
Iván Oliva Arias
Cinvestav-Mérida, Depto. de Física Aplicada, Mérida
J. V. Cauich-Rodríguez
Centro de Investigación Científica de Yucatán, Mérida
William J. Folan
Centro de Investigaciones Históricas y Sociales, Universidad Autónoma de Campeche
María del Rosario Domínguez Carrasco
Centro de Investigaciones Históricas y Sociales, Universidad Autónoma de Campeche

During the last few decades, the analysis of skeletal remains has become an increasingly powerful analytical tool for reconstructing the life and death of ancient Maya royals (Buikstra et al. 2004; Demarest et al. 1991; Tiesler et al. 2002, 2003, 2004; Tiesler and Cucina 2005, 2006; Wright 2005). A general awareness of the importance of osteological studies on the ancient Maya was raised in the late 1960s and the 1970s with Haviland (1967), Saul (1972), and Stewart's (1975) seminal approaches to the study of human skeletal series from the sites of Dzibilchaltún, Tikal, and Altar de Sacrificio. More recently, Maya research has received direct input from bioarchaeological agendas. This also holds true for dynastic research, which draws increasingly from sophisticated interdisciplinary tomb studies that integrate detailed taphonomic and biovital information from skeletons (Bell et al. 2004; Tiesler and Cucina 2006). The integration of skeletal research in the reconstruction of ancient rulers' lives and deaths has been actively promoted by Jane E. Buikstra. Her important work on the Classic-period aristocracy of Copan, Honduras, and Palenque, Mexico, benefits from combining detailed conventional studies and sophisticated new analytical tools (Buikstra et al. 2004; 2006; see also Price, Burton et al. 2006; Price, Tiesler et al. 2006). Examined jointly with narrated schemes of life histories that are warranted by the ancient written sources, this holistic approach allows powerfully detailed accounts of individual pre- and postmortem trajectories that facilitate cross-examination with the broader iconographic and archaeological record.

The present study, which analyzes residues adhering to two royal skeletons from Calakmul, Mexico, builds on and expands Buikstra's approach. It sets out the idea that, apart from a skeleton itself, substances adhering to skeletal surfaces also provide important sources of information that shed light on the breadth of posthumous treatments that ancient rulers received as part of public mourning and commemoration (García Moreno 2005; Hall 1989; Michelet et al. 1999; Pereira and Michelet 2004; Tiesler 2004; see also Duday 2006). Presented during the symposium "The Dead Tell Tales: Jane E. Buikstra and Narratives of the Past," this study was inspired by our quest to explore new technical applications and innovative interdisciplinary, bioarchaeological approaches, following in the footsteps of Jane E. Buikstra's pioneering integrative research on the cutting edge between archaeology and human biology. The comprehensive, collaborative approach advocated here intends to provide a fresh look at the possible roles and techniques of different posthumous body preparations of Maya royals—specifically pigmentation, wrappings, and biers—by reanalyzing tomb burials 1 and 5 from Calakmul in Campeche, Mexico, originally investigated during the 1980s by the Autonomous University of Campeche. Our results add information to earlier lab analyses on these and other elite tombs from the site conducted by Xelhuantzi-López (1985), García Vierna and Schneider Glantz (1996), García-Moreno and Granados García (1999), and García Moreno (2005), with whom we seek to develop broader insights into the postmortem timing and forms of ancient Maya elite corpse coloring and wrapping.

TWO DYNASTIC TOMBS FROM THE CLASSIC-PERIOD URBAN CENTER OF CALAKMUL

The site of Calakmul represents a major regional and urban center in northern Petén (now in the Mexican state of Campeche). It lies along the limits of the Laberinto Bajo, which once controlled a good part of northern Petén and adjacent areas. Its 6,250 structures and more than 120 stelae were distributed over more than 30 km² of urban area populated by some 20,000 inhabitants (based on a 55 percent occupancy rate) during the Classic period (Figure 10.1). The site's urban space represents a concentrically organized core area divided into mosaics that extend several kilometers to the north and south and at least 10 km to the east of the central plaza (Fletcher et al. 2001; Folan et al. 1995; May Hau et al. 1990). Calakmul's aristocracy appears to have resided in the extensive acropolis areas in and around its core, where at least four royal tombs were discovered during the two closing decades of the twentieth century (Martin and Grube 2008). Two of these are the focus of this study.

Tomb 1 (Structure VII)

Previous studies indicate that the funerary chamber discovered in Structure VII dates to the Late Classic

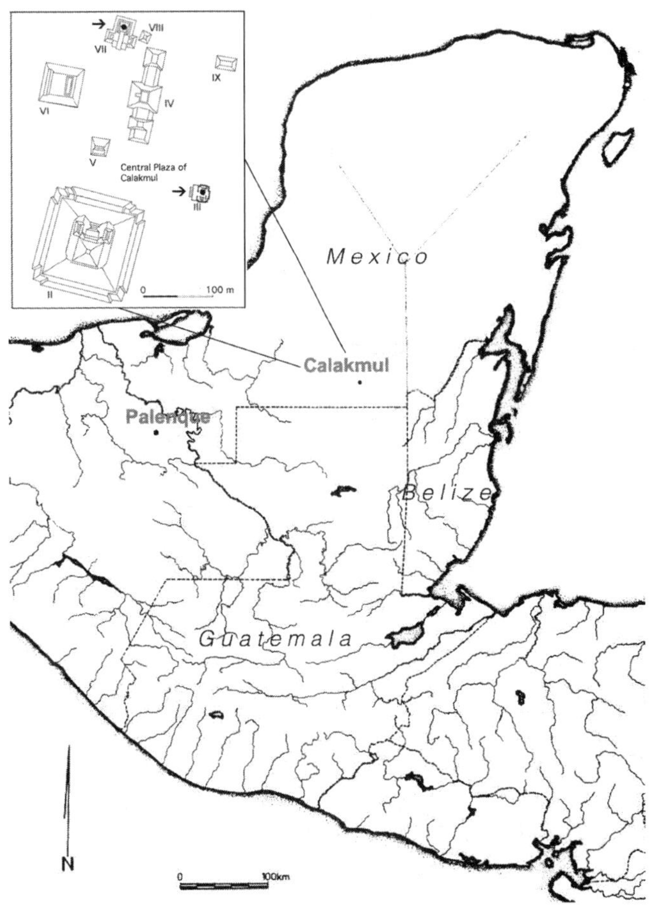

Figure 10.1. Map of the Maya area with sites described in the text, with locations of tombs from Calakmul indicated in inset (drawn by V. Tiesler).

period. Although the tomb is unidentified for lack of preserved inscriptions, its details clearly indicate the royal status of its occupant (Martin and Grube 2008:113). Structure VII is one of the massive vaulted structures that close Calakmul's central plaza to the north (Domínguez Carrasco 1994; Domínguez Carrasco and Gallegos Gómora 1989; Folan et al. 1995). The tomb contained the remains of a centrally placed body that had been laid out facing north. The corpse had been covered with red pigment and wrapped with several layers of a woven mat. Two tie holes formed of palm fibers were stabilized with *chaká* resin (*Bursera simaruba*) and with a jaguar skin with paws attached (Xelhuantzi-López 1985). Thick layers of what appeared to be a different material covered the lower extremities. The funerary bundle was laid on top of a line of four ceramic plates extended on a bed or mattress filled with *cheechém* seeds (*Metopium bownei*) (Xelhuantzi-López 1985). Before sealing, the chamber was packed with the dignitary's personal items and offerings—among them a splendidly crafted jadeite mosaic face mask; two pairs of engraved earflares; an engraved lip plug; a jadeite finger ring; and a pectoral. The body was also accompanied by several obsidian instruments, ceremonial recipients, and a small woven rectangular bundle of palm leaves placed diagonally over the thorax. Also, manta ray spines and other faunal remains were identified (Mauricio Enseñat, personal communication 1985).

The skeletal study indicates that the occupant was a male of medium height within the range of the pre-Hispanic Maya population (161 cm) who died between the age of 35 and 50. The remains, partly covered with red pigment, showed advanced deterioration due to rodent activity, which explains the disturbed arrangement of most of the skeletal segments at the time of discovery (Tiesler 1998; Tiesler et al. 2001; see also Coyoc Ramírez 1986; Lagunas Rodríguez 1985). Additional isotopic studies suggest a local origin for this ruler (Price, Tiesler et al. 2006).

Tomb 5 (Structure III)

This context consists of a large, roughly stuccoed, vaulted chamber, apparently conceived as a memorial to the royal founding ancestor of its residents during the Early Classic period (Folan 1969; Folan et al. 2001; cf. McAnany 1994). Structure III, known as the Lundell Palace after the 1931 discoverer of Calakmul (Lundell 1933), is an eight-room palatial structure, a vaulted building forming part of the Calakmul royal court (Folan et al. 2001). The tomb's occupant, who is still unidentified for lack of appropriate epigraphic texts, had probably been covered by a finely woven cloth held in place by a series of three pairs of *Spondylus sp.* shells (Figure 10.2). This cloth, similar to gauze, was registered on the front half of the cranium. The corpse had been adorned with a pectoral, ear flares, a necklace, and garments formed of thousands of small shells, including *Olivia spondae* (family Olividae) (Pincemin 1994). The body was then wrapped in a woven, mat-like material, with the right arm crossing the chest. It was laid out in a prone position on top of what might have been a wooden bier. Five ceramic plates had been placed underneath the body (Pincemin 1994; cf. Pereira and Michelet 2004). The dead ruler was also accompanied by a life-size jadeite face mask. A second, though smaller jadeite anthropomorphic mosaic mask was recorded at waist level, with a mosaic feline mask on the chest. A jadeite finger ring was also present. Other offerings consisted of a large-lidded polychrome vessel, a two-piece anthropomorphic vessel (thought to represent a portrait of the tomb occupant), and a cup in a vessel with a pouring spout. There were also the remains of polychrome stucco covering one of the supports of a tetrapod vase of perishable material, a manta ray spine, and several jadeite plaques inscribed with hieroglyphs.

The skeletal study indicates that the tomb's occupant was a robust, tall (166 cm) middle-aged male (35 to 45 years at death) who must have suffered from chronic arthritis and back ailments during the last years of his life. His cranium shows the effects of severe tabular oblique shaping, which left the forehead visibly inclined (Tiesler 1998, Tiesler et al. 2001; see also Coyoc 1992).

SAMPLING AND ANALYTICAL METHODS

Our analytical methods were designed to contribute new information on the structural properties of body pigmentation, support, and wrapping material found in the two chamber tombs. A total of 21 samples were selected from different parts of the bony surfaces of both individuals, along with residues of materials directly related to the remains. Thin sections of bone fragments and associated materials were elaborated and scrutinized by means of plain and polarized light microscopy. The slides were obtained after embedding, cutting, and polishing residue samples from both tombs following the protocol established for histomorphometric work (Tiesler et al. 2006). The structural characterization of

Figure 10.2. Hypothetical drawing of corpse positioning and equipment of Tomb 5 from Structure III at Calakmul (adapted and redrawn by V. Tiesler from Pincemin 1994, Figure 58).

the archaeological samples was carried out by Fourier transform infrared spectroscopy (FT-IR) and X-ray diffraction (XRD). The pigments were also analyzed in a pulverized form by X-ray diffraction after scratching the painted surface. This analysis was used to confirm the crystal structure of the pigment and to identify the mineral crystalline phases present in the pigment. The samples were registered with a diffractometer (Siemens D-5000) operated at 35 kV and 25 mA with a monochromatic Cu Ka radiation ($\lambda = 1.5418$Å). Measurements in a 2°–50° (2q) range were taken with a step time of 3s and a step size of .02°. Scanning electron microscopy (SEM) and chemical analysis by energy dispersive spectroscopy (EDS) were conducted with a JEOL 6360 LV microscope, and EDS analysis was performed on 120-x-120-µm^2 scanning areas.

Pigments, Supports, and Wrapping Materials

Tomb 1 (Structure VII)

While our analyses did not find evidence of textiles, they did confirm differences between the materials used for the two wrappings, as already observed during recovery, and they identified the red pigment as cinnabar by mineralogical X-ray diffraction analysis. Cinnabar (HgS) is a brick-red mercury sulfide, an exotic prestigious material imported from volcanic mountain mines of highland Guatemala and Honduras (Houston et al. 2009:57).

Some of the amorphous plaques found in the area of the lower extremities present a regular single surface with a slightly concave outline, probably due to contact with the corpse. Parts of the opposite surface show impressions of interwoven fibers. Microscopy of thin sections reveals a darker external and a lighter internal layer, both of which still preserve a smooth, rubber-like morphology suggestive of the wrap's original elastic properties (Figure 10.3). An interface can be clearly distinguished between the rigid, degraded external surface and the soft inner core. SEM images confirm the above impressions. The darker face exhibits an irregular surface with large amorphous areas and the presence of crater-like depressions in some parts (Figure 10.4). This rugged morphology could be related to degradation through time caused by changing humidity and temperature. Conversely, the lighter-colored surface presents several fissures, similar to those obtained when dehydration or crystallization occurs on a viscous material (Figure 10.4).

Additional EDS chemical analyses were performed on several pieces and on both faces of the wrap. Average atomic concentrations are shown in Table 10.1. The main elements—carbon (C; 53 percent average) and oxygen (O; 8 percent average)— point to an organic material. Calcium (Ca) and silicon (Si) were present in concentrations close to 3.4 percent, whereas mercury (Hg) averaged 1 percent. Calcium and silicon were present in natural minerals, as were quartz and gypsum, whereas the identified mercury is related to traces of cinnabar on the skeletal surfaces.

X-ray diffraction of both sides of the bundle and of the pulverized sample shows a wide amorphous band between 10° and 25° (2q) associated with the organic component of the wrap (Figure 10.5). Gypsum, albite, quartz, and traces of halloysite were recorded on the lighter side of the bundle, whereas only the last two were present on the opposite side. Since quartz and halloysite were detected on both sides, it is possible that these were intentionally added to the organic matrix of the bundle. On the other hand, it is not clear if gypsum and albite (a feldspar) are related to the stuccoed chamber walls or were added to the organic material to increase the resistance of the bundle. Cinnabar was not identified by XRD. Jointly with SEM and optical microscopy examination, the evidence points to the wrapping material being made from some type of latex sap, similar to other elite tombs documented from Calakmul (see, e.g., García Vierna and Schneider Glantz 1996).

The second wrapping material under study is less enigmatic and was identified as a mat made of plant fibers. The micrograph of the network of intertwined vegetable fibers confirms this interpretation. The interwoven fibers (of nearly 50 microns width) form a mesh network. XRD of the mat support showed an amorphous pattern (Figure 10.6) formed by two bands with maximum values at 14° and 20° (2q). The diffractogram

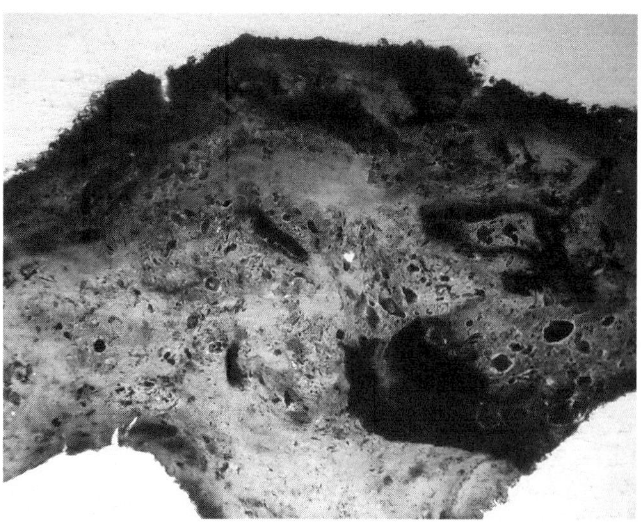

Figure 10.3. Thin section of the wrap from Tomb 1 (Structure VII), exhibiting an amorphous structure with distinctive eroded outer surfaces and an elastic, lighter inner core (x40 microscopy; photo by V. Tiesler).

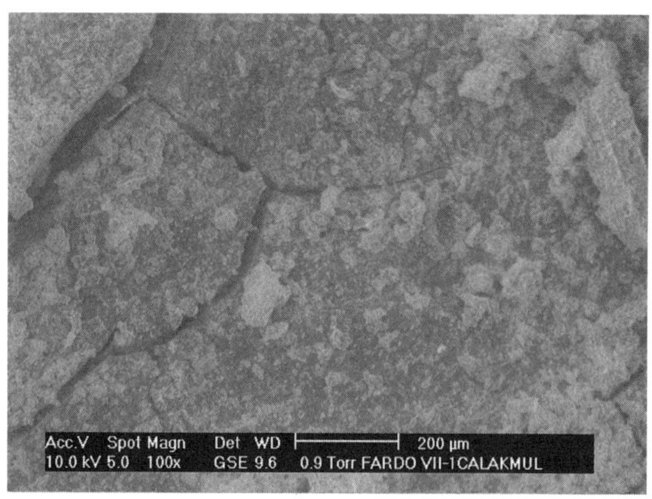

Figure 10.4. SEM image of the surface composition of the wrap (Tomb 1, Structure VII), exhibiting a fissured surface.

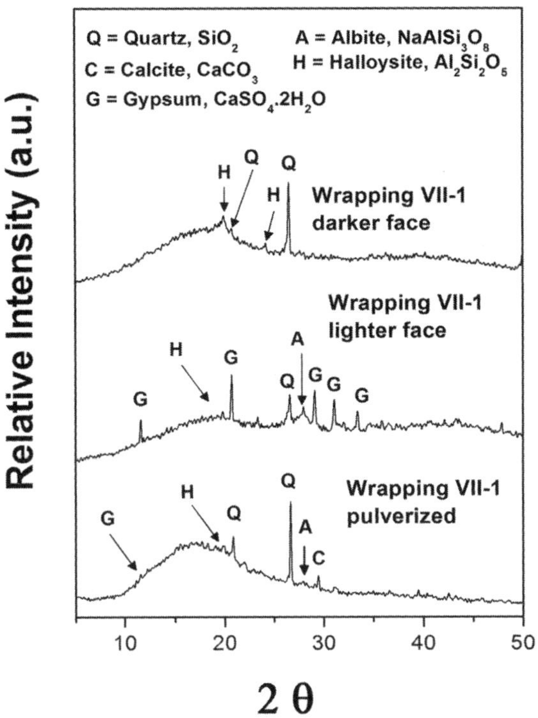

Figure 10.5. X-ray diffraction of the wrap (Tomb 1, Structure VII).

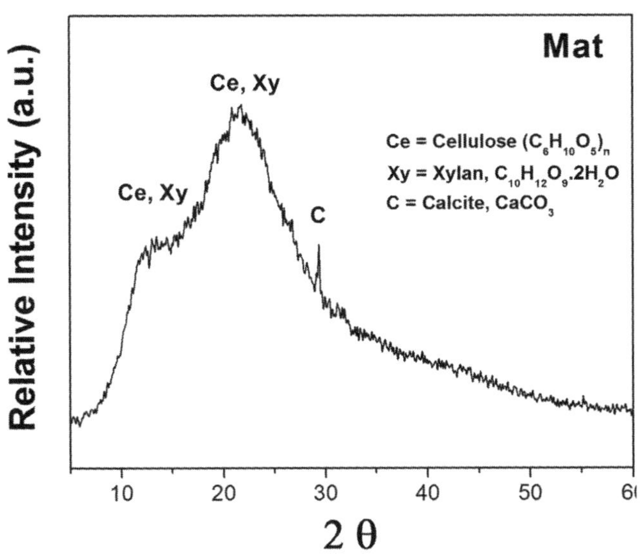

Figure 10.6. XRD pattern of the mat support (Tomb 1, Structure VII).

Table 10.1 Average Atomic Concentrations

Element	Wrapping VII-1 Average %	Fiber mat VII-1 Average %
C	53.01	44.92
O	38.09	39.27
Na	0.12	0.17
Mg	0.15	0.05
Al	0.49	0.05
Si	3.30	12.39
P	0.29	0.00
Hg	1.03	0.00
Cl	0.20	0.42
K	0.24	0.13
Ca	3.43	1.8
Fe	0.29	0.00
S	0.00	0.22

is similar to that of cellulose, $(C_6H_{10}O_5)_n$ and cellulose-derived patterns, such as xylan ($C_{10}H_{12}O_9.2H_2O$). Calcite was also detected. The chemical composition of the mat (Table 10.1) was of an organic nature, as oxygen and carbon were the main elements (44.92 percent and 39.27 percent), followed by silicon (12.39 percent) and calcium (1.8 percent).

Tomb 5 (Structure III)

The second case study refers to the chamber tomb from Structure III. As in the first tomb, no material textile evidence was preserved. We therefore focused for the residue analysis on the pigment concretions that covered most of the skeleton and the fragments of organic material identified as wood recovered beneath the remains.

A pigment nodule was sectioned in different orientations and the slides scrutinized with reflected light. The observed pattern exhibits a stratigraphy of alternating reddish and thin corrugated, amorphous, transparent to blackish layers (Figure 10.7). In this case, the vermillion pigment appears as a homogeneous, compacted deposit, which appears to have been applied together with a dark organic coating, possibly a vehicle to create a thick paste to be applied on the body. The total thickness of the layered red-and-black plaque ranges between 3 and 5 mm. As in Tomb 1, SEM and EDS analyses demonstrated that the red pigment was cinnabar. Additional X-ray diffraction of the pulverized pigmented sample on the wooden support (Figure 10.8) showed large amounts of

Figure 10.7. Thin section of alternating layers of cinnabar and organic black coating in the pigment concretion recovered from the support of Tomb 5 of Structure III (x25 microscopy; photo by V. Tiesler).

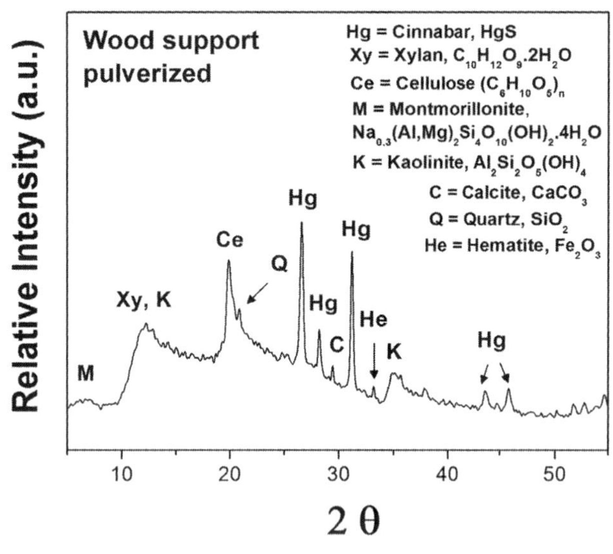

Figure 10.8. XRD of a powdered sample of wood support from Tomb 5 of Structure III.

Table 10.2 EDXS Analysis of Pigment

EDX		
WOOD B.III-9		
Elements (%W)	Dark seccion	Clear section
C	**27.48**	**9.21**
N	0.00	0
O	**31.13**	**26.96**
Na	0.14	0.00
Mg	0.21	0.17
Al	2.40	1.83
Si	**5.01**	**3.29**
P	0.80	0.00
S (Hg)?	0.00	0.00
Cl	0.00	0.00
K	0.26	0.00
Ca	2.76	1.99
Fe	1.53	1.21
Mo?	**7.35**	**13.24**
Hg	**20.93**	**42.11**

cinnabar along with calcite, clays such as montmorillonite and kaolinite, and traces of hematite. Hematite is a mineral of iron (III) oxide (Fe_2O_3) that was used in ancient Maya mortuary treatments as a substitute for, or in addition to, cinnabar (Bolio et al. 2012; Houston et al. 2009). Similar to cinnabar, hematite from mortuary contexts is red in appearance. Additional organic components of the wood, xylan, and crystalline cellulose (peak near 20° 2q), were detected. It should be noted that cellulose appears more crystalline in the wooden sample than in the mat of Burial VII-1. The EDS analysis of the pigment-covered surface and of the wood (Table 10.2) showed a higher content of mercury and carbon, respectively.

Discussion

Wrapped or elevated chamber burials of nobles such as the two from Calakmul were widespread in the Maya realm during the Classic period. Funerary bundles, some of which were very elaborate, were probably in use among the ancient Maya since the Preclassic period (Carrasco 2004; Pereira and Michelet 2004). At Calakmul, a large array of materials was employed to carry, cover, and wrap the deceased elite during the

Early and Late Classic periods. As previous studies have demonstrated, supports and bundles were tailored from textiles, resin-embedded fabrics, latex, straw mats, or a combination of materials, along with stuccoed wood for bier supports (Carrasco Vargas 2004; García Moreno 2005; García-Moreno and Granados García 1999; García and Schneider Glantz 1996; Pincemin 1994). In most elite tombs from Calakmul, where the identification of residues is hampered due to their advanced state of decay, there are taphonomic indications of bundling, as many of Calakmul's elite burials show vestiges of body "constriction" and elevation, leading to a characteristic skeletal distribution of the shoulders, pelvic girdle, knees, and ankles (Tiesler 2004). Here, as in other lowland Maya sites, the bundles could be laid on different kinds of supports, such as mattresses, wooden platforms, or "beds." Within the dominant sectors of Maya society, the use of elevated mortuary biers was especially popular during the Early Classic period (Hall 1989; Pereira and Michelet 2004). Bier elevation and wraps were probably reserved for selected ancestral shrines of the aristocracy, since commoners' filled-in graves seldom show signs of constriction or bier elevation (see, e.g., Medrano 2005). However, there survives no clear pattern in the elite mortuary record that might stand for any standardized posthumous procedures in this part of society. The observed diversity of individual body treatments suggests instead that the preparation and accommodation of a deceased body was family business.

More widespread than body wrapping in ancient Maya society was corpse pigmentation. We explored what role pigment covering might have played as part of the predepositional preparation of dead rulers by examining the consistency of applied pigments and the layering of pigments and wraps. Regarding the postmortem timing for ancient pigment application, there is still no agreement on whether it was applied directly on the dead body, on body wraps, or on already skeletonized remains. Classic-period Maya inscriptions refer to the painting of bones, pointing to the use of red pigment in secondary mortuary treatments (Eberl 2005). Other data, specifically the taphonomy of undisturbed primary burials, emphasize the coloring of freshly installed corpses rather than bones (Tiesler 2006).

For the two cases described here, along with others from Calakmul and Palenque (Tiesler 2004, 2006; Tiesler et al. 2002), we dismiss the hypothesis that the remains were painted after skeletonization, based on the pattern of pigment distribution on the bones and on placement between bones and body wrapping materials. Also, the undisturbed nature of both funerary chambers, as shown by the sealed roof and the anatomical distribution of skeletal segments, recorded during their recovery in the 1980s, rules out later entrances into the tomb and further handling of the remains. All this suggests that pigmentation did not involve skeletonized ancestral remains but instead formed part of corpse preparation, along with bundling prior to primary burial. This process is referred to in the epigraphic inscriptions as the *muhkaj* event (Eberl 2005). According to the mourning calendar, these pre-interment preparations could last several days. If we trust the epigraphy, the subsequent *muhkaj* ceremonies were performed up to 10 days after death. Since these festivities were probably public events, we can assume that the elaborate corpse preparations, like the ones studied here, would have held powerful symbolic and ostentatious functions.

A second question concerns the substances used for pigmentation, their forms of application, and their possible functions and meanings in ancient Maya ancestral treatments. Earlier studies have identified cinnabar and hematite in different proportions as the preferred colorants for painting the dead, although knowledge regarding the precise processes implied in pigment preparation and forms of application in ancient Maya mortuary treatment is still rather vague (Canto et al. 2004; Gazzola 2003; Tiesler 2006; Tiesler et al. 2004; Vázquez Negrete and Velázquez 1996; but see Houston et al. 2009). Specifically, the uses of cinnabar appear to have been restricted to elite mortuary treatments and sacred carvings and writings in temple contexts (Houston et al. 2009:57–65).

Additional substances, such as amorphic agglutinants, which we have documented in this study, could have been added as paint vehicles to improve durability and to facilitate application of the colorants as paint or paste. The alternating layers of cinnabar and dark organic coats that we recorded in one of our case studies are reminiscent of glazed blends of smooth pastes, directly applied on the skin of the deceased. This predepositional treatment is similar to what we have recorded for another Maya paramount from Palenque: Janaab'Pakal, whose body was laid to rest deep inside a monumental mausoleum in the Temple of the Inscriptions (Tiesler 2006). Here, the cinnabar showed organic and mineral impurities. It has up to five layers of coating alternated with a black organic substratum, identified as a carbon paste or bitumen, which looks similar to the pigment concretions associated with the remains of Calakmul's Tomb 5 in Structure III (Tiesler 2006).

Other forms of application, inferred in this and other studies, appear to range from powder sprinkling to blends of cinnabar and transparent organic adhesives of cinnabar and hematite (Bolio et al. 2012; García-Moreno and Granados 2000; Tiesler and Cucina 2006; Vázquez de Agredos 2006, 2007). Namely, our recent research on dynasts from the Maya Classic-period capitals of Palenque, Ek Balam, and Dzibanché has identified similarly high proportions of cinnabar as those documented in this study. In contrast, commoners' mortuary pigmentation, when present, apparently consisted of hematite, a more accessible substitute for the exotic cinnabar imports (Bolio et al. 2012).

Considering that cinnabar was employed together with different organic wrapping and support materials in the preparation of Calakmul's elite, it is reasonable to wonder whether its use in posthumous body pigmentation—like the use of latex, resin, or embedded fabric bundles—could have been employed not only for ritual but also for practical purposes, similar to the embalming techniques used in other ancient societies. (See, for example, David 2000 for materials used in Egyptian embalming techniques.) A compound of mercury and cinnabar is toxic and should have been helpful in slowing the incipient biological decomposition processes during corpse transportation or during the probably prolonged funerary ceremonies that preceded burial, which were undoubtedly public events of major importance. It is probably no coincidence that the body from Tomb 5 still had preserved hair strands below the plaques of vermilion pigmentation, a unique finding considering the generally poor preservation of hair on lowland Maya remains.

Further questions remain regarding the ritual meanings of funerary wraps, biers, and cinnabar pigmentation in local and regional traditions and their enactment according to the ritual calendar. The performance of royal corpse positioning, wrapping, binding, and concealing is itself powerfully reminiscent of the preparation of sacred bundles used for Maya ritual ceremonies (Guernsey and Reilly 2006). We think that cinnabar's exotic value and naturally occurring bright red color should have rendered it a remarkable ingredient in ancient royal ancestral rites, evoking life in the form of its primary living essence: blood. Its combination with the green jadeite ornaments on top of the royal corpse bundles expressed broader existential dualities of aristocracy, namely those of precious life and divine ancestry (Houston et al. 2009:82–83). Houston and colleagues also note the profoundly conservative quality of color choice in tomb decorations, a palette that remained essentially the same between the Preclassic and the Postclassic and that combined red and black tones on white surfaces (Houston et al. 2009). This profoundly primeval color scheme is also expressed in the cinnabar coatings we documented at Calakmul and Palenque, specifically the combination of black and red tones. These ancestral blends should have evoked the perpetual cycle of life, death, and ancestry, demise and resurrection, as expressed by the daily sunrise and sunset (Hammond 1989).

In closing, this study on ancient mortuary wraps and pigmentation among ancient Maya royals has strived to combine fruitfully the breadth of analytical tools and interpretational frameworks that the topic demands. The range of analyses presented here extends from material identification to microscopic and macroscopic morphological examination to taphonomic and behavioral mortuary analyses. These bring us to cultural interpretations of ancient Maya ancestral ideology and ritualized performance informed by coherent ideological frames and long-standing undercurrents of autochtonous Mesoamerican mortuary expressions. We were positively surprised that this study, which reexamines minute bone appositions three decades after excavation, was still possible. In this sense, we wish to encourage similar interdisciplinary inquiries of residues directly associated with skeletal remains, a source of information that we feel is still underexplored in Maya research.

Acknowledgments

The residues under study were recorded by the Calakmul Archaeological Project (Autonomous University of Campeche) under the direction of Dr. William J. Folan. The material science studies were supported by Conacyt projects 49275-F and 37743-H. We are thankful to J. E. Corona (Cinvestav-Mérida) and Rosana Vargas-Coronado (Centro de Investigación Científica de Yucatán) for the SEM and EDS analysis. A special thanks goes to Jane E. Buikstra for her helpful comments during the original session and, naturally, for all the invaluable scholarly inspiration she provided during the years we have had the honor of knowing her.

REFERENCES CITED

Bell, Ellen E., Marcello A. Canuto, and Robert J. Sharer (editors)
2004 *Understanding Early Classic Copan*. University of Pennsylvania Museum of Archaeology and Anthropology, Philadelphia.

Bolio Zapata, Catalina, Patricia Quintana Owen, Vera Tiesler, and Thelma Sierra Sosa
2012 Los pigmentos funerarios entre los antiguos mayas. In *Aplicaciones histomorfológicas en el estudio de restos humanos*, edited by Vera Tiesler, pp. 17–32. Universidad Autónoma de Yucatán, Mérida.

Buikstra, Jane E., George R. Milner, and Jesper L. Boldsen
2006 Janaab' Pakal: The Age-at-Death Controversy Revisited. In *Janaab' Pakal of Palenque: Reconstructing the Life and Death of a Maya Ruler*, edited by Vera Tiesler and Andrea Cucina, pp. 48–59. University of Arizona, Tucson.

Buikstra, J. E., T. D. Price, L. E. Wright, and J. A. Burton
2004 Tombs from the Copán Acropolis: A Life History Approach. In *Understanding Early Classic Copan*, edited by E. E. Bell, M. A. Canuto, and R. Sharer, pp. 191–212. University of Pennsylvania Museum of Archaeology and Anthropology, Philadelphia.

Canto, Ana Bertha, Patricia Quintana, J. José Alvarado Gil, Vera Tiesler, and Laura L. Díaz Flores
2004 Estudio por difracción de rayos x y espectroscopía infraroja de huesos humanos de la época prehispánica y colonial. In *La ciencia de materiales y su impacto en la arqueología*, edited by Demetrio Mendoza, Eva Brito, and Jesus Arenas, pp. 67–85. Academia Mexicana de Ciencia de Materiales A.C. CONACULTA-INAH, Mexico City.

Carrasco Vargas, Ramón
2004 Ritos funerarios en Calakmul: Practicas rituales de los mayas del clásico. In *Culto funerario en la sociedad maya: Memoria de la Cuarta Mesa Redonda de Palenque*, edited by Rafael Cobos, pp. 231–244. Instituto Nacional de Antropología e Historia, Mexico City.

Coyoc Ramírez, Mario A.
1986 *Algunas características antropológicas del personaje de la tumba I de la estructura VII de Calakmul, Campeche*. Información 11. Centro de Estudios Históricos y Sociales, Universidad Autónoma de Campeche, Campeche.
1992 *Características bioculturales en una muestra de restos óseos prehispánicos de Calakmul, Campeche*. Información 15. Centro de Investigaciones Históricas y Sociales, Universidad Autónoma de Campeche, Campeche.

David, Rosalie
2000 Mummification. In *Ancient Egyptian Materials and Technology*, edited by Paul Nicholson and Ian Shaw, pp. 372–389. Cambridge University, Cambridge.

Demarest, Arthur A., H. Escobedo, J. A. Valdés, S. Houston, L. E. Wright, and K. F. Emery
1991 Arqueología, epigrafía y el descubrimiento de una tumba real en el centro ceremonial de Dos Pilas, Petén, Guatemala. *U tz'ib* 1:14–28.

Domínguez Carrasco, María del Rosario
1994 *El Uso y Función de la Estructura VII de Calakmul, Campeche*. Investigadores de la Cultura Maya 2. Universidad Autónoma de Campeche, Campeche.

Domínguez Carrasco, María del Rosario, and Miriam J. Gallegos Gómora
1989 *Informe del trabajo del Proyecto Calakmul, 1984, Estructura 7*. Información 14. Centro de Investigaciones Históricas y Sociales, Universidad Autónoma de Campeche, Campeche.

Duday, Henry
2006 L'achéothanatologie ou l'archéologie de la mort (Archaeoethnoanatology or the Archaeology of Death). In *Social Archaeology of Funerary Remains*, edited by Rebecca Gowland and Christopher Knüsel, pp. 30–56. Oxbow, Oxford.

Eberl, Markus
2005 *Muerte, entierro y ascención: Ritos funerarios entre los antiguos mayas*. Universidad Autónoma de Yucatán, Mérida.

Fletcher, Laraine A., William J. Folan, Jacinto May Hau, and Lynda Florey Folan
2001 III Patrón de Asentamiento. In *Las Ruinas de Calakmul, Campeche, México: Un lugar central y su pasaje cultural*. Universidad Autónoma de Campeche, CIHS, SEP, FAMSI, and FOMES, Campeche.

Folan, William J.
1969 Dzibilchaltún, Yucatan, Mexico: Structures 384, 385 y 386: A Preliminary Interpretation. *American Antiquity* 34(4):434–451.

Folan, William J., Joyce Marcus, Sophia Pincemin, María del Rosario Domínguez Carrasco, Laraine A. Fletcher, and Abel Morales López
1995 Calakmul, Campeche: New Data from an Ancient Maya Capital in Campeche, Mexico. *Latin American Antiquity* 6(4):310–334.

Folan, William J., Joel D. Gunn, and Ma. del Rosario Domínguez Carrasco
2001 Triadic Temples, Central Plazas and Dynastic Palaces: A Diachronic Analysis of the Royal Court Complex: Calakmul, Campeche, Mexico. In *Royal Courts of the Ancient Maya*, edited by Takeshi Inomata and Stephen Houston, 223–265. Westview, Boulder, Colorado.

García Moreno, Renata
2005 Les sepultures royales de Calakmul, Mexique: Tecnologie, iconographie et symbolism. Unpublished Ph.D. thesis, Universidad de Paris I, Paris.

García-Moreno Rodriguez, Renata, and Josefina Granados García
1999 La restauración de la joyería y la vestimenta funeraria localizada en la tumba 4 de la subestructura II-B de Calakmul, Campeche. Unpublished B.A. thesis, Escuela Nacional de Conservación Restauración y Museografía, Instuto Nacional de Antropología e Historia, Mexico City.

García Vierna, Valeria A., and Renata Schneider Glantz
1996 El proceso de rescate, conservación, restauración y análisis como una fuente primaria de investigación antropológica: el caso de la tumba 1 de la estructura XV de Calakmul, Campeche. Unpublished B.A. thesis, Escuela Nacional de Conservación, Restauración y Museografía, Mexico City.

Gazzola, Julie
2003 El uso del cinabrio en Teotihuacan. Identificación en contextos funerarios. In *Contextos arqueológicos y osteología del barrio de La Ventilla: Teotihuacan (1992–1994)*, edited by Carlos Serrano Sánchez, pp. 81–88. Instituto de Investigaciones Antropológicas, Universidad Nacional Autónoma de México, Mexico City.

Guernsey, Julia, and Kent Reilly (editors)
2006 *Sacred Bundles: Ritual Acts of Wrapping and Binding in Mesoamerica*. Boundary End Archaeology Research Center, Barnardsville, North Carolina.

Hall, Grant David
1989 Realm of Death: Royal Mortuary Customs and Polity Interaction in the Classic Maya Lowlands. Unpublished Ph.D. thesis, Harvard University, Cambridge.

Hammond, Norman
1989 Maya Alchemy: Emic Understanding of Chemically-based Color Change in

Mineral Pigments in Preclassic and Classic Maya Culture. Unpublished paper on file at the Laboratorio de Bioarqueología, Facultad de Ciencias Antropológicas, Universidad de Yucatán, Mérida.

Haviland, William A.
1967 Stature at Tikal, Guatemala: Implications for Ancient Maya Demography and Social Organization. *American Antiquity* 32:316–325.

Houston, Stephen, Claudia Brittenham, Cassandra Mesick, Alexandre Tokovinine, and Christina Warinner
2009 *Veiled Brightness: A History of Ancient Maya Color*. University of Texas Press, Austin.

Lagunas Rodríguez, Zaid
1985 *La exploración de la tumba I de la Zona Arqueológica de Calakmul, Campeche*. Información 9. Centro de Estudios Históricos y Sociales, Universidad Autónoma del Sudeste, Campeche.

Lundell, Cyrus Longworth
1933 Archaeological Discoveries in the Maya Area. *Proceedings of the American Philosophical Society* 72(3):147–179. Reprint.

Martin, Simon, and Nikolai Grube
2008 *Chronicle of the Maya Kings and Queens.* 2nd edition. Thames and Hudson, London.

May Hau, Jacinto, Rogerio Cohouh Muñoz, Raymundo González Heredia, and William J. Folan.
1990 *El mapa de Calakmul.* Centro de Investigaciones Históricas y Sociales, Universidad Autónoma de Campeche, Campeche.

McAnany, Patricia
1994 *Living with the Ancestors: Kinship and Kingship in Ancient Maya Society.* University of Texas, Austin.

Medrano Chan, Lucy
2005 Tratamientos póstumos del cuerpo humano en la tradición funeraria de Xcambó, Yucatán. Unpublished B.A. dissertation, Facultad de Ciencias Antropológicas, Universidad Autónoma de Yucatán, Mérida.

Michelet, Dominique, Marie-Charlotte Arnauld, Philippe Nondédéo, Grégory Pereira, F. de Pierrebourg, and Éric Taladroire
1999 La saison de fouilles de 1998 à Balamku (Campeche, Mexique): Des avancées substantielles. *Journal de la Societé des Américanistes* 84(1):183–198.

Pereira, Gregory, and Dominique Michelet
2004 Gobernantes mayas en lechos de muerte: El caso de Balamkú, un patrón funerario del clásico temprano. In *Culto funerario en la sociedad maya. Memoria de la Cuarta Mesa Redonda de Palenque,* edited by Rafael Cobos, pp. 333–368. Instituto Nacional de Antropología e Historia, Mexico City.

Pincemin, Sophia
1994 *Entierro en el Palacio: La tumba de la Estructura III, Calakmul, Campeche,* Universidad Autónoma de Campeche, Colección Arqueología, Campeche.

Price, T. Douglas, James H. Burton, Vera Tiesler, Simon Martin, and Jane E. Buikstra
2006 The Companions of Janaab' Pakal and the "Red Queen": Evidence from Strontium Isotopes. In *Janaab' Pakal of Palenque: Reconstructing the Life and Death of a Maya Ruler,* edited by Vera Tiesler and Andrea Cucina, pp. 91–101. University of Arizona, Tucson.

Price, Douglas T., Vera Tiesler, Richard Burton, and Jane E. Buikstra
2006 Evidencia isotópica sobre el sitio de Calakmul, Campeche. In *Los Investigadores de la Cultura Maya* 14, pp. 87–94. Universidad Autónoma de Campeche, Campeche.

Saul, Frank P.
1972 *The Human Skeletal Remains of Altar de Sacrificios: An Osteobiographic Analysis.* Papers of the Peabody Museum of Archaeology and Ethnology Vol. 63. Harvard University, Cambridge.

Stewart, T. Dale
1975 *Human Skeletal Remains from Dzibilchaltun, Yucatan, Mexico, with a Review of Cranial Deformity Types in the Maya Region.* Middle American Research Institute No. 31. Tulane University, New Orleans.

Tiesler, Vera
1998 *Prácticas bioculturales entre los antiguos mayas del norte del Petén.* Los Investigadores de la Cultura Maya 6. Universidad Autónoma de Campeche, Campeche.
2004 Maya Mortuary Treatments of the Elite: An Osteotaphonomic Perspective. In *Continuity and Change: Maya Religious Practices in Temporal Perspective,* edited by Daniel Graña Behrens, Nikolai Grube, Christian M. Prager, Frauke Sachse, Stefanie Teufel, and Elisabeth Wagner, pp. 143–156. Anton Saurwein, Markt Schwaben, Germany.
2006 Life and Death of the Ruler: Recent Bioarchaeological Findings. In *Janaab' Pakal of Palenque: Reconstructing the Life and Death of a Maya Ruler,* edited by Vera Tiesler and Andrea Cucina, pp. 21–47. University of Arizona, Tucson.

Tiesler, Vera, and Andrea Cucina
2005 Las enfermedades de la aristocracia maya del Clásico. *Arqueología Mexicana* 74:42–47.

Tiesler, Vera, and Andrea Cucina (editors)
2006 *Janaab' Pakal of Palenque: Life and Death of a Maya Ruler.* University of Arizona Press, Tucson.

Tiesler, Vera, Andrea Cucina, and Arturo Romano Pacheco
2002 Vida y muerte del personaje hallado en el templo XIII-sub, Palenque: I Culto funerario y sacrificio humano. *Mexicon* 24:75–78.
2003 Vida y muerte del personaje del templo XIII-Sub, Palenque, Chiapas. Una mirada bioarqueológica. In *Culto funerario en la sociedad maya: Memoria de la Cuarta Mesa Redonda de Palenque,* edited by Rafael Cobos, pp. 455–482. Instituto Nacional de Antropología e Historia, Mexico City.
2004 Who Was the Red Queen? The Identity of the Female Maya Dignitary from the Sarcophagus Tomb of Temple XIII, Palenque, Mexico. *HOMO* 55(1–2):65–76.

Tiesler, Vera, Andrea Cucina, and Margaret Streeter
2006 *Manual de histomorfología en hueso no descalcificado.* Universidad Autónoma de Yucatán, Mérida.

Tiesler, Vera, María Rosario Domínguez, William J. Folan, and Mario Coyoc
2001 Los entierros: Funerarios y extra-funerarios. In *Las ruinas de Calakmul, Campeche, México: Un lugar central y su paisaje cultural,* edited by William J. Folan, Laraine A. Fletcher, Jacinto May Hau, and Lynda Florey Folan, pp. 77–80. Universidad Autónoma de Campeche, Campeche.

Vázquez Negrete, Javier, and Rodrigo Velázquez
1996 Análisis Químico de Materiales Encontrados en Excavación, Dos Casos: Porta-Incensarios Tipo Palenque y Cinabrio Usado en Prácticas Funerarias. In *Eighth Palenque Round Table 1993,* vol. 10, edited by Merle Greene Robertson, pp. 103–106. Pre-Columbian Art Research Institute, San Francisco.

Wright, Lori E.
2005 In Search of Yax Nuun Ayiin I: Revisiting the Tikal Project's Burial 10. *Ancient Mesoamerica* 16:63–87.

Xelhuantzi-López, María Susana
1985 Reporte de la identificación de restos botánicos, Calakmul, Campeche. Unpublished report on file, Universidad Autónoma de Campeche, Campeche.

11

AN ISOTOPE STUDY OF CHILDHOOD DIET AND MOBILITY AT COPAN, HONDURAS

LORI E. WRIGHT
DEPARTMENT OF ANTHROPOLOGY, TEXAS A&M UNIVERSITY

IN THE 1970S, BIOARCHAEOLOGY EMERGED AS a new field with goals both in archaeology and physical anthropology. With its name coined by Jane E. Buikstra, bioarchaeology emphasized populational approaches to ancient human biology (Buikstra 1977:69; Buikstra and Cook 1980) and stood in contrast to the descriptive osteobiography of the most prominent skeletal studies on the ancient Maya at that time, which served more narrowly archaeological goals (Saul 1972). Yet bioarchaeology began at the same time archaeologists of the ancient Maya emphasized settlement pattern studies over the study of tombs and temples. Truly populational approaches to the study of ancient Maya remains have been hindered by the small size of most Maya skeletal series and by the poor preservation of bone in the humid tropical lowlands of the Maya area. While populational studies of Maya remains have produced meaningful (and often highly debated) interpretations of ancient Maya health and adaptation (Wright and White 1996), osteobiographic approaches have recently found new relevance to Maya bioarchaeology. For instance, Buikstra's recent work in the Maya area reconstructs life histories of key elite skeletons at Palenque (Buikstra et al. 2006) and Copan (Buikstra et al. 2004). It is not coincidental that this renewed interest in life history followed the revolution in decipherment of the Maya hieroglyphic writing system that emerged in the 1980s and 1990s. The rich epigraphic culture-history of the Maya area tempts us to reconstruct individual lives of those few named participants of the ancient past, many of whose identities and family histories are better known now than they were during the growth of populational bioarchaeology. Moreover, bone chemical methods now offer a new approach to reconcile the historical reconstructions of Maya dynasties with the silent remains in royal tombs (Wright 2005b).

Stable isotopes can now be used to reconstruct diet at precise ages through the life span, permitting quite detailed resolution of individual dietary histories. In the last decade, we have added stable oxygen ($\delta^{18}O$) and strontium ($^{87}Sr/^{86}Sr$) isotopes to our analytic tool kit, bringing the opportunity to evaluate place of residence in addition to diet. For Sr, this is fairly straightforward because Sr comes into the body via foods. Its isotopic ratio is determined by that of the geological substrate and thus the soils on which foods are grown. In Mesoamerica, the dramatic geological differences between highlands and lowlands allow fairly good $^{87}Sr/^{86}Sr$ discrimination between these varied geological homelands (Price et al. 2000; Price et al. 2007). Although the trade of foods and sea salt (Wright 2005a) may confound this picture, there is considerable homogeneity within the Maya lowlands themselves (Hodell et al. 2004), and sorting out these influences is relatively straightforward for $^{87}Sr/^{86}Sr$.

Oxygen isotopes seemed at first to be good discriminators of geographic origin, as they vary with the composition of rainwater across the landscape. For instance, White et al. (1998) were able to identify outliers among Teotihuacan skeletons, and $\delta^{18}O$ values can be shown to vary dramatically between central

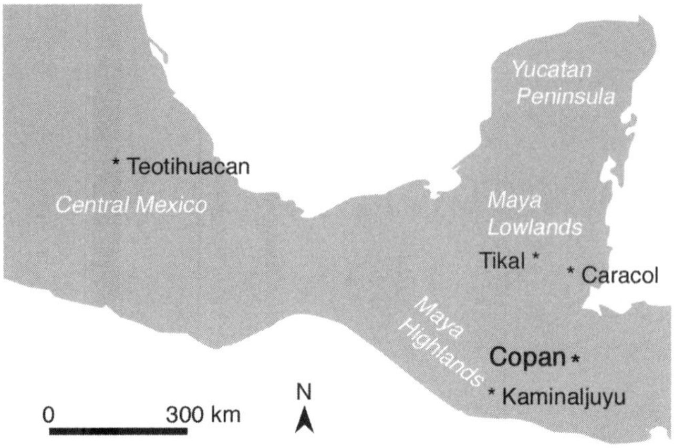

Figure 11.1. Map of Mesoamerica indicating the location of Copan and other key sites mentioned in the text.

Mexico, Oaxaca, and the Maya area (White et al. 2002). However, interpreting $\delta^{18}O$ data is a more complicated endeavor than interpreting $^{87}Sr/^{86}Sr$ data because $\delta^{18}O$ can be affected by much more than geographic variability and food trade. In this chapter, I aim to illustrate some of these complications using a small series of elite skeletons from the Classic-period (A.D. 250–900) Maya city of Copan in Honduras (Figure 11.1). My work with these remains is one component of Buikstra's multidisciplinary life history study in the region. In another publication, Price et al. (2010) found the oxygen isotope data to be less useful than strontium isotopes for studying mobility at Copan. To further explore this issue, I consider variability of both oxygen and carbon isotopes within individual teeth as well as between teeth.

Oxygen Isotopes and the Study of Geographic Provenance

The $\delta^{18}O$ ratios of bones and teeth are determined largely by the composition of water imbibed by an individual at the time the tissues formed (Kohn 1996; Longinelli 1984), offset by a fractionation that is dependent on the body temperature of the organism. The $\delta^{18}O$ of meteoric water, or rainfall, is determined primarily by the paths that weather systems take from their origins over the oceans (where rain clouds form from the evaporation of seawater) and the gradual rain-out of the heavier isotope, ^{18}O, as clouds move across continental land forms. Newly formed over the ocean, tropical clouds (and rainfall) that contain relatively more ^{18}O are referred to as heavy because they contain more of the heavier isotope, while rain from clouds that have already lost much of their ^{18}O is referred to as isotopically light.

The rainwater $\delta^{18}O$ of a given location is thus influenced by its latitude, elevation, and distance from the ocean (Rozanski et al. 1993). These geochemical principles are the basis for the suggestion that $\delta^{18}O$ in human remains might shed light on geographic provenance (Schwarcz et al. 1991; White et al. 1998). The $\delta^{18}O$ of human tissues may differ from that of rain falling in the landscape where people live due to a variety of factors.

Rainwater $\delta^{18}O$ is seasonally variable, both in temperate latitudes and in tropical areas with marked dry and wet seasons. For instance, Stuart-Williams and Schwarcz (1997) documented seasonal variations of 4‰ in Canadian beaver (*Castor canadensis*) dental enamel. The amplitude of the seasonal fluctuations was much smaller than that shown in rainwater (10‰) due to mixing of rainfall with existing surface waters, as well as mixing of water imbibed with the body water reservoir of the beavers. In the tropics, seasonal fluctuation in $\delta^{18}O$ is determined more directly by seasonal variation in the amount of rainfall (Rozanski et al. 1993). Figure 11.2 illustrates the weighted mean $\delta^{18}O$ of precipitation at Ilopango, El Salvador. The inverse relationship between $\delta^{18}O$ and precipitation levels is clear; rainy-season $\delta^{18}O$ averages 7‰ lighter than the meager dry-season rainfall. Naturally, this seasonality in meteoric water carries through to water available in soils and thus available to plants. In Costa Rica, Monteverde cloud forest trees show a 9‰ seasonal variation in wood $\delta^{18}O$ (Anchukaitis 2007).

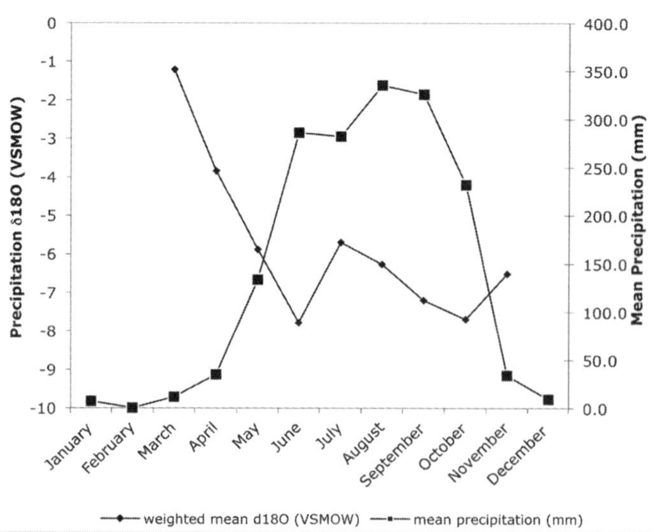

Figure 11.2. Monthly mean precipitation and weighted mean $\delta^{18}O$ of rainwater at the Ilopango weather station, El Salvador, 1968–1984. (Data are from the Global Network of Isotopes in Precipitation database (IAEA 2006).)

Rainfall levels also vary from year to year, contributing to variability in $\delta^{18}O$. Interannual fluctuations in $\delta^{18}O$ are evident in the larger Global Network of Isotopes in Precipitation database for the Ilopango weather station, with values reported ranging from zero to -13‰$_{SMOW}$ (IAEA 2006). This interannual variability is undoubtedly a major contributor to the broad variability of $\delta^{18}O$ values seen at a given site. Climate fluctuation has been shown in $\delta^{18}O$ of ostracods from lake sediments throughout the Maya area. These fluctuations are up to 2‰ over the long term and 1‰ within less than a century (Hodell et al. 1995; Rosenmeier et al. 2002). Though climate change occurs on longer-term cycles than the lives of most individuals, even skeletons buried within a single chronological period can be expected to vary somewhat due to climate fluctuation.

Rainfall recharges the natural and artificial reservoirs that were used by the ancient Maya for drinking water and for culinary needs. The degree to which seasonal variation in rainfall $\delta^{18}O$ will affect drinking water sources depends in part on the size of water reservoirs exploited by humans and their evaporation/recharge ratios. Larger water bodies show less fluctuation than small ones, and less evaporative enrichment. Cultural activities are an unknown contributor to $\delta^{18}O$ variability. In complex societies, social classes may obtain water from different sources; elites may have exclusive access to specific reservoirs, streams, or caves that can differ in evaporation/recharge rates and thus have different $\delta^{18}O$ than water imbibed by the populace at large. Cultural behaviors may also contribute to varied ratios. For instance, extended boiling can be expected to raise the $\delta^{18}O$ of beverages slightly.

At highland Kaminaljuyu, Wright and Schwarcz (1998) documented an average decline in $\delta^{18}O$ of .7‰ between first molars and third molars—probably a consequence of weaning: a dietary change from ^{18}O-enriched breast milk to water. However, we know that children nurse for hugely variable periods and intensities, and the proportions of milk and water they imbibe vary accordingly. While nursing behaviors are culturally shaped, there is substantial variability among infants and mothers within each culture (Dettwyler and Fishman 1992), and this should be expected in the isotope signatures.

These natural and cultural factors contribute to variation in $\delta^{18}O$ over time at any given site and among individuals. Moreover, considerable variability may be expected among the teeth of a single individual (Wright and Schwarcz 1998) or indeed within a single tooth. Since most permanent teeth form over the span of two to four years, seasonal fluctuations in $\delta^{18}O$ may well be visible in dental $\delta^{18}O$ values, if samples are sufficiently precise. Wright and Schwarcz (1998) analyzed samples that spanned from the cervical margin to the cusp of the tooth, thus averaging intratooth fluctuations. However, we should expect considerable variation between cervical and cuspal enamel within a single tooth due to cultural and dietary reasons alone. Hence, the precision of dental sampling is an important issue when comparing the results of oxygen isotope data collected in differing ways. As sampling methods continue to be refined, seasonality, annual fluctuations, and child feeding practices will need to be given more attention in oxygen isotope reconstructions.

In this chapter, I report inter- and intratooth variability in both $\delta^{18}O$ and stable carbon isotopes ($\delta^{13}C$) in tooth enamel from the ancient Maya city of Copan, Honduras. Maize was the primary C4 food consumed by the Maya, thus the $\delta^{13}C$ of the enamel carbonate measures the proportion of carbon that came from maize in the whole diet. Thus $\delta^{13}C$ ratios could highlight gross dietary differences that may also distinguish a foreign skeleton. The goals of this work were twofold: to determine whether or not the oxygen isotope values of the teeth would identify any of the skeletons as nonlocal to the Copan Valley, and to examine variability within and among teeth from an individual skeleton that might be due to climatic, seasonal, or dietary shifts. Because considerable variability was found in the isotope ratios, this small sample provides an interesting cautionary tale.

Copan and the Skeletal Remains

Ancient Maya civilization flourished in the tropical lowlands of Central America during the first millennium A.D. The Classic-period (A.D. 250–900) city of Copan lies in the eastern margin of the Maya lowlands in the valley of the Copan River. The city is well-known for the elaborate sculptural decoration of the monumental architecture located in the city center. The acropolis consists of successive constructions of temples and platforms containing the tombs of several of Copan's epigraphically known rulers. As the decipherment of ancient Maya writing has enabled archaeologists to learn the dynastic history of the kingdom, and as acropolis excavations have revealed elaborate iconography on buried temples and in tombs, questions have arisen about the relationship of the Copan dynasty with distant Maya cities such as Tikal and with other non-Maya states in Mesoamerica such as Teotihuacan (Bell, Canuto, et al. 2004). Thus bioarchaeological techniques that permit the identification of foreign individuals in the tombs gain relevance to a broad archaeological readership.

Tooth samples were collected from eleven skeletons from Copan by Jane E. Buikstra as part of a larger study of life history among Early Classic (A.D. 400–600) Copan elites (Buikstra et al. 2004). The skeletons were excavated from structures in the acropolis of the ancient Maya city by archaeologists from the University of Pennsylvania and Harvard University. The tomb occupants include rulers, female consorts, and perhaps other members of the royal courts, as well as possibly sacrificial victims of unknown origin. Many of these burials were accompanied by elaborate funerary goods, many implying long-distance contacts. Further details of the excavations and funerary contexts can be found elsewhere (Bell, Sharer, et al. 2004; Fash et al. 2004; Price et al. 2010; Williamson 1996).

Burial 95-2 is also known as the Hunal Tomb. Found in a lavish masonry tomb within Structure 10L-16, the skeleton is thought to be the epigraphically known founder of the Copan dynasty, K'inich Yax K'uk' Mo', and the stratigraphic context of the grave is consistent with his reign in the mid-fifth century A.D. (Bell, Sharer, et al. 2004). The skeleton is that of a male, who was older than 50 years at the time of his death, and it shows a number of injuries consistent with trauma inflicted either in battle or perhaps in the ancient Maya ball game (Buikstra et al. 2004). The elaborate structure built over this tomb shows iconographic connections with Tikal, in the central Petén, and with Teotihuacan, in central Mexico, as do the artifacts interred with the skeleton.

Burial 93-2 is commonly known as the Margarita Tomb. It was located within Structure 10L-16 and is slightly later in date than the Hunal Tomb. This tomb had two chambers: an inner mortuary chamber where the skeleton lay, and an outer chamber that contained numerous offerings, including a hieroglyphic monument known as the Xukpi Stone. This monument describes a funerary rite and mentions both Yax K'uk' Mo' and the second ruler of the city. The skeleton in the inner chamber is that of a woman, aged more than 50 years at death. Archaeologists speculate that she may have been the spouse of Yax K'uk' Mo'.

Burial 94-1 has been referred to as the Northern Guardian because this grave was located at the northern entry to the Margarita Tomb. It was probably deposited around A.D. 465 as an intrusive deposit into the Mitzil Platform. The skeleton was not accompanied by any grave goods (Bell, Sharer, et al. 2004). The remains were placed in a seated, bundled position and are those of a male, aged 30 to 50 years at death (Buikstra et al. 2004).

Burial 95-1 was found in an unlined cist, intrusive into a later Early Classic platform called Allamanda that was superimposed over the Margarita structure. It was accompanied by three ceramic vessels, five obsidian dart points, and two shell circles placed over the eyes (Bell, Sharer, et al. 2004). These "goggles" resemble the iconographic depictions of the central Mexican deity Tlaloc, hence the skeleton is sometimes nicknamed the Tlaloc Warrior. The skeleton is male, probably aged 40 years or older; however, the bone preservation was poor (Buikstra et al. 2004).

Burial 92-1 contained the disarticulated remains of a young adult male, aged 18 to 25 at death (Buikstra et al. 2004). The grave was located in the so-called Teal Platform, for which it is sometimes named. Located at the northern limit of the early acropolis and the southern margin of the Northeast Court group, the grave was a simple pit dug into structure fill below the floor of Patio 5B (Bell, Sharer, et al. 2004). The grave contained the dismembered and poorly preserved remains of an adult male.

Burial 93-1, referred to as Uranio, was a flexed interment of a single adult male skeleton located beneath an early platform below the early development of the acropolis. Associated with some burned jade offerings, the skeleton was not accompanied by further grave goods and was not deposited in a formal grave structure.

Burial 92-3 lay below a structure on the west side of the East Court 2B of the acropolis. Bell, Sharer et al. (2004:151–153) identify this grave as containing the remains of the eighth ruler in the Copan dynasty, whose name, Wil Ohl K'inich, is given in the inscriptions on the stairway of the structure containing the tomb. Commonly known as the Subjaguar Tomb, this grave was found below the sculptural Jaguar Stairway, which was added to the structure at a later time. Inscriptions indicate that Ruler 8 died in A.D. 551 after reigning 19 years (Bell, Sharer et al. 2004). However, there is no epigraphic evidence in the tomb itself to identify the occupant, so the identification is not certain. Accompanied by elaborate offerings, the grave contained the poorly preserved remains of an adult skeleton that may have been male. Age can be only roughly estimated, by the advanced state of dental attrition, as older than 35 (Buikstra et al. 2004). (Note: the Subjaguar Tomb was incorrectly published as Burial 92-2 [Bell, Sharer et al. 2004] but should correctly be Burial 92-3 [Price et al. 2010]).

Burial 37-8 is better known as the Motmot Tomb. The grave is from the earliest level of construction of Structure 10L-26, which in its final phase was decorated with an elaborate hieroglyphic stairway. Excavated into the earliest phase during a renovation, the cylindrical stone-lined cist contained the grave of a young adult female (Burial 37-8). The tomb style and seated position are reminiscent of burials at Teotihuacan. Later the grave was reopened and a fire ritual was performed. At this time, three decapitated skulls were added to the grave (burials 37-7, 37-9, and 37-10), and the cist was capped with a circular hieroglyphic monument, the Motmot Stone. Its inscriptions and context indicate that the reopening of the tomb coincided with a calendrical ritual carried out by Ruler 2 on the date 9.0.0.0.0. (A.D. 435) (Buikstra et al. 2004; Fash et al. 2004).

Sampling and Stable Isotopic Methods

Table 11.1 lists the teeth sampled from each skeleton, along with the stable carbon and oxygen isotope results. Dental samples were selected primarily for the purposes of strontium isotope analyses (Figure 11.3) (Buikstra et al. 2004; Price et al. 2010) and aimed to include a tooth that develops in early childhood as well as a third molar (M3)—which forms between 9 and 13 years of age—from each individual. M3s were sampled by cutting a section of enamel spanning from the cusp tip to the cervical margin, 1–2 mm wide, which was ground and homogenized. First molars (M1) develop between birth and 3.5 years of age. A 2-mm-wide span of enamel from the cusp to the cervical margin was removed from the M1s and divided into three samples, each approximately 2 mm wide, of equal length along the dentoenamel junction. These samples were labeled A, B, and C, with A being the cuspal sample, B the mid-coronal sample, and C the cervical sample. For several skeletons, a lateral incisor (I2, which develops from .5 to 4 years) was sampled, and the section was similarly divided into three samples. Two maxillary central incisors (I1) were sampled; because of the longer crown height of these teeth, the samples were divided into four sections of equivalent length. For some teeth, one or more of these components of the section was missing, and all samples could not be analyzed for each tooth. This is admittedly a crude sampling method, but it gave large enough samples for acid treatment to remove diagenetic carbonates. In view of the development of the teeth, each sample corresponds roughly to a year of growth.

The enamel was ground to a fine powder in an agate mortar and pestle and passed through a 50-µm sieve. The powdered enamel was soaked overnight in 1 ml of 1.5 percent sodium hypochlorite solution to remove any organic materials. After rinsing three times with distilled deionized water, the enamel was soaked in 1 M acetic acid, buffered with sodium acetate to pH 4.5, for one hour, with periodic agitation. The enamel was rinsed to neutrality with deionized water and dried at 70°C. Mass spectrometry of the enamel samples was carried out at the Department of Geology and Geophysics at Texas A&M University. The enamel was reacted with orthophosphoric acid at 80°C in a Kiel II carbonate device, and stable isotope ratios were measured on the evolved gases in a Finnegan MAT 251 mass spectrometer. The $\delta^{13}C$ and $\delta^{18}O$ were corrected to the PDB standard by comparison with aliquots of the NBS-19 carbonate standard analyzed in each run.

Stable Isotopes in Copan Tooth Enamel Carbonate

Figure 11.3 illustrates the $\delta^{18}O$ and $^{87}Sr/^{86}Sr$ of those teeth sampled for which Buikstra et al. (2004) and Price

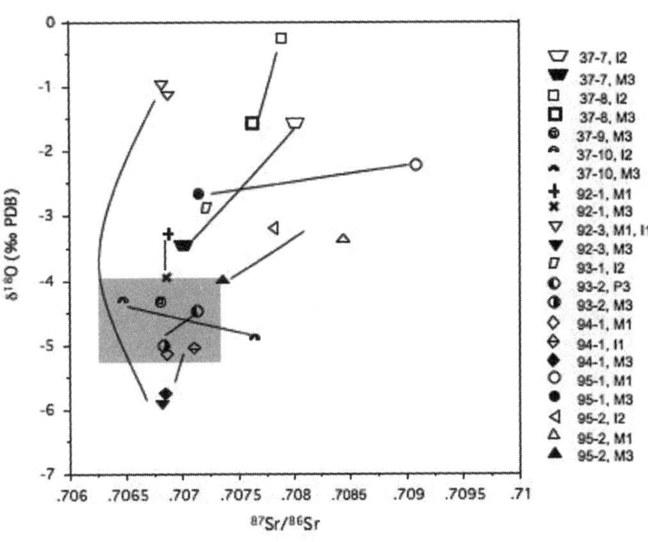

Figure 11.3. Stable oxygen and strontium isotope ratios in tooth enamel carbonate from Copan. Strontium isotope ratios are from Buikstra et al. 2004.

Table 11.1. Stable Isotopes in Early Classic Copan Tooth Enamel Carbonate.

Burial	Nickname	Tooth	Sample	$\delta^{13}C^{1}$	$\delta^{18}O$
92-1	Teal	M1, mand R	A	-.51	-3.19
92-1	Teal	M1, mand R	B	-.25	-3.25
92-1	Teal	M1, mand R	C	-.21	-3.70
92-1	Teal	M3, mand R	whole	-.88	-3.99
92-3	Subjaguar	I1, max R	A	-4.93	-1.10
92-3	Subjaguar	I1, max R	B	-5.94	-.99
92-3	Subjaguar	I1, max R	C	-6.20	-.88
92-3	Subjaguar	I1, max R	D	-4.96	-.25
92-3	Subjaguar	M1, max R	A	-5.23	-1.16
92-3	Subjaguar	M1, max R	B	-5.54	-1.16
92-3	Subjaguar	M1, max R	C	-5.73	-.76
92-3	Subjaguar	M3, mand L	whole	-3.30	-5.96
93-1	Uranio	I2, mand	A	-3.77	-2.81
93-1	Uranio	I2, mand	B	-3.59	-2.97
93-2	Margarita	P3, mand L	whole	-1.86	-4.52
93-2	Margarita	M3, mand R	whole	-2.99	-5.01
94-1	N. Guardian	I1, max R	A	-3.26	-5.03
94-1	N. Guardian	I1, max R	B	-3.04	-5.05
94-1	N. Guardian	M1, mand R	B	-3.46	-5.15
94-1	N. Guardian	M1, mand R	C	-3.09	-5.56
94-1	N. Guardian	M3, mand L	whole	-2.99	-5.77
95-1	Tlaloc	M1, mand L	A	-5.45	-2.28
95-1	Tlaloc	M1, mand L	B	-5.21	-2.21
95-1	Tlaloc	M1, mand L	C	-5.90	-2.29
95-1	Tlaloc	M3, mand L	whole	-4.09	-2.66
95-2	Hunal	I2, mand L	whole	-4.50	-3.17
95-2	Hunal	M1, mand L	A	-4.56	-4.10
95-2	Hunal	M1, mand L	B	-4.40	-3.39
95-2	Hunal	M1, mand L	C	-4.65	-3.36
95-2	Hunal	M3, max R	whole	-2.53	-4.02
37-7	37-7	I2, max	A	-4.47	-1.38
37-7	37-7	I2, max	B	-4.23	-1.66
37-7	37-7	M3, mand	whole	-3.27	-3.44
37-8	Motmot	I2, mand	A	-2.90	-.27
37-8	Motmot	M3, max L	whole	-4.95	-1.63
37-9	37-9	M3, max	whole	-4.63	-4.35
37-10	37-10	I2, mand	A	-3.69	-4.38
37-10	37-10	I2, mand	B	-3.01	-4.52
37-10	37-10	I2, mand	C	-2.40	-4.86
37-10	37-10	M3, max	whole	-2.14	-4.96

Note: Values for $\delta^{13}C$ and $\delta^{18}O$ are given in units permit, relative to the PeeDee Belemnite standard.

et al. (2010) published $^{87}Sr/^{86}Sr$ ratios. For M1s and incisors, the mid-coronal B sample is shown. Samples from the same skeleton are shown with similar symbols and are joined by lines. In $^{87}Sr/^{86}Sr$, Price et al. (2010) define a local range for Copan as .7063 to .7074, based on both commoner human remains and faunal remains, a range that reflects Copan's location on volcanic soils. Lower values (.704–.706) are found in the more recent volcanic soils of highland Guatemala, as at Kaminaljuyu, and in central Mexico at the important early Classic city of Teotihuacan. Higher values (.707–.709) characterize the core of the lowland Maya area, in the sedimentary limestones of northern Guatemala and the Yucatán Peninsula (Hodell et al. 2004; Price et al. 2008).

Price et al. (2010) report $\delta^{18}O$ values on M1 enamel carbonate from eight Copan commoner burials. These average -4.3 ± 0.3‰$_{PDB}$ and exclude two outlying values that must be migrants. Since these M1 values are presumably enriched by nursing, we can consider a local range for Copan enamel to be -4.0 to -5.3‰, to include teeth formed at both breastfeeding and weaned ages. Almost all the skeletons sampled by multiple teeth, including burials 37-10, 92-1, 93-2, 94-1, 95-1, and 95-2, show a $\delta^{18}O$ decline of less than 1‰ between early and later developing teeth, which is consistent with weaning from breast milk to water. This local range is illustrated by a gray box in Figure 11.3. However, its margins should be interpreted with some uncertainty. This range is only slightly higher than the local range measured for Kaminaljuyu (-5 to -6‰$_{PDB}$; Valdés and Wright 2004), probably due to the lower elevation at Copan. Local values at Tikal overlap this range but average higher ratios (-3.2 ± 1.2‰$_{PDB}$; Wright unpublished data), while Teotihuacan (-8.3 to -5.4‰$_{PDB}$ converted from phosphate data) and Monte Alban (-10.3 to -8.2‰$_{PDB}$) show much lower $\delta^{18}O$ (White et al. 1998).

Teeth from burials 93-2 (Margarita) and the early-forming teeth from 94-1 (Northern Guardian) clearly fall within the local box for both isotopes. The M3 for 94-1 is lower and approaches the range measured at Teotihuacan, but the skeleton cannot be definitively identified as foreign based on the $\delta^{18}O$ alone. Certainly, the strontium isotopes identify it as a local skeleton. The M3 of one of the decapitated skulls in the Motmot Tomb (37-9) also shows a local value. Burial 92-1 (Teal) is slightly higher in oxygen than the local box, but given the consistent Sr value, and the fact that the M1–M3 difference is that expected for weaning, it may also be a local oxygen value.

Several individuals show considerable change between the early teeth and the M3 in one or both isotopes. From the Motmot Tomb, a second cranium (37-10) shows a local I2 value but is higher in $^{87}Sr/^{86}Sr$ for the M3, implying a move to another locale for adolescence and a return to Copan in later life. The third cranium from this tomb (37-7) is high in both $^{87}Sr/^{86}Sr$ and $\delta^{18}O$ in the I2, with M3 values close to the local box and equivalent to those of 92-1.

For skeleton 95-2 (Hunal), both I1 and M1 values are higher in $^{87}Sr/^{86}Sr$ and $\delta^{18}O$ than the local range and match values for both isotopes measured at Tikal. However, the M3 falls at the margins of the local box and may be consistent with an adolescence spent at Copan while the M3 was forming. Bone $^{87}Sr/^{86}Sr$ reported by Price et al. (2010) is lower than the M3 value. Accordingly, they interpret Hunal's move to Copan as happening after adolescence. For Hunal, the finding of a foreign childhood is significant in that it confirms iconographic evidence that Hunal was a foreign ruler sent to Copan from another Maya polity. Although the data are consistent with an origin at Tikal, and most discussion emphasizes links with Tikal, Price et al. raise the possibility that Hunal may have spent some time during childhood at Caracol because a reference on Copan Stela 63 seems to suggest he came from there (Stuart 2007). Caracol $^{87}Sr/^{86}Sr$ averages are slightly lower than at Tikal; however, we have no $\delta^{18}O$ data from the site.

The skeleton decorated with Tlaloc goggles (95-1) and placed outside the tomb of Hunal's wife shows high $\delta^{18}O$ for both teeth sampled—higher than the Copan box but in the range of central Petén—and a dramatic $^{87}Sr/^{86}Sr$ decline to Copan. The higher $^{87}Sr/^{86}Sr$ for this individual is beyond the range for Tikal and suggests an origin on quaternary soils or very high consumption of marine foods (with $^{87}Sr/^{86}Sr$ of .7092), as found on the north coast of the Yucatán Peninsula.

Skeleton 92-3 (Subjaguar/Ruler 8) shows local $^{87}Sr/^{86}Sr$ in all teeth sampled. However, the $\delta^{18}O$ of his early-forming teeth is 5‰ heavier than that of the M3, which falls slightly below the local Copan box (but approaches the range of Teotihuacan), indicating a dramatically different source of water in early childhood than adolescence, which may well have been spent at Copan. It is difficult to ascertain where these very high I1/M1 $\delta^{18}O$ ratios would match. One possibility is a Caribbean coastal area with volcanic soils, perhaps in Honduras. The strontium isotope ratios rule out Pacific coastal Guatemala, and the limited $\delta^{18}O$ data from that region are also lower than this. Price et al. (2010) discount the oxygen data for this individual as not reliable in view of the very consistent strontium ratio. Note that if the oxygen isotopes are considered, both of the suspected rulers appear not to have been born at Copan. However, little is known of Ruler 8's ancestry or reign (Martin and Grube 2000).

The M3 of the female in Burial 37-8 (Motmot) is also higher in both $^{87}Sr/^{86}Sr$ and $\delta^{18}O$ than local Copan burials, also suggesting a foreign origin, and is consistent with an adolescence spent in the central or northern Maya lowlands. Of the three skulls, only Burial 37-7 shows comparable values, with a foreign incisor value and a local M3 value. Although the strontium data are consistent with Tikal, the oxygen values are probably too high for the central Petén. Very high values are reported for coastal Belize (Metcalf et al. 2009) though not yet adequately published, so this may be a possible homeland for this royal female.

Thus it seems that more than half of the acropolis burials are those of foreigners who came to Copan from several distant places. The higher $^{87}Sr/^{86}Sr$ identifies most of these as being from areas with Cretaceous limestones (95-2, 37-7, 37-8) or perhaps coastal quaternary deposits (95-1). The higher $\delta^{18}O$ of some of these skeletons may also imply a coastal origin, though the values are quite variable and comparative data is weak.

Figure 11.4 illustrates the relationship between carbon and oxygen isotopes in the tooth enamel of the Copan skeletons, including all the data in Table 11.1. Skeletons are distinguished by symbols, and samples are joined together in order of formation, with lines that stop just short of the M3 data point. There is a broad range in both $\delta^{18}O$ and $\delta^{13}C$; the $\delta^{13}C$ variability is both broader and heavier than that reported for bone apatite (-5.5 ± 1.0‰; n = 27) of adult burials from elsewhere at Copan (Gerry 1993). Oddly, the skeletons with enamel $\delta^{13}C$ consistent with this range are primarily those identified by $\delta^{18}O$ or $^{87}Sr/^{86}Sr$ to be migrants (92-3, 95-1, 95-1). By contrast, the "local" skeleton consumed significantly more maize in childhood than the presumably local adults of Gerry's sample. It is not clear if this is an age or social distinction in diet, however, since Gerry's sample includes few elites.

As described earlier, in Figure 11.3, several skeletons show a slight drop in $\delta^{18}O$ between early developing teeth and M3s, generally less than 1‰, a drop that would be consistent with weaning. However, the age at which this shift occurs is quite variable. Some (95-1, 37-7) show little change among the M1 or I2 samples

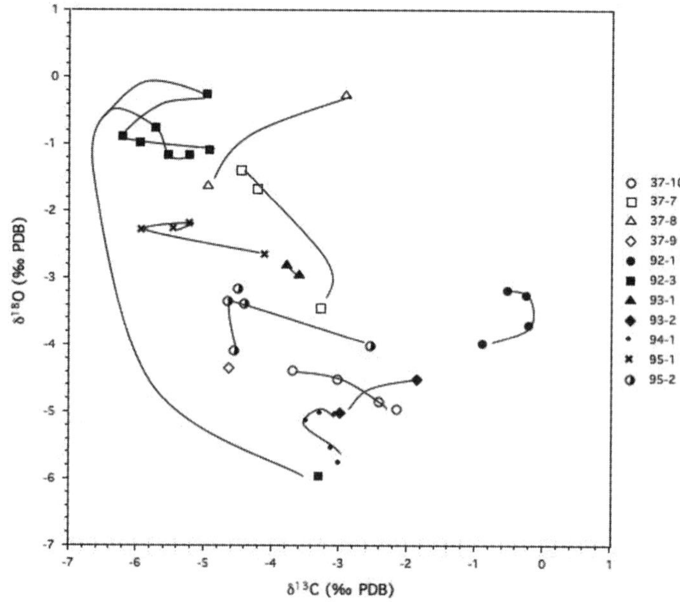

Figure 11.4. Stable oxygen and carbon isotope ratios in tooth enamel carbonate from Copan.

but a larger drop in the M3, while others (92-1, 94-1, 37-10) show greater decline between the mid-coronal and cervical samples of the early teeth, consistent with an earlier weaning age. Interestingly, skeleton 95-2 (Hunal) shows a marked rise between the cuspal and mid-coronal M1 samples, which might be explained if the cuspal sample was formed in utero in this individual and thus reflects the $\delta^{18}O$ of maternal tissues rather than consumption of ^{18}O-enriched breast milk. Given that the samples used in this study presumably average a year of enamel growth or more, seasonality is not likely a huge contributor to this anomaly, though interannual fluctuation in rainfall $\delta^{18}O$ might well be a factor.

In addition to the oxygen isotope changes, carbon isotope changes within and between teeth are variable. Some skeletons show a shift of up to 2‰ in $\delta^{13}C$ between early teeth and the M3, but the direction of this shift is not consistent, indicating quite variable dietary change with age. Among them, several of the migrants (37-7, 37-8, 92-3, 95-2) show quite large $\delta^{13}C$ changes between early teeth and the M3, corresponding to a dietary change that might reflect new dietary customs in the new home, as well as age-related dietary changes. Indeed, the local skeletons show much narrower ranges of $\delta^{13}C$, suggesting less age-related diet change among individuals who remained at Copan throughout childhood.

IMPLICATIONS FOR OXYGEN ISOTOPE STUDIES AND FOR THE MAYA

Interpreting the $\delta^{18}O$ values of Copan tooth enamel is much less straightforward than interpreting $^{87}Sr/^{86}Sr$ data. The oxygen data confirm foreign status for several skeletons, especially that of Copan's first ruler, Yax K'uk' Mo' (95-2); a royal woman (37-8); and the Tlaloc Warrior (95-1), as well as a local origin for several others (93-2, 94-1, 92-1). However, $\delta^{18}O$ values conflict with an apparent local status as shown by $^{87}Sr/^{86}Sr$ in all teeth for the Subjaguar skeleton (92-3), which may be that of Copan's eighth ruler. When compared to his M3 values, the divergently heavy $\delta^{18}O$ and light $\delta^{13}C$ ratios of this individual's M1 and I1 suggest a childhood spent elsewhere and a move to Copan between ages four and nine. He may have come from somewhere in the southeastern Maya area, where $^{87}Sr/^{86}Sr$ is comparable to that at Copan but where $\delta^{18}O$ is substantially higher, but it is difficult to imagine where that might be. Alternately, given his high social status, he may have consumed water from a very different source (evaporatively enriched?) than other Copanecos. However, the shift seems far too large to be explained by either seasonality or local climate change at Copan. Little is known epigraphically of rulers 6, 7, and 8, so there is no reason to rule out a foreign origin for this individual (David Stuart, personal communication 2009). While they appear at times to be at odds with the strontium data, the oxygen isotope results draw attention to possible migrants from areas that are geologically similar to Copan. Although the strontium isotope data alone confirm the epigraphic identification of Copan's first ruler as foreign, only the oxygen isotope data raise the possibility that the probable ruler buried in the Subjaguar tomb may also have been foreign. Thus the data reported here both support the epigraphic record that the city's royalty was tied through marriage and migration to distant parts of the Maya area, and perhaps beyond, and shed light on political history during times that are poorly documented in the inscriptions. Although long-distance contacts between Maya cities, and indeed the exchange of elite marriage partners (Molloy and Rathje 1974), have been known since the earliest decipherments of Maya hieroglyphics, isotope studies provide the first means to identify individual migrants and to reveal the life histories of specific skeletons. The case of Copan is especially important because of its well-documented dynastic history and the recovery of so many elite skeletons.

Unlike strontium isotopes, for which local values can be inferred from bedrock geology (Hodell et al. 2004) or from nonhuman faunal samples (Price et al. 2002), local oxygen isotope signatures should be inferred only from human data. The offset between oxygen isotope ratios in bone and imbibed water differs between animal species because it is dependent on body temperature as well as variable contributions from food and physiological effects (Kohn 1996). Price et al. (2010) have observed that $\delta^{18}O$ does not vary in a simple geographic pattern across Mesoamerica. Although altitude and mountain rain shadow effects provide some predictable patterning on a large scale, within the Maya lowlands, local effects, such as reservoir size and recharge, may be more important. Perhaps due to the substantial interannual variability in $\delta^{18}O$ and the short time (months to a few years) represented by each dental sample, Maya sites studied to date show very broad, overlapping ranges. Thus better mapping of variability in $\delta^{18}O$ from human samples across Mesoamerica is needed. Stable oxygen isotope ratios in teeth should be considered a means to identify the outlying values of nonlocal skeletons rather than a means to identify a specific foreign homeland for those outliers. Although the small numbers of commoner skeletons analyzed to date from Copan help constrain the local ratio for the city, they also illustrate significant mobility in lower social classes of this city (Price et al. 2010), and they emphasize the need for large sample sizes.

Together, these Copan data paint a somewhat confusing picture of early childhood diets and water sources. The carbon isotope data indicate considerable variability in childhood diets and hint that childhood diets differed among sites, given that the migrants show different $\delta^{13}C$ ratios than the local children. In addition to broad overlapping $\delta^{18}O$ ranges among sites, the variability seen in $\delta^{18}O$ among samples from a single individual is marked. As yet, we have no way to determine the contribution of seasonality, climate change, or reservoir size and recharge to variability among $\delta^{18}O$ data from a single skeleton. While it is tempting to interpret individual isotope patterns in terms of life history events, such as weaning and migration, many possible factors could result in the erratic patterning of intratooth $\delta^{18}O$ that we see in this small sample. Undoubtedly, these burials are *not* representative of Copan's population at large, or even of Copan's elites, but they do illuminate the variability in water sources and childhood diets that can complicate the interpretation of isotopic life histories from teeth. Obviously, we must analyze larger numbers of skeletons to identify patterning in life histories using tooth enamel. It will be quite challenging to integrate these individual lives back into a populational perspective on ancient Maya bioarchaeology. Future work should emphasize large samples of skeletons from diverse social contexts to first define local ranges and then to identify outliers. Given the significant interannual variability, and the dramatic changes shown here within individual teeth, consistent and precise sampling of enamel is necessary to ensure comparable data.

Acknowledgements

Clearly, this research would not have been possible without Jane E. Buikstra, whom I also thank for her guidance through the years. I also thank Doug Price and Jim Burton for the strontium isotope data, as well as Bob Sharer and Bill Fash for access to the remains analyzed here. Thanks are especially due to Ethan Grossman, in whose isotope lab the carbonate analyses were completed.

REFERENCES CITED

Anchukaitis, Kevin John
2007 A Stable Isotope Approach to Neotropical Cloud Forest Paleoclimatology. Unpublished Ph.D. dissertation, University of Arizona, Tucson.

Bell, Ellen E., Marcello A. Canuto, and Robert J. Sharer (editors)
2004 *Understanding Early Classic Copan*. University of Pennsylvania Museum of Archaeology and Anthropology, Philadelphia.

Bell, Ellen E., Robert J. Sharer, Loa P. Traxler, David W. Sedat, Christine W. Carelli, and Lynn. A. Grant
2004 Tombs and Burials in the Early Classic Acropolis at Copan. In *Understanding Early Classic Copan*, edited by Ellen E. Bell, Marcello A. Canuto, and Robert J. Sharer, pp. 131–157. University of Pennsylvania Museum, Philadelphia.

Buikstra, Jane E.
1976 Differential Diagnosis: An Epidemiological Model. *Yearbook of Physical Anthropology* 20:316–328.
1977 Biocultural Dimensions of Archeological Study: A Regional Perspective. In *Biocultural Adaptation in Prehistoric America*, edited by Robert L. Blakely, pp. 67–84. Southern Anthropological Society Proceedings No. 11. University of Georgia Press, Athens.

Buikstra, Jane E., and Della C. Cook
1980 Palaeopathology: An American Account. *Annual Review of Anthropology* 9:433–470.

Buikstra, Jane E., George R. Milner, and Jesper L. Boldsen
2006 Janaab' Pakal: The Age-at-Death Controversy Revisited. In *Janaab' Pakal of Palenque: Reconstructing the Life and Death of a Maya Ruler*, edited by Vera Tiesler and Andrea Cucina, pp. 48–59. University of Arizona, Tucson.

Buikstra, Jane E., T. D. Price, L. E. Wright, and J. A. Burton
2004 Tombs from the Copán Acropolis: A Life History Approach. In *Understanding Early Classic Copan*, edited by E. E. Bell, M. A. Canuto, and R. Sharer, pp. 191–212. University of Pennsylvania Museum of Archaeology and Anthropology, Philadelphia.

Dettwyler, Katherine A., and C. Fishman
1992 Infant Feeding Practices and Growth. *Annual Review of Anthropology* 21:171–204.

Fash, William L., Jr., Barbara W. Fash, and Karla L. Davis-Salazar
2004 Setting the Stage: Origins of the Hieroglyphic Stairway Plaza on the Great Period Ending. In *Understanding Early Classic Copan*, edited by Ellen E. Bell, Marcello A. Canuto, and Robert J. Sharer, pp. 65–83. University of Pennsylvania Museum of Archaeology and Anthropology, Philadelphia.

Gerry, John Phillip
1993 Diet and Status Among the Classic Maya: An Isotopic Perspective. Unpublished Ph.D. thesis, Harvard University, Cambridge.

Hodell, David A., Mark Brenner, George Kamenov, Rhonda Quinn, and S. C. Anton
2004 Spatial Variation of Strontium Isotopes ($^{87}Sr/^{86}Sr$) in the Maya Region: A Tool for Tracking Ancient Human Migration. *Journal of Archaeological Science* 31:585–601.

Hodell, David A., Jason H. Curtis, and Mark Brenner
1995 Possible Role of Climate in the Collapse of Classic Maya Civilization. *Nature* 375:391–394.

IAEA
2006 Isotope Hydrology Information System database. Electronic document, http://www.iaea.org/water, accessed March 14, 2008.

Kohn, Matthew J.
1996 Predicting Animal $\delta^{18}O$: Accounting for Diet and Physiological Adaptation. *Geochimica et Cosmochimica Acta* 60(23):4811–4829.

Longinelli, A.
1984 Oxygen Isotopes in Mammal Bone Phosphate: A New Tool for Paleohydrological and Paleoclimatological Research? *Geochimica et Cosmochimica Acta* 48:385–390.

Martin, Simon, and Nikolai Grube
2000 *Chronicle of the Maya Kings and Queens: Deciphering the Dynasties of the Ancient Maya*. Thames and Hudson, London.

Metcalf, Jessica Z., Fred J. Longstaffe, and Christine D. White
2009 Method-Dependent Variations in Stable Isotope Results for Structural Carbonate in Bone Bioapatite. *Journal of Archaeological Science* 36:110–121.

Molloy, John P., and William L. Rathje
1974 Sexploitation Among the Late Classic Maya. In *Mesoamerican Archaeology, New Approaches*, edited by Norman Hammond, pp. 431–444. University of Texas Press, Austin.

Price, T. Douglas, James H. Burton, and R. A. Bentley
2002 The Characterization of Biologically Available Strontium Isotope Ratios for the Study of Prehistoric Migration. *Archaeometry* 44(1):117–135.

Price, T. Douglas, James H. Burton, Paul D. Fullagar, Lori E. Wright, Jane E. Buikstra, and Vera Tiesler
2008 $^{87}Sr/^{86}Sr$ Ratios and the Study of Human Mobility in Ancient Mesoamerica. *Latin American Antiquity* 19(2):167–180.

Price, T. Douglas, J. H. Burton, Robert J. Sharer, Jane E. Buikstra, Lori E. Wright, Loa P. Traxler, and Katherine A. Miller
2010 Kings and Commoners at Copan: Isotopic Evidence for Origins and Movement in the Classic Maya Period. *Journal of Anthropological Archaeology* 29(1):15–32.

Price, T. Douglas, James H. Burton, Lori E. Wright, Christine D. White, and Fred Longstaffe
2007 Victims of Sacrifice: Isotopic Evidence for Place of Origin. In *New Perspectives on Human Sacrifice and Ritual Body Treatments in Ancient Maya Society*, edited by V. Tiesler Blos and Andrea Cucina, pp. 263–292. Springer/Elsevier, New York.

Price, T. Douglas, Linda Manzanilla, and William. D. Middleton
2000 Immigration and the Ancient City of Teotihuacan in Mexico: A Study Using Strontium Isotope Ratios in Human Bones and Teeth. *Journal of Archaeological Science* 27:903–913.

Rosenmeier, Michael F., David A. Hodell, Mark Brenner, Jason H. Curtis, and Thomas P. Guilderson
2002 A 4000-Year Lacustrine Record of Environmental Change in the Southern Maya Lowlands, Petén, Guatemala. *Quaternary Research* 57:183–190.

Rozanski, K., L. Araguás-Araguás, and R. Gonfiantini
1993 Isotopic Patterns in Modern Global Precipitation. In *Climate Change in Continental Isotopic Records*, edited by P. K. Swart, K. C. Lohmann, J. A. McKenzie, and S. Savin, pp. 1–36. Geophysical Monograph. American Geophysical Union, Washington, D.C.

Saul, Frank P.
1972 *The Human Skeletal Remains of Altar de Sacrificios: An Osteobiographic Analysis*. Papers of the Peabody Museum of Archaeology and Ethnology Vol. 63. Harvard University, Cambridge.

Schwarcz, H. P., L. Gibbs, and M. Knyf
1991 Oxygen Isotope Analysis as an Indicator of Place of Origin. In *Snake Hill: An Investigation of a Military Cemetery from the War of 1812*, edited by Susan Pfeiffer and Ronald F. Williamson, pp. 263–268. Dundurn Press, Toronto.

Stuart, David
2007 The Origin of Copan's Founder. In *Maya Decipherment: A Weblog on the Ancient Maya Script* Vol. 2009. Electronic document, http://decipherment.wordpress.com/2007/06/25/the-origin-of-copans-founder/, accessed October 4, 2012.

Stuart-Williams, H. L. Q., and H. P. Schwarcz
1997 Oxygen Isotopic Determination of Climatic Variation Using Phosphate from Beaver Bone, Tooth Enamel and Dentine. *Geochimica et Cosmochimica Acta* 61(12):2539–2550.

Valdés, J. A., and L. E. Wright
2004 The Early Classic and Its Antecedents at Kaminaljuyu: A Complex Society, with Complex Problems. In *Understanding Early Classic Copan*, edited by E. E. Bell, M. A. Canuto, and R. J. Sharer, pp. 327–346. University of Pennsylvania Museum, Philadelphia.

White, Christine D., M. W. Spence, F. J. Longstaffe, H. Stuart-Williams, and K. R. Law
2002 Geographic Identities of the Sacrificial Victims from the Feathered Serpent Pyramid, Teotihuacan: Implications for the Nature of State Power. *Latin American Antiquity* 13(2):217–236.

White, Christine D., M. W. Spence, H. L. Q. Stuart-Williams, and H. P. Schwarcz
1998 Oxygen Isotopes and the Identification of Geographical Origins: The Valley of Oaxaca Versus the Valley of Mexico. *Journal of Archaeological Science* 25(7):643–655.

Williamson, R. V.
1996 Excavations, Interpretations, and Implications of the Earliest Structures Beneath Structure 10L-26 at Copan, Honduras. In *Eighth Palenque Round Table, 1993*, edited by M. G. Robertson, M. J. Macri, and J. McHargue, pp. 169–175. Pre-Columbian Art Research Institute, San Francisco.

Wright, Lori E.
2005a Identifying Immigrants to Tikal, Guatemala: Defining Local Variability in Strontium Isotope Ratios of Human Tooth Enamel. *Journal of Archaeological Science* 32(4):555–566.
2005b In Search of Yax Nuun Ayiin I: Revisiting the Tikal Project's Burial 10. *Ancient Mesoamerica* 16:63–87.

Wright, Lori E., and H. P. Schwarcz
1998 Stable Carbon and Oxygen Isotopes in Human Tooth Enamel: Identifying Breastfeeding and Weaning in Prehistory. *American Journal of Physical Anthropology* 106(1):1–18.

Wright, Lori E., and Christine D. White
1996 Human Biology in the Classic Maya Collapse: Evidence from Paleopathology and Paleodiet. *Journal of World Prehistory* 10(2):147–198.

12

MOBILE BODIES, EMPTY SPACES

WENDY ASHMORE
DEPARTMENT OF ANTHROPOLOGY, UNIVERSITY OF CALIFORNIA–RIVERSIDE

JANE E. BUIKSTRA CONTRIBUTES FUNDAMENTALLY to bioarchaeological understandings and, indeed, to shaping the conduct of far more than this merged domain of biological anthropology and archaeology. I welcome this opportunity to celebrate our collegial friendship and shared interests in the meanings of space in the lives of peoples of the past and present. Whereas Buikstra examines bodily presence in space, the subject here is bodily absence: places where archaeologists anticipate the presence of interred bodies yet none are encountered. Such instances are often appropriately recognized as reflecting acts of disinterment. But in this exploration, I want to consider a wider range of situations that could lead to absence of bodily remains, focusing specifically on a case at the Classic Maya site of Quirigua.[1]

Attention to spatial aspects of mortuary practices has a long history, with tremendously productive expansion in recent years (e.g., Chesson 2001; Goldstein 2006). Perhaps the developments most pertinent here are an enhanced appreciation for the complexity of burial programs, and conjoined issues of social memory and emplaced social identity. Amid these advances, explanations for absence of anticipated human remains center on three alternatives: (1) that soil conditions were not conducive to bone preservation; (2) that subsequent removal took place in ancient or recent times; or (3) that no corpse had ever been interred.

Just as Buikstra and her colleagues mix science and humanism to infer cosmological meaning from Hopewell earthwork construction (Buikstra et al. 1998), I too seek meaning in the material. In this instance, I draw as well from Parker Pearson's (2002:145) comments: "Many monuments and buildings have a funerary or mortuary purpose even though they contain no human bones or bodies—cenotaphs, war memorials, and ancestor shrines are examples. One of the problems for prehistoric archaeologists is how to recognize the funerary dimension of structures and monuments that contain no corpses or body parts."

Not surprisingly, identifying ancient cenotaphs is seldom straightforward. For example, although the spectacular ship burial in Mound 1, Sutton Hoo, initially appeared to lack human remains, prevailing scholarly opinion now holds that acid soils destroyed the remains of an early-seventh-century East Anglian king (Carver 1992, 1998). Even the inclusiveness of a cenotaph *category* is not without challenge. The label *cenotaph graves* at fifth-millennium Varna is reserved for instances where grave goods are arranged as if accompanying an inferred body; when life-size clay masks stand in for human bodies at the same site, the term *mask graves* is used (Chapman 1996; Taylor 2002). Do the latter not fit the definition of cenotaphs? Where do the decedents' remains rest? At Abydos, Egypt, scholars debate which among chambers lacking bodies are "dummy tombs," which are chapels, and for which the term *cenotaph* is appropriate (e.g., Aldred 1984; O'Connor 1998, 2009; Wilkinson 2000). In short, for all these cases, what evidence suffices to infer a "funerary dimension"?

In studies of the pre-Columbian Maya, too, neither the presence nor absence of human remains suffices alone for imputing ancient intent. At Tikal, for example, investigators have grappled for decades with the ambiguity in distinguishing "burials" (that is, deliberate human interments) from "caches" (customarily interment of objects other than human remains). Becker (1992) suggested that all constitute a continuum of expressive forms and considers them alternative expressions of offerings to the earth. Building from his work, Bell (2007) proposes formalizing the neutral term *placed deposit* to encompass this range, leaving inference of meaning to detailed analysis. Among the range of documented Maya placed deposits, Freidel and Guenther (2006) recently reviewed instances they believe are cenotaphs. That is, where royal burials were anticipated, excavation either encountered none or encountered the expected decedent in a separate location. In these cases, the authors highlight particular royal accoutrements—especially jade earflares—as metonyms for corporeal remains, and they consider lidded pottery vessels potential emblems of "soul caches" (compare Houston, Stuart, and Taube 2006; Houston and Taube 2000). Even if the metonyms and lidded containers are adequate and reliable indicators of Maya funerary acts, however, they would seem unlikely to exhaust the options for such expression.[2]

Quirigua SD 6 and Classic Maya Mortuary Ritual

Let me now introduce the crypt whose emptiness prompted this paper topic (Figure 12.1). The chamber in question—Special Deposit (SD) 6—was encountered in 1976 excavations at Structure 3C-2, an earthen mound at the Classic Maya site of Quirigua, in a compound adjoining one of the civic center's two large public plazas (Ashmore 2007; Sharer et al. 1979). Structure 3C-2 was likely part of a domestic compound, found through subsequent research to overlie early civic architecture, masonry construction that Structure 3C-2 postdated by probably more than a century. Despite clear stratigraphic disjuncture, this observation hints further at importance for the location and at special social standing for its occupants.

When the capstones of SD 6 were removed, the chamber's observed contents comprised three pottery vessels (Figure 12.2). The size, form, and construction style of the chamber make it a close counterpart to contemporary burial crypts known at nearby Copan and other settlements in and beyond the region.[3] But to our great surprise at that time, no human remains were encountered. No trace of secondary removal was evident, and preservation elsewhere at Quirigua argues against simple disintegration (e.g., Ashmore 2007; Jones

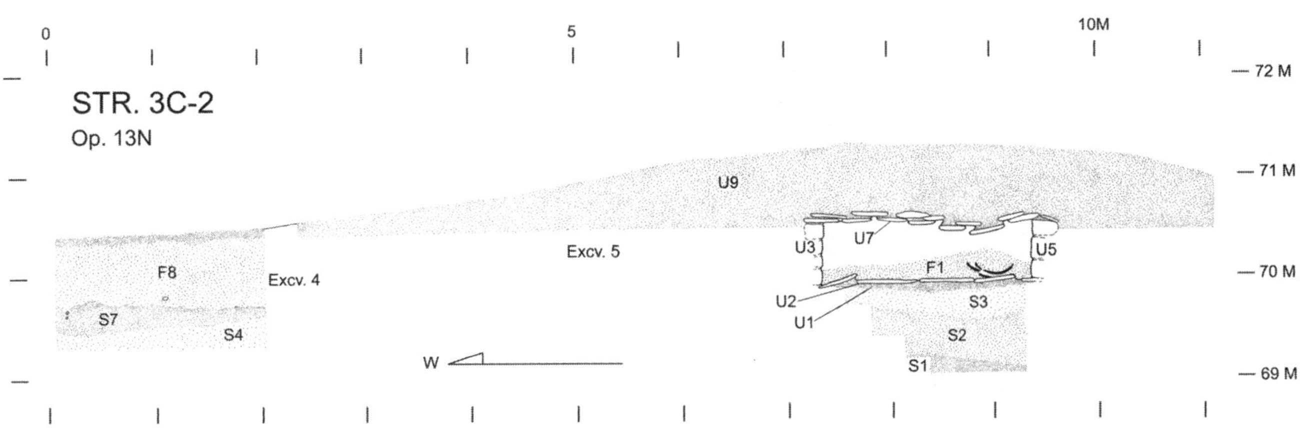

Figure 12.1. Structure 3C-2 excavation section (reproduced by permission of the University of Pennsylvania Museum, from Ashmore 2007:CD Figure 3C.3).

et al. 1983; Sharer et al. 1979). Why, then, would local residents, presumably members of the same family group, have constructed and stocked this relatively elaborate chamber if no corpse were to be interred?

To address that question, let me return to Buikstra, specifically to her critiques of a one-stage "mortuary paradigm." In collaboration with Rakita, she argues that mummification is not necessarily the mechanical step Hertz had envisioned in 1907, one completing the physical processing of corpses. Instead, Rakita and Buikstra suggest that Chiribaya mummies mark a stage in an *extended* mortuary program, whose aim and consequence is to "bridge in an uninterrupted way the divide between the world of the living and the afterworld and continue to structure the lives of [the] descendants" (Rakita and Buikstra 2005:106).

Figure 12.2. Quirigua SD 6 crypt with three vessels, from the southwest. Chamber interior 2 m by .7 m by .6 m (reproduced by permission of the University of Pennsylvania Museum, after Sharer et al. 1979:Figure 9c).

MAYA MORTUARY BELIEF AND PRACTICE

Returning to the ancient Maya, mortuary programs most commonly tied decedents to houses or shrines. And the interment act related simultaneously to passage of the decedent beyond the mundane world of the living and to continuity of the worldly domestic unit, the social house, or the polity (e.g., Geller 2004, 2006; Gillespie 2002).

Drawing from differing but complementary evidence, Fitzsimmons (2002) and Geller (2004) have detailed the intricate processes that most plausibly attended ancient Maya death, mourning, departure of multiple souls, and—in all—social transformation of both the decedent and the living. Notably, these diverse processes and stages potentially extended almost indefinitely in time, material evidence for which includes reentry of burial chambers and frequent removal of select elements of the skeletal remains. At least for royal cases, hieroglyphic texts sometimes explicitly attest to one or more liminal periods separating death, interment, and ritual commemoration of the death, the stated intervals ranging from three days to an extraordinary span slightly exceeding 24 years (e.g., Fitzsimmons 1998; McAnany 1998; Reese-Taylor et al. 2006). These varied spans supported ritual, social, and physical transformations of the corpse, souls, and mourners. We turn now to the location of the decedent while the transformations occurred.

MOBILE BODY ELEMENTS

Particularly important here are material punctuations bounding liminal periods: Maya customs of reentry and removal insofar as these acts relate to empty or emptied chambers. Many documented instances involved multiple, sequential interments, widely viewed as "additive" acts reaffirming social continuities. Such entries are documented both in relatively simple, small-scale interments and in elaborate crypts and tombs (e.g., Bell 2002, 2007; Chase and Chase 1996; Geller 2004; McAnany 1998).

In other cases, however, reentry allowed *removal* of body parts. Fitzsimmons (2002:368) evocatively describes the situation at Caracol as one "where skeletal remains [were] fluid in their transport over the landscape." Across the Maya world, femora, fingers, and especially skulls or faces were those elements removed with greatest frequency. Whether at Caracol or elsewhere, and especially for members of the royalty, the elements removed could be kept as "heirlooms," worn in attire of descendants, and displayed and handled during rites of ancestor veneration or earth offerings (e.g., Becker 1992; Fitzsimmons 1998; Joyce 2000; McAnany 1995; Mock 1998).

Alternately, elements could be removed before and separately from an individual's death, or held in reserve at the time of interment. "Reserving" skulls and face elements would necessarily accompany or follow death; these elements were particularly potent possessions, whether removed in reverence or triumphal capture (Duncan 2005). Epigraphy, iconography, and ethnohistoric sources indicate the paramount significance of the human head, including its standing for the person as a whole (Houston, Stuart, and Taube 2006). Other body parts held strong meaning and could mark antemortem acts. Danien (1989), for example, describes ethnographic accounts of Ixil Maya mothers severing one of their own fingers at the death of a child. Whether or not reflecting such practices in antiquity, what Chase and Chase (1998) call finger caches are numerous enough in their occurrence to be a recognized category of ritual deposition at Late Classic Caracol.

Maintaining connections between the dead and the living was critical to centering ancient Maya society at multiple scales, from house to polity. Increasingly, however, Mayanist scholars recognize that intact bodies were only one reference point for contact and *that their presence was not an absolute requirement*. Body parts, especially but not solely skulls and faces, were powerful material remains for curation and display, to venerate ancestors and as demonstration of social continuity (e.g., Freidel and Schele 1989; Joyce 1998, 2000; McAnany 1998). It becomes increasingly clear, however, that *nonmaterial* remains were equally important, especially the heritable and conjurable names, titles, and *souls* of the deceased (Geller 2004; Gillespie 2002; Taube 2004). The locale of such recognition can materialize the memorialized (Hendon 2000:50). For the Maya, discussions of soul caches certainly come to mind here (Freidel and Guenther 2006; Houston, Stuart, and Taube 2006). If and when the body or its individual elements were unavailable, the deceased could still be acknowledged. Moreover, if the lack of a corpse were due to capture or other violence, the crypt's material recognition as a place for connection and recollection could assume added importance (e.g., Duncan 2005; Metcalf and Huntington 1991). Recalling Parker Pearson's words, cenotaphs, war memorials, and ancestor shrines exemplify commemoration in the absence of bodily remains; from this observation, he urges that archaeologists more often allow for the possibility of such monuments.

Cenotaph commemoration has no single material form, and among the ancient Maya it need not take the specific form outlined earlier. For example, consider the case of Copan's thirteenth ruler, Waxaklahun-Ubah-K'awil. Classic Maya texts indicate his death in A.D. 738 at the hands of the subordinate lord of neighboring Quirigua. Although archaeologists have documented an impressive set of royal tombs at Copan, that of Waxaklahun-Ubah-K'awil has not been found. His remains might lie undetected in areas untouched by excavation. Or it might be that his death at Quirigua deprived heirs and subjects of his formal interment. Half a century later, however, the sixteenth Copan king, Yax Pasaj Chan Yopaat, acknowledged his revered if unfortunate predecessor—his dynastic ancestor—to a degree that some have characterized as near obsession (Stuart 1992). The later sovereign likely commissioned the imposing compound where the earlier king was celebrated in ritual acts and permanent architectonic display of a text bearing his name, royal title, and a date plausibly marking an anniversary of his death (Ashmore 1991; cf. Fitzsimmons 1998; Houston and McAnany 2003; McAnany 1998). That architectural compound, now known prosaically as Copan Groups 8L-10 and 8L-12, ultimately might have sheltered remains of his skull, plausibly returned by later, repacified lords of Quirigua (Figure 12.3) (Ashmore 1991; Ashmore and Geller 2005; Carrelli 1990). At least until that point, however, his memory and acknowledgment had to be maintained in other ways.

QUIRIGUA CENOTAPH

This returns discussion to SD 6, the apparent cenotaph at Quirigua. In contrast to theoretical inferences at the time of field research in 1976, it now seems highly likely that the chamber was material commemoration for an individual whose bodily remains were wholly unavailable for interment. The pottery in the undisturbed crypt tentatively places its construction in the seventh or early eighth century A.D., and pottery types, together with masonry construction and the chamber's location adjacent to a long-standing civic arena, suggest that the decedent was a prominent member of an important Quirigua family (Ashmore 2007).

Figure 12.3. Copan burial XLII-5, Group 8L-10. Cranial fragments were encountered in a vessel in the southeastern corner, at upper left. Chamber interior 1.7 m by .75 m by .6 m (photo by author).

Figure 12.4. Vessel 13N/48-1 from Quirigua Structure 3C-2, SD 2. Height: 8.9 cm; diameter: 15.0 cm (photo by author).

More precisely, the style of one of the three vessels suggests high, if not royal, social and political standing for the person commemorated (Figure 12.4). Although location of the chamber and the structure housing it is beyond the likely physical extent of Quirigua's royal court, at least one of the vessels suggests a gift from that court or perhaps directly from overlords in the Copan court (e.g., Houston, Stuart, and Taube 1992; LeCount 1999). Of the three simple white vessels of SD 6, one was a low cylinder (Ashmore 2007). Not only is this type of cylinder rare in the Quirigua assemblage and in its counterpart version at Copan (Bullard and Sharer 2004; Willey et al. 1994), but also this particular vessel is noteworthy for its potential political message.

The relatively squat cylinder rests on *tau*-shaped feet, recalling distinctive fifth- and sixth-century cylinders emblematic of ties with the great central Mexican city of Teotihuacan (e.g., Reents-Budel et al. 2004; Sharer and Traxler 2006). Such pottery modes are now well-known from a small set of Early Classic Maya capitals, each with further material reference to Teotihuacan—especially its fourth- and fifth-century shaping of dynastic history at Tikal and Copan (Sharer et al. 2005; Stuart 2000; Taube 2004). Copan, in turn, oversaw fifth-century establishment of the Quirigua dynasty, retaining sovereignty over Quirigua until the aforementioned rebellion of A.D. 738. In the interim, prestige goods, as well as utilitarian items and tribute, likely moved between the two capitals and their support populations (e.g., Schortman et al. 2001). Chemistry identifies at least six vessels in a sixth-century royal tomb at Copan as "likely made in workshops at or near Quirigua" (Reents-Budet et al. 2004:185). Lacking chemical signatures for the SD 6 cylinder, its association with upper echelons of Quirigua-Copan society is nonetheless likely, and its role as a gift recognizing an important local person seems probable.[4]

Putative commemoration in SD 6 clearly implies considerable investment of energy and materials. Resultant archaeological traces mark only one episode in what was plausibly a more extended mortuary program. They do so in a manner that we can now understand as materializing the social memory and identity of the decedent, respectful mourners, and determined celebrants of the continued life of the person, the family, and the intricate web of sociopolitical relations of which they were part.

So a puzzle at the time of its excavation has now acquired at least tentative explanation. It is precisely the mobility of Maya bodies that can explain the empty spaces of the chapter's title. That inference is due in significant measure to new thinking and new findings within studies of the Maya past. Its relevance to this volume is the broader set of advances in understanding mortuary practices and the spaces and places of the dead, domains we collectively comprehend better in large measure because of Jane E. Buikstra's work. As the volume editors suggest, the dead *do* tell tales. And it is to Buikstra's skills in reading and translating those tales that we owe much of our ability to learn from them.

Acknowledgments

I thank María Cecilia Lozada and Barra O'Donnabhain for inviting my participation in celebrating Jane E. Buikstra's life and career contributions.

Research at Quirigua (1974–1979) was pursued under contract between the Instituto de Antropología e Historia (IDAEH), Guatemala, and the University of Pennsylvania Museum. William R. Coe and Robert J. Sharer directed research for the University of Pennsylvania Museum, with funding from the National Geographic Society, National Science Foundation (BNS 7602185, 7624189, 7603283), University of Pennsylvania Museum (Francis Boyer Museum Fund), Ford Foundation, Tikal Association, Guatemalan Ministry of Defense, Museum Applied Science Center for Archaeology (University of Pennsylvania Museum), Department of Anthropology (University of Pennsylvania), Landon T. Clay, Alfred G. Zantzinger, and Dr. John M. Keshishian. At IDAEH, I thank directors Dr. Luis Luján Muñoz, Lic. Francis Polo Sifontes, Arq. Marcelino Gonzalez Cano, and our extremely capable foreman, Sr. Enrique Monterroso R. In the field and after, I also thank Bob Sharer, Ed Schortman, Pat Urban, Chris Jones, and Mary Bullard for collaboration and sharing insights. I am grateful to Elin Danien, Ginny Fields, Pamela Geller, Chris Kitchin, Ellen Bell, Gordon Rakita, Christina Halperin, and Tom Patterson for fruitful conversations and helpful critiques. Most of all, I thank Jane E. Buikstra for her many fundamental professional contributions, her stunningly innovative research, her profoundly critical insights, her deeply caring mentoring—and frankly for being such a wonderful colleague and friend.

Notes

1. The Classic period is here defined as circa A.D. 250–950. Pertinent divisions within it are Early Classic (circa A.D. 250–600) and Late Classic (circa A.D. 600–950).

2. An empty chamber at fifth-century Copan, for example, suggests relation to funerary activities at the heart of the early dynastic center, but it remains unclear whether the distinctly smoke-smudged chamber remained completely unused, was emptied of placed deposits, or was a setting for subterranean rituals connected with the nearby tomb of the dynasty's founder (Bell 2007:312; Sedat and López 2004:94–95; Sharer et al. 2005:166; Taube 2004).

3. Only two formal interments were encountered in Quirigua Project research (1975–1979). While neither resembled SD 6, the latter finds close counterparts at Guaytan (Smith and Kidder 1943) and among the hundreds of interments documented at Copan (e.g., Bell et al. 2004; Longyear 1952).

4. Three points about the shape, decoration, and number of supports on the SD 6 cylinder invite further comment. First, while the significance of their *tau* shape and incised design is not certain, it is certainly reminiscent of the Maya glyph *ik'*, which refers to "wind" or "breath" (e.g., Houston, Stuart, and Taube 2006:142–150). The latter is associated strongly with the living soul in Mesoamerica, death being the termination of both breath and soul (Freidel and Guenther 2006; Houston and Taube 2000:267; Houston, Stuart, and Taube 2006:142; Taube 2001:105). For the Maya, wind and the breath soul are identified further with quintessentially precious new green entities—"jade jewels, flowers, and even the occasional green quetzal plume"; moreover, in Maya texts, the "*ik'* [breath] sign . . . typically occurs with the floral sign in the death expression" (Houston, Stuart, and Taube 2006:147).

The second point is that the number of supports on this vessel is unusual; pottery cylinders in Mesoamerica during this time are customarily tripods (cf. Bell 2007; Bullard and Sharer 2004; Longyear 1952; Willey et al. 1994). The unusual tetrapod set on this vessel might represent the four world directions, a pervasive idea with varied iconic expression (Coggins 1980). The distinctive markings, however, suggest intentional choice; I propose that the four *tau* supports of the SD 6 cylinder are meant as *ik'* signs.

This leads to a third point, positing that the vessel design was explicitly part of courtly Maya funerary expression. Taube's remarks about a different Classic Maya context, the text of Naranjo Altar 1, may be pertinent as analog; he calls attention to a "complex glyph composed of four *ik'* signs surrounding a sky glyph, representing the four celestial winds. On closer inspection, it can be seen that these signs are actually the earspools of the wind god" (Taube 2001:109). In other cases, *ik'* signs (including sets of four) adjoin iconic images of flowers, indicating their "breathlike fragrance," and Classic Maya earspools (or earflares), especially those crafted in jade, are material icons for flowers (Houston, Stuart, and Taube 2006:147; Taube 2001:108–109). This recalls Freidel and Guenther's (2006) contention that earspools served as body metonyms in royal Maya cenotaphs. The apparent conjunction of referents—putatively to breath (*ik'*) and thereby implicitly to souls, flowers, and possibly earspools—allows at least tentative inference that this SD 6 vessel owes its form to courtly Maya mortuary expression.

References Cited

Aldred, Cyril
1984 *The Egyptians*. Revised and enlarged ed. Thames and Hudson, London.

Ashmore, Wendy
1991 Site-planning Principles and Concepts of Directionality among the Ancient Maya. *Latin American Antiquity* 2:199–226.
2007 *Quirigua Reports*. Vol. 4, *Settlement Archaeology at Quirigua, Guatemala*. Museum Monograph 126. University of Pennsylvania Museum, Philadelphia.

Ashmore, Wendy, and Pamela L. Geller
2005 Social Dimensions of Mortuary Space. In *Interacting with the Dead: Perspectives on Mortuary Archaeology for the New Millennium*, edited by Gordon F. M. Rakita, Jane E. Buikstra, Lane A. Beck, and Sloan R. Williams, pp. 81–92. University Press of Florida, Orlando.

Becker, Marshall J.
1992 Burials as Caches, Caches as Burials: A New Interpretation of the Meaning of Ritual Deposits Among the Classic Period Lowland Maya. In *New Theories on the Ancient Maya*, edited by Elin C. Danien and Robert J. Sharer, pp. 185–196. Museum Monograph 77. University of Pennsylvania Museum, Philadelphia.

Bell, Ellen E.
2002 Engendering a Dynasty: A Royal Woman in the Margarita Tomb, Copan. In *Ancient Maya Women*, edited by Traci Ardren, pp. 89–104. AltaMira Press, Walnut Creek, California.

2007 Early Classic Ritual Deposits Within the Copan Acropolis: The Material Foundations of Political Power at a Classic Period Maya Center. Unpublished Ph.D. dissertation, University of Pennsylvania, Philadelphia.

Bell, Ellen E., Robert J. Sharer, Loa P. Traxler, David W. Sedat, Christine W. Carelli, and Lynn. A. Grant
2004 Tombs and Burials in the Early Classic Acropolis at Copan. In *Understanding Early Classic Copan*, edited by Ellen E. Bell, Marcello A. Canuto, and Robert J. Sharer, pp. 131–157. University of Pennsylvania Museum, Philadelphia.

Buikstra, Jane E., Douglas K. Charles, and Gordon F. M. Rakita
1998 *Staging Ritual: Hopewell Ceremonialism at the Mound House Site, Greene County, Illinois.* Kampsville Studies in Archeology and History No. 1. Center for American Archeology, Kampsville, Illinois.

Bullard, Mary R., and Robert J. Sharer
2004 *Quirigua Reports.* Vol. 6, *Ceramics of Quirigua.* Museum Monographs. Manuscript on file, University of Pennsylvania Museum, Philadelphia.

Carrelli, Christine W.
1990 Mortuary Practices in Groups 8L-10 and 8L-12, Copan, Honduras. Unpublished B.A. honors thesis, Rutgers University.

Carver, Martin
1992 The Anglo-Saxon Cemetery at Sutton Hoo: An Interim Report. In *The Age of Sutton Hoo*, edited by Martin Carver, pp. 343–371. Boydell Press, Rochester, New York.
1998 *Sutton Hoo: Burial Ground of Kings?* University of Pennsylvania Press, Philadelphia.

Chapman, John
1996 Varna. In *The Oxford Companion to Archaeology*, edited by Brian M. Fagan, pp. 739–740. Oxford University Press, New York.

Chase, Diane Z., and Arlen F. Chase
1996 Maya Multiples: Individuals, Entries, and Tombs in Structure A-34 of Caracol, Belize. *Latin American Antiquity* 7:61–79.
1998 The Architectural Context of Caches, Burials, and Other Ritual Activities for the Classic Period Maya (as Reflected at Caracol, Belize). In *Function and Meaning in Classic Maya Architecture*, edited by Stephen D. Houston, pp. 299–332. Dumbarton Oaks, Washington, D.C.

Chesson, Meredith S. (editor)
2001 *Social Memory, Identity, and Death: Anthropological Perspectives on Mortuary Rituals.* Archaeological Papers 10. American Anthropological Association, Arlington, Virginia.

Coggins, Clemency C.
1980 The Shape of Time: Some Political Implications of a Four-Part Figure. *American Antiquity* 45:727–739.

Danien, Elin C.
1989 Looking Down a Long Time Line: Ixil Vocabulary and Maya Iconography. In *In Love and War: Hummingbird Lore and Other Selected Papers of LAILA/ALILA's 1988 Symposium*, edited by Mary H. Preuss, pp. 23–27. Labyrinthos, Culver City, California.

Duncan, William N.
2005 Understanding Veneration and Violation in the Archaeological Record. In *Interacting with the Dead: Perspectives on Mortuary Archaeology for the New Millennium*, edited by Gordon F. M. Rakita, Jane E. Buikstra, Lane A. Beck, and Sloan R. Williams, pp. 207–227. University Press of Florida, Orlando.

Fitzsimmons, James L.
1998 Classic Maya Mortuary Anniversaries at Piedras Negras, Guatemala. *Ancient Mesoamerica* 9:271–278.
2002 *Death and the Maya: Language and Archaeology in Classic Maya Mortuary Ceremonialism.* Ph.D. dissertation, Harvard University, Cambridge. University Microfilms, Ann Arbor.

Freidel, David A., and Stanley Paul Guenther
2006 Soul Bundle Caches, Tombs, and Cenotaphs: Creating the Places of Resurrection and Accession in Maya Kingship. In *Sacred Bundles: Ritual Acts of Wrapping and Binding in Mesoamerica*, edited by Julia Guernsey and F. Kent Reilly, pp. 59–79. Boundary End Archaeology Research Center, Barnardsville North Carolina.

Freidel, David, and Linda Schele
1989 Dead Kings and Living Temples: Dedication and Termination Rituals among the Ancient Maya. In *World and Image in Maya Culture: Explorations in Language, Writing, and Representation*, edited by William F. Hanks and Don S. Rice, pp. 233–243. University of Utah Press, Salt Lake City.

Geller, Pamela L.
2004 Transforming Bodies, Transforming Identities: Corporeality among the Pre-Columbian Maya. Unpublished Ph.D. dissertation, University of Pennsylvania, Philadelphia.
2006 Maya Mortuary Spaces as Cosmological Metaphors. In *Space and Spatial Analysis in Archaeology*, edited by Elizabeth C. Robertson, Jeffrey D. Seibert, Deepika C. Fernandez, and Marc U. Zender, pp. 37–48. University of Calgary Press, Calgary.

Gillespie, Susan D.
2002 Body and Soul Among the Maya: Keeping the Spirits in Place. In *The Space and Place of Death*, edited by Helaine Silverman and David B. Small, pp. 69–78. Archaeological Papers 11. American Anthropological Association, Arlington Virginia.

Goldstein, Lynne
2006 Mortuary Analysis and Bioarchaeology. In *Bioarchaeology: The Contextual Analysis of Human Remains*, edited by Jane E. Buikstra and Lane A. Beck, pp. 375–387. Academic Press, Amsterdam.

Hendon, Julia A.
2000 Having and Holding: Storage, Memory, Knowledge, and Social Relations. *American Anthropologist* 102:42–53.

Houston, Stephen D., and Patricia A. McAnany
2003 Bodies and Blood: Critiquing Social Construction in Maya Archaeology. *Journal of Anthropological Archaeology* 22:26–41.

Houston, Stephen D., David Stuart, and Karl Taube
1992 Image and Text on the "Jauncy" Vase. In *The Maya Vase Book*, vol. 3, edited by Justin Kerr, pp. 498–512. Kerr Associates, New York.
2006 *The Memory of Bones: Body, Being, and Experience Among the Classic Maya.* University of Texas Press, Austin.

Houston, Stephen D., and Karl Taube
2000 The Archaeology of the Senses: Perception and Cultural Expression in Ancient Mesoamerica. *Cambridge Archaeological Journal* 10:261–294.

Jones, Christopher, Wendy Ashmore, and Robert J. Sharer
1983 The Quirigua Project: 1977 Season. In *Quirigua Reports*, vol. 2, edited by Robert J. Sharer, Edward M. Schortman, and Patricia A. Urban, paper 6, pp. 1–38. University Museum Monograph 49. University of Pennsylvania, Philadelphia.

Joyce, Rosemary A.
1998 Performing the Body in Pre-Hispanic Central America. *Res* 33:147–165.
2000 Heirlooms and Houses: Materiality and Social Memory. In *Beyond Kinship: Social and Material Reproduction in House Societies*, edited by Rosemary A. Joyce and Susan D. Gillespie, pp. 189–212. University of Pennsylvania Press, Philadelphia.

LeCount, Lisa J.
1999 Polychrome Pottery and Political Strategies in Late and Terminal Classic Lowland Maya Society. *Latin American Antiquity* 10:239–258.

Longyear, John M.
1952 *Copan Ceramics: A Study of Southeastern Maya Pottery.* Publication 597. Carnegie Institution, Washington D.C.

McAnany, Patricia A.
1995 *Living with the Ancestors: Kinship and Kingship in Ancient Maya Society.* University of Texas, Austin.
1998 Ancestors and the Classic Maya Built Environment. In *Function and Meaning in Classic Maya Architecture*, edited by Stephen D. Houston, pp. 271–298. Dumbarton Oaks, Washington, D.C.

Metcalf, Peter, and Richard Huntington
1991 *Celebrations of Death: The Anthropology of Mortuary Ritual.* 2nd ed. Cambridge University Press, Cambridge.

Mock, Shirley Botelier
1998 The Defaced and the Forgotten: Decapitation and Flaying/Mutilation as a Termination Event at Colha, Belize. In *The Sowing and the Dawning: Termination, Dedication, and Transformation in the Archaeological and Ethnographic Record of Mesoamerica*, edited by Shirley B. Mock, pp. 115–123. University of New Mexico Press, Albuquerque.

O'Connor, David
1998 Abydos, North, *ka* Chapels and Cenotaphs. In *Encyclopedia of the Archaeology of Ancient Egypt*, compiled and edited by Kathryn A. Bard, pp. 100–103. Routledge, London.
2009 *Abydos: Egypt's First Pharaohs and the Cult of Osiris.* Thames and Hudson, New York.

Parker Pearson, Michael
2002 Placing the Physical and the Incorporeal Dead: Stonehenge and Changing Concepts of Ancestral Space in Neolithic Britain. In *The Space and Place of Death*, edited by Helaine Silverman and David B. Small, pp. 145–180. Archaeological Papers 11. American Anthropological Association, Arlington Virginia.

Rakita, Gordon F. M., and Jane E. Buikstra
2005 Corrupting Flesh: Reexamining Hertz's Perspective on Mummification and Cremation. In *Interacting with the Dead: Perspectives on Mortuary Archaeology for the New Millennium*, edited by Gordon F. M. Rakita, Jane E. Buikstra, Lane A. Beck, and Sloan R. Williams, pp. 97–106. University Press of Florida, Orlando.

Reents-Budet, Dorie, Ellen E. Bell, Loa P. Traxler, and Ronald L. Bishop
2004 Early Classic Ceramic Offerings at Copan: A Comparison of the Hunal, Margarita, and Sub-Jaguar Tombs. In *Understanding Early Classic Copan*, edited by Ellen E. Bell, Marcello A. Canuto, and Robert J. Sharer, pp. 159–190. University of Pennsylvania Museum, Philadelphia.

Reese-Taylor, Kathryn, Marc Zender, and Pamela L. Geller
2006 Fit to Be Tied: Funerary Practices Among the Prehispanic Maya. In *Sacred Bundles: Ritual Acts of Wrapping and Binding in Mesoamerica*, edited by Julia Guernsey and F. Kent Reilly, pp. 40–58. Boundary End Archaeology Research Center, Barnardsville, North Carolina.

Schortman, Edward M., Patricia A. Urban, and Marne Ausec
2001 Politics with Style: Identity Formation in Prehispanic Southeastern Mesoamerica. *American Anthropologist* 103:312–330.

Sedat, David W., and Fernando López
2004 Initial Stages in the Formation of the Copan Acropolis. In *Understanding Early Classic Copan*, edited by Ellen E. Bell, Marcello A. Canuto, and Robert J. Sharer, pp. 85–100. University of Pennsylvania Museum, Philadelphia.

Sharer, Robert J., Christopher Jones, Wendy Ashmore, and Edward M Schortman
1979 The Quirigua Project: The 1976 Season. In *Quirigua Reports*, vol. 1, edited by Robert J. Sharer and Wendy Ashmore, paper 5, pp. 45–73. Museum Monograph 37. University of Pennsylvania Museum, Philadelphia.

Sharer, Robert J., David W. Sedat, Loa P. Traxler, Julia C. Miller, and Ellen E. Bell
2005 Early Classic Royal Power in Copan: The Origins and Development of the Acropolis (ca. A.D. 250–600). In *Copan: The History of an Ancient Maya Kingdom*, edited by E. W. Andrews and W. L. Fash, pp. 139–199. School of American Research Press, Santa Fe, New Mexico.

Sharer, Robert J., and Loa P. Traxler
2006 *The Ancient Maya.* 6th ed. Stanford University Press, Stanford, California.

Smith, A. Ledyard, and Alfred V. Kidder
1943 *Explorations in the Motagua Valley, Guatemala.* Publication 546, Contribution 41. Carnegie Institution of Washington, Washington, D.C.

Stuart, David
1992 Hieroglyphs and Archaeology at Copan. *Ancient Mesoamerica* 3:169–184.
2000 "The Arrival of Strangers": Teotihuacan and Tollan in Classic Maya History. In *Mesoamerica's Classic Heritage: From Teotihuacan to the Aztecs*, edited by Davíd Carrasco, Lindsay Jones, and Scott Sessions, pp. 465–513. University Press of Colorado, Boulder.

Taube, Karl A.
2001 The Breath of Life: The Symbolism of Wind in Mesoamerica and the American Southwest. In *The Road to Aztlan: Art from a Mythic Homeland*, edited by Virginia M. Fields and Victor Zamudio-Taylor, pp. 102–123. Los Angeles County Museum of Art, Los Angeles.
2004 Structure 10L-16 and Its Early Classic Antecedents: Fire and the Evocation and Resurrection of K'inich Yax K'uk' Mo'. In *Understanding Early Classic Copan*, edited by Ellen E. Bell, Marcello A. Canuto, and Robert J. Sharer, pp. 265–295. University of Pennsylvania Museum, Philadelphia.

Taylor, Timothy
2002 *The Buried Soul: How Humans Invented Death.* Beacon Press, Boston.

Wilkinson, Richard H.
2000 *The Complete Temples of Egypt.* Thames and Hudson, New York.

Willey, Gordon R., Richard M. Leventhal, Arthur A. Demarest, and William L. Fash
1994 *Ceramics and Artifacts from Excavations in the Copan Residential Zone.* Papers of the Peabody Museum of Archaeology and Ethnology Vol. 80. Harvard University, Cambridge.

13

Andean Life Transitions and Gender Perceptions in the Past:

A Bioarchaeological Approach Among the Pre-Inca Chiribaya of Southern Peru

María Cecilia Lozada
Department of Anthropology, University of Chicago
Gordon F. M. Rakita
Department of Sociology and Anthropology, University of North Florida

Life stages represent socially and biologically constructed phases during the life span of an individual. The definition of individual stages, and the criteria for transition between them, is culturally defined by societies and often perceived through the lens of biological changes. The result is context-specific age classifications that reflect important elements of the societies that create them. An understanding of such life transitions can serve as a window into the roles and status given to individual members of society, or more broadly to society as a whole (Bernardi 1985; Stewart 1977). Within the studies of life cycles, a very important dimension is the analysis and interpretation of gender (Nemerowicz 1979). As with social age, gender has a socially constructed dimension that often dictates the roles that men and women are to fulfill in life. These gender roles are malleable and in many contexts interwoven with chronological age, social age, biological transitions, and cultural ideals. Despite the prevalence of gender studies, few researchers have examined the relationship between age and gender from past societies using archaeological contexts (Effros 1999; Sofaer 1997).

During the past several decades, mortuary archaeology has been dominated by research focused on the reconstruction of social structure, beliefs about the dead, and treatment of the body (Rakita and Buikstra 2005). In a similar vein, bioarchaeological and mortuary research, interpreted within the context of ethnohistorical data, can be used to understand life cycles and gender construction in the past. These studies may help answer key questions regarding the way societies structured their communities and enforced gender roles.

We are quite fortunate in the Andes to have a wealth of detailed ethnohistorical accounts written during and after the Spanish conquest of Peru that comment on social age and gender construction in precolonial Andean societies. Of course, historical narratives from single authors may result in biased accounts; however, colonial administrative documents and censuses from the Andes appear to be less biased and provide more objective testimonies that may be used to frame individual accounts (Dean 2001). All together, these documents are a valuable source of information that can be used to produce more contextualized models of analysis for the archaeological interpretation of past societies.

To evaluate issues of social age and gender, we have examined the pre-Hispanic Chiribaya society of southern Peru. This coastal group centralized its power on the southern coasts of Peru in approximately A.D. 700–1200 (Figure 13.1). Our previous research demonstrated that the group was a large sociopolitical unit that consisted of economically specialized communities of farmers and fishermen under the authority of a

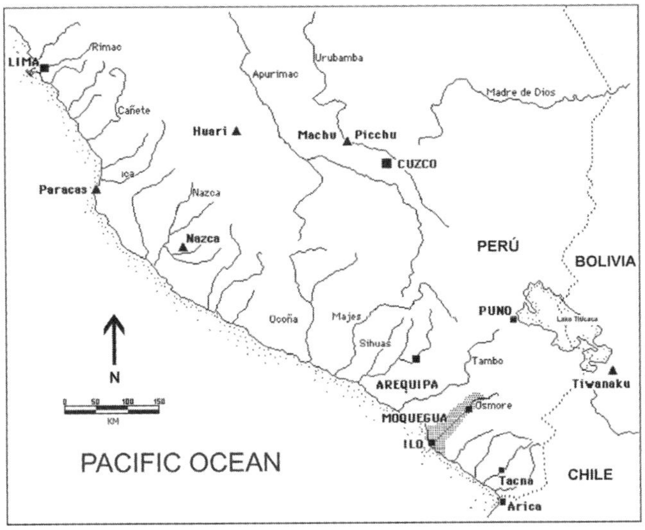

Figure 13.1. Location of the Osmore drainage in southern Peru.

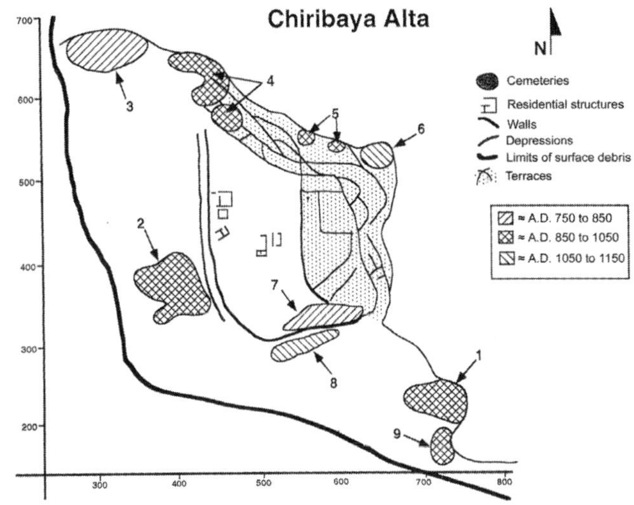

Figure 13.2. Chiribaya Alta, the Chiribaya capital in southern Peru.

paramount lord (Lozada and Buikstra 2002). This type of sociopolitical organization echoes ethnohistorical models of political economy as proposed by Peruvian historian Maria Rostoworowski de Diez Canseco and a number of other Andean scholars. This extensive bioarchaeological study incorporated mortuary data, biological distance studies, analysis of cranial modification styles, and dietary patterns. The fishing community symbolized its group identity by adopting the circumferential type of cranial modification, distinct from the fronto-occipital style used by the agrarian farmers. The cultural differences between fishers and farmers were codified in the body and were reinforced by distinctive dietary patterns, as well as the overall mortuary program (Lozada and Buikstra 2002). For instance, inland communities of farmers consumed more agricultural products, while the fishers' diet was based mostly on marine resources (Tomczak 2003). In addition, the fishers lived close to the shores of the Pacific Ocean and were buried with their fishing tools, while the farmers were excavated from their cemeteries within their communities in the valley.

As stated above, we were interested in studying life transitions and gender construction in this pre-Inca society. With this goal in mind, we examined a collection of 234 individual burials from Chiribaya Alta (Figure 13.2). Due to its size and complexity, the site has been characterized as the center of political power in this coastal society in southern Peru. The mortuary assemblages are extensive, and there is excellent preservation of both organic and inorganic material. The site was excavated by the Chiribaya Project, which was directed by Jane E. Buikstra, with detailed documentation for each of the mortuary contexts.

Through a complete analysis of this collection of burials, we sought to address two main questions:

1. Can material culture be used to identify key transitions in the life of the Chiribaya peoples?
2. Can grave goods aid in the identification of gender construction and/or gender roles in this society?

As mentioned above, life cycles are often related to specific biological or social transitions during the course of an individual's life. The Andean chronicler Guaman Poma de Ayala, born immediately after the conquest of Peru, circa 1550, describes the categories into which the Inca population was divided in both graphic depictions and short narratives. His descriptions are based on Inca census categories called *calles*, or "paths of life." There were 20 total—10 for males and 10 for females (Guaman Poma de Ayala 1988 [c. 1615]:179–189, 201–209). More importantly for our study, these categories help define the features that distinguish one age category from another, both among males and females. As noted by several specialists, these groups do not follow a clear chronological sequence. In fact, Poma's first category is composed of those individuals who contribute the most to the community, either socially or biologically. This group includes males and females between 33 and 50 years, and this classification appears to have been determined in large part by either a person's gender-specific economic activity or by key biological events. In the Inca system, life stages were not marked solely by chronological years but by changes in the functional status of individuals, resulting in a more fluid and less regimented system of age and gender categories. Tables 13.1 and 13.2 summarize the division of women and men by age groups and tasks by this chronicler.

As can be seen from the tables and descriptions, the Inca system of population classification for girls and boys under five years, when children were considered to be dependent on their parents, was mostly related to biological changes. Gender-specific roles appear to develop in Calle 8, after five years of age, when individuals were expected to contribute to their households and society at large. However, Poma depicted baby girls and baby boys differently in all the *calles*, indicating that sexual biological distinctions were very much recognized at birth and remained important throughout an individual's life.

The remaining categories were mostly based on physical activities and duties within specific gender spheres. For instance, females were involved in the production of textiles throughout most of their lives, even if they were sick or old. Females were also responsible for the production of an Andean beer called *chicha*. On the other hand, males had multiple roles, mostly outside the household realm. From Poma's depictions, males were responsible for hunting, herding, warfare,

Table 13.1. Male Life Age Categories According to Poma de Ayala.

Calle Number	Age or Status	Definition of Group
1	33–50 years	Selected group of warriors and active men
2	60 years	Old people who were not obliged to pay tribute but were still able to contribute to agricultural activities
3	> 80 years	Individuals who were inactive due to old age and sickness. If possible, they took care of small animals such as guinea pigs and ducks.
4	With a handicap or birth defect or very sick	Males, young or old, who were handicapped or sick and thus not able to work
5	18–20 years	Males who worked as messengers, took care of animals, and assisted warriors and lords
6	12–18 years	Young males who took care of animal herds, caught birds, and selected feathers for royal garments
7	9–12 years	Male children who were taught to hunt small birds, herd animals, dry meat, and cure animal skins
8	5–9 years	Children who helped their parents with household chores and the care of younger siblings
9	1–5 years	Unweaned children who could crawl
10	Just born	Breast-fed infants under the care of mothers

Table 13.2. Female Life Age Categories According to Poma de Ayala.

Calle Number	Age or Status	Definition of Group
1	33 years	Married and widowed women, responsible for the production of fine textiles for nobles and the production of ordinary textiles for the community
2	50 years	Old woman responsible for the production of ordinary textiles for the community. They also assisted in the household.
3	> 80 years	Old women who mostly slept and ate. If possible, they produced textiles for the community and assisted in the household.
4	With a handicap or birth defect or very sick	Women with birth defects or disabilities. They were expected to reproduce and if possible produce textiles.
5	30 years	Virgin women who married warriors. They were asked to participate in rituals for the sun and temples.
6	12–18 years	Young women who helped their parents and learned to produce textiles while assisting noblewomen. They took care of animals and helped with the production of chicha.
7	9–12 years	Girls who collected flowers and terrestrial and aquatic plants. They prepared dye from the flowers to dye threads for textile production.
8	5–9 years	Girls who helped their parents with household activities and assisted with the care of younger siblings, the production of chicha, and spinning
9	1–2 years	Girls who crawled
10	Just born	Breast-fed infants taken care of by their mothers

and agricultural activities. These life stages among the Inca of precolonial Peru were based on specific tasks and contributions to society, not on strict chronological categories (Rowe 1958). In addition, there are some indications that this system had its roots in pre-Inca populations, which is helpful for our analysis of the Chiribaya (McEwan 2006).

As mentioned by many chroniclers, pre-Hispanic Andean societies routinely buried the deceased with their own belongings, such as their tools of production and other personal items (Cieza de León 1922 [1553]). With this in mind, an analysis of grave goods vis-à-vis the skeletal age of an individual may help identify the life cycles described by Poma. To assess this hypothesis, all Chiribaya skeletons were aged and sexed following standard procedures in physical anthropology (Buikstra and Ubelaker 1994).

Burial items were classified into 1 of the 15 categories that incorporated all types of materials buried with individuals. The presence or absence of each artifact type was registered for each burial. These categories included typical Andean accoutrements found in mortuary contexts, such as bowls, cups, containers for water or *chicha*, pots, *keros* (ritual drinking cups), pitchers, wooden spoons, baskets, textile bags, corn, musical instruments, guinea pigs, gourds, small model boats, and textile tools.

It was possible to identify roughly 8 of the 10 categories described by Poma within the Chiribaya Alta skeletal collection. Calle 4, which included the disabled and individuals with birth defects, was excluded, as none of the skeletons exhibited any osteological evidence of such conditions. We recognize that individuals within this *calle* may have existed within Chiribaya society; however, archaeologically and osteologically this category is extremely difficult to identify, and notions of disability have to be carefully contextualized and analyzed. In addition, calle 5 and calle 1 were combined, since in Guaman Poma's system there is some overlap in the description of the roles of both men and women within these stages of life. A total of 234 skeletons were included in this study, and Table 13.3 illustrates the number of individuals by category.

In the following analyses, males, females, and individuals with undetermined sex were combined and placed into one of the above categories. Differences in associated artifacts between age categories were explored statistically using Fisher's exact test, using a bootstrapping technique to calculate significance. This statistical analysis did not reveal any correlations between types of funerary goods and specific age groups.

Table 13.3. Chiribaya and Poma de Ayala Age Categories.

Chiribaya Age Group	Chiribaya Sample	Guaman Poma's *Calle*
< 1 year	27	10
2–5 years	45	9
6–9 years	19	8
10–12 years	8	7
13–18 years	16	6
19–33 years	53	5 and 1
34–50 years	55	2
50 +	11	3

Although material culture does not appear to have reflected differences in a Chiribaya individual's life cycle, we found interesting differences between the specific age categories and the manner of burial. As illustrated in Figure 13.3, the dominant mortuary pattern among children less than six years was burial in urns. These clay containers were excavated from most of the Chiribaya Alta cemeteries; however, we found no examples of adults buried within these urns.

Apart from his graphic depictions, Guaman Poma did not discuss age categories in much detail. However, in her study regarding children in the Andean colonial period, Caroline Dean indicates that one of the most important periods in the life of an individual was when he or she was weaned and became less dependent on society both physically and socially (Dean 2001:44). In addition, current ethnographic studies in the Andes specific to children suggest that girls and boys between five and six years of age go through an important ritual that marks their social transition into the community. For instance, they are baptized in the traditional Andean sense, in a ceremony called *rutuchikuy*, by having their hair cut for the first time. For this ceremony, the hair is braided and each of the braids has a godfather and a godmother. In addition to monetary gifts, parents give children their own animals and tools of production to help ensure economic integration into the household (Isbell 1997; Portugal Catacora 1988). In sum, while grave goods do not seem to reflect life cycle stages among the Chiribaya, the very important integration of children into society is reflected by the manner in which they were treated at death; children older than six were buried following the ritual used for adults, thus integrating them into the realm of adulthood and productivity.

Although current ethnographic observations and historical records do not describe the use of urns for

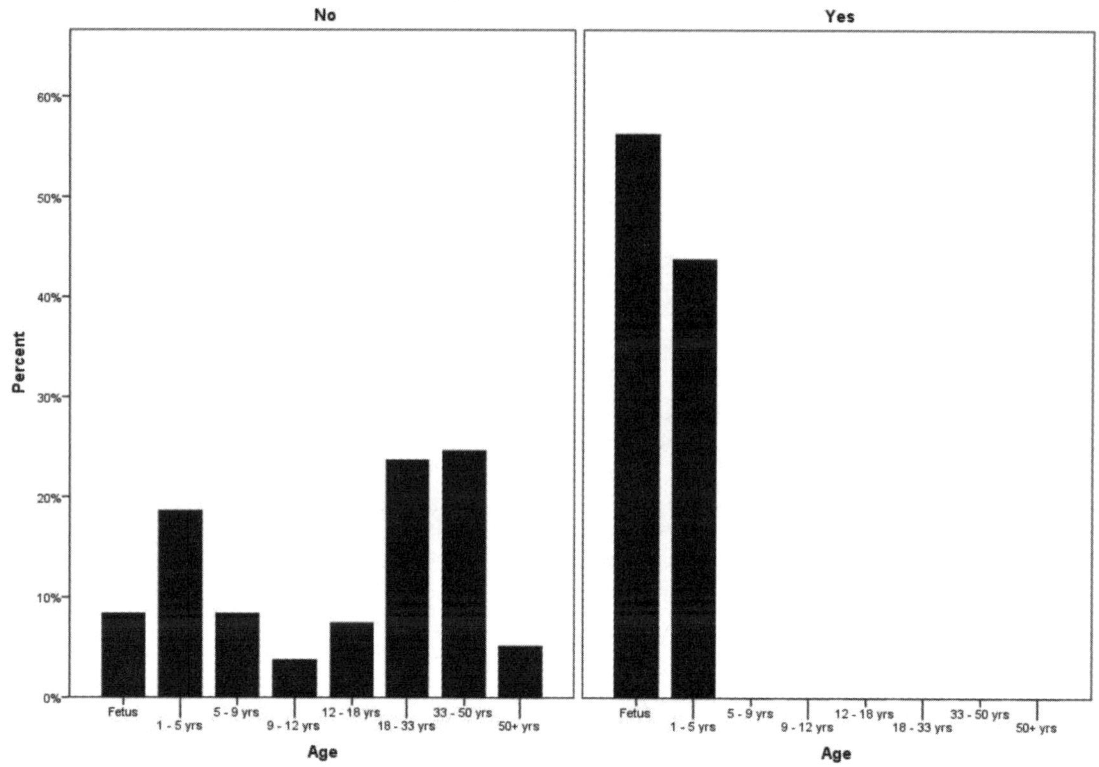

Figure 13.3. Urn burial practice by skeletal age.

the burials of children, we propose that these round clay containers, in which children were buried in a fetal position, can be seen as conceptual "wombs." In fact, in Guaman Poma's chronicles, the first five years of a child's life are characterized as periods without purpose or usefulness, and this idea may parallel the perception of children below the age of five as social "fetuses" who are entirely dependent on their immediate families and larger communities for their social, if not biological, livelihood. Altogether, this Chiribaya study highlights the importance of a multidisciplinary approach to the study of life cycles in pre-Inca societies. These patterns suggest that children were expected to transition to adulthood around age five or six. Although these important events in the lives of Andean people have been documented in contemporary and colonial studies (Dean 2001; Portugal Catacora 1988), this study shows similar ideologies regarding the development children and perceptions of adulthood among the coastal Chiribaya society in southern Peru.

As stated earlier, life cycle transitions are often interwoven with notions of gender. Some of the pioneering research in this area of study has taken place in the Andes, including studies that incorporate ethnohistorical and archaeological data. Researchers such as Joan Gero (2001) and Carolyn Dean (2001), for example, have proposed new methodologies and interpretations about gender in the prehistoric Andes, while researchers such as Isbell (1976) and Harris (1980) stress the dualistic nature of gender constructions, in which one gender is only meaningful when viewed relative to its complement. Furthermore, ethnographers in the Andes have documented the profound importance of gender opposition in indigenous Andean society and link gender differentiation to a person's biological sex. As with the first part of this paper, I would argue that bioarchaeological analyses allow researchers to examine specific nuances of gender behavior in past societies that might not be accessible otherwise.

As noted above, Guaman Poma de Ayala depicts specific roles that both males and females were expected to have as early as five years old, when a child engaged in household chores and became an adult and a "productive" member of society. According to Poma and paralleling modern ethnographies, females produced textiles throughout their lives. As stated earlier, they were also responsible for cooking and the production of *chicha*. Based on these descriptions, researchers have proposed that women kept their work within the household sphere (Dean 2001).

Table 13.4. Association Between Chiribaya Grave Goods and Skeletal Sex.

Artifact Class	Female (n = 73) % Present	Male (n = 51) % Present	Significant P-Value
Bowl	53.4	54.9	
Cup	1.4	39	
Water container	15.1	23.5	
Cooking pot	2.7	0	
Kero	**4.1**	**25.5**	**.006**
Pitcher	42.5	33.3	
Wooden spoon	42.5	43.1	
Basket	31.5	33.3	
Textile bag	26.0	37.3	
Corn	27.4	21.6	
Musical instrument	**1.4**	**15.7**	**.04**
Guinea pig	20.6	15.7	
Miniature boat	15.1	19.6	
Gourd	43.8	43.1	
Textile tool	**34.3**	**3.9**	**< .0001**

On the other hand, men were hunters, herders, and *chasquis* (official carriers) and were involved in warfare. In contrast to women in pre-Hispanic Peru, males ventured abroad, although as "seniors" they might help with some household chores. Can our analysis of funerary goods provide information regarding the gender roles described by Poma? To address this question, we conducted additional statistical tests to see if an item or a group of items was closely associated with either skeletal sex category. In this part of the study, we included only individuals whose skeletal sex was definitive: 73 females and 51 males. Using the same statistical method described in the analysis of age categories, differences in artifact frequency between males and females were explored for the 15 artifact classes. As can be seen in Table 13.4, statistical analysis revealed significant differences between males and females in three types of items.

Male individuals were associated with *keros* and musical instruments, while females were associated with weaving implements (Figures 13.4 and 13.5). These findings are in line with some of Poma's depictions of certain male and female activities in ancient Peru and reflect widespread burial practices throughout the Andes that incorporated gender-specific tasks and identity.

These findings suggest that there were gender-specific activities for males and females among the Chiribaya and that these gender distinctions were represented by the inclusion of certain artifacts in mortuary assemblages. In the Andes, *chicha* is a highly symbolic beverage mostly prepared by women. Among the Chiribaya, its consumption appears to have been exclusive to men, as manifested by the presence of *keros* in male contexts. In pre-Hispanic Peru, this alcoholic beverage, made from corn or *molle* (*Schinus molle*), was used for rituals and feasting both at the community and domestic levels (Bauer 1996; Goldstein 2003; Goldstein et al., 2009; Valdez 2006).

While Poma does not describe the nature of musicians in his work, ethnographic records in the Andes indicate that the use of musical instruments was associated with men (Harris 1980, Stobart 2008). Furthermore, in other archaeological contexts, such as Sipan in northern Peru, musical instruments are exclusively associated with men (Alva and Donnan 1993). Finally, the production of textiles in the household was a female task in pre-Columbian Peru and remains so in the current Andean household. This role seems to have been equally prevalent among Chiribaya women. These patterns of mortuary offerings are highlighted in the burial of a Chiribaya lord accompanied by two adult women. The lord was buried with *keros*, weapons, and musical instruments. In contrast, both females were interred with a vast number of textile implements (Lozada et al. 2009). It is key that we see the same fundamental gender distinctions between males and females in burials across all social strata of Chiribaya society.

Botanical studies by John Dendy (1991) add an additional perspective on the gender distinctions among the burials of Chiribaya Alta. For instance, *lucuma* (*Pouteria lucuma*), an indigenous Andean fruit, was more frequent in female burials. In the Andes, chroniclers document that the fruit was linked with women's fertility. It is said

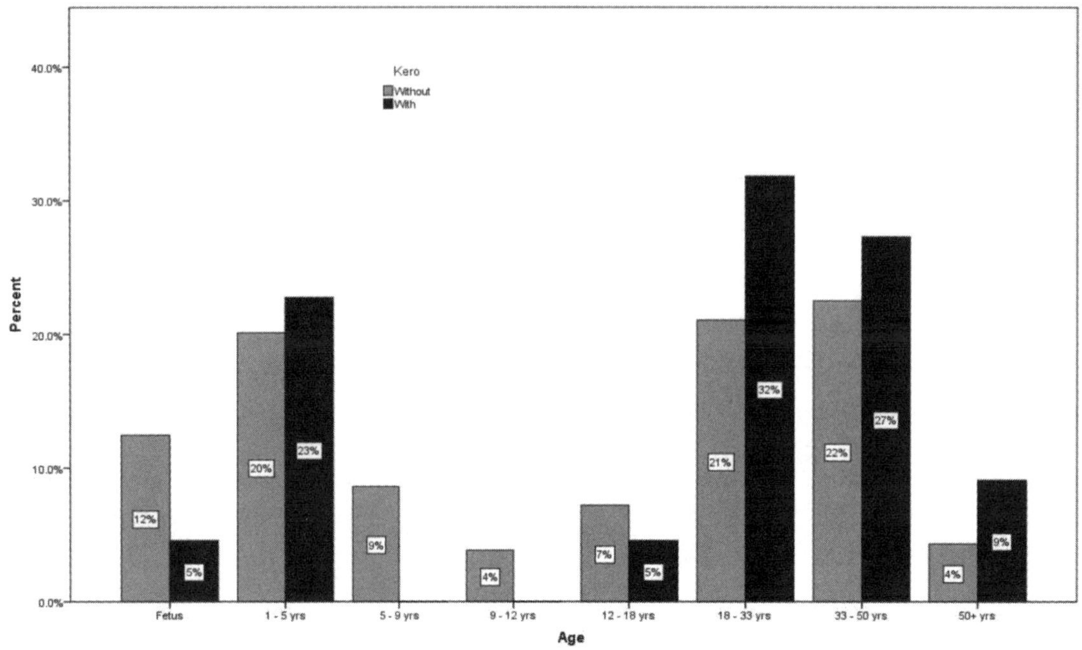

Figure 13.4. Association between keros and age categories.

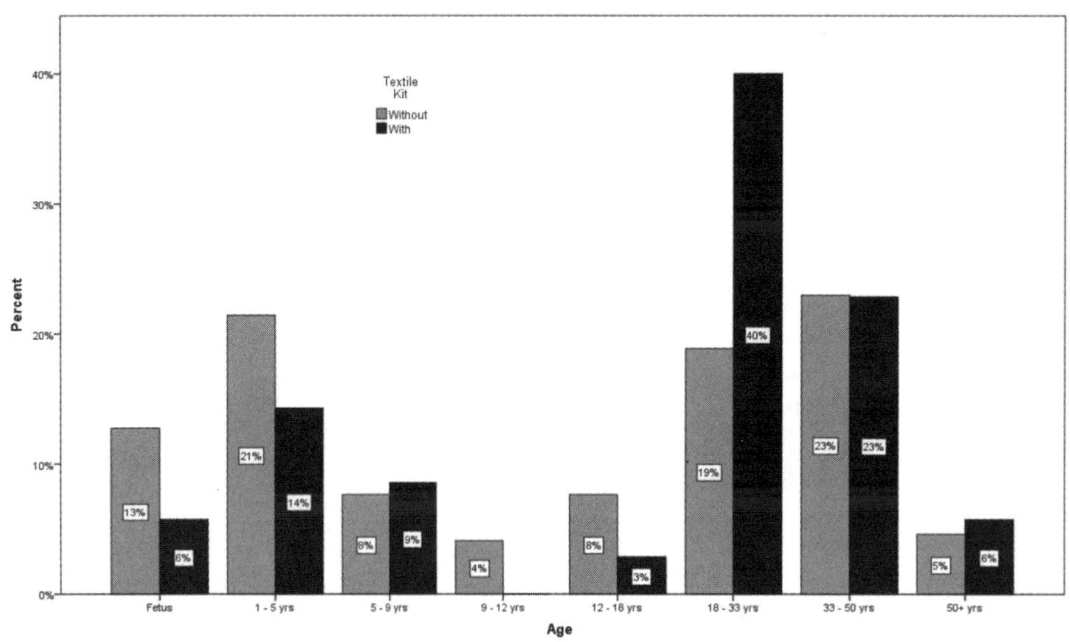

Figure 13.5. Association between textile tools and age categories.

that its form, similar to a female breast, served to nurture the world (Balbi and Cabieses 2003). This symbolic relationship between women and *lucuma* may have been important among the Chiribaya as well. Dendy (1991) also indicates that *molle* berries, also known as Peruvian pink pepper, used in the preparation of *chicha*, were more common in female burials. In this respect, and following Poma's accounts and current ethnographic studies, Chiribaya women were likely responsible for the production of this highly important ritual beverage in their communities.

Although in many cultures children are seen as genderless, it is apparent from Poma's depictions of Andean children that clear distinctions were drawn between males/boys and females/girls. In fact, ethnographic studies in contemporary Andean societies indicate that rituals designed to separate males and females begin as early as the birth of a child. For instance, after birth, the family buries the placenta of a baby boy by the right side of the front door to the home. If the baby is a girl, the placenta is interred on the left side of the door. Furthermore, in certain modern Andean communities it is believed that dreams, interest in particular foods, and the shape of the mother's stomach during pregnancy are all associated with the sex of the newborn baby (Portugal Catacora 1988). We examined burial inclusions with individuals below the age of six, specifically those interred in urns, and found that gender-specific items, similar to those found in adult burials, were included with fetuses and young children, suggesting that even though children under six may not have been active participants in Chiribaya society, distinctions between sexes were recognized early on in life and marked by specific material culture (Figures 13.4 and 13.5). None of the items associated with either adult males or adult females were found together, indicating that there were no cases of mixed gender identity from a cultural standpoint. Of course, short of using a DNA analyses to assess biological sex, it is not possible to assess these relationships further at the present time. With respect to gender construction among the Chiribaya, our results echo ethnohistorical and ethnographic accounts. Specifically, gender distinctions in the Andes appear to be based on biological sex and appear to remain constant throughout the life span of a Chiribaya person.

These two studies of social age and gender have relied on written material, archaeological data, and human biological information to assess social and biological factors that may explain differences between individual burials at Chiribaya Alta. In particular, this multidisciplinary approach underscores the need to move beyond rigid "universal" categories of both age and gender by including contextualized perceptions of individuals and society in the Andes. Furthermore, this study illustrates the fundamental sense of gender duality widespread in Andean societies long before the Spanish conquest of Peru.

References Cited

Alva, Walter, and Christopher B. Donnan
1993 *Royal Tombs of Sipán*. Fowler Museum of Cultural History, University of California Press, Los Angeles.

Balbi, Mariela, and Fernando Cabieses
2003 *Lúcuma un Legado de Sabor Prehispánico* [A Legacy of Pre-Hispanic Tastes]. Ediciones del Autor, Lima.

Bauer, Brian S.
1996 Legitimization of the State in Inca Myth and Ritual. *American Anthropologist* 98(2):327–337.

Bernardi, Bernardo
1985 *Age Class Systems: Social Institutions and Polities Based on Age*. Translated by D. I. Kertzer. Cambridge University Press, Cambridge.

Buikstra, Jane E., and Douglas H. Ubelaker (editors)
1994 *Standards for Data Collection from Human Skeletal Remains: Proceedings of a Seminar at the Field Museum of Natural History*. Arkansas Archaeological Survey Press, Fayetteville.

Cieza de León, Pedro de
1922 [1553] La Crónica del Perú. In *Los Grandes Viajes Clásicos* 24:217–221. Editorial Calpe, Madrid.

Dean, Carolyn
2001 Andean Androgeny and the Making of Men. In *Gender in Pre-Hispanic America: A Symposium of Dumbarton Oaks, 12 and 13 October, 1996*, edited by Cecilia Klein and Jeffrey Quilter, pp. 143–182. Dumbarton Oaks Research Library and Collection, Washington D.C.

Dendy, John. H.
1991 A Descriptive Catalog and Preliminary Analysis of Botanical Remains from Archaeological Excavations at Chiribaya Alta, Lower Osmore Drainage Perú. Unpublished master's thesis, Department of Anthropology, Washington University, St. Louis.

Effros, Bonnie
1998 Skeletal Age and Gender in Merovingian Mortuary Archaeology. *Antiquity* 74:632–639.

Femenías, Blenda
2005 *Gender and the Boundaries of Dress in Contemporary Peru*. University of Texas Press, Austin.

Gero, Joan M.
2001 Field Knots and Ceramic Beaus: Interpreting Gender in the Peruvian Early Intermediate Period. In *Gender in Pre-Hispanic America: A Symposium of Dumbarton Oaks, 12 and 13 October, 1996*, edited by Cecilia Klein and Jeffrey Quilter, pp. 15–55. Dumbarton Oaks Research Library and Collection, Washington D.C.

Goldstein, D. J., Robin C. Coleman, and Patrick R. Williams
2009 Reconstructing Middle Horizon (500–1000 C.E.) Social Dynamics Through Paleoethnobotanical Interpretation of Fermented Beverage Production and Consumption at Cerro Baúl, Moquegua, Perú. In *Drink, Power, and Society in the Andes*, edited by Justin Jennings and Brenda J. Bowser, pp. 133–166. University of Florida Press, Gainesville.

Goldstein, Paul S.
2003 From Stew Eaters to Maize Drinkers: The Chicha Economy and the Tiwanaku Expansion. In *The Archaeology and Politics of Food*

and Feasting in Early States and Empires, edited by Tamara Bray, pp 143–172. Kluwer Academic/Plenum Publishers, New York.

Guaman Poma de Ayala, Felipe
1988 [c. 1615] *El primer nueva corónica y buen gobierno*. 2nd ed. Edited by John V. Murra and Rolena Adorno. Translated by J. L. Urioste. Siglo Veintiuno, Mexico City.

Harris, Olivia
1980 The Power of Signs: Gender, Culture and the Wild in the Bolivian Andes. In *Nature, Culture, and Gender*, edited by Carol MacCormack and Marilyn Strathern, pp. 70–94. Cambridge University Press, Cambridge.

Isbell, Billie Jean
1976 La Otra Mitad Esencial: Un Estudio de Complementaridad Sexual en los Andes. In *La mujer en los Andes*, edited by June Nash, pp. 37–56. Revista de Estudios Andinos Vol. 5, No. 1. University of Pittsburgh, Pittsburgh.
1997 Inmaduro a Duro: Lo Simbólico Femenino y los Esquemas Andinos de Género. In *Mas Allá del Silencio: Las Fronteras del Género en los Andes*, edited by Denise Y. Arnold and A. Spedding, pp. 267–314. ILGA and Institute of Amerindian Studies/Artes Gráficas, La Paz.

Lozada, Maria C., and Jane E. Buikstra
2002 *El Señorío de Chiribaya en la Costa Sur del Perú*. Instituto de Estudios Peruanos, Lima.

Lozada, María C., Juana Lazo Mogrovejo, and Jane E. Buikstra
2009 El Señor y el Curandero: Patrones Funerarios Chiribaya en el Extremo Sur del Perú. In *Arqueología del Area Centro Sur Andina: Actas del Simposio Internacional 30 de junio–2 de Julio de 2005, Arequipa, Perú*, edited by Mariusz S. Ziólkowski, Justin Jennings, Luis Augusto Belan Franco, and Andrea Drusini, pp. 97–110. Boletín del Centro de Estudios Precolombinos de la Universidad de Varsovia. Warsaw University Press, Warsaw.

McEwan, Gordon. F.
2006 *The Incas: New Perspectives*. ABC-CLIO, Santa Barbara, California.

Nemerowicz, Gloria Morris
1979 *Children's Perceptions of Gender and Work Roles*. Praeger Publishers, New York.

Portugal Catacora, José
1988 *El Niño Indígena*. Artex Editores, Lima.

Rakita, Gordon F. M., and Jane E. Buikstra
2005 Introduction. In *Interaction with the Dead: Perspectives on Mortuary Archaeology for the New Millennium*, edited by Gordon F. M. Rakita, Jane E. Buikstra, Lane Beck, and Sloan Williams, pp. 1–11. University of Florida Press, Gainesville.

Rowe, John H.
1958 The Age Grades of the Inca Census. In *Miscellánea Paul Rivet Octogenario Dicata*, pp. 499–522. XXXI Congreso Internacional de Americanistas Vol. 2.Universidad Autónoma de México, Mexico City.

Sofaer, Joanna R.
1997 Age and Gender at the Site of Tiszapolgar-Basatanya, Hungary. *Antiquity* 71:875–889.

Stobart, Henry
2008 In Touch with the Earth? Musical Instruments, Gender, and Fertility in the Bolivian Andes. *Ethnomusicology Forum* 17(1):67–94.

Stewart, Frank Henderson
1977 *Fundamentals of Age-Group Systems*. Studies in Anthropology. Academic Press, New York.

Tomczak, Paula
2003 Prehistoric Diet and Socio-Economic Relationships within the Osmore Valley of Southern Perú. *Journal of Anthropological Archaeology* 22(3):262–278.

Valdez, Lidio M.
2006 Maize Beer Production in Middle Horizon Perú. *Journal of Anthropological Research* 62(1):53–80.

14

A Bioarchaeological Perspective on Inca Imperialism

Kenneth C. Nystrom
Department of Anthropology, State University of New York–New Paltz

Jane E. Buikstra's research is epitomized by broad, holistic projects that integrate the tools and methods available to biological anthropologists, and theory derived from mortuary archaeology. Such a research design provides researchers the opportunity to consider both the biological and cultural consequences of the interaction between groups. There is considerable data, both archaeological and ethnohistorical, regarding the Late Horizon (A.D. 1470–1532) Inca Empire and how administrative policies influenced the sociopolitical infrastructure (Bauer 2004), economics and production (Hastorf 2001; LeVine 1987), and demographics (D'Altroy 2003:273; Grosboll 1993; Murra 1982; Rostworowski and Morris 1999) of conquered groups. To supplement these efforts, I will discuss how Inca imperial policies impacted population history and mortuary behavior in the Chachapoya region of northern Peru. Late Chachapoya (A.D. 1100– 1470) population structure will be reconstructed utilizing a relationship (R) matrix that provid es estimates of genetic differentiation among samples (F_{ST}) and of extralocal gene flow (Relethford and Blangero 1990; Relethford et al. 1997; Steadman 2001). Determinant ratios, which characterize the differences in multivariate variance between groups (Konigsberg 1988; Schillaci and Stojanowski 2003; Stefan 1999), will be used to discuss changes in regional heterogeneity following conquest. The Inca impact on mortuary behavior will by examined by evaluating the evidence for imperial modification of postmortem body-processing techniques. The integration of these sources complements the archaeological and ethnohistorical records and grants archaeologists a fuller appreciation of Inca imperialism.

The Chachapoya and the Inca: Archaeological and Ethnohistorical Data

The people referred to ethnohistorically as the Chachapoya inhabited a large region in the eastern watershed of the Andes in the northern highlands of Peru (Figure 14.1).[1] The broad brushstrokes of early colonial descriptions depict the region as being inhabited by several different tribes, yet they obeyed a single chief during times of war (Sarmiento de Gamboa 1999 [1572]:47) and called themselves by a single name (Garcilaso 1966 [1609]:154). Archaeologically, there appear to be regionwide similarities reflected in architectural construction, symbolic language, and ceramic traditions, yet internal social differences may have manifested in a north–south division of architectural design motifs (Lerche 1995) and mortuary structures (von Hagen 2002).

The predominance of ethnohistorical descriptions revolves around the Chachapoya and their relationship with the Inca. Several authors describe the valiant resistance offered by the Chachapoya (Cieza de León 1998 [1553]:98; Vásquez de Espinosa 1966 [1629]:385), their inevitable defeat (Garcilaso 1966 [1609]:222;

Figure 14.1. Map of the Chachapoya region, with the location of the skeletal samples analyzed and major sites discussed in this chapter indicated.

Sarmiento de Gamboa 1999 [1572]:140; Vásquez de Espinosa 1966 [1629]:387), and the severe consequences of rebellion (Garcilaso 1966 [1609]:220; Pachacuti Yamqui 1927 [1613]:222; Sarmiento de Gamboa 1999 [1572]:163). Though potentially biased, the ethnohistorical records provide insight into imperial policies that could have impacted population structure. In reference to the Chachapoya, the ethnohistorical records indicate significant internal rearrangement of groups and the exportation of large numbers of laborers (Schjellerup 1997).

Archaeological evidence attests to the significance and pervasiveness of the Inca presence, yet imperial control in the province appears to have been variable. Architectural evidence points toward more direct control in the central region, epitomized by the administrative center at Cochabamba (Schjellerup 1997, 1998). Given the size of the site and its limited storage capacity, the primary function of Cochabamba may have been military in nature rather than serving as a collection or redistribution point (Schjellerup 1998). Another site, Inka Llacta, in the northeastern periphery of the Chachapoya region, may have served as a secondary- or tertiary-level administrative center, facilitating the extraction of local resources (Schjellerup et al. 2003). Alternatively, evidence of such direct control is limited in the southern region surrounding Los Pinchudos and Gran Pajatén (Church 1997). Los Pinchudos was constructed in the Late Horizon, and while Inca-style ceramics were recovered, there is no evidence of Inca architectural influences (Morales et al. 2002). Such intraregional variability may reflect a gradual process of increasing imperial influence and consolidation through time. Evidence of an Inca presence or influence has also been noted at Kuelap (Ruiz Estrada 1969), Congona (Ruiz Estrada 1985), Laguna de los Cóndores (Guillén 1998; von Hagen 2002), Papamarca, and a number of Inca *tambos* in the Chuiquibamba region (Schjellerup 1997).

Skeletal samples drawn from mortuary contexts provide the foundation for evaluating the biological and cultural consequences of Inca conquest. Craniometric analyses allow us to consider how the loss of large numbers of individuals due to bloody wars of (re)conquest, compulsory urbanism, and the importation and exportation of laborers would have affected regional phenotypic heterogeneity. The exceptional degree of soft and hard tissue preservation in the region allows for the reconstruction of mortuary behavior and in particular how the body was treated after death.

MATERIALS

Craniometric phenotypic data were collected from three Late Chachapoya (A.D. 1100–1470) skeletal collections (Reichlen, Laguna de los Cóndores, and Laguna Huayabamba) and one Late Horizon skeletal sample (Los Pinchudos).[2] Discussion of changes in mortuary behavior rest upon published data (Guillén 1998, 2003, 2004; Morales et al. 2002) and original observational data from the Laguna Huayabamba sample.

During the course of an archaeological survey of the Chachapoya region, Reichlen and Reichlen (1950) developed a relative chronology of what they considered to be three different cultural periods: Kuelap (circa A.D. 1000–1200), Chipurik (circa A.D. 1200–1400), and Revash (circa A.D. 1400–1470).[3] While craniometric data were generated from all the available crania, those assigned to Kuelap and Chipurik were not used in statistical analyses due to small sample size. The Revash culture was named after a collection of *chullpas* that architecturally and stylistically appear to be of typical Chachapoya construction. Unfortunately, given the nature of the recovery and the relative chronology, the allocation of this sample to the Late Chachapoya period must be considered provisional.

The site of Laguna de los Cóndores consists of a residential component exhibiting Chachapoya, Inca, and colonial-period influence (von Hagen 2002) and a funerary site consisting of six *chullpas* (von Hagen 2002). The remains of approximately 1,000 skeletonized individuals (Guillén 2003) attributed to the Chilchos, a Chachapoya ethnic group (Guillén 1998; von Hagen 2002), were recovered from two *chullpas* (von Hagen 2002).[4] Undecorated bundles, often containing skeletal material from several individuals, were also recovered (Guillén 2003). Based on a series of radiocarbon dates (Guillén 2003; Wild et al. 2007), the investigators consider these forms of body treatments to reflect typical Late Chachapoya mortuary behavior (Guillén 1998; von Hagen 2002). The mummy bundles from the site are described as anthropogenic because of evidence for evisceration and chemical treatment of the skin (Guillén 1998:47) and have been dated to A.D. 1410–1640 (Guillén 2003; Wild et al. 2007). According to the original investigators, following Inca conquest, the Chachapoya remains were relocated to two *chullpas* (Guillén 1998; von Hagen 2002). The Incas then elaborated and reused the remaining *chullpas*, interring Cuzco bureaucrats and *mitmaq* as well as local lords and their kin (von Hagen 2002:143).

The site of Laguna Huayabamba also consists of a residential and a funerary component. There is no architectural or ceramic evidence of Inca presence or influence (Muscutt et al. 1994). The mummified and skeletonized remains examined in this research were recovered from a tomb enclosed by a masonry stone wall (Briceño and Muscutt 2004) and date to the Late Chachapoya period (Fernandez-Davila 2008). Craniometric data were generated from 17 individuals, while examination of the mummified remains provided observational data on mortuary behavior (Nystrom et al. 2010).

Los Pinchudos is a Late Horizon mortuary site with no evidence for a pre-Inca presence (Morales et al. 2002). Contrary to the mortuary site at Laguna de los Cóndores, there is no suggestion that the Inca modified or influenced Chachapoya mortuary architecture. While an earlier report (Kauffmann 1980) depicted several mummy bundles, no mummies were recovered by Morales and colleagues during their more recent excavations (Morales et al. 2002), and only skeletonized remains were available for study (Bracamonte 2002). Morales and colleagues (2002) suggest that the remains were the result of a secondary interment ritual.

Summary data for the three Late Chachapoya skeletal samples examined for this research are provided in Table 14.1.

Biological and Social Consequences of Inca Conquest

To discuss how Inca conquest affected the Chachapoya, we must have an understanding of Late Chachapoya population structure. As mentioned previously, current archaeological interpretation suggests that the region was inhabited by a semi-independent confederation of groups that united only in the face of their common enemy. Measures of regional subgroup genetic differentiation are high (F_{ST} = .09; Table 14.2). The groups also differed in the degree of connection to external gene flow. The residuals in Table 14.2 indicate that the Laguna Huayabamba and Laguna de los Cóndores populations may have had stronger genetic interaction with extraregional sources. On the other hand, the individuals represented by the Reichlen collection were receiving less than average external gene flow (Table 14.2). Taken together, these results suggest that the Inca may have collapsed genetically and phenotypically heterogeneous subgroups. Imperial administrative units were presumably predicated upon some externally derived criteria, and while intraregional differentiation may have existed, the Inca considered the Chacapoya to be a single group and seemingly treated them as such.

The results of the determinant ratio analysis suggest that there was a decrease in sex-specific phenotypic

Table 14.1. Summary Data for the Three Late Chachapoya Skeletal Samples Examined for This Research.

Sample Name	n	Date	Reference
Vira Vira	17	A.D. 1000–A.D. 1150	Fernandez-Davila (2008)
Laguna de los Cóndores	151	A.D. 1100–A.D. 1420[1]	Guillén (2003)
Reichlen	78	A.D. 1350–ca. 1470[2]	Reichlen and Reichlen (1950)

1. The radiocarbon date reported by Guillén (2003) was derived from secondarily reconstructed bone bundles found in the same burial towers as the crania examined for this research.
2. This is the date range originally reported by the Reichlens for the Revash cultural period, to which the crania examined for this research have been attributed.

Table 14.2. Regional Phenotypic Distances to Centroid (r_{ii}), Observed Mean Variance ($\bar{v}_i$), Expected Mean Variance ($E_{(\bar{v}_i)}$), and Residual Variance ($\bar{v}_i - E(\bar{v}_i)$) for Late Chachapoya Populations with Trait Heritability = .55.

	r_{ii}	$(\bar{v}_i)$	$E_{(\bar{v}_i)}$	$\bar{v}_i - E(\bar{v}_i)$
Vira Vira	.2433	.931	.724	.207
Cóndores	.1108	1.006	.851	.154
Reichlen	.0348	.821	.924	-.102
F_{ST} = .0902, se = .0129				

Table 14.3. Between-Time-Period Sex-Specific Determinant Ratios.

Sex	Time Period Comparison	Determinant Ratio	More Variable Period	P-Value
Female	Late Chachapoya–Late Horizon	17.131	Late Chachapoya	.518
Male	Late Chachapoya–Late Horizon	2,034	Late Chachapoya	.394

variability following Inca conquest (Table 14.3). Though not statistically significant, the observed trend toward a loss of phenotypic variation sheds light on the impact of Inca conquest on Chachapoya populations. The most obvious social processes accompanying imperial conquest and consolidation that would have decreased genetic variation are deaths due to violent conflict and the exportation of large numbers of laborers. Indeed, ethnohistorical documents describe the loss or exportation of thousands of Chachapoya.

The exercise of ideological power was a significant theme in Inca consolidation policies (Conrad and Demarest 1984). The modification of local ideology and cosmology would have been a significant means of establishing their legitimate claim to resources. Indeed, it has been suggested that the Inca introduced anthropogenic mummification into Chachapoya. Evidence from two sites, Los Pinchudos and the Laguna de los Cóndores, suggests that pre-Inca Chachapoya mortuary behavior involved secondarily interred skeletal remains. As discussed above, Guillén (2002) suggests that at the Laguna de los Cóndores, the Inca removed the skeletonized remains of the Chachapoya, replacing them with their own anthropogenically mummified ancestors. A series of radiocarbon dates from this site provides evidence for a sequence of mortuary behavior, with skeletonized remains and the undecorated bone bundles preceding anthropogenic mummification (Wild et al., 2007).

Two points are worth considering in relation to this reconstruction (Nystrom et al. 2010). First, evidence from the Laguna Huayabamba indicates that some form of mummification existed in the Chachapoya region before Inca conquest (Fernandez-Davila 2008). While full internal examinations were not conducted, evidence of prolapsed rectums suggests that these mummies were not eviscerated in the same manner documented at the Laguna de los Cóndores (Nystrom 2005b, Nystrom et al. 2010).

Secondly, rather than viewing each type of body processing (for example, secondarily manipulated skeletal remains, bone bundles, anthropogenic mummies) as a discrete and bounded phenomenon, perhaps they should be viewed as phases within a more cohesive mortuary program that involved continued interaction with and manipulation of the remains. At the most basic level, the *chullpas* contain several generations of individuals. The dead could be physically moved, cared for, or, alternatively, destroyed by subsequent generations. Indeed, Guillén (2003:163) notes evidence of rewrapping and the presence of funerary bundles containing the remains of multiple individuals, both of which indicate long-term interaction with and manipulation of the dead. It is equally parsimonious to interpret the sequence of radiocarbon dates as indicative of continued manipulation of the ancestors, resulting in their gradual transformation from fleshed mummies to dry bones (Brown 1981). As new mummy bundles were placed within the *chullpas*, older mummy bundles may have been moved, manipulated, or even rewrapped (Guillén, 2003:163).

CONCLUSIONS

Inca expansion had more far-reaching effects than alteration to local economy or political structure. The same imperial policies that resulted in the construction of administrative centers or the relocation of conquered populations would necessarily have affected population biology. In the Chachapoya region, the impact of these policies can be seen in their effect on regional phenotypic heterogeneity. In other regions, imperial administration affected consumption and diet (Burger et al. 2003; Hastorf 1990; Hastorf and Johannessen 1993); health, trauma, and disease patterns (Andrushko 2007; Murphy 2004; Santoro et al. 2003; Torres-Rouff and Costa Junqueira 2006; Verano 2003); residential mobility (Andrushko et al. 2009); activity patterns (Andrushko et al. 2006; Toyne 2002); and even sacrifice (Eeckhout and Owens 2009). Importantly, the same samples that provide evidence on the biological consequences of conquest allow the opportunity to discuss the cultural impact of conquest, and it is the integration of these data with archaeological and ethnohistorical sources that provides a fuller understanding of the mechanisms and impact of Inca conquest.

Acknowledgments. Funding was provided by the National Science Foundation Doctoral Improvement Grant (BCS-0242941), the Student Resource Allocation Committee, the Office of Graduate Studies, and the Latin American and Iberian Institute of the University of New Mexico. I would like to thank Barra O'Donnabhain and Nene Lozada for organizing the original SAA symposium. And, of course, I would like to thank Jane E. Buikstra for her support and friendship.

Notes

1. Chachapoya refers to the prehistoric province and those populations that inhabited the region. Chachapoyas refers to the modern-day capital and political department.

2. For a more thorough discussion of the steps taken to prepare the craniometric data for analysis, see Nystrom (2005a, 2006). The Reichlen skeletal material has been denoted as "Kuelap" in these publications.

3. It has been suggested that the Revash is only a modification of the Chipurik tradition. Dates are approximate and based on a chronological diagram in Schjellerup (1997:219).

4. The craniometric data utilized in this research was generated from these crania.

References Cited

Andrushko, Valerie A.
2007 The Bioarchaeology of Inca Imperialism in the Heartland: An Analysis of Prehistoric Burials from the Cuzco Region of Peru. Unpublished Ph.D. dissertation, University of California, Santa Barbara.

Andrushko, Valerie A., Michele R. Buzon, Antonio Simonetti, and Robert A. Creaser
2009 Strontium Isotope Evidence for Prehistoric Migration at Chokepukio, Valley of Cuzco, Peru. *Latin American Antiquity* 20(1):57–75.

Andrushko, Valerie A., Elva C. Torres Pino, and Viviana Bellifemine
2006 The Burials at Sacsahuaman and Chokepukio: A Bioarchaeological Case Study of Imperialism from the Capital of the Inca Empire. *Ñawpa Pacha* 28:63–92.

Bauer, Brian S.
2004 *Ancient Cuzco: Heartland of the Inca*. University of Texas Press, Austin.

Bracamonte Ganoza, Florencia
2002 Los Pinchudos: Un Estudio Preliminar de du Población. *Sian* 8(12):14–15.

Briceño, Jesús, and Keith Muscutt
2004 Fardos funerarios Chachapoya en la Laguna Huayabamba. *Sian* 9(15):6–7.

Brown, James A.
1981 The Search of Rank in Prehistoric Burials. In *The Archaeology of Death*, edited by R. Chapman, I. Kinnes, and K. Randsborg, pp. 25–37. Cambridge University Press, Cambridge.

Burger, Richard L., Julia A. Lee-Thorp, and Nikolaas J. Van der Merwe
2003 Rite and Crop in the Inca State Revisited: An Isotopic Perspective from Machu Picchu and Beyond. In *The 1912 Yale Peruvian Scientific Expedition Collections from Machu Picchu: Human and Animal Remains*, edited by Richard L. Burger and Lucy C. Salazar, pp. 119–137. Publications in Anthropology 85. Yale University, New Haven.

Cieza de León, Pedro de
1998 [1553] *The Discovery and Conquest of Peru: Chronicles of the New World Encounter*. Edited and translated by Alexandra P. Cook and N. David Cook. Duke University Press, Durham, North Carolina.

Church, Warren B.
1997 Mas Allá del Gran Pajatén: Conservando el Paisaje Prehispánico Pataz-Abiseo. *Revista del Museo de Arqueología, Antropología e Historia* 7:205–248.

Conrad, Geoffrey W., and Arthur A. Demarest
1984 *Religion and Empire: The Dynamics of Aztec and Inca Expansionism*. Cambridge: Cambridge University Press.

D'Altroy, Terence N.
2003 *The Incas*. Blackwell Publishing, Malden, Massachusetts.

Eeckhout, Peter, and Lawrence Stewart Owens
2008 Human Sacrifice at Pachacamac. *Latin American Antiquity* 19:375–398.

Espinoza Soriano, W.
1967 Los señoríos étnicos de Chachapoyas y la alianza hipano-chacha: Visitas, informaciones y memorials ineditos de 1572–1574. *Revista Histórica* 30:224–283.

Fernandez-Davila, D.
2008 Architecture and Landscape in Vira Vira: Marking Dualisms on an Andean Ridge. Unpublished master's thesis, University of Leicester. England.

Garcilaso de la Vega, Inca
1966 [1609] *Royal Commentaries of the Incas*. Translated by Harold V. Livermore. University of Texas Press, Austin.

Grosboll, Sue
1993 . . . And He Said in the Time of the Ynga, They Paid Tribute and Served the Ynga. In *Provincial Inca: Archaeological and Ethnohistorical Assessment of the Impact of the Inca State*, edited by Micheal A. Malpass, pp. 44–76. University of Iowa Press, Iowa City.

Guillén, Sonia E.
1998 Laguna de los Condores: Donde Viven los Muertos. *Bien Venida* 6:43–48.
2002 The Mummies of the Laguna de los Cóndores. In *Chachapoyas: The Lost Kingdom*, edited by Elena González and Rafo León, pp. 345–387. AFP Integra, Lima.
2003 Keeping Ancestors Alive: The Mummies from Laguna de los Cóndores, Amazonas, Perú. In *Mummies in the New Millennium: Proceedings of the 4th World Congress on Mummy Studies*, edited by Neils Lynnerup, Claus Andreasen, and Joel Berglund, pp.

162–164. Greenland National Museum and Archives and Danish Polar Center, Nuuk, Greenland.
2004 Artificial Mummies from the Andes, supplement, *Collegium Antropologicum* 2:141–157.

Hastorf, Christine A.
1990 The Effect of the Inka State on Sausa Agricultural Production and Crop Consumption. *American Antiquity* 55:262–290.
2001 Agricultural Production and Consumption. In *Empire and Domestic Economy*, edited by T. N. D'Altroy and C. A. Hastorf, pp. 157–178. Kluwer/Plenum Publishers, New York.

Hastorf, Christine A., and Sissel Johannessen
1993 Pre-Hispanic Political Change and the Role of Maize in the Central Andes of Peru. *American Anthropologist* 95:115–138.

Kauffmann Doig, Frederico
1980 "Los Pinchudos": Exploración de Ruinas intactas en la Selva. *Boletin de Lima* 7:26–31.

Konigsberg, Lyle W.
1988 Migration Models of Prehistoric Post-Marital Residence. *American Journal of Physical Anthropology* 77:471–482.

Lerche, Peter
1995 *Los Chachapoya y los simbolos de su historia*. Ediciones y Servicios Gráficos César Gayoso, Lima.

LeVine, Terry Y.
1987 Inka Labor Service at the Regional Level: The Functional Reality. *Ethnohistory* 34(1):15–46.

Morales, Ricardo G., Luis V. Alvarez, Warren B. Church, and Luis C. Tello
2002 Los Pinchudos: Un estudio preliminary de su población. *Sian* 8(12):1–41.

Murphy, Melissa Scott
2004 From Bare Bones to Mummified: Understanding Health and Disease in an Inca Community. Unpublished Ph.D dissertation, University of Pennsylvania, Philadelphia.

Murra, John V.
1982 The Mit'a Obligations of Ethnic Groups to the Inka State. In *The Inca and Aztec States 1400–1800: Anthropology and History*, edited by George A. Collier, Renato I. Rosaldo, and John D. Wirth, pp. 237–262. Academic Press, New York.

Muscutt, Keith, Vincent R. Lee, and Douglas Sharon
1994 Vira Vira: A "New" Chachapoyas Site. *South American Explorer* 39:5–30.

Nystrom, Kenneth C.
2005a The Biological and Social Consequences of Inca Conquest of the Chachapoya Region of Northern Perú. Unpublished Ph.D. dissertation, Department of Anthropology, University of New Mexico, Albuquerque.
2005b Chachapoya Mummies from the Laguna Huayabamba. Proceedings of the 5th World Mummy Congress, Turin, Italy. *Journal of Biological Research* 80:197–200.
2006 Late Chachapoya Population Structure Prior to Inka Conquest. *American Journal of Physical Anthropology* 131:334–342.

Nystrom Kenneth C., Jane E. Buikstra, and Keith Muscutt.
2010 Chachapoya Mortuary Behavior: A Consideration of Method and Meaning. *Chungará Revista de Antropologia Chilena* 42:477–495.

Reichlen, Henry, and Paule Reichlen
1950 Recherches Archéologiques dans les Andes de du Huat Utcubamba. *Journal de la Société des Américanistes* 34:219–251.

Relethford, John H., and John Blangero
1990 Detection of Differential Gene Flow from Patterns of Quantitative Variation. *Human Biology* 62:5–25.

Relethford, John H., Michael H. Crawford, and John Blangero
1997 Genetic Drift and Gene Flow in Post-Famine Ireland. *Human Biology* 69:443–465.

Rostworowski, Maria, and Craig Morris
1999 The Fourfold Domain: Inca Power and Its Social Foundations. In *The Cambridge History of the Native Peoples of the Americas*. Vol. 3: *South America*, edited by Frank Salomon and Stuart B. Schwartz, pp. 769–863. Cambridge University Press, Cambridge.

Ruiz Estrada A.
1969 Alfareria del Estilo Huari en Cuelap. *Boletin del Seminario de Arqueologia* 4:60–65.
1985 Los Monumentos Arqueológicos de Leimebamba. *Boletin de Lima* 7(42):69–82.

Santoro, Calogero, Sheila Vinton, and Karl J. Reinhard
2003 Inca Expansion and Parasitism in the Lluta Valley: Preliminary Data. *Memórias do Instituto Oswaldo Cruz* 98:161–163.

Sarmiento de Gamboa, Pedro
1999 [1572] *History of the Incas*. Translated by Clements Markham. Dover Publication, Mineola, New York.

Schillaci, Michael A., and Christoper M. Stojanowski
2003 Postmarital Residence and Biological Variation at Pueblo Bonito. *American Journal of Physical Anthropology* 120(1):1–15.

Schjellerup, Inge
1984 Cochabamba—An Inca Administrative Centre in the Rebellious Province of Chachapoyas. In *International Congress of Americanists, Manchester 1982*, edited by Norman Hammond and Jeanette F. Peterson, pp. 161–187. BAR International Series 210. BAR, Oxford.
1997 *Incas and Spaniards in the Conquest of the Chachapoya: Archaeological and Ethnohistorical Research in the North-eastern Andes of Perú*. GOTARC Series B, No. 7. Götebotg University, Gothenburg, Sweden.
1998 Aspects of the Inca Frontier in the Chachapoyas. *Tawantinsuyu: Una revista internacional de estudios Inkas* 5:160–165.

Schjellerup Inge, Mikael Kamp Sørensen, Carolina Espinoza, Victor Quipuscoa, and Victor Peña
2003 *The Forgotten Valleys: Past and Present in the Utilization of Resources in the Ceja de Selva, Perú*. Ethnographic Monographs No.1. National Museum of Denmark, Copenhagen.

Steadman, Dawnie W.
2001 Mississippians in Motion? A Population Genetic Analysis of Interregional Gene Flow in West-Central Illinois. *American Journal of Physical Anthropology* 114:61–73.

Stefan, Vincent H.
1999 Craniometric Variation and Homogeneity in Prehistoric/Protohistoric Rapa Nui (Easter Island) Regional Populations. *American Journal of Physical Anthropology* 110:407–419.

Torres-Rouff, Christina, and María A. Costa Junqueira
2006 Interpersonal Violence in Prehistoric San Pedro de Atacama: Behavioral Implications of Environmental Stress. *American Journal of Physical Anthropology* 130:60–70.

Toyne, Marla
2002 Tales Woven in Their Bones: The Osteological Examination of the Human Skeletal Remains from the Stone Temple at Túcume, Perú. Unpublished master's thesis, University of Western Ontario, London, Ontario.

Vásquez de Espinosa, Antonio
1966 [1629] *Compendio y Descripción de las Indias Occidentales*, Vol. 231. Biblioteca de Autores Españoles, Madrid.

Verano, John W.
2003 Human Skeletal Remains from Machu Picchu: A Reexamination of the Yale Peabody Museum's Collections. In *The 1912 Yale Peruvian Scientific Expedition Collections from Machu Picchu: Human and Animal Remains*, edited by R. L. Burger and L. C. Salazar, pp. 65–117. Yale University Publications in Anthropology 85. Yale University, New Haven.

von Hagen, A.
2002 Chachapoya Iconography and Society at Laguna de los Cóndores, Perú. In *Andean Archaeology*. Vol. 2: *Art, Landscape, and Society*, edited by Helaine Silverman and William H. Isbell, pp. 137–155. Kluwer Academic/Plenum Publishers, New York.

Wild, Eva Maria, Sonia Guillén, Walter Kutschera, Horst Seidler, and Peter Steiner
2007 Radiocarbon Dating of the Peruvian Chachapoyas/Inca Site at the Laguna de los Cóndores. *Nuclear Instruments and Methods in Physics Research* 259:378–383.

PART IV

BIOARCHAEOLOGICAL RESEARCH IN EUROPE, AFRICA, AND THE MIDDLE EAST

15

A Brief History of Soft Tissue Paleopathology

Arthur C. Aufderheide
University of Minnesota Medical School, Duluth

The early history of studies on mummified human remains is inseparable from the struggle for public acceptance of human body dissection as part of the search for knowledge of human anatomy. Whatever the gifts of ancient Greece and Rome to modern civilization, these societies did not sanction the dissection of human corpses. The only exception was the famous library at Alexandria in Egypt. The usurpation of Egypt's crown early in the career of Alexander the Great included the construction of a port city in the Nile Delta, appropriately called Alexandria. After Alexander's death in 323 B.C., his principal general, Ptolemy, marched to Alexandria, appointed himself pharaoh, and built a huge library/museum. He attracted the most educated and creative scholars of the day, housed them there, and commanded only a single charge: "Create knowledge!" In the area of human anatomy, he provided his professional staff with the corpses of executed criminals for the purpose of dissection. In spite of later multiple raids and fires, this arrangement endured about seven centuries. Tragically, none of their publications dealing with human anatomy survived the vandalism of the early medieval period. The 50 generations of the Middle Ages were doomed to live their lives with an erroneous concept of disease that provided them with little if any useful medical knowledge (Long 1965:9–11; Lyons and Petrucelli 1987:399; Porter 1996:60).

It was the universities of northern Italy at Bologna and Padua that implemented the freedom of thought that swept through Europe in the 1500s. Human dissection—attended not only by physicians and anatomists but also by artists—soon became a standard option in their curriculum. Its impact is still evident in the muscular images on the Vatican's Sistine Chapel ceiling.

By the 1700s, occasional, isolated mummies were being dissected. In 1763 the British physician John Hadley (1764) unwrapped an Egyptian mummy. In 1794 John F. Blumenbach "unrolled" several Egyptian mummies, at least one of which was an ancient fraud. The physician Augustus Granville (1825) records a number of such somewhat casual examinations of Egyptian mummies by others. He himself found a large ovarian cyst in a mummy.

While the mid-nineteenth century in Europe is most well-known for advances in medical knowledge resulting from the human dissections of hospital deaths (autopsies) in Vienna and Berlin (Long 1965:102–106; Malkin 1993:114), it also documents a shift in medical viewpoints. This shift reflected awareness that mummies might be capable of adding to the developing medical database. In Britain, hucksters entertained paying customers by unwrapping Egyptian mummies in theaters and halls. Some people, however, explored mummy bodies in a serious effort to gain medical knowledge. Thomas J. Pettigrew, a British physician, taught university courses built around autopsy-based medical seminars. These included five lectures (one to two hours each) about Egyptian and other mummies, plus what today we would call a laboratory session. The latter consisted of unwrapping a mummy, followed by a meticulous dissection of the thoracic and abdominal viscera. By 1834 he had accumulated enough knowledge to share it with the public in a different form—a book (*A History of Egyptian Mummies*) that also included Gaunche mummies from the Canary Islands, as well as some Peruvian mummies, Burma priest mummies, and catacomb mummies from the Capuchin monastery of Palermo, Sicily. The intellectual climate was now receptive to the new field of mummy studies.

The Pioneers

Marc Armand Ruffer

If the field of mummy studies has a specific founder, it is Sir Marc Armand Ruffer. He was born into an aristocratic family in Lyon, France, in 1859, was educated at Oxford, and became a physician at University College in London. He was appointed professor of pathology in Cairo's new medical school in 1896 (Moodie 1921).

Ruffer's arrival in Cairo coincided with a surge of interest in Egyptian archaeology. Indeed, worldwide interest during this period is often termed Egyptomania. In 1881 a cache of pharaonic mummies was found in the Valley of the Kings, and nine more were found in 1898. Ruffer was invited to study these bodies, though only minimal dissection was permitted. In many of these mummies, however, portions of the corpse had suffered focal areas of decay that allowed Ruffer access to viscera, which could be sampled with minimal destructive effects. Most of Ruffer's diagnoses were based only on gross examination. Ruffer attempted to carry out microscopic tissue studies. He developed a method for rehydrating tissues and embedding samples in paraffin. Though his efforts had partial success and his method is still employed today, his histological observations made only modest diagnostic contributions to paleopathology. The list of diseases he identified would certainly have been much longer had he not suffered an untimely death in 1917, when, returning from a consultation dealing with public health problems in Greece, his ship was torpedoed. His principal contribution was the demonstration of the presence of information of medical interest in ancient, mummified human remains. After his death, his friend Roy Moodie (1921) collected his writings and published them in book form under Ruffer's name (*Studies in the Paleopathology of Egypt*).

Grafton Elliot Smith

Smith was a contemporary and colleague of Ruffer. A British-trained Australian neuroanatomist, Smith was head of the Department of Anatomy in the Cairo Medical School from 1900 to 1909. He was asked to examine all the royal Egyptian mummies. His enthusiastic response subsequently included not only most of those but also a vast number of other mummies. He is often credited with "examining" 30,000 Egyptian mummies (Dawson 1938), though he left us few descriptions or records of individually studied mummies outside of those of the pharaohs. Although Smith had an interest in diseases, his principal contribution to Egyptology was his focus on the methods employed by ancient embalmers to preserve corpses' soft tissues. His book (coauthored by Warren R. Dawson) *Egyptian Mummies* (Smith and Dawson 1991 [1924]) remains a classic.

Alfred Lucas

The British chemist Alfred Lucas applied his chemical knowledge to many aspects of Egyptian life as a member of Egypt's Department of Antiquities. He tested and identified coffin wood, textiles, foods, ornaments, and many other items. Compared to today's chemistry data bank, his chemical tools were primitive. Yet his book *Ancient Egyptian Materials and Industries* (1926) is even today a source of reliable information.

In spite of the exuberance that fueled the study of mummies during the first three decades of the twentieth century, a variety of factors combined to direct attention and activities away from mummy studies. Probably the most significant exception was what became known as the Manchester Museum Mummy Project (Murray 1910). That museum housed a large collection of Egyptian mummies. In 1910 its curator, Margaret Murray, launched an investigative study on two mummies that initially appeared to be well preserved. Although unwrapping their bodies revealed a degree of preservation much less than anticipated, a major examination of the textiles was a rich reward for the effort—sufficient to permit Murray's ultimate successor, Dr. Rosalie David, in 1975 to expand the project into what today is probably the largest mummy study program in the world outside of Egypt (David 1979). (For the contribution of Egyptology to paleopathology, see also Amelagos and Mills 1993.)

PALEOPATHOLOGY ORGANIZATIONS

The technological explosion following World War II spawned revived interest in mummies. A. T. Sandison (1955) plunged into a histological study of mummy tissue, while Brothwell and colleagues' *Science in Archaeology* (1963) focused interest on potential study methods for mummy diseases. Brothwell and Sandison collaborated to produce *Diseases in Antiquity* (1967), a book that summarized the state of mummy studies at that time. In recognition of the creative role played by research during World War II and its civilian applications in postwar life, Western nations structured funding sources for public projects, as did private companies. This work also rejuvenated interest in mummy studies, beginning in the early 1970s and resulting in the emergence of a number of organizations. Among the first was that founded by Marvin Allison, an infectious disease specialist in the Department of Pathology at the Medical College of Virginia, and pathologist Enrique Gerszten. Their annual visits to arid sites in Peru and northern Chile were spent dissecting human mummies, focusing particularly on infectious diseases. The Paleopathology Club, which they founded, published case reports of ancient mummies with tuberculosis, *Paracoccidioides brasiliensis*, osteomyelitis, Pott's disease, actinomycosis, congenital polycystic kidney disease, and more (Allison 1981).

Another organization devoted to mummy studies also began in the 1970s. British epidemiologist Aidan Cockburn and his wife, Eve, pursued an interest in the evolution of certain infectious diseases. Out of this grew the Paleopathology Association (Cockburn 1978). The initial group of about a half dozen scientists carried out autopsies on Egyptian mummies and published results principally in medical journals (Cockburn et al. 1975). Michael Zimmerman of the University of Pennsylvania, one of the group's leaders, studied mummies from arctic regions as well as temperate areas.

The third organization dedicated to mummy studies, the World Congress on Mummy Studies, met first in 1992 to study Gaunche mummies on the Canary island of Tenerife. It has been meeting every three years at different venues since then.

The fourth organization, the Institute for Mummies and the Iceman, evolved through the efforts of Albert Zink and others related to the Iceman mummy. Funded by the European Research Academy, its first meeting was held in March 2009 at the museum housing the Iceman mummy in Bolzano, Italy.

Membership in these organizations is growing. About 125 people attended the 2007 Meeting of the Sixth World Congress on Mummy Studies. Noteworthy was the broad array of scientific disciplines represented at the meeting.

METHODS FOR MUMMY STUDIES

Validation of Mummy Study Methods

Before plunging into discussions of methods employed in mummy studies, a brief but vital warning is applicable. "Blind" application to a mummy tissue sample of a technique originally designed for use on a specimen of a living individual runs the risk of producing unreliable results. For example, the lead content of a bone from a living or recently deceased person can be predictive of certain social features of that individual. These features were the product of that person's lifetime exposure to lead. In the 1990s a series of such studies on ancient bones was reported by Aufderheide et al. (1992). Some of their interpretations of the results are viewed today with a jaundiced eye because we know now that buried bone can absorb enough lead from groundwater to obliterate the antemortem values. Furthermore, the diagenetic lead cannot be separated analytically from the antemortem absorbed lead. Lesson learned: Validate the test's behavior on mummy tissues before relying on its results.

Emphasis on Mummy Soft Tissues

By the middle 1990s, the newly formed mummy study organizations had delivered a massive stimulus to research studies on mummies. Initially, the majority of studies consisted of descriptions of pathological lesions that were large enough to be detected and identified by gross observations. During the first few years after the founding of the Paleopathology Club, its newsletter featured case reports on such lesions as sinus mucocele, lung foreign bodies (projectile points), generalized hyperostosis, polycystic kidney disease, cardiomegaly, fibrinous pericarditis, skull and tibia treponematosis, and other gross pathological alterations. These were characteristic of articles reporting soft tissue paleopathology during this period.

Pseudopathology

Many articles were devoted to detailed descriptions of intact mummies, emphasizing features that revealed the various alterations that led to their soft tissue preservation. Nevertheless, investigators had to adapt to the reality that, unlike with hospital autopsies, they were seeing advanced, untreated, end-stage disease states. In addition, loss of water caused all mummified tissues to have a similar density and uniformly brown color, complicating the recognition of organs. Researchers also needed to deal with what I call organ migration, when partial decay causes an organ to detach from its normal location and move to a different location when the body is handled (Aufderheide 2003). Using a gross pathology approach, bog bodies, Chinese burials, Aleut burials, and many Egyptian burials were described with emphasis on their mummification methods.

Radiological Imagery

Early "flat plate" X-rays had a major limitation: superimposition of bones and soft tissues. This was a minor problem in supine bodies, but in a flexed body the superimposition of arms, legs, ribs, spine, and other structures profoundly reduced the amount of information one could derive from the study. This limitation was eliminated by the development of computerized tomography (CT), which effectively minimized superimposition by positioning detectors so as to generate an image equivalent to a body "slice." This technology became even more useful when the entire irradiated body area could be reconstructed as a three-dimensional image. While the use of portable X-ray machines in the field is practical, portable CT scanners are quite cumbersome, making it easier in most cases to bring the mummified body to the scanner rather than vice versa—although, as O'Brien et al. (2009) have pointed out in a review of the literature on imaging of mummies, the application of this kind of technology is most beneficial when it is hypothesis driven.

Just as postmortem changes by mummification mechanisms can cause an investigator to misjudge the nature of an altered tissue, leading to a misdiagnosis, X-rays can also produce unfamiliar changes that may lead a radiologist to erroneous diagnoses. Lynnerup (2007) has published a summary of such "diagnostic traps" in radiological image interpretations that can be avoided by an informed interpreter. Magnetic resonance imaging (MRI) designed for the study of hydrated tissues is ineffective when applied to desiccated mummies.

Elemental Analysis

Strontium isotope ratios differ in various geographic areas. With appropriate sampling of selected mummy tissue and soil (or rock) specimens in regions of interest, it may be possible to identify an individual's sites of residence in youth and in later life (Knudson et al. 2007). Measurements are performed using mass spectrometry.

Chemical Dietary Reconstruction

Isotope ratios of carbon and nitrogen as measured by mass spectrometry on mummy tissues are predictive of certain antemortem features of a mummy's diet during life (vegetal/meat fractions, dietary protein content, and terrestrial/marine diet sources) (Ambrose 1993). Postmortem compound degradation can introduce variables that can be avoided by carrying out the measurements on "purified" extracts of certain lipids that are known to resist such alterations (Evershed et al. 1999). Instrumentation employs gas chromatography and mass spectrometry.

Hair Studies

Removal from the blood of certain chemicals that circulate through hair roots results in incorporation of such chemicals into the hair shaft. After emergence of the hair shaft from the skin, the shaft can be cut and subjected to analysis. Cartmell et al. (1991) have validated both radioimmunology and mass spectrometry to quantify the amount of cocaine in hair samples from South American mummies who chewed or ingested cocaine-containing coca plant leaves in life.

Ancient DNA Studies

DNA in mummies is extensively fractured and degraded to the degree that commonly less than 1 percent of the DNA found in living persons is present in mummy tissues. Fortunately, polymerase chain reaction (PCR)—a technique for amplifying this amount to a concentration similar to that of living organisms—became available in the early 1980s (Mullis 1990). While routine recovery of ancient nuclear DNA is not yet predictable, that of mitochondrial DNA is common. The types of data studied fall into two broad groups: migration reconstruction, and detection of the presence of an ancient infectious agent in a tissue specimen of an ancient mummy. The hazards of error threaten the analyst at every step of the procedure; the principal problem is specimen contamination. In routine research laboratories, this risk is minimized by hoods with airflow controls and by carrying out certain steps in dedicated, separate rooms. When studying human DNA, the best success is experienced in laboratories that have been specifically constructed for that purpose. Identifying bacteria, viruses, and other infectious agents in mummy tissues carries less danger of contamination because DNA in mummies is not as ubiquitous in a laboratory as is DNA in living humans.

The list of applications of DNA is open-ended. Identification of DNA of the tubercle bacillus in a 1,000-year-old South American mummy established the presence of tuberculosis in the New World 500 years prior to European contact (Salo et al. 1994). A similar approach made it possible to trace the behavior of American trypanosomiasis (Chagas disease) over the past 9,000 years in South America (Aufderheide et al. 2004). Recent whole-genome sequencing methods have greatly expanded the applications of ancient DNA technology (Gilbert et al. 2008).

Proteometric Methods in Mummy Studies

Efforts to detect proteins in tissues have shown potential. To date, these employ the principle of protein digestion of tissue samples, then separation and identification of resulting peptides using mass spectrometry. Though the work is promising, it is probably too early to know what, if any, role it will play in routine ancient mummy studies.

Endoscopy

While the rigidity of desiccated ancient tissues imposes distinct limitations on the use of endoscopic applications in mummies, some bodies have yielded much useful data with this technology (Beckett et al. 2008).

THE FUTURE OF MUMMY STUDIES

Restrictive Legislation

In general, ethical concerns about mummy study activities are expressed in direct proportion to the degree to which a population or subpopulation perceives itself to be direct descendants of the studied mummies. Currently, legislation restricting mummy studies to some degree exists in the United States, Australia, and Israel. However, history indicates that once a source of knowledge has been identified, its study cannot be suppressed forever. Experience suggests that we need to be patient, but the Renaissance teaches us to actively seek our objectives if we expect to reach them. I am positive that the present impetus of mummy studies will be appropriately harnessed and lead us to our goals.

Funding

Funding is a critical factor for the future of mummy studies. The National Science Foundation and the National Institutes of Health in the United States are already struggling to meet their current needs. It will be a major challenge for leaders in the field of mummy studies to convince public funding sources such as these that mummy studies fall within their mandate. This work requires organized efforts at all levels.

Organization

It is possible but unlikely that the field of mummy studies will ever be large enough to be an independent scientific discipline. Thus, to survive and flourish, the field will need to join a related discipline. The current mummy studies organizations could bring a large number of attendees into a single, fused group. Physicians would need to learn more physical anthropology, while physical anthropologists would need to become more medically knowledgeable. Some educational supplementation would be needed to bring this about, but these concerns certainly would not prohibit progress. In addition, such a structured group would need a predictable source of mummies for training and research during summer field trips. This, too, can be arranged.

Due to their spectacular nature, mummies have often been decontextualized, because interest in the preserved body has overridden the importance of archaeological contexts. Integrative, hypothesis-driven, multidisciplinary approaches as advocated by Jane E. Buikstra are essential to a more holistic understanding of these remains. It has been my good fortune to work with Buikstra, and as a result of this collaboration, we have charted the societal impact of diseases such as primary tuberculosis, Chagas disease, osteosarcoma, and others from the Osmore drainage in Peru.

CONCLUSIONS

The scientific aspects of mummy studies have already justified their existence by demonstrating that mummies house both medical and anthropological information and that such information can be extracted and integrated with the broader databases of these disciplines. These data can be obtained from no other sources. Soft tissue paleopathology now has all the required features of a scientific subdiscipline; thus its future is promising.

REFERENCES CITED

Allison, Marvin J.
1981 Case No. 7: Polycystic Kidney Disease. *Paleopathology Club Newsletter* 9:2.

Ambrose, Stanley H.
1993 Isotopic Analysis of Paleodiets: Methodological and Interpretive Considerations. In *Investigations of Ancient Human Tissue*, edited by Mary K. Sandford, pp. 59–130. Gordon and Breach Science Publishers, New York.

Armelagos, George. J., and James O. Mills
1993 Paleopathology as Science: The Contribution of Egyptology. In *Biological Anthropology and the Study of Ancient Egypt*, edited by W. Vivian Davies and Roxie Walker, pp. 1–18. British Museum Press, London.

Aufderheide, Arthur C.
2003 *The Scientific Study of Mummies*. Cambridge University Press, Cambridge.

Aufderheide, Arthur C., George Rapp, Lorenz E. Wittmers, Roberto Machiarelli, Gino Fornaciari, Francesco Mallegni, Robert S. Corruccini
1992 Lead Exposure in Italy: 800 B.C.–700 A.D. *International Journal of Anthropology* 7:9–15.

Aufderheide, Arthur C., Wilmar Salo, Michael Madden, John Streiz, Jane Buikstra, Felipe Guhl, Bernardo Arriaza, Colleen Renier, Lorentz E. Wittmers Jr., Gino Fornaciari, and Marvin Allison
2004 A 9,000-Year Record of Chagas' Disease. *Proceedings of the National Academy of Sciences of the United States of America* 101(7):2034–2039.

Beckett, Ronald, Gerald Conlogue, and David Henderson
2008 Moving Toward Data Acquisition Standards for Endoscopic and Reflectance Applications in Anthropological Studies. In *Mummies and Science*, edited by Pablo Atoche Peña, Conrado Rodriguez-Martin, and Angeles Ramirez Rodriguez, pp. 425–432. Academia Canaria de la Historia, Santa Cruz de Tenerife.

Blumenbach, John Frederick
1794 Observations on Some Egyptian Mummies Opened in London. *Philosophical Transactions of the Royal Society of London*, ser. B, 84:177–195.

Brothwell, Don, and A. T. Sandison
1967 *Diseases in Antiquity*. Charles Thomas, Springfield, Illinois.

Brothwell, Don, Eric Higgs, and G. Clark
1963 *Science in Archaeology*. Basic Book, New York.

Cartmell, Larry W., Arthur C. Aufderheide, Angela Springfield, Cheryl Weems, and Bernardo Arriaza
1991 The Frequency and Antiquity of Prehistoric Coca Leaf-Chewing Practices in Northern Chile: Radioimmunoassay of a Cocaine Metabolite in Human Mummy Hair. *Latin American Antiquity* 2:260–268.

Cockburn, Aidan
1978 Paleopathology and Its Association. *Journal of the American Medical Association* 240(2):151–152.

Cockburn Aidan, Barraco Robin A., Theodore Reyman, and William H. Peck
1975 Autopsy of an Egyptian Mummy. *Science*, n.s., 187:1155–1160.

David, Rosalie A.
1979 *Manchester Museum Mummy Project*. Manchester University Press, Manchester.

Dawson, Warren R. (editor)
1938 *Sir Grafton Elliot Smith*. Jonathan Cape, London.

Evershed, Richard P., Stephanie N. Dudd, Stephanie Charters, Hazel Mottram, Andrew W. Stott, Anthony Raven, Pim F. van Bergen, and Helen A Bland
1999 Lipids as Carriers of Anthropogenic Signals from Prehistory. *Philosophical Transactions of the Royal Society of London* 354(1379): 19–32.

Gilbert, M. Thomas P., Lynn P. Tomsho, Snjezana Rendulic, Michael Packard, Daniela I. Drautz, et al.
2008 Whole-Genome Shotgun Sequencing of Mitochondria from Ancient Hair Shafts. *Science* 317:1927–1930.

Granville, Augustus Bozzi
1825 An Essay on Egyptian Mummies; with Observations on the Art of Embalming Among the Ancient Egyptians. *Philosophical Transactions of the Royal Society of London* 1:269–316.

Hadley, John
1764 An Account of a Mummy, Inspected at London, 1763. *Philosophical Transactions of the Royal Society of London* 54:1–2.

Knudson, Kelly
2008 Tiwanaku Influence in the South Central Andes: Strontium Isotope Analysis and Middle Horizon Migration. *Latin American Antiquity* 19(1):3–23.

Knudson, Kelly, Arthur Aufderheide, and Jane E. Buikstra
2007 Seasonality and Paleodiet in the Chiribaya Polity of Southern Peru. *Journal of Archaeological Science* 34:451–462.

Long, Esmond R.
1965 *A History of Pathology*. Dover Publications, New York.

Lucas, Alfred
1926 *Ancient Egyptian Materials and Industries*. Edward Arnold, London.

Lynnerup, Niels
2007 Mummies. In *Yearbook of Physical Anthropology* 50:162–190. Wiley InterScience, New York.

Lyons Albert S., and Joseph Petrucelli
1987 *Medicine: An Illustrated History*. Abradale/Abrams, New York.

Malkin, Harold M.
1993 *Out of the Mist*. Vesalius Books, Berkeley, California.

Moodie, Roy
1921 Biographical Sketch. In *Studies in the Paleopathology of Egypt by Sir Marc Armand Ruffer*, edited by Roy L. Moodie, pp. xiii–xvi. University of Chicago Press, Chicago.

Mullis, Kary
1990 The Unusual Origin of the Polymerase Chain Reaction. *Scientific American* 262(4):56–61, 64–65.

Murray, Margaret Alice
1910 *The Tomb of Two Brothers*. Sherratt and Hughes, Manchester.

O'Brien, J. J., J. J. Battista, C. Romagnoli, and R. K. Chem
2009 CT Imaging of Human Mummies: A Critical Review of the Literature (1979–2005). *International Journal of Osteoarchaeology* 19(1):90–98.

Pettigrew, Thomas Joseph
1834 *A History of Egyptian Mummies*. Longman, Rees, More, Brown, Green & Longman, London.

Porter, Roy
1996 *The Cambridge Illustrated History of Medicine*. Cambridge University Press, Cambridge.

Ruffer, Marc Armand
1921 *Studies in the Paleopathology of Egypt by Sir Marc Armand Ruffer Kt, C.M.G., M.D.* Edited by R. I. Moodie. University of Chicago Press, Chicago.

Salo, Wilmar L., Arthur C. Aufderheide, Jane E. Buikstra, Todd A. Holcomb
1994 Identification of *Myobacterium tuberculosis* DNA in a Pre-Columbian Mummy. *Proceedings of the National Academy of Sciences, USA* 91:2091–2094.

Sandison, Andrew T.
1955 The Histological Examination of Mummified Material. *Stain Technology* 30:277–283.

Smith, G. Elliot, and Warren R. Dawson
1991 [1924] *Egyptian Mummies*. Reprinted. Kegan Paul International, London. Originally published 1924, George Allen & Unwin, London.

16

Social Aspects of the Bioarchaeology of Leprosy

Charlotte A. Roberts
Department of Archaeology, Durham University

This chapter aims to offer perspectives on the social aspects of leprosy (or Hansen's disease) in medieval Europe, and Britain in particular, but by necessity grounds itself in the clinical literature. It is of course dedicated to Jane E. Buikstra, whose extensive interest in and research on the bioarchaeology of mycobacterial disease, particularly tuberculosis, inspired the author. However, her attendance at the "Past and Present of Leprosy" conference in the United Kingdom in 1999 (Roberts et al. 2002) proved she had an interest in mycobacterial infections beyond tuberculosis. Buikstra's tremendous contributions to bioarchaeology (in the widest sense) over more than 40 years of working in anthropology are breathtaking. However, of particular note has been her constant strong emphasis on contextualizing skeletal data, something that has been slow to develop in some parts of the world. Her research has included the publication of excavated funerary sites, incorporating both biological and archaeological data admirably (e.g., Buikstra et al. 2004); landmark works on specific health problems (e.g., Buikstra 1981); and invaluable contributions to the standardization of the recording of human remains, which have shaped the world of bioarchaeology (Buikstra and Ubelaker 1994). She has also provided bioarchaeology with a key text on its development (Buikstra and Beck 2006), as well as one on paleopathology in particular (Buikstra and Roberts 2012). Her involvement in fieldwork in the Americas and in parts of Europe is particularly illustrated in her long publication list, a list that shows the wide variety of collaborations she has nurtured at all levels and in many disciplines. Buikstra is a team player who has encouraged a great number of people in bioarchaeology, including this author, and continues to be an inspiration to all.

"It's hard to catch, easy to cure and ought to be on its way into the history books by now. So why is leprosy still blighting millions of lives?" (Nelson 2005:28). Why indeed? Leprosy is a chronic infectious disease that has plagued human populations for hundreds of years (Roberts and Manchester 2005). The first truly convincing evidence in skeletal remains comes from the Dakhleh Oasis in Egypt and dates to 250 B.C. (Dzierzykray-Rogalski 1980), although accepted documentary evidence from 600 B.C. is seen in the *Sushruta Samhita* from India (Dharmendra 1947). In some parts of the world, leprosy remains a devastating problem for many; India carries two-thirds of the world burden of leprosy (Young 2001). The problem should be considered particularly from the viewpoint of the social milieu in which many people with the disease are forced to live (Joseph and Rao 1999). This paper considers leprosy from a social perspective by comparing the present and the past, with a focus on the perception and treatment of people with leprosy in medieval Europe. However, the bioarchaeological aspects of leprosy need first to be grounded in what is known about the infection clinically.

CLINICAL LEPROSY

What Is Leprosy?

Leprosy is a chronic infectious disease that affects humans. However, it has also been recorded, although inconsistently, in other animals, such as the nine-banded armadillo (Truman et al. 1991). It is caused by *Mycobacterium leprae*, is of high infectivity but low pathogenicity, and primarily affects the peripheral nerves and secondarily the skin and other tissues, such as the eyes, testes, kidneys, bones, blood vessel endothelium, and upper respiratory tract (Jopling 1982). The main method of contracting the infection is via inhalation of bacteria-laden droplets. Therefore, prolonged close contact between affected and unaffected people is necessary for transmission; population density may play a role here. Nevertheless, leprosy is difficult to contract, unlike the related infection tuberculosis. Key to whether the infection is transmitted is the strength of the individual's immune system toward *M. leprae*. A person with a low resistance to the bacteria will develop lepromatous or multibacillary leprosy; one who is highly resistant will develop tuberculoid or paucibacillary leprosy—but there are other levels of immunity between these extremes. Leprosy can have a long incubation period, from three months to 40 years (Bryceson and Pfaltzgraff 1990), but two to five years is usual (Dayal et al. 1990). Leprosy can now be cured with antibiotic therapy, but it is important to treat it early, otherwise considerable disfigurement and disability can result.

How Does Leprosy Affect the Human Body?

Leprosy affects the body in a number of ways. In non-lepromatous leprosy, one or more skin lesions on the cooler parts of the body (buttocks, limbs, or face) are seen (Jopling 1982). In lepromatous leprosy, papules and nodules occur bilaterally and symmetrically on the face, earlobes, buttocks, and limbs, and they contain many bacilli. *M. leprae* also affects the peripheral nerves and prefers the cooler more superficial areas (Jopling 1982). Paraesthesia (pins and needles), pain, anesthesia, and paralysis also occur, with paralysis potentially affecting the face, hand, lower leg, or foot. The sensory, motor, and autonomic nerves can all be affected, usually in combination. Loss of sensation in the skin tends to occur (Bryceson and Pfaltzgraff 1990), and autonomic nerve damage affects blood vessel functioning. Loss of the ability to sweat and osteoblast-osteoclast balance, along with medullary cavity-width reduction, occurs in the metatarsals, metacarpals, and phalanges. Claw hand and foot (motor nerve damage and paralysis) and collapse of the foot arches develop. Sensory loss, repeated trauma, and bruising lead to ulceration of the soft tissues. Plantar ulcers enable secondary bacterial infection to develop, leading to osteomyelitis and septic arthritis of the bones and joints of the hands or feet. There can be multiple and varied changes in the hand and foot bones, described in Roberts and Manchester (2005). Essentially, the person may experience disintegration of the hand and foot structures, including dislocation of joints. *M. leprae* also infects the soft tissues in the nose and mouth; this process can lead to damage to the palatal and turbinate bones and the septum of the nose (pitting, perforation, new bone formation) and to the loss of maxillary alveolar bone around the incisor teeth, the anterior nasal spine, and the nasal aperture. The signs and symptoms of leprosy are variable and described in Dayal et al. (1990), onset usually being gradual and dependent on the person's resistance to leprosy.

Leprosy Today

In 1991 the World Health Organization (WHO) resolved to eliminate leprosy by the end of 2005, while the World Health Assembly agreed to set 2000 as the deadline. This meant a reduction of the global incidence to less than 1 registered case per 10,000 people. In 2001 the WHO said it had reached its target but admitted that leprosy was still a problem in parts of Asia, Africa, and South America. The WHO felt that by the end of 2005, leprosy could be totally eliminated. Now, the most prevalent endemic countries have reached elimination (World Health Organization 2012). The WHO has seen more than 14 million cases diagnosed and treated and a drop in numbers from 12 million to about 460,000 over 20 years. The WHO reports that the prevalence of leprosy at the beginning of 2011 was 192,246 cases, with newly detected cases during 2010 being 228,474. The main countries yet to reach elimination at the national level are Angola, Brazil, the Central African Republic, the Democratic Republic of Congo, India, Madagascar, Mozambique, Nepal, and the United Republic of Tanzania. Progress in elimination has been due to the use of multiple antibiotics (dapsone, rifampicin, and clofazimine), which are given free to anybody suffering from leprosy. Vaccines, particularly of BCG (tuberculosis), have also been used for preventing leprosy, but efficacy varies (Fine 1995). With a better understanding of the molecular nature of *M. leprae* (Cole et al. 2001) and the human response to infection, new vaccines will be developed. However, even if cured leprosy patients are increasing, thousands still continue to suffer the debilitating physical, social, economic, and psychological consequences (Scollard et al. 2006). Meima et al. (2004) suggest that leprosy's consequences will be with us for many years.

Unlike most other diseases, leprosy attracts much stigma and misunderstanding (Jopling 1991). This makes the social milieu in which affected people live particularly challenging, and they are often ostracized. This misunderstanding stems partly from a mistranslation in the Hebrew version of the Bible of the word *tsara'ath*—a word now accepted as being associated with any disfiguring skin disease or state of ritual uncleanliness.

Gussow and Tracy (1970:426) suggest, "Stigma is said to be worse than the disease itself," but Noordeen (1993:517) emphasizes, "Without the disability-producing potential, leprosy would not merit the attention it gets," although people disagree about how stigmatized leprosy is or was (Navon 1998). Prior to a cure for leprosy, reactions to leprosy were ambivalent. Once treatment had been developed, leprous sufferers could keep their illness a secret, but successful treatment also meant an improvement of patients' social acceptance. Disappearance from the public eye then led to the figurative use of leprosy in the English language; the word *leper* continues to be associated with social rejection, which has led to irrational perceptions of leprosy. Cochrane (1963) even suggested that charities helping those with leprosy perpetuated the negative image of leprosy in their fund-raising campaigns. More recently, the media, artists, and authors have also been accused of propagating the link between sensationalism and leprosy. A recent "educational" novel about leprosy in Greece by Hislop (2005) is a sympathetic and balanced treatment of the impact of leprosy on people in the twentieth century. Nevertheless, it is clear that stigma affects a person's lifestyle and position in society. For example, a study of people with leprosy in Nigeria found that males had problems securing and holding jobs, which led to loss of income, and divorce was usually instigated by males with leprous wives (rather than by wives of leprous men) (Awofeso 1995). Of relevance to discussions in bioarchaeology are numerous varied examples of how people view leprosy and how it affects populations (Barkataki et al. 2006). For example, Skinses (1964) notes that in China, leprosy was seen as a punishment from heaven, and it was thought to be transmitted through sexual intercourse or inherited. He records that if a person sat on a chair that was still warm from a person with leprosy using it, the sitter would be expected to contract leprosy; in one village, people kept special chairs in the rafters of houses and brought them down for healthy visitors. Concepts of leprosy in parts of the world appear strange to the Western eye but are highly relevant to the potential success of eradication programs, including acceptance of, and compliance with, treatment.

THE BIOARCHAEOLOGY OF LEPROSY

The way leprosy affects the body, and how leprosy is viewed and treated, is globally variable. This variability is highly relevant to our understanding of leprosy in the past and how it affected society, something that is often forgotten when we're faced with a skeleton with bone changes caused by leprosy. It is important to remember that "our skeletons" were once living, breathing people who functioned within societies with particular cultural values and attitudes toward disease. But how early do we see leprosy reflected in the bioarchaeological record, and how do we recognize it skeletally?

Skeletal Changes of Leprosy

Leprosy affects the skeleton in only about 5 percent of people with the disease (Resnick and Niwayama 1995), and depending on where on the leprosy immune spectrum the individual lies, these bone changes will vary in manifestation. Detection of leprosy in skeletal remains is based on the diagnostic criteria of Vilhelm Møller-Christensen, a Danish doctor who was interested in archaeology and paleopathology and who excavated and analyzed skeletons from medieval Danish leprosy hospital sites (Bennike 2002). Møller-Christensen first described bone changes in medieval Danish skeletal remains in the 1950s (1953); his criteria were extended mainly by Andersen and Manchester in a series of papers (cited in Roberts and Manchester 2005).

The facial bone damage, described above, has been called facies leprosa (Møller-Christensen 1978) and, more recently, rhinomaxillary syndrome (Anderson and Manchester 1992). This damage is considered pathognomonic for leprosy, but other disease processes may cause similar changes (Cook 2002; Manchester 1994). In lepromatous leprosy, bone damage to the nasal area and palate is seen, but in tuberculoid leprosy it is absent. In lepromatous leprosy, changes to the hands and feet are usually symmetrical, but they are asymmetrical in tuberculoid leprosy (Manchester 2002). Damage to the hands is less common than to the feet, and in archaeological contexts this is also the case, possibly because ulceration of the hands is noticed more often because of ease of observation for those living with leprosy (Manchester 2002).

Tibial and fibular new bone formation (periostitis) in leprosy is believed to be due to infection in the foot extending upward into the legs, but it has also been seen in living leprous sufferers without foot damage (Manchester 2002). In a bioarchaeological study, Lewis et al. (1995) documented 38 percent (76) of leprous individuals from a medieval leprosy hospital in Chichester, Sussex, England, with periostitis of lower leg bones, but 19 percent (60) of the non-leprous individuals also had periostitis. It is a nonspecific change that has multiple causes (for example, trauma, treponemal disease, scurvy, tuberculosis), but recent work has attempted to use histological analysis to differentiate the causes of periostitis (Schultz and Roberts 2002; but see Weston 2009).

How Common Was Leprosy in the Past?

All skeletal evidence for leprosy comes from the Old World; evidence in the New World should have appeared with colonization in late contexts. At the time of European voyages to the east coast of the Americas in the late fifteenth century, leprosy was declining in Europe; it is unlikely that lepromatous leprosy would have reached the Americas via European contact (Roberts and Manchester 2005). This is because leprosy is one of the least contagious of the transmissible infectious diseases; if it had been transported across the Atlantic, it would not have had as severe an impact on the native populations of the Americas as other infectious diseases (Browne 1970). The story of the bioarchaeology of leprosy in the New World is therefore considerably shorter than in the Old World. In the United States, leprosy was introduced to southern Louisiana by French settlers when they were expelled from Nova Scotia in 1755. In 1884 a State Board of Leprosy Control was directed to find a "leper home." Following passage of a bill to create a national leprosarium (1917) by the U.S. Congress, the Louisiana Home for Lepers was founded in 1921 at Carville, 85 miles northwest of New Orleans (at an abandoned plantation called Indian Camp). It became a sanctuary for people with leprosy throughout the United States, with admission on a voluntary basis. In the 1940s, researchers at Carville discovered the first effective antileprosy drug (promin). Leprosy is now a minor endemic disease in the states of Louisiana and Texas.

In recent years, comparative genomic research has been used to establish genealogical relationships in disease. Monot et al. (2005) suggested that *M. leprae* has undergone extensive reductive evolution and that leprosy probably originated in eastern Africa or the Near East and then spread as people moved around the globe. Early data from a third-century B.C. Chinese bamboo book suggest that leprosy was present in China (Skinses 1980), but skeletal remains indicate that by the first millennium A.D. it was likely present in Uzbekistan in west-central Asia (Blau and Yagodin 2005). Based on historical data, it has long been suggested that leprosy was brought to the Mediterranean from the Indo-Gangetic Basin by the armies of Alexander the Great (356–323 B.C.) returning from the Alexandrian campaign; there have been recent debates about this theory, however (Mark 2002). However, it is only recently that suggested bioarchaeological evidence for leprosy in India has been reported and dated to 2000 B.C. (Robbins et al. 2009), although the earliest evidence of leprosy in historical documents (*Sushruta Samhita*) is dated later, to to 600 B.C. (Dharmendra 1947), as mentioned above. Evidence from skeletal and mummified remains has also been observed in Israel and Egypt. Dzierzykray-Rogalski (1980) describes leprosy in four people from the Dahkleh Oasis of Egypt (250 B.C.), and Molto (2002) discusses more recent data at the Roman Kellis 2 cemetery (two leprous males, early to mid-fourth century A.D.).

In France and Italy, the earliest evidence of skeletal leprosy comes from the Roman period (third to 7th century A.D.—Belcastro et al. 2005; Blondiaux et al. 2002; Mariotti et al. 2005). In Britain, bioarchaeological data show leprosy increasing from the early to late medieval periods (fifth to sixteenth centuries A.D.) (Roberts 2002). In Scandinavia it is seen also in Denmark (Boldsen 2005; Boldsen and Mollerup 2006; Møller-Christensen 1953, 1969), and leprosy was present until the middle of the twentieth century in Norway (Richards 1977). While leprosy has been reported in Poland, Germany, and the Czech Republic (infrequently), in Hungary Marcsik et al. (2007) describe the first evidence for leprosy, which is dated to the seventh to ninth centuries A.D.

Despite early historical sources indicating leprosy in India and China, no bioarchaeological evidence has been found in China. The only possible skeletal evidence from Southeast Asia comes from Thailand (two skeletons dated to 300 to 200 B.C., and one to the first two centuries A.D.) (Tayles and Buckley 2004), along with evidence from Micronesia (seventh to fifteenth centuries A.D.) (Trembly 1995). On the basis of the skeletal evidence to date, leprosy has early foci in northern Europe and the Mediterranean, specifically Egypt and Nubia. If the data from India and Thailand are accepted, then early foci for leprosy are also noted in these areas. There are later appearances of leprosy in Micronesia and in other parts of northern Europe and the Mediterranean. However, it is not until the later medieval period that we see a rise in the frequency of the disease in northern Europe. Leprosy then declined from the fourteenth century onwards in Europe, possibly due to the rise of tuberculosis and the nature of cross-immunity between the two infections (Chaussinand 1953; Manchester 1991), but this possibility continues to be debated (Leitman et al. 1997; Wilbur et al. 2002). The disease has been maintained in some parts of the Old World today, as we have seen, but also in the Americas. Clearly, the movement of our ancestors enabled leprosy to be transmitted around the world, a factor that continues to affect the spread of infectious disease (Armelagos 1998; Bhatia et al. 2001).

How Was Leprosy Viewed, Diagnosed, and Treated in the Later Medieval Period?

Our understanding of leprosy in the late medieval period, and prior to Armauer Hansen's discovery of *M. leprae* (1873), is colored by those who wrote about and illustrated it, and perceptions were not helped by the mis-assignment of the infection to descriptions in the Bible (see above). As Rawcliffe (2006:17) states, "Just as cancer and AIDS have become iconic diseases of the late twentieth century, so leprosy has often been projected as representative of the 'Dark Ages,' when prejudice and superstition marched hand in hand with ignorance." Authors and artists instilled shock and fear of the leprous into society because they had found a disease that was dramatic and perceived of as dangerous. It was viewed as a punishment for immoral or unclean activities, including sexual intercourse, which led to strange diagnostic and therapeutic regimes. However, attitudes toward leprosy varied considerably around the world. For example, in the medieval crusader states, stretching from Egypt to Asia Minor, society was much more accepting of leprosy (Mitchell 2000).

A range of people—laypeople, physicians, barber-surgeons, apothecaries, monks, and the clergy—felt qualified to diagnose leprosy around Europe. They took their knowledge from works that had been translated from Latin, but, as Rawcliffe (2006:168) indicates, there was generally a common pool of knowledge that people could access regarding diagnosis and treatment, and diagnosis probably took some time and involved a combination of "medical knowledge and simple pragmatism." Diagnosis by examining blood, feces, and urine was particularly common. Cule (1970) describes the Welsh practice of dropping of a raven's egg into a person's blood. If it hardened, the person was deemed leprous. In contrast, Richards (1990) describes the French surgeon Guy de Chauliac and his *Inventarium* of 1363. Here he divided clinical features into "certain" and "uncertain" and described three stages of diagnosis: suspicion (observe at home and review continually), strong suspicion (stricter isolation at home), and certain diagnosis (consign to hospital), with anybody declared free of the disease receiving a certificate. "Certain" signs were eyebrow thickening, disfiguration and obstruction of the nostrils, scarring around the eyes and ears, and a harsh nasal voice. Clearly, many diagnostic tests were related to mythical perceptions of the disease, which then extended to treatment.

The basis of medieval European medicine lay in the doctrine of the four humors as described by Hippocrates (fifth century B.C.). A disturbance in the balance of blood, phlegm, black bile, or yellow bile was believed to lead to disease. Related to the four elements (fire, earth, air, and water) and the fundamental qualities (hot, cold, moist, and dry), the humors were also affected by astrology, especially in the fourteenth and fifteenth centuries A.D. (Rawcliffe 1997). In the later medieval period (the twelfth to sixteenth centuries A.D.), treatments for ailments, including leprosy, involved specific diets, herbal remedies, laxatives, diuretics, bloodletting, cautery, and bathing, along with treatments that seem unintelligible to the developed Western world, such as eating dead infants' flesh in China (Skinses 1964). These treatments took heed of astrology and the influences of the planets and heavens. Levels of heat, cold, dryness, and moisture associated with medications were very important (Rawcliffe 1997).

Apart from the range of potential remedies available to those with leprosy, one of the main suggested "therapies" was segregation once diagnosed; if society was afraid of people with leprosy, this was a way to rid society of leprosy. Richards (1990) describes, now controversially (see Rawcliffe 2006), that in the later medieval period in Europe, the leprous were considered dead once diagnosed and were isolated into leprosy hospitals via symbolic funerals. They had no marriage rights or property, were stripped of their citizenship, were prohibited from attending church, and were made to wear specific clothing and to carry clappers to warn people of their presence. (A full description of the rules regarding segregation is provided in Clay 1966.) Whether these rules applied to all those diagnosed in later medieval Europe is questionable. However, Rawcliffe (2006) argues that the view of leprosy was reinforced by nineteenth-century rewritings of medieval history in England by people who favored compulsory isolation. Both Rawcliffe (2006) and Demaitre (2007) emphasize the variability of reactions to leprosy in the premodern era (prior to treatment being available) and that we must not assume that everybody with leprosy was stigmatized, ostracized, and segregated. While historians are now developing more accurate views of how the leprous were treated in the past by scrutinizing historical documents more closely, bioarchaeologists are also reconsidering their data (see below).

Historical data indicate that in Europe, leprosy hospitals were founded by benefactors, usually on the edge of towns and cities and outside the walls. They rose in frequency from the eleventh century A.D., and their "popularity" was attained in the twelfth and thirteenth centuries, with a decline from the fourteenth century and with many being used as general hospitals from that time (see Roberts 1986 for a view of leprosaria in Britain). There may have been more than 200 founded in Britain between the eleventh and sixteenth centuries, but it is unlikely that everybody admitted to a leprosarium was leprous, and one certainly cannot take the number of leprosaria as indicative of the disease's frequency. Richards (1990) notes that leprosy hospitals in Britain were small and had a staff of about three people, with room for about 10 patients, but there were some larger hospitals. (Harbledown, Canterbury, Kent, for example, had room for 100, and Sherburn, County Durham, had room for 65.) Even if all the hospitals were full, there would have been a maximum of 3,000 to 4,000 leprous individuals in a population of 3 million in the late medieval period. The perception until recently was that life in leprosaria was unpleasant. However, Rawcliffe (2006) is clear that life was probably quite acceptable compared to prediagnosis living conditions: there was a guarantee of security and protection, regular food, warmth, clothing, a set routine, and even contact with the outside world. There are even suggestions that people wished to be segregated so that they had access to care and sustenance.

With respect to segregation in medieval Europe, several factors could have affected whether somebody with leprosy was diagnosed and segregated. First, the strength of a person's immune system would determine the type of leprosy he or she contracted. A person with the high-resistant type might not have shown any outward signs and therefore might have remained undetected. It is suggested that only the lepromatous leprous (low-resistant) were segregated into leprosy hospitals, and Ell (1986) argues that fourteenth-century medical writers advocated a conservative approach to leprosy diagnosis, selecting the most extreme cases. Certainly, the lepromatous leprous are seen in leprosy hospital cemeteries of the later medieval period (for example, at St. James and St. Mary Magdalene in Chichester, Sussex—Magilton et al. 2008), but people with no bone changes of leprosy at all were also buried there. Those people without evidence of leprosy may have been misdiagnosed, perhaps with skin lesions that were not related to leprosy, or they may have had high-resistant leprosy and thus no bone changes when they died. People in leprosy hospitals and buried in their cemeteries may have also had totally different diseases.

How effective leprosy hospitals were at segregating people with leprosy and controlling the infection is highly debatable. Because of its long incubation period, people with leprosy could have remained in the community long after contracting it and thus transmitted it to others. Some reports say that segregation was not strict in hospitals and that people could go to markets, have visitors, or even be expelled for bad behavior (Macarthur 1953). One also has to explore the social responses to leprosy through time and in different geographical contexts and cultures to understand how varied those responses were and can be. In bioarchaeology, the main avenue of investigation into society's response is the way the leprous were treated in death, along with the evidence of hospitals (see above). On the basis of bioarchaeological evidence, the idea that all society in later medieval Britain (or Europe as a whole) viewed the leprous with fear cannot necessarily be upheld if one considers skeletal evidence for leprosy and the cemeteries where leprous people were buried (Roberts 2002). Of the 27 archaeological sites where leprous skeletons had been found at the time of the research, only four were leprosy hospitals. There were no instances where the body had been treated in an unusual fashion (for example, a prone burial) or any evidence of a violent cause of death. This could suggest that society in general at this time tolerated those with leprosy or that they had not been detected and diagnosed and segregated (for reasons stated above). Nevertheless, one must also consider the challenges of interpreting disease from skeletal remains (Wood et al 1992). Other bioarchaeological studies have found the same picture, for example in Uzbekistan (Blau and Yagodin 2005) and during the crusading period in the Middle East (Mitchell 2000). Our Western views of past social attitudes toward leprosy, a subject with a complex picture even in developing countries today, are undoubtedly often assumed and may be inaccurate.

CONCLUSIONS

Any study of historical responses to disease "must venture far beyond the scrutiny of a particular virus or microbe and its impact on bone and tissue. It must embrace . . . the spiritual and intellectual *milieu* of the afflicted. . . . If the picture that emerges is sometimes contradictory, challenging and fragmented then it surely reflects the nature of human life itself" (Rawcliffe 2006:357). From the preceding dialogue, we have seen an infectious disease that remains prevalent in some parts of the world today and is often still poorly understood. Frequently people with leprosy are ostracized from their communities because they are stigmatized. Although there are exceptions, very little has changed over time from attitudes in late medieval Europe to today, despite better knowledge of both the clinical and social aspects of leprosy and the availability of successful treatment. However, this fact does illustrate, both from a contemporary and a bioarchaeological perspective, that people dealing with the leprous today and bioarchaeologists studying human remains of the past must consider the social milieu (in its very broadest sense) in which diseases thrive to understand the real impact of diseases on individuals and communities. Without a multidisciplinary and holistic approach, we cannot start to understand how our ancestors coped with devastating diseases.

REFERENCES CITED

Anderson, Johs G., and Keith Manchester
1992 The Rhinomaxillary Syndrome in Leprosy: A Clinical, Radiological and Palaeopathological Study. *International Journal of Osteoarchaeology* 2:121–129.

Armelagos, George J.
1998 The Viral Superhighway. *Sciences*, January/February:24–29.

Awofeso Niyi
1995 Effect of Socio-cultural Beliefs on Patients' Perception of Leprosy. *Tropical and Geographical Medicine* 47(4):175–178.

Barkataki, Pramila, Sheo Kumar, and P. S. S. Sundar Rao
2006 Knowledge of and Attitudes Among Patients and Community Members: A Comparative Study in Uttar Pradesh, India. *Leprosy Review* 77:62–68.

Belcastro, Maria Giovanna, Valentina Mariotti, Fiiorenzo Facchini, and Olivier Dutour
2005 Leprosy and a Skeleton from the 7th Century Necropolis of Vicenne-Campochiaro (Molise, Italy). *International Journal of Osteoarchaeology* 15:431–448.

Bennike, Pia
2002 Vilhelm Møller-Christensen: His Work and Legacy. In *The Past and Present of Leprosy: Archaeological, Historical, Palaeopathological and Clinical Approaches*, edited by Charlotte A. Roberts, Mary E. Lewis, and Keith Manchester, pp. 135–144. British Archaeological Reports International Series 1054. Archaeopress, Oxford.

Bhatia, Shushum, Tsegyal Dranyi, and Derrick Rowley
2001 Tuberculosis Among Tibetan Refugees in India. *Social Science and Medicine* 54:423–432.

Blau, Soren, and Vadim Yagodin
2005 Osteoarchaeological Evidence for Leprosy from Western Central Asia. *International Journal of Osteoarchaeology* 126:150–158.

Blondiaux, Joël, Jean Dürr, Lahchen Khouchaf, and Leslie E. Eisenberg
2002 Microscopic Study and X-ray Analysis of Two Fifth-Century Cases of Leprosy: Palaeoepidemiological Inferences. In *The Past and Present of Leprosy: Archaeological, Historical, Palaeopathological, and Clinical Approaches*, edited by Charlotte A. Roberts, Mary E. Lewis, and Keith Manchester, pp. 105–110. British Archaeological Reports International Series 1054. Archaeopress, Oxford.

Boldsen, Jesper L.
2005 Leprosy and Mortality in the Medieval Danish Village of Tirup. *American Journal of Physical Anthropology* 126:159–168.

Boldsen, Jesper L., and Lene Mollerup
2006 Outside St. Jørgen: Leprosy in the Medieval Danish City of Odense. *American Journal of Physical Anthropology* 130:344–351.

Browne, Stanley G.
1970 How Old Is Leprosy? *British Medical Journal* 3(5723):640–641.

Bryceson, Anthony, and Roy E. Pfaltzgraff
1990 *Leprosy*. 3rd ed. Churchill Livingstone, Edinburgh.

Buikstra, Jane E.
1981 *Bio-Archaeology at the Koster Site: The Multidisciplinary Approach of Modern Archaeology*, vol. 2, no. 1, *Koster*. Peoria, Illinois.

Buikstra, Jane E., and Lane A. Beck (editors)
2006 *Bioarchaeology: The Contextual Analysis of Human Remains*. Academic Press, New York.

Buikstra, Jane E., T. Douglas Price, Lori E. Wright, and James A. Burton
2004 Tombs from the Copán Acropolis: A Life History Approach. In *Understanding Early Classic Copan*, edited by Ellen E. Bell, Marcello A. Canuto, and Robert Sharer, pp. 191–212. Museum of Archaeology and Anthropology, University of Pennsylvania, Philadelphia.

Buikstra, Jane E., and Charlotte A. Roberts (editors)
2012 *The Global History of Palaeopathology: Pioneers and Prospects*. Oxford University Press, Oxford.

Buikstra, Jane E., and Douglas H. Ubelaker (editors)
1994 *Standards for Data Collection from Human Skeletal Remains: Proceedings of a Seminar at the Field Museum of Natural History*. Arkansas Archaeological Survey Press, Fayetteville.

Chaussinand, Roland
1953 Tuberculosis and Leprosy: Mutually Antagonistic Diseases. *Leprosy Review* 24:90–94.

Clay, Rotha Mary
1966 *The Mediaeval Hospitals of England*. Frank Cass and Co., London.

Cochrane, Robert Greenhill
1963 *Biblical Leprosy: A Suggested Interpretation.* 2nd ed. Tyndale Press, London.

Cole, S. T., K. Eiglmeier, J. Parkhill, K. D. James, N. R. Thomson, P. R. Wheeler, N. Honoré et al.
2001 Massive Gene Decay in Leprosy Bacillus. *Nature* 409:1007–1011.

Cook, Della Collins
2002 Rhinomaxillary Syndrome in the Absence of Leprosy: An Exercise in Differential Diagnosis. In *The Past and Present of Leprosy: Archaeological, Historical, Palaeopathological and Clinical Approaches*, edited by Charlotte A. Roberts, Mary E. Lewis, and Keith Manchester, pp. 81–88. British Archaeological Reports International Series 1054. Archaeopress, Oxford.

Cule, John
1970 The Diagnosis, Care and Treatment of Leprosy in Wales and the Border in the Middle Ages. *Transactions of the British Society for the History of Pharmacy* 1(1):29–58.

Dayal, Rajeshiwar, N. A. Hashmi, P. P. Mathur, and R. Prasad
1990 Leprosy in Childhood. *Indian Pediatrics* 27:170–180.

Demaitre, Luke
2007 *Leprosy in Premodern Medicine: A Malady of the Whole Body.* Johns Hopkins University, Baltimore.

Dharmendra
1947 Leprosy in Ancient Indian Medicine. *International Journal Leprosy* 15:424–430.

Dzierzykray-Rogalski, Tadeusz
1980 Palaeopathology of the Ptolemaic Inhabitants of Dakhleh Oasis (Egypt). *Journal of Human Evolution* 9:71–74.

Ell, Stephen R.
1986 Leprosy and Social Class in the Middle Ages. *International Journal of Leprosy* 54:300–305.

Fine, Paul E. M.
1995 Variation in Protection by BCG: Implications of and for Heterologous Immunity. *Lancet* 346:1339–1345.

Gussow, Zachary, and George S. Tracy
1970 Stigma and the Leprosy Phenomenon: The Social History of Disease in the 19th and 20th Centuries. *Bulletin of the Social History of Medicine* 44:446–447.

Hislop, Victoria
2005 *The Island.* Headline Book Publishing, London.

Jopling, William H.
1982 Clinical Aspects of Leprosy. *Tubercle* 63:295–305.
1991 Leprosy Stigma. *Leprosy Review* 62:1–12.

Joseph, Geetha A., and P. S. S. Sundar Rao
1999 Impact of Leprosy on the Quality of Life. *Bulletin of the World Health Organisation* 77:515–517.

Leitman, Tom, Travis Porco, and Sally Blower
1997 Leprosy and Tuberculosis: The Epidemiological Consequences of Cross-Immunity. *American Journal of Public Health* 87: 1923–1927.

Lewis, Mary E., Charlotte A. Roberts, and Keith Manchester
1995 Inflammatory Bone Changes in Leprous Skeletons from the Medieval Hospital of St. James and St. Mary Magdalene, Chichester, England. *International Journal of Leprosy* 63(1):77–85.

Macarthur, William P.
1953 Mediaeval Leprosy in the British Isles. *Leprosy Review* 24:8–19.

Magilton, John R., Francis Lee, and Anthea Boylston (editors)
2008 "Lepers Outside the gate." Excavations at the Cemetery of Hospital of St James and St Mary Magdalene, Chichester, 1986–87 and 1993. Research Report 158 and Chichester Excavations Vol. 10. Council for British Archaeology, York.

Manchester, Keith
1991 Tuberculosis and Leprosy: Evidence for Interaction of Disease. In *Human Paleopathology: Current Syntheses and Future Options*, edited by D. J. Ortner and A. C. Aufderheide, pp. 23–35. Smithsonian Institution Press, Washington, D.C.
1994 Rhinomaxillary Lesions in Syphilis: Differential Diagnosis. In *The Origin of Syphilis in Europe: Before or After 1493?* edited by O. Dutour, G. Pálfi, and J-P Brun, pp. 79–80. Centre Archeologique du Var, Editions Errance, Toulon.
2002 Infective Bone Changes of Leprosy. In *The Past and Present of Leprosy: Archaeological, Historical, Palaeopathological and Clinical Approaches*, edited by C. A. Roberts, M. E. Lewis, and K. Manchester, pp. 69–72. British Archaeological Reports International Series 1054. Archaeopress, Oxford.

Marcsik, Antónia, Erika Molnár, and Brigitta Ősz
2007 *Specifikus fertőző megbetegedések csontelváltozásai történeti népesség körében.* JETE Press, Szeged, Hungary.

Mariotti, Valentina, Olivier Dutour, Maria Giovanna Belcastro, and Fiiorenzo Facchini
2005 Probable Early Presence of Leprosy in Europe in a Celtic Skeleton of the 4th–3rd Century BC (Casalecchio di Reno, Bologna, Italy). *International Journal of Osteoarchaeology* 15: 311–325.

Mark, Samuel
2002 Alexander the Great, Seafaring, and the Spread of Leprosy. *Journal History of Medicine* 57:285–311.

Meima, Abraham, W. Cairns, S. Smith, Gerrit J. van Oortmarssen, Jan H. Richardus, J. Dik, and F. Habbema
2004 The Future Incidence of Leprosy: A Scenario Analysis. *Bulletin of the World Health Organisation* 82:373–380.

Mitchell, Piers D.
2000 The Evolution of Social Attitudes to the Medical Care of Those with Leprosy within the Crusader States. *Cahiers du GRHIS* 11:21–28.

Møller-Christensen, Vilhelm
1953 Location and Excavation of the First Danish Leper Graveyard from the Middle Ages. *Bulletin of Medical History* 17:112–123.
1969 Provisional Results of the Examination of the Whole Naestved Leprosy Hospital Churchyard—ab. 1250–1550 AD. *Nordisk Medicinhistorik Årsbok* 4:29–36.
1978 *Leprosy Changes of the Skull.* University Press, Odense, Denmark.

Molto, J. E.
2002 Leprosy in Roman Period Skeletons from Kellis 2, Dahkleh, Egypt. In *The Past and Present of Leprosy: Archaeological, Historical, Palaeopathological and Clinical Approaches*, edited by C. A. Roberts, M. E. Lewis and K. Manchester, pp. 179–192. British Archaeological Reports International Series 1054. Archaeopress, Oxford.

Monot, Marc, Nadine Honoré, Thierry Garnier, Romulo Araoz, Jean-Yves Coppée, Céline Lacroix, Samba Sow et al.
2005 On the Origin of Leprosy. *Science* 308:1040–1042.

Navon, Liora
1998 Beggars, Metaphors, and Stigma: A Missing Link in the Social History of Leprosy. *Social History of Medicine* 11:89–105.

Nelson, Bryn
2005 The Plague That Will Not Die. *New Scientist*, July 16:38–41.

Noordeen, S.K.
1993 Leprosy 1962-1992. 4. Epidemiology and control of leprosy—a review of progress over the last 30 years. *Transactions of the Royal Society of Tropical Medicine and Hygiene* 87:515–517.

Rawcliffe, Carole
1997 *Medicine and Society in Later Medieval England.* Sutton Publishing, Stroud.
2006 *Leprosy in Medieval England.* Boydell Press, Woodbridge.

Resnick, D., and Niwayama, G.
1995 Osteomyelitis, Septic Arthritis and Soft Tissue Infection: Organisms. In *Diagnosis of Bone and Joint Disorders*, edited by D. Resnick, pp. 2448–2558. W. B. Saunders, Edinburgh.

Richards, Peter
1977 The Medieval Leper and His Northern Heirs. D. S. Brewer, London.
1990 Leprosy: Myth, Melodrama and Medievalism. Fitzpatrick Lecture 1989. *Journal Royal College of Physicians of London* 24:55–62.

Robbins, Gwendolyn, Vena Mushrif Tripathy, V. N. Misra, R. K. Mohanty, V. S. Shinde, Kelsey M. Gray, and Malcolm D. Schug
2009 Ancient Skeletal Evidence for Leprosy in India (2000 BC). *PLoS ONE* 4(5):1–8.

Roberts, Charlotte A.
1986 Leprosy and Leprosaria in Medieval Britain. *Museum Applied Science Center for Archaeology Journal* 4:15–21.
2002 The Antiquity of Leprosy in Britain: The Skeletal Evidence. In *The Past and Present of Leprosy. Archaeological, Historical, Palaeopathological and Clinical Approaches*, edited by Charlotte A. Roberts, Mary E. Lewis, and Keith Manchester, pp. 213–222. British Archaeological Reports International Series 1054. Archaeopress, Oxford.

Roberts, Charlotte A., Mary E. Lewis, and Keith Manchester (editors)
2002 *The Past and Present of Leprosy: Archaeological, Historical, Palaeopathological and Clinical Approaches*. British Archaeological Reports International Series 1054. Archaeopress, Oxford.

Roberts, Charlotte A., and Keith Manchester
2005 *The Archaeology of Disease*. Sutton Publishing, Stroud.

Schultz, Michael, and Charlotte A. Roberts
2002 Diagnosis of Leprosy in Skeletons from an English Later Medieval Hospital Using Histological Analysis. In *The Past and Present of Leprosy: Archaeological, Historical, Palaeopathological and Clinical Approaches*, edited by Charlotte A. Roberts, Mary E. Lewis, and Keith Manchester, pp. 89–104. British Archaeological Reports International Series 1054. Archaeopress, Oxford.

Scollard, David M., Linda B. Adams, Tom P. Gillis, Jim L. Krahenbuhl, Richard W. Truman, and Diana L. Williams
2006 The Continuing Challenges of Leprosy. *Clinical Microbiology Reviews* 19:338–181.

Skinses, Olaf K.
1964 Leprosy in Society III. The Relationship of the Social to the Medical Pathology of Leprosy. *Leprosy Review* 34:175–181.
1980 Leprosy in Archaeologically Recovered Bamboo Book in China. *International Journal of Leprosy* 48:333.

Tayles, Nancy, and Buckley, Hallie R.
2004 Leprosy and Tuberculosis in Iron Age Southeast Asia? *American Journal of Physical Anthropology* 125:239–256.

Trembly, Diane L.
1995 On the Antiquity of Leprosy in Western Micronesia. *International Journal of Osteoarchaeology* 5:377–384.

Truman, Richard W., J. A. Kumaresan, Colleen M. McDonough, Charles K. Job, and Robert C. Hastings,
1991 Seasonal and Spatial Trends in the Detectability of Leprosy in Wild Armadillos. *Epidemiology and Infection* 106:549–560.

Weston, Darlene A.
2009 Brief communication. Paleohistopathology and pathological museum specimens: can periosteal reaction microstructure explain lesion etiology? *American Journal of Physical Anthropology* 140:186–193.

Wilbur, Alicia K., Jane E. Buikstra, and Christopher Stojanowski
2002 Mycobacterial Disease in North America: An Epidemiological Test of Chaussinand's Cross-Immunity Hypothesis. In *The Past and Present of Leprosy: Archaeological, Historical, Palaeopathological and Clinical Approaches*, edited by Charlotte A. Roberts, Mary E. Lewis, and Keith Manchester, pp. 247–258. British Archaeological Reports International Series 1054. Archaeopress, Oxford.

Wood, James W., George R. Milner, Henry C. Harpending, and Kenneth M. Weiss
1992 The Osteological Paradox: Problems of Inferring Skeletal Health from Prehistoric Skeletons. *Current Anthropology* 33(4):343–370.

World Health Organization, Leprosy Today. Electronic document, www.who.int/lep/en/, accessed October 9, 2012.

Young, Douglas
2001 Leprosy and the Genome: Not Yet a Burnt-Out Case. *Lancet* 357:1639–1640.

17

"Damnatio ad Metallum": Investigating the Origin and Role of Phaeno Mining Camp Residents Using Multiple Chemical Techniques

Megan A. Perry
Department of Anthropology, East Carolina University
Drew Coleman
Department of Geological Sciences, University of North Carolina–Chapel Hill
Abdel Halim al-Shiyab
Faculty of Archaeology and Anthropology, Yarmouk University, Jordan

In 1977 Jane Buikstra coined the term *bioarchaeology* to refer to a multidisciplinary, problem-oriented, population-level perspective of human skeletal data (Buikstra 1977:69). One of the major tenets of bioarchaeological research was to consider multiple lines of evidence to understand the past, including utilizing different skeletal analysis techniques and considering historical, archaeological, cultural, and political contexts. In her work on the nineteenth-century Grafton Cemetery in Grafton, Illinois, Buikstra presented a critical assessment of how researchers working with historical populations incorporate textual data into their bioarchaeological results. She notes that bioarchaeologists rarely treat documentary data as fallible and biased and simply add their bioarchaeological interpretations to historical evidence (Buikstra 2000:16). Scholars instead should look to developments in anthropological archaeology and historical archaeology, which espouse a critical assessment of all data and the exploration of *why* the stories they tell may not match (Buikstra 2000:16; see also Perry 2007).

This historical-bioarchaeological case study exploring the role and origin of mining camp residents presents one example of combing historical and bioarchaeological data. Historical sources (e.g., Diodorus, *Library of History*; Pliny the Elder, *Natural History*) describe the success of the Roman and Byzantine empires in garnering and controlling resources from many points within their territories. Minerals recovered below the earth's surface were no exception. Mining camps under Roman and Byzantine imperial control were notoriously unpleasant, however. Who were the unfortunate souls sent to work in this context? Historical sources (e.g., Eusebius, *Ecclesiastical History* 8.8, 8.10; Eusebius, *Martyrs of Palestine* 7.4, 8.1, 13.1–3; Strabo, *Geography* 12.3.40) imply that a majority of individuals working in the mines were there for punitive reasons. Strabo also notes that the prisoners in the Mount Sandaracurgium mines in Anatolia were overseen by a *publicanus*, or public contractor (Strabo *Geography* 12.3.40). Other individuals affiliated with mining operations, and support staff as well prisoners, thus likely resided near the mines. In this paper, the historical information on life in Byzantine-period prison camps is combined with bone chemistry data derived from a cemetery associated with one of these camps in southern Jordan. Strontium isotope analysis and concentrations of copper and lead in skeletal systems are used to elucidate the administrative structure of Roman and Byzantine labor camps, in addition to the origin of the mine workers.

THE MINING CAMP AT PHAENO

The Phaeno mines are associated with the archaeological site of Faynan, along the eastern escarpment of Wadi Araba in southwestern Jordan (Figure 17.1). The 12 km^2 area surrounding Khirbet Faynan contains more than 250 copper mines that were extensively exploited from the fifth millennium B.C. until at least the thirteenth century A.D. (Figure 17.2) (Grattan et al. 2007; Hauptmann 2000; Hauptmann and Weisgerber 1987, 1992; Mattingly et al. 2007). A number of cemeteries from different periods, including the Byzantine-period (fourth-to-sixth-century A.D.) Southern Cemetery, partially excavated in 1996 (Abu-Keraki 2000; el-Najjar and al-Shiyab 1998; Findlater et al. 1998; Mattingly et al. 2007), are also associated with the site. Extensive looting had damaged approximately 40 percent of the estimated 1,200 graves in the Southern Cemetery (Findlater et al. 1998:71). Forty-five undisturbed primary burials were excavated during the 1996 season. Grave goods recovered with these burials include remnants of textile shrouds, leather sandals, and personal jewelry, with the exception of graves 105 and 107, which also contained glass vessels, wooden kohl tubes, and plaster disks (Findlater et al. 1998). Additionally, many burials were marked with grave stelae inscribed with personal names and/or Christian crosses.

Historical references describe the grim conditions for laborers at Roman and Byzantine mining camps such as Faynan. Eusebius of Caesarea famously details the fate of Christian martyrs at Phaeno during the great persecutions of the early fourth century A.D., describing their gouged-out eyes, cut Achilles tendons, and shackled and bound legs (Eusebius, *Ecclesiastical History* 8.8, 8.10; Eusebius, *Martyrs of Palestine* 7.4, 8.1, 13.1–3). This cheerless existence was not limited to early-fourth-century Christian prisoners. Diodorus of Sicily provided an even more dismal picture of second-century B.C. mines, describing miners, old and young, men and women, working continuously despite repeated beatings until they dropped dead (Diodorus, *Library* 18.69.2–69.9).

According to Eusebius, most of the fourth-century prisoners at Phaeno came from the Palaestina provinces in the Levantine region and Egypt. Condemnation to *metallum* in the Roman and Byzantine empires purportedly involved transportation of prisoners over long distances, imperial expenditures that reflect, to some scholars, the seriousness of their crimes (Millar 1984:139). We would therefore expect that some

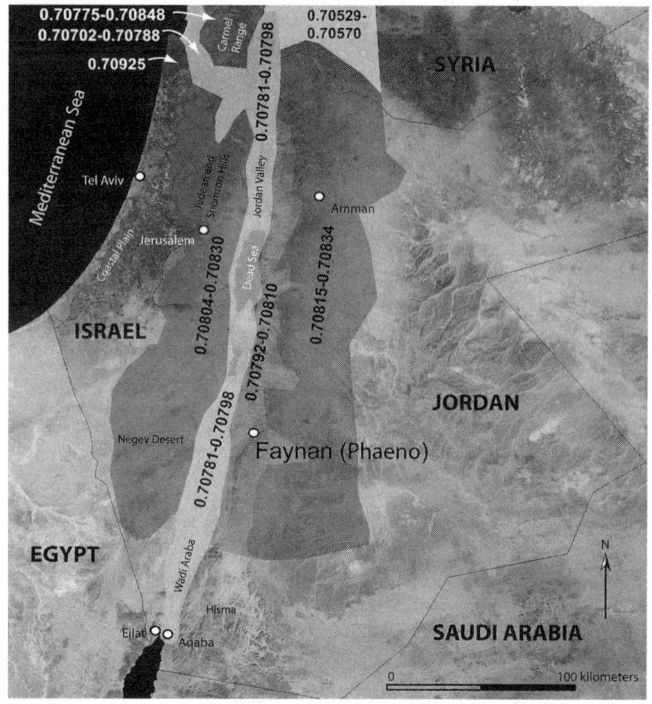

Figure 17.1. Map of the region showing the location of Khirbet Faynan (Phaeno) and $^{87}Sr/^{86}Sr$ variation based on samples of archaeological and modern fauna and modern flora (Perry et al. 2008; Shewan 2004). Unshaded areas of the map indicate insufficient strontium isotope data for these regions.

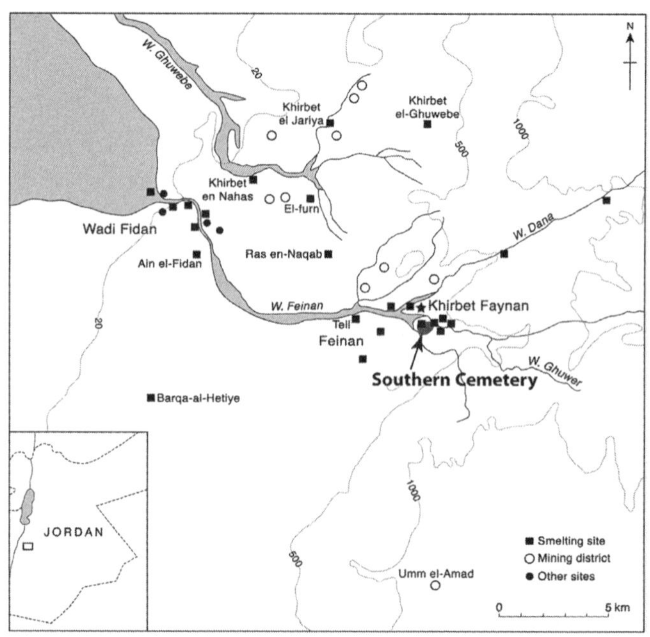

Figure 17.2. Map of Khirbet Faynan and Wadi Fidan, including location of the Southern Cemetery (from Grattan et al. 2007).

individuals in the Faynan cemetery were prisoners who had been transported to Phaeno from other regions. However, with a few exceptions, historical sources do not discuss other individuals who may have worked at the Phaeno camp, such as administrative staff, local laborers there for economic reasons, or their families.

Testing for levels of copper and lead in Faynan skeletal material by Grattan, Pyatt, and colleagues (Grattan et al. 2002; Pyatt et al. 2000, 2005) provides another indication of these individuals' roles in the mines. Bioaccumulation of lead and copper could have resulted from residing in contaminated areas surrounding the mines or from inhalation of metalliferous dusts and flue gasses generated by mining, quarrying, ore preparation, and smelting (Grattan et al. 2002, 2007; Pyatt et al. 1999, 2000). Even ancient writers recognized the health risks involved in mining activities (Lucretius, *De Rerum Natura* 6.808–815; Pliny, *Natural History* 31.49, 33.31; Strabo, *Geography* 12.3.40; Vitruvius, *De Architectura* 8.6.11). Faynan's unhealthy environment apparently persists to this day; as a result of ancient mining activity, toxic levels of copper, lead, and radon exist in local sheep and goats, bedouin tent floors, geological sediments, and plants (Grattan et al. 2003, 2004, 2007; Pyatt and Grattan 2002; Pyatt et al. 2000, 2005). Levels of copper and lead in the ancient skeletons suggest that 44 percent of these individuals were exposed to toxic concentrations of these heavy metals (Grattan et al. 2002). Tests of soil surrounding the burials (Grattan et al. 2002) and patterns of lead and copper partitioning throughout portions of the humerii and skeletons as a whole (Grattan et al. 2005) suggest that these levels do not reflect diagenetic contamination. Grattan, Pyatt, and colleagues thus surmise that individuals with high levels of lead and copper exposure actually had worked longer in the mines or resided longer at the site, while people with lower values died soon after arriving in the area.

The origins of individuals dying at Faynan and their possible role in the mines were explored through bioarchaeological data on exposure to toxic heavy metals and migration. If these individuals were mining camp prisoners, one would expect evidence for a nonlocal origin and *less* exposure to heavy metals due to childhoods spent in uncontaminated regions and death soon after arriving at the mining camp resulting from the poor working conditions described in historical sources. These data will illuminate the reality of Byzantine administrators regularly transporting criminals over long distances to mines such as Phaeno.

The Geologic Settling of Faynan

The site of Phaeno is located along the eastern edge of Wadi Araba, the southern portion of the Rift Valley system that dominates eastern Israel, the West Bank, and western Jordan. Faynan sits at the confluence of wadis Dana, Ghuwayr, and Shegar, which continue as Wadi Faynan into Wadi Araba. The sediments within these wadi systems vary slightly according to the bedrock lining each channel (Barker et al. 1998; Hunt et al. 2007; McLaren et al. 2004), although in general they are composed of Holocene-period alluvium, colluvium, and aeolian sediments eroded from Middle and Lower Cambrian dolomite limestone and shale, in addition to sandstone formations lining the escarpment and wadis (Bender 1974; Hunt et al. 2007).

Characterization of strontium isotopes based on archaeological faunal dental enamel shows that western Jordan can be split into three north–south zones: the Rift Valley ($^{87}Sr/^{86}Sr$ = .70781–.70786), the western highlands ($^{87}Sr/^{86}Sr$ = .70815–.70834), and the wadi and mountain systems in between the valley and the highlands ($^{87}Sr/^{86}Sr$ = .70792–.70810) (Perry et al. 2008). Faynan is situated within the geologically complex mountain and wadi systems that line the eastern escarpment of the Rift Valley, which includes the Jordan Valley, the Dead Sea basin, and Wadi Araba (Perry et al. 2009). The local range at the site was established through testing faunal dental enamel and snail shells recovered from a nearby site (Figure 17.3). Individuals with a $^{87}Sr/^{86}Sr$ signature outside of ± 2 standard deviations from the sample mean would therefore be identified as nonlocal.

Methods

To investigate migration into Faynan, dental enamel samples were collected from 31 burials from the Byzantine cemetery (Table 17.1). Additionally, one rodent dental enamel sample and eight land snail shells from Jebel Hamrat Fidan, about 10 km east of Khirbet Faynan, were used to establish a "local" $^{87}Sr/^{86}Sr$ value. Researchers have demonstrated homogeneity in land snail shell and faunal values within a site (Blum et al. 2000). Land snail shells were sampled from across Fidan to best reflect the local strontium, since land snails have a smaller home range than small mammals. The archaeological human and faunal dental enamel

Table 17.1. Results of $^{87}Sr/^{86}Sr$ Analysis of Archaeological Human Dental Enamel from Faynan.

Context	Age	Sex	Corrected $^{87}Sr/^{86}Sr$[1]	Tooth Sampled	Copper (µg/g)[2]	Lead (µg/g)[b]
Grave 11	35–39	F?	.707976	RM_1	9.8	1.8
Grave 12	50+	F	.707869	RM_1	8.6	112.3
Grave 25	40–44	M	.707849	M^1	109.1	170.0
Grave 63	35–39	F	.707992	LM_1	–	–
Grave 67	6 years ± 24 months	?	.707896	PM_1	181	289.2
Grave 69	Adult	?	.707979	RPM_2	17.1	27.6
Grave 70	25–29	F	.707854	RPM^2	5.0	1.0
Grave 71	20–25	F	.707906	LM^1	–	–
Grave 72	25–29	M	.708006	LM^1	3.0	13.0
Grave 73	30–34	F	.707971	UPM^2	296.2	19.1
Grave 75	45–49	F	.707939	RPM^1	7.0	42.0
Grave 78	7–9	?	.707975	?	20.0	12.8
Grave 80	35–39	F	.707978	RM^1	6.3	37.7
Grave 81	30–35	F	.708009	LM^1	7.0	27.9
Grave 83	45–49	F	.708004	LPM_2	11.0	28.9
Grave 84	35–39	F	.707926	PM	–	–
Grave 87	30–34	M	.708005	LPM^1	2.4	4.7
Grave 88	Adult	M?	.708030	LM^2	135.6	75.6
Grave 96	20–25	M	.707842	RM^1	90.7	44.3
Grave 97	20–24	F?	.707921	PM_1	5.7	13.7
Grave 99	3 years ± 12 months	?	.707952	Rm^1	–	–
Grave 100B	3 years ± 12 months	?	.708087	Lm^1	–	–
Grave 102	30–34	M	.708301	PM_1	27.5	75.6
Grave 104	7 years ± 24 months	?	.707755	LUc	43.1	17.01
Grave 105	10 year ± 30 months	?	.708006	RM_1	17.9	37.1
Grave 107	30–39	F	.707809	RM_1	–	–
Grave 108	Adult	?	.707925	LPM_1	–	–
Grave 109	25–29	M	.707853	LM^1	–	–
Grave 112	45–49	?	.707830	RPM_1	5.9	14.4
Grave 115	Adult	F	.707905	RM_1	–	–
Grave 117	30–35	F	.707913	RM^1	22.4	93.7

1. NBS 987 Standard
   Running mean .710270
   2σ standard deviation .000014
2. From Grattan et al. 2002.

samples were processed and mechanically cleaned in the Bioarchaeology Laboratory at East Carolina University. The 31 human dental enamel, one faunal dental enamel, and seven snail shell samples were then chemically cleaned, and the strontium was extracted and measured using a VG Micromass Sector 54 TIMS in quintuple-collector dynamic mode at the Isotope Geochemistry Laboratory in the Department of Geosciences at the University of North Carolina–Chapel Hill. Samples were prepared by dissolution in 7N HNO^3, dried, and redissolved in 3.5 N HNO^3 for ion-exchange column chromatography. Strontium was isolated using Sr-specific resin from Eichrom Technologies. Purified Sr was loaded on single Re filaments with TaCl and analyzed with ^{88}Sr = 3V (10^–11 ohm resistor) in triple dynamic mode. All Sr data are normalized to $^{86}Sr/^{88}Sr$ = .1194. Total procedural Sr blanks during these analyses was less than 30 pg Sr. The UNC–Chapel Hill ratios are reported relative to a value of .710270 ± .000014 (2σ) for the NBS 987 standard. Internal precision for strontium runs is typically ± .00012 to ± .00018 percent (2σ) based on 100 dynamic cycles of data collection. Fourier transform infrared (FTIR) spectral analysis on 14 randomly selected teeth discovered that tooth microstructure is minimally altered and that isotopic data are unlikely to be modified by diagenesis (see Perry et al. 2009).

Results

The estimated local $^{87}Sr/^{86}Sr$ signature at Faynan based on the faunal bone and shell sample mean (± 2σ) ranges between .707929 and .708144 (Table 17.2) (see also Perry et al. 2009). While less than half of the tested human samples fall under this range, there is no distinct cutoff in the distribution of these values indicating clear "local" versus "nonlocal" individuals (Figure 17.3). Therefore, it is likely that the faunal values do not accurately reflect the full range of Sr isotope variation at Faynan and that most of these individuals are local. Removing the one outlier (Grave 102) from the sample results in a normal distribution with no outliers (see Perry et al. 2009).

It thus appears that the individual from Grave 102 is the only nonlocal individual in the sample and that the other burials contain locally derived residents of Faynan. The Grave 102 burial had a $^{87}Sr/^{86}Sr$ value much higher than the local range, one mirroring strontium isotope ratios from the coastal region and foothills of the Galilee Range in Israel (Perry et al. 2008; Shewan 2004), although presumably other areas in the Levant have this value as well.

Copper and lead skeletal concentrations were compared with $^{87}Sr/^{86}Sr$ values to determine if local versus nonlocal origin could predict the exposure level of

Table 17.2. Results of $^{87}Sr/^{86}Sr$ Analysis of Archaeological Fauna from Jebel Hamrat Fidan.

Context	Corrected $^{87}Sr/^{86}Sr$[1]	Sample Type
1999 H 120 L. 1039 B.14345	.708071	snail shell
1999 H 120 L. 1052 B. 149412	.708005	snail shell
1999 Y 120 L. 1248 B. 35129	.707984	snail shell
2000 H 120 L. 2081 B. 56282	.707948	snail shell
2000 H 120 L. 2100 B. 56850	.708040	snail shell
2000 H 120 L. 2106 B. 57089	.708085	snail shell
2000 H120 L. 2107 B.57107	.708105	snail shell
Area C, Grave 701	.708053	rodent dental enamel

1. NBS 987 Standard
Running mean .710270
2σ standard deviation .000014

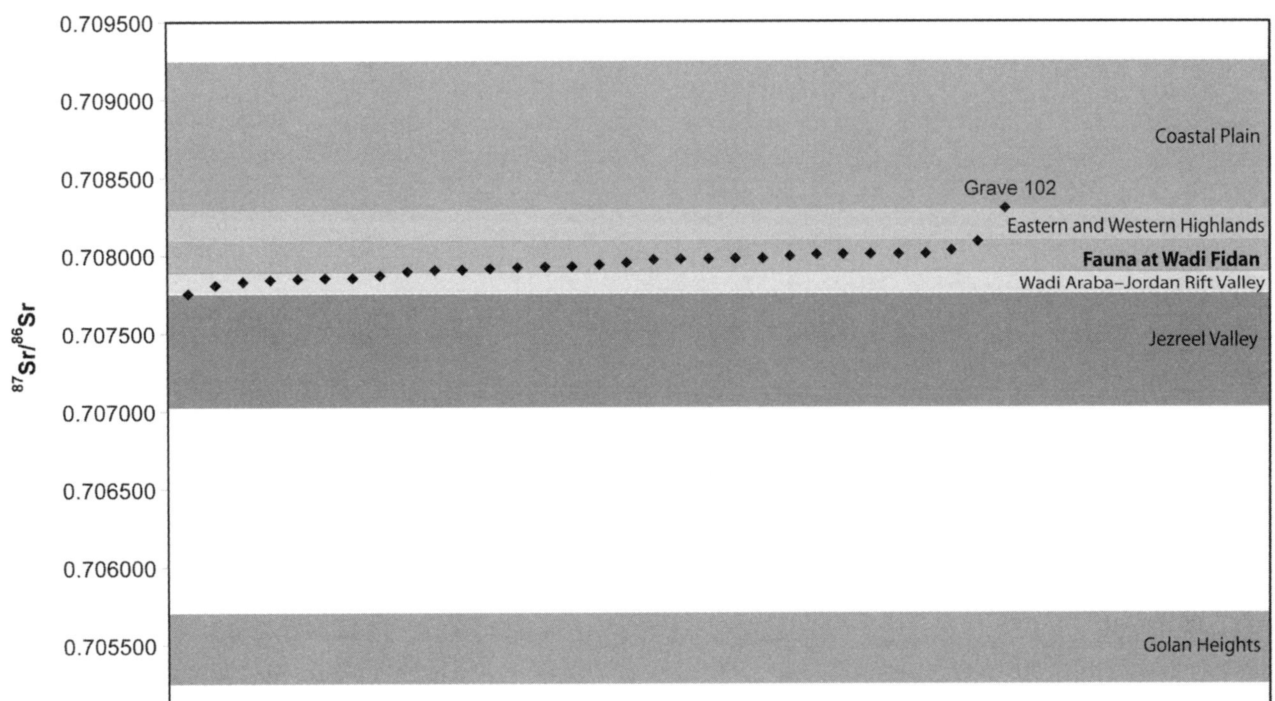

Figure 17.3. $^{87}Sr/^{86}Sr$ values of burials from Faynan compared with the range established by local archaeological faunal samples from Jebel Hamrat Fidan.

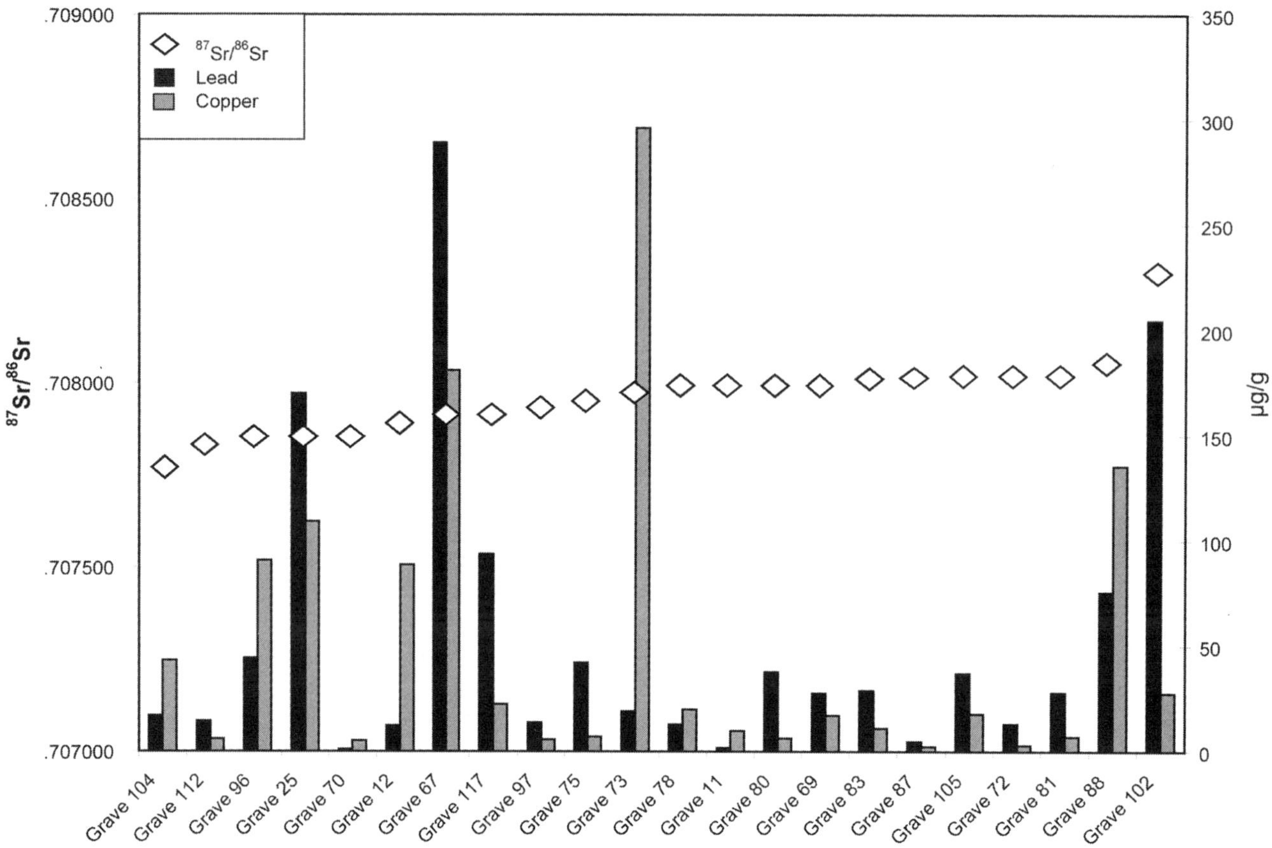

Figure 17.4. Archaeological human $^{87}Sr/^{86}Sr$ values from Faynan compared with skeletal copper and lead concentrations.

individuals to the mining environment based on their lead and copper skeletal levels (Figure 17.4). The one nonlocal individual had the second-highest lead level in the sample and a slightly elevated copper level. The local individuals, on the other hand, had a range of copper and lead levels in their skeletons. Some individuals had slightly elevated levels; others had extremely high amounts compared with a reference sample mean (see Grattan et al. 2002:301). Compared with a reference sample with "normal" copper and lead levels, 10 individuals from Faynan had copper levels greater than 2 standard deviations of the reference sample mean, and 22 had lead levels more than 2 standard deviations of the reference sample mean. These data imply that individuals of local origin carried out diverse roles at the mining camp that resulted in varied exposure to environmental pollutants.

Discussion

The Faynan sample was expected to contain a mix of locally and nonlocally born individuals. Many individuals residing at the site, however, remain invisible in historical sources. The camp certainly contained administrative staff or free mine laborers and their families, and possibly the families of prisoners. The fourth-to-sixth-century A.D. cemetery, for instance, contains children under the age of seven years, whom Byzantine courts would have exempted from many crimes (Prinzing 2006; Robinson 1995). They thus lived at Faynan because their parents resided there for employment or punishment.

Analysis of the strontium isotope data reveals only one nonlocal individual in the sample, possibly originating from the Mediterranean coast, the origin of many Phaeno prisoners during the early fourth century according to historical sources. Most burials instead likely are of individuals originating from the areas immediately surrounding Faynan or other geologically similar areas. Therefore, the most parsimonious explanation is that during the fourth to sixth centuries, Faynan residents primarily were locally born individuals, there for economic or social rather than punitive reasons. The Byzantine Empire in the later fourth century additionally may have considered the transport of prisoners from afar to the mines an unnecessary expense and sent only local miscreants to Phaeno for punishment.

These data further suggest that local individuals had varied exposure to copper and lead contaminants. Investigations at modern Faynan identified an environment markedly enriched with copper, lead, and other metals that presumably existed in antiquity (Grattan et al. 2003, 2007; Pyatt et al. 1999, 2000, 2002), suggesting that most residents of Faynan would have been exposed to a polluted environment. In fact, most Faynan individuals in this sample had elevated skeletal copper and lead concentrations, and 21 individuals had extremely elevated copper and/or lead levels. This may indicate that while everyone who lived at Faynan had slightly elevated copper and lead levels due to environmental exposure, some residents were particularly susceptible due to their direct involvement in industrial mining activities. Grattan and colleagues (2007) recently reported that varied patterns of anthropogenic, aeolian, and colluvial deposition of heavy metal pollution resulted in heterogeneous intrasite environmental copper and lead concentrations. Therefore, some differences in lead and copper concentrations should exist between site residents.

The children at Faynan displayed particularly toxic concentrations of copper and lead. Although no children under the age of 6 (± 24 months) were tested for lead and copper concentrations, three out of four children between 6 (± 24 months) and 10 (± 30 months) had extremely elevated lead levels, and half had enhanced copper levels. These high concentrations could have resulted from the primarily gastrointestinal absorption of contamination seen in children (e.g., Carrizales et al. 2006; Paoliello et al. 2002; Simon et al. 2007) or from the higher absorption of lead into the body by children's blood compared with adults' blood (Leggett 1993; O'Flaherty 1995). Another possibility is that the less mineralized and more porous subadult bones could be affected by digenetic contamination reflected as higher Cu or Pb levels (e.g., Guy et al. 1997; Lambert et al. 1979; Sandford et al. 1988). None of these individuals were tested by Grattan and collegues for diagenesis via assessing the partitioning of Cu or Pb in the humerus or soil samples from the grave context (Grattan et al. 2002). The presence of enhanced copper and lead concentrations in juvenile skeletons must be interpreted with caution.

The Faynan labor structure therefore included individuals not directly involved with industrial activities. These primarily locally born individuals could have been involved in administration or logistical support, which put them at decreased risk for lead or copper exposure. For instance, an extensive survey of agricultural fields surrounding Khirbet Faynan discovered that after the Roman period, fields were managed together, likely at the state level, for feeding administrative personnel and the labor force (Barker et al. 2000). The ancient sources' focus on the prisoners sent to mining camps therefore does not fully represent the labor structure of these camps. Emphasis on the terrible fate to befall someone sent to the mines likely served to instill fear and obedience in potential criminals or to glorify the sacrifices of Christian martyrs.

The role that individuals buried in the Faynan cemetery played in the Phaeno mining camps increasingly emerges through bioarchaeological analyses. Historical sources emphasize the grim reality of life in the mines, which frequently served as the final resting place for slaves and lower-class convicts in the Byzantine East. Researchers assume that burials in the Byzantine cemetery contain prisoners sentenced to the mines under circumstances similar to Eusebius's description. Bone chemistry tells a different story, however.

Researchers suggest that residence in the area would lead to elevated bioaccumulation of heavy metals due to the contaminated environment. Instead, individuals identified as "local" by their $^{87}Sr/^{86}Sr$ signature had varied lead levels and copper levels. This suggests that increased bioaccumulation of copper results from greater exposure to the mining environment rather than simply residing at Faynan. Strontium isotope data also do not identify wide-scale transport of prisoners to the mine, although punishment of locals at Phaeno remains a possibility. The cemetery therefore contains individuals with varied roles at the site.

Acknowledgements. The authors would like to thank Fawwaz al-Khraysheh, former director-general of the Department of Antiquities of Jordan, for facilitating this research. We also would like to thank Tom Levy and Adolfo Muñiz of the University of California–San Diego for providing the faunal samples from Jebel Hamrat Fidan. The Faynan South Cemetery excavations were cosponsored by the Faculty of Archaeology and Anthropology at Yarmouk University and CBRL-Amman. Funding for this research was provided by an East Carolina University CRA Award and an ACOR CAORC Senior Fellowship.

References Cited

Abu-Karaki, Lotus Omar

2000 Skeletal Biology of the People of Wadi Faynan: A Bioarchaeological Study. Unpublished M.A. thesis, Yarmouk University.

Barker, Graheme A., Russell Adams, Oliver H. Creighton, D. Crook, David D. Gilbertson, J. P. Grattan, Chris O. Hunt et al.

1999 Environment and Land Use in the Wadi Faynan, Southern Jordan: The Third Season of Geoarchaeology and Landscape Archaeology (1998). *Levant* 31:255–292.

Barker, Graheme A., Russell Adams, Oliver H. Creighton, Patrick Daly, David D. Gilbertson, Chris O. Hunt, David J. Mattingly et al.

2000 Archaeology and Desertification in the Wadi Faynan, Southern Jordan: The Fourth (1999) Season of Wadi Faynan Landscape Survey. *Levant* 32:7–52.

Barker, Graheme A., Russell Adams, Oliver H. Creighton, David D. Gilbertson, John P. Grattan, Chris O. Hunt, David J. Mattingly et al.

1998 Environment and Land Use in the Wadi Faynan, Southern Jordan: The Second Season of Geoarchaeology and Landscape Archaeology (1997). *Levant* 30:5–25.

Bender, Friedrich

1974 *Geology of Jordan*. Translated by M. K. Khdein, U. Wilkening, and D. Parker. Gebr. Borntraegger, Berlin.

Blum, Joel D., E. Hank Taliaferro, Marie T. Weisse, and Richard T. Holmes

2000 Changes in Sr/Ca, Ba/Ca and $^{87}Sr/^{86}Sr$ ratios between Trophic Levels in Two Forest Ecosystems in the Northeastern U.S.A. *Biogeochemistry* 49:87–101.

Buikstra, Jane E.

1977 Biocultural Dimensions of Archeological Study: A Regional Perspective. In *Biocultural Adaptation in Prehistoric America*, edited by Robert L. Blakely, pp. 67–84. Southern Anthropological Society Proceedings No. 11. University of Georgia Press, Athens.

2000 Historical Bioarcheology and the Beautification of Death. In *Never Anything So Solemn: An Archeological, Biological, and Historical Investigation of the Nineteenth-Century Grafton Cemetery*, edited by J. E. Buikstra, J. A. O'Gorman, and C. Sutton, pp. 15–20. Kampsville Studies in Archeology and History No. 3. Center for American Archeology, Kampsville, Illinois.

Carrizales, Leticia, Israel Razo, Jesús I. Téllez-Hernández, Rocío Torres-Nerio, Arturo Torres, Lilla E. Batres, Ana-Cristina Cubillas, and Fernando Díaz-Barriga

2006 Exposure to Arsenic and Lead of Children Living near a Copper-Smelter in San Luis Potosi, Mexico: Importance of Soil Contamination for Exposure of Children. *Environmental Research* 101:1–10.

Diodorus Siculus

1954 *Library of History*. Translated by R. M. Greer. Harvard University Press, Cambridge.

el-Najjar, Mahmoud, and Abdel Halim al-Shiyab

1998 Skeletal Biology and Pathology of the People of Wadi Faynan in Southern Jordan. *Mu'tah lil-Buhuth wad-Dirasat* 13(3):9–39.

Eusebius of Caesarea

1927 Ecclesiastical History and the Martyrs of Palestine. Translated by H. J. Lawlor and J. E. L. Oulton. Macmillan, New York.

Findlater, George, Mahmoud el-Najjar, Abdel-Halim al-Shiyab, Margaret O'Hea, and Edward Easthaugh

1998 The Wadi Faynan Project: The South Cemetery Excavation, Jordan 1996: A Preliminary Report. *Levant* 30:69–83.

González-Reimers, Emilio, Javier Velasco-Vázquez, M. Arnay-de-la-Rosa, Veronica Alberto-Barroso, L. Gilando-Martín, and Franciso Santolaria-Fernández

2003 Bone Cadmium and Lead in Prehistoric Inhabitants and Domestic Animals from Gran Canaria. *Science of the Total Environment* 310:97–103.

González-Reimers, Emilio, Javier Velasco-Vázquez, M. Arnay-de-la-Rosa, Francisco Santolaria-Fernández, and L. Gilando-Martín

2001 Paleonutritional Analysis of the Pre-Hispanic Population from Fuerteventura (Canary Islands). *Science of the Total Environment* 264:215–220.

Grattan, John P., David D. Gilbertson, and Colleen O. Hunt

2007 The Local and Global Dimensions of Metalliferous Pollution Derived from a Reconstruction of an Eight Thousand Year Record of Copper Smelting and Mining at a Desert-Mountain Frontier in Southern Jordan. *Journal of Archaeological Science* 34:83–110.

Grattan, John P., Gavin K. Gillmore, David D. Gilbertson, Bryan Pyatt, Colleen O. Hunt, Sue J. McLaren, P. S. Phillips, and A. Dennan

2004 Radon and "King Solomon's Miners": Faynan Orefield, Jordanian Desert. *Science of the Total Environment* 319:99–113.

Grattan, John P., Steven Huxley, Lotus Abu-Karaki, Harry Toland, David D. Gilbertson, Brian Pyatt, and Ziad al Saad

2002 "Death . . . more desirable than life"? The Human Skeletal Record and Toxicological Implications of Ancient Copper Mining and Smelting in Wadi Faynan, Southwestern Jordan. *Toxicology and Industrial Health* 18:297–307.

Grattan, John P., Steven Huxley, and Bryan Pyatt

2003 Modern Bedouin Exposures to Copper Contamination: An Imperial Legacy? *Ecotoxicology and Environmental Safety* 55:108–115.

Grattan, John P., Abu Keraki, D. Hine, Harry Toland, David Gilbertson, Ziad al-Saad, and Brian Pyatt

2005 Analyses of Patterns of Copper and Lead Mineralization in Human Skeletons Excavated from an Ancient Mining and Smelting Centre in the Jordanian Desert: A Reconnaissance Study. *Mineralogical Magazine* 69:653–666.

Guy, Hervé, Claude Massett, and Charles-Albert Baud

1997 Infant Taphonomy. *International Journal of Osteoarchaeology* 7:221–229.

Hauptmann, Andreas

2000 *Zur frühen Metallurgie des Kupfers in Fenan/Jordanien*. Deutsch Bergbau Museum, Bochum, Germany.

Hauptmann, Andreas, and Gerard Weisgerber

1987 Archaeometallurgical and Mining-Archaeological Investigations in the Area of Feinan, Wadi 'Arabah (Jordan). *Annual of the Department of Antiquities of Jordan* 31:419–437.

1992 Periods of Ore Exploration and Metal Production in the Area of Feinan, Wadi 'Araba, Jordan. In *Studies in the History and Archaeology of Jordan IV*, edited by M. Zaghlou, K. 'Amr, F. Zayadine, and R. Nabeel, pp. 61–66. Department of Antiquities of Jordan, Amman.

Hunt, Chris O., David D. Gilbertson, and Hwedi A. El-Rishi

2007 An 8000-Year History of Landscape, Climate, and Copper Exploitation in the Middle East: The Wadi Faynan and the Wadi Dana National Reserve in Southern Jordan. *Journal of Archaeological Science* 34:1306–1338.

Lambert, Joseph B., Carole B. Szpunar, and Jane E. Buikstra

1979 Chemical Analysis of Excavated Human Bone from Middle and Late Woodland Sites. *Archaeometry* 21:115–129.

Leggett, Richard

1993 An Age-Specific Kinetic Model of Lead Metabolism in Humans. *Environmental Health Perspectives* 101:598–616.

Lucretius

1924 *De Rerum Natura*. Translated by W. H. D. Rouse and M. F. Smith. Harvard University Press, Cambridge.

Mattingly, David, Paul Newson, Oliver Creighton, Roberta Tomber, John P. Grattan, Chris O. Hunt, David D. Gilbertson, Hwedi el-Rishi, and Brian Pyatt

2007 A Landscape of Imperial Power: Roman and Byzantine *Phaino*. In *Archaeology and Desertification: The Wadi Faynan Landscape Survey, Southern Jordan*, edited by G. Barker, D. D. Gilbertson, and D. Mattingly, pp. 305–348. Oxbow Books, Oxford.

McLaren, Sue J., David D. Gilbertson, John P. Grattan, Chris O. Hunt, Geoff A. T. Duller, and Graeme A. Barker
2004 Quaternary Palaeogeomorphologic Evolution of the Wadi Faynan Area, Southern Jordan. *Palaeogeography, Palaeoclimatology, Palaeoecology* 205:131–154.

Millar, Fergus
1984 Condemnation to Hard Labour in the Roman Empire, from the Julio-Claudians to Constantine. *Papers of the British School at Rome* 52:124–147.

O'Flaherty, Ellen
1995 Physiologically Based Models for Bone-Seeking Elements. V. Lead Absorption and Disposition in Childhood. *Toxicology and Applied Pharamacology* 131:297–308.

Paoliello, Monica Maria Bastos, Eduardo Mello De Capitani, Fernanda Gonçalves da Cunha, Tiemi Matsuo, Maria de Fátima Carvalho, Alice Sakuma, and Bernardino Ribeiro Figueiredo
2002 Exposure of Children to Lead and Cadmium from a Mining Area of Brazil. *Environmental Research Section A* 88:120–128.

Perry, Megan A.
2007 Is Bioarchaeology a Handmaiden to History? Developing a Historical Bioarchaeology. *Journal of Anthropological Archaeology* 26:486–515.

Perry, Megan A., Drew Coleman, and Nathalie Delhopital
2008 Mobility and Exile at 2nd Century A.D. Khirbet edh-Dharih: Strontium Isotope Analysis of Human Migration in Western Jordan. *Geoarchaeology* 23:528–549.

Perry, Megan A., Drew Coleman, David L. Dettman, and Abdel Halim al-Shiyab
2009 An Isotopic Perspective on the Transport of Byzantine Mining Camp Laborers into Southwestern Jordan. *American Journal of Physical Anthropology*, doi:10.1002/ajpa.21085.

Pliny the Elder
1947 *Natural History*. Translated by W. H. S. Jones. W. Heinemann, London.

Prinzing, Gunter
2006 The Status of Children and Adolescents in Byzantium Under Law and in Court. Paper presented at the Byzantine Studies 2006 Spring Symposium, Dumbarton Oaks, Washington, D.C.

Pyatt, Andrea J., Graeme Barker, P. Birch, David D. Gilbertson, John P. Grattan, and David J. Mattingly
1999 King Solomon's Miners: Starvation and Bioaccumulation? *Ecotoxicology and Environmental Safety* 43:305–308.

Pyatt, Andrea J., and John P. Grattan
2002 A Public Health Problem? Aspects and Implications of the Ingestion of Copper and Lead Contaminated Food by Bedouin. *Environmental Management and Health* 13:467–470.

Pyatt, F. Brian, Gavin Gillmore, John P. Grattan, Chris O. Hunt, and Sue J. McLaren
2000 An Imperial Legacy? An Exploration of the Environmental Impact of Ancient Metal Mining and Smelting in Southern Jordan. *Journal of Archaeological Science* 27:771–778.

Pyatt, F. Brian, Andrea J. Pyatt, C. Walker, T. Sheen, and John P. Grattan
2005 The Heavy Metal Content of Skeletons from an Ancient Metalliferous Polluted Area in Southern Jordan with Particular Reference to Bioaccumulation and Human Health. *Ecotoxicology and Environmental Safety* 60:295–300.

Robinson, O. F.
1995 *Penal Practice and Penal Policy in Ancient Rome*. Routledge, London.

Sandford, Mary, David Repke, and A. Earle
1988 Elemental Analysis of Human Bone from Carthage: A Pilot Study. In *The Circus and a Byznatine Cemetery at Carthage*, vol. 1, edited by J. Humphrey, pp. 285–296. University of Michigan, Ann Arbor.

Shewan, Louise
2004 Natufian Settlement Systems and Adaptive Strategies: The Issue of Sedentism and the Potential of Strontium Isotope Analysis. In *The Last Hunter-Gatherers in the Near East*, edited by Christophe Delage, pp. 55–94. BAR International Series 1320. BAR, Oxford.

Simon, David L., Edward J. Maynard, and Katherine D. Thomas
2007 Living in a Sea of Lead: Changes in Blood- and Hand-Lead of Infants Living near a Smelter. *Journal of Exposure Science and Environmental Epidemiology* 17:248–259.

Strabo
1930 *Geography*. Translated by H. L. Jones. Putnam, New York.

Vitruvius
1931 *De Architectura*. Translated by F. Granger. Harvard University Press, Cambridge.

18

Taphonomy and Funerary Practices in Collective Cemeteries:

A Prehistoric Case from Menorca (Balearic Islands, Spain)

Vicente Lull
Departament de Prehistòria, Universitat Autònoma de Barcelona
Rafael Micó
Departament de Prehistòria, Universitat Autònoma de Barcelona
Cristina Rihuete
Museu Arqueològic de Son Fornés, Molí d'en Fraret, C/ Emili Pou s/n, 07230 Montuïri, Mallorca
Robert Risch
Departament de Prehistòria, Universitat Autònoma de Barcelona

This chapter deals with "collective burials" as a category applied to the treatment and final disposal of the dead. These burials are characterized by the following main archaeological features: the absence of individual funerary containers and a lack of any apparent order or patterning in the spatial distribution of skeletal material.

Millennia of funerary activity in many European caves and rock shelters have produced thousands of archaeological sites from different chronological periods where remains of several dozen or even hundreds of people are mixed together. These sites include not only natural or artificially made caves (hypogea, or rock-cut tombs) but also megaliths and other monuments. Many of these graveyards, spanning from the Neolithic until historical times, have been interpreted as ossuaries, implying the accumulation of secondary inhumations. Needless to say, most of them were discovered and excavated a long time ago, with little sensitive attention paid to the recovery of material remains other than artifacts and with sketchy stratigraphic/contextual information. However, more recent works have also failed to provide a proper record regarding the treatment and disposal of the dead through the time span of cemetery use. As a result, categories of mortuary analysis end up being based more upon assumptions and speculation than on positive evidence. On the other hand, collective burials have traditionally been conceived as an attribute of, in processual terms, nonstratified societies, also called small-scale segmentary societies (Renfrew 1976). The term *collective* is often understood as synonymous with *homogeneous*, and other possible dimensions of variability are frequently neglected. Clearly, this oversimplification will hardly help us explore the expected wide array of social organizations developed by extinct societies.

Our perspective, which aims at searching for meaningful patterns, has a lot to do with the pioneering work of Jane E. Buikstra in promoting an integrated bioarchaeological approach to the study of funerary practices. Our research projects on Argaric Bronze Age societies in southeastern Spain (Buikstra et al. 1990, 1995; Castro et al. 1999; Lull 2000; Lull et al. 2005) have benefited much from her expertise and collaboration. In the case study we present here, her role as the mentor of one of us (C. Rihuete) in osteological analysis has had a major influence in shaping the general approach to the funerary record under consideration.

CÀRRITX CAVE

Menorca is located in the western Mediterranean and is the northernmost island of the Balearic Islands. Although it was peopled relatively late (by the end of the third millennium B.C.), it is extremely rich in archaeological sites. (For an updated review of the prehistory of the island, see Guerrero 2007; Micó 2005, 2006.) Menorca's geography is characterized by a flat landscape with a series of gorges running southward and with steep cliffs hollowed by numerous caves, either natural or artificially made. Difficult access, lack of close spatial relationships among settlements, and ritual use throughout prehistory are constant features in the cave record of the island.

The Càrritx Cave (Figure 18.1), lying some 30 m above the basin of the Algendar Gorge, fits the pattern of a natural cave whose entrance had been closed by what is traditionally known as a cyclopean wall, leaving a narrow space for a doorway as the only possible access. It was discovered by chance in 1995, and results of the subsequent research program have been fully published (Lull et al. 1999a, 1999b, 2002; Rihuete 2003a, 2003b, 2005). Geostratigraphical analysis has demonstrated that a collapse of the rock wall above the entrance, which happened not too long after the final abandonment of the necropolis, sealed off the archaeological deposit and contributed to the extraordinary state of preservation at the site.

The cave, with a total length of 210 m, has seven different chambers, but the cemetery was restricted to the first one: a two-level space of 32 m^2 (Figure 18.2). This funerary space contained thousands of human bones along with scattered pottery fragments, faunal and botanic remains, items of clothing, tools, and ornaments that had accumulated over 600 years (circa 1450–850 cal B.C.).

Human remains were primarily disarticulated. The total collection comprises almost 35,000 elements from 210 individuals (MNI) corresponding to a normal demographic profile (both sexes and all age categories

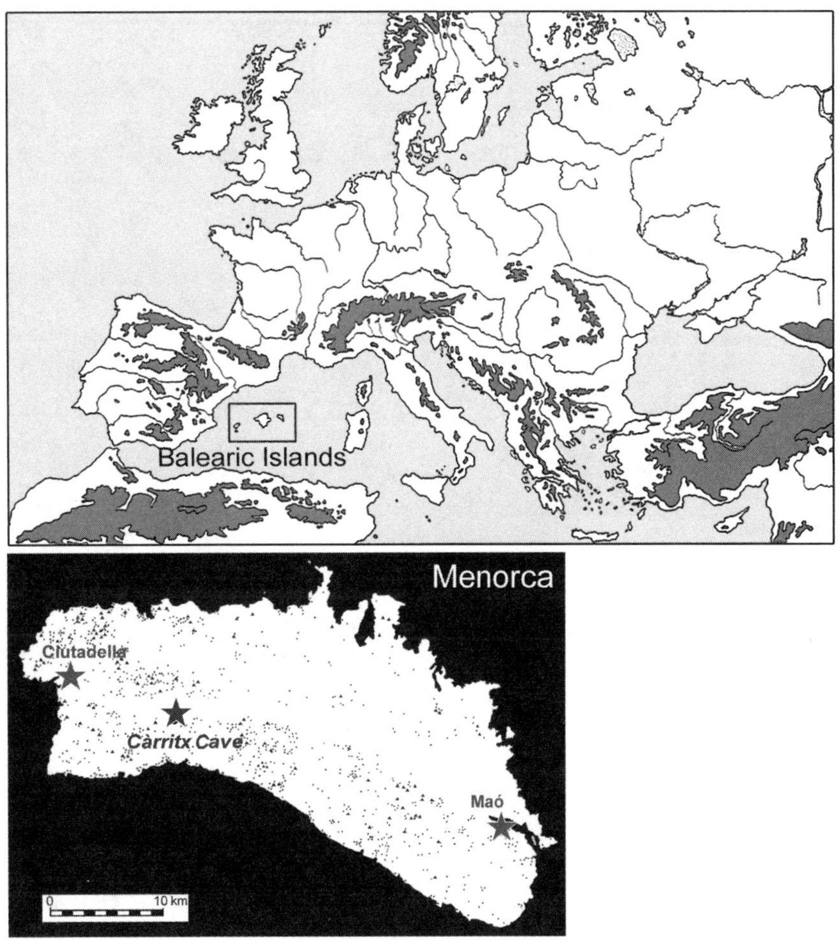

Figure 18.1. Location of Càrritx Cave.

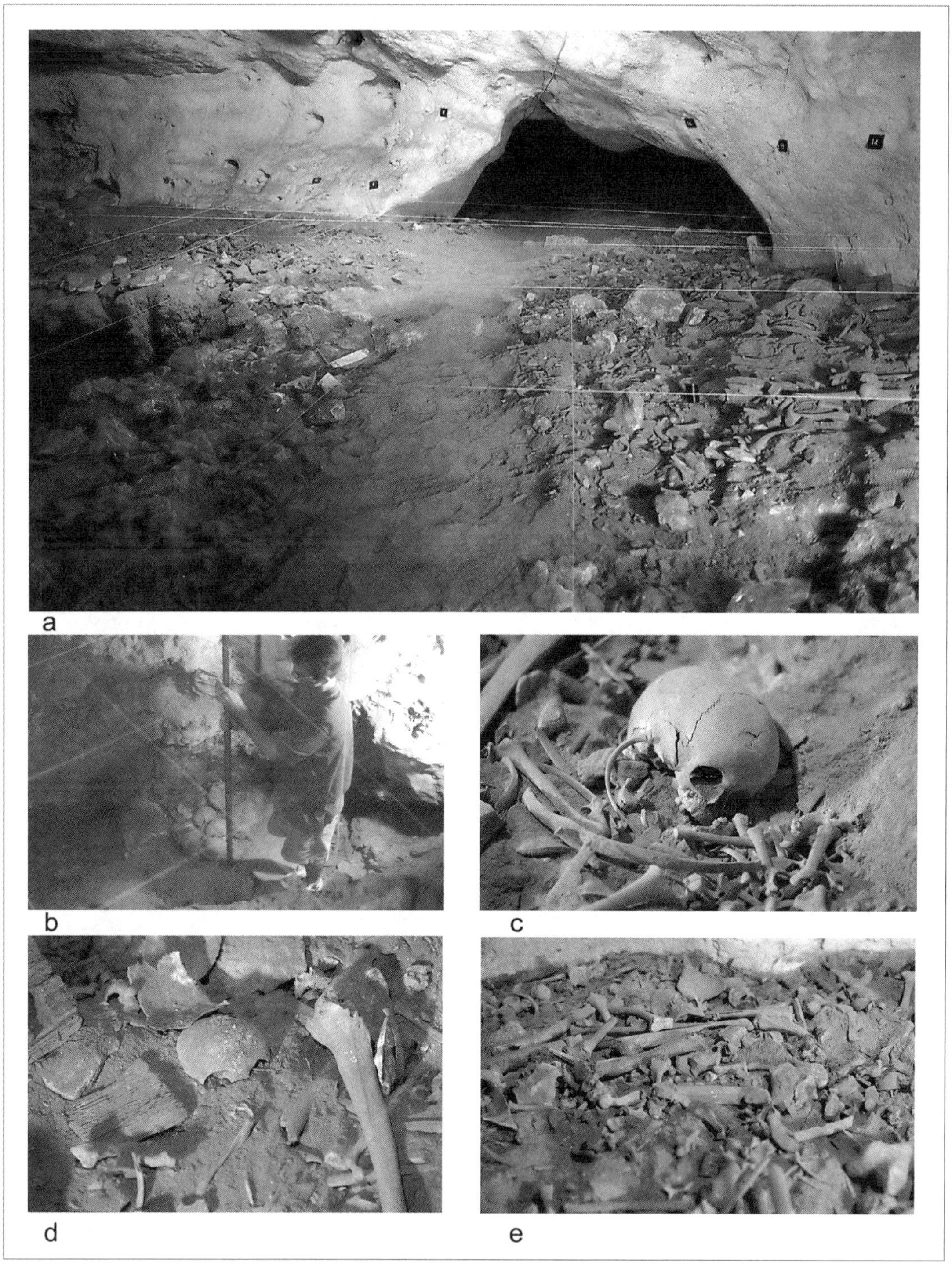

Figure 18.2. Burial chamber: (a) general view of the upper level; (b) lower level with cluster of skulls; (c–e) different aspects of the burial chamber upon its discovery.

included, except for fetuses and neonates). Some bones were burned, others appeared partially articulated, and still others, mainly skulls, were removed from their original locations and grouped together. The questions posed by these evidences can be summarized as follows:

- Were there multiple choices of burial?
- Was cremation an alternative to inhumation?
- Were commingled remains the product of spaced but continuous primary interments or the expected result of secondary inhumation in its proper sense?
- If body parts had been segregated and relocated, would that account for a differentiation among individuals?
- Were there any changes through time that would explain changes in mortuary procedures?

Cremation Versus Inhumation

In the Balearic Islands, cremation has been reported for other sites. The most well-known example comes from Son Matge (Mallorca), a rockshelter closed with a cyclopean wall during its use as a collective graveyard by the end of the second millennium cal B.C. (Waldren 1982). Some burned bones, albeit in low frequencies (2.8 percent), along with burned archaeological artifacts, charred seeds, and charcoal, were found in Càrritx. Therefore, the question arose as to whether cremations had taken place as an alternative to inhumation, either as a new type of rite or as a treatment restricted to certain individuals, or if burning of body parts was intended to accelerate decomposition as part of a process of secondary deposition.

Bone surfaces and lines of fracture showed a great variation in color, from dark brown to gray and white, which indicates different degrees of heat intensity (Etxeberría 1994). However, all burned bones showed the striation patterning typical of dry state conditions (Botella et al. 1999; Guillon 1986,), meaning that in all cases fire had acted upon already skeletonized remains. Therefore, bodies were not cremated. On the contrary, artifact, botanic, and spatial data offer a rather different explanation: accidental contact with fire. The small hearth located right at the entrance provided the first clue for this interpretation. There was also enough evidence of lighting devices in the form of wooden torches and pottery lamps scattered among the human remains. Finally, the identification of a wide array of bushes and aromatic plants, such as *Rosmarinus officinalis*, *Malva* sp., *Silene* cf. *gallica*, *Cistus* sp., and *Pistacea lentiscus* (Stika 1999), provides further support for the performance of rituals where fire must have played a prominent role in providing smoke, specific scents, and other essences.

Primary or Secondary Burials?

Now that it has been established that inhumation was the rule, let's turn to the ossuary status of the cemetery. It is true that human remains were primarily disarticulated, but body part representation (with high frequencies of hand/feet elements and other bones such as the hyoid) and the complete absence of defleshing marks are indeed sound indicators that the cave was a locus for primary inhumations. Moreover, the remains of three individuals in anatomical position (two adult males and a child, all of them located at distant points of the cemetery) also indicate that full bodies were brought into the cave.

In a situation of multiple, successive burials, we would expect the removal of previously skeletonized remains, and in that case the three skeletons preserved in anatomical position would have been the last corpses taken into the burial chamber. This supposition was contradicted by the results from absolute dating, since those individuals stand as the oldest ones for the whole cemetery, and, most interesting, two of them had their skulls and lower maxillae in place. The importance of this observation lies in the fact that many skulls (n = 32) had been carefully lined up at the junction of the floor and cave walls, sometimes arranged in rows four skulls deep. No other meaningful selection of skeletal items could be identified. The skulls correspond to both men and women and all age categories, and not a single one had its mandible in place, which means that heads were fully skeletonized when they were moved from their original positions.

As noted earlier, systematic osteological analysis of the whole skeletal sample in search of decapitation, disarticulation, and any other type of defleshing marks has produced not a single positive instance. Contrary to that, animal activity is confirmed (carnivore/scavengers and rodents), but in very low frequencies (2.4 and .1 percent, respectively) and spatially restricted, probably due to some occasions in which the cave had remained accidentally open. On the other hand, skulls appeared without mandibles, a body part that would have come along if removal of the head had taken place in a fresh condition. Thus the most likely explanation is that segregation and relocation of skulls against the cave walls were performed after natural decomposition and imply a new ritual episode that had to take place sometime after corpses had been transferred to the cave. Environmental conditions of the burial chamber such as high humidity levels (90 percent on average) and darkness (guaranteed by the closing wall and also inferred by the presence of nocturnal birds of prey), as well as clothing worn by the deceased (attested by V-perforated buttons), would have contributed to a more or less rapid disintegration of soft tissues, as forensic taphonomy has shown in comparative cases (Clark et al. 1997).

Finally, a careful spatial analysis of all archaeological materials supports the idea that successive depositions had produced a horizontal stratigraphy expanding from the area of prime exposure, which was identified by means of differential distribution and fragmentation frequencies at the northwestern corner. Funerary practices themselves were, then, the prime agent responsible for the general state of disarticulation. Full corpses were brought in the cave, but mortuary procedures involved new rites performed on the skeletons and focusing upon their heads.

STATIC VERSUS DYNAMIC: DIACHRONIC CHANGES

A series of 19 ^{14}C dates sampled from skeletal material of 18 different individuals (almost 10 percent of the MNI) shows that the cemetery was used from around 1450 to 850 cal B.C. (Figure 18.3). Uniform distribution of dates and lack of hiatus can be taken as an indication of a slow, continuous rate of deposition, without episodes of crises (higher death rates) or abandonment. Sex and age-at-death distributions account for a normal sample, and there are no archaeological reasons to believe that the cemetery is anything other than the accumulation of the deceased from a single community, either kinship or territorially based.

Contemporary settlements are found in open-air cyclopean boat-shaped structures (*naviformes*), most suitable for small residence groups. These dwellings

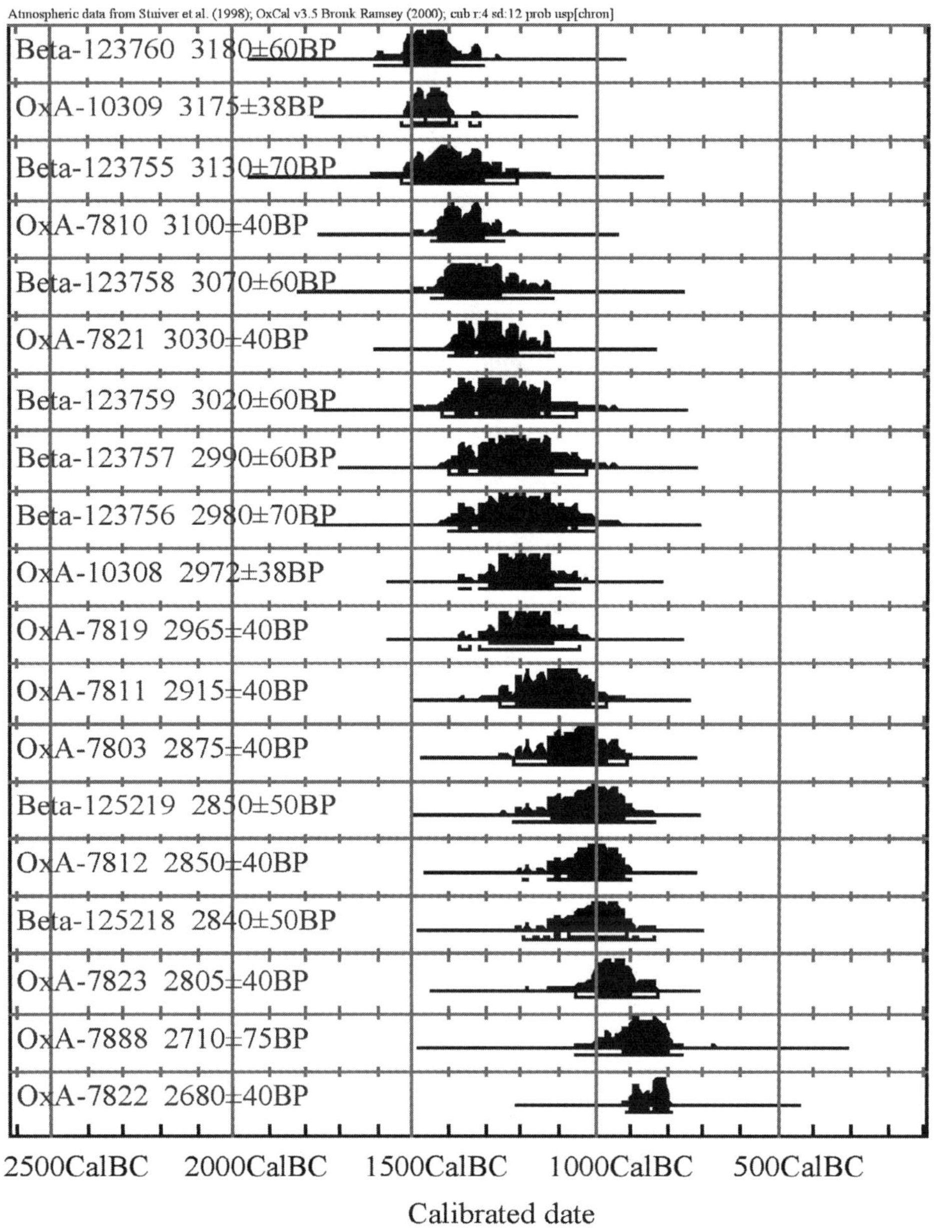

Figure 18.3. Graph of Càrritx ^{14}C probability sum from skeletal samples.

show a process of aggregation/nucleation ending up, by the middle of the eleventh century cal B.C., in new types of villages that incorporate the first attempts at monumental supradomestic towerlike buildings (Gili et al. 2006; Lull et al. 1999b, 2004). Throughout this period of 600 years there is not a single settlement unequivocally connected to its cemetery, and funerary sites display a great typological variability: natural caves, walled caves, rock-cut tombs, and open-air structures (tumular graves and *navetes*). The reasons for that variability aren't quite understood yet, especially because no detailed data on funerary practices are available. However, the sites all seem to have been used as places for communal burial and provide some interesting comparative data for the investigation of other possible dimensions of funerary variability.

In Càrritx, absolute dating and horizontal stratigraphy strongly support the idea that removal and relocation of skulls, a practice that emphasizes at a symbolical level the main physical attribute of the individual (the head), was not performed from the beginning but was introduced by the turn of the millennium. Other sites of similar recent date, such as *navetes*, have been reported as having groups of skulls clustered against chamber walls (Plantalamor and Sastre 1991:165; Veny 1976:228, 1987:447), whereas some walled caves not used after the end of the second millennium (Forat de Ses Aritges) lack evidence of this practice (Lull et al. 1999b:183).

Further support for newly introduced rites matching the chronology of changing settlement patterns and related social transformations by about 1100/1000 cal B.C. is also to be found in Càrritx. In a hidden place some 80 m away from the cave entrance, an amazing set of objects was discovered. These again focused upon the head of the deceased, but now in relation to a few individuals whose hair was dyed, cut, and finally stored in specific containers (Figure 18.4). The wealth of information retrieved from this context has a lot to do with the preservation of organic materials, namely wooden and horn artifacts, as well as human hair itself, but also with a thorough study of different sorts of evidence that allowed linking both chronologically and functionally the cemetery to the cache during the last centuries of its use. Hair and wooden containers from Càrritx were sampled for ^{14}C dating. The results provide further proof about rituals performed on the head of the deceased being introduced by the end of the second millennium. Hair containers of the same type have recently been discovered at another Menorcan burial cave, with unusual preservation of organic matter (Guerrero 2007:184). Carved lids for those containers, but made out of bone, were already known in other contemporary Balearic contexts from Menorca—Calescoves (Veny 1982) and Naveta des Tudons (Pericot 1972:79)—and from Mallorca—Son Matge (Waldren 1982). They all seem to demonstrate that hair manipulation of the deceased was not the rare habit of just one community but part of the normative rituals restricted to certain individuals and performed by the Balearic society in a time of deep social change.

Finally, the same chronological differentiation applies to a set of grave goods, namely a small number of bronze, iron, and lead ornaments found in Càrritx. Again, they all date to the last centuries of the cemetery's use, and again their association is not to an anonymous collectivity but to some specific individuals who seem to have deserved a new, special treatment unknown in previous times.

Conclusions

Following Hertz's seminal essay (1907), "secondary interments" is the corresponding category frequently used to account for mixed, disarticulated human remains in cave burials. However, a research strategy designed to account for taphonomic processes and different dimensions of variability might challenge the assumed homogeneity implied in those interpretations.

In our case study, even though collective inhumation was a standing tradition throughout the cemetery's history, uniformity in the treatment of the dead shifted to a pattern of individual differentiation whose ultimate explanation has to come from nonfunerary contexts. At a certain point, the community probably experienced remarkable changes that might have even implied a change of residence, but it continued burying its members in the same graveyard. Nevertheless, the introduction of new ritual practices in a context of multiple-stage burials seems a reliable symptom of the disintegration of the former social order.

As has been shown, research on collective burials must face the investigation of site formation processes *and* should never forget that any social practice is historically determined. Furthermore, it is our opinion that this perspective should be considered as a prerequisite of any serious investigation aimed at: (a) moving from intrasite analysis to regional scale studies and (b) providing an adequate data set for a genuine archaeological assessment of the social, political, and economical organization of past societies.

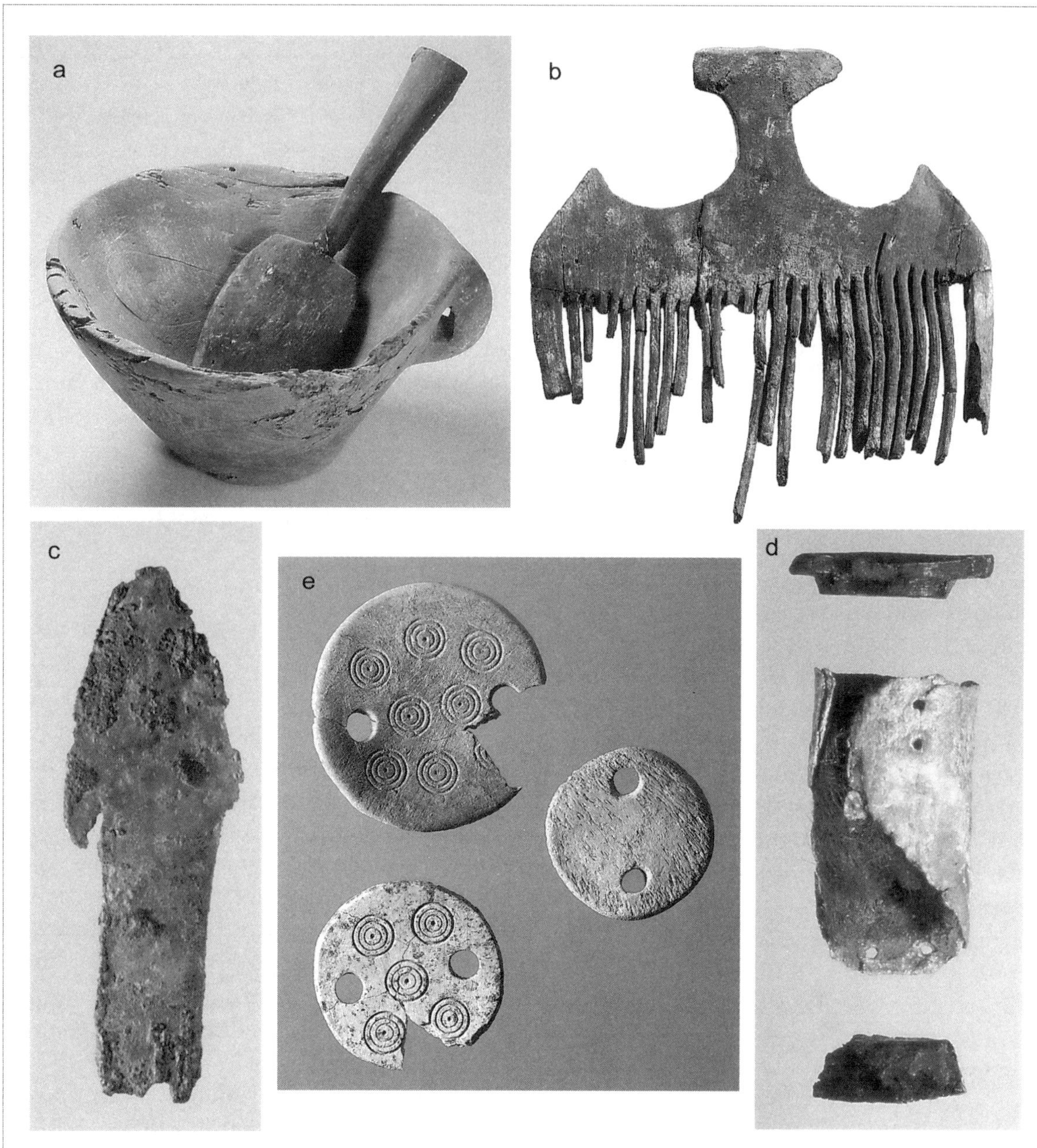

Figure 18.4. Some of the objects from the cache. Hairdressing tools: (a) wooden bowl and spoon; (b) wooden comb; (c) bronze razor. Hair containers: (d) horn container with dyed hair still inside; (e) container lids.

Acknowledgments

This research is part of our investigations as the Social Archaeo-ecology of the Mediterranean Research Group, supported financially by Direcció General de Recerca de la Generalitat de Catalunya (2005SGR01025, 2009SGR778) and Dirección General de Investigación del Ministerio de Educación y Ciencia, Spain (HUM2006-04610).

REFERENCES CITED

Botella, Miguel C., Inmaculada Alemán, and Sylvia A. Jiménez
1999 *Los huesos humanos. Manipulación y alteraciones*. Ediciones Bellaterra, Barcelona.

Buikstra, Jane E., Pedro V. Castro, Robert W. Chapman, Paloma González, Lisa Hoshower, Vicente Lull, Rafael Micó, Robert Risch, Matilde Ruiz Parra, and Mª Encarna Sanahuja
1995 Approaches to Class Inequalities in the Later Prehistory of Southeast Iberia: The Gatas Project. In *The Origins of Complex Societies in Late Prehistoric Iberia*, edited by Katina Lillios, pp. 153–178. International Monographs in Prehistory ARC 8. University of Michigan, Ann Arbor.

Buikstra, Jane E., Pedro V. Castro, Robert W. Chapman, Paloma González, Lisa Hoshower, Vicente Lull, Marina Picazo, Robert Risch, and Mª Encarna Sanahuja

1990 La necrópolis de Gatas. In *Anuario Arqueológico de Andalucía* 1990:261–276.

Castro, Pedro V., Robert W. Chapman, Sylvia Gili, Vicente Lull, Rafael Micó, Cristina Rihuete, Robert Risch, and Mª Encarna Sanahuja

1999 *Proyecto Gatas. 2. La dinámica arqueoecológica de la ocupación prehistórica*. Arqueología Monografías. Junta de Andalucía Consejería de Cultura, Seville.

Clark, Michael A., Michael B Worrell, and John E. Pless

1997 Postmortem Changes in Soft Tissues. In *Forensic Taphonomy: The Postmortem Fate of Human Remains*, edited by William D. Haglund and Marcella H. Sorg, pp. 151–164. CRC Press, Boca Raton, Florida.

Etxeberría, Francisco

1994 Aspectos macroscópicos del hueso sometido al fuego. Revisión de las cremaciones descritas en el País Vasco desde la Arqueología. *Munibe* 46:111–116.

Gili, Sylvia, Vicente Lull, Rafael Micó, Cristina Rihuete, and Robert Risch

2006 An Island Decides: Megalithic Burial Rites on Menorca. *Antiquity* 80:829–842.

Guerrero, Víctor

2007 Prehistoria de las Islas Baleares. BAR International Series 1690. Archaeopress, Oxford.

Guillon, François

1986 Brules frais ou brules secs? In *Anthropologie physique et Archéologie*, edited by Henri Duday and Claude Masset, pp. 111–134. CNRS, Paris.

Hertz, Robert

1907 Contribution à une étude sur la représentation collective de la mort. *Année Sociologique* 10:48–137.

Lull, Vicente

2000 Argaric Society: Death at Home. *Antiquity* 74:581–590.

Lull, Vicente, Rafael Micó, Cristina Rihuete, and Robert Risch

1999a *La Cova des Càrritx y la Cova des Mussol. Ideología y Sociedad en la Prehistoria de Menorca*. Consell Insular de Menorca, Barcelona.

1999b *Rituales de vida y muerte en la Prehistoria de Menorca. La Cova des Càrritx*. Consell Insular de Menorca, Barcelona.

2002 Social and Ideological Changes in the Balearic Islands During the Later Prehistory. In *World Islands in Prehistory: International Insular Investigations*, edited by William H. Waldren and Josep A. Ensenyat, pp. 117–126. BAR International Series 1095. Archaeopress, Oxford.

2004 Los cambios sociales durante el II milenio en las Islas Baleares. *Cypsela* 15:123–148.

2005 Property Relations in the Bronze Age of South-western Europe: An Archaeological Analysis of Infant Burials from El Argar (Almeria, Spain). *Proceedings of the Prehistoric Society* 71:247–268.

Micó, Rafael

2005 *Cronología Absoluta y Periodización de la Prehistoria de las Islas Baleares*. BAR International Series 1373. Archaeopress, Oxford.

2006 Radiocarbon Dating and Balearic Prehistory: Reviewing the Periodization of the Prehistoric Sequence. *Radiocarbon* 48(3):421–434.

Pericot, Luis

1972 *The Balearic Islands*. Thames and Hudson, London.

Plantalamor, Lluís, and Jaume Sastre

1991 Excavació d'urgència de la naveta de Binipati Nou (Ciutadella). *Meloussa* 2:163–172.

Renfrew, Colin

1976 Megaliths, Territories and Populations. In *Acculturation and Continuity in Atlantic Europe*, edited by Sigfried J. de Laet, pp. 198–220. De Tempel, Brugge.

Rihuete, Cristina

2003a *Bioarqueología de las prácticas funerarias. Análisis de la comunidad enterrada en el cementerio prehistórico de la Cova des Càrritx (Ciutadella, Menorca), ca. 1450–800 cal ANE*. BAR International Series 1161. Archaeopress, Oxford.

2003b Esqueletos humanos en la investigación arqueológica de la diferencia sexual. In *Morir en femenino: Mujeres, ideología y prácticas funerarias desde la Prehistoria hasta la Edad Media*, edited by Mª Dolors Molas and Susana Guerra, pp. 17–50. Col. Breviaris 7. Edicions Universitat de Barcelona, Barcelona.

2005 Salud y cargas laborales en una comunidad prehistórica menorquina. In *Nuevas Perspectivas del Diagnóstico Diferencial en Paleopatología*, edited by Antonio Cañellas Trobat, pp. 124–140. Asociación Española de Paleopatología, Mahón.

Stika, Hans-Peter

1999 Los macrorestos botánicos de la Cova des Càrritx. Appendix in *La Cova des Càrritx y la Cova des Mussol. Ideología y Sociedad en la Prehistoria de Menorca*. Consell Insular de Menorca, Barcelona.

Veny, Cristóbal

1976 Excavación de la naveta de Son Morell (Menorca). *Noticiario Arqueológico Hispánico* 5:223–228.

1982 *La necrópolis protohistórica de Cales Coves, Menorca*. Bibliotheca Praehistorica Hispana, Madrid.

1987 Las navetas de Menorca. In *Atti del 3° Convegno di studi "Un millennio di relazioni fra la Sardegna e i Paesi del Mediterraneo*, pp. 443–472. Selargius-Della Torre, Cagliari, Italy.

Waldren, William H.

1982 *Balearic Prehistoric Ecology and Culture: The Excavation and Study of Certain Caves, Rock Shelters and Settlements*. BAR International Series 149. Archaeopress, Oxford.

19

IMMIGRANT AND INDIGENOUS: COLONIAL ENCOUNTERS IN EARLY HISTORIC IRELAND

BARRA O'DONNABHAIN
DEPARTMENT OF ARCHAEOLOGY, UNIVERSITY COLLEGE CORK

BENEDIKT HALLGRÍMSSON
DEPARTMENT OF CELL BIOLOGY AND ANATOMY, UNIVERSITY OF CALGARY

ARCHAEOLOGICAL ANALYSES OF ANCIENT colonial encounters tended until relatively recently to be modeled on European expansion of the post-Columbian era. This fixation on relatively recent experiences resulted in representations of colonial relationships characterized by asymmetry. Interactions between immigrant and indigenous were typically understood in terms of significant imbalances of power. A mismatch was also central to understandings of the relationship between points of origin and destination, which tended to be portrayed as metropolitan core and colonial periphery, with the former usually identified as the innovator and exporter of cultural influences and the latter as a passive consumer of such. Recent scholarship (e.g., Dietler 2005, 2009; Gosden 2004; Stein 2005) has suggested that this focus on the interactions of the last few centuries is inadequate as a means of understanding colonial encounters in earlier periods. Dietler (2005, 2009), for example, has made the fascinating suggestion that these approaches in part reflect the colonization of modern Euro-American consciousness by the classical world as a result of the central place given to the classics in the education of European and American elites over the last five centuries. He has further argued that the practices of recent colonialism grew out of selective interpretations of the narratives of the imperial expansions of classical Greece and Rome and that the resulting imbrications of ancient and modern colonial situations present archaeologists with considerable challenges in reconceptualizing earlier interactions.

Dealing with these challenges involves explicit theorization and a reflexive approach to implicit assumptions that can condition interpretation. Dietler (2005) also stressed the active role of material culture and consumption in past encounters where novel cultural sensibilities were negotiated, primarily through habituated practices. He focused on the importance of historical contingency and exhorted archaeologists to examine the diversity and uniqueness of responses among both immigrant and indigenous in colonial encounters that predate what he referred to as modern Euro-American colonialism. Gosden (2004) has also stressed the role played by material culture and has argued that colonialism is produced by a desire for things that grips the minds and bodies of people, moving them across space and producing power structures to fulfill this desire. Other recent works have focused on the body as a contact zone in this process and on the role of the intimate in the construction of colonial self (e.g., Ballantyne and Burton 2005; Creed and Hoorn 2001; Stoler 2002).

Bioarchaeology, as defined by Jane E. Buikstra (1977:69; Buikstra and Beck 2006), involving as it does the contextualized analysis of the remains of individual participants in past social processes, provides an ideal lens with which to view the complex relationship between material culture, bodies, and the movement of both through space that characterized colonial encounters. Specifically, the analysis of biological distance by means of the study of patterns of cranial nonmetric traits in archaeologically retrieved skeletons can be used to reveal patterns of morphological variability between groups. As the work of Buikstra and others has shown, morphological variability is related to genetic variability, albeit not in a linear manner (Cheverud and Buikstra 1981; Saunders 1989; Saunders and Popovich 1978), and can be used to discriminate between different populations (Stojanowski this volume; Stojanowski and Schillaci 2006). In this chapter, we use morphological variability as a basis for discussion of the nature of the relationship between immigrant and indigenous groups in Ireland during the period of Viking expansion between the end of the eighth century and the twelfth century A.D. In keeping with the contextualized approach advocated by Buikstra, this variability is considered in combination with historical and material culture data to draw inferences about the nature of the encounter between native and newcomer. In keeping with Dietler's exhortation, we begin with a brief examination of the historiography of constructions of "Irish" and "Viking" in the archaeological discourse of Ireland. Given the tainted history of physical anthropology in the construction of colonial–imperial relations, such a critical approach is particularly important in a context that considers the biological remains of past populations. Studies of the genetic affiliations of earlier "peoples" that proceed without explicitly theorizing concepts such as "Irish," "Gaelic," and "Viking" run the risk of replicating essentialist conceptualizations and perpetuating the colonial worldview. A critical approach can contribute to unmasking the prejudices and assumptions that have created dominant visions of the past. It can thereby contribute to a more well-rounded understanding of the dynamics of earlier societies while also challenging the legitimacy of ideologies that have assumed the mantle of universal truths.

Situating Irish and Viking

The use of omnibus labels such as *Irish* and *Viking* to describe early medieval societies is potentially problematic. These labels promote a view of homogenous, bounded, and self-identifying populations and project this view into the past. The term *Irish* is used here to refer to the population that was extant on the island of Ireland on the eve of direct contact with Scandinavian peoples in the eighth century A.D. The population of Ireland is not conceptualized in terms of unilineal descent from any particular earlier population that can be defined in terms of language, material culture, or biology. The population of the island is not considered as a bounded or isolated group, as significant cultural interchanges have been documented in the Irish Sea area, while contacts along the Atlantic facade of Europe may also have been significant. It is likely that these interactions facilitated both acculturation and gene flow, so it would be unsafe to assume that the island's precontact population was culturally or genetically homogenous.

We use *Viking* and *Norse* here interchangeably to refer to peoples of Scandinavian origin who settled in many areas of western Europe between the end of the eighth century and the eleventh century A.D. These terms are understood to indicate heterogeneous groups from a wide geographical area who may also have had considerable interactions with other European populations prior to and during their interactions with populations in Ireland. Contemporary early historic sources in Ireland recognized the heterogeneity of the Vikings. Since the nineteenth century, this heterogeneity has been explained in terms of diversity of origins within Scandinavia (Norway versus Denmark), but it is recognized that other processes may also have contributed to it. These could include the possibility of gene flow as a result of contacts with other European populations, while the ranks of the Vikings may have also been swelled by the accretion, either voluntary or coercive, of personnel drawn from a variety of such populations.

The earliest historical reference to contact between the inhabitants of Ireland and Scandinavian peoples is from A.D. 795, when an entry in the *Annals of Ulster* mentions that the monastery at Rechru had been raided by "heathens" (Mac Airt and Mac Niocaill 1983). The *Annals of Ulster* form part of the corpus of record keeping by early medieval clerics in Ireland, and in recent centuries this body of literature came to the fore in the formation of ideas about the Vikings in Ireland. Ambrosiani (1998) has written of the tendency among non-Scandinavian historians and archaeologists, particularly those from Ireland and Britain, to consider Scandinavia as a single, homogenous unit during the Viking Age. He has argued that this represents a misunderstanding of the cultural, linguistic, and political diversity of the region in the early historic period and reflects the homogenizing influence of the dominant image of the Vikings in the historiography of Ireland, Britain, and France prior to the 1970s: the demonic "other." The success and longevity of this image is a classic instance of where the pen has proved to be mightier than the sword in that the dominant perception of "Viking" in the Anglophone and Francophone worlds is the one promoted by early medieval clerics in the partisan and ideologically charged historical record they left behind. That record was mostly forgotten in the centuries following the reconquest of Ireland by England at the time of the Reformation and the imposition of a new colonial ruling class. Yet prior to the 1840s, most archaeological monuments in Ireland were attributed to the Danes. This was part of the colonialist narration of the Irish past, where external agents were recruited to explain cultural innovation and historical change. As a model of the past, that involving the Danes was one imported directly from Britain, specifically England, where early historic interactions with Scandinavian peoples primarily involved groups of Danish origin. The use of *Dane* as a synonym for *Viking* served to universalize the English/Danish experience, and the process of Scandinavian interactions with the early historic population of Ireland was assumed to mirror the experience of Anglo-Saxon England. Traditional attributions of archaeological monuments to the Danes were first challenged in the 1840s with the editing and publication of the more substantial of the early historic Irish ecclesiastical manuscripts. The political import of the accounts they contained was immediately recognized. In 1843 the constitutional nationalist leader Daniel O'Connell eulogized the Irish struggle against the Vikings as a role model for his generation's struggle against British domination. This nationalist interpretation was to form a strong current in the mainstream of historical research for nearly a century and a half after O'Connell's time.

In the twentieth century, archaeology played a central role in the emergence of revisionist narratives of Irish–Viking interactions. Excavations of the Viking core of the city of Dublin began in 1962 under the auspices of the National Museum of Ireland. The first serious reappraisal of the nationalist-inspired view of the Vikings came from an archaeologist, A. T. Lucas, who was intimately connected with the Dublin excavations as director of the National Museum (Lucas 1966, 1967).

The archaeological data accrued since the 1960s indicate that unlike the situation in Britain and northern France, Viking territorial gains in Ireland were limited to a small number of coastal enclaves, and the nucleated settlements established at these footholds are considered the first truly urban communities on the island. Urbanism was in its nascent stages in contemporary Scandinavia but would have been encountered by Viking groups elsewhere in western Europe. The Irish coastal towns were integrated into wider Viking trade networks and became an important source of exotic material culture for elites of both colonial and local groups (Valante 2008). Viking material found in Ireland is typical of the distinctive range of objects found among émigré Scandinavian communities in the North Atlantic (Larsen and Stummann Hansen 2001). Established on the east coast of the island in the late ninth century A.D., Dublin was the largest and most powerful of these settlements (Figure 19.1). Archaeological investigations of the medieval core of the city have provided detailed, even intimate, insights into the daily life of its inhabitants between the tenth and thirteenth centuries (Fanning 1994; Geraghty 1996; Heckett 2003; Knudson et al. 2012; Lang 1988; McCutcheon 2006; Mitchell 1987; Wallace 1992). Interpretations of the evidence across an eclectic range of material culture elements tend to agree that by the eleventh century, a considerable degree of assimilation had occurred between Irish and Scandinavian groups (Hurley 2010; Hurley et al. 1997; Wallace 1992, 2008), with the result that the archaeology of the period is referred to as Hiberno-Norse. This archaeological narrative of acculturation contrasts with the contemporary historical record in which Irish chroniclers tended to portray the Scandinavians in negative terms. Yet political and military alliances between Norse and Irish are mentioned from the ninth century, while dynastic marriages are mentioned from the tenth (Ní Mhaonaigh 1998). Readings of the archaeological, historical, and linguistic data are suggestive of processes of acculturation from an early stage in the interactions between the two groups, with a concurrent maintenance of some degree of social distance.

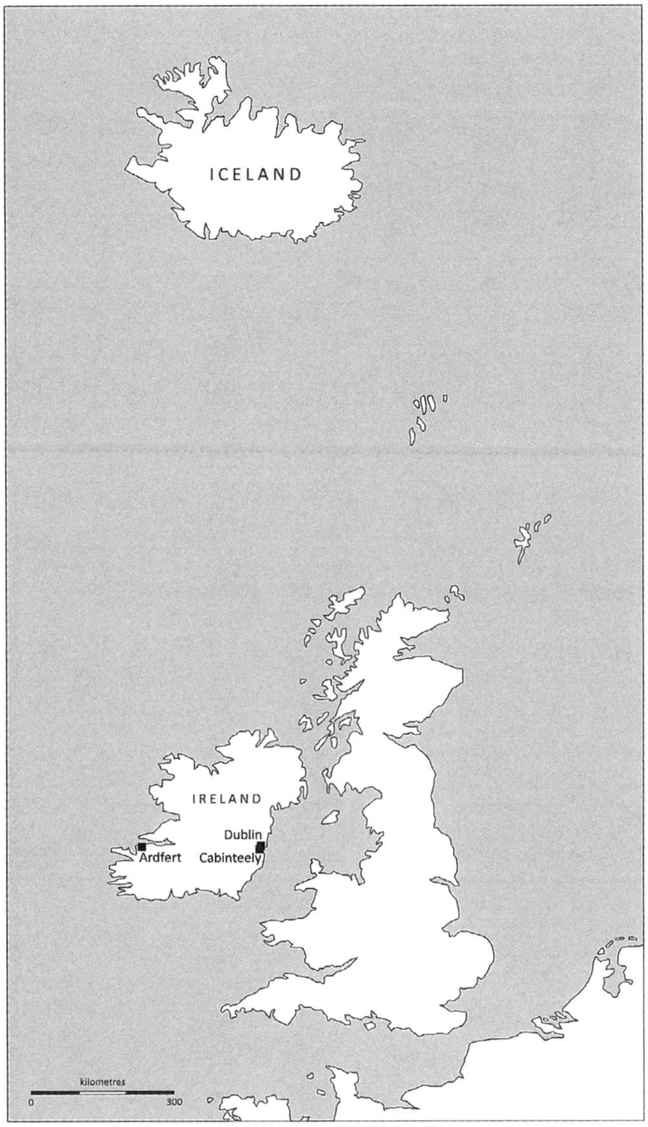

Figure 19.1. Locations mentioned in the text.

Morphological Variability in Early Historic Ireland

In a series of studies (Hallgrímsson et al. 2004; O'Donnabhain 2001; O'Donnabhain and Hallgrímsson 2001), we have interrogated the biological data to see if the flow of cultural elements was matched by a flow of genetic material between the populations. The methodologies and results of these studies are detailed elsewhere (Hallgrímsson et al. 2004), and the main results are summarized in the tables and figures below (Tables 19.1–3; Figures 19.2, 19.3). Samples of early medieval human skeletal remains from Ireland, Iceland, and Norway were analyzed, as was a later group of Inuit from Greenland that was used as a control. The Irish samples that are the focus of this discussion included skeletons from fifth-to-eighth-century levels of a cemetery at Cabinteely, a site located 10 km south of Dublin (Figure 19.1). This group (n = 101) represents the precontact population of the region in which Dublin was to develop. Skeletal remains have been found in a variety of different contexts during many excavations carried out in tenth-to-twelfth-century levels of Dublin. These represent the largest group of Viking-related human remains from Ireland that is available for study (n = 93). The bulk of this material consists of isolated bones that were found scattered in the general matrix of a number of mostly contiguous sites in the core of the medieval town. Some complete skeletons and portions of skeletons were also recovered. The latter were not found in cemeteries or areas that are likely to have been regarded by the inhabitants of the town as formal areas for the disposal of the dead. Most of the more complete remains came from excavations at Wood Quay, where most of the skeletons were found in what are best interpreted as mass graves. In contrast, the sample from Ardfert was recovered from a formal cemetery. The village of Ardfert is located on the west coast of Ireland, 1.5 km inland from the Atlantic on the flat and fertile coastal plain of north County Kerry and about 200 km southwest of both Dublin and Cabinteely (Figure 19.1). Ardfert was an important ecclesiastic and administrative center in the early Middle Ages and has a large medieval cathedral and associated cemetery. Excavations undertaken at the cathedral in advance of conservation work produced burials dating from the tenth century, while four building phases have been identified in the church beginning in the eleventh century. The skeletons analyzed (n = 64) predated the remodeling of the cathedral in the mid-thirteenth century. While there are no direct accounts of Viking attacks on or other interactions with Ardfert, it is likely that the Scandinavians were familiar with the site, as there are Viking-related sites in the general vicinity and the church site was close to sea routes connecting Viking settlements.

Analysis of biological distance indicated that the remains recovered from the Viking Age levels of the Dublin excavations were not significantly different from the local precontact population from Cabinteely or from the contemporary population on the southwest coast at Ardfert (Table 19.1; Figure 19.2). In contrast, there were significant differences between the Dublin remains and a sample of pre-Christian (that is, ninth-to-eleventh-century) burials from Iceland (n = 121), as well as from a sample of Viking Age skeletons from Norway (n = 110).

Table 19.1. Matrices of Frequency Distances Among Sites.

A. MATRIX OF MMD VALUES FOR ALL GROUPS.

	Pre-Christian Iceland	**Christian Iceland**	**Pre-Viking Norse**	**Viking Age Norse**	**Hiberno-Norse**	**Pre-Norse Irish**	**Late Medieval Irish**	**Greenland Inuit**
Pre-Christian Iceland		.875	1.865	1.980	**2.844**	**2.970**	**3.113**	**4.730**
Christian Iceland	-.003		**2.389**	**3.775**	**4.227**	**5.543**	**5.157**	**7.030**
Pre-Viking Norse	.038	**.050**		1.515	**2.763**	**4.108**	**3.143**	**4.457**
Viking Age Norse	.029	**.056**	.019		**2.524**	**3.608**	**2.317**	**5.154**
Hiberno-Norse	**.085**	**.122**	**.092**	**.066**		1.058	1.038	**4.326**
Pre-Norse Irish	**.071**	**.112**	**.156**	**.084**	.013		1.374	**6.872**
Late medieval Irish	**.089**	**.132**	**.115**	**.057**	.005	.014		**6.153**
Greenland Inuit	**.143**	**.161**	**.163**	**.143**	**.166**	**.226**	**.241**	

Note: The lower diagonal contains the MMD values, and the upper diagonal contains the standardized MMD, calculated as described in the text. The standardized MMD is considered significant at the .05 level if it exceeds 2 (Sjøvold 1977b). Significant values are bolded.

B. MATRIX OF HARPENDING-JENKINS DISTANCES.

	Pre-Christian Iceland	**Christian Iceland**	**Pre-Viking Norse**	**Viking Age Norse**	**Hiberno-Norse**	**Pre-Norse Irish**	**Late Medieval Irish**	**Greenland Inuit**
Pre-Christian Iceland		.328	.065	**.006**	**p < .001**	**p < .001**	**p < .001**	**p < .001**
Christian Iceland	.026		**.007**	**p < .001**	**p < .001**	**p < .001**	**p < .001**	**p < .001**
Pre-Viking Norse	.077	**.077**		.435	**p < .001**	**p < .001**	**p < .001**	**p < .001**
Viking Age Norse	**.060**	**.077**	.056		**p < .001**	**p < .001**	**p < .001**	**p < .001**
Hiberno-Norse	**.134**	**.159**	**.146**	**.112**		**.011**	.109	**p < .001**
Pre-Norse Irish	**.113**	**.141**	**.193**	**.120**	**.067**		.117	**p < .001**
Late medieval Irish	**.129**	**.157**	**.156**	**.093**	**.066**	.064		**p < .001**
Greenland Inuit	**.205**	**.202**	**.219**	**.191**	**.232**	**.278**	**.298**	

Note: The lower diagonal contains the H-J distance values while the upper contains the p-values as obtained by the randomization method described in the text. Significant values are bolded.

Table 19.2. Univariate Measures of Within-Group Variation.

Group	n	σ	p(1-p)
Pre-Christian Iceland	121	.142	.139
Christian Iceland	265	.150	.149
Pre-Viking Norse	51	.141	.137
Viking Age Norse	110	.139	.137
Hiberno-Norse	93	.162	.157
Pre-Norse Irish	100	.148	.145
Late medieval Irish	69	.145	.142
Greenland Inuit	59	.164	.161

Table 19.3. Multivariate Individual Mean Deviation Variances for All Groups.

Group	n	Mean Number Observable Traits per Individual	σ of IMD
Pre-Christian Iceland	72	22	.0055
Christian Iceland	174	26	.0047
Pre-Viking Norse	36	26	.0054
Viking Age Norse	81	27	.0036
Hiberno-Norse	36	26	.0082
Pre-Norse Irish	74	21	.0053
Late medieval Irish	50	23	.0046
Greenland Inuit	58	29	.0048

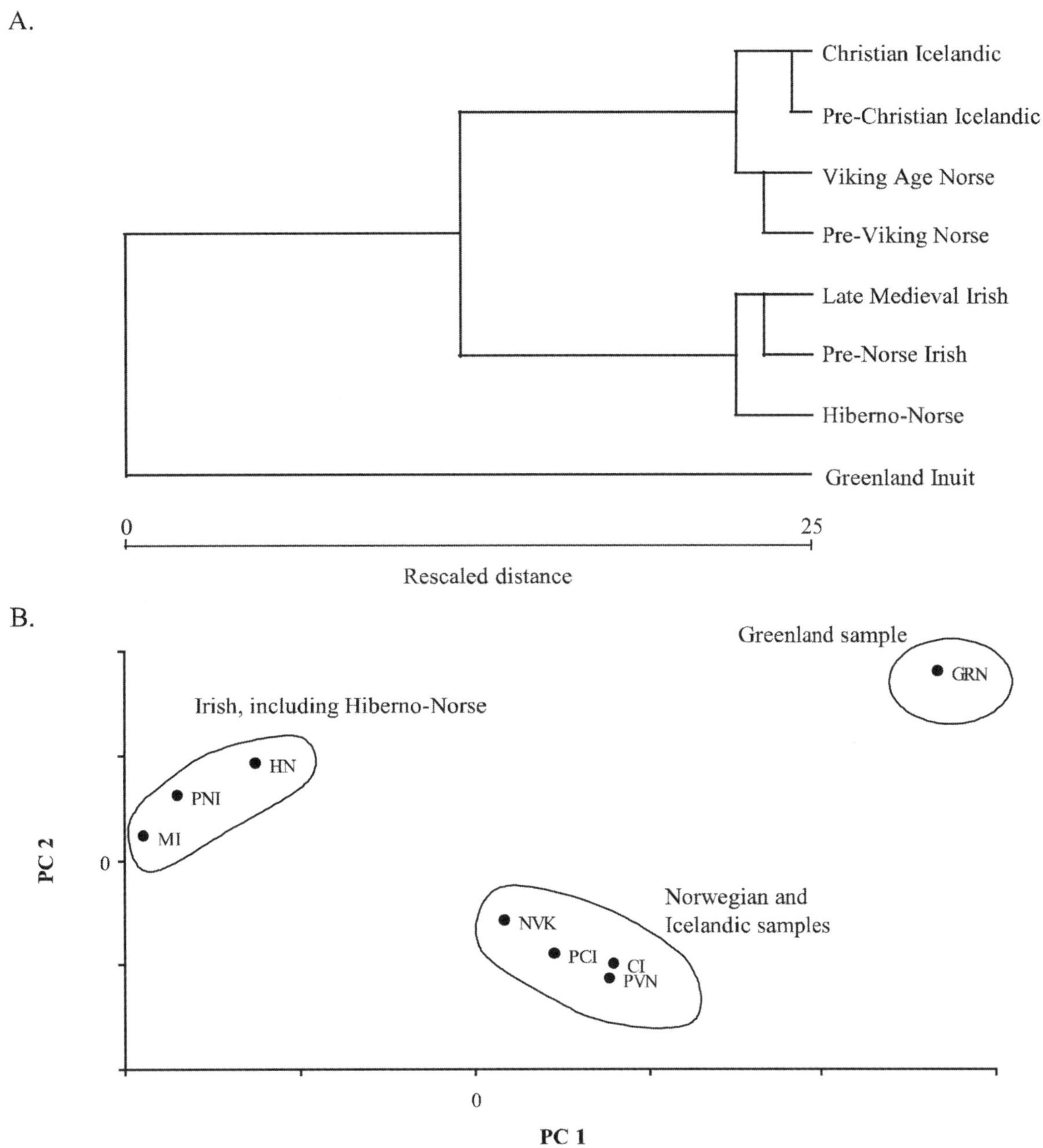

Figure 19.2. Results of principal components analysis of the R-matrix for the major groups in this study: (A) dendrogram of Ward's hierarchical cluster analysis using eight principal component scores derived from the R-matrix; (B) component score 1 plotted against component score 2; (CI) Christian Icelandic; (PCI) Pre-Christian Icelandic; (PVN) Pre-Viking Norse; (NVK) Viking Age Norse; (HN) Hiberno-Norse; (PNI) Pre-Norse Irish; (MI) late medieval Irish; (GRN) Greenland Inuit. Both A and B illustrate the phenetic groupings implied by the R-matrix values.

This suggests that local communities made a significant contribution to the population of the colonial outpost at Dublin and were to some degree ancestral to the skeletal collection recovered from the enclave.

Analyses of the within-group variability between the samples indicated that the collection from Dublin was the most heterogeneous of all the groups considered. This heterogeneity of the Viking Age sample from Dublin contrasted with the relative homogeneity of the precontact population of the region. A population of mixed geographic origins is a likely explanation of the marked heterogeneity of the Dublin sample. This does not conflict with the suggestion made on the basis of the biological distance analysis of a relatively high level of affinity with the local precontact population. It indicates rather that the latter group was only partially ancestral to the sample of the tenth-to-twelfth-century inhabitants of Hiberno-Norse Dublin.

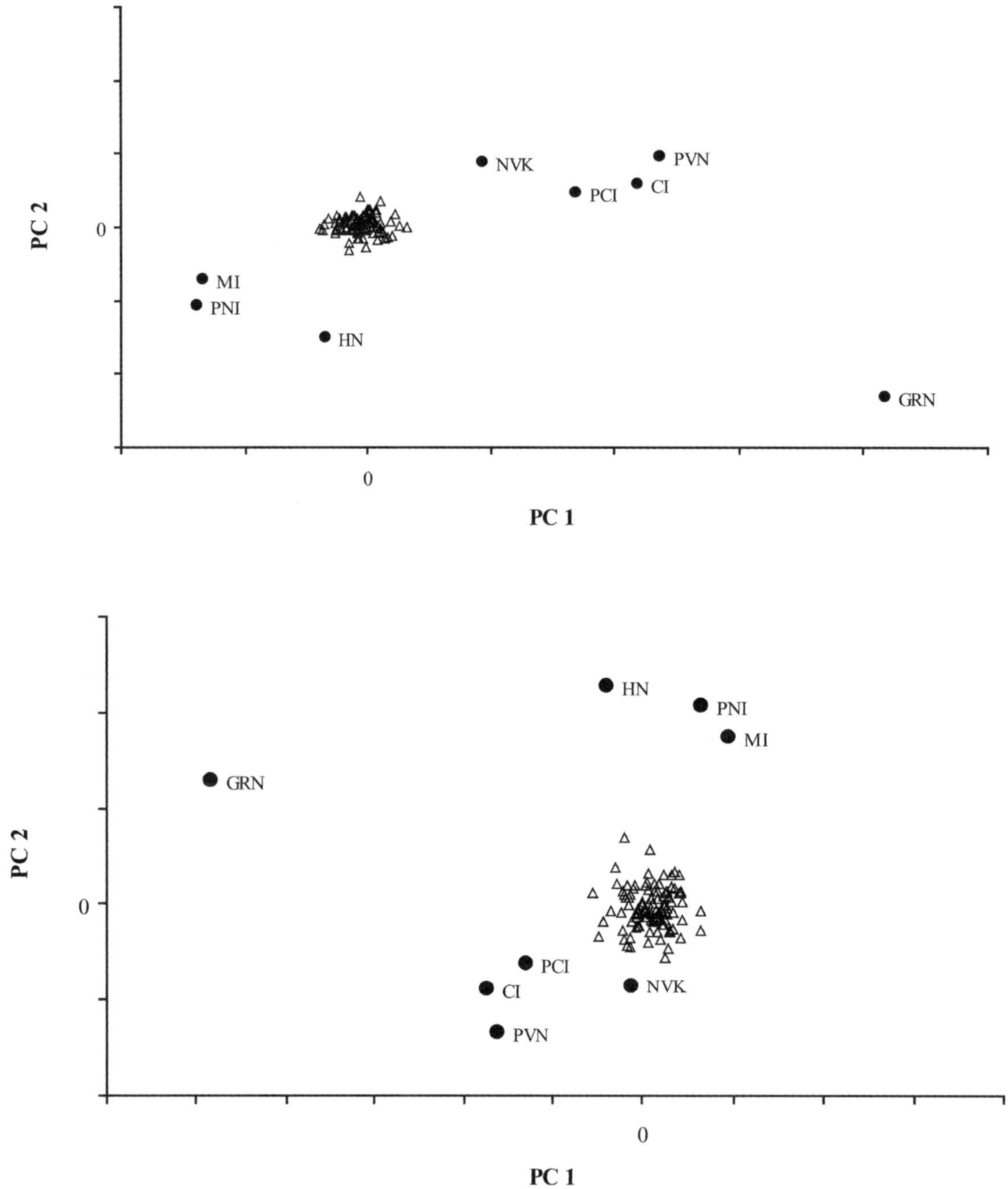

Figure 19.3. Plot of principal component scores 1 and 2 of the R-matrix for the original data and the resampled 50 percent and 66 percent hybrid populations between NVK and PNI (100 iterations). This distribution of triangles illustrates the expected position of the settlement Icelandic population (PCI) if it represented a mix of Irish (PNI) and Viking Age Norwegian (NVK). Abbreviations are the same as in Figure 19.2.

The Construction of the Colonial Self in Early Historic Ireland

The close relationship, spatially and morphologically, between the precontact sample from Cabinteely and that from Viking Dublin and the marked heterogeneity of the latter group are consistent with the occurrence of a process of gene flow between the immigrant and local populations. The results from the west coast sample from Ardfert are also consistent with such a scenario of interbreeding between native and newcomer. However, there are marked differences in material culture traditions between Dublin and Ardfert. There was no evidence of Hiberno-Norse traditions at the latter site. In contrast, Dublin maintained a distinct material culture tradition long after the period of most intense Viking activity in the North Atlantic and even after direct contacts with Scandinavia had ceased. This suggests that cultural responses to biological admixture proceeded in different ways in Dublin and Ardfert. Such admixture could have taken many forms, and explanations could range from coercion to the development of cultural proximities, sympathies, and intimacies. It is also possible that there were voluntary changes in ascription by cohorts of, in the case of Dublin, the local population or, perhaps in the case of Ardfert, the immigrant group. In Dublin, transformations in self-definition by local groups that may have chosen to identify with the economic goals and ideological values of the colonists might have been encouraged by the opportunities, economic and social, offered by a community such as the Viking Age town. The urban setting, a novel and experimental entity in tenth-century Ireland, may have presented opportunities to some segments of the local population that might not have been attainable in the context of the rigidly hierarchical society described in the early medieval Irish law tracts (Kelly 1988).

The archaeological data from Dublin and the other Viking ports suggest that their inhabitants maintained a distinct political and cultural identity up until the Anglo-Norman invasions of Ireland in 1169 and probably beyond that date. Not only did the population of Dublin maintain a distinctive material culture with a strong Scandinavian flavor, but the persistent use into the twelfth century of terms such as "Gall Átha Cliath"—the foreigners of Dublin—by writers of the Irish-language chronicles of the same period indicates that the attitudes and behaviors of those living outside the Viking settlements contributed to the maintenance of this social distance. Yet the biological data suggest that boundaries were transgressed and that there was a flow of genes across the cultural cordon. The maintenance of a distinctive lifestyle by some subgroups within early historic society in Ireland despite evidence for significant gene flow is a reflection of the dynamic, opportunistic, and pragmatic nature of identity construction and sense of ethnic affiliation (see also Stojanowski this volume). In the context of the fragmented and cellular political landscape that characterized early medieval Ireland, the privileging of a particular set of roots of the family tree at the expense of other kinship ties could have been an effective device in the maintenance of political and economic autonomy. This suggests that identity construction in Hiberno-Norse Dublin was located in the past. The representation of the past can be a source of power in the present. A dominant version of the past, irrespective of it being fictive or characterized by selective amnesia, can be a powerful tool in the legitimation of a particular set of social relations and the political status quo. In a context of increasing biological and linguistic entanglements, this selective privileging of a Scandinavian past had both overt and nondiscursive symbolic expressions that would have been meaningful to all the cultural groups who shared the island. These expressions ranged from the maintenance of distinctive settlement forms and economic strategies to the use of material culture items whose exotic nature and decorative styles evoked particular genealogical origins. These symbolic expressions also operated at the level of the individual inhabitants of the Viking enclaves. In this way, a distinctive Hiberno-Norse self was cultivated and affirmed through mundane sets of habitual activities. Daily actions with a particular material culture were not only microsites in which a distinctive identity was maintained and affirmed. Habituated practices were also the means by which distinctive Hiberno-Norse bodies were molded by the "natural" modus vivendi of the inhabitants of Dublin.

Nationalist fantasies, essentialist conceptualizations of "Viking" or "Irish," and asymmetrical models of colonization based on post-Columbian European expansion provide inappropriate lenses with which to view the cross-cultural and colonial encounters that occurred in Ireland toward the end of the first millennium A.D. The distinctive material culture of the Viking West suggests that the process of colonization was less about core–periphery relationships than about a novel network for circulating objects, ideas, values, and people. The encounters between colonists and locals in Ireland are perhaps best understood in terms of a meeting of equals where individuals and groups, operating with different cultural logics, interacted and were agents of change, transforming the values of all those involved as new cultural sensibilities were forged in the colonial setting. Not without considerable stress, both immigrants and indigenous created an elaborate network of economic, political, social, and genetic ties to meet the demands of their particular historical situation. The strategic, innovative, and symbolic use of material culture was central to this process, and through interbreeding and habituated practices, the political and the personal were enmeshed, with the result that the bodies of the inhabitants of the Hiberno-Norse enclaves can be seen as an archive of this particular colonial encounter.

The different cultural responses to processes of interbreeding seen in Ireland imply that material culture change was not a predictable outcome of biological admixture and that identity was not necessarily constructed solely around biological descent. Daily actions as visual performances of identity involving material culture and bodies' habitual activities were critical to the self-conscious construction of identity on both sides of the cultural divide in early historic Ireland. The colonial encounter resulted in processes of syncretism that left influences in technology, art, language, and social practices, as well as in the gene pool. All participants were radically changed by the experience, which was less about a mismatch between core and periphery and more about the transformation of bodies and minds.

References Cited

Ambrosiani, Björn
1998 Ireland and Scandinavia in the Early Viking Age: An Archaeological Response. In *Ireland and Scandinavia in the Early Viking Age*, edited by Howard B. Clarke, Máire Ní Mhaonaigh, and Raghnall Ó Floinn, pp. 405–420. Four Courts Press, Dublin.

Ballantyne, Tony, and Antoinette Burton (editors)
2005 *Bodies in Contact: Rethinking Colonial Encounters in World History*. Duke University Press, Durham, North Carolina.

Buikstra, Jane E.
1977 Biocultural Dimensions of Archeological Study: A Regional Perspective. In *Biocultural Adaptation in Prehistoric America*, edited by Robert L. Blakely, pp. 67–84. Southern Anthropological Society Proceedings No. 11. University of Georgia Press, Athens.

Buikstra, Jane E., and Lane A. Beck (editors)
2006 *Bioarchaeology: The Contextual Analysis of Human Remains*. Academic Press, New York.

Cheverud, James M, and Jane E. Buikstra
1981 Quantitative Genetics of Skeletal Nonmetric Traits in the Rhesus Macaques on Cayo Santiago II: Phenotypic, Genetic and Environmental Correlations Between Traits. *American Journal of Physical Anthropology* 54:51–58.

Creed, Barbara, and Jeanette Hoorn (editors)
2001 *Body Trade: Captivity, Cannibalism and Colonialism in the Pacific*. New York: Routledge.

Dietler, Michael
2005 The Archaeology of Colonization and the Colonization of Archaeology. In *The Archaeology of Colonial Encounters*, edited by Gil Stein, pp. 33–63. School of American Research Press, Santa Fe, New Mexico.
2009 Colonial Encounters in Iberia and the Western Mediterranean: An Exploratory Framework. In *Colonial Encounters in Ancient Iberia: Phoenician, Greek, and Indigenous Relations*, edited by Michael Dietler and Carolina López-Ruiz, pp. 3–48. University of Chicago Press, Chicago.

Fanning, Thomas
1994 *Viking Age Ringed Pins from Dublin*. Royal Irish Academy, Dublin.

Geraghty, Siobhan
1996 Viking Dublin: Botanical Evidence from Fishamble Street. Royal Irish Academy, Dublin.

Gosden, Chris
2004 *Archaeology and Colonialism: Cultural Contact from 5000 BC to the Present*. Cambridge University Press, Cambridge.

Hallgrímsson, Benedikt, Barra Ó Donnabháin, G. Bragi Walters, David M. L. Cooper, Daníel Guðbjartsson, and Kari Stefánsson
2004 Composition of the Founding Population of Iceland: Biological Distance and Morphological Variability in Early Historic Atlantic Europe. *American Journal of Physical Anthropology* 124:257–274.

Heckett, Elizabeth Wincott
2003 *Viking Age Headcoverings from Dublin*. Royal Irish Academy, Dublin.

Hurley, Maurice F.
2010 Viking Elements in Irish Towns: Cork and Waterford. In *The Viking Age: Ireland and the West*, edited by John Sheehan and Donnchadh Ó Corráin, pp. 154–164. Four Courts Press, Dublin.

Hurley, Maurice F., Orla M. B. Scully, and Sarah W. J. McCutcheon
1997 *Late Viking Age and Medieval Waterford: Excavations 1986–1992*. Waterford Corporation, Waterford.

Kelly, Fergus
1988 *A Guide to Early Irish Law*. Dublin Institute of Advanced Studies, Dublin.

Knudson, Kelly J., B. O'Donnabhain, C. Carver, R. Cleland and T. D. Price
2012 Migration and Viking Dublin: paleomobility and paleodiet through isotopic analyses. *Journal of Archaeological Science* 39: 308–320.

Lang, James T.
1988 *Viking-Age Decorated Wood: A Study of Its Ornament and Style*. Royal Irish Academy, Dublin.

Larsen, Anne-Christine, and Steffen Stummann Hansen
2001 Viking Ireland and the Scandinavian Communities in the North Atlantic. In *The Vikings in Ireland*, edited by Anne-Christine Larsen, pp. 115–126. Viking Ship Museum, Roskilde, Denmark.

Lucas A. T.
1966 Irish-Norse Relations: Time for a Reappraisal? *Journal of the Cork Historical and Archaeological Society* 71:62–75.
1967 The Plundering and Burning of Churches in Ireland, 7th to 16th century. In *North Munster Studies: Essays in Commemoration of Monsignor Michael Moloney*, edited by Etienne Rynne, pp. 172–229. Thomond Archaeological Society, Limerick.

Mac Airt, Sean, and Gearoid Mac Niocaill
1983 The Annals of Ulster (to AD 1131). Dublin Institute for Advanced Studies, Dublin.

McCutcheon, Clare
2006 Medieval Pottery from Wood Quay, Dublin. Royal Irish Academy, Dublin.

Mitchell G. Frank
1987 *Archaeology and the Environment in Early Dublin*. Royal Irish Academy, Dublin.

Ní Mhaonaigh, Máire
1998 Friend and Foe: Vikings in Ninth- and Tenth-Century Irish Literature. In *Ireland and Scandinavia in the Early Viking Age*, edited by Howard Clarke, Máire Ní Mhaonaigh, and Raghnall Ó Floinn, pp. 381–402. Four Courts Press, Dublin.

O'Donnabhain, Barra
2001 Immigrants and Indigenes: Morphological Variability and Irish-Viking Interactions in the Early Historic Period. Unpublished Ph.D. dissertation, Department of Anthropology, University of Chicago.

O'Donnabhain, Barra, and Benedikt Hallgrímsson
2001 Dublin: The Biological Identity of the Hiberno-Norse Town. In *Medieval Dublin II*, edited by S. Duffy, pp. 65–87. Four Courts Press, Dublin.

Saunders, Shelley R.
1989 Nonmetric Skeletal Variation. In *Reconstruction of Life from the Skeleton*, edited by M. Y. İşcan and K. A. R. Kennedy, pp. 95–108. Alan R. Liss, New York.

Saunders, Shelley R., and Frank Popovich
1978 A Family Study of Two Skeletal Variants: Atlas Bridging and Clinoid Bridging. *American Journal of Physical Anthropology* 49:193–203.

Sjøvold, Torstein
1977 The Occurrence of Minor Non-metrical Variants in the Skeleton and Their Quantitative Treatment for Population Comparison. *Homo* 24:204–233.

Stein, Gil J. (editor)
2005 *The Archaeology of Colonial Encounters: Comparative Perspectives*. School of American Research Press, Santa Fe, New Mexico.

Stojanowski, Christopher M., and Michael A. Schillaci
2006 Phenotypic Approaches for Understanding Patterns of Intracemetery Biological Variation. *Yearbook of Physical Anthropology* 49:49–88.

Stoler, Ann Laura
2002 *Carnal Knowledge and Imperial Power: Race and the Intimate in Colonial Rule*. Berkeley: University of California Press.

Valante, Mary
2008 *The Vikings in Ireland: Settlement, Trade and Urbanization*. Four Courts Press, Dublin.

Wallace, Patrick F.
1992 *The Viking Age Buildings of Dublin*. Royal Irish Academy, Dublin.
2008 Irish archaeology and the recognition of ethnic difference in Viking Dublin. In *Evaluating Multiple Narratives: Beyond Nationalist, Colonialist, Imperialist Archaeologies*, edited by J. Habu, C. Fawcett and J. M. Matsunaga, pp. 166–183. Springer, New York.

20

Trauma in the Medieval to Early Modern Sortebrødre Skeletons from Odense, Denmark

George R. Milner
Department of Anthropology, Pennsylvania State University

Skeletons are the primary source of information on the health of people who lived during the prehistoric and early historic periods, and they contribute much to knowledge about workload, cultural customs, social organization, and intergroup relations. Collectively, this research is commonly referred to as bioarchaeology, following Jane E. Buikstra's (1977:69) use of the term more than 30 years ago. With regard to the disease experience of past populations, the work undertaken over the past few decades has tended to focus on two pivotal transformations in human existence: the origins of agriculture and the emergence of complex societies, commonly called chiefdoms and states. Of particular interest are the effects of changes in dietary content, breadth, reliability, and sufficiency; settlement size and duration; population size and density; differential intragroup access to food and exposure to occupational hazards; and interaction among variously constituted groups at local and regional levels.

Since the early 1980s, it has been widely accepted that these two watershed events came at a great biological cost to our ancestors, with consequences rattling down to the present day (Armelagos et al. 1991; Cohen 1989, 2008; Cohen and Armelagos 1984; Cohen and Crane-Kramer 2007; Gibbons 2009; Larsen 1995; Steckel and Rose 2002; Steckel et al. 2002). Each step along the way is thought to have been accompanied by poorer nutrition, greater exposure to a wider array of infectious diseases, higher mortality, and a heavier workload for most people. In the fullness of time, the quality of life worsened as populations grew and regional densities increased. Infectious diseases became a major problem when settlements got larger and were inhabited for longer periods, fostering the contamination of local soil and water supplies and allowing more people to have regular face-to-face contact that facilitated direct pathogen transmission. Malnutrition became more common as diets changed and their breadth diminished when ever-greater reliance was placed on domesticated animals and plants. Finally, most people eventually came to be dominated, and thereby disadvantaged, by a privileged few who enjoyed disproportionate access to the necessities of life, often forcibly acquired from a downtrodden majority.

Not all researchers, however, agree that a simple stepwise deterioration in the human condition adequately captures the complexities of what took place. One major difficulty with what can now be characterized as Conventional Wisdom—that health progressively deteriorated as people began to farm and, later, to live in large, hierarchically organized societies—is that individual skeletal samples are treated as representative of entire ways of life subsumed within a few stages defined by subsistence strategy or sociopolitical system. Comparisons are drawn between hunter-gatherers and subsistence agriculturalists, or other such categories, as if societies in each group were similar with respect to the many aspects of cultural behavior and natural settings that influence disease experience.

The way Conventional Wisdom is framed poses difficulties, as there is in fact no reason to imagine that any one such society, often represented by a single cemetery, was the same as the next in terms of whether people were particularly healthy or not. One might just as easily expect considerable variation in disease experience within a societal category such as subsistence agriculturalist (that is, Neolithic). After all, differences that affected pathogen transmission and nutritional adequacy surely existed among groups classified as belonging to the same societal, archaeological, or temporal category.

If that was indeed the case—if variability, not uniformity, in disease experience was the norm within broadly defined societal categories—then there is much to be said for investigating thoroughly what took place in individual communities before using skeletons to construct grand narratives about trends in disease experience. An initial focus on communities and what happened within them conforms to Buikstra's (1977) call for a contextually nuanced approach to bioarchaeology. This theme is identifiable, however faintly, in a few early osteological studies that set a high standard for subsequent work (Angel 1971; Hooton 1930; also see overviews by Beck 2006; Ubelaker 1982).

Focusing first on variation in disease experience within communities is of special interest because overall frequencies of pathological bony lesions, as generated from cemetery samples considered in their entirety, might well mask much of what we would like to know about life in the distant past. That is true even if data are presented according to sex or long age intervals such as juvenile and adult. Such aggregated data are likely to obscure the diverse life experiences of various segments of past communities. It is precisely this diversity that our archaeological colleagues would like to know something about when reconstructing what took place in ancient societies and why it did so. An additional twist to the tale centers on using mortality samples (skeletons) to describe the disease experience of past populations (living people). This difficulty, a result of the selective effect of mortality, is sometimes referred to as the osteological paradox, after the title of an article where the issue was first discussed in depth for a bioarchaeological audience (Wood et al. 1992).

Intragroup heterogeneity in life experience with regard to age and sex is explored in this chapter using skeletons from a graveyard associated with the Sortebrødre (Black Friars) Monastery in Odense on the Danish island of Fyn. Some skeletons might date to as early as the thirteenth century, but the majority of them are from people who probably died in the sixteenth century following the Reformation (Boldsen and Mollerup 2006). One of the principal objectives of the pilot study, conducted in 2000, was to determine if it would be worth pursuing the subject of trauma further with the human remains available from this period in Denmark. Trauma was chosen as the focus of study because broken bones are relatively easy to identify in archaeological skeletons, the damage and bony response are correspondingly unlikely to be mistakenly attributed to some other cause, and fractures in archaeological samples are reasonably common relative to many other pathological conditions. The age distributions of broken bones were of special interest because they potentially provide us with perspectives on the experiences of different segments of past populations. Of particular concern was the reasonable, but not necessarily correct, assumption that examples of healed fractures simply accumulate with age in cemetery samples.[1]

CONVENTIONAL WISDOM

For the most part, comprehensive bioarchaeological studies focusing on the health of past peoples have been undertaken only over the past several decades. Yet the assumption underlying much of this work—that things got worse with the advent of new ways of life—has deep and tangled roots in Western thought. There are, in fact, distinctly eighteenth-century Rousseauian (1950 [1755]) overtones in much of the modern scholarship that generalizes from osteological findings. Most important in this regard is a unidirectional stepwise degradation in the human condition that is said to have accompanied the adoption of new subsistence strategies and sociopolitical systems, and all else that followed in train. There is also a political advocacy dimension. Even raising methodological concerns over using skeletons to infer whether one group of people were healthier than another, and thereby questioning the factual basis of Conventional Wisdom, invites accusations of "prostate" or "procivilization" agendas, as shown by Cohen's (1992:359) response to Wood et al. (1992).

Conventional Wisdom—that things got bad when people started growing crops and tending animals, and deteriorated still further when societies got larger and more complex—resembles in one important respect the frequently and rightly criticized notion of progress over time toward ever-improving conditions. Both ideas feature universal unidirectional change, only one represents an improvement in people's lives whereas the other is quite the opposite. These essentialist positions rest squarely on the identification of disease experiences that are said to typify certain classes of societies, however they might be defined.

Osteological support for Conventional Wisdom comes from individual cemeteries that are explicitly or implicitly treated as representative of particular types of societies classified by archaeological culture (distinguished by artifacts and architecture), time period (perhaps spanning many centuries or even millennia), sociopolitical stage (such as band or chiefdom), or subsistence strategy (including hunter-gatherer or subsistence agriculturalist). Such classifications imply the existence of readily separable sets of societies, considerable uniformity in each category, and clear distinctions between those groups. Regardless of how useful such categories might be as deliberate simplifications of messy reality, they each encompass considerable variation in community size, population density, residential mobility, technological sophistication, dietary practices, sociopolitical organization, intergroup relations, environmental productivity, subsistence security, and much else. These dimensions of variability no doubt had an effect on nutritional adequacy, pathogen transmission, and habitual activities, and hence what might be seen in skeletons. But treating individual cemeteries as singularly representative of larger categories of societies means that truly interesting differences in the health of roughly contemporaneous, geographically proximate, and culturally similar groups remain underappreciated.

Not all osteological studies, however, conform neatly to Conventional Wisdom, indicating that the situation is more complex than commonly depicted. Using various skeletal proxies for infectious disease load and nutritional status, researchers have noted exceptions to a progressive deterioration of health, as well as variability among roughly equivalent societies from the same general area and time horizon (Cook 1984; Douglas and Pietrusewsky 2007; Jackes et al. 1997; Meiklejohn and Babb 2011; Milner 1992; Pietrusewsky and Douglas 2001; Smith and Horwitz 2007; Wittwer-Backofen and Tomo 2008). Even when health is thought to have declined over time within a particular region, there could be considerable variability among populations inhabiting different local settings (Ubelaker and Newson 2002). So whatever happened in such an area during the shift from hunting-and-gathering to agricultural economies, it must be interpreted within the context of the specific groups of people, represented by mortality samples, that took part in the transition (Wittwer-Backofen and Tomo 2008). Yet despite acknowledging mixed results, especially in close examinations of multiple skeletal collections from culturally well-characterized regions, the general trend—things got bad, and then they got worse—is still touted as the essential story (Cohen 2008; Cohen and Crane-Kramer 2007).

Archaeologists, in particular, are understandably chary about broadly defined societal stages, since they are acutely aware of the considerable variability that exists in the nature and success of adaptations to local settings among societies otherwise similar in size, cultural background, sociopolitical organization, economic underpinnings, group mobility, and technology. Moreover, long-term cultural change within particular areas with well-documented archaeological sequences was not always in the same direction (for example, toward greater sociopolitical complexity). Given such diversity, it follows that one cannot assume uniform responses to what, in the fullness of archaeological time, were more intensive subsistence practices, elaborations in sociopolitical and economic systems, and greater numbers of people.

A prelapsarian state of good health followed by several millennia when people were sicker and died earlier is difficult to reconcile with a trend toward a larger global population. After all, large numbers of individuals can be considered a measure of a species' success. If Conventional Wisdom is correct, then people who were generally worse off than their ancestors managed to produce enough offspring to offset whatever losses resulted from early death. In short, sicker people routinely out-reproduced their healthier ancestors, and they did so within shorter life spans. Perhaps that is indeed what happened, but then it would have to be explicitly accommodated by our models of cultural evolution, including the eventual replacement of hunting-and-gathering ways of life by those based on agriculture.

General Trends Versus Local Circumstances

In any generalization of what took place over great periods of time, there is a problem with reconciling overall trends with specific samples, including skeletons from cemeteries associated with individual communities.

What tended to happen over several millennia across entire continents, or large portions of them, was not necessarily the same as what occurred locally over a few decades, generations, or even centuries. Since cemetery samples are for the most part drawn from one or at most a few nearby settlements, they necessarily represent little more than local conditions. Differences in pathogen exposure, dietary adequacy, and activity patterns can be expected to have been present among geographically, temporally, and culturally similar populations, as living conditions would not have been identical from one place to the next.

It might be imagined that more intensive subsistence systems, once widely adopted, resulted in transitory periods of plenty before increases in population once again dampened growth by pushing hard against production capacity ceilings (Wood 1998). Thus it is conceivable, even likely, that in any particular region, periods of growth alternated with stasis (or even decline), and people's health tended to vary accordingly. The general model—it features elements of both Malthus's (1970 [1798]) and Boserup's (1965) insights into the relationship between population size and productive capacity, and its consequences (Wood 1998)—gains some archaeological support from the American mid-continent. Two thousand years ago, there was a marked shift to a heavier use of native cultigens that, from an archaeological perspective, took place rather suddenly, and it was accompanied by greater interregional contact, more permeable territorial boundaries, and a dampening of intergroup hostilities despite general population increase (Milner 1999, 2004). To judge from this single preindustrial example, more people do not necessarily mean a correspondingly poorer quality of life, at least as measured in this instance by cultural conditions that influenced whether fights would break out among groups (a Malthusian misery). If a scenario such as the one proposed by Wood (1998) indeed characterizes what generally took place, we would expect alternating periods when people were better or worse off, and their skeletons would presumably show it. That sort of temporal variation in health within particular regions would produce a picture quite different from Conventional Wisdom, in which health inexorably and universally deteriorated with the adoption of new ways of life.

Before sweeping conclusions are made about the biological impact of changes in sociopolitical and economic systems, it would seem prudent to start with contextually secure, fine-grained snapshots of what took place in individual communities. That is because extrapolations from single cemeteries, or just a few of them, to broadly defined archaeological groups, cultural stages, or temporal horizons risk mischaracterizing general conditions. In part, the problem stems from the archaeological samples available for study. Cemeteries are rarely, if ever, systematically chosen for excavation from a well-characterized universe of sites—that is, numerous sites where it is possible to control for variation in function, size, duration, and the like. So osteologists must base their conclusions on samples composed of whatever has been excavated for any number of reasons. That is because excavations, especially large and expensive ones that yield many skeletons, are often undertaken as a result of circumstances that have little to do with a research question, since fieldwork is frequently dictated by modern land-use needs.

Saying it is necessary to have a thorough understanding of specific settings and populations before constructing grand narratives about the past should not be misinterpreted as a retreat to particularism. Instead, it is acknowledgment that we must be thoroughly familiar with the nature of our samples—the specific cultural and environmental circumstances that conceivably affected past communities, and hence skeletons—before treating cemetery samples as representative of general cultural types (for example, hunter-gatherer). In fact, community-focused skeletal studies nicely complement archaeological investigations of societal change that emphasize the interplay of cultural and environmental conditions within historically contingent contexts.

Living Populations Versus Mortality Samples

There are also methodological problems with interpreting the skeletal data widely regarded as supporting Conventional Wisdom. The difficulty in going from pathological features of skeletons to the characteristics of once-living populations, the fundamental point of the osteological paradox, boils down to how well a mortality sample reflects the population from which it was drawn (Wood et al. 1992). That is, we must ask ourselves what can truly be said about a group of living people when all we have available are those who happened to have died (excavated skeletons). While various aspects of this problem have been discussed in the literature, there is no consensus over the magnitude of its effect and how to deal with it effectively (Byers 1994; Cohen 1992, 1994,

1997, 2008; DeWitte and Wood 2008; Goodman 1993; Jackes 1993; Ortner 1991, 1998; Saunders and Hoppa 1993; Usher 2000; Wood and Milner 1994; Wood et al. 1992; Wright and Yoder 2003).

By their very nature, mortality assemblages are highly selected samples of people who were once alive at a given age. That is because each individual does not experience the same risk of dying at each age. So cemeteries are filled with the weakest, sickest, and most vulnerable members of every cohort at each step along the way from birth to the maximum life span. As a group, people who died in a particular age interval, say between 5 and 10 years, are not the same as those who survived for a while longer only to die at some later age. It follows, therefore, that the frequencies in skeletons of pathological lesions that are related in any way to a greater risk of dying do not equal the prevalence of those same lesions among the living (Wood et al. 1992). There is nothing original or surprising about such a statement, yet it is curiously what remains controversial about the osteological paradox. Cohen, for example, recently claimed that "straightforward interpretations of *relative* pathology frequencies in two or more past populations can generally be made from their cemeteries without concern for paradoxical interpretations" (2008:495; emphasis in original). The emphasis on *relative*, presumably in contrast to *absolute*, does not allow us to skirt the fundamental issue. The distinction between mortality samples and the population from which they were derived is important because we are interested in the life experiences of people in the past. Skeletons are of concern only insofar as they provide the primary data used to reconstruct what life was once like.

There are, of course, other issues that must be tackled, most importantly estimating the ages of skeletons without bias (Bocquet-Appel and Masset 1982; Chamberlain 2000, 2006; Hoppa and Vaupel 2002; Konigsberg and Frankenberg 1994; Konigsberg et al. 1997; Milner et al. 2008). The age estimation issue is particularly problematic for adults, especially the elderly. It too is the subject of continuing research, and some promising new directions are being pursued (Chamberlain 2006; Hoppa and Vaupel 2000; Milner et al. 2008; Weise et al. 2009).

Intracommunity Distinctions

A natural outgrowth of treating individual cemetery samples as representative of particular types of societies is the tendency to consider past communities as essentially homogenous except to the extent that skeletal samples are crudely broken down by sex, age (commonly juvenile and adult), and social status (typically an elite group in contrast to everybody else). Archaeologists, however, would welcome greater attention being directed toward within-community heterogeneity to identify the differential effects of infectious disease, nutrition, and workload on various segments of society.[2] Such an emphasis is consistent with one of the principal aims of archaeologists: to understand the functioning of past societies, including the opportunities and hazards faced by variously constituted social, activity, age, and sex groups. A firm understanding of how people were actually living—specifically, who became sick and died and what effect that had on households and communities—would seem desirable before making sweeping generalizations about human health. At the very least, closer attention to what happened in particular populations complements the archaeological interest in characterizing life experiences in individual communities, as well as the variation that existed among those local groups.

Excessive reliance on summary figures when comparing one cemetery sample to another does not encourage an examination of untested beliefs about what mortality samples indicate about the lives of past people. One such assumption is that signs of nonlethal (healed) skeletal trauma simply accumulate with age in archaeological samples. At first glance, that seems to make sense—the numbers of broken but healed bones would be greater in individuals of advanced age simply because older people have more years in which to accumulate injuries (Buzon and Richman 2007; Glencross and Sawchuk 2003; Lovejoy and Heiple 1981; Mays 1991, 1998; Torres-Rouff and Junqueira 2006; Tung 2007). Yet that seemingly reasonable assumption need not be correct, because, once again, osteologists derive their data from death assemblages (Wood et al. 1992). If having experienced injuries earlier in life was in any way associated with an increased risk of dying, then healed fracture frequencies will not necessarily increase with age in graveyard samples. One must keep in mind that people do not need to have died from such an injury—only that the presence of a healed fracture marks someone who for any number of biological or cultural reasons experienced a higher risk of dying than many other members of his or her cohort.

It is certainly true that for any single individual, the chances of ever having had a broken bone increase with advancing age; that is a function of years of exposure to conditions that might result in severe trauma. But it does not necessarily follow that in mortality samples the skeletons of old people, in aggregate, must have more healed fractures than those of younger adults. In the death assemblage, young to middle-age adult skeletons could show more signs of injuries than the skeletons of elderly people if survivors of trauma, those with healed fractures, experienced a greater risk of dying than other members of the community who were the same age. Should that occur, the individuals at each age who were most likely to enter the morality sample would include many with healed fractures. People with previously broken bones would be winnowed out of the population, leaving behind those who, for the most part, were free of fractures.

SORTEBRØDRE SKELETONS

The Sortebrødre sample consists of numerous partial to complete skeletons. Many additional bones were also found scattered through grave fill. That was because when new graves were dug, people often disturbed old ones; the bones that were encountered were simply tossed into open holes as they were subsequently filled. A few bones even have marks made when gravediggers chopped through earlier skeletons. During the pilot study, all the adult bones were examined, yielding a sample of 8,640 complete bones: frontal bones, parietals, occipitals, temporals, zygomatics, maxillae, nasals, mandibles, clavicles, scapulae, humeri, radii, ulnae, ilia, ischia, pubic bones, femora, tibiae, and fibulae.[3] They were for the most part well preserved, although many were broken postmortem.

With regard to trauma, attention focused on various kinds of bone fractures and damage from weapons such as swords. The latter featured distinctive smooth surfaces where heavy, sharp-edged weapons had cut cleanly through bone. Healed and unhealed examples of both fractures and blows from swords or other sharp weapons, such as axes, were recorded. Several instances of trauma that lacked signs of remodeling—that is, there was no evidence of survival in the form of bone resorption or proliferation at the sites of injuries—resulted from blows with sharp weapons. In contrast, people survived most injuries that produced ordinary fractures, as indicated by extensive remodeling where broken bones had healed. Healed fractures were typically poorly aligned, sometimes resulting in a noticeable shortening of a bone relative to the corresponding one on the opposite side. It is possible that some perimortem bone fractures were not recognized, so deaths directly related to severe trauma would be underestimated accordingly. It is unlikely, however, that many such fractures were overlooked since these breaks tend to have a distinctive appearance that is unlike the damage that can take place long after death through pressure exerted by grave fill, tree roots, or building foundations.

Ages at death were estimated on the basis of standard osteological measures, along with other age-informative skeletal characteristics (Buikstra and Ubelaker 1994). The ages used here are best regarded as experience-based estimates because they depart from a strict, mechanistic application of one or more formally described age-estimation methods. Osteologists have generally shied away from relying heavily on such estimates because of a concern over their accuracy and replicability. Yet as a first approximation of age—and in the absence of age-estimation refinements currently undergoing development (Weise et al. 2009)—experience-based estimates can be considered adequate for the present purposes. That is, they are sufficient to judge from blind tests on hundreds of known-age skeletons of people who died from the nineteenth to twenty-first centuries, such as the Bass Donated Collection at the University of Tennessee (Milner 2010). Estimates of sex were based primarily on pelvic and cranial structures summarized in Buikstra and Ubelaker (1994). Long bone dimensions, most notably the sizes of the heads of femora and humeri, also contributed to these assessments.

For convenience, adulthood was broken down into 10-year age intervals. Skeletons that did not entirely fall in a single age interval were apportioned among the appropriate age categories. The principal advantage of long age categories is that having many bones in each interval dampens the quirky effects of a rather small number of specimens showing signs of trauma despite an examination of several thousand bones. In short, the coarse intervals are a reflection of the size of the data set that could be collected within the time constraints of a pilot study.

SKELETAL TRAUMA

The people buried in the Sortebrødre cemetery had survived most injuries that caused fractures, as indicated by broken but healed bones (Figure 20.1). Some

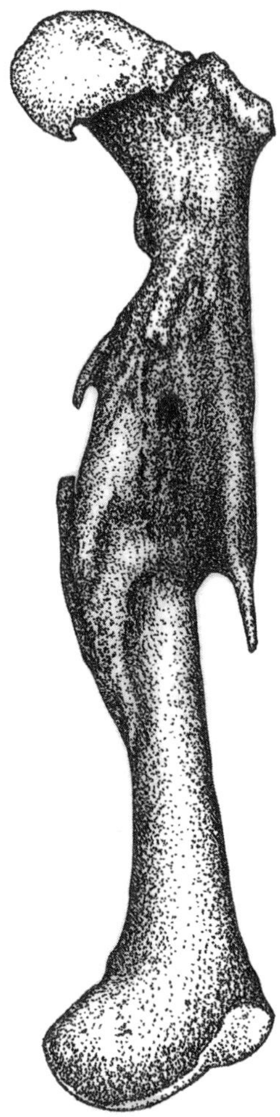

Figure 20.1. A healed but poorly aligned fracture of a left femur from a man's skeleton in the Sortebrødre graveyard. Quite remarkably, this individual survived major injuries that resulted in a number of badly fractured bones, probably attributable to the same incident (Jakobsen 1978).

of them, however, died immediately from their injuries or soon thereafter. Four of five people with evidence of unhealed trauma, all on crania, were male. Three young to middle-aged men had been struck with sharp, heavy weapons such as swords or axes. Two others, a man and a woman, had massive cranial fractures consistent with blunt-force trauma. Both were somewhat more than 50 years of age, so they were older than the men hit with sharp weapons.

As expected, many more bones showed signs of having healed after injuries had taken place. So for the most part, people survived trauma that was severe enough to affect the skeleton. Of the entire sample of complete bones, about .9 percent (81 of 8,640) had been broken and subsequently healed. Turning to long bones and combining both sexes and sides, radii were broken most often (3.1 percent; 15 of 478). Other commonly fractured long bones were clavicles (1.9 percent; 10 of 532), fibulae (1.5 percent; 6 of 407), and ulnae (1.1 percent; 5 of 469). Humeri (.6 percent; 3 of 516), femora (.5 percent; 3 of 596), and tibiae (.2 percent; 1 of 585) were broken less often.

Men and women were not equally likely to experience trauma that ended in broken bones that healed. Combining cranial bones and the major long bones of the upper and lower limbs, the men had more fractures that had subsequently healed than women: 1.6 percent (58 of 3,576) of male bones and .7 percent (22 of 3,339) of female bones ($p < .001$, chi-square test). The sample age distributions, however, are not the same: under 40 years, males 39.9 percent, females 49.6 percent; 40 to 65 years, males 54.1 percent, females 43.1 percent; greater than 65 years, males 6.0 percent, females 7.3 percent. While different age distributions complicate matters, they are not dissimilar enough to account for males having twice as many fractures as females. So discrepancies in bone fracture frequencies cannot be attributed to an equally great disparity in sample composition, at least in terms of age. It is reasonable to conclude, therefore, that males had a different experience with serious trauma than females.

Looking more closely at age, frequencies of broken but healed bones generally increase with advancing years for adult males (Figure 20.2). The pattern for women is similar, except in old age when there are relatively few broken bones.

Combining all fractures, regardless of origin, is not the best way to proceed because different injuries, with presumably different causes, are lumped together. It is, of course, usually impossible to determine precisely what caused a bone fracture in an archaeological skeleton. Nevertheless, some injuries likely resulted from intentional violence, most clearly blows from swords

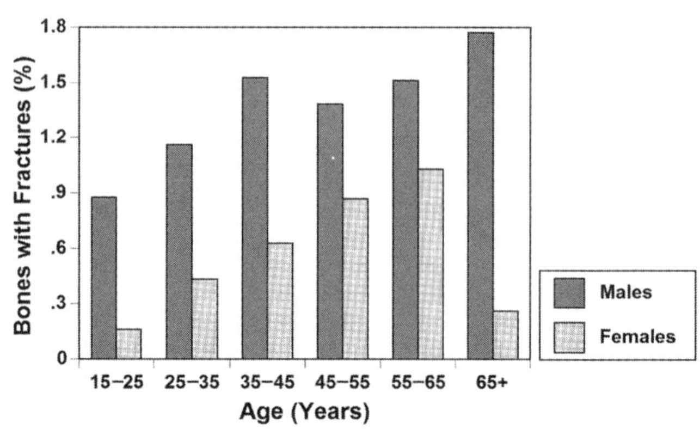

Figure 20.2. Age distributions of fractured but healed bones for males and females.

or axes, but also many examples of blunt-force cranial trauma, broken noses, and so-called parry fractures of ulnae. The majority of the other fractures probably came about through various accidents. Many clavicles and radii, for example, might have been broken when people fell (for example, Colles' fractures of radii). Falls were presumably common, as people would have routinely walked across uneven and at times slippery surfaces, frequently in poor light. The separate tabulations of fractures presented below, however, should not be taken to imply that all broken bones in each category occurred during either a fight or an accident. All that is intended is that many fractures allocated to one group, perhaps the majority of them, were attributable to interpersonal violence, whereas the other category likely had a larger proportion of fractures caused by accidents.

When frontal bones, parietals, nasals, and ulnae are combined—many of these bones could have been broken in violent encounters between people—healed fractures were observed in 3.9 percent (33 of 846) of male and .9 percent (8 of 859) of female bones ($p < .001$, chi-square test). A similar result is obtained when crania as a whole are examined rather than skull bones tabulated individually. Counting only individuals with at least three-quarters of the frontal and parietals present, 11.2 percent (18 of 161) of the males had some form of healed trauma, in contrast to only 3.6 percent (6 of 165) of the females. So men as a group experienced more trauma of this sort than women ($p < .01$, chi-square test). This tendency is accentuated when the five cases of unhealed cranial trauma, four of them occurring on men, are also included.

The distribution by side of frontal bone trauma is consistent with the intentional nature of many injuries. When examples of unhealed and healed trauma are combined for both sexes, the left side of the frontal bone was struck more often than the right: left 3.5 percent (12 of 345) and right 1.2 percent (4 of 343). While the patterning of injuries is consistent with victims facing right-handed assailants, and this difference approaches statistical significance, the sample size precludes definitive statements about whether one side showed more signs of trauma than the other ($p > .05$, chi-square test, correction for continuity). Trauma frequencies on the left and right parietals, however, were essentially identical: left 2.6 percent (9 of 341) and right 3.0 percent (10 of 337) ($p > 0.05$, chi-square test). A strong tendency toward one side or the other was not expected for the parietals since some people struck on the sides of their heads might have been hit from behind, whereas others could have been facing their attackers or were oriented sideways to them.

When the frontal bones, parietals, nasals, and ulnae are considered together and divided into 10-year intervals, the frequencies of healed bones for men vary somewhat throughout adulthood, although there is no clear trend one way or the other (Figure 20.3). Women show a different pattern: trauma frequencies increase early in adulthood and then decline. Neither men nor women show a tendency for these forms of trauma to increase steadily throughout the entirety of adulthood.

Turning to bones likely to have been broken in accidents, a difference between the sexes is not apparent for healed fractures of clavicles and radii. For these two bones, the difference between males at 2.8 percent (15 of 539) and females at 2.2 percent (10 of 453) is negligible ($p > 0.05$; chi-square test). So when only sex, not age, is taken into account, men were no more likely than women to break these two bones and to survive their injuries.

The skeletons of both sexes show an increase into middle age of broken, but healed, clavicles and radii (Figure 20.4). Overall patterns of increase, however,

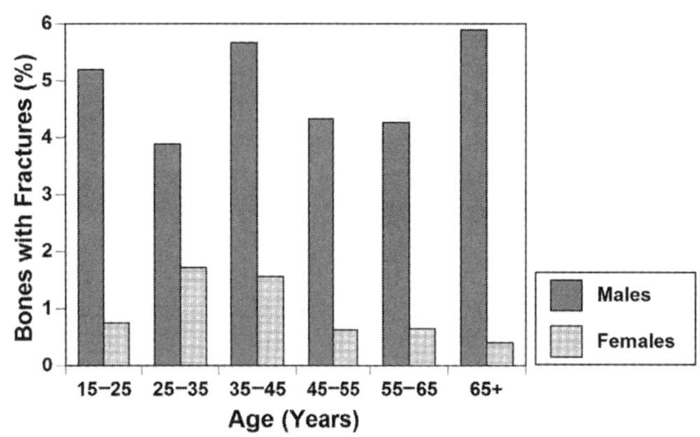

Figure 20.3. Age distributions of fractured but healed frontal bones, parietals, nasals, and ulnae for males and females.

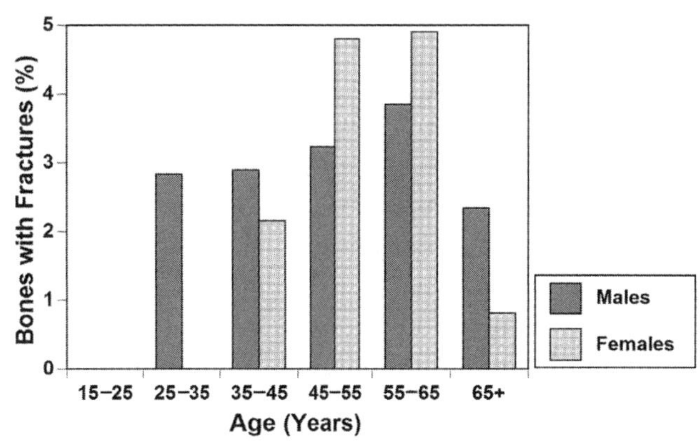

Figure 20.4. Age distributions of fractured but healed clavicles and radii for males and females.

appear to be different for men and women. Healed fractures in young men began higher relative to the middle-aged maximum than they did in women. Female skeletons also show more trauma concentrated in the 45-to-65-year period than those of males. In contrast to the skeletons of middle-aged people, those of the elderly had fewer healed fractures of clavicles and radii. Thus old-age fracture frequencies for both sexes depart from what would be expected if signs of trauma simply increased with age in individuals comprising the mortality sample. So it seems likely that many people with broken but healed bones were removed by death from the living population before they had reached old age.

The Community

Studies of European early to late medieval cemeteries indicate that male skeletons often show more signs of trauma than those of females, although that does not always occur (Angel 1974; Arcini 1999; Djurić et al. 2006; Gejvall 1960; Grauer and Roberts 1996; Judd and Roberts 1998, 1999; Mays 1991, 2007; Møller-Christensen 1982; Roberts and Cox 2003; Stirland 1996; Stroud and Kemp 1993; Weber and Czarnetzki 2001). The people buried in the Sortebrødre graveyard, therefore, conformed to a common pattern. The magnitude of the difference between male and female fracture frequencies varied from one place and time to another, as did the distribution of trauma throughout the skeleton. Assuming that such variation is not entirely an artifact of differential bone preservation, sex estimation, trauma identification, sample age composition, and burial circumstances—that is, to the extent information gleaned from separate studies is directly comparable—then there were measureable differences in the likelihood of suffering from severe trauma across medieval Europe. That conclusion is not at all surprising considering the diverse life experiences of people in rural and urban settings, regional differences in ways of life, and changes in life experience over several centuries. Nor is it new to this study. But it does underscore problems with treating only one skeletal sample, or at most a handful of them, as characteristic of entire ways of life or particular time horizons.

Overall trauma figures, however, do not tell the entire story. The Sortebrødre men were more likely to experience injuries that were probably often a result of intentional violence, specifically those affecting crania and ulnae. All five healed fractures of ulnae were from men (2.1 percent of 244 male ulnae). Although all of these fractures were not necessarily defensive injuries, the fact that males also experienced by far the largest proportion of cranial trauma is consistent with at least some ulnae being broken when fending off blows. In contrast, individuals of both sexes commonly fractured their clavicles and radii, probably most often in falls. In fact, these were the two most frequently broken bones when both sexes are combined. So it seems that women as well as men were prone to accidents, but men were far more likely to suffer from interpersonal violence that was serious enough to result in visible damage to bones.

The number of people who died when attacked or shortly afterward is too small to say anything definitive about which segments of society were most at risk. Yet the fact that four of five individuals with unhealed trauma were men suggests that they were more likely than women to be killed in such a fashion. Interestingly, the three men struck with sharp weapons were less than 50 years old. Old people, those over 50, were still vulnerable to attack, as shown by the man and woman with unhealed blunt-force trauma. These individuals, however, were struck with weapons that would have been available to everyone, perhaps staffs, cudgels, or even sticks. So it appears that the people most likely to fall victim to swords, axes, or other such weapons were men in the prime of life. But anybody, including the elderly, might be knocked about by whatever was readily at hand.

For the people who ended up in the Sortebrødre graveyard, the distribution of trauma by age shows that men and women did not experience the same chances of suffering from severe injuries throughout life, age-specific risks of dying associated with healed injuries, or both. Teasing these possibilities apart is not an easy task. Yet it is clear from these skeletons that healed fractures in mortality samples need not simply accumulate with advancing age; nor is the patterning of trauma by age for males and females the same.

Previous studies of adult skeletons from various places have likewise reported either no marked increase in fracture frequencies with advancing age, or old-age declines in whatever terminal, open-ended age interval is used (Buzon and Richman 2007; Judd 2002, 2004; Jurmain 2001; Lambert 1997; Robb 1997; Stroud and Kemp 1993; Walker 1989). In other skeletal collections, trauma of one kind or another increases with age. A mixed picture is precisely what is expected, as the skeletal samples no doubt represent diverse life experiences. So perhaps the only things we can be confident about are that the chances of breaking various bones over the course of a lifetime varied among these societies and that survivors of trauma did not face the same risks of dying at each age throughout life. Whatever real variation existed among these populations is complicated by differences in the kinds of data collected, how they were compiled, and the ways the resulting information was reported.[4] Published figures are also affected to some unknown extent, presumably some more so than others, by biases in age estimates, especially an underestimation of the elderly.

To judge from the Sortebrødre skeletons, everyone in medieval to early modern Denmark was hounded by death, but the people who survived earlier bone fractures were often weeded out of the population before they reached what at the time passed for old age. That is true even of injuries that today might be considered to have had little lasting consequence, such as fractured but healed clavicles and radii.

For the clavicles and radii, frequencies of trauma increased through middle age but then decreased. The early increase is consistent with the traditional interpretation that healed fractures in skeletal samples accumulate with age. That would not be surprising because of what might be regarded as the comparatively minor consequences of these injuries, at least when compared to fractures of other bones. It could also be the case that previously injured people experienced a somewhat higher mortality during that part of adulthood. But as long as the chances of breaking bones and surviving exceeded any increase in the risk of death if previously injured, each age interval would still have more skeletons showing evidence of trauma than the preceding one.

Whatever differences might have existed between men and women, the old-age picture for radii and clavicles is the same for both sexes (Figure 20.4). Healed fractures marked people who for one reason or another were removed from the population before reaching advanced age (greater than 65 years). Relatively few skeletons from old people showed signs of broken bones.

It is interesting that the skeletons of 45-to-65-year-old women had more fractures than their male counterparts. In medieval to early modern Denmark, that time of life (starting in the fifth decade) was when many women had osteoporosis that was far enough advanced that it can be noticed by simply picking up their bones. Mortality seems to have acted selectively on these middle-aged women, so their skeletons appear commonly in cemeteries (Jesper L. Boldsen, personal communication 2000). Perhaps women with bone loss or fractures, including those stemming from comparatively weak bones, were the ones most likely to have been culled from the population in middle age. The contrast between male and female fracture frequencies from 45 years onward indicates a stronger selection against women with healed clavicles or radii in the 45 to 65 interval, so fewer survived to the oldest age category (65-plus years) relative to men.

A decline in fracture frequencies for crania and ulnae throughout much of adulthood is seen in women (Figure 20.3). That patterning is only likely to occur if women who survived such trauma experienced a greater risk of dying than those who had not been similarly injured. For male crania and ulnae, there is no apparent increase in trauma frequencies with age. Yet men who had survived earlier violent encounters must still have experienced a somewhat higher risk of dying than other men if it is assumed that this kind of trauma might occur at any point throughout adulthood. The other possibility—that fractures of crania and ulnae were mostly restricted to the youngest age interval and that having healed trauma was not associated with an increased risk of dying in subsequent age intervals—is inconsistent with the few men with unhealed trauma where it is known when the injuries took place (death occurred at the time of the injury or shortly thereafter).

Thus it seems bones that had broken but healed have more to tell us than that some greater or lesser fraction of a cemetery sample experienced severe trauma at some point in their lives. Partitioning the sample by age across all of adulthood permits one to identify differences in the life histories of men and women (Boldsen 1997). Furthermore, it should be possible to use trauma—or, for that matter, any frequently occurring pathological condition—to identify segments of societies that faced a greater risk of dying because they were either biologically compromised, culturally disadvantaged, or both. Whatever happened to these people, they did not experience the same age-specific mortality patterns as other segments of society.

That finding, of course, is not unexpected, and it has been detected in other skeletal samples. For example, people killed in ambushes involving members of a late prehistoric village in the American Midwest were not representative of their community as a whole (Milner and Ferrell 2011; Milner et al. 1991). Individuals with prior conditions that interfered with their capacity to fight or flee were more likely to die in attacks than villagers who were, on average, more fit. It is precisely this heterogeneity within populations that is of real interest when trying to characterize the life experiences of people in the past and when untangling the effects of social, political, and economic conditions on groups defined in various ways. By adopting such a community-based approach, more can be learned from skeletons than just saying that one population was, in aggregate, sicker than another, even if such a statement could be made with some assurance.

Conclusion

The distribution of trauma by age is but one example of the counterintuitive consequences of dealing with mortality samples (archaeological skeletons). Although the Sortebrødre trauma sample is small, the commonly assumed increase-with-age scenario is not supported. The results are instead consistent with survivors of injuries being more likely to succumb to earlier death in comparison to many other members of their community, at least during some parts of the life span. People typically survived trauma that led to fractures, but these unfortunates tended to be among the ones who experienced a greater risk of dying as they passed through subsequent age intervals.

Such patterning, which says much about what took place within communities, is the sort of richly nuanced appreciation of the past that captures the spirit of Buikstra's (1977) sense of bioarchaeology. At the very least, this kind of information is of great interest to archaeologists as they strive to identify what life would have been like for people in the distant past.

In the best of circumstances, a skeletal collection drawn from a single cemetery would be a representative sample of deaths that occurred in the nearby area, quite possibly a single community. Whatever happened to these people when they were alive, it took place within the context of local cultural and natural settings. It is possible, perhaps even likely, that the particular challenges they faced bore only a tangential relationship to what might be said to characterize broadly defined types of societies. To the extent that is true, it is arguably best to start with well-characterized samples to understand life in specific communities before using the skeletons to bolster grand narratives of the human experience. While frequently couched in terms of the origins of agricultural economies and, later, organizationally complex societies, changes in morbidity and mortality patterns across these major transformations in ways of life quite likely resulted from a combination of alterations in population size and density, group mobility, purposeful and unintentional modifications of local settings, dietary composition and sufficiency, and intergroup contact. Identifying what had the greatest effect on disease experience in specific circumstances will require close attention to what took place in archaeologically well-characterized communities, as well as in cultural sequences within particular geographical regions.

Perhaps some version of Conventional Wisdom will one day be shown to be essentially correct. By that I am referring to the overall direction and timing of changes in health, not the way that conclusion is reached by simply counting skeletal lesions in mortality samples and using age-estimation procedures that yield biased results. But even if that is the case, the research question as it is commonly expressed is inherently limiting, as it does not naturally lead to more sophisticated questions. Little remains to be done once it is demonstrated to everyone's satisfaction that the situation got progressively worse over time, and that is how the situation is typically portrayed in current scholarly and popular writing.

In contrast, exploring temporal and geographical variation in health in relation to the wide variety of economic and sociopolitical systems, ecological settings, and population densities that once existed is a more interesting endeavor than setting out to show that conditions simply deteriorated with the introduction of new ways of life. It is also more amenable to studies that explore models of the rate and processes of cultural change (e.g., Wood 1998). Those kinds of analyses are precisely what will provide deeper insights into the conditions and events that contributed to cultural change, including the benefits and costs to human health of different ways of life.

Acknowledgements. The opportunity to examine these skeletal remains would not have been possible without the able assistance and wise advice of Jesper L. Boldsen and Ulla Freund of ADBOU, the Institute of Forensic Medicine, Syddansk Universitet, Odense. Funding for this pilot project was provided by the American-Scandinavian Foundation. This chapter is a somewhat updated version of a conference paper presented in 2006 in recognition of Dr. Jane E. Buikstra's many contributions to bioarchaeology.

NOTES

1. To my knowledge, Buikstra (1975) was one of the first to explore the effects of sample origin on fracture frequencies, in her case how a group of macaque skeletons were collected.

2. In this context, *heterogeneity* is arguably better than the more commonly used archaeological terms *hierarchy* and *heterarchy* because it refers to both, and it encompasses biological as well as cultural dimensions of variability.

3. There were also many incomplete bones, but they are not discussed here.

4. Such problems crop up whenever previously published skeletal information, no matter how meticulously collected, is used for comparative purposes, as pointed out by Ortner (1991) and Wittwer-Backofen and Tomo (2008), among others.

REFERENCES CITED

Angel J. Lawrence
1971 *The People of Lerna: Analysis of a Prehistoric Aegean Population.* Smithsonian Institution Press, Washington, D.C.
1974 Patterns of Fractures from Neolithic to Modern Times. *Anthropologiai Közlemények* 18:9–18.

Arcini, Caroline
1999 *Health and Disease in Early Lund.* Archaeologica Lundensia 8. Department of Community Health Sciences, Medical Faculty Lund University, Lund, Sweden.

Armelagos, George J., Alan H. Goodman, and Kenneth H. Jacobs
1991 The Origins of Agriculture: Population Growth During a Period of Declining Health. *Population and Environment* 13:9–22.

Beck, Lane A.
2006 Kidder, Hooton, Pecos, and the Birth of Bioarchaeology. In *Bioarchaeology: The Contextual Analysis of Human Remains*, edited by Jane E. Buikstra and Lane A. Beck, pp. 83–94. Elsevier, Amsterdam.

Bocquet-Appel, Jean-Pierre, and Claude Masset
1982 Farewell to Paleodemography. *Journal of Human Evolution* 12:353–360.

Boldsen, Jesper L.
1997 Estimating Patterns of Disease and Mortality in a Medieval Danish Village. In *Integrating Archaeological Demography: Multidisciplinary Approaches to Prehistoric Population*, edited by Richard R. Paine, pp. 229–241. Occasional Paper 24. Center for Archaeological Investigations, Southern Illinois University, Carbondale.

Boldsen, Jesper L., and Lene Mollerup
2006 Outside St. Jørgen: Leprosy in the Medieval Danish City of Odense. *American Journal of Physical Anthropology* 130:344–351.

Boserup, Ester
1965 *The Conditions of Agricultural Growth.* Aldine, Chicago.

Buikstra, Jane E.
1975 Healed Fractures in *Macaca mulatta*: Age, Sex, and Symmetry. *Folia Primatologica* 23:140–148.
1977 Biocultural Dimensions of Archeological Study: A Regional Perspective. In *Biocultural Adaptation in Prehistoric America*, edited by Robert L. Blakely. pp. 67–84. University of Georgia Press, Athens.

Buikstra, Jane E., and Douglas H. Ubelaker
1994 *Standards for Data Collection from Human Skeletal Remains.* Research Series 44. Arkansas Archeological Survey, Fayetteville.

Buzon, Michele R., and Rebecca Richman
2007 Traumatic Injuries and Imperialism: The Effects of Egyptian Colonial Strategies at Tombos in Upper Nubia. *American Journal of Physical Anthropology* 133:783–791.

Byers, Steven N.
1994 On Stress and Stature in the "Osteological Paradox." *Current Anthropology* 35:282–284.

Chamberlain, Andrew
2000 Problems and Prospects in Palaeodemography. In *Human Osteology in Archaeology and Forensic Science*, edited by Margaret Cox and Simon Mays, pp. 101–115. Greenwich Medical Media, London.
2006 *Demography in Archaeology.* Cambridge University Press, Cambridge.

Cohen, Mark N.
1989 *Health and the Rise of Civilization.* Yale University Press, New Haven.
1992 Comments. *Current Anthropology* 33:358–359.
1994 The Osteological Paradox Reconsidered. *Current Anthropology* 35:629–631.
1997 Does Paleopathology Measure Community Health? A Rebuttal of "the Osteological Paradox" and Its Implication for World History. In *Integrating Archaeological Demography: Multidisciplinary Approaches to Prehistoric Population*, edited by Richard R. Paine, pp. 242–260. Occasional Paper 24. Center for Archaeological Investigations, Southern Illinois University, Carbondale.
2008 Implications of the NDT for World Wide Health and Mortality in Prehistory. In *The Neolithic Demographic Transition and Its Consequences*, edited by Jean-Pierre Bocquet-Appel and Ofer Bar-Yosef, pp. 481–500. Springer, New York.

Cohen Mark N., and George J. Armelagos
1984 Paleopathology at the Origins of Agriculture: Editors' Summation. In *Paleopathology at the Origins of Agriculture*, edited by Mark N. Cohen and George J. Armelagos, pp. 585–601. Academic Press, Orlando.

Cohen, Mark N., and Gillian M. M. Crane-Kramer
2007 Editors' Summation. In *Ancient Health*, edited by Mark N. Cohen and Gillian M. M. Crane-Kramer, pp. 320–343. University Press of Florida, Gainesville.

Cook, Della C.
1984 Subsistence and Health in the Lower Illinois Valley: Osteological Evidence. In *Paleopathology at the Origins of Agriculture*, edited by Mark N. Cohen and George J. Armelagos, pp. 235–269. Academic Press, Orlando.

DeWitte, Sharon N., and James W. Wood
2008 Selectivity of Black Death Mortality with Respect to Preexisting Health. *Proceedings of the National Academy of Sciences* 105:1436–1441.

Djurić, Marija P., Charlotte A. Roberts, Zoran B. Rakočević, Danijela D. Djonić, and Aleksandar R. Lešić
2006 Fractures in Late Medieval Skeletal Populations from Serbia. *American Journal of Physical Anthropology* 130:167–178.

Douglas, Michele T., and Michael Pietrusewsky
2007 Biological Consequences of Sedentism: Agricultural Intensification in Northeastern Thailand. In *Ancient Health*, edited by Mark N. Cohen and Gillian M. M. Crane-Kramer, pp. 300–319. University Press of Florida, Gainesville.

Gejvall, Nils-Gustaf
1960 *Westerhus: Medieval Population and Church in the Light of Skeletal Remains.* Håkan Ohlssons Boktryckeri, Lund, Sweden.

Gibbons, Ann
2009 Civilization's Cost: The Decline and Fall of Human Health. *Science* 324:588.

Glencross, B., and L. Sawchuk
2003 The Person-Years Construct: Ageing and Prevalence of Health Related Phenomena from Skeletal Samples. *International Journal of Osteoarchaeology* 13:369–374.

Goodman, Alan H.
1993 On the Interpretation of Health from Skeletal Remains. *Current Anthropology* 34:281–288.

Grauer Anne L., and Charlotte A. Roberts
1996 Paleoepidemiology, Healing, and Possible Treatment of Trauma in the Medieval Cemetery Population of St. Helen-on-the-Walls, York, England. *American Journal of Physical Anthropology* 100:531–544.

Hooton, Earnest A.
1930 *The Indians of Pecos Pueblo: A Study of Their Skeletal Remains.* Papers of the Southwestern Expedition 4. Yale University Press, New Haven.

Hoppa, Robert D., and James W. Vaupel (editors)
2002 *Paleodemography: Age Distributions from Skeletal Samples.* Cambridge University Press, Cambridge.

Jackes, Mary K.
1993 On Paradox and Osteology. *Current Anthropology* 34:434–439.

Jackes, Mary, David Lubell, and Christopher Meiklejohn
1997 Healthy but Mortal: Human Biology and the First Farmers of Western Europe. *Antiquity* 71:639–658.

Jakobsen, Anna-Lise L.
1978 A Cripple from the Late Middle Ages. *Ossa* 5:17–24.

Judd, Margaret A.
2002 Ancient Injury Recidivism: An Example from the Kerma Period of Ancient Nubia. *International Journal of Osteoarchaeology* 12:89–106.
2004 Trauma in the City of Kerma: Ancient Versus Modern Injury Patterns. *International Journal of Osteoarchaeology* 14:34–51.

Judd, Margaret A., and Charlotte A. Roberts
1998 Fracture Patterns at the Medieval Leper Hospital in Chichester. *American Journal of Physical Anthropology* 105:43–55.
1999 Fracture Trauma in a Medieval British Farming Village. *American Journal of Physical Anthropology* 109:229–243.

Jurmain, Robert
2001 Paleoepidemiological Patterns of Trauma in a Prehistoric Population from Central California. *American Journal of Physical Anthropology* 115:13–23.

Konigsberg, Lyle W., and Susan R. Frankenberg
1994 Paleodemography: "Not Quite Dead." *Evolutionary Anthropology* 3:92–105.

Konigsberg, Lyle W., Susan R. Frankenberg, and Renee B. Walker
1997 Regress What on What? Paleodemographic Age Estimation as a Calibration Problem. In *Integrating Archaeological Demography: Multidisciplinary Approaches to Prehistoric Population*, edited by Richard R. Paine, pp. 64–88. Occasional Paper 24. Center for Archaeological Investigations, Southern Illinois University, Carbondale.

Lambert, Patricia M.
1997 Patterns of Violence in Prehistoric Hunter-Gatherer Societies of Coastal Southern California. In *Troubled Times: Violence and Warfare in the Past*, edited by Debra L. Martin and David W. Frayer, pp. 77–109. Gordon and Breach, Amsterdam.

Larsen, Clark S.
1995 Biological Changes in Human Populations with Agriculture. *Annual Reviews of Anthropology* 24:185–213.

Lovejoy, C. Owen, and Kingsbury G. Heiple
1981 The Analysis of Fractures in Skeletal Populations with an Example from the Libben Site, Ottawa County, Ohio. *American Journal of Physical Anthropology* 55:529–541.

Malthus, Thomas R.
1970 [1798] *An Essay on the Principal of Population.* Penguin, New York.

Mays, Simon
1991 *The Medieval Burials from the Blackfriars Friary, School Street, Ipswich, Suffolk (Excavated 1983–85).* AMP Report 16/91. Centre for Archaeology, English Heritage, Portsmouth.
1998 *The Archaeology of Human Bones.* Routledge, London.
2007 The Human Remains. In *Wharram: The Churchyard*, by Simon Mays, C. Harding, and C. Heighway, pp. 77–192. Archaeological Publications 13. York University, York.

Meiklejohn, Christopher, and Jeff Babb
2011 Long Bone Length, Stature and Time in the European Late Pleistocene and Early Holocene. In *Human Bioarchaeology of the Transition to Agriculture*, edited by Ron Pinhasi and Jay T. Stock, pp. 153–175. Wiley-Blackwell, Chichester.

Milner, George R.
1992 Disease and Sociopolitical Systems in Late Prehistoric Illinois. In *Disease and Demography in the Americas*, edited by John W. Verano and Douglas H. Ubelaker, pp. 103–116. Smithsonian Institution Press, Washington, D.C.
1999 Warfare in Prehistoric and Early Historic Eastern North America. *Journal of Archaeological Research* 7:105–151.
2004 *The Moundbuilders.* Thames and Hudson, London.
2010 Transition Analysis and Subjective Assessments of Age in Adult Skeletons. In *ADBOU 1992–2009: Forskiningsresultater*, edited by Jesper L. Boldsen and Peter Tarp, pp. 15–27. ADBOU, Syddansk Universitet, Odense, Denmark.

Milner, George R., and Rebecca J. Ferrell
2011 Conflict and Death in a Late Prehistoric Community in the American Midwest. *Anthropologischer Anzeiger* 68:415–436.

Milner, George R., Eve Anderson, and Virginia G. Smith
1991 Warfare in Late Prehistoric West-Central Illinois. *American Antiquity* 56:581–603.

Milner, George R., James W. Wood, and Jesper L. Boldsen
2008 Advances in Paleodemography. In *Biological Anthropology of the Human Skeleton*, 2nd ed., edited by M. Anne Katzenberg and Shelley R. Saunders, pp. 561–600. Wiley-Liss, New York.

Møller-Christensen, Vilh
1982 *Æbelholt Kloster.* Nationalmuseet, Copenhagen.

Ortner, Donald J.
1991 Theoretical and Methodological Issues in Paleopathology. In *Human Paleopathology: Current Syntheses and Future Options*, edited by Donald J. Ortner and Arthur C. Aufderheide, pp. 5–11. Smithsonian Institution Press, Washington, D.C.
1998 Male-Female Immune Reactivity and Its Implications for Interpreting Evidence in Human Skeletal Paleopathology. In *Sex and Gender in Paleopathological Perspective*, edited by Anne L. Grauer and Patricia Stuart-Macadam, pp. 79–92. Cambridge University Press, Cambridge.

Pietrusewsky, Michael, and Michel T. Douglas
2001 Intensification of Agriculture at Ban Chiang: Is There Evidence from the Skeletons? *Asian Perspectives* 40:157–178.

Robb, John
1997 Violence and Gender in Early Italy. In *Troubled Times: Violence and Warfare in the Past*, edited by Debra L. Martin and David W. Frayer, pp. 111–144. Gordon and Breach, Amsterdam.

Roberts, Charlotte, and Margaret Cox
2003 *Health and Disease in Britain: From Prehistory to the Present Day.* Sutton, Stroud, Gloucestershire.

Rousseau, Jean-Jacques
1950 [1755] What Is the Origin of Inequality Among Men, and Is It Authorized by Natural Law? In *The Social Contract and Discourses*, edited and translated by G. D. H. Cole, pp. 175–282. Dutton, New York.

Saunders, Shelley R., and Robert D. Hoppa
1993 Growth Deficit in Survivors and Non-Survivors: Biological Mortality Bias in Subadult Skeletal Samples. *Yearbook of Physical Anthropology* 36:127–151.

Smith, Patricia, and Liora K. Horwitz
2007 Ancestors and Inheritors: A Bioanthropological Perspective on the Transition to Agropastoralism in the Southern Levant. In *Ancient Health*, edited by Mark N. Cohen and Gillian M. M. Crane-Kramer, pp. 207–222. University Press of Florida, Gainesville.

Steckel, Richard H., and Jerome C. Rose
2002 Patterns of Health in the Western Hemisphere. In *The Backbone of History: Health and Nutrition in the Western Hemisphere*, edited by Richard H. Steckel and Jerome C. Rose, pp. 563–579. Cambridge University Press, Cambridge.

Steckel, Richard H., Jerome C. Rose, Clark S. Larsen, and Phillip L. Walker
2002 Skeletal Health in the Western Hemisphere from 4000 B.C. to the Present. *Evolutionary Anthropology* 11:142–155.

Stirland Anne
1996 Patterns of Trauma in a Unique Medieval Parish Cemetery. *International Journal of Osteoarchaeology* 6:92–100.

Stroud G., and R. L. Kemp
1993 *Cemeteries of St. Andrew, Fishergate*. Medieval Cemeteries 12. York Archaeological Trust, York.

Torres-Rouff, Christina, and Maria A. C. Junqueira
2006 Interpersonal Violence in Prehistoric San Pedro de Atacama, Chile: Behaviroal Implications of Environmental Stress. *American Journal of Physical Anthropology* 130:60–70.

Tung, Tiffiny A.
2007 Trauma and Violence in the Wari Empire of the Peruvian Andes: Warfare, Raids, and Ritual Fights. *American Journal of Physical Anthropology* 133:941–956.

Ubelaker, Douglas H.
1982 The Development of American Paleopathology. In *A History of American Physical Anthropology 1930–1980*, edited by Frank Spencer, pp. 337–356. Academic Press, New York.

Ubelaker, Douglas H., and Linda A. Newson
2002 Patterns of Health and Nutrition in Prehistoric and Historic Ecuador. In *The Backbone of History: Health and Nutrition in the Western Hemisphere*, edited by Richard H. Steckel and Jerome C. Rose, pp. 343–375. Cambridge University Press, Cambridge.

Usher, Bethany M.
2000 A Multistate Model of Health and Mortality for Paleodemography: The Tirup Cemetery. Unpublished Ph.D dissertation, Pennsylvania State University, University Park.

Walker, Phillip L.
1989 Cranial Injuries as Evidence of Violence in Prehistoric Southern California. *American Journal of Physical Anthropology* 80:313–323.

Weber, Jochen, and Alfred Czarnetzki
2001 Neurotraumatological Aspects of Head Injuries Resulting from Sharp and Blunt Force in the Early Medieval Period of Southwestern Germany. *American Journal of Physical Anthropology* 114:352–356.

Weise, Svenja, Jesper L. Boldsen, Jutta Gampe, and George R. Milner
2009 Calibrated Expert Inference and the Construction of Unbiased Paleodemographic Mortality Profiles. Abstract. *American Journal of Physical Anthropology Supplement* 48:269.

Wittwer-Backofen, Ursula, and Nicolas Tomo
2008 From Health to Civilization Stress? In Search for Traces of a Health Transition During the Early Neolithic in Europe. In *The Neolithic Demographic Transition and Its Consequences*, edited by Jean-Pierre Bocquet-Appel and Ofer Bar-Yosef, pp. 501–538. Springer, New York.

Wood, James W.
1998 A Theory of Preindustrial Population Dynamics. *Current Anthropology* 39:99–121.

Wood, James W., and George R. Milner
1994 Reply. *Current Anthropology* 35:631–637.

Wood, James W., George R. Milner, Henry C. Harpending, and Kenneth M. Weiss
1992 The Osteological Paradox: Problems of Inferring Prehistoric Health from Skeletal Samples. *Current Anthropology* 33:343–370.

Wright, Lori E., and Cassidy J. Yoder
2003 Recent Progress in Bioarchaeology: Approaches to the Osteological Paradox. *Journal of Archaeological Research* 11:43–70.

Index

UCLA COTSEN INSTITUTE OF ARCHAEOLOGY PRESS

MONOGRAPHS
Contributions in Field Research and Current Issues in Archaeological Method and Theory

Monograph 76 *The Dead Tell Tales: Essays in Honor of Jane E. Buikstra,* Edited by María Cecilia Lozada and Barra O'Donnabhain
Monograph 75 *The Stones of Tiahuanaco: A Study of Architecture and Construction,* Jean-Pierre Protzen and Stella Nair
Monograph 74 *Rock Art at Little Lake: An Ancient Crossroads in the California Desert,* Jo Anne Van Tilburg, Gordon E. Hull, and John C. Bretney
Monograph 73 *The History of the Peoples of the Eastern Desert,* Hans Barnard and Kim Duistermaat (eds.)
Monograph 71 *Crucible of Pueblos: The Early Pueblo Period in the Northern Southwest,* Richard H. Wilshusen, Gregson Schachner, and James R. Allison (eds.)
Monograph 70 *Chotuna and Chornancap: Excavating an Ancient Peruvian Legend,* Christopher B. Donnan
Monograph 69 *An Investigation into Early Desert Pastoralism: Excavations at the Camel Site, Negev,* Steven A. Rosen
Monograph 68 *The Chanka: Archaeological Research in Andahuaylas (Apurimac), Peru,* Brian S. Bauer, Lucas C. Kellett, and Miriam Aráoz Silva
Monograph 67 *Inca Rituals and Sacred Mountains: A Study of the World's Highest Archaeological Sites,* Johan Reinhard and Maria Costanza Ceruti
Monograph 66 *Gallinazo: An Early Cultural Tradition on the Peruvian North Coast,* Jean-François Millaire with Magali Morlion
Monograph 65 *Settlement and Subsistence in Early Formative Soconusco,* Richard G. Lesure (ed.)
Monograph 64 *The South American Camelids,* Duccio Bonavia
Monograph 63 *Andean Civilization: A Tribute to Michael E. Moseley,* Joyce Marcus and Patrick Ryan Williams (eds.)
Monograph 62 *Excavations at Cerro Azul, Peru: The Architecture and Pottery,* Joyce Marcus Monograph 61 *Chavín: Art, Architecture and Culture,* William J Conklin and Jeffrey Quilter (eds.)
Monograph 61 *Chavín: Art, Architecture, and Culture,* William J Conklin and Jeffrey Quilter (eds.)
Monograph 60 *Rethinking Mycenaean Palaces II: Revised and Expanded Second Edition,* Michael L. Galaty and William A. Parkinson (eds.)
Monograph 59 *Moche Tombs at Dos Cabezas,* Christopher B. Donnan
Monograph 58 *Moche Fineline Painting From San José de Moro,* Donna McClelland, Donald McClelland, and Christopher B. Donnan
Monograph 57 *Kasapata and the Archaic Period of the Cuzco Valley,* Brian S. Bauer (ed.)
Monograph 56 *Berenike 1999/2000,* Steven E. Sidebotham and Willeke Wendrich (eds.)
Monograph 55 *Roman Footprints at Berenike: Archaeobotanical Evidence of Subsistence and Trade in the Eastern Desert of Egypt,* René T. J. Cappers
Monograph 54 *Advances in Titicaca Basin Archaeology 1,* Charles Stanish, Amanda B. Cohen, and Mark S. Aldenderfer
Monograph 53 *Us and Them: Archaeology and Ethnicity in the Andes,* Richard Martin Reycraft
Monograph 52 *Archaeological Research on the Islands of the Sun and Moon, Lake Titicaca, Bolivia: Final Results from the Proyecto Tiksi Kjarka,* Charles Stanish and Brian S. Bauer (eds.)
Monograph 51 *Maya Zooarchaeology: New Directions in Theory and Method,* Kitty F. Emery (ed.)
Monograph 50 *Settlement Archaeology and Political Economy at Tres Zapotes, Veracruz, Mexico,* Christopher A. Pool (ed.)
Monograph 49 *Perspectives on Ancient Maya Rural Complexity,* Gyles Iannone and Samuel V. Connell (eds.)
Monograph 48 *Yeki bud, yeki nabud: Essays on the Archaeology of Iran in Honor of William M. Sumner,* Naomi F. Miller and Kamyar Abdi (eds.)
Monograph 47 *Archaeology in the Borderlands: Investigation in Caucasia and Beyond,* Adam T. Smith and Karen S. Rubinson (eds.)
Monograph 46 *Domestic Ritual in Ancient Mesoamerica,* Patricia Plunket (ed.)
Monograph 45 *Pathways to Prismatic Blades,* Kenneth Hirth and Bradford Andrews (eds.)
Monograph 44 *Ceramic Production and Circulation in the Greater Southwest,* Donna M. Glowacki and Hector Neff (eds.)
Monograph 43 *Pottery of Postclassic Cholula, Mexico,* Geoffrey McCafferty
Monograph 42 *Pompeian Households: An Analysis of the Material Culture,* Penelope M. Allison
Monograph 41 *Rethinking Mycenaean Palaces: New Interpretations of an Old Idea,* Michael L. Galaty and William A. Parkinson (eds.)
Monograph 40 *Prehistory of Agriculture: New Experimental and Ethnographic Approaches,* Patricia C. Anderson (ed.)
Monograph 39 *Recent Advances in the Archaeology of the Northern Andes: In Memory of Gerardo Reichel-Dolmatoff,* Augusto Oyuela-Caycedo and J. Scott Raymond (eds.)
Monograph 38 *Approaches to the Historical Archaeology of Mexico, Central and South America,* Janine Gasco, Greg Charles Smith, and Patricia Fournier-Garcia
Monograph 37 *Hawaiian Adze Production and Distribution: Implications for the Development of Chiefdoms,* Barbara Lass
Monograph 36 *New Light on Old Art: Recent Advances in Hunter-Gatherer Rock Art Research,* D. W. Whitley and L. L. Loendorf (eds.)
Monograph 35 *Pottery of Prehistoric Honduras: Regional Classification and Analysis,* J. S. Henderson and M. Beaudry-Corbett
Monograph 34 *Settlement Archaeology of Cerro de las Mesas, Veracruz, Mexico,* Barbara Stark (ed.)
Monograph 31 *Investigaciones Arqueológicos de la Costa Sur de Guatemala,* David S. Whitley and Marilyn P. Beaudry (eds.)
Monograph 30 *Archaeology of the Three Springs Valley, California: A Study in Functional Cultural History,* Brian D. Dillon and Matthew A. Boxt